MARINERS, MERCHANTS AND THE MILITARY TOO

1. ORIGINS OF AN EMPIRE

Even though modern political correctness and deliberate revisionism might sometimes regard a pride in our nations past as a highly negative and backward looking attitude to take, it is still sometimes hard to believe that less than a hundred years ago, the relatively small collection of islands that now form the modern United Kingdom were once at the centre of a global Empire that extended its reach throughout much of the known world. Reportedly the largest Empire that has ever existed throughout human history, at its height the British Empire was reported to have ruled over some four hundred and fifty millions subjects, a quarter of the world's population at the beginning of the 20th century and controlled an estimated thirteen million square miles of territory, around 25% of the world's total land surface.

However, within half a century of having reached the absolute zenith of its power, much of its power and prestige, along with virtually all of its larger overseas possessions were gone and the vast British Empire, which had evolved and been fought over for well over four hundred years, began to pass into a collective memory. Perhaps even more sadly, over the past sixty years, even these national recollections and celebrations of Britain's glorious past have been almost entirely expunged from British national life for fear of being seen as racist, imperialistic or undemocratic, such is the overwhelming desire for our United Kingdom to be seen as a multi-cultural, egalitarian and forward looking modern state. Even though Britain's great and expansive Empire has long since been consigned to the history books, even today it continues to divide opinion, with some critics accusing it of being the root cause of modern day Africa's political malaise, founders of the world's first infamous concentration camp systems and the world's first major exploiter of other nations and of the earths vast natural resources.

Clearly though, such criticisms are almost always seen from an entirely modern perspective, they take little account of how the world was, many decades or even centuries ago and should therefore always be treated with a great deal of scepticism, or even disdain. Applying 21st century values, opinions and explanations to events which took place between the 16th and 19th centuries is patently absurd, given that the religious, military, political and cultural imperatives of those particular times were probably informed by prevailing late medieval values, more than they were by our more modern and educated ones. Additionally, it also seems to be a common and deliberate mistake, to link the indigenous peoples of Britain to the wider and much larger Empire that was in and of itself an entirely political and economic union, a creation which had little in common with lives, traditions, values and customs of the native populations of England, Scotland, Ireland and Wales.

Although the Roman's knew our islands as their province of Britannia, earlier Greek explorers were thought to have known them as "Albus", meaning "White", a name that was said to have derived from the sight of the white cliffs of Dover, which early mariners may well have seen as they approached Britain from the south by sea. This early Greek name is also speculated to be the origins for the later and occasionally used name "Albion", which has often been associated with both the English and British nation. According to modern day geneticists, the very earliest inhabitants of Britain were the hunter gatherers and settlers who originated from both the Iberian Peninsula and from the Basque region of Europe, both of whom were thought to have been trapped by the eventual rise in sea levels that separated Britain from continental Europe, creating what we now call the English Channel and Irish Sea.

King Aethelred

King Harold II

King William I

The Celtic influences that were native to England, Wales, Scotland and Ireland are thought to have their earliest roots within the Iberian and French regions, although over centuries these had been added to and supplemented by the languages and cultures of other migrants groups, such as the Picts, Gaels and numerous others, who eventually evolved into the pre-Roman native tribes of Britain such as the Ordovices, Silures, Brigantes and the Deceangli, the tribesmen who populated various regions of Britain in the centuries prior to the Roman arrival. In fact, throughout its long history, Britain was thought to have been occupied by an almost endless succession of foreign migrants, most of who arrived here in relatively small numbers, along with those who participated in the three major military invasions of the country, all of which have helped to shape the language, culture, character and traditions of Britain and its native peoples. The first of the military invaders were the Roman's, who conquered much of southern Britain and Wales during the First Century AD and who through their northern defensive walls, helped to create and define the northern boundaries of Roman Britain, at the same time helping to mark the boundaries of the countries that would later become England and Scotland. During the Roman occupation of Britain, much of England, Wales and Southern Scotland were known to have come under legionary control, whilst Northern Scotland and Ireland remained outside of the Roman sphere of influence, allowing them to retain many of their original Celtic traditions, languages and customs.

By the 5th and 6th centuries and with the professional legions having been withdrawn to Europe, post Roman Britain subsequently found itself at the mercy of raiding bands from Ireland, Scandinavia and Europe, forcing Romano-British leaders to call on continental Anglo Saxons for military aid in helping to defend their national borders. However, either through sheer opportunism, or in revenge for being cheated out of their agreed reward, the Anglo Saxons mercenaries, including the Angles, Jutes and Saxons, began their own invasion of Britain, driving many of the native Briton's westward to Cornwall, Wales, Cumbria and back into continental Europe, most notably into the region of France, now known as modern day Brittany. Over time the native peoples of southern post-Roman Britain were thought to have either been driven out, or simply absorbed by the new Anglo Saxon society that had taken over significant parts of the country, later developing into the seven petty kingdoms of Wessex, Mercia, Northumbria, East Anglia, Essex, Sussex and Kent. Although these seven kingdoms, or Heptarchy, were said to have existed as individual realms for an extended period of time, towards the end of the 8th century those that were located on the eastern side of Britain eventually fell victim to the Viking people, Scandinavian raiders and settlers who established their own separate state in Britain, which became known as the Danelaw.

With Britain divided, by the end of the 9th century the remaining western Anglo Saxon kingdoms of Britain, including the largely independent British kingdom of Wales had been unified under the Lordship of King Alfred of Wessex who had managed to stem the Viking tide. However, it was thought to be his royal successors, including Edward the Elder, Athelstan, Edmund, Eadred and finally Edgar who finally managed to bring much of southern Britain back under Anglo Saxon control and helped to create the unified kingdom that would eventually become known as "Angle-land", which later became England. During these turbulent centuries, the Brythonic language of the native British people was thought to have been largely replaced by that of the Anglo Saxons, save for enclaves such as Wales and Cornwall, where elements of the ancient British tongue were thought to have survived. Elsewhere, Viking names and expressions were thought to have entered into everyday use and they too were eventually absorbed into what commonly became known as Old English, a native tongue for the newly formed kingdom of England.

In the last quarter of the 10th century and right through to the first half of the 11th century England once again found itself under sustained attack by Scandinavian leaders, who sought to exploit the weakness of the Anglo Saxon ruler Aethelred and usurp him from the English throne. Although there were later attempts to restore an Anglo Saxon ruler to the English throne in the form of Aethelred's son Edmund Ironside, his early death prevented a return to Anglo-Saxon rule, leaving the Crown to fall into the possession of the Norwegian ruler King Canute, who then went on to reign over a European Empire consisting of England, Norway and Denmark. However, on his death, the Crown of England was temporarily passed to his sons, but in 1042 it was subsequently reclaimed by the Anglo Saxon leader Edward the Confessor, whose later refusal or inability to produce a legitimate heir, as well as his own political manoeuvrings eventually led to the third and final military invasion of mainland Britain shortly after his death in 1066.

Following Edward the Confessor's death, there were thought to be at least three main contenders for the English throne, Harold Godwinsson of Wessex, Harald III of Norway and Duke William of Normandy, all of whom claimed to be the legitimate heir of the late Anglo Saxon monarch. Initially Harold Godwinsson was reported to have ascended the English throne with the approval of the Witan, the council of Anglo Saxon advisors and noblemen, whose support was vital to any potential monarch, although almost immediately Harald III of Norway was said to have brought a Scandinavian army to England, in order to pursue his own claim through force of arms. In September 1066 Harald III landed in the north east of the country with an estimated force of around fifteen thousand men, including Earl Tostig, Harold Godwinsson's estranged brother and having assembled their army, set out to pursue Harald's claim to the English Crown. In the meantime however, the Anglo Saxon monarch, King Harold II, or Harold Godwinsson was said to have been informed about the Norwegian threat and having mustered his own army set out to meet and defeat the foreign invaders, at the Battle of Stamford Bridge in Yorkshire, which was fought on the 25th September 1066.

Unfortunately for Harold II of England, despite having secured his kingdom from this Scandinavian threat, a far more serious danger to his Crown was said to have landed in England just three days after the Battle of Stamford Bridge had been fought. On 28th September 1066, a large Norman army led by the ruthless Duke of Normandy, who was often referred to as William the Bastard, because of his reported illegitimacy, landed at Pevensey in England, to pursue his own claim on Edward the Confessor's English throne. Although Harold Godwinson and the remnants of his victorious army were thought to be still recovering from their earlier battle with Harald Hardrada, having been informed about the new threat to the country they were left with little option but to undertake a forced march across the country, in order to confront this new foreign danger. Unfortunately, whilst Harold and his exhausted troops were marching to meet them, Duke William was said to have been busily preparing his position on the English coast and off-loading one of his greatest weapons, the specially trained warhorse.

In the two weeks that it was said to have taken for King Harold II and his army to travel from Yorkshire to East Sussex, via London, the Norman forces of Duke William were said to have been busy raiding and terrorising the local countryside, as well as preparing themselves for the battle that lay ahead. When the two armies finally did meet on the 14th October 1066, it was reported that they were fairly evenly matched, despite the fact that Harold's troops had already fought one major battle and then been forced to travel down the country at speed, in order to face yet another military opponent. According to some historians, both Norman and English armies were thought to have numbered around ten thousand men, although there are also suggestions that Duke William's force was actually about twice that figure. Either way however, later reports indicated that as the battle raged, the balance of power swung precariously between the two armies, with neither able to deliver a single decisive blow against the other. In fact, it was only when the Norman forces began to turn away from the shield wall of their enemy that the indiscipline of the English troops began to show, breaking their own defensive lines in order to pursue their fleeing enemy. It was at this point and as an act of sheer desperation that Duke William was reported to have ordered his archers to fire over the shields of Harold's troops, an action that resulted in the English monarch being struck in the eye by one of the flying missiles and finally turning the battle in Duke William's favour. Although the warhorses of the Norman army were undoubtedly a contributing factor during the confrontation, it was only when the English shield wall began to fragment and collapse that horse and rider could become more effective, helping to drive the English ranks further apart, as the Norman knights pressed home their advantage with lance and sword.

With Harold Godwinsson dead and no other native Anglo Saxon leader to replace him, Duke William's victory was said to have been complete and within a short time the English troops had either been scattered or killed. Initially the Norman Lord was said to have waited close to the site of the battle, in the expectation that the English nobility would come and willingly submit to his rule, but having waited for nearly two weeks eventually realised that the English nobles were not so easily inclined to grant him their submission, leaving him with little choice but to march on London. However, even this relatively straightforward task was thought to have been problematic for him, as sporadic attacks by Anglo Saxon forces on his columns and outbreaks of sickness spreading through the ranks of his soldiers, required Duke William to halt and bring in fresh recruits from the continent in order to reinforce his army. Eventually however, the "Conqueror" and his army did reach London and did receive the reluctant submission of England's Anglo Saxon aristocracy, being crowned as King of England on 25th December 1066. Interestingly however, despite having received the submissions of the great and the good of England, William and his Norman forces were still required to spend the next five years having to suppress numerous native rebellions that were said to have occurred throughout much of his new English kingdom.

Although Anglo Saxon England is often reported to have been a highly uncivilised place, a country wracked by petty internal disputes and dissent, with little local government and a marked lack of centralised control, not all historians share this view of the Anglo Saxon period. It has been suggested that in fact, both church and state exercised considerable administrative control and legal authority over most parts of the country, with local Anglo Saxon Earls and noblemen being charged with the security of their own particular regions, whilst centrally appointed administrators were made responsible for the collection of taxes, duties and debts. Even common men were thought to have fared well under the feudal Anglo Saxon system, with extensive lands granted to those men who were prepared to help defend the country from all of its potential enemies, both foreign and domestic. For those that were willing and able to work, the prospect of improving their own personal situation and providing for their families was thought to have been aided by the fact that most Anglo Saxon noblemen and large landowners of the age, actively encouraged widespread land use, simply because of the benefits it brought, not only to the national treasury, but also to the individual nobleman's own personal coffers.

King Malcolm III   Edgar of Scotland   King William II

Rather than William's subsequent victory at Hastings being the result of a failure of Anglo Saxon England at a local or regional level, it was undoubtedly the actions of the monarch, Edward the Confessor and his nobles that brought about its almost inevitable downfall. Although Edward was reportedly a well respected and fairly able monarch, it was thought to be his own personal prevarication over the subject of his royal successor, nominating Earl Harold Godwinsson on the one hand and William, the Duke of Normandy, on the other, which ultimately caused the confusion and dissent over who exactly was Edward's legitimate heir. On his death in 1066, the question of the royal succession was further complicated by the royal claims of the Norwegian king Harald Hardrada, who believed that he too had a legitimate claim to the English throne, a claim he was more than happy to pursue through force of arms. With no large standing Anglo Saxon army to call upon, Harold Godwinsson, later Harold II, was forced to rally his troops, before setting out to confront Hardrada at Stamford Bridge. However, having defeated this Norwegian threat to his kingdom and without the benefit of having large numbers of reserve troops to call upon, the new Anglo Saxon monarch was then forced to march halfway down the country to confront Duke William's invasion force, which had landed at Pevensey. Most contemporary reports of the conflict at Hastings have suggested that the battle itself was an extremely close fought affair, one that might have gone either way, but was ultimately decided by the death of Harold Godwinsson and which was brought about by the flight of a single Norman arrow or crossbow bolt. Rather than reflecting a failure of Anglo Saxon England itself, the events of 1066 were said to be simply the results of bad luck, poor planning and poor personal judgement on the part of those that had been charged with the protection of their kingdom.

For Duke William's part, his own claim to the English throne, which has often been thought to be spurious at best, was said to have been accompanied by four significant pieces of good fortune, which ultimately helped him to secure the Crown of England. Firstly, his invasion fleet faced no opposition from the fledgling English navy, which had reportedly been withdrawn in order to re-supply its limited number of ships, thereby allowing the Norman fleet to reach its destination relatively unmolested. Secondly, the absence of a standing English army, which might have otherwise opposed Duke William's forces, not only allowed the Norman landing at Pevensey, but also permitted William to prepare both his men and defences in readiness for the later arrival of King Harold's forces which were rushing southward to meet them. The third and most pivotal piece of good fortune that attached itself to the Norman leader's campaign was the unidentified stray arrow or bolt that somehow found its way through Harold's personal defences during the battle, hitting him in such a way as to bring an end to both his life and his short reign. The fourth and final piece of good fortune that presented itself to the Norman Duke, immediately after the Battle of Hastings, was the almost complete absence of a replacement Anglo Saxon leader who might otherwise have stood against his invasion force, but as no such person came forward, instead it was left to a generally leaderless Anglo Saxon nobility to make their peace with the Norman leader as best as they could.

As a result of William's successful conquest of England, so the borders of his new kingdom became more defined, with vast areas of both Scotland and Wales initially lying beyond day-to-day Norman control, save for occasional military campaigns around the periphery of these two native states. However, unlike the earlier Anglo Saxon conquerors of England, who came to settle the country, the Norman's who arrived with Duke William had little interest in simply settling there, or indeed adopting its native peoples culture, language, customs and traditions. Instead, most of the continental knights and noblemen who had accompanied William to England were solely interested in acquiring whatever wealth, lands, titles and possessions that might be earned in return for their military support. It has been reported that in the twenty years, from Hastings in 1066, to the compiling of William's great Domesday Book in 1086, virtually all of the lands, titles and possessions which had been previously held by the Anglo Saxon population, had been seized and given over to members of the new Norman administration, or their attendant followers. In order to ensure that the largely subjugated English population remained compliant to their will, almost immediately the Norman aristocracy started to build the many hundreds of castles that continue to stand as a lasting memorial to this particularly bloody phase of England's early history. Even the Anglo Saxon's earlier religious houses did not escape the Norman's attention, although perhaps these changes are often seen in a more positive manner, with countless early Churches, Abbeys and Monasteries demolished, to make way for the far larger and much more grandiose buildings that continue to grace the English countryside even today. Often rebuilt on the orders of individual noblemen who hoped to save their immortal souls, even here new changes were introduced, with the earlier Anglo Saxon clergy often being summarily replaced by new foreign orders and appointees who were more acceptable to the tastes and practices of the new Norman elite.

Although largely untouched by the initial invasion of the Norman's, the northern kingdom of Scotland almost inevitably became embroiled in the conflict, largely because the country became a safe haven for large numbers of Anglo Saxon refugees, who despite being driven out of England, remained determined to carry on the fight against the continental invaders. One of most notable of these Anglo Saxon lords was said to be Edgar (the) Aethling, the last surviving male heir from the House of Wessex, who despite being proclaimed King of England, by some of his supporters, was never formally recognised or indeed crowned as such. Fleeing to the independent Scottish Court of King Malcolm III, along with his family and entourage, Edgar quickly formed an alliance with the Scottish king, who not only agreed to offer support to the ousted Anglo Saxon leader, but also took Edgar's sister, Margaret, as his wife, in order to further cement the alliance between the two families.

Despite having suppressed much of southern England within a relatively short space of time, Duke William's forces were thought to have faced much stiffer resistance in the north of the country, where the descendants of much earlier Scandinavian settlers were said to have lived. These people refused to simply submit to the rule of the Norman invaders and supported by fighters from countries like Norway, Denmark and from Scotland, they were said to have played a significant role in helping English resistance to the Norman's, much of which was said to have been centred round the former Viking capital at York. However, William's response to their resistance was thought to have been both swift and brutal, gathering his forces and travelling northward, he and his heavily armoured troops were said to have systematically destroyed everything and everyone that stood against him, in a bitter campaign that later became known as the "Harrying of the North". People, shelter, crops and animals were all decimated by the advancing ranks of Norman troops, with no quarter offered or indeed being given, until at last they reached the gates of York itself. Even when the city surrendered itself to him, he was said to have remained merciless and was reported to have burnt much of the city to the ground, even ordering that it's ancient religious Minster should be destroyed, as an example to those that might consider standing against him in the future.

Recognising that Scotland was being employed as a safe haven by many of his political and military opponents, in 1072 William was said to have launched an invasion of the northern kingdom, forcing its ruler, Malcolm III, to recognise him as his overlord, which the Scottish monarch eventually did. However, despite having offered his submission to King William I of England, Malcolm was said to have continued to allow his lands to be used as a base for the dispossessed Anglo Saxon rebels, who were raiding along both kingdoms shared border, including the ousted Anglo Saxon leader Edgar Aethling. Perhaps realising the futility of Edgar's continuing campaigns against the Normans, in 1074 Malcolm was said to have persuaded his new brother-in-law to finally make peace with William, bringing an end to the ongoing troubles. Although Edgar was thought to have effectively resigned his historic claims to the English throne by publicly submitting to William's authority, for which he was said to have received scant reward, the Anglo Saxon leader would continue to be a central character in the history of the Scottish Court for many years to come.

Further conflict broke out between the neighbouring kingdoms of England and Scotland in 1093, when fighting erupted between Duke William's successor, William II of England and King Malcolm III of Scotland, during which the Scottish monarch was said to have died. Malcolm's brother, Domnall, was said to have temporarily ascended the Scottish throne following the king's death, but he was then reported to have been usurped by William II of England's choice for Scottish king, Duncan, a son of Malcolm's first marriage. However, unfortunately for Duncan he was reported to have been murdered and Domnall was restored to the throne, only to be usurped for a second time, by Edgar, the eldest son of Margaret and Malcolm, who finally ascended the Scottish throne in 1097. When Edgar died in 1107, he in turn was succeeded by his younger brother, Alexander, who ruled until 1124, when he was too was succeeded by a younger sibling, David, the youngest of Malcolm and Margaret's four sons. It was said to be this fourth son, King David I of Scotland, who essentially secured an independent Scottish nation through his willingness to embrace the political changes introduced by the Norman's and by inviting a number of highly influential Norman knights and noblemen to settle within his kingdom, which helped to guarantee his own position on the Scottish throne. It was also said to be during David's reign that many of the Scottish Isles, which had previously been under Norwegian ownership and therefore outside of immediate Scottish control, were finally brought under King David's authority, creating the unified Kingdom of Scotland that would remain largely independent of England right through to the beginning of the 18th century.

The Old English language, which was thought to be largely a product of the Anglo Saxons, once again began to evolve and develop, with new Norman French words being absorbed into the English vocabulary, although within the Royal Court itself, only Norman French was said to have been used in daily conversation. According to some historians, much of the English language that is both written and spoken today originates from the generations immediately following the Norman Conquest of England, when common French words were introduced and subsequently amalgamated into the earlier English tongue, accounting in part for the sometimes confusing, but extremely rich language that is so widely used throughout the world today. However, Two of the greatest changes that the Norman's introduced to England, were thought to be the Domesday Book, derived from the Day of Judgement, and perhaps more importantly, the relocating of Norman power from England to William's home region of Normandy in France. Although nominally a vassal of the French Royal Court, Duke William was said to have been such an important military and political figure in Western Europe that his lordship of England was considered to be of secondary importance, to the role that he played within the wider continent itself. Because of this, the new King of England was reported to have spent little time in his new kingdom, leaving much of its security and administration to the various noblemen and court officials that he himself had appointed to take care of such matters. One of his greatest legacies, the Domesday Book, which was thought to have been compiled purely for the assessment of royal taxes, was reported to have been completed in 1086 and even today is generally regarded as one of the most important historic documents relating to England's early history. Likewise, the international link which was made between England and the French region of Normandy would remain as a lasting testimony to Duke William's early reign, with both territories later becoming part of the much larger Angevin Empire of Henry II.

Prior to 1169, the only links between England and Ireland were thought to have been almost entirely commercial or cultural, with both countries early settlers having only extremely tenuous contacts with one another, an entirely separate and divisive relationship caused in part by the existence of a vast and seemingly impenetrable expanse of water that lay between them, which is commonly known as the Irish Sea. Although occasional contacts were made between the two neighbouring territories, these were thought to be highly uncommon affairs, brought about by exceptional seamanship, blind curiosity or as a result of entirely accidental landings on one another's coastlines. Even though each of the three early invasion forces that had conquered Britain, later creating England, Scotland and Wales, undoubtedly knew about the island of Ireland, or Hibernia, neither the Romans, nor the Anglo Saxons had thought them worth the effort of invasion. It was only the Vikings who were thought to have considered the rugged, windswept lands of Ireland, worthy of invasion and settlement and only then to the west of the country, which not only offered them safe anchorage, but perhaps more importantly, easy access to the much richer settlements and more important trade routes that lay to the west of England and Wales.

However, Norman England's attitude to Ireland was said to have fundamentally changed in 1169, when a group of Cambro-Norman mercenaries arrived in Ireland with the express purpose of creating their own private fiefdoms within what appeared to be a completely unexploited and largely unprotected lands. Reportedly invited by a native Irish Chieftain called MacMurrow, who had previously been dispossessed of his own native kingdom, a relatively small, but extremely well armed Norman force, under the command of Richard de Clare, the 2nd Earl of Pembroke, who was commonly known as "Strongbow" landed in Ireland and quickly overcame the local Irish defenders, who had little knowledge of, or defences to, Norman armour and their highly trained warhorses. As in Wales, Ireland at that time was said to have been largely composed of numerous petty kingdoms which were ruled over by disparate local chieftains, who spent much of their time fighting and squabbling with one another and were therefore unable, or unwilling, to launch a coordinated attack against the well armed and highly mobile Norman forces, including Welsh archers, who had come into their midst.

King David I

King Alexander

King Henry II

Faced by this highly professional Norman force, even the usually martial Viking and Danish settlers who had established themselves along the east coast of Ireland, in places like Dublin, Waterford and Wexford, found themselves unable to resist the invaders. Within a matter of months, De Clare and his allies had not only taken control of these cities, but had also restored MacMurrow to his lands, for which De Clare was said to have received the chieftain's daughter in marriage and been nominated as the Irish leader's legitimate heir. Concerned and outraged by these events, the other native Irish leaders were said to have attacked the newly acquired Norman territories, in a determined effort to recover their rights, but were subsequently repulsed by De Clare and his troops, who just about managed to defeat the united Irish tribesmen. At the same time, back in England, Henry II was reported to have become increasingly concerned over the state of affairs in Ireland, believing that its invasion and colonisation by De Clare and his followers might eventually represent a threat to his own royal position, a threat that he was not prepared to risk. Despite having initially given his permission for the Earl of Pembroke to intervene on behalf of MacMurrow, possibly believing that the venture would accomplish little, by 1171 Henry was said to have been so concerned that he ordered all of his Norman knights in Ireland to return to England by Easter of that year. Unfortunately for De Clare, securing his new Irish possessions had unexpectedly delayed his departure from Ireland, causing him to miss the royal deadline and incur the English monarch's wrath. Stripping the Earl of Pembroke of his new titles, Henry II subsequently sailed for Ireland with his own English army, dispossessed many of those Normans knights who had seized lands there and put his own appointees in their place. Naming himself as Lord of all Ireland and having established his own authority over much of the country, Henry returned to England having spent some six months in his new kingdom, although many of his knights and nobles would subsequently have to return to Ireland, to help suppress a series of revolts and rebellions that would mark much of the period, including De Clare, who was said to have recovered the County of Kildare, only to die fighting there in 1174.

According to some historic sources, the 12th century Norman Conquest of Ireland represented the very first English colonisation of what was essentially a foreign country, preceding the later colonisation and settlement of Ireland by English forces by some three hundred years. It has also been suggested that the Norman's deliberately misrepresented the case for their invasion of Ireland, claiming that the native people there were little better than savages, who were not only uncivilised pagans, but also practiced cannibalism. However, it is worth noting that such blatant public propaganda was not unusual, given that the Roman's had used similar tales to justify their own military invasion of Britain in the 1st century AD. Regardless of such considerations however, the invasion of 1174 inexorably drew the kingdom of Ireland into the Norman sphere of influence and established that country as a fundamental part of the many conflicts and confrontations that would dramatically affect the development of the English, Irish, Scottish and Welsh nations for the following six hundred years.

It was thought to be during the thirty five year reign of Henry II that England once more became a monarchical kingdom, with day-to-day power being taken back from the Barons, Earls and Churchmen who had previously held control of the country; and put back into the hands of the king and his council. It henceforth remained a sovereign state until around 1194 when it temporarily became a vassal of the Holy Roman Empire, following the capture of the English monarch, Richard the Lionheart, who was returning home from the Crusades. Richard's royal successor, King John, was thought to be both an unfortunate and unpopular ruler of England, who not only lost many of his country's possessions in France, but so antagonised his nobles and subjects that he was finally forced to sign the Magna Carta, which limited his personal powers and authority, at Runnymede in 1215.

King John's son and successor Henry III ascended the English throne when he was only nine-years-old and as a consequence the kingdom was largely administered by his guardians and a number of England's leading noblemen. Unfortunately for the young king many of his more influential court advisors were reported to have French sympathies, which caused a great deal of unrest amongst members of the English nobility, resulting in Henry's reign being marked by internal unrest and fractiousness within both England and the neighbouring principality of Wales. Throughout much of his rule Henry was reported to be at odds with the rulers of France, the native Princes of Wales as well as a number of England's leading Barons, including Simon de Montford, the 6th Earl of Leicester, who led a rebellion against Henry and his son Prince Edward; and very nearly managed to steal the English throne from them. Fortunately for King Henry, his son and successor, later Edward I, managed to escape his captors, rally his supporters and together with his father later defeated De Montford and his allies at the Battle of Evesham in 1265.

King Edward I succeeded his father Henry III to the English throne in 1272 and began a period of consolidation for the English Crown, beginning with a widespread reorganisation of the country's administrative, political, financial and legal systems, which resulted in many new statutes and regulations being introduced by the astute young monarch. First and foremost however, Edward was a military leader, as well as being a skilled politician and what he could not achieve through bluff and bravado, he was quite happy to achieve through military force. Although he is commonly referred to as the "Hammer of the Scots" he was far less successful against that particular kingdom than he was against the native Princes of North Wales. A significant part of the principality was already subject to the will of the English Marcher Lords who had held power from the time of the Norman Conquest, but much of the north remained under the control of the native Princes of Gwynedd. During the Baron's War, which was led by Simon De Montford and his allies, these Welsh rulers were reported to have supported the rebels and despite De Montford's defeat at the hands of Henry III and Edward, they still refused to accept the sovereignty of the English Crown.

Richard de Clare   King Henry III   Simon de Montford

Finally and perhaps in frustration, in around 1276 Edward was said to have deliberately engineered a conflict with the Welsh Prince, Llywelyn ap Gruffudd, ostensibly over the Welsh Prince's intention to marry Eleanor de Montford, the daughter of the rebellious Simon, who had very nearly managed to usurp Edward and his father from the English throne. Although Edward was reported to have assembled a massive army to invade North Wales, in actual fact there was no major confrontation between the two sides, as Llywelyn and his supporters quickly realised that they had little choice but to accept the English king's demand for homage, for fear of having their homelands destroyed by the impatient Plantagenet king. Under the terms of the resulting Treaty of Aberconwy, signed in 1276, Llywelyn retained his lands in Gwynedd, along with his title of Prince of Wales, but lost many of the possessions that lay outside of his native lands, thereby reducing his power and influence in the region. For the next six years Edward was reported to have imposed English Law within much of Wales and introduced significant numbers of English colonists and supporters to the principality, much to the alarm of the native population. This simmering unrest was said to have been exploited by the Welsh Prince Dafydd ap Gruffudd, brother of Llewellyn, who was said to have been unhappy with the settlement he had received as a result of the Treaty of Aberconwy in 1276. Before long this general unrest had erupted into a full-blown rebellion, which was soon joined by Llewellyn and a number of other Welsh leaders, who initially enjoyed some degree of military success against the resident English colonies and settlements. Once again Edward was reported to have assembled his English army to confront the rebellious Welsh leaders, although this time he was said to have little intention of simply reaching an amicable settlement with them, but was instead determined to conquer Wales once and for all and bring the erstwhile principality completely under his authority.

Even though the native Welsh forces were said to have enjoyed the occasional success against English commanders on the ground, many of their actions were said to have been primarily aimed against the numerous and sometimes isolated English towns that were located either within Wales itself or on the border of the two countries. The Welsh rebellion was fatally undermined though, on the 11th December 1282, when Prince Llewellyn was lured into a trap by a member of his entourage and was killed at the Battle of Orewin Bridge. Although his brother Prince Dafydd subsequently took over as the leader of the rebellion, it has been suggested that was not as capable as his sibling and was eventually captured by Edward's forces in June of the following year and executed as a traitor later in the year. In 1284 Edward introduced the Statute of Rhuddlan, whereby the principality was formally incorporated into England, bringing with it English laws and administration, along with an increasing level of English colonisation and construction of Edward's "ring of steel", the series of English held castles that were used to keep any future rebellions in check. These greatest of these English fortresses, built at Harlech, Beaumaris, Conwy and Caernarfon continue to stand today as a reminder of Edward's military policies and his utter determination to crush the independence of the native Welsh people and to finally bring them under the control of the English Crown.

To the north of Edward's English kingdom, Scotland remained an entirely separate nation, ruled over by the Scottish monarch Alexander III, who was said to have paid homage to Edward, but only for those English lands he held with the approval of the Plantagenet king. Accordingly, Edward was reported to have had made no direct claims on Scotland up until 1290, when the legitimate heir to the Scottish throne, Princess Margaret, who was known as the Maid of Norway, died on her way to her new kingdom. Reportedly three-years-old at the time of her death, she was said to be the daughter of Alexander's own daughter Margaret who was married to King Eric II of Norway. From a purely English perspective, young Margaret's death ended any hopes of a planned marriage between King Edward's own son, Edward of Caernarfon, the new Prince of Wales and the later Edward II, who had been promised to the ill-fated Princess Margaret, effectively creating a union between the royal houses of England and Scotland. Although in normal circumstances Edward I would have had no further involvement in the Scottish succession, with the most obvious royal heiress now dead, a significant number of potential contenders now pressed their claims to the crown of Scotland and requested that Edward arbitrate the matter. Eager to renew the possibility of English sovereignty over Scotland, which would have been the case, had Edward of Caernarfon actually married the young Princess Margaret, Edward agreed to settle the matter of the Scottish succession, provided that the new monarch was happy to recognise Edward's feudal lordship over them. The various Scottish lords and many of the contenders for the Scottish throne were unable to give such an undertaking to the English monarch, but given that Edward was the nominated arbiter on the matter of the royal succession, they rather foolishly passed control of the entire kingdom to him, until such time as he made his final decision on which of the possible candidates should actually succeed to the Scottish throne.

Although a large number of contenders were thought to have declared themselves as the legitimate heir to the Crown of Scotland, in reality only two of them, Robert Bruce and John Balliol could make any real claim to that high office. After lengthy investigations and consideration, in November 1292 Edward finally made his decision in favour of Balliol, although the actual reasons for his final choice are still a matter of debate even today. It remains a significant factor that even after Edward had made his decision and Balliol was publicly declared as the legitimate heir, the English monarch constantly interfered in what should have been purely Scottish affairs and even saw fit to hear appeals on cases which had already been judged by the Scottish Court of Guardians who had governed the country so well during the royal absence. Not only did this cause a great deal of antagonism amongst the Scottish nobility, but also helped to undermine the position and authority of the new Scottish monarch John Balliol. Even though Balliol was crowned as King of Scotland at Scone on 30th November 1292, St Andrew's Day, right from the outset he was thought to have been little more than a vassal of King Edward I, who was reported to have taken every opportunity to both exploit and humiliate the new Scottish king, perhaps suggesting why Balliol had become Edward's choice of candidate for the Scottish throne in the first place. Finally in July 1295, a large number of Scotland's leading noblemen, frustrated and angered by Balliol's apparent inability to cope with Edward, usurped the remaining power of the beleaguered Scottish king and created a new Panel of Guardians, which consisted of twelve of the country's wisest and most able lords, who were willing and able to resist the growing demands of the English monarch. When Edward demanded Scottish troops for his military campaigns against France, his request was ignored and in clear defiance of the English king, the new Scottish Council signed an accord with Edward's French enemies, creating what would become the "Auld Alliance", a relationship that would bring Scotland into armed conflict with England on a fairly regular basis over the coming centuries. As if to reinforce their own resistance to his perceived sovereignty, Scottish forces were said to have raided the English border town of Carlisle, which resulted in King Edward attacking Berwick in a particularly bloody fashion. At the subsequent Battle of Dunbar, Edward's army effectively crushed their Scottish opponents and then went on to confiscate the Stone of Destiny, the coronation stone of Scotland and had it transported to Westminster in London. The ill-fated John Balliol was quickly deposed by Edward and taken as a prisoner to the Tower of London, where his family's coat of arms and regal insignia were physically torn from his tunic, creating the rather cruel nickname "Toom Tabard", an epithet that often brought howls of derision amongst Edward's closest allies, as they related to one another, how easily they had conquered and humiliated the Scots. Unfortunately for Edward and his courtiers, later events in Scotland would ultimately prove just how badly misplaced his early optimism had been, as some of Scotland's ablest warriors would eventually come to the forefront of Scottish history and prove once and for all that Edward's almost pre-planned conquest of Scotland was not going to be that easy, or indeed, something that would be achieved in his own lifetime.

King Edward I

Robert Bruce

John Balliol

By the end of 1296 and following the Battle of Dunbar, much of southern Scotland was thought to be under English control, although significant parts of the country, particularly in the northern areas were said to have remained largely outside of Edward's immediate influence. Unlike those Scottish lords who had chosen to swear fealty to the English Crown, in return for lands, titles and other royal favours, other noblemen such as William Wallace chose to fight the annexation of their country, conducting raids against English troops and foreign interests that they believed were gradually overtaking their native lands. Having achieved such a decisive victory at Dunbar, Edward was said to have regarded rebellious Scotsmen like Wallace, more as an inconvenience, rather than as a serious threat to his military stranglehold of Scotland. However, on the 11th September 1297, a relatively small Scottish army, under the command of William Wallace, Andrew Moray and others, met and defeated a much larger English force under the command of John de Warenne and Hugh de Cressingham at Stirling Bridge. The defeat of the English force was said to have initially shocked Edward, who was otherwise occupied in France, but ever the militarist he immediately began to plan for a second much larger campaign against the Scottish lords. On the 22nd July 1298 the two armies were said to have finally met one another at the Battle of Falkirk and although Edward's forces won the day, ultimately he failed to crush his adversaries, which resulted in Wallace and his allies returning in the following year to recapture Stirling Castle. Although there were no further major military engagements between Edward and his Scottish opponents, the next six or seven years were said to have been marked by occasional raids against English interests on both sides of the border, which were also accompanied by a gradual erosion of the nationalist support that William Wallace and his allies had initially enjoyed in 1297. By 1304 most of those nobles who had earlier lent their support to the Scottish cause, had come to terms with Edward and now pledged their loyalty to him, often in return for new lands and titles, or simply to preserve their own family's holdings. In 1305, the Scottish nationalist cause was further damaged by the capture of Wallace, who was said to have been betrayed by a fellow countryman and subsequently handed over to the English authorities, who transported him back to London where he was later publicly hung, drawn and quartered.

Following Wallace's death and with most of the Scottish nobility either bribed or threatened into compliance, King Edward once again left the government of Scotland in the hands of specially appointed Englishmen and a number of collaborative

Scottish noblemen. Sadly for Edward however, his long hoped for settlement proved to be short-lived, as in February 1306, Robert Bruce, grandson of the royal claimant in 1290, unexpectedly seized the Scottish throne and had himself crowned King of Scotland in March 1306. As well as being a highly astute politician, Bruce was also a skilled military leader and a pragmatist, this latter trait testified to by the fact that he chose to secure his family's holdings, rather than risk them in support of earlier rebellions, such as those led by William Wallace. However, once he had made the decision to break with King Edward, he eventually managed to rally the various clans of Scotland to his cause and free his kingdom from English control. Fortunately for Bruce, on 7th July 1307 King Edward reportedly died of dysentery as he made his way north to oversee the military campaigns being waged against his new Scottish adversary. Although Edward's body was taken south to London for burial, his son and heir, Edward II, was said to have remained in Scotland to continue the military campaign against Robert Bruce. Unfortunately for England, Edward II was nothing like the military leader that his father had been and having spent a matter of weeks conducting fairly fruitless operations against the Scots, he later turned south and travelled back to London, where he was crowned as the new King of England on the 25th February 1308.

Under the generally ineffective leadership of their new monarch, Edward II, English holdings and interests in Scotland were eventually and inextricably lost, as the much more militaristic Scottish leader Robert Bruce regained complete control of his country, leading his forces to a great victory over the English at the Battle of Bannockburn in 1314. Unlike his father, Edward II was not thought to be a great military leader, politician, lawmaker, or administrator, but rather preferred to spend much of his time communing with his favourite courtiers, or indulging in more mundane pursuits, rather than the jousting, hunting, archery and swordplay that might have been expected of a soldier king. In fact his reign was said to have been marked by a series of long running political conflicts brought about by his own inability to control the English nobility, many of whom readily exploited his inherent weaknesses, along with those who feared for the country's future because of them. Within the English Court itself, a number of England's leading nobles were said to have regarded Piers Gaveston, the King's long standing personal companion, as a major threat to their own interests and so arranged for his capture and murder, although Edward was thought to have replaced him soon afterwards, with yet another male companion, a young man called Hugh Despencer.

William Wallace   **King Edward II**   **King Edward III**

Surprisingly perhaps, Edward's stuttering and rather uneventful reign was said to have been brought to an end, not by a jealous male rival for his throne, but by his Queen, Isabella, who was reported to have returned from her French homelands accompanied by both her lover, Roger Mortimer and a military force with which to usurp her ineffectual husband. Although a relatively small army to begin with, it quickly attracted support from the largely disenchanted English nobility, who were keen to see an end to Edward's reign. Recognising the impending threat, the King was thought to have fled the capital, leaving his new companion Despencer to face the wrath of Isabella and her army, who quickly had the unfortunate royal attendant tried and executed for his numerous wrongdoings. Before long, Edward himself was in custody, charged with breaking his Coronation Oath and committing other wrongs and was ordered to be held in Gloucestershire pending his trial. Unfortunately for the ill-fated monarch, there appears to have been little intention of putting him on public trial, as he was reportedly murdered whilst in custody, presumably on the orders of Isabella and Mortimer, or possibly by one of the many English noblemen who Edward had previously offended.

With the fairly disastrous nineteen year reign of Edward II brought to a sudden end, his son and heir, Edward of Windsor, later Edward III, succeeded to the throne of England and began a fifty year reign that would see him regarded as one of the most effective and successful monarch's ever to sit on the English throne. Crowned King of England on 1st February 1327 when he was only fourteen years old, initially his new kingdom was governed by his mother Isabella and her lover Roger Mortimer as joint Regents, although in reality, Mortimer was said to have taken over the role as de-facto ruler of England. On the 24th January 1328, fifteen year old Edward was married to Philippa of Hainault at York Minster and in June 1330 produced a male heir, much to the consternation of Mortimer, who believed that his position as Regent was likely to become less and less tenable as the young Edward neared his majority. Mortimer was said to have grown rich and powerful through his Regency, acquiring lands and titles at the expense of other English noblemen and as a result was disliked and even despised by many within the English Court.

Mortimer was also said to have made a personal enemy of the young Edward III, not only by deliberately and regularly undermining the authority of the young King, but also because of his part in the earlier death of Edward II, actions that would not be forgotten, or indeed forgiven by the seventeen year old Edward III. In October 1330, supporters of the young monarch were reported to have entered the inner precincts of Nottingham Castle, where Mortimer and the by now pregnant Isabella were staying, broke into Mortimer's bedchamber, arrested him in the name of the king and took him away to the Tower of London. Charged with assuming royal authority over England, Mortimer was stripped of all of his lands and titles, before being sentenced to death by Edward, who refused all please for mercy from both Mortimer and Isabella. Within a month of the royal command, Mortimer was dead and Isabella was reportedly confined to Castle Rising in Norfolk, where she was said to have miscarried her unborn child. With this threat to his throne removed and the death of his father avenged, King Edward III now set about restoring the fortunes of his English kingdom to their former glories, as they had been during the time of his grandfather, Edward I.

Even though he had undoubtedly inherited many of his grandfather's better qualities, the young Edward III also shared a highly combative and aggressive approach to the subject of Scotland and ultimately suffered a similar fate to that of his ancestor, fighting a series of expensive battles that ultimately achieved very little and gave him few territorial gains. Ever since the death of Edward I, the Scottish kingdom had largely been restored and expanded during the reign of Robert

Bruce, later Robert I of Scotland, who upon his death in 1329 had been succeeded by his young son, David II of Scotland, who now found his own royal lands under threat from the demands of an English king. During the Regency of Roger Mortimer and Isabella, the two countries had signed the Treaty of Northampton, settling the earlier territorial disputes between the two countries, but this agreement had subsequently been repudiated by Edward III, inevitably leading to further conflicts between the two neighbouring states. Initially Edward's English forces had enjoyed some military success against the Scots, recovering the town of Berwick and beating a Scottish army at the Battle of Halidon Hill in 1333. Edward was even thought to have attempted to repeat his grandfather's plan of placing a member of the Balliol family back on the Scottish throne, in return for extensive land grants in the south of Scotland, although many of these gains and proposals were ultimately reversed as the supporters of King David II began to gain ground over the Balliol party and its English supporters. Despite the large numbers of English troops being employed in Scotland, by 1337 much of the country was back in Scottish hands, save for a number of heavily fortified positions at Edinburgh and Stirling. Perhaps recognising, as his grandfather had, the near futility of trying to conquer Scotland completely, by the beginning of 1339, Edward III was said to have changed his priorities in Scotland, from one of total conquest, to simply consolidating what few gains he had actually made up until that time.

Although Scotland remained an important target for Edward, he was not blind to the fact that France represented an equal prize for and danger to his English kingdom. The fact that Scotland and France were historic allies, under the terms of the "Auld Alliance", meant that England faced potential enemies on two distinct fronts, one to the north and one to the south. As well as offering political and logistical support to David II of Scotland, who was being quartered in the French Court, the French monarch, Philip VI, was also thought to have authorised a number of attacks on several towns along the English south coast and had already confiscated English possessions on the French side of the Channel. However, rather than trying to reach an accommodation with the French King, Edward was said to have challenged Philip's right of succession to the French Crown, claiming that he himself was the rightful heir and even went as far as to incorporate the French royal symbol, the Fleur de Lys, into his personal coat of arms. In the series of battles and conflicts that were fought against the French, which together became more commonly known as the Hundred Years War, Edward was said to have made a number of military alliances with individual French Princes and Noblemen, who all had their own reasons for opposing Philip VI. Despite such foreign coalitions however, Edward III was reported to have made few territorial gains through his military adventures, although he was said to have caused a great deal of unsettlement, both within his own royal court and within the English economy. As a result, in 1340, he was said to have returned to England to carry out a complete reorganisation of his royal administration, bringing some sort of order to the country, but singularly failing to solve the financial problems affecting his treasury, which caused him to default on the enormous loans that he was thought to have owed to a number of his most important investors.

By 1346 Edward was reported to be back in continental Europe, this time accompanied by an army of some fifteen thousand men and more determined than ever to pursue his claim against the French monarch Philip VI. Landing in Normandy, his forces quickly overcame the town of Caen and in August of the same year met and defeated a large French army at the Battle of Crecy, before moving on to besiege the port of Calais, which finally surrendered to him some 12 months later, in August 1347. Meanwhile back in England, an English force under the command of William Zouche, the Archbishop of York, was said to have resumed the military conflict with Scotland, meeting and defeating a Scottish army, which was led by King David II of Scotland, who had returned from the French Court, at the Battle of Neville's Cross and during which the Scottish monarch was taken prisoner. The unfortunate King David II would remain a prisoner of his English neighbour for the next decade, only being released in 1357 after a large ransom was agreed with the Scottish nobility, though in reality, very little of this money was paid because of the perilous condition of the national treasury. The restored Scottish monarch was to continue his rule until 1371, but without producing a natural heir of his own and on his death was succeeded by his nephew, who later became Robert II of Scotland.

Following Edward's capture of Calais in 1347, the Black Death had swept across Europe, decimating the populations of most nation states and bringing an end to most of the military campaigns on the continent, including those of the English king Edward III. According to most estimates, the Black Death was thought to have reduced Europe's population by between 30% and 50%, with the resulting shortage of manpower leading to greater demands on the native workforces and as a result higher wages. The height of the plague was said to be between 1348 and 1350 with most cities, towns and villages around Europe feeling the effects from the contagion. However, once the blight had passed most of the conflicts and territorial disagreements between the competing states of Europe began once again and King Edward's eldest son, Edward the Black Prince, was reported to have won a great victory over the French army at the Battle of Poitiers in 1356, where the English Prince not only defeated a much larger enemy force, but also captured the French monarch, King John II. More English victories followed, but despite this, Edward III seemed unable to achieve an outright military victory that would give him the French Crown. Finally, in 1360 King Edward III decided to reach a political agreement with the French Court, under the terms of which, he would renounce all claims to the French Throne, but would receive full sovereignty over those French lands that were already in his possession. This period was thought to have been the height of Edward's reign, with English military power unchallenged in Europe, the French king in his possession and with Edward proclaimed as master of great swathes of France's continental territories. Unfortunately, his dominance failed to last, as first, a number of his most trusted military lieutenants and advisors died, as did the French monarch King John II, who had remained in English custody since 1356. Edward's second son, Lionel of Antwerp unsuccessfully tried to suppress the Anglo Irish lords of Ireland and Edward's youngest son, John of Gaunt, was heavily defeated by the new French monarch, Charles V, who by 1375 had recovered virtually all of the French territories that had previously been lost to the English, save for the coastal towns of Calais, Bordeaux and Bayonne. Back in England, both Edward and his eldest son, Edward the Black Prince, were reported to have been indisposed during the period, leaving John of Gaunt in nominal control of the country, a highly divisive figure who would later play a fairly significant role in the government of England. During the following year, Edward the Black Prince, who was King Edward's legitimate successor, was reported to have died on 6th June 1376 and was followed to his grave some four months later by his father King Edward III, who was said to have passed away as the result of a stroke on the 21st June 1377.

Upon his death Edward III was succeeded by his grandson Richard II, the son of Edward the Black Prince and an individual who would later prove to be as divisive and as unpopular as his great grandfather, Edward II had been. Significantly, young Richard would also be the second member of his family line who would suffer the pain and humiliation of being deposed by his fellow countrymen, only this time at the hand of his first cousin, Henry Bolingbroke, the Duke of Lancaster, who would later ascend the throne as Henry IV. The reigns of Edward I and his grandson Edward III are thought to mark the clear divide between the Norman England of William the Conqueror, who regarded England simply as an adjunct to his European territories, from the independent nation state that would later play such a significant role in the development of Western Europe. Under the two Edwards, England, the English language and a distinct English identity began to emerge from the shadow of the great Franco-Norman dynasties that had dominated the country for the previous two centuries. Both men are thought to have been similar in their demeanour and in their interests, skilled soldiers who were politically adept, capable of great cruelty, but also of great generosity. Each of them was said to have been feared and respected by their subjects, although neither was thought to have craved popularity directly, but simply chose to follow their own instincts in helping to secure their kingdom for their immediate heirs. Both Edward I and his grandson were reported to have been instrumental in helping to frame some of the earliest aspects of English Law, particularly those aspects relating to criminal and property matters, helped to create and reform England's fledgling Parliamentary system and introduced some of the country's first national taxes. Both men also appear to have shared a common desire to bring all of Britain under their personal control, an objective that was only partially completed by Edward I, following his conquest of Wales at the end of the 13th century. Although it has been suggested that Edward I may well have been driven by a personal desire to replicate the long since disappeared Roman province of Britannia, with himself as some sort of Emperor, to many historians this seems highly unlikely. It is thought to be much more probable that ongoing border disputes between England and Scotland over territory, along with the "Auld Alliance" made between the Scottish and French Courts, may well have posed such a serious threat to the English Crown that both Edward I and his grandson Edward III felt compelled to deal with in the most direct way possible.

King David II   King Philip VI   King Richard II

Just as Edward III was thought to have shared many of the more positive attributes of his grandfather, Edward I, so his own grandson, Richard II, the son of the late Edward, the Black Prince, shared very few. Ascending the English throne in 1377 at only ten years of age and therefore in his minority, he was said to have been guided and counselled by a group of the kingdoms most able noblemen, who were all keen to avoid the young monarch falling under the influence of a single individual. His uncle, John of Gaunt, the youngest son of Edward III might well have been appointed Regent, but he was thought to be such a divisive figure within the English Court that a Council was appointed instead, although Gaunt remained a highly influential figure regardless. It was during these early years of Richard's reign that England was rocked by a generally large civil uprising, the Peasants Revolt, which had resulted from the introduction of three Poll Taxes between 1377 and 1381 that were intended to pay for a number of largely unsuccessful English military campaigns in Europe. Although the taxes themselves were thought to have precipitated the rebellion, the root cause was said to be the widespread restriction on labour that had been introduced after the Black Death swept across Europe between 1348 and 1350, effectively creating a form of slavery that was abhorrent to most poorly paid agricultural workers. Beginning in Kent and Essex, where tax collectors were said to have been driven out of various towns, large numbers of protestors were said to have congregated together, creating two entirely different gatherings in the two counties, both of which began to move inexorably towards London. During May and June of 1381 these two disparate groups were reported to have begun merging in the capital, much to the consternation of the young king and his council, who had few regular forces with which to resist the crowd, should it choose to attack the royal palaces. Throughout the city, many buildings, particularly those associated with the government and unpopular public figures, such as John of Gaunt, were reportedly attacked and destroyed by the increasingly angry mobs. Perhaps motivated by a belief in his own invulnerability or venerated status, the young Richard II was said to have ridden out with a group of noblemen, along with William Walworth, the Lord Mayor of London, to meet one of the leaders of the revolt, Wat Tyler, at Smithfield. Unfortunately, this meeting did not go well and Tyler was reportedly struck down, first by William Walworth and then by one of the king's royal supporters. Fortunately for Richard, these events were said to have occurred a little way from the main body of the rebellious crowd, so that Richard was able to convince them that all was well and that Tyler would meet them later in the day. Promising that all their demands would be met and asking that they reassemble at St John's Field, Richard watched as the crowd began to disperse and then ordered his men to arrest the remaining ringleaders of the rebellion. With the leadership of the revolt in custody, most of the rebels simply drifted back to their villages and homes, whilst their former leaders, including John Ball and Jack Straw were either imprisoned or executed. Confident that there would no further reoccurrence of these events, Richard II simply withdrew all of the promises that he had made and the much hated labour restrictions remained in place

Following the revolt and for the remainder of his minority, Richard was said to have become increasingly dependent on a relatively small group of personal advisors, most of whom were deeply suspect in the eyes of England's established noblemen. These concerns were undoubtedly reinforced after 1385, when the young monarch achieved his majority and began appointing "outsiders" and "lesser people" to positions of authority within the English Court, as well as trying to make peace with England's historic enemy, France. Although he was thought to have pursued a number of traditionally masculine activities, such as jousting and hunting, Richard II was not a soldier, in the same way that his father, grandfather and great grandfather had been, as he lacked the martial acuity and comradeship that they had possessed in abundance. In 1385 Richard was said to have led a largely inconclusive campaign into Scotland, but returned to England having never even engaged the Scottish forces in battle, a fact that further undermined his military credentials, especially as his kingdom was still threatened by the possibility of a French invasion.

In the following year and with the threat of a French attack still hanging over the country, Richard's Chancellor, Michael de la Pole, a favoured royal appointee who was deeply resented by the established aristocracy, requested significant tax increases, in order to pay for the defence of the country. However, the English Parliament, no doubt influenced by a number of the traditional Earls refused to consider any such request until De la Pole was dismissed from his post, a demand that the young monarch was initially reluctant to meet. Although he initially refused to be dictated to, when faced with the possibility of his own deposition, Richard was said to have eventually complied with the noble's demand and dismissed his unpopular Chancellor. Having been forced to bow to the will of his Parliament and a number of

England's leading Earls, Richard was said to have remained unhappy about the outcome of the dispute and set out to bolster his own personal support in the country, in the event that such a situation should happen again. He was said to have appointed another of his court favourites, Robert de Vere, as Justice of Chester and began to recruit troops there, most notably Cheshire archers, who would later form part of the monarch's personal bodyguard. When he returned to London, Richard was reported to have found the Earls of Warwick, Arundel and Gloucester waiting for him, with charges of treason against De la Pole and a number of the kings other appointees, who they demanded should be tried for their crimes. However, rather than simply comply with their demands, Richard was reported to have deliberately prevaricated over the matter, giving his ally, De Vere, time to travel from Cheshire with military support, although De Vere and his forces were subsequently intercepted at Radcot Bridge in Oxfordshire by troops led by Henry Bolingbroke, the Earl of Derby and the eldest son of Richard's uncle, John of Gaunt.

Realising that he had no choice but to accede to the Earls demands, simply because he had such little military support of his own in the country, Richard was subsequently forced to pass death sentences on a number of his favourite courtiers, even though most of them had already fled the country and so were sentenced in their absence. By 1388 most of Richard's unpopular inner circle had been removed from court and although the young king was said to have been particularly outraged at this challenge to his personal authority, he was thought to have been patient enough to wait and wreak his revenge on those that offended him. For much of the next decade Richard was said to have ruled the country in a generally harmonious manner, apparently putting past differences between him and his Earls behind him, even though they disagreed with his policy of trying to make peace with the French Court. In 1394 Richard had even led a military campaign to Ireland, in support of the Anglo-Irish lords who were finding themselves under increasing pressure from the native Irish chieftains there. Travelling with a force of some eight thousand men, the English king was thought to have managed to achieve some measure of success in Ireland, receiving the submissions of a number of leading Irish lords and refortifying some of the Anglo-Irish settlements that were said to have been under threat. Having seemingly consolidated his position in Ireland, even though this ultimately proved to be a temporary situation; and having convinced himself that his authority in England was now absolute, in 1397 Richard began to wreak his revenge against those noblemen who he believed had treated him so badly in 1388. Announcing that there was a plot to overthrow him, Richard was said to have ordered the arrests of Gloucester, Warwick and Arundel and in June 1397 put Arundel on trial, after which the unfortunate nobleman was executed. Gloucester was reportedly killed on Richard's orders in the port of Calais and the Earl of Warwick was reported to have been found guilty of the trumped up charges, but was simply exiled from England, along with a number of other royal opponents. Having cleared his court of any opposition, Richard was then reported to have moved his attention to the wider country, removing those retainers who were reportedly loyal to the historic Earls and replacing them with people that were entirely dependent on him for their new lands, titles and position.

Henry Bolingbroke

Hotspur Percy

Owain Glyndwr

Unfortunately for Richard, the one great political figure who still posed a threat to him was his uncle, John of Gaunt, the Duke of Lancaster and the youngest son of Edward III, who had his own legitimate claim to the English Crown and therefore represented one of the most powerful family's in the country. However, rather than confront his uncle directly, Richard was said to have used a disagreement within the Royal Court, between John of Gaunt's son, Henry Bolingbroke and the Duke of Norfolk to exile his cousin from the country, essentially removing Bolingbroke as a potential rival for the English throne. Although he was initially exiled for ten years, when John of Gaunt, the Duke of Lancaster died in February 1399, King Richard was said to have exiled Bolingbroke for life, in an attempt to remove the family from the line of succession forever. However, rather sadly for Richard, on hearing of his father's death, Henry Bolingbroke was thought to have requested permission from the French Court to return to England in order to pursue his claim to his family's inheritance. As a result, in June 1399 and accompanied by a small military entourage, Bolingbroke was reported to have landed at Ravenspur in Yorkshire where he was met by Sir Henry "Hotspur" Percy, regarded by many as the most able and chivalrous English knight of the age, who had come to fear and question the tyranny of Richard II. Having received Bolingbroke's oath that he only wished to regain his family's lands and titles, but would make no claim to the throne itself, Percy agreed to support the newly returned nobleman and together they made their way to London to rally further support against the king. King Richard himself was reported to have been away in Ireland at the time of Bolingbroke's return, so few of his supporters were present at court as Bolingbroke and Percy entered London, although many of those that were, very quickly transferred their allegiance to the newly arrived Duke of Lancaster, who they regarded as an entirely legitimate replacement for the increasingly unpopular Richard II.

When Richard did finally return from Ireland in July 1399, he was thought to have been met at Conwy in North Wales by Henry Percy, who advised him of his cousins return and the demands that he was making. Perhaps recognising the hopelessness of his situation, Richard subsequently agreed to meet with Bolingbroke at Flint Castle in August 1399, where the two cousins had their first meeting together. According to some reports, the exiled Duke of Lancaster made it plain to Richard that his situation was hopeless and that he had little support amongst the nobility, leaving the hapless monarch with little choice but to surrender his crown to his most immediate and legitimate heir, Henry Bolingbroke. Initially transported to Chester Castle as a prisoner, King Richard was later transported to the Tower of London, then later on to Pontefract Castle in Yorkshire. Although removing the deposed monarch from the Tower of London was said to have been to prevent royalist sympathisers from freeing him, there is also a suggestion that the ill-fated Richard was placed in an isolated location, where it was impossible for his supporters to determine his fate. Even though there was a reported plot to murder Bolingbroke and restore Richard, by those that the deposed king had promoted, ultimately any such schemes came to nothing, as he was said to have been starved to death at Pontefract Castle sometime around February 1400.

Despite his earlier insistence that he had no desire to claim the Crown of England, Henry Bolingbroke did eventually ascend the English throne on 13th October 1399, even though he was not the most legitimate royal heir that might have held that position. Edmund Mortimer, the Earl of March, was thought to have been the next legitimate candidate for the role, being the eldest son of King Edward III's second son, Lionel of Antwerp. However, by cleverly manipulating the rules of succession, Bolingbroke was said to have finally managed to convince the Royal Court that he was the legitimate successor to Richard and was therefore crowned as Henry IV of England. The chivalrous knight, Henry Percy, would ultimately regret the support that he had initially shown to Bolingbroke, as he discovered far too late that the Lancastrian leader had always intended to usurp King Richard II, despite the oath to the contrary he had given to Percy at Ravenspur in June 1399. In later years, Percy would come to oppose the rule of Henry IV and in 1403 was said to have met his death fighting the usurper king at the Battle of Shrewsbury, an encounter that was said to have been watched by the future Henry V, the son of Henry Bolingbroke, who would later try and atone for his fathers underhanded actions by having the earthly remains of Richard II transferred from the relative obscurity of Kings Langley and reburied at Westminster Abbey, to lie alongside his late queen, Anne of Bohemia. For the next fourteen years of his reign, Henry IV was said to have been a generally unlucky and unsuccessful monarch, suffering from persistent physical ailments, constantly refuting claims that his predecessor Richard II was still alive; and dealing with occasional plots against both himself and his family's claims to the English throne. Although there were only two significant rebellions during his reign, both of these only failed thanks largely to the abilities of his oldest son and heir, Henry of Monmouth, who later ascended the throne as King Henry V. It was Bolingbroke's son and successor, who was the next significant monarch to govern England, even though his own reign was a comparatively short on, lasting just over nine years.

Reported to have been born around 1387 at Monmouth Castle in South East Wales, the young Prince Henry was said to have been a highly gifted soldier who learned much of his military craft from the likes of knights, such as Henry "Hotspur" Percy and the other leading noblemen of the age. When his father, Henry Bolingbroke, was exiled by King Richard II in 1398, the young Henry of Monmouth was reportedly taken into the king's care and even accompanied the monarch on one of his many campaigns to Ireland. Like his paternal ancestors he was first and foremost a soldier and was said to have honed his military skills under the tutelage of knights like Percy, who were often called upon to defend England's northern borders from occasional Scottish incursions. According to some reports the two young knights were said to have been friends, although in later years their friendship was said to have become increasingly fraught, especially after Henry Bolingbroke's deposition of his cousin, Richard II, from the throne of England in 1399. It has been suggested that the young Henry of Monmouth rode with Percy to Chester in 1403, in the hope of persuading his friend not to rebel against the king, Henry IV, but failed to prevent the almost inevitable battle that took place at Shrewsbury on 21st July 1403. Prior to the military engagement Prince Henry was said to have returned to his father's side and along with his personal entourage, formed part of the king's army that faced Percy's rebel force across a field of peas, just outside the Shropshire market town. With both sides seemingly irreconcilable in their differences and numbering around the same amounts of men, by the late morning of that day, battle was said to have been joined by the two armies. According to some contemporary reports from the time, initially Percy's forces were thought to have gained the upper hand over the king's forces, largely through the use of Percy's highly skilled Cheshire archers, whose arrows were reported to have decimated the royal ranks and caused a number of the King's troops to flee. However, just as victory seemed to be within the rebel army's grasp, their leader Henry "Hotspur" Percy was reportedly struck down by an arrow fired by one of the king's archers, killing the rebel knight instantly. With their charismatic young leader dead, the rebel force were thought to have quickly fragmented, allowing Henry IV to claim victory and secure the English throne for himself and his son. Even during the battle itself, Bolingbroke was said to have been extremely lucky, as his heir, Henry of Monmouth was said to have been struck in the head by an arrow fired by one of Percy's archers, but fortunately, the king's surgeon was able to withdraw the projectile and save the young prince's life.

Ultimately, the Battle of Shrewsbury was thought to have been won and lost through a combination of both good fortune and sheer bad luck which affected both sides on that historic day. Bolingbroke, Henry IV, was fortunate in that the arrow that hit his son in the temple did not prove to be immediately fatal and that he had a skilled surgeon that was able to save his royal heir. He was also said to have been fortunate in surviving a charge by Henry Percy, which was directed at his royal standard and that resulted in a number of the king's immediate entourage being killed or wounded. On the other side, Henry Percy and his supporters suffered nothing but poor fortune on the day, a fact that resulted in their almost inevitable defeat. The rebels had hoped to have the military support of the Welsh leader, Owain Glyndwr and his troops at the Battle of Shrewsbury, but through a lack of communication by both sides Glyndwr failed to arrive in time for the conflict. Percy's own personal character also proved to be a significant factor on the day, as his own bravado once again got the better of him, resulting in him launching a head-on attack against Bolingbroke and his royal entourage, which in normal circumstances might easily have cost him his life. However, it was thought to be the rather foolish act of lifting his visor, to better see where his enemy was located, which would prove to be his undoing, as a stray arrow found its way through this gap in his personal protection and instantly ended his life and the rebellion that he was leading.

The Welsh leader Owain Glyndwr, despite being an opponent of Henry IV, was said to have failed to join Percy at Shrewsbury, principally because he was unaware of Hotspur's plans for the battle and was already engaged in military operations against the king's forces in Wales. The descendant of native Welsh lords from the border region of Wales, during his formative years Owain was reported to have been well schooled and was later sent for training in London, before being employed in the military service of the English King, Richard II. Seeing limited service with the monarch in France and Scotland, Glyndwr was later knighted by the king before becoming a squire to Henry Bolingbroke, although he was eventually to become involved in a political dispute with another Marcher Lord and fell somewhat out of favour at the English court. Initially retiring to his estates in Wales, the emerging royal conflict between Richard II and Henry Bolingbroke drew him back into political life, especially when the border county of Cheshire chose to support Richard II in the dispute for the English Crown. The usurper Bolingbroke was said to have stationed himself at Chester Castle whilst awaiting the return of King Richard from Ireland and whilst there was reported to have executed one of Richard's main supporters in the county, Sir Piers Legh. This nobleman's death was said to have caused such uproar in and around the border fortress at Chester that Glyndwr was either persuaded, or was simply proclaimed as Prince of Wales by a number of his supporters, immediately putting him at odds with the new king in waiting, Henry Bolingbroke, his former employer. Military confrontations between Owain's supporters and those loyal to Bolingbroke were said to have intensified during 1400 and by the following year, much of North and Central Wales was reported to be under the native Welsh leader's control.

Glyndwr's later military ally and the then Constable of Wales, Henry "Hotspur" Percy, was appointed by Bolingbroke, by then King Henry IV, to bring order to those part of Wales that were outside of the Crown's immediate control. As a result, Hotspur was thought to have promised an amnesty to all of those involved in the rebellion, save for the leadership, which included Owain Glyndwr, Rhys ap Tudor and his brother, Gwilym ap Tudor, both of whom were thought to be ancestors of the later King Henry VII of England. Despite the offer of royal pardons however, the rebellion continued and between 1401 and 1402 the Welsh forces were reported to have achieved a number of military successes over their English adversaries, including the capture of Edmund Mortimer, the Earl of March, a legitimate claimant to the English throne. For their part, the English authorities, rather than trying to find a solution to the rebellion, simply made matters worse, by passing anti-Welsh legislation, which simply drove even more Welshmen into Glyndwr's camp. By 1403 it was reported that many hundreds of Welsh born students, workmen and soldiers were simply abandoning their posts in England, in order to join Glyndwr's cause, a concern that was added to by news that French troops might well be brought into Wales to help strengthen the anti-English movement, as was said to have been the case in Scotland. The situation was thought to have become much more serious for the English monarch, Henry IV, in 1404, when Glyndwr gathered his Welsh Court at Harlech Castle and ordered that a Parliament be held at Machynlleth in Mid Wales, where he was formally crowned as Prince of Wales. Announcing an independent Welsh nation, with its own Parliament, Glyndwr was reported to have called for a return to traditional Welsh society, where historic laws, customs and traditions would be restored to the people of Wales. Thousands of the great and the good of Wales were said to have flocked to his banner and the new Welsh leader was even said to have set out a new vision for both England and Wales, which would have seen the borders of the Welsh homelands extended and England divided between the Mortimer and Percy families. Despite this particular vision being largely unfulfilled, Glyndwr's rebellion against the English Crown continued to cause problems for King Henry IV and his court, especially during 1405 when a formal treaty was made and signed between the kingdoms of Wales and France. Later that same year a French military force was reported to have landed at Milford Haven in Wales and subsequently marched through large parts of Herefordshire and into Worcestershire, before being checked by English troops just a few miles outside of Worcester. However, rather than the two sides engaging one another, both military forces were reported to have remained apart for well over a week, before withdrawing from the area. This rather curious confrontation was thought to have been the result of negotiations that were taking place between the English and French Courts, with both sides agreeing to withdraw troops from highly sensitive areas of one another's territories.

King Henry V

Henry Beaufort

Anne of Bohemia

Despite the best efforts of Glyndwr and his allies, to generate more support from England's traditional enemies, including the French, Scots and the Irish, little aid was forthcoming, save for individual privateers, suppliers and militarists who tried to personally benefit from the ongoing dispute. The rebellion was said to have been further undermined by a change of approach by the English Crown, which chose to employ the strategy of a tactical blockade on Wales, rather than an out-and-out military assault. Although the Isle of Anglesey was taken by force, elsewhere the English chose to starve their Welsh opponents of supplies, by employing a number of those English built castles still in their possession to isolate individual areas of Wales and prevent their local populations from transferring much needed foodstuffs and arms from place to another. Even though this proved to be a much more drawn out strategy from an English perspective, it was thought to have been effective nonetheless and by 1410 most of the former Welsh strongholds were said to have submitted to English demands, as the architect of the plan, Prince Henry of Monmouth, assumed that they would. For his part, Owain Glyndwr, the last formally recognised Prince of Wales, was thought to have continued to evade capture by the English, even though many of his most important supporters, including Edmund Mortimer, were either caught or killed by the English forces of Henry IV. According to some reports, the last time that Glyndwr was seen alive, was at Brecon in Mid Wales around 1412, when he ransomed one of Henry's leading Welsh supporters, but after that time no definitive sighting of the Welsh leader was ever made. In the following year, 1413, King Henry IV died and was succeeded to the English throne by his son, Henry of Monmouth, who was subsequently crowned as Henry V. Despite the lives and money that the Welsh rebellion had cost, the new English monarch was reported to have been very forgiving to those that had participated in the revolt, offering pardons and granting freedom to many of his former adversaries. As for Glyndwr however, following his completely unexplained disappearance, his name was thought to have been largely forgotten over the next four centuries, except amongst those nationalist groups that continued to celebrate Welsh traditionalism. However, during the 19th century, the name, life and achievements of this medieval Welsh patriot began to be openly celebrated by the wider Welsh public; and today he is generally regarded as the father of Welsh nationalism, with street names, parks and public spaces all recalling his life and achievements.

Because of his father's failing health, the young Henry V was said to have been given nominal control of the kingdom around 1410, some three years before he was officially crowned as King of England and along with his uncles, Thomas and Henry Beaufort, was already implementing royal policy well before that date. Officially crowned on 20th March 1413, Henry already had many of his own policies in place, by the time he ascended the throne, although not all of them were thought to be the same as his late father's, who was said to have bitterly opposed a number of his young son's proposed changes. Keen to correct some of the wrong's that he believed his father had committed during his reign, the young King Henry V was said to have ordered the body of Richard II be re-interred where it properly belonged, in Westminster Abbey, to lie alongside the body of his queen, Anne of Bohemia. Henry also tried, where possible to reinstate the lands, titles and estates of those noblemen who had been wrongly dispossessed by his father and even took under his personal protection, Edmund, the young son of Roger Mortimer, the 4th Earl of March, who had died during the Welsh rebellion. Even though he was thought to be an extremely generous and forgiving king, for those who chose to oppose or threaten his rule, he was said to have been merciless, as was proved to be the case in 1414, when he ordered the burning of a nobleman who he deemed to be dangerous to England. He was also thought to be the first English monarch to order that all government business should be conducted in English, as opposed to the Anglo-French or Latin, which might have been usual in previous years. Not only did he insist that English be used within government, but was also thought to be the first monarch to use English for his own personal correspondence, the first time this had happened in the three centuries, since William the Conqueror had first invaded the country. For most of his relatively short reign, England itself was said to have been settled, with no major outbreaks of violence or rebellion and the whole country, including Wales, seemingly at peace for the first time in many years.

Like many of his royal predecessors, Henry continued to assert his rights over the French throne, a claim undoubtedly strengthened by the fact that the French monarch of the time, Charles VI, was reportedly prone to regular outbreaks of mental instability and his heir was regarded to be generally ineffective. To pursue his longstanding claims to the French throne, in 1415 Henry V was reported to have crossed the English Channel and besieged, then captured the French fortress at Harfleur in September of that same year. He was then thought to have moved his army across the country to capture the port of Calais, but as they travelled across the French countryside, they were said to have been intercepted by a large French force, just outside the village of Agincourt on the 25th October 1415. Heavy rains, coupled with the local ground conditions, were said to have turned the local fields into quagmires, which proved to be death-traps for the ranks of heavily laden French knights and troops that attacked the English force. Accompanied by significant numbers of more lightly equipped English and Welsh archers, Henry was said to have used these men to decimate the ranks of French soldiers and horsemen who were increasingly slowed by the soft muddy ground. Those who were not struck down by the showers of English longbow arrows were said to have been hacked to death by the English men-at-arms, who attacked them from every quarter and offered no mercy to their struggling French adversaries. Henry's reported order to his own troops to offer "no mercy" to their French opponents was thought to have been both highly unusual and surprisingly cruel, given the prevailing military etiquette of medieval warfare, which would have been common practice at that particular time. Usually, those knights or fighting men who asked for quarter would be granted mercy by their opponent and either imprisoned or held for ransom, especially those noblemen who were thought to have extensive estates or wealthy families that would pay handsomely for their safe return. However, in this specific instance, Henry was reported to have ordered that no prisoners were taken, simply because their subsequent care and security might and would have represented a direct threat to his own army's safety. Although his order may well have been based on such concerns, it has also been suggested that Henry's orders and actions were also intended to send a message to his French adversary, Charles VI that he would be both merciless and unremitting in his pursuit of the French Crown.

Having defeated the French forces so decisively at Agincourt, Henry was then reported to have spent some considerable time consolidating his gains, replenishing his supplies and renewing his depleted and exhausted army. However, these plans were said to have been threatened and interrupted by the arrival of a Franco-Genoese naval fleet in the Channel, which threatened, not only to cut off his lines of supply and communication to England, but could also be used to land French troops to the rear of his forces, essentially trapping him between two enemy armies. In 1416, this is exactly what happened, when a Franco-Genoese fleet was said to have landed French troops close to the recently captured fortress at Harfleur, where they quickly began besieging the English garrison there. In response to this, Henry was reported to have sent his brother back to England to raise an English fleet that could disperse the Franco-Genoese naval threat. Having returned home to England, within a relatively short time, Henry's brother, John of Lancaster, was said to have mustered and provisioned a sizeable English fleet, which then set sail in August 1416 and within 48 hours had met and dispersed the Franco-Genoese navy, allowing the English garrison at Harfleur to be relieved and Henry's supply lines to be secured once again.

Following his emphatic victory over the French, Henry and his army were said to have remained encamped in France for nearly two years, patiently preparing for their next great military expedition, the conquest of France itself. Beginning in 1417, Henry's English army slowly but surely brought much of the French countryside, along with its major towns and cities under their direct control. Where outright surrender was not offered by the local populations, the English army would attempt to starve the French communities into submission, sometimes using tactics that further blackened the name and reputation of the young Henry V. The city of Rouen for instance, the historic capital of the Normandy region, which lay along the route of the River Seine, was said to have been besieged by Henry and his army during 1418, after the local authorities refused to surrender the city to the English monarch. As the days, weeks and months passed, conditions within the city were said to have become increasingly desperate, to the point where the French authorities in Rouen took the decision to expel all of the women and children, in the belief that the English troops would allow them safe passage through their siege lines. Surprisingly, Henry was said to have refused to allow the starving refugees to pass through his lines, whilst at the same time, the French defenders would not allow them back into the city. In a scene that recalled the earlier tragedy of the Battle of Alesia, which was fought between the native leader Vercingetorix and Julius Caesar, both sides were thought to have waited for the other to change their minds, but neither relented and as a result, all of the entirely innocent women and children were said to have perished of starvation and disease. Even though such incidents were later used to taint the reputation of the English monarch, it has also been suggested that both sides at Rouen were deserving of criticism, by choosing to employ completely innocent non-combatants as pawns in the ongoing war of nerves that were a feature of such medieval siege warfare. It has also been reported that Henry was determined to inflict his revenge on the peoples of Rouen, who had not only hung captured English prisoners from the walls of the city, but who had called for his excommunication from the church. Clearly though, such matters appear to be trifling, when laid against the indifference shown by both the English king and the French authorities towards the starving and dying inhabitants of Rouen, which should also be considered in relation to Henry's previous orders at Agincourt, where no mercy was offered or indeed shown to enemy troops.

Whatever Henry's personal reasoning for his military tactics however, by January 1419, the city of Rouen was reported to have finally fallen to the English troops who had been besieging it; and Henry was finally able to exact his full revenge on those who had refused to yield to him. By August of the same year, his forces were reported to be outside the walls of the French capital, Paris, where a number of its leading citizens and noblemen were thought to have thrown themselves on the English king's mercy. After a period of negotiation, they were said to have agreed to recognise Henry as the legitimate heir to the French throne and appointed him as Regent of France, settling the matter further, by arranging for Henry to marry the French King's daughter, Catherine of Valois. With his long demanded entitlements finally granted to him and with much of France seemingly under English control, Henry eventually returned to England towards the end of 1420, although he was thought to have spent little time there, being compelled to return to France some six months later, to begin what would be his final military campaign there. Reportedly crossing the English Channel once again in June 1421, to help suppress a French rebellion that was centred on the historic walled French town of Meaux, located just outside of

Paris, Henry called for the local authorities to submit to him, but they were said to have refused his calls outright, leaving him with little option but to mount a blockade of the town. Having besieged the heavily fortified town for some months, outbreaks of dysentery and smallpox were said to have regularly swept through the English ranks, although this did not prevent the siege from being imposed, or indeed proving successful. Unfortunately, Henry himself was said to have become the most notable victim of the dysentery epidemic and was reported to have died from the disease on the 31st August 1422 at the Chateau de Vincennes just outside Paris. The body of the still comparatively young thirty five -year-old king was subsequently returned to England and later interred at Westminster Abbey in November 1422. During his brief marriage to his French queen, Catherine of Valois, the royal couple had only one son, Henry, who would later ascend the English throne as King Henry VI. During his brief but glorious reign, Henry V was thought to have turned England from a divided and uncertain nation state, into one of the most feared and unified in all of Western Europe, protected and promoted by some of the most effective troops of the age, the English Longbow archers. Although he had undoubtedly achieved his own longed for goal of successfully restoring his family's claim to the throne of France, he was never formally crowned as King of these new possessions; and it was his son Henry VI who finally received the French Crown in December 1431. Unfortunately, for all that Henry V had done to unite his English kingdom and restore the English Crown's rights over France; much of this would be undone by the weakness of his successor Henry VI, as well as the rise of the iconic French heroine Joan of Arc, whose life and death would inspire her nation to rise up against enforced English rule.

Charles VI of France   John of Lancaster   Catherine of Valois

The infant Henry VI was only nine months of age when his father died in France, an event that was said to have been followed two months later by the death of his maternal grandfather, Charles VI, the king of France, thereby creating the young English prince as the potential monarch of that European kingdom too. As his mother, Catherine of Valois was French; she was said to have been treated with enormous suspicion by members of the English Court, who immediately appointed a council to govern the country, naming Henry V's brother, John of Lancaster as senior Regent in France, whilst another brother, Humphrey, the Duke of Gloucester, was put in nominal charge of English affairs. Matters were thought to have become much more complicated later one, when Catherine began an intimate relationship with the Welsh nobleman, Owen Tudor, by whom she had two sons, Edmund and Jasper, who automatically became half-brothers to the English king Henry VI. In recognition of their noble births, both of these two brothers were subsequently granted the title of Earl, through which one of them, Edmund, would later see his own son, Henry Tudor, ascend to the English throne as Henry VII.

Henry VI was reported to have assumed control of his English kingdom in 1437 and like others before him quickly surrounded himself with a small number of favoured nobles, often to the exclusion of some of the more influential and experienced aristocrats who had helped guide the kingdom during his minority. In the fifteen years since his father's death, his most trusted advisor in France, his uncle John of Lancaster, was reported to have died and French forces had been dramatically inspired by their young Maid of Orleans, Joan of Arc, who had helped to stifle English expansionist ambitions there. Under the influence of his less traditional advisors, King Henry VI was reported to have preferred a peaceful settlement with France, as opposed to those who were advising him to impose a purely military solution. English ambitions there and Henry's rule of the foreign country were being challenged by the increasingly powerful Valois family, ancestors of Henry's mother, Catherine, who considered themselves to have a greater legitimacy to the throne of France than the English monarch Henry VI did. In order to resolve the conflict between the two sides, a marriage was arranged between Henry and Margaret of Anjou, the niece of the Valois king, Charles VII, although the union itself in 1445 was said to have been highly unpopular amongst much of the English aristocracy generally. As part of the marriage agreement made between the two royal houses, Henry was said to have relinquished the English held regions of Maine and Anjou to the Valois king, but did so without confirming this to his opponents in England. However, when the English aristocracy discovered the truth, a number of England's leading noblemen, including the Dukes of Gloucester and York, were said to have been absolutely outraged, but were unable to do little about it. Recognising their vehement opposition to his actions, King Henry was said to have ordered the arrest of Gloucester, who subsequently died during his captivity and sent the Duke of York into virtual isolation in Ireland, hoping no doubt that their removal would end any further hostility towards the Crown. Unfortunately for Henry, the next few years of his reign were said to have been constantly dogged by allegations of corruption, uncertainty and unfairness, along with increasing losses of English interests and territories in France, all of which helped to erode confidence amongst the aristocracy that Henry would come to rely on in future years. In common with a number of his other royal appointments, Henry was said to have chosen his favourite noblemen to hold important posts, rather than those best qualified for doing the job itself. Two in particular, the Dukes of Suffolk and Somerset both proved to be disastrous for Henry, with Suffolk arranging his marriage to Margaret of Anjou and Somerset leading the English forces in France, only to suffer one military reverse after another. Eventually and no doubt under pressure from his Parliament, Henry was finally forced to remove the Duke of Suffolk and exiled him from the kingdom, although the unfortunate aristocrat ultimately failed to find a safe haven elsewhere, as he was reportedly murdered as he made the Channel crossing to France. Somerset proved to be equally unlucky for the English king, as from the date of his appointment in 1449, leading English military forces in France, he was said to have lost virtually all of the territories that Henry V and his armies had struggled so hard to win. At one point he was even said to have managed to lose French territories which had been held by England since the reign of Henry II, some two hundred and fifty years earlier, leaving Henry VI with only the port of Calais to call his own.

By 1452 many within the English nobility were said to have been seeking alternatives to the highly erratic and unfortunate Henry VI, with Richard Plantagenet, the Duke of York, who had been sent to govern Ireland, seen as the most legitimate replacement to the hapless Henry. Persuaded to return to England by a number of the country's leading nobles, Richard was thought to be a highly popular choice amongst the British people and quickly rallied significant numbers to his cause, although initially they chose little more than to demand the arrest of the largely incapable Somerset and the settlement of other outstanding grievances. However, despite his widespread unpopularity, Henry still managed to garner sufficient support to protect his throne and though initially inclined to grant the unhappy noblemen's requests, interference by his wife, Margaret of Anjou, caused Henry to quickly withdraw his agreement, a decision that was no doubt swayed by the announcement that his French queen was pregnant. Although in the short term it seemed that Henry had weathered the political storm, the news that the English held region of Bordeaux had finally fallen into French hands in 1453, was said to have crushed what remaining good sense the inept English monarch had retained. On hearing the news he was reported to have slipped into a mental malaise that would continue to affect him for the foreseeable future, even while his throne was being stolen away from him. His maternal grandfather, the French king, Charles VI, was said to have suffered similarly dark episodes throughout much of his own life, so many historians believe that Henry's mental infirmity originated from that specific side of the royal bloodline. Unfortunately, his indisposition was also thought to have been marked by a period of particularly significant political intrigue, with his closest rival and potential heir, Richard Plantagenet, receiving the support of Richard Neville, the Earl of Warwick, who was reported to be one of the richest and most influential noblemen of his age and who subsequently became known as the "Kingmaker".

By the time that Henry was thought to have recovered his senses at the end of 1454, much of the power within the kingdom had already begun to move away from Henry and towards the Duke of York, who was first suggested as a Regent, but then later as king in his own right. A younger son of King Edward III, Richard Plantagenet, the Duke of York, was to play a pivotal role in forcing the deposition of his relative Henry VI from the throne of England, in the series of Yorkist Lancastrian conflicts that raged between 1454 and 1461. Although Henry VI was largely absent from many of these military conflicts due to his recurring bouts of mental illness, Richard was said to have been opposed by the highly militaristic Margaret of Anjou, Henry's queen, who was determined to retain her husband's place on the throne of England. It had always been intended that Richard himself would succeed Henry to the English Crown, but the death of his oldest son, Edmund, followed by his own early demise, meant that it was his second son, Edward of York, who would eventually ascend the English throne as Edward IV in 1461. Unfortunately for Edward and his followers, they were reported to have failed to secure Henry and Margaret, who both subsequently escaped to Scotland where they found a safe haven and a base from where they could continue to fight the Lancastrian cause. Margaret particularly was said to have made use of those northern and Welsh noblemen that were still sympathetic to her cause, although her husband, Henry, was reportedly captured by Edward's forces in 1465 and transported to the Tower of London where he was held until 1470. In the intervening period, Edward IV and his main supporter, the Earl of Warwick, were reported to have had a severe disagreement with one another, allowing Margaret and her own supporters to strike a deal with the disgruntled Earl. Warwick subsequently lent his considerable military support to Henry's cause and having joined with Margaret to defeat the Yorkist forces of Edward IV, put the largely incapable Henry VI back on the throne of England in October of 1470. Unfortunately, the years of mental illness and the strains of being imprisoned were thought to have left Henry as a mere shell and it was thought to be Warwick and Margaret who ruled in the king's place. However, their hold on power was thought to have been relatively short-lived as their military forces were later defeated by the ousted Edward IV at the Battle of Tewkesbury in May 1471, during which the Earl of Warwick and Henry's son, Edward of Westminster, were both reportedly killed. The victorious Edward IV then simply resumed his position as King of England, ordering that his rival, Henry VI, should once again be imprisoned in the Tower of London, where he died in May 1471. It has been suggested that Henry may well have died of melancholy, having been informed about the death of his son, Edward of Westminster, at the Battle of Tewkesbury some two or three weeks before. However, most reports seem to suggest that Henry VI was in fact murdered on the orders of Edward IV, in order to prevent any further Lancastrian claims on the English Crown.

King Henry VI

Margaret of Anjou

King Edward IV

The military conflict between the two royal houses of York and Lancaster for the throne of England, which became more commonly known as the "War of the Roses", was a civil war that not only divided the English nobility, but also the general population of England and Wales as well. Under the sometimes chaotic reign of Henry VI, England was said to have become a much more unsettled kingdom, simply because of the monarch's poor choice of royal appointees, as well as his later and regular bouts of mental incapacity. Edward IV on the other hand was thought to be a much more stable individual, a skilled soldier, administrator, politician and businessman, for most of England's native population he would always have been the preferred choice for king, which he eventually became for the second and final time in April 1471. Having secured his throne, in 1475 Edward was reported to have declared war on France, although he quickly came to terms with his French adversaries after they agreed to pay him an annual royalty, on the understanding that he avoided becoming involved in the day-to-day running of the country. He was also said to have involved himself in Scottish politics, by backing Alexander Stewart, the younger brother of the Scottish monarch James III, in his claim for the Crown of Scotland. Edward was reported to have despatched his brother Richard, the Earl of Gloucester, along with an English army, to Scotland in 1482, where they quickly captured the city of Edinburgh and the Scottish monarch, James. Unfortunately for Stewart, his whole position was entirely dependent on him receiving the continued support of Edward IV, who had not only demanded lordship over Scotland, but also significant territories in the south of the country. Stewart also needed national support within Scotland itself, primarily from the great nobles of that country, who, by tradition could be extremely reluctant to change their allegiances. Although Stewart's position was generally secure while Gloucester remained in Scotland, the English Earl was said to have returned to England in early 1483, before Stewart's political negotiations had been fully completed. Richard of Gloucester's return was thought to have been caused by King Edward's sudden illness, which resulted in most of England's leading nobles making their way to the English capital, anxious to ensure that the country remained calm and that any possible succession, should that become necessary, was carried out as quickly and as painlessly as possible. Unfortunately for Alexander Stewart, the impending royal crisis in England was immediately followed by resurgent support for the Scottish monarch, James III, who was now able to fully contest his younger brother's claims, by force of arms if necessary. With the tide of events now flowing against him, Stewart soon found his position in Scotland becoming increasingly untenable and after Edward's unexpected death in April 1483, any lingering hopes that he might have held, of retaining the Scottish Crown were very quickly undone, once and for all. For the English too, Edward's initially successful foray into Scottish affairs had suffered a similar fate to those that had gone before, where initial English success had very quickly been undone by other unforeseen factors, although the one success they did gain from the whole affair was thought to be the ownership of Berwick, the border town, which the two neighbouring countries had fought over for centuries.

Back in England, the death of Edward IV was thought to have been deeply mourned by a large section of the population, who regarded his comparatively short second reign as a highly successful and peaceful period for the English people. Although supporters of the largely extinct Lancastrian cause, in the north of the country, undoubtedly celebrated his early demise, the possibility of him being succeeded by his 12-year-old son, as Edward V, held out the hope that these earlier national wounds might be healed once and for all by the ascension of an entirely innocent boy king, who might promise much for the future of England. Unfortunately for the young Prince, who would and should have ben king, along with his younger brother, their futures were not determined by any right of succession, but by the machinations of their uncle, Richard of Gloucester, the late king's brother, who had secretly determined that it would be him that would sit on the throne of England, in place of the young prince who he had sworn to advise and protect. Richard was the youngest son of Richard Plantagenet, the 3rd Duke of York, the nobleman who had hoped to replace King Henry VI as monarch, but who along with his eldest son, Edmund, had been killed at the Battle of Wakefield, one of the many conflicts fought during the War of the Roses. When Richard Plantagenet's second son took the English Crown as Edward IV, his younger brother, Richard of Gloucester was subsequently created the Earl of Gloucester and granted extensive lands and titles in northern England, where he maintained control of the country for and on behalf of the king. Throughout his brother's reign, including those periods when Edward IV was temporarily exiled from England, Richard was said to have remained loyal to his older sibling, even when the two brothers had had to flee to Burgundy, to escape the wrath of Henry's queen, Margaret of Anjou. Once Edward IV had been permanently restored to the English throne in 1475, Richard was said to have remained entirely faithful to him, showing no sign that he was unhappy with or opposed to Edward's right to hold the English Crown. However, upon his brother's death, Richard's loyalty to Edward's legitimate successor, the twelve-year-old Prince Edward, was thought to have quickly evaporated and those that publicly supported the young prince's claim were either isolated or arrested and subsequently executed on trumped up charges, brought by Richard. Appointed by the late King Edward IV as the two young princes Lord Protector, Richard almost immediately accommodated Edward V and later his younger brother, the Prince Richard, the nine-year-old Duke of York, in the Tower of London, ostensibly because of the supposed threats that were being made against their lives.

With the young princes effectively isolated and under his own personal control, Richard was said to have initiated a widespread public propaganda exercise, which suggested that Edward's marriage to his wife, Elizabeth Woodville, mother of the two young princes, was invalid and therefore Prince Edward and his brother, Richard, were not legitimate heirs to the English Crown. Further evidence was produced, suggesting that Edward had bigamously married Elizabeth, despite already being married to a Lady Eleanor Butler, who was still alive, at the time of his marriage to the prince's mother, Elizabeth Woodville. As a result of this highly questionable campaign and other rather spurious evidence, the two princes, who were still being held in the Tower of London, were excluded from the right of succession and Richard himself became the legitimate heir to his late brother. Shortly after his coronation as Richard III of England at Westminster Abbey on 6th July 1483, the two royal princes were reported to have mysteriously disappeared from the Tower of London, although most sources suggest that being of no further use to their conniving uncle, they were both killed and their bodies disposed of. Described and thought of by many, as a deeply religious and pious individual, Richard III's subsequent reign as King of England was said to have been marked by significant royal endowments to a number of important religious and secular centres, including York Minster and two major Cambridge universities. However, despite such good deeds, Richard was said to have been distrusted and even despised by large sections of the population, most notably by those who had been attached to the old Lancastrian cause and who had now been joined by those Yorkist supporters of Edward IV that considered Richard III to be little more than a murderous usurper. Regardless of such simmering discontent however, those who were opposed to Richard appeared to have no ready made alternative to rally around, as the House of Lancaster was thought to have been largely extinguished following the death of Edward of Westminster, Henry VI's son, at the Battle of Tewkesbury in May 1471 and both royal families were instinctively divided by tradition anyway. That situation had begun to change however in 1483, when the young Henry Tudor was reported to have made a pledge in Rennes Cathedral to marry Elizabeth of York, the eldest daughter of the King Edward IV, thereby uniting the two major political factions, which had previously divided the kingdom. This personal oath was thought to be acknowledging the generally known fact that the two, by now supposedly illegitimate, sons of Edward IV, who had been imprisoned in the Tower of London, were in fact dead by December of that same year. Tudor was formally recognised as a descendant of Owen Tudor and Catherine of Valois, the former queen of Henry V and was also related by blood to the Dukes of Lancaster, through to John of Gaunt, the youngest son of King Edward III. The English Parliament had legitimised the children of Owen Tudor and Catherine of Valois as early as 1452, so along with his accepted ties to the House of Lancaster, Henry Tudor was and became the most legitimate royal challenger to King Richard III and therefore an acceptable candidate for those who were opposed to Richard's continuing rule.

Henry Tudor's popularity in northern England was said to have been further strengthened by his Welsh heritage, with much of the principality being instinctively sympathetic to the long since suppressed Lancastrian cause, which had largely been stalled since the death of Henry VI in the Tower of London. Although some claims of Henry's lineage were undoubtedly exaggerated by his supporters, his obvious Welsh heritage was said to have helped him gain much support amongst the local population there and gave him a relatively safe haven from which to launch his military campaign against Richard III. Having received significant financial and military support from a number of disparate sources, including the French, the Scots, the Woodville family and many others, Henry was reported to have landed at Pembrokeshire in Wales and quickly rallied a large number of troops to his standard, including men from Lancashire and Wales. With this force behind him, Henry began his journey into England, where he hoped to meet Richard III in battle and deprive him of his throne. Despite being aware of this new threat to his throne, Richard was said to have been confident about defeating Henry Tudor and his relatively small force of rebels and foreign mercenaries. He quickly raised his own royal army, half as big again as Tudor's force and set out to meet his adversary, which he finally did at Ambion Hill, just outside the village of Market Bosworth on 22nd August 1485. As both sides faced one another, Richard was said to have been convinced that his much larger force would easily overcome Tudor's relatively small mixed army, although he was completely unaware that there was dissention within his own ranks that would prove to be pivotal to the outcome of the battle. As fighting broke out, a number of Richard's allies, including Thomas Stanley, the 1st of Earl of Derby, along with his younger brother Sir

William Stanley and Henry Percy, the 4th Earl of Northumberland all deserted Richard's ranks, either by switching sides completely, or by simply refusing to fight against Henry Tudor's forces.

According to most contemporary reports of the ensuing Battle of Bosworth, the loss of his allies significantly weakened Richard's military position, reducing his numerical superiority quite dramatically and giving his enemies a morale raising advantage over his own army. Despite this however, Richard was said to have charged almost recklessly into the fray, striking out at anyone that stood before him and attempting to identify and defeat Henry Tudor himself, in order that his death might discourage the rebel force and force them to yield. Unfortunately for the English monarch, it was said to have been him who ultimately succumbed to his enemies attack, being struck down in the heat of battle and thereby granting victory to his royal adversary, Henry Tudor. Richard's death at Bosworth was notable for several reasons, the first being that the outcome of the battle essentially brought and end to the English War of the Roses, the series of conflicts that had been fought between the great houses of Lancaster and York and which were only subsequently united by the marriage of Henry Tudor and Elizabeth of York. Secondly, Richard III became the last reigning English monarch to die on an English battlefield, joining the Anglo Saxon king Harold II and Richard I as the only three English monarchs to have ended their lives in that particular fashion. Thirdly, with Richard's death the Plantagenet dynasty that had ruled over England for well over three hundred years and been represented by some fifteen different rulers was said to have come to a rather unfortunate and less than glorious end. Reported to have been founded by Geoffrey of Anjou in the 12th century, the Angevin dynasty was the foundation of both the House of Lancaster and the House of York, both of which would inevitably become such bitter rivals for the English Crown in later centuries. Although the Plantagenet claim was said to have died with Richard III at Bosworth in 1485, he was thought to have been survived by a nephew, Edward, the Earl of Warwick until 1499 when he too passed away, although an illegitimate line of the family were also thought to have continued through the later Beaufort family. Finally and most importantly, Richard's passing was also notable, in that it facilitated the dawn of a new noble dynasty, one that would come to dominate England for the next century or more, the Tudor's. It was said to be the ascension of this particular English royal family, along with their notable heirs, who would finally begin the process of developing England's naval, military and commercial interests, into some of the most formidable that the world would ever see.

King Richard III   Henry Tudor   Elizabeth of York

Marrying Elizabeth of York at Westminster on 18th January 1486, Henry Tudor was reported to have ordered the creation of a new crest or symbol for the newly conjoined houses of Lancaster and York, the "Tudor Rose", a merger of the two historic symbols, which had once signified division, but now illustrated the unity of the two great families. In order to further strengthen his own hold on the throne, Henry VII, as Tudor would become, introduced legislation to limit the military power of England's great Baron's, restricting their authority and opportunity to recruit personal retainers, effectively preventing them from amassing private armies that might pose a threat to his own position in the future. He also made sure to settle amicably with any potential enemies, pardoning those that were prepared to offer him their loyalty and submission, including those surviving members of the Plantagenet family who might have been used as a focus for any future insurrection against him. Although his subsequent reign was thought to have been marked by occasional outbreaks of revolution, only two of these were said to have represented a potential threat to his rule and both of were quickly suppressed by the king. The first of these potential challenges was said to have occurred in 1487, when a commoner, Lambert Simnel, was publicly proclaimed as the Earl of Warwick, supposedly a legitimate grandson of the former king, Edward IV. In fact, the young man in question, Simnel, was simply being exploited by Richard III's closest heir, who Henry had previously created the Earl of Lincoln. The matter was said to have come to a head on 16th June 1487 at the Battle of Stoke, when Henry's English army faced a largely Yorkist rebel force under the Earl of Lincoln, who was subsequently killed during the battle, essentially bringing the revolt to an immediate end. The young man at the centre of the dispute, Lambert Simnel, was said to have been captured by Henry's forces, but rather than punishing the generally inept imposter, the Tudor king was said to have arranged for him to be employed in the royal kitchens, where he could be cared for, for the remainder of his life.

The second more serious challenge to Henry Tudor's throne was said to have occurred in 1490, when a young Fleming called Perkin Warbeck publicly claimed to be Richard of Shrewsbury, the Duke of York, the youngest son of King Edward IV, who had previously been imprisoned in the Tower of London by his uncle, Richard III. Although the young prince was assumed to have died in the Tower, along with his older brother, the missing Edward V, the fact that their deaths could not be completely confirmed, meant that such a claim might well be treated seriously. Having announced his supposed identity in 1490, the young pretender was reported to have sailed for Ireland, in the hope that he might gain some material support there, although his arrival and subsequent claims were thought to have met with little interest amongst the local population and he was forced to sail back to Europe having achieved very little. However, his royal claims later came to the attention of the French Court and more importantly to Margaret of Burgundy, a sister of the late Edward IV, who perhaps for her own reasons decided to officially recognise Warbeck as the real Richard of Shrewsbury, thereby giving the imposter a significant degree of legitimacy. With Margaret's connivance, the young pretender was then thought to have spent many months being escorted around and introduced to a number of Europe's leading noblemen, presumably in the hope that they might choose to support him in his claim to the English throne.

Warbeck was said to have attempted his first visit to England in 1495, when a relatively small foreign expedition was landed in Kent, but was immediately intercepted and routed by English forces, even before the pretender himself had managed to step ashore, leaving a significant number of his foreign troops lying dead on the English coastline. Retiring to

Ireland once again, Warbeck was reported to have sought aid there and was said to have been offered some support by the Earl of Desmond, who was already in dispute with Henry VII and therefore happy to help the imposter in his royalist campaign. With Desmond's help, Warbeck was reported to have temporarily laid siege to the English held port city of Waterford in the southeast of Ireland, but meeting stiff resistance from the military garrison there, he was said to have quickly retired from the area and travelled across the Irish Sea to Scotland and the court of James IV. Accepting that Warbeck might well be a legitimate heir to the English Crown, James was thought to have welcomed the young pretender and even permitted him to marry his cousin, Lady Catherine Gordon, who was related to James I of Scotland and to other members of the English Beaufort family. However, having attempted a brief military foray into England, which met with little success, James IV was said to have quickly lost interest in the pretender, who clearly had very little support within England itself. Forced to leave Scotland, Warbeck then made his way back to Ireland, but even there he was thought to have found little interest in his cause and within a week or so was being hounded out of Ireland, hotly pursued by an English fleet, which had been ordered to capture him and bring him back to England.

Fortunately for Warbeck he managed to reach the safety of Europe before being captured by the English ships and was thought to have spent the next months trying to garner further support amongst sympathisers in the various Royal Houses there. By September of 1497, he was reported to be ready to try yet another landing in England, this time in Cornwall, where he hoped to find support amongst the disaffected inhabitants of that region who had already rebelled against Henry VII some weeks earlier and been brutally suppressed as a result. This time his reception in England was thought to have been far more welcoming and having gathered a sizeable rebel army about him was ceremonially proclaimed as Richard IV by his new supporters before they began the march towards London. Unfortunately for those who had chosen to support his cause, as soon as Warbeck was informed that an English force, under the command of Lord Daubeney, was marching to intercept him, the young pretender was said to have lost his nerve completely and unceremoniously abandoned his supporters, leaving them to face the king's troops, whilst he made good his escape. Unfortunately for Warbeck, he was subsequently captured by English troops at Beaulieu Abbey in Hampshire and transported back to London to be held in the Tower, while his now largely leaderless army were forced to surrender to Henry VI, who ordered a number of the ringleaders executed and many other participants fined.

Having been held in the Tower of London, along with Edward, Earl of Warwick, the genuine nephew of Richard III, the royal pretender, Perkin Warbeck, was said to have successfully escaped custody, along with his fellow inmate, during 1499, although both men were quickly recovered and placed back into captivity. Warbeck was thought to have been thoroughly interrogated by the English authorities regarding his claims to the throne of England and it was said to be under this rigorous questioning that he admitted his true identity, of being the son of a French official and his wife, rather than being any sort of English royal heir. As a result of this subsequent confession, which essentially amounted to high treason, the rather foolish imposter was reported to have been dragged on a hurdle from the Tower of London to the public gallows at Tyburn, on 23rd November 1499. Having arrived at his place of execution, Warbeck was permitted to read out a statement, admitting his wrongdoings to the watching crowd, before being hung by the neck, bringing an end to his public claim to be Richard of Westminster, one of the Princes in the Tower.

Lambert Simnel

Perkin Warbeck

King James IV

Despite such occasionally serious challenges to his Crown and the fact that he had won the throne through direct military action, Henry VII was thought to be, first and foremost, an administrator and a politician, a man who much preferred to secure his kingdom's future prosperity through peaceful alliances, rather than fighting highly expensive wars. England's traditional enemy, France, was reported to have been extremely helpful to Henry in his claim to the English throne, so he was not therefore easily inclined to resurrect old antagonisms between the two nations. However, neither was he discouraged from using the threat of military force in order to achieve a better settlement for England in negotiations between the two countries, which he was said to have done in November 1492, when he sent a token military contingent into Brittany, simply to compel the French Court to conclude a formal peace treaty with him. Although King Henry VII clearly recognised the value of this early form of "gunboat diplomacy" to try and enforce settlements on the other party, so too he saw the need for a strong English navy that could be employed to protect his nations vitally important commercial trading routes. It was Henry who was said to have authorised and financed the construction of England's first shipbuilding dry dock at Portsmouth in 1495, reportedly the first of its kind anywhere in Europe and the oldest surviving dock of its type in the world. In conjunction with his desire to improve England's maritime strength, the Tudor monarch was also reported to have authorised a number of highly speculative and generally risky naval expeditions, all of which were designed to expand the English Crown's knowledge of and influence over lands beyond its own national borders. Employing highly skilled foreign navigators, such as John Cabot and others, Henry VII was reported to have granted royal charters to a variety of English merchant adventurer companies, all of whom were keen to explore and exploit the unknown lands that lay to both the east and west.

The emergence of English overseas exploration and commercialism aside, much of Henry's reign was reported to have been marked by the consolidation of his own family's position in relation to England's throne, as well as neutralising many of the political, economic and judicial problems that had beset most of his predecessors. As well as reducing the personal and military power of England's great aristocratic families, by appointing Justices of the Peace in every Shire and ensuring that national legislation was employed to curb excessive practices, Henry was also thought to have brought both uniformity and oversight to every corner of his kingdom. In addition to such locally based instruments of control, the

Tudor monarch was also reported to have also established the Star Chamber, a national court composed of Privy Councillors and Judges who would preside over matters relating to both Civil and Criminal matters that had been laid against the great and the good of England, who might in normal circumstance have avoided being tried by local courts. It was said to have been held in secret and although it did not call witnesses in person, it was said to have received all of the evidence in writing and handed out sentences that could not be appealed. Regarded more as an inquisition than as a Court of Law, the Star Chamber later evolved into an instrument of terror, rather than simply being a judicial tool, but nonetheless was thought to have done much to help reduce the historic authority of those noblemen who believed themselves to be above the law.

In other areas Henry was thought to have been equally astute, especially in matters relating to foreign policy and relations, which continued to be a cause of concern for English monarchs for many decades to come. Eager to cement an ongoing and equitable relationship with the Scottish monarchy, in 1502 Henry was said to have arranged the marriage of his daughter Margaret to King James IV of Scotland, an alliance that would physically unite the Crowns of England and Scotland in the person of James Stuart at the beginning of the 17th century. Henry was also thought to have agreed a series of treaties with the newly emerging Spanish kingdom in 1489, arranging for his eldest son, Arthur Tudor, to marry the Spanish princess, Catherine of Aragon, who also later became the wife of Arthur's younger brother Henry, later Henry VIII. Although such skilfully arranged marriages and alliances were thought to have helped reduce international tensions within Europe, more importantly they were said to have brought great financial benefit to England's developing economy and particularly to Henry's royal treasury, allowing the Tudor king to amass a personal fortune, which could only have been dreamt about by his royal predecessors. The only major setback for the king in the later years of his reign was the unexpected death of his eldest son, Arthur Tudor, who died suddenly at Ludlow Castle in 1502, leaving his younger brother Henry, the Duke of York as his heir apparent. Arthur's death was also thought to have threatened the alliance between England and Spain, and as Arthur's young widow, Catherine of Aragon remained the most suitable and obvious match, King Henry VII was still keen to unite the two royal houses through a union with his surviving son, Prince Henry, later Henry VIII. Unfortunately, the match initially seemed to be unlikely, until the king subsequently acquired a papal dispensation that permitted the marriage, although the couple were not thought to have actually married until after Henry VII's death in 1509. When he did finally pass away at Richmond Palace on the 21st April 1509, Henry Tudor was succeeded by his surviving son Henry VIII, whose later marital activities would help to undo many of the alliances that his father had built, but who would ultimately play his own significant role in the development and expansion of the English nation and the later British Empire.

In the fifteen hundred years that had passed since the death of Christ, the lands that had once been called Albion, had evolved into three separate and distinct nations, England, Scotland and Wales, which in turn had unavoidably been linked to the land of Hibernia, the island of Ireland. The native peoples of these four disparate lands had variously been subjected to instances of fire, flood, famine, drought, disease, military conflict and foreign invasion, as well as seeing their languages, cultures, traditions and heritage inexorably altered by the passage of time, the settlement of foreign migrants and the invention of new technologies. Beginning with their prehistoric ancestors, each of them had evolved into a sovereign nation state, which had been forged through natural events, human conflict and by the imagination and sheer will of individual men. Although Ireland and Wales had partially fallen under the control of English authority, by the time of Henry VII's death in 1509, the history and character of its native peoples remained unchanged; and it was these unique attributes, along with those of the English and the Scots, which would later be harnessed to create the uniquely "British" identity that would go on to spread its influence throughout much of the known and the as yet undiscovered world.

MARINERS, MERCHANTS AND THE MILITARY TOO

2. EXPANSION AND EXPLORATION

Britain's expansion beyond its own territorial waters is generally thought to have begun during the "Age of Discovery", which is said to have started during the 15th century, most notably with the voyages of John Cabot in 1497 and continuing with the likes of Drake, Raleigh and Cook in the following centuries. The seaborne exploration of the globe was said to have been preceded by entirely land based expeditions, from Europe through to Asia, many of which were led by Italian explorers, who were often privately employed by the heads of the various medieval Italian city states. The most famous of these explorers, Marco Polo, was reported to have travelled throughout Asia during the 13th century and became a guest of the great Chinese leader Kublai Khan. His experiences, many of which were recorded at the time as personal travel logs were thought to have been read widely all over Europe and helped to give the impetus for other north European adventurers to explore the wider, but still relatively unknown world.

As an island kingdom, which is surrounded by water on all sides; and with no direct land route to the European continent, British exploration of the lands beyond its native shores was thought to have been entirely limited by the naval technology of the age. Unlike its foreign counterparts, many of whom had ready access to the profitable eastern trade routes first laid down by the Mongol traders of the 13th century, Britain was generally thought to be a consumer of the rare and exotic products that originated in the far east, rather than a supplier; and it was only with development of bigger and faster ocean going vessels, which finally allowed British merchants and traders to explore the wider world, seeking out new commercial opportunities. Another major factor, which was said to have helped inhibit the widespread exploration of the Asian trade routes, was thought to be their domination by the emerging Turkish Ottoman Empire in the late 15th century, which was determined to protect its virtual monopoly of the valuable spice and silk trades, by preventing other competing trading nations from gaining access to these generally isolated manufacturing centres.

The first north European nation to attempt to break this Ottoman monopoly of the Spice and Silk routes were reported to be the Portuguese, who launched a number of seaborne expeditions, most of which were said to have been authorised and financed by their Prince, Henry the Navigator, at the beginning of the 15th century. Prior to this, the Portuguese, in common with most other northern European countries were thought to have been limited to trading within their own territorial waters, as well as in the more northerly seas, which had been known to them and their predecessors for generations. However, with the ascendancy and insistence of their ruler Prince Henry, Portuguese seafarers were said to have pushed out from their traditional trading routes, discovering the Madeira Islands in 1419 and the Azores in 1427, both of which they subsequently went on to settle. Despite these new territorial acquisitions however, Henry's main interest was thought to have been in gaining access to the highly lucrative slave and gold markets of West Africa, which were reported to have run through the western Sahara Desert and been controlled by a number of generally hostile Muslim states based in North Africa. By searching for alternative sea routes, Henry hoped to bypass these largely unfriendly Arabic tribes and still gain access to the lucrative markets of the Indian Ocean and the Far East. Having received permission from the Pope, to establish a trade monopoly on these newly accessed lands and market places, for his part, Prince Henry was said to have promised the Pontiff that he would ensure the spread of Christianity to the native peoples of these newly discovered lands, thereby helping to extend the church's influence well beyond its traditional European kingdoms.

King Henry VIII

John Cabot

Henry the Navigator

Within twenty years of having sent out his first ships, Henry's explorers were said to have discovered a new sea route, which essentially by-passed the Arab Muslim states and created a new trade in both African slaves and native gold, bringing great wealth to their country and their royal rulers. Later, more extensive explorations by the Portuguese was thought to have seen them establish new trading posts in what is now both modern day Senegal and the Congo by 1482; and within another five years they were said to have discovered yet another trade route, this time around the southern tip of Africa, giving their country free access to the Indian Ocean and its limitless supplies of spices, silks and much, much more. Portugal's Iberian neighbour, the kingdom of Castile, which later merged with the kingdom of Aragon to form what would later become modern day Spain, did not begin to explore the wider world until the latter part of the 15th century, although up until 1492 was regularly trading in African goods with the Moorish kingdom of Granada. However, following the conquest of Granada by the merged Spanish kingdoms of Castile and Aragon, virtually all of this trade was reported to have been lost, leaving the rulers of Spain with little option but to begin looking for their own new trading opportunities, much the same as Portugal had done more than half a century before. As a result of their need to replace these earlier trading routes, the joint monarchs of Spain, were said to have funded a number of expeditionary voyages, including that of Christopher Columbus, which they hoped might give them access to Asia from the west, rather than from the traditional eastern routes that were dominated by their Portuguese neighbours. However, rather than discovering a new route to the well known Asian markets, Columbus ultimately discovered a "New World", which eventually evolved into the modern day regions of South, Central and North America, which in later years would be fought over by most of Europe's leading nation states.

The Portuguese too had begun to look west at around the same time and in 1500 an explorer called Cabral was reported to have discovered and explored new lands in what is now modern day Brazil. With both countries seeking out new lands and trading opportunities to the west, there was always the possibility that conflicts might arise between Portugal and Spain, over who owned particular trading rights and lands, so in 1494 a Papal Treaty was agreed and signed between the two countries. Portugal was granted exclusive rights over Asia, Africa and Brazil, whilst Spain was granted control over everything to the west, much of which was still undiscovered, as well as the islands of the largely unexplored Pacific Ocean. Ultimately, the Spanish were probably the most fortunate of the two great explorer nations, as once they began to explore the interior of the Americas and most notably that of the modern day South America, they discovered a number of native Empires, including the Aztecs in Mexico and the Inca's in Peru, both of which they exploited for their treasures and natural resources. In exchange the Spanish "conquistadors" were said to have given the people of these great native civilisations European diseases, which ultimately devastated the indigenous tribesmen and led to their society's almost inevitable collapse and destruction.

As for the Portuguese, in May 1498 their mariners were said to have reached India and within a decade were reported to have conquered the region of Goa. In the west, around 1500, their seafarers were thought to have sighted the coast of Brazil, in 1501 a Portuguese ship was said to have discovered Madagascar, in 1506 Ceylon was reached and in 1507 Mauritius was first discovered by their seamen. Under the Portuguese monarch, Manuel I, they were said to have opened up new sea lanes and trade routes throughout Africa and the Far East, establishing trading forts and military outposts along the Gold Coast, Mozambique, Zanzibar, Mombasa, Calcutta, Goa, Bombay, Macau and Timor. Mainland China and Japan were also reported to have been reached by 1514 and in the following year they were said to have seized ports in the Persian Gulf region, thereby establishing a trading relationship with Persia, the historic name for modern day Iran. In 1521 the Portuguese were thought to have conquered Bahrain, beginning an 80 year rule there and in 1522 a ship commanded by one of Portugal's most famous sons, Ferdinand Magellan, was reported to have been the first vessel to complete a voyage around the world. It is worth pointing out however that Magellan himself was said to have been killed before this feat was accomplished and as he had previously taken on Spanish citizenship, he was therefore technically in the pay of the Spanish Crown, rather than in the employment of his native Portugal. These achievements by the two competing Iberian neighbours did not come without a cost however; and despite the terms of the Papal Treaty of 1494, the exploration of and discoveries made in the Pacific Ocean region was said to have led to almost a decade of squabbling and military skirmishes between the two nations, as they both fought for control of the newly discovered lands and the riches that they were thought to possess.

Although English merchant adventurers were thought to be rather late in launching their seaborne expeditions beyond their traditional home waters, the first of these journeys was recorded to have been commanded by the seasoned Italian seafarer John Cabot in 1497. Sailing west, Cabot was reported to have been searching for a fabled Northwest Passage that was said to link the Atlantic Ocean to the Pacific, but ultimately he only succeeded in discovering the east coast of the New World, at a place they chose to call "Newfoundland". Despite his failure to find the elusive sea passage, linking the world's two great oceans, this first voyage of Cabot seems to have given England's merchant adventurers the necessary impetus to launch themselves and their ships into the vast expanse of the Atlantic and Pacific oceans and to challenge the existing trading monopolies of their Southern European competitors, Portugal and Spain. Cabot was said to have been employed by King Henry VII of England in March 1496 and *"given free authority, faculty and power to sail to all parts, regions and coasts of the eastern, western and northern seas under our banners, flags and ensigns, with five ships or vessels of whatever burden and quality they may be; and with so many and with such mariners and men as they may wish to take with them, in the said ships and at their own proper cost. We further charge them to find, discover and investigate whatsoever islands, countries, regions and provinces of heathens and infidels in whatever part of the world, which before this time was unknown to all Christians"*

Christopher Columbus   King Manuel I   Ferdinand Magellan

According to some sources, Henry's decision to employ men like Cabot was as a result of the Treaty of Tordesillas of 1494, which had been authorised by the Pope and which had divided the globe between Portugal and Spain. Having received his Royal Warrant, Cabot was said to have travelled to Bristol, at that time England's second largest seaport, where he hoped to find additional financial backers for his expedition and by May 1497 was reported to have found a number of interested merchant adventurers and set sail with them on the ship "Matthew". Sailing due west, past Ireland and into the Atlantic, the Matthew and its crew were thought to have encountered few real problems and according to most reports were thought to have reached land on June 24th 1497, although exactly where they landed is still a matter of some debate, more than 500 years later. Depending on whose accounts you prefer, the Matthew was said to have landed its crew at St John's in Newfoundland, in Nova Scotia, Labrador or possibly at Maine in the United States, although according to both Canadian and British official accounts, the crew first came ashore at Cape Bonavista in modern day Newfoundland. Whichever place is right however, most sources agree that this landing was thought to be the first time that North Europeans had set foot on American soil since the age of the Vikings. Landing only to take on fresh supplies of food and water, Cabot and his companions were said to have formally claimed these new lands for King Henry VII and the Holy See, before embarking aboard the Matthew once again to map the coastline of these new territories. Having completed this task, the crew were then reported to have set a course for home, content that their first expedition had been entirely successful, although poor navigation on the return leg of the journey resulted in them landing at Brittany in France, rather than their home port of Bristol, which they finally reached in August 1497.

Cabot was said to have undertaken a second maritime expedition in May 1498, this time with a fleet of five ships, although according to some sources, this journey was largely unsuccessful, with one ship damaged during a storm and forced into an Irish port, whilst the remaining four, including Cabot's own vessel were reported to have been lost in the Atlantic. However, other reporters suggest that Cabot and his remaining ships actually did make a second successful landing in North America; and then spent the next year or so exploring the interior of the country, before returning home to England in 1499. Although there is some uncertainty as to whether or not Cabot actually returned to England in 1499, the fact that his pension was still being paid up until that year, suggests that he did indeed complete the return journey, but died in England a short time later. Although Cabot has long been credited with being the first Northern European to set foot in North America since the age of the Viking's, the first Englishman to achieve that feat is thought to be a merchant adventurer called William Weston, a contemporary of Cabot's, who was reported to have led an expedition to the Americas in 1499, once again supported by the English monarch Henry VII. England was not alone is reaching out beyond its own shores, as the Age of Discovery also saw the emergence of both French and Dutch influence throughout the wider world, who like England, were equally anxious to acquire new lands and free access to the new foreign markets. As well as exploring the vastness of the largely undiscovered Pacific Ocean, these three leading European nations were said to have taken the lead in challenging Spain and Portugal's trading monopolies in and around the Indian Ocean; and as they grew in strength and influence, so the former two trading superpowers saw their power wane. This was thought to have been especially true of the Portuguese, who found their historically valuable holdings constantly threatened and reduced by the growing maritime and military strength of the English, French and Dutch Empires.

England's first steps towards what would later become a worldwide Empire is thought to have its foundations during the reign of King Henry VIII, the monarch who is widely credited with creating the basis for England's first professional navy, which would ultimately play such a pivotal role in the early development of what would eventually become the all powerful British Empire. No doubt brought about by Henry's own decision making processes, which were based almost entirely on his own personal whims and desires, he was thought to have had little choice, but to have his kingdom sink or swim in its dealings with the wider world and especially those countries that were allied to the church in Rome, most notably Spain and Portugal. Even after Henry's own death, the antipathy between England and her two main European rivals, France and Spain, along with their mother church did not abate, but in fact worsened, following the execution of the Roman Catholic monarch Mary Queen of Scots, by the English Queen, Elizabeth I. This act alone was thought to have set the seal on centuries of conflict between the two states, which England would eventually win, but only by becoming the leading sea power of the age. It was also thought to be through this need for a strong naval deterrent, which saw the inexorable rise of the professional English seafarer, rather than the wealthy amateur, men who saw the world as a mysterious place; and were determined to discover its untold riches, for the good of England; and of course, for their own personal enrichment.

One of those early leading adventurers that helped to forge England's maritime reputation during the 16th century was said to have been Sir Francis Drake, who was born at Tavistock in Devon in 1540 and who died off the coast of Panama in 1596. He was variously described as a Sea Captain, Privateer, Explorer and Slave Trader, as well as being a leading political figure of the Elizabethan era. Regarded by the Spanish as little more than a common pirate, who regularly raided their treasure ships that were crossing the Atlantic, to and from the New World, Drake was generally seen by the English populace as a heroic sea commander, who was deservedly knighted by Queen Elizabeth I in 1581. However, according to other sources, Drake's military actions against Spanish interests were reported to be as the result of the personal antipathy he felt towards Spain generally, rather than the more obvious and far simpler patriotic fervour that has sometimes been attributed to him. According to some historic reporters, Drake had first visited the New World in 1563 and five years later, on an entirely separate raiding expedition, he and his men had been trapped by the Spanish forces that were stationed there. Although it isn't entirely clear, exactly what happened to affect him so badly, but it was said to be after this incident that Drake's personal feelings towards his Spanish adversaries radically changed, turning from a simple dislike, to an intense burning hatred.

In 1572 Drake was reported to have led yet another raid against the Spanish Main, the historic name for modern day Panama, the place where the Spaniards loaded their looted gold, silver and other treasures onto galleons that were destined for Spain. His attack on the base was initially a success, but sheer bad luck, illness and bad weather all conspired to snatch defeat from the jaws of victory, leaving Drake and a large part of his crew fortunate to escape with their lives, let alone a portion of the Spanish treasure. It was only through Drake's daring leadership and natural seamanship that he and crew were able to rejoin their ship and sail back to England, with enough treasure to make them all wealthy men. Five years later, in 1577, Drake was reported to have undertaken yet another naval expedition, this time against the Spanish holdings on the Pacific west coast of South America. Landing first at San Julian, now in modern day Argentina, Drake and his three surviving ships were thought to have remained ashore for a significant period of time, before setting out for the Magellan Straits at the southern tip of South America. However, by the time his small flotilla had made its way into the Pacific Ocean, only his own ship, The Pelican, was fit enough to continue the voyage and so, renaming it the Golden Hind, he sailed north along the west coast of the New World, attacking Spanish ports and bases along the way, relieving them of their stores and treasure. It was said to be during this particular raiding campaign that Drake attacked and sacked the Spanish port of Valparaiso in modern day Chile, capturing two Spanish treasure ships, one of which, the Caca Fuego, was reported to have been laden down with gold, silver and jewels destined for Spain's national treasury.

With the Golden Hind loaded down with the stolen Spanish treasure, Drake was then said to have headed west across the Pacific, stopping first at the Molucca's Islands, now Indonesia, before beginning the slow and exhausting journey towards the east coast of Africa. Having rounded the Cape of Good Hope, the Golden Hind was reported to have stopped once more, this time in Sierra Leone, where Drake and his crew were reported in July 1580. Within a matter of weeks however, they were said to have been back on English soil, with an enormous bounty for the Queen's treasury, one that was said to have equalled the Crown's entire income from all other sources and enhancing Drake's personal reputation throughout the country. Awarded a knighthood by Queen Elizabeth I, ostensibly for being the first English sea commander to successfully circumnavigate the globe, Drake was now such a wealthy and influential figure in England that he was thought to have purchased Buckland Abbey in Devon and settled down to become a leading politician of the age. Unfortunately, despite his hopes for a much quieter personal life, in 1585 he was reported to have been drawn back to the sea, following the outbreak of war between England and Spain, which saw the highly experienced Drake returning to the Americas and attacking the various Spanish possessions there. He was reported to have sacked the ports of Santo Domingo and Cartagena and on his way back to England also captured the Spanish fort of San Augustin in Florida, actions which were thought to have encouraged the outraged King Philip of Spain to plan for the full-scale military invasion of England.

Elizabeth and her closest advisers were said to have been fully aware of the Spanish plans for the invasion of her kingdom by sea; and in a daring move Drake and his ships were reported to have sailed into both Cadiz and La Coruna, two of

Spain's main shipping ports and destroyed a large number of the military and supply vessels that were being prepared for the attack on England. Although these pre-emptive raids did not stop the Spaniard's preparations for the invasion of England, they did however, delay the threat for well over a year, giving the English navy time to prepare for the battle that was to come. In the meantime, English commanders like Drake were reported to have continuously patrolled along the Iberian coastline, seeking out, seizing and often destroying any Spanish controlled vessels that they happened to come across. The two fleets would eventually meet in battle in July 1588, with the English forces commanded by Lord Howard of Effingham and with Drake's own ships in close attendance. Although there was no out-and-out sea battle as such, a combination of good fortune, poor weather conditions and the smaller, much more manoeuvrable English ships helped Elizabeth's fleet to disperse the Spanish galleons, essentially putting an end to any invasion plans that King Philip may have held. In the year following the defeat of the Armada, Drake and Sir John Norrey's were thought to have been ordered to hunt down and destroy any surviving Spanish ships that remained at sea, a task that they were more than happy to perform. By 1595 Drake was said to have returned to the Americas, where once again he began raiding any and all Spanish interests that he came across in the region. Less successful than in earlier times, Drake was reported to have suffered at least two notable defeats during his final expedition, at both San Juan and Puerto Rico, which may have been as the result of his own failing health. In 1596, while his ship was anchored off the coast of Porto Belo in Panama, Drake was thought to have been struck down by a severe case of dysentery from which he subsequently perished. Perhaps typically of the man, before breathing his last, he was said to have insisted that he was to be buried at sea and in full fighting armour, with his body being placed within a lead coffin and buried off the coast of Panama.

Drake was also reported to have played a minor part in the first attempted British settlement of America in around 1585, although his role seems to have been limited to helping with the evacuation of the colony's surviving settlers, during one of his intermittent raids against the Spanish ports and bases in the region. It was actually thought to be his fellow Englishman and explorer, Sir Walter Raleigh, who was the main driving force behind the colonisation of Roanoke Island in 1585, a small islet located off the coast of modern day North Carolina. The man in overall charge of the expedition, Sir Richard Grenville, a relative of Raleigh's, was said to have appointed a Master Ralph Lane to take charge of the new settlement, while he, Drake and the rest of the fleet returned to England. The intention seems to have been that Grenville and a supply ship would return on a regular basis to bring new settlers and provisions to the Roanoke Colony, but war with Spain had prevented this from happening and the colony was eventually abandoned by the English settlers. Fortunately for those that did manage to survive the fairly arduous conditions, Drake was said to have been campaigning in the region and was able to rescue them from their perilous situation and return them to England aboard his own ships. However, despite the failure of this first English colony and the obvious hardships that future settlers were likely to face, in 1587 Grenville was said to have tried once again to establish an English colony on Roanoke, on much the same basis as the first. Sometime after this second colony had been established, a member of the community was said to have returned to England, with the intention of bringing back much needed supplies to the settlement, but once again their return was said to have been delayed by a shortage of ships, most of which were being used in the ongoing war with Spain, so no contact with the Roanoke colony was made until 1590, when the whole settlement was found to be deserted, with no trace of the inhabitants ever being found. Although it was suggested that the colonists may well have left the island through their own choice, no conclusive evidence of their fate was ever found and they eventually became known as the "Lost Colony" a title which continues through to the modern day.

Francis Drake   Richard Grenville   John Hawkins

Although Walter Raleigh is often regarded as one of England's most successful Elizabethan seafarers, in reality most of his naval expeditions ultimately proved to be failures and it was his own personal involvement in the courtly politics of the day that not only made him a leading figure of the age, but also led to his unpopularity and relatively early death. Born sometime around 1553 in Devon, Raleigh was said to have been the youngest of five sons born to Catherine Champernowne, who was also the mother of yet another notable Elizabethan mariner and explorer, Humphrey Gilbert, making the two men half brothers. Brought up as an ardent Protestant, Raleigh was said to have developed a hatred of the Roman Catholic religion during his formative years, creating a personal intolerance that would shape his future dealings with the majority population of Ireland during the latter part of the 16th century when Raleigh was posted to Ireland during the Desmond Rebellions of the early 1580's. He was alleged to have played a major part in the massacre of unarmed Italian and Spanish troops in Ireland following the Siege of Smerwick in 1580, where some several hundred papal soldiers and Irish Roman Catholics were systematically beheaded by English forces, before their decapitated bodies were thrown into the sea. As a reward for his service in Ireland, Raleigh was reported to have been granted several thousand acres of land in Munster, although his inability to attract sufficient numbers of English settlers there was thought to have resulted in the property remaining unprofitable, to the point that in 1602, he was said to have sold the properties to Richard Boyle, the 1st Earl of Cork.

As previously mentioned, in both 1584 and 1587, Raleigh was said to have been the main driving force behind early English attempts to colonise the New World, specifically in the region that was then known as Virginia, now represented by the modern day American states of Virginia and North Carolina. Both of these unsuccessful English colonies were centred on Roanoke Island, off the eastern seaboard of North America, although each of them in turn were thought to have failed to survive, largely due to the hardship of the terrain, the ferocity of the local tribes and the inability of the settlers to fully adapt to life in the Americas. Ultimately, the failure of what later became known as "The Lost Colony" of Roanoke was said to have proved to be costly for Raleigh, not only financially, but also for his general reputation, although as a personal favourite of the English monarch, Queen Elizabeth I, the failure of these expeditions were not thought to have hurt his standing at court. Awarded several titles by the monarch, Raleigh was said to have become a significant figure of the age, both as a Member of Parliament and as a military officer, being appointed as Vice Admiral in two separate counties, Lord Lieutenant of Cornwall and Warden of all the mines within Cornwall and Devon. No doubt as a result of his well paid and prestigious appointments, Raleigh was said to have personally commissioned the construction of a brand new warship called the "Ark Raleigh", which was later purchased by the Crown and renamed as the "Ark Royal", a famous name which has been carried by several vessels within the Royal Navy, from the time of Queen Elizabeth I, right through to the modern day.

In 1588, the year of the Spanish Armada, unlike Drake, Frobisher, Newport and Adams, who were preparing to defend England at sea, Sir Walter Raleigh was reportedly ordered to organise the kingdom's southern coastal defences, in readiness for the planned Spanish barges and ships that were expected to try and land on England's shores. However, thanks largely to good fortune and bad weather the great Spanish fleet ultimately failed to safely navigate its way through the English Channel and collect the thousands of Spanish troops, which had been assembled to attack England. With Elizabeth's kingdom safe; with the Spanish Armada largely dispersed and the English fleet victorious, at least in the short term, life in the English Court was reported to have returned to normal, with Walter Raleigh resuming his role as a favourite of the increasingly confident Tudor Queen. Unfortunately for Raleigh, his later romantic entanglement with one of Elizabeth's own ladies in waiting contrived to rob him of his most favoured status, especially after Raleigh secretly married, Elizabeth Trockmorton, without having first obtained the permission of the Queen, who was said to have been so outraged by the secret and unauthorised marriage that she dismissed Bess Throckmorton from her court and ordered Raleigh to be imprisoned for his deliberate transgression. Although he was subsequently released from prison on Elizabeth's order, Raleigh remained out of favour at court and so contented himself with managing his vast estates and involving himself in English politics, as well as settling down to raise his and Bess' two young sons. However, in 1594, Raleigh was reported to have come into possession of a written account about a golden city called Manoa, which was said to have been located in the region of South America, now marked by the modern day states of Guyana and Venezuela, causing him to travel to the Americas in pursuit of this mythical "El Dorado". Unfortunately, having spent some time there and uncovered no conclusive evidence relating to the mythical golden city, Raleigh was said to have returned home to simply write about his great adventures in these faraway lands, reportedly helping to create the myth of the city of El Dorada, which thousands of treasure seekers would pursue over succeeding centuries. Back in England though, he was said to have returned to royal favour, being appointed as the Governor of Jersey where he set about refortifying the island's defences and building a new defensive fortress, Elizabeth Castle, although as his work there came to an inevitable end, Queen Elizabeth I was reported to have died, leaving Raleigh with little if any support in the English court and made him susceptible to the scheming of those courtiers who had envied him his apparent closeness to the former Tudor queen. Elizabeth's royal successor, James VI of Scotland, was the son of the Roman Catholic monarch Mary Queen of Scots, a choice of heir that Raleigh was said to be instinctively opposed to, given his own personal hatred towards Catholicism in general. Although the new James I of England had been brought up in the Protestant faith and vowed to protect it as part of his royal oath, the new king was thought to be far more forgiving towards the Catholic Church than men such as Raleigh and was therefore more likely to be less tolerant of the rabid anti-Catholic rhetoric as practiced by the likes of Raleigh and others. As a new Scottish born monarch, it was always likely that James would be suspicious of the English royal court and its officials, including those that had previously served, or who had found favour with Elizabeth and who James would almost certainly replace or displace, as soon as he took his rightful place on the combined English, Scottish and Irish thrones. According to most sources, James had always intended to try and reduce the historic and costly religious tensions that had previously existed between Protestant England and its main Catholic neighbours, France and Spain, a policy that did not find favour with the likes of Raleigh, who had spent much of their lives fighting against these two enemy European states.

It was thought to be because of his own personal antipathy towards King James that Raleigh's enemies tried to implicate him in a number of plots against the new English monarch, the most serious of which was said to be the Main Plot of 1603, a conspiracy that was supposedly aimed at removing James from the English throne and replacing him with his cousin, the Roman Catholic heiress Arabella Stuart. Although the idea of the staunchly Protestant Raleigh becoming involved in a plot to put a Roman Catholic on the English throne would appear to be completely absurd, all the same, Raleigh was charged with being involved with the conspiracy and forced to defend himself against the accusations. However, despite the lack of any real evidence against him in terms of the Main Plot itself, it was thought to be Raleigh's own personal dislike of James I and his public grumblings about the new king, which ultimately helped to convict him of the charges and led to him being sentenced to death. Fortunately, King James I was not so convinced of Raleigh's guilt and refused to confirm the death sentence passed by the court, although the nobleman was said to have been imprisoned for the next decade or more, during which time he remained in the Tower of London. It was only in 1616 that James I finally ordered his release and only then, so that he could lead a second English expedition in search of the fabled, gold rich city of El Dorado, which Raleigh still believed existed along the banks of the Orinoco River. However, before being despatched on his voyage to South America, Raleigh was said to have been given explicit instructions to avoid any sort of direct military conflict with Spanish forces that he and his men might encounter, thereby ensuring that the peaceful relations between the two countries, promoted by James himself, would remain undisturbed. With these instructions clearly understood, Raleigh and his English expedition, which included Raleigh's own son, who was also called Walter, set out on their search for the mythical South American city, arriving in the region of Guiana later in the same year.

Unfortunately, having anchored off the coast of Guiana, Raleigh himself was reported to have been taken ill and was therefore obliged to allow one of his lieutenants, Lawrence Keymis, along with his son Walter to lead the English expedition upstream, requesting that they simply reconnoitre the region before reporting their findings back to him. As they made their way further into the hinterland, occasionally stopping to investigate particular sites that might be suitable for mining, the English party were thought to have found little of value, leading to a growing frustration amongst both the men and their leaders. At some point along the way the Englishmen were said to have encountered the Spanish held settlement of San Tome' de Guyana along the banks of the Orinoco, where, for some unknown reason the two sides came into conflict with one another, resulting in Raleigh's son Walter being killed, along with a number of other men, both English and Spanish. Eventually, Keymis was able to safely lead his party back to Raleigh's headquarters, where he informed the English commander about the death of his son and the conflict with the Spanish outpost. For Raleigh personally, the expedition had proved to be a complete disaster, as he not only lost his eldest son, but his men had also engaged in combat with the Spanish, in clear defiance of King James' instructions. Even though he had not been present at San Tome', as the overall commander of the English expedition, it had been his responsibility to ensure that such an action did not take place and knew that he was certain to face the consequences upon his return to England. Things might well have been different, if Raleigh and his men had actually managed to discover the supposedly lost golden city of El

Dorado, although given that no such place was thought to have existed, he and his men were subsequently forced to return to England with little to show for their endeavours, or indeed for their losses.

By the time Raleigh and his men returned to England in 1618, news of the attack on the Spanish outpost at San Tome' had already reached Europe, with the Spanish Ambassador in London, Count Gondomar, angrily demanding Raleigh's execution in reprisal for the unwarranted English attack on his country's settlement. Unfortunately for Raleigh, the question of his own culpability in relation to the events at San Tome' became a part of a much larger political intrigue, with Gondomar and the Howard family lobbying for a much more pro-Catholic approach to England's European alliances, causing Raleigh's fate to become inextricably linked to a continuing peace with Spain, something that James I was desperate to maintain. Having previously and erroneously been found guilty of treason in 1603, Raleigh was said to have carried the suspended death sentence over his head for nearly thirteen years, before the Spanish Ambassador called for James I to implement the sentence, in response to the San Tome' incident. Eager to ensure future peaceful relations between England and Spain; and no doubt at the instigation of his closest pro-Catholic advisers, eventually and perhaps a little grudgingly King James was said to have signed Raleigh's death warrant, condemning him to be executed on 29th October 1618. According to legend, in the hours before his death on the scaffold at Whitehall, Raleigh was said to have been relatively calm about his impending demise, an attitude that was no doubt influenced by the earlier death of his eldest son in Guiana, a personal loss that was thought to have had a significant affect on the English nobleman's character. Following his execution, Raleigh's decapitated head was reported to have been embalmed and presented to his wife, Elizabeth, who was said to have displayed it to the numerous friends, visitors and supporters who frequented her family home in later years. It was also reported that many influential people of the time were extremely unhappy about the way in which Sir Walter Raleigh had been dealt with, making their feelings known, especially to the likes of Count Gondomar and others who had actively lobbied for the nobleman's death, with pamphlets and posters being produced, publicly condemning their actions. Nearly thirty years after his execution and following Elizabeth Frockmorton's own demise, Raleigh's severed head and body were finally reunited, being reinterred in St Margaret's Church, Westminster, where it remained as a site of special interest and religious pilgrimage. Somewhat interestingly, it was thought to be only after his death that Raleigh began to achieve the level of public recognition that has helped to turn him into something of a national icon, which in reality is probably undeserved, given that some of his credited actions and innovations had little to do with him in the first place.

Walter Raleigh

Queen Elizabeth I

King James I

Despite the earlier failures at colonisation in the Americas, English explorers and settlers continued to be carried across to the New World in the hope of finding new lands and trading opportunities, which might benefit not only themselves, but also the English Crown. The first successful English colony to be formally founded in these new lands was said to be Jamestown in Virginia, both of which were named after successive English monarchs, Virginia after the "Virgin Queen" Elizabeth I and Jamestown after King James I, Elizabeth's royal successor. One of the men responsible for the discovery, establishment and ultimately the commercial success of Jamestown, was thought to be the English privateer and adventurer, Christopher Newport, the captain of the "Susan Constant", one of the three English ships that carried these first permanent settlers to the New World. Born in London in 1561, Newport was said to have spent most of his adult life as a sailor and privateer, primarily raiding the Spanish and Portuguese ships that regularly travelled between Europe and the New World, carrying supplies and treasures across the Atlantic, to and from Spain and Portugal's far flung outposts. Although Newport was thought to have achieved some notable success in his role as English privateer, for the most part, many of the ships that he managed to capture were often carrying general cargoes, either supplies for the individual colonies, or commodities being sent back to Europe for sale. However, in 1592, Newport and his crew were reported to have captured the Portuguese treasure ship, the "Madre de Deus", which was said to have contained one of the largest treasure cargoes ever seized by an English privateer, an estimated five hundred tons of valuables, including spices, gemstones and precious metals. Even though his share of the treasure would have allowed Newport to retire in some comfort, given that he was still a comparatively young man, it was perhaps no surprise that he chose to continue his seafaring career, accepting a commission from the Virginia Company of London in 1605 to establish a new settlement in the Americas. Beginning their journey in December 1606, Newport and the crews of the "Susan Constant", the "Godspeed" and the "Discovery" were reported to have set sail across the Atlantic and in April 1607 made landfall at what later became known as Cape Henry in the area of Chesapeake Bay. Over the next few weeks, Newport and newly appointed council member, Captain John Smith, along with a number of other English colonists were said to have set out to identify a likely spot for their new settlement, eventually choosing what later became known as Jamestown Island, although not for the most obvious reasons.

Initially choosing the site for its location, which was highly defendable, rather than for its more vital resources, such as a ready supply of fresh water, plentiful game and access to good growing land, ultimately the site chosen for the new settlement would prove to be an ill-fated decision for many of the early colonists. However, by June 1607 Newport and his ship "Constant Susan", along with the "Godspeed" were reported to have departed for England, taking with them a cargo of various minerals that had been discovered in the area, including Iron Pyrite, or Fools Gold, a poor return for the financial investments and human losses that the venture would eventually cost before the settlement finally became a commercial success in later years. Over the next year and a half, Newport was said to have made two return journeys to the new English settlement, ostensibly to re-supply the colony, which was reported to have been struggling to survive in the generally harsh and unfriendly conditions. Newport's third supply voyage to America in 1609 proved to be his most arduous and life threatening, as his fleet of nine ships was reported to have been struck by an enormous tropical storm that not only dispersed his fleet, but also damaged his own ship, the "Sea Venture", forcing the leader of the expedition Sir George Somers to order the ship grounded on the then uninhabited island of Bermuda. Despite attempts to repair the ship, Somers and Newport were compelled to cannibalise the "Sea Venture" in order to construct two smaller vessels, the "Deliverance" and the "Patience", which were both subsequently used to carry the survivors onto Jamestown, where they found the settlement devastated by a shortage of food, disease and Indian attacks. With very few food stores between them, finally the decision was made to abandon the new settlement entirely and return to England onboard the two newly built, but generally unsuitable ships, the "Deliverance" and Patience".

Fortunately, just as the ships were about to begin their journey downstream to the Atlantic Ocean, they were said to have sighted a supply fleet under the command of a new English Governor, Baron de la Warre, who was said to have been accompanied by more colonists, food supplies and a doctor, much to the enormous relief of Newport, Somers and the surviving Jamestown settlers. Although De la Warre's carried a significant amount of stores to maintain his own ships crews and passengers, the additional demands of the Jamestown survivors and Newport's own seamen meant that these supplies would not last for very long. Consequently, Newport and Somers were compelled to sail back to Bermuda where the supplies from the ill-fated "Sea Venture" were said to have been stockpiled immediately after the ship was beached on the local reefs. Somers was thought to have subsequently perished on Bermuda, reportedly as a result of eating too much meat, although Newport was still said to have recovered many of the much needed stores but also those few survivors from the "Sea Venture" who had been left behind on Bermuda, returning them all to Jamestown a few weeks later, thus ensuring the survival of the English colony there. It has also been reported that one of the people that Newport rescued from Bermuda was a man called John Rolfe, a Norfolk businessman with a particular interest in tobacco, a crop that he intended to grow in the New World. Although Rolfe was said to have lost both his wife and baby daughter during the arduous journey across the Atlantic and been forced to bury them together on Bermuda, eventually he did continue his journey to Jamestown, carrying the vitally important tobacco seeds on which the colony would build its future prosperity. This journey to Jamestown, proved to be the final sea voyage for the English seafarer Christopher Newport, who was said to have returned to England a short time later, never to visit the settlement again. However, he did return to the sea, taking employment with the emerging East India Trading Company, which had just begun regular trading expeditions to Asia and the Indian subcontinent, including the island of Java, where Newport was reported to have died in 1618, at fifty seven years of age.

At around the same time that Christopher Newport was involved with establishing England's first colonial settlement in Jamestown, one of his contemporaries, Henry Hudson was said to be leading an expedition financed by the Muscovy Company to discover a northern route from Europe to the Pacific, allowing western sea traders to reach the Spice Islands, via what was commonly referred to as the North East Passage. Reportedly born in London sometime around 1565, Hudson was thought to have been born into a family of merchants, with his grandfather, who was also called Henry Hudson, thought to have been a founding member of the Merchant Adventurers Company that was first established in 1551. Later evolving into the Muscovy Trading Company, this particular merchant company was said to have been granted exclusive trading rights with Russia, under the terms of which, the company was said to have sought the elusive North East Passage that might link Europe with the faraway lands of China and Japan. Although little evidence of his early life remains today, for most historians it seems likely that Hudson would have received a relatively good education and might well have spent his formative years working as a cabin boy on one of his family's ships, learning his trade and working his way up to the rank of captain, following which he would have been given his own command. Certainly by 1607 he was reported to have achieved that rank, as it was in that year that Hudson was given the task of trying to find the passage, via the North Pole, to Japan and China, having been given command of the "Hopewell", a relatively small vessel that was reported to be old by the time he received command of it. However, despite the age and condition of the ship, on 1st May 1607, Hudson and his ten man crew were reported to have left Gravesend, reaching Greenland in the following month. Sailing north towards the Arctic Circle, the "Hopewell" were thought to have encountered large numbers of whales on their journey, although the presence of heavy pack ice soon prevented them from travelling further north, forcing them to turn south and return to England, arriving in Tilbury in September 1607, some four months after they had left.

Despite failing to find the North East Passage, in the April of 1608 Hudson once again took command of the "Hopewell", which was thought to have been re-provisioned and repaired for a new attempt to find the northern channel, with the ship reportedly departing from St Katherine's Dock in London, in April of that year. Sailing northward, Hudson steered his ship past Norway and towards Russia, although increasingly severe weather conditions, which caused his crew to threaten mutiny, forced Hudson to abandon the attempt and turn south again, returning to Gravesend in August 1608. In spite of his earlier failures however, Hudson was determined to try once again to find the elusive northern passage, although by this time English financiers were said to be unwilling to back a further expedition, leaving Hudson with little option but to seek financial support elsewhere. Fortunately for him, the Dutch were also said to be actively seeking a similar sea route to Asia, so in January 1609 Hudson was said to have signed an agreement with the Dutch East India Company, under the terms of which the English sea captain would supply them with full details of his expedition and any discoveries that he made during his journey. Unfortunately, the Dutch merchants were thought to have been as miserly, or as unconvinced about the expedition as their English counterparts, supplying Hudson with the "Half Moon" (or Halve Maen), an equally ancient and inappropriate vessel as the "Hopewell". Sailing with a mixed English and Dutch crew, Hudson was reported to have sailed the ship northward towards Norway and Russia, but once again the bitter weather conditions and the crews growing antagonism over their perilous situation caused the English sea captain to abandon this attempt at finding the northerly route to Asia. However, rather than face the ignominy of having to return home with little to show for his voyage, Hudson was said to have turned the "Half Moon" westward towards the marginally warmer waters of the North American territories of Newfoundland and Nova Scotia. By July 1609 Hudson and his crew were said to have arrived off the North American coast, where he and his men went ashore to explore the region and to trade with the local Indian tribesmen, who Hudson later described as savages, despite there having been quite friendly negotiations between them. After a few days the captain and his crew were reported to have embarked on the ship once again, moving south towards the Delaware River, which Hudson attempted to explore but found some stretches too shallow to navigate. Moving on again the "Half Moon" and its crew proceeded to the mouth of the Hudson River, where they passed what would later become known as Statten and Coney Islands, claiming all these previously unknown territories for his new masters in Holland. Throughout much of September 1609 Hudson and his crew were reported to have continued upstream, navigating the river, surveying the lands and making occasional contact with the local Indian tribes, who for the most part he found to be friendly and trusting, although in one instance a skirmish was said to have ensued and one of his English crewmen was killed.

By the beginning of October 1609 and having logged an extraordinary amount of information for his employers back in Holland, Hudson decided to set course for home, but rather than sailing to a Dutch port was reported to have sailed the

"Half Moon" back to the English port of Dartmouth, from where he sent a communiqué to his Dutch backers asking them to finance a second expedition. Unsurprisingly perhaps, the Dutch East India Company were not so easily inclined to meet his request, but instead demanded that Hudson and his crew return to Holland immediately, but before he could respond to their message he had been arrested by the English authorities for sailing under a Dutch flag. Charged with exploring to the detriment of his own country, although the "Half Moon", its Dutch crew and Hudson's logs were subsequently returned to Holland, the English sea captain himself was prevented from doing so and he never visited the country again. However, as a result of his reports and charts the Dutch East India Company were reported to have despatched more of their ships into the region and along the length of the Hudson River, eventually settling the lands that would later become known as New Amsterdam and later still, the British held territory of New York. Even though he was brought before the king, James I, for his seemingly unpatriotic behaviour, by 1610 Hudson's personal reputation was thought to have been generally restored and the Muscovy Company once again decided to appoint him as Captain of one of their ships, the "Discovery", which was to set sail in April 1610, departing from the River Thames. This time however, Hudson was ordered to search for a North West Passage to Asia, as opposed to the earlier North East channel which had previously eluded him, requiring the "Discovery" and its crew to travel north of Greenland, Iceland and into the perilous regions towards the Arctic Circle. Having left England and travelled past Northern Canada, the ship and her crew were said to have become trapped in thick pack ice in Hudson Bay, a situation that resulted in their having to cope with some of the very worst winter conditions and creating a great deal of antagonism between Hudson and his crew. As the "Discovery" was finally released from the ice, the majority of the crewmen onboard wanted to return home, although Hudson insisted that they should continue on in search of the sea passage that they had been ordered to find. Perhaps recognising that mutiny was their only logical course, on the 22nd June 1911 the crew of the "Discovery" were reported to have cast Hudson, his young son John and eight loyal members of the crew into an open boat and cast them adrift, essentially condemning them to almost certain death. With their captain abandoned, the remaining crew were then reported to have set sail for England, where they arrived back in London in October 1611, although surprisingly there seems to have been little action taken against them, despite the best efforts of the Muscovy Company directors. It was only in 1618, some seven years after the event that the surviving mutineers were brought to trial on charges of murder, rather than mutiny, but with little evidence against them and any potential prosecution witnesses already dead, the trial was quickly done with and the men subsequently acquitted.

Christopher Newport   Sir George Somers   Henry Hudson

Whilst Christopher Newport and Henry Hudson were sailing north and west to settle the New World, or discover the almost mythical Northwest Passage, other English mariners, such as Sir James Lancaster were reported to be undertaking some of the earliest voyages eastward, taking the more conventional route around the southern tip of Africa and into the Indian Ocean. Although reportedly born in Basingstoke, for much of his early life, Lancaster was said to have lived and worked as a trader in Portugal, one of Europe's main centres of exploration and international trade, which allowed him to gain significant experience in international trade. However, by the second half of the 16th century he was thought to have returned to England and served under Sir Francis Drake in his battle with the Spanish Armada in 1588, commanding the English ship the "Edward Bonaventure" during the conflict. Three years later, in April 1591, Lancaster was said to have led a fleet of three ships, the "Edward Bonaventure", the "Penelope" and the "Merchant Royal" on the first formal voyage to trade with the East Indies, an expedition that would last for some three years, from 1591 to 1594. However, having rounded the Cape of Good Hope an outbreak of sickness amongst the crews of all three English ships was said to have resulted in the "Merchant Royal" having to return to England with all of the incapacitated crewmen on board, leaving the "Edward Bonaventure" and the "Penelope" to continue on to their final destination. By February 1592, the two ships were said to have reached the island of Zanzibar, where they were able to refit and re-provision the vessels before continuing on with their journey. By May of 1592, Lancaster's two ships were reported to have rounded the southern tip of India, arriving at Penang on the Malay Peninsula in the following month, where they began trying to trade with the local merchants. Unfortunately, their main cargo of English Broadcloth, proved to be highly unpopular with the local population, who found it to be far too heavy for their needs, leaving Lancaster with little to trade with and facing the real possibility of the expedition turning into a complete commercial disaster. However, according to some sources the English sailors subsequently overcame this problem by raiding other European ships, such as Portuguese and Dutch vessels that were operating in the region, relieving them of their cargoes, which the English crews could then trade for various exotic goods that could be taken back to England. Having managed to complete a fairly successful trading expedition to the East Indies, Lancaster had intended to spend some more time in the region, although owing to the length of the voyage and the serious depletion of his crew due to sickness and disease, in September 1592 he was reported to have set sail for England, reaching his home port of Rye in May 1594. Opinions differ, as to whether or not Lancaster's initial voyage to the East Indies was a financial success or not, given that he was said to have lost so much in terms of the expeditions actual monetary cost. However, from the point of view of establishing England's first trading links with this largely unknown, but potentially valuable region, then James Lancaster's original expedition proved to be highly successful, regardless of its initial financial outcome.

It was said to be almost entirely as a result of Lancaster's voyage in the Edward Bonaventure that in 1596 another fleet of three English ships was despatched to the region, although all of them and their crews were subsequently lost at sea. Despite this catastrophe however, investors and merchants remained convinced of the potential riches that awaited them if they could establish regular trade routes between England and the East Indies. Consequently, two years later, in September 1598, English merchants and their financial backers once again raised a substantial amount of money in order to form a trade corporation that might finance future expeditions to the eastern regions. Convinced that their efforts would eventually prove to be successful, in December 1600, members of the new merchant company requested permission from the monarch, Queen Elizabeth I, to grant them a Royal Charter, guaranteeing them a trading monopoly in these new territories for a period of fifteen years. With little to lose and much to gain, on the 31st December 1600 the queen was said to have granted the new, Governor and Company of Merchants of London trading with the East Indies, their fifteen year patent, marking the birth of the trading organisation that would subsequently evolve into the British East India Company. With this new royal charter in their possession and having previously purchased more ships especially for the purpose, it simply remained for the company to provision and man their new vessels, as well as appoint their expedition's leader, with James Lancaster, the only English navigator to have successfully performed the task, being assigned to lead this new naval expedition in April 1601.

Commanding the flagship, "Red Dragon", Lancaster's small trading flotilla was reported to have included the "Hector", "Ascension", "Susan" and a small supply ship called the "Gift". The outward journey for the small fleet was reported to have been both harsh and slow, ostensibly because of adverse weather conditions and the regular occurrence of scurvy and other contagious illnesses amongst the crew, although Lancaster was said to have reduced the instances of scurvy amongst the crew of the "Red Dragon" by ensuring that they took regular doses of lemon juice. Having reached the southern tip of Africa, the fleet was said to have remained anchored there for several weeks, allowing the crew to acquire new supplies and to regain their strength after the arduous voyage, in preparation for the second half of the voyage to the East Indies. Even though a significant number of sailors were thought to have been lost during the first part of the journey, by the time the fleet left southern Africa the remaining crews were thought to have been reasonably well, having been allowed time to recuperate during their stopover in southern Africa, although Lancaster was forced to order yet another layover on the island of Madagascar in December 1601, after members of the crew began suffering from scurvy once again. Despite these unexpected delays however, by June 1602 the English fleet was reported to have arrived off the coast of Sumatra, where Lancaster began negotiations with the local native ruler, who agreed to waive all of the usual custom charges, although the region failed to offer sufficient goods for the English traders to fill their holds. Despite this, over the next few weeks Lancaster's ships were reported to have acquired additional cargoes from waylaying passing Portuguese merchant vessels, transferring their goods to his own ships, before allowing the Iberian traders to go on their way. Having collected a sufficient amount of cargo, Lancaster then loaded it all aboard the "Ascension" which was then ordered to return to England, loaded down with its rich cargo of exotic textiles and spices. A short time later the "Susan" was similarly ordered to set sail for home, laden with a cargo of peppers and spices, whilst Lancaster took the "Red Dragon", "Hector" and the "Gift" further north, towards Java.

James Lancaster

William Adams

Shogun Ieyasu

Arriving at the Javanese port city of Bantam in what is now modern day Indonesia, in December 1602; Lancaster immediately presented himself to the local ruler who was said to have warmly welcomed the English traders, allowing them to trade freely and establish their first trading factory on the islands. Over the next few months the few remaining English goods brought with them from home were thought to have been exchanged for local produce, including bags of peppers and spices, which were subsequently loaded aboard the three remaining ships ready for their return journey. In February 1603 the three English ships began their homeward voyage loaded down with fresh provisions and their cargoes of exotic spices and peppers, as well as a letter of friendship from the ruler of Bantam to Queen Elizabeth I of England. Apart from the loss of a rudder, which might have resulted in the loss of Lancaster's flagship, but which was subsequently repaired, the journey home was thought to have been relatively straightforward, apart from a stopover at the island of Saint Helena, where repairs were made to the ships and fresh provisions brought on board. Arriving back in England in September 1603, although the expedition was judged to be both a commercial and national success, in that the voyage had achieved all of its initial objectives, such was the volume of products brought back by the fleet that much of the cargo failed to sell, making the voyage a financial failure. For Lancaster personally, despite there being little by way of monetary reward for all of his efforts, such was the national acclaim that the journey had caused in England itself, he was subsequently knighted by Elizabeth I for his diplomatic and commercial endeavours. For much of his later life Lancaster was reported to have remained involved with the fledgling British East India Company, largely as a company director and as a proponent of future commercial expeditions, both to the East Indies and in search of the highly elusive Northwest Passage. At least one of these exploratory journeys, under the command of William Baffin resulted in the naming of the northern waterway, now known as Lancaster Sound, in celebration of the expedition's supporter, Sir James Lancaster, in July 1616.

In the same year that Queen Elizabeth I had granted her royal charter to the Merchants of London trading with the East Indies, initiating the trade links that would ultimately lead to Britain's control of the Indian subcontinent, another Englishmen, William Adams, was reportedly arriving in the relatively undiscovered island kingdom of Japan. Born on 24th September 1564, in Gillingham, Kent, Adams was reported to have been orphaned at a fairly young age and as a result was apprenticed to a shipbuilder, who trained the young William for a career at sea. At the time of the Spanish Armada in 1588, when he was around twenty four years old, Adams was said to have commanded a supply ship attached to Sir Francis Drake's naval force and was a notable witness to England's subsequent military victory over the Spanish fleet. For the next decade the young mariner was thought to have been constantly employed at sea, participating in various arctic expeditions in search of the fabled Northeast Passage and commanding vessels that were travelling between England and the northern states of Africa, for the English based Barbary Company. However, reportedly anxious to extend both his knowledge and his experience, in 1598 Adams was said to have resigned his position with the Barbary Company and accepted the post of Pilot Major with the Dutch East India Company, who were planning a five ship expedition to the Far

East, a region that the thirty four year old English captain was eager to explore and experience. Embarking on the Dutch ship "Hoope", Adams was said to have departed Rotterdam in June 1598, with the fleet sailing due south, along the west coast of Africa, where they were forced to take on fresh supplies from one of the outlying islands.

Crossing the Atlantic, the Dutch East India fleet was reported to have been scattered by a series of storms, so that by the time the first of the vessels reached the tip of South America, ready for their voyage through the Magellan Straits, only three of the five ships had managed to survive the journey intact. First discovered by the navigator Ferdinand Magellan in 1520, these straits were said to have offered the safest route between the world's two great oceans, the Atlantic and the Pacific, as well as providing an alternative link between Europe and Asia. One of the Dutch ships was said to have been captured by the Spanish, whilst another was forced to return to Holland with a much reduced crew, the majority of its men having died through sickness and disease. Two of the ships, the "Hoope" and the "Liefde" were said to have anchored off the Chilean coast in the first part of 1599, whilst they waited for the other ships to arrive in the region, during which time Adams was thought to have transferred from the "Hoope" to the "Liefde", a move that would later prove to be a lifesaver for the English mariner. Despite losing a number of crewmen to native attacks on the outlying Chilean islands, the two vessels were thought to have continued with their voyage, navigating the Magellan Straits and entering the Pacific in the first half of 1599, from where they travelled to what were described as "certain islands", where a small number of the crew were reported to have deserted the expedition. Having repaired and re-supplied the ships, the two vessels were then said to have sailed on with the intention of reaching Japan, where they hoped to sell their surviving cargo for silver, before moving on to the Spice Islands. Unfortunately, a severe tropical storm was thought to have caught the two remaining Dutch ships at sea, resulting in the loss of the "Hoope" and her entire crew, a disaster that caused Adams to give thanks for his earlier decision to swap ships before travelling through the Magellan Straits. However, even though the "Liefde" had managed to survive the tropical typhoon, it was thought to have not only sustained major damage, but also suffered substantial losses amongst its crew, with only a handful of them surviving through to April 1600, when the vessel finally anchored off the Japanese island of Kyushu.

For those Portuguese traders and missionaries who had already established themselves in Japan, the sudden and unexpected appearance of a Dutch ship, along with its small and bedraggled crew was generally seen as posing a real threat to their own positions, causing them to accuse William Adams and his surviving crewmates of being pirates, largely in the hope that they would then be executed by the local authorities. Fortunately for the English seafarer and his Dutch comrades, the Japanese authorities were thought to be curious about their new foreign visitors and rather than simply take the Portuguese word for their being pirates, arranged for Adams and his shipmates to be held in Osaka Castle where they might be questioned more thoroughly. Their principal inquisitor was reported to be Tokugawa Ieyasu, the royal guardian of Japan's young ruler, who would seize control of the country later in the same year and who held power in the country right through to his death in 1616. Seemingly fascinated by Adams' knowledge of navigation, mathematics and shipbuilding, Ieyasu was said to have ignored the Portuguese demands for Adams and his comrades to be executed, perhaps recognising that these calls were entirely motivated by personal antagonisms, rather than for any other rational or lawful reason. Ordering that Adams' ship be removed to Edo, which is now known as Tokyo, the capital of Japan, the "Liefde" was said to have barely survived her final voyage, as having finally been sailed into Edo harbour, the by now rotten and heavily damaged vessel was thought to have simply sank beneath the waters of the Japanese port. In the meantime, Adams and his comrades were thought to have become subjects of interest for the Japanese Shogun, Ieyasu, who saw the advantages of exploiting their knowledge and expertise, particularly in the areas of shipbuilding, navigation and seamanship, subjects that he was keen to develop amongst his own people, allowing Japan to become independent of other foreign traders, including the Portuguese. Finally, some four years after Adams and his few surviving comrades had come ashore in Japan; Ieyasu ordered the Englishmen and his shipmates to be taken to the port of Ito where they would help design and construct a new western style sailing ship, which could be employed by the Japanese navy. Although relatively small in scale, this first vessel was thought to have been such a success that the Shogun ordered a larger version to be built, which was also well received by the Japanese ruler, who subsequently came to regard Adams as a trustworthy adviser and confidante, whilst the other surviving members of the "Liefde's" crew were also thought to have been treated extremely well by their Japanese hosts.

Clearly recognising Adams' value, not only as a skilled navigator and shipbuilder, but also as an adviser on foreign affairs and trading matters, it was perhaps little surprise that Ieyasu was reluctant to allow the Englishman to leave, even though most of the Dutch crewmen had been given permission to leave the country by 1605. However, despite not being allowed to leave Japan, Adams was reported to have been treated extremely well and with great courtesy by the Japanese Shogun, who bestowed on the Englishman a number of titles and offices that gave him an elevated status within the native community. Having spent so many years at the royal court, Adams eventually became fluent in the Japanese language, becoming the Shogun's official interpreter in matters of trade and foreign affairs and was often employed as Japan's chief negotiator with various merchant companies that arrived in Japan to trade. It was also around the same time that Adams was said to have been elevated to the status of a Samurai, was granted substantial estates by the Japanese Shogun and even took a Japanese woman as his wife, despite already having a wife back in England, who he continued to support and communicate with up until his death in 1620. It was thought to be largely as a result of his high status and personal relationship with Ieyasu that Adams was able to contact agents of the Dutch East India Company in an attempt to develop Japan's international trade, as well as reduce the influence of the Portuguese traders, who had previously controlled much of the country's overseas trade, often to their own advantage. Arriving in Japan in 1609 the Dutch agents had to negotiate with Adams for equitable terms, although in a short space of time the two sides were reported to have reached an agreement, which would allow the Dutch merchant company to establish their first trading post in Japan, at better rates than were being offered to the Portuguese, ostensibly because of Adams' personal involvement in the negotiations.

However, even though Adams had arrived in Japan as a servant of the Dutch East India Company and therefore owed them his commercial loyalty and allegiance, he was first and foremost an Englishman and would therefore have been inclined to help his fellow countrymen to establish new trading links with his adopted Japanese homeland. According to some sources, it was said to be the presence of a formal English trading settlement in Indonesia that initiated contact between Japan and the British East India Company, after Adams had requested the English traders to pass along messages to his family in England, as well as advising them about the establishment of Dutch trading interests in Japan. As a result of his first communiqué, the British East India Company was said to have despatched one of their ships, under the command of Captain John Saris, to visit Japan and begin negotiations for trade between the two countries. Arriving at Hirado in Japan in 1613, Captain Saris' initial impressions of Adams were thought to have been negatively affected by the Englishman's decision to meet them wearing traditional Japanese clothing, his refusal to stay in English accommodations and his reported exaltation of everything "Japanese", which Saris felt made Adams appear more native than European. However, despite such early and plainly obvious reservations on the part of the English trade delegation, Adams was reported to have shown them every kindness and even took the time to show Saris and his officers some of the most notable sights in Japan, before accompanying them to a meeting with the Japanese Shogun, Ieyasu and his son Hidetada. As a result of these meetings, the British East India Company was said to have been granted significant trading rights in Japan, as well as managing to retain the services of Adams himself, which they were said to be willing to pay handsomely for, reportedly at twice the normal rate of pay. Despite the best efforts of Adams however, for the most part the British East India Company was said to have sent few commercial shipments to Japan and those that they did were reported to be of poor quality and of little interest to Japanese consumers, who preferred to trade with neighbouring China, leaving Adams to try and support the English trading post through his own commercial enterprise.

For the final few years of his life, Adams was reported to have spent much of his time trying to organise various exploratory expeditions, both for the British East India Company and for himself, although always with the interests of his adopted Japanese homeland in mind. Trading with Siam, China and other neighbouring Asian states, Adams continued to try and make the English trading post a success, although much of the profit generated by the company's Japanese factory was largely the result of Adams and the resident English traders own efforts rather than through any help they received from England. When his employer and friend, the Japanese Shogun, Ieyasu, died in 1616, it was feared that much of Adams' status and authority might disappear, but Ieyasu's successor, Hidetada reaffirmed all of the Englishman's earlier titles and offices, ensuring that Adam's could continue with his commercial activities as before. However, at the age of fifty five and having lived a highly arduous life, in May 1620 Adams suddenly became ill and was reported to have died on the 16th of that month at Hirado in Japan. In his will, the English mariner, shipbuilder and royal adviser was said to have left his estate to be equally divided between his two families, the one in England and the one in Japan, with all of his Japanese trading rights being conferred on his son, Joseph, who was born out of Adams' marriage to his Japanese wife Oyuki.

Captain John Smith   William Dampier   Abel Tasman

The other great region of exploration, albeit in a limited form, for most of the leading western European states was the coastal areas of the African continent, where gold, ivory and slaves could be purchased by seaborne traders and then sold at home, or in the New World, where Portugal, Spain, Britain, France and the Netherlands were beginning to establish their overseas empires. One of the earliest English explorers of the region and therefore one of England's first slave traders was said to be John Hawkins, who was thought to have followed the example of other merchants, John Lok and William Towerson, who were reported to have purchased a small number of Black African slaves during the middle of the 16th century. However, Hawkins was said to be different from these earlier traders, in that he purposefully set out to purchase slaves, with the expressed intent of making a profit from each leg of what became commonly known as the Triangular Trade. Setting out on his first voyage in 1555, Hawkins was reported to have directed his three ships towards the west coast of Africa, with the intention of purchasing slaves, gold dust and ivory from the region later called Sierra Leone, although in the event he was said to have captured a Portuguese slave ship carrying some three hundred or so Black African slaves, which he subsequently stole from the unfortunate Portuguese traders. Setting off across the Atlantic and having reached the New World, Hawkins was reported to have sold his human cargo to the Spanish authorities in Santo Domingo, making significant profits, both for himself and his financial backers in London. As a consequence of his having arrived in the New World with a cargo of slaves, a business dominated by themselves and the Portuguese, the Spanish authorities in the West Indies were reported to have later banned their American colonies from trading with visiting English merchants. Reportedly making a second voyage across the Atlantic to trade for African slaves in 1563, Hawkins returned to the Americas with his second human cargo, which he was said to have sold to planters in the Caribbean, before beginning the long voyage home to England, where he was warmly welcomed by his financial backers. In the following year, the English seafarer was reported to have organised yet another voyage to West Africa, this time with the support of the Tudor monarch, Elizabeth I, who was equally keen to benefit from this new and highly lucrative trade, even providing Hawkins with a 700 ton ship called the "Jesus of Lubeck", which could be used to carry an even larger human cargo. Once again though, rather than trading for African slaves, Hawkins was reported to have simply waylaid those Portuguese slave ships that he came across on the west coast of Africa, relieving them of their cargoes, which he later transported and sold in Venezuela and Columbia, making himself and his backers a tidy profit in the process. On at least one occasion, local Spanish officials were said to have tried to prevent Hawkins from selling his slaves for a profit by threatening to impose swingeing taxes on the transaction, although the English captain's subsequent threats to burn down their town, were thought to have resolved the issue in the Englishman's favour, allowing him to retain his ill-gotten gains, which he later returned with to England.

Having returned home in September 1566 with huge profits for everyone, including the Queen and himself, Hawkins quickly began to make arrangements for another voyage in the following year. Although he was thought to have traded for his own slaves during the expedition, he was also reported to have captured the Portuguese slave ship, the Madre de Deus, en route, bringing his total number of slaves to well over four hundred, all of whom were then transported across the Atlantic to be sold in Spain's South American colonies. Unfortunately, having arrived off the coast of Mexico to sell his slave cargo, Hawkins ships were said to have been chanced upon by a large Spanish naval force, which quickly began to attack the smaller English fleet, causing the loss of four of Hawkins ships and forcing the English privateers on the other two vessels to flee for their lives. Having lost two thirds of his fleet and most of his profits, Hawkins and his surviving crews were forced to retire to England, with only a handful of the sailors who had originally set out and with nothing to show for all of their efforts and losses. Ultimately though, this disastrous voyage did little to damage Hawkins reputation, or indeed his future prospects, as he later played a significant role in helping to protect Elizabeth I from the various military threats that were made against her life during her long reign. According to some historians, it was his later reorganisation of the English Navy that helped to create the basis of the modern and highly effective naval force, which faced the enormous Spanish Armada in 1588 and subsequently destroyed it, raising England's status from a small and besieged island state, to become one of Europe's naval superpowers.

Following in the footsteps of the likes of Drake, Raleigh, John Smith and the many others, a new generation of British maritime explorers and traders came to replace them, although not always achieving the level of public recognition, or acceptance that these earlier, much more notable seafarers ultimately received. As time progressed and attitudes changed, so the status of Britain's privateers became inexorably altered, putting them outside of the law and thereby lessening their contribution to Britain's maritime expansion and the country's knowledge of previously unidentified and unclaimed lands. One of the earliest of these late 17th and early 18th century explorers was William Dampier, who was reportedly born at East Coker, Somerset in August 1651 and went on to be acclaimed by some, as the greatest post Elizabethan explorer of his age, a title he was thought to have held until the later voyages of the legendary Englishman, James Cook. Beginning his naval career as a teenager aboard a merchant ship sailing to North America, Dampier later travelled to Java in modern day Indonesia before returning home to join the Royal Navy as a twenty two year old, although his service was said to have been temporarily cut short after he became seriously ill and was forced to return home to recuperate. However, rather than immediately returning to sea, Dampier was reported to have travelled to the Caribbean where he had relatively short and unsuccessful careers as a plantation manager and then as a logger in the forests of Mexico. In 1679 he was reported to have returned to the sea, joining the crew of the English buccaneer, Captain Bartholomew Sharp, who was said to have been operating in and around the Caribbean and South America, targeting Spanish ships that were travelling in and out of the region. Having spent some years with Sharp, Dampier was then said to have made his way north to Virginia, where he became involved with another band of privateers and buccaneers, including Edward Davis and Charles Swan, during which time he was said to have travelled as far as the East Indies, where they visited the islands of Guam and Mindanao, as well as navigating the coasts of China, Indonesia and Australia.

It was thought to be during these voyages that Dampier began to record his observations about the flora and fauna of these exotic lands, as well as reporting on the indigenous peoples that he happened to encounter, creating a personal record that would prove to be so valuable to those scientists and intellectuals who were interested in such matters. It was said to be during these extensive voyages that Dampier was reported to have taken his leave of the privateers, being deliberately abandoned by his former comrades on one of the Nicobar Islands in the midst of the Indian Ocean, from where he was forced to make his way to Sumatra and eventually home to England. Arriving back in 1691, Dampier was said to have earned a living by exhibiting two slaves, a mother and daughter, who he had acquired on his travels, although for the mariner these were only a temporary means of earning a living, while he waited for the records of his adventures to be published as the "New Voyage Round The World", which was eventually produced in 1697. Almost instantly Dampier's tales were thought to have attracted the interest of the British Admiralty, who were eager to employ the former buccaneer in their service, offering him command of the ship "Roebuck" in 1699, with a commission to explore the east coast of New Holland, the lands, which were later to become Australia. Setting out in January 1699, although Dampier had originally planned to reach New Holland (Australia) via Cape Horn, at the tip of South America, given the date of his departure he was forced to travel by the more conventional route, via the Cape of Good Hope in Southern Africa. Following the usual trade routes of the time, the "Roebuck" and its crew were reported to have reached the southern Pacific by the middle of 1699 and on 26th July were said to have arrived at the mouth of Shark Bay in Western Australia. Within days of their arrival Dampier was said to have gone ashore and began documenting the various flora and fauna that existed in these new territories, before beginning a voyage northward, collecting examples of the numerous plants, shells and wildlife that he could find, all of which were meticulously recorded by Dampier and his assistants. Further north again, by December 1699 the "Roebuck" was reported to have reached New Guinea, where Dampier recorded and charted the coastlines of the various islands, as well as collecting whatever specimens he could manage, which were added to the already vast collection stored onboard his vessel. Although he had intended to explore the east coast of Australia, as per his original commission, the rotten state of the "Roebuck", allied to an incompetent ships carpenter prevented this, forcing him instead to begin the return journey home, well before he had intended. Unfortunately, by the time the ship had rounded the Cape of Good Hope and sailed into the Atlantic the vessel it was said to be leaking heavily, leaving Dampier with little option but to deliberately run the "Roebuck" aground on Ascension Island, stranding the crew and its precious cargo. With the carpenter unable to make the ship seaworthy again, Dampier and his men were reported to have been marooned on the island for well over a month, before a passing ship called at Ascension and was able to return the crew to England, where they arrived in August 1701, some two and a half years after they had first left there.

Although much of his cargo and many of his records were thought to have been lost as a result of the ships poor condition, enough were saved to make the expedition worthwhile, especially the charts and records he had made regarding trade winds and tidal currents in the South Pacific. Sadly for Dampier, his earlier removal of a crewman from the ship, which resulted in the man being jailed, came back to haunt him, as the seaman in question returned to England and made a formal complaint regarding Dampier's action. As a consequence, when Dampier returned home in August 1701 he was charged with cruelty by the Admiralty, found guilty and dismissed from the Royal Navy, leaving him with no wages for his work and with no immediate prospect of a career. However, once again he was able to publish stories of his expedition to the Pacific, particularly his adventures in Australia, which he titled "A Voyage to New Holland", although according to some reports the outbreak of the War of the Spanish Succession in 1701, also provided a new form of employment for the unemployed mariner, who was said to have simply resumed his career as a British privateer. Appointed as the commander of a British ship "St George" in 1703, Dampier was said to have operated in conjunction with a second ship, the "Cinque Ports" raiding against both French and Spanish vessels that they happened to encounter at sea, during which they were said to have captured a number of enemy vessels. Sometime later however, as the two English privateers sailed along the Pacific coast of North America, the two vessels parted company, with the "Cinque Ports" reported to be in such poor condition that she was later reported to have sunk, having previously abandoned the seaman Alexander Selkirk on a remote island, because of his continuous complaints about the vessels poor condition. Interestingly, the writer Daniel Defoe was said to have later used Selkirk's experiences as the basis for his novel "Robinson Crusoe", which told the story of a castaway trapped alone on a tropical island. As for Dampier, as the war progressed, he was reported to have been employed as sailing master aboard the "Duke", under the command of Woodes Rogers and was thought to have been responsible for rescuing the abandoned Alexander Selkirk from his uninhabited island, as well as taking prizes worth in excess of £200,000, which Rogers and his crew would have shared once they returned to England. Sadly for Dampier though, he never received a penny of his share of the prize money, as he was reported to have died in London in 1715, just before the monies were awarded. Although he failed to gain the level of public recognition that was lavished on the likes of Raleigh, Drake and later Cook, Vancouver, etc. Dampier's voyages and his skilful recording of the flora and fauna of the Pacific region, were thought to have informed, inspired and underpinned the later expeditions of people such as Charles Darwin and James Cook, as well as causing the voyage of the HMS Bounty, famous for its commander William Bligh and his mutinous assistant, Fletcher Christian, who initially set out to find specimens of "bread fruit" from the Pacific region.

Ultimately, the Age of Discovery is thought to have simply resulted in the widespread exploitation of the planet's natural and human resources, in part through the foundation of the Transatlantic Slave Trade, the growth of the spice and drugs trades, as well as the extensive exploitation of the earth's naturally occurring mineral deposits. It also said to have marked the introduction of new and previously unknown crops into Europe, such as maize and molasses, potatoes and tobacco, which would ultimately earn great wealth for those involved with their cultivation and importation. Sadly, this period also marked the start of large scale land seizures from the native tribes of the various subject countries and the spread of Christianity which would go on to supplant many of the native religions that had existed in their home countries from the beginning of time. For England's seafarers, by the middle of the 17th century many of the world's previously unknown regions had already been discovered, if not fully explored, although many would continue to be fought over in the following centuries, as the competing leading European powers sought to extend their influence over as much of the known world as possible. The only region of the world that was reported to have remained largely undiscovered by the first half of the 17th century was the far southern ocean, where it was speculated an unknown continent existed. For hundreds of years, scientists, explorers and cartographers had claimed that unknown lands existed in these faraway waters, although in most cases there was little to support the claims, other than legend, speculation and even mathematical calculations. However, in 1603 the Dutch explorer, Willem Janszoon, was thought to have been the first European to have sighted the coastline of Australia for the first time, although he made no attempt to investigate the local waters, or to land there. Three years later though, Janszoon was said to have returned to the region, with the intention of mapping this previously undiscovered coastline, beginning his journey around the modern day region of Queensland, where he and members of his crew were reported to have landed. Unfortunately, it later transpired that the Dutchman ultimately failed to recognise the territory as being part of an entirely separate continent, but simply believed that it was a yet another part of the New Guinea chain of islands.

Captain James Cook   **Tobias Furneaux**   **George Vancouver**

The next European explorer to report on the existence of these southern territories was another Dutch navigator Abel Tasman, who was reported to have circumnavigated the lands that he later named as "New Holland" in 1644. Tasman was also credited with being the first European to launch an expedition to the island that he subsequently called Van Diemens Land, which was later renamed Tasmania, in honour of the explorer who first brought these southern lands to the world's attention. Despite these initial Dutch voyages to explore the new southern continent however, ultimately it was the British and a Royal Navy officer called James Cook who would explore, colonise and develop these southern lands, helping to create the modern day Commonwealth nations of Australia and New Zealand. Born in October 1728, in the village Marton, North Yorkshire, James Cook was the second child of a local farm labourer, who was fortunate enough to catch the attention of his father's employer, the local landowner, who paid for the young James to attend the local school, thereby guaranteeing him the benefit of a formal education. Having been employed as a farm worker, then as a shop assistant, around 1746 the young James Cook was said to have made the acquaintance of a local ship owner called Walker, who owned a fleet of vessels in the port of Whitby. Having taken a liking to the 18-year-old James, Walker subsequently offered him a position as an apprentice on one of his colliers that regularly shipped coal up and down the English coast, allowing James the opportunity to escape the drudgery of his previous employment. Over the period of the next few years Cook was said to have served on a number of the company's vessels, learning the practical skills that would serve him so well in his later naval career, along with the vitally important subjects of astronomy, trigonometry, geometry and navigation. Having completed his three year apprenticeship with the company, Cook was then able to serve on bigger, more widely ranging vessels that operated in and around the Baltic region, allowing him to gain even greater experience within the British merchant marine service. However, by 1755 and with the prospect of war with France looming on the horizon, Cook was said to have made one of the most important decisions of his life and applied to join the Royal Navy and was accepted into the service in June 1755.

Progressing quickly through the ranks, Cook was said to have successively held the post of master's mate, boatswain, as well as temporarily holding the position of master on a number of occasions, when he was put in charge of smaller naval vessels. During the Seven Years War, which was fought between 1756 and 1763 and that was generally waged in and around the territories of North America, Cook was reported to have distinguished himself through being involved in several notable engagements against the French. His own particular skills in navigation and cartography were also thought to have been noted, allowing British forces to identify possible lines of approach in their attacks along the St Lawrence River, for which Cook gained significant personal recognition. With a peace treaty signed in 1763, Cook's abilities as a map maker, navigator and surveyor were thought to have been put to good use when he was asked to map the entire coastline of Newfoundland, a task that he was said to have completed so well that he quickly came to the attention of the Admiralty, who were keen to obtain as many detailed maps of the world as possible. As a direct result of his work in North America, in 1766 Cook was promoted to the rank of Lieutenant and was given command of a Royal Society expedition to the Pacific Ocean, principally to track the transit of Venus across the Sun, although it was clearly a voyage that would also allow him to map the coastlines of the South Atlantic and Pacific islands as he travelled to his ultimate destination. Setting out from

England in 1768, the Royal Navy expedition was said to have travelled south across the Atlantic, down past Cape Horn and west to the island of Tahiti, where they arrived in April 1769, just in time for their astronomical observations to be made.

However, although the observations they made were later reported to be inconclusive, it was whilst they were in the Pacific region that Cook was reported to have mapped the entire coastline of New Zealand, as well as the whole length of Australia's east coast, the first time the region had ever been recorded by a European explorer. It was said that it was during these initial investigations into the coastline of Australia that the first sightings of the indigenous peoples, the Australian Aborigines, were reported, although it was only after he landed in Botany Bay on the 29th April 1770 that they had their first full encounter with the native tribes of the new continent. Having spent a brief time exploring the area around this first landfall, during which various specimens were collected for the British societies, Cook and his crew turned the HMS Endeavour northward and began the long journey home, although they were subsequently delayed after the ship was accidentally grounded on a reef, requiring some remedial work to be undertaken. However, with the vessel repaired they were said to have resumed their voyage, stopping briefly in Indonesia, before rounding the Cape of Good Hope and sailing northward to England, which they were reported to have reached in July 1771, some three years after they had first set out.

Following his successful return to England, Cook was subsequently promoted to the rank of Commander and was almost immediately commissioned by the Royal Society to search for the legendary lands known as Terra Australis, an as yet undiscovered southern land mass first proposed by the Greek philosopher, mathematician and scientist, Aristotle. Believing that New Zealand was simply the northern tip of a much larger continent, the fact that Cook had already disproved this theory by sailing around the islands did little to undermine the idea that this mythological land did actually exist. This time in command of "Resolution", which was accompanied by the "Adventure", under the command of Tobias Furneaux, the British expedition set out to circumnavigate the globe, taking a route that would see them sailing close to the Antarctic in January 1773. Along the way Cook was said to have claimed South Georgia for Britain, although whilst sailing in the Southern Oceans the two British ships were reported to have become separated in heavy fog, with the "Adventure" first arriving in New Zealand where it lost a number of men to Maori attacks, before beginning the long voyage home to England. For his part, Cook was said to have continued with his Antarctic explorations, once again sailing to the ice bound continent, but turning back to Tahiti just before he reached the frozen wastes. However, determined to put an end to the rumours of an unknown southern continent, Cook subsequently returned to the icy waters of Antarctica, if only to satisfy himself that no such place existed, which he was finally able to do by 1774, having charted and mapped most of the region. As they set their course for home the crew of the "Resolution" was reported to have stopped at a number of the Pacific islands, where the ship was re-provisioned and their charts updated.

Having returned safely to England aboard "Resolution", such was the scope, accuracy and length of his well charted voyages that James Cook was said to be regarded as the foremost European explorer of the age, an accolade that earned him yet another naval promotion, this time to the rank of Captain. However, simply because of his public value and his age, the British Admiralty were thought to have retired him from active service, although Cook himself was said to have been keen to carry on with his career. As a result, when in 1776 a new expedition was planned to try and discover the fabled Northwest Passage the great explorer was eager to be the man to lead it. Commanding "Resolution" once again, he was accompanied on his third voyage by "Discovery", which was captained by Charles Clerke, a seasoned mariner who had previously sailed with Cook on his earlier journey to the Pacific. Travelling first to the Pacific to return his Tahitian guide to his home island, Cook then turned north, visiting the Hawaiian Islands, becoming the first European to do so, before travelling on in search of his objective. Turning northeast, the two ships were reported to have travelled along the west coast of America, north towards the strait leading to Vancouver Island, where the crews were said to have spent several weeks exploring the hinterlands. Whilst they were there Cook and some of his men were thought to have made contact with the local Yuquot people, who although pleasant enough were not entirely trusted by all of the English crewmen. Having left the area after about a month the vessels then proceeded along the Bering Straits, which Cook and his officers mapped, creating some of the most complete maps of the region and helping to fill in some of the gaps that had existed on all previous navigation charts. However, so severe were the conditions along the route of the Bering Straits that Cook and his ships were unable to fully navigate the entire length of the route, causing immense frustration for the English commander, which he was said to have visited on his crew, whenever he was sick or melancholic.

Returning to Hawaii in 1779, Cook and his ships were said to have spent some weeks in the area, having been warmly received by the local tribesmen, who were thought to have treated the Englishmen with quite high regard. Eventually though the crews returned to their respective ships in order to resume their exploration of the Northern Pacific, but almost as soon as they got underway, one of the masts on "Resolution" broke, preventing the ship from continuing on and forcing it back to Hawaii for repairs. Even though they had only just left the island, as they landed once again, the mood of the local people was reported to have been far more belligerent, causing tensions to arise between the two sides. The situation was then said to have been worsened, when one of the English crew's boats was stolen by some of the islanders, much to the annoyance of Cook, who was said to have tried to hold the local chief hostage, until such time as the stolen boat was returned to him. Unfortunately, not only were they unsuccessful in trying to capture the native ruler, but their attempt was said to have caused the local islanders to attack Cook and his shore party, forcing them to retire to the beach, where they attempted to board their small boat in order to return to "Resolution". However, as he turned his back on the approaching native warriors, the explorer was reported to have been struck on the back of the head and having fell face down on the beach, was subsequently stabbed to death by one of the local natives. The remaining members of Cook's landing party only just managed to escape, although four of the marines who had accompanied him to shore were also thought to have died, while two others were seriously wounded by the islanders, preventing the crew from rescuing their commander's lifeless body, which was subsequently dragged away by the victorious islanders. In the aftermath of their leader's death, the British expedition was said to have come under the command of Charles Clerke, who was said to have made one last attempt at navigating a route through the Bering Straits, although with equally unsuccessful results. Unfortunately, Clerke too was reported to have perished before the two English ships finally managed to make their way home, arriving in England in October 1780, under the command of John Gore and James King, two more of Cook's most capable subordinates.

Despite the loss of Captain Cook however, the Royal Navy's exploration and mapping of the world's great continental coastlines continued unabated, with a succession of navigators, astronomers, cartographers and scientists continuing to try and identify the new lands, waterways, plants and animals that existed in these foreign lands, thereby adding to their own knowledge of the natural world. Even though most of the earth's oceans were thought to have been visited and most of the world's main nation states identified by the time of Cook's death in 1779, still vast internal regions of these various waterways and massive continental areas remained mysterious, uncharted and therefore potentially attractive to those explorers and merchants, who were prepared to risk all for the for the possibility of finding something that was of great interest, beauty or value. By the second half of the 18th century Britain was said to have emerged as the pre-eminent European sea power of the age, largely as a result of having destroyed the naval power of the competing French and Spanish empires, allowing British navigators free reign over many of the world's oceans, inland waterways and coastal sea lanes. Although James Cook rose to become the foremost naval explorer of his generation, even to the point of being granted free passage by Britain's enemies, his work and the development of scientific organisations such as the Royal Society had created an imperative, to see that every part of the known world was visited, charted, catalogued and reported.

One of James Cook's many Royal Navy contemporaries was said to be George Vancouver, who was reported to have commanded a number of exploratory expeditions in and around North America's Pacific region, Alaska, Hawaii and the southern coast of Australia. Born in June 1757, Vancouver was thought to have served aboard Cook's ship "Resolution" during his second voyage between 1772 and 1775, with the teenage Vancouver serving as a midshipman on the English survey vessel. Similarly he was said to have been part of the famous navigator's third voyage between 1776 and 1778, although this time serving on the "Discovery" and in company with his shipmates was present in Hawaii when Cook was killed by local tribesmen. When the two English vessels returned to Britain in 1779 the young George Vancouver was subsequently promoted to the rank of Lieutenant and posted to the "Martin", which was assigned the task of mapping various Pacific coastlines for the Admiralty and Royal Society. However, during the time the vessel was at sea, Spain was reported to have sent their own naval expedition into the northwest region of the Pacific, not only to chart the area, but also to reassert their own sovereignty and trading rights there. Having arrived in the region of the Columbia River and Sitka Sound, the Spanish force immediately seized those British merchant vessels found operating there, leading to the British authorities demanding compensation for their loss, which the Spanish subsequently refused to pay, leading to the possibility of war between the two nations. As part of the Royal Navy's presence in the Pacific, Vancouver was reported to have been transferred to a British warship, in readiness for a military confrontation with the Spanish, although as it turned out a diplomatic solution was found that prevented all out war between the two European neighbours, resulting in the signing of the Nootka Convention in 1790. With the dispute having been resolved peacefully, Vancouver was transferred yet again, this time to the Royal Navy vessel "Discovery" and was ordered to take possession of Nootka Sound, on the west coast of British North America, in what is now the Canadian province of British Columbia and survey the coastline of the new British territory. Having undertaken the task, during which time the large island off the west coast of British North America was renamed Vancouver Island, in honour of the naval commander, he and his crew aboard "Discovery" subsequently returned home to England to await their next assignment. In April 1791 George Vancouver left Britain once again, with two Royal Navy vessels after having been instructed to carry out further exploration of the Pacific Ocean, which resulted in the ships visiting southern Africa, Australasia and the Far East, before beginning a voyage northward along the west coast of America, passing by the coastline of Oregon and on towards British controlled North America, in particular the previously visited Vancouver Island. Even though he was undoubtedly one of the leading British explorers of the age, Vancouver has largely been overlooked because of the achievements of his contemporary, James Cook, one of the main reasons why he would subsequently die in relative obscurity, with his name being almost forgotten by all but the most interested parties.

James Bruce   Mungo Park   Richard Burton

Around the same time that the likes of James Cook and George Vancouver were exploring the world's oceans and coastlines, other Britons, including the Scottish explorer, James Bruce, were beginning to investigate the hinterlands of these previously unknown and uncharted lands. Born at Kinnaird, Stirlingshire in December 1730, Bruce was thought to have been born into a wealthy landowning family, with an expectation that he would marry well and settle down into some or other profession, possibly as a lawyer. However, despite marrying the daughter of a wealthy local merchant, her unexpectedly early death soon after they were married and then the later loss of his father, ultimately provided Bruce with the freedom and means to pursue an alternative career, first as a diplomat and then as a traveller and writer. Posted to Algiers as a British Consular official in 1763, he soon began to explore the historical ruins of the region, particularly those remaining from the Roman Empire, which he examined and recorded, beginning an interest that remained with him for the remainder of his life. Having visited a large number of the ancient sites in Algeria, Bruce subsequently travelled overland from Tunis to Tripoli, before taking ship to Heraklion in Greece, although he was reported to have been shipwrecked off the coast of Libya and forced to swim ashore to the port of Benghazi in Libya. Having recovered from his ordeal he was then said to have travelled onto Crete and then Sidon in the Lebanon, before making his way to Syria, where he visited the ancient cities and once again studied and sketched the architectural remnants of the once great ancient civilisations.

Having determined to discover the source of the Nile River, in 1768, Bruce was thought to have travelled to Alexandria in Egypt and enlisted the aid of the local ruler, Ali Bey Al-Kabir, who helped the Scottish explorer cross the desert to Jeddah in Saudi Arabia, where he remained for some weeks before crossing the Red Sea to the Ethiopian port city of Massawa, which was temporarily held by the Turks. Travelling to the then capital of Ethiopia, Gondar, where he was reported to have been warmly welcomed at the Ethiopian court, so much so that he was thought to have remained there for very nearly two years, during which time he was able to record the lives of the native peoples there. By October 1770 Bruce was said to have resumed his journey to find the source of the Nile and a month or so later was reported to have arrived at Gish Abay, the source of the Blue Nile, which was located in Central Ethiopia. Believing himself to be the first European to have visited the source of the Blue Nile, in December of the following year, Bruce was said to have set out on his second expedition, to find the confluence of the Blue and White Nile Rivers, a journey that required him to travel from the region of Sennar in Northern Sudan, to the region of Nubia, which was divided between Northern Sudan and Southern Egypt. Despite the difficulty of the terrain, eventually Bruce and his travelling companions were said to have found the meeting of the two ancient rivers, although their subsequent journey out of the region and back to Cairo was thought to have been both fraught and highly dangerous, with Bruce only narrowly escaping threats to his life on a number of occasions. However, thanks largely to good fortune and the efforts of his local associates, in January 1773 Bruce managed to reach Cairo, where he subsequently took ship for Europe, arriving back in France, where he soon met up with former acquaintances who were anxious to hear about his travels and adventures. When he returned to Britain in 1774 however, the stories of his travels and his subsequent journeys to the source and confluence of the Nile Rivers were thought to have been dismissed by many experts who thought them to be too fantastic to be believed. Even when he published his exploits in 1790, there were many so called experts who continued to doubt his reports of the regions, although in later years virtually all of his reports and recordings would prove to be relatively accurate, thus restoring his reputation and credibility somewhat. It was only after some of his work and findings were confirmed and authenticated that Bruce was eventually accepted as one of the leading explorers and travel writers of his age, adding much to his successor's knowledge of this previously unknown part of the world.

Back on the North American continent and particularly in the region of what would later become British North America, or Canada, one of the earliest and most successful British explorers was thought to be David Thompson, an English born trader, surveyor and cartographer, who helped map a significant proportion of Britain's North American territories. Born at Westminster, London in April 1770, when he was two years of age Thompson's father was reported to have died and as a result, he and his brother were placed in a Church of England boarding school for the poor, where the young David was reported to have shown such an aptitude for learning that he was selected to receive additional education, including mathematics and the associated subjects of astronomy, trigonometry and navigation. As a consequence of having learned these highly valuable skills, when the teenage Thompson turned fourteen years old he was apprenticed to a commercial enterprise, The Hudson Bay Company, where his skills might be put to some good use and his future employment ensured. However, as this particular company was specifically engaged in the exploration and exploitation of the still relatively unknown North American continent, his employment with the company almost inevitably led to Thompson being transported across the Atlantic, never to see his homeland, or indeed his family again. Having arrived in Manitoba by the middle of 1784, Thompson was said to have spent the next four years of his life employed as a clerk in a number of the Hudson Bay Company's offices and outposts. However in December 1788 he was said to have suffered a serious leg injury that confined him to Cumberland House where he came to the attention of the company's chief surveyor, Philip Turnor, who was said to have taken a particular interest in the young apprentice and helped develop his surveying, astronomical and mathematical skills. Having completed his seven year apprenticeship by the end of 1790, he was then formally employed by the Hudson Bay Company as a fur trader, although having requested a set of surveyor's tools on completion of his apprenticeship, during his first expedition as a fur trader, he was said to have surveyed his journey, creating the first formal map of the route to Lake Athabaska and as a result earning himself a promotion to the role of company surveyor. However, over the period of the following three years, Thompson was said to have become increasingly dissatisfied and disillusioned with the policies of the Hudson Bay Company, which eventually led him to resign his post with them and to take up a post with the rival North West Company, where he continued to pursue his interest in surveying the territories that would ultimately become the modern state of Canada. In 1797, the same year he began work for his new employer, Thompson was thought to have been sent to the area of the US Canadian border, where he was reported to have spent much of the year mapping the region, helping to resolve many of the geographical issues that had previously remained outstanding between the rival British and American governments. Over the next few years the surveyor was also reported to have undertaken a number of expeditions for the company, during which he managed to chart large areas of the previously unmapped hinterland, although he continued to trade in furs and establish new trading posts in and around the region's many waterways and great lakes.

In 1806, the North West Company asked Thompson to undertake a survey to identify a trade route through to the Pacific Ocean, in response to the earlier American backed Lewis and Clarke expedition, which had been undertaken between 1804 and 1806. The North West Company's young surveyor was reported to have begun his exploration of the entire length of the Columbia River in 1807, having first crossed the Rocky Mountains and was said to have spent much of the next few years exploring and mapping the region of the Columbia River basin, as well as establishing a number of new trading posts for his employers. Travelling through what would later become Western Canada, Northern Montana, Idaho and Washington, Thompson's expeditions not only resulted in some of the most detailed maps of the various regions, but also helped the North West Company extend their trading operations over a much wider area, helping them to become one of the most successful merchant company's in all of North America. Thompson was thought to have continued his career right through to 1812, when at the age of forty two, he returned to his family home in Montreal to begin work on his greatest achievement, an almost complete map of the interior of North America, which was thought to be so accurate that it continued to be used for the next century or more. However, despite having compiled one of the most important and truly accurate maps of the age by 1815, Thompson subsequently continued with his exploration and charting of his homeland, so that by 1843 he was able to produce the most comprehensive map of the North American region, stretching from Hudson Bay in the east, to the Pacific Ocean in the west. Unfortunately for the great explorer and cartographer, in later life his failing eyesight prevented him from continuing with his work from around 1851 and for the remaining six years of his life he was thought to have been unable to complete many of the projects that had been so important to him. One of these was his proposed book recalling his lifetime as a fur trader and explorer in North America, although in later years Thompson's numerous diaries and notebooks were recovered by the academic J B Tyrell, who was finally able to publish an account of the late cartographer's career and life. As is sometimes the case with history's most notable people, Thompson was reported to have died in relative obscurity, being cared for by his daughter and her family, who had been forced to offer him a home because of his abject poverty and subsequent poor health. Despite being one of the principal figures in exploring and developing the territories of North America, when he died in 1857, Thompson's passing was thought to have gone largely unnoticed, even to the point of his body being interred in an unmarked grave in a Montreal cemetery. However, when his memoirs were finally published by J B Tyrell in 1916 Thompson's life was subsequently brought back to the public's attention once again and demands grew for the great explorer to be publicly recognised for his enormous achievements, with a monument being placed on his grave by the Canadian Historical Society in 1926. Latterly regarded as one of the greatest explorer of his age, the work of David Thompson is thought to have inspired any number of subsequent explorers, navigators and cartographers, who have all tried to emulate the achievements of the fatherless boy from London, who played such a pivotal and significant role in helping to establish many of the modern day states of North America, including the now independent nation of Canada.

Back across the Atlantic, in continental Africa, a Scottish born explorer, Mungo Park, was thought to be one of the first Europeans to travel into the interior of West Africa, reportedly becoming the first westerner to view the River Niger in what is now the African state of Mali. Born in September 1771 near Selkirk in Scotland, Park's parents were said to be reasonably wealthy tenant farmers, who had been able to provide their thirteen children with a fairly good level of education, allowing the young Mungo to find employment as an apprentice to a local surgeon, Thomas Anderson, as a result of which he later attended Edinburgh University in 1788, where he was said to have studied medicine and botany. Completing his medical studies by January 1793, Park was said to have been appointed as the assistant surgeon aboard the vessel, "Worcester", which was sailing to the port of Bengkulu, on the island of Sumatra, in what is now modern day Indonesia. Having returned safely from his initial voyage, the twenty three year old Mungo was said to have offered his services to the African Association, which was otherwise known as the Association for Promoting the Discovery of the Interior Parts of Africa, a club dedicated to the exploration of West Africa. Ostensibly aimed at discovering the source of the Niger River and the legendary city of Timbuktu, purportedly the "lost city of gold", the Association was happy to accept the young Mungo Park's application and by June 1795 he was thought to have arrived at the Gambia River, ready to begin the two hundred mile journey to the isolated British outpost located close to the Mandingo homelands. Having reached this last western settlement, Park and two native guides reported to have set out into what were then largely undiscovered territories, in order to find the source of the Niger River, although the journey itself was said to have proved to be extremely difficult and ultimately resulted in the Scottish explorer being captured by a local Moorish leader, who held him prisoner for several months before Park's was finally able to escape. Unfortunately, his capture had left him alone in foreign lands, but armed only with a compass and a horse he was said to have navigated his way to the Niger River in Mali, a remarkable achievement considering his own limited circumstances. Beginning his return journey by following the course of the river as far as possible, Mungo was said to have avoided further problems with the native tribesmen, although given the conditions and his lack of supplies, by the time he reached Bamako, the capital of Mali, he was said to be seriously ill and forced to rely on the kindness of local people who were reported to have cared for him over the next few months until he had fully recovered from his illness. Finally making his way back to a British settlement, Park eventually managed to return to Scotland by December of 1797, where his return was greeted with disbelief by his family and friends who had previously thought him to be dead. His employers, the African Association were also very quick to report his discovery of the Niger River, an event that not only caused much excitement within the British establishment, but also amongst the British public who were fascinated by the young explorer's tales of adventure in the African continent.

Safely back home with his family and friends, Park was reported to have married and settled down as a doctor in the town of Peebles, on the Scottish borders, where he was offered the occasional post overseas, although none of them interested him sufficiently for him to leave his family, home and practice. However, having spent some three or four years practicing medicine, in 1803 he was offered the opportunity to lead a second expedition to the Niger River, an offer that he was inclined to accept, although only after he had learned to speak Arabic, a priceless skill that would undoubtedly be needed on any such journey. Having been taught by an Arabic acquaintance, by 1804 Park was said to have been fluent enough in the language to satisfy his own high standards and subsequently travelled to London, to begin making arrangements for the forthcoming expedition. Departing from Portsmouth in January 1805 with a party of fellow explorers, Park sailed to West Africa and arriving at the British outpost of Goree on the outskirts of Dakar in Senegal met up with the main body of his expedition, including a contingent of thirty six British soldiers and a handful of British seamen who were to accompany Parks and his fellow explorers on their journey to the Niger River. Unfortunately, by the time the expedition finally reached the Niger by the middle of August 1805 only a dozen or so of the original party had managed to survive the treacherous journey, with most of the others having died or become incapacitated through disease, most notably dysentery. However, having reached the Malian capital of Bamako and been granted permission to travel down to Sengou, Parks and his surviving comrades were reported to have travelled down the Niger by boat, although virtually all of them were reported to have been in extremely poor health and in no real condition to undertake the arduous journey. Regardless of their situation though, Parks and his surviving European colleagues were said to have pressed on along the length of the Niger, in search of Timbuktu, despite being regularly attacked by native tribes as they sailed through the various tribal homelands. Rather foolishly perhaps, instead of asking for help from the local peoples, the British explorers were thought to have pressed on alone, until finally their boat became stuck on a rocky outcrop and could not be released through their own efforts. Being attacked by local tribes and with no escape by boat, Parks and his few remaining men were said to have jumped into the river in an attempt to escape their predicament, but given their weakened condition were simply swept away and drowned in the fast moving river. Although it was some time before the fate of Mungo Park and his fellow travellers was known, investigations by the British authorities, later confirmed that all of the European explorers had indeed perished, despite the fact that some people continued to believe that they had survived, only to be held prisoner by one or other local ruler. Ultimately though, despite Parks' career as an explorer being relatively short lived and his own final demise immensely tragic, his initial search for the Niger River and his seemingly heroic travels on the African continent ensured his elevation to the status of a hero within the British Empire, creating an example that many others would continue to follow throughout the 19th and early 20th centuries.

John Hanning Speke

Mary Kingsley

Isabella Bird

Along with Livingstone, Stanley and Speke, one of the other most notable successors to Mungo Parks was thought to be Richard Francis Burton, a former East India Company officer who would not only make a name for himself as a noted British explorer, but also as a bit of a social renegade, who defied convention as easily as he placed himself in harms way. Born at Torquay in Devon on 19th March 1821, Burton was born to a serving British officer and his wealthy heiress wife, who travelled widely, which resulted in their three children receiving much of their early education from a variety of nannies and private tutors. It was thought to be as a result of this extensive travelling that the young Richard Burton became interested in the study of various foreign languages, including Italian, French and Latin, which he was said to have picked up at a fairly early age, a linguistic ability that would serve him so well in later years. Although he was known to have received a reasonably good standard of formal education, both at Preparatory School and at Trinity College, Oxford, the young Francis was reported to have found the strict social conventions of these academies difficult to bear, not least because of his personal interests in other less formal subjects such as riding, falconry and later pursuing the fairer sex, interests that ultimately led to him being expelled from college in 1842. With few ideas of what particular career to pursue and no doubt influenced by his father's own military background, eventually Burton was said to have chosen a career with the British East India Company, the merchant venture company that offered the promise of travel, excitement and action, as well as being the place where many of his closest friends had also found employment. Although he was thought to have been posted to India at a time when no major conflicts were being fought by the company, the subcontinent was said to have appealed to him purely because of the various languages and dialects that were spoken there, allowing the linguistically gifted Burton to involve himself in the traditions and customs of the different indigenous peoples, a practice that was said to have brought him much criticism from those colleagues who considered themselves to be superior to the native tribesmen of India.

As he became increasingly interested in the languages, habits and customs of the local tribes and ethnic groups, so Burton was reported to have commonly adopted the guise of a native tribesman, regularly travelling in local native quarters and amongst westerners to see if anyone could identify him as a European in native clothing, which in most cases they could not. It was thought to be as a result of his ability to disguise himself as a native that he was occasionally employed by British military commanders to infiltrate local areas, or to act as a spy within suspected tribal groups, to find out what was happening. In fact, Burton was said to have been so confident about his ability to pass as a native Muslim that he even travelled to Medina on a "Hajj", a religious pilgrimage undertaken only by Muslims, who would have killed any Christian within their ranks, although Burton was said to have successfully completed his subterfuge and later wrote about his exploits. Having returned to India in 1854 and rejoined his regiment, Burton was subsequently posted to Aden where he was assigned to lead an expedition supported by the Royal Geographical Society, designed to explore the hinterland of Somalia, where a number of great inland lakes were rumoured to exist, a series of tales that Burton was particularly interested in investigating. It was during this expedition that Burton first met Lieutenant John Hanning Speke, who shared Burton's love of adventure and who would later join him in some of his most notable explorations and discoveries. However, as the expedition arranged to set out on their journey, they were reported to have been attacked by a band of several hundred Somali warriors, who killed and wounded a number of the party before being driven off. Speke was said to have received numerous wounds as a result of the action, although he survived them to undertake further adventures, whilst Burton was reported to have been struck in the head by a spear, which penetrated one cheek and exited through the other, leaving a significant wound that he would carry for the rest of his life. Following the failure of the expedition, in 1855 Burton rejoined his army unit once again and was posted to the Crimea where he hoped to see action, although the regiment he was attached to was subsequently disbanded following a refusal to obey orders, a mutinous act that somehow attached itself to Burton's reputation, although there was no direct evidence of his own involvement in this particular incident.

Having been cleared of any wrongdoing in the previous expedition, in 1856 Burton was once again asked to head a Royal Geographical Society survey mission to Africa, this time to investigate the existence of some reported inland lakes, with the expedition leaving from the East African territory of Zanzibar. Although the principal objective of the journey was to investigate and identify these rumoured inland lakes, it was also suggested that the party might search for the source of the Nile River, although this was not thought to be a specific aim of the expedition. Burton was once again joined on the journey by John Hanning Speke, who was said to have recovered from the wounds he had received during their last expedition together and who was a more suitable companion for the often irascible Burton, who some companions, including Speke, found to be extremely difficult to deal with. For Burton too, Speke might not have been his first choice of companion, as he was said to be the sort of Englishman that Burton despised, brash, arrogant and totally indifferent to the beliefs and traditions of the native peoples, who Speke considered to be inferior to himself. Hiring local guides and bearers after they had first arrived on the east coast of Africa in June 1857, initially the expedition was said to have progressed reasonably well, although as time passed and the journey continued both Burton and Speke were thought to have suffered fairly serious illnesses and a good deal of their equipment was thought to have been lost due to the desertion of their local guides and bearers, or through just plain theft. However, some eight months after they began their expedition the two explorers were reported to have finally reached the shores of Lake Tanganyika, where they were able to rest and try as best as they could, to survey the region, an almost impossible task given the loss of much of their equipment and continuing instances of illness that affected both men. Because of their differing states of health, Burton was unable to continue with the journey, whilst Speke continued to explore on his own, although his inability to speak any native languages meant that he was forced to rely on a native translator, which given his own superior and imperialistic attitudes proved to be extremely difficult for him.

Despite his own continuing health problems and the difficulties caused by his own personal demeanour, as part of the same expedition, Speke was reported to have later gone on to locate one of Africa's greatest inland waterways, which he named Lake Victoria, but again he was unable to survey the region properly, because of the lack of adequate equipment. As they made their way home, the tension between the two men were reported to have been palpable and having returned safely to the coast, both of them were said to have returned to England separately, with Speke reaching Britain first and thus receiving much of the public acclamation that was due to both men, although personal rivalries quickly ensured that Speke tried to play down the part that Burton had actually played in the expedition. Yet again, Burton's perceived sympathies towards and understanding of the indigenous peoples of both Africa and India were used to undermine him and his reputation, by those people who took a much more superior, imperialistic attitude towards these supposedly uncivilised continents and their native inhabitants. Interestingly though, despite the best efforts of his enemies, who went to great lengths to destroy his personal and professional reputation, Burton continued to be seen as a notable and knowledgeable figure in 19th century Britain, especially by those who shared his interests in the native peoples, traditions and histories of the strange and exotic lands that were being brought to the public's attention. Although Speke would later go on to complete a second expedition to Africa's great lakes, lending weight to the assertion that the Nile River emanated from Lake Victoria, ultimately his many achievements seem to have afforded him little in the way of personal satisfaction, or indeed peace of mind. In September 1864 Speke was supposed to have participated in a public debate with Burton, but just before it was due to begin, he was reported to have jumped up from his chair, declaring that he could not stand the situation anymore and simply walked out of the hall, much to everyone's surprise. Having retired to Neston Park in Wiltshire, later the same day Speke's lifeless body was found near a wall on the estate, with a bullet wound in his chest, which almost immediately led to claims that he had committed suicide rather than face public scrutiny, not only by Burton, but also by the wider general public. However, despite such fanciful theories, ultimately the local Coroner determined that Speke had accidentally shot himself whilst climbing over the wall, which given his intemperate nature was probably the most likely explanation of his sudden and completely unexpected demise.

Although Burton would never undertake another major exploratory expedition again, during the second half of the 19th century, he was reported to have begun a diplomatic career that saw him posted to various destinations, which allowed him to engage in his passion for exploring and studying the native peoples, traditions and religions of these faraway lands. Initially posted to Equatorial Guinea, on the west coast of Africa, as a British Consul in 1861, although his work there was reported to be relatively unimportant, it allowed him time to continue with his personal exploration of the west coast of the great continent, journeys that he would subsequently commit to paper. However, given the rigorous nature of the climate there, Burton's wife, Isabel, was not able to accompany him and had to remain in England, although in 1865 the couple were finally reunited when Burton was assigned to a new diplomatic post in Brazil, where once again he was given ample opportunity to pursue his interests in travelling, journeying through the country's central highlands and canoeing down many of Brazil's biggest rivers. Four years later, he and Isabel were reported to have moved to Damascus in Syria, where his knowledge of the country's language, traditions and religions proved to be a major benefit to the new British Consul and his wife. Unfortunately, his regular habit of failing to pander to the interests of certain favoured groups, eventually led to calls for his removal from Syria, with the authorities back in London arranging for him to be transferred to Trieste in northeast Italy, where he was once again able to pursue his interest in travelling and writing. Knighted by Queen Victoria in 1886, much of Burton's later career was thought to have revolved around his love of writing, with the explorer penning any number of travel books, poetry, anthropological studies, some of which were considered pornographic at the time, as well as a series of books that he had translated from earlier native manuscripts, dealing with a variety of subjects, from religion to sexual and social matters. It was said to be while he was working on his final book that Burton suffered a heart attack and died, on the 20th October 1890, bringing an end to the life of one of Britain's most colourful and divisive characters.

Even though for the most part, early British explorers and adventurers were almost entirely male, increasingly during the Victorian period a small number of women began to explore Britain's vast imperial territories, bringing their own unique perspective to the subject of the world's numerously diverse peoples, cultures, traditions and histories. One of the most notable of these early female travellers and reporters was said to be Mary Henrietta Kingsley, who gained considerable recognition for her journeys in and writing about the African continent and the indigenous peoples that she encountered there. Born at Highbury, London in October 1862, Mary was said to have come from a family of writers, her father being engaged in that profession and her uncle Charles Kingsley being the author of the famous "Water Babies", a literary classic that enthralled generations of book reader's right through to the 20th century. Despite her family's literary background though, the young Mary was thought to have received very little formal education, but was said to have learned much from her father's extensive library of books, as well as from her father himself, a man who was thought to be highly critical of the increasing unfairness of the great powers, including Britain and the United States, in their treatment of the native peoples, both at home and abroad. Unfortunately, because she was restricted by the social conventions of the time, which insisted that young women should occupy themselves with more trivial matters, such as embroidery, housekeeping, running a home, or caring for sick and elderly relatives, it was only when both her parents had passed away that Mary was finally able to pursue her own interests in travel and adventure. Having inherited a reasonable sum of money from her late parent's estate in 1892, within a year the thirty year old Mary was reported to have arrived in the West African state of Sierra Leone, with the stated intention of accumulating information on the cultures of the native peoples of Africa, for a book her father was said to have started, but which he had never actually begun. For many within the resident European community in Africa and indeed for many of the local natives, the sight of a young western woman travelling alone was said to have caused a great deal of interest and concern, although Mary herself was thought to be largely indifferent to such matters and continued with her adventures nonetheless.

Travelling next to Nigeria, she was then said to have made arrangements to move south along the west coast of Africa, eventually arriving in Angola, where she was reported to have spent some months living with the local people, who not only taught her some of the skills needed to survive in the jungles of Africa, but also allowed her to witness the traditional customs and religious practices that guided their everyday lives, exactly the sort of things that Mary had come to Africa to learn. As a trained nurse and with her newly adopted skills, for much of the time she spent in West Africa, Mary was said to have travelled into various regions of the hinterland, seemingly unconcerned about the possible dangers that might present themselves, but confident in her own ability to deal with them, whatever they may be. However, after spending some months in Africa, in 1894 she was said to have returned to England, but only with the intention of gaining additional support for her work, which she was said to have found with the aid of the British Museum and the publisher George McMillan, who agreed a publishing deal with the highly unusual young Englishwoman. Returning to Africa in December 1894, Mary was said to have revisited Sierra Leone and then Gabon, before becoming aware of the work of another single white female who was working with the native Efik people of Calabar in modern day Nigeria, the Scottish missionary Mary Slessor. A devout Christian missionary, working for the United Presbyterian Church of Scotland, Slessor was said to have spent much of her time in Africa trying to suppress the local tribal practice of killing twins at infancy and preventing incidents of cannibalism amongst some of the native peoples. Believing that twins were the result of the Devil impregnating a normally pregnant woman with a second "evil" child, as there was no clear way of identifying which of the two babies was the Devil's seed, local tribesmen were thought to have simply killed both, in order to remove the perceived threat to their village. Slessor was determined to stop this practice, along with the not so common instances of local people eating human flesh, a campaign that she was said to have successfully completed before her untimely death in 1915 and for which work she was later given a state funeral in Nigeria. Mary Kingsley was said to have spent some time with Slessor and was thought to have been inspired by the Scottish missionary, although the two were thought to have disagreed over the matter of women's rights and suffrage, which Kingsley considered to be a distraction from her real goal, of highlighting the positive influences and practices of the native African tribes.

Although the prevailing attitudes of the time suggested that most of the indigenous people of Britain's vast Empire were "uncivilised savages", travellers, explorers and writers such as Mary Kingsley were highly critical of such attitudes, believing that they were almost entirely the result of misinformed reports often created by Christian missionaries who were following their own evangelical agenda. She also believed that most westerners were ill equipped to pass judgement on the lives, customs and beliefs of the Black African people, simply because, unlike herself, they had no first hand knowledge of such matters, save for the information they received from a largely sensationalist press and the fairly rabid Christian community. Mary was said to have been particularly scathing about the missionaries habit of trying to eliminate the common native practice of polygamy, which allowed native men to have a number of wives, all of which he took responsibility for, along with any resulting children. The Christian ideal of a monogamous relationship that saw one man, one wife and their children, as a preferred family unit, was openly criticized by Kingsley, who was a first hand witness to the misery caused, as newly converted African men subsequently abandoned their additional wives and children, leaving them to rely on good fortune or charity as a sole means of survival. Such was the public interest in women like herself that when Mary returned to England in November 1895, there was an immediate clamour by newspapers, societies and the public alike to hear her talk about her adventures in Africa, although the subject of women's rights also proved to be a major distraction to her main objectives. Even though she was a single woman pursuing her own career, in the most unusual circumstances; and despite having strong views on a number of issues, Mary was not thought to be a supporter of the Women's suffrage movement, although it remained a subject that she preferred not to talk about if given a choice. That was not the case regarding her own personal attitude towards Britain's imperialist approach to the native peoples of its vast overseas possessions, a subject that was said to have caused a number of newspapers and periodicals to refuse to publish or indeed promote her work, for fear of undermining the Empire's purportedly benign attitude towards its foreign subjects, which many believed to be little more than a public pretence. However, despite these occasional attempts at censoring her work, Kingsley's stories and reports about the lives of the native peoples of Africa were said to have been fairly well received by most people, particularly those groups and societies who shared her concerns about the pervasive influence of British Christianity and Imperialism on the indigenous peoples of the Empire. She was said to have made her final journey to Africa, around the same time as the Second Boer War broke out in 1899 and immediately travelled to Cape Town in South Africa to offer her services as a nurse. Posted to Simon's Town Hospital, which was located at False Bay on the Cape Peninsula, Mary was reported to have spent some months treating wounded Boer prisoners of war, before succumbing to the effects of typhoid, a common disease within most of the hospitals and camps, which finally claimed her life on 3rd June 1900, with her body later being buried at sea, as she had previously requested. Even though Mary Kingsley remains relatively unknown to most modern day Britons, she and her work are still recalled through a number of associations and groups that were formed as a direct result of her efforts, including the later Royal African Society formed in 1968, as well as a medal awarded by the Liverpool School of Tropical Medicine, which even today continues to bear her name.

Francis Younghusband

Mary Slessor

Middle East Travels

At the same time that Mary Kingsley was exploring and writing about the peoples and places of West Africa, yet another Englishwoman, Isabella Bird, was travelling the world, producing travelogues for a number of newspapers and magazines, which helped describe and explain the many exotic lands that she visited. Although not a dedicated supporter of the rights of the world's indigenous peoples, Isabella might be more properly described as one of Britain's first civilian global travellers, a feat in itself given the available modes of transport at the time and made even more remarkable by the fact that she was a woman, at a time when women did not generally travel abroad alone. Unlike her contemporaries, Mary Kingsley and Mary Lessor, who were thought to have been driven by social conscience and religious fervour respectively, Isabella Bird was said to have simply wanted to travel, purely for the purpose of seeing the world and the people and places that it contained. Born at Boroughbridge, North Yorkshire in 1831, she was said to have been the daughter of a Church of England clergyman who was posted to several parishes within England, but who spent most of her formative years at Tattenhall in Cheshire. Reportedly a sickly child, Isabella was said to have remained in fairly good health, but became ill after a tumour was found on her spine, forcing doctors to carry out an operation to remove it, which was only partially successful. However, following the removal of the growth she was said to have undertaken her first trip abroad in 1854, when as a twenty three year old she travelled to America to visit relatives and remained there until her money ran out. Whilst there she was reported to have recorded her journey and arranged for it to be published anonymously under the title of "The Englishwoman in America", which was first released in 1856. It was in 1856 that her father was reported to have died, after which Isabella, her mother and her younger sister decided to relocate themselves to Edinburgh, where Isabella was thought to have undertaken a tour of Scotland and the Highlands, as well as making several more trips to North America and one to the Mediterranean.

Seemingly unable or unwilling to settle for any period of time, Isabelle was thought to have turned to writing as a way of supporting her desire to travel and following the death of her mother in 1868, the number of excursions and journeys she undertook was said to have increased significantly. Travelling to Australia in 1872, she quickly moved on to the islands of Hawaii, which were more commonly known in Europe as the Sandwich Islands, where she was reported to have climbed Mauna Loa, the largest volcano on earth, as well as meeting Queen Emma, the consort of the Hawaiian ruler. Having spent some weeks on the island, Isabella then travelled to the United States, where she visited the newest of the American states, Colorado, which was reported to have the ideal climate for those of a frail disposition, something that she believed herself to be. Whilst travelling around the wide open countryside, she was reported to have ridden considerable distances on horseback, adopting the straddled male riding position, rather than the conventional side-saddle posture, more usually employed by female riders. It was during her time in Colorado that Isabella was said to have met and become involved with an outlaw called Jim Nugent, who was reported to have become equally enamoured by the rather unconventional Isabella, although ultimately the relationship ended when she moved on to San Francisco, whilst Nugent himself was purportedly shot and killed in the following year. Rather than returning home to England, Isabella was then said to have left for a trip to the Far East, to visit a number of Asian countries, including Japan, where she was thought to have visited the northern region of Hokkaido and stayed with members of the local Ainu tribe. Later on she was said to have travelled to Singapore, Malaysia, Vietnam and China, although her journey there was thought to have been cut short in 1880 when she had news of her sister' being seriously ill, which forced her to return home. Back in Britain and following her sister's death from Typhoid, she was said to have married the doctor who had cared for her sister, John Bishop, who despite offering her a home, security and company, failed to satisfy her desire to travel, or address many of the psychological and health issues that regularly affected her. However, within a few years of their marriage, Bishop was said to have died, leaving her alone once again, but also allowing her the freedom to resume her travels, although this time with a purpose in mind, rather than just for pleasure.

Having undertaken some medical training, Isabella determined to travel to India as a missionary and set out for the subcontinent by ship, arriving there in February 1889 and was said to have spent the rest of the year visiting various missions, as well as setting up the Henrietta Bird Hospital in Amritsar and the John Bishop Hospital in Srinigar. She then travelled to the neighbouring states of Iran, Kurdistan and Turkey, before joining up with a Major Herbert Sawyer who was travelling from Baghdad to Tehran and accompanied him to the Persian capital, although both were said to be barely alive by the time they reached the city. Having recovered from the arduous journey, Isabella was thought to have taken her leave of Sawyer and then spent the next six months travelling the border regions of Iran, Kurdistan and Turkey at the head of her own camel caravan. Returning home to Britain in 1892, she was said to have met with the British Prime Minister, William Gladstone and with various parliamentary committees regarding the plight of the Armenians in the Middle East who were said to be suffering enormous injustices. Throughout her time in India, Tibet, Iran, Iraq and Turkey she was said to have continued her writings about the regions and the peoples she encountered there, which not only helped to maintain her public profile as a noted explorer and travel writer, but also helped to have her inducted into the Royal Geographical Society in 1892. Two years after receiving this huge honour, Isabella was reported to have undertaken her last great adventures, travelling to Yokohama in Japan, before sailing along the Han River in Korea, where she was forced to flee the country following the outbreak of the Sino-Japanese War, which eventually led to the annexation of Korea by the Japanese Empire. From there Isabella was said to have travelled along the Yangtze River in China, before going across land to the province of Sichuan, where she was attacked by a mob of local people who accused her of being a foreign devil and besieged her in a house that they subsequently set fire to. Fortunately she was said to have been rescued at the last minute by a detachment of soldiers who escorted her to safety, although in another instance, she was said to have been knocked unconscious by another crowd, but once again managed to survive the assault. Returning to Britain briefly, in 1901 Isabella was said to have visited Morocco, where she was said to have travelled with the Berber peoples and was later presented with a black stallion by the local Sultan, who was said to have held the highly unusual Englishwoman in very high regard. Returning home to Edinburgh in 1904, despite being seventy three years of age, Isabella was thought to be already making plans for yet another journey to China when she was suddenly taken ill and died on October 7th of the same year; bringing an end to the life of one of Britain's most notable and widely travelled Victorian female explorers.

For the most part though, most Victorian explorers and adventurers continued to be men, simply because their careers in the military, merchant marine, commerce and diplomatic services allowed them the opportunity to travel throughout Britain's expansive empire, a facility that was thought to have been denied to most women of the age. It was also thought to be the case that many of the men who went on to become noted explorers and adventurers came from a small number of career backgrounds, either religious, as in the case of men like David Livingstone, or military, as was the case with the previously mentioned Richard Burton. In a similar vein, other British military officers and missionaries began to venture out into the hinterlands of Central Africa and Asia, into regions that had previously remained largely undiscovered and which were inhabited by any number of previously unknown and unreported ethnic groups. One such explorer and adventurer was said to be Francis Younghusband, a British Army Officer, who was born at Murree in modern day Pakistan in 1863, but sent back to and educated in England, where he later attended the Royal Military Academy at Sandhurst, before being commissioned in the 1st King's Dragoon Guards, when he was nineteen years of age. Although his cavalry regiment was said to have seen active service in South Africa's First Boer War, it seems likely that Younghusband would have spent much of his early career stationed on the Indian subcontinent, carrying out whatever military duties were required of him. However, in 1886, the young Francis was reported to have been on leave from his regiment when he undertook his first major expedition, travelling through Manchuria, Mongolia, across the Gobi Desert and identifying a route from Kashgar in China, through to India, across the Karakoram Range, via the Mustagh Pass. At the same time he was said to have discovered the Aghil Mountains, as well as proving that the Great Karakoram was the water divide between India and Turkestan, achievements that later earned him membership of the Royal Geographical Society and the organisations gold medal award. Returning to his regiment with his reputation much enhanced, two years later Younghusband was reported to have been promoted to the rank of Captain and in the same year, 1889, was ordered to lead a detachment of Ghurkha's to the Kashmiri province of Ladakh, where raiders from the neighbouring area of Hunza were said to have been disrupting the trade route between China and India, activities that the young captain and his men eventually managed to suppress. In the following year, he was sent on a diplomatic mission to the neighbouring Chinese province of Turkestan, now Xinjiang, along with George McCartney, an Anglo-Chinese diplomat who acted as Younghusband's interpreter; and who would later be appointed as the British Consul-General in the Chinese province of Kashgar. Having spent the winter in Kashgar and leaving McCartney behind to begin his consular work, Francis was reported to have returned to India via the Parmir Mountain range, where close to the Afghan border he was said to have been confronted by Russian troops who forced him to leave the area. This particular incident was thought to have been one of many that revolved around the competing imperial ambitions of the British and Russian Empires, both of which were trying to gain influence in the Indian subcontinent, in what became known as "The Great Game". From a British perspective, the presence of Russian troops in the border regions of India, Afghanistan and some of the more northerly Princely states that were continually resisting British control, simply underpinned the belief that Russia was supplying some of the most anti-British native states with guns and ammunition, with which to fight British forces. This was thought to be especially true with the Hunza and Nagar peoples, who were openly opposing Britain's control of the northern territories, forcing the British authorities to send troops into the region, in what became known as the Hunza-Nagar Campaign of 1891, which the British were finally able to win, but with significant human losses.

A gifted artist and writer, Younghusband was thought to have written expansively about his love of the Kashmir region and in his book "Kashmir" he was said to have provided many of the publication's illustrations, helping to bring the beauty and history of the area to a much wider public audience. He was also said to have been an active participant in "The Great Game", becoming involved in the political and military "hide and seek", which was carried out by both Russia and Britain in the mountainous border regions of India and Afghanistan, as both powers battled for influence over the native states of the area. Whilst he was on leave in 1895 Younghusband was said to have acted as a correspondent for the London Times, covering the relief of the isolated British outpost at Chitral, where he himself had once been stationed and met the future British Viceroy of India, George Curzon, who was thought to have been travelling in the region. It was said to be through his friendship with Curzon that Younghusband found himself appointed as the British Commissioner for Tibet, a post he was thought to have held from 1902 until 1904; and during which he was said to have been involved in the military invasion of Tibet, along with the associated massacre of Tibetan monks. According to some reports, in 1903, the British

Viceroy of India, Lord Curzon, was said to have authorised a military invasion of Tibet, ostensibly to settle a border dispute between Tibet and the neighbouring Indian state of Sikkim, although in reality, the operation was designed to allow Britain complete control of the country of Tibet itself. British forces having crossed the Tibetan forces and advanced deep into the country were then said to have been confronted by a Tibetan militia force comprised mainly of monks, who were subsequently attacked by the combined British-Bhutanese forces, leaving a large number of the Tibetan militia either dead or wounded. Even though Younghusband was later awarded a number of honours for all of his many positive achievements in India, the infamous massacre at Guru was thought to have remained a stain on his character, as people on both sides of the argument continued to differ as to the actual cause of the incident; and more importantly, about the numbers of Tibetans who actually died there.

However, regardless of that particular issue, for the remainder of his career in India he was reported to have played much more of a political role, although he was said to have still found time to survey the Brahmaputra, Indus and Sutlej Rivers, as well as making three separate attempts to climb the largest of the Himalayan peaks, Mount Everest. He was eventually appointed as the British representative in Kashmir, a post he was thought to have held for four years before returning home to England, where he later became the president of the Royal Geographical Society, involving himself in several attempts to conquer Mount Everest, something that was never achieved in his own lifetime. According to some later historians, Younghusband was typical of his generation, in that he was a dutiful and courageous individual, who actively sought out adventure, taking great pleasure in exploring and visiting places that no European had ever visited before; and reporting them in both pictures and words. However, in other ways he was completely untypical of many of his contemporaries, in that he was said to have been deeply sympathetic to the needs, traditions and spiritual beliefs of the native peoples of the subcontinent, views not shared by many Europeans at that time. He was also reported to have accepted the need for self government in India and was no doubt gratified to witness the emergence of India's own fledgling democratic parties, even though he would never see the country achieve its formal independence in 1947. Whilst speaking to a meeting of the World Congress of Faiths in Birmingham, in July 1942, Younghusband was reported to have suffered a stroke, which did not immediately prove to be fatal, although having been released into the care of his long time lover, he then suffered a major heart attack on the 31st July 1942, which ultimately ended his life, at the age of seventy nine.

MARINERS, MERCHANTS AND THE MILITARY TOO

3. THE PLANTATION OF IRELAND

The historical relationship between Britain and Ireland is a famously troubled one and can generally be seen in the context of certain notable events, beginning with the Norman invasion of Ireland in 1169, which was reported to have been led by the Cambro-Norman knight Robert de Clare. At the same time that the east of Ireland was said to have been held by both Norman Lords and English monarchs, large parts of western Ireland was said to have remained in the hands of a number of native Irish Princes, often Catholics, who were constantly at odds with the predominantly Protestant English Crown. Inevitably the national, cultural and religious differences of the parties were thought to have led to direct military conflict between the two sides, as each fought for dominance over the other, finally leading to the Tudor invasion and settlement of Ireland during the most of the 16th century. It was said to be these same underlying causes that would ultimately lead to centuries of simmering discontent and warfare between Britain and Ireland, cause the deaths of hundreds of thousands of people on both sides of the argument, a conflict which would only finally be resolved at the start of the 20th century, some 400 years later.

King John

Henry Sidney

William Pelham

According to most sources, prior to 1169 the English people were said to have had little interest, or indeed involvement in Ireland, save for the regular commercial trading that took place between the two countries, which was thought to have been in existence for hundreds of years. It was only in the second half of the 12th century that a Norman nobleman called Richard de Clare or "Strongbow" was said to have arrived there, following an invitation from an Irish chieftain called MacMurrow, whose lands had been stolen from him, thereby creating a situation that would inevitably lead to English involvement in that country. It was said to be in response to De Clare's arrival in Ireland that the English King, Henry II, led his own military expedition to the island in 1171, ostensibly to contest the Norman noblemen's rights to rule there. It has also been suggested that Henry was also attempting to pre-empt any future challenge to his own rule in England, although having overcome De Clare and his allies, Henry was then reported to have passed his new Irish territories to his younger son Prince John, the brother of King Richard I, who later ascended to the English throne. Even though Prince John was widely recognised and accepted as the King of Ireland by most of the subject Irish people and English settlers, his royal possessions there were said to have been almost entirely limited and restricted to the east coast of the island, from Waterford in the south to Ulster in the north, whilst the western part of the country continued to be held by a number of native Irish Lords as individual Petty Kingdoms, who paid homage to their overlord Prince John. According to some records, John was said to have visited Ireland on at least two occasions, in 1185 and 1210, during which time he was reported to have campaigned against the native Irish rulers and where possible sought to replace them with his own candidates.

The last few remaining Norman interests, which continued to exist within Ireland, were thought to have continually clashed with the native Princes there, each side trying to strengthen their position at the expense of the other. From the middle of the 13th century there was reported to have been nearly a century of intermittent hostilities between the two parties, which resulted in large swathes of English and Norman lands falling back into the hands of the Irish families who had owned them prior to De Clare's invasion of 1169. The English and Norman communities were said to have been further weakened by the arrival of the Black Death in Ireland in around 1348, which saw the remaining settlers from both groups pushed farther back to well defended enclaves along the east coast of the country, essentially handing even more lands back to the native Princes, who were only too happy to exploit the relatively unexpected withdrawal of these foreign forces. By the end of the 15th century, English control over Ireland was thought to have been virtually non-existent, save for the immediate areas outside of the heavily defended English port enclaves, which the English had just about managed to retain control of. With England itself divided by the War of the Roses, many of their former possessions in Ireland were reported to have reverted back to the control of the native Irish lords, especially the Fitzgerald family, the historic Earls of Kildare, who were said to have controlled much of the country by force of arms. Along with a number of other subordinate Irish families, much of Ireland was thought to be under Irish control, although the English authorities in Dublin remained in place, albeit in a non-functioning form. Perhaps because of this, in 1494 the English was reported to have withdrawn its government ministers from Ireland altogether and decided to administer its foreign possessions from London.

Full English involvement in Ireland was only thought to have started in the first half of the 16th century, during the reign of King Henry VIII, whose Reformation of the church in England, immediately put him at odds with the Catholic Church of Rome, which was then the predominant faith in Ireland, therefore making its native Roman Catholic population a potential threat to Henry's new Protestant Church. Beginning in 1536, successive and largely Protestant English monarchs were said to have waged a series of often brutal and religiously inspired military campaigns against the Catholic majority in Ireland, culminating in the colonisation of captured native Irish lands by tens of thousands of English Protestant settlers, whose allegiance was first and foremost to the English Crown and its associated Anglican Church. This extended period of religious and military conflict, running from 1536 to around 1691, is often referred to as the "Plantation of Ireland", a process that saw tens of thousands of both English and Scottish settlers forcibly introduced into Ireland, generally at a direct cost to the native Roman Catholic peoples and ultimately leading to generations of sectarian violence, which remains there even through to the present day. King Henry's decision to re-conquer Ireland in 1536 and bring that country back under full English control was not just because of different religious beliefs, but was also said to have been caused in part by the Fitzgerald's decision to employ Burgundian troops in Ireland to help maintain control of the country. In conjunction with the arrival of this foreign mercenary force, the Irish leader's reported decision to anoint one Lambert Simnel as the de facto King of England in 1487, undoubtedly made it imperative for Henry to suppress all of Ireland, not least to ensure that they could not be used as a base for a foreign invasion of England, then or in the future.

In 1541 Henry was said to have upgraded Ireland's status from that of a colony, which was under the control of an appointed Lord, to become a kingdom in its own right, which he could then rule as a legitimate monarch. At the same time, a new Irish Parliament was reported to have been constituted and many of the leading Irish Princes and Norman Lords, who held possessions throughout Ireland, were then engaged in helping to administer Henry's new kingdom. Although there were said to have been several isolated regions within Ireland that continued to operate outside of the monarch's immediate control, for the rest of his reign Henry was said to have worked towards bringing these generally independent regions into his new Irish kingdom, either by negotiation, but more generally through force of arms. It was only during the 5 year reign of Henry's eldest daughter, Mary Tudor that the Roman Catholic's plight in Ireland was significantly improved, as the English Queen, along with her Spanish consort, Philip of Spain, who were both Roman Catholics, mercilessly suppressed the Protestant minority in Ireland, a situation that was said to have continued right through to Queen Mary's death in 1558 and the ascension of her half sister, Elizabeth, to the English throne in the same year. It was only during the reign of Henry's youngest daughter, Elizabeth I that her father's plans for Ireland were fully achieved, but even then, not before several bitterly fought rebellions and conflicts had brought further bloodshed and social division to the kingdom of Ireland. The Desmond Rebellions, the grounding of the ships from the Spanish Armada and the Nine Years War were thought to have been just three of the notable events that wracked the country and its native peoples, before the English authorities in Dublin finally established some degree of overall control in 1603. Unfortunately for all parties concerned though, the ongoing religious intolerance of both Protestant and Roman Catholic faiths; and in particular the English attempts to convert Roman Catholics to the Protestant faith simply helped to deepen the resentment that Catholics in Ireland felt towards England, its Queen and its largely Protestant population.

The Desmond Rebellions were reported to have been named after a series of revolts that took place in Ireland between 1569 and 1583, which were said to have been led by two notable Catholic families in the country, the Fitzgerald's who were the Earls of Desmond and the Geraldine's. As was perhaps typical of the time, in their simplest form these uprisings were brought about by the ongoing and seemingly insurmountable differences that existed between Protestant England and Catholic Ireland, with the Butler family representing the unwelcome influence of England within the Irish homelands. During the 1560's, Queen Elizabeth, who was keen to extend her influence throughout the country, was said to have ordered her Lord Deputy of Ireland, Henry Sidney, to establish a number of Lord Presidencies, or local military Governors, in order to maintain the Queen's Peace and thereby reduce the power and influence of the Catholic landowners, such as the Fitzgerald's and Geraldine's. In 1565 the Earl's of Desmond and their Protestant contemporaries, the Butler's, were said to have fought a pitched battle with one another in clear defiance of Elizabeth's orders and were consequently summoned to England to explain themselves to the English monarch. Butler, who was a cousin of the Queen, was thought to have been subsequently pardoned for his actions, whereas the Fitzgerald brothers, Gerald and John, were both reported to have been arrested and held in the Tower of London. With the leaders of the clan imprisoned, it then fell to another member of the Fitzgerald family to take over the day-to-day control of their holdings and assets in Ireland, in order to ensure that the family fortunes remained intact. James Fitzmaurice Fitzgerald was thought to have previously lost lands to the English and was a fervent Roman Catholic, who hoped to see the Protestant Elizabeth, removed from the throne of England as quickly as possible and by whatever means necessary. Possibly with this aim in mind and perhaps rather foolishly, James was thought to have approached the Spanish king, Philip II, requesting military support for a planned revolt in Ireland, which he hoped would be supported by other leading Irish Catholic landowners. According to a number of sources, James was said to have eventually managed to persuade a number of local clans, including the McCarthy's, O'Sullivan's and O'Keefe's to join his proposed uprising and even more surprisingly was said to have been joined in the potentially dangerous enterprise by two disillusioned members of the Butler family.

Fitzgerald was reported to have launched his rebellion in June 1569 by attacking an English settler colony just outside of Cork, after which his forces moved on to attack the main town itself, following the local landlord's failure to support his revolt. He was then thought to have besieged the town of Kilkenny, home to the Earl of Ormonde, whose family name was Butler, a relative of the two Butler's who were actually accompanying Fitzgerald and the same man who had previously been summoned to London by Queen Elizabeth and was still there. Unfortunately for James Fitzgerald, Henry Sidney, the Queen's Lord Deputy of Ireland very quickly raised a force of some six hundred men, who was supplemented by a further four hundred men landed by sea and then moved south to begin attacking the lands of Fitzgerald and his allies. Sidney was subsequently joined by Thomas Butler, who had travelled back from London and who had managed to persuade his two erstwhile relatives to abandon their part in the revolt. The English Lord Deputy's forces were further added to by Humphrey Gilbert, the newly appointed Governor of Munster, who joined in the attacks on the rebels estates, forcing many of Fitzgerald's allies to abandon the cause, in favour of returning home to defend their own properties and essentially leaving him to face the English forces alone. Humphrey Gilbert particularly was said to have been a notoriously cruel and vindictive man, infamous for killing innocent civilians indiscriminately and setting up the severed heads of his victims at the entrance to his headquarters. Finally forced back into the mountains of Kerry, Fitzgerald was reported to have initially tried to wage a guerrilla campaign against his English adversaries, a campaign that was reported to have lasted for very nearly three years and even as each of his allies were lost or gave up the cause, he was said to have carried on regardless. Finally, in February 1573 and with less than one hundred men at his command, Fitzgerald was thought to have been compelled to accept the English commander's terms, receiving a pardon for his life, but very little else. By 1574 he was said to have been landless once again and sometime during that year he was reported to have left Ireland destined for France, where he hoped to find support from the Catholic monarchs of Europe, in order to continue his fight against the English Crown.

In the meantime, Gerald and John Fitzgerald, who had previously been incarcerated on the orders of the English Queen, had been released from their imprisonment to help stabilize the political situation in southern Ireland. However, the English authorities, eager to avoid any repetition of the Catholic led revolt, were said to have introduced new laws in order to limit the size of the military forces that could be retained by private landowners, reducing it down to a maximum of twenty horsemen. Individual tenants that would have previously owed military service to their nobleman landowner now had to pay rents instead, helping to ensure that any such private armies remained relatively small and therefore posed little threat to the English authorities. By the end of the rebellion, the biggest beneficiary was thought to have been the Butler family, the Dukes of Ormonde, who were said to have gained extensive power and influence within southern Ireland, thanks largely to their continuing support for the English Crown. Even though the first Desmond Rebellion was thought to be over by 1575, the actions of certain English Lords continued to cause great anger and resentment amongst the general population and most notably within the Catholic majority. William Drury, the Lord President of Munster was reported to have hung several hundred Catholic men years after the rebellion had actually ended and at the same time, a number of Gaelic customs, including those which celebrated Irish identity were said to have been outlawed by the authorities. These actions and the increasing numbers of English colonists, who were arriving in Ireland to settle former native held lands also continued to be the cause of underlying bitterness between the two communities, ensuring that hostilities would be an ongoing feature of Irish life for many years to come.

In 1579 the exiled James Fitzmaurice Fitzgerald was reported to have returned to Ireland accompanied by a mixed contingent of Spanish and Italian Catholic troops; as well as funds supplied by the Roman Catholic Pontiff in Rome. Once ashore, James was thought to have quickly gained support from his relative, John Fitzgerald, the brother of the Earl of Desmond, along with many other disaffected landowners, soldiers and clansmen, who were willing to risk all, for the chance to overthrow English rule in Ireland. Unfortunately for all concerned, James was thought to have been killed shortly after returning to his homeland and control of the rebellion passed into the hands of his relative John Fitzgerald, a far less charismatic figure than James. Although the Earl of Desmond, Gerald Fitzgerald, was not thought to have played any sort of significant role in this second Desmond Rebellion, it was undoubtedly because of his brother's leadership of it that Gerald too was also labelled as a traitor by the English authorities in Ireland. Having been accused of wrongdoing, the Earl, who had little to lose, was then reported to have actively participated in the revolt and helped the his fellow Irishmen to sack a number of English-held towns and their outlying settlements, with the intention of driving the largely Protestant settlers out of Ireland forever. With this sudden and unexpected escalation of the revolt, Elizabeth was reported to have despatched additional English troops to Ireland, under the command of William Pelham, with orders to suppress the rebellion as quickly and as ruthlessly as possible. Upon his arrival in Ireland, Pelham was also said to have been able to raise a large force of local Irish levies, which, along with his main body of English troops were quickly able to bring much of southern Ireland back under the Crown's control.

Thomas Fitzgerald   Pope Pius V   Mary Queen of Scots

With the second Desmond Rebellion seemingly over, life in Ireland began to return to normal, but the Queen's peace was suddenly shattered once again, when the revolt was thought to have been reignited in Leinster, by a number of local clan chiefs and other anti English groups. A second English military force was immediately sent into the region to put down the revolt, but this force, under the command of Earl Grey de Wilton, was reported to have been ambushed by the rebels at Glen Malure in August 1580 and up to eight hundred men were said to have been lost in the attack. The situation, from an English perspective, was thought to have worsened in the following month, when some six hundred Papal troops were said to have been successfully landed at Smerwick in Ireland. Unfortunately for the Irish rebels these foreign troops were said to have played no significant part in the rebellion as they were subsequently bombarded into submission by English troops and the Papal forces who survived the onslaught and surrendered, were reported to have been massacred by the English soldiers shortly afterwards. These events were thought to have marked a turning point in the revolt, with the uprising having been partially crushed by the English authorities, army commander's now adopted a scorched earth policy, which they hoped would deprive the remaining Irish rebels of food supplies and local support, by destroying any useable foodstuffs within their areas of operation. Although this was thought to have been a common feature of military warfare for hundreds of years, almost inevitably, the real victims of such policies were thought to have been the local people, who despite being entirely innocent of any wrongdoing, nonetheless suffered for the actions of their fellow countrymen. By the middle of 1581, the rebellion was thought to have been largely over, as many of the Irish rebels had chosen to accept the Queen's Pardon and the leader of the initial revolt, John Fitzgerald, was reported to have been killed at the beginning of 1582, an event that further undermined the will of the remaining rebels to continue their fight with England. The Queen however, was said to have been unwilling to extend her royal pardon to the Earl of Desmond, Gerald Fitzgerald, who she believed had betrayed her and as a result he was said to have been relentlessly pursued by the English authorities in Ireland for well over two years, from 1581 to 1583. Almost inevitably though, Gerald was thought to have finally been caught by members of the Moriarty clan in November 1583, who later claimed the £1,000 reward for the "traitor's" head, which had previously been offered by the English Queen.

Ultimately, this particular uprising, along with the first Desmond Rebellion and the many other revolts that took place in Ireland during the Tudor period, were said to have brought nothing but misery, starvation and death to the largely innocent population of the country, who saw their crops destroyed and their people displaced. The scorched earth policy, which had been adopted by the English forces, was thought to have caused the deaths of many thousands of innocent Catholic workers, either through simple starvation or its associated diseases. Earl Grey de Wilton, one of the main architects of the policy, was said to have been recalled to England shortly afterwards, ostensibly because his methods were deemed to be too severe and might just cause a backlash amongst the Catholic population, who were suffering through his personal actions. Unfortunately, the removal of English extremists such as De Wilton was thought to have been a case of too little, too late, as the authorities had already begun a new round of colonising Irish lands and "planting" thousands of English Protestant settlers throughout Ireland. Many of these Irish lands were said to have formerly been in the ownership of the Fitzgerald's and Geraldine's; and had subsequently been seized by the English Crown, in recompense for those noble family's rebellious acts. It was precisely because of such actions that Ireland would continue to remain as a country that was rife with insurrection for generations to come and within a decade was once again reported to have been wracked by murderous rebellion in the form of the Nine Years War, or alternatively as, Tyrone's Rebellion.

It is perhaps worth noting that both Elizabeth I and her successor James I had good reason to fear the Roman Catholic faith and some of its more radical followers. On the 25th February 1570, the Pontiff, Pope Pius V was reported to have issued a Papal Bull, calling for the removal of Queen Elizabeth from the English throne and reportedly exonerating any Roman Catholic, who happened to be involved with assassinating the English monarch. According to most sources, Elizabeth was thought to have taken a generally quite pragmatic about the Roman Catholic faith and believed that so long as it was practiced in private, rather than publicly, she had few personal problems with people practicing their faith, in whatever fashion they chose. However, the later issue of the Papal Bull and the planned assassination of her by a group of English Catholic noblemen, headed by the Duke of Norfolk, who planned to replace her with the Roman Catholic, Mary, Queen of Scots, was said to have changed Elizabeth's attitude markedly; and from that point onwards, she was thought to have taken a far less tolerant attitude towards Catholic's generally. Her royal successor, James I of England, was also thought to have his own reasons to fear the Roman Catholics in England, following the attempted plot to blow up the English Parliament, with him in it, which took place on 5th November 1605. Led by one Robert Catesby, the actual implementation of the plot was said to have been left in the hands of one Guy Fawkes or Guido Fawkes, a member of a Catholic extremist group, fighting against the suppression of Catholicism in England. Interestingly, the English Parliament of the time, was reported to have contained a significant number of leading Roman Catholics within its ranks, who were presumably considered expendable, as far as Catesby and Fawkes were concerned and would certainly have perished had the plotters not been discovered, prior to their plan being carried out.

Although the colonisation or "Plantation" of Ireland was reported to have started during the reign of Henry VIII, it is more commonly associated with Queen Elizabeth I and her royal successors, the Stuart family. Reminiscent of the colonisation of Wales by Edward I in the late 12th century, the practice of colonising generally unfriendly territories was a strategy that was thought to have been used for hundreds, if not thousands of years, prior to England's use of the tactic in Ireland during the 16th and 17th centuries. Not only did colonisation offer new, much needed lands to the victorious monarchs and their peoples, but also ensured that the conquered populations were constantly monitored for signs of future insurrection and perhaps more importantly, reduced the need for a large standing army to watch over them. Although the strategy of colonisation has been attacked by some modern day historians and compared to the "ethnic cleansing" of more recent years, it should be remembered that applying current standards of behaviour to historic events is not only inappropriate, but serves little purpose, other than to deliberately revise ancient events and practices in order to mislead current generations and help create largely misinformed opinions. Elizabeth's deliberately planned plantation of Ireland certainly increased Catholic antagonism towards the English generally, as previously held Irish lands were seized and subsequently handed over to English and Scottish Protestant settlers. Under the terms of these English colonisation plans, native Catholic workers and former landowners were forbidden from owning or renting lands in these plantation areas, or indeed from labouring on them, leaving many farm workers destitute and family members dispossessed of their hereditary land holdings. As a consequence of these new laws, large numbers of Catholic noblemen were reported to have been compelled to leave Ireland, forcing them to sell their estates to new settlers, often at rock bottom prices; such was the fear of the lands being seized by the English authorities, in which case they may well have received nothing at all. It was thought to be as a result of such treatment that a significant number of these same leading Catholic noblemen were later reported to have become highly active opponents of English rule in Ireland and in some cases undertook military service with Elizabeth's main European enemies, Spain and France.

The last great Irish revolt that took place during the final years of Elizabeth's reign and through to the ascendancy of her royal successor James I, was the Nine Years War, which is otherwise known as Tyrone's Rebellion and that raged from 1594 through to 1603, the final year of the Tudor Queen's life. Led by Hugh O'Neil, the second Earl of Tyrone and Hugh Roe O'Donnell, these two noblemen were reported to have taken up arms against the increasing number of English settlers being brought into Ireland generally, although in reality, much of their resistance was fought in and around the province of Ulster, in the north of the country. This particular rebellion was said to have been notable for the numbers of English troops that were employed in helping to suppress the revolt, around 18,000 at its height, reportedly the largest number of English soldiers ever employed there up until that time. Unsurprisingly perhaps, the uprising was thought to have had its roots in the increasing numbers of English settlers being brought into Ireland as part of the Elizabethan plantation of the country and their advance towards and into the historically native held lands of the Irish Catholics, including the O'Neil's, O'Donnell's and numerous other titled families. Hugh O'Neil himself was said to have come from one of these noble families, but their rights and entitlements had been usurped by another member of the clan in earlier years. Despite this and using what few possessions he had, O'Neil was said to have built a series of cleverly crafted alliances and used his political astuteness to recover many of these lost family assets, eventually taking his rightful place as head of the O'Neil clan throughout Ireland. However, having restored his family's fortunes and his rightful place in society, Hugh was reported to have tried to extend his influence by making new and sometimes dangerous alliances, most notably with the Spanish king, Philip II, the leading Roman Catholic of the age and a sworn enemy of the English queen, Elizabeth I. King Philip was said to have provided O'Neil with much needed funds and arms, with which to protect his lands and it was thought to be as a result of such allegiances that Hugh was said to be able to field an army of some 8,000 men, armed with the very latest muskets, something that was unprecedented for an Irish Catholic nobleman of the age.

Direct conflict between the Earl of Tyrone and the English authorities was said to have first arisen during the early 1590's when Queen Elizabeth's Lord Deputy in Ireland attempted to bring the north of the country, including Tyrone's own home region, under full English control. His imposition of a provincial President and Sheriffs was reported to have been resisted by a number of local Irish landlords, including the McMahon's, O'Farrell's and O'Reilly's, as a result of which, some of them were arrested, tried and executed, as well as having their lands sequestrated by the English authorities. Although it had been intended that both the O'Neil and O'Donnell homelands would eventually be brought under central control, geographical factors were thought to have prevented this from taking place. Naturally occurring features such as marshes, mountains and sometimes impenetrably thick woodlands meant that the O'Neil and O'Donnell lands were generally well protected from any form of military attack and those passes that did offer access to them, could be easily be defended by the well equipped forces of the native Irish lords. During 1592 and 1593 there were said to have been a number of minor skirmishes in the north of Ireland, with English Sheriffs regularly being driven out of Irish held territories and reciprocal attacks being launched against isolated English settlements, which had previously been established in these generally unregulated border areas. At the same time that these minor military engagements were taking place, O'Neil was reported to have been negotiating with Elizabeth's royal agents, in the hope of persuading the English monarch to appoint him, as Lord President of Ulster, although Elizabeth was said to be distrustful of O'Neil, fearing that if she appointed him to the post, then he would almost certainly unilaterally declare himself Prince of Ulster once his position was secure.

Perhaps realising that the English Queen would never officially appoint him to the post, in 1595 O'Neil was thought to have ended any attempt to negotiate a settlement, choosing instead to take a more direct military approach to the problem, by simply joining his neighbours, the O'Donnell's and the O'Connor's in physically opposing English forces in Ulster.

Recognising perhaps that negotiation was the best way of resolving the impending problem; the English authorities were reported to have tried finding an equitable solution with O'Neil in 1596, but failed to agree terms with the Earl, so subsequently tried unsuccessfully to take control of Ulster by force of arms. The English forces were thought to have tried several times to subjugate the lands of Tyrone and his allies, but each time were said to have been beaten back by the large native Irish army ranged against them, most notably the highly professional musketeers, who were said to have been employed by Hugh O'Neil. Having survived innumerable attempts to dislodge him, the Earl of Tyrone and his allied force then appear to have gone on a political and military offensive, appointing his own agents around the country and causing the rebellion to spread throughout the whole of Ireland, especially in the north, where thousands of dissident Irishmen were said to have rallied to his cause. Attacking English held estates and forcing the Protestant settlers to flee for their lives, much of O'Neil's support was reported to be in the centre of the country, where the English had few major fortified garrisons to oppose him. However, the situation was thought to have been entirely different around the coast of Ireland, where a large number of well established and highly defended settlements, some dating from the 12th century and generally allied to English interests, refused to support O'Neil's uprising, despite any sort of overtures that the rebel Earl made to them. According to some reports, such negotiations were not always undertaken out of choice, but often through sheer necessity, as Tyrone's lightly armed forces, generally lacked the equipment to physically storm the rugged defences of these English held ports and towns, so trying to persuade the inhabitants to join him, was often the only option left open to Hugh O'Neil.

Finally in 1599, Elizabeth was said to have despatched Robert Devereaux, the second Earl of Essex, to Ireland, along with over 17,000 English troops, to put an end to the rebellion. Unfortunately for the queen, Devereaux was not a gifted military strategist and having spread his troops throughout Ireland, with the larger garrisons often billeted in the most unsanitary conditions, he very quickly began to lose thousands of his men to ambushes, direct military engagements, typhoid, dysentery and desertion. In what appears to have been an act of blind panic and desperation, Devereaux then appears to have made the ill-fated decision to try and negotiate with O'Neil, rather than to confront him militarily, a move that would lead to him being publicly criticised and even ridiculed back in England. Not content with making what was clearly the wrong decision, he was then thought to have compounded his error, by leaving Ireland and returning to England, without Elizabeth's permission, a clear breach of Court and military etiquette. Always a highly divisive figure within the English Court, Devereaux then tried to silence his critics within royal circles through force of arms, a move that was not only unsuccessful, but one which ultimately cost him his life. Devereaux was said to have been replaced in Ireland by Lord Mountjoy, who immediately appointed two highly experienced military commanders, George Carew and Arthur Chichester, to continue the English campaign against O'Neil and his rebellious allies. By 1601 this change in English leadership was reported to have radically changed the military situation in Ireland, with Carew's forces having regained control over much of the north of Ireland and forced large numbers of O'Neil's foreign mercenaries to flee the country. It is also clear that much of O'Neil's private land, which had previously been relatively inaccessible to the English and thus provided a safe haven for the rebels, could now be attacked by Mountjoy's troops, following seaborne landings at the English held towns of Derry and Carrickfergus. Tyrone and his allies were said to have been further undone by the actions of rival families to the O'Neil's and O'Donnell's who were keen to see Hugh O'Neil's power and influence reduced, which led them to ally themselves with the English in devastating the Earl's lands, depriving him of necessary supplies and his supporters of the will to fight.

Hugh O'Neil   Robert Devereaux   Lord Mountjoy

However, despite such setbacks, it was not all bad news for O'Neil and his followers, as in 1601, some 4,000 professional Spanish troops were reported to have landed at Kinsale in the south of Ireland, having been despatched by the Spanish king Philip II. Unfortunately for the Earl of Tyrone, the English commander, Lord Mountjoy, had already been informed about the landing and immediately moved to besiege these troops in the south, essentially leaving the two Roman Catholic forces located at opposite ends of the country. Realising the situation, O'Neil was then reported to have gathered his remaining forces and moved south, towards his besieged Spanish allies and perhaps hoping to launch a surprise attack against Mountjoy, leaving him trapped between the two Catholic armies, who were intent on his destruction. As he marched his army south, O'Neil was said to have tried to recruit new men to his cause and devastated the lands of those noblemen who were opposed to his military venture. Finally reaching Kinsale in January 1602, once again O'Neil's campaign was said to have suffered a setback, as his approach to the town had been monitored by Mountjoy's English forces, who promptly launched a full scale assault on the Irish Earl's generally exhausted army at the Battle of Kinsale, which O'Neil and his supporters subsequently lost.

Having been defeated by the English force, the remnants of O'Neil's Irish army was thought to have retreated north, being further diminished by cold, starvation and disease, before they were essentially destroyed as a credible fighting force during the Siege of Dunbuy, which was commanded by one of Lord Mountjoy's lieutenants George Carew. With the rebellion fatally undermined, one of O'Neil's leading allies, Hugh O'Donnell, was reported to have left Ireland and sought refuge in Spain, where he was said to have died later the same year. As for Tyrone himself, he was reported to have carried on his revolt, largely conducting a guerrilla campaign against the English and spending much of his time trying to avoid the English forces of Mountjoy and his subordinates. For Tyrone personally, the rebellion was thought to have been a disaster, as not only had his military campaign been generally undermined through bad choices and equally bad luck, but his vast private holdings in Ireland were now generally lost to him. Not only had his home estates been systematically devastated by the English and their Irish allies, but perhaps more significantly, the O'Neil family's inauguration stone, the symbol of the clan's history and prestige in Ireland, was reported to have been smashed into pieces at Tullahogue. Famine was said to have been widespread, as the effects of the English force's scorched earth policy began to impact on the local population, with some reporters suggesting that local people had even resorted to cannibalism, such was said to be the desperation to simply stay alive. In fact the oppression meted out by the English, was thought to have been so severe that even the staunchest of O'Neil's allies, felt compelled to accept the terms being offered to them by the English and even Tyrone himself, finally had to admit defeat in March 1603, when he surrendered on terms to the English commander, Lord Mountjoy.

Rather fortunately for Hugh O'Neil, just one week before he had surrendered himself to the English commander, Queen Elizabeth I was reported to have died and had been succeeded by James I, a monarch who was keen to see an end to the highly expensive rebellion in Ireland, which according to some reports, had very nearly bankrupted the English treasury. As a result of James' pragmatism, O'Neil and his allies were said to have been granted full pardons by the new king and in 1604 Lord Mountjoy was reported to have issued a full amnesty to all rebels throughout Ireland. Despite these acts of public forgiveness however, those that took part in Tyrone's Rebellion were never entirely trusted by the English authorities again. With their status and personal holdings severely reduced after the revolt, a large number of these men were said to have left Ireland in around 1607 in what later became known as the "Flight of the Earls". According to some sources the original intention had been that they would travel abroad to raise support for a future Catholic invasion of Ireland, but ultimately found their plans undone by subsequent peace treaties signed between England and its historic enemy, the Catholic kingdom of Spain. As a result, the lands owned by these largely absentee Irish lords were eventually confiscated by the English Crown and used to settle even more English colonists in Ireland, which almost inevitably led to future conflicts between the suppressed Catholic majority and their incoming Protestant neighbours. Although no definitive death toll could ever be established for the period of this particular rebellion, which is commonly known as the Nine Years War, but it has been suggested by some modern academics that around 100,000 people, English and Irish, were likely to have perished during the conflict, most of them succumbing to disease, cold and starvation, rather than through battle injuries. In addition to the numerous military campaigns, which the English Crown was reported to have waged in Ireland, political and land reforms were also thought to have been introduced, which were specifically designed to reduce what little influence was left to Ireland's Roman Catholic majority, including the reorganisation of the country's local boroughs in 1613, which took local political control away from the native Catholics and put it in the hands of the English Protestants instead. Other reforms followed and by the end of the 17th century Roman Catholics were reported to have been barred from being directly elected to the Irish Parliament, despite making up some 80% of the country's total population.

The 17th century in Ireland, was also thought to have been notable for the two Civil Wars that were fought there; the first between 1641 and 1653 and the second between 1689 and 1691, both of which saw the suppressed Catholic majority rebel against English interests and which resulted in many thousands of people being killed on both sides of the argument. Generally known as the period of the Irish Confederacy, these wars were said to have been fought against a background of the highly divisive English Civil War, which saw an anointed English king come into direct opposition with his own Parliament, as a result of which, the monarch, Charles Stuart, would ultimately lose his head. Depending on whose version of events one chooses to follow, the 1641 rebellion in Ireland was said to have been caused through the vengeful Protestants and Puritans of England who regarded the Catholic population in Ireland as allies of their own national enemy, Charles I, who was seeking to undermine and destroy the authority of the English Parliament; and as such the Catholic community in Ireland were generally regarded as enemies of the Parliamentary cause. Alternatively, from the Irish Catholic's perspective, the English Civil War, which was just beginning to rage across the Irish Sea, was generally regarded as an event that might be used to their own advantage, allowing them to support the king, in return for a lessening or repeal of those previously enacted English laws that tended to disadvantage the Roman Catholic's in Ireland. However, the actual truth of the matter probably lay somewhere in the middle, with some Catholics leaders recognising the benefit of supporting King Charles I, in the hope of regaining their status and previously sequestered lands within Ireland under a victorious Stuart monarchy, rather than under a generally antagonistic British Parliament. Additionally, even in the event that Charles Stuart was unsuccessful in his conflict with Parliament, it also seems that these leading Catholic lords in Ireland, also saw the English Civil War as an opportunity to re-establish their own high status and influence in their native land, while the English authorities had "taken their eye off the ball", so to speak.

Either way, it was undoubtedly as the result of these mutual misgivings and general opportunism, which saw the first uprising launched by the Catholic leadership in 1641 and the formation of the Catholic Confederacy in the following year, which ultimately became the de facto government of Ireland for an extended period. Possibly because of promises made by the increasingly desperate King Charles I, who was no doubt keen to retain his regal authority in England at any cost, a number of Ireland's leading Roman Catholic noblemen were said to have joined his military campaign against Parliament, in an alliance that would ultimately have catastrophic results for them personally and for Ireland. It has also been suggested that a number of the Irish nobles that took part in the rebellion were the very same men, or at least the successors of those, who had been forced to flee Ireland during Queen Elizabeth's reign, when large swathes of Catholic owned lands were seized by the English Crown. Initially some of them were thought to have hoped that the rebellion would be a relatively bloodless affair, given that the English were involved in killing one another in the battles of the English Civil War. Unfortunately for everyone involved however, the Catholic plans to seize control of Ireland were thwarted when an informer advised the Protestant authorities of the planned rebellion, leading to a number of the potential rebels being seized before they could put their plans into action. Other members of the plot however, were able to carry out their roles, seizing English held possessions throughout Ireland, although this was said to have led to a gross overreaction by the English authorities, who despatched two Protestant military commanders, Charles Coote and William St Leger, to suppress a rebellion that did not really exist and who were later accused of using excessive force and sheer brutality against any Irish Catholic who was unfortunate to cross their path. In fact, according to some historians, it was said to be the overreactions of Coote and St Leger which actually caused the Irish rebellion of 1641 to dramatically escalate, turning it from a relatively small outbreak of disorder into a widespread Catholic Uprising, which would costs thousands of lives on both sides.

In the province of Ulster, which was one of England's main plantation areas in Ireland, the lack of local military control, was said to have led to widespread attacks on Protestant settlers by outraged Catholic workers. Although the leaders of the rebellion were thought to have tried to prevent such unwarranted attacks, they were said to have found it almost impossible to control the local farm workers, who often gave vent to their long held grievances by attacking any English colonists that they happened to come across. Almost inevitably, word of these local insurrections was said to have spread throughout the country and because the English authorities seemed to be unable to stop them, being forced back into their fortified settlements such as Dublin, other local Catholic workers assumed that they too were safe to carry out similar sectarian attacks in their own areas. In most cases Protestant workers, settlers and landowners were simply driven off their lands by gangs of marauding Roman Catholics, although in some cases where the Protestant settlers resisted the mob, tempers were said to have flared and blood was spilt. The reasons for the Catholic majority's sudden outburst of anger were thought to be many and varied, but generally obvious, given the actions that had been taken against them by the English state in previous decades. Dispossessed of their own lands and often poorly treated by the incoming English settlers, not only had they suffered starvation, poverty and disease, but also faced the real prospect of having their faith and native language taken away from them by an occupying foreign force. In addition to these causes, there were of course just plain and simple human reasons for the sometimes violent antagonism that people felt towards one another, where personal grudges could be settled, or a neighbour's property stolen, through sheer opportunism.

As always, propaganda was said to have played a large and important role in both sides argument, as to who was right or wrong, who was guilty or innocent, with both parties anxious to gain and hold the moral high ground. English Parliamentarian pamphlets of the time claimed that up to 200,000 English and Scottish settlers had been killed by Catholics during the rebellion, although in reality only some 5-10,000 colonists were thought to have lost their lives, with around half of that number succumbing to enemy actions and the rest lost through disease, cold or starvation. Clearly though, such deliberate misinformation not only helped to stiffen English resolve to settle the Irish problem once and for all, but also helped to explain and excuse some of the atrocities that were later said to have been committed by English troops and their military commanders. The reality of the situation, according to most scholars, was that during the revolt, the general pattern of events was that in most cases Catholic rebels would simply beat and rob the English settlers, before burning their properties and evicting them from their lands. It was only very occasionally that settlers would physically resist the mob and the situation would escalate to a point where reason was lost and people would be attacked and killed. It is perhaps also worth remembering that at this point in time, most information was conveyed almost entirely by word of mouth, as most common people would have been illiterate and so their news would have received orally, rather than in a written form. Also, unlike today where conflicts are generally monitored by objective reporters, such independent points of view were almost non existent during the 16th and 17th centuries, so notable or catastrophic events were almost always reported by those who were predisposed to support one side or the other from the outset.

Even though the 1641 Irish rebellion is generally seen in the context of Catholics attacking the English Protestant settlers who had colonised their lands, any idea that such unprovoked and sometimes lethal outbreaks of violence were always initiated by the Catholics is entirely incorrect. At Lisnagarvey in November 1641 and following a failed rebel raid on the largely Protestant township, several hundred Catholics, who were reported to have been captured by the settlers, were later said to have been murdered in cold blood. This act was said to have contributed to the Portadown massacre and the killing of settlers and their families at Kilmore, whilst English settler families were also said to have been murdered in County Armagh and County Tyrone, as well as those lost in the infamous Shrule massacre of 1642. Such ferocity by both sides during the rebellion ensured that neither party would ever fully trust the other again, or that Catholics would be given a share of political power in any future government of Ireland by their Protestant neighbours. Despite the fact that Roman Catholics still formed the majority of the population, this highly antagonistic attitude on the part of the largely nervous Protestant minority, tended to overlook the fact that criminal acts had been perpetrated by both sides during the rebellion, including the slaughter of Catholics around the town of Newry by supposedly professional English soldiers.

George Carew

Oliver Cromwell

Henry Ireton

At the outbreak of the English Civil War, large numbers of soldiers were said to have been withdrawn from Ireland in 1642 in order to support both sides in the conflict and Ireland was thought to have been generally left in the control of Government militia's and rebel forces, who were both left to sort out the situation between themselves and which ultimately resulted in a military stalemate. It was said to be during this lull in military activity that the rebel Catholic leaders and their respective armies came together to form the Catholic Confederation, which before too long became the de facto government of Ireland, established under the auspices of the Catholic Church and two of the leading rebel lords, Viscount Gormanstown and Lord Mountgarret. By the middle of 1642 however, the rebellion as such was over and the country was generally divided between the rebels, who controlled much of the countryside and the generally besieged English authorities, who continued to hold their fortified settlements at Dublin, Cork and in Ulster. This particular period of the Catholic Confederacy is thought to be notable for its ill-fated decision to side with Charles I in his dispute with the English Parliament; and who was reported to have offered Self Government and full Catholic Rights to the Confederacy, once he had gained victory over his Parliamentary adversaries. Unfortunately for Ireland, Charles' Royalist forces were subsequently defeated by the Parliamentarians and in 1649 Oliver Cromwell was reported to have brought his professional New Model Army to Ireland to restore English Protestant control to the country, a campaign that continued there through to 1653 and which was said to have resulted in even greater repression of the Catholic majority, along with more Protestant land ownership in Ireland. By the end of the English Civil War, Parliament was now in complete charge of England and they had instructed Cromwell to take his new army to Ireland to restore their authority there and crush the Catholic Confederation that still held large parts of the country. The fact that the Catholic Confederation had previously allied itself to King Charles I, supported the royalist claims of Charles II and believed in a heretical Papist religion, was said to be, in Cromwell's view, sufficient grounds to treat members of the Confederacy with complete contempt, which according to some accounts, was how he led his military campaigns in Ireland.

Prior to his arrival in Ireland however, the Confederation forces in Ireland were said to have given their allegiance to Charles II, the son of the executed Charles I, whose aim was to restore his family to the throne of England and undermine the authority of the English Parliament. To this end, Royalist officers and men who had fled England following the defeat of their armies, were reported to have arrived in Ireland, to train and command elements of the Catholic Confederate army that existed in the country. James Butler, the Duke of Ormonde was said to have travelled to Ireland to take overall command of these Irish forces, which they hoped might restore the Crown of England to Charles Stuart. Even though some members of the English Parliament were thought to be largely unconcerned about the future of Ireland, many others regarded that country as being an integral part of the English kingdom and were therefore determined to recover those lands, either through negotiation or by force of arms. Also, there were thought to be a significant number of leading Protestant politicians who wanted the Roman Catholic's punished for the suffering they were deemed to have inflicted on the Protestant settlers and for their harbouring of privateers, who were reported to have attacked English shipping during the previous civil conflict, operating from the Catholic held ports of Wexford and Waterford. However, in all probability, the real reason for Parliament's overwhelming desire to recover Ireland was thought to be much more basic, the repayment of the huge war debts the government had accrued during it civil war with King Charles I. Amounting to some £10m, the Parliamentarians were reported to have borrowed heavily in order to support their armies and were said to be intent on repaying these massive debts through the seizure and sale of Catholic held lands in Ireland.

By the time Cromwell and his New Model Army were ordered to Ireland in 1649, the only remaining southern Irish port still in English hands was said to be at Dublin, which was held under the command of a notable Parliamentary officer, Colonel Michael Jones. Aware that any English force would have to land there, the Catholic and Royalist armies in Ireland, under the control of the Duke of Ormonde, knew that to secure their borders they would have to take control of Dublin, thereby depriving the English of a major Irish port and making any subsequent military invasion extremely difficult, if not impossible. Ordering his mixed forces to converge on the outskirts of Dublin, Ormonde's plans were thought to have been undone by a pre-emptive strike engineered by Colonel Jones, whose forces attacked the rebel army at Rathmines, killing over two hundred of their number, capturing two thousand more and scattering the remainder throughout the wider area. Retreating in some disarray, Ormonde and his remaining forces were said to have fallen back to the rebels own fortified strongholds along the east coast of Ireland, ostensibly in the hope that Cromwell's newly arriving force would be sufficiently weakened by military action, hunger and disease, before Ormonde had to finally face him in battle. Although the Confederation army still held several port towns along the east coast, which might have been a hindrance to an English army travelling across the Irish Sea, the Royalist fleet that might have interrupted the Parliamentary supply lines and which was thought to be under the command of Prince Rupert of the Rhine had its own problems to deal with. Based at Kinsale harbour in the south east of Ireland, an English fleet under the command of the outstanding Parliamentary Admiral Robert Blake, was reported to have blockaded Prince Rupert's ships at Kinsale, preventing him from lending any sort of aid to his Royalist comrades further north, or indeed from interfering with the transportation of Parliamentary troops from England to Ireland.

With any and all immediate military threats having been removed, Cromwell and his forces were able to land safely at Dublin and having assembled his forces moved them towards the east coast, where the Duke of Ormonde and his combined Royalist and Catholic garrisons were reported to have been waiting to meet him. The first rebel town that Cromwell and his army were said to have arrived at and subsequently attacked was Drogheda, a place that even today is remains infamous for the actions of the English commander and his Parliamentarian forces, who were reported to have massacred almost its entire population, supposedly as an act of barbaric revenge against those who had chosen to oppose them and as a dire warning for those he had yet to meet in battle. According to some sources, having arrived outside of Drogheda, Cromwell ordered its outer defences stormed; and this having been achieved, instructed his men to sack the town, which ultimately resulted in the unnecessary deaths of hundreds of enemy troops, Irish civilians and even a number of Catholic priests who were said to have been present in the town. There is often a suggestion, sometimes from the same sources that the "massacre" at Drogheda was somehow a total annihilation of the population of the town, which would no doubt fit with the particularly nationalist reporting of these historic events. Modern expressions such as "genocide" and "ethnic cleansing" have also been applied to Cromwell's campaigns in Ireland, with the capture of towns such as Drogheda and Wexford, used to exemplify the Parliamentary leader's uncompromising and sometimes vicious attitude towards the Irish Catholic population in Ireland. Historic records of the time do seem to suggest that Cromwell was unapologetic about the methods he employed in his military campaigns in Ireland and in his later reports to Parliament, he makes it exceedingly clear that the sacking of both Drogheda and Wexford were highly deliberate military acts, designed to strike fear into his adversaries and make any future enemy think twice about resisting him. The fact that other reports of the time suggest that many hundreds of Catholic and Royalist troops, captured at Drogheda, were later transported to the West Indies, as indentured prisoners would seem to make a lie of the idea that the whole garrison was mercilessly slaughtered on Cromwell's orders. If one accepts that there had been a total Royalist and Catholic contingent of some 3,000 men at Drogheda, then clearly the fate of the remaining 2,000 plus troops is open to question. Did they die in battle, or were they killed having already surrendered to Parliamentary troops? Almost inevitably there will be claim and counter claim over the events that took place at any significant battle, including the treatment or mistreatment of captured prisoners and it would be absurd to suggest that in every case the civilities of war were adhered to by all parties and in all instances.

Having captured Drogheda and its Confederate garrison, Cromwell and his main force then moved towards the Irish port towns of Wexford, Waterford and Duncannon, all of which were still held by native Irish forces. At Wexford, Cromwell was reported by some sources to have deliberately broken a truce, ordering his troops into the town while negotiations were still taking place to arrange the town's surrender. According to these same sources, the combined Catholic and Royalist garrison, numbering some 2,000 men and the civilian population of around 1,500 people were all attacked and in most cases killed by the English Parliamentary troops, who later set fire to the town. Although most informed sources generally accept that Cromwell did not personally order the sacking of Wexford, as he was busy actually negotiating its surrender, his apparent failure to control his officers and men, who committed the acts, makes him, in most people's eyes, equally culpable for the murderous slaughter that subsequently took place there. It seems remarkable that such an astute military commander and politician like Cromwell would not have been aware of the damage that reports of such atrocities could do to him personally and to his ongoing military campaign in Ireland. It has been suggested that the kind of actions undertaken at Drogheda and Wexford represented a gamble by the Parliamentary leader in his conflict with both the Royalist rebels and the native Catholics of Ireland. By appearing to be merciless, he would undoubtedly be feared by his enemies, but any obvious refusal on his part to make terms with his opponent, would leave them with little option but to fight to the death, a situation that was both time consuming and highly unpopular with the country at large. Events at

Wexford, whether with Cromwell's implicit connivance or not, ultimately proved to be a gamble that he lost, as it often served to simply stiffen Irish resistance to Cromwell, his army and the English cause generally. Later rebel towns like Limerick and Galway were only thought to have been taken by the Parliamentarians after stubborn resistance from their Irish garrisons, whilst others like Duncannon and Waterford refused any calls for their surrender and were only defeated by siege, holding out until 1650. This was not always the case of course, as one or two other rebel towns surrendered quite quickly, equitable terms having been reached with the besieging English forces. Ultimately though, Cromwell's tough and uncompromising approach was probably a failure, as he and his army were forced into a second year of campaigning in Ireland, which compelled them to face the intervening winter in the country, during which many hundreds of English troops were thought to have died as a result of enemy action, cold, starvation and disease.

By the beginning of 1650, Cromwell's army was said to have been back on the campaign trail and within a short time had suppressed the main Confederate headquarters at Kilkenny, but only after terms had been reached with its Royalist and Catholic defenders. Their next target, the rebel centre at Clonmel, proved to be much more troublesome, with valiant defending and seemingly insurmountable defences reportedly costing the lives of some 2,000 English troops, before the defending garrison agreed to surrender their town on terms. These formal surrender terms are thought by many to be completely at odds with the treatment of enemy garrisons meted out by Cromwell at both Drogheda and Wexford, where little quarter was given and according to some historians, none was asked for by the defenders. The subject of terms being agreed between the two warring parties has often been used to explain the reported massacres that took place during Cromwell's invasion of Ireland during the 17th century, a time when much earlier chivalrous pleasantries were still in existence and commonly offered in most European conflicts. According to the most reliable academic sources, during the 17th century, an enemy garrison that was called upon to surrender and which subsequently refused, forcing the attackers to storm their defences could expect no mercy, as and when their fortifications were finally taken. However, where the defences were substantial enough to resist cannon and shot, or could not otherwise be overcome, then it would not have been unusual for the besieging army to make several calls for the garrison to surrender, until such time as they actually chose to do so, or the defences were finally defeated. It is on the basis of these accepted protocols and the reported refusal of the two garrisons, at both Drogheda and Wexford, to accept the Parliamentary terms that is commonly used as a reason for the carnage that subsequently followed.

The military campaigns in Ireland were said to have been fundamentally altered in May 1650 by two separate events that ultimately affected both sides involved in the ongoing conflict. The Catholic Confederacy was rocked by the news that Charles Stuart had decided to repudiate the alliance made by his late father, Charles I, with the Confederation and switch his support to the Scottish Covenanters who were fighting in Ulster, taking many of his Royalist forces away from the fight with Parliament in the south. Around the same time, Cromwell was thought to have returned to England to lead the third English Civil War against Charles II and his Covenanter and Royalist supporters on the British mainland. Fortunately for the English forces in Ireland, Cromwell's replacement, Henry Ireton was said to have been an equally capable military leader who was left to complete the destruction of the Catholic Confederacy. In June 1650 elements of Ireton's army, under the command of the previously mentioned Charles Coote, was reported to have met a mixed Catholic and Royalist force of around 6,000 men in what later became known as the Battle of Scarrifholis. Some 2,000 troops from the rebel army were reported to have been killed during the engagement and a number of their officers captured, many of whom were later executed for their actions. Over the next two years the last two remaining rebel strongholds, at Limerick and Galway, were said to have been captured, both after long sieges, essentially bringing an end to any large scale military resistance in the south of Ireland. Interestingly, many troops on both sides did not actually perish from fighting one another, but rather were thought to have succumbed to cold, starvation and disease, with typhus and dysentery being the most common killer, the latter claiming one of the most notable victims of the conflict, the English Parliamentary commander, Henry Ireton, who reported to have died from the disease just outside Limerick in 1651.

King William III   Henry Gratton   Robert Peel

With most of the regular Catholic and Royalist forces defeated or withdrawn from the field, the English troops now found themselves under occasional attack by Irish guerrilla forces, a tactic that Catholic troops were said to have regularly employed since 1651. In response to these attacks, the Parliamentarian forces were reported to have adopted a scorched earth policy, depriving the raiders of food supplies and local support, but indirectly causing food shortages and destroying the lands of the local, generally law abiding population. Occasionally, whole communities and their livestock were reported to have been relocated from rebel held areas, to lands that were under English control, preventing their being exploited by the dissidents and further reducing the rebel's access to food and other vital stores. Where rebels were unfortunate to be captured, those who were not executed or imprisoned for lengthy terms, were often sentenced to transportation to Barbados as indentured prisoners, with an estimated 12,000 Irish Catholics said to have suffered this particular punishment. The years of famine, war and disease were thought to have proved to be costly for everyone involved in them, especially the generally peaceful rural population who were said to have endured great suffering through no fault of their own, but often because of the actions of others. In total, it has been suggested that some 500,000 people died as a direct result of the Catholic Confederacy and the subsequent military campaigns led by Cromwell and his Parliamentary lieutenants. Almost two-thirds of these deaths were reported to have been borne by Ireland's Catholic community, with the majority of them being caused by war, cold, starvation and disease.

Although rebel elements were thought to have remained in Ireland well after the Catholic Rebellion, much of the tension in the country was said to have been reduced in 1652, when the Parliamentary Authorities in Ireland issued national terms, which allowed Irish Catholic combatants to leave the country unmolested. As in previous times, many thousands of these men, who were essentially forced to ply their trade abroad, later offered their military services to England's foreign enemies, particularly France and continued to play a role in opposing the English occupation of their homeland. The small numbers of regular troops, both Catholic and Royalist that remained in Ireland in defiance of this amnesty were said to have been hunted down and either chose to lay down their arms, or in some cases join the English forces. The only other force of note that remained in the country, were those individual groups who had chosen to turn their military talents to banditry and were known to have been raiding the country for their own financial benefit. However, slowly but surely even these disparate groups were said to have been identified by the authorities, hunted down by English troops; and subsequently dealt with. With an end to the Irish rebellion, the English Parliament now sought ways of recovering the cost of fighting both of the expensive conflicts that had very nearly bankrupted the country, the successive English Civil Wars and the Catholic revolt in Ireland. Additionally, the Protestant led government was also said to have been keen to punish the Catholic population of Ireland for their perceived support, real or not, of the rebellion and the Catholic Confederacy, which had done so much to damage English interests in Ireland. Anyone who was known to have actively participated in the rebellion was said to have been identified, brought to trial and in most cases executed, with many hundreds of individuals thought to have been maliciously implicated by their English settler neighbours, who had a personal score to settle, or were anxious to increase their own land holdings at the expense of their entirely innocent Catholic contemporaries.

Actual members of the Confederacy and their supporters, including many of the leading titled and wealthiest Catholics in the country were said to have had their lands seized; assets sequestrated and in a large number of cases found themselves transported to the West Indies to serve out long sentences as indentured prisoners or slaves. In Ireland itself, Roman Catholics were reported to have been forbidden from living within the towns that had previously been their homes and attempts were made to ban Catholicism in the country, with the severest penalties being levied against those that broke these new laws. Catholic priests, the perceived teachers of this despised and heretical religion, were thought to have been a particular target for the English authorities in Ireland, with those that were unfortunate enough to be caught likely to be executed, in scenes that were reminiscent of the extreme religious purges of the previous century. Prior to the various rebellions that had wracked the country over the period of 120 years, from 1536 to 1653, land ownership in Ireland was said to have changed dramatically, with Catholic ownership dropping from over 60% to around 10% by the time that King Charles II had been restored to the English throne in 1660. Much of this missing Catholic land was said to have passed into the hands of former English soldiers, who had fought for the Parliamentary cause, as well as the merchants and money lenders who had actually financed England's wars, with the rest being held by some of the leading political figures of the Commonwealth period, who had been granted their new estates with the grateful thanks of the victorious English Parliament.

Even the restoration of the previously sympathetic Charles II did not significantly improve the plight of the Roman Catholic majority in Ireland, as their share of the land was only reported to have risen to 20% during Charles' reign and often then only to those Catholic Royalists who had been instrumental in helping him to regain his Crown. The vast majority of Catholics though, saw no improvement in their own personal situations and remained barred from holding public office, but were permitted to sit in the Irish Parliament. Catholic hopes for a return of their status and lands were no doubt heightened with the ascendancy of James II to the English throne in 1685, even though much of the political power within the country remained within Parliament's hands. A Roman Catholic monarch, who chose to appoint likeminded individuals to key posts, often without Parliamentary approval, James was generally disliked and mistrusted by the English legislature, who saw the new monarch as a threat to their own political authority, much the same as Charles I had been some forty years earlier. Although there was never any question of removing the king in a similar fashion to Charles I, it was said to be because of the fears of a resurgent Catholic church and all that that entailed; that some members of Parliament began to actively seek out an alternative to James. The most obvious candidate for the English throne was thought to be Mary, James' daughter, who was married to Europe's leading Protestant prince, William of Orange. Initially it was hoped that Mary might become Queen of England, Scotland and Ireland in her own right, but possibly because of her subservience to her husband's will and William's obvious reluctance to invade England, without gaining the crown, eventually led to a tacit agreement being made, where William and Mary would rule England and its dependencies as joint monarchs, thereby ridding the country of its unpopular Catholic monarch and finally bringing an end to the Stuart claim to the throne. At the time, William was also known to be at war with King Louis XIV of France, a Roman Catholic ally of James II, so the opportunity to take control of England, her army and navy, which might then be used in his military conflict with France, was yet another benefit of William accepting the offer being made by the English Parliament. Consequently, as a result of these secret negotiations and with Parliamentary support generally agreed beforehand, William and his Protestant army sailed for England, with the intention of deposing his father-in-law, the legitimate monarch, King James II.

Unsurprisingly perhaps, the largely Protestant population of England was said to have warmly welcomed the Dutch monarch and his foreign troops, regarding them as liberators and within a short time most of the great and the good of the country had declared for the new foreign king and his queen. For the Roman Catholic James II however, the situation was extremely grave and no doubt recognising that his cause had little support within his own country, he subsequently chose to abandon his kingdom for the relatively safe haven of France, ruled then by his fellow Roman Catholic monarch, King Louis XIV. Louis had been in almost continual religious and military conflict with William of Orange for a number of years, so when the opportunity to support James II, a fellow Roman Catholic, in a confrontation with his enemy presented itself, it was an obvious way to further his own cause. Granting James and his family sanctuary, as well as a place where the ousted English monarch could rebuild his fragmented military forces, Louis was also reported to have furnished James with arms, men and equipment, which might be used in any future confrontation with the new Protestant king and queen of England. From all over Europe, from England, Scotland and Ireland, thousands of Roman Catholics, exiles and royalists were said to have rallied to James' cause, not least the many Irishmen who had lived, served or been born in France, since the last great exodus from that country, following the unsuccessful Confederate Wars and Cromwell's subsequent suppression of the Catholic majority. It was to the island of Ireland that the ousted James instinctively looked, to provide the men and the military bases, from where he could launch his campaign to restore his family to the throne of the three kingdoms, England, Scotland and Ireland. For those Irishmen who rallied to his cause in what became known as the War of the Two Kings, the hope of restoring a Roman Catholic monarch to the English throne, also promised the possibility of sequestrated lands being returned to their rightful owners and the repeal of discriminatory laws that had helped to oppress the native peoples of Ireland. The Catholic's support of the Stuart dynasty was thought to have been a well established connection throughout this period of English history, with many Irishmen having fought for both Charles I and Charles II in their various conflicts with the English Parliament, even though, ultimately, they achieved few if any of their long term aims under either monarch.

Around the same time that William and Mary were arriving in England to be crowned as the new joint monarchs, the Lord Lieutenant of Ireland, appointed by and completely loyal to James, was said to have been taking action in order to secure the country for the usurped Stuart king. By appointing Roman Catholics to command strategic ports and towns throughout the southern half of the country, he was able to secure that part of Ireland for James. Unfortunately for the ousted king however, his Lord Lieutenant was not able to complete his defence of the country in the Northern provinces, where the majority of the population was Protestant and therefore loyal to the new Dutch administration. Fortunately for the Jacobites, the name commonly given to James' supporters, the only military garrison that might have offered any sort of opposition to the Catholic forces in Ireland was at Derry, which by December 1688 was being besieged by a large Jacobite force. Although it was not obvious to its commanders at the time, the majority of this Catholic force was said to have been made up of young untrained farm workers, who would ultimately prove to be completely unreliable, when it came to fighting in the pitched battles that would almost inevitably follow.

Back in France, James had now managed to gather around him a sizeable force of suitably trained and equipped men who might provide the core of an army with which to oppose his adversaries and one that had been supplemented by several thousand seasoned French troops, assigned to James by his ally King Louis XIV. Significantly and rather oddly perhaps, Louis was said to have assigned these troops on some sort of exchange basis, with an equal number of Irish troops being transferred to France, to fight in Louis' continental wars and establishing what later became known as the Irish Brigade, a formidable fighting unit that faced their English adversaries on a number of occasions and whose loss to England was even thought to have been bewailed by the future English king George II. Finally in March 1689, James and his mixed Jacobite forces were reported to have boarded a fleet of French ships and having avoided the English navy which was patrolling the coast of Ireland, arrived at the Irish port Kinsale on 12th March 1689, where he received an extremely warm welcome from the local population. Having assembled his forces, James was then reported to have marched his Irish army north to join those forces besieging the Protestant enclave of Derry; and having reached the outskirts of the town was said to convened what later became known as the "Patriot's Parliament", a gathering comprised mostly of Irish Catholic gentlemen, during which he was reported to have passed several declarations, promising the restoration of Catholic rights, as well as proclaiming that the English Parliament had no right to pass laws affecting Ireland.

In June 1689, a number of English warships, completely loyal to William and Mary, were reported to have arrived off the coast of Derry, ostensibly to relieve and re-supply the Protestant garrison there, but deterred by the presence of Jacobite gun batteries, were unable to bring their men and provisions ashore immediately. According to contemporary reports of the time, it was only after a change of leadership amongst the English fleet that the ships were finally able to break through the Jacobite siege and re-supply the desperate loyalist garrison. Elsewhere in Ireland, the arrival of James' army and the raising of Catholic Jacobite forces were thought to have caused great alarm amongst the Protestant communities that were spread throughout the country, causing them to raise their own irregular militia units, with which to defend their homes and properties. One of the most effective of these was reported to operating around Enniskillen, just south of Derry and was thought to be such a threat that a similarly raised Catholic militia was sent north to confront them, only to be heavily defeated by the Protestant force at the town of Newtownbutler in July 1689. The large numbers of untried and untrained farm workers amongst the Catholic militia was said to have been a vital factor in this defeat, as most were reported to have retreated as soon as the first shots were fired and never came close to actually engaging the Protestant's in battle.

Daniel O'Connell

Charles Trevelyan

William Smith O'Brien

In August 1689, one of William's leading military commanders finally arrived in Ireland to drive James' army out of the country and suppress those native Catholic forces that were supporting him. Landing in County Down and then capturing Carrickfergus, the Duke of Schomberg was reported to have set out for Dundalk with his forces, being attacked occasionally by the Jacobites, but avoiding an all out battle with his enemy, who seemed content to monitor the English military columns, rather than confronting them directly. Eventually, with the year drawing to a close and in common with the military practices at the time, both sides were said to have identified and settled into their respective winter quarters, where both stores and men could be re-supplied and preparations made for the following years campaigns. Although few if any serious military engagements were thought to have taken place during the winter months, Schomberg's troops were thought to have been seriously depleted and psychologically undermined by the deaths caused by cold and disease, as well as the shortage of necessary supplies. In part, this shortage of stores was said to have been caused by their Catholic adversaries who routinely destroyed crops as they retreated, leaving little if anything for the Protestant troops to forage upon. Although such tactics generally proved to be successful in limiting the effectiveness of King William's foreign troops, perhaps more importantly they proved to be catastrophic for the local population, who relied on such crops for the coming winter and ultimately suffered a far heavier penalty than any of the warring soldiers did. With seemingly little progress being made in the conflict and no doubt aware of the effects such deprivations might have on his troops in the long term, in June 1690 William himself was reported to have arrived in Ireland to take overall command of the campaign there. Arriving in Belfast with a large fleet of ships and some thirty-odd thousand men, mainly English, German, Dutch and Danish troops, the English king was said to have moved his army south towards Dublin, only to encounter a large Jacobite army on the south bank of the River Boyne. Sending his highly professional troops across the river at several different crossing points, they quickly unnerved the massed ranks of largely inexperienced and outclassed

Catholic soldiers facing them, forcing them to break ranks and flee, for fear of being surrounded, ignoring the protestations of their officers who urged them to stand and fight. Although this "battle" could never really be regarded as an outright victory, or defeat, for either side, it proved to be a pivotal moment in the conflict nonetheless. Not only had the Catholic forces retreated like a rabble, but their retreat ultimately proved to be watershed for James' royal ambitions, forcing him to turn away to the south and eventually to take ship for France, bringing an end to any hope of his ascending the throne of England again.

Even though James had abandoned his Catholic army in Ireland, this large Jacobite force was still thought to have represented a significant danger to William's position as king of England, Scotland and Ireland, meaning that it had to be dealt with. However, finding an equitable solution to the insurrection was more problematic, given William's absolute refusal to offer a pardon or surrender terms to the Jacobite leadership, or their followers. Many of the leaders of the uprising were reported to have been landed Catholic aristocracy and Royalist officers who had much to lose if they simply surrendered to the king, leaving them with little option but to continue with their rebellion, until such time as they were guaranteed more favourable terms regarding their lives, property and religious freedom. By the August of 1690, the Jacobite army was reported to have been forced back to Limerick, which they were said to have refortified, allowing them to consolidate their position and repel several attacks that were launched by William's forces. Over time, this defensive enclave was thought to have been extended to include much of the Connacht region and was so large that the Protestant forces were pushed further east, leaving large parts of the west of Ireland in Jacobite hands. With much of the country pacified however, William subsequently returned to England to prepare for the resumption of his conflict with France, leaving one of his most trusted commanders, General de Ginkell, to complete the military campaign in the west of Ireland. By the following year, de Ginkell and his troops were reported to have managed to break through the defences of the Jacobite enclave and began moving towards the two rebel strongholds of Galway and Limerick. The French commander of the Jacobite force, the Marquis de St Ruth, was said to have taken the decision to confront De Ginkell's forces near the town of Aughrim in Galway, but either through misfortune or misjudgement, found his troops seriously outmatched by the General's mixed English force and was said to have lost up to half of his 8,000 men in that one single engagement. With many of the rebels killed, wounded or captured, including their commander St Ruth, the way now lay open for De Ginkell's troops to push forward into the Galway region, leaving only the rebel held town of Limerick to be confronted.

Initially commanded by a French military officer, the rebel stronghold of Limerick at first refused to surrender to William's forces, possibly because the French officers in charge recognised that they were likely to face the same fate as their Irish and Royalist counterparts. However, a number of these junior officers, mostly Catholic or Royalist, could now see that the revolt was over and their cause could not be won, leaving them with little option but to seek their own terms with William's field commanders. Overthrowing their French officers, they were then thought to have sought their own terms from De Ginkell, in return for which, they would surrender the town and in doing so bring an end to the rebellion. Surprisingly; and despite William's explicit orders that terms should not be offered to the rebel leaders, De Ginkell was prepared to offer fairly generous terms to those still holding Limerick, provided that they promised to remain in Ireland and swore an oath of allegiance to King William. In return, they were offered tolerance of their religious practices and full legal rights within Ireland, far more than the rebel officers might have hoped to achieve in normal circumstances. Unfortunately, the terms offered by William' General, De Ginkell, were far more generous than even his employers, King William and the Parliament, were prepared to afford the rebel leaders and they were all subsequently rescinded by the Irish legislature, which was at that time dominated by Protestant politicians. Instead, rather than offering settlement terms that were fair and equitable to all communities, the Parliament simply introduced another round of updated penal reforms, which discriminated against the Catholic majority, thereby increasing the level of bitterness felt by members of that community towards both Protestants and their English protectors.

Following the surrender of Limerick and the end of the Jacobite uprising in Ireland, an estimated 14,000 Catholic and Royalist supporters of the Jacobite rebellion were reported to have left Ireland to resettle in Catholic France, in what became known as the "Flight of the Wild Geese". Often accompanied by their wives and children, many of these fighting men would help to form the basis of the French army's famous Irish Brigade, along with those soldiers who had previously been swapped by James II for the French troops that had formed part of his unsuccessful campaign in Ireland. Although these men ostensibly formed part of James' army in exile, upon his death they were thought to have been absorbed into the French regular army, becoming a favoured Brigade of that country's monarchy. Despite James' untimely retreat from Ireland, which was said to have earned him the nickname of "James the Shit" in some Catholic circles, most of the Irish Brigade members were said to have remained loyal to the Stuart claim to the English throne, with elements of this same fighting force reported to have been present at the Battle of Culloden in 1745. The end of the Jacobite rebellion in Ireland was also thought to have marked the beginning of the Protestant Ascendancy there, a period when Irish Catholics and Presbyterians were systematically denied equal rights, by members of the minority Protestant ruling class, who held almost complete authority in the country. This wholly unrepresentative national administration was said to have enforced a period of grudging peace throughout Ireland, during which time fundamental changes were made to the country's economy and political structure, as well as enacting laws that were often highly discriminatory in their nature, particularly towards those of a Catholic or Presbyterian persuasion.

By the beginning of the 18th century, Catholic land ownership in Ireland was reported to have fallen dramatically, from around 15% during James II reign to only 5% under William and Mary, due mainly to the fact that those who had fought for James' cause, had seen their lands confiscated, in retribution for supporting the ousted Roman Catholic monarch. Even those landowners who had managed to avoid becoming embroiled in the conflict were thought to have paid a high price for their religious beliefs, as the Protestant dominated legislature introduced a series of bills, all of which were designed to limit the wealth, power and influence of the Catholic landowners. Not only were they prevented from holding public office or military commissions, but were also now barred from sitting in the Irish Parliament entirely. The Protestant administration also ensured that Catholic held lands could not be passed on intact to a single heir, but could only be inherited by all of the landowner's sons, or alternatively, sold to Protestant settlers or landowners, as Catholics were now forbidden from buying new lands and estates. Not only did these measures serve to limit the amount of land that an individual Catholic landowner might own, but ultimately led to their lands becoming less and less productive, as the size of their holdings inevitably shrank over time. From a Protestant point of view, such anti-Catholic legislation was necessary, not only to limit the ability of such landowners to finance and support future rebellions, but also to safeguard their own communities and possessions. Pointing to the fact that previous revolts had been supported, militarily and financially, by wealthy Catholic noblemen and landlords, who possessed both the means and the men to unlawfully launch such a revolt against the elected representatives of the country, it was a potential threat that the Protestant minority were determined to eliminate once and for all.

At the same time that legislation was being used to control the lives of the Roman Catholic majority within Ireland, English and Irish Protestant landowners were also reported to be systematically altering the agricultural base of the country and making changes that would prove to have catastrophic results for the population in the years ahead. Driven almost entirely by profit, landowners were said to have cleared thousands of acres of previously untouched woodlands, forests and wilderness in order to create new pastures for the cattle, pigs, sheep and horses that were being raised to satisfy a growing demand in England and continental Europe. Although large areas of land were still given over to the cultivation of cereal crops, these too were generally destined for foreign markets and along with the animals raised in Ireland were seen as little more than "cash crops" for the wealthy landowners and merchants who were said to be putting up to 25% of Ireland's total revenue into their own pockets, often to be spent in England or elsewhere, rather than in the country in which it was produced. For the few remaining Irish Catholic landowners who had somehow managed to retain their large estates, often by converting to Protestantism, these changes in land use was not that much of a problem, as their lands remained much as they had always been. For the smaller landowners however, those whose lands had been legally divided into smaller and smaller plots by the new inheritance legislation, they were said to have found it increasingly difficult to survive in the new agricultural economy of Ireland, often managing just to feed themselves and their families with the limited crops that they could grow on their depleted lands. However, the most unfortunate of all agricultural workers were thought to be the tenant farmers and estate workers, whose livelihood and very existence often depended on the goodwill and patronage of the English or Irish Protestant landlord that owned the land that they lived and worked on. With the best of the lands having been given over to crops or pasture, these tenant farmers and estate workers were often reported to have worked for little if any pay, but rather for a plot of marginal estate land, on which they lived in the most dire circumstance and grew their one and only staple food, the potato. Introduced to Europe during the 16th century, ostensibly as a garden crop, the plants ability to grow in the very worst of soils, without any sort of intensive husbandry, whilst at the same time delivering large numbers of potatoes from a single plant, made it an ideal subsistence crop, especially for those workers that had little else to support them.

The widespread practice of farming animals, or the production and export of cereal crops to England and elsewhere, rather than producing food for the local population, was said to have had a highly negative effect on the native peoples of Ireland and seriously limited their ability to withstand any sort of natural disaster that might inevitably occur. That natural disaster did occur in the second half of 1739, when severe weather was reported to have affected much of northern Europe, bringing freezing temperatures and driving rain to much of the continent and especially Ireland. The extremely cold weather was said to have been exacerbated by widespread fuel shortages, brought about by the freezing of coal stocks, mining equipment and even commercial docks, which prevented the movement of fuel throughout Britain, the main source of Irish coal supplies. This shortage was said to have been compounded by the lack of natural fuels within Ireland itself, where the trees and hedges that might have been used as alternatives, had either been removed to create new open pasture, or had simply died back because of the time of the year. As usual, the poor tended to suffer more, as a result of poor weather than the middle or upper classes did, who were often able to buy what little fuel supplies existed and which became increasingly expensive as time went by. Furthermore, the Irish population and economy were adversely affected by a slowdown in industry caused by the weather, which was reported to have resulted in waterwheels, canals and commercial harbours being brought to a standstill, as the freezing water slowly but surely turned to ice. Fortunately perhaps, both the Irish and British governments, despite being largely Protestant led, were quick to recognise the seriousness of the situation that was affecting their fellow countrymen and began to make provision for the very poorest citizens. The Duke of Devonshire was reported to have closed Irish ports to the export of Irish grown grain to anywhere but England, thereby preserving stocks for Ireland and England alone. This recognised the fact that the staple food for many of the population was the potato, which due to the freezing weather had been particularly hard hit by frost and snow, destroying much of the crop that had not yet been harvested, or which had been intended as a seed crop for the following year.

Patrick Pearse **Michael Collins** **Roger Casement**

The cold weather of the winter months in 1739 was then said to have been followed by an unexpectedly long drought throughout much of 1740, which caused crops to wither and animals to die from thirst. Not only did this limit the amount of food being grown within Ireland itself, but also caused the price of basic commodities to rise to extortionate levels, making them generally unaffordable to the poorest working man. Almost inevitably the suppliers of such foods became the target for riotous crowds who attacked their warehouses and storerooms and tried to seize the much needed supplies for themselves. Local officials alarmed by such unlawful behaviour began to prohibit the sale of these stores to any overseas destination, with one Scotland bound ship at Drogheda being forcibly prevented from leaving harbour by local people who boarded it. In fact, in some places local unrest was said to have escalated to such a degree that the local authorities were forced to call out troops in order to control the troublesome crowds, with at least four people being killed in one instance where rioting got out of control. Another noticeable feature of the food shortages was said to be the migration of thousands of people from the worst hit areas of the country, to the larger towns and cities, where reports suggested that many of the itinerant and hungry farm workers threw themselves on the charity of the city dwellers or simply resorted to begging in the streets. Thanks in part to a large portion of the previous year's Irish grain harvest having survived the worst of the weather and the regular shipment of cereals from overseas, eventually stocks and perhaps more importantly prices began to stabilize, reducing the outbreaks of violence and making food supplies more affordable for the common working man. However, this provided only temporary relief to the Irish population, as later in 1740 the bad weather returned, with freezing temperatures, incessant rain and heavy snow once again bringing food production, transportation and industrial manufacturing to a halt. Unsurprisingly, these events were thought to have caused a rise in food prices yet again, with large numbers of the poorest families struggling to feed themselves and bringing about a resurgence of the food riots and raids that had seemingly been eradicated earlier in the year.

Although the authorities continued to use troops to quell the worst of these riots, it soon became increasingly clear to the Government in Ireland that much more needed to be done to establish both food and work programs, so that those left hungry and penniless by the adverse weather conditions might be fed and occupied. In response to this dawning realisation, Government, religious groups and individual philanthropists all began to set up food and work programs that helped to house, feed and occupy the large numbers of destitute people that had been affected by the famine, at least until circumstances improved. Significantly, grain stores and food prices were only reported to have stabilised once the weather began to improve, at the beginning of 1741. Sadly, many did not live to see the end of the famine, with some sources suggesting that up to 300,000 people may have died as a result of the cold, starvation and disease that beset the country between 1739 and 1741. Tens of thousands more were thought to have abandoned Ireland forever, choosing to emigrate to Britain, Europe and North America, rather than face the continuing rigours of their native lands. It has also been suggested by some historians that Ireland's population took very nearly a century to recover from the effects of the 18th century famine, just in time for it to be decimated once again, by what later became known as The Great Famine.

By the second half of the 18th century and no doubt following the disastrous famine and the collapse of the Jacobite cause at Culloden in 1745, it was reported that many of the previously enacted and fairly Draconian anti-Catholic laws in Ireland began to be relaxed, as fears of further rebellions started to ease. Indeed by the latter half of the century, these political and religious reforms began to see the economic development of the country, with new trade agreements being framed between Britain and Ireland and the country's first signs of an industrial infrastructure being laid, with commercial docks, canals, roads and manufacturing centres being constructed. It has also been suggested that by the end of the 18th century many of the Anglo-Irish settlers, initially planted there by the English authorities, had begun to regard Ireland as an entirely separate country, rather than simply as a satellite state of Britain. A number of leading Irish politicians, including the likes of Henry Gratton, began to lobby for a greater level of Irish autonomy for Ireland's own Parliament and for more equitable trading terms between the two countries. Part of this same campaign also called for the emancipation of the Catholic majority in Ireland, which was partially achieved in 1793, although Catholics were still prevented from standing for the Irish Parliament, or indeed, being employed as Government officials.

Despite the improving situation for Roman Catholics, a large number of Irish nationalists were said to have been unhappy about the speed of change within their homeland and in 1791 formed the Society of United Irishmen, a group dedicated to the military overthrow of British rule in Ireland. The final bloody phase of the French Revolution, which saw the execution of King Louis XVI and his queen Marie Antoinette, along with thousands of other innocent citizens began in 1793 and provided a stark warning to many European countries, about the dangers of the revolutionary cause. Undoubtedly fearful of the new Catholic organisation and its ultimate aims, Protestants in Ireland were said to have soon rallied together to form the Orange Order, an organisation dedicated to the preservation of their loyalist ideals and the protection of their communities in Ireland. Their fears of a nationalist inspired revolution, similar to the one that had occurred on the continent were no doubt realised in 1796, when an abortive raid was launched by French Revolutionary troops at Bantry Bay, reportedly in support of the United Irishmen. As a result of this perceived threat, the Irish authorities began to actively suppress the Society, purportedly using torture and executions to bring an end to the nationalist movement. However, despite the failure of the French raid and the oppressive methods being used against them, the United Irishmen were thought to have continued with their organising and ultimately bringing about yet another national rebellion that was said to have lasted several months, cost thousands of innocent lives and achieved none of its stated aims.

Surprisingly perhaps, this society, the United Irishmen, was thought to have been founded by a small number of political radicals from all the various communities within Ireland, who wanted to establish a non-sectarian republic, similar in fashion to that which had previously been created in France. Unfortunately for the original founders of the group, the uprising of 1798 saw multiple instances of sectarian violence, as personal and religious scores were thought to have been settled by the disparate groups involved in the rebellion, with Catholics killing Protestants and Protestants killing Catholics. Perversely, it was thought to be this revolt, as much as anything that ultimately persuaded, or possibly forced the English and Irish Parliaments to introduce the Act of Union, which was enacted in 1801 and that abolished the independent Irish legislature, leaving the island of Ireland to be governed directly from Westminster. Even though this Act was thought to have been achieved mainly through the use of bribery, corruption and coercion, nonetheless it proved to be a pivotal moment in Ireland's history and was one that would undoubtedly contribute to the death and misery of hundreds of thousands of Irish people some forty-odd years later, when the Great Potato Famine struck Ireland. The Act was also known to have helped define the politics and policies of the two main religious communities that then existed within Ireland, with Roman Catholics mainly leaning towards the ideals of a completely independent Irish state and Protestants seeking even greater union with Great Britain. Ultimately, it was said to have been these two opposing aspirations that would set the tone for Irish politics for the next century or more and eventually lead to the partition of the country in the first part of the 20th century.

Although the Act of Union, which created the United Kingdom of Great Britain and Ireland, was initially intended to include a provision that would offer Roman Catholics full rights in their own country, the English monarch, George III, a staunch Protestant, refused to sanction this specific change, ostensibly because it violated his coronation oath with regard to defending the Church of England. Even though Irish MP's were still elected by their national electorate, they were now required to sit in the combined British and Irish Parliament based at Westminster. However, Roman Catholics remained banned from sitting in this Parliament as well, at least until 1829, when the Catholic Emancipation Act was finally passed, partly due to pressure from the likes of Daniel O'Connell, the Irish politician, lawyer and a member of the Repeal Association. However, as only generally wealthy Roman Catholics were entitled to vote in the first instance, full democracy was not really returned to Ireland until much later. What seems to have been particularly irksome to the largely dispossessed Catholic majority in Ireland, was the practice of some English landowners, who feared the simmering unrest of the Catholic community, to absent themselves from their Irish estates, leaving them in the hands of private agents, who were charged with maximising the incomes from the lands, regardless of the cost that these practices might have on the common working man, who were mostly Catholic. As a consequence, tenants who couldn't afford their rents, or workers who were too sick to work, were simply evicted from their homes, to a largely unknown fate. Although the existence of these absentee landlords was not thought to have been unique to Ireland, the Act of Union 1801 was thought to have substantially increased their numbers, as politically active landowners removed themselves to Britain and the new combined Parliament.

Although little political progress was thought to have been made during the first half of the 19th century, the great landowning classes of Ireland, who were still typically English and Protestant, continued to be a highly contentious issue within the country. Their continued ownership of huge tracts of land, primarily used for the cultivation of cereal crops and the raising of animals, took absolutely no account of Ireland's burgeoning native population, who had more and more mouths to feed, despite the fact that there was little additional land to be had. As a consequence, by the beginning of the 19th century, up to one third of all Irish smallholders were said to have been unable to feed their families and were often on the brink of starvation. According to most historians, there were a number of factors that had led to this situation, including the fact that Ireland's young people married earlier, couples had more children so they might be supported in their old age and the Catholic Church categorically forbade any form of contraception, which might have otherwise limited the number of children to young couples. As before, the majority of the rural poor relied almost entirely on the potato for their staple diet, along with perhaps turnips, other root vegetables and occasionally the odd lamb or pig that the family had somehow managed to acquire or raise. Their homes, more commonly known as cabins, were generally thought to be of very poor construction, as many landlords made little if any investment in their workers accommodations, regarding it as an unnecessary expense and a drain on their own personal resources. Where rent was due on these small parcels of land, the smallholders would generally grow a cereal cash crop, like wheat or barley that could then be sold to meet this annual cost, as well as being used to buy everyday items like clothes, shoes, furniture, etc.

Although any number of commissions, inquiries and resulting reports were said to have been made into the state of Ireland in previous years, very little was thought to have been done to improve the lives of its poorest citizens, often because vested interests in the British legislature had deliberately hampered or rejected any widespread reforms. It was commonly reported that by the first half of the 19th century, where Britain's working classes were beginning to benefit from better education, laws, wages and working conditions, in Ireland, nearly three-quarters of the working population were unemployed, housing conditions were deplorable and most Irish peoples standard of living fell way below that of their European neighbours. Ostensibly, many of these problems were the result of a lack of both public and private investment in industrial development, education, housing and general infrastructure, which by the early 1800's had left Ireland in an almost medieval condition, with few factories, mills or transport links helping to drive the country forward. According to some sources many of these problems were thought to be as a direct result of the great land holding culture that continued to exist in Ireland and which allowed much of the income derived from its agricultural industry to be taken out of the country and spent in England. It was said to be against this background of large scale exploitation, indifference and extreme poverty that the rural population of Ireland, the very poorest of people, were reported to have been visited by yet another famine during the mid 1840's, which would make all those that came before and after, almost pale into insignificance, such was the scale of its effects. Although the potato, the staple crop of Ireland's poorest inhabitants was known to suffer from occasional bouts of disease, such as Dry Rot and be susceptible to extremes of weather, like cold and flood, it was generally a reliable crop nonetheless and one that might be expected to survive any natural calamity relatively intact. However, in 1844 a previously unknown disease, which subsequently became known as "potato blight" was said to have crossed the Atlantic in a shipment of potatoes from America and spread quickly through the native crops of mainland Europe. In Ireland, a noted nationalist writer of the time, John Mitchell, was reported to have warned the British authorities about the possibility of famine in Ireland, due to this unknown threat to the European potato crops, but seems to have been largely ignored by the British authorities, who no doubt believed that Mitchell was simply scaremongering. Some 17 years later and having been proved right, Mitchell was said to have written "The Almighty sent the Potato blight, but it was the English who created the famine", damning words that were later said to have earned Mitchell a 14 year prison sentence, after the British authorities charged him with Felonious Treason.

Benjamin Disraeli **Lord Russell** **Queen Victoria**

By the middle of 1845 the "blight" was reported to have been present in the potato crops of England, Belgium, Holland and France, devastating large parts of each nation's countryside and leaving growers, landowners and governments completely perplexed as to what had caused it and more importantly how to deal with it. By the September of 1845, this completely unknown and seemingly untreatable disease had finally made its way to Ireland and by the end of the year, was said to have already destroyed up to one third of the country's total potato crop. For a rural population that even in good years was bordering on starvation, the loss of these vital crops was reported to have created real hardships, but somehow most people were thought to have survived, no doubt hoping that the following year, 1846, would see an end to the blight and a restoration of their crops. Unfortunately, they were to see neither of these things, as the next year was reported to have been even worse, with up to three quarters of the national potato crop lost to the disease; and the first instances of deaths from starvation being reported in Ireland. With an estimated three million people relying in whole or in part on the potato for their very survival, the British Prime Minister, Robert Peel, was reported to have tried to alleviate the worst of the effects in February 1846 by purchasing stocks of corn from India and America, which could be used to feed the starving population. Sadly, Peel seems to have failed to take into account the actual nature of the grain that his government was purchasing, which required extensive milling, before it could be used by the population and Ireland at that time had a limited number of mills, which slowed the process considerably. The fact that Peel and his government had chosen to import foreign grain, when Ireland itself had a surplus of food, in the form of Irish grain, cattle, sheep and pigs was later pointed to as a failure of his administration to fully grasp the seriousness of the situation, as well as British indifference to the suffering of their Irish neighbours.

Although some historians have maliciously claimed that Peel's Government was driven by some sort of genocidal desire to punish and reduce the largely Catholic native population through starvation, such claims are not only thought to be absurd, but also a complete distortion of the truth. Britain at that time, was and always had been a mercantile economy, driven almost entirely by the vagaries of the marketplace, embracing the idea of demand and supply, all of which was commonly embraced within a Laissez Faire, or a "leave it alone" economic approach. Unfortunately for the people of Ireland, Peel's belief or possible hope that the markets would ultimately provide a solution to the crop failures in Ireland proved to be completely misinformed and his own miscalculations and later mismanagement of the crisis ultimately led to the deaths of hundreds of thousands of people. Even in Parliament itself, the subject of the impending and actual famine caused great divisions amongst its political representatives, with some members openly declaring that the situation was being overstated and exaggerated, whilst others claimed that up to 15,000 people a day were dying of starvation in Ireland. It was even publicly stated by individual MP's that any suggested relief schemes would prove to be detrimental to the people of Ireland, as it would encourage idleness amongst the population, with many who were capable of work choosing to beg relief from the state instead; and therefore setting a dangerous precedent for the future. It is worth noting however that many of the representatives who spoke against giving aid to Ireland and who dismissed the very idea of a crisis in the country, had more often than not, failed to visit Ireland to see for themselves the true level of poverty there, but relied instead on rumour and word-of-mouth to help create their supposedly informed opinion.

It was often within the political maelstrom of the British Parliament that both national and religious intolerance served to distract members from creating an equitable and effective solution to the problems affecting Ireland. This was particularly evident in the attitude of some English MP's who openly accused Irish Catholic representatives, especially Daniel O'Connell, of being dishonest in their reporting of the calamitous situation in their homeland. Citing the collection of money from Catholics in support of O'Connell's Repeal Association, they used this instance to throw doubt on the severity of the famine in Ireland, claiming that this "Catholic Rent" would undoubtedly be used to feed the poor, if indeed matters were as bad as O'Connell claimed. In reply, the Irish MP stated that this money was in fact collected and used for the express purpose of fighting legal injustices that still existed within Ireland and that it would continue to be used for that specific purpose. Although, there is little doubt that the attack on O'Connell and his Association was almost certainly politically motivated, distractions such as this, almost inevitably slowed government actions and swayed both political and public opinion. Yet another declaration, made by a sitting MP, suggested that Irish grain merchants were deliberately inflating their prices on the same day that those employed on Government Work Programs were paid, keeping prices artificially high and maximising their own profits at the expense of the poor. It was also claimed that these same merchants were deliberately adulterating grain supplies with beans and other fillers, reducing the nutritional value of the food and gaining greater profit from each ton sold. On the other side, it was suggested that in parts of Ireland, the poor were being ordered, sometimes under threat of physical violence, not to cultivate their land, but to leave it alone and force the British authorities provide them with food. Even though such reports and accusations were generally incidental to the human catastrophe that was occurring in large parts of Ireland, such suggestions almost inevitably help to divide opinion and thus delay much needed aid to the people.

The British Parliament of the time, much as it always had been, was said to have been divided over what steps should be taken for the relief of Ireland's poor and destitute, the people worst affected by the famine. On the one hand, some were said to have argued that the government should intervene financially to support both the people and the economy, with much, if not all of the cost being borne by the British taxpayer through the exchequer. However, the counter argument to this was that the cost of supporting the very poorest of Ireland's people should be met by the Irish economy itself, by taxing the wealthy landlords and landowners, those who were drawing the greatest financial benefit from the country. The obvious problem with this particular solution was that many of these same landlords and landowners were members of the British legislature, sitting in either the Commons or House of Lords and were therefore unlikely to support any potential legislation that might make them financially liable for the crisis in Ireland. This fact had been particularly noted by Benjamin Disraeli as early as 1844 when he stated that "Ireland has a starving population, an absentee aristocracy and the weakest executive in the world", words that ultimately summed up much of what was wrong with Ireland at that particular time. Absentee landlords such as Lord Lucan, William Beecher and Lord Kilmaine were three of those specifically mentioned in Parliamentary debates, publicly charged with failing to prepare for the almost inevitable famine in Ireland, by not ensuring that there were adequate food stocks on their own estates until it was too late. Once the famine had fully arrived in Ireland, these men were then accused of looking for relief from England, rather than from their own private resources. Lord Lucan was also said to have failed to pay all or part of the rates levied against his holdings in Ireland, although according to a acquaintance of the lord, this was because he had been incorrectly assessed by the authorities and he had in fact, paid all that was due on his estates. This particular nobleman is generally regarded as being typical of the absentee landlords who held great status and influence within Ireland; and was just one of those later accused of authorising the mass evictions that took place during the worst of the famine years. According to one Member of Parliament during a debate on Ireland, such landlords should have been expected to contribute some £1.5 million to the British exchequer, comparable to their English counterparts, which could and should have been used for the relief of the Irish population. However, only a small proportion of this money was ever collected, as large numbers of landowners found reasons not to pay their rates, often claiming that their own incomes had fallen due to tenant's rent not being paid to them.

Ironically perhaps, it was not Peel's failure to deal with the famine that saw his party lose control of the British Parliament, but rather his attempts to deal with it, by repealing the protective tariffs which had been imposed on foreign imports of grain, known as the Corn Laws. Peel's government was subsequently replaced by that of Lord John Russell, who, although publicly sympathetic to the plight of the Irish people, ultimately presided over an administration that was not only highly ineffective, but according to some, was totally indifferent to the obvious suffering in Ireland, an attitude manifested by a number of the British officials in Dublin charged with finding solutions to the problems affecting the country. Like his predecessor, Russell was said to have been a supporter of the free market, Laissez Faire economy, which required little if any government intervention in the day-to-day running of the country's industry, manufacturing, food production, or indeed anything else. However, it was clear to Russell and his ministers that some sort of government involvement was going to be required in Ireland, such was the seriousness of the food shortages and it's potential to cause death and disease amongst the people there. Once again though, like Peel, Russell was thought to have ruled out any suggestion of closing Ireland's ports to food exports and allowing those stores to be used to feed the native population, as he considered that such an action would be detrimental to the Irish economy, as well as to the British businesses and customers that received many of these exports. Instead, Russell chose to implement a Public Works program in Ireland, based on the idea that those who were unemployed, homeless or starving could be employed on essential construction projects, in order to earn money, which could then be spent within the Irish economy and allowing the free market to operate as usual. In principle, the idea was relatively sound, but Russell and his ministers failed to grasp the severity and length of the food shortages that were actually affecting the whole of Ireland. They also failed to ensure whether or not many of the projects that were put in place were absolutely necessary in the first place, as in some cases, it was reported that people were being employed on fairly pointless tasks, such as building roads that did not lead anywhere. It has also been suggested that in some cases, being employed on such projects became a form of local lottery, as people were chosen for work purely on the basis of their religion, through knowing the foreman, or sometimes through simple bribery and corruption. It is also clear that such schemes were generally dogged by poor administration, much of which was controlled in Dublin by Chief Secretary, Sir Charles Trevelyan, who was said to have insisted on personally overseeing every minute detail of the scheme, no matter how small and who through his interference undoubtedly delayed the implementation of the scheme in the worst hit areas of the country.

Charles Trevelyan, the man who was reported to be ultimately responsible for implementing government initiatives in Ireland, including presumably both the Public Works and Famine Relief programs, is often regarded as one of those people who played a part in creating the catastrophic famine that actually occurred in Ireland. A distinguished civil servant and diplomat who had served in other parts of the British Empire, Trevelyan was known to have been highly sympathetic to the needs, religious beliefs and rights of other native peoples within the Empire, yet was reported to have been generally antagonistic towards the needs and rights of the Irish people generally. It was said to be his personal inaction and interference, supposedly tainted by his own personal antipathy towards the Irish that caused many of the problems, which would culminate in hundreds of thousands of people dying from highly preventable starvation and disease. Reputed to have stated that he "saw the famine as a mechanism for reducing the Irish population" Trevelyan was also quoted as saying that "he regarded the famine as the judgement of God, a calamity sent to teach the Irish a lesson". Whether or not Trevelyan ever uttered these words is generally immaterial, given that the policies he was meant to implement for the benefit of Ireland's population ultimately proved to be highly ineffective, resulting in tens of thousands of unnecessary deaths and becoming a mark against his reputation that would never be fully removed. Even though the government's Public Works Program was generally regarded as being ill thought out, badly administered and actually achieved little with regard to improving Ireland's national infrastructure, nonetheless it did provide employment for some hundreds of thousands of people, saving them from the worst effects of the famine that was raging all around them. In London, Russell and his government were said to have become increasingly concerned by the large numbers of farm workers that were being employed by such schemes and how their absence from the land might affect the next year's harvest, which had yet to be planted. No doubt acting on advice from his officials in Ireland, including Chief Secretary Trevelyan, the decision seems to have been made to scale back the size and numbers of the government's Work Program's, essentially forcing an estimated 500,000 people back onto the land, without the guarantee of a regular income or indeed a necessary food supply.

Charles Parnell

Joseph Plunkett

Black & Tans

As the famine became increasingly worse, so the English press began to publish stories about the plight of the Irish people and the relatively poor government response to the crisis. Perhaps to guard against any further criticism, which might be levelled against them, Russell's Government decided to establish a number of schemes, including a Poor Union and Soup Kitchens to help feed the young, old, poor and homeless that now existed in Ireland in ever increasing numbers. In order to spread the financial burden caused by these new organisations and schemes, it was also decided that some of the cost should be borne by the private landowners themselves, through locally imposed rates, through aid from religious groups such as the Society of Friends and from charitable donations made by individuals, groups, monarchs and even countries. Once again though, what should have been a relatively straightforward aid program was thought to have been made even more complicated by political and religious interventions that resulted in often unreasonable addendums, such as the Gregory Clause, being added to the Poor Law legislation. These sections of the Bill prohibited anyone who owned land from receiving relief, whereas the unemployed and indigent could, forced many small farmers to make a choice between retaining their land and starving to death. Because of such nonsensical rules, over a quarter of a million people were reported to have been forced to off the land during the period of the famine, leaving hundreds of acres of land untended in the process. It was also reported that a high proportion of these former smallholders had been evicted from their land by unscrupulous landlords, who had suddenly been made liable for the upkeep of their poverty stricken tenants by the new legislation. With falling rents and even greater government demands on their dwindling profits, some landowners or their agents saw the opportunity to limit their financial liability by removing tenants, either through the courts or by other more illegal methods. Landlords suddenly became liable for the rates on any plot that paid less than £4 a year in rents, consequently encouraging landlords to evict the smaller tenants and amalgamate a number of these smaller plots into much larger units that would ultimately pay for themselves. Large scale evictions were said to have become more common during 1847, by which time most small tenants had fallen into serious arrears with their rents, having had to make the choice between paying the landlord and buying food for their families.

The Irish Relief Unions which resulted from Lord Russell's government and that were supposed to be funded by the rates levied against landlords, never appear to have been as successful as the authorities had initially first hoped, largely because the size and scale of the famine seems to have been wildly underestimated by those that were organising the Unions. Although many existing workhouses were said to have been converted and enlarged, new buildings constructed and easier administrative systems introduced, it soon became clear that not only was there a shortage of such centres, which in most cases were under-funded, but little if any thought had been given to the control of the diseases that were spreading relatively unchecked. At one point, some 10% of the entire population was said to be at risk from Cholera alone, with Dysentery and Typhus presenting equal dangers to a population that was now being forced together by starvation, making a bad situation even worse. It was perhaps little wonder then that so many people ultimately perished, as many thousands of hungry, but otherwise healthy people, were forced to expose themselves to a number of highly infectious diseases in order to get fed. It was also the case though that even where people, who were so desperate, chose to run the obvious risks and apply for entry to the workhouse; this was not always a guarantee of a regular meal. Many instances are thought to exist of individual workhouses, hospitals and hostels that were unable to offer their residents any sort of food for many hours or even days at a time, although whether this was entirely due to simple mismanagement, deliberate decision making, a shortage of necessary funds or some other unspecified reason, is not entirely clear. That having been said though, it is perhaps worth remembering that virtually all of these Unions were actually administered by a Board of Guardians, a committee comprised of local landlords, merchants, clergymen and no doubt the local doctor. It was these people that generally made the decision, as to whether or not an individual and their families could be admitted to the workhouse, essentially giving them the power of life or death within each and every Irish community.

It has also been suggested that the decision to locate such workhouses within electoral districts, as opposed to a carefully considered central point within a particular district, proved to be yet another fatal mistake by the authorities, especially in the more rural parts of Ireland, where the effects of the famine were said to be at their greatest. Numerous tales exist of starving individuals, families and whole communities being unable to access the relief that was available, simply because of the travelling distances involved, which could be as much as 30 miles each way. It is little wonder then that reports existed of many bodies being found along the roads and tracks of Ireland, some that were crudely deposited in the nearby ditches and fields, ultimately preventing accurate numbers of the dead from ever being recorded. In most instances it was left to the local clergy to keep a record of those parishioners who had food, those that did not, those that had simply abandoned their lands and those that were known to have perished as a result of the famine. Throughout Ireland, individual accounts exist of people walking ten miles or more to apply for relief from the local Board of Guardians, only to be told that they had left for the day and to return the following day or the next week, forcing them to walk the ten miles home, with no food, no money and little hope of immediate salvation. Of course it would be completely wrong to assume that every landlord treated their tenants in an equally cruel fashion, as that was clearly not the case. Most students and historians tend to make a clear distinction between the resident landowner and the absentee landlord, with each generally representing the extremes of the treatment meted out to individual tenants. Most resident landlords were reported to have been generally sympathetic to the plight of their tenants and tried whenever possible to alleviate their suffering by providing them with food, money and healthcare. In fact, in a number of instances, some of these same landlords were said to have been so desperate to help that they eventually bankrupted themselves and even succumbed to instances of disease, which had been caught from the sick tenants that they had visited.

The absentee landlords on the other hand were regarded by many to be culpable parties in the disaster that blighted Ireland, either through their limited intervention or complete indifference to the plight of their tenants. Although most of these landholders were fully aware of the extent of the disaster that was occurring throughout Ireland and particularly on their own great estates, it seems that the maxim "what the eyes don't see, the heart doesn't grieve over" was adopted by many of these English landowners, who were purely concerned with how the disaster might affect their own personal profit margins. With land agents and estate managers acting on their behalf, most landlords were thought to have been largely indifferent to the human catastrophe that was taking place in Ireland, although one or two of these vast estate holders were reported to have sent money, so that their tenants and their dependents might be fed. Unfortunately, such instances were thought to have been extremely rare and in most cases it was the profit driven agent and manager who decided what actions were taken on individual estates and often such decisions were made to the detriment of the tenant farmer, rather than the landlord or his agent. Although no definitive figure exists for those that died during the Great Famine, the most commonly accepted figure is in the region of 750,000, most of who were thought to have died from hunger, cold and disease. Another one million people were reported to have been forced to abandon Ireland altogether, a large number of whom were said to have been transported abroad by ruthless landlords, who often hired unsuitable and sometimes quite dangerous ships to carry these reluctant immigrants to the New World. Commonly known as Coffin Ships by some historians, reflecting the often high mortality rate amongst its passengers, a large number of these cargo vessels were reported to have been destined for both Canada and the United States, where the surviving migrants were finally disembarked to begin their new lives, away from the poverty of Ireland. Large numbers of these Irish passengers were known to have been seriously ill when they arrived in their new homelands, often suffering from hunger-related diseases, as well as cholera, dysentery and typhoid which were said to have spread throughout the ship's companies at an alarming rate. Hundreds were said to have died on route, being buried at sea and even those that made it to land, were reported to have found the authorities in the New World completely unprepared for the numbers of sick people arriving in their ports.

Although most informed authorities tend to accept that hundreds of thousands of people died as a result of the Irish Potato Famine, it is thought that far more died from disease than from actual starvation. The most common victims of the famine were reported to have been the young and the old, who often succumbed to disease, as a result of starvation and their weakened systems which were unable to fight off the infections that abounded at the time. The rate and scale of the outbreaks of communicable diseases, such as cholera, dysentery and typhus was undoubtedly exacerbated by the fact that people were actively being encouraged to gather together at the Poor House, Soup Kitchens and Feeding Stations in order to be housed and fed. It has also been claimed by some sources that the depopulation of Ireland, through death and enforced immigration, was in fact deliberately engineered by the British government and its officials, to fundamentally limit their liability in respect of the native population. The main reasons given for this supposedly genocidal approach was reported to be the political and religious intolerance of the ruling classes of Britain, primarily Protestant, who saw the famine as an opportunity to severely reduce the Catholic majority, allow private landlords to restructure their landholdings in Ireland, as well as limiting Britain's financial and social responsibilities to the very poorest people of that country. However, more balanced historians have tended to regard the Great Famine as a purely natural disaster that was compounded by executive mismanagement and neglect, rather than as any sort of deliberately malicious action on the part of the British Government and its agents. It is also worth noting that at the same time Ireland was suffering the worst of the Potato Famine, so was most of Europe, including large parts of Scotland. The likes of Belgium, Denmark, Sweden, France, Holland and Spain were some of the other European countries that suffered as a result of the blight, but through their reduced level of dependency on the potato and preventative measures taken by their respective governments, suffered far less loss of life than Ireland did. A reported 100,000 people throughout Europe were said to have died as a result of the blight, a fraction of those that succumbed in Ireland, although just how many chose to abandon their homelands and emigrate to the New World, like their Irish counterparts, is unknown.

In Scotland though, as many as one million people were thought to have left the country during and immediately after the potato famine there, with many being helped to emigrate by their English and Scottish landlords, who arranged passage for them to Canada and the United States. Death rates, through starvation and its associated diseases were reportedly much lower in Scotland because of the introduction of Public Works programs, sponsored largely by the Government and that were seemingly far more successful than those established in Ireland. Possibly the biggest difference however, was the existence of large industrial towns and cities throughout mainland Britain that could easily accommodate many of those who had been forced off the land by the blight, thereby tempering the worst effects of the potato famine amongst the Scottish highland clans. Although no-one can doubt that the Great Famine was a human disaster, virtually unparalleled in either British or Irish history, some modern day reporters have deliberately chosen to misinterpret a series of historic events in order to squarely place the entire blame on the British Empire, its various monarchs, governments and therefore by implication its own native people. Pointing to early events such as the Statutes of Kilkenny, enacted in around 1366 to preserve and protect English customs and culture within the communities that had settled in Ireland, some historians have suggested that these statutes indicate English intolerance and disregard for the native Irish culture, which was beginning to infiltrate the isolated English communities that were located in Ireland. However, the fact that these statutes failed to prevent mutual assimilation between the two disparate communities would appear to undermine any suggestion that the English colonists were actively trying to eradicate Irish culture or customs, as it was them who were ultimately absorbed by the native culture and customs of Ireland, not the other way round. The same sources further point to instances such as the depiction and verbal descriptions of the Irish population as little more than monkeys, or lesser men that were featured in various publications over a particular period of time, comparing them in some way to the propaganda issued by Nazi Germany in their public campaigns against the Jewish communities of Europe during the 1930's and 1940's. Of course what they fail to mention, is that in most cases such depictions and descriptions are generally individual instances, which reflected a specific writers, artists or publisher's personal hatred and intolerance to a specific racial group, as opposed to a centralised and wholly pervasive campaign that was waged by the National Socialists in Germany. If such individual instances were true then it might follow also that every person in America, including those involved in the Abolitionist campaign were fundamentally racist, simply because pictures and articles of the time depicted Negro's as ape-like creatures, or less intelligent than a white person, suggestions that are patently absurd.

Finally, it has been claimed that the English authorities deliberately suppressed the Irish language, culture and economy to such a degree that it was unable to withstand natural disasters such as the potato blight and had lost much of its native language and culture by the beginning of the 19th century. Reporting various trade embargos and legislation that had been introduced over a period of several centuries, these historians have stated that this continued economic, cultural and industrial suppression of the Irish people is indicative of a centralised campaign by the British authorities to deliberately and systematically destroy, in whole or in part, an ethnic, racial, religious or national group within Ireland. In other words to commit genocide against the Irish people, or at least the Roman Catholic majority, by ethnically cleansing that section of the population through the use of murder, rape, torture and the forced removal of those people from their native lands. In fact, so sure are some historians and reporters of Britain's guilt in this matter that they have publicly accused the former British Empire of both genocide and ethnic cleansing, even to the point of one US State declaring the Great Famine in Ireland a holocaust deliberately perpetrated by the British authorities. Of course, to accept that such a proposition were true, one would also have to accept that this supposed act of genocide and its associated ethnic cleansing had been planned and operated over a period of more than 300 years, from the reign of Elizabeth I in 1558, right through to that of Queen Victoria in 1837. Clearly any such suggestion is an absolute absurdity, given that during that time any numbers of British monarchs, both Catholic and Protestant, had sat on the throne of England and governments of all persuasions had held power in the English Parliament.

During the period of the Great Famine, the Irish population was reported to have fallen from some eight million people, to around four and a half million, with most of the missing millions falling victim to starvation and disease, or more likely choosing once again to leave their native homelands for Britain, Europe, America, or Australia. Given such enforced hardships and the involvement of the British government, it was little wonder perhaps that a number of relatively small scale revolts and full blown rebellions were said to have occurred in Ireland throughout the 19th century. In 1803 Irish Republicans were reported to have staged a number of smaller localised revolts, whilst in 1848 the Young Irelanders were reported to have organised yet another rebellion, which is more commonly referred to as the Famine Rebellion, due to its occurrence towards the latter end of the Great Potato Famine that had gripped the country for the previous three years. Reportedly led by a number of Irish intellectuals and fervent nationalists, some sources suggest that a number of the revolt's leadership had previously been connected with Daniel O'Connell's Repeal Association, but eventually came to disagree with O'Connell's political methods and long term aims for the future of Ireland. Although not specifically dedicated towards an armed insurrection, this group of young men, calling themselves the Irish Confederation, were reported to have been led by William Smith O'Brien and Thomas Francis Meagher, both of whom had dedicated themselves to the overthrow of British rule in Ireland. Initially, they had hoped to achieve this by uniting the Irish landowners and native population in opposition to Britain's day-to-day running of the country, in an attempt to make Ireland virtually ungovernable. Unfortunately for members of the Confederation, the British Government was thought to have viewed their activities so seriously that they imposed strict measures on the country, including the suspension of the Habeas Corpus Act, thus forcing the Confederations leadership to make a choice between fight and flight. As a result, a number of leading figures in the nationalist movement were reported to have been arrested and held without trial, whilst some chose to flee the country and yet others decided to carry on with their campaigns, being prepared to meet violence with violence if the situation so demanded.

In March 1848 a number of the Confederation's leadership were reported to be canvassing support throughout Wexford, Kilkenny and Tipperary, most notably amongst local farm workers and small landowners. By July of that year William Smith O'Brien was said to have been visiting the village of Commons, where he was due to meet local miners, when a number of Policemen, intent on arresting him and his supporters, unexpectedly appeared on the outskirts of the village. Recognising that the large numbers of workers represented a potential risk to him and his men, the officer in charge of the Police unit was reported to have immediately withdrawn his men across the outlying fields of the town and sought refuge in a local house, which was occupied by a widow and her family. Perhaps angered by the unexpected Police presence, O'Brien and his followers, rather than make good their escape, or continue with their campaigning, were reported to have pursued the Police unit across the fields, until their quarry was forced to take refuge in the home of the entirely innocent Widow McCormack, who along with her five young children was subsequently held hostage by the besieged Policemen. Having barricaded themselves in Mrs McCormack's home, the policemen were said to have refused to release the homeowner or her children for fear that they would then be attacked by O'Brien and his supporters. Eventually, after what was said to have been an extended standoff, O'Brien began to negotiate with the besieged officers and finally the two sides were said to have agreed terms with one another. Unfortunately, as the agreement was finally made, an unidentified party from one or other side was thought to have opened fire, causing a ferocious exchange of gunfire between the two parties, during which one of O'Brien's men was shot and killed. As the nationalist's withdrew from the property, another member of their party, who had been positioned close to the house, was said to have been spotted by the Police, trying to rejoin his retreating colleagues and he too was shot and fatally wounded. Having withdrawn to a safe distance and with two of his men shot, O'Brien and his supporters were reported to have regrouped to consider their next move, although any further attacks on the house were thought to have been prevented by the sudden arrival of the local Parish Priest who set about trying to bring an end to the confrontation. Ultimately, O'Brien's decision was made for him, with the imminent arrival of a second Police unit who were intent on rescuing their colleagues from Mrs McCormack's house. Although the nationalist group were said to have opened fire on this second Police unit, in order to prevent them from aiding their colleagues, a combination of failing light and a shortage of ammunition, was thought to have finally forced O'Brien and his supporters to withdraw from the area. A number of the republican leaders who were involved in the incident were said to have been subsequently arrested, tried and found guilty of sedition; and although they were initially sentenced to death, all of these sentences were later commuted to transportation to Van Diemen's Land, in modern day Australia.

Less than twenty years later, in 1867, the Irish Republican Brotherhood was said to have initiated yet another rebellion, although as with most of these uprisings ultimately it proved to be a catastrophe, largely because of poor planning, lack of support from the general population or through pre-emptive actions on the part of the British authorities. Commonly referred to as the "Fenian Rising" this poorly organised and badly executed rebellion was said to have initiated by the Irish Republican Brotherhood, but sponsored and supported by Irish Nationalist groups in the United States, including a number of American military officers who had fought on both sides of the Civil War there and were keen to bring their personal expertise to the republican "cause" in Ireland. Many of these Irish American officers, having found themselves essentially unemployed after the end of the American Civil War, were thought to have been recruited by the likes of the Irish Republican Brotherhood, which had been established, funded and organised by Irish immigrants who were resident in a number of major US cities. Beginning in 1866, a series of paramilitary raids against British interests in Canada, were reported to have been launched by these groups, purportedly with the unofficial connivance of the US Government, who were keen to repay Britain, for her material support of the Confederacy during the American Civil War. Although a number of these raids were thought to have achieved some degree of success, ultimately they were said to have simply served to harden attitudes within the British establishment and proved to be a highly divisive issue amongst those Irish settlers living in Canada, who were often called upon to defend their new North American homelands from these Irish American raiders. Significantly, it was reported to be during these same paramilitary raids that the title of the Irish Republican Army was first officially used by the nationalist movement.

Lloyd George **Eamon De Valera** **Sean Treacy**

Unlike a number of the earlier revolts and rebellions, the Fenian Rising of 1867 was said to have brought the subject of Irish independence to the streets and cities of the British mainland, notably in this case, to Chester, Manchester and London, where paramilitary operations were reported to have been carried out by supporters of the largely nationalist led rebellion. The ancient city of Chester and its magnificent Castle complex was said to have become a target for the rebels, simply because of the thousands of arms and rounds of ammunition that were reported to have been held there by the British military. The abortive raid was said to have called for hundreds of Fenian supporters from Liverpool and Manchester, to congregate in the city, seize the Castle's armoury, hijack a train and use it to transport the stolen weapons to the North Wales coast, where a ship would carry the arms shipment back to Ireland. Unfortunately for the raiders however, the plot was uncovered almost immediately, thanks largely to the actions of an informer, who advised the authorities in Chester about the planned raid, allowing the local army garrison and militia's to be mobilised in order to counter the impending threat. In Manchester, the local authorities were also thought to have arrested two Fenian leaders that were found in the city and both men were subsequently remanded into Police custody. Keen to free their comrades a group of nationalist sympathisers in the city were said to have hatched a plan to release the two Fenian organisers, Thomas Kelly and Timothy Deasy, as they were being transported from prison to the courts. Once again though, poor judgement and sheer bad luck seems to have plagued the Fenian cause, resulting in the death of Police Sergeant Charles Brett, who was shot and killed during the freeing of the two Irish organisers. Three of the men who freed Kelly and Deasy were reported to have been subsequently captured by the local authorities and were charged, tried and executed for the murder of Sergeant Brett. The third notable event associated with the Irish Rebellion of 1867, was the attempted freeing of a Fenian leader, Richard Burke, in September of that year from Clerkenwell Prison in London. The Irish republican's who were involved in the breakout from Clerkenwell, were reported to have placed a quantity of gunpowder on the outside of the prison wall, in order to blow a hole in the perimeter wall, through which Burke and any other prisoners might make their escape. Unfortunately, once again poor planning and possibly sheer stupidity resulted in far too much gunpowder being used which caused twelve people being killed by the blast and more than one hundred others suffering various degrees of injury. A Fenian activist called Michael Barrett was later charged, tried and convicted of the outrage and subsequently executed by the British authorities.

Land ownership, which was known to be one of the biggest causes of dispute in Ireland since the 16th century, was one issue that was said to have been partially resolved by the British Government during the second half of the 19th century. Thanks largely to the lobbying campaigns waged against the absentee landlords who held many of the great landed estates in the country, a series of Irish Land Reform Acts were introduced, which resulted in the breaking up of these vast historic holdings and ensuring that smaller properties were returned to private individual ownership. Around the same time, politicians such as Charles Stewart Parnell were founding the Irish Parliamentary Party, which along with the likes of the

English Parliamentarian William Gladstone, attempted to gain Home Rule for the Irish State in 1886 and 1893, although both ultimately proved to be unsuccessful. The Irish Parliamentary Party was thought to have evolved from the earlier Irish Home Government Association, which had been founded by Isaac Butt in around 1870, before becoming the Home Rule League that campaigned for limited Irish Home Rule, but with Ireland continuing to remain a part of the United Kingdom. In 1898 the British Parliament eventually passed the Local Government (Ireland) Act, which finally broke the power of the private landlords, allowing local political control to pass into the hands of locally elected officials. During the latter half of the 19th century and well into the first decades of the 20th century, Irish Home Rule was probably the most significant and contentious issue relating to Ireland and the one that most polarised opinions amongst the native population of that country. On the one hand, there were the nationalist groups who believed that Ireland should be an independent state, free from all ties to Britain and comprised of all thirty two counties. On the other side of the argument, were the Protestant Unionists, who believed explicitly in the Act of Union and considered the island of Ireland to be an intrinsic part of Britain, the same as the historic kingdoms of Scotland and Wales had inevitably become. Perhaps surprisingly, most of Irelands Roman Catholic majority seem to have been largely indifferent to the separatist arguments of the nationalist political parties, choosing instead to vote for the traditional Liberal and Conservative representatives, who generally argued for the maintenance of the historic ties that linked Britain and Ireland together. Protestant politicians on the other hand, continued to argue that full independence for Ireland, would almost inevitably lead to Civil War, telling their supporters that any future Irish Government would be largely Roman Catholic in nature and therefore unsympathetic to the sizeable Protestant minority, who would have little choice, but to defend their religion and properties through force of arms.

However, despite their concerns, real or otherwise, by 1910, Home Rule for Ireland was virtually guaranteed, given that the Irish Parliamentary Party held the balance of power in the Westminster Parliament; and in 1912 the third Home Rule Bill was introduced. Despite opposition from the same Unionist and Conservative representatives, who had previously blocked similar Home Rule Bills, this time the legislation successfully negotiated the British legislature and was finally passed onto the statute books in September 1914. Reacting to this news, the Protestant leadership in Ireland were reported to have formed the Ulster Volunteers, an organisation founded specifically to oppose the Independence movement and in response to this threat, the Roman Catholic leadership in Ireland was said to have founded the Irish Volunteers. Even though the third Home Rule Act for Ireland had been passed by the British Parliament in September 1914, the outbreak of World War I was reported to have caused its implementation to be delayed until such time as hostilities were ended. At the beginning of the war, it had been widely assumed that the conflict would only last a matter of months, but as it turned out, this Great War would eventually last for four years, claim millions of lives on both sides and rob Europe of an entire generation of its bravest and brightest young men. Despite their religious and political differences, it was reported that large numbers of both Irish Catholic and Protestant men chose to serve in Britain's armed forces during the Great War, often in direct opposition to a number of leading Irish politicians, who were vehemently opposed to supporting Britain's war effort in any form. Regardless of such unpatriotic voices though, the British authorities were said to have been bound and determined to press ahead with Home Rule for Ireland, with two abortive attempts being made to implement the plan during the war itself, although both attempts were said to have failed because of disagreements between Catholic and Protestant parties who remained divided over the future of the predominantly unionist region of Ulster.

Perhaps through sheer frustration at Protestant political obstinacy, but probably through ill judged political opportunism, in 1916, the Irish Republicans, a Roman Catholic group, staged what later became known as the Easter Rising. Members of this paramilitary group were reported to have seized a number of Government buildings in Dublin and other major centres and declared independence for Ireland, no doubt hoping that the Catholic majority throughout the country would rally to their cause and force the British Parliament, busy as they were with the war in Europe, to acquiesce to their demands. Unfortunately for those involved in the uprising, once again there seems to have been little public appetite to support their cause and the revolt was quickly suppressed. However, Britain's reaction to the event and to those who were involved in the rising, was said to have been so severe and extreme that they quickly lost a good deal of the public's goodwill, which then quickly swung behind the republicans cause. A revolt of one sort or another was thought to have first been proposed by the Irish Republican Brotherhood in around 1914, with the intention that some sort of rebellion would take place before the war in Europe had ended. Although typically opportunist, given that Britain's main focus was on the bitter continental war being fought in Europe, it has been suggested that the leaders of the planned uprising restricted their planning to a small number of trusted activists, rather than making them known to the wider republican membership. Whether or not this was to reduce the chances of the plot being disclosed to the British authorities or not is unclear, although the fact that many thousands of Irish soldiers were serving with the British Army may have been a significant factor in their decision making process. It also seems clear that the committee charged with organising the revolt, were quite willing to accept help from any outside source, including the Germans, who as Britain's main military opponent in Europe were only too happy to support a nationalist revolutionary movement that might distract the British Government and its armed forces from events taking place on the Western Front.

Significant members of the Irish Republican Brotherhood's original planning committee were reported to have included Tom Clarke and Sean McDermott, although they were later joined by the members of the Irish Volunteers and the Irish Citizen's Army, including the likes of Patrick Pearse, Joseph Plunkett, Thomas McDonagh and Eamonn Ceannt. Plunkett, along with Roger Casement, was even said to have even visited Germany to interview captured Irish prisoners to try and persuade them to join their ill-fated insurrection against the British authorities in Ireland. Of the thousands of Irish prisoners held by the German, only around fifty-five were thought to have volunteered to take part in the uprising, with most of them probably agreeing to join, simply to escape from German captivity. Plunkett and Casement were also reported to have tried to arrange for a German expeditionary force to be landed in Ireland, in order to divert British troops away from Dublin, whilst the planned uprising was taking place. As it turned out however, the poor planning, lack of communication and sheer bad luck that had beset virtually all previous revolts in Ireland occurred once again, suggesting perhaps that nationalistic fervour alone, was never a good substitute for a professional, well planned approach. Having agreed to launch the uprising in the Easter week of 1916, the republican's planning committee was said to have arranged for members of the Irish Volunteers to take part in a series of parades, although the fact that the Volunteer's leadership had not been fully consulted about the matter, very nearly resulted in their being withdrawn from the plot; and it was only the promise of an arms shipment being brought in from Germany that persuaded its leadership to lend their support to the plan. Unfortunately, as it turned out, the German arms shipment was said to have been lost, when the trawler skipper bringing it into Ireland was said to have ordered it dumped overboard, presumably to avoid being caught by the British authorities. Matters were thought to have been further complicated when Roger Casement, one of the main organisers of the uprising, was subsequently captured by the British authorities, sometime after he was landed back in Ireland by a German U-Boat, which ultimately resulted in him later being charged, tried and executed for treason.

A final contributing factor to the outcome of the uprising, was said to have been the fact that one of the leaders of the Volunteers, who was thought to be unaware or opposed to the action, had instructed his own men to ignore anyone else's orders and stand down, preventing them from playing any significant role in the uprising.

Even though the British authorities in Dublin, had seemingly anticipated some form of rebel action during the course of the war, there was not thought to have been any sort of definitive indication, as to when or how such an event might take place. Rather than making arbitrary and wholesale arrests amongst the leadership of the Irish Volunteers, which would have undoubtedly caused a great deal of anger amongst the general population, the Lord Lieutenant of Ireland, Lord Wimborne, chose to wait until after Easter Monday 1916, before taking any sort of affirmative action, by which time the armed rebellion had already begun. On that particular Monday morning, several units of the Irish Volunteers, along with a number of their other nationalist allies, were reported to have taken up positions in various government buildings throughout Dublin, including the Four Courts, Dublin City Hall and the General Post Office. Having taken control of their objectives, the leaders of the rebellion, were then reported to have raised two flags above the General Post Office building, whilst Patrick Pearse read out the rebel's declaration of an independent Irish Republic on the steps of the city's Post Office. Although the British forces in Dublin were thought to have been slow, to respond to the rebel uprising, this was ostensibly due to the fact that a number of senior British officers were either on leave or could not be contacted by their junior officers. Eventually though, the local military garrison's were said to have been partially mobilised to deal with the rebels, who were reportedly holding several government buildings, although initial reports regarding their strength and armaments were obviously unknown to the soldiers that had been sent to deal with the problem. This lack of intelligence is clear from the fact that many of the British units sent to retake these buildings were obviously ill-prepared for the well defended rebel positions that they encountered, which in the first instance forced many of the British soldiers to withdraw under heavy fire and led to the death and injury of a number of British troops. In fact, it was only when British troops brought Lewis Guns and heavier artillery pieces to bear on the rebel positions that they were able to confront the Irish Volunteers with overwhelming firepower and in some cases re-take the occupied government buildings. Over the next few days there were thought to have been almost continuous exchanges of gunfire between the two sides and it was only thanks to the heavier armaments of the British that allowed them, eventually, to start to take control of the situation. Almost inevitably perhaps, the rebel forces were eventually pinned down to such a degree that Pearse, the overall commander of the revolt, finally issued an order for all of his men to lay down their arms and surrender themselves to the authorities. Throughout the rest of Ireland, actions by the Volunteers had been generally sporadic, consisting mainly of individual guerrilla attacks on isolated military and Police outposts, although most of these proved to be largely unsuccessful.

Kevin Barry   Dan Breen   Eamonn Ceannt

With the rebellion over, the British military commander, General Maxwell, was said to have ordered the arrest of all known Sinn Fein members, regardless of whether or not they had taken place in the uprising, which was thought to be the case for most of those that were subsequently arrested. In the weeks following the uprising, around three and a half thousand people were reported to have been arrested by the British authorities, although the vast majority of these were later released, once it became apparent that they had played no part in the revolt. Possibly because of the times and the state of war that existed between Britain and Germany, those implicated in the plot were said to have been tried by military courts, under the Defence of the Realm Act of 1914, rather than through the usual civilian judicial system and faced a military tribunal rather than a jury of their peers. Of those that were said to have been brought before these Court Martial panels some ninety individuals were said to have received a death sentence, although ultimately only fifteen people, including the seven men who had signed the Proclamation of Independence, were executed by a British firing squad. Unfortunately, a number of those who were sentenced to death, were thought to have been entirely innocent of participating in the Easter Rising, but were said to have been executed for other acts they had committed, some at the same time as the rising and others prior to it. Either way, it was thought to be the execution of the rebellion's leaders that did much to damage the British cause with the Irish population, who might usually have expected that those involved in the revolt would subsequently have their sentences commuted to long prison terms, rather than the death penalty actually being applied.

A later contributing factor to this Irish backlash against the British authorities was thought to be the threatened conscription of young Irishmen, who it was said, were to be drafted into the British forces to help defeat the German armies in Europe. Although towards the end of the war, Britain was known to have been desperately short of fit young fighting men, having lost so many since 1914, the government of the day was thought to have attempted to link the subject of conscription in Ireland, with the political issue of Home Rule, which essentially ended the political coalition that had existed up until that point. As it turned out however, there was no compulsory conscription introduced into Ireland, but much political goodwill was said to have been wasted as a result of such ill-conceived planning, allowing smaller peripheral political groups, such as the Republican's Sinn Fein, to benefit from the Irish publics general dissatisfaction and anger. However, with the war eventually won, Irish politics continued to illustrate the underlying public resentment to British involvement in the island of Ireland and in the 1918 General Elections, the Republican's main political party, Sinn Fein, was reported to have won 75 of the 105 Irish seats in the British Parliament. During this period, the legitimately elected Republican MP's were also reported to have refused to take their seats within the British Parliament, regarding it as a foreign and wholly unrepresentative legislature for the electorate of Ireland. Interestingly, this same action was repeated during the 20th century when Sinn Fein MP's refused to sit at Westminster, having been elected to represent Roman Catholic sections of the electorate of Northern Ireland. In January 1919, twenty-six Sinn Fein MP's were reported to have met at the Mansion House in Dublin and unilaterally established their own Irish Parliament, a move that was said to have been generally ignored by the British authorities initially. Set firmly on having a 32 county Independent Irish Republic, the Sinn Fein MP's simply refused to negotiate the future of Ireland on any other basis and as if to underpin their resolve, decided to arbitrarily declare that a state of war existed between England and Ireland, as well as announcing that henceforth the Irish Volunteers would become known as the Irish Republican Army. Perhaps to signal their intentions for future campaigns, in the same month that the twenty-six Sinn Fein representatives were declaring their new Republic, two IRA members, Sean Treacy and Dan Breen, were thought to have shot two Policemen in South Tipperary, an event that is often regarded as the beginning of the armed conflict between the IRA and the British authorities.

In response to this unprovoked attack, the British authorities were thought to have made South Tipperary a special military area and therefore subject to the Defence of the Realm Act 1914, which gave both the Police and Military special powers over the local population. Almost inevitably, the IRA responded to this announcement by carrying out guerrilla attacks throughout the country, attacking British interests and assassinating prominent officials, including magistrates and Police Officers, much the same as they would do some sixty-odd years later in Northern Ireland. By attacking such high profile targets, most notably policemen, the IRA not only hoped to undermine the morale of the Irish Constabulary, especially those posted in fairly isolated stations, but also used such attacks to acquire additional arms for their own republican arsenals. In conjunction with these guerrilla campaigns, the Republican movement was also reported to have organised numerous workers strikes, as well as acts of public disobedience and non-cooperation, which were designed to make Ireland virtually ungovernable by the British authorities. For her part, Britain was said to have countered these nationalist campaigns by threatening to withhold financial subsidies to the organisations which were strike bound, essentially depriving strikers of their wages and possibly their whole employment. Known strike organisers were arrested or had their movements severely restricted by the authorities, in an attempt to prevent further strikes being planned, although all of these measures ultimately proved to be largely ineffective against a nationalist community who were becoming increasingly sympathetic to the Republican cause. As more and more of the day-to-day routines of government were usurped and removed by Sinn Fein; and its supporters, who deliberately targeted Tax Offices and Police Stations for destruction, so the British Government found it increasingly difficult to maintain overall control over the running of the country. Although Britain might well have considered imposing Martial Law throughout the whole of Ireland, the investment of both men and materials, along with the political ramifications of such a course of action, was thought to be too high a price to pay for a country that was still recovering from being bled dry by four years of bitter warfare.

By destroying the administrative and legal infrastructure of the country, the Republicans were able, in part, to replace these seemingly important British assets with their own nationalist courts, tax raising offices and even an Irish Republican Police Force, which was reportedly founded in 1920. Ultimately, their hope was that by depriving the British authorities of their officials, Policemen and more importantly, the tax revenues that paid them, then the British position in Ireland would become largely untenable, which would force them to relinquish political control of the whole country to the Republican's. Unfortunately for the nationalists however, the IRA's continuing guerrilla campaign against the judiciary, Police and military, simply hardened the British authorities attitude towards the Republican cause generally; and the IRA specifically. Instances of individual IRA men, real or suspected, being assassinated by members of the Police or Armed Forces became common events, as did the reprisals meted out by the Republican themselves. In Westminster, this hardening of attitudes was represented in the legislation that was passed by the government of Lloyd George, which saw the suspension of local Coroner's Courts, which were commonly being used by the Republican's to indict the British Government, its Ministers and its Armed Forces for any and all nationalist deaths that were brought before them. In addition to these measures, British military courts were also thought to have been given complete authority over the whole of the country and were entitled to use Capital Punishment and Internment as legitimate methods of controlling or punishing nationalist wrongdoers.

Active membership of the Irish Republican Army was only thought to have numbered some 10-15,000 people throughout the whole of Ireland, which explains why the organisation would not and could not fight the British military in any sort of conventional sense. Despite calls from some Irish nationalist leaders for the IRA to confront the British Army in the open, any and all such suggestions were quickly dismissed by the Republican's military council, who recognised that to do so, would almost certainly invite the complete destruction of the movement by the military superiority of a professional British Army. Instead, the Republican leadership chose to conduct a clandestine war against Britain, which allowed its members to form themselves into independent active service units that were led by local commanders, who carried out their own guerrilla operations, with little if any authority from their central military council. Although it is clear that the vast majority of the Irish population were largely indifferent or directly opposed to the guerrilla tactics employed by the IRA, there were thought to be a significant number of people, specifically within the nationalist community in the south of Ireland, who were quite willing to offer both explicit and tacit support to their long term aims. Not only were they willing to feed, finance and harbour Republican's who were conducting military operations against the British, but they rarely disclosed any sort of information which might prove to be useful to the British authorities or indeed their agents. In fact, it was widely thought that there were a large number of isolated towns and villages where the local police had been forced out, under threat of death or violence; where Republican groups held such sway that they essentially controlled the local population, either through similarly held convictions or simply by intimidating them into compliance.

With the Irish Police Force, the RIC, seemingly under pressure from Republican guerrilla units and unable or unwilling to deal with them directly, the British Government was said to have embarked upon a recruitment campaign, in order to create two new paramilitary units of their own, the infamous Black and Tans and the not so well known Auxiliaries. Established primarily to support and strengthen the weakened and largely ineffective ranks of the Irish Police, most of the men recruited for these new British units were reported to have been veterans of the First World War, as well as professional British Army Officers with experience in intelligence gathering. The British Government's decision to employ these two groups, was thought to have been largely based on the idea that paramilitary Police units would prove to be less inflammatory to the local population, than regular soldiers, which might well have been true, had the command structure within these two groups been as disciplined as in the regular British Army. Unfortunately for everybody concerned, it was precisely because these two groups lacked such discipline and any sort of centralised oversight that they ultimately proved to be such an unmitigated disaster, not only for the British Government, but the British Army, the Irish Police and the people of Ireland themselves. The Black and Tans were reported to have been raised in England, primarily from former English and Scottish soldiers, who had fought during the First World War, but who had been discharged once the conflict was over. Their name, the "Black and Tans" is reported to have derived from the uniforms that members of the unit commonly wore, a combination of army khaki and black Police uniforms, which was said to have been caused by a shortage of regular Police dress, rather than any sort of predetermined design. Renowned for their poor discipline, drunkenness and arbitrary acts of violence against both members of the IRA and the often entirely innocent Irish population, rather than helping to reduce Irish hostility to the British Government, the Black and Tans were said to have simply made a bad situation even worse. With few quality officers within their ranks to oversee unit discipline, the Black and Tans were said to have "to responded in kind" to any IRA atrocity that was committed against them or the Irish Police, with instances of IRA suspects being brutally attacked, individual houses or whole villages being burned and even claims that the British paramilitary group assassinated suspected Republican leaders. This unofficial unit creed of "fighting terror with terror" ultimately helped to make the Black and Tans one of the most feared and hated symbols of British rule in Ireland and even today the memory of the unit continues to reviled in most parts of the modern day Irish Republic.

The second paramilitary unit established by the British authorities in 1920 was the Auxiliaries, which generally comprised a number of former military officers, who were said to be highly effective in taking on and dealing with the IRA's own active service units. Although a far superior force than the Black and Tans, even the auxiliaries were thought to have contained individual members who occasionally demonstrated instances of ill-discipline and brutality, bringing about events that would ultimately result in their being equally hated by the IRA and the law abiding Irish population. Interestingly perhaps, even though the Black and Tans, the Auxiliaries and the Irish Constabulary were entirely independent units, in the minds of many Irish people, they all came to be seen and reported as Black and Tans, which undoubtedly accounted for the number of outrages that the unit was ultimately blamed for. Probably one of the most infamous incidents that involved all three organisations and which came to signify their obvious lack of discipline, was the attack on an entirely innocent and unarmed crowd of spectators who were gathered at Croke Park to watch a Gaelic football match, an event that later became known as the First Bloody Sunday. It would be wrong to see this specific event, as an isolated incident, as that was not the case. Rather, the attack in Croke Park was simply the culmination of a series of events that was said to have been initiated by the deaths of three Republican prisoners, who had starved themselves to death while in British custody, a course of action that was repeated some 50-odd years later by Republican prisoners in Northern Ireland. In retaliation for these deaths and possibly because of the British authorities' continuing success in countering the IRA's ongoing guerrilla campaigns, Michael Collins, the IRA's chief military strategist, was reported to have planned an operation, which would eventually lead to the assassination of fourteen British Intelligence Operatives in Dublin and the wounding of five more. Many of these men were thought to have been former Army and Police Officers, who because of their experience and intelligence gathering skills, represented a real threat to the IRA and it was hoped their elimination would prove to be critical loss to the British authorities in Ireland.

Thomas Meagher   Thomas McDonagh   Royal Irish Constabulary

The first assassinations were said to have taken place on the morning of 21st November 1920, on what later became known as Bloody Sunday and it was thought to be as a direct result of this murderous assault that all of the subsequent events took place. Reportedly enraged by the assassination of their colleagues, members of the Black and Tans, Auxiliaries and the Royal Irish Constabulary, were said to have received information that some of the IRA gunmen, who had been involved in the attacks, had infiltrated the football crowd at Croke Park, intent on hiding their weapons and leaving the city as part of this entirely innocent gathering. Generally reported as simply being Black and Tans, the British forces that arrived at the stadium, were actually thought to be members of all three units, the Black and Tans, Auxiliaries and the Irish police, although for most of the spectators who were present on the day, they were all one and the same. Most of the later reports of the events at Croke Park suggest that the Police and military units who initially arrived at the stadium, had initially intended to surround it, ensuring that no potential suspects escaped; and then search every member of the crowd as they exited the arena. However, as they approached the entrance to Croke Park, a couple of men were reported to have entered the stadium, presumably to warn other members of the crowd about their arrival, which then caused a number of the British paramilitaries and Police units to hurriedly follow them into the stadium, with their guns drawn and in a state of high anxiety. It was also later reported that these same British units had driven their trucks into the stadium, although exactly how many and where they were placed is unclear, but some Republican claims that one of these vehicles was an armoured car later proved to be untrue, as this particular vehicle was known to have taken up a position outside of Croke Park, rather than inside the stadium.

Almost inevitably, given the highly tense situation which had been created by the arrival of a number of heavily armed and highly agitated paramilitaries in a stadium packed with a generally hostile crowd, the likelihood of a disaster taking place was almost a guaranteed certainly. Exactly what specific incident caused the British units to open fire on the crowd has never been completely identified, whether it was a look, a movement, a hostile word or simply an overreaction by an overanxious British paramilitary, regardless of the cause, by the time the shooting had stopped some fourteen people were dead or dying and over sixty more were said to have been wounded. For both the British authorities and the Irish people, the massacre at Croke Park proved to be an unmitigated disaster, as it not only further stained Britain's reputation in Ireland, deprived innocent people of their lives, but also ensured that the armed conflict between Britain and the Irish Republican cause became marked by even more bitterness and brutality on both sides of the struggle. Even though the Croke Park massacre would have been infamous in its own right, what became known by Republicans as "Bloody Sunday" did not finish at the football stadium, but rather at Dublin Castle, later on in the same day. Three Republican prisoners, who were being held at the castle, were reported to have been killed whilst trying to escape from custody, although in reality it seems likely that they were simply murdered by unidentified members of the British military services, who were keen to avenge the deaths of the British intelligence officers earlier in the day. These two events together are commonly remembered as Bloody Sunday, a day that is marked as a national day of mourning within Republican circles, as well as one of British brutality, although interestingly, the killing of the fourteen British military officers and policemen is often overlooked by nationalist supporters, who are keen to avoid any suggestion that their movement bears a degree of responsibility for the catastrophe that occurred on that day.

Within a week of Bloody Sunday, the IRA had once again initiated large scale reprisals against the British authorities, when they were reported to have ambushed an eighteen man Auxiliary patrol in County Cork, killing all but one of them. It was thought to be as a result of these continuing attacks that British forces were tacitly authorised to use reprisals against members of the general population who were suspected of colluding with and supporting these IRA active service units. The method of reprisal generally involved the burning of the people's houses and in one case in Cork; British forces were reported to have fired their weapons to prevent local fire-fighters from extinguishing the flames. In the following months, dozens of such incidents were said to have taken place and hundreds of people were reported to have died, as both sides fought a largely indiscriminate war against each others supporters. Hundreds, if not thousands of Republican sympathisers were said to have been interned by the British authorities and of the hundreds of Republicans that died, some twenty four men were known to have been executed by the authorities, including the famed Kevin Barry, who was later immortalised in word and song, becoming one of the many Republican martyrs celebrated by the nationalist cause. It was said to be partly due to the successful propaganda, issued by the Republican cause that Britain was prevented from finding any sort of definitive military solution to the Irish problem. Along with the occasional outrages perpetrated by their agents, the Black and Tans, Auxiliaries and Irish Police, the British Governments apparent inability to fully and publicly refute many of the more outrageous claims of the nationalists, most notably in the United States, proved to be highly damaging to Britain's image abroad. This particular factor was also thought to have been instrumental in the British Government's decision not to employ regular troops to suppress the whole of Ireland; as such an act would undoubtedly have been totally unacceptable to the wider international community. Eventually it was thought to have been this absolute refusal to impose an entirely military solution on Ireland, along with the successes and failures of both sides that saw the Irish conflict essentially fought to a standstill, with neither party being able to deliver the final telling blow to the other one's position.

Despite many members of the main Republican Party refusing to negotiate the future of their country, the British Government, Protestants and other Irish Nationalist parties continued to do so, pressing ahead with plans for Irish Home Rule and seeing the fourth Government of Ireland Act passed through the British Parliament in 1920. This final draft would see the island of Ireland divided into two distinct areas, Southern Ireland and Northern Ireland, the same division that continue to exist to the present day. It also seems clear that the British Government quickly realised that with no chance of a military solution being found to the troubles in Ireland, then the obvious answer was to settle the matter through negotiation. Having ended the policy of burning houses as an act of reprisal, Britain then proposed peace talks with the main nationalist parties, initially represented by Raymond de Valera, who was said to have met with Lloyd George in order to arrange a temporary military truce and set out terms for future negotiations. In the following year, the Anglo Irish Treaty was reported to have been signed by both the British and Irish Governments, with Arthur Griffiths and Michael Collins acting for the Irish Party. This treaty was thought to have formally abolished the Irish Republic, replacing it with the Irish Free State, a self governing dominion of the Commonwealth of Nations and holding a similar status to that of Australia and Canada. Although the division of Ireland was a compromise too far for many Republican's, who had seen their comrades fight and die for a complete and united Republic, most nationalists regarded the new arrangement as being in everyone's best interests, as it finally brought an end to British rule in Ireland after some 700 years. Under the terms of the treaty, the six states that constituted Northern Ireland, were said to have been given the choice of opting into the Irish Free State or remaining as part of Great Britain. Bearing in mind that the majority of the people within these six counties, were Protestant by religion and Unionists by preference, it was hardly a surprise when they opted to stay as part of Great Britain, the province being noted in the title Great Britain and Northern Ireland and their own independent Parliament coming into force in June 1921.

In 1922, both British and Irish Parliaments were said to have ratified the treaty, giving independence to the twenty six southern counties of Ireland, which then became the Irish Free State. Almost immediately though, the divisions, which were thought to have existed between those Republicans who supported the treaty and those that were opposed to it erupted into violence, with the outbreak of the Irish Civil War, which raged between 1922 and 1924. Reported to have cost more Irish lives than the preceding War of Independence, which had been fought against British involvement in Ireland, this particularly bitter conflict was said to have resulted in the deaths of many leading nationalists, including one of the main architects of the Anglo Irish Treaty, Michael Collins, who was assassinated by a member of the anti-treaty republican movement. Ultimately though, the Civil War was said to have been won by the pro-treaty Republicans and in 1937 the Irish Free State renamed itself as Ireland. Twelve years later, Ireland was reported to have unilaterally declared itself as an independent Republic, becoming the Republic of Ireland and at the same time choosing to leave the British Commonwealth of Nations. Although nobody would claim that England's, later Britain's involvement in Ireland was in anyway a picture perfect example of Imperial rule, but as with most historic events, it should be seen in the right context, rather than in some modern, politically correct atmosphere, which bears little resemblance or connection to these earlier times.

MARINERS, MERCHANTS AND THE MILITARY TOO

4. BRITAIN AND THE SLAVE TRADE

The British Empire's active participation in the Transatlantic Slave Trade, which saw millions of Black Africans forcibly transported from their homelands to the Americas, where they were simply sold as chattels, is undoubtedly one of the darkest and least honourable episodes of Britain's long and generally distinguished history. Commonly used to undermine Britain's enormous and undoubted contribution towards creating the modern world that we all now inhabit, along with the supposedly wholesale destruction of numerous native societies, the capture, imprisonment, transportation and abuse of millions of Black Africans, remains first and foremost the biggest single charge laid against the founders of Britain's great Empire. Interestingly however, those who are generally quick to point to Britain's early and extensive involvement in the Transatlantic Slave Trade, appear to be reluctant to publicise the fact that it was Britain, which ultimately played a leading role in helping to outlaw the generally barbarous trade by the first half of the 19th century.

It is also perhaps worth noting from the outset that slavery, in one form or another, is known to have existed throughout much of the ancient world and was reported to have been a common feature of most of the great human civilisations of the past, from the Greeks to the Romans, from the Persians to the Mongols. Even in Western Europe, the Roman legions were reported to have regularly enslaved hundreds of thousands of people from the territories that they conquered, often transporting them against their will to the various villas, houses and amphitheatres of Rome, where they would serve out their days for the comfort or amusement of the Roman elite, yet few historians are thought to be critical of that fact. Even after the fall of the great Roman Empire, slavery was said to have continued within numerous individual states and countries, where captured prisoners of war, or the indigenous population were simply sold into slavery, often being transported to slave markets in North Africa and the Middle East, where the buying and selling of human cargoes, was reported to have been a relatively commonplace event. In Britain, as elsewhere in Western Europe, large numbers of its native peoples, who were conquered by the likes of the Barbary Corsairs, Mongols, Anglo Saxons and even the fearsome Vikings were all thought to have been stolen away from their family, friends and homelands to be sold into permanent servitude in foreign lands, where strange languages and unknown customs were thought to have surrounded them for the remainder of their lives.

Slave Caravans

Slave Plantations

Slave Ship

Even before, during and after the Roman settlement of Western Europe, large numbers of slaves were reported to have been taken from the countries that had been invaded by the legions of Roman, principally to serve the citizens of Rome or the Empire's other great cities, who regarded the ownership of slaves, as an obvious indication of their own personal wealth and status. It has even been suggested by some historians that up to 25% of the entire population of the vast Roman Empire were slaves, including those convicted of debt, prisoners-of-war, orphans and the children of slaves, who by their very birth were automatically delivered into slavery. The Romans themselves were said to have inherited the idea of slavery from the earlier Greek Empire, who undoubtedly inherited it from even earlier peoples and Empires that had existed hundreds, if not thousands of years before the Greek Empire ever came into being. For both the Greeks and the Romans, slavery was not only an economic imperative, but was also thought to have become an essential part of their social structure, as in the case of the gladiators who fought in their arenas, the prostitutes who serviced their troops and the personal sex slaves who were owned by individual citizens. According to early Roman law, a slave was said to have been defined as anyone whose mother was a slave, anyone that had been captured in battle, or anyone who sold themselves into slavery, in settlement of a debt. Significantly, even early Christian leaders of the time, rather than attacking the concept or practice of slavery, were known to have supported it, telling their followers who were slaves to "obey their masters and dedicate their suffering to God", suggesting that their enslavement was both a common and entirely legal process that the early church had little interest in overturning.

With the almost inevitable demise of the Roman Empire, much of Europe was then reported to have descended into chaos, with weaker countries exploited by their much stronger neighbours, a part of which would have involved their populations being snatched away to be sold in the thriving slave markets of the east, or within the aggressor nations own territories. In addition to the generally domestic western raiders, like the Anglo Saxons and Vikings, most of Europe's leading western nations were thought to have been ravaged by marauding bands of sea borne Arab slave traders who would attack coastal communities on a fairly regular basis, robbing, burning and stealing away their citizens, particularly women, who would be carried away to the eastern slave markets, to be sold as domestic servants, or worse still, as prostitutes or sex slaves. Even in England itself, prior to the 11th century, slavery was thought to have been fairly common, especially with the early Anglo Saxon's who had invaded Britain in the 5th and 6th centuries. However, with the arrival of William the Conqueror in 1066, the practice was said to have been generally outlawed by the new English ruler, although even by 1086, the time of the Domesday Book, at least 10% of the native English population were still thought to have been enslaved in one way or another. Chattel slavery, as an outright form of ownership, was said to have been formally abolished in England around 1102, although bonded slavery, indentured service and serfdom were all thought to have continued after that date. Of the three forms of service, serfdom was said to be the most common, as it inextricably tied a common individual to the lands of a particular overlord or landowner, leaving them at the beck and call of that particular nobleman. Unlike a chattel however, serfs could buy and sell land, acquire personal possessions, get paid for their labours and generally enjoy many of the rights and freedoms that any free man might expect. This was thought to have remained the case throughout much of Britain's history, with English Common Law, generally protecting the rights of the common man and curtailing the excesses of the nobles; and it was only in the 16th and 17th centuries that this protection was said to have been removed, but even then, only for those that were outside of Great Britain and Ireland.

That is not to say however that the British population were immune from the effects of the Slave Trade, especially that which was being operated by foreign traders, such as the Vikings and the Barbary Corsairs. For many hundreds of years, numerous British and Irish citizens were thought to have been stolen away from their coastal communities, which were rarely protected by the native forces and were therefore left to defend themselves from such seaborne assaults. The Vikings of northern Europe were known to have been particularly adept at raiding throughout the wider region, although after 1000 AD they were thought to have become less and less of a problem, as they chose to settle around the British Isles and were eventually absorbed into the native British communities, adding their own distinctive language and culture to the country. According to some sources, the Vikings tended to follow regional Scandinavian rules, in relation to the taking and treatment of slaves, which dictated that native slaves could not be sold abroad, yet foreign slaves could. Additionally, slaves were only ever accorded equal rights to any other chattel or possession, which meant that they had no human rights as such and therefore the killing of a slave, was not generally regarded as being a serious offence within the Norse community, with the offender only being required to compensate the owner for the cost of the slave, much the same as if a common farm animal had been unlawfully slaughtered.

The Barbary Pirates or Corsair's, were reported to have been a largely North African and Mediterranean sea-based confederation, which raided the coastal communities of North Africa, the Mediterranean and Northern Europe between the 16th and 19th centuries, taking thousands of people captive, either for ransom or for sale in the eastern and African slave markets. In a single Corsair raid, which was said to have taken place in June 1631, these seaborne pirates were reported to have attacked the Irish community of Baltimore in County Cork; and stolen away almost the entire population of the town, who were subsequently said to have been delivered into a life of slavery in North Africa or the Middle East. Hundreds of individual European ships, along with their crews, as well as many thousands of coastal dwelling people from throughout the Iberian and European region were said to have been snatched away by these raiders, who were only finally suppressed when the western nations sent their combined navies into the pirates strongholds and destroyed them.

Before looking at the actual history of Britain's involvement in the Transatlantic Slave Trade, perhaps it is worth clarifying exactly what the situation was before a single English ship ever sailed anywhere near the west coast of Africa. It is also worth reiterating that human bondage is thought to have been an integral part of all of the great civilisations, be they early or late, east or west, Christian or non-Christian, rich or poor. Where great strength and weakness exists, there is almost always the potential for the strong to exploit the weak, an aspect of human nature that can be seen in the histories of the world's greatest empires and kingdoms, including the Greeks, Egyptians, Romans, Portuguese, Spanish and of course the British. It is also worth recalling that from the late 12th century onward, Britain was not a slave owning society, even though indentured service or serfdom was known to have existed for hundreds of years. Unlike many parts of the world, including the far flung British colonies of the Caribbean and North America, the question of chattel slavery in Britain remained largely ignored, simply because it did not affect the lives of most everyday citizens, be they rich or poor, educated or uneducated. There were undoubtedly chattel slaves in Britain, who were brought back with their owners from the foreign lands that they visited, but in most cases, such human property would have been hidden away from the public gaze, in the fancy houses or on the great estates of their affluent masters. Owning slaves was thought to be as much about personal choice, as it was about the local culture that accepted chattel slavery as a normal, everyday occurrence, something that was not the case in Britain from the 16th to 19th century, when the Transatlantic Slave Trade was operating. Instead it was only a commonly accepted form of ownership in those British colonies that were permanently isolated from their motherland by great distances and where the social structure was very different to that which operated in Britain itself. Even though the British colonies of the Caribbean and parts of North American were known to be lands of great financial opportunity, it was usually only the most daring or desperate who would actually leave Britain to live there, such was the poor reputations of such regions.

Not only had these lands and islands been initially settled by adventurers, but later more permanent settlements were thought to have been populated by large numbers of convicted criminals or political prisoners, who the British establishment in London had been glad to see the back of. Added to, by any number of outcasts from many of the western European nations and large numbers of businessmen and speculators who saw the potential profits from the various commercial opportunities that presented themselves, these were the social classes that often made up the ranks of the British communities in places like Barbados and Jamaica. In common with Ireland, much of the land of these great plantation estates was thought to have been owned by a relatively small number of absentee landlords, who delegated the running of their Caribbean businesses to appointed agents, who had little interest in anything else, but making a profit for his employer who was back in Britain. With this one single financial imperative in mind, it is perhaps small wonder that all other considerations, including the treatment of his slaves, would automatically have become secondary to this primary aim. Notable British absentee landlords of the time were said to have included William Beckford, Lady Home, Erle Drax, Sir Peter Parker, Lord Maynard and Admiral Rodney. Although a significant number of the sugar cane producers and their families were known to have lived on their foreign plantations, it was probably the case that many of them had originated from the convicts and indentured servants who had been brought to the islands many years before. Often with questionable characters to begin with, their own treatment and hardships undoubtedly helped to shape their own attitude to the African slaves that now worked on their own estates, highly negative views that were no doubt reinforced by a belief that they were somehow superior to their non-European workforce. It is also likely that such attitudes and beliefs would have been passed from one generation of planters to the next, with levels of discrimination and indifference becoming stronger and more deeply engrained as the planters children became more and more deeply imbued with the often racist and highly intolerant attitudes of their own parents.

It should also be remembered that for much of its known history the African continent has been exploited for its natural resources, its animals, its mineral deposits, its valuable metals, as well as its rich resource of people. Firstly, the native peoples of Africa were said to have been exploited by one another, the military strong preying on those that were militarily weak, delivering tens of thousands into continental slavery and sometimes death. The tribes of Africa were then said to have been exploited by the great civilisations of Egypt and Rome, then by the Arab states of North Africa and the Middle East, with millions of black Africans having been taken from their native homelands, before a single European foot ever touched the soil of the so-called "Dark Continent". Of course, it would be foolish to deny that racial prejudice or religious dogma has not played a part in the exploitation of Africa's native people, especially amongst other non-African nations. But such prejudices are not simply modern themes, but are known to have existed for hundreds, if not thousands of years and have even been the subject of debates based on biblical scriptures that experts continue to argue over, even through to the modern day. It is often these historic debates, interpretations and beliefs that have supposedly informed western nations about the black African and ultimately determined their approach to and treatment of the peoples of Africa. Clearly the subject of religion was a major factor for most western Christian nations during and after the 15th century, the very time that the lands of Africa were first being explored by western European nations like the Portugal and Spain. The fact that most native African tribes of that time, were reported to have still held to a pagan or native belief system, inevitably helped European Christians to justify their treatment of native Africans, views that were often endorsed by biblical teachings or by individual Pontiffs. In the opinion of some early biblical scholars, both the Old Testament and the New Testament advocated the use of slavery, although it is worth noting that just as many people disagree with this interpretation, which is why the subject has been the subject of heated debate for hundreds of years and remains so today.

Those who believe that the Bible endorses slavery, generally point to certain ancient texts, which supposedly state that enslavement of another person is not unchristian, provided that it is along the lines of what later became known as indentured service, rather than outright chattel slavery. A number of these early Christian sources believe that slaves or servants should be released from their service after a specified number of years and given parting gifts to celebrate their release and to help them start a new life for themselves. However, there are an equal number of early Christian saints and evangelists who condemned any form of slavery or servitude outright, but at the same time accept that slavery could and did play a normal part of everyday social practice. Christian doctrine as advocated by Christ's representative on earth, the Pope, has been mixed on the subject of slavery throughout the early history of the church. It seems that most early Popes, preachers and ministers took the view that although slavery was not ideal, it was a natural occurrence and state within most human societies and could not therefore be condemned or abolished outright. In America, church leaders refused to condemn slavery or those that were involved with it right through until the middle of the 19th century when the practice of slavery was outlawed by statute. But even then, ministers in certain slave owning states still refused to condemn the practice of slavery up until the middle of the 20th century when national legislation finally outlawed any sort of discrimination within the United States. Such was the divisive nature of the slavery debate that even churches were reported to have split in two, having disagreed over the moral right and wrongs of the practice of enslavement, divisions that remain within those communities to this very day.

Captain Hugh Crow   **Middle Passage**   **Thomas Golightly**

Likewise, the slave trades, both Arab and European, undoubtedly owed much to basic racial discrimination, which like its counterpart; religious intolerance, has been a feature of human civilisation from the very earliest times. However, it would be wrong to suppose that such virulent racism is an entirely white characteristic, as this is not the case. Even in early religious literature, which was largely thought to have been written by Arab or Middle Eastern scribes, black people were generally seen as being descended from the biblical character "Ham", the sinful son of Noah, who had been cursed by God. The ancient Empire of Egypt was equally damning about black people, who they believed to be less civilised and less lawful than their Arabic counterpart. This theme was thought to have continued well beyond the time of the pharaohs, with the 15th century Arab historian Al-Abshibi stating that "when the black slave is sated, he fornicates and when he is hungry, he steals". Other Arabic scholars were equally disparaging about the abilities of black people, with one of their number comparing black Africans to dumb animals "who lived in thickets and caves, ate herbs and unprepared grain, as well as occasionally eating one another" Most historians agree that virtually every major African city and town had a slave market, where captured prisoners-of-war, convicted criminals and society's troublemakers were offered for sale to their fellow Africans, or to the Arab slave merchants who regularly attended such markets. It seems clear that slavery within Africa itself was a common practice before the Portuguese, Spanish or indeed the English had even begun to explore the continent in the late 14th and early 15th centuries. That having been said, then Europeans cannot be blamed for introducing the basic principle of slavery itself into Africa, but are simply guilty of somehow industrialising a process that was endemic to the continent in the first place.

For hundreds of years, prior to the first Portuguese ship sailing into African coastal waters, native Africans had regularly been traded in large numbers, by the Arab tribes of North Africa and by merchants based in the Middle East. Through historic Saharan routes, across the Red Sea and Indian Ocean, millions of black Africans were reported to have been transported by both land and sea, in a trade that was said to have existed from the 9th century, right the way through to the 19th century, representing a millennium of exploitation and misery. According to some sources, even the Arab Slave Trade was thought to have begun as a supplementary feature of the trade in gold, ivory and pepper, which had already existed in the region for hundreds of years. Likewise, some historians have also suggested that the Arab Slave Trade was at least equal to, if not greater than the Transatlantic Slave Trade, which both followed and accompanied it. Significantly, the Arab Slave Trade is thought by some reporters to have had much more an impact on the female population of Africa, simply because African women were in generally greater demand within the Arab world, both as domestic workers and as both prostitutes and sex slaves. This is thought to be the opposite effects, as was caused by the Transatlantic Slave Trade, where strong young African males, were very much in demand, due to their ability to work long hours in the fairly arduous conditions of the sugar plantations, gold mines, etc. Clearly both the Arab and the Transatlantic Slave Trades impacted heavily on both sexes, of the native African population; and it would be wrong to simply assume that Arabs only enslaved women or the European slavers only men, as both parties were known to have taken both, although according to some reporters in disproportionate numbers.

According to some sources, the Indian Ocean slave route, had begun as a relatively small scale operation in the 9th century, but was one that developed substantially over time, eventually accounting for tens of thousands of African slaves being taken into the Middle East for similar reasons as elsewhere. The port of Zanzibar, on the east coast of Africa, was reported to have been the largest and most important slave trading centre in the whole of Africa, with a reported 50,000 slaves being traded and passing through the port during the height of the trade in the 19th century. The African Slave Trade was also known to have played a significant part within early African societies and of course their regional economies, with some native kingdoms employing roving bands of warriors, to attack and capture neighbouring tribesmen, who would then be sold into captivity. For some tribal monarchs, the slave economy allowed them and their peoples to accumulate great wealth, as was said to be the case of the predominant tribes of modern day Ghana and Nigeria, who became rich by selling their fellow Africans. Even though the capture and selling of neighbouring tribesmen was a major financial benefit of such inter-tribal warfare, fundamentally such conflicts were thought to have been precipitated for the same reasons as elsewhere, which was regional dominance, land or border disputes, access to and acquisition of natural resources such as water, etc, or simply as the result of personal and tribal vendettas. Prior to the advent of both the Arab and Atlantic though, some of these tribal captives were reported to have been ritually killed in annual native ceremonies, rites and punishments, which were thought have become far less common as the slave trades developed and expanded. Although the majority of slaves were not thought to have been subjected to such ritual ceremonies, prior to their sale to the European slave trading nations, most captives were thought to have been employed as farm workers, soldiers, domestic servants and occasionally public servants, such as civil servants or administrators. With the large scale development of both the Arab and Atlantic slave trades however, so such native captives were less commonly used within the native African kingdoms, but were more commonly traded to the European nations.

Within many of these early African societies however, the concept of slavery was thought to have been regarded in an entirely different way, as were the captives themselves. Unlike western nations, where captives might commonly be treated as a chattel, being the possession of a particular master, in some African societies, slaves were said to have been treated reasonably well, occasionally being paid for their labour, being allowed to accumulate possessions and wealth; and sometimes even being able to buy their freedom from the person who had originally purchased them. This was in complete contrast to most Arab and European slave owners, who generally took the view that African slaves were a possession that could be bought and sold in the same way that one might buy or sell an animal, which had absolutely no rights whatsoever. But of course it would be wrong to over-simplify, what was in reality a much more complex set of circumstances that laid the basis for the Transatlantic Slave Trade, which ultimately proved to be so lucrative for some and so catastrophic for others. Primarily the reasons behind the establishment and large-scale development of this inhumane trade was said to have been the greed and acquisitive natures of those that drove it forward, both the African tribal leaders who sacrificed their fellow Africans for their own prosperity and the Europeans who not only chose to disregard the rights of their human cargoes, but deliberately exploited native African traditions of enslavement, for their own financial and national benefit. According to some experts on the subject, up to 80% of those traded into slavery, had been taken captive by other African tribes, as a result of neighbouring wars or disputes and were therefore commonly regarded as booty by the victorious warriors. Of the remaining 20%, some were reported to have been sold into slavery as a punishment for their own wrongdoing, while others were simply child slaves, sold into captivity by their parents, who were either unwilling or unable to care for them. Some, although not all, of this early slave trading was also thought to have been as a result of a native caste system, which continues to exist in parts of the world today, most notably in parts of Africa, the Indian Sub-Continent and in Asia. Within the African continent, the largest number of slaves was reported to have been taken from the region now occupied by the modern day states of Congo, Angola, Ghana, Sierra Leone, Madagascar, Mozambique and Cameroon. One of the main African slave trading nations within the continent, were reported to be the Ashanti people, whose territories included the modern day states of Ghana and Togo; and who were said to be one of the principal suppliers to the western European slave trading nations. Reportedly at their height, between the 17th and 19th centuries, from 1670 to 1870, the Ashanti were thought to have become one of the principal slave trading nations through the use of the modern weapons which had originally been supplied by the likes of Britain and Holland. According to some sources the main African tribes who were said to have fallen victim to slave traders were the Bakongo, Igbo, Mande', Wolof, Akan, Fon and Makua peoples who were generally thought to be natives of the African states which were previously noted.

The Igbo people for example, were said to have originated from the south east region of the modern state of Nigeria and were thought to have been enslaved during the period of the Transatlantic Slave Trade and transported from the area then known as the Bight of Biafra. The Bakongo or Congolese people were said to have been members of the much larger Bantu people, who originated from the west coast of Africa, including the area of modern day Angola. Reportedly, some of the earliest African people to have established trading links with the Portuguese around the 15th century, initially the merchandise exchanged between the two sides, was said to have included ivory, copper and slaves, who were undoubtedly prisoners-of-war, or criminals who had first been enslaved by the Bakongo themselves. The Makua people were thought to be yet another offshoot from the much larger Bantu people, who were taken as slaves from their tribal homelands of both Mozambique and Tanzania. The kingdom of Dahomey was reported to have been formed by a combination of the Aja and Fon peoples in Western Africa, who, during the 17th century were thought to have been ruled by an individual called Wegbaja. Native rituals within this particular tribal society were said to have included human sacrifice, especially during times of war, pestilence, natural disaster or even the death of a monarch, when hundreds and possibly thousands of captives were reported to have been sacrificed by having their heads removed. It was said that these human sacrifices were killed in order to provide the dead king with servants in the afterlife and they joined the late monarch's many wives who were reportedly buried alive to await their ruler husband in the next world. On one occasion, several thousand prisoners-of-war were said to have been killed in celebration of the Dahomey's victory over a neighbouring tribe. King Wegbaja was reported to have been actively involved in the sale of slaves, to the Western European nations, who visited his kingdom during the 17th century and was thought to have become extremely wealthy and powerful through the Transatlantic Slave Trade.

Even before the rise of the kingdoms of Dahomey and Ashanti, much of the region now occupied by the modern states of Nigeria, Benin and Togo was said to have been dominated by the Oyo Empire of the Yoruba people, who were reported to be a highly skilled and militaristic tribe that subjugated many of the smaller native kingdoms and made them their vassal states. The Oyo Empire was reported to have been actively involved with the supply of slaves to the newly arrived western European traders, as well as other commodities such as gold, ivory and textiles. However, as their military strength and political influence eventually declined, the Yoruba people themselves were said to have been suppressed and exploited by the emerging kingdoms of both the Dahomey and the Ashanti, who enslaved many of their former oppressors and delivered them into the hands of the transatlantic slave traders, forcing them to share a similar fate, as had many of their former captives. Other native tribes that were thought to have been complicit in the Transatlantic Slave Trade were the Imbangala from Angola and the Nyamwezi of Tanzania, both of whom were said to have involved themselves with the sale of captured Africans, as well as participating as roving slave catchers. The Imbangala were thought to be a native African people who originated from the coastal and highland regions of what is now modern day Angola. Said to have been a highly aggressive and militaristic tribe, they were reported to have been traditional raiders who roved throughout their home regions attacking neighbouring tribes, seizing their possessions and enslaving their people. Interestingly, this early tribe has also been accused of forcibly recruiting child soldiers to fight in their ranks, a practice that continues to be employed in parts of Africa even through to the present day, especially in many of the inter-tribal conflicts that have wracked the continent during the past fifty years or so. It was also been reported that many of the Imbangala's war captives were occasionally sacrificed to their native deities and worse still perhaps, some members of the tribe were thought to have been cannibals, who not only killed their prisoners, but ate them as well. The first European nation to contact the Imbangala, was said to be the Portuguese in the early 17th century; and although initially appalled by some of the Imangala's native rituals, went on to form extensive trading links with the native tribe. Over time and undoubtedly because of the Portuguese' influence with members of the tribe, many of their less attractive practices were thought to have been abandoned, with war captives generally being transported to the Americas, rather than being killed, or even eaten.

The Nyamwezi people were reported to have originated from western Tanzania and were yet another tribe that was said to have been involved in supplying native Africans to the Transatlantic Slave Trade between the 17th and 19th centuries. Reportedly famed for their individual slave and cattle holdings, the Nyamwezi were noted for their highly acquisitive society, where any means of acquiring personal wealth, was deemed to be acceptable. Members of this tribe were also reported to have been renowned ivory traders, who slaughtered significant numbers of African elephants, in order to supply the demand for such "elephant's teeth", which was said to have been driven by traders from both the east and the west. Although they were said to have retained many captive African slaves, for use as porters and manual workers, the Nyamwezi were also thought to have transported large numbers of enslaved Africans to the west coast slave ports, for sale to the western European Europeans who were based there. Likewise, the Mali Empire was yet another native African kingdom, which was thought to have believed in and practiced a culture of human enslavement, with captives commonly being employed as bearers or even units of trade. One 14th century Imperial ruler of the Mali Empire was said to have routinely travelled with a large contingent of female slaves, who were thought to have been used as payment for foreign trade goods, although gold, ivory or gemstones might just as easily have been used. As a largely Islamic society, the Mali Empire has generally been more commonly associated with the much larger North African Empire, which was dominated by Arab traders. However, the Portuguese were reported to have made contact with the rulers of Mali in the second half of the 15th century; and traded quite extensively in a range of goods, including slaves. By the middle of the 16th century though, the Mali Empire was beginning to be undermined by the emergence of the neighbouring Songhai Empire, which would eventually go on to dominate that particular region of the African continent.

Thomas Leyland   **William Beckford**   **William Wilberforce**

Linked to this early Mali Empire, were the Mandinka people, reputedly one of the largest tribal groups throughout the whole of western Africa. According to some reports, members of the Mandinka tribe were thought to have been some of the most heavily exploited by those nations that were actively involved in the Transatlantic Slave Trade and were said to have been indigenous to a large number of west African states including Gambia, Guinea, Mali, Sierre Leone, Ivory Coast, Senegal, Liberia, Niger, Mauritania and Chad. Between the 16th and 18th centuries, large numbers of the Mandinka people were said to have been forcibly transported across the Atlantic to work on the sugar cane plantations that were being established by the leading European states. According to most historic reports, the Mandinka people were mainly farmers by tradition, which might well account for their susceptibility to attack by other well armed and more militaristic African tribes. However, there were also thought to be significant numbers of skilled artisans among the various Mandinka communities that were raided by African slave traders, including woodworkers and metalworkers who were said to have been much prized within the Slave Trade. The final two native African slave trading nations who are undoubtedly noteworthy were the kingdoms of Whydah (Ouida) and Bonny. Whydah was reported to have been a prominent slave trading society up until 1695 when it was finally overrun by the rival kingdom of Dahomey. Even though it only had a 10 mile stretch of coastline facing the Atlantic, which later became part of the infamous Slave Coast, between 1692 and 1700 the kingdom of Whydah was estimated to be delivering in excess of one thousand slaves per month to the Transatlantic Slave Trade. For its part, the kingdom of Bonny was reported to have been populated by the Ibani people, who were said to have been prominent slave owners and traders from the 15th to the 19th centuries and was centred around the region of modern day south east Nigeria.

It has often been suggested that many of the native African slave traders were completely unaware of the type of service that they were selling their fellow countrymen into, believing that they were being transported elsewhere to undergo the relatively benign kind of indentured servitude that was common within many African societies. However, it is now evident that most prominent slave traders were fully aware of the privations, hardships and cruelty that was being commonly inflicted on their neighbours, but continued to supply them nonetheless. During the 17th century, a number of African ambassadors were known to have travelled the Transatlantic Slave Trade route, on their way to the royal courts of their European partners; and were reported to have visited the Caribbean plantations, as well as witnessing the degrading and cruel treatment inflicted on the black African slaves, which they undoubtedly would have reported back to their own particular tribal leaders. Yet despite what they had seen; and the obvious inhumanity that was being levied against their countrymen, they continued to supply hundreds of thousands of their fellow Africans to the European traders, making any subsequent pleas of ignorance highly improbable at best. Even a number of today's leading African academics accept that such claims of ignorance on the part of those African's, who actively participated in the enslavement of other native tribes are generally unlikely. They also tend to accept that even if the likes of the Ashanti, Imbangala, Nyamwezi or the Dahomey had initially been unaware of the Europeans intentions towards and treatment of black African slaves, then these same native slave traders and catchers would almost certainly have continued to supply slaves regardless. This is testified to by the fact that they did not stop catching and trading millions of slaves with the European nations, or destroying thousands of the native communities that they attacked, but chose instead to enhance their own power and influence, whilst at the same enriching themselves at the expense of their fellow Africans. Of course, this was not a one-sided bargain and the European powers too, were equally culpable in the establishment, organisation and continuance of this barbaric trade. It is clear that where the western nations chose to directly involve themselves in Africa, it was generally to support a native monarch or tribe, who were sympathetic to their needs for black African labour, often supplying these same allies with arms or other goods that would not only enrich them, but also help them to subjugate even more of their African neighbours.

However, it should also be pointed out that some native African tribes could and did refuse to participate in the enslavement of black African people. The Xhosa people of southern Africa for example, were reported to have been contacted by European slave traders, who were seeking new regions to exploit, but were rebuffed by the Xhosa leaders and consequently had to look elsewhere for their labour supplies. There are no reports of the Xhosa people having suffered as a result of their outright refusal, suggesting that these European traders did not feel compelled to press their request through military force, which seems to have been the case throughout much of Africa. This can only lead to the presumption that the Transatlantic Slave Trade could and would not have existed without the direct complicity of certain African tribes, who were more concerned with improving their own positions, than they were about the fate of their fellow Africans. Such a presumption, of equal culpability on the part of both native Africans and certain western European states, would therefore fundamentally undermine any modern day claims for financial reparations that are regularly being made by some leading African nations. It seems to be common knowledge that the state of slavery was recognised as being legitimate by most African kingdoms and societies before, during and after the 15th century, as was the practice of transferring ownership of a human being from one person to another. Although some historians have suggested that many of the tribal leaders who actively participated in the slave trade did not necessarily agree with the western idea and practice of chattel slavery, they seem to have done little to prevent it, possibly by refusing to supply slaves to the European nations, so their opposition to such practices can only really be regarded as anecdotal. The rulers of the kingdom of Congo for instance, were said to have been deliberately enticed into the slave trade, by western traders who would only exchange their valuable and exotic goods for slaves, rather than anything else. However, such suggestions seem entirely improbable, when one considers that other native African goods such as gold, ivory and gemstones would have been available for trade at the same time, so the idea that European traders would have refused such items, in favour of a human being, seems highly implausible.

Slavery was known to be an acceptable form of punishment under Congolese law, so was not an invention of the European nations or their representatives in Africa by any means. One of the principal tribes of the kingdom of Congo were thought to be the Lunda people, who were reported to be active participants in the enslavement of other African tribesmen, before, during and after the period of the Transatlantic Slave Trade, but most notably during the 17th century. The king of Congo himself was reported to have sent several gifts of up to fifty slaves to Portuguese representatives in the first quarter of the 16th century, which suggests that the practice of gifting human beings to other people was a fairly commonplace practice within Congolese society, as opposed to being any sort of foreign custom that had been adopted by the African monarchs. It is also known that a number of the first Portuguese traders to visit Congo visited the local slave markets and purchased native Africans, who were then taken out of the country and back to Portugal, with absolutely no objections being raised by the local Congolese authorities. In fact the only restriction that seems to have been placed on these early Portuguese traders by the Congolese was that they refrained from purchasing female slaves, although the exact reason for this particular restriction is unclear. In addition to allowing outsiders to buy African slaves, the Congolese monarchy was also said to be paying for foreign trade goods with enslaved Africans, who were subsequently taken out of their homelands, presumably to be employed in the sugar cane plantations of the Portuguese empire. What makes this trade in native Africans more interesting, are reports from the beginning of the 16th century which state that African states were regularly paying for foreign trade goods with shipments of copper, ivory and native textiles, suggesting that other forms of payment were available and indeed acceptable, other than enslaved African people.

Where there were disagreements between the Portuguese and Congolese authorities with regard to the trading in African slaves, these tended to be about numbers, rather than the trade in human beings itself. According to some sources, the Congolese monarch publicly expressed his concerns to the Portuguese representatives that some European traders were enslaving all African citizens, regardless of whether they were free or not, actions that might well have ended the relationship between the two parties. It was thought that many of these incidents had involved renegade slave traders, who chose to ignore local customs; and simply seized any African that they happened to come across and through their actions put the whole trading relationship at risk. However, despite these occasional contraventions of local trading practices, both sides seem to have been reluctant to allow such instances to bring an end to their mutually beneficial trading arrangements. For the Portuguese, continuing a trade that gave them access to an unlimited supply of African labour, as well as gold, ivory and other exotic trade items was essential. For the Congolese monarch and his noblemen, who were reported to be getting richer and more powerful through the trade, the prospect of losing access to the guns, ammunition and western goods that helped to make their people so respected and even feared in the region, was not something that they were likely to give up easily.

Even though retrospective and sometimes extremely slanted reporting of the Transatlantic Slave Trade might suggest that many of the native slave traders of Africa were somehow coerced or forced to participate in the trade, this does not appear to have been the case in most instances. Had the Western European nations wanted to enslave the native African states by force, then they were more than capable of doing so, much the same as the Spanish conquistadors had done in the New World. However, rather than land large numbers of heavily armed troops onto the continent and suppress the local tribes by simply military means, instead they chose to establish equitable trading relationships with the local tribal leaders, who appear to have been equally keen to develop such trade links. According to most contemporary reports, early western traders went to great lengths in order to avoid upsetting local leaders and even adopted the usual trading customs, then being practiced by the indigenous people of Africa. It was only after good trading relations had been established that the European states began to construct the westernised port facilities and protective forts that were required and even then it was only with the express agreement of the local monarch or tribal leader. The only major exception to these usual practices was said to have taken place when the Portuguese were reported to have landed a large number of troops in the region of modern day Angola, in response to a military dispute with the local tribes.

The first western European nation to actively engage in the African slave trade was said to be the Portuguese in the 15th century and it was they, along with their Spanish neighbours who were said to have inaugurated what became commonly known as the Triangular Trade. The first black Africans to be traded in the Caribbean by the Spanish were said to have been sold there in 1518, during the reign of the Spanish monarch Charles I, who was reported to have granted a licence to a member of his royal household, to import some 4,000 African slaves to the Americas. These slaves were thought to have been landed in the area of Hispaniola, later Haiti and the Dominican Republic, before being shipped on to the Spanish held regions of Mexico, Venezuela and Chile, where they were principally employed in mining for the gold and other treasures that had first brought the Spanish to the New World. However, it was not just the Spanish gold mining industry that required large numbers of manual labourers, but also the sugar cane plantations of Mexico, Colombia, Peru and the Antilles, the cocoa plantations of Venezuela, grape and olive farms in Peru, as well as the wheat growing farms of Chile. Spanish exploration, exploitation and settlement of the New World, South America, North America and the Caribbean had begun in the latter half of the 15th century, following the voyages of Christopher Columbus. Initially, the Spanish Conquistadors were said to have enslaved the native tribes of South America to carry out these duties, but their population had subsequently been decimated, both by the Old World diseases such as Smallpox, Typhus, Measles and Influenza, brought by the Spaniards and by the sheer overwork levied upon them by their new masters, leaving the Spanish with no effective workforce.

Arab Slave Trade   Arawak Indians   Barbary Pirates

Portuguese planters were known to have been employing black African labour since the early 15th century, on a number of sugar plantations located on volcanic islands to the west of Africa, most notably the islands of Madeira, the Azores and Cape Verde. In common with the rigorous climate of the New World, some of these Atlantic islands were thought to be generally unwelcoming for most European settlers, so African labour was employed to help plant, harvest and process the sugar cane crops grown there. Parts of the Cape Verde islands were thought to have been discovered by Portuguese mariners, as early as 1456, although it was said to have been after 1496 that the first settlers and first black African slaves were brought to the region to help cultivate and colonise these new lands. The island's geographical position, alongside some of the main Transatlantic Slave routes also helped them to become synonymous with the trade and to bring great prosperity to these new Portuguese territories in the 16th and 17th centuries. The Azores were said to have been discovered by Portuguese seafarers as early as 1427 and like the Cape Verde islands, along with Madeira was not thought to have been settled immediately, but were eventually colonised over a period of time. Madeira itself was reported to have been discovered by the Portuguese in the first half of the 15th century, with most sources suggesting a date of around 1420. The first colonists, who were said to have included sugar planters, were thought to have arrived there in around 1455 and by 1490 large numbers of African slaves were reported to have been employed there to plant, cultivate and harvest the sugar cane crops that had become a vital part of the island's economy. It was also thought to be the same Portuguese planters who had first settled and farmed these islands that later moved across the Atlantic and set about farming in the Americas, bringing with them the black African labour force, which would eventually help to build the New World's economy. It was said that modern day Brazil was first settled by the Portuguese in 1516 and within thirty-odd years had become the principal sugar exporting country in the New World, as well as being the largest importer of African slave labour. In fact, according to some sources, of the 11 million or so Black African slaves landed alive in the Americas throughout the period of the slave trade, some 38% of the total were said to have been transported to Brazil, with 51% being employed by the Spanish, British and French in their Caribbean and South American colonies. Of the remaining 11%, some 6% were reported to have been sent to the North American colonies and the other 5% put to work in the Caribbean colonies of the Dutch, Danes and the Swedes.

It is perhaps surprising to note though that although the Spanish Empire employed a great number of slaves, very few were actually transported to the Americas by Spanish owned ships. Instead, it seems that Spain commonly bought slaves that had been transported by other European nations, including the Portuguese, Dutch, French and of course the English. However, this possible reluctance or refusal to actually carry enslaved Africans aboard Spanish ships seems to have changed around 1700, when they were thought to have become actively engaged in all aspects of the Triangular Trade, including the Middle Passage.

Typically, the first leg of the Triangular Trade was said to have involved slave merchants stocking their ships with a plethora of trade goods, including cloth, beads, pots and pans, alcohol and armaments, all of which were manufactured in the factories of Britain, France, Holland and India. Not only were these factories able to produce a wide variety of goods, but were also able to manufacture them in comparatively large numbers, unlike the native African tribes who tended to produce most of their own necessary goods on a fairly local ad-hoc basis. Iron, Copper and Brass items were thought to have been particularly popular trade items, as were the brightly coloured Cowry shells, which were often used by local tribesmen as personal adornments. Likewise, guns were said to have been a highly prized trade item for most local African tribes, as not only were they unusual items in themselves, but also offered the recipient the chance to dominate their home regions, often at the expense of their neighbours who did not have such advanced weaponry. For the European suppliers of such armaments, allowing one particular tribe to achieve military dominance had its obvious benefits, as these tribes were then able to attack and capture neighbouring tribes with increasing regularity, providing even more African captives who could then be transported into slavery.

Major West African slave trading regions were thought to have included the Upper Guinea Coast, or Senegambia, now marked by the modern area that lies between the Senegal and Gambia rivers, the Ivory Coast, marked by modern day central Liberia and the Lower Guinea Coast, now marked by today's Ivory Coast. The region of the Slave Coast was identified as the area of modern day Togo, Benin and Western Nigeria, with Gabon and Angola reportedly supplying almost half of the total slave numbers transported across the Atlantic during the trade. Of the thirteen million black Africans thought to have been transported across the Atlantic between 1650 and 1860, some three million were said to have been shipped from ports and forts in the area of Congo and Angola, one and a half million from the Gold Coast, two million from the Slave Coast, two million from Benin and one million more from the Mozambique and Tanzania regions. The kingdom of Benin, which was reported to have flourished from the 14th century through to the 17th century was said to have been heavily involved with the slave trade, principally through its principal tribal group, who were known as the Edu people. Just under half of the thirteen million slaves reportedly shipped from these African ports, around six million people, were thought to have been destined for work in the sugar plantations of the Caribbean and South America. Another two million were thought to have been sent to the coffee plantations of South America, with the majority of the remaining five million African slaves said to have been employed in various tasks such as mining, planting, harvesting and production of both cotton and cocoa, as well as other general construction work.

It also seems clear that shipping numbers were largely spread over a period of some 350 years, from 1450 through to 1900, with a peak of activity between 1700 and 1900. From 1450 to 1600 an estimated 500,000 black African slaves were thought to have been transported across the Atlantic, mostly by Portuguese and Spanish traders who were supplying workers to their own nation's new South American and Caribbean colonies. Between 1601 and 1700 a further one and a half million Africans were reportedly shipped across the Atlantic by a number of European nations, including the Portuguese, Spanish, Dutch, Swedes and the English. From 1701 to 1800, up to seven million Africans were thought to have been forcibly transported across the Atlantic with the vast majority being transported by Portuguese, French, Dutch and English ships, in order to supply the ever increasing demands from South America and the Caribbean region. Even though the Transatlantic Slave Trade was said to have been largely abolished by most of the leading European nations by the beginning of the 19th century, between 1801 and 1900, an estimated three and a half million Africans were said to have been carried across the Atlantic, often by illegal slave traders or by the ships of those nations that had chosen to ignore the widespread abolition of the trade. At least one other source has suggested that between 1651 and 1807, British ships were reported to have carried an estimated two million Africans across the Atlantic, whilst in the same period French ships transported one and a half million and the Dutch an additional half a million black slaves, most of who were destined for work in the Caribbean.

In virtually all of the previously mentioned African regions, there thought to have been were numerous forts and ports, which were used as trading posts by the western nations, although slaves might just as easily be transferred to the western trading ships, from inland River Stations that could be accessed via local creeks and rivers. According to some contemporary reports, it was also common practice for slaves to be held for months in secure stockades called "Barracoons", or on various coastal beaches, before being delivered to the ships on specially built coastal vessels that were capable of carrying up to 200 enslaved Africans below their decks. It has also been reported that up to 40% of the slaves captured from their native villages, were thought to have died on the journey from their place of captivity to these river stations, coastal beaches or western slave forts, which is said to account for the deaths of several million Africans, who died before ever reaching the western traders, who were waiting to transport them across the Atlantic. If these reported figures are anywhere near accurate, then that would mean that some eight million Africans died before they could be traded to the western nations, as opposed to the one million or so, who were thought to have died during the Middle Passage, or those that died once they had reached the New World. Clearly, such massive loss of human life is a tragedy, but the fact that a greater number of Africans were thought to have died at the hands of their fellow Africans, rather than the financially driven white Europeans is a point worth noting, when considering the whole subject of the African Slave Trade and more importantly who was most responsible for the huge loss of life that resulted from it.

The series of European "forts" that were said to have been built at various sites along the western coast of Africa, were primarily constructed to serve a number of purposes, including securing trade items that were being brought in and out of the country, as well as providing a secure defensive redoubt for those white Europeans, who lived and worked in the region. Although most of these bases were thought to have been constructed with the express permission of the local reigning monarch or tribal leader, conditions and people often changed, so it was necessary for traders to have accommodations that might offer them a secure position, until the next European ship visited the area and was able to rescue them. Originally built of timber, over time, these trading forts were generally reconstructed on highly defendable areas of open ground and rebuilt using stone and rocks that were sometimes specifically imported for that particular purpose. As such centres were redeveloped and became more and more sophisticated, so they began to include large covered warehouses, where trade goods could be stored, jetties and wharves which allowed merchandise to be ferried to and from the various ships that sat offshore, as well as dungeons or yards, which could be used to hold the tens of thousands of black African slaves that would almost inevitably pass through their gates. In what is now modern day Ghana, the Cape Coast Castle, was reported to have been one such European constructed trading fort, which was originally built by Swedish explorers and traders, sometime before the first half of the 17th century. By around 1665 however, the fort was thought to have fallen into a British trading company's hands and was then used as a defensive position and trading centre to secure their interests in the region. Imported trade items such as guns, rum and tobacco, were reported to have been brought into the castle, to be traded with the local tribes, in exchange for locally sourced gold, ivory, pepper, coffee, corn and of course black African slaves.

Possibly the earliest of these European trade forts, was thought to have been Elmina Castle, which was reported to have been constructed by Portuguese explorers and traders in around 1482. Built to protect the goods that were being brought in and out of the region, as well as the Portuguese trading monopoly, the base later fell into the hands of Dutch traders around 1637 and remained in their possession, until well after the Slave Trade had been abolished by most western nations in the early 19th century. A trade fort with one of the most interesting names was reported to have been Fort Metal Cross, which was said to have been originally built by the British based Royal African Company in around 1692, although the base itself was reported to have relatively uncompleted until 1698, due to ongoing hostilities with local

African tribesmen. The base was said to have been so vital to British interests in the region, which were constantly under threat from other European nations that its garrison took great care to ensure its security, including the emplacement of some twenty-odd canons around its perimeter, which were employed to deter any would-be attackers, be they black or white. The rather odd sounding name is thought to have been a legacy of its later Dutch inhabitants, who were thought to have occupied the base sometime after 1867, when its days as a slave trading centre were long since over. However, one of the most infamous and notable slave trading centres that was employed by a number of British mercantile companies was thought to have been Bunce Island, which was located only some twenty miles or so, from what later became Freetown in Sierre Leone. This river based island was reported to have first been occupied by the British in 1670, by agents of the Royal African Company and the Gambia Adventurers Company, both of whom were seeking to exploit the natural and human resources of the region. However, despite the best efforts of these early traders and explorers, the base was said to have been generally unsuccessful and by around 1740, the site was said to have been abandoned by its original inhabitants.

Spanish Conquistador

Elmina Castle

Jamaican Maroons

Within a few years though, Bunce Island was reported to have been reoccupied by two more London based British trading companies, Grant, Oswald and Company, along with John and Alexander Anderson, who between them were said to have made the base an extremely profitable enterprise for all of those concerned. Trading in slaves and other native goods, Bunce Island was thought to have been used as a transit point for tens of thousands of captured black Africans, who were later transported against their will to the New World, most notably to the region of the British and French West Indies. Notable British families who were reported to have participated in the Bunce Island slave trade include the likes of the Caulkers, Tuckers and the Clevelands, all of whom were said to have made their fortunes from the misery of the native African tribesmen that they processed within the base. One of the main indigenous tribes within the area of Sierra Leone, were thought to be the Mende people, who were reported to be farmers and hunters by tradition, although elements of the Mende, were also said to have been actively involved in the slave trade, whilst others became victims of it. Some of the families that were directly involved with the slave trade were thought to have been of Anglo-African descent; their white fathers have married or formed relationships with black African women by whom they had children. One of these families was said to be the Sherbro Tuckers, who were said to have originated from an English slave trader called Tucker, who married an African Sherbro princess and went on to form his own dynasty of slave traders and merchants. The Sherbro were an indigenous African tribe that had formed extensive trading links with both the Portuguese and British traders that came to West Africa in search of riches. When the first English explorers and merchants visited Sierre Leone in around 1620, it was the Sherbro that were one of the first people that they encountered and with whom long-term relationships were formed, ultimately creating families like the Tuckers. Likewise, the Caulkers of Sherbro were said to have been yet another Anglo-African family group, who benefited from slave trading within the region of Sierre Leone and one that was said to have employed the previously mentioned Mende people to help enslave other native African tribes for the Transatlantic trade.

In the meantime, onboard the slave ships, the ships carpenters would have been busily altering the internal structure of the ship, by reconstructing slave decks within the holds that would eventually hold the expected cargo of unwilling passengers. This human cargo ultimately replaced the merchandise, which had been traded for their freedom; and in order to maximise their profits, ship's crew were said to have packed slaves into these claustrophobic and unsanitary conditions, regardless of the hardship and loss of life that they caused. Once the ship had reached the Americas and off loaded its cargo of African slaves, these slave decks would commonly be removed by the ship's carpenter, in order that the holds could be used for the transportation of more usual trade commodities, which were then taken back to Britain to be sold.

Perhaps typical of the men who were involved in the Transatlantic Slave Trade was the Welsh sea captain, John Phillips, who was reported to have commanded the Royal African Company ship, "The Hannibal" and who sailed from London to Guinea on the west coast of Africa, with a cargo of guns, gunpowder, cloth and other goods, which could then be traded for slaves. Having exchanged these items for a cargo of individually selected slaves, Phillips was then thought to have sailed his newly laden ship, across the Atlantic to St Thomas' and Barbados in the Caribbean, where the African slaves were off loaded and then sold to local agents and planters. "The Hannibal" having been cleaned and made ready for sea, Phillips then had a cargo of sugar loaded into the holds, which was then carried back across the Atlantic to his home port of London. Yet another slave ship captain was said to be Hugh Crow, a one-eyed Manxman, who was known to have made several voyages to West Africa during his long and colourful career and to have carried African slaves across the Atlantic. Despite his involvement with the slave trade however, Crow was reputed to have been a generally kind and Christian-like man, who took great care of his human cargoes, although he was said to have been deliberately vague about the day-to-day running of his ship, when publishing his life story some years later. Having witnessed the tribal sacrifice of a dead African king's wives, presumably to accompany their lord to the after-life, Crow was said to have come to the conclusion that far from enslaving black Africans, European traders were in fact saving them from their highly primitive and cruel lives in their homelands. Whether or not he actually believed this or not is unclear, but it does seem as though Captain Crow experienced mixed feelings over the rights and wrongs of the slave trade, much of which was informed by his own limited experience of it. Although he undoubtedly witnessed first-hand, some of the more extreme cruelties of the native

African cultures that he visited, he obviously had little, if any knowledge, of the fairly brutal lives he was delivering them to in the Caribbean.

The common practice of trading African slaves for European merchandise seems to have been a fairly lengthy process, being largely dependent on meeting the right African agent or "factor", selecting the appropriate number and type of fit and healthy slaves, who might be expected to survive the long and arduous journey across the Atlantic and agreeing terms with the local tribal leader or king through his appointed agent. Sufficient food and water supplies also had to be arranged by the captain and his crew, so that everyone on board might be adequately fed and watered throughout the lengthy voyage and it was often the most inexperienced seafarers who happened to misjudge this aspect, leading to starvation amongst the slaves. Most experienced sea captains tried to ensure that they carried sufficient food supplies for cater for everyone on board, both the slaves and his own crew. They would have also taken onboard a surplus of both food and water, which might keep the ships company fed and watered during any unexpected delays caused by damage or adverse weather conditions. Reports from the time suggest that supplies of local foodstuffs were commonly taken aboard the ship, to specifically cater for the African palette, including rice, peppers, corn, palm oil and potatoes. It was also thought to have been common practice for some captains to include stocks of rum, cheese and salt, as well as occasional luxuries such as coconuts that could be distributed amongst both the crew and their captives.

Where an inexperienced or over-confident sea captain was in charge of a vessel and the ship subsequently faced unforeseen delays in its transatlantic journey times, then it was often the slaves who starved, especially when additional food stores had not been loaded onto the ship beforehand. Although not specifically relating to the matter of food stores, the Royal African Company was reported to be one of the worst performing companies in terms of slave survival rates aboard their ships. Between 1680 and 1688 the company was said to have lost around 15,000 of the 60,000 Africans that they shipped across the Atlantic, a full 25% of their total human cargoes. Although whole ship losses might have accounted in part, for this extremely high mortality rate, it seems just as likely that such high death rates, were actually caused through overcrowding, a wilful lack of care, disease and malnutrition, all of which might have been avoided if financial profits had been a secondary consideration to common humanity. In at least one notable case, the captain and crew of the slave ship "Zong", were known to have deliberately cast over 130 African slaves over the side of the ship and to their certain deaths, purportedly to save the rest of the ships company from disaster. The ships owners then made a claim against their insurers for the loss of the slaves, a claim that was successfully upheld by the British courts. The fact that a ship's captain could essentially murder 130 human beings and yet not face charges, whilst at the same time receive compensation for their loss was a clear and damning indictment, not only of the trade, but also of some of the men and legal system that were involved with it. Often though, the treatment that each cargo of slaves might receive from the crew of a particular ship was entirely dependent on the nature of the master who was in control of the vessel. Some were generally good natured men who despite their involvement in the slave trade, tried to make the journey bearable, whereas there were also those who saw the captives, as little more than animals and treated them in a similar manner. It has also been suggested that often the differences in treatment, which African slaves experienced, was sometimes just determined by the captain's personal financial involvement with the cargo. A master who owned and operated a ship at his own expense, was thought to have a far greater interest in the health and well-being of his cargo, than did the master, who was simply employed on a fixed wage to take a vessel full of slaves across the Atlantic, but had little financial interest in whether or not they arrived there dead or alive.

European Slaves

Arab Slave Sale

Slave Branding

The actual process of selecting slaves was said to have been just the first of many humiliations that would be suffered by those Africans who had been captured by their neighbouring tribesmen. Typically, selections were reported to have been carried out by the ships doctor, or surgeon, who in conjunction with the ships captain, would inspect all of the available slaves and choose the most suitable. Aside from looking for any obvious injuries or deformities that might reduce the financial value of the slave, the ships surgeon would also inspect each individual, looking for signs of communicable diseases, including any venereal disease that might be passed from one slave to another during the long sea voyage. Once the agreed number of physically fit slaves had been chosen, each of them would have been branded, either with the name of the ship or their new owner's initials. Generally these brands would be placed on the African slave's breast or on their shoulder and was possibly the first of many such marks that they might receive during their lifetime.

The second leg of the Transatlantic Slave Trade, which was commonly known as the Middle Passage, was often the most dangerous and potentially fatal part of the journey, for both the ships crew and their human cargo, as they were far away from land and unlikely to be saved, if the ship suffered damage, or was caught in adverse weather conditions. As most ships crews were generally far smaller, than the numbers of African slaves actually aboard the ship, there was also the danger of the vessel being taken over by their unwilling passengers, so great care and even extreme measures were taken to ensure the European crew's safety. Often fettered by the feet and joined by the wrists, the African slaves were thought to have often been brought above decks, weather permitting, to allow the clearing of the holds, with the unhygienic accumulation of bodily fluids being washed away and the dead and dying slaves simply deposited into the vastness of the Atlantic Ocean, happily spared from the future horrors, which awaited their fellow passengers once they had reached the New World. These sessions, which were said to have occurred maybe once or twice a week, also allowed the slaves to be exercised, often at the end of a whip, for those slaves who refused to participate in such activities. It also appears commonplace for the ships weapons to have been primed during these exercise periods, so great was the risk of rebellion, by the enslaved Africans and numerous occurrences have been reported where crews had to suppress revolts by enraged African slaves, often at the point of a cutlass or the barrel of a gun. Although conditions were generally thought to have been fairly deplorable during the Middle Passage, with men, women and children all accommodated in relatively confined areas, according to some reports women and children were often given more freedom than their adult male counterparts. Perhaps believing that the women and children posed significantly less risk to the safety of the ship and its crew, than the African men, they were sometimes allowed to roam the ship, helping to prepare meals for the slaves or carrying out the more mundane tasks for the captain and his crew. Female slaves however, also regularly faced the risk of being sexually abused by the crew of the ship, who saw little wrong in raping the slave women who were aboard and it was sometimes only the intervention of a fairly strict captain that might have helped prevent such attacks.

The length of time taken to cross the Atlantic was said to have been subject to a number of different factors, including the actual port of departure and the ship's final destination, as the greater the distance, the greater the journey time. The actual size and basic speed of each individual ship were also thought to have been determining factors in journey times, as was the sorts of weather that the ships encountered, as they crossed the vastness of the Atlantic Ocean. During the 16th century, basic ship design was thought to have limited the speed of most ships, which typically took several months to cross from Africa to the New World. However, by the 18th century, journey times were said to have been cut in half, from twelve or fourteen weeks, down to six or eight weeks, with much of this reduction having been brought about by improved maritime technologies in the field of ship design and building. Fortunately these technological improvements were also thought to have had a direct effect on the mortality rates amongst the African slave cargoes, reportedly reducing death rates among the slave cargo from around 15-20% to 10-15% on average, with quicker transatlantic journeys, having a less negative effect on the health and well-being of the ships company. Having spent several weeks at sea, during which time unknown numbers of their fellow slaves would have died from diseases such as dysentery, smallpox, malaria and scurvy, as well as desperation leading to suicide, the remaining Africans would have been landed in one of the many slave ports that had been established throughout the Americas. It was only towards the late 1700's and as the value of individual slaves increased that national governments, such as the British and French, began to enforce legislation upon the slave traders and their ships. Insisting that each ship carried a doctor, to care for the slave cargoes that they transported across the Atlantic, making slave numbers proportionate to the size of the ship; and specifying a minimum amount of space and headroom for slave holds, were all reported to have become legal obligations imposed by the various national authorities. However, it seems likely that it was more the financial value, rather than any sort of human consideration, which saw these new regulations introduced and the rigours of Middle Passage improved, so that the previous death rates amongst the human cargoes were steadily and significantly reduced. Clearly, by the beginning of the 18th century, more and more ships captains were starting to reduce the numbers of slaves that they carried on each voyage, in order to more adequately preserve their precious cargoes, by reducing occurrences of deaths caused by disease and depression. Although unscrupulous slave traders would continue to overload their ships, regardless of any changes demanded by the various national governments, most slave traders did try to reduce the stress and strain on their unwilling passengers by adopting these new measures. Interestingly, the slave ship "Brooke" is commonly used to illustrate the typical layout and size of most transatlantic ships, showing the African cargo being tightly packed and with little room given over to each individual slave. It has also been regularly reported that most ships employed for the purpose, offered as little as 18" of headroom to each confined person, which was not only clearly claustrophobic, but also prevented slaves from being able to turn over easily. However, although the "Brooke" was generally typical of its type, it did not follow that it was completely representative of every ship that plied this particular trade, as not every ship's captain could or would allow his ship to be loaded in such a way. Although there were undoubtedly cramped areas of the slave deck, most illustration, pictures and paintings of the time, show decks that were several feet high and with adequate room for slaves to move around, albeit in a fairly limited way. Rather than all slave ships handling many hundreds of captured slaves, there are numerous reports of European ships actually only carrying tens or dozens of enslaved Africans, who clearly would not have been subjected to the sort of cramped and inhumane conditions, so often considered to be the norm. In fact, it has now become clear that the widely used image of the slave ship "Brooke" was deliberately chosen and used by the Abolitionist movement, to both shock the general public around the world, as well as to underpin their own campaign against the Transatlantic Slave Trade generally.

Having been disembarked in the New World, each shipment of African slaves were thought to have been taken to a holding area, typically a stockade, until such time as an auction was arranged for them to be sold. It was probably during this period that slaves were "seasoned" by the slave traders, acclimatised to the foreign climate and taught their place in the New World, often at the end of a whip or a cane. Commonly the slaves would have been displayed naked, or perhaps with sufficient clothing to save offending the sensitivities of those European ladies who might be present. In order to ensure that the potential workers were of good quality and not suffering from any sort of disease or physical weakness, they would have been carefully inspected by each of their would-be purchasers before the auction began. It has also been reported that most slaves were regularly ordered to prove their fitness, by running and jumping about, so that their future owners might check them for any unseen infirmity. Even though entire families were often transported across the Atlantic, little consideration was thought to have been given to keeping friends and relatives together, although for some slave owners it was said to have been common practice to deliberately separate companions, so that the individual slave was thoroughly isolated from their family, language and culture; and therefore more likely to adapt to his or her new circumstances. This generally indifferent approach to maintaining the integrity of African family units was thought to have been carried out, even where slaves had become settled on a particular plantation and had raised new families together. Many stories exist, of young slave children, fathers, and mothers being separated from one another, either because the owner had died; and their estates were subsequently divided up amongst their relatives, or simply because the owner had received an offer, on one or another of the family members.

Even after having suffered the confusion and indignity of the slave auction, where they were paraded before a crowd of strangers and sold in the same way as a prize steer or horse might be, their humiliation and bewilderment often continued. Having been purchased by an owner, who had absolutely no regard for them as a human being, they were then said to have been transported to their new plantation home, often walking tied to the back of their new master's horse or cart. Having reached the plantation they would then have been put in the hands of the plantation's head overseer or one of his lieutenants, who would have been able to converse with the slave and explain the routines of the plantation and their particular duties there. They would have been given European clothing to wear, which was often replaced annually, although slave children were generally not provided with any sort of clothing by their owners, until such time as they became economically viable for the owner, or if their parents could somehow acquire clothing from elsewhere. It also seems likely that many of the slaves who would already be carrying a brand on their skin, a reminder of their initial capture in Africa; would be marked once again, this time in order to identify them if they ran away from their new owners. Slave accommodations on most plantations were thought to have been generally poor quality affairs, often built of wood, mud, or wattle and daub walls and covered by a rudimentary thatched roof. Most of these quarters would have contained no furniture to speak of and in most cases slaves were required to provide their own furniture and fittings, either by making them themselves, or by bartering the food that they were allowed to grow on their individual plots of land. Although most slaves were given a basic food allowance each day, this had to be supplemented by the individual slaves growing their own additional products, seeds for which, were often provided by their owner and tended to on a Sunday, the one day a week that slaves would generally be allowed to have off, largely due to the Christian ideal of "resting on the seventh day". Although there was little time given over to leisure and relaxation, occasional Christian feasts throughout the year, sometimes allowed slaves to rest and celebrate, with some more reasonable plantation owners even providing additional rations to their slaves in order to mark the event.

Day to day control of the slave workforce on most plantations was thought to have been left in the hands of the owners head overseer and his lieutenants, the slave drivers. These men were often slaves themselves, but those who were willing to control and discipline their fellow slaves, in order to make a better life for themselves. The head overseer or plantation manager, was almost always a white European, who was employed by and answerable to the plantation owner directly; and in his turn had complete day-to-day control over the lives of the entire slave population, only deferring to the owner in the most serious circumstances, such as when a slave committed a serious offence or ran away from the plantation. Even within the plantations slave community itself though, a hierarchy was reported to have existed, with domestic slaves being far more important and influential, than those that were employed on the outside of the master's house. This was largely due to the fact that they were often in day-to-day contact with the slave owner and his family, which allowed them to form relationships with the master himself, his wife and very often his children, who sometimes regarded their slaves as members of the immediate family and made little distinction between people that were black or those that were white. Outside in the fields however, there were thought to have been even further classification of slaves, with field slaves, those that worked at harvesting the sugar cane or cotton crops, deemed to be the lowest of the low. Above them, were the slaves who worked in the sugar factories, those who helped process the raw sugar crop and turned it into molasses, the basic product that helped to fund their master's lifestyle. Because they possessed these specific production skills, they were considered to be of a slightly higher value than their field-working counterparts; and as such were only inferior to the artisan slaves, who were reported to have been a much prized assets by most slave owners. Skilled wood and metal workers, these slaves generally represented the best sort of investment by any slave owner, as they could often be hired out to other farmers and plantation owners for a fee, generating an additional income for the master, as well as saving him the cost of having to employ expensive outside tradesmen. According to some historians, these highly skilled slaves were often allowed to take on their own work and to earn money from their own labour, offering some of them the opportunity to eventually buy their freedom from their own individual slave owners.

From a British perspective, the first recorded English explorer to acquire African slaves was thought to have been a man called John Lok, who was said to have brought five black Africans back to Britain in 1555. However, these captives were not thought to have been acquired for sale, but rather to be taught English, so that they could then act as interpreters for future English expeditions to Africa, where Lok and his fellow traders were trying to source gold, ivory and pepper. Traders like John Lok were said to have been joined by the likes of William Towerson, a British trader who was reported to have traded relatively small numbers of African slaves during his voyages of 1556 and 1557. Interestingly though, Queen Elizabeth I, who was reported to have helped facilitate a number of these expeditions, does not appear to have supported the taking and selling of African slaves as commodities, publicly admonishing those that did and ordering that all "Negroes and Blackamores" be arrested and sent out of her kingdom. The main reason for the Queen's actions was thought to be a growing concern amongst her own citizens of places like London, about the increasing numbers of black people, both free and enslaved who were being seen in and around the capital city. However, the monarch was also known to have granted a Royal Charter to the African Company of Merchant Adventurers in 1588, ostensibly allowing its merchants to trade for anything but slaves, although in all likelihood, the trade in black African slaves probably continued unabated, but without it actually being brought to the Queens personal attention. The first English Sea Captain to actually engage in the Transatlantic Slave trade proper was said to have been Sir John Hawkins, who is credited with this dubious honour, having managed to make a profit from the three voyages he undertook over a six year period. According to most sources, Hawkins was said to have transported around twelve hundred African slaves to the Caribbean, where he subsequently sold them to the Spanish authorities there. The first of these voyages was said to have been marked by the capture of a Portuguese slaving ship in 1562, which Hawkins caught transporting some three hundred African slaves to the New World. Adopting the view that this human cargo should be treated in exactly the same as any other enemy prize, the English sea captain was reported to have completed the transportation of the unfortunate captives across the Atlantic, where he subsequently sold them to Spanish slave merchants in San Domingo in the Americas.

Having purchased a mixed cargo of pearls, animal hides, sugar and ginger, Hawkins was then reported to have returned to England and having sold these goods there was said to have made a 60% profit on the expedition. With such profits to be made from the trading of human cargoes, Hawkins and his partners were said to have immediately organised a second expedition to the African continent, which was known to have sailed in 1564. However, rather than simply relying on good fortune to deliver him yet another Portuguese slaving ship, this time Hawkins was reported to have dealt directly with the native African slave traders, trading then English goods for another four hundred slaves. With his ships holds stocked with his new cargo of enslaved Africans, Hawkins then set sail once again, selling his valuable cargo once again to the Spanish authorities in the New World and returning home to England with yet another cargo of highly prized goods that could be sold in English cities. His third voyage was said to have taken place in 1567 and despite being intercepted by the Spanish, Hawkins still managed to transport a further four hundred Africans to the New World and make a handsome profit from the expedition. Following this trip, Hawkins was said to have written an account of his exploits, promoting the potential profitability of the slave trade and no doubt laying the basis for the extensive trade that was to follow. According to most reports Britain was thought to have participated in the Transatlantic Slave Trade for a period of some 245 years, from 1562 through to 1807, when the trade was finally abolished by the English Parliament. During that two and a half centuries British slave ships were said to have made several thousand Triangular Trade journeys and transported anything up to three million Africans into slavery. Aside from the early expeditions made by the likes of Towerson, Hawkins, etc. the vast majority of these thousands of slaving journeys were made, principally to supply the new and emerging British colonies in the New World, rather than the general slave trade at large. Between 1560 and 1590, British ships were thought to have played no significant role in the Triangular Trade, mainly because Britain had no colonial interests in the New World to speak of and British mariners were said to have concentrated on delivering goods across the Atlantic, between Africa and the Americas. In 1618, the Guinea Company was reported to have been founded with the permission of King James I, to trade for Gold, Ivory and Pepper with the native tribes of Africa. However, the surplus of captive slaves and the profits that could be made from trading them in the New World quickly persuaded a large number of merchants to trade almost exclusively in human cargoes, rather than the more usual commodities. Even the king himself, was said to have recognised the potential wealth that might be made in the trade, reportedly founding the Company of Adventurers trading into Africa at that time. In the following year, the first waves of African slaves were reported to have been sent to the British colony of Jamestown in Virginia, to work on the burgeoning tobacco plantations that had been established by the English settlers there. In 1631, James' royal successor, Charles I was reported to have granted a monopoly to the Guinea Company to trade in Africa, which included the wholesale trafficking of black African slaves into the Americas.

Sugar Cane Cutters **Sugar Cane Mill** **Sugar Plantation**

In order to be perfectly clear regarding the status of slaves during this period, it is perhaps worth remembering that slavery as we understand it today was only one type of slave ownership, which saw Black African's bought, sold and treated as chattels, the same as any other common possession. In addition to this outright and commonly accepted form of slavery, other various forms of enforced service were thought to have existed at the time, albeit in a much more restricted and legally enforceable format. Indentured service for example, was thought to be a type of contractual enslavement, often made willingly between one individual person and another, by which the first individual sold his labour to the second party for a specific period of time and under certain previously agreed terms. So for example, an individual unable to pay for the cost of a voyage to the New World might agree a contract with a ships master that saw the individual carried to the Americas, provided that he agreed to several years of indentured service to the Master. Typically, such contracts provided for the ships master, to then transfer or sell these "services" to other people, such as mine owners or plantation owners who were always looking for new sources of labour. Significantly, such contracts of indentured service did not always guarantee how the servant was to be treated by their master, only that they should be given adequate housing, food and clothing for the period of their service. The obvious difference though, between this form of indentured service and outright chattel slavery was that the person had some sort of legal entitlement and that once their term of service was completed then they were free to get on with the rest of their lives, often with a small sum of money, or parcel of land, with which they could build their own fortune. Indentured servants though, black or white, were not always immune from harsh treatment that might be meted out by their employer and contemporary reports from the time suggest that many were treated extremely badly. Being punished through physical beatings, starvation and temporary imprisonment were all said to have been common occurrences on a number of New World plantations, which undoubtedly accounted for a marked decline in the numbers of white settlers who were prepared to undertake such employment.

Perhaps surprisingly, it was typically this form of service that was offered to both black and white workers prior to the middle of the 17th century; and it was only after that time that African slaves began to be treated differently, eventually simply turning them into chattels, the status which we commonly associate with the Transatlantic Slave Trade and its victims. Despite the fact that many tens of thousands of Africans were reportedly stolen away from their homelands in the first century of the trade, it has been suggested that many thousands more were actually employed on a similar basis to that of indentured service, where they worked for a specific period of time, before being given their freedom by their owners, along with a small plot of land where they might spend the rest of their lives. It was said to be because of this having to regularly replenish their worker numbers that first introduced the idea of depriving African workers of their basic human rights and fundamentally altering their status from indentured servant to that of personal chattels. The main change in African workers status' was reported to have originated in the British colony of Barbados in 1661, when a Slave Code was first introduced by the authorities on the island. This legislation was said to have established that African slaves were chattels, rather than free people and as such had no more rights than any other possession. Although this piece of legislation claimed to be a guide for slave owners, designed to help them with the "proper" treatment of their servants, in reality it merely helped to make most slaves lives even more miserable and harsh. By failing to specify how slaves should be fed and housed, or to specify the conditions under which slaves might be employed, it simply gave some slave owners free rein to treat their slaves in the most inhumane fashion. The Slave Code deliberately denied African slave's rights that they might have expected under English Common Law, including the right to life, which then allowed some owners to simply kill their slaves with virtual impunity. Unfortunately for future generations of Africans that were subsequently shipped across the Atlantic, these Slave Codes were said to have been adopted by the colonial authorities throughout much of the Caribbean, South America and the Northern States, essentially condemning millions of black slaves to live out their lives as the possessions of other people, rather than as human beings in their own right and with all of the rules pertaining to that status.

Many of these punitive Slave Codes were reported to have been introduced into North America during the second half of the 17th century, just a few years after they had first been issued by the British administrators in Barbados. In 1662 for example the colonial authorities in Virginia issued a statute that declared *"all children born in this country shall be held to be bond or free, according to the condition of its mother"*. In other words, if the child's mother was a slave, then so were all those children born to her while she was enslaved, even if those children were fathered by a white man, either willingly or unwillingly. Two years later, the legislature of Maryland declared that *"any white woman, who married a slave, would herself be deemed to be a slave, until such time as her husband died. In addition to this, if any children were born to the woman whilst she was enslaved, then these children too would be deemed to be slaves"* In 1667 Virginia added to its earlier statute by declaring *"any slave children, regardless of whether or not they were baptised into the*

Christian Church remained a slave", which fundamentally swept away any earlier ideas or spiritual teachings that it was sinful for one Christian to hold another in bondage. The same Assembly then declared in 1682 *"that all Negroes, Moors, Mulattoes or Indians that had not been Christians at the time of their enslavement or purchase, were deemed to be slaves and therefore might be used as such"*. In 1705 the Virginia legislature was reported to have clarified this previous stature by announcing a rider to it, which stated that *"such slaves were to be held as Real Estate"*, presumably as opposed to being held as human beings in their own right. The Virginian Assembly also stated that *"if any slave resists his master and if when correcting the slave the master shall happen to kill him, then the master shall be free of all punishment, as if such an accident had never happened"*. Clearly, this particular piece of legislation later became a common defence for those owners who maliciously injured or even killed their slaves, relatively safe in the knowledge that there was little that the law would do to punish them, if they did happen to accidentally or deliberately kill a slave.

Other states too began to adopt their own new laws and regulations pertaining to the status and treatment of African slaves, including the General Assembly of South Carolina, which declared in 1712 that *"all Negroes, Mulattoes or Indians that were bought, sold, or taken to be slaves, were in fact slaves, as were their children"*. At the same time the Assembly also declared that *"No master, mistress or overseer that has the care of any Negro or Slave shall give their Negro or Slave leave to go out of their plantation without a ticket. Any Negro or Slave found outside his master's plantation without a ticket shall be whipped"*. Statutes such as this were generally designed to limit and account for all slave movements within the colony; and were undoubtedly the result of concerns expressed by the minority white communities who felt threatened by the black African slaves who lived amongst them. These concerns also led to much more repressive legislation being enacted by a number of the southern colonies, including the likes of Louisiana, which declared in 1724 that *"any slave who strikes his master, mistress or their children and causes a bruise or the shedding of blood on their face will suffer capital punishment"*. Despite such discriminatory legislation however, it would be wrong to believe that all blacks had absolutely no rights whatsoever, because that is incorrect. Neither is it true to say that all black African slaves were owned by white people, because that too is incorrect. Freed black slaves were entitled to and often did buy, sell and own other African slaves, who they employed on their own plantations and farms. A notable example, although certainly not a rarity, was said to have been a freed black slave called Anthony Johnson who was reportedly captured from his homeland of Angola in around 1620. He was said to have been indentured to a white planter called Bennett in 1621 and once his contract had been completed Anthony was reported to have established his own farm, presumably with money or land that had been provided by his former employer Mr Bennett. It was also reported that at the same time that Johnson was freed by Bennett, the white slave owner also freed Johnson's wife, so that the two freed slaves could live and work on their own land together. The reason that Johnson's name and situation are so well known, is largely due to the fact that Johnson then went to court to confirm his own ownership of a black African slave called John Casor, who the court decided was Anthony Johnson's slave for life. It is also clear from the reports of the case that Johnson owned a number of black slaves, who were all said to have been imported directly from Africa.

As if to clarify and limit the numbers of slaves that were then being held by black farmers and plantation owners, the Virginian Assembly subsequently enacted statutes that expressly forbade any Negro or Indian from owning any Christian, which presumably meant any white person. However, these statutes did not prevent freed black farmers from buying, selling or owning *"any of their own nations"*, in other words, other black slaves. Unsurprisingly perhaps, most black slave holders were generally thought to have been far more humane than their white counterparts, in their treatment of Negro or Indian slaves and in some cases deliberately purchased their friends and family members in order to save them from white ownership. Often though, such purchases were thought to have been just a precursor to or even a pretext for the black slave owner, to grant the purchased slave his or her freedom, by allowing them to buy their liberty by working off the debt on the black farmers lands. However, perhaps alarmed by these practices and the increasing numbers of freed black slaves who were now inhabiting the various white communities, a number of state legislatures were said to have introduced statutes that specifically prevented freed Negroes from acquiring permanent ownership of slaves, other than husbands, wives or children, unless they were acquired by descent, that is, passed from one generation of the family to another.

It is thought that large scale British colonisation of the West Indies or Caribbean, only really began in the first half of the 17th century, with the island of Barbados reportedly being settled by colonists in 1627. The following year, the island of Nevis was settled and four years later, in 1632, Antigua and Montserrat were said to have received their first English settlers. However, all of these islands were thought to have initially been inhabited by a collection of small farmers, who were cultivating crops such as tobacco and therefore had little need for large numbers of workers. It was only in later years, when some of these same planters made the change to the much more labour intensive sugar cane and cotton production that large numbers of both white indentured and then African slave workers were said to have been introduced into the various islands. Although the Portuguese were said to have been the first people to introduce both the sugar beet and sugar cane to the Americas in the 15th century, it was thought to have been the Dutch who helped to make it such a popular crop throughout the 17th century Caribbean, by persuading many tobacco and cotton farmers that there were greater profits to be made from the planting, harvesting and processing of sugar cane. In fact, they were said to have been so successful in changing Caribbean planters minds regarding sugar that by the end of the 18th century around 85% of the sugar consumed in Europe was said to have come from the West Indies. However, it should also be noted that many tobacco and cotton planters in the Caribbean were said to have made the switch to sugar production, not only for the extra profits they could make, but also because of the additional competition that they were beginning to face from the fast emerging cotton and tobacco growers in the North American colonies.

By the latter half of the 17th century, the numbers of white European indentured servants was reported to have declined significantly, due in large part to improving living standards in Britain and the increasingly harsh conditions that were said to have been prevalent on these West Indies plantations. It was for these reasons that the numbers of black Africans being forcibly imported into the islands, was said to have increased so markedly during the same period. The sugar cane industry was said to have been particularly rigorous during the harvesting period, when slaves were thought to have had to work up to twenty hours a day, which inevitably led to many living relatively short lives, often only between eight and ten years, after which they had to be replaced by the plantation owners. Along with other European held colonies, such as Antigua, Martinique and Guadalupe, the British colony of Barbados was reported to have been one of the first major slave holding societies throughout the Caribbean; and by the middle of the 18th century both it and Jamaica were said to be two of the largest and most brutal slave societies in the entire region. As has been previously noted, the callous and often inhumane treatment of African slaves meted out to them by the white European plantation owners, managers and head overseers, was often thought to be a symptom of a white Caribbean society that was operating on the very margins and occasionally crossing the lines of generally accepted western civilised behaviour. As in other far flung places, societies that operated at the very fringes of the known world, were often extremely lawless places, where the idea and practice of "might is right" tended to hold sway, over the lives of the people that lived there. Long established legal controls and accepted social conventions often only came to places like the Caribbean over time and in response to the development of a traditional western society, which in places like Barbados, Jamaica and the other British held Caribbean islands was extremely hard to find. With a minimal white European population, controlling a large enslaved black majority, usually through fear and abuse, it was never likely that the communities of islands such as Barbados, Jamaica, etc could or would ever be deemed to be conventional British societies and as a consequence never developed the sort of legal and social protections that operated in Britain itself. Rather, it appears that the British authorities in London chose to hand overall control of the Caribbean, to military or civilian Governors, who were very often complicit in producing island societies, which were purposely racist, inhumane and intolerant.

Ironically perhaps, it was thought to be these same uncivilised attitudes and practices, which ultimately led to both the decline and then the later abolition of the slave owning societies that had dominated these British held islands since the beginning of the 17th century. Because of their reputations for hardship and cruelty towards workers, planters and farm owners in places such as Barbados, Jamaica, etc found it increasingly difficult to attract new European settlers, preventing the more widespread development of the islands economy. Added to this was the increasing influence of and competition from other European Caribbean colonies, which not only undermined British planter's ability to source workers, thereby increasing such costs, but also helped to reduce the potential profits that could be made by these same planters and their associated London merchants. According to most reputable sources, the number of African slaves employed on Britain's Caribbean possessions decreased significantly over time, ostensibly because of their relatively short lives, which was undoubtedly a result of the extreme conditions under which they laboured. In normal circumstances and with more liberal employment, it has been suggested that the British slave communities on these islands would have regularly replenished themselves through usual reproductive methods, but this does not appear to have been the case. Long hours, along with arduous work, minimal food and regular acts of infanticide were all thought to have contributed to a steadily falling birth rate amongst the slave community, requiring more and more to be spent on replacing those Africans that almost inevitably succumbed to the rigorous conditions under which they worked. Still born babies were thought to have been common feature amongst slave women, as were failed pregnancies and a high rate of infant mortality generally, all of which were thought to have been caused by a combination of poor diet, extremely hard work, long hours in the fields and often squalid living conditions.

Transatlantic Ship

US Slave Auction

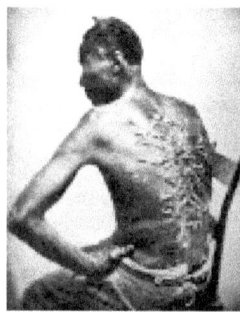
Slave Punishment

Although numerous British ships were undoubtedly involved in the enforced transportation of black Africans during the early part of the 17th century, they were not thought to be one of the principal slave trading nations at that particular time. Rather, it seems that most of the African workforce supplied to Britain's early Caribbean holdings, were actually supplied by the Dutch, who had taken over large parts of the Portuguese holdings on the African continent. According to some reporters, it was these same Dutch interests that had helped to develop Britain's evolving sugar and cotton industries in the West Indies, having well established markets for these new commodities on the European mainland, as well as in Britain itself. However, in both 1651 and 1660 the English Parliament introduced legislation to fundamentally reduce the involvement of other European nations in supplying slaves to the emerging Caribbean colonies that Britain was acquiring. Two different Navigation Acts passed in those years specifically forbade other European slave trading nations from supplying black African labour to the new English colonies, thereby granting British ships a monopoly on that particular area of trade. Bermuda was said to have first been settled by the British in 1612, although the island was thought to have first been discovered by a group of shipwrecked English sailors in around 1609. It was also reported to have been a small number of these early British settlers who left Bermuda to colonise a small group of islands that later became known as the Bahamas. Prior to the widespread Western European exploration of the Americas, the island of Bermuda was also said to have been home to an indigenous people called the Arawak, but most of their population was thought to have been removed by Spanish explorers in the 15th and 16th centuries to work in their mines scattered throughout the region of Hispaniola, where most of them were thought to have subsequently perished.

The first African slaves landed in the mainland United States were thought to have been brought to Jamestown in Virginia in 1619, although demand for cheap labour was thought to have escalated dramatically during the next few years as Britain settled the West Indies and Barbados during the first half of the 17th century. These first two hundred enslaved Africans were thought to have been introduced into the colony by a Dutch sea captain, who had captured a Portuguese slave ship crossing the Atlantic and relieved it of its human cargo. Having seen his ship damaged by storms, this Dutch trader was then said to have arrived in the Americas with a damaged ship, but with a valuable cargo to sell, which is exactly what he did, selling the slaves in order to have his ship repaired. Although the fate of the two hundred African slaves in unknown, it has been suggested that most of them were subsequently sold into indentured service, as opposed to outright slavery; and were later freed, having served the usual terms of service for their new American owners. Barbados was known to have been captured in 1624-5, with the first slaves being introduced within a couple of years; and St Kitts was said received its first African slaves in 1626, the island having first been settled in 1623. It has also been reported that a large number of African slaves were brought to Charlestown in South Carolina in 1670, having been transported there by their owners, a group of colonists who had originated in Barbados and had brought their slaves as a labour force to help establish their new plantations in mainland America. Although no large numbers of African slaves were reported to have been brought into England at any time, small numbers were said to have been transported back to Britain on a fairly ad-hoc basis, most notably during the 17th century. In 1621 the first black Africans were said to have been traded in Britain, when a William Bragge was reported to have claimed monies from the East India Company for thirteen Negroes or Indian people, although whether or not these people were actually sold into slavery in Britain itself is unclear.

However, it would be wrong to believe that the demand for slaves was entirely met from the forced importation of people from Africa alone, as that was not the case. Between 1610 and 1660 an estimated 100,000 white servants, primarily from Britain and Ireland, were reported to have been transported both to the Caribbean and North America by the British authorities, having been sentenced to varying terms of indentured service and imprisonment. These numbers were thought to have largely comprised of Irish nationalist rebels and Royalist supporters, who were transported to the New World both by the English Crown and the Parliamentary authorities, before, during and after the English Civil War. It was thought to be as a result of the labours of both black and white servants that helped Barbados harvest its first successful sugar crop in 1640, a cash crop on which much of the Caribbean would come to rely in the future. According to some sources Oliver Cromwell's military campaigns in Ireland during the late 1640's was reported to have resulted in some 500,000 Irishmen being transported to the British held Caribbean islands to serve out their sentences, with very few of them ever making it back to their native homeland. It has also been suggested that in addition to the hundreds of thousands of British, Irish and Scottish citizens who were transported into penal servitude, there were thought to have been an even greater number of British people who volunteered to undertake indentured service in order to escape the poverty and religious persecutions that were rife in Britain during the 16th, 17th and 18th centuries. A number of other groups were thought to have been transported out of Britain in order to serve as indentured servants on the plantations in the New World, including convicted criminals, the nations indigent, as well as those that were "pressed" into service by gangs of men, specifically employed to shanghai unwitting and unwilling volunteers, who in most cases woke up to find themselves aboard a ship destined for the Americas.

Although white European labour was thought to have formed a significant part of the wider slave trade during the 16th and 17th centuries, by the second half of the 18th century the numbers of white European's available for such work was thought to have fallen quite dramatically, as civil and religious conflicts within Europe reduced and standards of living improved. It is also likely that many of the indentured servants and prisoners who had originally formed part of the plantation labour force had subsequently been released from their service and now became landholders and slave owners in their own rights, creating an even greater demand for cheap labour. Even for those former indentured servants that chose to remain in the New World as simple workers, with their enforced service at an end they still expected to be treated better than the black Africans who had taken their place. It was possibly because of the higher wage demands of the white Europeans, the increasing numbers of land owners and the increasing demands for their products that led many plantation owners to look for new sources of cheap manual labour. Rather than pay higher wages and have to invest in improved accommodations for their labour force, who were generally employed on legally enforceable contracts, most plantation owners chose to exploit the human resources of places like Africa, buying slaves at a one-off price and then owning them for ever more, or at least until they died. For the plantation owners, a change in the legal status of the African slave's own children also made them a far more attractive long-term investment. Commonly a child's legal status would be determined by the father's status, meaning that children born out of a sexual relationship between a white European freeman and a black slave woman, even in the case of rape, would have resulted in the child being regarded as free. However, by altering the law to make the child's status dependent on the mother, then children born out of such relationships automatically became enslaved themselves and thus increased the slave owners own holdings. Sex crimes such as rape were thought to have been common events on certain plantations, where white European males exploited their authority over female slaves, safe in the knowledge that they were generally immune from prosecution and in some cases had the added benefit of increasing the numbers of slaves that they owned, without owing any sort of legal responsibility to the resulting child.

Formal royal recognition of the African Slave Trade, as opposed to the generally ad-hoc trading expeditions for gold, ivory, spices, etc. was thought to date from April 1671, when the Royal Africa Company was first established under a Royal Charter, granting a monopoly to a number of London merchants, by the then English monarch King Charles II. This charter authorised the *company "to set to sea, as many ships, pinnacles and barks as thought necessary, for the buying, selling, bartering and exchanging of, for or with any gold or silver, Negroes, slaves, goods and wares"*. Between 1672 and 1698, the period of the company's actual trading monopoly; the Royal Africa Company was reported to have shipped around 100,000 African slaves to Britain's Caribbean and North American colonies. Many of these native people were thought to have been transported from the forts and ports located along the coastlines of the modern day African states of Senegambia and Angola. The previously noted Bunce Island Slave Castle was thought to have been just one of these English built forts, which were not only constructed as defensive redoubts, but also included a holding area, for those slaves who had been captured throughout the region. Built somewhere around 1670, this particular trading post was thought to have operated right through to the turn of the 19th century, when the abolition of the slave trade essentially made the fortress virtually obsolete. The Royal Africa Company was said to have been almost entirely established to deal in the purchase, transportation and selling of African slaves, solely for the purpose of making a profit off the trade; and was thought to be an enterprise almost entirely instituted and operated by members of the Stuart family, who sat on the English throne during most the 17th century. Originally known as the Company of Royal Adventurers Trading in Africa, the business was said to have first been established in 1660, under a charter granted by King Charles II, but generally led by his brother, the Duke of York, who later ascended the throne as James II. Despite the loss of the company's trading monopoly in 1698, the new English monarch's William and Mary having ended it in that year, the Royal African Company continued to trade in these same human cargoes and by 1700 was reported to have shipped around 175,000 Africans to a number of England's overseas possessions. Some 25,000 of the slaves taken out of Africa were said to have been destined for the Caribbean island of Barbados alone, where most of them were said to have employed in the extremely arduous sugar cane industry, often in the most inhumane circumstances. The enormous profits generated by the slave trade were said to have been further increased by the Royal African Company's exploitation of the native gold deposits found within the continent, much of which was thought to have found its way into the Royal Mint. Interestingly, this African gold was reported to have been identified by the image of an elephant being inscribed below the usual monarch's head on the individual coins; and is also thought to be the source for the now generally defunct English guinea coin.

Although the withdrawal of the trade monopoly was largely thought to have been as the result of political lobbying by influential merchants in both Liverpool and Bristol, the fact that the Royal African Company had been founded, headed and operated by a highly unpopular Roman Catholic monarch, who had subsequently been forced to abandon his throne, was undoubtedly a factor in the decision made by King William and Queen Mary. Although the London merchants who were involved in the slave trade, no doubt suffered as a result of the trade being opened up to rival ports, the trade itself was said to have escalated dramatically after 1698, as both Liverpool and Bristol hosted their own fleets of slave ships, which were destined for the African continent. As even greater numbers of merchants became involved in the trading of African slaves, to meet the increasing demand on the emerging Caribbean and American plantations, so greater demands were thought to have been made on the native population of Africa itself, forcing the slavers to venture deeper and further into the African interior. For the most part, these slaving expeditions would have been carried out by African tribesmen, rather than white Europeans, who were generally susceptible to native diseases, unfamiliar with the terrain and more likely to be viewed with suspicion and distrust by the indigenous peoples of the African interior. Having conducted a successful slaving campaign though, African captives would still be brought back to the European held forts and ports on the west coast of the continent, where they would be forcibly embarked on the ships destined to transport them to foreign lands and an unknown future.

With the opening up of trade in 1698, the numbers of English ships involved with the Transatlantic Slave Trade was said to have significantly increased and by 1740 some thirty-odd slave ships were reported to be operating from the English port of Liverpool, which was beginning to dominate the trade in Britain. However, it has also been suggested by some commentators that British ships were making many thousands of journeys every year to trade slaves between Africa and the New World, which seems highly unlikely given that each voyage often took the best part of a year to complete; and would therefore have taken several hundred, or thousand of ships to achieve that largely unsubstantiated target. According to more reliable sources, between 1695 and 1807 the number of slave trading voyages made by British ships, from each of the three main slaving ports in England was; 5300 from Liverpool, 3100 from London and 2200 from Bristol. Totalling some 10,600 voyages, over a period of 112 years, which gives an average number of some ninety five voyages each year, although Liverpool ships were said to have been making significantly more journeys than their counterparts elsewhere. Liverpool's growing slave trading activity was indicated by the increase in the numbers of voyages being undertaken by ships based at the port, with a reported fifteen ships sailing out in the 1730's, fifty ships in the 1750's and over one hundred vessels in the 1770's. As a result, it has been suggested that Liverpool based ships actually transported around one million African slaves to the New World during the period that the Slave Trade operated, which based on the previously noted 5300 voyages from the port, would have actually worked out at some 208 slaves per ship's voyage; and is thought to be a more generally accurate figure for the port as a whole. Mersey based vessels such as the "Lively", the "Blessing" and the "Liverpool Merchant" were all thought to have been employed in the transportation of black Africans across the Atlantic and Liverpool merchants such as James Gregson, Thomas Golightly and James Penny, were thought to be just three of those, who made their fortunes from the trade in human cargoes. The last of these three men, James Penny, was said to have subsequently achieved even greater fame, not only in his home city, but throughout the world, when the Beatles wrote the song "Penny Lane", although in recent years there have been calls for the street to be renamed, ostensibly because of Penny's participation in the Transatlantic Slave Trade.

Slave Collar

African Slave

Child Soldiers

Another major English seaport that was thought to have been involved with the Transatlantic Slave Trade, albeit in a much smaller way, was the port of Plymouth, which was said to have played host to a relatively small number of slave ships after 1698. Plymouth based ships such as the "Michael" and the "Rochester" were reported to have carried a mixed cargo of various commodities, such as tobacco and metal goods to trade with the tribes of Africa. Both of these vessels were thought to have carried up to 280 slaves on each of their voyages to the New World, making handsome profits for both their owners and the captains who commanded them. Other trade goods carried by the ships, included drugs that could be used to treat common illnesses amongst the African tribesmen, as well as seeds that might be used for planting and the more common items such as guns, ammunition and textiles. Although the trade through Plymouth was always thought to have been a fairly minimal part of the city's commercial business, by around 1750, only one ship, was said to be operating out of the port, so any benefits gained by the Transatlantic Slave Trade were thought to have been negligible.

It was said to be between 1740 and 1807 that the Transatlantic Slave Trade was at its greatest height, with an estimated 60,000 Africans being brought into the Americas, for work on the expanding rice, tobacco, sugar and cotton plantations that were the financial hub of the Caribbean and European colonies. Even prior to this, Britain's status as one of the slave trades leading participants was thought to have been reinforced by the Treaty of Utrecht, signed in 1713, between the governments of Great Britain and Spain, which gave British slavers exclusive rights to supply African labour to the Spanish colonies in the Americas for a period of 30 years. It was largely as a result of such treaties; and the continuing development of the British plantation system throughout the Americas that helped Great Britain gain the unenviable reputation of being the biggest slave trading nation from 1730 onwards. This position was thought to have been strengthened after 1763, when Britain acquired even more Caribbean possessions, in the form of Grenada, Tobago, St Vincent, Dominica, Cuba, Demerara and Trinidad, most of which were already occupied by other European plantations; and that regularly required new slave workers to replace those that had died. However, it should also be pointed out that according to some reporters, between 1698 and 1775, the North American colonies were also importing large numbers of African slaves on their own account and on their own ships, directly from Africa, rather than from the British West Indies, which had been the usual practice prior to that time. Operating from ports such as New York, Boston and Newport, Rhode Island, these entirely American slave ships, were reported to have carried slaves directly from Africa to the American colonies, where they were auctioned off and put to work on the burgeoning tobacco, rice and cotton plantations. Although direct imports of slaves did not end in 1775, following the American War of Independence, a number of new slave ports were reported to have sprung up, with Newport, Boston and Charleston becoming the principal points of entry for African slave labour. Interestingly however, after 1783, the newly established United States of America was also said reported to have been importing its own African slaves, largely through the use of its own slaving ship, as opposed to the former colonial powers, such as England. It has also been noted that by 1860 most of the four million black slaves, still in enslavement within the US, had actually been born within the borders of that country and were therefore American citizens rather than true native Africans.

Despite its pre-eminence amongst the by now well established trade and the military might which Britain employed throughout its emerging Empire, the slave trade was also thought to have presented many problems to the British authorities, most notably through a series of Slave Rebellions, which were said to have occurred on the main Caribbean island of Jamaica. Between 1730 and 1739 a series of armed revolts, led by a "Cameroon" leader called Cudjoe were reported to have erupted throughout the island, leading to the deaths of a number of European plantation owners and English administrators. As England found herself unable to fully suppress these revolts through entirely military means, eventually a Peace Treaty was agreed between the two sides, although it obviously failed to address many of the slaves basic demands, as reoccurrences of the revolt were known to have taken place during the 1760's and again between 1794 and 1796. Between 1655 and 1807 there were reported to have been a total of around thirty slave revolts on the island of Jamaica alone; and there were thought to have been numerous other slave uprisings and rebellions throughout the Caribbean in succeeding years. The Maroons of Jamaica were a colony of runaway slaves, who had either escaped from or been abandoned by, their former Spanish masters prior to Britain seizing the island in 1655. Rather than risk being enslaved by the new British occupiers, the Maroon's chose to establish their own free community in the mountains of Jamaica, under the leadership of the self styled Captain Cudjoe, who was said to have been aided in his work by a supposedly magical matriarch called Queen Nanny. Although their mountain hideaway was said to have provided these freed slaves with most of their basic needs, generally they were thought to have relied on guerrilla raids against British plantations, to supply them everything else, including new black recruits. Although the British authorities had initially been fairly tolerant towards the Maroon's, their increasing habit of attacking British owned plantations, stealing foodstuffs, money and weapons, as well as encouraging other slaves to abscond from their owners, eventually became too much for the local authorities, who decided to put a stop to the Maroons once and for all.

Unfortunately for those British military commanders who were ordered to suppress the rebels, the Maroons were said to have been a highly mobile guerrilla force, which was adept at disappearing into the islands interior, only to reappear somewhere else, to begin attacking British interests once the military had withdrawn. In fact, the rebels were thought to have been so successful in their campaigns that British plantation owners, such as George Manning and Colonel Thomas Brooks, continually lost property and more perhaps importantly, workers to the Maroons over a period of years, leading them to eventually abandon their plantations for fear of losing their own lives. Things were said to have become so serious on the island that the British authorities even employed native Indian trackers and regular British troops from Gibraltar, to try and chase down the elusive rebels, but all to no avail. Finally though, British political pragmatism was used to deal with the situation; and a Peace Treaty was eventually agreed between the two sides in 1739. This Peace Treaty was reported to have granted the Maroons land and financial incentives, provided that they returned British owned runaway slaves to their masters, which the rebels agreed to do, but only as and when they chose to do so. For the British authorities though, their commonly employed tactic of divide and conquer, had once again provided a temporary solution to their immediate problems.

In the first few decades of the transatlantic trade, African slaves were thought to have been treated fairly badly; and following the introduction of the Barbados Slave Code in 1661, they were thought to have been treated little better than animals. Because of their lowly status, slaves who transgressed the rules and regulations of the individual plantation, could expect to be punished severely, often by being whipped mercilessly by one of the many overseers. For the slave owner, this form of punishment was intended to reinforce his power over the slaves, inflict a painful lesson on the individual transgressor, but without restricting their ability to work on the plantation. Occasionally, an overzealous overseer might inadvertently beat a slave to death, but from the owner's perspective, this simply reflected the loss of a possession, rather than representing any sort of illegal act, as at the time, slaves had few if any legal rights. For more serious infringements of the rules, such as absconding from the plantation, other far more serious punishments might well have been meted out to the individual offender. It was not uncommon for runaway slaves to have part of their limbs amputated by the owner, or to have their hamstrings deliberately cut, in order to ensure that the slave did not run away for a second time. It has also been reported that both starvation and solitary confinement, were regularly used to teach erstwhile slaves a lesson, which along with the implicit threat of being whipped or losing part of a limb, tended to keep each plantation's slaves in a permanent state of passive servility. However, as time passed some plantation owners were said to have adopted a much more humane attitude to the slaves that they owned, even regarding them as fellow human beings, with inherent rights, feelings and aspirations. By the latter part of the 18th century, many slaves were being regarded as trusted retainers by their owners, who often took on the task of educating and advising their slaves, so that their lives were as pleasant and as contented as they could be, albeit within an enslaved environment. Unfortunately, despite the best intentions of these much more forward thinking plantation owners, resentment and antagonism still existed within many slave communities and outbreaks of rebellion and violence were still thought to have been commonplace during the period, requiring increasingly stronger measures to be taken by the authorities, in order to suppress them.

The latter part of the 18th century, was also thought to have marked the beginning of the Abolitionist movement within both the United States and in Britain, an anti-slavery lobby which was thought to have significant support amongst the Quakers communities of both countries. In 1765, the first in a series of cases, were reported to have been brought before the English Courts in order to challenge the legality of the Slave Trade and in 1772 a landmark ruling in the English Courts, declared slavery in Great Britain and Ireland illegal. Also, in 1774, the Quaker leader, John Wesley, was said to have published an anti-slavery booklet that was widely distributed and supported by the Society of Friends. However, the outbreak of the American War of Independence in 1775 ensured that the subject of the Transatlantic Slave Trade was largely forgotten over the next two years, as Great Britain and its revolutionary colonists fought for control of the North American states. By 1787 and with control of the North American colonies settled, in favour of the newly founded United States of America, the subject of slavery once again became a subject for discussion within Britain. That same year was said to have seen the establishment of a committee, dedicated to the ending of the Slave Trade, which was founded in London, by a number of Britain's leading social and religious groups, including the Society of Friends, although it would be another twenty years before any real change was made to the trade, when in 1789, the abolitionist movement did see improvements under the terms of the Dolben Act. This particular piece of British legislation was said to have laid down strict rules and regulations, pertaining to the transportation of African slaves, stating how many could be carried on ships of a particular size and helping to reduce some of the worst conditions which had been common prior to that.

A related issue that stemmed from the conflict between Britain and its rebellious American colonists was that of the thousands of black Afro-American slaves who had chosen to support the Imperial cause during the military dispute. Serving with both the British army and navy, most of these former slaves were said to have chosen to take up arms against the American settlers in return for the Crown's guarantees for their future freedom. Unfortunately for everyone on the British side, the American colonists ultimately proved victorious in the American War of Independence and many of these same black soldiers and sailors were left little option but to resettle themselves elsewhere. Although some were reported to have made their way back to Africa or stayed on to make new lives in the northern states of America, large numbers were reported to have chosen to relocate themselves to other Caribbean islands, or to mainland Britain. The great maritime ports of Britain were often the final destinations for many of these former black soldiers and sailors, including the likes of London, Liverpool and Bristol, although many of them were reported to have failed to thrive in these largely urbanised areas. Since 1722, all black men and women entering Britain were deemed to be free persons, following the landmark ruling made by Chief Justice Mansfield in the case of a black fugitive slave called Somerset. Even though Mansfield's legal opinion failed to uphold the rights of the millions of black slaves, who were being held on British owned plantations in the Caribbean, the judgement did clarify the legal position of those former slaves that were resident within Britain's national borders and defined their rights as individuals under English law. Although only dealing with the case of the slave known as Somerset, Mansfield's decision is also thought to have set a precedent that would ultimately lead to the abolition of the slave trade some thirty-odd years later. Sadly, such legal determinations failed to address many of the issues and prejudices that continued to affect most black people who lived and worked in late 18th century Britain. Although some managed to find both employment and accommodations in the great urban centres, many more found that they were largely unwelcome in some parts of the country and unable to find work, so were subsequently forced to beg in the streets to keep themselves alive. Such discrimination was also thought to have been the reason why so many immigrants, including many of these former slaves found themselves forced into racial ghettoes, where conditions were often not only appalling, but lives were short and poverty was rife.

It was thought to be as a result of such obvious black poverty that numbers of local benefactors, charitable foundations and supporters for the abolition of slavery came together to form the Committee for the Relief of the Black Poor. Dedicated to finding a long term solution to the problems faced by the black poor in cities such as London, although the committee dedicated themselves to feeding and accommodating many of the poorest black citizens, its primary aim seems to have been to establish a colony, where these former slaves might build a new life. Initially though, such proposals were said to have met with very little support amongst members of Britain's black communities and it was only after a number of assurances had been given, relating to their continued British citizenship and future security that a number of these former black soldiers and sailors agreed to be relocated to the region of modern day Sierra Leone. Taking with them a number of white women, who were reported to be the wives and girlfriends of these black settlers, the first contingent of London's black poor were reported to have been transported to the site of a former slave market in Sierra Leone in 1787. Joining a group of freed black American slaves who had established their own colony there some years earlier, initially everything seemed to have gone very well for the new community. However, following a series of disputes with the indigenous tribes of West Africa, the original settlement was said to have been burned down in 1789, with a large number of the black British settlers being killed as a result of the ongoing conflict. In 1792 a second wave of immigrants were brought to the area, but this time the new settlement was thought to have been rebuilt in an entirely different, but much more defendable position, with the surviving members of the first colony forming part of this new community. Although this second British settlement still faced considerable hardships and the risk of native attacks, it future was said to have been virtually guaranteed after 1807, when the Royal Navy units which were employed to suppress the Transatlantic Slave Trade, were reported to have used the site of the British black settlement, later to be called Freetown, as its main base of operations.

Lord Mansfield   Slaves For Sale   Child Labourer

The British MP William Wilberforce was said to have been one of the main advocates for ending the Transatlantic Slave Trade and was reported to have dedicated much of his working life to see the trade suppressed. It was in 1790 that Wilberforce first attempted to guide a bill for the Abolition of Slavery through the English Parliament, but the bill was subsequently defeated, largely it is said, because of the vested interests within the House of Commons and the House of Lords, particularly those members who were themselves Plantation and slave owners. Two years later, in 1792, the British authorities were said to have first founded the colony of Sierra Leone in Africa, principally for those black slaves who had fought alongside Britain during the American War of Independence. Two years later, in 1794, France became the first western European nation to formally abolish slavery within its Empire, largely as a result of the revolutionary zeal that was said to have been spreading throughout the country. However, slavery was also said to have been reinstated by the Emperor Napoleon Bonaparte in 1802, although its widespread reintroduction was thought to have been fairly limited, due to a lack of support within the general populace and the inability of Napoleon to enforce the law in a number of France's overseas colonies. In 1804, the former Spanish colony of St Domingue was said to have become the first independent black state outside of continental Africa, having been established by the successors of the original African slaves who had been brought there by the Spanish and continues to exist today as the nation of Haiti.

Finally, beginning on 1st May 1807 the British Parliament eventually passed the Abolition of Slavery Act into law, thereby outlawing the trade in slaves and preventing British merchants and their ships from participating in the enforced abduction, transportation and sale of indigenous peoples from anywhere in the world. Initially the terms of the Act was designed to abolish slavery within the United Kingdom of Great Britain and Ireland, as well as any of the colonies, islands, dominions, or territories belonging to, or in his majesties possession, or occupation. Although this particular piece of legislation did not outlaw slavery completely, it was said to have helped to establish the basis for future legislation, passed in 1833, which would finally put an end to slavery within the British Empire and in much of the wider world. Having generally introduced the idea of bringing an end to the Transatlantic Slave Trade, the British authorities then began to take practical steps to physically enforce the new legislation on the High Seas, through the use of Britain's formidable Royal Navy. A dedicated naval taskforce, the West Africa Squadron, was reported to have been established to patrol the traditional slave trading routes along the west coast of Africa and use their military might to stop and seize any suspected slave ships, arrest the captain, along with his crew and free those slaves found aboard. Working within some of the most perilous and disease ridden conditions, these Royal Navy crews were reported to have suffered heavy losses whilst performing this particular duty, but ultimately carried on with their mission, in helping to bring an end to the gruesome international trade. According to some reports, the West Africa Squadron was said to have stopped and seized several hundred ships that were transporting captured Africans and in total were thought to have freed several thousand slaves from captivity. British sanctions against slave traders were said to have been significantly increased after 1827, when the British Parliament followed the lead of the US authorities, who in 1820, had made slave trading an act of piracy, punishable by death. The Royal Navy was said to have been particularly successful in the seizure of ships destined for the Portuguese colony of Brazil, reportedly the largest importers of African slaves since the trade had been inaugurated. Not only did the Royal Navy stop and search many hundreds of ships, but was thought to have freed many thousands of imprisoned Africans, who were destined to be enslaved throughout the Americas. It was also reported that the British authorities tried to suppress the trade at source, by persuading local tribal leaders within Africa itself, to desist from participating in the trade, threatening them with sanctions if they failed to comply. It has also been suggested that where incentives, or the threat of trade sanctions, failed to stop individual tribesmen from engaging in the slave trade, then the British authorities were not averse to using direct military action to achieve their goals.

Even though most of the western slave trading nations came to see the slave trade as a highly immoral and fundamentally inhumane business practice, some of the most serious objections to its cessation were thought to have come from the slave trading kingdoms of Africa itself. At least one of these slave suppliers was reported to have complained bitterly about the end of the trade, proclaiming publicly his outrage that a trade "ordained by God" was being stopped by the British. Along with a number of other tribal leaders, this chieftain had obviously become rich, through the enslavement of his fellow Africans and now saw his principal source of income being inextricably brought to an end. The Slavery Abolition Act of 1833 was said to have been the second piece of formal legislation passed by British Parliament, designed to end the enforced enslavement of native peoples within the Empire, although the law itself was thought to have only come into force in the following year. Perhaps because of the presence of significant numbers of slave owners and traders within the legislature itself, the Act was thought to have contained a number of legal "fudges", which ultimately prevented the widespread and immediate release of the hundreds of thousands of African slaves still held on British owned plantations. Rather than simply releasing them straight away, an "apprenticeship" clause was said to have been inserted into the Act, forcing the former slaves to remain on their owners plantation for a period of years, which caused a great of resentment amongst those being held, who often had little trust in their British masters. Consequently, the vast majority of the slaves being held on the British Caribbean islands were not actually released until 1838. It was also in response to the 1833 Act that the British Government tried to ensure compliance on the part of the Caribbean plantation owners and slave holders, by appointing local magistrates to oversee the treatment of slaves, most of whom had now become apprentices to their former owners. Instructed to regulate local conditions and the planter's treatment of their workers, in reality these magistrates tended to be largely ineffective and planters continued to treat their former possessions much the same way as they had always done. With some of these newly appointed officials either under the influence or even in the pay of local landowners, most former slaves still found their lives as miserable and harsh as before, although the customary and arbitrary levels of ill-treatment imposed on workers was said to have been partially reduced, simply because of the planters real fears of being prosecuted for seriously injuring or even killing a worker.

Even after much of the Transatlantic Slave Trade had been rigorously suppressed by the British and American Navies, this did not end the trafficking of Africans within the region, as the Arab Slave Trade was said to have continued for many years after the legislation had first come into force. In fact, according to some sources, the trade was said to have expanded substantially in the first few years after the Atlantic trade had been stopped, largely because there was thought to be a surplus of black Africans being held by the slave takers. However, this trade too, was reported to have eventually been brought under control as a result of the increasing European colonisation of Africa during the 19th century by a number of Western Europe's leading powers, who employed their own armed forces to suppress the trade. Unfortunately for many hundreds of thousands of Africans, the trade was almost impossible to eradicate completely and despite the best efforts of numerous countries and agencies, human slavery is still thought to exist in Africa to this present day. Significantly, the practice of human slavery is still thought to be most common in those native states and countries, which are deemed to have generally failed, where central government and law enforcement agencies either do not exist, or are largely ineffective.

Even though most modern historians and reporters unanimously agree that the Transatlantic Slave Trade had a highly detrimental effect on the African continent generally, the same sources tend to differ, when it comes to how much effect the trade had on the subsequent development of those nations that were the victims of slavery. Clearly for most of the Europeans, who were directly involved in the practice, the slave trade proved to be a highly lucrative business, but one that was incredibly dangerous for those involved in the practical aspects of it, such as the agents and ships crews, who ventured onto the unknown coasts of West Africa and traversed the Atlantic Ocean. Even today, many experts are thought to remain divided over the actual long term effects of the slave trade, particularly those that were felt by the smaller and weaker African tribes, who saw many millions of their youngest and most vital men and women snatched away by the stronger slave traders of Africa. Some critics of the trade, point to the fact that it was precisely the loss of these young, vibrant people, from the regions "gene-pool" that has been the greatest loss to continental Africa, although whether or not these losses have proved to be catastrophic to the African continent as a whole, is still very much open to conjecture. The most serious charge made by some critics of the Atlantic Slave Trade though, is that the trade and those involved with it, are guilty of the wholesale destruction of African culture, language and religion within certain areas of the continent, acts that might be seen to represent early forms of both genocide and ethnic cleansing by the western nations, which were involved in the trade. However, any such claims can only ever be regarded a being spurious at best, as history tends to indicate that those who were involved with the slave trade at source, had no such deliberate aims in mind, but were simply dedicated to making money out of the trade, rather than shaping the social, economic or belief systems of the native tribes of Africa.

Finally, it is also worth noting that although slavery per se is generally regarded as a historic practice and one that was best consigned to the history books, in reality versions of such a barbaric trade are still thought to exist throughout the world to this present day. In virtually all parts of the globe, slavery exists in most forms, from outright chattel slavery to bonded service, from domestic bondage to the sex slaves of Eastern Europe, the Middle East and Asia. Even in Africa, the continent which has undoubtedly suffered more than most from the depravities of wholesale human enslavement, chattel, bonded, sex and child slavery still exist within various supposedly modern societies, often with complicity of the law enforcement and civil government agencies that are supposed to oppose them. In places like Mauritania, Sudan, Benin and Ghana, where poverty and unemployment are widespread, modern day enslavement is still reported to exist and is still practiced by African traffickers, who specifically target young children, who are much more easily transported throughout the continent to be sold to those rich African families, who still value the ownership of another human being. Often these children are sold by their own parents, who wrongly believe that they are selling their child into a better life, one where they will be fed, clothed and educated, but where, in reality, they will often be subjected to domestic drudgery and sexual abuse. Common destinations for these trafficked children are reported to include the Ivory Coast and Gabon, although in all likelihood many can end up in any number of countries, both inside and out of continental Africa.

It is also worth noting perhaps that in many of Africa's numerous post-colonial civil wars and disputes, tens of thousands of children and young people have been forcibly abducted by one or other side of a national dispute and used either as child soldiers or as sex slaves. A number of these same conflicts have also thought to have been marked by levels of barbarity that could hardly have been matched by any period or any person related to the Transatlantic Slave Trade itself. Horrific tales of pregnant women and their unborn babies being bayoneted to death, people's limbs being hacked off by machete's, or whole villages being massacred, are just three of the atrocious methods that have been employed by various militant forces, which have vied for control of a particular region of Africa. Likewise, thousands of indigenous Africans are reported to have been forced to labour under the most intolerable conditions to excavate diamonds, or other precious elements, which can then be traded for more guns, or arms, as well as to simply enrich the African leaders of some or other tribal rebellion. Some modern day African leaders tend to blame the great colonial powers for such appalling incidents and the state of the continent generally, pointing to the white colonisation and settlement of Africa, as well as the much earlier Transatlantic Slave Trade, for modern day Africa's many troubles. The argument generally runs that the great colonial powers have prevented African society from developing in a much more traditional manner, first by forcibly removing so many of its youngest, fittest and most promising young people through the Transatlantic Slave Trade. The second factor is said to have been the imposition of colonial rule throughout much of Africa, by the great European powers, including, Portugal, France, Germany, Belgium and of course Britain. These same leaders suggest that by depriving the native peoples of Africa of their right to self determination and self government, the great powers have produced societies, which are not only entirely dependent, but one's that are largely devoid of native traditions and customs. However, as is reported in other chapters of this book, even though most of the African continent was and has been colonised at one time or another by the leading European states, for the most part, Africa has been under African leadership for well over fifty years and yet much of the continent continues to remain under the shadow of poverty, disease and perhaps more significantly, inter-tribal violence, exactly the same sorts of circumstances which had allowed the slave trade to exist in the first place.

MARINERS, MERCHANTS AND THE MILITARY TOO

5. INDIA AND THE SUBCONTINENT

Most of the foremost western European empires that have existed throughout human history have known, used and appreciated the various exotic spices, herbs, oils and metals that man had learned to exploit from the very earliest times. Indeed, even at the time that Christ was reputedly born, gifts of gold, frankincense and myrrh were reported to have been delivered to the newly born "King of kings", by the three wise men, who had travelled across the Middle East, to welcome the new and legendary saviour of mankind. Likewise, supplies of black pepper, cinnamon, cardamom, ginger and turmeric were all thought to have been traded in various regions of the world, along with other equally unusual and highly prized materials, such as ebony and ivory, silks and other native textiles.

The Greek and Roman Empires were reported to have commonly used such items, as had the Persians and the Egyptians before them and it was through the trade routes established by these great human civilisations that such rare and valuable commodities came to be known throughout most of western Europe, even though such goods were typically too expensive for the everyday citizen to buy. Supplies of such prized goods was said to have become even much more limited and expensive following the decline of the Roman Empire, which allowed control of the Spice and Silk roads to fall into the hands of Arab traders by the 7th century, creating supply monopolies that were tightly controlled by a generally small number of Islamic kingdoms, who were keen to exploit their monopolistic position to its very limit. By limiting supplies of these highly valuable commodities, to a small number of European traders, such as the Venetians, these Arab suppliers not only ensured high profit margins for themselves and their partners, but also that they continued to exercise almost complete control of the marketplace throughout the period. This situation was thought to have remained relatively unchanged for the best part of eight hundred years, until in the 15th century, the Turkish Ottoman Empire began to emerge and evolve, allowing it to take control of the well established overland trade routes and putting in place, their own restrictive trading practices that limited the supplies and price of such goods being brought into western Europe. It was thought to be as a result of these restrictions and practices that the greatest European maritime nation of the age, the Portuguese, began to look for alternative, more direct trade sea routes, which would allow them to access these highly prized items at their source, effectively circumventing the Ottoman blockade of the eastern states and helping Portugal to become the main western supplier of these highly valued trade goods.

Vasco da Gama **Akbar the Great** **Emperor Jahangir**

Although the Portuguese were known to have been exploring the world's oceans for a number of years, it was only thought to be around 1498, when the explorer Vasco Da Gama first set out with a small flotilla of ships, determined to establish a trade route to the eastern states which supplied these highly prized products. Following traditional sea routes down the western side of Africa and around the southern tip of the continent, Da Gama and his small fleet were reported to have made their way into the Indian Ocean and in doing so established a Portuguese trading monopoly that was said to have lasted for the next century or more. It was thought another twenty years before Portugal's larger Iberian neighbours, Spain, would set out to establish its own trading links with the eastern states, initially choosing to sail westward under the command of Christopher Columbus and Ferdinand Magellan; and on the way discovering the previously unknown American continent and the straits of Magellan, which provided access from the Atlantic to the Pacific oceans. Beginning his voyage in 1519, Magellan was reported to have discovered the passage that allowed his ships access between these two great bodies of water and eventually reached the legendary "Spice Islands", now marked by parts of modern day Indonesia and the Philippines, in 1521. The following year Magellan was said to have returned to Spain, his ship laden down with a cargo of Cloves and Nutmeg, his voyage deemed a huge financial success and with yet another new trading route established.

The Dutch were also thought to have sent a flotilla of their own ships to trade with the Spice Islands in both 1595 and 1598, although it was only the second of these Dutch missions, which was thought to have returned home in 1599, laden down with goods and spices from these new found lands. Although British traders had attempted to establish trade routes with the Indian Ocean region between 1583 and 1594, all of these journeys were reported to have been generally small-scale private enterprises, which met with only varying degrees of results. It was said to be in 1591 that a small fleet of British ships, including the Edward Bonaventure, which was under the command of Captain James Lancaster, finally succeeded in completing the voyage that ultimately put in place regular trading routes and which would eventually lead to Britain's formal and wholesale involvement in the Indian sub-continent. Of the three ships that departed with Lancaster in 1591, only his own survived the arduous journey, returning to England in 1594, loaded down with foreign merchandise and colourful reports of the fabulous wealth that existed in these faraway lands. However, Britain's first formally authorised voyage to the region of the Spice Islands was only really initiated by the formation of a joint stock company, called the Governor and Company of Merchants of London Trading with the East Indies and the granting of its official Charter by Elizabeth I on the 31st December 1600. The trading company was reported to have been established by a relatively small number of London's leading merchants, all of whom were keen to investigate and trade with the foreign lands that they were slowly but surely becoming aware of. The man that the Company chose to lead its first official expedition was none other than Captain James Lancaster, who was tasked to lead the Company's fleet of ships to Sumatra in 1601. Carrying a mixed cargo of gold, silver, lead, ironwork and textiles with which to trade, Lancaster was said to have returned home to England in 1603 with a cargo of mixed spices and other exotic merchandise, said to be worth in excess of a million pounds. Despite its later evolution into a semi-autonomous Imperial agency, it seems unlikely that there was ever any intention on the part of these early traders, merchants or mariners to actually conquer the region that they were destined for, but rather they had simply set out to build and develop new trading links with a previously unknown and unexplored part of their world.

The Mughal Empire, which was said to have controlled vast areas of the Indian subcontinent, was reported to have emerged in the first half of the 16th century, under the leadership of the Timurid Prince, Babur, who was thought to have originated from the region of Asia, now marked by the modern day state of Uzbekistan. In 1526 Babur and his armies were said to have defeated the forces of the last native Indian Sultan of Delhi, Ibrahim Shah Lodi and set about establishing a dynasty that would last for the next two centuries. Four years later however, Babur was said to have been succeeded by his son Humayun, who was a far less effective than his father and who was reported to have lost much of the fledgling Mughal Empire in a series of military conflicts with the neighbouring Pashtun tribes. For most of the next two decades the new Mughal Emperor was thought to have been in virtual exile and it was only sometime after 1550 and following the death of his greatest adversary, Sher Shah Suri that Humayun was finally able to raise a large enough army to defeat his enemies and regain the city of Delhi. Unfortunately for Humayun, he was said to have died in 1556, little more than a year after his final victory and whilst his Empire was still relatively young and unsettled. Control of the Mughal states was then said to have passed into the hands of Humayun's young son, Jalaluddin, who was more commonly known as Akbar, or Akbar the Great, who would go on to rule the Empire for well over forty five years, from 1556 to 1605. Said to have been a far more capable and pragmatic ruler than his father, Akbar was thought to have been extremely tolerant of his subjects different religious beliefs, which helped to reduce the historic tensions amongst the disparate ethnic communities that made up much of his vast Empire. He was also said to have made a number of alliances with neighbouring Rajputs and even appointed Hindu officers to hold positions of command in his largely Muslim army, further strengthening bonds between the two main religious faiths. In 1605, Akbar was reported to have died and was then succeeded by his son Jahangir, the Emperor who would initially welcome the first English merchants into his kingdom and that inadvertently set in place relationships, which would allow the British East India Company to become the de-facto rulers of the Indian subcontinent in later years.

The first English ships to reach mainland India proper were reported to have reached Surat in August 1608, under the command of the notable English sea captain Sir John Hawkins, who had come not only to trade, but also to seek permission to establish a permanent English presence in the region. Unfortunately for Hawkins, the regional administrator informed the seafarer that only the Mughal Emperor himself, Nuruddin Salim Jahangir, could give permission for a permanent presence in the country and so Hawkins was forced to travel to the Emperor's palace at Agra to seek permission for the trading post. Luckily for the Captain and his employers back in Britain, the Emperor Jahangir was said to have taken an immediate liking for Hawkins, not only welcoming the English trader with the gift of an Armenian girl, who Hawkins later married, but also appointing the Englishman as a paid advisor to the Mughal Court. However, precisely because of his popularity with Jahangir, Hawkins was said to have earned the antipathy of the local Portuguese trade representatives, who saw the Englishman as a direct threat to their own commercial opportunities and immediately began trying to undermine his position at court. Not only did these foreign agents deliberately try to poison the relationship between Hawkins and the Mughal ruler, Jahangir, but were even reported to have tried to assassinate the English sea captain, although fortunately their attempts were said to have been unsuccessful. It soon became clear to Sir John that the only way to reduce Portuguese influence was through a display of superior British sea power, which might also help to convince the Mughal Emperor that Britain was in fact a much stronger military ally than their rivals, thereby strengthening the British position within India itself. As it turned out, a number of relatively small skirmishes at sea, which saw British ships defeat their larger Portuguese adversaries, helped to convince the Mughal Emperor that Britain was in fact a far greater military ally than the Portuguese and in 1612 he gave Hawkins permission to establish the first ever British trading post or factory at Surat. This new trading relationship was reported to have been followed up sometime later by the appointment of Sir Thomas Roe as the English ambassador to India, thereby formalising diplomatic relations between the British and Mughal courts. Roe was said to have been sent as a personal emissary to the Mughal Court by the British monarch James I, who was reported to have made several previous attempts at establishing diplomatic relations with the Emperor Jahangir, but had had no obvious success through these. Fortunately, Roe proved to be a highly effective ambassador to the Indian Court, as his less than deferential style was said to have appealed to the Mughal Emperor, Sir Thomas having correctly identified that Jahangir had little respect for the majority of the English traders, deliberately took a less than accommodating approach, which proved to be a highly successful strategy and led to Britain gaining even more trading posts throughout the Indian continent. When Jahangir died in 1627, he was reported to have been succeeded by his son, Shah Jahan, who was said to have inherited the greatest Empire in the world at that particular time. It was Jahan who was known to have authorised the construction of the Taj Mahal in Agra between 1630 and 1653, a building that remains as one of the world's most iconic structures even today, some 350 years after it was first completed. Designed and built principally as a tomb for the Emperor's wife Mumtaz Mahal, who died giving birth to his 14th child, the monument was said to have been designed by the leading Persian architect of the age, Ustad Ahmad Lahauri. According to an associated legend however, Shah Jahan was said to have been so deeply moved and impressed by the monument that he ordered the architects hands to be cut off, so that he could never design a more beautiful building in the future.

During Shah Jahan's reign, from 1628 to 1658, the British were thought to have been equally welcome as they were during his father's time and continued to expand their commercial operations throughout the limits of the Mughal Empire. In fact, the years between 1600 and 1647 were thought to be the most successful period for the company's trading operation in the region, with factories being established at Masulipatam on the east coast of India in 1611, Surat on the west coast in 1612 and at Hoogly, on the east coast in 1640. In 1639 the Company established a trading post in Madras, at Bombay in 1668 and at Calcutta sometime around 1687. Notably though, Bombay Island was not thought to have required the express permission of the Indian Emperor's to establish the trading post, as this particular possession was reported to have been granted to the English Crown as part of the wedding dowry of Catherine of Braganza, the Portuguese bride of the British monarch Charles II. However, even by 1647 the East India Company was reported to have established around twenty three such trading centres throughout the wider subcontinent, with each of them under the direct control of a "Factor" or master merchant who supervised all trade business and oversaw all of the local native employees. The largest of these early trade posts were said to have later evolved into the protective "Presidencies" of Fort William in Bengal, Fort St George in Madras and the Bombay Castle, all of which were run by individually appointed British Governors. However, the last of these three great forts, Bombay Castle, eventually became the main headquarters for the Company's operations within India, being moved there from Surat in 1687.

When he died in 1658, Shah Jahan was reported to have been succeeded by his son Aurangzeb, who was said to have received the Mughal Empire at the height of its existence, with most of modern day India, Pakistan and Afghanistan subject to his rule. According to most historians, Aurangzeb was the last of the great Mughal Emperors, as it was thought to be during his reign that the vast Indian Empire initially began to contract, a process that would inevitably lead to its collapse at the beginning of the 18th century. However, despite the long term improvements in Anglo-Indian trade generally, elsewhere in the wider region things were not going so well for British traders, largely because of outside competition. Even though Portuguese interests had largely been suppressed by British naval superiority, one of Britain's other European neighbour, the Dutch, were said to have emerged as an equally effective military force in the Indian sub-continent and were now challenging Britain's position in the region. Despite being allies in the European theatre, in India, both nations were reported to have adopted a highly aggressive approach to one another, with the Dutch having a marked naval superiority over British ships. This mutual antagonism was said to have been specially marked in the area of the Spice Islands, the place where Britain had first arrived in the region, but where Dutch influence now largely prevailed. Seemingly unable to confront the Dutch on an equal naval footing and following the killing of a number of English traders there in 1623, British interests were said to have withdrawn from the immediate area and fallen back to the Indian mainland, where they would now concentrate their efforts. For much of the next century, British interests through the offices of the East India Company were said to have grown steadily, despite the fact that towards the end of the 17th century the Mughal Empire was slowly beginning to disintegrate throughout much of India. This decline was thought to have allowed a number of European countries and various native princely states to expand their own holdings and influence within the limits of the old empire, not least of which was the British East India Company itself. Along with the British, both Dutch and French imperial interests battled for control of the vast and decaying Mughal Empire and its many possessions. Britain was said to have been fortunate though, in that one of the last Mughal Emperor's, Shah Alam, was reported to have formally appointed the British East India Company as his official agents in the region of Bengal, one of the most valuable and important regions within his extensive Empire.

The term British "Raj", which is thought to be derived from the Sanskrit word "Raja" meaning "king", is only really thought to refer to the period between 1858 and 1947 when the British Government of the day officially took overall control of the Indian subcontinent, replacing the East India Company, who had held power there as an agent of the Crown since 1600 and which was replaced in that role following the Indian Sepoy Mutiny of 1857. According to some sources, the British East India Company was said to have controlled increasingly larger parts of India between 1612 and 1757 and between 1757 and 1857 was largely engaged in consolidating its earlier gains, during which time it was simply referred to as "the Company". However, it is also reported that the term "Raj" had been in common use within India for a considerable period of time and well before the British Crown actually took over responsibility for the country as a whole. By the latter half of the 17th century the Company's position on the sub-continent was said to have been substantially strengthened; and they were reported to be regularly exporting large amounts of cotton, silk, spices, indigo dye, saltpetre and tea back to Britain, products that were then distributed throughout Europe and to most of Britain's other overseas colonies. Even during the Protectorate of Oliver Cromwell, the Company's legal charters were thought to have been renewed and enforced and even following the Restoration of King Charles II in 1660, its position was further improved and enhanced. In fact, the restored Stuart dynasty in Britain, even went so far as to grant the East India Company permission to mint its own money, command its own fortresses, recruit its own troops, to make war and peace at its own discretion, as well as exercising civil and military jurisdiction over the territories that it then held. By the beginning of the 18th century the Company had even managed to establish several factories outside of the Indian sub-continent, with a trading post reportedly established at Canton in China in around 1711.

Sir Thomas Roe

Shah Jahan

Mumtaz Mahal

Within the Indian mainland itself and following the death of the last of the great Mughal Emperor, Aurangzeb, in 1707, the Empire was said to have deteriorated fairly rapidly, largely because of expansionism by other ethnic tribal dynasties and regular border incursions by neighbouring kingdoms based in both Persia and Afghanistan. The greatest threat to the crumbling Mughal Empire though, was thought to have come from the emerging Marathas and Sikh Empires, both of which sought to take advantage of the Mughal Court's inability to defend its own historic borders. The fragmentation of the old Empire was thought to have been so rapid that in less than a century, the vast lands of the Mughals had been reduced to a relatively small enclave surrounding the city of Delhi, which was then ruled by the elderly, blind and comparatively powerless ruler, Shah Alam II, who out of pure desperation was said to have requested help from the British East India Company to defend his embattled kingdom. Never a business to miss an opportunity, the Company were thought to have been quite happy to lend their support to the ailing leader and even allowed Shah Alam II to retain his position of authority over the kingdom, although in reality the Company themselves now held power there. When the old ruler died in 1805, he was reported to have been succeeded by Akbar Shah II, who held the throne for the next twenty seven years, although without wielding any real power or control over his kingdom. Following the death of the elderly and infirm Mughal Emperor, Shah Alam II, the British East India Company and its forces were reported to have held the real power in the region, with Akbar Shah II and his son, Bahadur Shah Zafur, both being little more than puppets or figureheads of the East India Company.

Such was the wealth generated by the trading activities of the East India Company that shareholders were thought to have used some of their profits to lobby the British Parliament for even greater rights, which would help the Company become even richer and more influential. Despite such political overtures however, in 1694 the British Government was said to have passed an Act, which would permit other private merchant companies to trade in the Indian sub-continent, undermining the East India Company's historic monopoly and creating some level of commercial competition within the region, although the East India Company still managed to maintain its dominance of the region. Four years later, Parliament was said to have passed yet another piece of legislation, which allowed for the establishment of a second, much larger trading company, one that had the potential to seriously threaten the East India's domination of the eastern markets. However, Company shareholders were quick to identify this potential threat to their profits and began buying stock of the new mercantile business, eventually owning a sufficiently large enough share of it that they could dictate how the new venture was operated and thereby reducing the risks to the East India Company itself. For the next decade, these two great trading companies were reported to have actively competed against one another in the highly lucrative Eastern markets, until 1708, when the decision was made to amalgamate the two great trading companies, creating The United Company of Merchants Trading to the East Indies. In order to secure its immediate future, this new company was reported to have made a loan of some three million pounds to the British Government, in return for being granted exclusive trading rights for the following three years, after which the arrangement would be reviewed. Although the shareholders of the new trading company would have preferred a much more permanent arrangement with the British Parliament, in respect of their trading rights in India, Britain's national legislature was unwilling to offer any long term agreements to the Company. As a consequence, throughout much of the 18th century a continuous stream of Acts and Amendments were thought to have been passed by Parliament, specifically relating to the Company's business activities on the Indian sub-continent. According to some sources this reluctance by the British government to agree long term trade rights in India, was thought to have been heavily influenced by Britain's generally troublesome relationship with its European neighbour France, who British ministers feared, might pose a threat to their interests in these far-off foreign lands. However, the largely hostile relationship between Britain and France also presented a financial opportunity for the government; and when military conflict erupted between the two nations in 1756, marking the beginning of the Seven Years War (1756-1763), monies paid by the Company, for extending their trading rights in India, were said to have been used by the government to fight the war against their European neighbour. Fortunately for the East India Company, many of the battles of the Seven Year War were largely centred on both countries overseas colonies, most notably in the Americas, the Caribbean and elsewhere. Although the conflict between the two European states inevitably encroached into the region of the Indian sub-continent, overall French military incursions and political interference failed to damage British trade interests to any serious degree. East India military officers, such as Robert Clive, were also thought to have ensured that French ambitions in and around the Indian sub-continent went largely unfulfilled; and by 1763 France's expansionist policies had been well and truly halted by the forces of the British Crown, who emerged victorious after almost seven years of military conflict between the two nations.

The private shareholders of the British East India Company and members of the then ruling British Government were said to have been well placed to exploit the deterioration of the Mughal dynasty, largely through the use of the Company's own private army in India. Under the control of the likes of Colonel Robert Clive, later known as "Clive of India", the Company's forces were able to gain military control of various regions from the middle of the 18th century onwards, a position that became increasingly secure following the Battle of Plassey in 1757. Over the period of the next century the East India Company would eventually go on to establish almost total control over the majority of India and in the process inexorably laid the foundation for an Anglo Indian society within the country. Prior to 1757, the East India Company was reported to have simply controlled a relatively small number of "factory" areas, where trade was conducted between Indian and British businesses. After Clive's victory at Plassey however, the Company was said to have gained control of much more significant areas of the country, including West Bengal, Orissa, Bihar and the areas of modern day Bangladesh, which were substantially added to following the Company's victory at the Battle of Buxar in 1764, when the Company forces defeated the native Mughal Emperor, Shah Alam II. Between 1766 and 1818, the Company was also said to have acquired even more lands and assets to its burgeoning company portfolio, through a series of battles and conflicts, which saw them take almost complete control of the southern Indian states and provinces. In 1772, the Company were said to have added East Bengal, allowing them to create the combined Presidency of Bengal, which was added to between 1773 and 1785 with the creation of the Bombay Presidency, following the annexation of other native lands. By 1799 and following the defeat of the Indian ruler, Tipu Sultan, a significant part of his former native homelands were said to have been given over to the creation of the Madras Presidency, the third of the great trading and administrative areas created by the East India Company. By the beginning of the 19th century the Company's practice of amalgamating captured territories had not only led to the creation of the Presidencies of Madras, Bombay and Bengal, but also to the regions of the Central Provinces, North Western Provinces, the Punjab and a variety of smaller districts and provinces. Most of these provinces and regions were said to be under the day to day control of various British Governors, or Chief Commissioners, who were directly responsible to the Governor General. A number of Princely States were also known to have co-existed within these great British held administrative regions and although they were often described as being semi-autonomous or independent, in reality they were little more than puppet regimes that were answerable to the British authorities in Delhi.. Most of the Raja's or Maharaja's who ruled these nominally independent Princely States were thought to have chosen to reach an accommodation with the British, rather than have their lands stolen, or seen themselves replaced by a relative with a more pro-British attitude.

Following the death of the Mughal Nawab or Governor of Bengal in 1757, his relative Siraj-Ud-Duala was said to have succeeded him to the throne and almost immediately began to attack British interests in the region, reportedly with the connivance and encouragement of Britain's greatest European enemy, France, who was said to have gained influence over the new and relatively young native ruler. The Mughal Nawab's forces were said to have captured the British base at Calcutta, imprisoning a number of British officers and men, along with native Sepoys in a small and claustrophobic room, where a significant number were reported to have died. Later becoming the basis for the infamous "Black hole of Calcutta", which has become a common description for any dark, dismal and generally airless room, many historians have questioned the actual authenticity of the story itself, suggesting that the facts of the incident were deliberately misrepresented by one of the East India Company's officers who was imprisoned there, but more particularly by elements of the British press. The Battle of Plassey itself took place on 23rd June 1757 and involved the forces of the British East India Company, under Colonel Robert Clive and native Bengali troops, under the command of the rebellious Indian Nawab, Siraj-Ud-Duala. The battle was said to have taken place at Palashi in West Bengal, where the much smaller British company army was said to have been faced by a far greater native Bengali force, whose numbers had been reinforced by a small contingent of French artillery. The Seven Years War, had only just begun between Britain and France; and though the French were keen to usurp British control in the Indian sub-continent, their leadership never committed sufficiently large enough numbers of regular French troops to supporting those political and military aims; and so they remained completely unfulfilled. According to some sources, much of the French involvement in the Indian sub-continent only ever amounted to general scaremongering and other local political intrigues, much of which was initiated by their Governor General in the region, a man called Joseph Dupleix, although occasionally France did lend actual military support, often in the form of heavy French artillery.

However, the British commander, Robert Clive, was known to have been an extremely capable military leader and a highly astute politician, who immediately recognised that at least one of Siraj-Ud-Duala's leading army chiefs, Mir Jafar, had become largely disaffected by Ud-Duala's rule, not least because he had been demoted by the Nawab, an act which caused him a huge loss of face within the Bengali native army. Clive was said to have been quick to exploit these potential divisions between the Mughal Nawab and one of his leading Lieutenants, sending agents to meet with Mir Jafar, prior to the battle, to see if some sort of accommodation could be made between the two parties, which they eventually managed to achieve. As the battle raged and after the British had effectively neutralised the French artillery, Ud-Duala was said to have launched a full-scale attack on the British lines, in the expectation that Mir Jafar and his forces would support him in the move. However, Jafar and his men were reported to have deliberately held themselves back from the fight, leaving the Nawab without these vitally important troops and helping sway the battle in the British army's favour. With the fight effectively lost, Siraj-Ud-Duala was thought to have had little choice but to retreat and withdraw from the region, although he was reportedly captured and executed by Mir Jafar's son, Miram, in July of 1757. This victory at the Battle of Palashi, which was known by the British as Plassey, was said to have been significant, in that Robert Clive's generally smaller East India Company force had managed to overcome a much larger Bengali army, albeit it through connivance as much as military might. Said to have comprised some one thousand Europeans, two thousand native Sepoys, along with a small number of artillery pieces, they had managed to overcome a Bengali force estimated at some fifty thousand men, who were being supported by around forty French gunners and their equipment. Of the estimated fifty thousand native troops facing Clive's relatively small Company force, around twenty thousand were said to have followed Mir Jafar's lead and withheld themselves from the fight, effectively cutting the native army numbers by 40%. These unforeseen developments for Siraj-Ud-Duala and his forces were said to have been compounded by a highly fortuitous strike by the East India Company's gunners, who managed to kill and wound a large number of the Nawab's military commanders all in one go, completely undermining the resolve of the native Bengali soldiers who were relying on them for leadership.

As per the previous agreement made with Robert Clive, Mir Jafar subsequently succeeded to the Governorship of Bengal, becoming the new native Nawab, with the permission of the British East India Company, although according to some it was a position he failed to hold for an extended period of time. Like his predecessor, he soon found himself opposing British policy in Bengal and in response to these unwarranted developments, rather foolishly invited the Dutch East India Company to intervene against the British interests. Unfortunately for Mir Jafar, the Dutch military force that was reportedly sent to help him was said to have been decisively beaten by a Company force under the command of a Colonel Ford at Chinsura in November 1759, which then led to the traitorous Nawab being deposed by the British in the following year. Mir Jafar was subsequently replaced by his son-in-law, Mir-Kassim-Ali-Khan, although he too was said to have showed far too much independence for the Company's taste and was likewise deposed after the Battle of Buxar in 1764. Perhaps surprisingly, the British were then said to have re-appointed Mir Jafar as Nawab of Bengal, although this time with a much reduced authority with which to challenge the Company's policies in the region; and much of the executive power left in the hands of local military officers and civil administrators. Aside from the British East India Company itself, the greatest beneficiary of the Company's operations in India around this time, was said to be Colonel Robert Clive himself. Appointed as Baron of Plassey in 1762 and then appointed as Governor of Bengal in 1764, he was said to have amassed an enormous personal fortune as a result of his adventures in India, levels of wealth that would make him a multi-millionaire in today's terms. However, questions have always remained as to the true source of his personal wealth, with many critics believing that much, if not all of his riches were acquired through less than legitimate means. In what might be seen by some as an ironic twist of fate however, Clive's fame, riches and titles were thought to have afforded him little personal luck, as he was reported to have committed suicide after becoming addicted to Opium, a drug that was reported to have been grown and traded by his own employer, the British East India Company.

Catherine of Braganza   **Aurangzeb**   **Akbar Shah II**

Famine was reported to have been a regular feature of the Indian sub-continent, before, during and even after the British became involved there, although according to some Indian historians, the trading practices and agricultural management of the East India Company was said to have made a number of these regular food shortages far worse and more extensive than they normally would have been. The first of a handful of famines that were said to have occurred during the East India Company's rule of the sub-continent was in the province of Bengal between 1769 and 1773; and was said to have resulted in the deaths of up to fifteen million people, mostly in the Indian states of Bihar and Orissa, which are marked today by West Bengal and Bangladesh. Much of this region of India had previously been ruled by a Nawab, or Governor, who ruled on behalf of the Mughal Emperor's, although after 1757 and the previously mentioned Battle of Plassey, was said to have been held by the British East India Company, by their nominated Nawab. The region had once again been drawn into conflict in 1764, when the Company's forces met and defeated yet another native Indian force at the Battle of Buxar, giving the British company almost complete control over this region of India. Following this second battle, the East India Company was said to have introduced swingeing new land taxes, which not only drove large numbers of people off the land, but also allowed them effective control of the local population. In 1768, a series of what appeared to be; largely insignificant crop shortages were reported to have affected the region, which in the first instance were not thought to be that serious. However, in the following year, 1769, there were more crop shortages, as well as an extended period of drought, which added to these initial problems and started to make the situation seem a little more serious. However, local officers from the British East India Company, who should have taken notice of these conditions, were said to have failed to act and generally ignored the impending problem until it was far too late. By 1770, there were said to have been reports of people starving in some parts of the region and it was even claimed that some inhabitants were resorting to cannibalism, so great was their hunger. Added to this, reports also began to come in to the authorities that cases of smallpox and other contagious diseases were spreading throughout the local population, adding to the escalating native death toll. In the latter part of 1770, monsoon rains began to fall in the region, which initially seemed to alleviate some of the starvation problems, but once these rains had stopped and the drought resumed, then the death toll amongst the native population began to rise once again.

One of the main symptoms of such devastating agricultural conditions was thought to be that such famines tended to drive hundreds of thousands of people out of the region or off the land altogether, as they searched elsewhere for food, or for alternative employment so that they could feed their families. Although a figure of some fifteen million deaths has been attributed to the Bengal Famine of 1769, no-one has been able to accurately estimate just how many actually died as a result of the event, simply because nobody was actually reporting the deaths and most reports were thought to be anecdotal at best. Although there is no doubt that millions of people died through what was an entirely foreseeable and manageable event, millions more would have undoubtedly left the region to find food elsewhere, or found alternative supplies of nutrition. Another side-effect of the famine was thought to have been the widespread abandonment of the land by those small scale farmers and landowners, who would have had no spare resources, which might have carried them through until the next rains. An associated problem with this large-scale depopulation of the region meant that it soon became inhabited by roving bands of robbers and raiders, who used the vast open spaces to launch attacks on unsuspecting travellers or those villages and towns that had managed to escape the worst of the famine. This problem was said to have become so serious in some parts of Bihar and Orissa that the East India Company had little choice but to send military units into the areas to locate and suppress these roving bands of robbers, campaigns that often took many days or weeks to complete. A number of modern day historians, including many from the sub-continent itself, believe that this famine, along with other subsequent ones, were caused as a direct result of the East India Company's own particular agricultural policies in the region, although other sources believe that these were simply contributing factors, as opposed to their root cause. In reality however, it was thought to be naturally occurring weather conditions, allied to the Company's profit driven policies, which made, what were regularly occurring regional crop failures and food shortages, far worse than they might normally have been. The weather condition known as "El Nino" has officially been recognised since the 19th century, although some scientists believe that this naturally occurring event was evident as early as the 16th century and may well have existed well before that date. Extremes of weather throughout the world are thought to be a major feature of the "El Nino" effect, causing a range of natural catastrophes, from drought to flooding and are thought by some climatologists to be the root cause of the many natural disasters that have and continue to blight large parts of Africa, Asia and the Indian Ocean region.

Prior to any sort of European involvement in the region, the largely rural Indian population would have undoubtedly faced such occasional climatic catastrophes and put measures in place to try and off-set the worst effects of these extended droughts or widespread flooding. However, it would be wrong to conclude that high mortality rates did not occur during such events, as they almost certainly did and it would have been the poorer agricultural classes, who would have borne the brunt of such crop failures and associated food shortages. As in later centuries, a high proportion of the rural population would have been employed on the land, either planting or harvesting the various food crops that the wider country relied upon and often would have been paid in kind, rather than in cash. Being paid in rice, maize, etc. would have made such workers even more dependent on a successful harvest and if that failed, then not only did they not get paid, with no food to carry them through to the next harvest, but would also have lost their jobs, as there was no work for them to do. It would be absurd to suggest that widespread loss of life did not exist on the Indian subcontinent prior to the arrival of European traders in the 16th and 17th centuries, as even Indian records suggest that it did. However, it was thought to be the actual levels of such losses that are sometimes attributed to European involvement within India, in particular the British East India Company, who are accused of fundamentally interfering in native land use, thereby making the effects of such naturally occurring events even worse. As the Company gradually took control of the various regions of India, they were said to have significantly increased the levels of tax applied to the agricultural lands in these areas, sometimes increasing them by up to reported 500%. Part of the reason for the introduction of these often exorbitant land taxes, was thought to be the Company's policy of deliberately acquiring large swathes of land on which to grow the much more profitable crops that happened to be in demand throughout the European marketplace. Those landowners who were unable to meet the Company's often ridiculous tax demands, very quickly found their land and properties being seized by the authorities and turned over to growers, who would plant and harvest these alternative crops. Even those who managed to meet the tax demands, were thought to have been pressured to switch their crops, although just as many native farmers, who were keen to exploit the demand for these new agricultural products, were said to have willingly adopted the new more profitable crops. The major problem with these new policies and practices however, was that many of these new cash crops, although vitally important to the Company's profit margins, were not suitable for feeding the local populace if there happened to be poor harvest, which was said to have been a common occurrence on the subcontinent.

It was also thought that prior to the rule of the British East India Company much of the revenue earned from the growing of staple foodstuffs had remained within the region where it was originally grown, but with the later change to entirely cash crops, which were being grown purely for export, a significant amount of the total revenue now went back to Britain and to the shareholders of the East India Company. This often had a highly negative affect on a number of regional economies, which were now largely centred on a single cash crop, often at the expense of other far more necessary foodstuffs. Along with the vast amounts of money, which was being taken out of each local economy through the new land taxes levied by the Company, many areas found it increasingly difficult to invest for the future, or indeed for the possibility of as yet unseen emergencies. From a purely agricultural point of view, one of the worst reported policies of the East India Company was said to have been its prohibition on local farmers from storing reserves of rice, something that was said to have been done for many generations, simply to counter the worst effects of any food shortages that might and often did arise. All of these policies were said to have contributed to the severity of the famine that began in 1769 and continued on and off until 1773, which was said to have culminated in the deaths of several million people during that time. According to some reporters, the East India Company's profits were said to have doubled over the same period, with much of their money coming from land taxes, the sale of largely inedible cash crops grown within the famine regions and even the export of foodstuffs that were being grown in India itself. However, it would be wrong to believe that such obviously thoughtless and inconsistent practices only ever occurred on the Indian subcontinent, as they clearly did not. During the mid 19th century similarly poor planning measures and a lack of emergency aid, were thought to have been a characteristic of the British government's response to the Irish Potato Famine, which was said to have occurred during that same period. Although it could never be suggested that there was a deliberate policy of starving people to death, a rigidly held belief in; and reliance on the prevailing economic theories of the day, which dictated that private enterprise would meet any and all demands, even for food, during periods of famine, was fatefully flawed and as a result, millions of starving people died.

Although the British East India Company were undoubtedly partially complicit in the deaths of those many Indians who died of starvation during the Bengal Famine of 1769 to 1773, it is also worth pointing out that the millions of dead referred to, are extremely rough estimates at best and even then, include those that not only died of starvation, but also its associated diseases, such as cholera and typhus. It has also been suggested by a number of reporters that large numbers of the local population within the Bengal area would have abandoned their homes and travelled to neighbouring regions in search of food and shelter, much as they have continued to do through to the present day. The British East India Company themselves, were first and foremost, a commercial operation that had little experience with the care and social administration of a large native population, a fact that was witnessed by its abject failure to both foresee and deal with the Bengal Famine in India. It was only in later years and following the increasing involvement of the British government in the Company's business practices that a centralised administration, more suited to deal with such civil emergencies, was actually put into place. It is also worth noting that a second famine, one that was reported to have blighted the regions of Uttar Pradesh, Eastern Punjab and Kashmir, occurred some after the Bengal Famine, between 1783-4. Known as the Chalisa Famine, this civil emergency was said to have caused the death of large numbers of the local population, although significantly these particular regions were reported to have been ruled by a number of native princes, rather than by British commercial interests.

Robert Clive   Siraj-ud-Duala   Mir Jafar

Yet another significant famine that was said to have blighted India in the final years of the 18th century was the Doji Bara or Skull Famine, which affected large areas of southern Asia, including India, from 1789 to 1795. Reportedly called the "Skull Famine" because of the sheer numbers of dead bodies that resulted from starvation, according to most sources, the large scale failure of crops throughout the region was thought to have been caused by a widespread drought brought on by El Nino weather conditions that affected the region between 1789 and 1795. As on other occasions, these adverse climatic changes were said to have combined with other factors, to create a human catastrophe of generally unparalleled scale, although in some areas of India, the effects were said to have been less severe due to the prompt actions of the East India Company, who were thought to have learned some lessons from earlier famine disasters and put emergency measures in place. Despite this however, large areas of the country were said to have been temporarily depopulated, until eventually the worst effects of the drought had passed away. During the 1866 famine, which affected the regions of Bengal and Orissa, the British authorities were reported to have responded in a fairly mixed and haphazard way, with relief supplies being brought into some areas, but failing to provide them in others, until it was much too late. In Bengal the British response was thought to have reasonably good, whereas in Orissa it was said to have been extremely poor, although according to the British administrators there at the time, a contributing factor to the famine, was reported to have been the unexpected closure of the regions main harbour, which prevented relief food supplies being brought in as quickly as they would have liked. Although the authority's failure to properly estimate the level of need, was a central factor to the resulting loss of life, the fact that the British authorities actually tried to bring in some ten thousand tonnes of food, of which only a fraction was delivered, points not only to their incompetence, but also to their absolute sincerity. By 1874, the British response to the prospect of an impending famine was reported to have been much more successful and widespread starvation was thought to have been avoided. Two years later however, the British Viceroy, Lord Lytton, was said to have applied his own personal views to the threat of yet another crop shortage, by suggesting that the market alone, should be relied upon to feed those that were starving, the same policy, which had earlier been applied to Ireland; and once again resulting in the same disastrous loss of life. Although most British Viceroy's were not quite as short-sighted as Lord Lytton, even after he had been replaced in his post the actual amount and level of famine relief generally remained in the hands of the individual British representative. A later holder of the office, Lord Curzon, was reported to have introduced means testing for those who required famine relief and as a result of his strictly enforced limits; millions of more starving people were thought to have died. Despite the personal initiatives and theories of men like Lytton and Curzon though, the latter part of the 19th century was thought to have marked a period of change and development, in the way that the British authorities dealt with the issues and causes of these regularly occurring famines. The widespread construction of canal and irrigation systems within the country undoubtedly helped to reduce the twin threats of drought and flood, whilst at the same time, far greater importance was said to have been given to the storing of food reserves, which could be used during times of need. From 1902 onwards the incidents of widespread famine and starvation was thought to have been significantly reduced within India, with only the 1943 famine, replicating the worst levels of earlier shortages. It is also perhaps worth noting that Britain's experience with famines, undoubtedly helped the British authorities to develop the "famine mix", which was successfully used towards the end of World War II, to help feed the many thousands of malnourished inmates, who had been rescued from the Nazi Concentration Camps at Bergen Belsen and elsewhere.

Right through to the end of the 18th century, the Company continued to expand its operations throughout the sub-continent and in 1799 the region of Mysore, which previously been supported by French interests, fell to the military forces of the East India Company, after its legendary ruler Tipu Sultan was killed in battle. Traditionally known as the "Tiger of Mysore", Tipu Sultan was renowned in India, for being the only native Indian prince that ever dictated terms to the British East India Company, after he and his father had fought the British to a standstill during the Second Mysore War. Following his succession to the throne of the Mysore Sultanate however, he was reported to have fought and been defeated in two subsequent campaigns against the British East India Company, who had by then allied themselves with neighbouring states and traditional enemies of the Sultan. He was said to have been a devout Muslim, but a man who was prepared to respect the rights and beliefs of his Hindu countrymen, although most modern historians are highly divided on this particular subject, with some believing that most of the negative stories relating to the ruler, are little more than British inspired propaganda, which was designed to excuse their later punitive actions against him. Either way, there is little doubt that Tipu Sultan was one of the most famous and capable military rulers that ever held power within the Indian subcontinent, who ruthlessly and effectively defeated most of the native armies that ever faced him in battle and who was only finally beaten when his enemies combined to destroy him. Reportedly dying on the battlements of his capital, Srirangapattana, in May 1799, at the age of 48, Tipu Sultan's memory would later come back to haunt his British adversaries some years later, when his son would become the figurehead for native rebels during the Vellore Mutiny of 1806. Elsewhere, the Company's forces under the likes of Arthur Wellesley, later the Duke of Wellington, were helping to overcome the Marathra Dynasty, which helped British interests to acquire the city of Bombay. By the dawn of the 19th century, much of southern India was reported to have been under the Company's complete control, with only northern parts of the mainland still held by their traditional native rulers, although many of these, were either being cajoled, coerced or threatened into making agreements with the British East India Company. In what was and remained common practice for the Company, an underlying policy of "divide and conquer" was thought to have been used in dealing with these native states, ensuring that they could never mount a unified opposition to British interests, which as it turned out, proved to be a highly effective and profitable strategy for the East India Company and its representatives.

However, despite its virtual monopoly of the eastern trading routes and markets, by the last quarter of the 18th century the East India Company was said to be seeing its profit margins dwindle, as worldwide demand for its products, shareholder dividends, British taxes and increasing interest payments on its massive loans, began to cut away at its bottom line. It also seems clear that the actual cost of defending and administering these vast lands, was proving to be a daily drain on the profits actually being earned from their ownership. Although the Industrial Revolution had initially helped to introduce greater efficiencies and profits for many companies, it had also brought with it a commercial depression, caused in part by the huge overabundance of manufactured materials that were being produced, forcing some companies into bankruptcy and forfeiture. In response to this, the directors of the East India Company, along with their Parliamentary lobbyists were said to have approached the British government and asked for help from their financial difficulties. As a result of this request, in 1773 the Company were granted some relief on the Tea Tax, imposed by the British legislature, which helped to benefit the shareholders of the Company, but at the same time disadvantaged other tea traders who found their businesses seriously undermined by these cheaper Company supplies. American tea merchants especially, were said to have been outraged by the preferential treatment offered to the East India Company, which was now importing this tax exempt tea into ports like Boston and effectively undercutting local American tea supplier's prices. Although the British government which had initially agreed the deal undoubtedly wondered what all the fuss was about, it was thought to be this incident, along with other taxation issues, which would ultimately lead to the loss of Britain's North American colonies and the subsequent foundations of the United States.

Even though the Company had been granted an exemption on the Tea Tax, the British legislature in London also introduced a series of new regulations that gave them greater oversight and authority over the Company's trading activities, despite some resistance from Company directors, shareholders and lobbyists. The biggest change saw a formal understanding of the East India Company's implicit subservience to the British Crown and Britain's ultimate sovereignty over the lands that the Company held under its own control. Rather than these possessions being assets of the Company, it was clearly understood that they were in fact British Crown possessions, leased to the East India Company at a cost of around £40,000 for every two years that they were held. The British government also insisted that a new Governor General was appointed in Bengal to hold both administrative and legislative control over all of India, thereby centralising the Company's operations in these eastern territories. Finally and in addition to these other changes, the Government set out to establish a new Council, which was designed to oversee the behaviour of the new Governor General and to help install a new judicial system, which would be staffed by British personnel, sent out specially to achieve this task. However, despite all of these regulatory and administrative changes, it was stressed that the British East India Company would remain as the de facto head of the Company's day-to-day operation in the Indian sub-continent, with the government back in Britain playing little part in its commercial activities. Unfortunately for those who had been involved with this restructuring of the Company's role, its financial fortunes still continued to decline, a situation that was not helped by the additional levy of £20,000 per annum, which was imposed on the balance sheet by the government of the day. As a result, in 1784, further regulations were applied to the Company's role, with a new Board of Commissioners being appointed to oversee the political and civil control of the Indian sub-continent, which included the introduction of a new centralised administrative bureaucracy, a feature of Indian life that would remain and evolve well into the 20th century. Two years later in 1786 a further Parliamentary Act was passed, which essentially put both the political and military control of India in the hands of the Governor General, who then became the military Commander-in-chief of the Indian sub-continent.

By 1813, the East India Company was reported to have pretty much taken full control of the Indian mainland, with the exception of the Punjab, Sindh and Nepal regions, as most native rulers by that time, had chosen to become vassals of the Company, rather than remain independent and risk conflict with the British. However, the cost of making such alliances, were thought to have proved to be expensive for the East India Company and around the same time, they were reported to have gone back to the British government once again for financial help. This time however, government aid was said to have cost them their trade monopoly within India, with the exception of their tea trade, their trade links with China, as well as agreeing to open India up for numbers of western missionaries, who were keen to begin spreading the word of God amongst the population of this largely unknown country. Although the Company obviously failed to recognise the problems that such evangelising individuals might cause them in the future, it was thought to be this act, as much as any other, which would help to bring instability and rebellion to India that, would culminate in the deaths of thousands of people. Some twenty years later, the East India Company's financial situation was said to be still relatively poor and was said to be failing to benefit from the widespread laissez faire economics that the Industrial Revolution was thought to be offering elsewhere in Britain's colonies. As a result the Company had to go once more "cap in hand" to the British government for help, this time sacrificing its remaining trade monopolies in the region, allowing the Board of Trade to take overall control of its activities, permit the increased centralised administration of India, as well as allowing more political and military control to be vested in the person of the Governor General. Despite its loss of control and authority over Indian affairs however, such agreements with the British government were said to have allowed the Company to keep going, so that by 1845 it had managed to recover some of its financial losses, most notably by extending its trading links and influence into countries such as the Philippines, China and Java.

Although the British East India Company was thought to have been generally successful in trying to extend its influence and its trading operations, in and around the Chinese mainland, unfortunately for them, trade with this great untapped marketplace was disproportionately weighed in the Chinese traders favour, with the East India Company buying huge amounts of Chinese Tea for the European markets, but lacking the products to import into China itself, in order to redress this critical trade imbalance. As a result the Company was thought to be using vitally needed funds, to purchase tea stocks, rather than trading their other manufactured goods for them, a situation that might eventually prove perilous for the Company's financial survival. However, it soon became apparent to the East India Company that there was one product that the Chinese would take in trade and that was Opium, widely used for medicinal purposes, but a highly addictive drug, which the Chinese Quing Dynasty was desperately keen to control. Regardless of such concerns however, the Company was said to have established extensive poppy growing centres in northern India, often in spite of local opposition, which were then processed and shipped to China, in order to balance the Company's trading figures with the region. Eventually the amount of Opium being delivered into China was said to have been so enormous that its uses went well beyond general medical use and was commonly being used by the Chinese population for recreational purposes. However, given the addictive nature of the Opium, it soon became apparent to the Chinese authorities that its widespread availability, was extremely damaging both to the national economy, but also to society generally and immediately put in place legislation to outlaw the importation and sale of the drug. In 1838 a new Chinese Governor, Lin Zexu was appointed to stamp out the trade and introduced new legislation, which meant that those found guilty of trafficking in Opium, faced an automatic death sentence, which not only helped to suppress much of the illicit trade, but also posed a real financial threat to the future of British East India Company. As a result, armed conflict between the two sides soon broke out, leading to a series of Opium Wars between 1839-1842 that resulted in the creation of several Treaty Ports on the Chinese mainland, as well as the seizure of Hong Kong by the British.

Although individual and generally isolated incidents of rebellion by native Indian troops or Sepoys, were known to have occurred on a fairly regular basis during the long rule of the British East India Company, most of which were caused by the Company's own high-handed and thoughtless approach to the local population, in most cases, these outbreaks of violence were quickly and easily contained by the Company themselves. However, the Indian Sepoy Mutiny of 1857 was thought to have been entirely different, both in terms of its viciousness and its scale; and was deemed to be so serious by the British Government in London that it brought to an end the Company's rule in India, after some 250 years. The most notable Indian Sepoy rebellion prior to the Great Mutiny of 1857 was the Vellore Mutiny of 1806, which is regarded by some as a warning that the British East India Company either deliberately, or accidentally missed, much to their own cost in later years. Occurring on July 10th 1806, this particular rebellion by native Sepoys, was said to have lasted for a single day, but resulted in a large number of deaths amongst both British troops and their Indian adversaries. The mutiny itself, was said to have resulted from resentment amongst the Sepoy ranks, caused by the East India Company enforcing a new dress code on its native troops, which not only banned traditional Hindu marks being worn on the face or forehead, but also insisted that Muslim soldiers shaved their beards and moustaches, all of which were likely to cause an affront to these deeply religious soldiers. Matters were said to have come to a head, when a number of the Sepoys refused to accept these changes and were immediately arrested and sent to the Company's headquarters at Fort St George for punishment. Of the troops sent to the fort, a Muslim Sepoy, along with a Hindu one, were chosen to be flogged as examples to the rest of their comrades, each of them reportedly receiving nine hundred lashes, before having their service with the Company terminated. A further nineteen Sepoys were also said to have been flogged, being given a reported five hundred lashes each, before being forced to beg for a pardon from the officers of the East India Company. The punishment inflicted on the men was thought to have caused even greater bitterness and resentment amongst the remaining Sepoys, a discontent that was easily manipulated and used by the sons of the defeated native leader, Tipu Sultan, who were being held captive in the base. They began to put in place, plans for an attack on the East India Company's post at Fort St George, a strategy that was helped by the fact that one of their sisters, who was also being confined within the base, was due to be married there, presumably with the Company's permission. On the pretext of attending the wedding, a number of plotters and their supporters were able to gain entry to the military compound; and on the afternoon of 10th July 1806 began to put their plans into action.

Lord Curzon

Lord Lytton

Tipu Sultan

Along with other native allies located outside of the base, the rebels immediately began attacking members of the garrison and any other European that they happened to come across. Their surprise attack was said to have been so successful that by dawn of he following day, the rebels had gained control over much of the fort and were reported to have raised the flag of the Mysore Sultanate over the British base and declared Tipu Sultan's second son, Fateh Hyder as their new king. Unfortunately for the rebels, their new ruler and their cause, one of the British officers from the fort had managed to escape and make his way to the East India Company post at Arcot and raise the alarm. Within thirty minutes of the alert being sounded, a relief force was reported to have been assembled and despatched to rescue any of the remaining British garrison at Vellore, a force headed by a highly capable military officer, Sir Rollo Gillespie. Under his command, elements of the 19th Light Dragoons and the Madras Cavalry were said to have galloped ahead of the main relief column and having reached the fort, Gillespie and a small contingent of his men managed to scramble over the battlements and link up with a small detachment of men from the garrison, who were being led by a number of NCOs and two military surgeons. This small group of men had been forced to take shelter on the ramparts during the rebel attack on the base, but were now completely out of ammunition and being increasingly threatened by the rebel forces, who had taken over the fortress. Gillespie immediately took control of the embattled party of survivors; and led them in a bayonet charge against the rebels, thereby relieving their position and preparing the way for the arrival of his own remaining men and the much larger British relief force.

With the arrival of his main force of Dragoons and Madras Cavalry, Gillespie reportedly ordered these men to blow open the main gates of the fort using their galloper guns and having done so they rushed forward to join Gillespie and the survivors. As they pressed further into the fortresses precincts, they were said to have cut down every rebel that they encountered and as they became aware of the merciless nature of the rebels own attack on the base, so they too were said to have been unremitting in their treatment of the rebel Sepoys. According to reports from the time, a group of around one hundred Sepoys who had previously taken refuge in a nearby palace, were said to have dragged from their hiding places, stood in front of the palace's walls and were despatched using canister shot. Even though some of the watching British officers were thought to have been appalled by the sight, most of them agreed that this was simply summary justice, no matter how terrible it might be. The swift and brutal retribution of the East India Company's forces was said to have brought an almost immediate end to the simmering discontent which had been behind the attack and that might have threatened the whole region had it been allowed to continue. By the end of the engagement, between six and eight hundred native Sepoys were thought to have been killed, with a further three hundred suffering some form of injury. The royal prisoners, the children of Tipu Sultan, who were said to have played a leading role in the rebellion, were subsequently transferred to new quarters in Calcutta, whilst the Company's local governor, William Bentinck, was thought to have been replaced. It was also reported that the changes in the Indian Sepoys dress code, which was thought to have caused much of the problem in the first place were subsequently rescinded and the practice of flogging native troops was also abolished. Unfortunately, the Company obviously failed to learn any long term lessons from this early bloody rebellion, as history later proved that it was many of these very same reasons, which brought about yet another mutiny some 50-odd years later.

The causes of the Great Indian Mutiny were thought to be many and varied, but were generally thought to have been brought about by the East India Company's unremitting interference in the religious, political and cultural life of the native population. The spark for the mutiny itself was said to have been lit amongst the ranks of the largely native troops who helped support the rule of the Company within India, men from all castes and both major religions, whose beliefs and allegiances were fundamentally challenged by the introduction of what appeared to be a fairly innocuous item, a new rifle cartridge. Although there were said to be a number of underlying causes for the mutiny, including resentment over pay and conditions, pensions and promotions, the new rifle cartridge was thought to be the final straw for many native of the native soldiers. The new cartridges for the Indian Sepoy's 1853 Enfield rifles were said to have required the soldiers to bite through the outer case of the gunpowder pack, before pouring the powder into the barrel of the rifle, ready to receive the shot itself. Almost immediately, rumours began to circulate amongst both the largely Hindu and Muslim troops that the cartridge cases had been greased with both cow and pig fat, both of which were untouchable to the native troops. Although there appears to have been little truth to these rumours, it was later thought that they had been started by local native leaders, who were bitterly opposed to British rule and knew that the mere idea of such animal products would make the cartridges unusable by the highly religious Indian Sepoys. The escalating situation was said to have been made worse, by the attitude of some Company officers, who tried to override the Sepoys concerns by simply ordering them to use the cartridge or face Company punishment. To make matters even worse, a military secretary was said to have issued an order, requiring all cartridges to be cleaned of grease, thereby confirming the suspicious Sepoys that their fears were well founded, even though in reality the animal fat probably never existed to begin with.

The issue of the cartridges themselves was just the last of many native grievances, which had been caused by the East India Company's administration and rule of the Indian sub-continent. Within the wider native community, the introduction of new legislation on inheritance, the arrival of large numbers of western Christian evangelists, the large scale seizure and acquisition of land and increasingly severe taxes all combined to cause a simmering resentment amongst the native peoples of India. Seemingly indifferent to local concerns, the Company were reported to have taken little action to curb the spread and influence of newly arrived Christian groups, who were keen to try and convert many of the mainly Hindu and Muslim believers, to their supposedly true faith. Even European officers within the Company's military forces, were said to have actively participated in this unwanted and unwelcome evangelical campaign, causing great consternation and suspicion amongst the ranks of the increasingly vital native troops. The local Indian leadership, many of whom were from the titled and landed classes, had already become disgruntled with British rule, not least because of the introduction of new legislation that was known as the Doctrine of Lapse, laws that related to local inheritance practices that were commonplace in Indian life and tradition. Historically, Indian landowners and rulers had been able to name their own heirs and successors, regardless of whether or not they were immediate relatives. However, without any sort of consultation with the native population, the East India Company was reported to have arbitrarily introduced new laws, which prevented the passing of lands and assets to anyone other than an immediate relative, or to those that the Company regarded as legitimate heirs, such as a son, etc. This meant that any landowner or ruler, who died without such a legitimate heir, would automatically surrender their lands and possessions to the East India Company, who grew increasingly rich and powerful through such highly questionable and probably illegal practices. As a result of such acquisitions, which saw many thousands of tenants, servants and soldiers thrown out of work and out of their homes, the Company inadvertently helped to create a simmering mass of resentment throughout large parts of India, a body of people who would help to fuel the fire of mutiny, when the army Sepoy's finally rebelled in 1857.

Although it seems unlikely that the Company deliberately exercised any sort policy that accounted for a climate of indifference or discrimination towards the native people of India, the old adage of "familiarity breeding contempt" seems to have become particularly applicable as time passed by. The longer that the Company retained control of the sub-continent and its people, so less concerned they were thought to have become regarding the treatment of those who had to live under their rule, especially if that population were seen to be hampering the Company's profit making aims. This approach was undoubtedly added to by widespread racial discrimination practiced by the European officers and men who were employed by the Company, many of whom were either simple adventurers, men of low repute, or soldiers who came from the lowest tiers of British society and who were keen to exploit their supposedly superior standing amongst the native Indian troops. Large numbers of British aristocrats and wealthy merchants were said to have sent their younger sons to pursue careers in the far-off and exotic lands of India, simply as a way of keeping them occupied. Often military commissions would be purchased by wealthy fathers, in order that their sons might be given the opportunity to make their own careers or fortunes in these mysterious faraway lands, regardless of whether or not the son had any military abilities at all, which in most cases they did not. By actively employing a "divide and conquer" approach amongst the various native "castes" which existed within the Indian military contingents, the officers and men of the European forces hoped to maintain their total control over the Company's native troops. It was also reported that native Sepoy's found it much more difficult to complain about their treatment, with the Company employing, a much more protracted complaints procedure for native troops than for their European counterparts, which led most native troops to have little confidence in their officers, or indeed the Company itself.

This perceived disregard of Indian culture, customs and practices, along with the increasing westernisation of Indian society helped to underpin a nationalist movement that wanted to see an end to British rule in India once and for all. However, it was only when these attitudes began to infiltrate into the ranks of the Indian Sepoy Army that local leaders could see their opportunity finally arrive. As Sepoy confidence in their officers began to wane, so instances such as the greased rifle cartridges were said to have gained even greater significance, increasing the likelihood that some sort of rebellion would break out amongst these armed soldiers. Local native Indian Sepoys, had been employed by the British East India Company from the very earliest days of trading in the sub-continent, with numbers rising exponentially as the Company increased its holdings and influence in the region. Typically such men were thought to have been recruited from the higher caste, more martial tribes of India, who were overseen and commanded by East India Company officers, many of whom had been trained at the Company's own military schools back in Britain. Traditionally trained British officers and experienced NCOs were said to have been present in relatively small numbers, with only around forty thousand European soldiers posted to the whole of India at their peak. The Company's combined military force of an estimated quarter of a million men were reported to have been broken down into three distinct regional armies, which were centred around three main areas, Bombay, Madras and Bengal. In common with the rest of Indian society, these native army units were based on and influenced by the social "caste" system, which regarded some native ethnic groups as being superior or inferior to other groups. These beliefs and practices were thought to have been a significant factor in the Mutiny of 1857, especially amongst the so-called higher caste soldiers of both major religions, who believed that their rights were being infringed. Although the Company was reported to have taken steps to protect the various rights of the Hindu and Muslim Sepoys, such as allowing them to dine separately and permitting them to practice their individual religious ceremonies, by 1857 an increased level of distrust was thought to have existed between the three main parties, the British, the Hindu's and the Muslims. Apart from changes to Indian life, introduced by the Company, including the infamous Doctrine of Lapse and the burgeoning number of Christian missionaries entering the country, changes to the Sepoy's previously agreed terms of service were also thought to caused great consternation amongst the ranks of these native troops. Previously, local Indian troops were not required to serve outside of their home regions, but with the expansion of the Company's operations throughout the wider sub-continent, to places like Burma, led to many of these Indian Sepoys being deployed to foreign parts, often without being properly consulted about it first or without being compensated for their foreign service.

The Indian Mutiny, otherwise known as the Great Mutiny, Sepoy Mutiny or by most Indians as, the First War of Independence was reported to have begun in the town of Meerut on 10th May 1857 and was started by previously loyal Sepoy's rebelling against the forces of the British East India Company. What began as a fairly limited local revolt, very quickly escalated into an almost national uprising, which culminated in tens of thousands of Indian soldiers, either refusing to follow orders or directly attacking British and European interests throughout mainland India. Out of a total of around two hundred thousand native troops employed by the Company at the time, only an estimated fifteen thousand were said to have remained loyal to the British administration and were prepared to follow orders. In Delhi, there were reports of European's being attacked and killed by roving bands of rebel soldiers who were often accompanied by large numbers of Indian civilians, who took advantage of the situation, in order to exact their own retribution on the foreign enclaves. Although the mutiny in Meerut was reported to have begun as a single act of rebellion by native Indian troops, its outbreak led to a series of associated revolts and uprisings throughout many of India's northern states including Uttar Pradesh, Bihar, Madhya, Pradesh and Delhi. The opening act of the mutiny was said to have occurred in February 1857, when native troops from the 19th Bengal Native Infantry were said to have become aware of the rumours regarding the new Enfield cartridges. Almost immediately both Hindu and Muslim troops refused to use the cartridges; and when their British commander was informed of this fact he threatened the Sepoy's with artillery and cavalry, if they failed to obey their orders. Fortunately, in this particular incident, commonsense was thought to have prevailed and the commander subsequently withdrew his threat, but not before deciding to cancel the regimental parade due to take place the following day.

The first clear act of defiance by native troops was reported to have taken place the following month, in March 1857, when a single soldier of the 34th Bengal Native Industry expressed his resistance to British rule and refused to take orders from his superiors. As he tried to incite his fellow Sepoy's to join his resistance, a British officer on horseback was said to have approached the soldier, who opened fire on the officer, but only managed to shoot the horse instead. The British company commander immediately ordered a native NCO to arrest the soldier, but he refused the order, although he made no move to support or join the first man's rebellion. As a result of their action and inaction, both the first Sepoy and his NCO, were reported to have been hung for their acts of defiance. Despite the limit of the revolt, which essentially comprised a single man, the East India Company were said to have made an example of the entire regiment, by disbanding the whole unit and publicly humiliating a large number of entirely innocent Sepoy's by stripping them of their uniforms and weapons; and sending them on their way to an uncertain future. According to some historians, many of these dismissed Sepoy's were thought to have returned to their homes seething with anger over their treatment by the British East India Company, with some of these same men later playing an active role in inciting the countrywide rebellion that gripped much of British India. During much of March 1857, there were thought to have been sporadic outbreaks of unrest throughout large parts of British controlled India, including in Agra, Allahabad and Ambala, with regular arson attacks on various military stations and government buildings. Anger and discontent about the new Enfield rifle cartridges continued to simmer amongst the ranks of the Company's Hindu and Muslim Sepoy's, although there were no reports of any armed rebellions, actually taking place at any of the Company's military bases. That situation suddenly and dramatically changed however at Meerut in April 1857, when a British Lieutenant-Colonel called Carmichael Smyth, who was commanding the 3rd Bengal Light Cavalry, ordered a detachment of his native troops to participate in a live firing drill, reportedly using the new and greased Enfield rifle cartridges. Only five members of the troop agreed to use the supposedly untouchable ammunition, with the remaining eighty five men refusing to do so. Two weeks later, virtually all of these Sepoys were said to have been brought before a military court and court-martialled for their refusal to obey orders, with most of them sentenced to ten years hard labour for their trouble.

However, not content with simply jailing them, the Company representatives seemed to have been bound and determined to make their suffering worse, by publicly parading the Sepoys in front of their former comrades, who were lined up in ranks to witness their humiliation. Having been stripped of their uniforms the chained prisoners were then marched away to begin their long jail sentences, but as they were being led away many of them were said to have publicly berated their former comrades, for failing to support them and for agreeing to use the reportedly tainted rifle cartridges. The following day, the 10th April 1857, was a Sunday and in common with most Europeans, many of the East India Company's officers and NCOs in Meerut were thought to have been off-duty, attending church services, spending time with their families and friends, or simply visiting the local bazaars and canteens for entertainment. Military command of Meerut was thought to have been left in the hands of a small number of junior officers, who began to receive reports from a number of loyal Sepoys that a number of disaffected Indian soldiers were planning to release those prisoners who had just been jailed by the military court, but despite being warned beforehand, the junior officers apparently took no action to reinforce the defences. On the Sunday evening, a number of rebel Sepoys suddenly rebelled against their officers, reportedly attacking and killing a number of the junior officers who tried to stop them. The rebel troops then began attacking and burning both military and civilian accommodation, during which an unknown number of local civilians, including men, women and children perished. In the town of Meerut itself, more rebel Sepoys, accompanied by crowds from the local Indian community, began attacking European soldiers and civilians who were visiting the town centre, or those that owned businesses there. Elsewhere, other members of the rebel Sepoy force were said to have broken into the local jail, freed their eighty-odd former comrades and also released several hundred other common criminals who were being held in the prison.

Although a large number of Sepoys were reported to have remained loyal to the East India Company, whilst others joined in the rebellion, there were those who ensured that their British officers and their families were safe, before finally abandoning their posts and joining in the revolt. However, some of those loyal Indians who were employed as house servants by the British families and who helped to steal them away from danger, were later thought to have paid the price for their faithfulness, by falling victim to the roving bands of vengeful rebels that were sweeping through the streets of the town. Even though the numbers and manner of European deaths as a result of the rebellion was comparatively small, as against total native Indian deaths, in the British controlled media of India and at home in Britain, the numbers and manner of these deaths were thought to have been greatly exaggerated leading to disproportionately vicious British reprisals later on. Even though more senior British officers soon became aware of the rebellion amongst the Indian Sepoy ranks, they were said to have been particularly slow to respond to the increasingly violent events, which was undoubtedly due in part to the fact that the most senior officer in the field, was a 70-year-old Major General Hewitt, a man who was reportedly in poor physical health and completely unprepared for the turbulent events that were happening around him. Possibly unsure of the level of support that he could rely on, it was said to be through his actions that those troops that he could muster were simply assembled around the military base and Company armoury, remaining there until the following morning, before setting out to confront the rebel Sepoys and their attendant civilian rioters. The only flaw with Hewitt's plan however, was that by the time his forces had left their compound, many of the rebel soldiers and their riotous supporters had already left Meerut and moved onto Delhi, where they could wreak even more death and destruction on the European settlers.

Rollo Gillespie   **William Bentinck**   **Bahadur Shah**

In the city of Delhi itself, large bands of rebel Sepoys, along with many thousands of rioters were said to have congregated beneath the walls of the Red Fort, home to their most obvious and highest profile native leader, the Mughal Emperor, Bahadur Shah, who they called upon to lead their fight against the British. However, Bahadur Shah was said to have been a skilful and pragmatic politician, who rather than risk alienating either the native people, or the East India Company, tried to play for time, until he could be sure which of the two competing parties was likely to be victorious in the unfolding conflict. Meanwhile, in the streets of Delhi itself, Sepoys and their supporters were said to be busy ransacking European owned businesses, attacking and killing Company officials and their dependents, as well members of minority religious groups, such as the Indian Christians. At least three other Bengali Infantry Battalions were reported to have been stationed in Delhi at the time and although many of these troops were said to have joined the rebellion, a significant number initially chose not to do so, choosing instead to stand aside and take no action whatsoever. However, by the afternoon of the same day, many more Sepoy's were thought to have joined the rebellion, a decision reportedly made after a local ammunition store was deliberately blown up by a contingent of British officers who feared that the arms might fall into rebel hands, although it was an act, which accidentally caused great death and destruction amongst the local community; and helped to push many undecided native soldiers firmly into the rebel camp. Even though the demolition of the arsenal prevented these particular munitions from falling into the rebel hands, elsewhere in the city, a number of ammunition stores did fall into the Sepoy's possession, with several hundred barrels of gunpowder and assorted arms being seized by the rebels and later used by these same native troops.

Panic was said to have gripped members of the European community living in Delhi, along with the many native Indians who earned their livings directly from them, many of whom were thought to have remained loyal to the families that they served. Both military and civilian personnel who managed to avoid the rampaging rebel mobs began to make their way to the Flagstaff Tower, a Company building, located on the outskirts of Delhi, where they hoped to create a defensive redoubt, in which they could take shelter until help arrived. Telegraph operators at the redoubt began sending out news of the rebellion to outlying stations, confident that these messages would be passed on to other British military forces that would come to their rescue. Desperate to escape the violence in Delhi some Europeans were able to get out of the city before the worst of the rioting began and made their way to the town of Karnal, whilst other Europeans who were unable to reach the Flagstaff Tower chose to make the way to Karnal as well, although a number of these refugees were said to have fallen victim to groups of rebellious Sepoys or fell into the hands of local bandits with the same fatal result. Back at Bahadur Shah's palace, the generally powerless Indian Mughal Emperor, was said to have finally made his mind up on the 12th May 1857, and decided to give his approval to the rebellion, although he was said to have been concerned about the levels of violence being used by some of the rebels. With or without Shah's knowledge on May 16th 1857 a group of around fifty Europeans, who were said to have been captured in by the rebels in Delhi, were killed in cold-blood by a number of Bahadur Shah's servants and their bodies later disposed of. The decision to support the uprising, ultimately proved to be a huge mistake for the last official Mughal Emperor of India, as following the suppression of the mutiny by

British forces, he was deposed and exiled to Burma in 1857, bringing an end to his family's three hundred year rule within the subcontinent.

In other parts of India, thus far immune to the rebellion, numbers of the East India Company's officers, both military and civilian, were reported to have abandoned their posts, in order to ensure the safety of their own family and friends. Such a noticeable level of desertion amongst the Company's military officers and civil administrators was said to have encouraged local Sepoys and political agitators in these particular areas, leading the rebellion to spread well beyond its original starting point. However, even in those regions where the local military forces and civil administrators remained in place, it was often difficult for the Company to keep control and prevent local instances of rebellion. This was because the Company was thought to lack any sort of co-ordinated and centralised strategy for dealing with this kind of large-scale emergency, simply because they were first and foremost a trading company, rather than a full-time civil and military administration. On the ground, some Company officers implicitly trusted their Indian Sepoys and made no move to disarm them, while elsewhere other Indian units, were forcibly disarmed by their European commanders, who were then left with no viable military force with which to maintain order. Despite the fact that the rebellion appeared to be quite widespread, reaching many parts of the Indian mainland, its actual aims and leadership were fragmented, with little agreement between any of the individual participants. These divisions helped to prevent the revolt becoming a total and unmitigated disaster for the Company and the many Europeans who were resident in the country and made their livings there. Fortunately for the British authorities, the numerous and historic antagonisms, which was said to have existed between the various tribal groups that inhabited the sub-continent, resulted in Muslims fighting Hindu's, Sikhs and Pathans and therefore preventing the rebellion becoming what the British feared most, a national and unified crusade aimed at driving them out of India altogether.

Fortunately, some of the country's leading martial tribes, such as the Sikhs, Pathans and Ghurkhas continued to actively support the British authorities, whilst many Muslim and Hindu troops also remained loyal to their British employers, regardless of the many insults and humiliations that had been heaped upon them by the administrators of the East Indian Company. For many of these men, who had sworn an oath of loyalty to the Company and therefore to Britain, the rebellion represented an extremely serious breach of faith by their countrymen and was an insult that had to be remedied. Of the three major standing armies employed by the Company, the Bengali Army was said to have seen the greatest number of losses, with many native soldiers joining the rebellion itself and many more units being quickly disbanded by an employer, who had started to question their reliability and their loyalty. Up to two thirds of the Army's infantry regiments were said to have disappeared, along with virtually all of the Bengali Light Cavalry regiments, most of who simply returned home and played no active part in the insurrection, although some undoubtedly did join the rebel forces. These losses contrasted markedly with the remaining two Company armies, which were based in and around the two main British trading centres of Bombay and Madras and which were reported to have suffered very few incidents of rebellion within their ranks. Of the twenty-odd regiments that made up the Bombay Army there were reported to be only a handful of incidents, where individual soldiers rebelled against Company rule and in the Madras Army there was said to be not a single instance of a Sepoy rebelling against his British commanders. Such levels of fidelity was thought to be a reflection of the actual troops employed within these military units, who included Ghurkhas, Sikhs, Punjabis and other various ethnic groups, who had been specifically recruited from the regions of the North West Frontier. Along with their own European officers and men the Company was said to have suffered few outbreaks of rebellion within the southern parts of India, which was a tribute to the faithfulness of the native troops that held these areas of the Indian sub-continent.

Gandhi   Reginald Dyer   Michael O'Dwyer

The two most infamous acts of brutality perpetrated by rebel Sepoys and their native leadership was thought to be the massacres of Cawnpore and Bibigarh, both of which helped to colour British attitudes and prejudices towards the rebellious troops and even towards the largely innocent Indian population as a whole. During the Sepoy Mutiny, the city of Cawnpore had been besieged by rebel forces, preventing a large number of Europeans from escaping the city and making their way to the safety of Allahabad. Having resisted the initial onslaught of the rebellious Indian forces, the local Indian leader Nana Sahib was reported to have agreed that the trapped Europeans, who included men, women and children would be given safe conduct to the local river, where they could embark on river boats and sail down the waterway to Allahabad. However, having reached the river and started to embark, gunfire erupted between the rebels and the European party, which resulted in most of the men in the party being killed or wounded. By the time the firing had stopped, virtually all of the men were dead and the surviving European women, along with their children were hauled back to Cawnpore and imprisoned in the courtyard of the local Magistrates house, which was called a Bibigarh. Although the rebel sources later denied that they had fired first, in British minds, there was no doubt that the rebels had initiated the firing and had fully intended to massacre the European party right from the outset. Meanwhile the party of around one hundred and twenty European women and children were said to have been joined in the Bibigarh, by even more foreign captives, who had subsequently been taken by the rampaging rebel forces. During the time that these two hundred people were being held prisoner at the Magistrates house, a significant number of the hostages were thought to have died of ill-treatment, disease and as a result of the wounds they had received at the riverbank massacre. Although it has often been suggested that the rebel leadership had initially intended to release the Europeans to sail down the river to Allahabad, as soon as the first shot was fired and the first European killed, then this plan had quickly unravelled and they were then at a complete loss as to what action to take. It seems likely that the rebel's revised plan, was to hold hostages as a bargaining chip with the British authorities, but even this idea soon went the way of the first. In the meantime, a British relief force was reported to have been despatched to suppress the rebellion around Cawnpore and to rescue the hostages that were being held by the rebels. Perhaps alarmed by this news and fearing the vengeance of the British forces, once they had discovered the evidence of the first massacre, the local native leaders then committed their second and even greater atrocity.

Recognising perhaps that the surviving women and children were eye-witnesses to the first massacre, the native leadership ultimately determined that they too had to die, in order to suppress the truth about the riverside killings. Initially, local Sepoys were asked to commit the odious task, but virtually all of them refused the order, ostensibly because they knew that it would be a criminal act that the British would be bound to avenge in the most terrible fashion. With none of the native rebels willing to commit such a heinous act, Nana Sahib was said to have looked elsewhere for willing assassins and were reported to have found them in the shape of two local butchers and some native peasants, who were all willing to overlook the moral implications of their actions, for a handful of treasure. Having entered the compound wielding a collection of cleavers, knives and hatchets, the killers were reported to have carved their way through the ranks of cowering hostages, massacring the men, women and children, until they were all dead or dying. To hide the evidence of their heinous crime, the killers were then said to have thrown the dead and the dying down a deep well, located in the courtyard of the Magistrates house and quickly made their escape. Unfortunately for them and their Indian paymaster, British forces quickly relieved the city and discovered evidence of this second murderous attack, which brought about a disproportionately severe round of reprisals against any rebels who were unfortunate enough to be captured and against the Indian population generally. Even in Britain itself, the wave of revulsion felt by the general public, once the crimes were discovered and publicly reported, meant that any sort of British reprisal was acceptable, given the type of crimes that had been committed at Cawnpore. The call "Remember Cawnpore" was said to have become a rallying cry for British interests in India and the vengeance of the British forces who had relieved the city, was both swift and severe. Hundreds of Indian rebels who were captured in and around the city were summarily hung for their rebellious actions and captured Sepoys suffered an even greater fate than that. As proven mutineers, the British deliberately chose to employ the historic Mughal punishment of blowing such traitorous soldiers from the mouths of the army's cannon, an extremely violent end, for any human being, but one that was guaranteed to send a clear and resounding message to any future rebels who might be tempted to oppose Britain's authority in India ever again.

Almost as soon as the first reports began filtering out of India, about the mutiny and the reputed attacks on European settlers, the British media began to report events, despite having only the scantest of information to rely on. Before long, deliberately exaggerated reports started to appear in parts of the British press, helping to fuel a completely unwarranted level of racial hatred against the Indian people and forcing the government of the day to completely overreact, to a generally uncertain situation. In response to the reported atrocities that were taking place in cities throughout India, the British were said to have despatched professional British troops to counter the insurgency and restore order to the country. Largely because of the lurid stories being published by an uninformed and generally sensationalist press, these troops were thought to have made their way to India determined to exact revenge on an Indian population, which were thought to be massacring every single foreigner in the country. As a result of this overtly jingoistic misreporting, many of those charged with suppressing the revolt were often guilty of far greater brutality, than had ever been practiced during the mutiny itself and leaving a legacy of deep-seated hatred that would never be forgotten by the native peoples of India.

Following the suppression of the Sepoy Mutiny by regular British troops, along with other loyal native soldiers, such as the Sikhs and the Ghurkhas, the British East India Company was said to have temporarily resumed its role as the administrative agent of the Crown, although it would prove to be a relatively short-lived resumption of its former position. In the short term and with central control restored, a thorough investigation by the government was reported to have taken place and as a result some of the more inflammatory practices introduced by the East India Company, such as the Doctrine of Lapse and interference in native religious affairs were either rescinded or abolished completely. These changes, it was hoped, would help to restore confidence in British rule and bring peace back to the regions, which had been disturbed by the rebellion. Within sixteen years of the rebellion, the East India Company itself was said to have been dissolved and its role as administrator of the huge continent passed to the British Crown, in the person of the Governor General and an Executive Council. Even though order had been restored and peace began to settle on the country once again the British authorities also made sure that India would remain secure in the future by increasing the number of regular British troops stationed there, by disbanding those native regiments that had proven themselves to be disloyal and recruiting more Sepoy's from those regions and ethnic groups who had remained steadfast throughout the emergency. Changes in attitudes towards native troops were also thought to be at the forefront of the British Crown's new policies in India. Where before, East India officers had remained aloof and distant from their native Sepoys, regular British forces were now encouraged to develop a good working relationship with their Indian comrades; and to rely on them when dealing with the local native population.

When full control of the Indian sub-continent was finally transferred to the British Crown in 1858, it provided for the appointment of a Cabinet Minister in London, who was responsible for overall control of these new imperial territories. This new Secretary of State for India was said to have been aided in the day-to-day governance of the country by the Governor General in Calcutta, later known as the Viceroy, who was himself advised by a fifteen member council of India, which planned, discussed and implemented policy, before passing them along to the various administrative centres of the numerous Indian states and provinces. The political and economic importance of India to Britain, was thought to have been further highlighted in 1876, when the British Prime Minister, Benjamin Disraeli declared Queen Victoria as Empress of the vast new empire, in an attempt to bring a cohesive figurehead to the vast sub-continent, which had been missing since the end of the Mughal Empire. Despite several instances of devastating famines and outbreaks of highly contagious diseases, which were said to have decimated large parts of the country during the 19th century, British government involvement in India was also thought to have helped to provide the country with a large number of beneficial changes that have continued through to the modern day, including the reorganisation of the Indian Army, the development of the Indian Railway and Canal systems, the building of Bombay, Calcutta and Madras universities, the creation of the Indian Police service in 1861 and the founding of the Indian Forestry Service in 1867. By the end of the 19th century and on into the 20th century the British authorities increasingly began to involve the native Indian population in the administration and governance of their own country, although without handing over any real executive control. Despite these politically driven restrictions however, small numbers of commercially successful and politically important Indian leaders were said to have been appointed to act as counsellors to the British Viceroy, as well as being elected to sit on the boards of various corporations and councils that helped to run the country. The Government of India Act 1909 also allowed for and encouraged native Indian's to be elected to both local and regional administrative councils and assemblies, although initially most of those elected to such bodies, were thought to have come from the higher echelons of Indian society, much as they had in the past.

However, it was thought to be the First World War, which fundamentally altered British attitudes towards the native peoples of India and set in place the basis for a highly organised and centralised Independence movement that would see its ultimate goal achieved some twenty-odd years after the conflict was over. When World War I erupted in 1914, Britain's Empire was reported to be at its height, with vast continental territories and their native peoples subject to its rule, the world's leading naval force at its disposal and supported by one of the most experienced and professional armies of the era. However, for the British Crown, the ownership and defence of such vast foreign territories inevitably meant that Britain's highly capable armed forces were stretched incredibly thin, leaving the government of the day with little option but to substantially increase army numbers from both home and abroad. From all over the Empire, millions of Britain's subjects were said to have answered the motherland's call to arms, as she faced the expansionist policies of an aggressive German nation and its equally warlike European allies. Native contingents from throughout Britain's sprawling Empire also answered this call for help and even though there was thought to be opposition to Indian participation in what was fundamentally a European conflict, tens of thousands of Indian men stepped forward to help defend the British Crown and its dependencies. According to some historians, it was precisely because of this willingness to fight and die for the British Crown, sometimes in the most outstandingly heroic fashion, which finally persuaded some people, to begin calling for and sometimes demanding an independent India. Although unwilling to grant full independence to its dominions within the Indian subcontinent, the British government of the day did accept that Indian participation during World War I should be recognised and the growing demand for independence neutralised. As a result, a new approach was taken by the British authorities, one that would significantly and substantially increase the role and status of native Indians within their own country. Increasingly, Indians were appointed to important administrative offices within the country, native soldiers were commissioned as officers within the British Indian Army and a number of the oppressive laws and taxes, so despised by large parts of the native population, were systematically removed.

However, despite these moves towards offering greater freedom and autonomy to the people of India, there still remained an underlying demand for a complete end to British rule and absolute independence for the peoples of India. These unfulfilled aspirations were thought to have been regularly exploited by Britain's enemies over an extended period of time, most especially by the Germans during World War I, when their agents on the subcontinent tried to promote native unrest within certain areas of the country, no doubt in the hope that such problems would undermine British control of the region, or at least divert badly needed troops away from the European theatre. As a result of such enemy inspired rabble-rousing and because of the actions of the more militant opponents of British rule, the authorities were said to have introduced a number of fairly draconian security measures, including the right to detain such people without trial, which was a measure that had been employed elsewhere within British controlled territories. By the end of World War I however, most Indian troops were reported to have had returned home and in common with many other returning combatants, they were said to have found their homeland radically different from how they had left it, with high unemployment, high food prices and a marked slowdown in international trade, affecting their everyday lives. The dissatisfaction that these problems caused within the civilian population of India made parts of the country highly receptive to the steady clamour and the agitation of the pro-independence groups, which were now emerging within mainland India and elsewhere in the subcontinent. Deeply concerned by the strengthening of these national independence movements and fearful that any or all of them might fall under the control of an unfriendly foreign power, the British authorities decided to retain some of the wartime emergency powers which had been introduced since 1914, under the terms of the Defence of India Act. This legislation allowed for the detention and imprisonment of political agitators, or anyone else who was thought to be trying to destabilise the country. Although such legislation undoubtedly suppressed the activities of certain political troublemakers, its often widespread and casual use by the authorities to stifle genuine political debate or argument, was said to have caused a great deal of resentment amongst the wider Indian population. In fact, rather than reduce the effects of the Indian independence movement, such heavy handedness by the authorities, simply served to heighten tensions in the country, leading to incidents like the Jallianwala Massacre of 1919 and bringing the likes of Mahatma Gandhi to the forefront of the Indian independence movement.

Alternatively known as the "Amritsar Massacre", the Jallianwala Massacre was perpetrated by a military contingent of the British Indian Army, under the command of Brigadier General Reginald Dyer on the 13th April 1919. As with many of the incidents, which took place on the Indian subcontinent, these killings were said to have been inextricably linked to the simmering anti-British sentiments that were prevalent within Indian society, as well as the superior and highly discriminatory attitudes displayed by some British officers, including unfortunately, Reginald Dyer. The background to this particularly bloody outrage was thought to have had its roots in the anti-British movement established around the beginning of the First World War and said to have been supported by ex-patriot Indians living abroad and by agents of the German and Turkish governments, who were all keen to undermine British control of India. During the Great War, it was reported that these anti-British elements tried to bring chaos to the region, by encouraging widespread upheaval and rebellion, including fomenting mutiny within the ranks of the British Indian Army. Fortunately for the British authorities in India, many of these planned military insurrections and civilian rebellions were reported to have been thwarted by Britain's own intelligence agencies, who warned the authorities before any serious damage could be done.

However, even after the First World War had ended, much of the Indian nationalist movement was thought to have remained in place and was increasingly fed by high unemployment, heavy taxation and widespread food shortages. Of these various nationalist groups, the National Congress Party was said to have been the largest of these politically active parties, which subsequently formed an alliance with the Muslim League, its Islamic counterpart, to campaign for Indian independence and an end to British rule on the subcontinent. Fearful of the growing influence of these two generally mainstream political parties, as well as a number of minor Indian parties, which had continuing links with German and Russian Bolshevik groups abroad, the British authorities introduced legislation to try and curtail the activities of all such nationalist parties. The Rowlatt Act of 1919 was reported to have been an extension of the Defence of India Act introduced in 1915, but was specifically aimed at identifying, prosecuting and suppressing incidents of sedition or treason within British India. Additionally, under the terms of this particular Act, the British authorities could arrest and hold people without trial, put them before special tribunals and control the content of the India's national media. The Congress Party's spiritual leader, Mahatma Gandhi, was said to be so outraged by the introduction of the Rowlatt Act that he called for nationwide demonstrations to oppose it, which resulted in tens of thousands of Indian supporters taking to the streets of the nation's major cities to show their opposition. Although the vast majority of these demonstrations were generally peaceful, in some places, groups of more militant Congress supporters were reported to have taken it into their own hands, to attack government buildings and infrastructure, as well as committing acts of sabotage against the country's telegraph and railway communication systems.

In Amritsar in the Punjab, thousands of people began marching through the city's streets, ostensibly to demand the release of two local nationalist leaders, who had been arrested by the regional authorities. With such large and generally unruly crowds sweeping through the streets of Amritsar, it was almost inevitable perhaps that some sort confrontation would take place, between the demonstrators and the local authorities, which it did later in the day. Members of a military picket, perhaps unnerved by the approach of a large crowd, were said to have opened fire on a group of demonstrators, killing several of their number and setting in motion quite a few hours of civil unrest, during which numerous government buildings were attacked and set on fire. Perhaps more seriously however, during the mayhem, a small number of Europeans, Indian Civil Servants and innocent civilians were said to have been killed, which then led to even more fairly indiscriminate shootings by local military units. Despite these deaths though, for the following two days the city itself was reported to have remained relatively calm, although throughout the Punjab region generally there were said to be several incidents of government buildings being burnt, telegraph and railway lines being cut, during which several more people, including a number of European's were killed. As a consequence of these violent anti-government attacks, the regional authorities were said to have lost patience with the demonstrators and decided to place the entire Punjab region under martial law, the terms of which forbade gatherings of more than four people in any one place. Unfortunately for all concerned, the actual notification of martial law being declared in the region, proved to be a relatively haphazard procedure, with most of the local Indian population being completely unaware of the orders, until such time as they were advised by the local authorities or happened to fall foul of those military forces that were actually implementing the orders on the ground.

Lord Chelmsford   Edwin Montagu   Winston Churchill

In Amritsar itself, thousands of Sikh families were reported to have begun arriving in the city to celebrate the Sikh New Year and to attend the annual harvest festival at the Jallianwala Bagh, or garden, which was located close to one of Sikhism's holiest shrines, the Golden Temple of Amritsar. Many of these people were thought to have been travelling from all over India for a number of days, in order to attend the festival and were therefore completely unaware of the prohibition order, which had been placed on the region by the British authorities. It was also reported that very little action had been taken by the authorities to actually advise arriving Sikh travellers that such meetings had been banned, a glaring oversight, which was to have tragic consequences for many of the unwitting celebrants. About an hour or so after the harvest festival had officially begun at the Jallianwala Bagh; and completely unnoticed by the thousands of Sikh's attendee's, a relatively small group of British Indian Army troops, mainly from Ghurkha and Punjabi infantry regiments, supported by two armoured cars, were said to have made their way to the Jallianwala Bagh and took up position at the garden's main entrance. Having readied their weapons and on the orders of their officer, Brigadier General Reginald Dyer, the soldiers were then reported to have started shooting into the unsuspecting crowd, causing them to break into a wild panic, during which many of their number were killed or wounded by being trampled underfoot. As the firing continued; and even more guests fell dead and dying, large numbers of the crowd were said to have tried to escape the carnage by running towards the parks alternative entrances, only to find that many of them were shut tight, forcing people to look elsewhere for shelter. Within the garden itself, there was known to have been a deep well, so rather than face the bullets of the British troops, many people were said to have leapt into the well, only to be crushed to death or drowned as other panic stricken guests jumped in on top of them. It was later reported that at least one hundred and twenty bodies were recovered from the well, over the following days, although most accept that this is probably an estimate and the real figure might well have been greater.

After a period of about ten minutes, the firing was said to have ceased and many of those surviving guests, who had somehow managed to escape the carnage relatively unscathed were quick to remove themselves and their families from the area as quickly as possible. Large numbers of survivors however, were thought to have remained in the garden, some to comfort the wounded and the dying, others to search for the bodies of their missing relatives and still others who had been so traumatised by the event that they had no clear idea of what they should do. As for the Indian troops who had committed the atrocity, they were thought to have been simply withdrawn by Dyer and offered no aid or succour to the dead or the dying, before returning to their military bases. By the end of the massacre and according to official British figures of the time, around four hundred people were reported to have died and several hundred more were said to have been wounded during the incident. However, Indian nationalist sources who later investigated the outrage and took evidence from a number of witnesses, subsequently announced that some fifteen hundred people had died at the Jallianwala Bagh, although most historians now agree that a true figure for those killed on the day will probably never be known. One other source who later gave evidence about the massacre, was reported to have been a Dr Smith, a civil surgeon at Amritsar who stated that according to his own calculations, around eighteen hundred people had either been killed or wounded during the event, although as with all of the other reports regarding the incident, Dr Smith's figures could not be independently confirmed and therefore remain highly speculative.

Despite the outrage that he had ordered his men to perpetrate, Brigadier General Dyer was said to have made no effort to render aid to the hundreds of people that his men had killed and wounded, later defending his decision by suggesting that the survivors could have gone to hospital, in spite of the fact that he knew that the whole city was under curfew; and so this solution was not available to the wounded and the dying. Immediately after the massacre, Dyer was thought to have reported to his superiors that his men had been confronted by a revolutionary army and that he and his men had taken appropriate action to deal with the perceived threat. Although clearly untrue, the Lieutenant Governor of Punjab, Sir

Michael O' Dwyer was said to have accepted Dyer's version of events without question and even declared his public support for the actions of his subordinate. O' Dwyer then requested permission from the Viceroy, Lord Chelmsford, to place all of the Punjab under martial law, which the largely misinformed Viceroy agreed to. Some critics of British rule in India, point to this decision as an attempt by both Chelmsford and O' Dwyer to suppress news of the massacre, although this seems to be highly unlikely, as within hours of the killings having taken place, news of the attack was already starting to filter around India and within days had spread around the world. With news of the killings making headlines in most corners of the world, the British government and its administration in India were thought to have come under increasing pressure to establish an independent inquiry into the events that took place in Amritsar. Within a matter of weeks, the Hunter Commission had been set up on the orders of the Secretary of State for India, Edwin Montagu, to investigate the incident and look into the actions of those who were involved in the massacre. When Reginald Dyer appeared to give evidence to the inquiry, he freely admitted that he had known about the gathering at the Jallianwala Bagh, some hours before the killings, but had taken no affirmative action to arrange for the dispersal of the crowd, had not prevented additional guests from joining the festival and had not even tried to stop the festival from continuing. He also admitted to the inquiry committee that he probably could have dispersed the crowd without the need for violence, but his decision was swayed by the thought that without a show of force, the crowd might well have ignored his order, making him, in his own words, *"look foolish"*.

Dyer was later asked, if he had considered using the machine guns on the armoured cars to help disperse the crowd, to which he chillingly replied that he would have done so, had the car been able to enter the park and train its guns onto the crowd. However, with these guns unavailable to him, he had had to rely on the arms carried by his mixed contingent of Ghurkha, Pathan and Baluch troops, who he ordered to keep firing, until such time as their total of fifteen hundred rounds of ammunition ran out. When he noticed that some of his men were deliberately firing over the heads of the crowd, he admitted that he had reprimanded them for not following their orders; and watched over them to make sure that they were firing into the main body of the crowd in front of them. When questioned about his failure to help aid the wounded and dying, Dyer simply remarked that *"it was not my job and the hospitals were open, so they could have gone there"*. It was significant to some observers at the time that the injured and the dead could not easily be removed from the park as a curfew was in place, which prevented medical aid from being given to the survivors of the attack, a fact that seemed to have escaped Brigadier General Dyer. By the time the Hunter Commission had listened to all of the evidence surrounding the events at Amritsar, there was at least, an expectation that someone would be held accountable to the deaths of several hundred entirely innocent civilians. However, although the inquiry was critical of Dyer and his actions on that particular day, no formal action was taken against him in the form of a criminal punishment. Where he was censured by the inquiry, they pointed to the actions he failed to take, as opposed to the ones that he did, criticising him for failing to issue a dispersal order to the crowd, failing to limit the amount of time that the crowd was fired upon and failing to attend to the dead and wounded after the shooting had stopped. However, despite the Hunter Commission's abject failure to hold Dyer accountable for his actions, a short time after their findings were announced, General Sir Havelock Hudson was said to have met with Dyer and informed him that he was being relieved of his command and would immediately revert to his former rank of Colonel. Dyer was later summoned to appear before General Sir Charles Carmichael Monroe, who demanded that the officer resign his post immediately; informing him that he would not be re-employed by the authorities in any capacity. Whether or not it was these particular events which brought about Dyer's subsequent bout of ill health is unclear, but it was reported that the former Brigadier General was eventually brought back to Britain on a hospital ship.

Although a small number of his fellow British officers were thought to have regarded Dyer's actions as fairly laudable, with some Peers in the House of Lords publicly commending his swift actions, for the most part, the former officer was publicly vilified for his actions at Amritsar, both in the House of Commons and in much of Britain generally. In the British Parliament, Winston Churchill was reported to have stated that *"this was an extraordinary event, a monstrous event and an event that stands out in singular and sinister isolation"*. Not only was Dyer's actions censured by the House, but the Labour Party, which was reported to have been holding its Annual Conference at Scarborough, unanimously passed a resolution condemning the Amritsar Massacre as a cruel and barbarous act and also called for two of the principal government officers in India, Lord Chelmsford and Sir Michael O' Dwyer to be recalled to Britain immediately. Herbert Asquith stated that *"there has never been such an incident in the annals of Anglo Indian history, nor I believe in the entire history of our Empire, since its very inception, down to the present day. It is one of the worst outrages in the whole of our history"*. Within India itself, there were said to have been large-scale protests at the deaths of so many innocent civilians, with even largely pro-British Indians demonstrating their anger at the events which had taken place in Amritsar. Rabindranam Tagore, a notable Indian leader was even reported to have returned his knighthood to the King Emperor, George V; such was his disgust at the atrocity that had been committed by supposedly friendly British forces. However, perhaps the biggest change which resulted from the Jallianwala Bagh Massacre was the way in which it helped to galvanise the anti-British and pro-Independence movement within India itself, thereby setting in motion a series of events that twenty eight years later would see an end to British rule on the subcontinent forever.

However, despite such widespread condemnation throughout much of British society, there were those who continued to condone Reginald Dyer's actions at Amritsar, including the few who contributed to a sympathy fund set up for him by the British Newspaper, The Morning Post, a conservative and highly imperialistic publication that later merged with the Daily telegraph. On Dyer's return to Britain on board the hospital ship, he was said to have been presented with a purse of £26,000, which had been donated by the readers of the Post and other supporters. Despite the widespread condemnation of his actions, both at home and abroad, Dyer continued to believe that he had acted in a proper manner and expounded his views in a national newspaper article, which he was subsequently asked to write. In this article, Dyer was said to have stated that he believed that the Indian people were not sufficiently enlightened to warrant free speech, or indeed a free media. He also believed that actions, such as his own, would become commonplace, in order to maintain the peace and stability of India; and even suggested that Indian leaders such as Gandhi could not lead India to capable self-government, as only a strong British Raj could carry out that function. In a way, Reginald Dyer was thought to represent the archetypal British Indian Army officer of his day, someone who had learned his trade during the great upheavals of Britain's Imperial adventures on the subcontinent, but who was unable to adapt to the new realities of the modern world. Although it would be wrong to say that Dyer was unique in this respect, as many British officers of the time shared his fairly patronising views about the native people's of Britain's sprawling Empire, few of them were thought to have been deliberate or arrogant enough, to allow such personal discrimination to influence their day-to-day actions.

Dyer was said to have been born in India, but was sent home to Ireland to be educated, before returning to the subcontinent as a British Army officer. In the early part of his military career, he was reported to have seen considerable military action in a number of campaigns and his conduct was thought to have been so exemplary that by 1915 he had risen to the rank of Colonel. In the following year, he was awarded the temporary rank of Brigadier General, having been appointed to lead a full brigade; and even after the events at Amritsar was said to have led his brigade for a short period, even being mentioned in despatches for his units actions elsewhere in India. However, despite his otherwise consummate military character, Dyer is considered by some to have been a highly inflexible individual, who had a rather low and suspicious nature regarding the Indian people themselves. Although he was not considered to be an out-and-out racist, there is a suggestion that Dyer, along with many other European's in India at the time, considered most Indian people to be little more than children and consequently treated them as such. As he made clear in his later newspaper articles, he certainly did not consider them enlightened enough or sufficiently capable to govern themselves. It also seems clear that his own personal attitudes, along with those of many others, was largely informed by historic events, particularly incidents like the Great Sepoy Mutiny of 1857, which led him and others, to believe that Europeans were at serious risk from mutiny or rebellion, if the Indian population were given too much freedom.

The second apparently similarly minded individual, whose actions and opinions were thought to have contributed to the massacre at Amritsar, was the Lieutenant Governor of the Punjab region, Sir Michael O' Dwyer. According to some historians, O' Dwyer was constantly troubled by the fear of Indian rebellions and mutinies and as a result tended to overreact to what were in reality, fairly innocuous events. It was said to be on his direct order that two relatively high profile nationalist campaigners were arrested by the British authorities and held at an undisclosed location, which then led to large numbers of their supporters taking to the streets of Amritsar. Almost inevitably these demonstrations were said to have led to violent clashes between the protestors and the authorities, during which a unit of panic stricken troops, were said to have opened fire on a crowd of demonstrators, killing and wounding several of them. In response to these killings, sections of the crowd were said to have begun attacking local businesses, government buildings and any Europeans that they happened to come across, killing several and wounding a good few more. It was said to be during these attacks that a Miss Sherwood, a teacher at a local school, was reportedly accosted by the members of a mob, as she cycled through the city. Fortunately for Miss Sherwood though, a number of local residents were able to rescue her from the crowd, before she was seriously injured; and managed to get her to comparative safety, although when Reginald Dyer learned of the attack he was said to have been outraged at her treatment. It has been suggested by some sources that it may well have been this particular incident which affected Dyer's behaviour later on in the day, when he took his troops into the Jallianwala Bagh and ordered his men to open fire on the crowd that was gathered there. The idea that Dyer was particularly angered by the attack on Miss Sherwood is supported in part, by later reports that the Brigadier General reportedly revisited the site of the attack on the school teacher and forbade any Indian from walking along the street. According to some sources, Dyer insisted that any Indian pedestrian who wanted to pass along the street, or who wanted to visit the various stores located there, had to do so by crawling along on their stomach's, although whether or not these events actually occurred is unclear. As part of the same legend however, it was also claimed that Indian shopkeepers located along the street, were forced to climb out of the rear windows of their shops, rather than face the humiliation of having to crawl in and out of their shops at the front. It was also reported that deliveries from suppliers were blocked for nearly a month, during which time no doctors or any other visitor, was allowed to enter the stores along the busy thoroughfare.

Herbert Asquith

Udham Singh

Jawaharlal Nehru

Reginald Dyer was reported to have died from a stroke in 1927, although his superior, Sir Michael O' Dwyer, the former Lieutenant Governor of Punjab, who was judged by some to be equally culpable in the Amritsar Massacre, suffered a much more violent end. When Dyer finally passed away in 1927, he was remembered by the Morning Post, as the man who had saved India, although most British newspapers of the day were far less kind to his memory. The Westminster Gazette wrote that *"No British action during the course of our whole history in India has struck so severe a blow to the Indian's faith in British justice than the massacre at Amritsar"*. Although some historians and sources at the time believed that Sir Michael O' Dwyer was actually complicit in the Amritsar Massacre, most independent reporters simply regarded him as being guilty of poor judgement and unreasonable support for his subordinates, including Brigadier General Dyer. Even though it had been O' Dwyer who had implemented martial law on the Punjab, in the mistaken belief that some sort of armed insurrection was about to take place, which clearly was not the case, it was thought to be yet another of his poor decisions, allied to the events in Amritsar, which finally caused his own downfall. During an outbreak of violence in the vicinity of Gujranwala, O' Dwyer was said to have ordered a British aeroplane to bomb and strafe the area, in order to suppress the disorder, although unfortunately for him, during the attack, a number of local civilians, including women and children, were reported to have been killed. At the same Labour Party Conference, which had publicly condemned Reginald Dyer, there were also calls for both O' Dwyer and his superior Lord Chelmsford to be recalled from India in order to account for their actions, which both men subsequently were and later relieved of their offices. On the 13th March 1940, some twenty years after the Amritsar atrocity, an Indian called Udham Singh was reported to have assassinated O' Dwyer as he attended a meeting of the Royal Central Asian Society at Caxton Hall in London. As well as ending the life of the former British Civil Servant, the killing of O' Dwyer by Udham Singh, once again raised the issue of British control of India, with many international voices calling for a formal end to colonial rule within the subcontinent. As for Singh himself, he was subsequently arrested, tried and executed for the murder of O' Dwyer, even though his execution simply served to highlight once again the continuing debate and divisions over the subject of Indian independence.

The Indian National Congress Party under its spiritual and political leaders, like Gandhi and Nehru were thought to have been highly problematic for the British authorities, as they commonly advised their followers to employ a non-violent and non-cooperative form of direct action against British interests, rather than the more usual forms of civil disobedience, which could commonly be dealt with by force. Even though large scale public demonstrations did occur, most were entirely peaceful affairs, comprised of nationalist supporters, who were keen to show their vocal opposition to the range of British enforced laws that most Indians believed to be both unfair and overtly authoritarian. However, despite the instructions of the Congress Party's leadership, occasionally such public demonstrations could and did become violent, forcing the regional authorities to employ local police or troops to disperse the crowds and to issue prohibition orders preventing further gatherings or demonstrations within the immediate area. This was thought to be the case at Chauri Chaura in February 1922, when a group of protesters were reported to have begun picketing a local liquor shop in the town, leading to a public demonstration that the authorities believed might become violent. In response to the demonstration a local police inspector was said to have sent a group of armed officers to disperse the crowd, although their sudden appearance on the scene, rather than suppressing the crowd's emotions simply seemed to have heightened tensions amongst the demonstrators. The presence of the police was thought to have incited certain troublesome elements within the crowd, to divert attention away from the liquor shop and towards the police officers themselves, who then became the target of the demonstration, being approached by the large threatening group, who now began chanting anti-government slogans at the increasingly nervous policemen. Obviously unnerved by the situation they now found themselves in, a number of the officers were reported to have fired into the air, in an effort to discourage the crowd from approaching their lines, but their actions were said to have simply incited the demonstrators to attack the policemen with stones and rocks that they had picked up from the street. Now being attacked directly, the officers then responded by firing directly into the demonstrators, reportedly killing three and wounding a number of others. Rather than halting the crowd though, their actions were said to have incensed the crowd to such a degree that they attacked the policemen even more vehemently, forcing the increasingly anxious officers to withdraw from the scene completely.

A slowly calculated withdrawal by the police soon became a full scale retreat, as the crowd pressed forward, bombarding the officers with whatever missiles they could lay their hands on. Finally, the policemen were reported to have made their way back to the relative safety of the local police station, where they hoped they might be safe from the anger and missiles of the demonstrators. Unfortunately for the officers involved in the incident; and their entirely innocent colleagues, who just happened to be in the station at the time, the crowd was said to be so furious about the deaths of their fellow protestors that they had no intention of leaving the matter alone. Within a relatively short time, the demonstrators had set alight to the station building and the twenty two policemen who were trapped inside, were said to have burned alive, having had no way of safely escaping the inferno. When the British authorities learned of the incident, they very quickly rounded up a number of those accused of leading the attack and put them on trial. Over one hundred and fifty people were subsequently arrested and charged with a variety of offences, most of which were related to the deaths of the twenty two policemen, although when they came to trial, not all of the accused were convicted of any offence. A reported nineteen demonstrators were found guilty of their crimes and subsequently received a death sentence; around one hundred people were convicted of lesser offences and were subject to varying jail terms, whilst the remaining demonstrators were reported to have been released through lack of evidence.

Despite their apparent inability or unwillingness to deal with the issue of independence, the British government continued with a legislative program which was aimed at increasing the involvement of the native population in the administrative, logistical and military control of their homeland. The Government of India Act 1919, was said to have swept away some of the more discriminatory practices that had previously prevented native Indians from holding public office, thereby providing new jobs within the national health and education ministries, as well as within India's burgeoning local government system, much of which was transferred out to the various regions and provinces of the massive country. This new Act was also thought to have seen control of many basic industries and services placed under the control of Indian ministers and civil servants, including the likes of the Indian Education Service, Agriculture, Transport and Local Government, all of which were said to have been run by Indians themselves. With most local schools now offering reasonable levels of education, most Civil Service jobs were available to and filled by local workers; and military service within the British Indian Army was reported to have become a highly popular career for many of the country's young men. Despite such improvements and advances in the Indian franchise however, the great state departments of India, defence, justice and foreign affairs, remained very firmly under British control, as did the vitally important departments which dealt with irrigation, taxation, law enforcement, prisons and the media. Virtually all of these highly significant political and economic agencies were held under the authority of the British Crown's representative in India, the Viceroy, albeit with the support of his Executive Council that was made up of both European and Indian advisors. Although the underlying demand for full Indian independence was thought to have been reduced somewhat, it was never fully silenced and the emergence of nationalist leaders like Jinnah, Gandhi and Nehru, ensured that the subject remained foremost in most people's minds. In 1935, the British government passed further legislative powers to the individual regions, under the terms of a new Government of India Act, which allowed for the creation of regional assemblies throughout India; and the devolution of even more power to the local Indian people and their representatives. It was also reported that this same Act, established the basis for the separation of Burma from the rest of British India, something that was finally achieved two years later, in 1937. Interestingly, in the first election held for these newly created regional assemblies in 1937, the largely nationalist Congress Party led by the likes Gandhi and Nehru, was reported to have gained political control of the majority of these assemblies, suggesting that the demand for Indian independence was still a major issue for most people within the country.

On the outbreak of the Second World War in 1939, the Viceroy of India, was said to have unilaterally declared war on Germany, without first consulting his Executive Council, or any of India's leading political leaders, causing most of the Congress Party's ministers to resign in protest. The leadership of India's Muslim League however, were reported to have supported the Viceroy's decision and some British politicians even went so far as to link Indian support, to the promise of future negotiations on India's own independence. Unfortunately, proponents of this particular campaign were said to have been largely undone by nationalist leaders such as Gandhi, who not only advocated a non-violent approach to Germany's policies, but was also accused by some of deliberately exploiting the situation to demand Britain's immediate withdrawal of its military forces from India itself in 1942. Believing that such suggestions presented a real danger to British interests; and to the region as a whole, the British authorities once again used its own security legislation to arrest and intern a number of the Congress Party's leadership, despite the fact that this led to some unrest within the civilian population, which was subsequently suppressed by the authorities. Once again though, tens of thousands of Indian troops were said to have rallied to Britain's cause, although this time, many of these same colonial soldiers would fight and die in their own region of the world, opposing Germany's far eastern wartime ally, the Japanese, who had already begun their own expansionist domination of the Far East. The Axis Powers, as Germany, Japan and their allies became known, were reported to have been aided in their attacks on the subcontinent, by an Indian nationalist leader called Subhos Bose, who arranged an alliance with the Axis Powers, ostensibly to free India from British rule. He was reported to have organised and led the Indian National Army, a military force made up of nationalists like himself and numbers of Indian regular troops, who had been captured and imprisoned by the Japanese following the fall of the British military base at Singapore. Bose was said to have formed a rebel led Provisional Government for the Freedom of India, although unfortunately for Bose and his supporters, most of the Japanese gains made on the subcontinent, were subsequently reversed by the Allies during 1945, with the Indian National Army surrendering at the recapture of Singapore in the same year. As for Bose himself, he was reported to have escaped British justice, but was killed in a plane crash sometime later.

Following the Allied victory in 1945, which saw both the German and Japanese forces defeated, in India itself, the subject of Independence once again became a topic for discussion, especially in view of the sacrifices that Indian troops had made in helping to defeat the Axis Powers. According to a number of sources, the defeat of Fascism in Europe and Japanese Imperialism in Asia, had fundamentally altered people's perception of the British Empire, altering it from a previously well thought of form of rule, to one that was not only potentially repressive, but largely undemocratic. Even back in Britain itself, there seems to have been little appetite for a return to a pre-war world, which was commonly ruled by class divisions and by Imperial ambition. Fighting almost alone, to preserve European democracy, had left Britain virtually bankrupt, its infrastructure and manufacturing base were almost shattered beyond repair and its population was struggling to survive in a post-war world of shortages and rationing. It was little wonder perhaps that the new Labour government which came to power at the end of World War II were generally more sympathetic to Indian demands for independence; and sent a delegation to India in 1946 to review the situation. In that same year, fresh national Indian elections were held and the Congress Party, led by the likes of Gandhi and Nehru were reported to have swept to power in three-quarters of the country's regional assemblies. However, these elections were also said to have been marked by inter-communal violence between the two main religious groups within India, the Muslims and the Hindus, a clash of religions and cultures that would erupt into even greater violence in the following year. Despite these incidents of regional violence however, the overall winner in the Indian elections was said to have been the Congress Party and in September of 1946, their political leader Jawaharlal Nehru was finally appointed as the country's first freely elected Prime Minister.

In Britain, the new Labour administration, was still struggling to cope with the structural and financial damage caused to the country during the war, whilst at the same time trying to play its part in creating a more peaceful and equitable Europe. In the meantime, its delegation were said to have returned from India, convinced that Indian independence was almost inevitable, a point of view that was reinforced by the lack of international support for Britain's continuing presence in the subcontinent. It has also been suggested that the British delegates were equally concerned about the reliability and loyalty of those Indian troops, who would ultimately be responsible for the security of the country and who were coming under sustained pressure to support Indian independence. With such factors affecting their decision, it was perhaps inevitable that the Labour administration eventually decided to press ahead with Indian Independence, despite the opposition of certain high profile opposition Members of the House. As the date set for India's independence approached, the country was thought to have become increasingly wracked by outbreaks of communal violence, ostensibly between the two largest religious groups, the Hindus and Muslims, although other ethnic groups such as the Sikhs, Christians, etc. all occasionally became victims of the rampaging mobs. Fundamentally, these outbreaks of violence were often caused by inter-communal tensions, founded on intolerance, fear and even instances of personal antagonism, which occasionally resulted in one group attacking members of another. A good deal of the violence though was thought to have been orchestrated by local community and religious leaders, who were keen to strengthen their own supporter's position prior to Indian independence. This was said to be especially true for the Muslim League, whose supporters were fearful of a non-Islamic government controlling India after independence; and who were primarily dedicated to creating their own Islamic state within the subcontinent. The provinces of Bengal and Punjab were said to have been at the centre of these religious and communal tensions, ostensibly because of their highly volatile and equally mixed populations, which helped to create a crucible of intolerance, hatred and fear amongst the various ethnic groups who inhabited these particular regions of India.

Muhammad Jinnah

Subhas Bose

Louis Mountbatten

Even prior to World War II, the leadership of the Muslim League had come to the conclusion that only the physical partition of India would guarantee their supporters some sort of fair representation within the subcontinent. Years of trying to negotiate some sort of equitable long term solution for the future government of an independent India, with the largely Hindu led Congress Party, had come to nothing and although this situation was caused by distrust and intransigence on both sides, neither could have imagined the bloodshed that would occur as a result of their failure to come to terms with one another. Between late 1946 and early 1947, the country was in complete turmoil and the remaining British military forces were simply unable to deal with the number of violent attacks which were regularly taking place throughout India. In order to try and settle matters as quickly as possible the last British Viceroy of India, Lord Louis Mountbatten was reported to have brought forward independence to August 1947, even though it would not be the independent and united India that many had long waited and fought for. In the months leading up to Independence Day, millions of native Indians, were reportedly displaced from their homes, as the two greatest provinces of the subcontinent, Bengal and Punjab, were divided between the soon to be Union of India and its neighbour, the Islamic Republic of Pakistan. Separated along largely religious and ethnic lines, as the date for the creation of these two new independent states approached, millions of Indians, who found themselves on the wrong side of this new racial and religious divide were forced to leave their homes and resettle on the right side of these new national borders, with refugees from both sides of the argument, having to endure the hardships and dangers that such a move involved. Countless tales exist of innocent travellers having their trains, refugee columns and caravans attacked by bands of religious zealots, from both the Muslim and Hindu communities, who murdered hundreds of refugees, simply because they were different from them. The new border which marked the dividing line between India and Pakistan was said to have been littered with the corpses of thousands of men, women and children, who were simply guilty of being Muslims, Sikhs or Hindus and for that reason alone, were mercilessly cut down by their attackers. Such outrages lived long in the memory and even today are thought to colour the relationship between the two modern nuclear states which day by day face one another in a military fashion, despite the fact that some sixty years have passed since those terrible events took place. According to some sources, anything between a quarter and half a million people were reported to have died during this transitional period, although in most people's minds, many millions more died as a direct result of partition. Either way, British involvement in the region which later became the Islamic republic of Pakistan officially ended on 14th August 1947 and the following day, 15th August 1947, the Union of India was officially born, bringing an end to over two hundred years of British involvement in the Indian mainland.

Although Indian Independence had been the fundamental objective of the native people of the sub-continent for hundreds of years, the solution that was finally agreed between the British administration, along with the competing Hindu and Muslim leadership singularly failed to provide an ideal solution, with British India later becoming India, Bangladesh and Pakistan, three separate states, which even today have a largely antagonistic and distrustful attitude towards one another. Even before full independence in 1947, the India of the East India Company had already been reduced and redesigned, with Burma, which had been seized by the Company in 1826, becoming a separate and independent province in 1937 and gaining full independence in 1948. Other countries that had once formed part of the vast British Indian Empire were the likes of British Somaliland, Singapore, Ceylon, along with independent states, kingdoms and protectorates, such as Nepal, Bhutan and the Maldives, all of which and in their turn were eventually granted independence by various British governments during the second half of the 20th century. The commonly used expression of India being Britain's "Jewel in the Crown" is sometimes thought to refer to the fabulous riches and especially the various gemstones that were said to have been acquired by Britain, both legally and illegally, during more than two centuries of British rule on the subcontinent. Although large amounts of treasure were undoubtedly looted from the great treasuries of India's historic Empires, the reference itself is actually thought to relate to India's location, its capacity to generate great wealth for the British economy and its vast resources of gemstones, precious metals, vital commodities and much needed foodstuffs. The expression itself is said to originate from a speech given by the British Prime Minister, Benjamin Disraeli, during the latter part of the 19th century, when he described Queen Victoria's Indian Empire as "the brightest jewel in the Crown". Some historians have also interpreted his remark as identifying India's continuing importance to Britain as a source of diamonds, cotton, wheat, indigo dye and its vitally important geographical location, which helped to act as a barrier to Russian expansionism during that period of time.

MARINERS, MERCHANTS AND THE MILITARY TOO

6. THE THIRTEEN AMERICAN COLONIES & BRITISH NORTH AMERICA

From an entirely modern European perspective, the New World, or the Americas was first discovered by Christopher Columbus in 1492, when during a voyage sponsored by the Spanish monarchs, Ferdinand II and Isabella I, he inadvertently landed on the islands that would later become known as the Bahamas, beginning what would eventually evolve into the widespread European colonisation of South, Central and North America, along with the islands of the Caribbean. However, although it was not generally recognised at the time, Columbus and the other western explorers who followed him, were not actually thought to be the first Europeans to have set foot on this new continent, with Norsemen or Vikings being largely credited with that momentous feat, particularly the explorer Leif Eriksson, who was thought to have discovered Newfoundland around 1000 AD, some five centuries before Columbus even sailed out of European waters.

The question of European discovery aside, the American continent itself, from Canada and Alaska in the north, to Peru and Chile in the south was reported to have already been inhabited by a multitude of native peoples, who according to some sources, were descended from a common mixture of central Asian settlers, who had crossed a long extinct ice bridge to the north and early travellers from the Pacific Ocean, who had used small craft to navigate their way to these new, largely undiscovered lands. Either way, for hundreds of years before either Eriksson or Columbus had ventured across the often wild Atlantic Ocean, the native peoples of these highly diverse lands, were thought to have evolved into their own disparate tribal groups, forming the great human civilisations of south and central America and the largely hunter-gatherer based tribes in the north. Although entirely distinct and separate from one another, all of these "Native American" peoples would ultimately share a common fate, once their lands had first been discovered by the 15th century European explorers, with war, disease and exploitation being introduced in equal measure over successive centuries, bringing death and disease to many of these earlier native American societies.

James Oglethorpe

John White

Sir John Popham

The subsequent division of the Americas, into its southern, central and northern regions was thought to have been as much a result of timing, as it was about geography, climate or natural resources. When Christopher Columbus first landed in the New World in 1492, he immediately and instinctively claimed these new lands for his employers, Ferdinand and Isabella. This assumed European right to claim any and all such unknown lands was subsequently employed throughout much of the continent, with Spain, Portugal, England and France all simply claiming ownership of the various territories, with little thought or consideration being given to the native peoples who happened to live there. For Spain particularly, the discovery of these new lands, some five years before any of its main European neighbours and competitors, proved to be vital, as it gave their explorers and traders sufficient opportunity to identify the most potentially profitable regions which might be brought under their immediate and absolute control. Reportedly fascinated by tales of the fabulously wealthy civilisations which lay to the south of their new territories, within a relatively short period, the Spanish Conquistadors were said to have searched for, found and conquered the great Aztec Empire, taking control of much of modern day Mexico, along with large parts of Central America and establishing the roots of their later extensive Spanish American colonies. Although the Spanish and Portuguese were known to have been at the forefront of the colonisation of the Americas, they were thought to have concentrated much of their efforts towards the area of modern day South America and rarely ventured much beyond what is now the US State of Florida. It is also generally accepted that the main drive behind the exploration and settlement of the wider world by these two Iberian neighbours, was the will of their individual monarchs, who were keen to expand their power beyond their own national borders, gain greater personal wealth and spread Christianity throughout the wider, but still largely unknown world. This was completely different to the English, Dutch and French, who were said to have been simply driven almost entirely by trade considerations, rather than any sort of religious or imperial zeal. The Spanish were reported to have been trying to establish settlements in the north of the Americas as early as 1526, when they founded the colony at San Miguel de Guadalupe, although that particular settlement was said to have failed to survive largely due to the harshness of the environment and outbreaks of disease. Two years later they were thought to have tried again, this time in what is now modern day Florida, but that colony was said to have failed as well, ostensibly because of similar problems and the unfriendliness of the local native tribes. They were then thought to have tried to establish a third colony at Pensacola in 1559, but that particular settlement was reported to have been destroyed by a hurricane in 1561, a natural and recurring phenomena which continues to dog this particular region of the United States even today, although with generally less catastrophic results. The fourth historic attempt by the Spanish to establish a presence in North America was reported to have been a colony which was established in what later became North Carolina in 1567, but this settlement too was thought to have failed after it was attacked by hostile native Indian tribes in 1569.

Even though England, in common with a number of other North European nations, began to explore the wider world sometime after the Spanish and Portuguese explorers, by 1497 and with the authority of the first Tudor monarch, Henry VII, John Cabot was said to have reached the shores of Newfoundland, on the east coast of North America. Although Cabot was said to have simply explored the coastline of these unknown lands, nonetheless he was said to have claimed them for the English king, Henry VII, returning to England with tales of shoaling fish, so vast and deep that a man might walk across them from ship to land. However, despite these initial exploratory forays into the oceans of the world, English territorial ambitions were thought to have remained largely unfulfilled for the next hundred years or more, mainly because of the national and military tensions which existed within Europe itself. Following the death of Henry Tudor in 1506, he was reported to have been succeeded by his second son Henry, who ascended the English throne as Henry VIII, one of the most notable monarch's ever to hold the position and one of the most divisive European kings of the period. A soldier by instinct, on his ascension to the English throne, Henry VIII was said to have continued the enlargement and development of the English navy that had first been begun by his father. Unfortunately, through his own personal philandering and ultimately, his decision to refute the authority of the Pope, England found itself at odds, not only with the great royal houses of Europe, but more importantly, with the Roman Catholic Church, one of the most powerful political forces of the age. By creating himself as head of the church in England, later the Anglican Church, Henry VIII, was said to have put himself, his heirs and most of his people, outside of the Roman Catholic faith, the dominant religion in medieval Europe, which essentially isolated England from many of its continental neighbours. For the next fifty years, from 1537 to 1588, England and its monarchy, including Henry VIII, Edward VI, Mary I and Elizabeth I, remained concentrated on entirely European matters, with only the largely Roman Catholic kingdom of Ireland, becoming the focus for large scale English conquest and colonisation.

It was only during Elizabeth's reign, from 1558 to 1603 that the English navy began to be rebuilt and reorganised to the sort of levels, it had been during the time of Henry VIII, but even then much of its influence was thought to have been due to the semi-autonomous privateers like Sir Francis Drake, who employed their own ships to raid Spanish treasure fleets or their American possessions, without the official sanction of the queen, but with her obviously secret connivance. However, it was only after the defeat of the great Spanish invasion armada in 1588 that England's naval power finally became to be seen as a potent maritime threat, allowing English ships to once again resume their exploration of the world's great oceans and establishing the conditions for the later successful colonisation of the great territories that lay beyond England's immediate shores. It was said to have been Elizabeth's successor, James VI of Scotland, later James I of England who ultimately reaped the rewards of his predecessor's strategy and investment in the English navy. It was also thought to be James I who first suggested the idea of "Great Britain", a conjoining of the three crowns of England, Ireland and Scotland into one United Kingdom, a grand alliance, which would be ruled over by him and his royal successors. In reality though, such a political entity would not actually exist for another century, with the kingdoms of England and Scotland only formally signing the Act of Union in 1707, creating the Union of Great Britain. For its part, the kingdom of Ireland was only finally brought under full British political control by the second Act of Union, which was reported to have been passed in 1800, thereby creating the kingdom of Great Britain and Ireland.

It was said to be during King James' reign that widespread English exploration and permanent colonisation was first thought to have begun, although debate continues over exactly where the first English colony, outside of Great Britain and Ireland was actually located. The first successful English colony on the North American continent was reported to have been the settlement at Jamestown in Virginia, which was officially founded in 1607, although there were said to have been two earlier unsuccessful English colonies, one at Roanoke in North Carolina, which was founded in 1587, during the reign of Elizabeth I; and a second one at Popham in Maine, which was founded in 1607, during the reign of James I, but both foundered within a year of their first being established in the New World. The English settlement, which is often known as the "Lost Colony of Roanoke" was said to have first been established in 1584, as the result of an expedition organised by the Elizabethan sea captain, Sir Walter Raleigh, who had been granted a charter by Queen Elizabeth I, giving him permission to colonise North America. The intention had been to establish an English settlement in the New World, so that these new territories might provide the Crown with much needed income, but also more importantly, to provide a base from where English privateers might operate against the Spanish treasure ships that were regularly operating between South America and Europe. The first expedition, which was said to have been led by Philip Amadas and Arthur Barlow, was said to have identified the best site for an English settlement and made contact with the local native Indians, whose help and expertise might prove to be vital to the new settlers. This part of Raleigh's plan was said to have been successfully completed by the spring of 1585, when a second, much larger contingent of settlers, under the command of Sir Richard Grenville, was said to have arrived at Roanoke, principally to help build the new settlement buildings; and to prospect for any valuable metals or minerals that might be present in the local area.

However, these first attempts at settling North America were said to have been adversely affected by the partial loss of the group's food-stores, which forced the settlers to postpone much of this intended work and begin instead to explore the wider area, including the local Indian villages. It was thought to have been there, at some point that a disagreement broke out between the English and their new Indian neighbours which resulted in Grenville's men burning down one of the villages and killing its tribal chief. It is worth noting perhaps that a number of the English settlers were former soldiers who had fought to impose English rule in Ireland, so were no doubt easily inclined to resolve disputes in a highly combative manner, rather than just ignoring or overlooking them. Despite this incident however, Grenville was reported to have decided to leave a sizeable contingent of settlers at Roanoke, whilst he and the remainder of the expedition returned to England to arrange for a fresh supply of stores, which he promised to bring in April of the following year. However, by the April of 1586 Grenville had still not returned with the supplies, so when Sir Francis Drake happened to stop at Roanoke in June of that year, on his way back to England from a successful raiding campaign in the Caribbean, he offered passage to the remaining settlers, which they all eagerly accepted. As it turned out, a little time after Drake had rescued the English colonists, the relief supply promised by Grenville in August 1585 finally arrived in the area, only to find the colonists gone and the buildings abandoned. With no settlers to re-supply and with English possession of the region under threat, Grenville was said to have left a small detachment of English troops at Roanoke, along with sufficient supplies and returned to England with the remainder of his men and stores.

The third and final attempt to establish a colony at Roanoke was reported to have taken place in July 1587, when some one hundred and seventeen men and women landed there, under the leadership of John White, a friend of Sir Walter Raleigh who had accompanied a previous expedition. Almost as soon as the colonists arrived, White was said to have tried to restore the settler's relationship with the local Croatan Indians, but his efforts were rebuffed and instead one of the colonists was reportedly killed by the local tribe. Fearing for their future safety, the remaining settlers asked that John White return to England and request help from the authorities. When he departed Roanoke in the latter part of 1587, White was reported to have left behind one hundred and fifteen colonists, including a new born baby girl, Virginia Dare, who had been born less than a month after the settlers had initially arrived. Unfortunately for those who had been left behind, White's decision to leave so late in the year, when winter storms turned the Atlantic Ocean into a churning maelstrom, proved to be fatal for the colonists, as did the political situation taking place back in England. Despite having survived the incredibly dangerous journey across the Atlantic and having managed to secure new stores and military support, White then found that he could not find a sea captain brave enough to face the winter storms in the Atlantic

Ocean. When he finally did find someone bold enough to undertake the journey, White then found there were no ships to be had, as virtually every seaworthy vessel in England had been appropriated to face the impending menace of the Spanish Armada, which was threatening to land foreign troops on England's shores during 1588.

It was thought to have been a full two years before the national emergency was completely over and English ships once again began to venture away from the European coastal waters, where they had been engaged for so long. Even then, the by now desperate White was reported to have been forced to accept passage on a privateer's ship that was sailing to the Caribbean to begin raiding Spanish possessions there, but who agreed to stop at Roanoke, to help determine the fate of the colonists. Arriving there in August 1590, White was said to have found the settlement abandoned, with many of its defences and buildings partially dismantled, suggesting that the colonists had carefully planned to leave the site for an unknown destination. Scratched onto one of the fort's timber posts was the word "Croatan", perhaps suggesting that the settlers had relocated to the villages of the native Indians, or possibly that the colonists had been attacked by them, although no evidence of either scenario was subsequently discovered. Pressed by the captain of the English privateer, who was anxious to complete his journey to the Caribbean; and the lucrative Spanish shipping lanes, White was left with little choice but to abandon his search for members of the "lost colony" and leave the area soon afterwards. Even though no definitive explanation regarding the fate of the Roanoke colonists has been offered or indeed accepted, most historians seem to believe that those men, women and children who survived after White's departure, were either killed or adopted by one of the local native Indian tribes. Many oral histories from various Native American tribes from the region are thought to make mention of the Roanoke colonists, although many have been simply dismissed as complete nonsense. In all probability though, it seems likely that seemingly abandoned by England, the colonists simply decided to relocate to the mainland of North America and formed an as yet unidentified English settlement there, where they continued to live out the rest of their lives in relative obscurity.

Further English colonisation of North America was thought to have been discontinued for the next sixteen years and for the remainder of Queen Elizabeth's reign, which finally came to an end in 1603. It was only under her successor, James VI of Scotland, James I of England that further permanent settlement was attempted, albeit under the auspices of two English commercial enterprises, the Virginia Company of London and the Virginia Company of Plymouth, both of which were granted identical trading charters for North America by James I in April 1606, with the express purpose of establishing English colonies in the New World. Allocated individual section of the same eastern seaboard of North America, both of these Joint Stock Companies were reported to have established new English colonies in their individually assigned areas during the following year, the London Company at Jamestown in May 1607 and the Plymouth Company at Popham in August of the same year. However, for a variety of reasons it was the Jamestown settlement that would ultimately prove to be successful, with the rival Popham colony finally being abandoned by its inhabitants, a little over a year after it had first been established, an event that eventually led to the dissolution of the Plymouth Company itself. Competition between the London and Plymouth Virginia companies was said to have been fierce, simply because, whichever of the two companies successfully settled the eastern coastline of North America, would be granted exclusive colonisation and trading rights there by the English monarch, James I. Although the Plymouth Company was reported to have launched an expedition to its North American possessions as early as August 1606, the company's ship, "The Richard", was reported to have been captured by the Spanish as it travelled within their sphere of influence and the ship, its crew and the colonists were subsequently taken prisoner. Despite this setback however, the Plymouth Company then arranged for a second expedition to be sent out in the following year, but this second contingent of settlers was said to have been beaten to the New World, by colonists despatched by the London Company, who landed on the American coast in May 1607, some three months before them.

However, despite having been beaten to their new homelands by the London Company's settlers, the one hundred strong Plymouth colony, under the command of their leader, George Popham, the nephew of one of the enterprise's main financial backers, Sir John Popham, quickly set about identifying the best location for their new base and once found, began building the protective fortress that would house them, complete with defensive ditches and cannon, with which to defend themselves. By October of 1607, the compound was said to have included a large number of buildings, including a Chapel, a guardroom, storeroom and living accommodations, all of which suggested that the colony was beginning to thrive. Unfortunately, the colonists generally late arrival in America and their failure to build successful relations with the native Indian tribes, who had had less than favourable dealings with European explorers in the past, meant that the settlers faced an increasingly arduous time as the American winter approached. Perhaps fearful of what the future held, a number of colonists were said to have decided to return to England on one of the company's ships that was returning home, leaving the settler numbers depleted. This situation was then thought to have been worsened further by an extremely rigorous winter, during which many of their supplies and a number of the fort's buildings were said to have been destroyed by fire, although the cause of these blazes was never fully explained. Finally, during the winter of 1607, dissent broke out amongst the colony, splitting the settlement into two opposing factions, each of which supported one of the two main leaders of the expedition, George Popham and Raleigh Gilbert, who were both thought to have argued over the best way forward for the colony.

Edward Wingfield

John Winthrop

Lord Baltimore

By the February of 1608, George Popham was reported to have died and had been replaced as leader by Gilbert, who was thought to have led the colony until the late summer of that year, when he received news of his entitlement to his late brother's titles and estates in England, which caused him to return home on the company's supply ship. With both of their leaders gone and facing the prospect of yet another miserable winter alone, the remaining colonists finally gave up on building a permanent settlement and returned home to England as well. Although the abandoned fort was visited occasionally for the next decade or so, there were no subsequent attempts to reoccupy the site by any future English colonies and over time it was thought to have simply crumbled back into the surrounding landscape. The financial backers of the Popham colony, the Plymouth Virginia Company, who had hoped to establish themselves as the principal trading company in North America, never recovered from the failure of the colony in 1608, which was said to have been followed a short time later by its own dissolution, leaving its rival, the London Virginia Company, as the main commercial agent in the region. Although both the Roanoke and Popham colonies are probably the earliest and best known of England's unsuccessful North American settlements, a number of others were reported to have been established by various trading companies during the reign of James I, although most of them failed to survive for any extended period of time. Examples include Cuper's Cove in Newfoundland, which was founded in 1610, but was subsequently abandoned sometime around 1620. Likewise, the settlement of Bristol's Hope was also established in Newfoundland in 1618, but failed to survive much beyond the early 1630's, both of these colonies being founded by the same company, the Society of Merchant Adventurers in Newfoundland. Elsewhere in the same region, the London and Bristol Company trading into Newfoundland was said to have established settlements at both New Cambriol and Renews between 1615 and 1617, although both had been abandoned sometime before 1637. In fact, between the 16th and early 19th centuries, any number of colonies and settlements were thought to have been established by the various English, Scottish, Irish and Welsh settlers who left their native homelands to help build the sprawling English, later British Empire.

The original Jamestown expedition, financed by the London Virginia Company, was said to have been led jointly by Captain John Smith and Captain Edward Wingfield, but unlike the Popham Colony did not have the most promising start. This was principally because the site chosen for the new settlement by Wingfield was poorly situated, plagued by mosquitoes from nearby swamps, had limited access to fresh water supplies, a lack of edible foodstuffs and a minimum amount of good arable land on which crops could be grown. Despite these initial problems though, the colonists were reported to have persevered and the enterprise was finally saved from disaster by the introduction of a tobacco crop that could be successfully grown and harvested in the generally limited land holding, so that by 1612, the community was reported to have exported its first American commercially grown crop. With this success behind them, the community at Jamestown continued to grow and develop throughout the 17th century, eventually emerging as the capital of the Virginia colony, a title it would hold until 1699 when a new capital, Williamsburg, was built and named in honour of the new English king, William of Orange. Unfortunately, the development of the tobacco growing industry was said to have become so successful and widespread that it helped to create the need for indentured servants, initially using those convicted of criminal offences in England, but later being serviced by the transatlantic slave trade in which most of the leading European nations actively participated.

The next significant influx of English settlers to North America were the colonists who later became known as the Pilgrim Fathers and who arrived off the coast of New England in November 1620. Having travelled across the Atlantic onboard The Mayflower, these new settlers were reported to have anchored off Cape Cod in modern day Massachusetts, prior to landing in the New World. Significantly, one of their advisors for the expedition was said to have been Captain John Smith, the same man who had led the Jamestown colony during 1608 and 1609. Described as a religious sect from England, who were trying to escape persecution in their European homelands, they were said to have set a trend for future religious settlements, by mutually agreeing a common set of rules for the governing of their new colony, which eventually became known as the "Mayflower Compact". Within a decade, several more English colonies had been established in North America, including those at Plymouth in 1628 and Salem around 1629. Earlier still, in 1623, two entirely separate groups of English settlers arrived in what is now New Hampshire, transported there by a Captain John Mason and establishing a fishing village near the Piscataqua River. In 1630, a group of colonists led by a John Winthrop arrived as part of the Massachusetts Bay Charter Company and went on to found the city of Boston, whilst in 1632 King Charles I was said to have granted a Royal Charter to Lord Baltimore, authorising him to found the English colony of Maryland, which was to be supervised by Baltimore's eldest son Cecil, although it was thought to be the nobleman's youngest son Leonard, who actually travelled to America with the group of English settlers in 1633 to build their new community. Along with the English, a number of other European nations began to explore and settle the New World, including the French, Dutch, Swedes and Germans, each of them establishing control over various neighbouring areas. The site of modern day New York was reported to have been inhabited by Dutch settlers as early as 1614, although they only officially purchased the land from the Native Americans, or Indians, in 1626, when they paid the seemingly paltry sum of $24 and renamed the site as New Amsterdam, the capital of the Dutch controlled region called New Netherlands. However, in 1664 the English monarch Charles II, decided to reclaim these lands by force and the Dutch leader in America, Peter Stuyvesant, was eventually compelled to hand the lands over to British control. King Charles subsequently passed his new possession into the hands of his brother, the Duke of York, who renamed the settlement as New York. Although the Dutch were thought to have made several abortive attempts to reclaim their former colony from the English, by 1674 the ownership of the settlement was said to have been beyond doubt and the area remained under English control right through to the American Revolution. These states, New York, New Jersey, Pennsylvania and Delaware were all reported to have become known as the middle states by the English; and despite their military control of them, were known to have been settled and inhabited by a mix of European colonists including the English themselves, the Dutch, Irish and Germans.

As the numbers of foreign migrants who had settled America continued to grow, so more and more settlements and colonies were said to have sprung up, as individual groups and people, decided to separate from their original communities. In 1636, an English settler called Roger Williams was said to have been driven out of the community of Salem in Massachusetts, because of his own personal religious beliefs, which seem to have been at odds with the general community there. However, rather than join another well established English community, or return home to England, Williams was said to have done neither, but instead negotiated the purchase of new lands from the native Narragansett Indians and laying down the foundations for the modern day Rhode Island. Likewise, a second English settler called Anne Hutchinson, was reported to have been expelled from her home community in Massachusetts and went on to help found the colony of Portsmouth in Rhode Island. Although the colony of Connecticut was originally founded by Dutch settlers in 1633, they were later said to have been joined by a group of English colonists in 1636, these people having previously been expelled from Massachusetts. Led by a clergyman called Thomas Hooker, by 1639 their new community was reported to have been established on the basis of formalised and fundamental orders that were used to govern the settlement. In 1638 an individual called Wheelwright, was reported to have founded a settlement called Exeter in New Hampshire, where all members of the colony signed a common compact to guide the day-to-day running of their new community. The colony of Delaware was thought to have first been settled by Swedish immigrants in around 1631, the European colonists who are largely credited with introducing the log cabin to the New World. In around 1655 the Swedes were then thought to have been displaced in part by the Dutch, who were themselves supplanted by the English in around 1664. The Dutch later briefly re-established control over the region in 1673, but by 1674 the English had once again regained control over the area, later passing it to William Penn and his Society of Friends in 1682, as settlement of a debt owed to Penn's father. Penn and his community were then reported to have held Delaware until 1701, when it finally gained independence. The other American territories granted to Penn in 1682, continues to carry its founders name through to the present day, in the form of the modern day Pennsylvania. The capital of this new possession, Philadelphia, was thought to have been planned in the same year that these colonists first arrived and in the following year, 1683, a group of German settlers were reported to have established their own colony of Germantown nearby.

Elsewhere, the region of South Carolina was said to have been settled by Europeans as early as 1526, when San Miguel de Guadalupe was originally established by colonists from Hispaniola. Unfortunately, due to an exceptionally high death rate amongst the settlers because of disease, most of the surviving colonists decided to return to Hispaniola sometime later. In 1663, the English monarch Charles II, under the terms of a Royal Charter, authorised the establishment of a new colony in the region, naming it Carolina after the Latinized version of his own name "Carolus". At the time, the region that was incorporated into this new colony was said to have included the lands of the modern day states of North Carolina, South Carolina and Georgia. Charles' Royal Charter was granted to a group of English merchants, known as the Lord Proprietors, whose intention was to develop the colony as a commercial rival to Jamestown in Virginia. Unfortunately for them, their new venture was reported to have been extremely slow to evolve into a commercial success, not least because it failed to attract sufficient numbers of English settlers to actually work the land. However, in around 1670 the Lord Proprietors were said to have financed an expedition, led by one John West, who discovered an area of extremely fertile land, which could be easily defended and on which the regions first major settlement could be built. The capital of this new colonial possession was Charleston or Charles Town, which was reported to have been established by a group of English colonists from Barbados, led by one Sir John Yeamans, a powerful plantation owner from those English held islands. According to most historical sources it was said to have been these settlers who first introduced African Slaves into the area, a labour source for which the southern states would later be condemned. Although the colony itself eventually proved to be a thriving commercial success, a series of military and political conflicts was thought to have caused the Lord Proprietors to sell their interests back to the English Crown, making England completely responsible for the day-to-day running and security of the region once again. Probably as a direct result of this, in later years, the English King George II was said to have granted these lands, now occupied by the modern day State of Georgia, to James Edward Oglethorpe, an English General and MP, in return for protecting England's North American possessions from its southern enemies. It was also said to be here that English convict labour was heavily employed by Oglethorpe and his agents to grow much needed crops, with the whole region being run along highly puritan lines. However, these restrictions on slave owning and drinking were thought to have inhibited investment in the colony and once they were removed, the colony as a whole was said to have thrived, becoming one of the most successful and profitable English colonies in all of North America. These lower colonies, Virginia, Maryland, North and South Carolina were reported to have been largely plantation states, which were generally located around the Chesapeake region and as previously noted, were later added to by the state of Georgia.

Peter Stuyvesant	Roger Williams	Thomas Hooker

It is perhaps worth pointing out that the European colonists who came to settle the New World were often a mixture of the rich and the poor, the skilled and unskilled, the educated and uneducated, in fact a microcosm of the societies from which they came, be they Spanish, Portuguese, English, French or indeed Dutch. These countries represented the five major European powers of the age and as such possessed the will, the military might, the manpower and more importantly, the maritime experience and ships to cross the world's oceans and exploit the wealth of these newly discovered lands. Individual settlers were reported to have been transported to America for any number of reasons, from those that were sentenced to penal "transportation", or a sentence of indentured service, to those that were simply seeking a new life, free from the poverty, which they had previously suffered in their native lands. Then there were the religious groups who were attempting to escape the persecutions that were thought to have been a common feature of Europe at that time, as well as those who simply wished to escape the wars and regional conflicts, which raged throughout the period. Added to these generally poorer migrants were the land speculators and gamblers, traders and merchants, all of whom were keen to exploit the commercial opportunities that the Americas might offer them, a chance to make them their personal fortunes. The most prominent and ultimately most successful of the European adventurers were said to have been those that were ordered or supported by the great European Royal Houses, who had the financial and military strength to both support their claims and hold their gains. In addition to these, were the Private Venture Companies or Joint Stock Companies, who established Mercantile Trade companies, often with the support or sometimes the connivance of European monarchs, who tacitly supported their claims and in some cases allowed them to raise private armies to protect their gains, as in the case of the British East India Company.

Following its successful colonisation at Jamestown, in 1609, the London Virginia Company was reported to have been granted a new Royal Charter by the English monarch, James I, which permitted the trading company exclusive rights over the territories of the now defunct Plymouth Virginia Company which had failed so disastrously at the Popham colony in Maine. With these new possessions in mind, in the same year, the London Company was said to have sent a significantly larger fleet of new settlers and supplies aboard nine ships, which were put under the command of Admiral George Somers, who was embarked upon his flagship, the "Sea Venture" ready for the journey across the Atlantic. Unfortunately, as the English fleet approached American territorial waters, a huge storm was said to have battered the fleet of ships, separating them and causing Somers' flagship "Sea Venture" to become dangerously waterlogged. Fearing for his ship and the lives of those onboard, Somers deliberately grounded his ship, on a reef, damaging his vessel, but nonetheless saving the lives of his passengers and their livestock. Somers and the ship's company were then said to have reconstructed his ship, into two smaller vessels which were subsequently used to deliver his passengers and their possessions safely through to Jamestown, which they reached in May 1610. The unoccupied islands that had provided the stranded English settlers with a safe haven during the ten month interruption to their voyage were subsequently named as the "Somers Isles" after the man who had saved the settler's lives, although in later years they were thought to have become better known as the English Caribbean possession of Bermuda. Unfortunately for many of those who had survived the arduous journey across the Atlantic and their fellow colonists who were already settled in the new territories around Jamestown, the previously friendly relations between the settlers and the native Powhatan people were already becoming fraught. From the Indian's perspective, they had initially been quite happy to welcome the foreign settlers, but as their numbers increased and they began to establish various settlements throughout the wider region, so their concerns grew. Matters were thought to have been made worse by the actions of some colonists who took it upon themselves to burn down and attack isolated Indian villages which happened to be located on lands that they wanted, as well as destroying native food crops, as a way of forcing the native Powhatan people off their traditional lands. Not only did this cause hardships and food shortages amongst the native Indians, but also hardened attitudes against them, which would inevitably lead to conflict between the two sides.

Finally recognising that the English settlers were not simply content to trade, but wanted to take over ownership of the land itself, in 1610, the Indian leaders were reported to have ordered their people to stop trading with the settlers and to offer them no further aid. Concerned by these developments and the increasingly poor relations with the native tribes, the London Company were then thought to have compounded matters by ordering their newly arrived Governor, Lord de la Warre, to suppress local Indian activity by whatever means necessary. Taking his orders quite literally, De la Warre was reported to have arranged for the local Indian tribesmen to be drawn into a carefully planned ambush and then he ordered them killed. Causing the first Anglo Powahatan War and using the life of the captured Indian princess, Pocahontas, to enforce English authority over the local tribes, for the next few years relationships between the two sides were thought to have remained tense, but relatively peaceful. The subsequent marriage of Pocahontas to the English colonist John Rolfe, was also hoped to heal the wounds between the English settlers and the native tribesmen, but ultimately achieved very little by way improving the overall situation. In reality, the uneasy peace was said to have been brought about through the will of the native chief, Wahunsonacock, who recognised the dangers that such a conflict might bring to his own people, although when he died in 1618, a much more militant native leadership began to come to the fore. The new native chief, Opechancanough, was said to have been bitterly opposed to the English settlers and carried a deep resentment of De la Warre's slaughter of his fellow tribesmen in 1610, both of which he was determined to avenge. His anger towards the English was said to have been increased in 1622, when one of his most trusted advisers was killed by an English settler, presumably for no real reason. Finally, in March 1622 he was ready to exact his revenge on the colonists and arranged for his men to launch simultaneous attacks on the various English homesteads and settlements that lay along the banks of the James River. Caught completely by surprise, the numerous English farmsteads, settlements and plantations were quickly overrun by the bands of rampaging Indians, who were reported to have killed around four hundred colonists, about one third of their of their total and carried away a number of female hostages, who were either subsequently ransomed or absorbed into the local tribes. Only the main, heavily defended settlement at Jamestown was reported to have escaped the carnage and only then, after the settlement had been forewarned by a local Indian boy, who was reported to have been concerned for an individual settler's safety.

For those several hundred colonists who managed to escape the unexpected and widespread attack, their safety was thought to have been assured by the Indian's failure to follow up on their surprise assault, wrongly believing that the settlers would simply leave, rather than face further violence. However, having worked so hard to develop their lands and with little in England to return to, the vast majority of the colonists were said to have decided to remain in Virginia, although they were also determined to build a much smaller number, of highly defended settlements, which might better protect them in the future. The leaders of the colony were also said to have tried to organise their own defence forces, or militias, which might be used to repel future attacks, although the significant loss of men during the Indian attack, meant that there were far more women and children in the main settlements, preventing this plan from being put into operation. When news of the attacks finally reached England, the authorities there were said to have been so outraged that they immediately sent military aid to the region to ensure that no such attacks could happen again and to mete out some form of retribution against the local Indian tribes. The colonists too, now reinforced by military forces, were also said to have taken it into their own hands to punish the local Indians, burning their crops, destroying their villages and in one particularly vicious case, even deliberately poisoning local Indians with tainted liquor, which was said to have killed several hundred of the local tribesmen. As a direct result of the Indian attack on the Virginian colonists, the English Crown finally took over formal control of the colony in 1624, essentially passing control of the land and its profits to associates of the monarch, James I, who also dissolved the Virginia Company of London in the same year. For the Powhatan people and their leaders, the future was equally bleak too, as their tribal chief, Opechancanough, who had led yet another raid on colonists in 1644, was subsequently captured, imprisoned and finally murdered by one of the colonist assigned to guard him. In what became a regularly occurring feature of the European's settlement of the North American continent, the Powhatan and their tribal neighbours subsequently found their native lands increasingly under threat and overtaken by continued colonial expansion, which inevitably led to even more armed conflict between the two sides, along with the associated bloodshed that the native Indian people themselves found to be largely unsustainable.

The English colony of Virginia officially became a Crown Colony in 1624 and although its overall administration and trading rights were thought to have been put into the hands of English aristocrats favoured by the monarch, James I, in reality day-to-day control of the colony remained in the hands of local administrators and elected officials. Within a decade of the Crown having assumed possession of the colony, English settlement was reported to have increased significantly, so much so that by 1634 the colony had been broken down into a number of different Shires, although this title was subsequently renamed County, a form of geographical identification still commonly used within much of the modern day United States. Large scale exploration of Virginia's unknown hinterland was thought to have been limited during the first half of the 17th century, most notably after a second massacre of colonist in 1644, although elsewhere in the region the colony's former dependency on tobacco was thought to have been reduced following the introduction and development of other valuable cash crops. The population of the colony was said to have swelled significantly, following the defeat of the English monarch, Charles I, by the Parliamentarian forces of Oliver Cromwell during the second half of the 17th century. Even though the Puritan authorities back in England were reported to have appointed their own representatives as governor of the royal colony, some of these former royalist supporters were said to have thrived in the New World and by the time Charles' son was restored to the English throne, they were thought to be some of the wealthiest and most influential of Virginia's landed families. For much of the remainder of the 17th century Virginia and her inhabitants continued to thrive, despite occasional outbreaks of disease and Indian attacks, along with fluctuating financial fortunes, affected by wider economic considerations. The most notable period of instability within the region however, was said to have occurred during the 1670's, when resurgent Indian raids, coupled with political infighting amongst the colonies leading figures, resulted in armed conflict between rival factions within the colony, which was only finally resolved by direct intervention by the English Parliament. Although Jamestown had remained the nominal capital of Virginia since its foundation and despite the many adversities it had faced over the years, including fire and Indian attacks, it was only in 1699 and following a fairly devastating fire that the capital was relocated to another part of the region and renamed as Williamsburg, in honour of William of Orange, the new English king. Interestingly, Virginia was also reported to have been one of the first American colonies to question the authority of the British Parliament to rule over the colonist's lives and lands following the imposition of new and generally punitive taxes and legislation. Beginning in 1763 many of Virginia's most prominent leaders were said to have been at the forefront of the American settler's later decision to establish and elect their own congressional movement, in opposition to the British Parliament in London.

Meanwhile, along much of the eastern seaboard of the later United States, the English Crown was thought to have held much of the country under its direct control and from 1670 onwards, began to claim sovereignty over the more northerly areas of Hudson Bay, Prince Rupert's Land and Newfoundland, through its royal agents, the Hudson Bay Company. These lands were said to have formed a significant proportion of the territories already claimed by French settlers as New France, which at the time stretched from Hudson's Bay in the north, to the Gulf of Mexico in the south, a huge swathe of land, running from north to south and covering the entire central section of the modern day United States. With English interests effectively restricted to the east coast and with French claims preventing any further expansion west, it became almost inevitable that the two sides would have to settle matters through force of arms. As a result of the two kingdoms competing claims in North America, England and France were reported to have fought a series of wars during the 17th and 18th centuries, which became parts of the much larger conflict known as the Seven Years War, which was fought between 1756 and 1763. As a result of this great Imperial contest; and under the terms of the subsequent Treaty of Paris, which was signed in 1763, France was compelled to cede most of its North American territories, including those in Upper and Lower Canada, to Britain, although those French colonies already established, were said to have been exempted from any British interference in their religious, cultural and political practices by statutes enacted after the conflict. Unfortunately for British interests, the gains that they had made since the founding of Jamestown in 1607, through to the defeat of French American interests in 1763, proved to be relatively short lived, as within a dozen years of its victory in the Seven Years War, the British Crown had been all but defeated by an irregular army, partially made up of descendants of the first English colonists who had set foot in the New World. Differences between the American colonial leadership and the British government were thought to have arisen following the successful completion of the French and Indian Wars, which was fought in North America between 1754 and 1763. Seen as part of the much larger and much more widespread Seven Years War between Britain and France, the French and Indian War was thought to have represented the North American theatre of this worldwide Imperial conflict and almost inevitably resulted in American colonists being compelled to carry arms in defence of Britain's American possessions. Not only did this general call-to-arms bring greater British military involvement in the day-to-day lives of the colonists, but amongst those who chose to rally to the British cause, it also helped to generate a sense of common unity and brotherhood which would ultimately re-emerge some dozen or so years later.

When the Treaty of Paris was finally agreed in 1763, it brought an end to the Seven Years War, as well as the associated French and Indian War which had been fought in North America, leaving Britain and its colonial allies in almost complete control of the American continent, from Hudson Bay in the north to Florida in the south. As peace eventually descended on the American colonies and with their national borders effectively secured by treaty, the British government began to steadily withdraw and reduce its military presence in North America. Although a significant part of the British military presence in North America was thought to have been in the form of regular troops, a much greater number was thought to have come from within the colonies themselves, often in the shape of local militia's, which were led and commanded by American born, but British trained officers, such as George Washington. As these military forces were reduced and other regular units were withdrawn, so the British government in London began to count the financial cost of having fought such a wide ranging and expensive war against France and its other European allies. Although Britain's burgeoning worldwide Empire was more than capable of absorbing the huge costs of such a military conflict, political and financial considerations in Britain itself conspired to create disharmony between the British government and their American subjects, which would not only lead to further military conflict, but also to the total loss of the thirteen American colonies from Britain's Imperial possessions. Ultimately, the root causes of these difficulties seems to have centred around money and moral authority, with both the British government and the colonial leadership claiming their own legitimacy over which of the two sides actually held the moral high ground in terms of the basic argument. From the British government's perspective, the financial cost of the Seven Years War against France, particularly the French and Indian War which had been fought in North America, had been almost entirely paid for by the British treasury, through the income it derived from both the British people and its other great Imperial possessions. It argued that its American colonies had paid disproportionately less to the costs of the conflict than any other British possession had; and was bound and determined to recover some, if not all of these costs from its newly extended and secured American colonies. However, the counter argument from the American colonial leadership, stated that British colonists had in fact, paid a much higher price in human lives than British regular troops and that the British government had also gained huge financial benefits from the new territories that it had gained as a result of their sacrifice.

Although such differences of opinions were not serious enough in themselves to cause actual conflict between Britain and its colonial subjects in America, it did represent one of a growing number of individual instances, legislative measures and political directives that almost inexorably began to divide the two great English speaking societies. Beginning in 1764, some dozen or more British Acts of Parliament were reported to have been imposed on the thirteen American colonies, including the Sugar Act of 1764 and the Tea Act of 1773, all of which severely damaged or disadvantaged American colonists and businesses in favour of their British counterparts. In and of themselves, these individual pieces Parliamentary legislation were not thought to have been fatal to Anglo-American relations, but as each subsequent Act was passed and added to the rest, so colonial resentment and antagonism towards the British authorities was said to have grown. Britain's decision to introduce these highly unpopular and often repressive Parliamentary Acts was thought to have been driven by two main political imperatives, the first to recover some of the financial costs incurred through its American based conflicts with France; and secondly, to impose complete British authority over the new and enlarged American colonies. For many of the American colonial leaders, British actions were deemed to be undemocratic, given that the British Parliament was passing legislation which affected the lives of all Americans, yet did not have a single American representative within that legislative body, which for most colonial leaders was a complete affront to the whole idea of the democratic process. Adopting the mantra of "No taxation, without representation" by 1772 a number of these American leaders, including lawyers and merchants, were already beginning to question and oppose the very idea of British rule, forming themselves into independent committees, which became part of much larger provincial or regional congresses, designed as alternative legislative assemblies which were fundamentally opposed to British authority and oppression. Over the course of the next two years similar congresses and councils were said to have been established throughout most of Britain's American colonies, allowing their leaders to formerly reject British Parliamentary authority and to establish their own centralised legislative body, the First Continental Congress, which was held in 1774.

With an alternative legislative body to look to, American merchants and businessmen soon began to ignore British imposed trade regulations, bringing them into direct confrontation with the regulators and tax collectors, who had been appointed on the British Parliaments authority. However, rather than trying to resolve their differences through negotiation, the British authorities in Boston, where such an incident took place, resorted to using regular troops to enforce Parliamentary authority, causing the American colonists to respond in kind by raising their own local militias. With the threat of military conflict between the two sides looming, American congressional representatives were said to have appealed to the British monarch, King George III, to help arbitrate an equitable solution. Unfortunately for the colonial leadership however, George III was reported to have been disinclined to interfere in the dispute, with the result that the American colonies were accused of being in open rebellion and their leaders regarded as being guilty of treason. With few options left to them, the colonial leadership were thought to have had little choice but to call a Second Continental Congress in 1776, following which they issued their historic Declaration of Independence, under which they rejected the authority of the British Parliament and its monarch, George III, effectively putting the two countries at war with one another.

William Penn Lord de la Warre Jacques Cartier

Depending on one's point of view of course, the conflict that followed is either known as the American Revolution, or as the American War of Independence. Either way and regardless of how it is sometimes reported, it was never simply a conflict between the British and American peoples, but was a war which involved Britain, America, France, Spain and Holland, as well as any number of North Americas native tribesmen and many thousands of black African slaves. Neither was the American Revolutionary War simply about the governorship of the North American continent, but was also about historic antagonisms, sheer opportunism, national revenge and personal antipathy. The five year period, from the Declaration of Independence in 1776, to Britain's last great military surrender at Yorktown in 1781, was said to have been indelibly marked by individual instances of great courage, cruelty, generosity and kindness. There were also numerous incidents of sheer bad luck, amazing good fortune, poor command decisions and even inspired leadership, all of which contrived to end British sovereignty over its thirteen American colonies and eventually led to an independent United States of America. Despite the loss of the thirteen American colonies however, British interests, both to the north and south, in Canada and the Caribbean remained relatively intact, essentially negating the overall effect of her colonial losses as a result of the conflict.

British interests in the far north of the American continent, in the area of modern day Canada, were said to have begun with two French Traders, who saw the opportunity for improving the existing trade routes for the northern fur trade, but having been rebuffed by the French authorities, travelled to Boston in Massachusetts, to put their proposals to American investors instead. As a result, a number of these well connected American merchants were reported to have sent the proposal to England, both for the necessary financial backing and for the acquisition of a Royal Charter from the English monarch, Charles II. Whilst waiting for the monarch to consider their proposals, the merchants themselves managed to find sufficient financial backing to send two ships to explore the Hudson Bay Area, although only one of the two vessels, the "Nonsuch", actually completed the journey and arrived in St James' Bay, where Fort Rupert was established by the explorers. Named Fort Rupert, after the main sponsor of the expedition, Prince Rupert of Bavaria, having conducted a successful season of trading with local fur trappers the "Nonsuch" was then reported to have returned to England in 1669. Finally given Royal approval in the following year, the Hudson Bay Company was said to have been officially incorporated by the English king in 1670, giving the company a complete monopoly over the fur trade in the north of America. Despite coming into dispute with competing French interests, who also claimed rights over the North American fur trade during the 17th century, which occasionally resulted in fighting between the two sides, by the beginning of the 18th century the Hudson Bay Company was generally regarded as the de facto government body in that area of America, a position accepted by the terms of the Treaty of Utrecht which was signed in 1713. Widely regarded as a contemporary of and similar to the British East India Company which held a similar position in both India and Asia, at its height the Hudson Bay Company was said to have controlled the region known as Prince Rupert's Land, which consisted of around 30% of modern day Canada and around 60% of modern day North America. On a day-to-day basis, the company was reported to have traded trapped furs for equipment and supplies needed by the European trappers, whilst their Native American competitors were only offered blankets in exchange for their pelts.

It is perhaps worth noting that in this particular region of the North American continent, recent evidence of early Norse settlement is thought to confirm suggestions that Viking explorers were the very first Europeans to reach the American Continent sometime around 1000 AD, although these first visitors were thought to have been subsequently expelled by the native Indian tribesmen who occupied the region. The Portuguese explorer, John Cabot, who was employed by King Henry VII of England at the time, was thought to have been the next European to reach these same eastern shores in 1497, even though it was his native homeland which claimed the same territories under the terms of the Treaty of Tordesillas. Signed in 1494, this treaty divided all of the unknown world between the kingdoms of Portugal and Spain, but as a creation entirely of their own making, was largely ignored by most other European states of the time. For most of the next decade, until around 1506, several Portuguese explorers were said to have made voyages in and around the coast of Newfoundland and North America, reinforcing their own nation's claim to the land and its territorial waters, which were regularly exploited by Portuguese fishermen, who even established temporary settlements on the coastline, although virtually all of these had been abandoned by the middle of the 16th century.

Around 1535 the French explorer, Jacques Cartier, was reported to have claimed parts of these northern territories for his monarch, King Francis I, who subsequently named these new lands, New France. Although French fisherman and explorers were said to have fished in local waters and made journeys into the hinterland of their new found territories, there were thought to have been few attempts to actually colonise these new lands, until such time as local agreements and alliances had been made with the indigenous peoples who inhabited them. By the beginning of the 17th century though, several thousand, largely French colonists, were thought to have settled in New France, many of whom were employed in the fledgling fur trade which had first begun in 1604. Within four years the capital city of these new French territories, Quebec, was thought to have been founded, resulting in further, more detailed exploration of the wider region, including its great lakes and rivers and the formation of new alliances with the local tribesmen, such as the "Huron". However, despite these French explorers and colonists having settled throughout extensive areas of the territories that later became Canada, their numbers were thought to have been relatively small and thinly spread, which prevented them from holding complete control over their vast new possessions. Whilst French interests were thought to have been largely concentrated to the east and south of Hudson's Bay, various British colonies were said to have been established in both Newfoundland and along the shores of Hudson's Bay, in areas where ownership was disputed by each of the European powers. From Quebec in the north east to New Orleans in the south, French claims included the later southern states of Louisiana and Illinois, along with all of those territories now occupying the centre of the modern day United States. To the northeast, the region of modern Canada, now marked by New Brunswick, Nova Scotia and Prince Edward Island, had originally been occupied by French explorers and settlers, who knew the region as Acadia, which was said to have changed hands between Britain and France during the 17th century. For much of the next century, until 1756 and the start of the Seven Years War, this French held region of Acadia was reported to have been a generally unsettled place, with parts of Nova Scotia passing into British hands in 1713 and the other areas of Acadia remaining the subject of both sides claims right through to the 1756. In 1758 British forces were reported to have attacked the main French military stronghold in the region, Louisbourg and having captured the fortress, completely demolished it, in order to prevent the French from re-occupying it in the future. With their main defensive position destroyed, the remaining French positions quickly fell, leaving Britain in complete control of the northeast region of the American coastline. In the remaining parts of French Canada, the end of the Seven Years War and the Treaty of Paris in 1763, saw France formally cede the remainder of their western territories to Britain, regions that would later form part of British controlled Canada.

Although these new possessions were not thought to have been permanently settled by British colonists until after the Seven Years War in 1763, loyalist immigrants were said to have begun arriving after that date and went on to form the basis for the local population. Their numbers were said to have been substantially increased in the late 18th century by large numbers of immigrants and refugees, who had travelled north from the thirteen former British colonies, which had previously declared themselves as the United States. Following the end of the American Revolution in 1781 and the resulting Treaty of Paris signed in 1783, between Britain and the United States, certain territories of British Canada were subsequently ceded to the new American Republic, including what later became the US states of Michigan, Illinois and Ohio, in return for the establishment of a formal border between the United States and British controlled Canada. Being on the border of the newly formed United States though, the southern regions of British Canada were also said to have been heavily involved during the war of 1812, which saw American and British forces confront one another again over their newly formed territorial borders. However, with a significant British naval presence based in Halifax and with the new American Republic lacking the ships and personnel to seriously threaten the region, eventually a peaceful settlement was found that both countries could accept. However, not content with having tried unsuccessfully to invade the British regions of Canada, a number of American republicans were reported to have tried to promote civil discontent in the largely French dominated region of Lower Canada, especially around the city of Quebec, where rebel leaders tried to foment rebellion against the British authorities. Although these revolts were thought to have been largely unsuccessful, nonetheless the British government were said to have sent a delegation to Canada to assess the situation and to determine the best course of action for the authorities to take. The main delegate, Lord Durham, was reported to have spent some months talking to local representatives, before returning to Britain to advise Parliament that Canada should be offered its own responsible government. Durham suggested that the regions of Upper and Lower Canada should be merged into one United Province of Canada, a suggestion that was incorporated into the Act of Union, which was passed by the British Parliament in 1840. Despite the reservations that were expressed by those Canadians opposed to the scheme, within eight years, systems of both local and national government were said to have been established in the newly united Province of Canada, which continued to operate right through to the 20th century.

Further political unity between the main part of British Canada in the west and the Maritime colonies in the east was thought to have become a much greater priority following the American Civil War, which occurred between 1861 and 1865. With diplomatic relations between Britain and the United States said to have been uneasy, largely because of tacit British support for the southern Confederacy and with North American connivance over Irish republican raids into British controlled Canada, there were calls for further cooperation between the various northern states that lay outside of American control. Although not all of these British colonies were amenable to the idea of any sort of political union, ultimately all of them were reported to have attended a conference at Charlottetown in 1864, where the subject of a much larger confederation of northern states was discussed by the various regional delegates. They subsequently agreed to meet in London, where the British North America Act of 1867 was discussed and eventually signed, ostensibly leading to the creation of a united Canada. According to most Canadians this first Act represents the date that their country became independent of the British Empire and although the act itself was subsequently modified in both 1949 and 1982, these later amendments were generally in response to specific French Canadian issues and Parliamentary procedures, rather than dealing with the day to day governance of the country, which had largely come into effect in 1867. During the 19th century the east coast of Canada was also thought to have become the destination for many hundreds of thousands of refugees from England, Scotland, Ireland and Wales who were driven from their homes by poverty or famine during the 1800's and who all added their own particular influences to the creation of the modern day Canadian nation. From 1867 through to the dawn of the 20th century, Canada was said to have continued its consolidation, with the colonies of British Columbia and Vancouver Island finally choosing to become part of the federated country in 1871, with Prince Edward Island following suit some two years later. Although this thirty-odd year period was generally regarded as one of growth and settlement, there were still occasional disputes with its southern neighbour, America, especially regarding the purchase of Alaska in 1867 and the subsequent gold rush there during the late 1890's, although both of these issues were said to have been finally resolved through negotiation.

As with many of Great Britain's self governing colonies and dominions, the outbreak of the First World War proved to be a pivotal moment in the history of these former Imperial territories, marking their change from being an historic dependency of the British Crown, to becoming a recognisable international state in its own right. Through its political decision making, but more importantly through the valour and commitment of its armed forces, Canada was reported to have finally emerged upon the world stage as an independent democratic nation which willingly submitted itself to upholding the ideals of freedom and democracy. As in the other great British colonies and dominions throughout the globe, including India, Africa, Australia and New Zealand, tens of thousands of young Canadian's, both men and women, were reported to have rallied to Britain's cause, willingly committing themselves to her defence. Despite only having a relatively small standing army of some several thousand men, within a matter of months, some thirty thousand Canadians were said to have volunteered to serve in Western Europe and were making their way across the Atlantic to take their place on the Western front. The first Canadian troops were thought to have arrived in France by the beginning of 1915 and elements of their 1st Division were reportedly some of the first allied troops to have been attacked with the poison chlorine gas which was commonly used by the German army. While large numbers of British and French troops were said to have fled the threat of this new weapon, the Canadians were thought to have quickly realised that the effects of the gas could be neutralised by the use of urine soaked rags being placed over their nose and mouths, helping them to hold their positions and preventing the enemy forces from advancing. However, even with their homemade defence against the poisonous clouds that were unleashed on their lines, it was still reported that some six thousand Canadian troops were affected by the gas, of which, a full third were thought to have died as a direct result of it being deployed against them.

Ferdinand II

Isabella I

Leif Ericsson

Canadian forces were also an intrinsic part of the allied force that was marshalled in 1916 in preparation for the Battle of the Somme, which ultimately resulted in the largest number of allied casualties ever suffered by British and Dominion forces, nearly fifty eight thousand men killed or wounded in a single day. As much the result of poor planning, communications and inadequate leadership, as it was of complete incompetence, such enormous human losses were thought to have become a common feature of the First World War overall, although for the Canadian's specifically, the Somme campaign alone was thought to have accounted for some twenty five thousand casualties, either killed or wounded. Despite such losses however, Canada's frontline troops, continued to enhance their military reputation, reportedly being prepared to take on any military assignment, seemingly regardless of the cost and earning the everlasting esteem of their civilian contemporaries, as well as their political masters in equal measure. Vimy Ridge was said to be just one of the many battles which saw the Canadian military divisions take their place in the vanguard of various allied operations, designed to capture the German army's well established defensive lines. Beginning on the morning of the 9th April 1917, a "creeping artillery barrage" was said to have cleared the way for the following Canadian troops, who then cleared the trenches of their German defenders, slowly, but surely moving the allied lines forward of their previous positions. By the afternoon of the following day the Canadian troops had not only taken a great deal of ground, but also captured several thousand German prisoners and killed many hundreds more. However, the victory had not come without a high price for Canada's own young troops, who were reported to have suffered some eleven thousand casualties, either dead or wounded, a figure which underpinned their utter determination to achieve the objectives that they had been given.

Seven months later and largely because of their tenacious reputation, Canadian troops were reported to have been redeployed to the Ypres area, in readiness for yet another allied offensive that later became known as the Second Battle of Passchendaele, which was fought between October and November 1917. In conjunction with British and Anzac troops, Canadian soldiers were tasked with pushing the German's front line back, allowing the allied positions to be advanced, so that the town of Passchendaele could be recovered by the allies. Although there were several instances of allied reversals and occasional failures to reach individual objectives, the operation itself proved to be successful, although the entire campaign was said to have cost some sixteen thousand Canadian casualties, with at least a quarter of that number being killed. Despite these losses though, Canadian troops were thought to have been so vital to the allied offensive strategy that they were intensively employed throughout much of 1918, most notably during the famous One Hundred Days Offensive, which saw Canadian troops and others, participate in the Battle of Amiens, Cambrai and the vital breaking of the Hindenburg Line which ultimately forced Germany to agree an Armistice on 11th November 1918. As with a number of other former British colonies, including Australia and New Zealand, by the end of the First World War, Canada's international reputation as one of the principal victorious allied nations, had been assured and the military worth of its fighting forces had likewise been enhanced. Back in Canada itself, its own people began to see themselves as an integral part of the international community, a country with its own culture, traditions and now with a reputation and standing that was equal to its previously more dominant American and British counterparts. Although Canada was thought to have been largely independent of Britain, since the beginning of the 20th century, its emergence after World War I, was thought to mark the period when most Canadians began to see themselves as Canadians, rather than being historically tied to or associated with Britain or indeed the United States. The almost inevitable separation of Canada from the British Empire was said to have been largely confirmed by the Canadian government's subsequent adoption of the Statute of Westminster 1931, which essentially granted the former dominion full legislative independence from the British Parliament in London. For some Canadians, the formal adoption of this 1931 Statute actually represents the true date of Canada's independence, as opposed to the North American Act of 1867, though either way this was only a matter of formality, rather than being a substantive issue. Interestingly though, despite Canada's decision to ratify the 1931 Statute, the neighbouring British dominion of Newfoundland refused to do so, a situation that was only changed in 1949, when political and economic circumstances effectively forced Newfoundland to become a province of Canada, a decision that was thought to have caused much bitterness and resentment within the local population at the time.

Although Canada was entirely independent of Britain by September 1939, when the Second World War erupted, the Canadian government declared war against Nazi Germany on 10th September nonetheless and the following day issued a similar declaration against Mussolini's Italy. As was the case elsewhere with many of the western allies, during the inter-war years Canada was thought to have put little investment into its armed forces and in common with its pre-First World War status had a relatively small full-time army of several thousand which was supplemented by a part-time militia, both of which were poorly trained and ill-equipped. In common with most democratic countries of the time, Canada, along with its former allies, Britain, France, Belgium, Australia, New Zealand, etc. had believed that the losses of the Great War would prevent such an event ever happening again, but as with all of the other allied nations, they were wrong. Fortunately for the allied cause, in common with the United States, Canada was reported to have had the capacity to become one of the world's greatest industrial producers and like its southern neighbour was able to mobilise these vast manufacturing facilities to produce materials for the war, including ships, aircraft and wheeled vehicles. However, according to some sources, the most important products supplied by Canada during the Second World War were the vast amounts of both aluminium and nickel, both of which were necessary components of the allied war effort. The first military supply convoy reportedly left Canada just days after war had been officially declared and by June 1940, the first Canadian troops were said to have been landed in Europe, in an attempt to reinforce the British and French forces that were being forced back to Dunkirk by the advancing German army. Unfortunately, the Canadian troops were thought to have reached France far too late to prevent the large scale evacuation of the allied expeditionary force and were subsequently forced to withdraw from Europe, back to the isolated British mainland. Rather frustratingly perhaps, for the Canadian troops, with Britain generally besieged and few foreign theatres in which to operate effectively against Germany and her Axis allies, most of these Canadian forces were thought to have been largely restricted to defending Britain's mainland from the threat of an impending German invasion, which never actually happened. Thanks largely to a British Air Force which contained numerous Commonwealth pilots from around the world, including many from Canada itself; the German Luftwaffe was prevented from gaining air superiority, which was a prerequisite for the planned military invasion of Britain. With the Battle of Britain won by the RAF and its limited numbers of pilots and planes, Germany subsequently turned its attention to Russia, fatally wounding its own long term military ambitions by fighting on two separate fronts, one to the east and one to the west.

Apart from the ill-fated and largely unsuccessful raid on the French port of Dieppe in August 1942, most Canadian troops had to wait until 1943 before they could become formerly engaged on the European continent, when they were fully employed in both the invasion of Sicily and later the Italian mainland. However, elements of the Canadian army were said to have been involved with one of the conflicts most notable Special Forces units, the Devil's Brigade, a mixed force made up of both American and Canadian troops. Although they were reportedly tasked for a number of extremely difficult missions, the unit's first high profile operation was reportedly against Monte La Defensa in Italy, during December 1943, where they were reported to have scaled a seemingly impenetrable cliff face to overcome German positions that were stationed there. Having overcome their initial target, the Brigade were then said to have been used to attack a number of similarly difficult mountain targets, as a result of which some 70% of the unit was thought to have been either killed or wounded. By January of the following year the Brigade was said to have been reinforced and put back into the frontline at Anzio, where they were first referred to as the "Devils Brigade", having terrified the life out of the German forces that were opposing them. With the approach of the allied invasion of mainland Europe planned for June 1944, the Canadian forces were said to have allocated their own section of the Normandy coastline, codenamed "Juno" beach, where they suffered heavy casualties as they hurled themselves ashore to begin the long awaited liberation of Europe. Despite incurring heavier losses than any other allied force on the day, with the exception of the American troops on "Omaha" beach, the Canadian troops were reported to have still managed to penetrate deeper into occupied France than any other allied soldiers, save for those paratroopers who had been deliberately dropped inland in order to disable German communication systems, thereby preventing them from reinforcing their coastal defences, which were being attacked and overrun by the allies. Canadian forces were later instrumental in helping to secure the port of Antwerp, leading a mixed British, Polish Belgian and Dutch force to secure the Scheldt estuary, which was still held by the Germans, thereby preventing the allies from using Antwerp as a supply point for their military operations in Europe. Suffering extremely heavy losses, of which some six thousand were reportedly Canadians, this force was said to have spent several weeks helping to secure the area around Antwerp, before turning their attention to the liberation of the Netherlands. Throughout the entire course of the Second World War, the Canadian people were reported to have contributed hundreds of thousands of their young men and women to the allied cause, who subsequently served in virtually every service, from the Army and Navy, to the Air Force and the auxiliary services, including Nursing and the Merchant Marine. Some one hundred thousand Canadian's were thought to have been killed or wounded during the conflict, amongst which a significant number of gallantry awards were said to have been earned by Canada's fighting forces, including several Victoria Crosses, the highest award that could be issued by the British military authorities.

MARINERS, MERCHANTS AND THE MILITARY TOO

7. BRITAIN IN THE CARIBBEAN

English and the later British colonisation of the Caribbean and West Indies, was reported to have begun in a meaningful way on Bermuda, otherwise known as the Somers Islands, in 1612, some three years after the islands had first been claimed for James I of England by Admiral George Somers. This first round of settlement was reported to have followed in 1623 by the colonisation of St Kitts and three years later by the permanent settlement of Barbados in 1627, both of which later became part of the Caribbean islands known as the West Indies. Once St Kitts was occupied it later became the launch point for the further colonisation of other nearby islands, including Nevis, Antigua, Anguilla, Montserrat and Tortola, which itself became the base for the later colonisation of the Windward Islands and the wider Caribbean region. Although the English were said to have shared the colonisation and use of St Kitts with French interests, this situation only continued until 1713, when complete control of the islands were said to fallen into British hands. However, following Britain's withdrawal from the thirteen colonies of North America, which later became part of the United States, British former interests in that region were thought to have been relocated southward to its historic Caribbean possessions and northward to the territories which later became part of an independent Canada. England's Caribbean possessions are said to be inextricably linked to the transatlantic slave trade, by virtue of the numerous sugar plantations that were reported to have been established in the region by various English/British landowners, merchants and traders, a subject that has previously been dealt with elsewhere.

Although the island of Bermuda was reported to have first been discovered by the Spanish navigator Juan de Bermudez in 1505, the man who gave the island its name, for much of the next century, between 1505 and 1609, it was said to have remained unoccupied, save for numbers of passing ships and shipwrecked sailors who were thought to have landed there to re-provision or repair their ships. It was only in 1609 that Bermuda was accidentally visited by Sir George Somers, an admiral of the English Virginia Company, whose ship the "Sea Venture" was reported to have been wrecked on the coast of the island, as it made its way across the Atlantic to the company's American colony at Jamestown in Virginia. It was said to be Somers who formally claimed the island for the English Crown, which was later incorporated into the territories of the Virginia Company, with its first settlers arriving there sometime around 1612, making it the oldest inhabited English colony anywhere in the New World, apart from those that now lie within the United States. Ownership of the island was said to have passed to the Somers Island Company in 1615, although its control of Bermuda was thought to have been revoked in 1684, mainly because of the company's insistence on the islands economy being almost entirely directed towards the production of tobacco, much to the local population's annoyance. Rather than having the island's economy turned over to entirely agricultural purposes, most of the local inhabitants were thought to have been employed within Bermuda's traditional shipbuilding industry, which had been established around its plentiful supply of native juniper trees, which were regularly replanted by the islanders to ensure a ready supply of wood. However, despite their best efforts in this respect, such was the scale of the shipbuilding industries on the island that before long, the thick canopy of trees which had once covered much of the island, was said to have been exhausted and the population began to look for alternative industries to maintain the islands economy. The natural replacement for the historic maritime industry was thought to have been salt production, although local people reportedly also turned their hands to whaling, fishing, shipping and even piracy to maintain Bermuda's local economy.

Following Britain's forced military withdrawal from the territories that later became the United States, Bermuda was said to have become the British Empire's main military base in the Caribbean and as such was developed to house a significant naval presence in the region. Not only did these new Royal Navy dockyards and military bases serve to protect Britain's valuable possessions in the Caribbean, but also provided a naval station from where the Royal Navy could patrol the waters of the eastern seaboard of the United States, restricting the international trade between America and Britain's greatest European enemy of the time, France. Not only did these restrictions limit the amounts of goods being transported to French ports, but almost inevitably had an adverse effect on the American economy, much to the irritation of the United States merchants whose businesses were slowly being strangled by Britain's unilaterally imposed trade sanctions. With the Royal Navy being expanded to meet the increasing danger posed by the French forces of Napoleon Bonaparte, there was reported to have been a shortage of experienced seamen to serve aboard these Royal Navy ships, leading to the widespread use of pressgangs to make up the shortfall in manpower. Although the use of the pressgangs was known to have been common practice in Britain, the increasing habit of the Royal Navy in forcibly abducting foreign sailors from ships which had been intercepted at sea, was said to have become a source of great contention for the American authorities, especially as many of their own British born seamen, or former Royal Navy personnel, were quite often the target for such recruitment practices.

Tecumseh

James Madison

Lord Liverpool

Elsewhere on the North American continent, Britain's continuing presence in both Upper and Lower Canada remained a source of irritation for those American leaders who were wholly dedicated to the complete removal of the British Empire from the New World. According to some historians, the still relatively new American Executive was said to have come under increasing pressure to invade these northern territories and bring them under the authority of the newly emerging

United States. For its part, Britain was said to be keen to develop a broad neutral border between itself and the new American Republic, an aim that it attempted to pursue by encouraging the independence of the various Native Indian tribes, whose homelands lay in the northwest frontier, now marked by the modern day American states of Indiana, Illinois, Michigan, Ohio and Wisconsin. Under the leadership of the Shawnee tribal chief, Tecumseh, a number of these frontier tribes, along with other displaced native peoples were thought to have allied themselves to the British cause in Canada, although the later loss of Tecumseh, during the Battle of the Thames in October 1813, was said to have ultimately ended this particular alliance. However, the American government's continuing belief that British held Canadian provinces would be a military walkover, allied to increasing resentment over Britain's control of its Atlantic trade routes, which was suppressing America's trade with Europe, eventually forced the American legislature to act. In June 1812, the US President, James Madison, made a speech publicly criticising Britain's treatment of the United States and its people, which subsequently evolved into a declaration of war against Britain and its Empire, a call that was later endorsed by both the Congress and the Senate, before being signed by Madison, on June 18th 1812. Advised of the declaration some weeks later, the time it took for news to cross the Atlantic, initially the British government was not thought to have been overly concerned by the American legislature announcement, confident that Britain's military forces in the Americas were more than sufficient to defend its existing possessions. More concerned with the danger posed to Europe by the forces of Napoleon Bonaparte, the administration of Lord Liverpool, were reported to have ordered British forces in America to maintain a defensive position, rather than taking any sort of proactive action against the United States, its citizens or its territories, which is exactly what they did. In July 1812 however, the American General, William Hull, was said to have led a contingent of around a thousand militiamen across the Detroit River and captured the relatively small Canadian town of Sandwich, where his force was subsequently joined by another five hundred men, many of them Canadians. Holding the town and the surrounding area for a matter of weeks, by August of 1812, Hull and his militia were said to have been forced back across the Detroit River, before being required to surrender to regular British troops who had been sent into the region to evict them.

By October of 1812, American militias launched yet another attack on Britain's Canadian territories, this time in the area of the Niagara Peninsula, but once again were forced to retire, although the engagement was said to have cost the life of the English Major General, Isaac Brock, the man who was charged with defending Upper Canada from invasion by the United States. Despite these initial setbacks however, American forces continued to push forward into the British held territories, with the capture of York, the provincial capital of Upper Canada, being one of their most notable victories during the entire course of the War of 1812. The attack reportedly began on 27th April 1813, when some sixteen hundred American militiamen, supported by a number of assorted warships, were thought to have come ashore, to be faced by a British garrison of around three hundred regular troops, who were themselves reinforced by a small number of Native Indians and a handful of local Canadian militiamen. Apart from being outnumbered, the British garrison were also reported to have been ill-prepared for and poorly led during the engagement, with significant numbers of men being lost to reckless charges and cannon fire which was launched from the supporting American warships lying offshore. Recognising the seriousness of the situation, the British officer in charge, Major General Roger Hale Sheaffe, was thought to have ordered the local ammunition store be blown up and that a ship being constructed in the local dockyards be burned, in order to deprive the American forces of their future use. With an American military victory imminent, Sheaffe decided to negotiate the surrender of the British base, although this reportedly took some time because of a reluctance by the American military commander, Major General Henry Dearborn, to come ashore from the warship, from where he was supposedly overseeing the military operation. However, eventually he did agree the surrender terms and promptly set about seizing the arms and stores that were held at York, as well as arranging for them to be sent away into American hands a few days later. It was said to be following the signing of the surrender that a number of the American militiamen began to carry out acts of plunder, looting several of the local houses and government buildings, before setting fire to them and causing a great deal of damage within the town itself. Although the American commander, Henry Dearborn, later denied any prior knowledge of or complicity in these actions, for most reporters, his unwillingness to restrain his troops was simply indicative of his own poor leadership. It was thought to be these particular actions that were said to have been used as justification for Britain's subsequent attack on and destruction of America's capital city, Washington DC, which occurred in August 1814.

Following the American attack on the British township of York, the Governor General of Canada, Sir George Prevost, wrote to the Royal Navy's commanders in Bermuda, requesting their help in responding to the American looting and burning of York, which even by their own standards were thought to have been outside the terms of normal warfare. Arriving off the east coast of America in August 1814, the British Royal Navy fleet which had been despatched from Bermuda was said to have contained a large infantry contingent under the command of Major General Robert Ross, who had been appointed to lead the punitive raid against the Americans, despite still recovering from an earlier injury received in France. Landing his troops at Benedict on the Patuxent River in Maryland on the 18th August 1814, elements of the British fleet were reported to have carried up along the river, whilst Ross and his troops marched to a point which allowed them to advance on both Washington and Baltimore, depending on which of the two cities was to be attacked first. Under persuasion from Rear Admiral Cockburn and other officers, Ross ultimately chose to attack Washington, having been convinced that a military raid on the American's capital city would have a much greater effect on the population at large, which certainly proved to be the case. Rather than launch an immediate attack on Washington however, Ross chose to rest and reorganise his contingent of some five thousand men, which was said to have been composed of marines, rocket brigades and engineers, along with their supplies of ammunition, rockets and field guns. Choosing a route that would more easily accommodate his forces, Ross initially headed towards the American township of Bladensberg in Maryland, a small commercial centre that lay at the crossroads linking Washington, with the much larger areas of Annapolis and Baltimore. The military defence of both Washington and Baltimore was reported to have been under the command of a local Brigadier General called William Winder, an American officer, who had not only been unfortunate enough to be captured by the British in an earlier engagement, but who was generally regarded as incompetent by most other American commanders. Having received sufficient notice about the advancing British forces, Winder was said to have sent for reinforcements from Washington and Annapolis, as well as alerting his own local militia, all of whom were reported to have arrived in the area, with sufficient time to prepare their own defences. Unfortunately for the American defenders though, Winder's decision making and failure to communicate with other commanders simply helped to ensure that the defensive positions held by the American forces, were neither effective, nor durable. As a result, the highly professional British commanders and their troops quickly identified the weaknesses of their opponent's positions and employed military tactics specifically designed to circumvent them. With many of his previously prepared positions essentially neutralised by the British forces, many of Winder's troops began to withdraw, a retreat that was reportedly hastened by Winder's own confused series of orders, which helped to further bewilder his already perplexed troops. It was largely because of his chaotic instructions that rather than reforming at an agreed central point, most of the American military force simply fragmented, with some units reforming immediately, others retreating towards the capital and yet others, simply heading back home. For the British troops, the Battle of Bladensberg was said to have represented a clear military victory, even though it was one that was aided and abetted by poor American planning on the part of its overall commander, William Winder. For the American authorities however, this relatively insignificant battle was thought to have been a complete disaster, as the failure of their forces to hold or defeat the British, essentially left their own capital city open to attack by a foreign army, albeit one that had little interest in holding it.

Within hours of defeating the American forces at Bladensberg, the British commander, Major General Ross, was reported to have moved his troops towards Washington, their advance unhindered by any further military actions by the American authorities, most of whom had chosen to flee into neighbouring states, rather than risk being captured by the British forces. It was also reported that prior to reaching the outskirts of Washington, both Major General Ross and Rear Admiral Cockburn had warned the British troops about their behaviour whilst in the city, threatening dire retribution on any man who failed to follow orders, or committed any unlawful act. As the British force slowly made its way through the suburbs of Washington, it was said to have met little resistance and it was only when Ross' advance party arrived near Capital Hill that shots were fired at them by a small number of American defenders. However, these men were quickly dispersed by the British troops, who subsequently burnt down the house which had been used by the attackers, in order to deter any further resistance. As Ross, Cockburn and the main body of British soldiers arrived in the area of the still incomplete White House, orders were given for it and other government buildings to be set alight, repaying the destruction that had been inflicted on the Canadian provincial capital of York some two years earlier. Amongst those prominent Washington buildings set alight was the Congressional Library, home to many of America's most important books and historic documents, some of which were only saved when a rainstorm developed, helping to extinguish the flames that would otherwise have destroyed everything, including the library building itself. At the much more iconic White House, the approach of the British forces were said to have been well anticipated and tales exist of the American First Lady, Dolly Madison, valiantly saving many of the buildings unique treasures, including a great portrait of George Washington, which was cut out of its frame, rolled up and carried away to safety. However, the reality of the situation was that much of what was saved was in fact carried away by members of the White House staff, who tried to rescue as much as they could, before the British troops arrived. When Ross and his men finally did arrive in the Presidential building, they were reported to have been confronted by a dining room devoid of guests, but replete with food and wine, which they were said to have happily consumed, before setting light to the building and leaving it to burn.

General Wm Hull   General Isaac Brock   Roger Hale Sheaffe

As well as the White House, Senate and other major government buildings, the British forces were also said to have set alight to the United States Treasury offices, as well as a number of other public buildings. Others however, including the US Patents Office and Marine Barracks were said to have been spared a similar fate, after requests for their preservation were made to the British commanders, who happily agreed to their protection. Elsewhere, the British troops had little need to attack and destroy certain targets, as they were destroyed by the American authorities themselves, with the Washington Navy Yard, along with its many ships, stores and arsenal all being deliberately wrecked by the local authorities, in order to prevent them from falling into British hands. Although a significant number of British troops were said to have been killed and injured whilst trying to destroy American munitions on the outskirts of the city on the 25th August 1814, having spent around twenty four hours in the capital, the arrival of a tornado, which resulted in the deaths of both American inhabitants and British soldiers alike, forced Ross and Cockburn to begin withdrawing their forces from Washington. Most historians tend to agree that the raid and the subsequent destruction of the capital's state buildings was only ever an act of reprisal for the destruction of York in Canada, by American forces some two years earlier. The fact that few if any private houses were damaged during the raid and that no American citizens were purposely killed, during those 24 hours, tends to reinforce the idea that the raid on Washington was simply an act of retribution by Britain for the earlier American actions, albeit one that was designed to help undermine America's largely undeserved self confidence in the wider region. Having withdrawn their remaining forces to the British ships anchored on the Patuxent River, some of which had suffered damage during the bad weather, Major General Ross and his forces were then assigned the task of attacking the American city of Baltimore. At the same time as Ross had been given the task of attacking Washington, a squadron of British ships, under the command of Commodore James Alexander Gordon, had been ordered to sail up the Potomac River to attack the American naval dockyards at Alexandria and Georgetown, both of which actions were primarily designed to distract American attention away from Ross' military assault on Washington. One of the main targets for Gordon's squadron was said to have been Fort Washington, a military station located along the Potomac River, which presented a threat to British navigation of the waterway, so therefore became a legitimate military objective for the British ships. The American commander, Major General William Winder, the same man who had organised the catastrophic defensive positions at Bladensberg, had also been responsible for the defence of Fort Washington, ordering the commander there, Captain Samuel Dyson, to destroy the fort and its stores, only if they were attacked by a superior number of British troops. However, Dyson seems to have been completely intimidated by the arrival of Gordon's naval squadron and as quickly as they began an opening salvo against the fort, Dyson ordered his own guns spiked and blew up the remainder of the station.

With this objective achieved, Gordon then sailed his fleet upstream to the large commercial centre of Alexandria, where the city's mayor agreed terms with the British commander, in order to spare the city from destruction. As a result, Gordon was able to take possession of a number of American merchant ships and their various cargoes, which included flour, cotton, tobacco, wines and other valuable commodities. Having achieved many of his military aims and rather than risk any unnecessary losses by continuing his advance to Georgetown, Gordon subsequently began to withdraw his naval forces back down the Potomac, to rejoin the main British fleet in Chesapeake Bay, taking all of his plunder with him. Despite efforts by American forces to hinder his progress down the river, nonetheless Gordon was able to rejoin the main British fleet by September 9th 1814, with most of his ships and captured booty intact. However, the delay caused by his squadron's relatively slow progress up to Fort Washington and Alexandria ultimately allowed the American defenders of Baltimore, the next most likely target for the British fleet, to more adequately prepare themselves for the arrival of the British force some few days later. The battle for Baltimore, from an entirely British perspective, was thought to have been important for several reasons, not least of which, was the belief that the large east coast port played host to many of the American privateers who regularly raided British ships in both the Caribbean and the Atlantic, as well as carrying on a clandestine trade with Britain's military enemy, France. Repeating the tactics which had worked so well in the raid on Washington, Robert Ross and his land forces were said to have been put ashore some distance from Baltimore, while the British fleet was sailed up into Baltimore harbour in order to besiege the city from the sea. Unfortunately for the British commanders however, the delays caused by Commodore Gordon's slow journey up and down the Potomac River, some few days earlier, had allowed the American defenders to fully prepare for such British tactics, with Major General Ross' land forces encountering heavy resistance from the Americans at a defensive position known as North Point. It was said to be there that the highly competent British commander, Robert Ross was shot and fatally wounded by an unknown American sniper, causing the less able and experienced, Colonel Arthur Brooke, to take over command of the British land forces, who promptly decided to hold his position, until such time as the seaborne attack on Baltimore was finally decided.

The main American stronghold in Baltimore was reported to have been Fort McHenry, a star shaped fortress positioned on a spur of land that stretched out into Baltimore Harbour, providing an all round defence for the city and its large commercial port. Although designed to resist a land attack by enemy forces, the fact that the British troops, now under the command of Colonel Brooke, were still some way outside of Baltimore, meant that the fort only had to contend with the salvoes were launched at it by the British ships located offshore. Having previously sunk a number of their own vessels to hamper the movement of the British ships in the harbour, the American defenders were thought to have been reasonably content to sit behind their newly built fortification, while the Royal Navy attempted to batter the American defenders into submission, which they singularly failed to do. After some twenty-odd hours of bombarding Fort McHenry and the surrounding positions to little effect, the British naval commander, Vice Admiral Sir Alexander Cochrane, was said to have ordered a landing to be made by British troops at a point a little way off Fort McHenry, in the hope that these forces might help relieve Colonel Brookes marines, who were still being held back by the American defenders at North Point. Unfortunately, these small British boats and their passengers were quickly identified by the defenders of Fort McHenry who brought their guns to bear on the Royal Navy's diversionary attack, forcing the remaining boats to retire to the British warships. Witnessing the failure of the attack, Colonel Brooke and his marines, who were still pinned down by American forces, were left with little option but to withdraw from the area and wait until such time as they picked up by the Royal Navy ships. By the morning of the September 14th 1814, the battle was over and having collected the marines the British fleet, complete with many of its captured American possessions withdrew from the Chesapeake Bay and set sail for the Caribbean. As for the valiant Robert Ross, who had led the British raid on Washington and was shot and fatally wounded by an American sniper, just prior to the Battle of North Point. Reportedly hit in the arm and chest, he was said to have died whilst being transported back to the fleet, although despite this, his body was returned to the ship nonetheless, to be stored in a large barrel of rum, for his final journey home to Halifax in Nova Scotia, where he was interred in the Old Burying Ground.

Even though the War of 1812 was largely caused by inflexibility and intolerance on both sides, arguments still persist as to which of the two protagonists actually won the war, although in reality, most historians agree that neither side won the dispute, because in practical terms it became an almost inevitable draw. Both sides achieved limited success during the conflict and likewise both suffered territorial losses and military failures, but overall both the United States and the British Empire were glad to see a final resolution to the dispute. By the time that the Treaty of Ghent was signed by both parties in December 1814 and introduced in the following February, the main loser of the conflict was thought to have been the Native Indian tribes of the northwest frontier, who had previously allied themselves to the British cause, in the hope that this would guarantee them continuing control of their historic tribal homelands, many of which were subsequently swallowed up by the later expansion of the United States and its burgeoning settler communities. The greatest winners by far, were thought to be the citizens of Canada, whose ongoing security was ensured by the British Empire's decision to oppose America's military expansion into these northern territories, allowing the modern state of Canada to evolve through to the present day. Two years after the Treaty of Ghent was implemented in February 1815, a new agreement, the Rush Bagot Treaty was said to have been signed between Britain and the United States, which formalised the territorial border between America and Canada, as well as arranging for the removal of those military installations that had been constructed by both nations, essentially creating a demilitarised zone between the two countries. Further treaties were signed between Britain and the United States in 1818, 1842 and 1846, all of which were designed to resolve any lingering territorial issues between the two nations, particularly those relating to the Oregon territories, which finally resulted in the land being divided between the US and Great Britain. With virtually all such land issues resolved, the border between Canada and the United States was thought to have remained relatively settled in later years, although the American Civil War, fought between the Union of northern states and the Confederacy of the southern American states, once again brought America and Britain into conflict with one another, albeit a largely political one. The southern Confederacy was said to have been eager for Britain or France to intervene in the national conflict, believing that with their help, they could easily defeat their northern opponents, although both European states were said to be instinctively against involving themselves in what was an entirely American military conflict. In order to try and force Britain and France to intervene, the southern authorities were reported to have initiated a ban on the export of cotton, a valuable and much needed commodity for the two European countries, although unfortunately for the confederacy, one that they could source from elsewhere in the world.

Even though there were many people in Britain and France who were generally sympathetic to the Confederate cause, few were prepared to risk all out war with the north, simply to help what was always likely to be an unsuccessful campaign for southern independence. However, the actions of one particular American sea captain, Charles Wilkes, might well have caused a military conflict between Britain and the United States during 1861, when he chose to intercept the British mail ship "Trent", which was conveying two Confederate diplomats from America to Britain, so that they could have talks with the British and French governments, in the hope that they might choose to officially recognise the new Confederate administration. Many within the British government were said to have been outraged at this illegal seizure of the mail ship and Captain Wilkes' decision to ignore Britain's neutrality, as well as the capture of the two diplomats, who were in effect in British custody. Demanding an apology from the American government and the immediate release of the diplomats, the

British authorities took immediate steps to upgrade its forces in both Canada and in the Atlantic, illustrating to the United States its annoyance at being dragged into the civil war politics of America. Eventually, the American President, rather than risk adding to his country's military worries, decided to release the two diplomats, but refused to offer a public apology over the matter, believing perhaps that Britain had in part been responsible for creating the situation, by allowing the two diplomats to take passage on a British mail ship in the first place. Although Britain was said to have considered trying to arbitrate between the two warring factions as early as 1862, it seems that any such negotiations would have proved futile, given that both governments were so far apart from one another in terms of their ultimate objectives, so the British government tried to maintain diplomatic relations with both sides, but without offering formal political recognition to the Confederacy, a move that would have permanently alienated the legitimate northern government.

Both before and after the War of 1812, the British held Caribbean island of Bermuda was regarded as vital to Britain's interests in both the Caribbean and the wider Atlantic region, leading to the military presence there becoming the most dominant feature of Bermuda's economy. Even greater development of the island's infrastructure and military defences were undertaken during the remainder of the 19th century, being constantly maintained right through to the middle of the 20th century and the end of the Second World War. Since then however, the island has reverted to largely civilian employment, relying on tourism and financial services to generate income, although a military presence still exists, but only in the form of the Bermuda Regiment, a conscripted force responsible for the defence of the island and its territorial waters. Although the large scale production of tobacco was attempted on Bermuda, ultimately it proved to be a largely unsuccessful industry and was soon replaced by shipbuilding, which then became one of the main economic drivers on the island. On the St Kitts and Nevis islands though, which were first settled by English colonists in 1624, tobacco and then sugar cane production were reported to be the main commercial products, with the latter requiring the importation of thousands of Black African slaves during the 17th and 18th centuries. Initially settled by a group of English colonists led by a Captain Thomas Warner in 1624, this seafarer and his crew were said to have originally been destined for the coastal region of Guiana, but having landed there quickly found their numbers devastated by foreign diseases, native attacks and lack of supplies. Rather than lose his entire expedition, Warner was thought to have left the area of Guiana, bringing his remaining colonists into the Caribbean, to search for a more suitable home, where they could settle themselves. Having explored a number of the unoccupied islands, eventually they arrived at St Kitts and having made a preliminary search of the island, during which they met the seemingly friendly natives and plenty of fresh water, Warner decided that this would become their new home. Returning to England to gather replacement colonists, by 1625 Warner and his newly reinforced settler community were said to have established the township of Saint Christopher, which is thought to be notable for being the first English community founded within the Caribbean.

In the year following the establishment of Saint Christopher, a French vessel, the only survivor of a Spanish naval attack, was said to have arrived in St Kitts and along with its crew were reported to be in such a pitiful state that Warner invited them to stay and establish their own colony on the island. However, as the two white European colonies increased in size, so their continued expansion was thought to have caused some resentment amongst the native Kalinago people, whose previously friendly disposition reportedly began to change. According to later reports, the tribal leader of the Kalinago, Tegremante, began plotting to eliminate the two settler communities, who were subsequently forewarned of his actions by a slave girl, who was fond of Warner and his family. As a result, the French and English colonists were thought to have combined together to attack the local tribesmen first, reportedly killing several hundred of their number and exiling the rest to neighbouring islands. The same year as this Indian massacre, 1626, was also said to have been marked by the formal division of the island between the English and French settlers, with each nationality being allocated their own particular areas of responsibility and authority. However, both groups suffered equally in 1629, when a Spanish naval force arrived at St Kitts, forcing most of the colonists to flee to outlying islands until such time as the pillaging Spaniards had left. Although they subsequently returned to reclaim their respective settlements, the two communities worked together to ensure that such an event would not reoccur, reportedly building a series of coastal defences around the island which might be used to prevent any future Spanish raids. Within thirty years, both the English and French communities had reportedly begun to spread out amongst the neighbouring islands of the Caribbean, with Nevis, Antigua, Montserrat and Anguilla being colonised by the English; and Martinique, Guadeloupe and St Croix by the French. It was also thought to be during the same period that the inhabitants of St Kitts began to experiment with the planting of tobacco, although as in the case of Bermuda, the domination of this particular marketplace by the English colony of Virginia, generally made its production on the Caribbean islands largely uneconomic, so they began to look for alternative cash crops. The most obvious substitute for the unsuccessful tobacco plant was said to have been sugar cane, although this subsequently required the importation of large numbers of Black African slaves to help plant, harvest and process this particularly valuable commodity, which almost inevitably led to the emergence of the slave owner, slave drivers and overseers, as well as many of the brutally depraved practices and conditions that were commonly associated with those people.

The neighbouring island of Nevis, which has formally been associated with St Kitts since 1671, was actually colonised by a group of settlers from St Kitts in 1628 and like there, quickly became dominated by the production of tobacco, making it one of Britain's most valuable possessions in the New World. In common with St Kitts, the colonists there were said to have been forced to flee their homes by the Spanish raid of 1629, although they quickly returned and resumed their cultivation of the valuable cash crop, before finally switching to sugar cane production in the 1640's. Within twenty years, Nevis was once again celebrated as the most profitable English possession in the New World, although it's perceived riches was thought to have made it a target for Britain's European competitors who were keen to add such a prized possession to their own international territories. In 1671, the British authorities were reported to have joined Nevis with St Kitts, Antigua and Montserrat, to form the Leeward Caribbean Island Government, a confederation which allowed each island full autonomy, but under the authority and protection of the British Empire. However, even the military protection of the Empire failed to prevent both islands from being attacked by French troops in 1705, when several thousand troops were landed on St Kitts, attacking the relatively small British military garrison there and holding the islands by force until 1713, when they were once again returned to Britain under the terms of the Treaty of Utrecht in that year. As St Kitts quickly regained its position as one of the British Caribbean's most valuable possessions, so the fortunes of neighbouring Nevis were beginning to decline, largely because of the planters over exploitation of the island's soils and the damage caused by the French occupation of the island. Interestingly though, this decline in the sugar cane industry was said to have had a positive effect on the fortunes of the Nevis islanders, who were forced to look for non agricultural uses for their lands, leading to the unlikely development of turning their economy towards tourism, rather than the more traditional Caribbean industries.

By 1776 St Kitts still remained one of the Caribbean's most profitable and most successful sugar producers, surviving numerous attacks by foreign states, the most serious of which was the attack on St Kitts by French forces in 1782, although Britain's supremacy over the island was finally accepted by the Treaty of Versailles, which was signed in the following year. The British authorities were reported to have reorganised its smaller Caribbean possessions yet again in 1806, when St Kitts, Nevis, Anguilla and the British Virgin Islands became one part of a much larger Leeward Islands Caribbean Government, a new confederation of semi autonomous islands, which was reported to have lasted from 1806 through to 1816. St Kitts and most of Britain's other sugar producing territories were said to have been adversely affected by the abolition of slavery within the Empire in 1834, legislation that subsequently freed hundreds of thousands of Black Africans from bondage and turned them into demanding paid workers. Although the end of this brutal trade was claimed by some, to signal the end of Britain's highly profitable sugar trade, in reality it was thought to be the development of sugar producing economies in India, Brazil and elsewhere which helped to reduce the Caribbean's influence in the worldwide sugar markets, as opposed to granting workers their freedom. Clearly, the demand to pay workers for their labour and to offer them suitable habitation and nutrition, did indeed adversely affect the profits made by private plantation owners and commodity merchants, but all the same, the sugar industry in the Caribbean continued nonetheless, albeit on a smaller, less profitable scale. Regardless of the changes brought about by international competition and the abolition of slavery however, much of the land on St Kitts and on many of Britain's Caribbean territories remained in private hands, ensuring that alternatives to sugar cane production were not only hard to find, but almost impossible to implement, unless the landowner chose to do so. It was this worldwide issue of land ownership, particularly in Britain's Imperial possessions that would continue to dominate the agenda of the Caribbean from the abolition of slavery in 1834, right through to the first half of the 20th century and the end of Empire. Sugar producing islands, such as St Kitts were reported to have been hit particularly hard by the collapse of commodity prices during the inter-war years, which adversely affected the jobs, wages and standards of living for many of the lowest paid workers on St Kitts, leading almost inevitably to the formation of trade unions and labour inspired political parties. From the 1940's through to the 1960's these parties were reported to have dominated St Kitts and Nevis political life, with the various administrations attempting to acquire failing or former sugar cane plantations, so that they could be put to more profitable use, as both islands began to change from an entirely agricultural economy towards a mixed industrial and tourism base. Although generally an independent nation since 1967, St Kitts and Nevis has been associated with Great Britain since that date, although the modern day United Kingdom has little practical involvement in the day to day governance of the country. Since being granted independence in 1967, the democratic process on the two islands has remained relatively stable, apart from an attempted coup by a neighbouring island in 1971 and the usual charges of inaccuracies and lack of representation by members of the losing political parties.

General Henry Dearborn

Sir George Prevost

General Robert Ross

Also associated with St Kitts and Nevis, at least in more recent years, was the Caribbean island of Anguilla, which was first settled by English colonists in 1650, during the period of expansion that immediately followed the colonisation of St Kitts in 1627. Initially occupied by English settlers from those two earlier English Caribbean possessions, in the mid 1660's Anguilla was reportedly seized by French forces and held for a period, before being handed back to Britain under the terms of the Treaty of Breda, which was signed in 1667. With English ownership re-established the island's settler community was said to have been subsequently reinforced with even more colonists, some of whom were thought to have come from Antigua and Barbados, bringing with them a number of Black African slaves as part of their own personal inventory. For much of its subsequent history, the main island of Anguilla, along with the numerous small islets that are associated with it, have been administered through the much larger territorial possessions of Antigua or St Kitts and as such, were subject to similar events as occurred elsewhere. However, during the 20th century and following the granting of national autonomy to St Kitts and Nevis in 1967, Anguilla was reported to have been incorporated into this new semi-autonomous territory, without the local population having been consulted. As a result, for the next two years, civil unrest was rife in Anguilla, a situation that was only resolved in 1971, when British authority was restored to the islands, although the underlying cause of the discontent, its enforced federation with St Kitts and Nevis, remained a topic for dissent. It was only in 1980 that Anguilla was able to finally secede from the confederation with St Kitts and Nevis, becoming a self governing British Overseas Dependency, for which the United Kingdom guarantees its ongoing security. Internally however, Anguilla remains an independent democratic state, governed by an elected legislature and an independent judiciary, with an economy largely based on tourism and offshore banking. In common with a number of its Caribbean neighbours, the lack of good arable soil and the regularity of severe tropical storms, including hurricanes, both serve to adversely affect and restrict the economic development of Anguilla, although for all those disadvantages the islands continue to thrive.

The year following Captain Warner's initial colonisation of St Kitts, an English sea captain called Henry Powell, was said to have landed on the Caribbean island of Barbados in May 1625 and almost immediately claimed the unoccupied lands for King James I of England. Although Powell's arrival on the island did not begin English colonisation of these newly found territories right away, within two years, an English expedition under the command of a Captain John Powell had been despatched to establish a colony there, taking with it around eighty settlers and a handful of young men who had been sentenced to transportation. Not unusually for the time, rights to these new territories were reported to have been granted to a London based merchant, by the English monarch, essentially making him the temporary owner of Barbados and the new settlers his tenants. Under this arrangement, the new settlers were to be provided with food and shelter, in return for helping to establish a new settlement, as well as the planting, cultivation and harvesting of the various cash crops that would be grown there. However, despite all of their hard work, virtually all of the profits that might be gained from the subsequent sale of these commodities belonged to the merchant, who would have been required to pay the English Crown for their continuing rights to the land, bear the cost of providing all of the necessary supplies for the settlers and arranging for goods to be transported between Barbados and England. However, this arrangement was reportedly altered in 1639, when control of Barbados was reported to have been handed to the Earl of Carlisle, a confidante to the monarch, who appointed his own agent as Governor of Barbados, much to the dissatisfaction of London's merchant community who branded this new arrangement as a robbery. Establishing a House of Assembly in order to assuage any possible resentment by local landowners, the new Governor, Henry Hawley, immediately set about trying to improve the efficiency of the islands agricultural output and began to look at the alternative crops which might be introduced in order to maximise the profitability of these new possessions. Initially, the new settlers and planters had concentrated on growing a mixture of cotton, ginger, indigo and tobacco, all of which were valuable cash crops that were increasingly cared for by white indentured servants brought in from England, Scotland, Ireland and Wales, who were bound by contract to serve for a determinate period of time. Although sugar cane production was reportedly introduced as early as 1637, it was only in 1640 that this new cash crop was more widely planted throughout the island, ostensibly to produce rum, which could then be sold for a premium. Within a relatively short time, the growing of sugar cane became the island's principal industry, with other earlier cash crops being replaced by increasingly large sugar plantations that were naturally labour intensive and extremely arduous to work on. As the availability of free land decreased, due to the amount of land being purchased by larger planters and investors, so the numbers of white indentured servants fell, as free land was often the incentive for poor Europeans to come and work in Barbados. Although these shortfalls were initially overcome by utilising convict labour, the harsh conditions, long hours and tropical diseases, were said to have decimated these workers, many of whom were in poor physical health and brutally treated to begin with. As an alternative to these unsuitable white European workers, so planters and landowners on Barbados began to look elsewhere for suitable labour, focusing first of all on the native Caribbean tribesmen, who had been continually exploited since the Spanish and Portuguese settlers had arrived in the New World in the late 15th century.

However, by the time English planters and landowners began to develop Barbados' sugar cane industry in the middle of the 17th century, there was already a well established slave route across the Atlantic ocean, the Transatlantic Slave Trade, which transported millions of ensnared Black Africans from their homelands, to the utter misery of the Caribbean sugar cane industry. Although the subject of the Triangular Trade has been dealt with more fully elsewhere, it has been reported that from the 1640's onward an increasing number of these Black African slaves were brought into Barbados to help service the ever expanding and highly lucrative sugar cane industry. For very nearly two hundred years, from 1640 to 1834, hundreds of thousands of Black slaves were thought to have worked on the vast sugar cane plantations that occupied vast areas of the island, a situation that was only finally resolved in 1834, when all such slaves were emancipated by legal statute. Even after the slave trade had finally been outlawed though, the many thousands of former slaves on Barbados were still thought to have been compelled to carry on with their extremely hard lives, albeit as free men, who were now being paid for their labour. Often, denial of paid work was said to have been a measure employed by some white landowners and planters to isolate or punish workers who demanded too much from their former owners, such was the monopoly operated by the sugar cane growers on Barbados and other Caribbean islands. As a result of their economic power, social standing and political influence, for much of the hundred years following their legal emancipation, the Black majority on most of Britain's Caribbean colonies were said to have had little if any voice in the governance of their island home, a situation that only slowly began to change in the 1930's. By the late 1930's and through the 1940's however, there was thought to have been an increasing level of representation for the Black majority of Barbados with the trade unions and their fledgling political wings being partly responsible for the introduction of adult suffrage on the island in 1951, which was later followed by the election of Grantley Adams, the leader of the Barbados Progressive League, who was elected as Premier of his country in 1958. By 1966 and under the leadership of Errol Barrow, one of the founders of the Democratic Labour Party in Barbados, the island was reported to have finally achieved full independence from Great Britain in November of that year, with Barrow becoming his nations first elected Prime Minister. Remaining a member of the Commonwealth of Nations, since independence, Barbados is thought to have generally allied itself to more regional bodies and confederations, including the Caribbean Community, Association of Caribbean States and the Organisation of American States, as well as membership of the United Nations. In common with a number of its former colonial neighbours, Barbados has moved its economy away from a complete reliance on the historic sugar cane industry, becoming instead a mixed economy, focused on both agriculture and tourism, helping to make Barbados one of the most successful democratic economies in the entire Caribbean region.

Some two years after Barbados was first discovered by Henry Powell in May 1625, the islands of St Vincent and the Grenadines were formally claimed by Britain, although due to the presence of a largely unfriendly indigenous population, no serious effort was made to colonise the islands. Instead that was left to French settlers who were said to have arrived there in around 1700 and despite native hostility managed to establish both a settlement and a number of plantations, growing a mixed crop of coffee, corn, indigo, sugar and tobacco, most of which were grown using the labour of Black African slaves. Although the ownership of St Vincent was reportedly a matter of continuing dispute between France and Britain from 1700 through to the 1780's, it was only with the signing of the Treaty of Paris in 1783 that the islands were formally and finally ceded to Great Britain. However, despite the French settlers having managed to establish a thriving agricultural economy, the presence on the islands of a highly resentful and menacing Carib community remained a problem that the British authorities would eventually have to deal with. Comprising a mixture of the native Carib people and escaped Black African slaves, who had made the islands their new home, often such groups would live in relatively isolated or naturally protected areas which prevented the local authorities from suppressing their unlawful activities. They were thought to have survived by raiding local plantations, robbing travellers and encouraging slaves from the island's plantations to join their communities, making them a real worry for local planters and landowners, who often lived a good distance away from the island's main settlement, where the local authorities were based. These Carib communities were thought to have presented a real threat to both the French and British throughout both countries control of the islands and were only finally dealt with by the British military commander, General Abercrombie in 1796, following a rebellion inspired by a revolutionary French politician and activist Victor Hugue, following which a significant number of the Carib community were said to have been exiled from St Vincent.

Although slavery was finally abolished throughout the British Empire in 1834, as elsewhere the lives of the former slaves on St Vincent and the Grenadines were not thought to have been significantly improved, forcing many to leave the islands and relocate themselves to other parts of the Caribbean. For the planters and landowners based on St Vincent, this exodus of workers was said to have presented them with a major manpower problem, forcing them to recruit paid labour from abroad, including many workers from Portugal and India, who were prepared to undertake the work, in the generally extreme conditions. Despite the arrival of these willing workers though, the sugar cane industry in the Caribbean was thought to have remained relatively depressed, right the way through to the 20th century, when an increase in world prices began to improve matters. Because of the island's size, economic importance and geographical position, the British authorities remained uncertain as to what action to take over the governance of St Vincent and its associated islands, initially federating it with others in the Windward Islands group, although its actual status was reported to have changed a number of times throughout the 19th and 20th centuries. Regardless of this executive uncertainty however, the islands were granted the usual democratic systems afforded to other British territories, including a representative assembly, colonial government, legislative council and adult suffrage, all of which were designed to prepare St Vincent and the Grenadines for independence. Finally, in October 1969 and in common with the likes of St Kitts and Nevis, St Vincent and the Grenadines were granted associated status by the British authorities, making it responsible for its own internal affairs, but under the protection of Great Britain. It was only in 1979 and following the outcome of a national referendum on the subject that St Vincent and the Grenadines were formally granted their independence by the United Kingdom. Unfortunately, due to a series of natural disasters, including a volcanic eruption and at least two hurricanes, which devastated much of the islands agricultural economy thousands of its inhabitants were said to have been forced to temporarily abandon the island, until such time as the island was made safe. In November 2009 moves were made to alter St Vincent and the Grenadines constitution, allowing the country to reform itself as a Republic, replacing the Queen as head of state with a president, although these suggestions were subsequently rejected by a majority of the voting population. However, the country remains a highly successful parliamentary democracy and has become an important member of a number of the Caribbean's regional political and economic institutions, including the Caribbean Community and Organisation of Eastern Caribbean States. Despite some of its later naturally occurring misfortunes, St Vincent and the Grenadines continues to develop into a model democratic state, one of a number of former British possessions that have successfully built on their nation's natural resources, to help create a highly stable and productive economy.

First identified and named by Christopher Columbus in 1493, the Caribbean island of Antigua was only first colonised by the English in 1632, when Captain Thomas Warner, the explorer more commonly associated with St Kitts, arrived on the island to establish the first European settlement there. Although previous attempts to colonise the territories were said to have been thwarted by the presence of the indigenous Carib people, Warner and the members of his expedition somehow managed to overcome their resistance to strangers and establish the first English colony there, with Warner being appointed as the first official Governor. These new English settlers were reported to have thrived on Antigua and within a short time were said to be raising several important cash crops, including ginger, indigo and tobacco, although most of these were later replaced by the much more valuable sugar cane crops. Even though Warner himself was known to have died in 1649, the colony remained largely unaffected by this, with more and more English settlers and investors arriving to make their fortunes on Antigua. In 1674 one of the most notable planters was said to have arrived there, establishing a large sugar cane plantation and leasing the neighbouring island of Barbuda as a place to raise provisions for his large slave labour force and his personal plantation household. Sir Christopher Codrington was reported to be the Captain General of the British held Leeward Islands, who established his own sugar cane plantation on Antigua during the late 17th century, a property that was later passed on to his son, also called Christopher, who later matched his father's military success by similarly being appointed as Captain General of the same British Caribbean dependencies. However, the younger Christopher Codrington was reported to have led a failed invasion of the French held territories of Guadeloupe in 1703, after which he resigned his military post and settled back into civilian life on Antigua, overseeing his sugar cane plantation and studying his books. Despite this seemingly benign lifestyle however, his plantation on Antigua was said to have gained a reputation for being particularly brutal, although all of these estates were later said to have passed into the hands of the Society for the Propagation of the Gospel in Foreign Parts, the SPG, with the intention that its income would be used for the funding and maintenance of a new college, Codrington College, which was built between 1714 and 1742, with the expressed intent of improving the physical and moral health of both the black and white communities of the Caribbean.

Admiral Cockburn   General Wm Winder   Admiral James Gordon

However, the continuing operation and ownership of the sugar plantation by this religious society was said to have done little to improve the daily lives of the Black African slaves who were tied to it, even after Codrington died in 1710. The day to day operation of the plantation was said to have remained in the hands of agents and managers, who then reported back to the Church of England authorities regarding the levels of productivity, purchase of new slaves and the overall profit and loss of the business, seemingly indifferent to the fact that the plantation's death rates were far higher than elsewhere in the Caribbean. As had been the case for well over a hundred years this religious society was reported to have used religious scripture to underpin its continuing use of human beings as slave labour, much as was the case with most of the other European states who engaged in the practice. Although the managers of the society's estates were later instructed to desist from the practice of branding their new slaves, during Codrington's time and for the first decade of the society's stewardship, all newly purchased slaves were branded with a red hot iron, first with Codrington's initials and then later with the word "Society". Once that practice was finally brought to an end however, the plantations new owners simply relied on iron collars or straight jackets, but more commonly the whip, which was used liberally to ensure compliance from the chattel workforce. By the end of the 18th century and through to the beginning of the 19th conditions on the former Codrington estates began to improve, no doubt in part because of better reporting of the day to day running of the site, but also through increasing pressure by the Christian fellowship to eradicate this dreadful practice entirely. Despite a growing recognition that slavery was in fact a wholly unchristian practice, the Church of England only finally released its slaves on the Antiguan plantations, when required to do so by statute, with the abolition of slavery within the British Empire having been announced in 1834. Even here though, the Church of England made sure that Codrington's College funds received full and fair compensation from the British government, for the loss of their enslaved workforce, although it was only in the 21st century that they finally issued a public apology to the descendants of these former slaves, for the part that the Church had played in the trade.

It was said to be largely Christopher Codrington senior's decision to introduce large scale sugar planting to Antigua which persuaded many other planters, landowners and investors on the island to follow his lead, creating even more misery for even greater numbers of enslaved Black Africans, who were taken from their native homelands to fill the growing demand. By the middle of the 18th century there were thought to be so many slaves on the island, many of them living in such intolerable conditions that unrest amongst them became almost inevitable, requiring only a particular incident or specific individual to spark a full blown revolt, an alarming thought for the then minority white population. The situation was not helped by the occasional killing of slaves by individual owners, who were bound by the terms of the Slave Act, passed in 1723, which forbade the arbitrary killing of slaves, but who often excused their actions by charging the unfortunate slave with some or other spurious crime, in order to condone what was in effect plain and simple murder. A case in point was reported to be that of a Black African slave called Hercules, who was said to have been hung, drawn and quartered, whilst at the same time, three more slaves were reported to have been burnt alive, all of them killed, for purportedly conspiring to kill their white owner and his family. Matters were said to have come to a head though in 1736, when a slave called Prince Klaas, or more properly named as Count, was thought to have been appointed as leader of the local slave population in a ceremony witnessed by local white settlers, who believed that the ritual was little more than a simple local tradition. According to some historians though, rather than just appointing some sort of community leader, the ceremony was said to have represented a declaration of war against the local white population, who were to be attacked and killed by members of the slave community. However, members of the white authorities were quickly made aware of the possible threat and subsequently arrested Prince Klaas and four of his supporters, sentencing them to be executed on the breaking wheel, a wagon wheel device, which allowed the victims body to be pummelled by a block or cudgel that passed through the gaps in the wheel, breaking whatever body part happened to lie in its path. Essentially, the breaking wheel was akin to strapping a body down and beating on it with a large block of wood or a hammer, with the obvious difference being that the body was rotated, although the damage done was fundamentally the same. Although Prince Klaas and four others were said to have met their deaths on this particularly brutal medieval device, another sixty-odd slaves were said to have been executed by equally gruesome methods, with some being hung from chains and others by being burnt at the stake.

Clearly the brutality demonstrated by some members of the slave owning community was a reflection of their own personal characters, pointing to their own individual indifference of the pain inflicted upon and suffered by their fellow human beings. However, given that some members of the white community considered Black African slaves to be little more than the basest sort of animal, then their attitude, no matter how despicable, is understandable nonetheless. For many others however, their decision to deliberately inflict pain, suffering and sometimes death on their black slaves has often been attributed to a demonstration of their own fears, believing that an illustration of severe retribution would more easily dissuade the restless and extremely large slave population from even considering revolt against their white owners. Although today, such a suggestion would not only be derided and even physically opposed, at the time it was thought to be a generally successful strategy and one that was employed throughout much of the Caribbean and other slave owning regions of the New World. Unfortunately for slaves such as Hercules, Prince Klaas and the many thousands of others who suffered equally igniminious ends, they did not live to see the demise of the Transatlantic Slave Trade, although by 1807 the treatment meted out to individuals like them, had begun to herald the end of the activity, which was finally abolished by the British Empire in 1834. As elsewhere in the Caribbean, Antigua's almost complete dependence on agriculture was said to have hindered the development of the country's economy, as well as its political evolution, with no obvious worker's representation present on the island until the beginning of World War II; and only then after a Royal Commission suggested that such a body was necessary. As on a number of these sugar producing islands, the economic power and political influence of the hereditary plantation owners dominated much of the islands subsequent social and economic development, a situation that was only altered by the emergence of a trade union movement during the 1940's. Since that time the country's political system has been largely dominated by the Antigua Labour Party, a sign of its widespread support within the nation, rather than any sort of restrictive political system. Granted full independence by Great Britain in 1981, Antigua and Barbuda continue to operate as a highly successful parliamentary democracy, playing a full part in the Commonwealth of Nations, as well as being active members of several regional trading federations.

The neighbouring island of Montserrat was said to have been initially settled by a small number of Irish colonists in 1632, after these former indentured servants had left Nevis, ostensibly because of anti-Catholic demonstrations that were taking place there. Over the course of the next fifty years or so a large number of sugar plantations were reported to have been established there, bringing about the importation of significant numbers of Black African slaves to Montserrat, who were employed in the planting, cultivation and processing of this highly valuable commodity, as well as the development of arrowroot and rum production. Because of its value as a financial asset to the British Empire, during the American Revolution, the island was said to have become a target for the United States military ally, France, who were reported to have temporarily seized control of Montserrat in 1782, although was subsequently compelled to return the territories to Britain, under the terms of the Treaty of Paris, signed in the following year. As elsewhere, slavery on the island was formally abolished in 1834 and in the second half of the 19th century the decline in world sugar prices caused a marked decline in the fortunes of the island and the European planter classes who had settled there. Fortunately for many of those inhabitants who had been adversely affected by the decline in the sugar industry, the arrival of the British philanthropist, Joseph Sturge, in 1869, was thought to have helped reinvigorate the islands fortunes through agricultural diversification. By buying up many of the former plantation lands which had either been abandoned, or that were no longer profitable, Sturge and his associates, were said to have divided these estates up into smaller parcels of land, which were then planted and cultivated by a new generation of smallholders, who helped to make the islands increasingly self sustainable.

For much of the next eighty-odd years Montserrat was thought to have developed rather slowly, remaining as a political and financial dependent of the British Crown, much as it continues to do, even through to the present day. Unfortunately, attempts to develop the island as a tourism destination and as a residency for high profile celebrities have been hampered by extreme weather conditions and the reawakening of the island's Soufriere Hills volcano, both of which have conspired to undermine these efforts. In September 1989, Hurricane Hugo, a Category 4 tropical storm struck the island, devastating virtually everything that it came into contact with, including the vitally important tourism and agricultural industries. Some six years later and with Montserrat having only recently recovered from Hurricane Hugo, the Soufriere Hills volcano, which had remained dormant throughout the island's recorded history, suddenly and inexplicably erupted into life once again, decimating significant areas of Montserrat's valuable agricultural land. As a result of the eruption, the island's capital, Plymouth, was said to have been completely destroyed, more than half the island was left uninhabitable and around half the population chose to leave Montserrat to resettle elsewhere, including in Antigua, the United States and Britain. Although the island's population and its economy have subsequently started to recover from these cataclysmic events, it is anticipated that some parts of Montserrat will remain uninhabitable for anything up to ten years and as such, will require further aid from Britain and elsewhere for many years to come.

The Bahamas are yet another collection of Caribbean islands that are steeped in the history of the British Empire's presence in the New World and inextricably linked with privateers, plantations and the Transatlantic Slave Trade. According to some sources, prior to the arrival of Christopher Columbus and the Spanish conquistadors, many of the Caribbean islands, including the Bahamas, were thought to have been inhabited by various indigenous tribes, most of whom were subsequently enslaved and carried away to work in the mines and plantations of the Spaniard's New World. As a result of this enforced exodus, many of these larger Caribbean islands were thought to have been largely devoid of human life, thereby encouraging their colonisation by the likes of the English and the French, who were keen to settle these new lands, both through economic imperative and for regional influence. Although the exact circumstances of the decision to colonise the islands of Barbados remain unclear, it is generally reported that the island of Eleuthera was initially settled by a group of English colonists, escaping from the religious intolerance and restrictive practices of Bermuda, which was becoming increasingly crowded and regulated. However, their arrival and settlement of the island, was thought to have been extremely difficult, with the loss of a ship and its cargo of vitally important stores reportedly causing great hardship among the first wave of settlers, many of whom chose to return to Bermuda, rather than struggle for survival. However, some of these early settlers did remain and were subsequently joined by new colonists, although even some twenty years later, there were only thought to be a couple of dozen families actually living around the island, grinding out a living from the generally harsh conditions.

On the neighbouring island of New Providence, a new wave of English colonists were said to have first arrived there in 1666, but unlike the farmers on Eleuthera, chose to establish their new settlements close to the coastline, where they could make a living from fishing, salvage, salt manufacturing and exploiting the natural resources of the island, including shells, turtles and ambergris, the intestinal secretion from sperm whales, much prized for its perfumed odour, which was often used in medicinal vapours. So successful was the colony on New Providence that before long, even more English settlers began to arrive, including farmers who were attracted by the widespread availability of land that could be employed to grow their crops, although a much more profitable benefit from these land clearances was said to have been the amount and variety of Caribbean hardwoods which could be used for a range of purposes, including shipbuilding, construction, furniture making, as well as being exported elsewhere. However, much of this early settlement and economic development was thought to have been largely unregulated and unlawful, given that none of the colonists had actually bothered to acquire any sort of legal authority to establish themselves on the islands of Eleuthera and New Providence. Although they had been living there since 1648, it was only in 1670 that the English Crown eventually handed control of the Bahamas to a recognised official body, when the proprietors of Carolina were reported to have been granted a legal patent to the territories, albeit some twenty years too late. However, when the Carolina authorities came to enforce their trading rights on the islands they were said to have encountered great difficulty in making the settlers actually accept their legal authority, which resulted in very little changing on the islands.

Despite having few legal rights to the islands, or to the resources that lay within their territorial waters, the colonists on New Providence were said to have continued to conduct their businesses much as before, although salvaging shipwrecks was thought to have become an increasing part of the local economy and a trade that would eventually lead the settlers into direct conflict with Spanish salvagers who also relied on the numerous wrecks to make a living. Matters were said to have escalated when the New Providence colonists began to drive off those Spaniards who had successfully retrieved goods from sunken wrecks and then stole their prizes for good measure, forcing the Spanish salvagers to call on their own national authorities in the region to remedy the situation. As a consequence, the Spanish military were said to have attacked both Eleuthera and New Providence in 1684, burnt the English settlements down and drove the colonists away from the area. However, by 1686, most of them were thought to have returned and rebuilt their settlements, with these coastal towns continuing to play host to a number of English privateers, who had previously occupied themselves with attacking French ships, while England was at war with France during the 1690's. By 1697 though; and with that particular conflict at an end, the privateers were said to have been at a loss for an enemy to attack, so many of them were thought to have joined the growing number of pirates who were beginning to establish themselves in the Bahamas, particularly in the main port of Nassau.

Grantley Adams

General Abercromby

Joseph Sturge

Despite being given responsibility for controlling the Bahamas, the authorities in Carolina were thought to have been, either unwilling or unable to stem the growth of the pirates in and around the Caribbean islands, causing many to suspect that the English authorities were actually complicit in the development of what was becoming a safe haven for these seafaring outlaws. Possibly as a result of such assessments, when war broke out between England and a Franco-Spanish coalition, Barbados and its pirate sanctuaries were said to have become an important target for a combined French and Spanish fleets, causing some of the more legitimate colonists to leave, the pirates to temporarily abandon their safe haven and the authorities in Carolina to discard all attempt at controlling the islands. However, once these enemy naval forces had left, the pirates simply returned to the Bahamas and resumed their normal trade, although by then, they were reported to be targeting any French or Spanish ships which were unfortunate enough to sail within their areas of operations. Even when hostilities between England and the Franco-Spanish coalition had ended, the pirate threat was thought to have remained and it was only with the appointment of Woodes Rogers, as the first British Governor of the Bahamas in 1718 that the situation began to change. As well as being instructed by the King to bring good government to the islands, Woodes Rogers, had also been granted a lease on the islands by the Carolina authorities, giving him a highly lucrative reason for finally settling the Bahamas once and for all. Publicly announcing his own appointment and intentions, Rogers was thought to have offered an amnesty to all pirates and privateers who would swear an oath to the king, although he had also brought a fleet of British warships with him in the event that there was any armed opposition to his plans. Having arrived in the Bahamas in 1718, within a relatively short time, most of the pirates opposed to his appointment and offer of amnesty, were thought to have left Nassau and were plying their trade elsewhere, whilst many others had accepted his offer and were settling down into more peaceful and law abiding employment. By the middle of the 1720's virtually all of the privateers and pirates were reported to have left the Bahamas forever, allowing Rogers to establish law and order to the islands and a colonial assembly, which was introduced by 1730.

For the next fifty years or so the Bahamas remained relatively peaceful, with its population increasing and more of the land being employed for growing crops, including sugar cane, which inevitably led to a large influx of Black African slave labour, along with its associated brutality and systems. Control of the islands was reported to have been temporarily lost, during the period of the American Revolution, when a Spanish force under the command of General Bernardo Galvez, were said to have taken advantage of the military situation in mainland North America and seized the islands in 1782, although they were subsequently recovered by loyalist forces from Britain's American colonies. Following the enforced military withdrawal of British troops from the region that later became the United States, many of the loyalist colonials who had supported the British cause during the war, were thought to have moved to the Bahamas, along with their slaves, significantly increasing the settler communities and adding to the diversity of the population that inhabits the islands through to the present day. The abolition of the slave trade within the British Empire by 1834 was also thought to have made the Bahamas a destination for hundreds of escaped Black African slaves during the American Civil War, as well being a base from where smugglers ran contraband to and from the besieged Confederate states. However, with the failure of a large scale agricultural industry, due to poor growing conditions, much of the Bahamas 19th century economy on the three main islands, Eleuthera, New Providence and Grand Bahama, was thought to have been centred around smuggling, tourism and the continuing military occupation of New Providence. During the late 19th century, the main British military installations and the numbers of personnel centred on Nassau were both beginning to be reduced, forcing the local economy to increasingly rely on its more traditional industries, such as fishing, shipping, tourism and smuggling. Although agriculture continued to play a significant role in the local economy, growing produce such as pineapples, etc. which were then exported elsewhere, much of the islands economy was thought to be inextricably linked to the sea, either through, fishing, shipping, salvaging or smuggling. By the beginning of the 20th century though and most notably during the period of prohibition in the United States, a number of Caribbean islands, including the Bahamas, were reported to have been used by rum-runners to smuggle alcohol into America, to fuel the illicit liquor trade, much of which was in the hands of organised crime syndicates. At the outbreak of the Second World War, both British and American forces were said to have employed the islands as the base for their anti-submarine operations which were conducted in the Atlantic Ocean, against the fearsome German U-boats that were attempting to destroy the vital supply lines between America and the embattled islands of Great Britain.

Following the end of World War II, a limited military presence was thought to have been maintained in the Bahamas, but not at the levels employed during the war, although increasing numbers of both wealthy American residents and tourists were reported to have begun arriving on the islands during the immediate post war period. Former military bases, including the main airfield at Nassau, were subsequently redeveloped for entirely civilian purposes, becoming a gateway for the evolving international airlines that were now able to carry passengers to and from any corner of the globe, many of whom were attracted by the clear blue waters and warm sands of the Bahamas. The closure of Cuba, to American interests in 1961, also proved to be beneficial to the Bahamian economy, as many of these US investors looked elsewhere in the Caribbean to re-establish themselves, bringing with them significant amounts of money for their various leisure, financial and tourism ventures, all of which proved to be highly beneficial for the economy of the Bahamas. During the 1950's, political parties and representative agencies were established in the Bahamas and in 1964 the islands finally became a self governing British colony, with the United Bahamian Party's leader Roland Symonette, elected as the first premier of the territories. Three years later, the Bahamian Progressive Liberal Party was reported to have won the country's first national elections, with its leader, Lynden Pindling, being appointed as premier of his country; although in the following year his title was changed to Prime Minister. In 1973, the Bahamas were finally granted full independence by the British authorities, but remained a member of the Commonwealth of Nations and continuing to recognise Queen Elizabeth II as their formal head of state. Since that time, the Bahamas have continued to thrive as a parliamentary democracy, with various and successive administrations helping to create a modern independent state that has an economy generally based on tourism and financial services. In more recent years, its relative proximity to the United States and the emergence of a thriving Caribbean drugs trade has seen the Bahamas earn itself an unwanted reputation as a major hub in the illegal narcotics trade, much to the dismay of the Bahamian authorities. Composed of around thirty different islands and over six hundred separate cays, or small sandy islets of varying sizes, the Bahamas, although not lying within the Caribbean itself are commonly associated with the region and therefore form an integral part of that particular grouping.

Some twenty two years after the first illegal English settlers had established themselves on the island of Eleuthera in the Bahamas, Britain's great empire was said to have been further enlarged by the acquisition of Jamaica and the Cayman Islands, both of which were reportedly settled in 1670. Although Jamaica was originally a Spanish possession, being claimed by Christopher Columbus in May 1494 and revisited by him in July 1502, it was only after his death in 1506 that the island, the third largest in the Caribbean, was permanently settled by the Spanish authorities. However, within a relatively short time of their arrival, the indigenous peoples of the island, the Arawak, were thought to have largely disappeared, ostensibly because of their enforced removal by the Spaniards, for use as slave labour, but also because of the many foreign diseases brought by the Spanish conquistadors, to which the native Indians had little or no immunity. Even though this provided Spain with an almost entirely unoccupied new territory, which they called Santiago, it also provided other settlers and explorers with the opportunity to settle on Jamaica, making the island a target for the numerous pirates and buccaneers who roamed the Caribbean, sometimes at the behest of foreign governments, but often in pursuit of their own interests, attacking Spanish ships and settlements and robbing them of every resource. For the best part of a century, the relatively isolated port settlement of Spanish Town was said to have been regularly attacked by English privateers or independent buccaneers, who terrorized the local population and seized whatever valuables they could lay their hands on, before sailing away with their booty of looted Jamaican treasures.

It was only in 1655 though, when two English Commonwealth Generals, William Penn and Robert Venables, who had earlier been instructed by Oliver Cromwell to seize the Spanish territory of Hispaniola, attacked Spanish Town on Jamaica, having failed to capture their original target. Despite the seizure of Jamaica being an unauthorised act, the two Commonwealth commanders and their forces were reported to have held onto these new territories nonetheless, resisting all attempts by the Spaniards and their Cameroon allies to retake the island and force the English garrison to retire. For much of the next fifteen years Spanish forces were said to have made repeated, but ultimately unsuccessful attacks on the English held island, with their efforts and forces continually thwarted, not only by the English themselves, but also by random fleets of English privateers, buccaneers and other disparate pirate groups. By 1670, the Spanish authorities in the New World were said to have finally come to the conclusion that Jamaica was not worth the time and effort being expended on its recapture, essentially handing ownership of the island to Britain, once and for all. However, even with Spanish claims to Jamaica having been abandoned, large parts of the territory were said to have remained outside of the law, with numerous pirates and privateers using the island as a base from where they could intercept ships that were sailing to and from the Caribbean, America and Europe.

Over time and with the intervention of the English authorities, who sent greater numbers of Royal Navy warships into the region to help suppress the pirate menace, Jamaica along with other British held islands were eventually brought under control, helping to attract investors, planters and private landowners there, who quickly began to clear the land and plant new cash crops which would help generate valuable revenues, both for themselves and the island's economy. Sugar cane and coffee were reported to have become the staple crops for the island, resulting in the widespread introduction of Black African slaves to work on the labour intensive plantations, clearing the land, tilling the soil, sowing and harvesting the crops, as well as processing the cane into molasses, which was then refined into sugar and rum. As was common elsewhere, conditions on many of these plantations was generally intolerable for the tens of thousands of slaves who were employed on them; and were thought to have been so severe that insurrections became almost commonplace, with the white authorities reacting to each of these, in an increasingly brutal fashion. The particularly high numbers of revolts, which took place on the island of Jamaica, were thought to have been caused, not only by the sheer number of Black African slaves who were enslaved on the island, but also by the underlying influence of a native Maroon community, who were escaped slaves that lived in isolated areas of Jamaica; and survived by raiding outlying plantations and communities. Apart from attacking these often isolated and unprotected homesteads, as well as the white settlers who lived there, it was also common for the maroons to encourage the plantations own slaves to abscond and join their raiding bands, adding to an already significant problem for the local authorities.

In response to the ongoing problem, white plantation owners were said to have begun to form themselves into local militias, which could be called together to defend a particular location, or to launch pre-emptive attacks on various maroon settlements, as and when they could be identified. The British authorities too, began to take a more serious view of the lawlessness, sending regular troops into suspected maroon territories, to try and recapture the escaped slaves and to arrest their leaders, who if caught, would often face the most severe sanctions. It was also reported that the authorities regularly paid certain maroon groups to help them trace and attack the more troublesome maroon bands and the other escaped slaves who were operating in Jamaica, in an effort to bring the worst of the offenders to book. In the latter part of the 18th century, the British authorities reportedly began a series of military campaigns against the various Maroon groups, which history now recounts as the Maroon Wars, indicating the seriousness of the conflicts from the British authority's perspective. During the 1790's, a large number of the captured Maroons, were reported to have been deported from Jamaica and sent to the new British colony of Sierra Leone in West Africa, where they helped to form part of that new nations resident community. Although discontent continued to exist in Jamaica throughout much of the late 18th and early 19th centuries, one of the largest and worst incidents of conflict between the Black slave community and the white plantation owners was reported to have been caused by the growth of the anti-slavery movement back in Britain.

Lynden Pindling

William Penn

Samuel Sharpe

As the abolitionist movement in Britain, led by the likes of William Wilberforce and a number of Methodist ministers became more popular in the country and in its Parliament, so the expectations of the enslaved Black African workforce throughout the British Empire began to grow. Reportedly believing that their emancipation was close at hand, in December 1831, a large number of Jamaican slaves were said to have waited for a declaration of their freedom to be sent from England and then announced to the white slave owners, who would have been forced to free all of their enslaved workers. Sadly, no such decree arrived in Jamaica, with the Governor explicitly announcing the fact that Black emancipation had not been granted by the British legislature and thereby dashing the hopes and expectations of the hundreds of thousands of Jamaica's slave community. Meanwhile, having pre-empted the expected announcement of freedom, a local Black preacher called Samuel Sharpe was reported to have had called on the enslaved Black community to stage a general strike, demand their immediate emancipation and the payment of a living wage to all of the islands three hundred thousand Black workers. A slave himself, Sharpe was thought to have gained a reasonable level of education, both through his own efforts and with the permission of his white owner, which had allowed him to gain a level of status within his native community, becoming a leader and a religious preacher. Having eventually become a Deacon at his local Baptist church, under its white minister, Reverend Thomas Burchell, Sharpe was thought to have been made aware of the abolitionist movement in Britain, which it was hoped would bring about the end of slavery within the British Empire forever. However, whether or not he had been misinformed by Burchell that anti slavery legislation was about to be passed in Britain is unclear, but either way, Sharpe was said to be confident enough to announce it to members of his own community, which proved to have fatal repercussions for him and many of his fellow slaves.

Unsurprisingly, perhaps, the white planters and landowners immediately rejected the slave workers demands for emancipation and a living wage, which caused some of the slave community to stop working altogether, which resulted in some of the slave owners carrying out brutal reprisals against their workforce. In response to the white planter's actions, other slaves were said to have damaged buildings and machinery, as well burning the valuable crops of sugar cane, causing the planters to adopt even more vicious methods of reprisal, all of which led to an escalation into a full blown slave rebellion. Over the period of ten days, beginning on the 25th of December 1831, some sixty thousand Jamaican slaves were reported to have participated in the uprising, which left some fourteen white settlers and several hundred Black African workers dead. At the end of the ten day revolt, which Sharpe had only ever intended to be a peaceful protest, the disturbances were thought to have finally been brought to an end by the local military forces and the mixed white militias, who were eager to punish those that they considered to be responsible for the disorder. Samuel Sharpe, along with a number of other reported ringleaders, were subsequently arrested, tried and hung by the Jamaican authorities for having instigated the revolt, although Sharpe himself was said to have announced that he would rather hang on the gallows, than spend another minute as a slave. For some time after the death of Sharpe and his fellow prisoners, a significant number of slaves were reported to have been hung by the local authorities, often on the say so of individual planters, or overseers who specifically targeted certain slaves, in an attempt to intimidate the rest of their own slave workforces.

Even though Samuel Sharpe himself did not live long enough to be freed by his white owner and even though it was his pre-emptive declaration that inadvertently caused the rebellion, ultimately it was that same insurrection, which was said to have been instrumental in bringing an end to slavery within the British Empire and in most parts of the civilised world. It was thought to be as a partial result of this revolt that at least two Parliamentary inquiries were launched in Britain, which ultimately resulted in the Abolition of Slavery Act 1833 being passed by the British legislature, in that same year and enacted in the following. Regarded as a national hero within Jamaica, Samuel Sharpe has since been celebrated with a posthumous title, the foundation of a college dedicated to his memory; and had his picture reproduced on one of Jamaica's major banknotes. However, despite the Black African workers of the island formally receiving their freedom in August 1834, the decision of the British authorities to include a mandatory apprenticeship scheme, possibly as a result of lobbying by the former slave owners, meant that many workers were not completely free until 1838; and even then their lives were not straightforward. For much of the next thirty odd years the Black African population of Jamaica remained largely disenfranchised because of their extreme poverty and the shortage of free land on which they could work or build, forcing them to remain reliant on the white landowning classes, who had previously been slave owners. Unable to vote and with very little formal representation, save for local civic leaders, rumour commonly became reality in the eyes of the generally uneducated population, whose tenuous employment and livelihoods were often affected by misinformation and highly questionable rumours. Such was the case in 1865, when towards the end of a long term drought, which had not only caused hardship to the local workforce, but had also reduced the profits of the local landowners, a rumour began to circulate that local employers were considering reintroducing slavery to the island, as a means of reducing their costs without losing their workforce.

Alarmed at the prospect of their freedom being denied them once again, the relationship between the Black workforce and the white planters was thought to have become increasingly fraught, despite reassurances from the local authorities that there was no suggestion or even possibility of slavery being reintroduced to Jamaica. The mistrust of the local white community, coupled with the unequal distribution of land, which prevented the Black community from working, let alone owning sections of land, remained as a source of tension between the two communities and almost inevitably played a part in the conflict that erupted at Morant Bay in Jamaica in October 1865. Despite being in control of the island, most within the white settler community recognised that they only retained their position of power, because of the enforced compliance of the Black majority through the threat of military force. However, following the Indian Sepoy Mutiny of 1857, which had resulted in hundreds of white settlers being attacked and killed, many of Britain's settler communities in the vast Empire were thought to have become increasingly worried about possible outbreaks of violence in their own communities and began putting plans in place, in order to deal with such an emergency. On the island of Jamaica, the already tense relationship between the majority Black community and the white settlers was reported to have been made far worse, by what at first glance, was a relatively innocuous incident, involving an individual Black worker and a piece of abandoned farmland.

Reportedly occupying and clearing an unused area of plantation land, the unknown Black worker, rather than just being ejected from the land, was said to have been arrested and imprisoned by the white authorities, causing a great deal of resentment amongst the Black community. As a result, a group of workers began to demonstrate against the man's continuing detention, leading to the authorities to arrest one of the demonstrators as well, which simply helped to escalate matters even further. In response, the remaining demonstrators were reported to have marched to the local jail and forcibly freed their fellow worker, causing the local white authorities to issue arrest warrants for all twenty eight of the workers involved in the incident, including the group's leader, a church Deacon called Paul Bogle. However, rather than just surrendering themselves to the police and accepting whatever punishment was meted out to them, Bogle and his fellow demonstrators were said to have marched on the local courthouse at Morant Bay, determined to air their grievances to the local magistrate, in the hope that the matter might be resolved in a more equitable manner. Unfortunately, having arrived on Morant Bay, the group of demonstrators found themselves confronted by a group of armed militia, who were said to be clearly alarmed by the sudden arrival of the black workers and began shooting at them, killing and wounding several of the group before retiring from the area. Outraged at the murder of their fellow workers, the group of demonstrators were then reported to have begun attacking the inhabitants of the township, killing a number of white officials and militiamen, before dispersing into the local countryside, where over the period of the next few days, several thousand Black workers were thought to have attacked local plantations and farms, forcing their white inhabitants to flee for their lives. The Jamaican Governor, John Eyre, on hearing about the violence was said to have immediately despatched regular troops into the area with orders to arrest all of those involved, particularly their leader, Paul Bogle, who was to be brought back to Morant Bay to stand trial. However, rather than arresting those that they believed to be involved in the outbreak of violence, some troops were said to have begun shooting at any worker that they happened to encounter, regardless of whether they had been involved in the Morant Bay incident or not. Several hundred Black workers were thought to have been killed by such actions, many of whom were almost certainly innocent of any crime, other than being a black worker, who was in the wrong place, at the wrong time. Within a matter of days though, the authorities were said to have arrested several hundred workers, who were thought to have been involved in the violence, including Paul Bogle, who along with a number of the other prisoners was subsequently executed, whilst the remainder were either jailed for lengthy terms, or were sentenced to be flogged.

In normal circumstances, what was little more than an isolated outbreak of civil unrest, would have never caused any great concern outside of Jamaica itself, although it was the wholly disproportionate response of the authorities and the Jamaican governor, John Eyre, in particular which ensured that the incident would gain such international prominence. Back in Britain, the incident quickly became the subject of party politics, with both of the country's main political groups lining up to either condone or condemn the erstwhile administrator, the Tory Party offering support and the Liberal Party inciting sanction. In fact, some public figures were even reported to have demanded that Eyre should be tried for murder, given the questionable and highly brutal methods he had employed in order to suppress the disorder, although in the end no such charge was brought against him. His actions however, did ultimately lead the private Charter Company to surrender it hold on Jamaica in 1866, ensuring that control of the island then reverted to the British Crown, leading to the appointment of a far more accountable administration there. In 1870, a legal case was brought against Eyre in the British Courts, to bring him to account for his actions in Jamaica, although ultimately the action was said to have failed, because of legislation Eyre had introduced as Governor of the island, which ensured that he remained largely unaccountable for his decisions, or indeed for his wholly unreasonable actions. With Jamaica having reverted to being a Crown Colony once again, the island and its community slowly began to move forward, with its capital being moved from Spanish Town to Kingston in 1872, the newer port city having evolved well beyond its historic counterpart. A decade later the islands legislative assembly was said to have been restored, with some of its members being elected by the local population, ensuring that some degree of self government was reintroduced to the island nation, a first step towards its almost inevitable and undoubtedly long awaited state of independence, which was finally achieved some ninety years later, in August 1962. In those intervening years though, Jamaica continued to suffer from occasional outbreaks of civil disorder, as the islands economic and political development were both hampered by the peaks and troughs of the worldwide commodity markets, as well as the intransigence of the country's minority white community. However, during the late 1930's and the early 1940's Jamaica's black majority finally began to gain limited political influence through the evolution and development of the country's first trade unions and their associated political parties, including the People's National Party, founded in 1938 and the Jamaica Labour Party, which was established in 1943. In the following year, the entire Jamaican adult population was able to vote in national election for the first time, although it was another eighteen years before the country finally gained official independence and saw its first Jamaican born Prime Minister elected to that high office, with Alexander Bustamante of the Jamaica Labour Party achieving that historic objective in 1962.

During the 1970's Jamaican politics were reported to have been extremely volatile, with supporters of the competing Jamaica Labour Party and the People's National Party vying with one another for control of the country's legislature. One of the most high profile figures of the period was the People's Party leader, Michael Manley, who was thought to have introduced a number of socialist measures to the country, as well as formalising diplomatic relations between Jamaica and Fidel Castro's Cuba, much to the annoyance of their much larger international neighbour, the United States. For much of the 1970's, whilst Manley was thought to have been locked in a political battle with his rival, the Labour Party leader, Edward Seaga, armed gangs, reportedly supported and financed by both of the main parties, were said to have fought running battles with one another in many of Jamaica's main towns and cities. Such was the level of violence in the country that a State of Emergency had to be called by Manley in 1976, although that did not prevent him from holding elections in December of the same year, despite the fact that many of his political opponents were being detained by his government's forces. Needless to say, Manley's People's National Party were returned to power, although by the time new elections were held in 1980, the Jamaica Labour Party was returned as the largest party and its leader Edward Seaga, appointed as Prime Minister. Although Jamaican politics became a lot more settled in later years, Manley himself was reported to have been re-elected as Prime Minister of his country in the early 1990's, albeit with a more enterprising, capitalist driven agenda, reflecting the failure of the communist ideals as previously practiced by the Soviet Union and its satellite states. Unfortunately for Manley however, his tenure as Prime Minister of his nation was said to have been generally short-lived, after he was diagnosed with cancer, a disease that he finally succumbed to in 1997.

Paul Bogle   John Eyre   Edward Seaga

Despite having once been described as one of the most dangerous places in the world and at one time having one of the highest murder rates of any country, tourism has been and remains one of the major industries within Jamaica. Apart from being home and a regular holiday destination for many of the world's elite people over the past few decades, more than a million tourists are thought to visit the country every year to experience its astonishing beauty, it unique culture and traditional lifestyle. Tourism apart though, Jamaica's economy is said to be highly diverse, allowing the country and its people to better weather the vagaries of the modern international markets, Based on industrial mining, manufacturing, tourism, art, as well as the highly lucrative financial services industry, Jamaica's economy is thought to be one of the most robust and successful within the Caribbean, an opinion supported by its continuing membership of a number of the regions commercial federations including, the Caribbean Community and the Caribbean Single Market Economy.

As part of the Treaty of Madrid, which was signed by both England and Spain in 1670 and which formally, passed possession of Jamaica into English hands, a smaller group of Caribbean islands, known as Caymans, were also transferred between the two European powers. Comprising Grand Cayman, Little Cayman and Cayman Brac, the English seafarer, Sir Francis Drake, was reported to have been the first European explorer to visit the islands in 1586, although Christopher Columbus was said to have sighted and recorded them some eighty years earlier. Originally called Las Tortugas, after the sea turtles that were seen swimming around the islands, their latter name of Caymanes, reflected the presence of the small Caiman crocodiles which also lived on the isolated islands, both of which animals were reportedly caught as foodstuff by passing ships. Even though they were formally handed to England in 1670, it was thought to be another thirty-odd years before any permanent English settlement was established on these new territories, a colony that was subsequently added to by a variety of shipwrecked sailors, escaped slaves, as well as religious refugees escaping persecution in Europe and elsewhere. For much of the period from 1670 to 1730, life on the islands was thought to have been quite turbulent, with the settlers regularly being attacked and driven off their lands by pirates and buccaneers who were said to have used them as bases from where they could raid passing trade ships. However, by the 1730's many of the

Caribbean's privateers and pirates had either been captured, or had agreed to settle down into more legitimate employment, helping to make the region more conducive for the law abiding colonists who were prepared to settle these new territories. For much of the time, the Cayman Islands were thought to have been treated as an adjunct to the far larger and much important island of Jamaica, with the authorities there administering the Caymans, albeit from a distance.

By 1831 though; and with a growing demand for increased autonomy on the islands, a new legislative assembly was reported to have been established on the Caymans by a number of its leading citizens, which helped to construct and enact local legislation for the islands and their inhabitants. Although overseen by the British governor in Jamaica, this assembly was thought to have acted as the main legislature for the Cayman's right through to 1962, when the islands link to Jamaica was finally severed and the islands reverted to the status of a Crown dependency. In the intervening years a series of magistrates, chief magistrates and commissioners were appointed to look after the day-to-day running of the territories, although following its separation from the newly independent Jamaica in 1962, the former post of commissioner was renamed as administrator, although that title too was abolished in 1971, when the Crown's agent was officially appointed as Governor of the dependency. Since that time, the Cayman Islands have been governed by a legislative assembly, comprising elected representatives from the local population, with the leader of the largest party, holding the position of Premier, as opposed to Prime Minister in most independent parliamentary democracies. Despite the formal severance of their earlier political and legal links with Jamaica in 1962, the Cayman Islands, along with their culture, people and to a degree, their economy, remain inextricably linked to their much larger Caribbean neighbour and will no doubt continue to do so in the future.

Because of their relatively low position in the waters of the Caribbean, the Caymans are thought to be particularly susceptible to the sort of flooding caused by exceptional events, which happened to occur in September 2004, when Hurricane Ivan struck the region. Although the islands were reported to have been extremely hard hit by the effects of the hurricane, financial concerns and the assembly's desire to avoid a panic by the Cayman's important financial investors, all contrived to help make the effects of the storm far more serious in the wider world. Keen to avoid the island's collateral damage being photographed by reporters, the ministers of the Cayman's took the extraordinary step of closing the islands to all outside traffic and help, including two Royal Navy warships which had rushed to the scene to render aid, causing the international community to belief that extensive damage had been caused to the islands infrastructure, but more importantly to its population. Fortunately, there were few losses amongst the population and what little damage that was done to the islands buildings and infrastructure was very quickly repaired and the Caymans were opened for business once again two days later.

In 1672, English forces were reported to have captured the Caribbean island of Tortola from the Dutch and by the end of the decade had also managed to annexe the neighbouring islands of Anegada and Virgin Gorda, along with a number of smaller uninhabited islets, creating the basis for the modern day British Virgin Islands, which even today remains as a British Overseas Territory. Originally sighted by Christopher Columbus in 1493, he was said to have named them, St Ursula and her eleven thousand Virgins, which over time became more commonly known as The Virgin Islands. Although Spanish explorers were never thought to have formally occupied any of the three main islands in the Caribbean chain, during the 15th and 16th centuries, assorted seafarers, pirates and privateers were thought to have landed on them, either to repair their ships, re-supply their stores, or simply to use the islands as a hideout from the various legal authorities. According to some reports, the English sea captain, Sir John Hawkins was said to have landed on the islands in both 1542 and 1563, having returned across the Atlantic with cargoes of Black African slaves that he intended to sell to the Spanish authorities in Hispaniola. It has also been suggested that a young Francis Drake accompanied Hawkins on one or both of the voyages, returning to the islands some twenty-odd years later with his own fleet, prior to his attack on the Spanish held territory of Santo Domingo in 1585. Drake was said to have returned to the islands once again in 1595, just prior to his fateful voyage to Panama in the following year, where he finally met his death, succumbing to a deadly bout of dysentery, after which he was said to have been buried at sea. The Virgin Islands were thought to have been used by the British once again in 1598, when George Clifford, the 3rd Earl of Cumberland was said to have used them as a staging post for his later successful attack on the Spanish Governor's palace, La Fortaleza in Puerto Rico. Although, his initial attack on the seemingly impregnable fortress was highly successful, he and his crew were subsequently forced to surrender their prize, after the local people started to rebel against the English occupation of the palace.

For much of the 17th century, most of the larger islands in the chain were thought to have been occupied by various Dutch interests, either private individuals or the Dutch West India Company, both of whom were said to have been in almost constant conflict with the Spanish authorities in the New World. As early as 1615 a Dutch explorer called Joost Van Dyk was reported to have held possession of Tortola, the largest of the islands and was said to have rendered aid to a Dutch fleet in 1625, as they made their way through the Caribbean to attack the Spanish possession of San Juan in Puerto Rico. In retaliation for this raid, the Spanish authorities were reported to have sent a naval force to the Virgin Islands to destroy the relatively new settlements there, forcing Van Dyk and the rest of the Dutch colonists to flee Tortola and take refuge on a number of the neighbouring islands. After the Spanish had left however, most of the Dutch settlers were thought to have returned to the main island and began rebuilding their homes, as well as replanting their vitally important cotton and tobacco crops which had been damaged during the raid. Much more importantly however, the Dutch West India Company began to construct large warehouse facilities on Tortola, where goods could be temporarily held on their journey from the Dutch territories in South America to their possessions in the North, most notably the Dutch settlement in New Amsterdam, later to become New York. For much of the decade between 1625 and 1635 the Dutch inhabitants of the islands were reported to have substantially strengthened their settlement's defences, constructing a series of forts and defensive redoubts in order to deter any further attacks on the territories, by any of the major European powers that were beginning to dominate the Caribbean region. The first real test for these new positions was thought to have occurred in 1640, when a Spanish force attacked the islands and completely overwhelmed the Dutch defences, killing most of the colonists that were on the main islands, but largely ignoring those that were occupying the smaller ones.

Having later reoccupied the islands, it has been suggested that rather than trying to develop them, the Dutch West India Company sought to reduce their own liability, by leasing the islands to individual investors, who would then be responsible for their security and settlement. By 1650 a small number of Dutch settlers were said to have been present on the island of Tortola, along with some Black African slaves, who were thought have been held there prior to being sold to plantation owners on one or more of the neighbouring Caribbean islands. As the numbers of pirates, privateers and buccaneers began to increase throughout the next ten or twenty years, so the Virgin Islands increasingly became the target for these seaborne outlaws, with various outlying islands being used by them as hideouts from the different national authorities, who were attempting to suppress their illegal activities. With growing numbers of pirates visiting and settling on the islands, so the numbers of law abiding Dutch settlers began to decline, leaving the likes of Tortola and its legitimate settlements at increasing risk of being attacked by one or more of these sea raiders, or even by another nation state. Almost inevitably perhaps, in 1665 an English privateer called John Wentworth was reported to have attacked the main Dutch settlement on Tortola, looting the various buildings, driving the local inhabitants out of the area and seizing a large number of Black African slaves from the island, who he later transported to and sold in Bermuda. It was probably because of such raids and the lack of a proper defensive capability that eventually forced most of the Dutch settlers to abandon the islands for good, leaving the territories to be annexed by the English commander, Colonel William Burt, in July 1672.

Michael Manley   George Clifford   Alexander Bustamante

Although some thought was given to the settlement of the islands, continuing disputes with the Dutch authorities over ownership of them were thought to have continued until 1694 when the largest of the islands began to be colonised by land hungry planters and individual farmers, who were keen to exploit the Caribbean climate for growing one or other valuable cash crop, with sugar cane being particularly suited to the local conditions. However, despite the growing population the British authorities seemed to remain uncertain of their intentions towards the islands, especially in terms of its long term development and governance. Seemingly without its own assembly, legislature or judiciary for well over seventy years, it was only in 1773 that such political and legal bodies were finally established on the Virgin Islands, bringing with them much needed representation and the rule of English law. Although a legislative assembly was initially granted in 1774, it was said to be a full ten years before any sort of statutory body was actually established and even then it failed to operate as elsewhere, such was the intransigent nature of the local people. With sugar cane being one of the islands earliest agricultural commodities, needless to say, the cultivation of such crops resulted in the forced importation of large numbers of Black African slaves, who laboured on these new plantations, often in the direst conditions. Both the main island of Tortola and the smaller Virgin Gorda (the Fat Virgin) were thought to have been the principal sugar cane production areas, which during the period from 1717 to 1756 was said to have seen a tenfold increase in slave numbers from around six hundred, to well over six thousand, far in excess of the local white population. An almost inevitable consequence of such a large slave community were the occasional revolts and disruptions which were reported to have caused widespread panic on individual plantations or through the white community as a whole, with the first of these occurring sometime around 1790, following rumours that Black emancipation had been granted on other British islands, but not on the Virgin Islands. Replicating the events that had taken place on Jamaica and on a number of other British possessions, these rumours ultimately proved to be unfounded, although for the ringleaders of such revolts the punishment remained the same, with execution being the typical result. Over the next forty years there were reported to be at least four more instances of slave revolts on the islands, all of which were subsequently suppressed by the British authorities, with the last of these, which occurred in 1831, requiring regular forces to be brought in to bring the situation under control. In part, later slave unrest was said to have been caused by the British governments own decision to outlaw the trade in slaves in 1807, even though the state of slavery itself continued to exist within the British Empire, right through to 1834. As a result, those African slaves who were freed by the Royal Navy's seizure of slave ships from 1807 onwards were often brought to British territories like the Virgin Islands and having served a fourteen year apprenticeship, were subsequently released as free men. For those Black African slaves, who remained the property of their white owners, the sight of freed Black Africans, who were able to live independent lives outside of the often cruel and almost endless plantation system, must have been the source of much anger and resentment amongst the captive slave community; a likely cause of later rebellions.

However, eventually on 1st August 1834, all of the black African slaves on the British held Virgin Island were finally emancipated, a declaration that was reportedly celebrated by a three day holiday amongst the local Black communities. Even though most of them were forced to endure a further four years as apprentices, doing the work that they had previously done, new restrictions regarding their hours of work, their treatment and living conditions were thought to have been introduced, as part of the new British legislation, ensuring that their lives were at least significantly improved on what had existed before. Although some reporters believe that the abolition of the slave trade within the British Empire was the root cause of the demise of the sugar cane industry in the Virgin Islands, others believe that it was simply a contributory factor, in what was an almost inevitable decline. The sugar cane industry on the islands was also thought to have been partially damaged by the widespread cultivation of sugar beets in both Europe and in the United States, increased sugar tariffs and regular occurrences of seasonal hurricanes and widespread droughts which helped to devastate much of the islands agricultural land. For the local population, particularly the black community, the steady decline of the sugar cane industry ultimately proved to have a dual effect, with the resulting loss of employment offset by an increasing availability of land, as a growing number of white plantation owners decided to surrender or sell off their properties on the islands. However, many of the benefits that might have helped the black population to develop and expand their emerging agricultural economy, were thought to have been hindered by the British government's decision to introduce a series of new tax burdens on many of its Imperial territories, including the Virgin Islands. These new levies having been introduced, by the late 1840's local resentment was said to have been running high on Tortola, not simply about the new taxes, but also because of the appointment of fifteen coloured officials, who had been recruited from outside of the Virgin Islands. Antagonisms over these particular issues was said to have been added to by the introduction of new legislation that penalised those Virgin Islanders found guilty of smuggling, which was generally regarded by most of the local population as a traditional industry and something that the island's economy had come to rely on. The author of these new laws was reported to be the local magistrate, Isidore Dyett, who was not popular with the islands urban population, but was said to have been fairly well regarded by most of the rural poor, whose support for the magistrate ultimately prevented any planned actions being taken against him by the local shopkeepers and the remaining white landowners.

Over the period of the next few years, the islands were said to have remained relatively peaceful, although the atmosphere amongst the local population was thought to have remained fairly tense, with an expectation that some or other event would almost inevitably cause the peace of the islands to be shattered. The event when it did come, was reported to have been both unexpected and entirely avoidable, had the relevant authorities given some careful thought to the measure that they planned to introduce and discussed it more fully with members of the local population. As it was, in March 1853 two local ministers asked for relief on the taxes which were being demanded of them, a request that was subsequently refused by the local assembly, causing the two preachers to threaten the members of the governing body with a popular rising against their rule. Although they were reportedly unconcerned about the prospect of the two ministers agitating against their government of the island, neither did members of the assembly give much thought to the root cause of the two men's dissatisfaction, which were high taxes and a depressed economy. Instead, rather than try and alleviate some of the problems which were affecting the local population, three months later they announced the introduction of yet another tax, this time on every head of cattle that was owned by individual islanders, which was to come into force on the 1st August 1853. As most cattle tended to be owned by the generally poorer rural black farmers, then the new tax would significantly affect them more than their white neighbours, although despite this, there was reported to be little direct opposition to the measure when it was first announced. It was only on the 1st August 1853 when the new tax actually came into force that a number of the island's black farmers marched into the main settlement of Road Town to demonstrate against the new levy, to which the authorities responded by reading them the Riot Act and arresting two of the demonstrators. Almost immediately, violence was said to have broken out between the two sides, with several of the local constables and the magistrate being attacked by the incensed group of farm labourers, who vented their fury by attacking and burning some of the settlements buildings, before moving off, to set fire to individual plantations and sugar mills, causing their white owners to scatter in fear for their lives. Within a day, virtually all of the white settlers were thought to have fled to the neighbouring island of St Thomas, where they remained, until such time as it was safe to return, although a number of the islands officials did stay behind to try and reason with the outraged Black workers. The President of the Virgin Islands, Lieutenant Colonel John Cornwell Chad, was reported to have remained on Tortola during the crisis, along with the island's doctor, a missionary and the local customs collector, all of whom were said to have met with the rioters on the 2nd August to try and negotiate a peaceful end to the disorder. Unfortunately, despite agreeing to convey the labourer's grievances to the island's legislative assembly, he could do little more, simply because most of the assembly members had already fled Tortola in terror and could not be persuaded to return, until peace was restored. As it turned out though, peace was finally restored to the island, after British troops from Antigua, were despatched to Tortola to bring an end to the disturbance by force of arms. As a result, several of the rioters were reported to have been sentenced to lengthy terms of imprisonment, while at least three others were executed for their part in the civil unrest.

Unfortunately, despite the restoration of law and order, the damage caused by the 1853 riot was thought to have had much longer term consequences for the islands and its peoples, with large numbers of white settlers being forced or choosing to abandon their homes forever. For many of them, the heavily mortgaged, but now largely destroyed plantations could never be rebuilt and so they chose to relocate themselves and their families elsewhere, a decision that was no doubt influenced by the declining economic value of their farms and the islands generally. As the island's fortunes diminished, so the bitterness and resentment of the local workforce increased, with the danger of armed insurrection an ever present danger, requiring military reinforcements to be brought to the islands in both 1887 and 1890. Despite such concerns however, elsewhere on the main islands, local communities continued to develop, with new schools being introduced for the islander's children, who it was hoped might be better educated and more successful than earlier generations had been. Towards the end of the 19th century, the Virgin Islands also saw the first coloured inhabitant of their country appointed as President of his homeland, when Frederick Pickering achieved that notable goal in 1884 and continued to hold the office until 1887. Sadly, this notable achievement was reported to mark the pinnacle of early self government, as in later years, the island's own assembly was dissolved by the British authorities and the administration of the Virgin Islands was put under the control of the Leeward Islands, who appointed their own candidate as British Commissioner. By the beginning of the 20th century, many of the Virgin Islands younger inhabitants were choosing to leave their homelands, ostensibly because of the lack of employment opportunities on their home islands, forcing them to look elsewhere for work, with the larger Caribbean islands, often benefiting from their labour skills. Unfortunately for the British Virgin Islands and many of the Empires other Caribbean possessions, the first half of the 20th century saw Britain's economic and military power drained by two World Wars and a series of economic depressions, all of which ensured that support for its numerous colonies, dominions and dependent territories overseas was always likely to be extremely limited. As a consequence, it was only in the late 1940's that Britain could once again begin focusing on the fate of these overseas territories, often with the clear intention of granting them some form of self government, if not full independence.

On the Virgin Islands themselves, any British proposals for the territories were thought to have been pre-empted by the campaigns of a numbers of its citizens, including Theodolph Faulkner, Isaac Fonseca and Carlton de Castro, three Virgin Islanders who began to lobby for; and demand some form of self government, which ultimately led to the reestablishment of a reconstituted Legislative Assembly in 1950. It was thought to be this new legislative body which helped move the Virgin Islands forward, so that throughout the 1950's and early 1960's the island's outdated road system was modernised and extended, the first elements of the islands fledgling tourism industry were established, new financial investment was found and the island's first airport was constructed. It was also during the term of the new assembly that the Leeward Island Federation was formally dissolved by the British authorities, as a number of its member states were granted some form of self government, prior to being granted full independence. For the British Virgin Islands this period was also marked by the implementation of a new formal constitution, which granted the territories even greater administrative powers, over the day-to-day running of their various islands, as well as the ability to make long term plans for the future economic development of the islands. Even though the islands tourism industry had started to evolve throughout the 1950's and 1960's, real change was only said to have occurred during the early 1970's, when American tax lawyers, began to see the advantages of registering their clients companies outside of the mainland USA, allowing the likes of the Cayman and British Virgin Islands to initially develop into the financial centres that they are today. As an addendum to the historic development of the British Virgin Islands, it is worth noting that despite England having gained control of the three Virgin Islands of Tortola, Anegada and Virgin Gorda by 1680, rival Dutch interests were said to have maintained their ownership of the neighbouring islands of St Thomas, St John and St Croix. By 1917 however; and with these islands providing them with little financial or political benefit, the Dutch authorities agreed to sell these Caribbean possessions to the United

States for the combined sum of twenty five million US dollars, after which the American authorities renamed them the United States Virgin Islands.

The Caribbean island of Dominica only formally came into Britain's possession in 1763, as part of the Treaty of Paris which was signed in that year, which brought an end to the Seven Years War that had been fought between Britain and France since 1756. Although the island of Dominica had been known about since 1493, when Columbus was said to have first given the island its name, the indigenous people were said to be so fierce that the Spanish made no serious attempt to settle it, other than to put men ashore to determine whether or not there was any gold there, which there was not. As a result, the island was generally left alone until the middle of the 17th century, when France, which already had possession of the neighbouring islands of Guadeloupe and Martinique, claimed ownership of Dominica in 1635, sending explorers and missionaries onto the island a short time later. However, initial contacts with the local Carib people were thought to have been less than successful, with the local tribesmen reportedly being as fierce as before, forcing the French to withdraw from their new territorial possession. As news of the highly combative Caribs became more widely known, both France and her greatest European competitor, England, mutually agreed to leave both Dominica and the island of St Vincent abandoned by both nations, with the local Carib people as their only inhabitants, an agreement that was reported to have lasted for the next century or more. However, by the first half of the 18th century, both Britain and France had substantially increased their holdings and influence in the Caribbean, with each nation seeking to exploit as much of the regions natural resources as was possible, which almost inevitably drew both countries back to the island of Dominica. With a growing demand on both sides for new sources of wood and land, each country was reported to have been sending their own expeditions and logging teams onto the island to exploit its previously untouched natural resources, although by the second quarter of the 18th century, French interests were said to be dominating the island, a situation undoubtedly helped by the close proximity of its other two Caribbean possessions, Guadeloupe and Martinique. From 1756 onward though, Britain and France were reported to have been fighting the Seven Years War, a conflict between the two European Empires that was generally fought in the New World, from Canada to the Caribbean. It was said to be during and largely because of this wider conflict that the British military began to target and attack French held territories in the Caribbean, including the contested island of Dominica. In June 1761, the Scots born British commander, Andrew Rollo, the 5th Lord Rollo, was reported to have landed his forces on the island; quickly attacked the French held capital of Roseau and took control of the territory for the British Crown. He was subsequently appointed as Commander-in-Chief of Dominica, although he was said to have taken part in both of Britain's military expeditions against Martinique and Cuba in February and June of 1762 respectively. Unfortunately, such was the arduous nature of these three major military campaigns that Lord Rollo subsequently fell gravely ill and was forced to return home to England later in 1762, where some three years later he was reported to have passed away, aged 62.

Andrew Rollo   Eugenia Charles   Maurice Bishop

Despite having agreed to cede Dominica to Britain under the terms of the Treaty of Paris in 1763, some fifteen years later and with the two nations opposing one another during the American War of Independence, the French authorities authorised a new invasion of the island, with the support of the largely French population. However, when a peace treaty was subsequently signed between Britain and the new America Republic, as well as its wartime allies, which included France, the return of Dominica to British control formed part of that particular agreement, the Treaty of Paris 1783. Having reluctantly agreed to return the island back to Britain in 1783, the French authorities subsequently attempted two further invasions of the territory in 1795 and 1805, both of which were unsuccessful. During Britain's first period of ownership, having been granted the island in 1763, the British authorities were said to have established Dominica's first legislative assembly, although this body only really represented the interests of the white community, with the wishes of the Black and native communities largely ignored. However, after Britain regained possession of the island in 1783, over the course of the next few decades, the composition and membership of the assembly inextricably altered, reflecting the changing attitudes in the British Empire towards the native peoples of these overseas territories. By 1832 and in line with these more liberal ideals, the Dominican assembly was reported to have at least three elected black representatives, whilst at the same time, the free black and native inhabitants of the island were said to be enjoying greater social and political freedom, than many of their contemporaries elsewhere. Such was the scale of change on Dominica that by 1838, the island's legislative assembly was thought to be controlled by its black membership, the only one in all of the Britain's Caribbean possessions during that highly volatile period. Unfortunately, the white minority, concerned about their own rights being eroded, began to agitate for more centralised control, demanding that Dominica be restored as a Crown Colony, thereby restoring some of their own influence over the fate of the island, a demand that was eventually met in 1865, when the British colonial office imposed a new legislature on the island. Six years later the British government authorised the island's reversion to a Crown colony, effectively bringing to an end the prospect of black majority rule for the best part of the next century.

It was only in 1961 that the Dominican Labour Party finally won control of the island's legislative assembly, although even then, it remained as part of the ill-fated and short lived West Indies Federation, which was put together by British administrators as a means of governing some of their smaller Caribbean possessions. However, this poorly planned and generally unpopular organisation was said to have failed to survive beyond 1964 and by 1967, Dominica along with other members of the federation had been granted authority over its own internal affairs. The Dominican Labour Party leader, Edward LeBlanc, who had led his party in the legislative assembly since 1961, finally retired from that post in 1974 and just four years later his country was granted its independence by Britain, with LeBlanc's successor, Patrick John, being appointed as his country's first Prime Minister in that same year. As with a number of Britain's former Caribbean possessions, Dominica was said to have been beset by many economic problems after independence, largely because of a British failure to invest in the island's infrastructure throughout its tenure of the country. As a result of these social and economic difficulties, progress in the newly independent state was said to have been slow and painful, causing a great deal of tension amongst the population which occasionally resulted in civil disturbances and even two attempted coups. Interestingly, one of the coups that attempted to overthrow the elected government of Eugenia Charles, the first female Prime Minister in the Caribbean, was supposed to have been led by an American mercenary group, with the support of the former Dominican Prime Minister, Patrick John, who had previously been voted out of office, but had then established his own Dominica Defence Force in order to usurp the legitimate government of the country. The American mercenaries were said to have been led by two men, Mike Perdue and Wolfgang Droege, who hoped to be given development rights on the island, following their successful takeover of the island. Unfortunately for all of those involved in the plot, one of the leaders of the American group, Mike Perdue was said to be little more than a con-man, who had completely misled many of the would-be mercenaries, who were even thought to have included a white supremacist leader called Don Black. Perhaps unsurprisingly, the plot failed after the ATF (Bureau of Alcohol, Tobacco and Fireams) was told about the planned coup beforehand and put the ringleaders under surveillance, arresting most of the group before they had even left the dock in New Orleans. Back on Dominica, the authorities there were also informed about the plans, which led to Patrick John being arrested, tried and jailed for twelve years, for his part in the attempted coup. As for the American and Canadian leaders of the would-be mercenary force, Perdue and six others, were subsequently found guilty of contravening America's strict neutrality laws and were sentenced to three years in prison.

In the year immediately following Britain's acquisition of Dominica in 1761 and as part of the same Seven Year War, which was fought between 1756 and 1763, the French held territory of Grenada also fell into British hands. Although the English had originally claimed and attempted to settle the island in 1609, the local Carib people were thought to have been so violently averse to the new colonists that these first explorers were driven off the island, leaving it largely in native hands for the next fifty years or so. However, in 1650 a French merchant company were reported to have purchased Grenada from the English Crown, determined to colonise the island regardless of the Carib's resistance; and having reinforced their numbers with French troops from Martinique, set about pacifying the local tribesmen, who refused to surrender to their authority. By 1705, these new French settlers were said to have begun construction of Fort Royal, which was intended to act as their main defensive position on the island, although ultimately, at least according to some sources, it was the British who completed the base, as Fort George in 1710. That discrepancy aside however, the French were said to have retained possession of Grenada until 1762, when it was attacked and captured by British forces, as part of the military actions taken during the previously mentioned Seven Years War. In common with the island of Dominica, as part of the resulting Treaty of Paris, signed between Britain and France in 1763, which brought an end to the Seven Year War, Grenada was formally ceded to the British authorities and remained in their possession until 1779, when the French once again seized control of the territory, taking advantage of British military weaknesses during the American Revolutionary War. That conflict having ended, as part of the resulting Treaty of Paris, signed by Britain, along with America and her military allies, Grenada was once again returned to British ownership, although France subsequently attempted to foment revolt on the island in 1795, a rebellion that ultimately proved to be unsuccessful.

In the final years of the 18th century, Grenada, unlike a number of other Caribbean islands, but in common with some others, saw its agricultural base altered by forward thinking planters and landowners, who were keen to diversify away from the sugar cane industry which had previously dominated the island's economy. Recognising the financial damage that could be done by investing in a single cash crop, which was subject to the vagaries of the Caribbean climate, a number of planters began to introduce alternative cash crops to their lands, including nutmeg, a spice advocated by Joseph Banks, the British monarch's botanical adviser and the cocoa plant, both of which proved to be ideal crops for the local conditions. The widespread introduction of these two valuable commodities, was thought to have ultimately proved to be extremely advantageous for local growers, as the sugar cane industry began to decline with the advent of sugar beet production in Europe and the United States, allowing more of Grenada's plantations to be broken up for smaller sharecroppers to grow even more nutmeg, cinnamon, cloves, ginger, and cocoa, helping Grenada's economy to flourish, whilst many other neighbouring ones struggled. In line with other British territories, slavery was finally abolished on Grenada in 1834; a year after the island had been placed under the authority of the British Windward Islands, from where the island was administered until the dissolution of that administrative body in 1958. Governorship of Grenada was then transferred to the short-lived Federation of the West Indies, although with the collapse of that body in 1962, the island was granted associated statehood by the British authorities, which was later extended to partial independence in 1967. As in most cases, these increasing levels of self government were designed to prepare the former colonies and dependent territories for full independence, which was finally achieved by the people of Grenada in February 1974.

Influenced by the British parliamentary system, Grenada's political executive was established as a multi-party democracy, overseen by a Governor General who acted on behalf of the British monarch, with the leader of the majority parliamentary party being elected as the Prime Minister of Grenada. The first Grenadian to hold that office after independence was said to have been Sir Eric Gairy, the leader of the Grenadian Labour Party, who had previously held the post of Premier, during the country's final period as an associate state. Unfortunately, Gairy's reputation had been damaged during the 1960's when he was dismissed from his post as Chief Minister, having been accused of corruption, although despite this, by the mid 1970's and with his country on the verge of independence, he had somehow managed to repair his reputation and gain favour once again with a majority of the Grenadian population. However, when new national elections were called in 1976 and Gairy's Labour Party won a parliamentary majority once again, opposition parties refused to accept the outcome, declaring the result fraudulent and inciting civil unrest throughout the country. Although Gairy managed to maintain political control of Grenada for a time, in March 1979, the New Jewel Movement, under the leadership of Maurice Bishop was reported to have launched an attack on the country's parliament and managed to remove Gairy and his party from power. The New Jewel Movement had originally been established as a legitimate political party in 1973 and for a number of years was said to have engaged in the regular democratic processes of Grenada, although without achieving any sort of success. By the late 1970's though; and possibly because of the worsening political climate and their own lack of success at the ballot box, the leadership of the New Jewel Movement were reported to have established the National Liberation Army, a small paramilitary force which was trained abroad, in preparation for the overthrow of the Grenada's elected Labour government.

The armed revolution of March 1979 was reported to have begun when Gairy was out of the country, with members of the New Jewel Movement, including those from the National Liberation Army, seizing police stations, military barracks, government buildings and more importantly, the country's radio station, from where they publicly announced the establishment of a new People's Revolutionary Government, with Maurice Bishop as Prime Minister at its head. Although concerned about the revolution in Grenada, most other countries were thought to have either noted their disapproval, or chose not to comment at all, although the United States was thought to have been deeply concerned over the Marxist-Leninist principles of the new Grenadian administration and began to watch developments in the country much more closely. Having consolidated their hold on the island, Maurice Bishop and his allies then began to introduce many of their own socialist ideologies to Grenada, which involved turning the country into a single party state, the discontinuation of national elections, the creation of a new, much larger Grenadian army and the appointment of likeminded individuals, to many key offices, both in the executive and in Grenada's newly enlarged standing army. However, despite many of these overtly undemocratic changes, which caused concerns for the United States and some of Grenada's Caribbean neighbours, within the wider international community, the situation on the small Caribbean island was thought to have remained relatively unimportant.

Although Maurice Bishop and his People's Revolutionary Government had forged links with America's long time adversary, Cuba, long before the revolutionary party even gained power in Grenada, following their takeover of the island in 1979, Fidel Castro's country was thought to have been one of the first Caribbean nations to offer both formal recognition and logistical assistance to the new Grenadian administration. Within a matter of month's significant numbers of Cuban military advisers, engineers, doctors, nurses, teachers and other personnel, were said to have arrived in Grenada, bringing with them new skills and equipment to help drive the country forward. From an American perspective however, it was the proposed development and expansion of Grenada's airport facilities which posed the greatest concern, leading some US politicians to conclude that these new airport facilities, apart from helping Grenada's economy to grow, might also represent a real military threat to the United States itself. Despite such obvious concerns though, both in America and the Caribbean generally, no affirmative action was taken against Grenada or its socialist government, save for those warnings which were transmitted through the usual diplomatic channels. However, by 1983 the People's Revolutionary Government was beginning to fragment, with a number of its more radical elements becoming increasingly concerned over Maurice Bishop's apparent failure to introduce some of the more extreme Marxist-Leninist ideas to Grenada. Failing to recognise that Bishop was in part constrained by the looming presence of the United States; and its instinctive distrust of anything that was deemed to be socialist, let alone communist, Bishop and his ministers were thought to have been compelled to shelve a number of policies that they would otherwise have introduced. Unfortunately, this brought Bishop into conflict with other members of the party, particularly Bernard Coard, his Deputy Prime Minister, who soon began plotting Bishop's removal from office, in order to allow some of the movement's more militant policies to be introduced to Grenada.

Bernard Coard **Ronald Reagan** **Margaret Thatcher**

Having planned Maurice Bishop's removal from office, Coard was then thought to have arranged for the ousted Grenadian leader to be placed under house arrest, until such time as a decision could be made regarding his future. Unfortunately for Coard and his allies however, despite having taken control of Grenada by force, Bishop remained extremely popular with large sections of the island's population, many of whom immediately began to violently demonstrate against his arrest, which ultimately led to Bishop escaping his guards and managing to make his way to the main Grenadian army headquarters on the island. Taking refuge in the building, along with a number of his fellow ministers, Bishop was reported to have tried to rally further assistance from elsewhere on the island, but with few ways of communicating and with much of the country in disarray, his attempts at rallying further support, proved to be largely unsuccessful. In the meantime, Bernard Coard had managed to bring in additional forces from another part of the island and launched an attack on the headquarters building where Bishop and his ministers were taking refuge. After a fairly lengthy gun battle, during which many innocent civilians were reportedly killed or wounded, Coard's troops were said to have finally managed to secure the building, capturing Bishop and his ministers and subsequently holding them in a small courtyard, while their fate was decided by Coard and his allies. Sometime later, a group of soldiers were reported to have entered the courtyard and simply turned their guns on Bishop and his fellow prisoners, one of whom was a pregnant female minister who was said to have begged for the life of her unborn child, but to no avail. Having murdered Bishop and his ministers, the leaders of the coup then announced the formation of a new military government under the control of Hudson Austin, who subsequently announced a nationwide curfew for the following four days, during which anyone found outside without permission would be shot.

Alarmed and outraged by the turn of events on Grenada, within hours, a number of nations in and around the Caribbean, including the United States, began discussing what action, if any, should be taken, in order to restore law and order to the island. The United States and its then President, Ronald Reagan, was thought to have been particularly disturbed by the developments on Grenada and within hours of the murder of Maurice Bishop and his ministers, was said to have authorised the use of American military forces to remove this far more dangerous new Grenadian regime from power. From an entirely diplomatic point of view, it was considered necessary for the United States to receive a request for their help from a third party, with Eugenia Charles, the Prime Minister of Dominica and Paul Scoon, the British Governor General of Grenada, both being named as the source of this international request for American military aid, which was subsequently used to justify the United States invasion of the island to the wider international community. As an aside to the subject of the American invasion generally, it is interesting to note that the subject of the new airfield on Grenada had previously been discussed by the Reagan administration, which refused to accept that its use was entirely civilian, or peaceful. In response to these ongoing concerns, an American Congressman, Ron Dellums, was reported to have visited the island in 1982 and issued a report categorically dismissing any suggestion that the airfield had a military purpose, although his findings were subsequently ignored by Reagan, who chose to continue with his own political scaremongering over the project. It is equally interesting to note that the planning and construction of the new airport, was said to have first been proposed by the British authorities as early as the 1950's and was then subsequently designed, financed and built by a number of countries, including the United Kingdom, Canada, Algeria, Libya and Cuba, at least two of which were direct military allies of the United States and therefore unlikely to participate in the building of what was purported to be a potential enemy asset.

The presence of American citizens on Grenada was also reported to have been used as a pretext for the invasion of the island, despite the fact that both Cuban and Grenadian authorities had repeatedly offered assurances regarding their continued wellbeing, guarantees that the Reagan administration ultimately chose to disregard. It is worth speculating perhaps, whether or not this particular aspect of the Grenada problem, was actually informed by a fear of repeating earlier events and the much publicized seizure of the American hostages in Tehran, which caused so much frustration and soul-searching in the United States and ultimately helped put Ronald Reagan in the White House. Either way, having made the decision to invade the island of Grenada, with or without any legal authority to do so, at five o'clock on the morning of 25th October 1983, some six days after Maurice Bishop and his fellow ministers were murdered, the first elements of the United States military taskforce were said to have stepped ashore on the Caribbean island. The operation, colourfully codenamed "Urgent Fury", eventually involved some eight thousand American servicemen, including Marines, Sailors and Airmen, along with other assorted ground troops, who were faced by a mixed force of around fifteen hundred Grenadian and approximately seven hundred Cuban troops, whose numbers were said to be supplemented by a few dozen military advisors, although these were later reported to be foreign diplomats, who actually played no part in the fighting. Needless to say, the United States forces eventually overcame the relatively small numbers of Grenadian and Cuban troops who were opposing them, after which the leading members of the New Jewel Movement were arrested and the islands Governor General, Paul Scoon, was asked to form an interim civil administration, which was supported by a US military presence which remained on Grenada for some months.

Almost as soon as the first American marine's boot landed on Grenada, condemnation of the United States invasion began, although in the US itself, the action was broadly approved of by most citizens, many of whom seemed to believe that the American students on the island had already been taken hostage, although clearly they had not. In what later became a fairly obvious absurdity, on the evening of the 25th October, some hours after the invasion had first begun, a group of the students were spoken to by telephone on a US television program, where they clearly stated that they were safe and had not considered themselves to be in any sort of danger. However, the following day, another group of medical students, who had been informed that they were being relocated to the United States to complete their studies, were keen to tell the interviewer and his listeners, how grateful they were for the intervention of the US Marines, who had undoubtedly saved their lives. Despite such clearly manipulated reporting however, in the wider international community, the wholly disproportionate and highly questionable American response, to what was an entirely internal matter for the Grenadian people, provoked a great deal of outrage, with the United Nations General Assembly passing a resolution deploring the United States flagrant violation of international law, by a vote of one hundred and eight in favour, against nine opposed. Both the governments of China and the Soviet Union were reported to have publicly criticized the invasion and although there was an attempt to introduce a vote against America's actions in the UN Security Council, this was ultimately vetoed by the United States own representative. The Conservative Prime Minister of Britain, Margaret Thatcher, was said to have been particularly outraged by the American invasion, not least because of the assurances given to her by Ronald Reagan that no immediate military action was likely, despite the fact that plans were already in place to attack the island. In common with most American leaders, ultimately Reagan's responsibility for maintaining the so-called and almost mythical "special relationship" between the United Kingdom and the United States only extended as far as it did not impede America's own self interest, an extremely one-sided agreement that continue to operate right through to the modern day.

The small collection of islands that now form the modern day British overseas territory of the Turks and Caicos Islands, were thought to have been known about since the beginning of the 16th century, when the Spanish explorer, Juan Ponce de Leon, was said to have first sighted them in 1512. As elsewhere in the Caribbean, a number of the larger islands within the chain were thought to have been inhabited by the native Arawak people, who were eventually displaced by the much more militaristic Caribs, who took control of the territories in later decades. Following the widespread colonisation and exploitation of the region by the Spanish conquistadors during the 16th century though, large numbers of these Caribs were reportedly captured and enslaved by the Spaniards, who subsequently used them to help build their new South American empire. With the Turks and Caicos island's essentially bereft of their indigenous peoples and with few if any natural resources to attract colonists, for much of the 17th century, their only visitors were thought to be a succession of pirates and privateers, who used the islands, both as a hideout and as a base from where they could attack any commercial ship that was unfortunate enough to pass their way. It was only in the final quarter of the 17th century that the first European settlers were thought to have arrived on the islands, seasonal salt manufacturers who had travelled from Bermuda, to take advantage of the islands shallow waters, which made them so suitable for salt production. Most of the people employed in the these salt industries were reported to have been African slaves, who were required to spend many hours every day standing in large salt pans raking or skimming the salt from the pools of slowly evaporating water, the liquid becoming increasingly saline as it dried. As a result of their almost constant exposure to this highly alkaline solution, the bare limbs of the slaves were said to have regularly become affected by blisters and ulcers, some of which could penetrate to the bone, causing life threatening infections that were often compounded by poor diets and ineffective treatments. The most notable of these slaves was thought to have been one Mary Prince, a young slave girl who was sent to work in the salt raking pans of the Turks and Caicos Islands; and later recalled her time there, in the memoir "The History of Mary Prince", which was widely used by members of the British Abolitionist movement to illustrate the depravity and brutality of the international slave trade.

It was said to be these same salt workers, along with a number of foresters, subsistence farmers and hunters who had accompanied them on their seasonal trips that began to clear away the island's historic trees and vegetation, opening the land up for cultivation. However, it was only towards the end of the 18th century that the first group of planters and growers arrived on these generally isolated British possessions, loyalist settlers from Britain's former colonies in the United States, who were said to have been granted these new lands in recognition for the support they had offered the British Empire during the American Revolutionary War. Cultivating a plant known as Sisal, a naturally fibrous plant commonly used in rope-making, etc. these few dozen planters were reported to have been responsible for introducing large numbers of black African slaves to the islands, who were subsequently employed in the planting, harvesting and processing of this unusual plant. Unfortunately, the development of this particular industry was thought to have been generally short-lived, as crops of Sisal were regularly affected by both natural pests and adverse weather conditions, which conspired to make the industry largely unprofitable, forcing many of the smaller planters to abandon the islands altogether. Although some of the larger investors reportedly switched their estates to salt production in later years, by around 1820 most of the loyalist settlers were thought to have moved elsewhere in the Caribbean, leaving many of their former slaves to survive on the islands as best as they could, which most did by hunting and fishing. Although Britain assumed territorial rights over the Turks and Caicos through its larger neighbour Bermuda, initially the Turks themselves were not regarded as a significant area in their own right and were not formally attached to Bermuda, but simply regarded as common ground for all of Britain's immediate territories. As a result of this, both Bermuda and the Bahamas laid a nominal claim to the islands, even though it was the Bermudians who expelled a mixed Franco-Spanish force which seized the islands in 1706, thereby strengthening their own title to ownership. Unfortunately, under British law, a Crown Colony could not own other colonies, which undermined the Bermudian claim and allowed the Bahamas to lay claim to the Turks and Caicos. The first attempt at adopting the smaller islands was said to have occurred in 1766, when the Kings agent on the Bahamas, Andrew Symmer, altered the colony's constitution to allow for the taxation of those Bermudians who were living or working on the Turks and Caicos, despite the fact that he had no authority to do so. The British Colonial Secretary, Lord Hillsborough, in response to Symmer's new constitution, immediately refuted the new constitution and ordered that all Bermudians on the Turks and Caicos should be permitted to work there without hindrance, forcing the Kings agent to rescind his new orders. As a result of Symmer's actions though, those Bermudians living on the Turks appointed their own commissioners to govern them, with the permission of the king's agent and even drew up their own regulations to ensure good government on the islands. However, not to be outdone, the Governor of the Bahamas subsequently drew up his own regulations for the islands, which ordered that no-one could work on the islands without having first agreed to his having authority there, by signing his unilateral declaration.

Clearly, with both Bermuda and the Bahamas claiming authority over the Turks and Caicos, it was only a matter of time before one or more Bermudian worker refused to sign the Bahamian governor's new working regulations and therefore brought the two sides into conflict over the issue. However, rather than the matter degenerating into any sort of physical conflict between the two colonies, it was referred to the Crown authorities, who refused to grant Bahamian authority over Bermudians living and working on the Turks and Caicos, which caused a great deal of dissatisfaction in the Bahamas, where the authorities had finally hoped to gain control of the islands highly lucrative salt manufacturing industry. Although workers from both Bermuda and the Bahamas visited the Turks to produce salt, in 1783 a contingent of French troops were said to have been temporarily landed on Grand Turk and held the island for a period, despite British military efforts to remove them, before they chose to withdraw of their own volition. Following this incident, salt makers from the Bahamas were reportedly reluctant to return to the island, even though their Bermudian counterparts returned almost immediately. As a result, the Bermudians were able to take full advantage of the islands vast salt resources, with increasing numbers of workers coming to Grand Turk, helping to make the industry even more profitable than it had been before. This proved to be particularly irritating for the Bahamian authorities, who were struggling to cope with the increasing financial costs of having to accept growing numbers of loyal settlers from North America, who were being relocated to the Caribbean following Britain's withdrawal from the regions which later became the United States.

Sir Eric Gairy

Paul Scoon

Roland Symonettec

In order to recover some of these costs, the authorities in the Bahamas once again tried to institute a levy on the salt producers of the Turks and Caicos Islands, insisting that all ships travelling there, should obtain a licence from the Bahamian authorities. Needless to say, virtually all Bermudian vessels chose to ignore this demand, causing the Bahamian authorities to begin seizing those ships which refused to obtain the licence, with the Crown authorities taking little affirmative action to discourage such seizures. However, it was the Bermudian authorities themselves, who ultimately gave sanction to the highly questionable Bahamian measures, by subsequently refusing to allow free trade between Bermuda and the Turks and Caicos islands, ostensibly recognising that the islands lay outside of their own territorial control. The abandonment of their earlier claims to the islands were further implied in 1806 when the Turks and Caicos Islands were attacked by a French fleet and the Bermudian authorities refused to help hunt down the attackers, or to send aid to the territories. The island's vitally important salt industry were said to have been further affected by the damage caused by two separate hurricanes which struck the islands in 1813 that not only decimated many of the buildings there, but also led to the loss of much of the salt stores that were being held on the islands, as well as a number of ships that were anchored offshore. The final straw for the salt industry on the Turks and Caicos Islands though, was thought to be the downturn in demand from the United States, which had been one of the industry's largest customers, but whom over a period of time, had developed their own sources and no longer needed to buy salt from the Caribbean.

It was little wonder perhaps that Bermuda became increasingly indifferent to the fate of the Turks and Caicos Islands, as their contribution to the Bermudian economy became less and less important. It was principally because of this situation that the Bermudian authorities were thought to have essentially abandoned any claim to the islands and the people that made their living there, by allowing the territories to be transferred to the authority of the Bahamas in around 1818. However, the island's only remained part of the Bahamas until 1848, when representatives from the Turks and Caicos Island's successfully appealed to the British government, to be granted the status of a colony, with its own legislative council, which would then be overseen by the Governor of Jamaica. For the next twenty five years the island's was thought to have remained as a separate colony, but due to its increasing costs, in 1873 the territories were passed into the authority of Jamaica, simply becoming a part of that particular imperial possession until 1962, when the larger Caribbean island was granted full independence by the British authorities. Although subsequently granted the status of Crown Colony, from 1965 the islands were then placed under the authority of the British Governor of the Bahamas, a situation that continued until 1973 when the Bahamas too were granted full independence by Great Britain. Since that time, the Turks and Caicos Islands have generally operated as a British Overseas Territory, ruled by an independent legislative council, whose representatives, appointments and elections are overseen by their own British Governor, who as the Queens representative is appointed by the British Crown.

In common with the Cape Colony in South Africa, Dutch interests in the New World also became a target for the British Empire during the late 18th century, following the French conquest of the Netherlands, with Britain keen to ensure that these Dutch possessions did not fall into French hands as well. In 1796, the Dutch colonies of Essequibo, Demerara and Berbice, which lay on the northeast coast of South America, were seized by British forces which had been despatched from Barbados, the Netherlands having submitted to French rule in 1795. For many of the Dutch and other European inhabitants of these territories, the British arrival was said to have been generally welcomed, guaranteeing as it did, that their farms and plantations would not fall under French authority and with the British having previously agreed to maintain and abide by the laws that were common to each of the individual colonies. However, in 1802 Britain agreed to return possession of these three territories to the new Batavian Republic, under the terms of the Treaty of Amiens which had been signed by Britain and France in March 1802, bringing a temporary respite to the ongoing dispute between the two countries that had been raging since 1793. However, within a year or so of signing the Treaty of Amiens, the two European neighbours were at war once again, as the Napoleonic Wars engulfed Europe, resulting in British forces once again taking possession of the three Dutch colonies in South America which would henceforth remain in British hands. Even though the colonies were only formally ceded to Britain in 1814, under the terms of the Anglo-Dutch Treaty of that same year, even before the territories were formally granted to Britain, the British authorities there had begun the process of amalgamating the three regions into a single colonial possession, although this was not fully achieved until 1831, when they formally became known as British Guiana.

Sugar cane was reported to have been the predominant agricultural crop of Britain's new imperial possession and remained so right through to the end of the 19th century, when a decline in sugar prices and the advent of the new sugar beet crops, both conspired to reduce the profitability of the New World plantations that had made their fortunes from this highly prized commodity. Needless to say, the dependency of this industry on manual labour had led to the mass importation of tens of thousands of enslaved black Africans to labour on these former Dutch and later British plantations, with resulting disquiet, revolts and even large scale rebellions being a regular feature of the territory's colonial history. The worst of these slave rebellions was reported to have occurred in 1823, in what has sometimes been described as the Demerara Rebellion, during which some two hundred or so slaves were said to have been killed, along with a white minister; and it became yet another event that helped underpin the argument of the Abolitionist movement in Britain. As had been the case elsewhere in the Caribbean, the root causes of the revolt was thought to be the general dissatisfaction of the large slave population in the British colony, which was exacerbated by the mistaken belief that the British authorities in London had already announced, or were about to announce, freedom for all slaves within the British Empire. In support of their demands for full emancipation and in order to highlight the atrocious conditions that some of the slaves endured, a small number of slaves, along with other free Blacks were reported to have organised a peaceful general strike for the 18th August 1823 which would bring the island's sugar cane industry to a halt. Although the leaders of the revolt had instructed their supporters to demonstrate in a peaceful fashion, almost inevitably some chose not to do so, but were determined to exact some form of retribution against their white masters and overseers. These more rebellious elements were said to have invaded the houses of the white farmers and plantation owners, searching out weapons that they could steal before locking their owners in rooms, or tying them up, before abandoning them with a promise to return and release them at a later date. The most serious attacks upon the white owners were thought to have involved their being forced into the plantation's stocks, a punishment that was commonly inflicted upon the slaves themselves, who were keen for their masters to share the experience first hand. Even though a few of the white community may well have been manhandled by their slaves, there was not a single incident of a white person being deliberately wounded or killed by the rebellious slaves, something that could not be said for the white community themselves.

According to most contemporary reports of the time, a leading member of the white community, a plantation owner called Simpson, had been informed about the strike at around six o'clock in the morning of the 18th August 1823, the same day that the action began. Simpson subsequently set out to advise the colony's governor of the planned strike, on the way stopping to alert his closest neighbours about the proposed event, before continuing his journey to see the governor, who immediately alerted the islands military forces, including cavalry units, to put down the insurrection. Declaring martial law throughout the colony, the governor was also reported to have mobilised his detachments of regular troops and local militias, who were both sent out to hunt down and suppress any and all lawbreakers, which they were said to have done by the afternoon of the 20th August 1823. Whilst most slaves had been rounded up and subsequently returned to their owners, a small number were said to have been shot, supposedly while trying to escape, although exactly how many slaves died during the first two days of the strike was largely unreported. In later confrontations between the two sides, once again relatively small numbers of slaves were thought to have been killed, although in total, some two hundred were reported to have died during the entire episode. By the 21st August 1823 the uprising had been suppressed and the authorities had most of the reported ringleaders in custody, being held awaiting trial, which was scheduled to take place on the 25th August, under the auspices of a court martial which had been constituted by the British Governor, John Murray. Rather typically for the time, the court martial, which was presided over by Lieutenant Colonel Arthur Goodman, was thought to have handed down severe sentences to those slaves who were found guilty of planning, or participating in the revolt. Quamina, a slave from the "Success" plantation was found guilty of leading the revolt and was executed for his crime, whilst his son, Jack, a slave who worked on the same plantation and who had been equally involved with the uprising was spared a similar fate, reportedly after one of the owners of the estate, Sir John Gladstone, father of William Gladstone, the British Prime Minister, wrote to the Governor, appealing for clemency. It was thought to be as a result of Sir John's intervention that Jack was spared a death sentence and was subsequently sold by his owners and deported from British Guiana. Amongst the other slaves, found guilty of various offences, some were sentenced to flogging, others to solitary confinement, whilst a good many others suffered the same fate as Quamina and were executed by the colonial authorities.

However, at least these particular slaves were reported to have been sentenced by a legitimate British court, albeit one that was ill-suited for the task for which it was constituted, but a British court nonetheless. Elsewhere in the colony, other slaves were thought to have fared less well, with reports of locally constituted trials being established on several plantations, where individual slaves were tried and sentenced for their purported wrongdoings, including some who were reportedly executed for their crimes by being shot in the head and later having their decapitated heads nailed to a post, or their corpse hung out on public view, presumably as a warning for the other slaves to heed. Aside from the previously mentioned slaves, Quamina and Jack, the most notable victim of Goodman's court martial was said to be John Smith, the English born Parson who had been sent to British Guiana by the London Missionary Society in 1817 and whose active campaigning for the slave community's religious rights, was reported to have caused the revolt to occur in the first place.

Charged with promoting unrest in the Negro community, inciting rebellion, communicating with named ringleaders of the revolt and failing to advise the proper authorities of the planned revolt, after a month long trial, Smith was subsequently found guilty of the charges against him and was sentenced to death. Almost immediately however, an appeal was lodged on his behalf, but not before he was transferred from the courthouse to the local prison, where he subsequently died of consumption. A little over a month after Smith had died, a Royal Reprieve was received by the British authorities in Guiana, who, rather than risk any further unrest amongst the local slave community, many of whom were extremely fond of the Pastor, decided to bury John Smith in an unmarked grave within the colony. Back in Britain though, news of Smith's death was said to have caused outrage within abolitionist circles, with several hundred petitions being sent to the British Parliament and many of the nations leading newspapers carrying notices of his demise, which allied to the deaths of the slaves in the colony, did much to stimulate the anti slavery movement in Great Britain, as well as attracting the interest of the great emancipator William Wilberforce.

A little over a decade after the Demerara Rebellion, slavery was finally abolished within the British Empire and although the former slaves were compelled to serve a period of apprenticeship before becoming completely free, new regulations regarding the treatment of former slaves ensured that there were some improvements in their lives, no matter how slight. However, because of the previously noted decline in the colony's sugar cane industry, the economy of British Guiana began to diversify, with rice production, mining and forestry becoming new sources of revenue and employment for the colonial population, although mining for gold and diamonds ultimately proved to be of limited use to the local economy as deposits of both were thought to be relatively small. Aside from the sugar cane industry, which remained as a mainstay of the local economy, the colony was thought to have been unable to develop any sort of large scale manufacturing industry, largely because of the lack of any significant natural resources. As a result, much of British Guiana's economy came to be dominated by a single commercial operation, the Booker Group of companies from London, who eventually owned all but three of the colony's sugar plantations and thereby became the largest employer in the country. It was only in later years that Guiana was found to have significant deposits of Bauxite, or aluminium ore which has become such a valuable revenue earner for this generally resource poor South American country. In keeping with the arrangement that had first been made in 1796, legislative control of the British colony closely followed the Dutch colonial model, which placed executive power in the hands of Crown appointees or the colony's largest, wealthiest and most influential landowners. It was only in 1928 that the British government finally abolished this Dutch based system, instituting the more usual British colonial model in its stead, with a typically British legislative assembly established and greater powers handed to the colonial Governor, changes that were not immediately welcomed by certain elements of the population. Fifteen years later, the legislative makeup of the colony was altered, creating a much more democratic assembly, with a majority of the seats being taken by truly elected representatives who came from all spheres of the local population. Although responsible for much of the day to day business of the region, this legislative assembly still had to defer to both the British Governor and his Executive Council, who maintained oversight and overall control of Guiana, right up until 1953, when the system was changed once again. It was only in that year that a more traditional and fully elected national assembly was established, with no property qualification being required for those standing for office. The colony's Upper House, or State Council was appointed by both the Governor and the national assembly, but had limited powers, thereby conveying greater authority to the fully elected members of the national assembly, in what became a forerunner to Guiana's own independent democratic system.

Errol Barrow   Edward Le Blanc   Sir John Gladstone

In the year following Britain's seizure of the former Dutch colonies that later became the independent nation of Guyana, Britain was also reported to have acquired the island territories of Trinidad and Tobago in the Caribbean. Seized by a fleet of British warships, under the command of Sir Ralph Abercromby, in February 1797, this same force was said to have been responsible for capturing the previously mentioned Dutch colonies of Demerara and Essequibo, along with the islands of Grenada, Saint Lucia and St Vincent. For virtually all of its later history, from 1498 through to 1797, Trinidad had been occupied by the Spanish, who were thought to have initially employed the islands native inhabitants as a source of slave labour for their new territories on the South American mainland. Although Spanish explorers and colonists reportedly settled the islands as early as 1530, according to some historians in the first half of the 16th century these few colonists were said to have only occupied small parts of the island, the remainder being heavily forested and inhabited by a variety of native Caribbean tribesmen, including the Caribs. By the second half of the 16th century however, more Spanish settlers were thought to have arrived there, being granted lands in various regions of the territory on which to settle themselves, creating the basis of the later settlement St Joseph and other townships. Although English privateers appear to have been generally disinterested in many of Spain's smaller Caribbean possessions, including the likes of Trinidad and Tobago, in 1595 the English sea captain Sir Walter Raleigh was reported to have attacked and captured the settlement of San Jose, before interrogating one of its founders, the Spanish explorer Antonio de Berrio, in order to discover information relating to Spain's most important and wealthiest settlements in the New World.

Even through to the early 1700's, Spanish settler numbers on Trinidad were said to have remained relatively small, which was said to have resulted in large numbers of foreign migrants being encouraged to relocate themselves, their families and their slaves to the islands, in order to consolidate the population, with each new settler receiving generous grants of land that they could then cultivate. These new migrants were thought to have included settlers from England, Scotland, Ireland, Italy, Germany, the Netherlands and France, with significant numbers of French colonists reportedly arriving on the islands in the aftermath of the French Revolution, bringing with them their experience of growing both cocoa and sugar, cash crops which would prove to be vital products for Trinidad's future economic development. In a little over twenty years, from 1776 to 1797, the population of Trinidad was reported to have expanded significantly, from a few thousand to nearly twenty thousand, of which nearly half were thought to be persons of colour, both free and enslaved. It was this peculiarly mixed population that was said to have come into British hands in 1797, when Sir Ralph Abercromby brought his squadron of British warships to the coast of the islands in February of that year, causing the Spanish Governor of the island to surrender the territory without resistance. Although he might ordinarily have offered some opposition to an enemy force, perhaps recognising that his forces were both outnumbered and outgunned, Governor Chacon quickly realised the futility of any armed defence, to his own forces, the islands settlements, but more importantly perhaps, to the local population. As it turned out, after negotiating the handover of the territories to the British forces, the islands subsequently became a British imperial possession, with a largely French speaking population, who were generally governed by traditional Spanish laws, a highly unusual set of circumstances given the times. For the next five years or so and despite the islands remaining under British control, actual ownership of Trinidad and Tobago continued to be disputed between the two European nations, with the matter only being settled in 1802 when the Spanish authorities finally and formally ceded them to the British Crown. It was only after this date that large numbers of British settlers began to arrive on the islands, both from Britain itself and from its other Caribbean territories, although even these new migrants failed to populate the islands as much as the authorities would have liked. Even though Britain was reported to have introduced its first piece of anti slavery legislation in 1807, in the intervening period, between 1802 and 1807, large numbers of black African slaves were thought to have been brought to Trinidad and Tobago to help develop the sugar cane plantations, which at the time, remained one of the most profitable industries in the Caribbean. However, the relatively small scale of the slave holding on these islands, as opposed to some of the other larger slave holding territories, was best illustrated by the numbers recorded as being owned there in 1838. Whilst Trinidad and Tobago was reported to have held some seventeen thousand black African slaves at the time of their emancipation on 1st August 1838, the neighbouring territory of Jamaica held some three hundred and sixty thousand lack African slaves, some twenty times the number, despite being only twice the size. Although the two islands of Trinidad and Tobago were thought to have been treated as entirely separate entities throughout much of their later history, from the 15th century to the middle of the 19th century, as territorial neighbours, ultimately the two islands were subsequently developed in tandem with one another, although it was only in 1889 that the two territories were finally bound together as a single British possession.

Because of the vast amounts of uncultivated land available on Trinidad and Tobago, unlike most of Britain's other slave holding territories, the newly freed slaves on the islands did not automatically remain on the European owned plantations where they had previously laboured, but instead established their own smallholdings, or followed other occupations on the islands. The resulting labour shortages on the generally white owned sugar cane plantations was reported to have led to yet another much needed influx of labourers, only this time indentured workers from Portugal, China and the Indian subcontinent, people who had agreed a fixed five year term contract with the authorities, after which they could return home, or remain on the islands and become a part of the resident population. Beginning sometime around 1845, the first of around several hundred thousand indentured workers were brought to Trinidad and Tobago, a form of migration that was only terminated in the second decade of the 20th century. This later curtailment of indentured workers was said to have been caused in part by the almost inevitable decline of both the cocoa and sugar cane industries during the first half of the 20th century, as a result of the economic depression that gripped the international community during the 1930's. However, some of the worst effects of the economic downturn were thought to have been offset by the rise of the islands petroleum industry, which had been established as early as 1857 by the American Merrimac Oil Company, although this particular aspect of the islands economy was thought to have only benefited a small section of the native population initially and it was only in later years that it helped to improve the lives of the wider Trinidadian population.

The former British Caribbean island of Saint Lucia was thought to have been one of the last territories acquired by the British Empire in 1803, having been argued about and fought over for the preceding one hundred and seventy years. First visited by Spanish explorers in the last years of the 15th century, French privateers were thought to have employed the island as a base for their activities during the 16th century, although it was the Dutch who were said to have established the first formal settlement there in 1600. English sailors and colonists were also reported to have landed on another part of the island a few years later, but disease and attacks by the native Carib tribesmen, were said to have reduced their numbers to such a point that they subsequently abandoned Saint Lucia, to settle elsewhere. Some thirty-odd years later the English tried once again to settle the island, but with similarly unsuccessful results, leaving French interests to claim and finally settle the island by the beginning of the 1650's. It was only a decade later that the English explorer, Thomas Warner, the son of Sir Thomas Warner, the Governor of St Kitts and Nevis, who brought a large and well armed force to Saint Lucia to contest French claims to the island. However, yet again this English expedition was significantly reduced by disease and conflict with the local tribesman, with only around 10% of his original thousand strong force surviving by the end of their two year occupation of the territory. Although both France and Britain maintained their claims to the island for much of the next decade, following the end of the Seven Years War between the two countries, the resulting Treaty of Paris, signed in 1763, eventually gave formal possession of Saint Lucia to France. With sovereignty over the island finally settled, albeit temporarily, French interests quickly began to colonise Saint Lucia, sending large numbers of indentured white servants to establish the first sugar cane plantations on the island, their noble owners keen to make a profit from the emerging sugar industry that was evolving throughout the Caribbean. Unfortunately, the later outbreak of the American Revolution, during which France chose to ally itself to the American cause, brought Britain and France into conflict once again and as a consequence, so too did the island of Saint Lucia. Britain captured the island in 1778, as part of this wider conflict and in April 1782, a Royal Navy fleet, commanded by Admiral Sir George Rodney, operating from Saint Lucia, was said to have engaged and defeated a French fleet which had been despatched to invade the British-held island of Jamaica. However, in the following year and as part of the Treaty of Paris 1783, which brought the American Revolutionary War to an end, Britain was compelled to return possession of Saint Lucia to France.

For the following six years, life on Saint Lucia was reported to have returned to normal, with the French owned plantations continuing with the planting and cultivation of their valuable sugar crops, helping to increase the fortunes of those merchants and noblemen who owned them. In 1789 though, France itself was rocked by the French Revolution, which brought a temporary end to the rule of the French aristocracy and the death of France's monarch Louis XVI, along with his consort, Marie Antoinette. On Saint Lucia, although the revolution was thought to have caused a great deal of concern and disruption, especially for those noblemen who had made their homes there, although the first major repercussion from these momentous events were only thought to have occurred in 1790, when large numbers of the plantations black African slaves simply stopped working for their owners and began tending their own lands. Almost inevitably perhaps the French Revolution eventually crossed the Atlantic and made its way to the plantations, estates and territories of the New World. In 1794, representatives of the new republican administration, eager to wreak revenge on those aristocrats who had so far escaped their scrutiny, were reported to have erected a guillotine on the island, in order to exact retribution against those unfortunate enough to be considered as enemies of the state. Fortunately for some of those plantation owners and noblemen who were resident on Saint Lucia, the presence of a British military force, capable of securing the island and its population proved to be extremely fortuitous, for those who managed to avoid the touch of "Madame Guillotine". Even with a large military presence in the region though, it was said to have taken until 1803 for Britain to finally secure Saint Lucia, her troops being violently opposed by French republicans and the many of the islands former slaves who were keen to avoid being placed back into bondage by the invading British forces.

However, having restored order to Saint Lucia by 1803, within four years Britain had passed the first of its anti-slavery bills through parliament, which forbade the transport of new slaves to the New World. Unfortunately, it would be another thirty years before the British authorities would finally condemn the state of slavery to history and even then, most former slaves were compelled to endure a further five years of apprenticeships to their former owners. In fact, it was only in 1838 that virtually all of Saint Lucia's slaves were finally free to follow their own paths, the same year that their island home was formally integrated into the British Windward Island administration, where it would remain until 1885, when it was transferred to the authority of Grenada. Together with Grenada, Antigua, Dominica, along with a number of the other smaller Windward and Leeward Islands, Saint Lucia was reported to have been included within the temporary Caribbean union known as the West Indies Federation. However, with the failure of that group in 1962, the British authorities developed an alternative form of self autonomy called associated statehood, which granted Saint Lucia and some of the other smaller territories internal self government, whilst remaining under the overall protection and external stewardship of Great Britain. As part of this arrangement and in preparation for its later independence, the colonial authorities were said to have established a fully elected representative body on the island, which eventually emerged as the chief legislature of the nation, when Saint Lucia achieved full independence from the United Kingdom on 22nd February 1979.

William Gladstone

Antonio de Berrio

Patrick John

Alternatively known as the Treaty of Paris 1783 and the Treaty of Versailles 1783, the agreement signed between Great Britain, the United States, France and Spain, brought an end to the conflict, known by some as the American War of Independence and others as the American Revolution, depending on one's particular point of view. Under the terms of this agreement, Britain was said to have been granted access to the Yucatan peninsula, to cut logwood, a source of dye for the European textile industry, although British loggers and privateers were thought to have been visiting and employing the region as a base since the late 1630's. Initially, British privateers were thought to have simply stolen the highly prized logwood from Spanish foresters and from their ships at sea, but by the 1660's Britain was said to have established their own bases in the area to make better use of the region's seemingly unlimited supply of the valuable resource. Unlike the Spanish, who moved in and out of the area, as and when they needed new supplies, British sailors and loggers were reported to have established permanent bases in the area, allowing them to make full use of their time and the availability of the stocks. However, this British exploitation of the logwood was thought to have caused enormous resentment with the Spanish cutters, resulting in the Spanish authorities attacking and expelling the British settlers from the region in 1717. Between 1756 and 1763, Britain and Spain were at war with one another in what became known as the Seven Years War, which was only officially ended with the signing of the Treaty of Paris in 1763 which returned Britain's right to harvest logwood, although with the territories remaining under Spanish authority. Unfortunately, when the two countries went to war once again in 1779, the territories were said to have become off-limits to British cutters and were not available to them until 1783, when the second Treaty of Paris was signed in that year.

By the time British settlers had finally returned to the region in 1784, the logwood trade was thought to have significantly reduced, forcing the foresters and loggers to seek out new woods to sell, including some of the regions tropical hardwoods. Having been explicitly ordered not to build any sort of formal defences, or establish any form of local ordinances, both of which might agitate the Spanish authorities, instead the British settlers were thought to have adopted an informal set of rules that were known only to themselves. However, the almost permanent presence of the British settlers over succeeding years inevitably caused a great deal of antagonism amongst the Spanish community, some of whom were reported to have organised a military raid in September 1798 ostensibly to drive the British settlers out of the region once and for all. The Spanish forces in Mexico, acting on orders from the government in Spain, which was in conflict with Great Britain as a result of the Napoleonic Wars, were thought to have sent a substantial force to attack the British settlement, but due to the arrival of British warships, weapons and reinforcements, the colonist were able to drive off the larger Spanish force, effectively bringing an end to Spain's claims to the territories. However, despite having affirmed their rights over the region, under the terms of the previously mentioned treaties, the settler's were still forbidden from establishing any form of political or legal infrastructure, nor were they permitted to plant or cultivate any crops there. In spite of these legal restrictions though, a number of the wealthiest British settlers conspired to establish their own ruling executive and judiciary, to rule over the settlements, impose levies and control the imports and exports to and from the region.

Although black African slaves were not thought to have been employed by the first British loggers and mariners who had visited the region between 1640 and 1720, by the mid 1720's relatively small numbers of slaves were thought to have been used to provide a labour force, their numbers growing to a few thousand by the following century. Unlike the plantations of the Caribbean and North America, the wood cutting industry of the later British Honduras, was reported to have required very few labourers, so most of those that were brought to the British settlements tended to be employed as house-workers, or in specialist roles such as blacksmiths, wheelwrights, carpenters, etc. However, despite their seemingly easier lives, bad owners still existed in these isolated British settlements, with instances of misuse and abuse just as common in British Honduras as they were anywhere else. When slavery was outlawed in the British Empire in 1833, as elsewhere, these former slaves were still required to serve a five year apprenticeship, designed to guarantee owners a labour force for the immediate future, but after which they were free to choose whatever particular path they wanted to follow. Although some of the freed slaves from British Honduras chose to remove themselves to neighbouring states, for the many that remained, their lives were not thought to have been significantly improved, largely because of a determination by the wealthiest white settlers that their former slaves should only have restricted access to land, money and property. For much of the period from 1784 through to 1862, the region of British Honduras was generally regarded as an isolated imperial territory, which Britain had given little thought to. However, during the middle of the 19th century, British and American proposals for Central America required both countries to avoid colonising this region of the continent, which from the United States perspective required Britain to withdraw from areas like Honduras, despite the fact that the settlements there were already well established and had been for the past century. In order to address this particular problem, Britain decided to establish a formal constitution for the region, by giving the territory its own legislative assembly and bringing it into line with other British overseas possessions. The assembly that was established in 1854 however, was unlike many others, in that it could not raise or refute any form of legislation, all of which was produced by the British colonial offices back in London. In truth, the assembly which was formed in 1854 was not designed to function as a legitimate legislative assembly, but was instead, simply formed as a way of circumventing the agreements which had previously been made with the US administration. This situation was only changed in 1871, when, following a number of military engagements with hostile Mayan tribes; and because of the inability of British community leaders in the region to agree a common policy for defending their settlements, the colonists requested that the region be granted formal colonial status by the British authorities. Although this request would inevitably lead to the imposition of formal controls over those areas previously managed by a clique of wealthy landowners and merchants, the benefits of increased security for themselves and their businesses was thought to have far outweighed the loss of privilege which would inevitably result from becoming a formal Crown Colony.

Consequently, the territories earlier legislative assembly, which had few if any law making powers, was reconstituted by the colonial authorities, into a new legislature that had full authority to govern the new British colony. This new assembly was overseen by a new Lieutenant Governor, who was aided in the governance of British Honduras by a council of nine officials, a move that finally removed day-to-day control of the settlements from the hands of the individual wealthy landowners in the region, to the colonial services back in London. Unfortunately, although this formal adoption of the region as a Crown possession delivered security to British Honduras, its economy was said to have become increasingly dominated by large corporate interests from outside of the colony, who purchased large areas of previously unused land in the territory, in order to exploit its natural resources. In similar fashion to the much earlier merchant companies which had contributed so much to the English and the British exchequers, the British Honduras Company, later the Belize Estate and Produce Company came to dominate the colony's landholdings and even its entire economic system. With the arrival and expansion of this particular corporation, many of the regions previous landowners, the wealthy and influential men who had earlier held sway over the colony's economic development chose to sell their holdings and leave the region, making the local economy even more dependent on the newly arrived corporations. However, despite their almost near monopoly on the regions lands and industry, profit-making opportunities were not always thought to have been that straightforward for these companies, as attempts to develop any sort of large scale agricultural operations, similar to the plantations of old, proved to be generally unsuccessful. Even the mahogany industry, which was reported to have been a mainstay of the regions economy for decades, proved to be highly susceptible to international demand, as well as being a finite resource which would eventually become exhausted through its continued exploitation.

MARINERS, MERCHANTS AND THE MILITARY TOO

8. BRITISH COLONISATION OF THE PACIFIC AND THE FAR EAST

With the possible exception of the Indian subcontinent, which was said to have first been visited by English traders in 1591 and who established their first trading post there in 1608, many of England's first attempts at exploration, or colonisation, was directed almost entirely towards the west and the comparatively undiscovered and unknown New World. The fledgling colonies of North America and the numerous islands of the Caribbean seem to have dominated English thinking for much of the 17th and 18th centuries, a national mindset that was only changed in the late 18th century, following Britain's enforced withdrawal from the eastern seaboard of the later United States.

Some seven years after Britain had failed to retain control over its thirteen North American colonies, on the other side of the Pacific, the British authorities were reported to have despatched a large scale expedition to the then relatively unknown lands that would eventually become known as Australia. Although British navigators had already explored the coastline and even landed at Botany Bay in April 1770, it was only in January 1788 that the first fleet of eleven British ships complete with some fifteen hundred colonists, eventually landed at Port Jackson in the territory now known as New South Wales. Despite the fact that these British colonists were thought to have been the first Europeans to try and settle these new and relatively unknown new lands, most modern historians accept that it was in fact a Dutch navigator, Willem Janszoon, who had made the first authenticated discovery of the new continent as early as 1606, although he was said to have made no serious attempt to actually explore the hinterland of these new territories. His initial discovery was reported to have been followed some thirty-odd years later by the exploratory voyages of his fellow Dutchman, Abel Tasman, who not only mapped the coastline, but also explored the lands that became known as Van Diemen's Land, which was later renamed Tasmania, in honour of their European discoverer. During his extensive expedition, Tasman and his fellow voyagers were thought to have discovered both New Zealand and Fiji, as well as making the first known notes regarding the native peoples of these various previously undiscovered territories. However, by the second half of the 17th century and despite the fact that explorers like Janszoon and Tasman had generally mapped the coastline of the Australian continent, none of the main European states had been inclined to claim, let alone settle, these faraway lands. According to most sources of the time, this reluctance to lay claim to these new lands was thought to have been largely informed by the belief that they contained very little of intrinsic value, so therefore would not warrant the cost of launching a large scale naval expedition, or indeed the even more expensive task of colonising these supposedly worthless lands.

Australian Aborigines   **New Zealand Maori**   **Willem Janzoon**

This general indifference to the new and unclaimed continent would undoubtedly have continued, had it not been for events elsewhere, which were thought to have been driven by the conflicting Imperial ambitions of Britain and France. This was particularly true in the second half of the 18th century, when both European nations were said to have been faced with the prospect of losing their extremely valuable North American possessions, initially to one another and then finally to the American settlers themselves. Between 1756 and 1763 the two imperial neighbours had fought one another for possession and control of various territories, but most notably, for those in North America, where Britain ultimately proved to be victorious, gaining much of Canada as a long term result of the conflict. However, less than twenty years later, Britain and France faced one another once again during the American Revolution, when French, Spanish and Dutch forces were reported to have joined with the fledgling American colonial army to overcome British military control of the territories which subsequently became the United States of America. It was said to be in between these two great military conflicts that the British navigator James Cook, aboard his ship "Endeavour", first discovered and landed at Botany Bay in April 1770, even though it would be almost another eighteen years before Britain decided to try and colonise these new lands. Despite a number of other European states having claimed the territories for themselves, none of them had actually committed colonists to settling their new possessions, which ultimately allowed Britain to lay claim to them, after nearly twenty years of prevarication and general disinterest. It is interesting to note however that an outline proposal for the colonisation of Australia was only completed and presented in 1783, the same year that the Treaty of Paris brought a formal and final end to Britain's historic possession of its thirteen American colonies. Additionally, it was also a significant factor that in the following year, this first proposal for the colonisation of Australia was said to have been amended, to allow for convicts to be transported to these new lands, people who would have previously been sent to the Americas to serve out their prison sentences.

It is generally suggested that there were a number of reasons why Britain eventually chose to colonise the relatively unknown lands which later became known as Australia. Although the loss of its thirteen American colonies to the descendants of their European founders was undoubtedly a contributing factor in the decision, according to other informed sources the main reasons for settling Australia was both economic and strategic. Norfolk Island, which lay within the territorial waters of these new lands, was said to have been identified as a ready made source of timber and flax, both of which were said to have been in much demand by Britain's Royal Navy and which up that time had been sourced from America and Russia. However, with the later loss of its American colonies and restrictions on hemp supplies being initiated by the Russian authorities, there was both a financial imperative and military need to find new sources for these vitally important commodities which Norfolk Island was said to meet. First visited by James Cook in 1774, it was subsequently decided that Norfolk Island should be partly colonised by convicted felons, who might provide a vital service to Britain by way of their working to harvest the necessary timber and flax, whilst at the same time serving out their sentences. Unfortunately for the architects of this particular scheme, the planned harvesting and processing of both timber and flax proved to be generally unsuccessful, as the convicts lacked the ability to produce suitable hemp; and the local pine trees were reported to have been generally unsuitable for use in the Royal Navy's ships. However, rather than abandoning the island completely the authorities were said to have simply turned it into a prison colony, where the inmates helped clear and develop the land, whilst at the same time building their own accommodations and growing their own food supplies, on which they could survive. Sadly though, these plans were reported to have come to little, as the prisoner's buildings and crops were each said to have been overcome, both by the local weather conditions and by naturally occurring pests, as well as regular outbreaks of disease. Despite these problems however and the increasing costs of maintaining the colony, calls for Norfolk Island to be abandoned, which first began around 1795, were said to have been resisted by a number of its supporters, particularly those former convicts, who had previously served their sentences and then stayed on to cultivate their own civilian settlements on the island. The future of the British presence, military, penal and civilian was thought to have been continually debated right through to around 1808, by which time most of the island's population had already been relocated to the much more convenient and economically viable Van Diemen's Land, which was later renamed Tasmania. Finally however, by 1814 the island was said to have been almost completely abandoned by its former British occupants, who had not only removed or slaughtered the colonist livestock, but also demolished all of the buildings, in an attempt to discourage any other would-be settlers from inhabiting the island.

Although its formal closure in 1814 should have represented a complete end to Norfolk Island's history, its isolated position and generally harsh environment, ultimately became the reasons for its later re-occupation by the British authorities. Even though most of the felons who were originally transported to Australia in chains, eventually settled into civil colonial life and played their own individual part in helping to build Australia's fledgling communities, almost inevitably there were those career criminals, who even after release, continued to pursue their felonious activities, or whose character was far too extreme for normal methods to apply. It was in response to this growing number of increasingly violent and habitual criminals that around 1825, the decision was made to reopen Norfolk Island as a penal colony for the very worst offenders within Australian society. The conditions and regime in this new prison settlement were said to have been so severe that following a mutiny in 1834, those convicts who were sentenced to death for their part in the revolt wept with joy, whilst those who received longer sentences or were cleared of the charges were reported to have wept with sorrow, at the prospect of having to continue their sentences there. Throughout much of the 19th century, inmates on Norfolk Island were said to have suffered the greatest levels of human degradation, torture and mistreatment at the hands of members of the prison authorities, as well as other felons. However, changes within Britain's own legal system, which ended the practice of transportation and the development of Australia's own prison service, both contrived to bring an end to the penal colony on Norfolk Island, which was finally closed in 1855. Interestingly, the last few people to actually occupy the island were said to have been settlers, who had been relocated from Pitcairn Island, the descendants of some of the "Bounty" mutineers and their followers from Tahiti, who had fled British justice, having taken over the "Bounty" from the reportedly tyrannical Captain Bligh. In what might be regarded as an ironic twist of fate, the mutineers descendants were said to have occupied some of the former prison buildings, where they remained for a number of years, carving out a whole new community from the sometimes arduous and always isolated environment.

Meanwhile, back on the Australian mainland and following the arrival of the English settlement fleet in 1788, the eleven ships, comprising a total of some fifteen hundred men, women and children were reported to have anchored, first at Botany Bay, then a few days later at Sydney Cove, which was found to be a much more convenient location for the settlers to be disembarked. Formally raising the British flag over the site chosen for their new colony on 26th January 1788, on the 7th of February the colony was officially declared as the colony of New South Wales, finally creating that territory in its own right. Almost immediately, a number of the over seven hundred convicts, who had been transported by the English fleet were said to have been put to work, under the watchful eye of the Royal Marines that were attached to the ships, who ordered the felons to begin clearing the land in preparation for the construction of the necessary buildings and the planting of essential crops. Unfortunately, most of the convicts who had been employed for the task had little experience of farming the land, so the settlers were reported to have become increasingly reliant on the limited foodstuffs which they brought with them from England. Although their extremely scarce supplies were sometimes supplemented by the Royal Marines and the settlers themselves by hunting local game, the lack of recognisable foodstuffs and the absence of any immediate supply ships, was thought to have very nearly caused these first colonists to succumb to starvation.

Fortunately, the settlers were ultimately saved by the timely arrival of a second fleet in 1790, which as well as bringing a fresh supply of settlers, convicts and military personnel, also brought much needed foodstuffs and supplies to help stave off the worst of the colony's shortages. It was also reported though that many of the convicts, who had been brought by this second fleet had been treated very badly during the voyage; and instead of being of benefit to the colony, actually proved to be a drain on its limited resources. Despite such setbacks however, a number of settlers soon began to come to terms with the local agricultural environment and started to grow crops that could be used to sustain the growing settler community. Much of the backbreaking work involved with clearing the land, ready for cultivation, was said to have been undertaken by the growing numbers of convict labourers who had been transported to Australia, often in the vilest of conditions, for the slightest of reasons and with very little hope of seeing their family or homeland ever again. Typically, for those prisoners who had no specialist skills, they would be assigned to individual settlers who would then employ them as indentured servants, for the period of their given sentence, after which they would be granted a parcel of land to settle on. In common with other forms of slavery, the convicts who were employed by English settlers might often be treated in the most appalling way, with little if any recourse to the law, if their employer chose to abuse them in some way or other. This was thought to be particularly true for those female convicts, who were transported to Australia, where little consideration of their gender and limited employment opportunities, usually compelled them to sell their bodies, purely as a means of survival. Discipline meted out to convicts, both male and female, was said to be extraordinarily harsh and for those who resisted or refused their settler employers orders, the future could prove to be even more bleak, with transfer to an increasingly violent penal colony, the usual result of such behaviour. Of them all, the previously mentioned Norfolk Island was said to be by far the very worst of these penal colonies, where death was often preferable to imprisonment, which was why so many prisoners were thought to have simply complied with their employer's instructions and waited for the end of their sentence.

The vast majority of those English and Irish convicts who had been unceremoniously discarded by the legal systems of their native lands, via the imposition of transportation, eventually became legitimate members of Australia's burgeoning population, although a number continued to live outside the law, despite having experienced the British judicial system at first hand. For those who were prepared to live law abiding lives though, the end of their prison sentence saw them granted their own parcels of land, on which they too might employ prison labourers, to do the same sort of backbreaking work, they themselves had undertaken in earlier years. A small number of these ex-convicts were even reported to have created highly successful lives for themselves and their families, founding individual farmsteads that over time developed into regional townships, which even today continue to recall these early pioneers in their modern day place names. Elsewhere in the newly settled continent, other British colonies, both civil and penal, were beginning to emerge, with the region of Van Diemen's Land officially becoming a colony in its own right in 1825. Although the area had first been settled as early as 1803, by a relatively small group of soldiers, sailors, settlers and convicts, this first colony was reported to have lasted for less than a year, finally being abandoned, when the site of the settlement proved to be largely unsustainable. By February 1804 though, a second colony was said to have been established at Hobart, only this time in the right location and with sufficient settlers, soldiers and convicts to ensure that it continued to succeed for the foreseeable future. For much of the next fifty years, Van Diemen's Land was said to have become the final destination for tens of thousands of English, Irish, Scottish and Welsh convicts, who were sentenced to varying lengths of imprisonment and transportation, with very few ever making the return journey back to Britain. In most cases, the only time these prisoners ever left Van Diemen's Land, which was officially renamed as Tasmania in 1856, was to be transferred to the even more terrible penal colony on Norfolk Island.

Over the course of seventy-odd years, from 1788 through to 1863, much of the mainland continent we now know as modern day Australia, was said to have been gradually populated and settled, first by convicts and colonists, then later by numerous waves of migrants busily escaping the hardships of the old world. Beginning with the establishment of Port Jackson in 1788, around the same time, the British authorities were reported to have founded the ultimately unsuccessful colony on Norfolk Island, although convicts and freed men remained there until 1814. In 1825, the first successful colonisation of Tasmania was said to have taken place with the founding of Hobart and two years later the region of Western Australia was formally occupied, with the establishment of the Albany colony at King George's Sound. By 1829, the new Swan River colony had also been founded there and in 1836 the state of South Australia was officially founded. In 1841 the islands of New Zealand were formally separated from the Australian state of New South Wales; and in 1851 the autonomous region of Queensland was similarly detached. Within each of these often highly distinctive regions, British colonists, convicts, soldiers and migrants eventually established their numerous settlements, townships, homesteads and farms, all of which were carved out of the local environment, sometimes at the cost of many lives. Although many coastal locations may have been identified and settled by sea, inland locations, which later became established British colonies, were typically discovered by individual adventurers, exploring the unknown hinterland of the Australian mainland. Such expeditions were known to have first begun as early as 1813 and as a result of these initial investigations, the Blue Mountains, along with the Darling and Murray rivers were discovered, opening the hinterland up to future settlement and development.

Capt William Hobson   **New Zealand WWI**   **Australian WWI**

With so much free land available for cultivation and habitation, by the middle of the 19th century increasing numbers of free men, as opposed to indentured servants and convicts, were beginning to arrive on Australia's shores, anxious to escape the poverty and hardship which existed in England, Scotland, Ireland and Wales at that time. Similarly, large numbers of European settlers were also arriving, driven by the prospect of providing themselves and their families with a better standard of living, than they might ever hope to enjoy in their native lands. Along with these generally poor colonists, successful investors and businessmen too, were said to have made the long and arduous journey to the far reaches of the globe, keen to invest in and exploit the new commercial opportunities which were presenting themselves in Australia. Within the ranks of the many thousands of new immigrants who arrived in the country, there were thought to have been a significant number of farmers and merchants, who quickly realised the potential of these vast new lands to raise huge numbers of cattle and sheep, animals which would ultimately bring huge financial benefits to this evolving fledgling nation. As in the New World though, such large scale European colonisation of the region was thought to have had a fairly catastrophic effect on the indigenous peoples of both Australia and New Zealand, who found much of their ancient tribal lands simply seized, altered and enclosed by these uninvited strangers. In common with elsewhere, many of the generally poor European settlers who arrived in Australia were thought to have brought with them a variety of diseases that helped to decimate the local Aboriginal peoples, who had no experience of or indeed defences to, these numerous communicable ailments. Although the relationships between early British explorers and the native Aboriginal peoples of Australia was thought to have been mixed, depending on how contact was initially made, commonly both sides were reported to have been highly suspicious of the other and there were a number of individual instances where people were killed or wounded on either side. However, as in North America, serious conflicts only began to occur when European colonists began to spread out from their initial coastal settlements, seemingly to threaten the historic hunting grounds and water supplies which the local Aborigines had used for thousands of years. Typically, most of these conflicts were thought to have been generally local affairs, partly as a result of the Aborigines having no obvious allegiance to or connection with a centralised tribal structure, as was often the case in the Americas, where federations of local tribes was not uncommon. Largely as a result of this lack of a coordinated strategy towards the European settlers, there were thought to have been very few large scale Aboriginal attacks on British interests, save for those instances where larger Aboriginal communities were thought to have launched one-off attacks on individual settlements or wagon trains that might be crossing their lands. Even here though, most of these attacks proved to be rather unsuccessful, as the Aborigines with their spears and clubs, proved to be largely ineffective against the columns of often well armed European settlers with their increasingly modern and sophisticated firearms.

For very nearly one hundred and fifty years, from 1788 through to 1933, there were thought to have been any number of individual incidents, where Aborigines and European settlers found themselves at odds with one another, during which people on both sides were either killed or wounded. It is also clear that over the same period, there were any number of individual atrocities or massacres carried out, many of which were perpetrated by groups of white Australian settlers, in response to Aboriginal attacks on their livestock, or sometimes because of their own personal racial hatred towards the native peoples of Australia. However, despite the law supposedly protecting the indigenous peoples, in the same way as it did the white settlers, proving cases of murder against white men, who were accused of killing native Aboriginals, was notoriously difficult, although there were thought to have been several instances of Europeans being found guilty of the crime and subsequently being hung for their actions. Overall though, many thousands of native Aborigine men, women and children were thought to have died as a result of these ongoing conflicts, with only a few hundred Europeans dying in similar circumstances, indicating the disparity in weaponry and community organisation between the two sides. Pressure on native Aboriginal homelands was said to have significantly increased during the second half of the 19th century, when gold deposits were reported to have been discovered in New South Wales in 1851, causing a rush of new migrants and prospectors from all over the world, but particularly from Britain and Ireland. This massive influx of generally law abiding people into Australia, was said to have forced the British authorities to introduce changes to the country's, previously limited legal, political and administrative systems, which had been designed to deal with a largely criminal based community, made up of a large convict workforce and with a significant number of ex-offenders living within the civil population. Faced with an increasing lawful and law abiding populace, local and regional administrators were said to have been forced to introduce more regular and much more easily recognised democratic systems, such as trial by jury, a free press and representative government, the basic instruments of a free and democratic society.

From around 1855 onwards, many of Australia's original colonies and regions began to be organised into the semi autonomous states that we would recognise today, governed by state legislatures, which were populated by elected representatives of the people. Trade Unions, so often despised by both governments and employers, began to be formed and the country's industrial base began to be created by the great entrepreneurs, who had been drawn to Australia's burgeoning population. Unlike the old world though, Australian workers and employers were said to have united behind the common aim of creating a vibrant and successful economy, from which all might benefit, with workers enjoying a level of benefits undreamt of by their European contemporaries. However, much of this late 19th century optimism and commercial expansion was thought to have been brought to a shuddering halt in the final decade of the century, as a worldwide depression caused a general slowdown in both demand and productivity. The subsequent loss of employment and benefits was reported to have caused a great deal of resentment and anger amongst the working classes, who, supported by their Trade Unions, began to organise behind new political party's that they felt might be more sympathetic to their demands. In addition, Australian workers were also reported to have begun campaigning against the large numbers of foreign workers, who had migrated to the work in the country's lowest paid industries, but who were now regarded as a direct threat to the native Australian workforce. The period was also thought to have been marked by a much more federalist movement within the country, which was accompanied by a growing Australian nationalism which vehemently opposed continuing British involvement in the continent. Much of the political unrest was reported to have centred on the obvious lack of centralised policies for the entire country, which often resulted in one state enacting laws and legislation that acted against the interests of the rest, as in the case of immigration, where some states were permitting new immigration, whilst others were preventing it. Defence too, was thought to another great concern for many of those that had been charged with protecting the continents borders, especially at a time when a number of often belligerent nations were expanding their influence throughout the world's oceans. Finally, by the last few years of the 19th century these concerns were thought to have led to discussions between Australian and British representatives which ultimately resulted in the formation of the Commonwealth of Australia in 1900, uniting the various states under a single governing body, which could then enact legislation for the whole country, much as it does today.

Despite the agreement that allowed the various Australian colonies or states to become part of a larger national federation, this was not achieved immediately, as one or two of the colonies, including New Zealand were thought to have been unsure as to whether or not they wanted to participate in the democratic exercise. Ultimately, whilst New Zealand chose not to participate in the end, yet another colony, Western Australia chose to join the federation, helping to create the Australian nation that we all know today. Although Melbourne was temporarily chosen as the site for the capital city, in which Australia's first national Parliament was opened in 1901, this was later replaced by the purpose built city of Canberra, which was said to have hosted its first federal Parliament in May 1927. Even though Australia only became completely autonomous in 1942, following the passing of Statute of Westminster Adoption Act by the British Parliament, its earlier creation as the Commonwealth of Australia, was thought to have been a far more significant boost to the country's nationalist aspirations, allowing its citizens to finally consider themselves to be true Australians, rather than British, English or Irish immigrants, etc.

In common with their counterparts in countries such as Canada, when the First World War erupted in 1914 and Britain's own security was threatened by foreign enemies, Australia's young men were reported to have rallied to her cause, determined to defend a mother country that many of them had never even known and in some cases, had been brought up to despise. Regardless of their personal motivations however, by the time that the Armistice was signed in 1918, a reported sixty thousand young Australians and New Zealander's were reported to have given their lives in defence of Britain's possessions, often in the most wasteful, but always in the most valiant circumstances. Prior to the outbreak of World War I, Australia had little need for a large standing army, but protected its possessions largely through the use of locally enlisted militias and a small regular military force, who were principally employed in defending the country's extensive continental coastlines. Prevented by statute from conscripting troops for use overseas, it was necessary for the Australian authorities to raise a fighting force which was specifically designed for and charged with, fighting in foreign theatres, with the resulting army becoming known as the Australian Imperial Force. Initially comprised of only volunteers, entry into this new force was said to have been incredibly difficult, with only the very best young men recruited into its ranks, making it one of the fittest and most proficient military forces that was ever put into battle during the war. With its first division formed by the middle of 1914, in November of the same year, they were reported to have set sail for Egypt, where they were to receive further training for service on the Western Front, although elements of the force were also reported to have been temporarily stationed at the Suez Canal, which was said to have been a potential target for Turkish forces. However, despite being held in Egypt for a considerable period of time and supposedly being given more training in trench warfare, it was only at the start of 1915 that the decision was finally made to re-task the combined

Australian and New Zealand units (ANZACS) to a new and secondary campaign in the Dardanelle's, which would allow unfettered access to Russian territories. Originally it had been hoped that a purely naval campaign might achieve this vital objective, but the presence of mobile Turkish artillery units and the mining of the local waters, meant that the task could only be achieved through the use of ground troops, including the ANZACS, along with other British, Indian and French soldiers, who were specially chosen to attack the Turkish defences in the region.

The planned attack on the Gallipoli peninsula, initially proposed by Britain's First Sea Lord, Winston Churchill, ultimately proved to be disastrous campaign which was dogged by both bad luck and poor judgement on the part of some military officers that culminated in the wholesale slaughter of allied troops, which might otherwise have been avoided. The eight month long Gallipoli Campaign, which was reported to have run from April 1915 to December of the same year, was reported to have achieved few of its planned objectives, yet resulted in an estimated two hundred thousand allied troops being killed or wounded during the ill-fated campaign, of which around thirty thousand were said to have been Australians and New Zealanders. The level of fatalities and wounded, suffered during this particular campaign was reported to have caused enormous resentment amongst the Australian population back at home, many of whom blamed poor leadership and planning for the high mortality rates, much of which was directed against Britain's government and its military chiefs, who were reported to have had overall command of the war. Interestingly though, virtually all of the allied units who were sent ashore during the Gallipoli Campaign were said to have suffered huge losses, with one Irish unit in particular losing some thousand men, who were either killed or wounded during the operation, which represented a 99% loss of their particular regiment. Likewise, other British units were reported to have lost up to 60% of their unit strength and such was the ferocity of the fighting by both sides that one Turkish unit was said to have been completely wiped out of existence, never to be reformed again.

Although most modern day historians generally accept that the Gallipoli Campaign was an unmitigated disaster from beginning to end, it is also widely accepted that much of its failure was due to initial bad luck, which was then compounded by poor judgement on the part of some commanders on the ground, as well as those Generals who were overseeing the whole campaign. For the ANZAC troops though, losses would have been especially hard, given that both Australia and New Zealand were relatively new countries and had little experience of such bitter national conflicts, which ultimately claimed so many of their brightest and best young men. Elsewhere, Australian and New Zealand forces were reported to have been employed in both the Middle East and along the Western Front, where they very quickly earned themselves a reputation for their bravery and their determination, qualities which helped to further underpin the growing national pride and international reputation of the ANZAC troops. Sadly though, many more Australians and New Zealanders would be killed or wounded during the remaining years of the Great War, with their soldiers distinguishing themselves at Fromelle, Bullecourt, Messines and Amiens, as well as participating in the third Battle of Ypres and the second Battle of the Somme. By the time that the Armistice was signed on the 11th November 1918, there were reported to be around one hundred and eighty thousand ANZAC troops stationed at various locations, including France, the Middle East and elsewhere, who were then able to look forward to the prospect of returning home and resuming their normal lives. By the end of 1919, most ANZAC troops had finally returned home, being helped by their government to resettle, retrain and resume their former civilian lives, with special provisions being made for those large numbers of troops who had returned home damaged by the conflict. Nearly half a million troops were said to have been mobilised during World War I, with some three hundred thousand of them serving overseas, all of them volunteers, of which some sixty thousand failed to return home and a further one hundred and forty thousand coming back with varying degrees of injury, a casualty rate of around 60%. Although clearly a massive loss for these two generally young nations, who could ill-afford to lose so many of their vitally important young men, ultimately the Great War and the significant role that both Australia and New Zealand played in helping to achieve an allied victory, became a source for great national pride and helped their peoples to fully recognise their own standing in the wider world, outside of Great Britain's control. A symbol of their national pride in their lost generation of young men was later acknowledged by the establishment of ANZAC Day, which is held on the 25th April each year, which recalls the day in 1915 that their troops first landed at ANZACS Cove on the Gallipoli Peninsula, marking the day that their country's sacrifice began.

Capt William Bligh

General Arthur Percival

John Curtin

In the years following the Great War and in common with most countries elsewhere, Australia and New Zealand were both thought to have been affected by the economic slowdown caused by the Great Depression, which had first begun during the late 1920's and continued into the next decade. Like many of the victorious allied nations that had helped curb German ambitions at the beginning of the 20th century, Australia and New Zealand both believed that the enormous human losses of the First World War would prevent further conflict and as a consequence of the world's economic downturn and the common belief that such a war could never reoccur, had made little investment in their own armed forces. Unfortunately, as the Nazi Party of Adolph Hitler began its gradual rise to power in Germany during the 1930's neither Britain, nor its allies, could have envisaged the carnage that his country would wreak upon the rest of the world, so most were largely unprepared for war when it finally came. Unlike the Great War however, much of Australia's and New Zealand's war effort would ultimately take place within their own region of the world, facing Nazi Germany's equally vicious military ally, the Japanese Empire.

Japanese Imperial expansionism in Asia, which was thought to have started as early as 1895 with the first Sino-Japanese War had seen Japan become the most powerful and influential country in the region, a position which was further strengthened by its defeat of Russian forces and interests that occurred between 1904 and 1910, effectively handing control of Manchuria and Korea to the Japanese. During World War I and with most colonial powers completely focused on the European theatre, Japan was reported to have declared war on Germany, ostensibly to lay claim to and seize a number of its Asian territories, including the Marianas, Caroline and Marshall Islands, along with German territories on the Chinese mainland. With their regional dominance reinforced by the end of the First World War, Japan subsequently demanded certain conditions were inserted into the League of Nations, giving them parity with the major western powers, demands that were generally ignored, essentially isolating Japan from the rest of the allied powers. These divisions were thought to have been exacerbated at the end of 1918 when Japanese troops who had previously formed part of a much larger allied force in Siberia were said to have occupied most of the Russian towns and ports that bordered Japan and remained there through to 1922, some four years after the First World War had finished. Much of Japan's regional expansionism was said to have been driven by any number of factors, including economic, military and political, with a shortage of raw materials on its home islands, its continuing reliance on the United States for essential supplies, the military presence of Russia and China along their common borders and Japan's influence in the wider world all contributing to drive the country's economic, military and political policies. What Japan could not achieve through trade, it often tried to achieve through diplomacy, sometimes even employing the gunboat variety. When it could not achieve its aims through threat and intimidation, then Japan would often resort to the use of force itself, although always being sure to avoid a direct confrontation with any of those great Western Powers, who had their own particular interests in the region.

By the beginning of the 1930's though, Japan was said to have begun a second round of Imperial expansionism, invading and conquering Manchuria in 1931 and then two years later invaded the bordering regions of China. By 1936 Japanese forces were reported to have seized a significant portion of Mongolia and in the following year invaded the rest of mainland China, during which hundreds of thousands, if not millions of Chinese people were reported to have been either killed or wounded during the period of World War II. In the Chinese city of Nanking alone, an estimated three hundred thousand people were said to have been killed by Japanese forces, although most sources suggest that this figure is, in itself, a serious underestimation of the true number of deaths. By contrast, in the following year a local dispute was thought to have erupted between Japanese and Russian troops, during which the Japanese force was very nearly annihilated by their Russian adversaries, forcing the Japanese to agree a ceasefire with their northern neighbours which later developed into a formal neutrality pact between the two sides. It was as a direct result of Japan's generally brutal military expansion during this period that relations between the Japanese and the great western powers, including America, Great Britain and France were said to have declined markedly, especially after French-Indochina became yet another victim of Japanese imperialist expansion in 1940. In response to this action, America was reported to have placed an embargo on all metals and oil being exported to Japan, much needed supplies that were vital to their ongoing military expansionism, but which would have required them to surrender their recently seized territories in Indochina, thereby losing face. However, rather than accept the American's ultimatum, the Japanese authorities simply continued to expand their new Asian empire and now sought to take over the British and Dutch colonies in Malaya and the East Indies. It was partially as a result of this decision and a growing recognition that they would ultimately have to face the military might of the United States that in September 1940 Japan was reported to have signed a mutual accord with Nazi Germany and its European ally Italy, both of whom were already at war with all but one of the major western allies.

In a sense, the common accord which was signed in September 1940, creating what would later become referred to as the Axis Powers, automatically put Japan at war with Great Britain and its allies, including Australia and New Zealand, if only through Japan's mutual support for Nazi Germany and Italy. Faced with the continuing embargo placed on it by America, in December 1941 the Japanese were said to have finally taken the fateful decision to enact a plan that had been prepared many months earlier, for a military attack on American interests in the Pacific, most notably in Hawaii, where the United States Pacific Fleet was stationed. The intention had always been to reduce American influence in the region through military means, in the hope that this would give Japan the time to take complete control of Asia, before America and her allies could respond, by which time Japanese forces would have consolidated their gains, thereby preventing the United States from regaining control of the Pacific region. Unfortunately for the Japanese Emperor, his military and his peoples, Japan's attack on the Hawaiian Islands and particularly Pearl Harbour on the 7th December 1941 was undertaken in such a way, as to outrage the American people and its leaders, who immediately declared war on the Japanese Empire and within days were also formally at war with Nazi Germany.

Although Australia and New Zealand had begun to mobilise their young men once again, following the formal declaration of war on Germany in September 1939, in this great worldwide conflict, many of their troops almost inevitably ended up fighting in North Africa, Asia and the Pacific, often confronting an enemy that was often more experienced and unforgiving than any they might have faced before. Significant numbers of Australian and New Zealand air crews were reported to have fought in Western Europe, where they played pivotal roles in the air war there, combating German bombers and helping to attack the industrial heartland and major cities of Nazi Germany. An estimated one hundred Royal Australian Air Force pilots were thought to have flown alongside Britain's Royal Air Force during the Battle of Britain in 1940; and many more participated in the subsequent Battle of the Atlantic, which saw Australian and New Zealand aircrews flying against the German U-Boats and Surface Raiders which were attempting to sever Britain's Atlantic supply lines. Australian and New Zealand naval ships were also reported to have played a vital role in the war at sea, escorting supply convoys across the Atlantic and patrolling the waters of the Caribbean, as well as the Mediterranean, where they were reported to have successfully engaged Italian ships in the early part of the military conflict. Four Australian destroyers were even said to have formed part of the operation to try and relieve the besieged island of Malta during 1942, although the operation subsequently failed in its objective, having come under sustained attack from German forces, which resulted in one of the Australian being scuttled, after it was seriously damaged by enemy bombers.

Close by, in North Africa and in Greece, Crete and the Lebanon, Australian and New Zealand army units were said to have been heavily involved in combating German forces who were trying to take control of the region. Involved from as early as 1941 and reportedly in the vanguard of the allied units who faced Rommel's forces in North Africa, Australian and New Zealand troops were some of those that were charged with mounting a valiant defence of Tobruk, an action that was said to have resulted in some two thousand of their men being killed or wounded. Australian and New Zealand units were also thought to have returned to the region in the middle of 1942, when they joined up with the British Eighth Army to confront German forces at a fairly innocuous railway siding that would come to mark the turning point for allied forces in North Africa, El Alamein. These Commonwealth units were said to have been involved in some of the heaviest fighting of the engagement, although they were thought to have been returned to Australia sometime later, as there was a shortage of replacements to make good the losses that these initial units had suffered. In the Pacific, the region closest to their homelands, Australia and New Zealand units were initially quite limited, given that the war had originally erupted in Europe, North Africa and the Middle East, which were the areas that attracted most military support. However, by the end of 1941 and following Japan's unprovoked attack on the US military installations at Pearl Harbour, the Australian authorities quickly began to make arrangements to reinforce their own national defences and to recall those units operating elsewhere. Unfortunately for the Australians, New Zealanders and for the British Empire generally, much of their shared defensive strategy was thought to have been built around the major British naval base at Singapore and the presence of a large British Imperial fleet, which was said to have been specifically designed to counter any Japanese aggression in both Asia and the Pacific. Sadly, many of these preparations and plans, which were supposed to stifle Japanese military aggression, ultimately proved to be ill conceived and poorly planned, with Japan's forces seemingly able to circumvent most of the defensive strategies employed by Britain and its allies. By February 1942 virtually all of the allied forces had been pushed back to their Singapore stronghold, but even there, poor thinking and over cautious commanders were reported to have fatally undermined the allies position, leaving the officer in charge, Lieutenant General Arthur Percival, to make the much criticised decision, to surrender the entire Singapore garrison, including the fifteen thousand Australian and New Zealand troops who had been caught in the same military trap.

The fall of Singapore was thought to have caused real fears for the safety of the Australian mainland itself, although it later transpired that the Japanese had no intention of invading there, for fear of over extending their own military forces. However, there was said to have been a clear policy of isolating Australia from the rest of the Pacific and from its closest geographical ally, the United States; and to this end there were plans to invade and secure all of the islands to the north of the Australian mainland, including New Guinea, the Solomon Islands, Fiji and Samoa. Fortunately, these plans were thought to have been undermined by the Battle of Midway, which took place between the 4th and the 7th June 1942 which saw an American carrier group meet and defeat a much larger Japanese carrier force, an outcome that essentially brought an end to Japan's immediate expansion and control within the Pacific region. 1942, was also notable for Australia's decision to finally ratify the Balfour Declaration of 1931, which declared that Britain's Dominions, including Australia, New Zealand, Canada, South Africa, the Irish Free State and Newfoundland were autonomous members of the British Empire and as such were free of any British legislative authority or political control. The Australian Prime Minister of the day, John Curtin, was said to have finally adopted the Statute of Westminster in 1942 following the fall of Singapore in that year and the increasingly close relationship that was being formed between Australia and the United States. In effect, Curtin's formal adoption of the Westminster Statute reaffirmed Australia's independence from Great Britain, in all internal and external matters, a situation that has continued through to the present day. For the remaining years of the Second World War, much of Australia's and New Zealand's war efforts were said to have been coordinated, first and foremost, with the United States, although various smaller ANZAC units continued to operate with their European military allies elsewhere. By the end of World War II though, it was estimated that some thirty thousand Australian and New Zealand troops had been captured by the various Axis powers, of which, some twenty one thousand had been captured by Japanese forces, with only fourteen thousand of these men surviving through to the end of the war. Those nine thousand remaining prisoners, who had been captured and held by the Germans generally managed to survive the war, largely because they were accorded proper treatment, under the terms of the Geneva Convention, which regulated the treatment of enemy combatants, something that the Japanese military largely ignored. In total, a reported thirty thousand Australian and New Zealand troops were thought to have died during World War II, approximately half the number who perished during the 1914-1918 conflict, but a significant level of human losses nonetheless.

Francis Light **Major Wm Farquhar** **Stamford Raffles**

Although New Zealand was thought to have originally been given its first name of Nova Zeelandia by Dutch map makers in the 17th century, it was said to have been the English seafarer and explorer, James Cook, who gave it the title New Zealand during his voyages of 1769-1770. When the first English settlement of Australia began in 1788, the north island of New Zealand, along with Tasmania was reported to have been included within the region of what is now New South Wales and although Tasmania became a separate colony in 1825, it would be another fifteen years before New Zealand achieved the same status, becoming an independent colony of the British Empire in May 1841. Its colonial status was reported to have been granted a year after the signing of the Treaty of Waitangi, an agreement made between Captain William Hobson, a representative of the British Empire and a number of local Maori Chieftains, which effectively gave Britain sovereignty over these new lands; and the Maori's full rights as British citizens, although the actual terms of the Treaty remain a subject of dispute even through to the present day. From the first arrival of British settlers in 1788, the islands of New Zealand were reported to have been visited by large numbers of European traders and whalers, who were seen to be rather troublesome and lawless, largely because of the lack of formal authorities there. There unregulated presence was also thought to have contributed to an increase in inter-tribal violence, with newly imported pistols and muskets reportedly being traded with local Maori tribesmen, who subsequently used these newly acquired modern weapons to attack and enslave their weaker neighbours. It was ostensibly because of these developments and the continuing lawlessness of the whalers and traders that Christian missionaries who began to arrive in New Zealand from the early part of the 19th century were said to have urged the authorities to act to suppress the violence and unlawful behaviour. In response the British government were thought to have appointed their own official representative to the islands in 1832, who advised the local Maori leadership to declare their independence, which they subsequently did in 1835. Although this declaration, did not immediately bring an end to the lawless and violent behaviour of the foreign visitors, it was said to have brought the problems to the attention of the British authorities, who then sent Captain William Hobson to New Zealand, to persuade the Maori chiefs to cede sovereignty to the British Crown, in return for their formal protection, something that Hobson was said to have achieved with the signing of the Waitangi Treaty in 1840.

Following the signing of the treaty in 1840, British control and protection was subsequently introduced to the islands, as too, were an increasing number of new European immigrants, mainly from the British Isles, but also from continental Europe as well. In 1852, the New Zealand Constitution Act was reported to have been passed by the British Parliament, effectively giving the islands the power of self government from that time, until the later enactment of the Statute of Westminster Act 1931, which essentially granted New Zealand independence from Britain. The discovery of gold deposits on the south islands during the latter part of the 19th century, was said to have brought many thousands of new migrants to New Zealand during the period, but eventually became such a problem that the authorities had to draw up legislation to discourage people from migrating there. The second half of the century was also thought to have been marked by great changes being wrought on the native Maori people, whose lifestyles, health and landholdings were all said to have been significantly affected by the massive waves of inward migration, reducing their numbers from around eighty thousand in 1800 to a low of some forty thousand by the end of the century, a 50% loss in their total numbers.

When the First World War broke out in 1914, New Zealand, along with its northern neighbour, Australia, immediately volunteered military support for Britain and her allies, despite being halfway across the world and still a relatively small nation. As part of the highly acclaimed ANZAC forces, many of New Zealand's young soldiers were reported to have served in the highly questionable and ultimately unsuccessful Gallipoli Campaign, where an estimated eight thousand Kiwi troops were either killed or wounded during the abortive operation. On the battlefields of the infamous Western Front, New Zealand's young troops were said to have once again distinguished themselves at the Battle of the Somme, Messines and at Passchendaele, which took place between July and November 1917. In total some fifty thousand New Zealand soldiers were said to have been either killed, wounded or captured during the military campaigns undertaken in Western France, around 50% of the total New Zealand contingent of one hundred thousand men, which had been raised from a total national population of an estimated one million people. Likewise, when the Second World War broke out in 1939, New Zealand once again rallied to Britain's defence, providing not only what little military material she had to offer, but perhaps more importantly supplying vitally needed ground troops, naval personnel and air crews that would prove to be invaluable for the future of Western Europe. Kiwi troops were said to have been involved with the unsuccessful defences of Greece and Crete, as well as in the much more successful operations in the Western Desert and Tunisia, where they were often in the vanguard of the allied opposition to Axis troops. In Britain too, New Zealand pilots and air crews were reported to have been at the forefront of Britain's wartime defence, with a number of New Zealand pilot's being directly involved in the Battle of Britain, as well as the reciprocal bombing raids over Germany. Elements of the New Zealand navy were also thought to have been instrumental in helping to protect Britain's vital sea routes from the threat of submarine and surface raider attacks, with the Kiwi ship "Achilles" actively involved in the harrying and ultimate destruction of the German pocket battleship "Graf Spee" in the Battle of the River Plate in December 1939.

In Asia and the Pacific, as with their Australian neighbours, New Zealand was thought to have relied for much of its own national defence on what proved to be the ill-fated and highly unsuccessful military centre at Singapore, which with its fall, left much of the region exposed to Japanese attack. However, following the pivotal and previously mentioned Battle of Midway in June 1942, where the myth of Japan's supposed military invincibility was completely destroyed, both Australia's and New Zealand's military forces played a generally supportive role to America's military strategies. With its massive industrial, logistical and manpower resources, the United States were able to re-supply and reinforce those allied forces within Asia and the Pacific, ultimately at a direct cost to Britain's former influence within the region. However, by the time the Second World War ended in 1945, New Zealand was finally able to count the human cost of his second great conflict of the 20th century, which was thought to have cost the country some twelve thousand of its very best and brightest young countrymen. In common with their Australian neighbours, New Zealand continues to celebrate ANZACS Day on 25th April each year, recalling their nations enormous sacrifice at Gallipoli, which is in addition to, the main allied Armistice memorial, which is held on the 11th November each year.

In the year following James Cook's exploration of the Australian coastline in April 1770, the agent of a British merchant company, based in Madras, was despatched to the Malay state of Kedah, to negotiate trading agreements with the ruling Sultan there. Although trading links between British India and the various states of the Malay Peninsula were thought to have been in place since the middle of the 18th century, no permanent trading post was thought to have existed in the native state of Kedah itself, a necessary facility for any of Britain's overseas merchant companies. The agent despatched to Kedah, Francis Light, was also an officer in the British East India Company; and as such carried the authority of that great commercial enterprise with him, along with its ability to negotiate for and on behalf of the British Crown. Meeting with the Sultan of Kedah, Muhammad Jiwa, in April 1771, Light requested permission for the British merchant company to establish a permanent trading post in the region, an appeal that was provisionally granted by the Sultan, but on very specific terms. As a relatively small independent state, Kedah along with other individual Malay territories was constantly under threat from its much larger neighbour, Siam, now the modern day nation of Thailand, which demanded tribute from the smaller vassal state of Kedah, often in the form of military recruits for Siam's ongoing disputes with Burma. Anxious to remove this threat to his kingdom, Muhammad Jiwa, agreed to allow the British company to establish a permanent trading post in Kedah, provided that Britain would guarantee his kingdom's future security against any further Siamese demands. Having gained this tentative agreement with the Sultan, Light subsequently relayed the native ruler's demands to the British authorities in India, who unanimously refused to sanction such an undertaking.

With little more to be done, for the following few years the situation was thought to have remained unchanged and it was only following the death of Muhammad Jiwa that his successor, Abdullah Mahrum, once again began discussions over the establishment of a permanent British trading post in Kedah. Francis Light was once again involved in these negotiations and with the new Sultan demanding the same guarantees as before, protection from both Siamese and Burmese intervention in his kingdom, needless to say, the British authorities in India, refused to sanction the agreement. However, depending on which version of events one chooses to believe, either Light himself, or the British East India Company deliberately misrepresented their intentions to the Sultan, by first landing on the island of Penang, the proposed site for the new trading post and then publicly reneging on their guarantees to protect the state of Kedah from Siamese and Burmese aggression. Outraged by the British trading company's obvious duplicity, the Sultan of Kedah, Abdullah Mahrum, attempted to regain possession of the island by military means, although ultimately these attempts proved to be unsuccessful, leaving the Malay ruler with little option but to formally lease the territory to the British for an annual rent of some six thousand Spanish dollars or pesos. With Penang now legitimately in his possession, Light subsequently set about constructing his employer's first trading post and port facilities on the island, ostensibly to lure traders away from the rival Dutch ports that existed in the region. Having renamed the territory, Prince of Wales Island and initiated the construction of its main base, Fort Cornwallis, he then began to try and recruit new British settlers to the island, offering land to those who were prepared to clear away the local trees and vegetation to help colonise the new British possession. Unfortunately for Light and many other settlers however, their continuing presence on the island ultimately proved to be fatal, as most of them subsequently succumbed to a range of tropical diseases, including malaria, which helped the territory to earn the local reputation of the white man's grave.

In order to offer the new British trading post additional security, in 1800 Major General Sir George Leith, the Lieutenant Governor of the island was reported to have secured a second area of land, which was acquired to help protect the main base on the Prince of Wales Island. Leased from the Sultan of Kedah, this territory was subsequently renamed as Province Wellesley, in honour of Arthur Wellesley, the Duke of Wellington, who had been involved in helping to prepare the defences of the main island. By 1826, additional territories had been added to these earlier British possessions, with Singapore and Malacca both being added, to what became known as the Straits Settlements, which along with Penang were administered from India, but came under direct colonial rule in 1867. The area of Malacca had previously been a Dutch colony and from the 17th century through to the early 19th century had remained under their control, save for the four year period between 1811 and 1815 when the Netherlands were under the control of Napoleonic France, forcing Britain to take control of many Dutch possessions. However, when the Napoleonic Wars ended in 1815, Malacca, along with other Dutch territories were thought to have been handed back by the British, although under the terms of the later Anglo-Dutch Treaty of 1824, their colony of Malacca was placed under British control once and for all.

Sir Harry Ord　　　　　　　　　William Pickering　　　　　　　　　Franklin Rooseveldt

Prior to Britain establishing its first trading post and port at Penang and before being ceded control of the former Dutch colony of Malacca between 1811 and 1815, the Dutch were thought to have had an unrivalled trading position in the Malay regions, a situation that ultimately led British merchant companies trying to establish the post in the region of Kedah. However, even with that base secured by 1800, the Dutch still retained significant control of the region's trade, a fact not lost on the likes of Major William Farquhar and Sir Stamford Raffles, colonial leaders who could see the need for yet another British trading post, which might help Britain, better contest the near monopoly enjoyed by their Dutch competitors. As a consequence, Raffles was reported to have begun searching for an alternative site for a second British base, in addition to the one already established at Penang, in 1818 he was said to have tentatively identified the Malay island of Singapore as a possible site for this proposed new base. Initially his efforts to reach an agreement with the local Sultan were thought to have achieved very little, ostensibly because the ruler was generally allied to the Dutch and was not prepared to sacrifice those pre-existing trading links, by allowing Britain to establish a new trading post in opposition to them. However, Stamford Raffles subsequently began talks with the Sultan's older brother, who might normally have inherited his father's position of ruler, but because of the peculiar nature of Malaysian law, had been usurped by his younger sibling, leaving him highly dissatisfied and a potential ally for British interests. Consequently, Raffles was reported to have reached an agreement with the dispossessed brother, whereby he would be formally recognised as the Sultan of Singapore, provided that he would grant permission for Britain to establish a trading post on the island. As a result, the older brother was given his own kingdom, albeit as a puppet of the British Empire and Stamford Raffles was finally able to establish the trading post that he hoped would reduce Dutch influence within the wider region. As things turned out however, the later signing of the Anglo-Dutch Treaty in 1824, which granted Britain full control of the Malacca region, effectively undermined the need for a second British base in the region, thereby negating the efforts made by Farquhar and Raffles in the first place.

Regardless of such considerations though, following the signing of the Anglo-Dutch Treaty in 1824, the British authorities were able to establish the Straits Settlements in 1826, with Penang as its capital, although this role was later transferred to Singapore in 1832. Initially this new British confederation was thought to have been administered by officers of the British East India Company, who in subsequent years also added the Cocos and Christmas Islands to their portfolio, all of which were later transferred to the London offices of the British Colonial services in 1867, following the dissolution of the East India Company in 1858. In common with their rule of the Indian subcontinent, both the East India Company and the later British Colonial authorities, were often said to have employed a divide and conquer approach to their dealings with the native states of Malaysia, a common range of policies that were applied to Northern Malaya, Siam and even to parts of Burma throughout much of the 19th century and even into the 20th century. In the same year that the East India Company was establishing the British Straits settlements, company officials were reported to have been holding secret negotiations with Siam, which recognised that country's sovereignty over a number of Malay states, but which guaranteed British trading access to those territories, all of which was agreed without the prior knowledge or indeed the agreement of the local Malay rulers. Even after the East India Company had been succeeded by the British colonial services, imperial representatives were not averse to using intimidation and connivance to threaten or cajole the rulers of native states, as well as Burma and Siam, to comply with British demands, many of which were purely made in pursuit of private commercial interests. Beginning with the Treaty of Pangkor, which was signed in 1874, over the period of the next twenty odd-years a number of Malay states had decided, or were persuaded, to adopt similar treaties with the British Empire, including Pahang, Selangor, Perak and Negeri Sembilan. Having eventually become the de facto ruler of these individual regions, in 1909, the declining Kingdom of Siam, later Thailand, was said to have been forced to cede a number of its own territories to British control, with Kedah, Kelantan, Perlis and Terrengganu all being adopted into the British sphere of influence. After nearly a century of involvement in the Malay Peninsula, Britain had finally become the dominant force in the region, with many of these previously independent states and regions having been formed into loosely controlled federations and unions by the British authorities, allowing it to exercise almost complete authority over much of the region.

However, despite the continuing existence of some un-federated regions, by the beginning of the 20th century many Malayan territories had already become formal British territories, including Singapore and the Straits Settlement. A number of Malayan states, including Pahang, Perak and Selangor had been formed into federated unions, whilst regions such as Johor, Kedah and Kelantan remained nominally unattached, with some form of semi-independent native government being advised by a British resident or advisor. It was said to be in order to rationalise this situation that the Colonial Office in London attempted to introduce a system which would help streamline and improve the administration of these territories, by creating the Federated Malay States, which included the regions of Negeri, Pahang, Perak, Selangor and Sembilan, with their new capital established in Kuala Lumpur. Although each of these former independent states and their tribal rulers, the Sultans, were said to have retained authority over their traditional customs and religious observances, ultimately they were forced to defer to the authority of the British Resident-Generals who controlled much of the day-to-day running of the regions. They in turn were guided by the authority of the Executive Council in Kuala Lumpur, who introduced new legislation, modernisation and new administrative systems, which allowed the native states to act in conjunction and in unison with one another, offering mutual aid, where once they would not have done so. For those regions that chose to remain outside of such unions, rather than having a Resident to take on the role of government, they were required to accept a British advisor, a non-negotiable term of the agreements made between the individual ruler and the British authorities. The advice offered by these British appointees was rarely ignored and although regional rulers may have regarded themselves as being outside of British control, the reality was very different. According to some historians, this inexorable reduction in the powers of the Malay Sultans ultimately allowed the country to move towards and adopt a more democratic form of government, although that particular objective would only finally be achieved some thirty-odd years later. In the short term, the relatively strict and highly centralised system of administration remained in place for a number of years and it was only in the inter-war years that such procedures were relaxed, in an attempt to persuade those non-federated regions of Malaysia to become full and formal members of a much larger political union.

As had been the case since the 18th century, during both the First and Second World Wars Malaysia's vast resources of tin were said to have made it an important objective for many of the world's great industrial powers, one that was utilised by Britain before and after World War I and one that subsequently seized by the military forces of the Japanese Empire in World War II. The later military history of Malaysia, specifically the period of the Second World War, is almost inexorably linked to the history and development of Singapore, the British Crown colony upon which much of the regions defence relied upon, but that was ultimately betrayed by a lack of investment, poor leadership and a highly imaginative military adversary. As has been previously mentioned, Singapore was thought to have been founded out of necessity, by a British East India Company that was determined to protect its trade with the Malay Peninsula, but more importantly with mainland China, the source of its valuable tea and silk trade and a consumer of the Opium cultivated by the company, to redress its disproportionately negative trade figures. Having connived and contrived to engineer a lease on the island of Singapore with the older brother of the local Sultan, Sir Thomas Stamford Raffles, the chief architect of the plan, reportedly signed the resulting treaty in 1819, before returning to resume his position as Lieutenant Governor of Bencoolen, leaving the subsequent construction and development of the new territory to his subordinate, Major William Farquhar. Although Farquhar was able to defend the territory from any potential military threat using the troops and artillery units that had accompanied him to Singapore, the prospect of actually building a new settlement and port from scratch, was thought to have presented Farquhar with a variety of problems, not least of which, was the need for a strong settler community to help populate the colony. However, attracting ships and merchants to the new British port and settlement ultimately proved to be relatively easy, given that Raffles had instructed Farquhar to operate the new base as a Free Port, which ensured that no duties or tolls were levied against visiting ships, unlike the neighbouring Dutch ports in the region who often charged high duties on each and every cargo brought through their own facilities. As a result, in less than a decade, Singapore was said to have surpassed the performance of the British port of Penang, which had been established some twenty years earlier and was also able to boast a resident population of around ten thousand people, as well as handling trade goods in excess of some £22 million sterling. However, when Raffles returned to Singapore in 1822, he was reported to have been alarmed at the conditions in the territory and Farquhar's earlier decision to raise revenues by selling gambling licences to individual traders and permitting the sale of Opium in the colony. As a result, Raffles immediately drafted a new series of local ordinances for Singapore, which regulated the types of businesses that could operate in Singapore, as well as organising the civilian settlement into ethnic and commercial divisions, features that continue to be represented in Singapore nearly two hundred years later.

Although initial Dutch resentment towards Singapore had largely dissipated by 1824, when the Anglo-Dutch Treaty was signed in that year, the success of the new settlement and its associated free port ensured that it remained at the heart of the East India Company's planning in successive years. In 1826, Singapore was joined together with Malacca and Penang to form the Straits Settlement, which was administered by the British East India Company and its officers. Four years later though, these administrative arrangements were altered once again, so that Singapore, Malacca and Penang became a single subdivision of the Bengal Presidency of the Indian subcontinent, reflecting their growing importance to the British merchant company and the British Crown. Singapore's continuing operation as a free port ensured that it remained at the forefront of the regions commercial development, with increasing numbers of cargo ships, passenger liners and travelling merchants, all visiting the port to take advantage of its almost non-existent taxes and tariffs. After 1869 the port was reported to have garnered even more trade, as ships travelling along the newly built Suez Canal were said to have arrived at and departed from Singapore in equal numbers, much to the annoyance and frustration of the competing ports of Jakarta and Manila, who continued to levy charges on each ship and consequently saw their business suffer. Within half a century though and partly through the traditional lack of investment, which became a trademark fault of the British East India Company, Singapore had become a victim of its own success. With many tens of thousands of ethnic Chinese, Malays, Indians and various European nationalities inhabiting the British territory, almost inevitably the stresses and strains on Singapore's administrative services began to overwhelm those who had been charged with governing the territory. Quite apart from the intolerable pressures put on the local utilities and the escalating public health issues, which began to manifest themselves with isolated outbreaks of Cholera and Smallpox, one of the biggest worries for the local authorities was the growing lawlessness within Singapore, with prostitution, gambling and illegal drugs all being controlled by a small number of crime syndicates, who regularly engaged in bitter turf wars with one another, leaving many hundreds of people dead and the whole territory in near chaos. By the end of the 1860's and with the territory close to collapse, community and business leaders in Singapore began to demand a change of administration, charging the British authorities in India with being guilty of indifference and mismanagement. As a result of such lobbying and because of growing concerns within the British legislature itself, in 1867 the British government began to make plans for the Straits Settlement in Malaysia to become a self governing colony in its own right, with its own Governor, who would be supported by an executive assembly and legislative council to help manage the burgeoning colony.

Sir Harry Ord was reported to have been appointed as the first colonial governor of the Straits Settlement in 1867, a post that he would continue to hold until 1873, a period marked by increasing tensions between the large Chinese communities and the native Malays. However, Ord was said to have been aided in his work as governor by William Pickering, a Chinese speaking official, who was able to communicate and negotiate with many of the ethnic Chinese leaders in Singapore and help ease community tensions. More importantly perhaps, with his command and knowledge of the various Chinese dialects, which allowed him to communicate with most of the resident immigrant communities, Pickering was able to undermine the influence of the colony's various Chinese criminal gangs, who had proved to be such a threat in earlier years. In fact, he was thought to have become so successful at reducing the power of these groups that on at least one occasion a gang member was said to have attempted to assassinate Pickering by attacking him with an axe, an attempt that he was fortunate enough to survive. By helping to minimise the worst excesses of the Chinese coolie trade, reducing the incidents of Chinese women being forced into prostitution and suppressing some of the most serious aspects of the Chinese gangs criminal activities, Pickering was at least able to make Singapore, a slightly safer place to live in the latter half of the 19th century.

Tomoyuki Yamashita

David Marshall

Sri Vikrama Rajasinha

Elsewhere in the colony however and despite the ports continuing commercial success, a lack of investment and local controls both contrived to ensure that public health, standards of living and housing conditions remained at relatively low levels, causing generally poor health and comparatively short life spans for many of those who were forced to live in these generally squalid conditions. Reportedly caused, at least in part, by the plans first introduced by the settlements founder, Sir Stamford Raffles, the local ordinances which clearly defined the colony's different ethnic neighbourhoods, undoubtedly caused many of the housing, health and public services problems that later affected Singapore, with increasing numbers of each individual ethnic group forced to live within a clearly defined and highly restrictive area of land. However, with little to be done to remedy the situation, for the remainder of the 19th century and throughout the first half of the 20th century, the colonial authorities were said to have simply contented themselves with maintaining the status quo, by providing good administrative government, ensuring the property and lifestyles of the white European community, maintaining the overall security of the colony and protecting the commercial prosperity of Singapore's harbours and ports. All of these considerations were thought to have been brought into much sharper focus though, in the aftermath of the First World War and were particularly affected by the emerging military power of the Japanese Empire, which was quickly recognised as a potential future threat to the whole of the Pacific region, including Britain's far eastern holdings. In response to this possible future danger, in 1923 the British government was reported to have first proposed the construction of a brand new naval establishment at Sembawang in Singapore, which would comprise the largest dry dock facilities in the world and shore facilities that would allow Britain's Royal Navy to remain in the region for anything up to six months at a time. However, as remains the case to the present day, although the project was initially seen as being vital to Britain's future defence of its far eastern territories and dependencies, including India, Malaysia, Australia and New Zealand, in a post war era dominated by talk of disarmament and appeasement, the need for a hugely expensive Naval Station became less of a priority for successive British administrations. Although construction work on the massive new defence project was reportedly undertaken during the 1920's, it was only in 1931 and following the Japanese invasion of Manchuria that the British authorities began to take the need for the base much more seriously, making significant amounts of money available, for what had once again become a vitally important strategic asset for the British Empire and its imperial possessions. Taking nearly eight years to complete, the highly impressive naval facility could not only support Britain's Royal Navy fleet, but was itself said to have been defended by a huge array of weaponry, including batteries of 15" naval guns at Johore, Changi and Buona Vista, a variety of smaller batteries at outlying bases and an assortment of RAF aircraft stationed at Tengah and Sembawang. With uninterrupted views of the local waters, its ability to house the greatest warships of the age and with a defensive shield that was thought to be capable of fending off any potential attacker, even the great British war leader, Winston Churchill, had been tempted to publicly acclaim Singapore as the "Gibraltar of the East", a celebratory epithet he would have cause to regret in little more than two years after the base had finally been completed.

For those men who had originally conceived the idea of turning Singapore into the main defensive hub of Britain's far eastern empire, the one military scenario that had obviously escaped them was the one where most of Britain's great imperial fleet would be based in Western Europe. For Britain's military planners, any Japanese aggression in the region that directly affected British interests should have been countered in the first instance by ships of the Royal Navy, which would have been based at Singapore. Unfortunately, the prospect of the British Empire having to fight a war in two entirely different theatres and at the same time, proved to be too much, even for the extremely large and versatile Royal Navy. Consequently, when Great Britain declared war on Nazi Germany in September 1939, most of the Royal Navy's ships were thought to have been withdrawn to the waters of Western Europe, where they were needed to counter the threat of German surface raiders and U-boats. By the middle of 1940, Britain itself was under direct threat of invasion and the need for the Royal Navy to stand by, to defend Britain's shores from the invasion barges of Nazi Germany ensured that all available ships were returned to Britain with the greatest possible haste. Between the 27th May 1940 and 3rd June 1940 significant numbers of Royal Navy ships and their crews were required to participate in the evacuation of the British Expeditionary Force, which had been sent to France in an unsuccessful attempt to protect Europe from the expanding Nazi menace. Driven back to Dunkirk by the highly disciplined and well armed German army, the BEF, along with its French and Belgian allies, comprising in excess of four hundred thousand men were subsequently trapped in and around the French port of Dunkirk, with little hope of being rescued. Faced with the prospect of losing the entire core of the British army in

Europe, along with the remainder of the French and Belgian armies, the British authorities quickly contrived a rescue plan, Operation Dynamo, to snatch as many of these troops from the coast of France, before they fell into German hands and became prisoners of war. Initially, the Royal Navy was expected to rescue some fifty thousand troops from the beaches, but in what was later described as the "miracle of Dunkirk", some dozens of Royal Navy destroyers, merchants ships and auxiliary craft, along with hundreds of little ships from all around Britain, were mobilised in a nine day operation that rescued some three hundred and forty thousand allied servicemen, nearly seven times the number that the British government had first expected. Although a large number of Royal Navy ships were either lost or damaged during the operation, as well as some of the little ships that had participated in the rescue, the recovery of nearly two hundred thousand British troops, who would later form the basis of a new army ensured that the Britain would remain free of the Nazi yoke; and would go on to play its part in liberating the rest of Europe, some five years later.

However, despite the need for Royal Navy units to return home to face the menace of Nazi Germany in late 1939 and early 1940, Britain's imperial possessions in the Far East were not simply stripped of their military protection, but instead saw them reduced, as the impregnability of "Fortress Singapore" increasingly grew to become a matter of faith, rather than a proven matter of fact. Always believing that any Japanese attack would come from the sea, which was well defended against by the massive 15" naval guns pointing out from Johore, Changi and Buona Vista, although some consideration had been given to a landward invasion from the north, the mountainous terrain and the presence of seemingly impassable jungle, had already convinced British commanders in Singapore that such an attack was unlikely, so they had made few preparations to defend the territory against it.

On the morning of Sunday 7th December 1941, the Imperial Japanese Navy launched a surprise and unprovoked attack on the American Pacific Fleet, anchored at Pearl Harbour in Hawaii, with some three hundred Japanese aircraft being launched against their target from six aircraft carriers at sea. By the end of the attack, some four American battleships had been sunk, four more had been damaged, three cruisers and several destroyers had either been sunk or damaged and several thousand American personnel had either been killed or wounded. The United States' response was immediate and unequivocal, with President Franklin D Roosevelt announcing the following day that his country was now at war with the Empire of Japan, because of their infamous and unwarranted attack upon his country's armed forces. On the same day that Roosevelt called his nation to arms, Japanese troops were said to have landed at Kota Bharu in northern Malaya, beginning a fifty five day military campaign which would see them sweep aside the extremely limited British defences and bring them to the outskirts of the supposedly impregnable fortress of Singapore. Just three days after the Imperial Japanese Fleet had launched their air attack against the United States base in Hawaii, the British battleship "Prince of Wales" and the cruiser "Repulse" had both been attacked and sunk by Japanese land-based and carrier-borne aircraft near Kuantan in Malaya. Part of the British Force Z, the original fleet of one aircraft carrier, one battleship, one cruiser and four destroyers was supposed to have been despatched to Singapore, ostensibly to deter Japanese aggression in Malaya, although the earlier Japanese attack on the American Pacific Fleet at Pearl Harbour had already signalled their true military intentions. According to some historians, in normal circumstances, Force Z would have been more than capable of matching the Japanese fleet, but the loss of the aircraft carrier "Indomitable", which had previously been damaged in Jamaica, ensured that the British flotilla was without air cover and therefore susceptible to attack by enemy aircraft, a weakness that was successfully exploited by the Japanese commanders on more than one occasion.

Sir Robert Brownrigg   Don Senanayake   Solomon Bandaranaike

Several factors resulted from the sinking of Britain's two great capital ships while they were at sea, not least of which, was the sudden realisation that air power had become the dominant feature of modern warfare, with those who controlled the skies, controlling the outcome of the battle, whether on land, or at sea. The action also proved the inadequacy of Britain's pre-war planning, which had assumed that in the event that Singapore was attacked, then the American Pacific Fleet might be relied upon to defend the port, if only for its own self interest. However, with the US Fleet critically damaged by the same sort of airborne campaign, both Winston Churchill and President Roosevelt came to recognise that in the short term, Japan ruled supreme over the Pacific Ocean, despite all of their previous assumptions, financial investment and strategic planning. For much of the next six months or so, both British and American navies were said to have been forced to avoid major confrontations with the larger Japanese fleets, especially those comprising aircraft carriers, which had so successfully wrought so much destruction on the extremely powerful allied ships. A major turning point for the allies only came in June 1942, when the surviving American aircraft carriers, Enterprise, Hornet and Yorktown successfully engaged a much larger Japanese Carrier Force, at what became known as the Battle of Midway, a three day battle that ultimately resulted in the destruction and loss of four Japanese aircraft carriers and other surface vessels. Although these losses did not immediately put an end to Japanese expansionism, it did limit Japan's ability to carry out offensive operations, robbed them of experienced personnel and gave the allies time to rebuild and consolidate their depleted forces ready for their own military initiatives against Japanese forces in later years.

However, in December 1941 and with no effective naval protection to prevent Japanese landings further north in Malaya, with their big 15" naval guns pointing out towards the sea and with few if any inland defences to protect its rear, the British base at Singapore soon became the target for Japanese military. Having landed ground forces at Kota Bharu on December 8th 1941, Imperial Japanese troops quickly began to move southward towards the British military base of Singapore, brushing aside many of the temporary and highly ineffective defensive positions that the British and their Malay allies had tried to construct to delay them. The presence of modern Japanese aircraft, including fighters and bombers, which were operating from both aircraft carriers and Japanese held airfields, proved to be too much for the ageing RAF aircraft sent up to challenge them and as a consequence quickly gained control of the skies over Malaya. Singapore was subsequently bombed and strafed on an almost daily basis, with the intention of not only reducing the base's fighting capabilities, but also to demoralise the local population, before the Japanese were even within striking distance of the port. Land tanks, which the British believed would be completely unsuitable for the highly mountainous jungle terrain of Malaya, proved to be a valuable military asset for the Japanese forces, whose light tanks were able to navigate the countryside quite easily, providing their crews with a well defended platform from which to attack the British defences. Surprisingly perhaps, one of the most important pieces of military equipment employed by Japanese troops during many of their eastern campaigns was the common bicycle, which allowed each soldier to carry enormous amounts of food and equipment that he might require during individual battle. By the 31st January 1942, some fifty five days after stepping ashore at Kota Bharu, elements of the Imperial Japanese Army were already establishing themselves on the outskirts of Singapore, bringing with them the light tanks and field guns that would eventually be used to batter the supposedly impregnable fortress of Singapore into submission.

The final defensive feature which was said to have barred the Japanese forces from the city of Singapore was the Straits of Johor, a stretch of water separating the British territory from the Malayan mainland and that was normally bridged by a large man-made causeway. However, with the impending arrival of Japanese forces on the outskirts of the port, British engineers were reported to have destroyed the causeway with explosives, in the hope that it might provide the city with one last, perhaps insurmountable barrier. Unfortunately, the highly experienced Japanese troops were reported to have simply used inflatable dinghy's to cross the waterway, despite being faced with a heroic defence by the waiting allied troops, who were eventually forced back, having expended thousands of rounds of ammunition in trying to break up the Japanese advance. Throughout the entire length of Singapore's northern defences, which were almost entirely constructed in response to the Japanese attack from the north, thousands of Commonwealth troops and even some civilians were prepared to meet the estimated 36,000 Japanese soldiers who had been landed in Malaysia. Over the period of some two weeks, the defenders of Singapore were reported to have found themselves engaged in some of the bitterest hand-to-hand fighting ever experienced by Commonwealth troops, whilst each day that passed, saw their actual numbers and their vital supplies of food, water and ammunition grow ever smaller. However, despite outnumbering the Japanese forces by some three to one, for the British commander of Singapore, Lieutenant General Arthur Percival, there were a number of stark realities to be faced. Even though he still commanded a large military force, both they and the civilian population of the colony were essentially isolated from the outside world by a superior military force, which held command of the land, sea and air, leaving him with little chance of being reinforced or indeed re-supplied in the immediate future. Had he chosen to maintain his defence of the city and port, no doubt the Japanese would have continued with their bombardment and siege of the base, bringing ever greater misery and casualties to the civilian population, who had already suffered a great deal over the preceding weeks. Having discussed the matter with his military subordinates and the civil administrators of Singapore, finally on the 15th February 1942, General Percival arranged to surrender the base to the Japanese military commander, General Tomoyuki Yamashita of the Imperial Japanese Army, essentially condemning large numbers of his Commonwealth troops to spend the next three years of their lives as slave labourers for the Imperial Japanese Empire. Although there was no way that Percival could have anticipated the particularly brutal treatment that his men would receive at the hands of the Japanese, with tens of thousands of them succumbing to fatigue, starvation, ill-treatment and even deliberate murder, many of them did fail to survive their three and a half years of incarceration. Likewise, the Japanese hatred of the Chinese people generally, was thought to have caused the deaths of up to fifty thousand native Chinese who lived in Malaya and Singapore, many of whom were reported to have perished in the aftermath of Singapore's collapse, a military calamity that could and should have been foreseen by successive British governments.

With both Malaya and Singapore occupied, the Japanese were then thought to have moved on to capture the territories of North Borneo and Brunei, which are dealt with elsewhere. On the Malay Peninsula however, rather than face an entirely hostile native population, the Japanese occupiers were reported to have made a clear distinction between the various ethnic groups in the country, treating Malays and Indians as oppressed native peoples, whilst the Chinese were generally regarded as foreign aliens, who were to be granted few, if any, rights. In order to consolidate their hold on the country, many of Malaya's state rulers, the Sultans, were eventually persuaded to support the Japanese occupation, often with the promise of being granted their freedom from British Imperialism, or the prospect of their territories being returned to their earlier status, of being vassal states to the neighbouring country of Thailand (formerly Siam). With little prospect of an immediate return of British troops, most of the native Malay states and their peoples were reported to have settled down to enduring the Japanese occupation, in the hope no doubt that it would end sooner, rather than later. For the Chinese population of Malaya, the Japanese occupation was not so easy, with their businesses seized, their schools burned down, their leaders imprisoned or executed and up to fifty thousand of their number perishing during the period. It was little wonder perhaps that many ethnic Chinese chose to resist the Japanese occupation through the Malayan Communist Party, which played a significant role in the activities of the Malayan People's Anti Japanese Army, a relatively small guerrilla force which was dedicated to opposing the occupation in whatever way it could. Initially offering little opposition to the highly experienced Japanese troops, as the occupation wore on and these resistance fighters became more skilled and better trained, so they began to offer more of a military challenge to the increasingly isolated Japanese forces, whose own lines of communication and supply were constantly being interrupted by the growing military presence of the allied war machine. Unfortunately, as Japan's military forces began to withdraw and collapse towards the end of World War II, the Malayan People's Anti Japanese Army, comprising a largely communist membership, became the largest irregular force in Malaya and quickly began to turn their attention to opposing a British return to the country. Although most native Malayan's did not openly welcome the prospect of a return to British Colonial rule, neither did they like the idea of their country being dominated, or indeed run by Chinese communists, a situation that almost inevitably led to violent clashes between the two ethnic communities, which almost brought Malaya to the brink of an all out civil war.

When the British were finally able to return to Malaya and Singapore in September 1945, they found a country devastated by three and a half years of Japanese occupation, during which time the local population and especially the Chinese community had been subject to the worst excesses of an invading army. Driven almost entirely by a need for raw materials and foodstuffs for their own national industries and population, the period of the Japanese occupation of Malaya and Singapore, was said to have been largely marked by a complete exploitation of the country's natural resources and people, the widespread destruction and devastation of the country's economy and infrastructure, along with an almost complete disregard for the local population's civil and human rights. As they once again took control of their former colonies, members of the British military administration were thought to have found a country with few reliable utilities, the electricity, water and telephone systems having been damaged and degraded by three years of abandonment and abuse. Likewise, the Singapore dockyards, on which much of the colonies prosperity and security had previously depended, was said to have been severely damaged, both by the Japanese themselves and by the allies, who had bombed the facilities, in order to prevent their use by the occupying forces of Japan. However, the greatest challenge facing the new British administration was to try and solve the problems within the local population, with malnutrition and disease affecting a significant proportion of the local populace, as a direct result of the shortages caused by the occupation. These problems, allied to personal frustrations, revenge and other issues resulted in the country seeing an escalation of violent behaviour throughout Malaya, which the newly returned British administrators were eager to suppress, although many of the root causes, including food shortages, lack of services and high unemployment almost inevitably took some time to resolve. Even by 1947 some of these same problems still existed, despite the best efforts of a British Empire that was still struggling to cope with the effects of the Second World War, both at home and abroad. In Malaya itself, frustration at the continuing shortages, unemployment and lack of services was said to have culminated in a series of strikes in 1947, with workers pressing the British authorities to do more to improve conditions in the country. However, even though the Malaysian economy began to recover towards the end of 1947, with the worldwide demand for both tin and rubber increasing in the post-war period, it would still take several more years for the country's trade figures to achieve their pre-war levels. More importantly however and in common with British attitudes elsewhere in the region, continuing imperial control of these native states came to be regarded in an entirely different way, both in Britain itself and in the wider international community. Britain's pre-war status as a major world power had been shattered by the events of World War II, which had not only proved the lie of her reputed military power, but also questioned the moral right of any single country to dominate so many individual nation states, who had themselves played such a vital role in overcoming the threat of the Axis Powers.

With a clear recognition of its reduced ability to maintain its imperial possessions in the Far East, as early as 1946 the British government accepted that some of its colonies, including the Straits Settlement in Malaya should be granted an increased level of self government, if only to assuage the growing demands for national independence. Consequently, in April 1946 the old Straits Settlement was formally dissolved and the British port territory of Singapore was reconstituted as a Crown colony in its own right, headed by an appointed Governor, who took overall responsibility of its daily administration. In the following year, entirely separate executive and legislative councils were established to help run the new colony, although for the most part, members of these new councils were appointed, rather than being elected by the people of Singapore. Of the six seats available on the colony's new legislative council, all of them were taken up by local businessmen or politicians, who had a vested interest in continuing British rule and were therefore unlikely to represent any sort of opposition to it. This rather limited form of self government was said to have continued through until 1953, when the British authorities in London, perhaps mindful of the new international climate, established a commission under Sir George Rendel to review the political situation in Singapore, as a result of which he recommended an extended form of self government for the colony. A new legislative assembly was constituted to replace the earlier legislative council, which would be comprised of some thirty two seats, twenty six of which would be held by elected representatives, chosen by the people of Singapore. As elsewhere, the new Chief Minister and Cabinet Ministers would be chosen from this largely elected body, allowing the relatively new Labour Front party to gain the largest number of seats in the new assembly and its leader, David Marshall, to become the first Chief Minister of Singapore in 1955.

Over the same period of time, beginning in 1946, the British government decided to amalgamate the remaining Malayan states, including Penang and Malacca into the Malayan Union, a single British Colony, in which all citizens, Malays, Chinese, Indian, etc would be granted equal status to one another, a proposal that met with considerable opposition from most ordinary Malaysians and their native rulers. As a result, nationalist leaders and political leaders in the country founded the United Malays National Organisation, which began to campaign for full independence from Britain, forcing the colonial authorities to quietly drop the idea of equal citizenship, which then allowed the new union to be formed. However, by 1948 and following further lobbying by these new Malaysian parties for the restoration of the earlier independent states, a new arrangement, the Federation of Malaya was formed, composed of the original independent states, all of which operated under British protection and supervision. Rather predictably though, Chinese leaders within the country were said to be outraged by the decision to refuse them equal status, publicly venting their frustration through groups such as the Malayan Communist Party, which subsequently reinvented itself as a legitimate political party. Calling for immediate independence and complete equality of all ethnic groups, unsurprisingly the aims of the MCP were completely at odds with the aspirations of the Malay majority, who regarded the Chinese with some suspicion. More worryingly perhaps for some, the MCP's ready access to its war time arsenal of weapons, made the largely communist organisation a continuing threat to the country's future stability and helped to heighten community tensions even further. With large numbers of sympathisers in Malaya's main trade unions and high schools, a general upsurge in Chinese nationalism throughout the Far East was thought to have forced a change of tactics on the MCP, from conducting an entirely political campaign, to taking more direct action, including armed conflict where necessary. Having initiated a guerrilla campaign against British interests in Malaya, including the assassination of local planters and officials, the British authorities subsequently declared a State of Emergency, banning the Malayan Communist Party and arresting several hundred of its supporters and activists. In response to the colonial crackdown on their activities, more militant members of the MCP were said to have retreated into Malaya's jungle hinterland, forming the Malayan People's Liberation Army, which conducted an armed insurgency lasting from 1948 through to 1960 and that became more commonly known as the Malayan Emergency. However, in what became one of the first instances of a modern counter insurgency campaign, the British authorities were reported to have managed to successfully isolate the rebel forces from their support base, tactics that were no doubt helped by the MPLA's later decision to kill high profile individuals, turning them from freedom fighters to terrorists and robbing the organisation of much of its needed support. Significantly, the fact that the insurgency was a communist driven campaign, the actions of the MPLA helped to harden local Malaysian attitudes against the concept of communism generally, helping to reduce British concerns over the future direction of Malayan politics and leading to the early granting of independence to the country on 31st August 1957.

Around the same time that the historic Dutch Empire first surrendered its possessions in Malaya to British custody, as a result of the French invasion of the Netherlands, the Prince of Orange, who was reported to have been a refugee in England, also handed control of the island of Ceylon to the British authorities. However, despite the territory being legally transferred to Britain by the ousted Dutch monarch, a number of Dutch merchants and political interests on the island were reportedly unhappy about the prospect of British rule and were thought to have favoured the idea of becoming an independent republic in their own right. Despite this local opposition though, in 1795 British forces began their occupation of Ceylon, beginning with the strategic port settlement of Trincomalee, along with a number of other vitally important assets in the region. Having consolidated these new territories on the island, these original British forces were subsequently reinforced with local Sepoys, or native troops, some of whom were thought to have been provided by local tribal rulers who were particularly keen to make alliances with the newly arrived British, sometimes for their own pecuniary advantage, or in order to settle an already outstanding ethnic conflict. However, it was thought to be the British attempts to outlaw Ceylon's traditional caste system and the people's servitude to the historic rulers of the island which caused the greatest antagonisms between the British and some of the larger, more established and largely independent Ceylonese kingdoms. During both the Dutch and earlier Portuguese occupations of the island, the native kingdom of Kandy was said to have generally remained outside of European control, save for those occasions where the interests of the two conflicted with one another and where the Kandyan kings would often defer to the more powerful European forces. Regardless of such occasional instances however, the kingdom of Kandy remained independent nonetheless and despite British overtures to form a mutual alliance, Britain's insistence on the Kandyan kings changing their traditional practices, meant that there was little likelihood of the two parties ever reaching an amicable and ongoing agreement

Controlling the more mountainous and generally inaccessible regions of Ceylon, ensured that any British attempts to enforce their will on the Kandyan kings would be exceptionally difficult, even for Britain's highly experienced and professional forces, especially against an enemy who had already successfully resisted both the Portuguese and Dutch military. Fortunately for the British though, the Kandy monarch, Sri Vikrama Rajasinha, was reported to be fairly unpopular with a number of his leading Sinhalese noblemen, who were said to have not only conspired against him, but also lent their tacit support to the British authorities and their colonial forces. Part of the difficulty for any British force attempting to confront the kingdom of Kandy was thought to have been the extreme nature of the local terrain, with mountains and jungles being added to by malarial swamps, which provided an almost impenetrable barrier for any invading army and required detailed knowledge of the region to navigate safely. Such detailed information was known only to members of the indigenous Kandyan people themselves and it was only having secured the services of such knowledgeable guides that two separate British forces were able to attempt any meaningful expeditions into the interior of the isolated kingdom. With the aid of these Kandyan scouts the first military expedition was reported to have been able to reach the Kandyan capital, Senkadagala, in February 1803, but the king and his courtiers, having been warned of the British approach had already abandoned the city. With little more to be done, the British commander, a Colonel Barbut, was said to have established a military garrison there and installed a rebellious Sinhalese nobleman, Muttusami, as the new puppet ruler of the kingdom of Kandy.

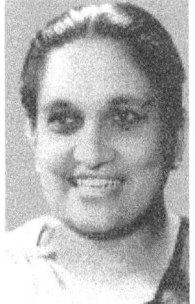  

Sirimavo Bandaranaike   **Rajiv Gandhi**   **Thenmuli Rajaratnam**

Unfortunately, both through having been misinformed by those rebels who were opposed to the Kanyan king, Sri Vikrama Rajasinha, as to the level of native resistance and to the difficulties they might face in actually holding the capital of Kandy, within a matter of months, the British hold on the region began to unravel. Reduced by disease and by desertions, the relatively isolated British garrison at Senkadagala, which had been left behind to maintain control of the region, was eventually overwhelmed by the native forces of the legitimate Kandyan king, with only a small number of survivors managing to make their way back to British lines. This defeat was said to have been compounded by further reverses in the region, with Britain's forces being pushed further back by the Kandyan troops who were reported to have waged an incessant guerrilla campaign against the British forces, much the same as they had previously done against their Portuguese and Dutch predecessors. Having defeated all successive efforts to conquer their mountainous homelands, the king of Kandy then ordered his forces to attack the British outside of his home territories, a move that ultimately proved to be extremely unsuccessful, as his guerrilla fighters were subsequently routed by the highly professional and well equipped British troops, who were now fighting on more familiar ground. Although the British were thought to have easily defeated the Kandyan forces and drove them back into their mountain retreat, ultimately the conflict between the two sides proved to be a military stalemate, which was only finally brought to an end by both sides failing to launch further operations against one another from around 1805.

Having now fully recognised the difficulties of overcoming both the natural and military defences of the kingdom of Kandy, the British authorities were thought to have reverted to their often more successful divide and conquer tactical approach, which involved the creation of new political alliances, thereby undermining their enemy's position. Having stopped any further military expeditions into the Kandyan kingdom in 1805, the British authorities then set about trying to change some of the religious and racial causes of Kandyan resistance, as well as supporting those groups who were opposed to the rule of Sri Vikrama Rajasinha, whose rule was said to have become more and more oppressive. Divisions within the Kandyan court were thought to have deepened in 1814, when the king's chief minister was reported to have become involved in an intrigue against the monarch and having been discovered, was forced to flee the kingdom and seek refuge with the British authorities. Outraged by the actions of his royal adviser, Sri Vikrama Rajasinha was said to have taken his revenge on the man's family, ordering their executions in a most brutal fashion, which caused many other Kandyan noblemen to publicly declare their own opposition to the king. With much of his own aristocracy now in open rebellion against him, Sri Vikrama Rajasinha was said to have fled his royal palace at Senkadagala and made his way to the fortress at Hanguranketha.

In an attempt to avenge himself on his still surviving and rebellious Chief Minister, Ehelepola, Sri Vikrama Rajasinha was reported to have despatched troops across the border into British controlled Ceylon, where they attacked the garrison at Sitawaka, an act which caused the British Governor, Sir Robert Brownrigg, to send a military expedition into the kingdom of Kandy after nearly ten years of peace. With most of the Kandyan aristocracy now welcoming a British intervention, if only to rid them of their highly unpopular monarch, British troops were thought to have entered the kingdom relatively unopposed and made their way to the capital Senkadagala, where they were said to have been welcomed by the local people. Having secured their hold on the region, within a short space of time, Sri Vikrama Rajasinha's hiding place at

Hanguranketha was discovered and the Kandyan monarch taken into British custody. However, rather than take any serious action against him, the Kandyan king was said to have been simply exiled, along with his entire Harem, to the city of Vellore in India, where he was reported to have lived out the remaining years of his life in relative comfort. As part of the ensuing Kandyan Convention, an agreement between the British authorities and the remaining Kandyan aristocracy, the British were careful to avoid offending the traditions and sensibilities of the local people. Although the late king and his successors were subsequently declared as fallen and deposed, with no future claim to the throne, at the same time, all forms of physical torture or mutilations in the kingdom were strictly forbidden. The Buddhist religion was restored and the people's right to practice their beliefs was enshrined within the treaty, as were the traditional practices and customs of the native peoples, although the British authorities retained the right to intervene in certain cases, should it become necessary. The signatories to this convention were reported to have been The British Governor, Sir Robert Brownrigg, the former Kandyan Chief Minister Ehelepola and the various tribal lords who together made up the aristocracy of the kingdom of Kandy.

The tribal chiefs and headmen, who had conspired together to rid themselves of the king of Kandy, had hoped to be left alone to rule over their various provinces and regions, with as little interference from the British as possible. Unfortunately for them, British interests were almost entirely driven by the Empire's own particular goals, which required them to ensure that all of their colonial territories were directed towards the common goals of centralisation, security, colonisation and profitability, with all of their efforts being directed towards achieving these basic objectives. Britain's administration of her colonial territories, which was often regarded as interference by the native peoples of those lands, often caused intense antagonism between the two parties, as these two diametrically opposed interests attempted to balance their opposing expectations, sometimes with tragic results. Such was the case by 1817, a little more than two years after the Kandyan Convention had first been agreed by the British authorities and the tribal chieftains of the now defunct Kandyan kingdom. The "Uva Rebellion" which is also commonly to as the Third Kandyan War was said to have begun in 1817, largely as a result of dissatisfaction amongst the ranks of the Kandyan aristocracy, who having conspired to rid themselves of their legitimate king, now tried to rid themselves of the British authorities, ostensibly to allow them a greater level of authority within their own homelands. Having launched yet another guerrilla war against the British, which had proved to be so effective in the past, unfortunately for the rebellious chieftains, the imperial forces in the region were now so well established and stationed in sufficient numbers as to easily defeat the native forces, with most of the rebel leaders later being eliminated or exiled, to ensure no future repetition of the revolt. The suppression of this final Kandyan revolt in 1818 is thought by many to mark the end of the kingdom of Kandy, royal territories that had once been ruled by Indian born aristocrats for well over four hundred years and which were subsequently dismantled by the British in the aftermath of this abortive insurrection. What had once been an isolated kingdom, protected by its mountains, forests and impenetrable undergrowth was very quickly opened up and exposed by the military roads and later railways of the British Empire and its colonial migrants, who cut down the trees, cleared the undergrowth and levelled the land for the cultivation of the tea, coffee and rubber plants, all of which would eventually become basic economic crops for Ceylon and its native population.

King Thibaw

Dr Ba Maw

General Aung San

With the entire island now under their control, the British authorities quickly began the process of essentially industrialising the agricultural output of Ceylon, with relatively small numbers of white planters being permitted to purchase huge tracts of land for their new tea, coffee and rubber plantations, which would be worked by the thousands of indentured Tamils brought in from Tamil Nadu on the Indian mainland. Treated little better than slaves on some plantations, eventually the Tamil community grew to represent some 10% of the island's total population, evolving into a highly independent ethnic group, whose political aspirations would almost inevitably lead to conflict with the majority Sinhalese population and result in the later Sri Lanka being dogged by decades of civil war. However, despite the European planters decision to introduce the Tamil workers in the first place, which has often been blamed for sowing the seeds of these later ethic quarrels, according to some sources, it was the treatment of these workers, by both the Europeans and the Sinhalese that actually laid the basis for the Tamil peoples later isolation and demands for greater autonomy. Although some of Ceylon's European and Eurasian communities were thought to have been granted greater autonomy as early as 1833, it was only at the beginning of the 20th century that a limited form of national government was introduced and even then, with the resulting legislature being controlled by appointed officials. By the 1920's this national assembly was said to have been populated by fully elected representatives, albeit those almost entirely drawn from the elite ranks of the native European, Sinhalese and Tamil communities, who could meet the necessary qualifications for standing for office. It was only a decade later, in 1931 that full voting rights were offered to the entire population and even then largely against the will of the native ruling classes, who were said to be horrified at the prospect of the common man being able to vote for their own particular representative.

The development of a Ceylonese independence movement was thought to have its roots in the aftermath of the ethic and religious riots that occurred on the island in 1915, which saw Ceylon's various religious communities, Muslims, Christians and Buddhists, clash with one another over a variety of issues, including commercial interests, social legislation and religious intolerance, forcing the British authorities to introduce martial law. Although these disturbances undoubtedly centred round particular ethnic tensions, there is also a suggestion that they also emanated from political opportunism as much as anything else, with British forces in Europe having suffered a number of military setbacks during the early part of World War I, which certain nationalist groups in Ceylon hoped to exploit for their own political ends. However, rather than undermining British control, the riots and the actions of the fledgling nationalist groups were said to have simply served to tighten Britain's control over the island, with many of Ceylon's most prominent pro-independence leaders being arrested, jailed and even sentenced to death, although most of these were later reprieved. By the end of the First World War, restrictions were reported to have been relaxed in the country, allowing the formation of the Ceylon National Congress, a political party campaigning for greater autonomy, but not full independence from Britain.

As a result of the Donoughmore Commission, which had been appointed by the British Government in 1927 to review the political and democratic systems in Ceylon, the first elected State Council of the country was officially opened in July 1931, although without the presence of some of the island's most experienced Tamil politicians, who chose to boycott the new assembly, because of their own objections to the introduction of universal suffrage. Under the terms of this new Donoughmore constitution, Ceylon subsequently governed itself for the next sixteen years, having full responsibility for its own internal self government and marking a period when there were few, if any incidents of inter-communal violence, although this constitution was later rescinded when the country attained full independence in 1947. However, despite having achieved a significant degree of self rule in 1931, Ceylon's new government was said to have been severely challenged by a number of natural disasters which were reported to have occurred between 1934 and 1935. In common with other regions in and around the Indian subcontinent, in 1934 Ceylon was said to have been affected by a widespread drought that helped to reduce the country's rice harvest, leading to severe shortages of this much needed crop for the local population. This loss was then thought to have been followed by completely unexpected seasonal floods, which not only washed away significant amounts of fertile soil, but also brought with them an uncommon number of mosquitoes and their associated malarial diseases that were then said to have caused the deaths of over one hundred thousand people. With the native peoples already suffering from varying degrees of malnutrition, caused by the rice shortage, the subsequent arrival of large numbers of mosquitoes undoubtedly helped to make what was a regularly occurring problem into a much more catastrophic event.

Partly as a result of these huge human losses, but mainly through the pervasive influence of the communist ideologies that were spreading around the world during the 1930's, in 1935 the Marxist inspired Lanka Sama Samaja Party, was said to have made the first public demand for Ceylon to declare itself independent of Britain. Although not supporting the actual aims and objectives of this particular communist group, a small number of other nationalist parties came to support their call for independence, although like the call for the official language of the Dominion to be changed from English to Sinhalese and Tamil, these demands were largely ignored by the British authorities, who believed that the country was not ready for full independence. In pursuit of the their calls for independence however, the Lanka Sama Samaja Party were thought to have employed the services of a former white planter called, Mark Anthony Bracegirdle, to publicly admonish the white European planters, who he accused of great cruelty against the native peoples of Ceylon. Outraged by Bracegirdle's flagrant and unsubstantiated denigration of their reputation, a number of white community leaders were thought to have made formal complaints to the British authorities in Ceylon, forcing them to deport Bracegirdle from Ceylon at the earliest possible convenience, before his rabble rousing actually led to serious community violence. Unfortunately for the white settler community and the British Governor, the move to deport Bracegirdle was found to be illegal by Ceylon's Supreme Court, who ruled that to do so would impinge Bracegirdle's right to free speech and ordered the authorities to release him immediately.

However, following the outbreak of the Second World War in September 1939 and after the Japanese attack on Pearl Harbour in December 1941, the British authorities were not so tolerant of anti-British, or indeed pro-Japanese sentiments that were sometimes expressed by several Ceylonese political leaders, or their parties. With some pro-Independence parties actively agitating against support for the British cause and even some Ceylonese government ministers holding discussions with Japanese representatives to help facilitate the forced removal of the British from the island, some form of British response became inevitable. In June 1940, a number of the leading independence activists were arrested by the British authorities and new legislation was introduced to prevent the public activities of the Lanka Sama Samaja Party, many of whose remaining leaders chose to go underground, rather than face arrest and internment. With Britain distracted by the European conflict with Germany and Italy, members of the Lanka Sama Samaja Party now chose to stir up unrest within the ranks of the native working population, organising strikes and disputes on Ceylon's plantations, its harbours, utility companies and transport systems, all of which were said to have affected the native population as much as it did the white community. The same party were also thought to be responsible for a failed mutiny on the Cocos Islands in May 1942, when native Ceylonese troops attempted to take control of the islands and then hand them over to the Japanese, so that they could be used against British interests. Unfortunately for the mutinous troops however, their failure to take complete and effective control of the military garrison, subsequently allowed loyal British forces to re-establish control on the islands and overcome the band of rebels. Three of the would-be mutineers were later executed for their actions, becoming the only three serving British soldiers to be executed for mutiny throughout the entire period of World War II, a fitting tribute perhaps for those who would have put their neighbours in harms way.

Although many anti-colonialists on the Indian subcontinent undoubtedly celebrated the losses suffered by the British Empire during the period of the Second World War, they forget of course the many thousands of Asian lives, which were freely given in its defence. Apart from the relatively small numbers of Indians and Ceylonese who turned their hands against the British during World War II, including those handfuls who mutinied on the Cocos Islands, tried to spy on Ceylon and participated in the ill-fated Indian National Army of Subhas Chandra Bose, the overwhelming majority of the subcontinents population were reported to have remained faithful to the ideals of the British Empire, confident in the knowledge that their independence would eventually and inevitably be achieved through more peaceful means. Such was the case in Ceylon, where despite the best efforts of the rabble rousers and other pro-Japanese supporters, wiser heads were said to have prevailed to bring the country to full independence. According to some of the more modern revisionist reporters of post war Ceylon, the struggle for independence was almost entirely won by the strikes and civil unrest initiated by the anti-British nationalist parties, as opposed to those political leaders who continued to remind the British authorities of the debt which was owed to Ceylon and its people for the active support they had shown the Allied forces during their war with Japan. Even as the war in the Far East raged, but more especially as it drew to a close, Britain and the Ceylonese authorities were thought to have been in regular discussion regarding the country's political future, with full Dominion status being agreed as the most obvious and next logical step in the process of granting full independence to Ceylon and its native population.

As a result of these lengthy and entirely peaceful negotiations, in 1947 Ceylon was granted self governing Dominion status by the British authorities, with its new constitution and independent standing being officially recognised on 4th February 1948. It is worth noting perhaps that the title of Dominion only formally recognised the role of the British monarch as the new country's head of state, in the person of the British Governor General, who played no significant role in the actual governance of these newly independent territories. The first Prime Minister of Ceylon was Don Senanayake, the leader of the coalition United National Party, which had joined together to lead Ceylon to political independence in 1947 and held that office from 1947 until 1952. Unfortunately, Senanayake's untimely death in 1952 and the failure of his two political successors to attract the popular support of their predecessor, ensured the electoral defeat of the United National Party, by yet another coalition, formed by the much more nationalistic and communist leaning Sri Lankan Freedom Party and the Lanka Sama Samaja Party, who immediately began to introduce changes which favoured the country's Sinhalese majority. Almost predictably perhaps, the Tamil minority were reported to have reacted violently to these clearly discriminatory changes to Ceylon's official language and educational systems, both of which disadvantaged them by insisting that the native Sinhalese tongue was used, as opposed to English or Tamil. Clearly, even though such changes were generally popular with the Sinhalese majority, the strength of feeling amongst the Tamil community was best expressed with the subsequent assassination of the Ceylonese Prime Minister, Solomon Bandaranaike, leader of the Sri Lankan Freedom Party and one of the main architects of these nationalist changes. Succeeded by his widow, as leader of the party and as the Prime Minister of Ceylon, the first female politician in the world to hold such a lofty position, Sirimavo Bandaranaike, subsequently arranged for the removal of all British military bases in the country, as well as the reorganisation of the country's land rights, giving increased access of privately owned estates to Ceylon's native agricultural workers.

However, despite such attempts to cultivate popularity amongst the working class Sinhalese majority, Mrs Bandaranaike's socialist policies ultimately led to even greater economic hardships for the country, not least because of her government's decision to nationalise foreign assets in Ceylon, which brought her into direct conflict with both the American and British authorities, whose companies were thought to have suffered most as a result of such seizures. Becoming increasingly unpopular abroad, the Bandaranaike government was also thought to be facing internal opposition from some of the more extreme political parties within the country, including the Marxist People's Liberation Front, who tried to overthrow her administration in 1971, which resulted in her government having to rely on British, Indian and Russian aid to help bring the situation under control. In the following year the country's status and name within the Commonwealth was altered by the Ceylonese government, changing it from an independent Dominion to that of the independent Democratic Socialist Republic of Sri Lanka, with the post of Governor General being replaced by the position of President. However, unlike the former Governor General, who was almost an entirely ceremonial figurehead, the president of the new Sri Lankan democracy is not only the head of the country's government, but also the commander-in-chief of Sri Lanka's armed forces, a variation of the more usual parliamentary and presidential systems that exist elsewhere in the world.

Interestingly though, despite Sri Lanka having evolved into a relatively stable and fairly successful democratic state, the extensive and extremely bloody civil war, fought between the Sri Lankan armed forces and the Liberation Tigers of Tamil Eelam, more commonly known as the Tamil Tigers, is perhaps the most significant feature and event associated with the modern Asian state. Thought by many observers to have its roots in the highly divisive social policies introduced by successive governments of the early to mid 1970's, this extremely bitter civil conflict is said to have raged, on and off, for very nearly thirty years, from 1983 to very nearly the present day. During this thirty year conflict, an estimated one hundred thousand people were said to have been killed and a small number of high profile individuals, including former Indian Prime Minister, Rajiv Gandhi, who was assassinated by a female suicide bomber, Thenmuli Rajaratnam, in May 1991, because of his perceived support for the largely Sinhalese Sri Lankan government. As the regional superpower in the region, India had chosen to involve itself in the dispute, ostensibly because of the large Tamil community within mainland India, many of whom were sympathetic to the cause of their fellow Tamils in Sri Lanka. According to some sources, in the initial stages of their involvement, the Indian authorities had tried to play the role of peacemaker between the two sides, a part of which saw them provide intelligence to the Sri Lankan military, whilst at the same time offering logistical support to those beleaguered Tamil communities, surrounded by Sri Lankan army units. However, almost inevitably India's own armed forces were eventually dragged into the affair, supplying troops for the Indian Peacekeeping Force, which it was hoped might provide a mutually acceptable barrier between the two warring sides in the north of Sri Lanka. Unfortunately, the later demands of this same peacekeeping force, for the Tamil separatist groups to lay down their weapons, in order for talks to take place, resulted in an armed conflict between the Indian and Tamil forces that led to heavy losses on the Indian side, which the later government of Indian Premier V P Singh were not prepared to accept.

Orde Wingate

Archibald Wavell

Walter Letaigne

British involvement in Burma is thought to be inextricably linked to the empire's presence in India, although at a much later date and in response to Burmese actions, rather than through any sort of pre-planned annexation of that previously independent state. When the neighbouring kingdom of Arakan was captured by Burma in 1784, it brought this huge country into direct contact with British held India for the first time; and when Burmese leaders crossed their own international border in 1817, 1819 and 1823 in an attempt to seize other independent states, the British Empire was said to have responded by sending a seaborne invasion fleet to seize the Burmese port of Rangoon in May 1824, where they met little resistance to their military forces. Having landed safely and moved inland, the British force was reported to have been confronted by a large Burmese army, which had reinforced the village of Kemmendine and that was only forced to withdraw, having come under sustained fire by British guns and naval cannons. However, the situation for the better equipped British troops was thought to have been made considerably more difficult by the retreating Burmese forces employing a scorched earth policy, which left few stores for the British Indian troops to requisition, leaving them susceptible to both hunger and disease, reducing their original numbers markedly. Despite such hardships and difficulties though, other British contingents that had fanned out throughout the rest of the country were reported to have been much more successful, bringing the Burmese provinces of Tavoy, Mergui, Martaban and Tenasserim under their control by the end of that first year. Recognising the seriousness of their situation, as more and more of the country came under direct British control, Burmese leaders were reported to have recalled most of the troops who had been previously occupying the neighbouring independent kingdoms, the invasion of which had brought them into conflict with the British in the first place. Unfortunately, even the addition of these highly experienced troops and the recall of their most formidable military leader, Maha Bandula, could do little to stem the British advance, with the strongholds of Danyubu and Prome, both falling to British forces during the first few months of 1825. The Burmese army's situation was thought to have become even more perilous in April 1825, when their noted military leader, Maha Bandula, was said to have been killed by a British mortar shell as he walked around his defences, trying to encourage his men to fight on against the overwhelming firepower of the British artillery. By the second half of the year, the British were said to have made further progress in pushing the native Burmese army back along the course of the Irrawaddy River and towards their last great military stronghold at Malun, where the British prepared to fight the final battle of the first Anglo-Burmese War. However, the planned assault on the fortress was reported to have been halted after the Burmese leadership requested a truce, so that negotiations could take place between the two sides, although the British commander, Major General Sir Archibald Campbell, was said to suspect that the appeal was little more than a ruse to delay the attack, which ultimately proved to be the case. Having offered terms to the Burmese king, which were subsequently ignored, on the pretext of the king not being available, Campbell was reported to have simply ordered a resumption of the attack on Malum, which was quickly taken by the well prepared and well equipped British troops. Although some Burmese survivors of this attack later were reported to have made a rather half-hearted defence of the city of Pagan, this too was eventually overcome by Campbell's troops, leaving the capital city of Ava at his mercy and forcing the Burmese monarch, King Bagyidaw, to accept the terms of the peace treaty which had been offered by Campbell.

The resulting Treaty of Yandabo, which was reported to have been formalised on the 24th March 1826, was signed at the village of the same name, just fifty miles outside the Burmese capital of Ava. Under the terms of the treaty, the Burmese provinces of Assam, Manipur, Rakhine and Tenasserim were all ceded to the British, in the form of the British East India Company and the Burmese agreed to refrain from interfering in the affairs of the states of Cachar and Jaintia. Additionally and in order to recompense the British company for their losses suffered during their campaigns, the Burmese authorities also agreed to pay the sum of one million pounds sterling, in four equal installments, as well as allow for the development of future trading relationships between the two sides. The final requirement of the treaty was for the exchange of diplomatic representatives between the two sides, with British agents being posted to the Burmese capital of Ava and Burmese agents being resident in Calcutta. According to some sources, this first Anglo-Burmese war was reported to have been one of the most expensive military campaign during Britain's rule of India, not only costing several million pounds to wage, but also costing the lives of an estimated fifteen thousand men amongst the British forces alone, not to mention the number of Burmese lives which had been lost as a result of the conflict. The human cost apart, this relatively unnecessary war was thought to have very nearly bankrupted both the Burmese nation and the British East India Company, as well as resulting in two further conflicts between Britain and Burma, which eventually saw the historic Burmese Empire finally brought under complete British control by 1886, when the country was formally annexed by Britain on the 1st January of that year. However, despite having generally suppressed Burma and deprived the country of its rightful monarch, King Thibaw, who was exiled to India along with his family, resistance to British rule was said to have continued right through to 1896, when the British military finally brought an end to the ongoing native insurgency.

Establishing a new provincial capital at Rangoon, the whole of Burma, both upper and lower, were subsequently governed as a single province of the much larger British Indian Empire, a situation that was thought to have remained in place until 1937, when Burma was formally founded as an entirely separate British colony in its own right. During this first half century of British rule, from 1886 to 1937, although Burma's economy and society were both undoubtedly developed by the new colonial authorities, as in neighbouring India, there was also thought to have been a great deal of exploitation carried out by various commercial interests, who had arrived in Burma in an attempt to secure new lands and exploit new commercial opportunities. This was said to have been particularly evident within the country's agricultural sector, where Burmese farmers were encouraged to grow bigger crops, often by borrowing money to buy more land, on which to cultivate them and inevitably creating a level of debt that most farmers were unable to afford. As a result, a great deal of Burmese farmland was reported to have come into the possession of European merchant companies, or private money lenders, both of whom subsequently employed cheaper indentured Indian farm labourers, to work on the land and thereby depriving Burma's own agricultural workers of much needed employment and income. Not only did these changes cause a great deal of economic hardship amongst the poorest sections of Burma's native population, but were also thought to have forced some individuals to turn to a life of crime, so severe were their personal circumstances, creating a situation where a career in illegal activities was thought to have been preferable to the prospect of utter destitution.

It was thought to be as a result of such outright exploitation and other discriminatory practices introduced by the British authorities, which saw large numbers of native Burmese being excluded from agriculture, the Civil Service and Armed Forces which almost inevitably ensured the successful foundation of Burma's first nationalist organisations. Although specifically political organisations were reported to have been prohibited by the colonial authorities, Burmese organisers were thought to have circumvented such restrictions by establishing what at first sight appeared to be religious associations, but which were in reality groups dedicated to lobbying for and delivering political change. The first of these organisations, the Young Men's Buddhist Associations, was said to have later evolved into the General Council of Burmese Associations, a largely political organisation that quickly spread throughout much of the country and found significant support amongst the millions of disenfranchised Burmese, who were desperate for change. It was said to be from the ranks of such nationalist groups that a new generation of Burmese political leaders were found, including a relatively small number of highly educated and well travelled individuals, who had not only studied nationalist movements elsewhere within the British Empire, but were determined to bring change to their own nation.

At the same time that these first Burmese leaders were beginning to organise opposition to British rule in Burma, so too the colonial authorities in London were starting to devolve increasing powers to each of their overseas territories and dominions. During the 1920's Britain was reported to have established a limited legislative assembly in Burma and even made efforts to ensure greater Burmese participation in the day-to-day governance of the province, mostly through the active employment of native born people in the regions civil service, although even these developments did not satisy those nationalists who were desparate for real change. As in a number of other Asian countries, the young and especially well educated students, were said to have been in the vanguard of the various public demonstrations that were organised to demand greater independence from British rule. Unfortunately, as had also been the case elsewhere, some nationalists, rather than simply demanding democratic reform through entirely peaceful means, chose to employ more violent methods to demand their freedom, forcing the authorities to bring in thousands of regular troops in order to suppress their campaigns and leading to the arrest and imprisonment of the movements leadership. Throughout much of the late 1920's and the 1930's Burma was reported to have been affected by numerous student strikes, which led to the formation of a number of new nationalist unions that were all dedicated to the single aim of achieving Burmese independence, although that particular objective would only finally be achieved some twenty-odd years later, in 1948. In the short term however, such campaigns and demonstrations were thought to have convinced the British authorities to formally separate Burma from its other Indian possessions in 1937, establishing the territory as a colony in its own right and with its own fully elected legislative assembly, in which the native Burmese were granted equal rights and status.

In the first Burmese elections for the new legislative assembly, Dr Ba Maw, a member of the Poor Man's Party, was said to have been elected as the first Prime Minister of his country from 1937 to 1939, having previously served as Burma's Education Minister. His premiership was said to have been relatively short because of his later decision to resign from the government, in protest at Britain's decision and therefore the empire's participation in World War II, a decision that Ba Maw continued to campaign against, even after he was arrested and jailed for sedition by the authorities. However, when Burma was captured by the Imperial Japanese Army in 1942, Ba Maw, having been released by the Japanese military leadership, subsequently agreed to lead a provisional government established by the Japanese authorities, called the Burmese Executive Administration, which was formally established in August 1942. Even prior to their attack on Pearl Harbour in December 1941, the Japanese were thought to have made contact with a number of the nationalist Burmese groups that had previously been campaigning for an end to British rule in Burma, believing that they might make suitable allies for Japan's future military objectives in the Far East. In the same month that Japan carried out its attack on the American Pacific Fleet, a number of Burma's leading nationalist dissidents, were said to have been transported to China to undergo formal military training in preparation for the Burmese conflict that lay ahead, with one of the leaders of the group, Aung San, publicly announcing the formation of the Burmese Independence Army, a native army that would ally itself with Japanese forces, in order to push the British out of Burma forever. Although in normal circumstances Britain might well have been able to defend its Far East possessions, including Burma, the differing theatres of World War II, which stretched from Western Europe to Australasia and which involved Britain confronting two separate and distinct enemy forces, ensured that her imperial forces were always likely to be tested to their absolute limits. As with Singapore and Malaya, the British defence of Burma, along with the rest of its Pacific territories was thought to have centred around the perceived invincibility of its powerful naval station at Singapore, the close proximity of her Indian Empire and the belief that British military forces would never have to fight on two entirely separate fronts, or in two different theatres, all of which ultimately to be incorrect. Britain's pre-war failure to fully comprehend the danger posed by the evolving Japanese Empire, the increasing threat of air power to the Royal Navy at sea and neglecting to prepare for a land based invasion of its imperial territories by Japan's military forces, all contrived to undermine the fairly limited preparations Britain had made in readiness to defend her Far East territories in the run up to war.

Renya Mutaguchi   **Chang Kai Shek**   **Sir Hubert Rance**

However, even though Britain's possession of Burma was thought to have been tenuous at best, given that her limited forces were facing both the Imperial Japanese Army and the Burma Independence Army, the fact that British forces in the region were largely composed of native Indian Sepoys, Sikhs and Ghurkha troops, some of the finest in the world at the time, ensured that the British Empire's defence of her eastern possessions was robust, ruthless and reinforceable. Initially, the Japanese were reported to have contented themselves with capturing the capital city of Rangoon, along with its highly valuable sea port, an offensive move which allowed Japan's military forces to sever the vital trade links between British India and China. Fortunately, those British forces defending the city had been ordered to abandon Rangoon just prior to the city being encircled by the main body of Japanese troops, who had hoped to capture the city's harbour and oil refinery intact, although both were subsequently destroyed by the British before they finally left the city on the 7th March 1942. However, for those allied servicemen who managed to escape from Rangoon, the general situation was said to have steadily worsened as the weeks went by, despite having been reinforced by an expeditionary force sent into Burma by the Chinese authorities, who were themselves at war with Japan. With few ways of being re-supplied on a regular basis and under increasing pressure from both Japanese and Thai regulars, along with Burmese nationalist troops, the British were left with little option but to withdraw back into India, all the time with the enemy at their heels. Given the abysmal conditions, with thousands of civilian refugees trying to reach the safety of India, along with their animals and household possessions, the allied troops who were withdrawing ahead of the Japanese were reported to have a torrid time, being short of food, reduced by disease and hampered by a lack of equipment and with vehicles that were completely unsuited for the purpose that they were being asked to contend with. In spite of all these difficulties however, eventually the surviving British forces were said to have reached Imphal in India just before May 1942, although it was said to have taken some time for the authorities in India to fully recognise the gravity of the situation at Imphal and deliver aid, or fresh supplies into the region.

Having driven the British forces back into India and with the Chinese expeditionary force having been largely destroyed, the Japanese and their Burmese allies then set about establishing a puppet regime under the leadership of Ba Maw and reorganising the Burma Independence Army as the Burma National Army, commanded by one of the country's leading nationalist figures, Aung San. Although the government of Ba Maw and the army of Aung San were supposed to be entirely independent bodies, in reality both were said to have been under the direct control of the Japanese Army commander in Burma, who was said to have promised full independence to the country's nationalist leaders, even though those offers had not been approved by the Japanese authorities in Tokyo, who would almost certainly have refused to endorse them, had the Japanese forces proved to be victorious during World War II. It was only towards the end of the conflict and as Japan's fortunes began to fail that these same Burmese leaders eventually began to recognise the insincerity of the Japanese offers of national independence and finally switched their allegiance to the allied cause, in the hope that the same nationalist objective might be achieved.

Despite having managed to save a significant proportion of their Burmese forces from the Japanese, the British authorities in London were thought to have been loathe to commit additional personnel to the recovery of Singapore, Malaya and Burma, while the threat of Nazi Germany continued to hover over Western Europe. As a result, Britain was said to have contented itself with securing India's borders, rather than planning for any sort of invasion of those temporarily lost imperial territories, which Britain hoped to recover once the war in Europe had been won. British efforts to secure India were also thought to have been hampered by a highly opportunistic Indian nationalist campaign, which demanded the immediate withdrawal of British forces from the country and the granting of independence by the British authorities in London, something that the government of the day were unable to do, given the extremely perilous military situation at the time. However, despite Britain's apparent inability, or reluctance to launch a full scale military campaign to recover Burma, Malaya and Singapore, smaller, more irregular forces, such as the Chindits, Special Operations Executive and other Special Forces were reported to have been ordered into these captured regions, to carry out saboutage, or to train local partisans. Unlike Britain's more regular forces, who were often unable to cope with the arduous conditions of the mountain and jungle terrains of South East Asia, only in the second half of the war did British military planners finally begin to see the worth of such specialist jungle fighters, who could meet and defeat their Japanese adversaries on equal terms.

The Chindits, which were more formally known as the 77th Indian Infantry Brigade, was said to have been the brainchild of Brigadier Orde Charles Wingate, a British officer who had first developed the idea of a long range irregular force that could operate behind enemy lines, during his military service in East Africa, whilst fighting the Italian army in the region. The "Gideon Force" was thought to have been so successful during its service in Ethiopia that the Supreme British Commander in the Far East, Archibald Wavell, asked Wingate to establish a similar unit for service in Burma, where it could operate against the Japanese, cutting off their supply routes, their lines of communications and generally making as much of a nuisance of themselves as possible. Unlike his unit in Ethiopia though, which was a mixed force of regular troops and partisans, Wingate chose to merge elements of a British unit, the King's Liverpool Regiment, with two other native Indian Regiments, the 2nd Ghurkha Rifles and the 2nd Battalion of the Burma Rifles, the latter unit being made up of men who had only just managed to escape from Burma in 1942. Bringing these formally trained British units together, Wingate was reported to have reorganised his troops into several distinct military columns, all of which could operate either independently, or as part of the larger combined force. All of the men who were selected to serve with this new Chindit force were trained to cope with the arduous terrain, along with the various dangers and maladies that the region might pose to their health, including malaria, snake bite, leeches, etc. The men were also trained to cope with the enormous amounts of equipment that they would have to carry on a daily basis throughout their extensive campaigns, although each column was reported to have had a number of mules to help carry the heaviest pieces of equipment, including mortars, anti-tank weapons and heavy machine guns.

In February 1943, just eight months after British forces had finalllly been driven out of the country, Wingate, along with his three thousand strong Chindit force crossed the border to begin their military operations in Japanese held Burma. Unfortunately, in their first three months of operations behind enemy lines, the Chindits were thought to have achieved few successes, save for disabling a main railway line for a week and killing an unknown number of enemy soldiers, a poor return for the eight hundred servicemen who were reported to have been killed, wounded or captured during the period of this first campaign. However, despite the overall failure of this first Chindit expeditionary force, the actual concept of such a military unit was soon thought to have found support at the very highest levels of government, with the British Prime Minister, Winston Churchill himself reportedly endorsing the continued use and equipping of Wingate's force. According to some sources, even the American military authorities were thought to have been convinced by the potential benefits of such specialist units, founding their own force, Merrill's Marauders, as a direct result of Wingate's implementation of the proposal. Having received backing from the very highest echelons of government, Wingate then began to plan for his next attempt at invading Japanese held Burma, although this time on a much larger and grander scale than before. Now with his own dedicated aircraft with which to land and re-supply his Chindits, Wingate was reported to have significantly increased the numbers of men attached to the force, enlarging it from around three thousand in February 1943 to a final total of around nine thousand in February 1944. In addition to these changes, Wingate and his superiors also began to alter the operational parameters of the Chindits, who were now being tasked to fly into Burma and establish semi permanent bases in the country, from where they could attack the Japanese, rather than simply conducting hit and run missions against the enemy over the period of a few weeks. By February 1944 Wingate's forces were ready to be deployed in Burma and the Allied Commanders in the region, General Slim and US Airforce General George Stratemeyer, gave the Chindits their final orders before departure, instructing them to inflict the greatest damage and confusion they could on Japanese forces in Northern Burma.

Over the period of a week, beginning on 5th February 1944, some nine thousand men and their equipment were reported to have been dropped onto designated landing sites in Burma, with defensive positions and temporary landing strips quickly constructed to allow heavy weapons and other materials to be landed in support of the operations. Within days and right through to the end of March 1944, the Chindits and their local Kachin allies were reported to have been engaged in bitter hand to hand fighting with elements of the Japanese army, who were only driven off, after the arrival of heavy artillery pieces that had been flown in by American support aircraft. Despite managing to establish themselves in the region though and having generally secured their positions through superior firepower, not all of their military objectives were achievable, as the Japanese were said to have rushed in reinforcements in order to defend their most important assets in the region. The Allied cause itself was thought to have suffered a major setback on 24th March 1944, when Wingate was unexpectedly killed in an unexplained air crash, which occurred as his plane was returning to Imphal in India. However despite the loss of their charismatic commander, the Chindit campaign was reported to have continued nonetheless, only now under the command of Brigadier Walter Lentaigne, a highly experienced officer, but one who instinctively lacked the vision and character of the man that he replaced, to the detriment of the Chindit forces in Burma.

Ultimately, the Chindits had only ever been envisaged as a temporary measure, until such time as the Allies could assemble a sufficiently large enough army to drive the Japanese forces out of Burma, Malaya and Singapore once and for all. As part of these preparations the British were reported to have begun massing troops and equipment around the Indian towns of Imphal and Kohima in the south east of the country, with fuel dumps, airfields and temporary troop accommodations all being built in readiness for the coming offensive. For the Japanese military, who were said to be coming under increased pressure throughout their extensive empire, the military threat posed by these British forces was thought to have been so important that rather than wait for the allies to advance, they decided to attack these positions as part of a wider invasion of the Indian mainland. Beginning in March 1944, a total force of some three Japanese infantry divisions and one tank division were reported to have launched a full scale attack on the much larger, but much more inexperienced British forces who were based at Imphal and Kohima, with the intention of destroying this allied army before it could be use against them. Believing that British and Indian armies were still inadequately trained to deal with the local conditions, which had been the case during the initial Japanese invasions of Burma, Malaya and Singapore, Japan's military commanders were also thought to have severely underestimated the allied use of supply aircraft, an oversight they would later have reason to regret. It has also been suggested that the Japanese launched their pre-emptive attack against India, despite having been informed about the presence of the British Chindit force at their rear, a military threat that some Japanese commanders were thought to have regarded as immaterial, given that their planned capture of the allied airfields in India would have ultimately denied the Chindits their vital airborne supply lines, causing their particular military threat to wither and die.

Clement Attlee

Thakin Nu

Lin Zexu

Initially the large scale attacks against the British forces along the Indian border were said to have gone well for the Japanese, largely because of a miscalculation by British commanders, who failed to withdraw their troops quickly enough to avoid the main enemy advance. As a result of these delays, British and Japanese forces were reported to have engaged one another in a series of extremely bloody battles throughout the entire length of the Manipur region's border area, with the Chindits playing their part by attacking the Japanese to the rear. During the first few weeks of the Japanese advance, both sides were thought to have suffered significant losses as a result of the bitter fighting, although this was thought to have affected the Japanese much more so, given their extended lines of supply and communications, whilst allied forces could rely on regular re-provisioning through the fleets of aircraft operating from Indian airfields. Throughout much of April 1944, the Japanese, despite suffering enormous losses and being without regular supplies were said said to have continued their advance on both Imphal and Kohima, possibly as a result of being reinforced by elements of the Indian National Army, a nationalist guerrilla group which had allied itself to the Japanese cause in return for the promise of Indian independence. However, despite the obvious bravery of some of these enemy troops, the allied use of aircraft for re-supplying their troops, the presence of American tanks and other heavy weaponry, along with the determined defence of the region by allied troops, ensured that none of the Japanese objectives were achieved and that their entire advance had been stopped by the 1st May 1944.

With the Japanese advance having been stopped in its tracks after some fierce resistance, the allies then immediately launched their own counter offensive, although this proved to be a much slower affair given the arrival of the seasonal monsoons, which turned the ground to mud and hampered relief efforts, even those that were delivered by air. Unlike the allied forces though, the invading Japanese forces, now much reduced by the weeks of bitter fighting, were said to have been on the verge of starvation and running short of other vital supplies, a situation which forced many of their units to abandon their positions, simply to go in the search for replacement food and ammunition. While the British and Indian troops were regularly being replaced by fresh fighting units, who had few such logistical and supply problems, Japanese commanders throughout the region were said to have become increasingly desperate to make a breakthrough, ordering their troops to carry out almost suicidal attacks on the newly strengthened allied lines and reducing their already limited strength, often to a point where the various units were no longer viable military contingents. Other commanders though were thought to have been far more realistic about the prospects of securing an overall victory, accepting that their position was indeed hopeless, but lacking the courage to tell their superiors of the futility of the Japanese forces true military situation. However, despite the fairly desperate positions of most of the Japanese troops, some of the more experienced units were said to have dug themselves into well prepared defences that defied all allied efforts to dislodge them; and it was only after some days of consistent bombardment by heavy field artillery that they were finally forced to withdraw, having lost many of their number to the allied shelling. Finally, at the beginning of July 1944 and having lost over fifty thousand men, either killed, wounded, or missing in action, the Japanese commander, General Renya Mutaguchi, formally ordered a withdrawal of his remaining forces, who then retreated back across the Chindwin River, into Burma. In a recreation of the earlier retreats suffered by the British forces in Burma, Malaya and Singapore, this time it was said to have been the Japanese forces who were forced to withdraw from the battlefield, leaving behind their abandoned vehicles, artillery pieces and those comrades too ill, or seriously wounded to carry with them. Although the successful allied defence of Imphal and Kohima did not represent the end of the Japanese threat in the Far East, for most reporters of the conflict, the victory there, did mark a turning point for the allied war effort, which would ultimately end with the Japanese Empire's unconditional surrender in the following year.

The Chindit force, as well as being involved in helping to lift the siege at Kohima, by diverting front line Japanese troops away from that particular operation, were also said to have been attached to the American commander, General Joseph "Vinegar Joe" Stilwell, who controlled the Northern Combat Area in Burma, where a mixed allied force of Chinese and American troops were confronting the Japanese. Although the American presence in this part of Burma was reported to have been minimal, with Chinese troops acting as the main military adversary to the Japanese, the American version of the Chindits, Merrill's Marauders, were known to have been one of the most effective military units in the region. They, along with the Chindits, were said to have been largely destroyed by Stilwell, who ordered them to take on a series of almost impossible military tasks which in normal circumstances could not have been achieved by any military force, but were eventually completed through sheer bloody mindedness and esprit de corp. Occasionally suffering casualty rates of over 50% and with their men suffering from all sorts of tropical diseases, including malaria, dysentery and malnutrition, by August of 1944 the last of the Chindits had been withdrawn from Burma, with the unit being formally disbanded in February 1945.

With the spearhead of the Japanese army in Burma having been broken by the allied forces at Imphal and Kohima, British, Indian, Chinese and American troops throughout the three main Burmese theatres of operations, north, south and central began to move forward, in an attempt to dislodge the Japanese from their well established bases there. In the south, large numbers of Japanese troops were reported to have died, rather than surrender their positions to the allies, a sacrifice that ultimately proved to be futile, in the face of the overwhelming forces which were being sent to capture their bases at Ramree and Cheduba Islands. In the north, Japans military forces were said to have been faced by a largely Chinese army that had been trained and equipped by the Americans, but which was limited in its operational uses, given the particular political agenda of the Chinese leadership under Chiang Kai Shek. The central region of Burma was thought to have been the main allied theatre of operations, as British, Indian and even native Burmese forces pushed forward towards the historic capital of Mandalay and the vital Japanese base at Meiktila, both of which were reported to have fallen into allied hands by March 1945. For those forces that were operating in the central theatre, the capture of the port city of Rangoon, before the onset of the seasonal monsoon, became the overriding consideration for allied commanders. However, for those Japanese forces withdrawing towards Rangoon, the port city also represented their most obvious escape route out of the country and as a result, a great deal of time and trouble was taken to protect it from allied forces. Mustering whatever irregular forces they could, Japanese commanders in Rangoon, were reported to have employed significant numbers of men to protect the outskirts of the city, allowing their main body of troops to escape by ship, although most of the defenders who had been left behind were subsequently killed, wounded or captured by the allies. In an attempt to capture the port intact, the British were reported to have even parachuted troops behind the Japanese defensive line, although upon their arrival in Rangoon found the city deserted by the enemy forces, but in a state of utter chaos, with levels of lawlessness and chaos that took them some time to contain. However, from the British perspective, the most important factor was that Rangoon was back in their possession, allowing it to be used for re-supplying those allied forces who were still engaged in military operations in other parts of Burma. Fighting between the two sides was said to have continued right through to July of 1945, although as British troops increasingly took control of the country, so the often isolated units of Japanese soldiers were either eliminated or captured by the allies, finally bringing an end to Japan's military presence in Burma and a restoration of British rule, albeit a fairly temporary one.

Charles Elliot   **Admiral Gordon Bremer**   **Sir Harry Parkes**

Following Japan's unconditional surrender to the allies, after the bombing of Hiroshima and Nagasaki in 1945, Japanese forces throughout Asia were ordered to lay down their arms, an imperial order that finally brought an end to the conflict in the Pacific. For Britain's Far East Empire, the war had not only exposed the fundamental weaknesses in the long held belief of British martial invincibility, but had also given fresh impetus to the independence movements within her various colonial territories, including India, Malaya, Singapore and of course Burma itself. As the war in Burma came to an end, many of those nationalists who had been involved in the Burmese National Army, the force that had initially allied itself to the Japanese war effort, in return for Burmese independence, remained as prominent figures within the post war nationalist struggle, including Aung San, the man responsible for operations of the Burmese National Army during the Japanese occupation of the country. However, as Japan's military forces came under increasing pressure from the allies from 1943 onwards, certain members of the nominally independent Burmese government, including Aung San, were said to have switched their allegiances to the Anglo American cause, playing a part in the later defeat of the Japanese forces in Burma. Rather than accepting a commission in the post war Burmese army established by the newly restored British authorities, Aung San was said to have returned to civilian life, involving himself in Burma's nationalist struggle for independence, by accepting the post of president of the Anti Fascist People's Freedom League, a loose coalition of the country's various socialist, communist and anti-fascist groupings within Burma. Repeating the tactics that had been tried during the nationalist struggles of the 1930's, a number of Burma's pro-independence groups were thought to have organised a number of nationwide strikes, most notably amongst the country's police force, which forced the British governor of the time, Sir Hubert Rance, to make concessions to the leadership of the nationalist groups, including Aung San. Appointed to Burma's newly constituted Executive Council, as its deputy chairman; and responsible for the country's internal and external defence, Aung San was not universally accepted by everyone involved with the reconstruction of Burma and his decision to even accept a seat on the Executive Council, was said to have caused deep divisions within the nationalist community, which would ultimately have dire consequences for Aung San in later years.

In the short term though, the nationalist leader was said to have become the de facto Prime Minister of his country, even though he was still subject to a British veto regarding certain vital aspects of the country's governance. However, despite such minor limitations, for the most part, Aung San was the leader of his country and the individual responsible for ensuring that Burma's achieved full independence from Britain in as short a time as possible. With a Labour government in London desperate to resolve the long standing issue of indigenous nationalism throughout the Indian subcontinent, when Aung San met with British Prime Minister, Clement Attlee, in January 1947, the Burmese leader received a firm undertaking that his country would be granted its independence within a year. Having returned to Burma with this promise of independence, Aung San very quickly received the agreement of other regional leaders for the creation of a unified Burmese nation, thereby circumventing any possibility of the country being fragmented by any future demands for regional autonomy or independence, as was sometimes the case elsewhere in Asia. The only exception to this nationwide accord, was thought to have been the Karen people of southern Burma, who were reported to have suffered significant persecution at the hands of Aung San personally and were not therefore inclined to accept his offer of a unified Burmese state, especially with him at its head. Although a relatively small ethnic group in relation to the rest of Burma, only representing an estimated 7% of the total population, the Karen's resistance to Aung San's centralised government state, was reported to have begun in 1949 and continued intermittently right through to the present day, a period of some sixty-odd years. Initially the Karen were thought to have demanded full independence from Burma, although these demands have subsequently been amended to demanding the introduction of a more federalist system, which might give them a greater level of regional autonomy. However, despite the reluctance of the Karen leadership to fuly embrace Aung San's vision of a new and independent Burma, in the national elections of April 1947, the Karen managed to elect 24 representatives to Burma's new national assembly, although this was dwarfed by the 176 seats won by Aung San's AFPFL party which subsequently took power in the country.

Unfortunately for Aung San, a few months after having achieved a fairly unanimous vote of confidence from the Burmese people, the deep divisions caused by his earlier decision to accept a role within the British led administration of Burma came back to haunt the leader of the AFPFL and a number of his fellow representatives. On the 19th July 1947 a group of gunmen, allied to the former Burmese Colonial Prime Minister, U Saw, were said to have broken into the government building in Rangoon, where Aung San and his cabinet were meeting; and assassinated the Burmese leader and six of his fellow ministers. In the aftermath of the murders, former Prime Minister, U Saw, was directly implicated in the attack and as a result was subsequently arrested, tried and executed for his part in the murders. Although, it has also been rumoured that certain British officials were involved in the murder of Aung San, with at least one military officer later being found guilty of supplying U Saw with weapons, whether or not these were the guns used in the assassination of the Burmese ministers is unclear. Although there were claims of further British involvement in this particularly murderous event, no evidence was ever produced to support these claims and in all likelihood there was never a conspiracy as such, but the assassination was simply the action of a small number of self serving individuals who had their own political scores to settle. Significantly, even though Aung San is still said to be revered throughout most of Burma, for much of the outside world, it is his daughter, Aung San Suu Kyi, who continues to dominate the Burmese political scene, most notably because of her lengthy and highly unreasonable imprisonment by the Burmese military authorities. Following Aung San's assassination in July 1947, the socialist leader, Thakin Nu, was subsequently asked by the British authorities in Burma to form a new national government, which he finally managed to do, leading his country to independence on the 4th January 1948 and inexorably setting Burma on the road to political turmoil, military insurgencies and undemocratic rule that has continued to mark Burma's history ever since the late 1950's.

Less than twenty years after the British Empire had begun its acquisition of the territories of the ancient Burmese Empire, Britain's military forces were said to have found themselves engaged in yet another military conflict, against an equally old and well established Asian dynasty. However, unlike the native invasion which had precipitated the British intervention in Burma, the 19th century wars that were fought against the vast Chinese Empire were almost entirely about trade, rather than any sort of defensive imperative on the part of British interests in the region. Although the British East India Company, along with a number of other European merchant companies, had been trading with China for many decades, by the end of the 18th century the British populations incessant demand for tea was said to have grown so large that the British company was having real difficulties in balancing its trade deficit with the Chinese markets. According to some sources, despite the widespread availability of mass produced items that were being manufactured in the newly industrialised cities of Britain, the Chinese population were said to have been generally disinterested in such everyday commodities, preferring instead unusual, or intrinsically valuable goods, such as gold, silver, watches, or musical boxes. Unfortunately, apart from such items being initially expensive to source, they were often quite difficult to find, leaving the East India Company in somewhat of a quandry as to the type and quantity of product that they had easy access to and that might be acceptable to their Chinese counterparts. Although Opium had undoubtedly been a trade commodity since the middle of the 18th century when the poppy producing regions of India had first been brought under British control, in the short term the amounts of the drug being traded with China were thought to have been relatively small. However, as the British demand for tea increased, so too did the amounts of opium being used in fair exchange, a troubling development for the Chinese authorities who recognised the highly addictive and disabling qualities of the product on their native peoples.

As early as the 1830's, the Chinese authorities were beginning to complain to the British government and to Queen Victoria herself about the increasing use of opium as a trade product, a criticism that was not well received by the British parliament, or indeed the monarch herself. For the Chinese commissioner, Lin Zexu, who had written to the British Queen expressing his government's concerns, the fact that little was done to suppress the trade, simply made him even more determined to bring an end to the opium trade, once and for all. In 1839, the same year that he had sent his correspondence to the British authorities, Lin Zexu was said to have seized an estimated twenty thousand chests of opium that had been delivered into Chinese ports by British ships and ordered the entire cargo to be destroyed, causing outrage within British government circles. As a direct result of Lin Zexu's decision to destroy the cargoes of opium, purportedly a clear violation of Britain's ancient right to trade, relations between British traders sailing into China's ports and local Chinese officials were reported to have become increasingly strained, with both sides regularly coming into conflict with one another, over a series of sometimes rather trivial incidents. However, matters were said to have come to a head in 1839 when the Chinese authorities began to insist that all foreign merchants sign an undertaking to refrain from trading in opium, on pain of death and to fully recognise the authority of Chinese laws whilst they were visiting the country. For Britain's trade representative in Canton, Charles Elliot, these demands were deemed to be generally unreasonable and as a result he ordered all British traders in Canton to withdraw from the port and forbade further trade with the Chinese merchant community there.

For those ship owners and captains who did not trade in opium and were willing to accept that they were bound by China's own national laws, the prohibition on Canton, placed on it by Britain's main trade representative, Charles Elliot, was thought to have caused a great deal of hardship and resentment. As a result, some of these merchants simply chose to make their own arrangements with the Chinese governor of Guangdong to unload their ships on the island of Chuenpee, which not only caused great personal irritation to Elliot himself, who saw his own authority being undermined, but also put the entire British trading position at risk. In order to ensure that Chuenpee and Guangdong did not become regular destinations for other British trade ships, Elliot was reported to have ordered a blockade of the main waterway, the Pearl River, in late October 1839 and within a matter of days the Royal Navy ships enforcing the blockade, were thought to have been called into action for the first time. On the 3rd November 1039, the British merchant ship, the Royal Saxon tried to reach Guangdong, despite being advised against it by the two patrolling Royal Navy ships, HMS Volage and Hyacinth that were enforcing Elliot's blockade of the waterway. Having had their hails ignored by the master of the Royal Saxon, the captains of the two British warships were forced to fire warning shots across the merchant vessel's bow, compelling it to comply with their demands to turn about. At the same time that the Royal Navy ships were attempting to divert the Royal Saxon, a number of ships from the Qing Navy were thought to have tried to interfere with Volage and Hyacinth's blockade activities and were subsequently sunk, although later Chinese reports of the action suggested that the Qing Navy had somehow achieved a victory over the two British ships.

Fearing Chinese retaliation for both the blockade and the subsequent destruction of the Qing Navy ships, Elliot was reported to have ordered all British ships to leave Chuenpee and remove themselves to the safer Portuguese held port of Macau. Unfortunately, the British were thought to have become so unpopular in China that the Portuguese governor of Macau, fearful that any support for the British, might be misconstrued by the Chinese authorities, refused to allow any British merchant ships to trade in Macau, irrespective of the financial incentives offered by Elliot. Back in London, the British government was said to be still unhappy about the earlier destruction of the East India Company's consignments of opium by the Chinese authorities, so the subsequent order of the Qing government in China for all foreigners to desist from rendering aid to British interests in the country proved to be the final straw for the by now completely exasperated British legislature. In June 1840, Britain's parliament authorised a military taskforce, comprising fifteen troop ships, four large steam powered gunboats, a fleet of smaller military vessels and up to five thousand marines, sailing from Singapore, to attack the Chinese province of Guangdong, including the port of Guangzhou. Having arrived off the coast of Guangdong in January 1841, the British gunboats began to bombard the local Chinese ports and within a short time were reported to have created a number of beachheads where the British marines and their equipment could be landed, ready for the move inland. Completely overwhelmed by the sudden arrival of this modern and well armed British force, local Chinese officials were thought to have quickly signed their own individual treaties with the British commanders, although when these were subsequently presented to the Qing authorities in Beijing for ratification, they were simply rejected out of hand and the officials punished for their failure to prevent the British military incursions.

Outraged by this attack on their sovereign territories, the Chinese authorities in Beijing were said to have sent reinforcements to Guangdong to help repulse the British invaders, although with the marines by now well entrenched, subsequent attempts by the Chinese forces to drive them off proved to be largely unsuccessful. By the end of May 1841, the British forces were said to have such a stranglehold on the region that local Chinese officials were forced into paying several million dollars in compensation, presumably for the loss of the earlier cargoes of opium, as well as the actual costs of Britain's military incursion into China, thereby adding even greater insult to the injury that China had suffered in the first place. What was said to have made the situation even worse, from a Chinese perspective, was the fact that even though compensation had been paid, elements of the British forces were reported to have looted a number of government buildings and private households as they retreated from the region, actions that were deemed to be both dishonourable and uncivilised. However, despite such events, eventually the British forces agreed to withdraw from the area, although as they did so, local Chinese forces reportedly attacked the withdrawing marines, forcing them to open fire on their attackers once again. Despite these intermittent engagements though, the British troops were finally able to complete their withdrawal by 1st June 1841 with relatively few losses, even though the Chinese leadership later reported that a large number of British troops had been killed, no doubt in an effort to play down their own military inadequacies and national humiliation.

Having begun their military attack on the main Chinese port cities in Guangdong province during January 1841, Britain's chief representative in China, Charles Elliot, was reported to have made an unopposed landing on Hong Kong Island on January 20th 1841, where Commodore Sir Gordon Bremer, officially claimed the territory as a British colonial possession in the following week, raising the Union Jack over "Possession Point" on 26th January 1841. At the same time that Hong Kong was seized by the British forces, a second island, Zhoushan, was also annexed, with the intention that it would be used as a staging point for British forces, although it was later handed back to the Chinese authorities, following the ceding of the Hong Kong territories to Britain by the Convention of Chuenpee, which was agreed in January 1841. Unfortunately, despite the convention being agreed between Charles Elliot and Qishan, the Chinese Governor of Guangdong province, the fact that neither of them had consulted their own governments regarding the actual terms of the settlement, ensured that it was never formally ratified, resulting in both men being subsequently dismissed from their posts by their respective governments. Elsewhere, British forces were also reported to have captured and temporarily held the walled Chinese port city of Ningbo, during October 1841, having previously captured the fortified town of Zhenhai, with Ningbo later becoming one of the five treaty ports which were granted to Britain under the terms of the Treaty of Nanking that was signed in August 1842.

Sir John Bowring

Lord Palmerston

Lord Elgin

Ultimately, for the British authorities, the Treaty of Nanking gave them much of what they had wanted from the Chinese government, five treaty ports from where they could ship their cargoes, in and out of mainland China, new colonial territories outside of Chinese control and a continuance of their highly questionable opium trade, which had caused much of the conflict between Britain and China in the first place. Although the American opium trade was later suppressed by the United States government, many traders were thought to have simply moved their operations to Hong Kong where the British authorities had few such qualms about the legitimacy of the highly profitable business. For the Chinese authorities however, Britain's continuing participation in the narcotics trade, which proved to be so damaging to China's native population remained a major concern, even after the Treaty of Nanking was signed in 1842 and was a major factor for the two countries going to war again in 1856, in what became known as the Second Opium War. Although the trade in opium was central to this second conflict between Britain and China, the dispute also involved the issue of trade and European access to China's vast population, which for French and British merchants, represented one huge untapped potential marketplace.

Britain, France and the United States were the three major exporters trading into China by the middle of the 19th century and although France and America had already established trade agreements that were due to be renegotiated, Britain had not, given that the Treaty of Nanking had only been signed in 1842. In an effort to ensure that it did not lose out to its two main trading competitors, Britain began to insist that the Chinese government agree to renegotiate the treaty, allowing for exemptions on trade tariffs, legalising the opium trade, establishing a permanent British diplomatic presence in Beijing and the precedence of the English language over Chinese in any trade treaties signed between the two countries. With the Americans and the French both demanding parity with the British, the Chinese authorities were faced with the real prospect of having to renegotiate three different treaties, on equally disadvantageous terms, so in the end refused to negotiate any of them, bringing themselves into conflict with three of the biggest military powers of the age. However, despite their refusal to discuss new terms, which could not be regarded as a legitimate basis for a new military conflict, the British authorities were thought to have waited for a situation to present itself that would give them legal grounds for imposing their will on the Chinese authorities. Consequently, when Chinese customs officials boarded a vessel called the "Arrow" in October 1856 and arrested a number of the crew on suspicion of being pirates, the British were inadvertently given the excuse they had been waiting for, to pick a fight with the Chinese authorities. Claiming that the ship had been sailing under British colours at the time of its detention, the British Consul in Canton, Harry Parkes, was said to have demanded the immediate release of the Chinese crewmen, which the Chinese Commissioner, Ye Mingchen, refused to do, especially when he found out that "Arrow's" British registration had expired some weeks earlier and was not therefore covered by the terms of the Nanking Treaty. Refusing to acknowledge the fact that he was in fact incorrect in his assertions, Parkes subsequently ordered the Royal Navy to bombard Ye Mingchen's palace, which they duly did, destroying it and parts of the city, causing significant numbers of casualties amongst the Chinese civilian population. Incensed by this act, in response to Parkes' actions, Ye Mingchen called on the people of Canton to unite in fighting the English criminals and offering a reward of one hundred dollars for the head of any Englishman brought to him.

Unfortunately for the Chinese, the fact that they had later returned the sailors in good order seemed to have made little impact with the British Governor of Hong Kong, Sir John Bowring, who rather high handedly was said to have ordered British military forces to carry out further actions against Chinese assets, including local forts and sailing vessels, which he later claimed presented a threat to British interests and personnel. Although Bowring was later publicly criticised for his actions, which were thought to have been wholly disproportionate, given that the supposedly British crewmen had already been released from Chinese custody the day before, which left little more to complain about. In normal circumstances the incident should have been resolved, although with the British actively seeking to create an international incident and the Chinese authorities diverted by their own internal Taiping Rebellion, things were never likely to be that straightforward. Back in Britain, reports of Harry Parkes' and Sir John Bowring's actions were said to have been met with outrage within the British parliament, with opposition members passing a motion of censure against the British Consul, Harry Parkes, whose actions were nonetheless supported by the British Prime Minister, Lord Palmerston, who having lost calls for an immediate inquiry into the matter, simply dissolved that particular sitting of parliament and went to the country in a new General Election, which his party subsequently won by a landslide. Having been returned to government with an increased majority and having seen his most vocal critics defeated at the ballot box, Palmerston then set about seeking redress from the Chinese authorities on the basis of the flawed information regarding the "Arrow". However, not content with simply confronting the Chinese with Britain's particular complaints, the British leader was reported to have sought support for his highly questionable actions, by seeking to include the demands of the United States and France in any final settlement with the Beijing government. Although America had tried to renegotiate its earlier trade agreement with the Chinese authorities without success, it seemed loathe to join any sort of military alliance with Britain and France, so simply contented itself with sending its own peace envoys to try and arrange an equitable agreement between the two sides. France on the other hand, was only too happy to lend its support to Britain's campaign, as it was already in dispute with the Beijing authorities over the execution of a French missionary, Father August Chapdelaine, by Chinese officials in Guangxi province, having been denounced by the relatives of a new Roman Catholic convert. With the two European nations forming a combined military expedition under Admiral Sir Michael Seymour, in 1857, a British force led by Lord Elgin and a French force under the command of the ambassador and diplomat Jean Baptiste Gros, were said to have attacked, captured and occupied the city of Guangzhou, capturing the Chinese commissioner Ye Mingchen, who was subsequently exiled to Calcutta in India where he later died. Holding the city and its surrounding regions for nearly four years, during this occupation of the Chinese mainland, both French and British forces were reported to have roamed at will, although by 1858 the European allies and the Chinese were thought to have reached some form of interim agreement that would satisfy the British, French and American demands, thus allowing the allied forces to withdraw from the region entirely.

By June 1858, a series of fairly punitive treaties were thought to have been drawn up by the three major western powers, Britain, France and the United States, which would have forced the Chinese authorities to accept greater western access to their national waterways, their main port cities and to previously closed areas of the country. In addition, the Chinese leadership was also expected to permit all foreign vessels to travel the Yangtze River unmolested, as well as paying the French and British governments millions in damages, or as insurance against any future conflict with the government in Beijing. These treaties were said to have been so severe from the Qing Court's perspective that initially they refused to ratify any of them, although eventually they were left with little option, but to agree to the clearly unequal agreements, in the hope that they might renegotiate or refute them at a later date. Almost as soon as the new treaties had been ratified, more militant members of the Chinese court were reported to have persuaded the Emperor to resist some of the more unreasonable demands of the western powers, including the appointment of diplomatic envoys to the closed city of Peking and the presence of armed foreign troops in Beijing. In the interim twelve month period, whilst waiting for Britain and France to send their new representatives, the Chinese courts were said to have arranged for their local defences to be reinforced, fresh troops to be brought in from its outlying provinces and the main waterway to Beijing to be blocked, thereby preventing foreign warships from threatening the city, its buildings, or its native population. Consequently, when the first of the new Anglo-French diplomats arrived in China in June 1859, accompanied by a Royal Navy flotilla of twenty-odd ships and several thousand men, as they entered the mouth of the Hai River, to continue their voyage to Beijing, their progress was prevented, not only by obstacles in the water, but also by the newly reinforced and rearmed Chinese forts that overlooked the waterway. The British commander of the naval force, Admiral Sir James Hope, demanded that the fleet be allowed to continue its journey unhindered, but the local Chinese commander insisted that the new western diplomats should disembark from their ships and travel to Beijing overland, without their military forces, who would not be permitted to travel to the Chinese capital. With neither side willing to compromise, the British fleet was reported to have remained at anchor for a number of days considering their next move, while the Chinese garrisons in the forts above them kept a close watch on the foreign fleet. Finally, on the night of the 24th June 1859, British troops onboard the Royal Navy ships were reported to have attached explosives to the obstacles barring the British fleet and simply blew them out of the way, creating a channel for the ships to carry on with their journey. However, almost as soon as the smoke had cleared and the fleet made ready to continue its voyage, the Chinese forts were said to have opened fire on the Royal Navy ships, sinking four and damaging a number of others over the next twenty four hours, forcing the British fleet to withdraw, under cover of fire from a nearby American squadron, which just happened to be in the area at the time.

Having been forced to retire from the area with considerable losses, the British and French governments immediately began to plan for a much larger force to resume military action against the Chinese authorities. Around twelve months later the European allies were said to have assembled a fleet of some two hundred naval vessels and some twenty thousand troops under the command of Generals James Grant for the British and Cousin Montauban for the French. Sailing from the newly established British colony of Hong Kong, within a relatively short time, the allied forces quickly captured a number of smaller Chinese port cities, before making a full scale landing at Beitang from where they could attack the well defended Taku forts that had proved to be so effective against the British fleet in the previous year. After a three week campaign, the Anglo French forces were said to have finally captured the forts, leaving the way open for the European troops to move against the Chinese capital of Beijing, an advance that forced the authorities in the city to send out peace envoys to try and arrange a truce with the allied commanders. Unfortunately, the Chinese government's decision to imprison those westerners who had remained in Beijing during the various conflicts, as well as the arrival of Chinese cavalry that tried to drive the Anglo French forces away from the city, ensured that no peace negotiations took place between the two sides, but rather led to the almost complete annihilation of the native cavalrymen who were no match for the well armed and highly disciplined European troops. With little reason to offer terms to the Chinese and with no credible military force to oppose them, by the beginning of October 1860, Anglo French troops were said to have entered the outskirts of Beijing, although by this time, the Chinese Emperor and his household were said to have fled the city. Intent on exacting revenge for the attacks on their forces, as well as the killing of several western hostages, who had been held by the Chinese authorities, the Anglo French commanders were then reported to have begun a concerted campaign of looting and destruction, purportedly to teach the Chinese leadership a lesson, although no doubt personal greed played a role in some cases, with valuable artefacts being spirited away by individual officers and soldiers.

General James Grant   Dowager Empress Cixi   Mao Zedong

Careful to avoid hardening Chinese attitudes even further, the allied commanders in Beijing were thought to ordered their forces to remain on the outskirts of the city, rather than entering its centre, where they might easily come into direct confrontation with the large native population. However, although they were said to have discussed the complete destruction of the "Forbidden City" as a possible punishment, in the end allied commanders were thought to have settled for the razing of the Emperor's Summer Palaces, including the many historic temples, royal apartments and fabulous artworks that existed within them. With the Chinese Emperor absent from the capital, it was left to his younger brother, Prince Gong, to actually ratify the new set of agreements, the Convention of Peking, which contained the terms demanded by the victorious Anglo French forces. For Britain, not only had the British Empire reinstated its rights under the terms of the Treaty of Nanking, but it had also added to its Hong Kong territories with the ceding of Kowloon to them by the Chinese government, as well as being compensated for their financial losses by the authorities in Beijing. The opium trade, which had been at the heart of Sino-British antagonism for so long, was finally legalised and those Christians living within China, both foreign and domestic, were also granted full and equal rights within the Chinese empire, including the right to evangelise, a practice that would continue to cause intolerance right through to the present day. However, perhaps the greatest effect of this Second Opium War, fought between Britain and China, was not so much the legalisation of the opium trade, or indeed the acquisition of Hong Kong as a British territory, but rather the catastrophic impact it had on the Chinese people themselves and the actual status of the country's historic Emperors, who had ruled the nation for nearly two thousand years and whose reign was finally ended in 1911, following the suppression of the Boxer Rebellion by an alliance of foreign powers.

With a formal end to the Second Opium War signed by Britain and China under the terms of the Beijing Convention in 1860, British possession of the Hong Kong and Kowloon territories was fundamentally assured, although it still required further negotiations between the two sides in later years. As these colonial possessions grew and evolved into one of the world's leading trading centres, so concerns over its future growth and defence became a matter of concern for its British administrators, leading to the signing of the Second Convention of Peking in June 1898, which granted Britain a 99 year lease on land that later became known as the New Territories. As part of wider Anglo Chinese talks that took place in 1984, a new agreement, the Sino British Joint Declaration, resulted in all of these former colonial territories being handed back to Chinese control on 1st July 1997.

In 1843 the British government constituted the first legislative council in Hong Kong, although as was common at the time, this first administrative body was almost entirely an advisory one, consisting of four members who simply advised the British Governor on matters pertaining to the running of these new territories. At the time that Britain first formally claimed Hong Kong Island for the British Empire, the territory was said to have been occupied by a relatively small number of Chinese fishermen and itinerant charcoal makers who made their living from the sea, or from the islands local resources. However, within a decade of Britain taking control of the island large numbers of ethnic Chinese workers, merchants, investors and even criminals were reported to have settled in the area, anxious to take advantage of the less stringent laws and commercial opportunites presented by the new European authorities. With the creation of the colony's new free port, as had been the case in Singapore, large numbers of traders, merchants, bankers and speculators, from both Asia and Europe were said to have relocated themselves to Hong Kong, bringing with them significant amounts of money to invest in the territory's evolving retail, wholesale and manufacturing industries. Shipbuilding, banking and the international trade in eastern textiles and spices, all became intrinsic parts of the Hong Kong economy, as did the development of the colony's immensely important military base, built to protect and enforce Britain's historic trading rights and far flung imperial possessions. By the second half of the 19th century, Hong Kong's ports were said to be handling around a quarter of all mainland China's exports and a full third of the country's imports, making the British colony one of busiest and most vibrant trading hubs in all of Asia, a reputation it would maintain right through to the present day, save for the period of the Second World War, when the territories were occupied by Japanese military forces.

Almost inevitably, Hong Kong, with its emerging trade and employment opportunities became a mecca for tens of thousands of China's poorest citizens, including those who had been dispossessed, or who had become disillusioned with the failures of the Qing dynasty in Beijing. However, as in Singapore, large numbers of these newly arrived immigrants were thought to have fallen prey to the already well established criminal gangs and slum landlords who made their livings from exploiting their own Chinese communities, through money lending, the drugs trade, or by ensnaring young women into the vice trade. For the British authorities in Hong Kong, even though great efforts were taken to suppress the criminal activities of these gangs, with large numbers of police being employed for the purpose, for the most part the colonial administration were thought to have contented themselves with keeping the worst aspects of such criminality from the European community, through the creation of ethnic neighbourhoods, or zones. As a result of this zoning system, clear demarcation lines were created between the native Chinese and European residential areas of the territory, with most westerners and wealthy Asians living apart from the squalour and poverty of the native quarters, where illness and death were an everyday occurrence. These divisions were often best illustrated by the various incidents of highly communicable diseases that were said to have visited the colony in the latter part of the 19th century, including an outbreak of bubonic plague in 1894, which was said to have spread through one of the colony's poorest neighbourhoods, killing an estimated one hundred people per day and forcing tens of thousands of refugees to flee the city.

However, despite the occasional catastrophic event that might endanger their lives in Hong Kong, for most of the native Chinese population who remained resident in the colony, life there was far more preferable to that which they might expect to endure back in China. As the 19th century gave way to the 20th, the Qing dynasty was thought to have been in serious decline, largely because of China's increasing importance to a growing list of foreign nations that all insisted on having preferential trading rights with the largely defenceless and beleaguered nation. In the half century since the British Empire, along with France and the United States had enforced a settlement on the Qing Emperor in China, in the aftermath of the First and Second Opium Wars, Japan, Russia, Germany, Italy and the Austro-Hungarian Empire had all helped to undermine, both the authority of the Emperor and the sovereignty of the Chinese nation. Each of these foreign states and particularly the British Empire were deeply resented by sections of the native Chinese population, who saw their presence in the country, as not only damaging to China's own historic traditions, but also as a potential threat to continuing Chinese unity. However, it would be wrong to assume that Britain alone bore the greatest responsibility for the events that took place in China, although clearly its military intervention to compel the Chinese authorities to accept opium as a legitimate trade commodity undoubtedly played a significant role in the almost inevitable decline of the Qing dynasty. It is also worth remembering though that even after the Second Opium War had been settled by the treaty of 1860, China continued to be wracked by a number of other internal rebellions and conflicts, including the Sino-French War of 1883 and the Sino-Japanese War of 1894, both of which saw the previously Chinese held territories of Vietnam and Korea eventually being lost to foreign powers. According to some within the Chinese government, there was a fear that the foreign states were conspiring to divide China into separate regions, which could then be taken over, colonised and governed by the various foreign governments, leading to the disappearance of the Chinese nation forever. Pointing to the unfair treaties imposed on the country by the likes of Britain and France, the continued importation of opium into China by the British authorities and the dangers posed by the increasing numbers of foreign missionaries arriving in the country, before long, anti-western feelings amongst the indigenous Chinese population was said to be on the rise. The situation was thought to have been made worse by the introduction of a series of liberal reforms by the Chinese Guangxu Emperor, largely at the behest of foreign advisers, which were regarded by some conservative elements as evidence of the Emperor's weakness in the face of outside influences, hardening Chinese attitudes even further. As a result of these unsuccessful reforms, the Emperor was reported to have been usurped by his mother, the Dowager Empress Cixi, who despite appearing to accept foreign interference in Chinese affairs, in reality encouraged much of the anti-western feeling that was slowly beginning to surface in the country. This native Chinese antagonism towards the foreign invaders was said to have been particularly strong amongst the Boxers, the Righteous Harmony Society, whose members were dedicated to ending colonial involvement in China, the removal of Christian evangelists from the country and the restoration of their nation's economic and political power. Unfortunately for China, eventually the Boxer Rebellion was suppressed by the foreign powers, who were said to have sent a large combined military force into the country, not only to rescue those foreign citizens trapped by the revolt, but also to exact revenge for those few hundred foreigners who were reported to have been murdered by the Chinese rebels. For the Dowager Empress Cixi, her armies, the country, but more importantly for the Chinese population, the rebellion proved to be a complete disaster, with the foreign powers imposing huge financial penalties on China's already impoverished economy and large numbers of entirely innocent Chinese citizens losing their lives, as foreign troops attempted to identify rebel leaders and bring them to justice. In a little over a decade following the unsuccessful Boxer Rebellion, the Dowager Empress and her Emperor son were both dead, their royal successor had been deposed and the country was divided between the military forces of a new republican movement and a number of individual warlords. By the early 1920's China was beginning to see the emergence of the Chinese Communist Party and the Chinese Nationalist Party, both of which would compete with one another for control of their homeland, pitting their respective leaders, Mao Zedong and Chang Kai Skek, in a struggle that would eventually culminate in the creation of the modern day states of the People's Republic of China (China) and the Republic of China on Taiwan (Taiwan).

For the British colony of Hong Kong, events in mainland China were said to have remained important, in that during the 19th century the deep water harbour of the colony was regularly employed as a base for the Royal Navy squadrons used to support British interests in the region. It was also said to be the case that Hong Kong's population ebbed and flowed with events in China, with times of trouble bringing increasing numbers of Chinese refugees across the border into British controlled territories, a trend that became just as commonplace in the post Second World War period, when the Communist Party of Mao Zedong rose to power in China, forcing large numbers of Chinese to permanently abandon their homes on the mainland to seek refuge in the comparatively small British enclave. However, despite its continued development as a major international trading centre and British military base during the first quarter of the 20th century, once again it was events elsewhere, along with the perceived invincibility of Britain's Royal Navy that would have the most significant impact on the colony during the second quarter of the century and see it suffer an equally disastrous period of occupation by the Japanese, as was to be the case in neighbouring Singapore. Although by 1912 China had finally rid itself of its historic Emperor's, the resulting fledgling republican movement, communist party and regional warlords ensured that the country remained divided and weak, to the point that there was little if any organised resistance to the rapidly expanding Japanese Empire, which was seeking to extend its own influence and control in the region, in direct competition to the British and Americans. Buoyed by their earlier successes against both China and Russia, the Japanese Empire was not only keen to exploit the military weakness of the Chinese state, but also its vast array of natural resources that might be used in the modernisation and military development of Japan, an objective that the British and Americans were seen to threaten. In 1931 Imperial Japanese forces were reported to have invaded Manchuria against little Chinese opposition and within a short space of time were reported to have established a puppet regime, known as Manchukuo, with the deposed Chinese imperial ruler Puyi, the "Last Emperor", as its head of state. Similiarly, five years later Japan's forces invaded the region of Inner Mongolia, renaming it as the province of Mengjiang and along with Manchukuo began to invite large numbers of Asians and Japanese into the region, resulting in the colonisation of the two areas by an estimated one million foreign immigrants, which helped to establish complete Japanese control over the regions.

In 1937 and having consolidated their control of both Manchuria and Inner Mongolia, the Japanese military were said to have invaded China proper, thereby creating a three-way conflict between themselves, the national forces of Chank Kai Shek and the communist forces of Mao Zedong, who had been fighting one another for the previous decade or more. Although in the early stages of this Second Sino-Japanese War, the nationalist and communists remained at odds with one another, along with opposing the Japanese, as the conflict developed the two Chinese forces were compelled to form an uneasy alliance with one another, until such time as the Japanese were defeated, allowing them then to continue with their own bloody civil war. For most of the native Chinese population, the sheer brutality of the Japanese military forces was thought to have allowed them to unify against a common enemy, with the Nanking Massacre being one of the most notably brutal incidents of the Japanese occupation of China. On December 13th 1937, the city of Nanking, the former capital of China surrendered to the Japanese, beginning a six week campaign of murder and rape that was reported to have cost the lives of anything between twenty thousand to two hundred thousand Chinese citizens, although these figures continues to be disputed by both sides even through to the present day. In the aftermath of the Nanking incident and with no concerted defence being offered by China's military forces, the Japanese quickly established yet another puppet regime in the country and began an occupation that was said to have cost around twenty million Chinese lives over the entire course of World War II.

Although all of these early Japanese military conquests had been undertaken in pursuit of their own imperial, military and economic ambitions, Japan's leaders had always known that their expansionist policies would inevitably bring them into conflict with the British and the Americans, the regions most dominant western nations. Japan's expansionist policies were reported to have alarmed both of these great powers, although Britain's problems in Europe with Nazi Germany and America's clearly defined policy of neutrality ensured that little had been done to physically challenge the increasing threat that the Japanese Empire posed to Asia generally. However, following Japan's invasion of China and then French Indo-China, the United States government was reported to have retaliated against the Japanese authorities by imposing a series of trade embargoes on the country, which forbade the exports of much needed raw materials that were vital to Japan's continuing war efforts. Recognising that Britain's far eastern forces had been weakened by the war with Germany, which formally began in September 1939, the Japanese government quickly realised that only the United States and its imposing Pacific Fleet stood in the way of their future military objectives, causing Japan's military strategists to begin planning for the American fleet's destruction. On the 27th September 1940, little more than a year after Britain had formally declared war on Germany, Japan signed the Tripartite Pact with Nazi Germany and Fascist Italy, agreeing between them to establish a new world order, with each of the three Axis Powers controlling their own particular regions of the globe and agreeing to mutually support one another if they were attacked.

Mark Aitchison Young

Takashi Sakai

Admiral Michael Seymour

Technically, this meant that Japan was at war with Great Britain, although in reality the presence of the United States Pacific Fleet at Pearl Harbour ensured that no significant military actions were likely to be undertaken against British interests until that particular threat had been neutralised by the Japanese. In September 1941 and with the American trade embargoes beginning to affect their war effort, Japan's chief military planners, Osami Nagano and Isoroku Yamamoto put forward their proposals for an attack on the American fleet based in Hawaii, which it was hoped would force the Americans to withdraw from the Pacific, leaving Japan free to consolidate its gains and take overall control of the region. Although Japan was thought to have tried to negotiate a settlement from a position of strength, given that it already held French Indo-China and much of the Chinese mainland, neither the United States, nor Great Britain was willing to acquiesce to the Japanese demands, leaving military action as the only possible means of achieving their long term aims. Consequently, on the morning of 7th December 1941 the Japanese military launched their surprise attack on the American naval base at Pearl Harbour in an attempt to destroy the United States ability to defend the Pacific region from Japan's expansionist ambitions.

Immediately following their infamous attack on Pearl Harbour, elsewhere in the region Japanese military forces launched a series of pre-planned assaults on other allied bases in and around the Pacific, including the British forces in Hong Kong,

Malaya, Singapore and American bases in the Philippines. Within days Japanese forces were reported to have begun their advance on the Malayan peninsula, moving south towards the British fortress of Singapore and on the 10th December 1941 Japanese aircraft attacked and destroyed the British ships HMS Prince of Wales and HMS Repulse, leaving the east coast of Malaya open to further attack. The day following Japan's unprovoked attack on Pearl Harbour, on the 8th December 1941, the British colony of Hong Kong was assaulted by Japanese forces operating from the neighbouring Chinese province of Guangzhou (Canton), beginning an eighteen day campaign that would ultimately result in the capture of the port colony by the Japanese Empire.

Hong Kong's security had been the subject of much debate by various British governments ever since the early 1900's, following the deposition of the Chinese Emperor's, the outbreak of the Chinese Civil War and a serious decline in Anglo-Japanese relations, any or all of which could have seriously threatened the future prosperity of the developing colonial port. Given the territory's position in relation to the Chinese mainland, the British military authorities in Hong Kong had always recognised the difficulties of defending the colony from any large scale and determined enemy attack that might be launched from China itself. Consequently, following Japan's invasion of the Chinese mainland during the 1930's some work was undertaken to construct new defensive positions that might protect the British territories from attack, although for the most part it was generally accepted that the position in Hong Kong would be largely untenable in the event of a full scale enemy assault. As a result, in the months and years leading up to the outbreak of war with Japan, the British military presence in Hong Kong was thought to have been kept relatively small, with only a minimal number of regular troops being stationed there, sufficient only to delay any planned invasion until such time as the colony could be reinforced, assuming of course that the British authorities chose to do so. For the Chinese nationalists who were already fighting the Japanese, Britain's apparent reluctance to allocate sufficient military resources to the defence of Hong Kong was said to have caused a great of anger and dismay, particularly with the nationalist leader Chang Kai Shek, who was said to have publicly criticised the British authorities for their failure to fully reinforce their port colony from the Japanese threat. As a result of such criticisms and the changing military situation in the region, especially Japan's increasingly war-like stance, in September 1941 the British Prime Minister, Winston Churchill, was said to have ordered a significant reinforcement of Hong Kong's military garrison, using some two thousand infantrymen who had previously been stationed in the Americas and therefore lacked any real frontline experience.

Because of this limited combat experience and the relatively small size of the allied forces in Hong Kong, when the Japanese finally launched their attack against the colony on 8th December 1941, the British, Canadian and Indian defenders were reported to have not only been outnumbered by nearly four to one, but were also being asked to confront three highly experienced Japanese regiments, supported by one of the best equipped airforces in the world at that time. Japanese aircraft very quickly overcame and destroyed the limited RAF presence in the colony, leaving the allied forces and the civilian population exposed to regular bombing and strafing by enemy aircrews, a situation that forced the remaining Royal Navy ships in Hong Kong harbour to withdraw from the area, rather than face almost certain destruction by the Japanese airforce. On the landward side of the colony, the limited defensive positions previously constructed by the British authorities proved to be highly ineffective barriers to a large scale and widespread Japanese advance, with the highly experienced Japanese troops simply using temporary bridges and boats to overcome the outlying rivers, streams and ditches that allied planners had hoped might stall any proposed enemy invasion of the territory. Even the carefully constructed defensive position known as the Gin Drinkers Line, comprising a series of interlinked and heavily constructed bunkers, field-gun emplacements, machine gun posts and trenches, which had taken the British two years to construct, was said to have been easily bypassed by the Japanese forces within three days of their initial attack, allowing them to overwhelm and surround the allied troops who were stationed there. With their main defensive line overcome, the allied defenders were subsequently pushed south across Kowloon and back towards Hong kong Island and its main population centres, allowing time for the authorities there to begin destroying many of the vital port facilities, thus preventing them from falling into Japanese hands. Within ten days of the attack having started, the Japanese forces were reported to have reached the northern end of Hong Kong Island itself and were said to be engaging those allied troops that were trying to throw them back, although with little real success. As they gained ground on the island, so instances of Japanese atrocities began to be reported, including the killing of a significant numbers of injured allied soldiers and medical staff, who had surrendered themselves to the Japanese military, only to be murdered in cold blood. Eventually though, sheer weight of numbers and the loss of the islands only fresh water reservoir was thought to have forced the allied commanders to consider surrendering the colony to the Japanese authorities, in the hope of preventing any further loss of life, both to the military forces and the civilian population. According to some sources, had the British authorities held out for a few days more, the outcome of the Battle for Hong Kong might well have have been entirely different, as there were said to be plans for a Chinese nationalist attack on the Japanese forces scheduled for New Years Day 1942, which would have seen both British and Chinese troops oppose the invasion of Hong Kong together. Unfortunately, the relatively sudden collapse of the British garrison in the colony, a little more than a week before the Chinese advance, ensured that Hong Kong fell into Japanese hands and remained that way for the following three and a half years.

Having managed to defend the colony for seventeen days during which time they had inflicted significant casualties on the Japanese forces, on the 25th December 1941, the British Governor of Hong Kong, Sir Mark Aitchison Young, formally surrendered the colony to the Imperial Japanese Army at the Peninsula Hotel in the city. As a result, in the following three and a half years of Japanese occupation, Hong Kong and its population would be subjected to a catalogue of indiscriminate murder, mass rape, widespread looting, ethnic cleansing and deliberate starvation of the local native and European populace. As was the case in Malaya and Singapore, as well as elsewhere, those in greatest danger from the Japanese military authorities were the native Chinese, who were systematically persecuted, expelled or murdered by the invasion forces, simply for being Chinese. However, it was from amongst the native Chinese community that much of Hong Kong's wartime resistance was said to have originated, with locally organised groups carrying out numerous acts of saboutage, killings and assassinations against the Japanese forces or those that collaborated with them, right through to the end of the conflict in August 1945. For those non-combatant westerners who had been trapped in Hong Kong, the surrender of the colony in December 1941 marked the start of nearly four years of internment, during which time they suffered enormous hardships and shortages, with many of them dying as a result of the malnutrition, disease and harsh treatment that was endemic to the Japanese prisoner of war camps.

The war in the Pacific and therefore the Japanese occupation of Hong Kong was only finally brought to an end on 15th August 1945, following the dropping of the world's first atomic bombs on the Japanese cities of Hiroshima and Nagasaki, on the 6th and 9th August 1945 respectively. At the same time that these two devastating weapons were unleashed on the civilian populations of Japan, the last great Japanese Army in China was reported to have been attacked by Soviet forces in Manchuria, ending all hopes that Japan might somehow manage to retain its hold on all of the territories it had previously brought under its control. In common with their allies in Western Europe, the Japanese military were keen to expunge all evidence of the many war crimes that had been perpetrated by their military forces throughout Asia, a national denial that continues to exist right through to the present day. However, the end of the war did bring some limited form of retribution and in Hong Kong, the Japanese commander of the invading imperial forces and later military commander of the occupation forces, General Takashi Sakai, was subsequently arrested, tried and executed for the numerous war crimes that he and his men had committed during the war. At the same time that the allies were planning for the new post war period, the British authorities were thought to be making arrangements for the recovery of their overseas territories, including Hong Kong, regardless of the American government's previously declared anti-colonial attitudes, which had seen the late President, Franklin D Roosevelt, promise the Chinese leader Chang Kai Shek that Hong Kong would be returned to Chinese ownership once the war was over, an outrageous promise for any leader to make, let alone one from a foreign state, who had no legal authority to make such an undertaking.

Admiral James Hope   **Prince Gong**   **Emperor Puyi**

Despite such unwarranted American interference in Britain's imperial affairs however, British colonial officials were quick to re-establish administrative control over Hong Kong following the Japanese surrender in August 1945, with the cruiser HMS Swiftsure arriving in Victoria Harbour on the 30th August of the same year to help reinforce the resumption of British rule. Although it was clearly understood by the British authorities that the world had been fundamentally changed by the events of the Second World War and that the old style of colonialism would no longer be tolerated by the native peoples of Britain's overseas territories, many of whom had fought against the Axis Powers, neither was Britain simply going to abandon these countries to an unknown fate, or indeed on the say so of its much larger military partner. It is perhaps interesting to note that Britain was not alone in adopting this particular colonial approach, as both France and the Netherlands were known to have set about re-establishing their own colonial controls over their former overseas territories at around the same time, albeit in an entirely different way and using entirely different methods. However, post war Hong Kong was entirely different from the port and city that the British had previously inhabited, not least because of the much smaller population and workforce, caused as a direct result of the war itself and the subsequent Japanese occupation of the colony. Although the numbers did begin to rise in the immediate post war period, it was only in the late 1940's and following the communist takeover of China by Mao Zedong and his party that large numbers of Chinese refugees once again began to arrive in Honk Kong, helping to swell the colony's population back towards its earlier pre-war levels. It was largely due to this huge influx of much needed labour that Hong Kong was able to develop its economy over the succeeding decades, restoring and then surpassing its previous position as one of the world's principal trading ports and passenger terminals.

Although it became one of the world's most important trading, manufacturing and financial centres, the impending handover of Hong Kong to the People's Republic of China, under the terms of the treaty signed by the Guangxu Emperor of China and the government of Great Britain, had agreed a ninety-nine year lease on the New Territories, beginning on 1st July 1898 and ending on 1st July 1997. Even though Hong Kong Island and Kowloon had been granted to Britain in perpetuity by the Chinese Emperor's following the end of the First and Second Opium Wars during the mid 19th century, from a Chinese perspective these were both unequal treaties, exacted by a dominant imperial power, from a failing Chinese court. The return of Hong Kong Island, Kowloon and the New Territories was and always had been an objective for the Chinese government ever since they had come to power in 1949 and they were therefore unwilling to renegotiate the lease on the New Territories, whilst at the same time challenging Britain's right to hold Hong Kong and Kowloon in the first place. For the British government, led by Margaret Thatcher, the imminent arrival of 1997, which would signal the end of the ninety-nine year lease on the New Territories presented a potential problem for the future prosperity of Hong Kong generally and risked future relationships with the People's Republic of China. Consequently, in 1984, Mrs Thatcher met with the Chinese Prime Minister, Zhao Ziyang, in Beijing and signed the Sino-British Joint Declaration, an agreement to introduce a "one country, two systems" series of practices that would see Hong Kong, Kowloon and the New Territories formally returned to China on 1st July 1997, but with Hong Kong becoming a Special Administrative Region. Under the terms of this agreement, the colony will retain its capitalist systems and its way of life until at least 2047, when the People's Republic of China will undoubtedly decide to introduce its own national socialist systems and policies into Hong Kong, effectively ending the territories Special Administrative status once and for all.

MARINERS, MERCHANTS AND THE MILITARY TOO

9. THE BRITISH IN AFRICA

Before the latter half of the 18th century and even into the first half of the 19th century, the continent of Africa was almost entirely seen in terms of the human, animal and mineral deposits that could be drawn from its shores, often from the hands of the continents own native peoples who knew its dark hinterland far better than any European explorer. However, thanks largely to pioneering adventurers like David Livingstone, Richard Burton and James Grant, to name but a few, by the second half of the 19th century, much of the continent's interior had been mapped, the immense Nile River had been explored and the great inland lakes discovered.

One of the first European countries to try and establish a new colonial settlement on the African continent were said to have been the Dutch, through their agents, the Dutch East India Company, who were reported to have founded their Cape Colony on the southern tip of Africa in 1652 and established their main settlement of Cape Town in the same year. Initially founded as a supply station for the numerous Dutch ships that were travelling between Europe, India and Asia, over time, this original supply depot was thought to have grown into a much more formal settlement, with Dutch farmers and settlers helping to expand the physical limits and actual purposes of this first European outpost. In the first instance, the local African tribesmen, the Khoikhoi, were said to have welcomed the new settlers, trading with them and providing the passing ships with much needed stores of meat that were necessary for such long sea voyages. However, as time passed and the Dutch settlers became even more eager to expand their territorial holdings, so the Khoikhoi were reported to have been pushed further and further away from their traditional grazing lands, which not only led to armed conflict between the two sides, but ultimately the impoverishment of the native African peoples. With their tribal economy severely undermined by the incoming European settlers, before long many of the local Khoikhoi tribesmen were thought to have been employed by the Dutch colonists to undertake much of the manual work in their new farms and settlements, a situation not helped by the widespread use of black African slaves from other regions of the continent. For the next one hundred and forty years or so, the Dutch colony was thought to have expanded well beyond its original limits, being further strengthened and settled by other European migrants, all of whom began to be shaped and formed by their adopted African homeland, ultimately helping to create the unique white race that referred to themselves as Afrikaans. However, despite their geographical and cultural separation from their historic homeland in the Netherlands, it was said to have been events back in mainland Europe that would ensure that this group of isolated colonists would inevitably become embroiled in the military turmoil which was to affect much of Europe in the last few years of the 18th century.

David Livingston   Henry Stanley   Boers

In 1795, Napoleonic France was reported to have invaded the seven European provinces of the Dutch Kingdom, causing fears within Britain that the new French Emperor might try to use Cape Colony as a staging post for an attack on British interests in India. In order to prevent such an action, British forces were reported to have occupied the Dutch settlement by sea later in the same year and after a brief military engagement took control of the region, primarily on behalf of the ousted Dutch monarch Prince William of Orange, who had been forced to flee to England. Nominal British control of the colony was reported to have lasted until 1803, when the region was temporarily returned to Dutch ownership, before being seized by Britain yet again in 1806, after which the decision was made to establish a permanent British colony in the area, with the town of Port Elizabeth being founded in 1820. Over the course of the next few decades, British settlement in Cape Colony was thought to have increased significantly, bringing with it the associated priests, evangelists and missionaries who were keen to convert the native peoples of Africa to their own particular faiths. Amongst this number, was a young Scottish missionary called David Livingstone, who had come to South Africa with the London Missionary Society in 1841, ostensibly to bring God's word to the native peoples of the continent. However, despite having spent his first decade there, attempting to convert various native African tribesmen to his faith, Livingstone was thought to have been largely ineffective in this particular respect and so began to look for an alternative role for himself in Southern Africa.

Having arranged for his wife and family to return to Britain, around 1852, Livingstone and a small party of native bearers were reported to have begun an expedition north of Cape Colony, into what were then still relatively undiscovered lands, where men and animal alike often fell victim to any number of strange diseases, such as malaria, dysentery and sleeping sickness. Beginning his journey at Luanda, in what is now modern day Angola, on the west coast of Africa, Livingstone and his party were said to have travelled eastward, along what is now the Zambian and Zimbabwe border, traversing the Zambezi River and becoming the first western European to witness the raw power and natural beauty of Mosi-oa-Tunya, "the smoke that thunders", which Livingstone subsequently named Victoria Falls. As he and his porters made their way towards Mozambique, on the east coast of the continent, the party were said to have encountered numerous native tribes, some of whom were highly suspicious of the party, but for the most part, were generally friendly towards Livingstone and his companions. As a committed Christian, Livingstone was said to have tried to introduce his beliefs to the various tribesmen that he met, but was always careful to avoid forcing his faith on them, for fear of alienating or antagonising them. Having successfully navigated his way across Africa, the young Scot was then reported to have returned to Britain, in the hope of raising additional funds for further exploration and development of the Zambezi River region, which he believed was the key to the future modernisation and civilisation of Africa's generally unknown interior.

Livingstone was said to have received additional financial and political backing from both the Royal Geographical Society and the British authorities in London, allowing him to continue his exploration of Africa, as a result of which, he was also said to have resigned from the London Missionary Society, recognising that he would have little time for his previous role as a full time Christian evangelist. His Zambezi Expedition, which was organised to explore and navigate the course of the Zambezi River, very nearly turned out to be an unmitigated disaster, after Livingstone and his wife were reported to have caused a certain amount of antagonism amongst the other European's who were participating in the venture. However, despite these particular problems and the expedition's obvious failure to find a navigable route along the full length of the Zambezi River, from a purely scientific point of view, the expedition was judged to have been generally successful. Unfortunately, for Livingstone personally, the Zambezi Expedition was said to have been very costly, with his wife, Mary succumbing to Malaria in April 1863 and a number of his closest friends, either dying from disease, or simply deserting him. The expedition was only finally brought to an end in 1864, when the British authorities recalled him to London, ostensibly because of the increasing financial costs and the failure of the expedition to identify an uninterrupted route into the African hinterland.

Two years later though, in 1866, Livingstone was reported to have returned to Africa, having managed to raise the funding for an expedition to determine the source of the River Nile, despite the fact that the explorers, Richard Burton and John Speke had already tentatively identified its source as being in the area of Lake Victoria sometime around 1858. However, Livingstone remained unconvinced about Burton and Speke's discovery, believing that the true source of the Nile actually lay further south of this identified spot. Accompanied by a number of native porters and two of his African assistants from previous expeditions, Livingstone was said to have travelled south to the great inland lakes of Africa, at the same time, losing numbers of his party to desertion and having many of his supplies, including vitally important medicines, stolen from him. Rather than return to Zanzibar though, Livingstone was said to have sent a message to his supporters there, to send fresh supplies to the town of Ujiji, an historic slave trading post in Western Tanzania, where he would arrange to collect them. Unfortunately, by November of 1867, the Scottish explorer was said to have been so sick that he was forced to ask for help from local slave traders that were operating in the region, who subsequently helped him to make the journey to Ujiji, where he hoped to pick up his new supplies and porters. It was said to be during this part of his journey that Livingstone first saw the Lualaba River, which he declared to be the real River Nile, but which was in fact just a part of the Congo River system and nothing to do with the Nile itself. By March 1869, Livingstone was reported to have finally arrived in Ujiji, only to find that his supplies and medicines had once again been stolen from him, leaving him with little option, but to rely on the kindness of the local slave traders, who then took him with them to Bambara. For the next two and a half years Livingstone was thought to have been transported throughout the vast African hinterland, only returning to Ujiji in October 1871, where he was said to have had his famous meeting with the American explorer and journalist, Henry Morton Stanley, who reportedly greeted the Scottish explorer with the immortal words "Dr Livingstone, I presume?" Despite being informed by Stanley that he had been reported dead some years before, Livingstone resisted all suggestions that he should return home, apparently determined to carry out his original mission of identifying the actual source of the River Nile. The two men were said to have remained in one another's company for some weeks, before Stanley finally left the region in March 1872, with Livingstone preparing to explore the Lualaba River, which he eventually realised had no connection with the Nile. For much of the following year, he was reported to have explored the various tributaries and wetlands of the region, seeking his elusive goal, before suffering once again from recurring bouts of malaria and dysentery, illnesses that would ultimately claim his life. Cared for by his faithful assistants in the final few days of his life, Livingstone was said to have passed away on the 4th May 1873 and was subsequently buried in a village on the shores of Lake Bangweulu in Zambia. However, the British authorities were said to have been particularly anxious to recover his body, so that the Scottish explorer could be given a proper Christian burial and his life properly celebrated in his native lands. Local African tribesmen though, were said to have been extremely reluctant to allow Livingstone's remains to leave Africa, believing that the continent had claimed him for itself; and it was only after careful negotiations that they agreed to let his body be taken home, although his heart was said to have been removed, to be re-interred near the place where he actually died.

In the south of the continent, as greater numbers of European settlers arrived in and around the former Dutch controlled Cape Colony which had been formally annexed by Britain in 1806, so the much earlier Dutch settlers, comprised mainly of Voortrekkers, and Trekboers were reported to have moved further away from the British held regions. Spreading out into the neighbouring homelands of the local African tribesmen, the Boers were said to have begun establishing brand new territories of their own, outside of British control, including the regions of Natal, which was said to have been established as early as 1839. Likewise, the Boer provinces or regions known as the Transvaal and the Orange Free State were similarly settled by members of the same white Afrikaan race, often at the expense of the native black Africans, who had little defence against the modern weaponry and cavalry tactics of these new white settlers. However, it would be wrong to suggest that black Africans were only dispossessed of their tribal homelands by the Boer farmers, who were seeking to escape the expansionism of British interests in the region. The discovery of gold deposits in southern Africa during the 1840's, followed by the unearthing of diamonds some twenty to thirty years later, was thought to have resulted in many thousands of European prospectors, explorers, miners and carpet baggers, arriving on the continent, determined to make their fortunes, regardless of the cost that it inflicted on the native tribes and the hereditary Boer peoples.

In response to these generally unregulated waves of immigration and at the behest of the British authorities, who were undoubtedly influenced by fairly obvious commercial interests, Great Britain was reported to have begun yet another round of seizures and annexations, taking military control of the tribal homelands of Basutoland in 1868 and Bechuanaland in 1885. Almost inevitably, British regular forces and the native Boer settlers were said to have finally come into conflict with one another over control of the region of the Transvaal, although initially Britain was said to have been more concerned with the military threat posed by the local Zulu people, a highly disciplined martial tribe, who would later prove to be a serious threat to British ambitions in the wider region. Both the Boers and the Zulu's were thought to have been competing for control of land from the late 1830's onwards and although both races were equally militaristic when necessary, from a British perspective, the fact that the Boers were pursuing their own expansionist policy in the region, which might have a detrimental effect on Britain's own Imperial ambitions, inevitably led the British authorities to support the Zulu cause. However, when British forces moved to annexe the Transvaal in 1877, instead of continuing their support for the Zulus, British representatives were reported to have ignored the demands of the Zulu king Cetshwayo, preferring instead to pacify the local Boer settlers, much to the annoyance of the Zulu peoples.

British representatives in the Transvaal and Natal, many of whom were reported to be personally antagonistic to the rule of the Zulu king Cetshwayo, were thought to have deliberately misrepresented a number of minor incidents that had occurred in and around the borders of the Zulu homeland. Although each of the incidents themselves were thought to have been internal matters for the Zulu people alone, the fact that the agreed borders, between the Zulu homeland and the British held territories of Transvaal and Natal had been crossed by Zulu warriors, who subsequently seized a number of their own native tribesmen, was said to have become the basis for a full scale diplomatic incident. Seemingly determined to provoke a conflict between the Zulu people and the British military, these same European representatives were then thought to have made sure that Cetshwayo was presented with a series of demands that he could and would not meet, thereby setting the stage for an armed conflict between the two sides. However, many of the British demands being made on Cetshwayo and his people, did not have the authority of the British Parliament back in London, but had been deliberately engineered by local administrators who were largely following their own personal agendas, which tended to paint the Zulu's as both troublesome and uncivilised. Despite Cetshwayo only being given the British demands on 11th December 1878, by January of the following year, a regular military force under the command of Lord Chelmsford was readying itself to cross the border into the Zulu homeland, without the permission of the British government, thereby setting in motion the First Anglo-Zulu War. Chelmsford's mixed force, which was reported to have included contingents of both English and native troops, of which, some ten thousand men, were to be broken down into three distinct forces which would then meet up to attack the Zulu capital at Ulundi. An additional five thousand troops were also said to have been assigned to defend the borders of neighbouring Natal, as well as other British interests in the area, although these forces were not intended to be employed in the main military assault on the Zulu kingdom itself.

Ready to meet any incoming British force, Cetshwayo was reported to have had some forty thousand Zulu warriors to defend his kingdom, although initially the planned incursion, led by Lord Chelmsford, was said to have been largely ignored by these native tribesmen. The British commander and his main force of an estimated four thousand troops, along with their associated supply train, were said to have made first for the small missionary station at Rorke's Drift in Natal, before crossing the border into the Zulu homelands and moving on to the isolated hilltop of Isandlwana, where the column was due to rest. Surprisingly perhaps, Chelmsford was reported to have failed to order camp defences to be raised, ostensibly because of the time involved in preparing such positions, although in reality the failure was undoubtedly due to his own mistaken belief that the Zulu's could not present a real enough threat to his well armed military force, an assumption that he would later have cause to regret. On the morning of 22nd January 1879, Chelmsford then committed his second great mistake, when he split his forces once again, riding out with just over half of his troops to look for the main Zulu army, at the same time leaving the remainder of his column, including his supply train, at Isandlwana, where they were commanded by one of his staff officers. Later that same morning, a contingent of native Natal cavalry, along with a rocket battery and under the command of a Colonel Anthony Durnford, were reported to have arrived at Isandlwana to support Chelmsford's forces, but finding the British commander away from the camp, made plans to attack the Zulu force that Durnford knew was approaching their position.

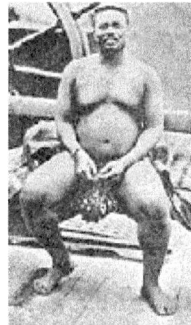

Cetshwayo **Anthony Durnford** **Henry Pulleine**

The main Zulu army meanwhile were reported to have completely outmanoeuvred the British forces, sending out diversionary units and scouts to both distract and monitor their enemy, whilst at the same time moving their main force of some twenty thousand Zulu warriors to a point where they might choose to engage Lord Chelmsford's main force. However, when the Zulu's army was accidentally discovered by British military scouts on the morning of the 22nd January, Zulu commanders immediately mobilised their huge native forces and moved them against the British positions at Isandlwana. Adopting the typical fighting form of a buffalo, with its head and encircling horns, the Zulu army began to move towards the British positions, who had by this time been warned by the retreating scouts of the danger that was rapidly approaching them. The British officer left in charge of the camp, Lt Colonel Henry Pulleine, immediately placed his regular British troops, six companies of the 2nd Warwickshire Regiment, armed with the latest Martini Henry rifles, in a position to meet the main part of the Zulu advance, the buffalo's head. Elsewhere both Pulleine and Durnford were said to have placed their remaining native troops in defensive positions, to help protect the camp itself and at the same time prevent the flanks of the regular British troops from being exposed to Zulu attack. The field artillery, comprising two cannons and the rocket battery that Durnford had brought with him that morning, were both initially employed with some success against the massing Zulu ranks, although the rocket's position, which was deliberately located away from the main body of the British forces, was reportedly later overrun, as the Zulu warriors began to press forward towards the British lines.

As the battle raged, the heavily outnumbered British forces were reported to have put up stiff resistance to the seemingly endless ranks of Zulu warriors who were attacking their lines, with the regular troops of the Warwickshire Regiment reportedly defending the camp with great valour and steadfastness. Elsewhere though, some of the native troops, who had less effective weapons and limited ammunition, began to desert their positions, eager to escape the field before they were completely overwhelmed by the Zulu hordes. With these defensive flanks becoming increasingly fragmented through injury, death and desertion, Pulleine was said to have been left with little choice but to order his regular British troops to make an orderly fighting retreat back into the main body of the camp, allowing the Zulu's flanking forces to push forward and begin encircling the whole British column. According to later reporters and modern day historians, the final hours of Chelmsford's forces at Isandlwana were thought to have been marked by a series of individual stands by the British forces and their native support troops. Massing together into several defensives positions, when their ammunition was expended, then fierce hand-to-hand fighting was said to have taken place between the two sides, until finally the remaining British troops were inextricably beaten down by the apparently inexhaustible ranks of the Zulu warriors.

Out of a total force of an estimated two thousand men at Isandlwana, only a few hundred survived, most of who were from the Natal native contingent, along with a handful of British officers who reportedly escaped being killed in the carnage, simply because their uniforms incorrectly identified them as civilians, rather than as combatants. As the battle at Isandlwana came to its inevitable end, a four thousand strong contingent of the Zulu army was said to have been detached to chase down any survivors and engage any other British forces that they might encounter, which they did at the isolated mission post at Rorke's Drift. Manned by around one hundred and thirty-nine British troops, who were supported by a small number of native auxiliaries, the commander at Rorke's Drift, Lieutenant John Chard, of the Royal Engineers, had been sent to the mission station, ostensibly to repair a pontoon bridge that crossed the Buffalo River. However, on the afternoon of the 22nd January, two native survivors of the Isandlwana disaster were thought to have arrived at Rorke's Drift and informed Chard of the impending arrival of the four thousand strong Zulu army, which was bearing down on his position. Quickly realising that a retreat from the area would be both foolish and unachievable, Chard and his fellow officers ultimately decided to reinforce their position and defend the station as best as they could, until such time as help arrived. Beginning at around five o'clock in the afternoon of the 22nd January 1879, the highly immortalised defence of Rorke's Drift was said to have begun, which although part of a much bigger military disaster, later became renowned as a place where British military discipline and valour, overcame insurmountable odds. Regarded as one of the foremost military defences of Britain's long and eventful martial history, the fact that between them, the defenders of Rorke's Drift were subsequently awarded eleven Victoria Crosses, along with a number of other bravery awards, is now regarded by some historians as an entirely inaccurate reflection of the events that actually transpired that day.

Rather than being given in response to the perceived victory at Rorke's Drift and the undoubted bravery of the eleven men who were subsequently awarded the Victoria Cross, the awarding of so many medals for a single action was later regarded as a deliberate act of misdirection by the military authorities, in the person of Lord Chelmsford and the British government, both of who were eager to distract the general public's attention away from the fiasco that had occurred at Isandlwana. Indeed, even a number of leading army officers at the time publicly criticised the granting of the awards, claiming that the garrison at Rorke's Drift had only remained there, not through duty, but simply because they had nowhere else to go. Had they chosen to flee the mission station, in all probability, they would have been pursued and cut down by the fast moving Zulu column, so their decision to remain within a potentially defensive position, required little in the way of bravery, but only a modicum of commonsense. In fact, many of the details of the battle of Rorke's Drift were thought to have been deliberately misrepresented by the authorities, probably in an attempt to mitigate the British defeat at Isandlwana and to publicly undermine the obvious military abilities of the Zulu warriors themselves. Interestingly, some later reports of the action at Rorke's Drift were thought to have mentioned that many thousands of Zulu's were killed by the valiant British defenders, whereas in reality only a few hundred native warriors were thought to have been killed or wounded during the ten hour assault on the station. Additionally, the fact that some several hundred wounded and captured Zulu's were deliberately massacred by British forces after the fighting was over, undoubtedly helped to swell the reported numbers of native warriors, who had violently assailed the walls of the British held compound, inadvertently becoming part of the legend that almost inevitably grew up around this particular engagement.

The man who was thought to have been directly responsible for this first illegal British incursion into the Zulu homelands was Sir Henry Bartle Frere, a career diplomat and administrator, who had received his training at the British East India Company in England. Initially employed as a civil servant in Bombay during the 1830's, he quickly progressed through the ranks of the British led administration in India and by 1850 he had been appointed as Chief Commissioner of Sindh Province, during which he was reported to have helped suppress the Great Indian Mutiny by sending troops into the Punjab. As a result of his actions there, in 1859 he was appointed as a member of the British Viceroy's Council and three years later was given the post of Governor of Bombay. Returning to England in 1867, Bartle Frere was subsequently appointed as a member of the Council of India, the advisory committee charged with the overall administration of the subcontinent, which advised the then British Secretary of State for India. In 1872 he was sent to North Africa, initially to help negotiate treaties with various Arab leaders that would help suppress the slave trade there. However, within five years he had been transferred to the south of the continent, where he was appointed as the British High Commissioner for South Africa by Lord Caernarfon, the man who had previously negotiated the confederation of Canada and who wanted to introduce a similar political union in the south of the African continent. Unfortunately for Caernarfon and Frere, there was said to be a great deal of political resistance to their plans for a federated South Africa, most notably from local politicians within Cape Colony itself, although Frere simply dismissed the locally elected politicians and appointed another British administrator to form a ministry, effectively circumventing any further political resistance. At the same time, Frere was also thought to be involved in the suppression of several regional disputes, one of which involved the native Xhosa people of the Transkei, where Frere employed both regular British troops and native auxiliaries to bring the area under Britain's immediate control.

It was thought to be in pursuit of his much larger objective, the confederation of South Africa that Frere decided to issue the Zulu leader Cetshwayo with his set of impossible demands in December 1878, in the full expectation that the Zulu leader would refuse them, allowing Frere and the British government to forcibly annexe the Zulu homelands. Rather oddly though, despite the fiasco at Isandlwana in January 1879 and calls from the British Parliament for him to be recalled from South Africa, Frere was said to have been simply censured by the British government, but allowed to remain in place nonetheless. Elsewhere in South Africa, the immediate problem of the Zulu homelands was said to have distracted Frere from other issues that were beginning to threaten his hopes for a single South African Confederation, most notably the Boers of the Transvaal, who were becoming more and more resentful of the British governments interference in their native lands. Although he was able to initially address the Boer leadership's main concerns about the future of their homelands, by 1880 these same concerns, allied to a growing frustration amongst the Boers generally, finally resulted in armed conflict between British farmers and the Boers own local militias. Seemingly underestimating the local peoples military abilities once again, the Boers subsequently inflicted severe military defeats on the British at several locations, which not only led to the formal establishment of an independent Boer Republic, but also the end of Lord Caernarfon's and Frere's dreams of a federated South Africa. In response to these events, other native tribes were said to rebelled against earlier legislation introduced by Frere, which prevented them from carrying arms and at the same time the Xhosa people of the Transkei revolted once again, bringing an unhappy and unsettled end to Frere's time in South Africa, as he was subsequently recalled by the new Liberal Prime Minister, William Gladstone, in August 1880.

Despite their military victory at Isandlwana in January 1879, the Zulu king, Cetshwayo, was said to have instinctively realised that the British would react to their military defeat, by simply returning with a bigger, much stronger force than before and one that his warriors would not be able to beat so easily. According to some sources, the Zulu army's greatest mistake had been to avoid crushing the entire British military expedition in the first place, rather than just settling for the defeat of the forces at Isandlwana. It has been suggested that the twenty four thousand strong Zulu "impi" (army), sent out by Cetshwayo could quite easily have overcome all of the British forces sent against his homeland by Frere, including the mobile force under the command of Lord Chelmsford, which only numbered some two and a half thousand men, who were lightly armed and with few provisions. It has been argued that had the Zulu Impi completely destroyed this force, then it might have given the British authorities cause to reconsider their whole approach to the Zulu people, forcing them to negotiate a settlement, which had been Cetshwayo's ultimate aim and preferred option. However, his failure to impose such a crushing defeat on British forces, allowing Chelmsford to simply withdraw and reinforce his shattered military forces, ultimately resulted in Cetshwayo's own demise, when Chelmsford returned in July 1879. Having been reinforced with regular troops from Britain and bringing with him a large number of cannon, cavalry and even the brand new Gatlin gun, the twenty five thousand strong British force that Chelmsford brought to Cetshwayo's royal kraal at Ulundi in July 1879 finally brought an end to the independence and the military power of the Zulu nation forever. What made this particular result even more tragic for those Zulu's that survived the destruction of their historic homelands was the later failure of Lord Caernarfon's and Bartle Frere's planned confederation of South Africa, the very reason for their illegal and clearly ill-thought out invasion of the Zulu homeland's in the first place.

In the year following the destruction of Cetshwayo's royal kraal and the suppression of the Zulu nation, British forces were said to have become involved in yet another armed dispute, this time with the Boers, the white African peoples whose forebears had first settled Cape Colony. For much of the 19th century and with increasing expansion by Britain and other disparate European settlers, the Boers homeland, known as the Transvaal, was thought to have become increasingly threatened by these various interests, so when Britain annexed the region in 1877, it created an enormous amount of bitterness and resentment within the native Boer community. Arguing that previous agreements and treaties had been violated by the British authorities, the Boer leadership initially tried to negotiate for their own independent homeland, but with their interests conflicting somewhat with Britain's policies in South Africa, it soon became clear that very little would be achieved through negotiation. The conflict that would later become known as the First Boer War was reported to have begun in December 1880 when the Boers unilaterally declared their independence from British control of southern Africa. In response to this announcement, the British authorities were said to have sent troop reinforcements to Pretoria, the Boer capital of the Transvaal, ostensibly to head off any form of armed revolt in the region. However, these troop reinforcements were said to have been intercepted by Boer militia, who ordered them to withdraw from the Transvaal and when they refused, the Boers opened fire, killing and wounding most of the British troops, including the convoy's commander, a Lt Colonel Anstruther, who died shortly after ordering the remainder of his troops to surrender to the Boers. With hostilities having officially begun, the Boer leadership then set about besieging or capturing the small number of British military bases that were located throughout the Transvaal, which were reported to have been garrisoned by a couple of thousand British regular and irregular troops at most.

In response to the Boer attacks on their forces, the British authorities were said to have authorised a Major General Pomeroy Colley to take control of the situation, but rather than wait for more regular troops to arrive, Colley was reported to have assembled a mixed force of foot soldiers and cavalry to help him relieve the besieged British bases. Unfortunately for this highly experienced British commander, the Boer militia who were opposing him were both skilled horsemen and sharpshooters, who had developed their skills fighting the indigenous tribes of southern Africa, including the fearsome Zulus, so were thought to have been more than a match for the irregular force that Colley had brought into the Transvaal. Within a matter of days the two forces were reported to have met one another in the Drakensberg Mountains, where Colley's forces attempted to break through the Boer positions which were barring their way to the besieged British garrisons, an action that resulted in Colley's forces being utterly decimated by volley, after volley of highly accurate Boer rifle fire. His force of some five hundred British troops having been reduced by a third, Colley was left with little option but to withdraw his remaining forces until such time as reinforcements might arrive to help his situation. The next day however, Colley was reported to have mistakenly decided to escort a convoy to Newcastle in Natal Province, ostensibly to keep his lines of supply open, but possibly to find reinforcements for his now depleted force. Unfortunately for Colley, the Boers decided to intercept him and his men as they accompanied the convoy, with a reported force of some three hundred Boers ambushing Colley and his troops close to the Ingogo River, killing and wounding around half of the British forces and forcing them once again to retire to their previous positions.

Lieutenant John Chard　　　　　　　Henry Bartle Frere　　　　　　　Lord Caernarfon

A week later, a ceasefire was thought to have been called between the two sides, to see if a peaceful solution could be found, during which time Colley's promised reinforcements were said to have arrived, helping to strengthen his own military position. When he heard that Britain was considering some form of conciliation towards the Boers, Colley reportedly took it upon himself to move his troops closer towards the Boer defensive positions overnight, occupying a knoll known as Majuba Hill, which overlooked the Boer lines. When daylight broke and the Boers realised that their positions were now under threat they were reported to have moved towards the bottom of Majuba Hill and using the natural cover of the land, began to advance on Colley and his troops. Using their knowledge of the local terrain, as well as their often superior marksmanship, before long the Boers too, were at the top of Majuba Hill, fighting directly with the British troops and through sheer weight of numbers forcing them to abandon their hilltop positions. A number of the British soldiers reportedly fell to their deaths during the struggle, with Major General Colley being the most high profile casualty within the British ranks. This defeat by the Boers was thought to have had such an impact on the British troops that in later conflicts with the same enemy, the cry "Remember Majuba" was often used to rally Britain's military forces. As it turned out though, Colley's unauthorised decision to occupy Majuba Hill actually achieved very little in the greater scheme of things, as the British and Boer leaderships later agreed a permanent settlement, based on the same terms which had been offered before Colley set foot on Majuba Hill, meaning that his death and those of his men were a complete and utter waste of time, in terms of actually achieving anything worthwhile.

Despite the Boers and British reaching some form of mutual agreement in 1881 to end the conflict known as the First Anglo-Boer War, almost inevitably events transpired to undo the treaty which had been made between the two sides. The first of these was thought to be the discovery of gold deposits in the Transvaal in 1886, which resulted in many thousands of foreign prospectors invading the Boer homelands, ostensibly to make their fortunes in the newly discovered goldfields, but inevitably putting pressure on the local Boer population, who very quickly found themselves outnumbered by the unregulated waves of foreigners. In order to prevent their republic being exploited and dominated by these large numbers of outsiders, in 1896 the Boer authorities in the Transvaal began to impose certain restrictions on the foreign migrants, insisting on a period of residency before mining rights were granted and levying high taxes on those foreign mining companies which had established themselves in the Boer Republic. Deeply resentful of these restrictions and their lack of representation in the Boer administration, before long a number of foreign businessmen and community leaders began to call for change, but when these demands were ignored by the Boer leadership, they very quickly began to plot for an armed solution to their problems. The British governor of Cape Colony, Cecil Rhodes, himself a wealthy mine owner and staunch British imperialist, was said to have conceived the idea of uniting the two independent Boer homelands, the Transvaal and the Orange Free State, into a single confederated state that would be controlled by Britain. However, Rhodes' imperial fervour was also reportedly tempered by his own commercial ambitions, with the highly lucrative Boer goldmines thought to be the main target of the greedy British industrialist, who was said to have set about trying to foment rebellion within the Boer homelands, using its resentful foreign migrants as a catalyst for his planned seizure of the Boer's gold and mineral deposits.

As part of his plans for a proposed Boer federation, Rhodes was thought to have organised an armed military force, which would invade the Transvaal from neighbouring Rhodesia, in support of a revolt initiated by the foreign workers who were based in the Boer homeland. Unfortunately for Rhodes and his commercial cohorts however, their plans were almost immediately called into question by the obvious reluctance of the migrant leadership in the Transvaal to participate in a highly illegal uprising and an outbreak of personal differences between the various ringleaders there. In the meantime, the mercenary force, paid for by Rhodes, but led by one Leander Starr Jameson, an employee within Rhodes' own trading company, was reported to have stationed themselves on the border of the Boer homeland, anxiously awaiting the foreign workers leadership in the Transvaal to decide whether or not they should incite a full scale revolt in the region. The basis of the planned invasion of the Transvaal, was said to have called for the foreign workers in and around the capital of Pretoria to rise up in revolt and to seize the local munitions depot in the city, in response to which, Jameson and his mercenary force would then cross the border, primarily to help restore law and order in the region. With the city under their control and with the aid of the rebellious foreign workers, Jameson and his forces would then go one to secure the valuable goldfields of the Transvaal, which could then be brought under the control of Rhodes and his commercial allies. However, this rather simple plan began to unravel almost immediately, when the leaders of the foreign workers failed to agree a common strategy, leaving Jameson and his men isolated on the Rhodesian border, unsure of what was going to happen next. Obviously not a patient man, finally in frustration, Jameson was reported to have unilaterally decided to complete his part of the plan, in the belief that his affirmative actions might somehow prompt the foreign workers in Pretoria to revolt. Informing his employer, Cecil Rhodes, of his intentions, Jameson's men then cut the local telegraph lines, preventing any recall of his forces and on the following day, 29th December 1895, he and his men crossed the border and invaded the Transvaal.

Perhaps indicative of the poor planning and amateurism of the entire enterprise, Jameson's decision to inform Rhodes of his planned action by telegraph ultimately proved to be his own undoing, as the Boer authorities were quickly advised of the operation and sent their own military units into the border area, waiting for the mercenary forces to cross. However, rather than engage the heavily armed force immediately, the Boer commandos were reported to have simply shadowed Jameson and his men until they were ready to intercept them, which they eventually did three days later. Although the mercenary forces survived the ambush, they were thought to have suffered sufficient losses to make them divert around the well prepared Boer positions, although even then, they were still followed by Boer observers who helped the authorities ready their defences to repulse Jameson's column. The second and final engagement between the Boers and Jameson's raiders was said to have taken place on the 2nd January at Doornkop, when Boer artillery effectively decimated the mercenary troops, forcing Jameson and his surviving men to surrender their arms and equipment, before being taken back to Pretoria as prisoners. Although much of the blame for this supposedly unauthorised raid into the Boer homeland was placed on Rhodes, Jameson and a number of other high profile administrators and individuals, according to some historians, the real architect of the scheme was said to have been Joseph Chamberlain, the British Colonial Secretary, who was known to be an avid supporter of British Colonialism and Imperialism. Despite publicly condemning the Jameson Raid itself, which was an illegal act, Chamberlain was said to have used the purported unequal treatment of the Transvaal's foreign migrants, who were mostly British, as grounds for creating a rift between Britain and the Boer homelands. With negotiations over and matters having failed to be resolved, in September 1899, Chamberlain was said to have issued the Boers a final demand, insisting that foreign workers in the Transvaal be given equal rights to native Boers, which their President, Paul Kruger, refused to do. Kruger subsequently called for all British forces to be withdrawn from the borders of the Boer homelands of the Transvaal and the Orange Free State, stating that a failure to do so would result in these two Boer states officially declaring war on Britain and its allies, which ultimately resulted in the outbreak of the Second Anglo-Boer War.

This second military conflict between the hereditary Dutch settlers and the British Empire, which is more commonly referred to as the Boer War, was initially marked by a number of military successes for the Boer commando units, who crossed the borders into both neighbouring Natal and Cape Colony, both of which were British held territories, where they managed to besiege the British garrisons of Ladysmith, Mafeking and Kimberley. In response to these incursions, British forces in southern Africa attempted to launch relief missions to each of these bases, but were soundly defeated by the Boers, who once again employed their fast moving commando tactics to attack the much slower British columns. All three sieges reportedly began during October 1899, with Boer forces isolating the British bases through the use of carefully prepared positions outside of their defences, employing both artillery and sniper fire to reduce the garrison manpower and undermine the defenders willingness to fight. Almost inevitably, shortages of food, fresh water and outbreaks of disease were reported to have further reduced each of these British garrisons, with Ladysmith being besieged for a total of 118 days, Mafeking for 217 days and Kimberley for 124 days. It was only following the arrival of additional regular troops, from both Britain and India that all of these bases were finally relieved in the first few months of 1900, allowing British forces to be consolidated, before they crossed the borders into the Boer homelands of the Transvaal and the Orange Free State. Despite the Transvaal's capital, Pretoria, being captured by June 1900, the native Boer forces were said to have continued their campaigns against the occupying British forces, once again employing the highly successful guerrilla tactics that had served them so well in the past. For most of the next two years, local Boer commandos were reported to have raided along the British supply lines, attacking trains, storage depots, troop columns and telegraph lines in an effort to disrupt and undermine Britain's control of their Boer homelands. Finally though, the British military commander, Lord Kitchener, in his determination to bring an end to the ongoing guerrilla campaign, was said to have initiated a scorched earth campaign, relocating the families and friends of the commandos from their farmsteads, burning and destroying their crops, as well as removing their livestock, all in an effort to deprive the Boer fighters of their support and sustenance.

Even though the wholesale destruction of the Boers homesteads, crops and sometimes livestock was deemed to be extreme by most independent reporters, it was the relocation of their wives and children to generally more secure, but often unsuitable locations that almost inevitably led to a public outcry over their treatment. Commonly referred to as "concentration camps", by those historians who already have a pre-determined view of the subject, there is a deliberate tendency to link these 19th century camps to the ones established by the Nazi authorities during World War II, which is not only blatantly unfair, but is completely absurd. Although nobody would doubt that the widespread employment of a scorched earth policy against the Boers and their families, by British commanders on the ground, was a highly questionable strategy to begin with, it seems to be widely accepted that ultimately it did achieve its principal aim, of ending the Boer commandos resistance to the British military occupation of their homeland. As to whether or not, the British invasion of the Transvaal and the Orange Free State was entirely justified, will always be a matter of debate and in all probability will remain so in the future. However, as for the resettlement camps, prisons or concentration camps, call them what you will, most independent reporters of the subject have a generally more balanced view of them. In common with most national conflicts, the largely innocent civil population of the land which is being fought over will undoubtedly suffer as a direct result of the fighting that takes place in and around them. As has previously been noted, there are numerous instances of civilians being driven off their lands and subsequently used as a weapon between two warring sides, both of whom refuse to take responsibility for the feeding and security of these non-combatants, for fear that would drain their own meagre resources, or otherwise slow down their military progress. In the Second Anglo-Boer War itself, there are suggestions that both the British and Boer forces refused to care for the landless and starving civilians, who were a result of their mutually harsh military objectives, both sides fearing that their own limited resources and necessary mobility would be adversely affected by accepting them into their care. It should also be remembered perhaps that British commanders were faced with a stark choice; either leave the Boer's rural communities intact and have them remain as a source of succour and supply for the native Dutch commandos, who would continue to raid, or simply destroy these potential bases and force the Boer fighters into submission.

Pomeroy Colley　　　　　Cecil Rhodes　　　　　Leander Starr Jameson

According to most sources, many of the estimated fifty or so camps established by the British authorities in both the Transvaal and in the Orange Free State were crudely built affairs, constructed in the most rudimentary fashion, in completely the wrong locations and lacking many of the basic facilities that would be required by their inhabitants. However, these camps were not built over an extended period of time, neither were they intended to offer any sort of permanent living accommodations for those that were incarcerated within them. For the most part they are described as being very similar to the refugee camps that have become a common sight in our own modern world, with poor sanitation, limited food supplies and with the people there, living in general squalor, susceptible to each and every communicable disease that was brought into the centre. Measles, typhoid, diphtheria and even scurvy were reported to be common ailments amongst most of the camps, passing from one susceptible person to another, as food and water supplies became limited or polluted over the course of time. Seasonal changes, many native to the African continent, including drought and flood, were all thought to have conspired to limit supplies of necessary foodstuffs, with the country's heat and cold, causing certain foods to spoil, all of which made the care of the Boer internees even more difficult. Some modern estimates of the numbers of Boers who died in these British internment camps, suggest that some twenty six thousand men, women and children perished during their confinement in various centres, a significant figure, regardless of the general circumstances. However, most contemporary reports from the time, suggest that most of these deaths were caused by largely preventable causes, including poor hygiene, outbreaks of disease and shortages of suitable nutrition. Initially, almost all of the camps had been built and run by the military authorities, who had little interest in, or knowledge of, running refugee centres, especially those that would be largely inhabited by women and children. It is probably also true to say that the British authorities of the time, as they do today, willingly embrace a culture of "make do and mend", which dictates that no money should be spent, until it is absolutely necessary. This seems to have been the case in South Africa, where policy and expenditure were both primarily aimed at achieving the political and military annexation of the Boer homelands of the Transvaal and the Orange Free State, rather than caring for the physical, medical and nutritional needs of their native peoples.

It was only when independent auditors and reporters began to make a political issue about the poor treatment and living conditions of the Boer civilian population that the British government in London began to take note of the problem. Much of the campaign to alert the British authorities to the impending civilian catastrophe in South Africa, was said to have been driven by Emily Hobhouse, a largely unknown spinster from England, who had become concerned about the fate of South Africa's women and children during the war and who had travelled to the continent, specially to visit the British refugee centres that had been established there. Completely appalled by the unsanitary conditions and the loss of life brought on by disease and poor nutrition, Emily was said to have returned to England with her own report on the camps, determined to improve conditions for those that were living there. By contacting the press, holding public meetings and petitioning various members of Parliament, her campaign very quickly gained momentum in Britain, with the government forced to act in the face of increasing public outrage. It is also worth pointing out; that it was during this part of Emily's humanitarian campaign that the highly emotive use of words like "extermination" were first used, not by Emily or her supporters, but by opposition politicians such as David Lloyd George, who were obviously eager to embarrass the government at each and every opportunity, so the use of highly emotive language inevitably became part of the ongoing political debate. Clearly though, the very use of such inflammatory language helped to harden attitudes on both sides, with the British and even foreign press, eager to uncover stories of the hardships and inhumane treatment suffered by the captive Boer population at the hands of the British authorities. Before long, stories of tragic loss and personal suffering, along with occasional pictures of skeletal internees, wracked by illness, found their way around the world, confirming the worst fears of those who were inherently antagonistic towards Imperial rule in the first place and outraging many who took such evidence at its face value. In reality, most of these stories and even some of the pictures were only part of a much larger story, with personal grievances, petty disputes and hidden antipathies, all contriving to help distort a wholly unplanned human catastrophe. Of course there were thought to be any number of incidents of callous indifference, unprofessional behaviour and even sheer incompetence by individual British administrators, but that does not mean that there was ever any sort centralised or systemic plan to hurt, let alone exterminate, the Boer people as a race.

According to some sources, of the twenty six thousand deaths which occurred in these British refugee camps, some 80% of them, around twenty thousand were thought to have been avoidable, had the authorities planned more carefully for their construction and future administration. A lack of planning in respect of their sanitation, healthcare, staffing, food supplies and administrative support, all combined to make them unsuccessful in the first instance, leading to high death rates amongst the refugee population. However, once resources, human, financial and logistical began to be invested in these camps, so the death rates were said to have plummeted, becoming lower in fact than those in many of Britain's biggest cities. Regardless of these earlier mistakes though and all that has been written about the Second Anglo-Boer War, Kitchener's scorched earth policy eventually proved to be a successful military strategy, in his conflict with the Boers, one that finally starved the local commando units into submission and to the negotiating table. Finally, it is also worth noting that the public outrage caused by the initially poor running of these camps, ultimately helped to secure the Boer people far greater concessions after the war, than might normally have been expected in any other conflict. In May 1902 the British and Boer leadership finally signed the Treaty of Vereeniging, which saw the two former Boer Republics in the Transvaal and Orange Free State absorbed into the British Empire. However, because of international and even British public indignation over the failure of the refugee camp system, which had cost so many unnecessary deaths, the British government was compelled to offer the Boer peoples significant concessions as part of the final agreement, as well as financial reparations for the damage caused to their homes and properties. Granted a fair degree of autonomy by the British state, ultimately this would lead to the formation of the Union of South Africa in 1910. Interestingly, a number of hard line Boer fighters continued to refuse to fully recognise the Anglo-Boer Peace Treaty and remained opposed to Britain for the remainder of their lives, later helping to form the South African National Party, who continued to wield significant political power and influence right through to the 1990's, at a time when the country was dominated by the now largely discredited Apartheid system.

One of the most influential, colourful and divisive figures in Britain's involvement in Africa during the late 19th and early 20th centuries was undoubtedly Cecil Rhodes, an English businessman, mine owner and politician, who was not only an ardent and vociferous Imperialist, but the man who also went on to found the former British colonies of North and South Rhodesia, which are known today as the modern states of Zambia and Zimbabwe. Born in July 1853 at Bishop's Stortford in England in Hertfordshire, Rhodes was reported to have been sent to Natal when he was a youngster, because of his sickly nature, his parents believing that the African climate would be beneficial to his health. Even at a comparatively young age, he was thought to be highly astute, establishing his own fruit business while still a teenager and later travelling to the newly discovered diamond fields at Kimberley when he was still only eighteen years old, to stake his own claim there. Two years later, Rhodes was thought to have returned to Britain to complete his education at Oxford, although his South African interests continued to occupy his mind, with further investments being made in new fields, including those on land occupied be the De Beer family. During the second half of the 1870's Rhodes and his business partners were said to have been occupied with the development and exploitation of these new diamond claims, as well as consolidating the South African diamond industry generally, which resulted in the formal establishment of the De Beers Mining Company in March 1880. With his financial future largely secured, Rhodes was then reported to have turned his attention to South African politics, recognising perhaps that executive power might well offer him the opportunity to extend his own personal influence, not only over the mining industry, but over the whole region generally. Entering public life as a representative in the Cape Parliament in 1880, Rhodes was and remained a staunch advocate of British expansionism, despite being elected to office by a largely Boer dominated electorate. In 1890 he was reported to have become the Prime Minister of the Cape colony and immediately set about introducing legislation and local statutes that directly benefited the South African mining industry and its investors, including local ordinances which allowed native Black Africans to be evicted from their homelands to make way for new industrial developments. It was also during his tenure as the First Minister of the Cape that Rhodes became involved in the planning and financing of the infamous Jameson Raid, a planned mercenary attack on the independent Boer Republic of the Transvaal, which not only cost Rhodes his position as Prime Minister of Cape Colony, but very nearly cost a number of his friends their very lives, as well as precipitating two subsequent African conflicts, including the Second Anglo-Boer War.

Even while he was involved in the politics of the Cape Colony itself, Rhodes continued to exert his own personal commercial influence elsewhere in the region, much of which with the expressed intent of increasing the power and wealth of his own company interests. In most cases, Rhodes or his local agents would try and arrange local mining agreements with the local tribal leaders, often without first explaining the full implications of the treaty that they were agreeing to. However, once the agreement had been signed, Rhodes could confidently expect to receive the full political and if necessary, military support of the local British authorities, if the local chief suddenly decided to renege on the previously signed agreement. Although this sort of creeping, commercially driven Imperialism was thought to have been frowned upon by many, from the British government's point of view there were few downsides to this type of expansionism, as it not only increased Britain's own sphere of influence, but required little in the way of financial outlay and more importantly, prevented their European competitors from gaining a foothold in the region. For many of the native African tribes however, Rhodes' habit of deliberately misrepresenting the terms of these agreements, often proved to be very costly, as they subsequently found their lands being occupied by increasing numbers of white Europeans, who in turn, brought greater development and industrialisation. As the mines and their associated buildings, communication systems and settlements grew ever bigger and began to spread beyond the limits of the previously agreed territories, so the native peoples commonly rebelled against further losses of their native homelands, which inevitably led to armed conflict between the two sides.

On the basis of such agreements, often gained through deliberately misleading the local native leadership, Rhodes was able to gain approval from the British government to set up his British South Africa Company in 1889, a commercial venture dedicated to the control, security and exploitation of Central Africa. It was this company, under Rhodes' instruction and with one of these agreements in hand that was said to have sent the first white settlers into the region that was known as Mashonaland, a part of what would later become the state of Rhodesia. Arriving in 1890, these first white settlers were reported to have founded their capital at Fort Salisbury, which today is known as Harare, the capital of the modern state of Zimbabwe, resulting in both the Mashonaland and Matabeleland regions being declared as British protectorates in 1891. Following this formal annexation of the territories by the British authorities in Africa, Rhodes and his associates then used the ongoing tribal disputes between the native Ndebele and Shona peoples as an excuse for attacking the Ndebele Kingdom, which was then ruled over by the native chief, Lobengula, the same man who had agreed to give Rhodes' company the rights to mine minerals in the country in the first place. The first military engagement between the British and the native tribesmen of the region was reported to have taken place in November 1893, when a British column, composed of some seven hundred British troops and native auxiliaries was attacked by a force of some two thousand native warriors, mostly armed with spears and rifles. Forming their wagons into a laager, a defensive ring, the British troops, who were armed with an assortment of weaponry, including modern rifles, field artillery and a number of Maxim guns, were reported to have quickly decimated the native ranks, forcing them to break off their attack. Even though Lobengula had a large native army, estimated at around ninety thousand warriors, he immediately recognised its limitations against a well equipped European force and having been informed that a British South African Police force, under the command of Leander Starr Jameson was on its way to his tribal capital of Bulawayo, Lobengula chose to withdraw, rather than face Jameson and his troops. However, before he left, the African chief ensured that there would be little left for the British forces to seize, ordering that his ammunition stores and anything else of value was blown up before Jameson and his men arrived in Bulawayo. With much of his capital being built of wood, the resulting explosion was said to have started numerous fires that burnt much of the tribal capital to the ground, leaving the British forces with little left to capture.

Despite his decision to withdraw from his tribal capital however, Lobengula did manage to achieve a small but notable victory over his enemy a few weeks later at the Shangani River. Pursued by a comparatively small unit of some thirty-odd British South African Police and their scouts, commanded by a Major Allan Wilson, Lobengula and his tribesmen were reported to have crossed the Shangani River and set up their camp. Wilson's small group of pursuers also managed to cross the river, before sending back three men to inform the larger British force of their location and to request reinforcements. Unfortunately for Wilson and his remaining troopers, having sent these three men back across the river, the Shangani River then rose during the night, effectively stranding them from any British reinforcements and leaving them at the mercy of the Ndebele king and his warriors, who were now aware of their presence. In the battle that followed, Wilson and his small band of British South African Policemen were reported to have put up a valiant defence to the mass of warriors who attacked their position, although all of them were subsequently killed as a result of the native assault. For later white European settlers in Rhodesia, the loss of the famed Shangani Patrol was said to have become their own version of the much more famous Custer's Last Stand, where a small number of predominantly white soldiers were said to have put up a valiant defence against an overwhelming number of native warriors. Eventually though, the Ndebele people were compelled to surrender to British authority in 1894, both by superior British weaponry and the ill-timed loss of their leader, Lobengula, who was thought to have died in rather mysterious circumstances in the same year. However, despite the British South Africa Company gaining control over the region, questions began to be asked in the British parliament over the company's involvement in the outbreak of the war, with some sources suggesting that Rhodes and his confederates had deliberately engineered the conflict for their own financial ends.

Joseph Chamberlain

Paul Kruger

Emily Hobhouse

With the country now largely under the British company's control and with its main shareholder having been so actively involved in the annexation of the region, the former native tribal homelands of Mashonaland and Matabeleland's were given the new title of Rhodesia in May 1895. Within a comparatively period, thousands of new white European settlers began to arrive in these new British controlled territories, building their own settlements in the former Ndebele capital of Bulawayo and introducing many hundreds of gold prospectors into the Shona homelands, all of whom were eager to exploit the natural resources of the land. Unfortunately for most of them, the anticipated riches of these native goldfields were thought to have been greatly exaggerated, leaving many of these early settlers with little option, but to look for alternative means of supporting themselves, which most eventually did through farming. Around the same time, the country was also divided into two separate and distinct areas, Northern Rhodesia being adopted in 1895, later becoming Zambia; and Southern Rhodesia simply becoming Rhodesia in 1898, later becoming Zimbabwe in the latter part of the 20th century. Although much of the country had been pacified following the death of Lobengula and the suppression of the Ndebele peoples through the use of modern western weaponry, dissent still existed within many regions of the new

Rhodesia, even by the beginning of 1896. The spiritual leader of the Ndebele tribe, a man called Mlimo, was said to have begun to foment revolution amongst both the Shona and Ndebele tribes, convincing them that the white European settlers were the cause of a number of natural catastrophes, including a plague of locusts, a lengthy drought and an outbreak of disease among the local native cattle herds that were affecting large parts of the country at the time. Luckily for the rebel leader, his calls for the African tribes to revolt against the European invaders was thought to have occurred around the same time that Rhodes, Jameson and the British South Africa Company forces were distracted by their own attempts to usurp the legitimate government of the Boer republics in the Transvaal and the Orange Free State.

Unfortunately, Mlimo's plans for a widespread and highly organised rebellion were thought have been undone by the premature actions of a number of his younger supporters, who took it upon themselves to begin the revolt, without their spiritual leader's approval or knowledge. Initially they began raiding throughout their own local areas, attacking and killing a number of white farmers and prospectors, as well as a local native policeman, whose deaths were said to have caused great alarm within the wider European community. Several thousand Ndebele warriors, along with a small number native police officers were thought to have joined Mlimo's revolt, arming themselves with a variety of weapons, including spears, clubs and axes, as well as single shot and repeater rifles. As they terrorized the local countryside, more Ndebele and Shona warriors were reported to have joined their force, driving more and more of the local European settlers and prospectors towards the settlement of Bulawayo, attacking and killing those who were too slow to avoid their general advance. Some several hundred white settlers were reported to have been killed in the tribal homelands of Matabeleland and Mashonaland, with dozens of farms, settlements, ranches and mines systematically destroyed as Mlimo's native army pushed the white Europeans further backward to their main settlements and towns. With significant numbers of British South Africa Company troops already involved with the abortive and illegal invasion of the Transvaal, the white settlers were more or less left to their own devices to try and protect themselves as best as they could. For those that managed to make their way to Bulawayo, the main priority was to defend the rebuilt tribal capital as best as they could, turning the town into one great laager, or defensive circuit, which could protect the settlers from the massing native army outside. According to some reports, every sort of conceivable defensive measure was used to protect the settlement, including dynamite, burning oil and broken glass, as well as the more conventional artillery pieces, rifles and machine guns that the inhabitants of Bulawayo had managed to lay their hands on. However, the experience of the First Matabele War and the loss of so many of their warriors to the British Maxim guns, was said to have had a deterrent effect on Mlimo's native army, who did not attempt to storm the laager at Bulawayo, but simply contented themselves with conducting raids in and around the well defended enclosure. Unfortunately for the native army though, none of their leaders, or indeed any of their warriors had thought to cut the telegraph lines leading in and out of Bulawayo, allowing the besieged settlers to send messages for help to the regional authorities. Although the relief forces that were despatched by both Rhodes and the British authorities, took some weeks to travel across Africa to the isolated settlement of Bulawayo, eventually they arrived in the region towards the end of May 1896 and immediately set about dispersing the rebel native forces, as well as relieving the township itself.

The Ndebele and Shona warriors, who had previously been besieging Bulawayo, were said to have fallen back into the Matobo Hills overlooking the settlement and began a guerrilla war with the British forces that had begun patrolling the area, conducting hit and run attacks on those columns which were foolish enough to enter their area of control. Perhaps realising that the native tribesmen would continue to rebel, as long as their spiritual leader, Mlimo, remained alive or at liberty, the authorities requested the American born scout Frederick Russell Burnham and local commissioner, Bonnar Armstrong to find Mlimo and either kill or capture him. Having received information from a local native informant, the two men were reported to have ridden into the Matobo Hills and made their way to the rebel leader's hideout and waited for him to return. When Mlimo did finally return to his cave, he was said to have been accompanied by a large number of his warriors, preventing Burnham and Armstrong from capturing him, so instead Burnham shot and killed him instead. Fleeing for their lives, they were said to have managed to avoid being caught by the incensed native warriors and made their way back to Bulawayo to inform the British commander, General Carrington; that Mlimo was indeed dead. However, despite the death of their spiritual leader, the combined Ndebele and Shona forces refused to disperse and continued to represent a threat to the region, although following Mlimo's assassination they were thought to have remained in their hilltop positions, only occasionally conducting raids against the local European settlers below. Even though the danger had largely passed, when Rhodes himself arrived at Bulawayo and was told about Mlimo's death, he proceeded to make his way up to the rebel army's main encampment unarmed and persuaded the majority of the warriors to lay down their arms and to return to their homes. Although this action effectively brought an end to the native resistance in the Matabele homeland, rebellion in the neighbouring Mashonaland was reported to have continued for some time afterwards, only finally being resolved when General Carrington took his regular army into the region and suppressed the rebellion by force of arms.

Rhodes ultimately became the Englishman most closely associated with Britain's involvement in the African continent, doing much to help create the modern day state of South Africa, which has become one of the most successful nations on the African continent. When he died in 1902, aged 48, he was reported to have been one of the wealthiest men in the world, with much of his fortune having been made by exploiting the human and mineral resources of Africa, often at a direct cost to its native peoples. Although there is little doubt that his legacy is still celebrated in certain parts of the continent today, through the likes of the Rhodes scholarship, Rhodes University and the various gardens and parks which he bequeathed to the South African people, in other parts of modern day Africa he remains the epitome of British suppression and imperialism. The suppression of Rhodes' legacy is no more obvious than in the modern day states of Zambia and Zimbabwe, which were formerly known as Northern and Southern Rhodesia respectively. Together with the territories known as Nyasaland, now called Malawi, these three territories eventually became individual British protectorates until 1953 when they were amalgamated to form the Federation of Rhodesia and Nyasaland. In 1964, all three states were reported to have been granted their independence by the British authorities, becoming Rhodesia, the Republic of Zambia and the Republic of Malawi. The only change to have occurred since that time was the renaming of Rhodesia in 1980, following the advent of majority rule in the country, which then became known as Zimbabwe.

British interests in Malawi were reported to have begun in the latter part of the 19th century, when Scottish missionaries and traders began to establish themselves in the region, founding various churches and the African Lakes Company, all of which helped to encourage further British settlement in the area. In order to formalise national relations between the British government and the local tribal leaders, in 1883 the region was newly designated as the British Central African Protectorate, effectively associating these new territories with its nearest colonial neighbour, Northern Rhodesia. In 1907 the British Central African Protectorate was renamed as the Nyasaland Protectorate, the name "Nyasa" being the Swahili word for Lake and in recognition of the regions ownership of the great inland body of water known as Lake Nyasa, now designated as Lake Malawi. Calls for independence were thought to have emerged during the early 1950's when the region was amalgamated with North and South Rhodesia to form the Federation of Rhodesia and Nyasaland. Although these calls ultimately failed to achieve little in the short term, other than to cause a number of the country's leading nationalist figures to be jailed for their activities, by the early 1960's Britain was actively encouraging nationalist aspirations within its various overseas territories, including Nyasaland. The most prominent nationalist figure in Nyasaland was thought to have been Dr Hastings Kamuzu Banda, a European trained physician, who had initially worked in Ghana, before being persuaded to return to his homeland to help lead the nationalist cause there in 1958. Becoming the leader of the Nyasaland Congress Party in the same year, Banda was originally jailed by the British authorities for his political activities, before being released in 1960 to help draft a new constitution for the country, which was a precursor to the native Africans taking control of the protectorates legislative council. By 1961, Banda's renamed Malawi Congress Party was said to have won a majority of the seats in the country's legislative council elections and two years later Banda became the first elected African Prime Minister of Nyasaland. Achieving its formal independence from Great Britain in July 1964, the country was subsequently renamed Malawi and by 1970 the country had become a single party state, run by Banda's Malawi Congress Party and with the former doctor holding office as President for life. For much of the next thirty years Banda was reported to have suppressed virtually all political opposition in his country, using whatever methods were necessary to extinguish any competition to his rule. He was also reported to have taken over much of the control of the country's fairly limited economy, using his own businesses to develop Malawi's fairly poor agricultural and industrial base, to the point where they became significant contributors to the country's overall economic performance. By 1993 and despite having ruled over a single party state for nearly thirty years, Banda and his Congress Party colleagues were eventually persuaded to grant their people additional political freedom, by allowing them to vote in a national referendum, which would bring multi party democracy back to Malawi for the first time in nearly thirty years. Following changes to the country's constitution, which essentially brought an end to Malawi's single party state, in 1994 the country was thought to have held its first democratic elections and since that time has continued to develop into a relatively stable African democracy, although it remains as one of the least economically developed countries in Africa.

Lord Kitchener

Lobengula

Major Allan Wilson

As previously mentioned, the modern day neighbouring state of Zambia emerged from the former British protectorate of Northern Rhodesia, which was formally adopted by Britain in April 1924, with Herbert Stanley being appointed as its first governor. Before that time, the territories had been operated as the separate administrative districts of Northwest and Northeast Rhodesia, both of which were controlled as charter colonies by the British South African Company, the commercial enterprise, created by Cecil Rhodes, ostensibly to exploit the natural resources of central Africa. He was reported to have first been granted possession of the territories that later became Northwest and Northeast Rhodesia in 1891, with both regions remaining associated with, but separate from one another until 1911, when the British South African Company chose to merge their two charter colonies into one, renaming the newly created colony as Northern Rhodesia, a designation it retained until 1964, when the independent African nation of Zambia was created. Surprisingly perhaps, given that these new territories had been placed under the control of Rhodes' highly exploitative British South African Company, which had a reputation for developing any sort of natural resource, very little was said to have been invested in these new northern possessions. Instead, it appears that the corporation simply employed both northern regions as sources for much needed manpower and agricultural production, but was not regarded as suitable regions for investment, or indeed for white settlement. As a consequence of this clear divide, between the poorer northern territories and the more affluent southern ones, when the company tried to unify the two regions in 1916, the plans were vehemently opposed by most southern white settlers, who baulked at the idea of having to bear the financial cost of supporting their poorer, generally black African neighbours. It was said to be as a result of this decision that the British South African Company began talks with the British government, which it was hoped would lead to these largely unwanted northern territories being formally adopted by the British Crown as a protectorate, thereby removing the South African Company's responsibilities for them. These talks ultimately led to Northern Rhodesia being adopted as a British protectorate in April 1924, with Herbert Stanley appointed as its first governor, but not before the South Africa Company had ensured that it retained any mineral rights to the region, as part of the final agreement.

Although copper reserves were known to have been found in Northern Rhodesia as early as 1895 and were subsequently mined by the British South African Company during their tenancy of the region, no large scale exploitation of these reserves had been undertaken, largely because of the company's reluctance to invest large amounts of money in the region. However, after the British Crown agreed to adopt the region as a protectorate and with their mining concessions guaranteed, the South African Company simply agreed terms with a number of international mining companies, who would then exploit the regions copper reserves and share the subsequent profits with the company and their investors. Between 1925 and 1931 the copper mining industry in Northern Rhodesia was said to have boomed, bringing a great deal of investment, development and modernisation to the region and even with a downturn in trade in 1931, these new mining interests still managed to produce a profit, albeit less significant than before.

In the region generally, a large number of white Europeans were thought to have migrated to Northern Rhodesia, attracted by the opportunities offered by the new copper boom, although the native peoples of the British held territories were also said to have benefited from the development of this new cash generating industry. However, unlike Southern Rhodesia, where the British South African Company and its mainly white settler communities still generally held control, in the north, the British colonial authorities were anxious to ensure that the rights and wishes of the black African majority took precedence over everything else. This idea was vehemently opposed by many of the white investors within Northern Rhodesia, who were thought to have used their influence in the British parliament to block any future moves towards greater African influence in the protectorate. As it turned out however, it was thought to have been the British government itself that caused the greatest dissent amongst the black African community, when they arbitrarily raised the level of the local Poll Tax in Northern Rhodesia, ostensibly to off-set the losses caused by those workers who had deliberately defaulted on the levy. Incensed by the disproportionate increase, a majority of the workers in the regions copper mines went out on strike to protest against the new tax, bringing much of the highly lucrative business to a complete standstill. Eager to guard against any sort of large scale demonstrations, the British authorities were reported to have brought in troops to protect the mines and in May 1935, soldiers attempting to disperse a large crowd of workers, lost control of the situation and opened fire on the workers, killing six of them and wounding many more. Although the strike was suspended following these completely unnecessary deaths, more importantly the event brought about the establishment of African councils throughout the region, which acted as arbitration and advisory bodies in disputes between the mine owners and their workers, allowing issues to be settled, where possible, in the most equitable and amicable manner. As these sorts of courts spread throughout the country, they were said to have evolved into rural and urban African councils, bodies that were often used to address issues and relieve tensions between the often conflicted white and black communities which existed within the various territories.

Unsurprisingly perhaps, given Northern Rhodesia's successful economy and subsequent development as a direct result of its buoyant copper industry, the subject of amalgamating the two Rhodesian territories, north and south, was once again revisited in 1936 by a number of the regions largely white politicians. However, in 1939 a Royal Commission set up by the British government, although sympathetic to the idea in principal, rejected the proposal, possibly because of the unsettled political situation in Europe, which was plunged into war some few months later, with Rhodesian copper reserves proving to be a vital resource in helping to win the war for the allied forces. It was thought to be during this worldwide conflict and in the immediate post way years that African nationalism in Northern Rhodesia began to emerge, initially as federated welfare societies, which eventually evolved into the Northern Rhodesia Congress, under the leadership of Godwin Lewanika, reportedly a native African aristocrat. At the same time that these welfare societies were beginning to emerge, the earlier regional African councils were also starting to amalgamate together, forming the African Representative Council, which became so influential in the country that two of its members were eventually invited to sit on the Northern Rhodesia's Legislative Council, the body that actually governed the colony. This direct native involvement in the running of the country was thought to have been added to by the post-war development of black African Trades Unions in Northern Rhodesia, which despite being opposed by many of the white settlers and mine owners, actually supported those political leaders who wanted to restrict the mining rights of the big conglomerates which were exploiting the country's mineral deposits for their own ends. Increasingly alarmed by the emerging power of the Black African majority in Northern Rhodesia, the still politically dominant white minority in the country, once again allied themselves with their fellow settlers in Southern Rhodesia and Nyasaland to reawaken the proposal for an amalgamation of the three territories, the very same idea that had been rejected by the British authorities in 1939. However, this time the prevailing Labour administration in London, were thought to have found the idea of reducing their colonial liabilities to be much more attractive and as a result in 1949 began to hold multi party talks aimed at creating the Federation of Rhodesia and Nyasaland, a political union that was finally achieved in 1953. However, despite becoming a single entity, the three regions of this newly federated British protectorate continued to act as semi autonomous areas in their own right, a situation that almost inevitably led to their later evolution as independent nation states. In part, this was said to have been caused by the decision of the British government to adopt a policy supported by most of the white minority communities in each of the separate countries, but one that was opposed by a majority of the individual Black African communities who lived there. As a result there was a continuous growth in the numbers of native peoples supporting the cause of Black Nationalism, a desire for independence that occasionally led to conflict between the white and black communities in both Northern and Southern Rhodesia, as well as in Nyasaland.

With increasing Black African involvement in each of the territory's legislative assemblies, so the inclination to secede from the British made Federation of Rhodesia and Nyasaland increased, to the point that in December 1963, the African dominated legislative assembly in Northern Rhodesia formally seceded from the union, essentially bringing an end to the political agreement. In January 1964, the people of Northern Rhodesia elected Kenneth Kaunda, leader of the country's United National Independence Party, as their Prime Minister for the first and only time, as later the same year, Kaunda redrafted the country's constitution and renamed Northern Rhodesia as Zambia, as well as declaring himself as its new President. Despite having achieved black majority rule and gained access to his country's highly lucrative mining industries, the new President quickly realised that the white minority community in Zambia remained a vital part of his nation's future economic and political development, so he was careful to avoid alienating them. Elsewhere though, his African nationalist sympathies were a little more evident and in the following years he was reported to have been an active supporter of the African National Congress in South Africa, the UNITA movement in Angola and the African People's Union in neighbouring Rhodesia. It was thought to be his support for these groups and in particular the Zimbabwe's African People's Union, who were fighting the white minority government of Rhodesia, which eventually brought him into direct conflict with his immediate neighbour.

The political, economic and military upheavals of the 1970's were reported to have been added to by a general downturn in the worldwide demand for copper, Zambia's main export, which resulted in the country becoming increasingly dependent on foreign aid, a situation that inevitably had a disastrous effect on the living standards of most Zambians. Although subsequent decades would bring resolution to many of the African nationalist conflicts that Kaunda had personally supported, thereby improving his own country's economic situation, the years of struggle for his people and a growing recognition of his failure to deliver real benefits for the country, led to demands for political change. During the late 1980's and early 1990's saw a resurgence of political opposition to Kaunda and his party, which despite his best efforts, refused to be bowed by intimidation or physical oppression. Having faced at least one potential coup in 1990, in the following year Kaunda authorised the reinstatement of multi party elections in Zambia and a new President, Frederick Chiluba, leader of the Movement for Multi Party Democracy, was elected to serve, holding the office from 1991 to 2002. He in turn was said to have been followed by Levy Mwanawasa, a highly skilled and well liked political figure who gained international praise for his handling of the country's economic problems, as well as his vocal opposition to the methods employed by the Zimbabwean President Robert Mugabe, who was re-elected to his office despite clear evidence of widespread vote rigging and intimidation of his political opponents. Completing one successful term of office in 2006, after which he was re-elected President, Mwanawasa reportedly then fell ill as the result of a stroke in 2008 and was temporarily replaced by Rupiah Banda, who subsequently won new elections in 2008 and continues to hold the office of President today.

The third and final member of Britain's 1953 Federation of Rhodesia and Nyasaland, which was formally dissolved in 1964, was the territory of Southern Rhodesia which later became more commonly known as Rhodesia, although today is generally identified as Zimbabwe. The history of this former British colony, which lies immediately north of and adjoining the modern day Republic of South Africa, was and continues to be at the very centre of the continuing debate over the European colonisation of the African continent during the 19th and 20th centuries. For many of Africa's leading nationalist supporters, modern day Zimbabwe and its highly controversial leader, Robert Mugabe, represent an independent nation state that has successfully freed itself from its colonial and imperial past, becoming instead a leading light in the ongoing battle for future African prosperity and individual empowerment. However, for many in the international community, modern day Zimbabwe and its President actually represent a betrayal of African nationalism, pointing to the almost complete collapse of the country's economic, social and political systems that has occurred since Robert Mugabe and his ZANU-PF party took control of the country in 1980.

The territories that later became Rhodesia were said to have been originally known as Southern Zambezia, principally because of their location, south of the Zambezi River, but from the 1890's onwards they were generally referred to as Rhodesia, in honour of the man who had first opened the territories up for European settlement and exploration, Cecil Rhodes. It was Rhodes, along with agents of his British South African Company, who were said to have negotiated the first concessions and treaties with King Lobengula of the native Ndebele people in 1888, which first allowed white migrants and miners to explore and settle these relatively unknown lands. As has previously been noted in the information relating to Rhodes himself, the deliberate distortion and misrepresentation of some of these treaties, ultimately allowed the British South African Company to receive a charter from Queen Victoria in 1889, which effectively annexed these new territories as a British protectorate, ruled over and controlled by Rhodes and his company agents. For much of the next decade, Rhodes, his British South African Company and the British authorities all became involved in a series of disputes and armed conflicts that have previously been noted, but which ultimately ended with the suppression of the native peoples and the establishment of a white minority administration that was specifically dedicated to the care of its European settler communities. By 1899 and with the insistence of the British authorities, the British South African Company had arranged for a legislative council to be established, to oversee the continuing development of the white settler communities and to provide oversight on the company's own industrial activities, even though in practice, the corporation actually remained in nominal control of the region anyway. However, as the white European communities continued to grow and diversify, so the demand for greater democratic accountability grew, leading to calls for the company's position as British administrator to be reviewed, a call that was further underpinned by a legal judgement expressed in the British Courts that lands not in legal ownership belonged to the British Crown and not the British South African Company, essentially making the Crown the largest landholder in the country and therefore responsible for its governance. By the start of the 1920's the white community in Rhodesia were said to have begun campaigning for responsible self government, which would bring an end to the rule of the British South Africa Company and that led to a referendum in 1922, which overwhelming came out in favour of self rule for the people of Southern Rhodesia. As a consequence of this decision, several members of the country's legislative council were said to have travelled to London in 1923 to request that the territories were granted the status of a self governing colony within the British Empire, a request that was subsequently granted by the British authorities, leading to Charles Patrick Coghlan becoming the first Premier of Southern Rhodesia in October 1923.

Frederick Burnham

Hastings Banda

Kenneth Kaunda

For much of the next thirty years Southern Rhodesia continued to expand and develop under the stewardship of the various elected representatives, with its economy, which was largely based on chrome and tobacco, variously expanding and contracting depending on the vagaries of the international markets. However, despite these occasional peaks and troughs the country continued to attract new European settlers, many of them drawn by the prospect of establishing themselves in the wide open spaces of the African plains and away from the desperate conditions in pre and post war Europe. However, in 1953 the British government reacting to increasing demands for African independence within many of its overseas colonies, decided to amalgamate the three adjoining territories of Nyasaland, Northern and Southern Rhodesia into a single federated body. The Central African Federation was said to have been created, in the hope that the three regions might eventually consolidate into a single political union, as had been the case in both Canada and South Africa, although this ultimately failed to happen. The Federation only lasted until the middle of 1964, when both Northern Rhodesia and Nyasaland seceded from the union and were subsequently granted independence by Great Britain, becoming the independent African states of Malawi (Nyasaland) in July 1964 and Zambia (Northern Rhodesia) in the following October. From the Southern Rhodesian's point of view, the end of the Central African Federation proved to be a mixed blessing, with its white minority government losing as much as it gained in terms of political, economic and military control. With both of its former northern federation partners becoming dominated by Black nationalist leaders, in the form of Kenneth Kaunda in Zambia and Dr Hastings Banda in Malawi, Rhodesia had now become a largely isolated frontline state, with only the apartheid South African government to the south, as its only real ally in the region. Although Britain had granted independence to both Northern Rhodesia and Nyasaland in 1964, this was largely on the basis of majority government being introduced into these former colonies, which was actually the case in Zambia and Malawi, where black majority rule was achieved, albeit in an initially undemocratic and dictatorial fashion. However, with Southern Rhodesia, no such undertakings regarding black majority rule were offered by the ruling white minority administration and in view of this refusal, the British government in London refused to grant any request for Rhodesian independence, leaving the white settlers there with little option, but to unilaterally declare itself independent of Britain on 11th November 1965. From an entirely British perspective, this act of UDI was regarded as being entirely illegitimate and although they took no direct action to regain control of the colony; neither did they support the white minority administration in the ongoing military conflicts that would beset the country for the next twenty-odd years.

Almost as soon as the then Rhodesian Prime Minister, Ian Smith, notified the British Labour government of its intention to declare itself independent of Britain, the authorities in London began a campaign to isolate Rhodesia from the rest of the international community, through the offices of the United Nations. As a result, the UN Security Council was reported to have imposed sanctions on the country, forbidding most types of trade and financial transactions with Rhodesia, in an attempt to force Ian Smith's white minority government to rescind its earlier decision. However, these restrictions and embargoes were not thought to have been universally adhered to, with countries such as South Africa, Portugal, Israel and a number of Arab states all continuing to trade with Rhodesia in one way or another, although mostly on terms favourable to themselves. Even the United States observance of the sanctions were thought to have been piecemeal, with products such as chrome and nickel being excluded from the terms of the trade embargo because of an amendment introduced by the American legislature. Such exceptions aside though, for much of the period between 1965 and 1979 Rhodesia's economic, industrial and military infrastructure was said to have been undermined by the refusal of the international community to fully recognise its white minority administration, or to trade with the country on an equal basis, if at all. Apart from the international isolation, Ian Smith's Rhodesia also faced military opposition from two separate nationalist guerrilla forces, ZANLA and ZIPRA, both of which were attached to their respective political parties, ZANU and ZAPU. ZANLA was the acronym for the Zimbabwe African National Liberation Army, which was the armed wing of the political party, the Zimbabwean African National Union, led by Robert Mugabe. ZIPRA was the acronym for the Zimbabwe People's Liberation Army, the military wing of Joshua Nkomo's Zimbabwe African People's Union. Although both party's were reportedly founded by different nationalist leaders, ZAPU was thought to have been established during the early 1960's, possibly as a direct result of the fragmentation of the politically inspired Central African Federation, which eventually led to the creation of the independent states of Malawi and Zambia. The first Black Nationalist guerrilla attacks in the latterly unrecognised state of Rhodesia were said to have occurred during the early 1960's, although they were often against isolated white owned farmsteads, rather than government or military targets. Large scale and organised attacks on the outcast Rhodesian administration by both ZANLA and ZIPRA guerrillas were only thought to have started during the early 1970's, ostensibly as a result of their gaining military and financial support from both China and the Soviet Union, who were said to have supplied both groups with money and increasingly sophisticated weaponry.

Initially, the generally well armed and well trained Rhodesian forces were able to contain much of the Black Nationalist's activities, although as the insurgency grew, so did the difficulties in trying to keep the country safe, especially for those settlers who had established themselves out in the Rhodesian countryside. As a result, the white authorities began to develop a network of defended settlements throughout the country, outposts where farmers and settlers could seek refuge and make a stand against the various nationalist insurgents who were reported to have drifted in and out of the country across the largely unprotected borders. It became commonplace for everyone within the minority white community of Rhodesia to learn how to use a gun and in most cases to carry one at all times, essentially reproducing the lives of the American pioneers who had settled the frontiers of the wild west some hundred and odd years before. Clearly though, with little logistical and military support from the international community, most of whom wanted a political settlement to the problem, the Rhodesian authorities were said to have come under increasing pressure to negotiate with the Black Nationalist parties, but Ian Smith and his ministers steadfastly refused. The situation was reported to have become even more severe in 1975, when Portugal finally gave up control of its Mozambique colony, having fought a bitter struggle to retain it, with yet another African Nationalist movement, FRELIMO, the Liberation Front of Mozambique, which was once again sponsored by both the Chinese and Soviet communist parties. When Mozambique eventually fell to the FRELIMO guerrillas though, it was thought to have removed the last relatively safe border for Rhodesia, save for that which linked them to the Republic of South Africa and as a result allowed both ZANU and ZAPU fighters to rest and train in the former Portuguese held territories. Surrounded by insurgents and with their economy, military forces and civilian populations under continuing threat, the conflict between the white population of Rhodesia and the Black Nationalist forces was said to have become increasingly bitter, with atrocities being committed by both side. Almost inevitably perhaps the human cost of the Bush War, as it became known, was thought to have been felt more acutely by the relatively small white population of Rhodesia, whose sons, daughters, fathers and mothers became legitimate targets in the nationalist's military campaign for Black majority rule. This was perhaps most graphically illustrated in the shooting down of Air Rhodesia flight 825 in September 1978, by ZIPRA insurgents using a surface to air missile. The aircraft, which was reported to have been on an internal flight, was severely damaged by the strike and crash landed in the African bush, with only eighteen of the fifty-six passengers onboard surviving the initial landing. A handful of the survivors managed to make it to a local village to search for help, but as they returned to the crash site they were said to have heard the sound of gunfire coming from the vicinity of the downed aircraft. It later transpired that a contingent of ZIPRA guerrillas had seen the aircraft come down and murdered ten of the survivors before looting the site. The head of ZAPU, the political wing of ZIPRA, Joshua Nkomo later admitted that his men had brought the aircraft down, but repudiated the charge that they had then murdered those passengers who had survived the crash. Nkomo's guerrillas were later reported to have repeated the act some five months later, when in February 1979, ZIPRA members using an SA-7 surface to air missile struck Air Rhodesia flight RH-827, causing it to explode in mid air and crash into the local countryside, killing all fifty nine people on board.

By the mid to late 1970's however, there was already a growing recognition within the Rhodesian minority government that some sort of settlement would have to be reached, although Ian Smith's administration were said to be reluctant to strike a deal with either of the two main nationalist parties that were involved in the guerrilla campaign. In 1976, both South Africa and the United States began to increase the diplomatic pressure on Rhodesia, with the white dominated government of South Africa deliberately reducing it logistical support to its northern ally, in an effort to force the Rhodesian administration's hand. Although Smith's government still retained a formidable array of offensive weapons and had a significant force of regular troops, police and paramilitary groups numbering around a quarter of a million people, much of its equipment was effective, but old, a result of the continuing sanctions being employed by the international community. Despite these limitations though, Rhodesia's armed forces still retained the capability to launch occasionally spectacular attacks against guerrilla bases in neighbouring countries, with Operation Dingo in November 1977, an attack on ZANLA bases in Mozambique, being one of the most effective during the entire conflict. Employing its ageing bombers, along with other aircraft and helicopters, a mixed Rhodesian force of paratroops and special operation units, totalling a few hundred men, were said to have attacked and destroyed two large ZANLA base at Chimoio and Tembue in Mozambique, killing an estimated three thousand guerrillas and wounding a further five thousand more. Suffering only one fatality and a handful of casualties, this Rhodesian raid was thought to have been one of the most spectacular military successes for the isolated Rhodesian state, although the claimed numbers of casualties on the ZANLA side remains a matter of debate even through to the present day.

Such occasional military successes apart though, the increasing pressures on the civilian population, as demonstrated by the shooting down of the two Rhodesian aircraft in 1978 and 1979, along with the subsequent murder of some of the first aircraft's surviving passengers, began to undermine the willingness of some of Rhodesia's white leadership to continue their opposition to black majority rule. As a consequence, Smith's government was said to have begun talks with a number of Rhodesia's black political leaders, who were not involved in the guerrilla campaign, negotiations which ultimately led to fresh national elections in April 1979, which saw the United African National Council Party, under the leadership of Bishop Abel Muzorewa, become the largest political party in the country and Muzorewa appointed as Rhodesia's first Black Prime Minister in June 1979. However, despite these moves towards majority rule and the formal recognition of the administration by the United States Senate, the fact that the two leading political groups, ZAPU and ZANU, were both excluded from the election, because of their continuing paramilitary campaigns, meant that a large section of the international community failed to see the election of Abel Muzorewa as entirely legitimate. Fortunately, or unfortunately, depending on one's view of subsequent events, the election of Margaret Thatcher, as Prime Minister of Britain, was reported to have brought fresh impetus to the search for a fair and equitable solution to the fourteen-year-old dispute. Inviting all of the parties to a peace conference, which was held at Lancaster House in London and chaired by Britain's Foreign Secretary, Lord Carrington, the British government attempted to arbitrate a lasting agreement that would offer both majority rule and much needed land reforms.

Eventually, after three months of talks, the Lancaster House Agreement was signed by all of the various interested parties, under the terms of which, Rhodesia's Unilateral Declaration of Independence would formally end, the country would temporarily return to its status as a British colony and new internationally supervised elections would be held in Rhodesia, with the previously excluded ZANU and ZAPU political parties standing for office as well. Taking place in early 1980's, these first free Rhodesian elections resulted in Robert Mugabe's ZANU party winning a majority of the vote, although many reports of the time suggest that this victory was largely achieved through violent attacks on and the intimidation of rival parties supporters. Despite such reports and continuing concerns over the veracity of the election results however, the British government and the international community generally accepted Mugabe's victory and welcomed his subsequent appointment as leader of Rhodesia, which was renamed as the independent Republic of Zimbabwe in April 1980. Within Zimbabwe itself, many within the often embittered white community were naturally cautious about the appointment of Robert Mugabe as their country's new political leader, with many thousands of them reportedly preparing to leave, almost as soon as the election results were announced. For Mugabe's fledgling ZANU administration, the potential exodus of thousands of Zimbabwe's white administrators, professional businessmen, farmers and other wealth generators would have been disastrous for his new nation's economy and for his own international reputation. Consequently he was forced to turn to his former adversary, Ian Smith, to try and persuade, not only the former white Prime Minister, but also the white community that they would be safe in the new Zimbabwe and that all of their rights offered by the Lancaster House Agreement would be guaranteed for the foreseeable future. However, despite such assurances, an estimated 60% of the white population of Zimbabwe reportedly left the country between 1980 and 1990, significantly damaging both the commercial and agricultural sections of the country's economy, a decline that has ultimately led to inflation rates as high as eleven million percent effectively making the national currency worthless. A major factor in this almost complete collapse of the Zimbabwean economy was reported to be the ZANU-PF's decision to involve itself in the war that erupted in the Democratic Republic of Congo between 1998 and 2002, which was estimated to have cost the Zimbabwean economy hundreds of millions of dollars that it simply could not afford.

Frederick Chiluba   **Charles Coghlan**   **Ian Smith**

Apart from the loss of the economically vital white settler colony, differences between the various ethnic groups within Zimbabwe have also played a part in helping to divide the country even further. Almost as soon as Robert Mugabe's ZANU party won the 1980 election, nationalist groups from within Matabeleland announced their opposition to his leadership, resulting in armed conflict between the two former guerrilla groups, ZANLA and ZIPRA, which are thought to have cost the lives of several hundred people and was only finally stopped by the intervention of regular troops. However, these initial outbreaks of violence were only thought to be a precursor of a much more murderous campaign which was undertaken by Robert Mugabe's infamous Fifth Brigade, who were said to have conducted a three year operation in the Matabeleland region, during which some twenty thousand opponents of his regime were massacred by this North Korean trained military unit. As a result of this campaign, the two opposing parties were reported to have agreed a truce, after which the ZANU party was renamed as ZANU-PF, the PF suffix being an acronym for the words Patriotic Front. In subsequent Zimbabwean national elections, held from 1990 onwards, the ZANU-PF party and its leader, Robert Mugabe have won a majority of the available seats, although in almost all cases the elections have been observed as being "neither free, nor fair", with violence and intimidation of opposition politicians and their supporters being regular occurrences. Aside from a serious decline in the living standards of the majority of the population, which has been marked by escalating food prices and non-payment of public service wages, the most high profile issue remains that of land distribution. These land reforms, which were a major election pledge by the Mugabe regime, have been handled so badly by the ruling administration that not only have they largely failed to deliver on the promise, but have also managed to destroy much of the agricultural sector of the country. Once hailed as the "bread basket" of southern Africa, today, Zimbabwe cannot even afford to feed it own population, but instead, relies on international aid to prevent its people from starving. Although nobody would dispute that the idea of 70% of the best arable land being in the hands of less than 1% of the population, who are predominantly white farmers, would be abhorrent to most civilised societies, so too is the idea that these lands should be forcibly seized by marauding gangs of government paid enforcers, who would rather see the lands lie fallow and unused, rather than it remain in highly productive and economically valuable white ownership. It also seems to have become common practice for former white owned farms to be turned over to leading members and supporters of the ZANU-PF party, including Robert Mugabe himself, who have little experience, or indeed interest, in using these sequestrated lands as productive farms, but rather as private retreats for themselves, their henchmen and their families. The most recent Zimbabwean elections, for both the office of President and Parliamentary seats were reportedly held in March 2008, which once again delivered what was widely accepted to be a flawed result, as a result of widespread ballot rigging and electoral fraud by the ZANU-PF party. However, despite their best efforts and possibly because of international observance, the outcome of the elections did not deliver a clear and outright winner, but did give an overwhelming mandate to the Movement for Democratic Change party, led by Morgan Tsvangirai. Unfortunately for the electorate of Zimbabwe however, the election result did not give Tsavangirai a sufficient share of the vote to finally displace Robert Mugabe, who chose to retain the post of President, although he agreed to his opponent being appointed as Prime Minister, ensuring beforehand that the post is relatively nominal and will not therefore deliver any real change to the country, or indeed threaten Mugabe's own position as President.

Elsewhere on the continent, British involvement in Africa was generally thought to have been divided into two other distinct spheres of influence, namely into British West Africa and British East Africa, both of which comprised individual colonies that later became sovereign nation states in their own right. On the west coast of Africa, the principal areas brought under British control, included Sierra Leone, Gambia, Ghana and parts of the present day Nigeria. On the other side of the African continent, to the east, British interests were said to have centred on the region of the modern day state of Kenya, although the region at the time also included parts of Uganda and the Great Rift Valley. England, later Britain was known to have had contact with Western Africa from as early as 1562, when the English adventurer and privateer, John Hawkins, was reported to have captured some three hundred black African slaves from a Portuguese slave ship and transported them across the Atlantic before selling them in the New World, thus beginning England's first involvement in that particularly odious trade. For the next one hundred and forty years Britain became increasingly involved in the Transatlantic Slave Trade, before becoming the principal agent behind the widespread suppression of the trade at the beginning of the 19th century. Significantly though, in 1787, Britain was also reported to have helped found one of its earliest formal settlements on the African continent, establishing a colony for those former Black slaves and servicemen, who had supported the British cause during the American Revolution. Initially, many of these men had left North America with the British, following the victory of the American colonists and their European allies, which had forced Britain to surrender its claims to the thirteen colonies of the later United States. However, for most of these black servicemen, Britain had little to offer, with most of their number only finding low paid work, abject poverty and discrimination on the streets of England's main cities, forcing them to rely on the charity of individual philanthropists, who used some of their great wealth to help the very poorest in society.

However, having recognised the plight of England's poorest black citizens, a number of leading white politicians, merchants and donors were said to have formulated a plan to establish a new British colony in Africa and help restore some of these former slaves to their hereditary homelands. Although it would be absurd to suggest that a desire to reduce the numbers of unemployed black beggars inhabiting the streets of England was a consideration for some, the fact that the first of these transports to West Africa also included white women and merchants would seem to indicate the sincerity of the planners. Intending to establish a free province for these mixed groups of settlers, the first ship was reported to have arrived off the coast of Sierra Leone in May 1787 and having disembarked, the colonists were thought to have immediately set about building their first colony. Unfortunately, this first batch of English settlers were said to have quickly fell prey to local diseases and the hostility of local tribesmen, who regarded the new migrants as a threat to their tribal homelands. However, later groups of settlers were thought to have fared a little better, after their new colonies were established in more suitable territories, where they could more properly defend themselves from possible attacks. Increasingly, as these new settlements became more established and successful, so they were said to have attracted greater numbers of new settlers, many of whom were black American slaves who had managed to escape their lives of drudgery and cruelty in the United States and make their way back to Africa. By 1799 the colonists in Sierra Leone were reported to be so well established and confident that they began to demand greater autonomy from the Sierra Leone Company, the corporate authority which had helped to found the second round of settlements in 1792. With the company refusing to allow individual settlers to own the rights to their own lands, most colonists were reported to have been uneasy about the fact that they could be dispossessed of the lands and properties, should the company choose to do so, a situation that almost inevitably led to conflict in 1799. The subsequent revolt was only finally suppressed with the arrival of some five hundred Jamaican Maroons, a group of runaway slaves, who were brought to Sierra Leone, via Nova Scotia, by the company a few months later. Eventually though, peace was finally restored and the British-led community continued to grow, with even more former slaves from the Americas arriving, each of them adding their own peculiar flavour to a social mix that would go on to become commonly known as Creole.

For much of its later existence from the end of the 18th century onwards, Sierra Leone was thought to have been a relatively peaceful place, save for the Hut Tax War of 1898, when the imposition of a tax on indigenous native dwellings was said to have caused armed conflict to arise in certain parts of the country. With limited military resources stationed in the region, the British authorities were reported to have initially struggled to suppress the revolt, resulting in significant numbers of people being killed, although the later capture and execution of many of the ringleaders ultimately brought a swift end to the rebellion. In later years the country remained generally calm and it was only in the 20th century, after independence from Britain that Sierra Leone began its slide into anarchy, with tribal and political divisions all helping to tear the country apart, resulting in several interventions by both African and United Nations peacekeeping forces. However, even these proved to be largely ineffective and it was only when British military forces entered the country, ostensibly to rescue a number of their own nationals that the British Prime Minister Tony Blair authorised the use of military force to restore order to the country, a move that was broadly welcomed by most of Sierra Leone's war weary population.

English involvement in the native African state of Ghana was thought to have originally begun in the mid 17th century, when British traders became interested in the gold deposits that were said to have existed there and as a result began referring to it as the "Gold Coast". Along with the French, who knew the same area "Cote d'Ivoire" or the "Ivory Coast", a number of Europe's leading trading nations, including the Portuguese, Spanish, Swedes, Danes and the Dutch were all reported to have established their own trading posts in the region, eager to exploit the vast natural resources of this particular part of the continent. However, it has also earned itself the epithet of the "White Man's Grave" due to the high incidents of the various native diseases, such as malaria, which led to the deaths and incapacity of many hundreds of foreign visitors. British domination of the region was reported to have begun after 1874, when the Dutch withdrew from the area, allowing Britain to declare the Gold Coast a protectorate, a claim to the region that was formally implemented in 1896 and lasted until Ghana gained independence in 1957. During this period of colonial rule, the British were thought to have fought four "wars" against the native Ashanti people, which became known as the Anglo-Ashanti Wars and that took place between 1823 and 1901. The first of the series of these conflicts was said to have erupted in 1823, when Brigadier General Sir Charles McCarthy, the Governor of West Africa, which included Sierra Leone and the Gold Coast (Ghana), refused to negotiate new borders with the Ashanti people, the hereditary rulers of the Gold Coast. Instead, McCarthy was reported to have organised a small expeditionary force, which he led into the tribal homelands, during which he was killed and his head taken as a trophy. Soon after, a second column of British troops which should have met up with McCarthy's original force was also attacked by the Ashanti tribesmen and was likewise destroyed, leaving a Major Laing to announce the news of the deaths to the British authorities. In the meantime, the victorious Ashanti tribesmen were reported to have overrun much of the surrounding region and its coastal area, before being stopped by an outbreak of disease within its own ranks, which prevented them from attacking any other neighbouring states. Despite British attempts though to fully engage the Ashanti forces in battle, it was only in 1826 that a well equipped British military column, armed with Congreve rockets, finally forced the Ashanti to withdraw away from the coast and back into their tribal homelands, after which a formal border was agreed between the two sides in 1831, thereby bringing an end to the dispute.

For the next thirty-odd years this earlier peace agreement was said to have held between the two sides, apart from a number of inter-tribal skirmishes that were regarded as being troublesome rather than serious breaches of the treaty. However, in 1863 the Ashanti were said to have sent a large armed party across the border in pursuit of a native fugitive, which resulted in fighting between the two sides and a number of deaths. The British governor was thought to have requested additional troops from England, but his application was initially declined by the authorities in London, who were reluctant to send troops until such time as they were actually required. As it turned out however, the local conditions proved equally hazardous to both the Ashanti warriors and the British troops, with each side losing more men to disease and sickness, than they did to enemy action, which eventually led to a military stalemate between the two adversaries. Nearly a decade later, the two sides were said to be at odds with one another again, this time over the disputed Gold Coast territories, formerly occupied by the Dutch, which Britain had previously purchased from their Western European neighbours. The region and in particular, the historic fort at Elmina, was subsequently claimed by the Ashanti, who having failed to secure the area through negotiation, chose to invade it and take possession by force. In response to this native incursion, Britain was reported to have assembled a force of some two and a half thousand regular troops and an equally large auxiliary force, which was put under the command of General Garnet Wolseley and despatched to the Gold Coast in 1873. Unlike previous campaigns, where British actions were said to have been largely unplanned and unreported, the notable Henry Morton Stanley, he of David Livingstone fame, was thought to have accompanied Wolseley and his troops, in order to report the war against the Ashanti. The campaign was also thought to be significant for the use of medical information that was given to the British troops to help reduce the incidents of sickness and disease, which had been so disastrous for earlier military expeditions. Having landed in the Gold Coast at the beginning of January 1873, in a little more than a month Wolseley was reported to have beaten the Ashanti in two separate battles and destroyed their tribal capital at Kumasi, after which they were forced to sign a fairly humbling peace treaty, which left them in a highly vulnerable military position. Although they were initially content to withdraw from the Ashanti homelands immediately after this third conflict, the British authorities soon realised that these tribal ands, including their rich deposits of gold, might now be susceptible to French and German overtures, a potential risk that the British were not prepared to take.

Robert Mugabe   Joshua NKomo   Abel Muzorewa

Having offered the Ashanti people the opportunity to become a British protectorate, which would neutralise any such future threat, this offer was refused, leaving the British authorities with little option but to impose the solution on the Ashanti. Using the excuse of fines and reparations, due after the third Anglo Ashanti War, having not been paid, Britain sent a second expeditionary force into the region in 1896, which eventually forced the tribal leadership to sign the protection treaty, before exiling them from their homelands forever. Although in normal circumstance that would have been the end of the matter, many of those Ashanti nobles, who had avoided being exiled by the British in the first place, later rebelled in what became known as the War of The Golden Stool, named after the historic throne of the Ashanti kings. Rather sadly however, once again they were defeated by the British forces and those found guilty of involvement in the rebellion were likewise exiled to the Seychelles, after which the Ashanti homelands were formally absorbed into the British Gold Coast territories in January 1902. Despite these less than friendly beginnings however, in subsequent years the relationship between Britain and the Ashanti people were said to have improved markedly, most notably when ceremonial control of Kumasi was finally returned to them in 1926 and the role of their tribal leader was reinstated in 1935. For much of the first half of the 20th century, the British Gold Coast, later renamed as Ghana, was governed by a British appointee, who in turn was advised by regional representatives and tribal councils. However, as Ghana's society improved, so a greater number of highly educated and extremely able Ghanaians began to mobilise into nationalist political groups who called for greater autonomy and more direct involvement in the government of their own country. As elsewhere though, independence would only finally be achieved in the second half of the 20th century, following the end of the Second World War, when British and international attitudes towards imperial control began to be questioned.

By the end of the 1940's a number of Ghana's leading public figures had begun to form their own democratic political parties, which garnered support from the large numbers of post war soldiers and professional workers who felt themselves perfectly capable of governing their own country. As a result of these growing demands for even more native independence, the British government began to devolve significantly more and more power to the people of Ghana, by appointing a fairer proportion of Ghanaians to the country's ruling Executive Council and other legislative bodies. In 1951 a new constitution was introduced, which allowed local politicians and nationalist leaders to stand for election as a nominal Prime Minister, a form of government that would eventually develop into the country's first formal Parliamentary system. By 1954, Ghana was being governed by a fully elected Legislative Assembly, headed by an elected Prime Minister, with only the country's defence and foreign affairs being determined by an appointed British governor. This form of staged independence was only finally brought to an end in 1956, when new national elections were held in Ghana in July of that year, with the intention of finding out if such a move was supported by a majority of the population. Some two thirds of the Ghanaian people were reported to have voted for independence parties, effectively ensuring that Ghana would finally become an independent democratic state, outside of British control, but linked through its Commonwealth of Nations. An addendum to Ghana's severing its historic ties with British rule was the decision over the future of the British and French protectorates of Togoland, which had been linked to the former Gold Coast protectorate since 1919. However, following a United Nations led referendum of the region, the majority of the inhabitants of British Togoland, who had historic tribal affiliations with the native peoples of Ghana, voted for union with their larger neighbour and were subsequently absorbed into that nation. Finally though, on the 6th March 1957, the Ghanaian Prime Minister, Kwame Nkruma, was able to announce to his people that Ghana was free forever, although for a significant part of the second half of the 20th century, the country was troubled by a number of military coups, at least one of which was reported to have been backed by the American intelligence services. Happily, since the early 1980's Ghana has returned to the democratic process and has since become one of the leaders of the African continent, a position that it continues to hold through to the modern day.

In common with a number of West African nations, the modern state of Gambia was said to have been visited by the Portuguese as early as the 15th and 16th centuries, ostensibly as a place of trade with the prevailing African Songhai Empire, who controlled the region at that time. However, by the second half of the 16th century, the power of this particular kingdom was reportedly beginning to wane and the Portuguese were able to exploit its decline to take overall control of the region. In 1588 though, a member of the Portuguese aristocracy was said to have sold the trading rights along the Gambia River to a group of English merchants, under a charter granted by the Tudor monarch, Elizabeth I. Her royal successor, James I, was said to have granted a second charter in 1618, allowing English merchants to trade in both Gambia and the Gold Coast, which latterly became Ghana. This arrangement was thought to have remained in place until 1651, when the region of Gambia was held and controlled by a European nobleman from the area of modern day Latvia, who held it in his possession until 1661, when Britain once again took the area back under its control. The most significant feature of the Gambian possession was the trading island, known by the previous European settlers as St Andrews Island, but renamed St James' Island by the British after 1661. Named after the Duke of York, who later became King James II, the fort that stood on the island was thought to have originally been built by Baltic traders who held the island from 1651 to 1661, who named it Fort Jacob, after Jacob Kettler, the Duke of Courland. After 1661, the fort was said to have been employed as a trading post by the English Royal Adventurers in Africa Company, which later evolved into the Royal African Company, as a centre for their trade in gold, ivory and finally slaves. By 1684 the Royal African Company was thought to have held complete control over the Gambia region, in terms of its trade and administration, although they reportedly lost possession of Fort James in 1695 to French forces, before they were restored in 1697. In fact, St James' Island reportedly changed hands several times during the late 17th and early 18th centuries, as the English, French, as well as local pirates all vied for control of the fortress, which had to be rebuilt several times as a consequence of these continuing disputes over its ownership. By the second half of the 18th century however, the island was once again under British control in the form of the Company of Merchants Trading in Africa, who not only held the trading fort, but also took over the administration of the entire region. Ironically perhaps, after 1816 the fortress was said to have been strengthened as a defence against those involved in the Transatlantic Slave Trade, which Britain had begun to suppress at the beginning of the 19th century.

An estimated three million black African slaves were thought to have been transported via the Gambia region over the period of some three hundred years, before the trade was finally outlawed by the British Empire, who employed significant elements of the Royal Navy to ensure compliance in West Africa. For much of the early part of the 19th century, Gambia was administered by the British authorities in Sierra Leone, but by 1888 it was thought to have become a colony in its own right, with its national boundaries being set in the following year. Just over a decade later, in 1901, Gambia was given its own legislative council, which marked the start of a staged program of increasing democratic change that would culminate in full independence being granted to the country in February 1965. Although in later years the country would be wracked by internal civil strife, which resulted in a number of military coups, at the present moment in time the Gambia does have an elected parliamentary government, which it is hoped will continue to offer a democratic choice to the inhabitants of the country. As Gambia is almost entirely surrounded by its much larger neighbour, the former French held territories of Senegal, it has often been hoped that some sort of confederation between the two countries might offer a solution to the problems affecting both nations. However, despite Britain having temporarily arranged a union between the two nations in the late 18th century, when it became known as British Senegambia, the two regions were later separated, with each returning to their respective British and French rulers. Since that time, a formal union, or political alliance has regularly been discussed by both countries, but as yet, no such agreement has been reached.

The final former British territory on the west coast of Africa is the modern day state of Nigeria, which is thought to be the partial result of the British mercantile organisation, the Royal Niger Company's involvement in this particular region of Africa. Principally the brainchild of a military engineer and civil administrator called George Taubman Goldie, who had first visited the area of the Niger River in 1877; he believed that British interests in Africa would be considerably enhanced by the inclusion of these largely unknown areas into Britain's Imperial possessions. Initially, Goldie set about trying to convince the British authorities in London to reinstate the idea of chartering a private mercantile company to act as a agent on behalf of the government, a system of control that had largely been discredited since the fall of the ill-fated British East India Company, which had previously ruled over much of the Indian subcontinent, with fairly catastrophic results. However, despite a general reluctance to adopt such a system again, Goldie continued on with his idea nonetheless, firstly by trying to consolidate all of the individual British commercial interests in the Niger region under one corporate body, a feat he achieved in 1879 when he founded the United African Company in that year. Two years later, he requested a formal trading charter from the British government of William Gladstone and despite a number of serious reservations and objections being raised by those opposed to the scheme; Goldie was able to provide surety enough for the authorities to grant him the necessary permissions. By 1884, the new United African Company had already established a number of trading posts along the Niger River and by the end of the same year Goldie and his associates had been able to buy out all of the other foreign traders in the region, leaving the British company in almost complete control of the entire River Niger waterway. At the same time that Goldie was securing the rights to the Niger's hinterland and its coastal ports, a number of the company's investors and agents were similarly securing trading agreements with the indigenous peoples of the region, essentially giving Goldie and his associates complete dominance over the regions entire trade resources. With all these things in place, the United African Company was then able to convince the British government to grant it its necessary charter, which resulted in the business being renamed as the Royal Niger Company in July 1886.

However, almost as soon as the new charter company had been established, its operations began to come under political and commercial pressure from some of its European competitors, most notable of which were the Germans, who were beginning to develop their own colonial interests there. Having gained trading rights in Chad, Cameroon and the lower Niger River basin, they regarded Goldie and the Royal Niger Company as a direct threat to their own colonial ambitions and commercial interests, so quickly began to foment trouble in the region in an attempt to hinder the British company's lucrative business operations, which ultimately resulted in a number of German representatives being arrested by the Royal Niger Company and expelled from the region, an action that outraged the German authorities back in Berlin. The main architect of Germany's colonial policies, Otto Von Bismarck, reportedly demanded that the British government compel the Royal Niger Company to surrender some of its territorial control, but Bismarck's later fall from office, effectively brought an end to the matter and in July 1890 a treaty was signed between Britain and Germany that brought a formal end to these territorial disputes. A much more significant danger to the company's trade were said to have been those posed by French colonial interests, who were already well established in the region of Congo and whose advance towards the borders of the Niger territories were thought to have been a cause of alarm for the Royal Niger Company. Despite signing a treaty with the British authorities in 1890, France was reported to have continued to foment trouble within the region and when a number of native Muslim Princes began to agitate along the Niger borders, Goldie was said to have taken a military force into their neighbouring kingdoms in 1897 and suppressed them by force. However, in the following year France once again initiated troubles along the borders, forcing the British government to intervene in the matter, which led to questions being asked about the Royal Africa Company's actual ability to protect such a valuable financial and territorial resource. With the charter company coming under regular pressure from state sponsored agencies in both France and Germany, the decision was eventually taken for the Royal Africa Company's assets to be purchased and taken over by the British state, an exchange that was formalised on the 1st January 1900, when the company's territories, along with a smaller protected coastal area were all merged together by the British authorities, to form the two protectorates of North and South Nigeria.

Morgan Tsvangarai   **Garnet Wolseley**   **Kwame Nkruma**

In 1914, the country was said to have been formally united as a single political and territorial entity, although the three distinct provinces of North and South Nigeria, as well Lagos were thought to have remained as entirely separate administrative regions, with individual differences being commonplace in each area. For most of the fourteen years, from 1900 to 1914, the British authorities employed the tried and tested formula of retaining regional, local and tribal government wherever possible, in an effort to minimise any disruption to the traditional methods of running the country. As elsewhere, local chiefs or noblemen were allowed to retain their authority, with British support, but with the proviso that certain essential British demands were met, including the ending of slavery and the acceptance of British rule and ownership over their native lands. For those who failed to accept or comply with such basic demands, then the local British representatives would generally organise their removal or detention, replacing them with another leader who took a much more pro-British approach. For the most part though, the majority of these District Officers were thought to have followed the orders and advice of the British High Commissioner, to interfere as little as possible with the native people's customs and traditions, but to ensure that British rules were generally followed. In 1916 though, the British Governor General, Frederick Lugard, established the Nigerian Council, a national consultative body which was composed of a number of the country's traditional leaders, to help represent the various parts of Nigeria. However, despite the intention for the council to be a method of unifying the country through common practice and legislation, it failed to achieve its main objective, largely because of Lugard's own personal habit of dictating issues, rather than discussing them. As a result, the three regions of Nigeria remained under the highly distinctive influences of their relevant Lieutenant Governors, as a result of which each of them progressed at different rates and in different ways, leading to divisions within the country itself. Despite these problems however, by the time that Lugard left his post of Governor General in 1918, Nigeria was reported to be one of the wealthiest, most commercially successful and settled British possessions in all of West Africa.

For much of the next forty years Nigeria continued to flourish commercially, although the tribal and regional differences previously hidden by British domination of the country were thought to have become more evident in the social and political development of Nigeria as the 20th century progressed. The most important event though, was reported to have occurred in 1956 when commercial deposits of oil were discovered in the Niger Delta, an event that has helped to fundamentally shape Nigeria since that time. Not only did the discovery of these oil reserves help to secure the country's financial future, but has also played a part in helping to exacerbate the rich-poor divide that has developed within modern day Nigeria, as well as damaging large parts of the country's coastal environment.

Full Nigerian independence was achieved on the 1st October 1960, after which the country became an independent parliamentary democracy, with power to determine its own defensive, foreign, fiscal and commercial policies for the first time in its modern history. In 1963 however, Nigeria declared itself a Republic, appointing its very own native President and setting in motion a series of events that would lead the country down the path to a bitter civil war. In January 1966 the first of a series of military coups, this one led by a small number of army officers from the native Igbo people, were reported to have assassinated the various regional leaders and overthrew the elected government. Within a matter of months these plotters too had been overthrown, although this second military junta were equally unsuccessful in restoring peace and stability to the country, especially after the massacre of thousands of Igbo citizens, had made the tribal divisions in the country even worse. In order to reduce these escalating ethnic tensions, the military government decided to divide the country into twelve semi-autonomous regions, which were intended to offer greater independence to the hereditary tribal areas, although this idea was largely rejected by those northern areas where the Igbo people dominated. In May 1967 a number of these northern states, under the leadership of Lieutenant Colonel Emeka Ojukwu, the military governor of the eastern region of Nigeria announced the secession of his region from the Nigerian Federation, declaring it as the newly formed Republic of Biafra and setting in motion the Nigerian Civil War, a conflict that would ultimately result in the deaths of more than a million Nigerian citizens, before the new Biafran Republic was militarily defeated in 1970. However, even after the war had finished and a united Nigeria had begun to rebuild its shattered infrastructure and society after the bitter conflict, by 1975 yet another military coup had swept the previous administration from power. This new junta, under the command of General Murtala Mohammed, set about ridding the country's civil service of the thousands of officials that he claimed were corrupt, replacing them with others, reportedly in preparation for new elections to be held in 1979.

Although General Mohammed was killed during yet another abortive military coup that was staged in 1976, new parliamentary elections were actually held in 1979, as a result of which a democratically elected civilian government was returned to the country for the first time in decades. Unfortunately, even this administration failed to survive for any length of time, as accusations of ballot-rigging and political corruption ended with the election results being challenged through the country's courts. Finally, with Nigeria's political system in tatters, the country's military once again stepped in to replace the elected civilian government and establish a ruling military council in its place. Its leader, Major General Muhammadu Buhari initially took over the government of the country, but in a little under two years he too had been replaced by another military officer, General Ibrahim Babingida, who promised the country fresh elections by 1990. Unsurprisingly, no such elections had been held, although yet another military coup had been attempted, leading to the execution of some sixty-odd officers who were tried by secret military tribunals. Though elections were eventually held in June 1993, even these proved to be problematic, with the unelected, General Ibrahim Babangida, annulling the results of the election, ostensibly because of some outstanding legal matters, but reportedly because the election failed to deliver the result he himself required. As a consequence of his decision, violence was said to have flared throughout the country and with little political or military support the General finally decided to appoint an interim government to run the country, until such time as new elections could be held. Unfortunately, even this decision could not prevent the social and economic turmoil within the country and with Nigeria facing an almost certain catastrophic collapse of its society and economy, it fell to the country's defence minister, Sani Abacha, to try and rescue the deteriorating situation. Rather sadly though, Abacha himself proved to be a highly ineffective leader, who replaced the regional civilian leadership with military officers and refused to lay out plans for future national elections, both of which measures helped to make the country's inhabitants even more desperate for change.

In response to Abacha's abject failure, both the international community and opposition leaders in Nigeria began to lobby hard for change, with the United States applying trade sanctions on the country and placing travel restrictions on many of the country's leaders and government officials, all of which were designed to increase pressure on the regime. Despite such measures though and the increasing levels of dissent within the country, Abacha's regime refused to hold fresh elections and took measures to crush any internal opposition from Nigeria's trade unions and political parties. A number of high profile labour leaders, opposition politicians and senior army officers were subsequently arrested, tried and executed, supposedly having been found guilty of plotting to overthrow Abacha's regime. His rule was only finally brought to an end in June 1998, when Abacha died from a sudden and fatal heart attack, leaving General Abdulsalami Abubakar to take over the reigns of power. Abubakar immediately ordered the release of many of the civilian political leaders imprisoned under Abacha's regime, setting in motion a return to the democratic process that had been missing for so long in Nigeria. Over the period of some several months, local, state, national and Presidential elections were all held in the country, which were contested by all of Nigeria's main political parties, representing most of the various ethnic groups within the country. In May 1999, Olusegun Obasanjo, a former military head of state, was elected as Nigeria's President, effectively bringing an end to fifteen years of consecutive military rule in the country, which by now was wracked by severe socio-economic problems that would take years to overcome. The new President immediately began to undo some of the corrupt practices that had been a feature of the preceding military regimes, by sacking corrupt officials, cancelling a number of contracts that were known to be questionable and attempting to recover the millions of dollars that had been hidden away in foreign bank accounts by certain military leaders and officials. In fact, the Nigerian military presented Obasanjo with his greatest challenge, as it continued to represent an ongoing threat to the newly emerging democratic process, often being led by a cadre of officers who were anxious to protect their own positions of authority. However, Obasanjo tried to reduce the potential for further military coups by retiring and sacking a number of the country's leading military officers, especially those that were linked to any of Nigeria's principal political parties, in an effort to finally separate the country's army from the executive process.

In the wider country however, although Obasanjo's reforms were beginning to stabilise the government, ethnic tensions and rivalries continued to exist, erupting into inter-communal violence on a regular basis between 1999 and 2001, during which many thousands of Nigerians died. Extreme poverty and religious militancy were also major headaches for the new President, who was re-elected to the office in 2003. Since that time though, Nigeria has elected two members of the People's Democratic Party to serve as President and Vice President, although it is the Vice President, Goodluck Jonathan, who is thought to wield much of the day to day power within the country, but without the level of popular support that the largely absent President, Umaru Yaradua, is said to enjoy. It is perhaps worth noting that the 2007 elections, which brought Yaradua and Jonathan to power, was said to have been marked by large scale electoral fraud, a charge that was said to have been confirmed by a number of the international observers who were brought in to monitor the process. What is particularly significant about Nigeria's more recent history, specifically those years since its independence from Great Britain in October 1960, is the loss of opportunity that has been experienced by the native peoples of the country. Potentially one of the richest countries on the African continent, ostensibly because of its huge natural resources, over the period of the past fifty years, Nigeria's vast wealth has been plundered and exploited by a small number of charismatic and greedy individuals, who have brought the country to the verge of anarchy. Although not a failed state, Nigeria is often regarded as a failing one, a country that regularly teeters on the precipice of complete turmoil, a nation that is oil rich, but where the majority of the population live on the equivalent of $2 per day. In spite of some claims that Nigeria's predicament is entirely the result of British colonialism, in reality; its fate has and always will be determined by its own people's failure to fully embrace the democratic process that they were first presented with in October 1960.

The former British colonies of West Africa are thought to have experienced similarly diverse histories to their eastern counterparts, with the present day states of Kenya, Uganda and Tanzania all having made the sometimes turbulent journey from former British colony, to modern democratic state. The first Western Europeans to visit the port of Mombasa in present day Kenya, were said to have been the Portuguese in 1593, when they established a trading base, Fort Jesus, to help facilitate their highly valuable trade with the Indian subcontinent. In later centuries however, their hold on the region became increasingly fragile, as Arab traders became more influential along the east coast of Africa, eventually coming to dominate many of the main seaports on the coast, along with much of their international trade. It was only at the beginning of the 19th century and largely in pursuit of illegal slave traders, who were thought to have been still operating in large parts of Africa that Britain began to become increasingly involved in the east coast of the continent, employing the Royal Navy as its main instrument of suppression. By the middle of the 19th century, European explorers and missionaries had begun to investigate and map much of the African hinterland, establishing trade links with the indigenous peoples for supplies of ivory and cloves, which were commonly shipped through these main eastern ports. The island of Zanzibar, lying just off the coast of East Africa, was reported to be one of the pre-eminent of these trading centres, its importance recognised by virtually all of the main western European nations, who all vied with one another for dominance in the region. In 1887, a British mercantile company, the British East Africa Company, were reported to have purchased the lease on a strip of land along the east coast of the African mainland, utilising it as a staging post for the various trade goods that it was bringing in and out of the continent. Stretching some one hundred and fifty miles along the east coast from the port of Mombasa, to the borders of the German East Africa territories, these new British holdings were said to have included a huge hinterland that would later form much of modern day Kenya and Uganda. Unfortunately, by the middle of 1895 the British East Africa Company was beginning to fail, leaving the authorities back in London, with little option but to take over the day to day running of the territories, which it did by declaring the entire region a British protectorate in July of 1895.

George Goldie

Frederick Lugard

Sani Abacha

By 1902, the territories that would later form the main part of Kenya and Uganda were incorporated together to form the British East Africa Protectorate, which were administered by Britain's colonial services, who began to set aside particular regions in the highlands of the country for white migrant settlers. Much of this inward migration was reported to have been organised by various private companies, most notably from the British South African Company, who requested grants of lands from the British authorities, ostensibly in an attempt to exploit the regions untapped natural resources. Other groups though made applications and elsewhere in these new British possessions, significant numbers of Indian settlers were reported to have populated the cities, ports and coastal areas of the new British territories, eventually becoming the largest migrant community in the country by 1920. Migration into the territories was said to have become such an issue by 1904 that serious questions were beginning to be asked by the British authorities, who feared that the indigenous Masai people and their tribal lands, might be adversely affected by such large numbers of foreign settlers. As a result, a number of new requests for lands were deliberately refused by the authorities in London, a decision which led to the resignations of certain local administrators who had been sympathetic to all new foreign applications. However, despite such minor disputes, by 1905 the capital of these new territories was said to have been relocated from Mombasa to Nairobi; and their first British governor, Lieutenant Colonel Hayes Sadler, was said to have been appointed to oversee the new protectorate.

One of the major reasons for the large inward migration of thousands of Indian workers and settlers was thought to have been the construction of the Kenya to Uganda railway line, which was designed to link the port of Mombasa to the territories of Uganda. Largely built to help in the development the Ugandan hinterland, some thirty-odd thousand Indian workers were said to have been employed in its construction, with many thousands more coming to help populate and modernise the relatively undeveloped region. The Highland region of Kenya, which was said to have some of the most fertile, but generally unused lands, were almost entirely given over to white settlement, where new revenue generating crops could be grown to help in part pay for the cost of building the new railway system. Although this program of foreign settlement and cultivation, almost inevitably led to some loss of native tribal homelands, this was often excused by the authorities, who believed that the introduction of modern medicines, as well as the widespread abolition of famine, witchcraft and slavery, would act as a balance to such minor territorial losses. Despite not having faced serious opposition from the local tribesmen, in terms of violent conflict, the British authorities did face a certain amount of dissent from local African chiefs and even from some white settlers, whose wishes were largely ignored by the appointed British governor, who ultimately decided policy for the protectorate. It was only in 1920, when the Kenyan territories were formally adopted as a Crown Colony and a representative council finally created that their views and opinions actually start to be taken fully into account.

Adopted as a Crown Colony largely because of the growing dissatisfaction at the higher taxes and lower wages caused as a direct result of the First World War, the 1920's was also to mark the beginning of Kenyan political nationalism, with a few fledgling groups, often led by the brightest and best educated Kenyans, lobbying for greater freedom from British control. The native peoples of Kenya, including the Kikuyu and the Masai were said to have become increasingly vocal in their opposition to British rule and settlement during the second quarter of the 20th century, particularly as new taxes, including the Hut Tax and price restrictions were imposed by the generally white dominated legislature, which drove many of Kenya's poorer subsistence farmers off the land and into the already heavily populated cities. The growing demand for greater involvement in their own country's government was thought to have increased significantly after the Second World War, during which an estimated one hundred thousand Kenyans participated in the British war effort, serving as "Askaris" with their commonwealth comrades. It was said to be just after the war that the young Jomo Kenyatta, first came to prominence, as chairman of the Kenyan African Union, a cross party political organisation which helped to drive forward demands for greater involvement of the Kikuyu and other native peoples in the governance of the country. In response to the political lobbying of individuals like Kenyatta and other African leaders, the composition of the country's legislative council was fundamentally altered to provide a greater say for Kenya's native African and Arab communities, which it was hoped would give them a greater voice in the running of the country. At the same time, the authority of the same executive body was reported to have been increased, so that it effectively supplanted the power of the Colony's governor, who for too long had been the final arbiter of Kenya's political and economic policies. Unfortunately for all of those involved, the suggested improvements in the numbers of representatives allocated to each ethnic group within Kenya, still discriminated in favour of the white European settlers, who despite numbering less than 1% of the native population, which was estimated at around five million people, were actually given nearly three times the number of council representative, a wholly disproportionate and unequal figure by any standards. Recognising perhaps that there was little chance of being offered any sort of real political involvement in the running of their own country, a number of Kenya's nationalist leaders were later said to have made the decision to pursue their objectives through armed struggle, rather than political persuasion, in what subsequently became known as the Mau Mau Uprising or Rebellion.

The root cause of much the native Kenyan antagonism was thought to have been the subject of land and its ownership, along with an implicit right for the farmer to grow the crops of his own choosing. Unfortunately, the relatively small numbers of white farmers, most of who had migrated from South Africa and Europe were reported to have owned or at least controlled the vast majority of the fertile lands within Kenya and through their economic strength generally determined policy within the Crown Colony. From their particular perspective, the ability to grow crops and then sell them at the best possible market price was essential, so the prospect of native farmers growing similar crops, but at much lower prices, encouraged the white settlers to try and eliminate their native competition. They were said to have achieved this largely by lobbying for legislation that outlawed or limited the cultivation of cash crops by the native Kenyan farmers, or by introducing local land taxes which financially crippled these smaller growers. An added bonus for the white farmers, was that such actions, not only forced many small growers out of business, but also compelled many of their formers workers to seek employment with the white farmer, who in turn could regulate the level of wages paid to these otherwise unemployed farm workers. Although not slavery in the most obvious way, over time this practice was said to have developed into a form of medieval serfdom that was completely out of place for the times in which it occurred.

The Mau Mau were said to have first emerged in 1951, when reports of a secret society, which was dedicated to the overthrow of British rule in Kenya, first came to the attention of the authorities there. According to these same reports, members of the organisation, who were said to have been largely recruited from the majority Kikuyu people, swore a sacred oath to help drive the white settlers out of their country forever. However, despite these early reports about the organisation, the first serious criminal act by the rebels was only thought to have occurred on 7th October 1952, when a local tribal chief, who was loyal to the British authorities, was reportedly killed by members of the Mau Mau. Over the period of about a month, several dozen more people were thought to have been murdered in Nairobi, which along with reports of the rebels having acquired significant numbers of firearms, forced the colonial authorities to request additional military aid from Britain and declare a state of emergency throughout Kenya itself. As part of these same emergency measures, a number of Kenya's leading nationalist figures, including Jomo Kenyatta, were said to have been arrested by the British authorities, even though there was little evidence of him having committed any crime. Elsewhere, hundreds of other suspected Mau Mau sympathisers were summarily arrested and interned by the authorities, whilst in the Kikuyu homelands, schools were said to have been closed down, in order to prevent the rebels from indoctrinating the local children and their families. By the following month, November 1952, Kenyatta was reported to have been formally charged with leading the Mau Mau insurgency in the country, despite there being little to link him to the rebels, as a result of which, he was thought to have been flown to an isolated region of the country and held there incommunicado. Within a matter of days, the leadership of the Mau Mau was said to have publicly announced its armed opposition to British rule in Kenya, as a result of which several thousand more suspected Mau Mau members were said to have been rounded up and imprisoned by the local authorities. For those Kikuyu people who were unfortunate enough to face the prospect of being forced to swear an oath to the Mau Mau cause, their refusal to attack or kill white settlers was said to have meant almost certain death, a position that was made even more difficult by the later announcement of the British authorities that anyone swearing such an oath would be automatically subject to the death penalty, leaving them condemned, no matter which path they chose to walk.

As the insurgency dragged on into the beginning of 1953, so the underlying tensions began to tell on the local white civilian population, who rightly or wrongly, believed themselves to be under siege by the native Kenyan people. Seemingly unconvinced by the measures being employed by the British authorities to suppress the Mau Mau threat and following the murder of a white farmer and his family, a number of the white settlers were reported to have established their own paramilitary commando forces, to combat the perceived threat. Unfortunately, certain members of these groups saw little difference between entirely innocent Kikuyu tribesmen and those who were involved with the insurgency, treating all native Kenyans with a level of brutality and indifference that simply helped to heighten tensions between the two communities even more. The fairly dire situation was reported to have been worsened by the use of highly emotive language by a number of the white community's leading citizens, including one who directly compared the incarcerated political leader Jomo Kenyatta, with Adolph Hitler, a statement that was almost guaranteed to cause even more antagonism between the black and white populations. For much of 1953 the British authorities were reported to have arrested large numbers of suspected Mau Mau members, most notably in and around the city of Nairobi, as well as conducting armed patrols in the Kenyan Highlands and Kikuyu homelands, where several dozen suspects were either killed or captured. It was also during the same year that the nationalist leader, Jomo Kenyatta, was finally brought to trial by the British authorities, being charged along with five other reported leaders of the insurgency and later sentenced to seven years hard labour by the Kenyan courts. Despite these successes for the authorities however, the Mau Mau themselves were thought to have enjoyed some partial military victories during the same period, mostly at the expense of local African forces who were employed by the British. Unfortunately, by the beginning of 1954, the Mau Mau's military campaign was said to have been further undermined by the capture of three of its leading figures, General China who was wounded and captured in January of that year and then in March 1954, Generals Katanga and Tanganyika both fell into British hands. Initially it was hoped that the capture of these men, especially General China, might offer the British an opportunity to bring the insurgency to an end, the General reportedly having agreed to contact the remaining Mau Mau military leaders to try and broker a deal. Sadly though, by April of 1954 it had become clear that no such agreement was likely to be reached, so the military operations against the rebels, was ordered to be continued.

In response to the failure to find alternative means to end the conflict, in April 1954, the British authorities were reported to have organised the biggest arrest of suspects ever arranged by Imperial forces, with some forty thousand Kikuyu tribesmen reportedly being arrested by a combined force of Imperial troops and policemen, numbering some six thousand men. Despite this overwhelming show of force and the arrest of so many suspects however, in the following month Mau

Mau insurgents still managed to burn down and destroy the Treetops Hotel, where Britain's then Princess Elizabeth learned of her father's death, despite having received an offer of an amnesty from the British authorities. This offer though, was quickly withdrawn in April 1955, when two English schoolboys were thought to have been murdered by Mau Mau fighters, who were subsequently caught, tried and executed for their part in the boy's deaths. These were just a few of the thousand or so Kikuyu men who would hang on the British gallows, during the entire six year period, from 1952 to 1958, with an estimated thirteen thousand native tribesmen reportedly being killed by British forces during the entire emergency. By comparison and despite the almost hysterical belief that white communities was being massacred by the Mau Mau insurgents, less than forty white farmers or settlers, were thought to have died as at the hands of the insurgents, whilst at the same time, some two thousand entirely innocent Kikuyu people were said to have been killed by the rebels. It is interesting to note however that a substantial number of "suspected" Mau Mau insurgents were thought to have been killed by the Kenyan Home Guard, a paramilitary force set up by the country's white settlers, with the approval of the British authorities. An estimated five thousand suspects were reported to have been killed by this mixed vigilante force of white farmers and loyal African retainers who were later accused of a range of offences including rape, theft and torture.

Jomo Kenyatta   **Dedan Kimathi**   **Daniel Arap Moi**

The beginning of the end of the insurgency was said to have begun in October 1956, when the self appointed Mau Mau Field Marshal, Dedan Kimathi, was captured by British forces and charged with the unlawful possession of a firearm and ammunition. Thought to have been a target for the authorities for nearly three years, Kimathi was tried and convicted for the firearms offences and was subsequently hanged by the British on 19th February 1957, effectively robbing the insurgents of one of their most prominent leaders. It was also around the same time that the British military authorities began to implement specific measures which were designed to target the Mau Mau fighters in their forest hideaways. Three particular measures which proved to be highly effective were the employment of pseudo rebel gangs that were staffed by former Mau Mau rebels, who were in the pay of the British, the use of widespread leafleting campaigns and the general harrying of the insurgents by British forces. The use of the pseudo gangs was thought to have been particularly successful, with these groups of former Mau Mau fighters, who had renounced their former allegiances and who were then led by British officers, deliberately tricking their former comrades into ambush sites, or providing intelligence for regular British forces, including aircraft, who would then attack the rebel bases. Likewise the widespread leafleting of rebel areas was also said to have been successfully employed, with thousands of leaflets being dropped by the Royal Air Force, in an attempt to persuade individual fighters to lay down their arms and accept the amnesty being offered by the British authorities. Almost inevitably though, the emergency was thought to have been brought to an end, both by sheer exhaustion and the inevitable need for dialogue to take place, in order to bring the conflict to an end. A contributing factor for the British authorities was said to have been the public outrage, caused by the killing of eleven Kikuyu prisoners by British guards in March 1959, simply because the prisoners refused to work. Very quickly the image of the native Africans being the aggressors in the conflict, was replaced by the idea of a subject native state being brutalised by a well armed and oppressive British Empire, a state of affairs that not only damaged Britain's international reputation, but also caused great controversy within London's political establishment. It was largely as a result of such occasional, but generally unrepresentative actions that the British government finally began to seek a political solution to the issue of the Kenyan situation, rather than just an entirely military one.

Beginning in November 1959, the British authorities formally ended the state of emergency in Kenya and began talks with the various political parties in the country, which culminated in the release of the imprisoned nationalist leader, Jomo Kenyatta, in July 1961, events that have since been reproduced in the white dominated state of South Africa, with the release of its own Black nationalist leader, Nelson Mandela. Following Kenyatta's release in July 1961, the Kenyan authorities were reported to have set in place the necessary executive measures for free elections to take place, which resulted in Kenyatta being elected as Prime Minister of his country in 1963. Within the space of seven months, Kenya was subsequently granted its independence from Britain, which was formally recognised on 12th December 1963, effectively bringing an end to over seventy years of British rule in the country. Having officially taken control of their own country, the Kenyan authorities almost immediately announced an amnesty for all of those Mau Mau rebels still in hiding and twelve months later, in December 1964, declared Kenya a republic, with Jomo Kenyatta as its first ever President.

Although there is little doubt that the period of the Kenyan Emergency and the measures which were employed by the British authorities left a legacy of bitterness for some of those involved, for many of the Mau Mau insurgents who fought Britain's colonial forces, the struggle achieved them little. According to most sources, the largely white administration of the British was simply replaced by its black equivalent, a class of well educated and often wealthy native businessmen and politicians, who filled the void left by the British community. Although a significant number of white European settlers and farmers left the country immediately following Kenyan independence, many were said to have remained in place and have continued to thrive right through to the present day. Ultimately though, Britain's actions during the emergency remain controversial, given that such low level insurgencies and their associated guerrilla tactics, were and are incredibly difficult for any regular military force to deal with, but were dealt with nonetheless, but perhaps not in the most satisfactory manner. Since independence in 1963 and its proclamation of a republic in 1964, Kenya has remained a relatively stable and representative democracy, led by Jomo Kenyatta until his death in 1978 and then by Daniel Arap Moi until 2002. Unlike a number of its African neighbours, fortunately, Kenya has not been subjected to the sorts of political turmoil which appear to be almost endemic to the continent generally; and apart from a single abortive coup attempt in

1982, which was quickly suppressed; it is widely regarded as one of the most successful African democracies of the 20th century.

In complete contrast to Kenya's relatively straightforward evolution from former British colony to independent nation state, the neighbouring territories of Uganda have been far less successful in developing into a modern democracy since being granted full independence by Britain in October 1962. In common with its neighbour, the territories that later became Uganda, were initially held by the private mercantile company, the British East Africa Company from 1887, until the business' decline in 1893, when its assets, including the native kingdom of Buganda, were transferred to the British Crown. The country subsequently became a British protectorate in 1894 and was eventually enlarged well beyond the historic borders of the earlier Bugandan kingdom, becoming formally identified as Uganda, the native Swahili word for the Bugandan kingdom, around the same time as the British authorities took over full control of the country. The fact that much of this new British protectorate was centred on the historic Bugandan kingdom, which had been highly supportive of Britain's territorial ambitions in the region, was a significant factor in the later development of the country. However, despite these earlier cordial relations between the British Crown and the Bugandan leadership, which led to the native African monarchs retaining much of their original authority in the region, later differences between the two sides were said to have resulted in the Bugandan king declaring war on Britain in July 1897, a conflict that the African tribesmen would lose within a matter of weeks. As a result of his actions, the Bugandan leader, Mwanga II, was subsequently arrested and interned by the British authorities, in order to maintain order, although he reportedly escaped in the following year, only to be recaptured and sent into exile on the Seychelles, where he was thought to have died in 1903.

Having incurred significant expense in suppressing the native tribes and building the extremely expensive Kenya to Uganda Railway system, the British authorities were eager to try and develop the country for commercial exploitation, in order to recover some of their initial outlay. Although the construction of the railway had inevitably opened up significant areas of the countryside for agricultural development and exploitation, the new British commissioner in Uganda, Sir Harry Johnson, was thought to have recognised that without regional controls and the agreement of the native peoples, then recovering the costs of settling the country and building its transport links would remain extremely problematic. However, by employing the same colonial systems which had been employed elsewhere in the British Empire, which involved local tribal leaders and native councils becoming the agents for the British colonial authorities, a system of regional administration was quickly established throughout much of Uganda. Unfortunately, Johnson was reported to be in such a rush to establish a settled and profitable British protectorate that he gave little thought to achieving a fair and equitable agreement for all of the various parties within the country, a failure which would ultimately have grave repercussions for its inhabitants in the future. As the largest and therefore most influential native tribe within Uganda, the Bugandan (or Bagandan) people were those largely appointed to carry out British policies, often at the expense and detriment of the smaller Ugandan kingdoms, such as the Toro, Ankole and Bunyoro, who achieved very few concessions from the British authorities and as such became increasingly disgruntled over time. The former independent African kingdom of Bunyoro was thought to have been particularly incensed by the appointment of their traditional enemies, the Bagandan's, as tax collectors and regional administrators, a situation that was reported to have led to a revolt by the Bunyoro people, which was only finally resolved after the British colonial authorities removed their Bagandan agents from the Bunyoro homelands in 1907. Although this helped to reduce the level of antagonism felt by the Bunyoro, throughout much of Uganda, the Bagandan's continued to enjoy a disproportionate level of authority, influence and financial security over their smaller tribal neighbours, which continued to cause resentment between the various ethnic groups, right through to the latter part of the 20th century.

Milton Obote **Idi Amin** **Julius Nyerere**

This apparent British favouritism towards the Bagandan people, was said to have been particularly evident with the establishment of the colonial capital in Kampala, at the heart of the former Buganda kingdom and the subsequent development and modernisation of this region, often at the direct expense of the smaller, less important tribal homelands, which lay on the periphery of the country. Uganda's thriving cotton industry was centred round Buganda, as was the development and expansion of the country's industrial and educational base, with numbers of new colleges and universities being established to help educate the children of the increasingly rich Bagandan administrators and entrepreneurs who were helping to drive the country forward. It was through these same schools and colleges that the new generations of civil administrators and officials were being trained, to take over the duties of the tribal chiefs and leaders, who had previously helped run the country. Supported by a new generation of British colonial officers, who appreciated the skills of these relatively well educated Black African administrators and officials, many of these young Bagandan leaders, soon began to press for independence from Britain, a desire that had growing support in Britain itself after World War II, where successive British governments were equally keen to dismantle the country's expensive, troublesome and generally unfashionable Imperial possessions.

During the early 1950's preparations began to be made for Ugandan independence; and as elsewhere within the dwindling Empire, a reorganisation of the colony's legislative system became a major priority for Britain's colonial services. The previous executive bodies in Uganda, which had previously favoured the white European minority, the merchant classes and the disproportionately influential native tribes, such as the Bagandan's, were reformed to include representatives from all of Uganda's tribal and ethnic regions, making these legislative bodies as representative as possible for a future parliamentary system. However, apart from creating a whole new range of political parties, who were anxious to be represented within these new legislative bodies, the changes were thought to have outraged those traditional groups, who had previously held a disproportionate amount of power within the country, especially those within the Bugandan community, who feared the loss of their own standing, within a parliamentary Uganda and began to lobby for a separate state of their own. In order to prevent this, once again British officials bowed to the threats of the Bugandan leadership, by allowing them undue influence in the country's democratic process, ultimately storing up problems that would prove to be catastrophic for the Ugandan people in future years. The political divisions within Uganda were thought to have become more evident as independence for the colony drew ever closer, during the late 1950's and early 1960's, with national opinion being polarised between those that supported Bugandan authority over the democratic process; and those that were vehemently opposed to it. Although the opposition parties had been largely fragmented up until 1960, in that year, virtually all of them rallied behind a single leader, a political organiser called Milton Obote, who founded the Uganda People's Congress as an umbrella group for all of the various groups that supported his opposition to the power of the Buganda people. Seemingly unable to find common ground between the two sides, the British government simply announced a date for Uganda's first elections, ostensibly in the hope that both parties would feel compelled to find a compromise, which they failed to do. When the first national elections were held in Uganda in March 1961, the Bugandan parties refused to stand and as a result handed seats to their political rivals, whilst Milton Obote's United People's Party gained the largest number of votes in the country as a whole.

In the aftermath of their ill-fated decision, the Bagandan political parties quickly recognised the futility of their decision not to field candidates and immediately began talks with the British government to try and retrieve the situation. As a result of these discussions, a compromise was said to have been reached between all of Uganda's political parties, whereby a federal form of government would be employed in the country, which guaranteed Buganda a significant amount of autonomy, whilst at the same time allowing its ruler, the Kabaka, to become the nominal and ceremonial head of the new Ugandan nation. With these agreements in place, Milton Obote, the Prime Minister of Uganda, was reported to have led his country to independence in October 1962 and in the following year, Frederick Walugembe Mutesa II, the Bugandan Kabaka, or ruler, was officially installed as the first President of Uganda. Unfortunately, Uganda's political unity failed to last more than a few years and in 1966, Obote was reported to have changed the country's constitution, removing the ceremonial positions of President and Vice President, effectively abolishing any sort of political oversight of his own office. The following year, he declared Uganda a republic and as well as abolishing the historic tribal kingdoms of his newly created republic, Obote then appointed himself as executive President, all of which was done without having called new elections in the country. For much of his decade in power, Obote was accused of having terrorized and tortured thousands of Ugandan citizens, especially those political opponents, who were critical of the abuse of power and the corruption that were said to be endemic to Obote's regime. However, it was only in January 1971, when Obote was out of the country attending a Commonwealth Heads of Government conference in Singapore that his greatest opponent, ultimately his political successor, felt confident enough to launch the coup that would finally bring an end to Obote's first period of office. That man was Idi Amin, a Ugandan army officer, who was initially well thought of by most foreign powers, but whose own brutal and chaotic rule, would ultimately prove to be a catastrophe for Uganda's economy, its people and its wider international reputation.

Although Amin's career was thought to have flourished under Obote's regime, largely because of his willingness to suppress the Ugandan President's political opponents, as is often the case with dictators, Amin's growing influence within the country and most notably within the army, eventually made him a potential threat to Obote's regime. As a result, just prior to his journey to Singapore in 1971, Obote was reported to have ordered that Amin and a number of his leading supporters should be arrested and held until he returned to the country. Unfortunately for the absent Ugandan President; and according to some sources, Amin was informed of his planned arrest by foreign agents, allowing him and his supporters to pre-empt Obote's orders and stage a military coup of their own and take control of the capital, Kampala. Having command of some of Uganda's most professional military units, Amin and his supporters quickly took control of the capital and of Uganda's Entebbe airport, thereby controlling movements in and out of the country. With these two targets having been secured, Amin quickly moved to eliminate any potential threats to his coup, reportedly ordering the arrest and executions of those pro-Obote supporters, who he believed might pose a danger to his tenuous hold on power. Publicly stating that he had seized power, purely to facilitate free and fair elections, Amin's new caretaker government was said to have been generally welcomed by most of his African neighbours, with Britain, Israel and the United States all officially recognising his new administration as the legitimate representatives of the Ugandan people. However, the one notable exception to this generally widespread acceptance of Amin's regime was said to have come from Tanzania, where it's President, Julius Nyerere, stubbornly refused to recognise the new Ugandan leader and even offered the ousted Milton Obote a home, helping the exiled President to remain a potential threat to Amin for the next eight years. Almost as soon as he took power, Amin began to put in place a number of the highly repressive agencies and statutes, which would help protect him from similar coups in the future and that were said to have cost an estimated three hundred thousand Ugandan lives during his eight year reign of terror. All of the country's surviving politicians, including those appointed by Amin to run his new administration, were subsequently placed under his military command, thereby ensuring that anyone who rebelled against the new leader would be dealt with in the most ruthlessly efficient manner possible, with little recourse to the countries judicial system. Equally oppressive measures were thought to have been applied to the general population of the country, with regional military commanders being appointed by Amin, to control the various districts of Uganda, men who were given his tacit permission to rule as independent warlords, using whatever methods they felt were appropriate, to keep the local population in check.

Replicating the sort of chaotic government that became a feature of the Nazi Party during World War II, Amin's administration was said to have very quickly evolved into a series of highly divided regions and government bodies which were ruled over by a series of highly ambitious individuals, who competed with one another for control of the country's resources. However, each of these men were careful to avoid becoming a threat to Amin himself, who was said to have eliminated anyone that displeased, opposed or threatened his position as ruler of Uganda, a character trait, which ultimately helped to rob him of his most able military commanders. Even here though, the occasional purges by Amin, against those he believed to be a threat to his rule, provided prospects for advancement for those opportunists who were willing to seize their chance, leading to a former telephone operator, running the Ugandan airforce and a former night watchman, becoming the unofficial state executioner. In fact, within the space of a few years, the country's armed forces were said to be in such an unreliable condition that only particularly trusted regiments were allowed to carry live ammunition; such was the level of distrust held by Amin and his entourage of largely incompetent lieutenants. However, rather than admitting any form of failure on the part of his own administration, in September 1972, Amin was said to have committed one of his most catastrophic decisions for his presidency, when he decided to expel Uganda's eighty thousand Asian businessmen, most of whom were directly responsible for helping to maintain the country's extremely valuable industrial and economic base. Although he publicly proclaimed that his action was for the benefit of the Ugandan people, whose lives would be supposedly improved by his decision, in reality, most of the former Asian businesses and companies stolen from their former owners, were subsequently gifted to his circle of sycophants and supporters, who very quickly ran Uganda's industrial and financial base into the ground, essentially destroying the country's economic power for the foreseeable future. Four years later, he committed a second, more atrocious act, by allowing a group of Palestinian terrorists, to land a hijacked Air France plane, filled with French and Israeli passengers, at Uganda's Entebbe airport, from where they demanded the release of fellow Palestinian prisoners held in Israel. For Amin, the opportunity to play the role of peacemaker, between the two sides, proved to be irresistible, although his own supposed neutrality was quickly questioned by the watching world and particularly by the Israeli government, who soon realised that an armed rescue of their citizens was the only realistic option left to them.

The subsequent Israeli rescue mission on Entebbe airport, was carried out on the night of the 4th July 1976, when one hundred commandos from the Israeli Defence Force, travelled some two and a half thousand miles from their homeland in the Middle East, intent on releasing their fellow Israeli's from the terminal building at Entebbe. Having crossed Uganda's border and landed their C-130 cargo aircraft on the runway of the airport, the commandos quickly spread out and began to secure the general area, while those tasked with attacking the terminal building, where the Israeli passengers were reportedly being held, prepared to launch their raid against the handful of Palestinian terrorists, who were holding the hostages at gunpoint. However, the commando's almost secret arrival was said to have been compromised by the actions of two Ugandan sentries, who had challenged the convoy of cars brought by the Israeli forces as a distraction, forcing one of the commandos to shoot them, possibly alerting both the terrorists in the terminal building and the remaining Ugandan troops, who were stationed at the airport. Fortunately, those Israeli troops specifically assigned to rescue the hostages, were already in place to launch their assault on the terminal building and within seconds they had burst through the main doors of the airport, announcing their arrival to the Israeli passengers who were being held there. Ordering the hostages to remain on the floor, the commandos then began to identify and eliminate the eight Palestinian terrorists, who were located around the terminal building, a task that was accomplished within a matter of minutes. Sadly, it was thought to be during these exchanges of gunfire that three of the Israeli passengers were fatally wounded, with a further ten receiving minor wounds, although all of these later made a full recovery. Having eliminated all of the terrorists, the commandos then set about getting all of the hostages, from the terminal building to the waiting planes which had been brought to take them back to Israel. Around the same time, more Israeli troops and armoured personnel carriers had been unloaded from other C-130 transport aircraft, principally to protect the freed hostages from Ugandan interference and to destroy any military aircraft that might be used by the Ugandan air force to intercept the Israeli aircraft after they left Entebbe. It was said to be during this final phase of the operation that the commandos came under sustained attack by regular Ugandan soldiers, who were garrisoned at the airport, which resulted in the death of Yonatan Netanyahu, the only Israeli military fatality of the entire operation.

Yonatan Netanyahu

Dora Bloch

Yoweri Museveni

Having taken some fifty-odd minutes from beginning to end, Operation Thunderbolt as it later became known, resulted in one hundred and two, out of, one hundred and five hostages being successfully rescued by the Israeli commandos, with only three fatalities. All of the eight Palestinian terrorists had been eliminated; some thirty to forty Ugandan troops were reportedly killed during the raid; and a dozen or so Ugandan military aircraft destroyed. An elderly Israeli passenger, seventy five year old Dora Bloch, who had been taken ill during the crisis and taken to a local hospital, was subsequently murdered on the direct orders of Idi Amin, in retribution for the Israeli raid on his country. According to later information, Mrs Bloch was said to have been dragged from her sick bed, before being shot dead by two Ugandan military officers, who then dumped her body in a remote sugar plantation, from where it was only finally retrieved in 1979. For Amin himself, the successful Israeli rescue operation was a complete and utter humiliation, with most of the leading western nations publicly applauding the action taken by the state of Israel and condemning Amin for his part in the crisis. Even worse for the Ugandan dictator, was the refusal of the United Nations Security Council to condemn the Israeli military action, despite Amin's claims that his country's sovereignty had been violated by their unlawful raid.

For the final three years of his reign Amin was thought to have become increasingly erratic and aggressive, characteristics that led him to order the killing of hundreds of Kenyans, who lived in Uganda, in reprisal for the Kenyan governments logistical support offered to Israel during the hostage taking crisis. Apart from further antagonising his immediate African neighbours, this action particularly was said to have isolated the Ugandan leader from many of his international supporters, who began to question the long term stability of the regime and its leader. By 1978, even some of his most loyal and steadfast supporters began to waver and with Amin's administration becoming more unstable each and every day, many of those who had exploited the country for their own financial benefit began to seriously reassess their own futures. As those about him started to question his suitability to continue as the country's President, so the various relationships between Amin, his ministers and his army chiefs began to fragment, with each of them having their own cadre of loyal supporters, who were constantly at odds with the various competing parties. Matters were said to have come to a head when Amin's vice President, General Mustafa Adrisi was reportedly injured in a car crash, which many of the general's troops believed to be the work of Amin's supporters, causing them to rebel against the dictator. In response, Amin sent his own forces to suppress the revolt, forcing many of the rebel troops to seek sanctuary across the border in neighbouring Tanzania, where they thought that they would be safe. However, Amin simply accused the Tanzanian leader, Julius Nyerere, along with ousted Ugandan leader Milton Obote, of being behind a plot to depose him and sent Ugandan troops across the border into Tanzania, where they annexed a region of the neighbouring territory. Outraged by this attack on his country's sovereign territory, the Tanzanian President, Julius Nyerere, immediately mobilised his own armed forces, who quickly forced Amin's troops to retreat back across the border, pursued by both the Tanzanian army and the exiled Ugandan forces under the command of Milton Obote. Despite receiving military aid from the Libyan dictator, Muammar al-Gaddafi, who had sent troops into Uganda to help support Amin's regime, by April of 1979, the combined Tanzanian-Ugandan invasion force was said to have reached the capital city, Kampala, forcing Amin and many of his supporters to flee the country. It was later noted that the speed of the collapse of Amin's military forces, was largely brought about by his soldier's tendency to loot an area before simply retreating from the advancing enemy troops, a characteristic that was said to be particularly prevalent amongst the remaining officers of the Ugandan armed forces, who were undoubtedly determined to escape the country with as many treasures as they could possibly carry away with them.

Escaping first to Libya, where he was initially welcomed by its leader Colonel Gaddafi, Amin later travelled to Saudi Arabia, where he was allowed to settle in Jeddah by the Saudi Royal family, on the understanding that he retained a fairly low public profile, in order to reduce any public criticism of the Saudi leadership for sheltering the former African dictator. However, in 1989 Amin was said to have attempted to lead an armed insurgency into Uganda, but was subsequently stopped at Kinshasa in Zaire, now the Democratic Republic of Congo and compelled to return to Saudi Arabia by the then Zairian President, Mobutu Sese Seko. For the remainder of his life, Idi Amin reportedly kept a relatively low profile in Saudi Arabia, although just prior to his death in 2003, the Ugandan authorities were asked for permission for the exiled dictator to return home, so that he could die peacefully in his homeland. Perhaps fearful that even a debilitated Amin might cause unrest in the country, Uganda's President, Yoweri Museveni, informed the dictators family that if he were to return home, then he would be brought to trial for his crimes, effectively bringing an end to any hopes for Amin's return to Uganda. As a result, Idi Amin remained in Jeddah until his death in 16th August 2003, when he was buried at Ruwais cemetery in Jeddah, bringing an end to the life of one of Africa's most infamous post colonial leaders.

Britain's third territory in East Africa, Tanganyika, was not a traditional imperial possession, but was reported to have been land granted to Britain in the wake of the First World War, being mandated to the British Crown by order of the victorious League of Nations, as part of the disposition of former German overseas territories seized by the Western Allies. As part of this redistributing of Germany's former African possessions, certain regions of the former Tanganyika territories were transferred to the Belgian controlled Ruanda-Urundi region, whilst at the same time, the islands of Zanzibar were granted to Britain to become part of the newly restructured Tanganyika. As an internationally mandated territory, the country was governed by an appointed Governor and Commander-in-chief for much of the period from 1920 until 1926, when a formal advisory legislative council was established, in order to help advise the Governor in his leadership of the territories. As part of these administrative changes and in pursuance of the colonial policies employed by the British authorities elsewhere, existing or tribal councils were employed throughout the country in order to help with the day to day administration of the country. For much of the 1930's and 1940's the British authorities were reported to have taken positive steps to develop Tanganyika's health and educational services, although both were said to have fell short of the huge investment made by the former German authorities in the country prior to the First World War. However, as Britain was gripped by food shortages during the Second World War, so significant investments were made to develop Tanganyika's agricultural industry and in particular its wheat production, much of which was destined for Britain's besieged wartime population.

It was thought to be as a direct result of this intensive agricultural development program that following the end of World War II, Tanganyika began to expand its co-operative farming systems, which allowed the country's economy to develop so successfully in the late 1940's and throughout the 1950's. It was also immediately after the Second World War that the country formally became a United Nations territory, under British control, ensuring that Tanganyika was allowed to progress towards self government and eventually full independence. In 1954, the man who would later become the first President of his country, Julius Nyerere, a former school teacher, was reported to have helped to found the Tanganyika African National Union, the same man and political party that would ultimately rule the country for well over twenty years, from 1961 to 1985. In December 1961, Tanganyika became an autonomous country within the British Commonwealth, with Nyerere becoming its first Prime Minister, although exactly a year later, the country was reconstituted as an independent republic, with Nyerere taking office as the new republic's President. Twelve months after Tanganyika became a new independent republic; in December 1963, the associated islands of Zanzibar were granted their independence as a constitutional monarchy, with the Sultan as their head of state. Almost immediately, this new nation was reported to have been rocked by outbreaks of ethnic violence, with the smaller Arab and Asian populations being attacked and killed by the Black African majority, whose leader, Abeid Karume, quickly installed himself as President of Zanzibar and chairman of its revolutionary council. Clearly concerned by these developments, in Tanganyika itself, the new President, Julius Nyerere, was also facing his own problems, as rebel elements within his own armed forces had chosen to revolt at the same time, leaving him with little choice but to request military assistance from the British authorities. In response, Britain immediately despatched Royal Marine Commandos from both England and from the aircraft carrier HMS Bulwark, who spent the next few months actively disarming rebel troops and securing the various military bases in the country. In order to ensure that such an event could not reoccur, in 1964 Nyerere and the leadership of Zanzibar agreed to unite the two states under the common name of Tanzania, with the islands retaining some level of local autonomy.

However, despite international hopes that the new state might prove to be a successful African democracy and perhaps because of the unexpected rebellion by his armed forces, almost immediately Nyerere began to implement a totalitarian doctrine, which used the country's carefully constructed constitution to suppress internal opposition to his rule. By employing his own personal brand of socialism within the country, Nyerere introduced legislation that allowed dissidents to his rule to simply "disappear", with many thousands of his political opponents reported to have been eliminated by his security services during his twenty-odd year reign. Like the now largely discredited system of the communist bloc, Nyerere was said to have introduced the idea of the collective farm into Tanzania, reducing what had once been a large number of highly successful privately owned farms, into a small number of state owned ones, which offered the farmers very little return for their labour. Similarly, many of the country's largest private industries were taken into state ownership, leading to the creation of a centralised public bureaucracy that was not only cumbersome, but was also rife with corruption. Although Nyerere eventually retired from Tanzanian politics in 1985, as is often the case with such totalitarian states, his successor, Ali Hassan Mwinyi, was an ardent follower of the former President and as such continued equally disastrous political and economic policies as his predecessor. This appears to be the case right through to the present day, with any form of dissent being crushed by the Tanzanian authorities and the country remaining almost entirely dependent on foreign aid.

MARINERS, MERCHANTS AND THE MILITARY TOO

10. BRITANNIA RULES THE WAVES

As an island race, the native peoples of England, Scotland, Wales and Ireland have always relied on having access to and use of the seas and coastal waters of the North Atlantic, both as a source of food, as well as a means of establishing permanent trade links between themselves and the indigenous tribes of the European continent. One of the earliest and best known forms of maritime transport of pre-Roman Britain was said to have been the coracle, which was thought to have been reported by Julius Caesar following his first military expedition to Britannia in the middle of the first century. Generally constructed in the shape of a half walnut shell, the coracle was said to have been made of a framework of tied willow rods, which was then covered by an animal hide, coated with a thin layer of tar that ensured it remained waterproof. Used throughout the British Isles, these early crafts have come to be more commonly associated with Wales and Ireland, although they were also reported to have been used in the south of England, often by local fishermen who would travel along local rivers, casting their nets from their sturdy native river crafts. It also seems to have been the case that the construction of these earlier river craft differed from region to region, suggesting that although the coracle had undoubtedly evolved from a much earlier single source, over time each region's boat builders had gradually adapted the crafts design to best suit their own watercourses and conditions. However, although the word coracle generally relates to the Welsh word "cwrwgl", both the Irish and the Scots tend to refer to their own versions as "currachs", even though according to some sources the "currach" was a much larger vessel than the coracle and therefore an entirely separate kind of boat. For some historians however, the distinction to be made between the two types of craft is that the coracle was generally an inland vessel, used primarily on inland waterways and rivers, whilst the larger, much more robust currach, was more suitable for coastal waters, being able to travel greater distances, in heavier seas and with larger numbers of crew.

However, one of the earliest sea going vessels ever discovered in mainland Britain is thought to be the craft known as the Dover Bronze Age boat, which reportedly dates from around 1500 BC and is deemed to be one of the most significant archaeological discoveries ever made in Britain. Along with three other Bronze Age boats, which were uncovered at Ferriby, Yorkshire in 1931, 1940 and 1963 respectively, all four of these early craft were said to have been examples of sewn plank vessels, designed to operate in and around the coastal waters of Britain, as well as the near continent. According to most informed sources, these craft, resembling punts, were thought to have evolved from the canoes and rafts that would have been the very earliest form of water transports designed by man. Described as being up to sixteen metres long, with a flat bottom and curved ends, like a traditional canoe, these early craft were thought to have been powered by a number of paddlers or oarsmen, who would have used the boats timber cross members to sit on. Constructed of several oak planks, often up to four inches thick, these were said to have been sewn together with yew or willow ties, with gaps between the shaped wooden planks being packed with moss, which was then kept in place with timber trims and tar, helping to make the entire hull reasonably watertight. Although it is unclear whether or not these early type of vessels employed masts and sails to propel them through the water, it is generally assumed, given the limitations of these early boats that sails were only employed when the wind was blowing in the right direction and for the majority of the time human muscle was required to move the craft forward in the water.

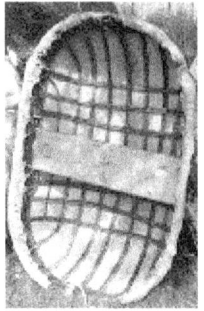  

The Coracle   The Currach   A Liburnian

At the same time that the Northern Europeans were just beginning to develop their skills at boatbuilding in order to explore their own coastal waters, to the south and most notably in the region of the Mediterranean, a number of native kingdoms and peoples had already perfected the arts of shipbuilding and maritime commerce. The Greek, Persian and Egyptian Empires were just three of the great civilisations that were known to have developed advanced shipbuilding techniques, which allowed them to construct vessels that could operate within their own regional waters, either as commercial cargo carriers, or as armed warships which could be used to confront their traditional enemies at sea. However, apart from the exploratory voyages undertaken by some early Greek mariners, who were anxious to learn about the wider world, few if any of these new and advanced marine technologies were thought to have found their way into northern Europe, where the native peoples were thought to be still using the most rudimentary techniques and designs to produce their own kind of sea going vessels. Although it is virtually impossible to attribute individual ship designs to any particular nation, the next significant step forward in British ship design was thought to have occurred as a result of the Roman invasion of Britain in the 1st century AD, with the introduction of the Empire's various galley-type ships, themselves a derivation of the earlier Greek and Persian designs, which were thought to have sailed the Mediterranean for thousands of years. Including Liburnians, Biremes, Triremes and Hemiolia, the Romans were thought to have come to Britain with a vast array of sea going vessels, which ranged from heavy warships, to much lighter scout and cargo ships, all of which were intended to support their land forces and protect their new northern territories from any seaborne pirates who might try to attack them. Although the Roman Navy was never regarded as being equal to its land based forces, as its Empire grew, so it became necessary to confront the threat of the numerous sea based piratical societies, who regularly began to attack their outlying provinces and extensive trade routes, forcing Rome's leaders to develop an effective maritime deterrent. This was thought to have been particularly true for its most northerly European province, Britannia, which was not only a source of great wealth for the expansive Empire, but also became a regular target for the marauding seaborne raiders who repeatedly attacked its Romano-British settlements. In response to these ongoing attacks, a number of Roman naval bases were reported to have been established throughout Britain to house the Classis Britannia, including those at Dover, London, Lancaster and Chester, to name just a few, whose job it was to protect, not only the coastline of Britain, but also the valuable merchant ships that plied their trade in and out of the various Romano-British ports.

The post-Roman period of Britain's maritime history was thought to have been notable for a number of reasons, including the advent of the Viking Longships and the emergence of England's first properly organised navy, which was said to have been ordered by the Anglo Saxon monarch, Alfred the Great, as part of his strategy to defeat the ongoing Viking menace. The term "longship" is thought to be a largely generic term, used to describe a variety of Viking crafts, which were often more slender and symmetrically built, giving the impression of being long, as opposed to the more usual, heavier and supposedly shorter ships of other European states. According to most historians, these longships were built and employed between the late 8th and late 11th centuries; and were employed as both raiders and general cargo carriers. For the Vikings themselves, their ships were often designed for specific purposes, with the largest of their vessels being called a "Knarr", an ocean going cargo vessel, measuring up to sixty feet in length and fifteen feet wide, with the capacity to carry a cargo of up to twenty-odd tons and a crew of anything up to thirty men. It was thought to be this sort of ship that regularly crossed the North Atlantic to Greenland, as well as to the Scottish Islands, its sturdy construction being able to cope with the most arduous weather conditions in the region, unlike some other smaller inland craft. In contrast to much earlier vessels, these Knarrs were thought to have relied heavily on their sail to power the ship, with its oars only being used when the prevailing winds were not in their favour. It has been suggested that it was this sort of ship that managed to cross the Atlantic in the 11th century, with its crew landing on the shores of Newfoundland, nearly five hundred years before Christopher Columbus first discovered America in 1492. Smaller ships used by the Scandinavian communities were said to have included the Karve, a cargo vessel with a relatively shallow draught that was commonly used to transport stores and livestock around the Vikings home regions; and which were thought to have operated in coastal waters, rather than in the open sea. For Viking mariners, the main benefits of their own native ships was said to be their speed, along with their ability to travel along coastal waters and shallow channels, which many of the heavier and deeper keeled European ships were unable to do, giving the Viking craft a number of major advantages over their rivals.

Following the end of the Roman occupation of Britain, the native British leadership were said to have requested military aid from European mercenaries in the form of the Angles from Angeln in modern day Germany, the Saxons who originated from the region of Lower Saxony in Germany and the Jutes, who were said to have come from the modern day region of Jutland, in Denmark. It is worth remembering perhaps that these post-Roman invaders would have come to Britain by ship and it is entirely likely that they brought with them shipbuilding designs and techniques that were not only different to those of the native British people, but also similar to those of the Viking boat builders of northern Europe. These similarities were thought to have been particularly evident, following the discovery of the Anglo Saxon "Sutton Hoo" ship burial in 1939, which contained the remains of an early 7th century vessel that had been interred there to hold the body of King Redwald, the Anglo Saxon king of the East Angles, who was said to have ruled between 599 and 624 AD. Although none of the ancient timbers had managed to survive through to the 20th century, when the burial mound was opened, stains in the sand had managed to preserve much of the vessels construction details and many of its iron rivets, used to hold the wooden planking together, had survived through to the modern day. From the remaining evidence, archaeologists were able to determine that the vessel had measured around ninety feet long and roughly fifteen wide, with a maximum depth of some five feet. Designed with a central keel board, the sides of the ship were said to have been constructed from a series of nine wooden planks on either side, with their overlaps fastened together with the previously mentioned iron rivets and the two sides supported by some twenty six horizontal bars that ran from one side to the other.

In the aftermath of their successful invasion of England during the 5th century, the next four hundred years was said to have seen the country divided into a series of regional kingdoms, including Mercia, Wessex, Northumbria, East Anglia, Essex, Kent and Sussex, which were commonly referred to as the Heptarchy. By the late 9th century, the kingdom of Mercia was said to achieved a degree of dominance, bringing much of the country under the authority of a single monarch, Alfred the Great, who would rule a united kingdom of England and begin the process of developing a national defence force, including a navy that would be formed to defend the country from the growing threat of the Viking menace. Widely credited with founding England's first official naval force, King Alfred was said to have reorganised his country's army and navy in order to resist the increasing incursions of Danish raiders, with the Anglo Saxon Chronicles recording that Alfred had introduced a number of longships, each with sixty oars in the year 896 AD. The King was reported to have created and paid for his new full-time English navy through the introduction of a new national tax, on areas called "ship sokes", which comprised some three hundred hides of land that were charged with providing the cost of a new ship. Likewise, other areas were ordered to provide the cost of a helmet, or the price of a smaller boat, which were then employed in the defence of the country, a scheme that saw every landowner in the country, large or small, make their own individual contribution to the formation of the country's first formal navy. However, following Alfred's death in 899 AD, the new English navy was said to have fallen into disrepair during the reign of Edward the Elder, who ruled between 899 and 925 AD, leaving his successor, King Athelstan, to revive the fortunes of the English fleet. It was said to have been under Athelstan that the early English navy reached its height, with some reports suggesting that anything up to one thousand ships could be mustered annually, although large numbers of these vessels were simply thought to be cargo ships, as opposed to warships that might be used to confront a foreign enemy. This Anglo Saxon fleet was said to have retained its strength through to the beginning of the 11th century, just as the Danish leader, Sweyn Forkbeard, began to cast an envious eye on the British Isles and set about planning for its military invasion.

Fortunately for the English monarch, Aethelred the Unready, the Danish raiders failed to launch any sort of full-scale attack on the country, although by 1000 AD many of England's leading military commanders were thought to have had little faith in the martial abilities of Aethelred, causing some of his most able mariners to defect to the Danish side. The forces of the Danish monarch, Sweyn Forkbeard, were reported to have begun carrying out raids in England in 1002, following the widespread massacre of Danish settlers in England on November 13th 1002, reportedly on the orders of the English monarch Aethelred, who was said to have feared their complicity in any future attack on his country. Unfortunately, one of the many innocent Danes who was said to have been killed during the slaughter was Gunhilde, the sister of Sweyn Forkbeard, an act that the Danish king was unlikely to forgive, or indeed forget. From 1002, right through to 1012 Danish forces were reported to have raided along the entire east coast of England, with property being seized, hostages taken and local inhabitants killed, all of which were thought to have been a preamble to the main Danish invasion that took place in 1013. Reported to have first arrived on English soil in July 1013, over the period of a few months Sweyne and his army were said to have swept across large areas of the east coast, taking control and receiving the submissions of several regional leaders, including those in Northumbria and East Anglia, before turning south to move on London. Although, initially rebuffed by the city's Anglo Saxon defenders, Sweyne and his forces were reported to have then turned their attention to the southwest of England, marching on the former Roman city of Bath, where the local lords were said to have submitted to him and offered hostages as guarantee of their future loyalty. It was thought to be as a result of this general surrender that Aethelred and his supporters in London finally recognised the hopelessness of their position; and agreed to surrender the city to the Danish monarch, with the Anglo Saxon monarch, Aethelred and his two sons, Edward and Alfred, being exiled to Normandy. Finally, on Christmas Day 1013, the Danish monarch, Sweyn Forkbeard, was formally recognised as the new King of England, a position he was said to have held for a mere five weeks, before he collapsed and died at Gainsborough in Lincolnshire, on 3rd February 1014, with his embalmed body later being taken back to his native Denmark, to be interred in the church at Roskilde.

Following the death of King Sweyn, his vast kingdoms were subsequently divided between his two sons, Harald and Canute, with Canute being granted sovereignty over the late Danish King's English possessions, beginning a royal line that would last for the next twenty six years. The Danish born Canute the Great, was said to have maintained only a small standing navy, comprising some sixteen ships, along with a one hundred and twenty oared flagship that was thought to have been used as his own personal transport. With the return of the Anglo Saxon Wessex dynasty to the English throne in 1042, in the person of Edward the Confessor, this relatively small number of ships was reported to have been reduced even further, with the English monarch only maintaining a handful of vessels and standing the remainder down, leaving England's defence almost entirely in the hands of individual nobles with the resources to fund their own private vessels. However, in later years these Earls were said to have employed their own naval forces to dictate terms to the king, as a result of which King Edward was able to use these English ships, to not only conduct military campaigns against the neighbouring Welsh and Scottish peoples, but also to deter further raids by the kingdoms of Norway and Denmark. These English naval forces were even thought to be in place in 1066, when Edward the Confessor died and his royal successor Harold Godwinsson ascended the throne of England, with a small number of vessels reportedly involved in the Battle of Stamford Bridge, when King Harold defeated the Norwegian invasion forces of Harald Hardrada. Unfortunately for the Anglo Saxon monarch, the naval forces which had previously been despatched to guard against an imminent attack from Normandy, the home of the Norman Duke, William the Bastard, had been forced to return to their home ports, in order to re-supply their stores, leaving the English Channel unguarded, at the same that the Norman leader decided to launch is his own bid for the English throne.

With no Anglo Saxon navy force to oppose his invasion fleet, Duke William and his armada of an estimated seven hundred ships were said to have been able to sail unhindered across the Channel to their final destination at Pevensey Bay in Sussex, beginning a chain of events that would eventually see him crowned King of England on 25th December 1066. For much of the next six years large parts of Britain were thought to have been in turmoil as the new Norman king sought to establish his authority of England, Scotland and Wales, employing whatever military resources were required to suppress the last remnants of Anglo Saxon resistance in the country, including those English ships which had been specifically built to resist foreign invaders such as himself. In 1072 William was even said to have despatched an English fleet to Scotland in order to demonstrate his military supremacy, although for much of the next century or so, the English fleet was thought to have played little part in the life of Norman England, save for protecting the vitally important English Channel, which divided England from the Norman's French homelands. It was only during the middle of the 12th century that the English monarch, Henry II, was reported to have assembled a large fleet to carry him and his forces to neighbouring Ireland, in order to prevent other Norman nobleman from seizing control of the territories, before sailing south to free the Iberian city of Lisbon, which had previously fallen into the hands of the Moors, North African Muslims who were beginning to dominate the southern regions of modern day Spain and Portugal. Although few significant voyages were undertaken by English ships during the period, the country's increasing reliance on its cross Channel trade routes led to the development of a specific naval force that was dedicated to protecting these vital supply lines. A series of ports were established to house and provision these ships, which later became commonly known as the Cinque Ports and that were required to provide an estimated fifty seven ships, each of which was operated by up to twenty seamen. More formally known as the Confederation of Cinque Ports, these five English ports included Hastings, New Romsey, Hythe, Dover and Sandwich, all of which were located at the eastern end of the English Channel, at the point where the crossing between England and France is at its narrowest.

A Trireme   Viking Longship   Sutton Hoo Ship

However, after the Plantagenet monarch, King John, contrived to lose the Normandy region of France in 1204, there was little further need for such a naval force, although in the immediate aftermath of these losses King John was said to have assembled a fleet of some five hundred ships to try and regain the territories, but with little success. Things were said to have become increasingly worse for the seemingly hapless English monarch, as even his right to sit on the English throne began to be contested by both foreign and domestic adversaries, which eventually erupted into the conflict that became known as the First Baron's War, which occurred between 1215 and 1217. Fought between King John and his supporters, against a coalition of rebellious English Barons and the future French King, Louis VIII, it was thought to be as a result of this impending war that the English fleet was substantially expanded by the Crown, with dozens of new galleys being constructed in order to defend the country's national borders from foreign intervention. Later Plantagenet rulers, including the highly militaristic Edward I, were thought to have regularly employed naval assets as part of their wider military campaigns, especially those in Wales, where English ships were said to have been regularly used in the monarch's disputes with the Principality's native Princes. Elsewhere, the English Crown was thought to have employed its navy in a number of roles, not only as troop carriers, but also as cargo ships and as blockade ships, preventing fresh arms and provisions being delivered by sea to the king's enemies within the mainland of Britain. Likewise it continued to be employed as a buffer to those foreign states that were in conflict with England, as well as patrolling the coastlines of England, Scotland, Wales and Ireland, helping to suppress the occasional pirate and slave trading ships that were reported to be operating in the region during the period.

The increasing formality of the English Navy was thought to have begun during the reigns of Edward I and his less able successor Edward II, with the office of Admiral reportedly being created in the latter part of the 13th century and that of Lord High Admiral of England first being recorded in 1408, all of whom were held to be responsible for the operation, manning and administration of all of England's naval assets, as well as for the occasional impressments of civilian merchants ships that might be needed to support the king's military ventures. The outbreak of the Hundred Years War, which was fought between the royal houses of England and France, between 1337 and 1453, was thought to have been marked by an increasing number of naval engagements, which were fought on a fairly irregular basis, over the entire one hundred and sixteen year period that the conflict eventually lasted. Largely involving merchant vessels that had been commandeered by the Crown, most of these craft were thought to have been oared galleys that usually carried cargoes, to and from the continent, although many of the English vessels were thought to be specially built warships manned by up to one hundred oarsmen, with archers and soldiers onboard to attack enemy vessels and their crews. Even though the English fleet was thought to have enjoyed considerable success during the various periods of conflict that made up the Hundred Years War, including aiding the successful military campaigns of Edward III and Edward V, ultimately the end of the war and pressure from the merchants whose ships were regularly being commandeered by the Crown, resulted in a significant reduction of the English naval forces. The fall in the numbers of English ships was said to have occurred in the latter part of the 14th and beginning of the 15th century, leading to increased incidents of piracy, in and around the English coastline, a development that was thought have caused such alarm in the country that in 1441 the English Parliament was forced to demand that the monarch authorise the building of eight "ballingers", relatively small ships with no forecastle, driven by a single sail and manned by approximately forty men, who could row or fight, depending on the circumstances.

Perhaps one of the most significant events of the early 15th century however, was the construction of England's first "great ships", including the likes of the "Grace Dieu", which along with a number of other vessels was said to have been constructed between 1413 and 1439, during the reigns of both Henry V and Henry VI. First commissioned in 1416 to compete with the Genoan carracks of continental Europe, the Grace Dieu was reported to be a three ply clinker built vessel, which was designed and laid down in Southampton where a dock was specially built for her subsequent construction. By the time the ship was completed in 1418, she was reported to have been one of the largest crafts of her type, measuring some two hundred and twenty feet in length and weighing something in the region of two thousand tons. Unfortunately, the Grace Dieu was said to have only undertaken a single voyage, being accompanied by two smaller ships, the Valentine and Falcon, on a journey to an unspecified destination, although the voyage was curtailed after a mutiny onboard, which resulted in the vessel being brought back home and laid up on the River Hamble. The ship was later said to have been de-masted and much of her equipment removed, a situation that was said to have continued until 1439 when the unfortunate vessel was reported to have been struck by lightning, causing a fire that ultimately destroyed much of her fabric. Even today the remaining portions of the ships structure are known to exist on the river bed of the Hamble, despite having been investigated by a number of archaeological teams, as a result of which it is now protected by legal statute.

Throughout the 14th and 15th centuries England's navy was known to have suffered a series of peaks and troughs in its fortunes, largely as a result of the prevailing political, military or royal considerations of the day and it was only with the emergence of the Tudor dynasty that England's rise to prominence as a major European seapower first began. It was said to have been Henry VII of England, the founder of the Tudor dynasty, who first arranged for his nations fighting ships to be financed through the introduction of an import levy, allowing him to order a series of newly subsidised vessels that could defend his kingdom's borders, without necessarily having to commandeer private merchant ships for the purpose. It was also Henry VII who was said to be responsible for the building of the first European and now the world's oldest surviving dry dock at Portsmouth in 1495, beginning a trend in English shipbuilding that would subsequently be copied by both his son Henry VIII and by his grand-daughter, Elizabeth I. By the time Henry Tudor ascended the English throne the most common design of ship included the Caravel and the larger Carrack, both of which were masted vessels, capable of harnessing the wind in order to create momentum and able to cross vast expanses of water, making them ideal for maritime exploration. In the footsteps of the previously mentioned Grace Dieu, English shipbuilders were said to have constructed a number of great masted ships, including the "Regent" and the "Sovereign", each of which was described as four-masted Carracks and weighing in excess of six hundred tons. However, the Regent was reported to have been lost following a battle with the French in 1512, whilst the Sovereign was later thought to have disappeared from the official records sometime after 1520, possibly as a result of her being damaged or dismantled in English waters.

Without intending to offer a full uninterrupted history on the development of the Caravel or Carrack, it is perhaps worth noting that both shared a common history and that the later Carrack was reported to be a successor to the much earlier Caravel, which had itself originated in the waters of the Mediterranean. According to some sources, the western European caravel, was thought to have originated from a variety of much earlier Arabic craft including the Arab Qarib, along with the Muslim Algarvian and Maghrebine, all of which were initially designed as relatively small, shallow draught vessels that were driven by one or two lateen-rigged sails (triangular shaped). Commonly used as cargo vessels, warships and troop carriers, initially it was thought that such was the importance of these ships to individual Mediterranean states that shipbuilders were forbidden from recording their designs, or indeed sharing them with outsiders, for fear that they might be copied or improved. However, almost inevitably, as these vessels travelled in and out of their home waters, so the eventually came to the attention of western European shipbuilders, including those in southern Spain and Portugal, regions that had been ruled by the Arab Moors right through to the 12th century. Using these early Mediterranean vessels as a template, over time the design of the ship was said to have been adapted and altered to better suit the heavier waters of the Atlantic coastline, with the ships becoming larger and more sails being added, in order for bigger crews and larger cargoes to be carried from one place to another. By the end of the 14th century, the Portuguese ruler, Henry the Navigator was ordering his mariners to venture out into the world's great oceans in the latest version of the Caravel, although given the size of the sails, which required a large crew, this often proved to be problematic, as the ships were very often unable to carry sufficient stores of food and water to supply the company over an extended period of time. As a result, the vessels were thought to have increased in size, requiring even more sails to drive them, which inevitably led to the introduction of additional masts to hold them, a situation that eventually led to the creation of the bigger, faster, two, three and four masted craft that would finally manage to circumnavigate the world.

As European ships increased in size and weight, as well as additional masts being added, so too the fundamental shape of these great ships was inexorably altered, with enormous forecastles and aftcastles being added, as well as larger areas of storage and accommodations, all of which were necessary to make the ship run efficiently and profitably. Where the earliest Caravels were thought to have weighed anything up to one hundred tons, towards the end of the 15th century, most ships commonly weighed some four, five or six times as much, while a much smaller number were even thought to have achieved weights of a thousand tons or more, a situation that inevitably led to the development of the much larger Carrack type of ship, both of which would come to dominate European seafaring for much of the 16th and 17th centuries. Where the Caravel was typically a one, two or three masted vessel, the Carrack was more commonly driven by at least three or four sets of sails, as well as having a high rounded stern, topped with an enormous aftcastle, whilst at the front of the ship there was an equally high forecastle, both of which were employed as observation points as well as fighting platforms. Employing a mix of square and lateen type sails, the Carrack was first and foremost an ocean going vessel, which was big enough to accommodate the amounts of stores and numbers of crew necessary for extended sea voyages, especially those that involved crossing the world's great oceans, where the journey could take many weeks or months. Although the smaller Caravels could and continued to be used for transatlantic journeys, the larger Carrack tended to be the vessel of choice for these longer sea journeys, simply because of its greater size and durability, important factors for early seafarers who were acutely aware of the many dangers they faced whilst sailing the open oceans. In England, the first great Carrack built by Henry V was the previously mentioned Grace Dieu, although in later years Scottish shipbuilders were reported to have constructed the "Great Michael", the largest vessel of its type in Europe at that time, an event that led the Tudor monarch Henry VIII to order the building of the "Mary Rose", "Henri Grace a Dieu" and the "Peter Pomegranate", three Carracks which ultimately suffered entirely different fates.

Carrack   **Caravel**   **Galleon**

The most famous of Henry VIII's carrack type warships, the Mary Rose' notoriety has almost inevitably been brought about by her sudden and unexpected loss in the Solent in July 1545, an event that was witnessed by any number of spectators, but yet became the subject of sometimes heated debate, as to what actually caused her calamitous loss, a topic of debate that has continued through to the modern day. The ship has also gained worldwide fame through the highly publicised salvage operation undertaken in 1982, which brought large sections of the vessel to the surface once again, to be preserved as a museum exhibit, allowing historians, archaeologists and the general public to gain an insight into the life and times of those many Tudor mariners whose existence was brought to a sudden and catastrophic end more than four hundred years earlier. First laid down in 1510, the Mary Rose was constructed at Portsmouth and officially launched in July 1511, before being towed to London, where she was said to have been fitted out with rigging, sails and the necessary armaments. Built in the traditional carrack style of the age, Henry's new warship was said to have included the usual high fore and aft castles, divided by the much lower open central deck, all of which sat above the three lower decks, where stores, cargo, guns and men were accommodated. Fitted with four masts, the ship was thought to have been able to carry anything up to ten sails when fully rigged, which would have included both square and lateen type sails, making her fast by the standards of the day, although incredibly slow and cumbersome by more modern standards. Designed as a warship, the Mary Rose was thought to have been built to incorporate a large number of gun ports along her sides, allowing a broadside to be delivered, but which according to some historians may well have played a significant part in her later loss. Even though gun ports were said to have been introduced as early as 1501, including them into the design of the ship could often prove to be damaging to the overall structure of the vessel, causing weaknesses to occur and allowing water to penetrate through the previously watertight hull. Throughout her career, not only was the Mary Rose subject to occasional changes in her layout and equipment, but in 1536 she was said to have undergone a major refit, in order to include some of the new technological advances that had been made since she was first constructed in 1511. Likewise, her armaments were also thought to have been altered on occasion, with periods of war and peace dictating the levels of weaponry that the ship and her crew would have carried, as well as the actual numbers of men who were on the ship at any one time, which might well have varied from twenty to some seven hundred, when armed troops were carried aboard.

First used in battle in a war against a French fleet in 1512, despite being at the cutting edge of marine technology, the Mary Rose was thought to have been accompanied by two much larger English carracks, the "Regent" and the "Peter Pomegranate", which between them, were reported to have been carrying an estimated five thousand men. In later naval engagements, the Mary Rose was said to have bombarded a French fleet causing it to withdraw, whilst the Regent was not so fortunate, reportedly being sunk by an explosion caused when an enemy ship's magazine blew up as the English carrack lay alongside. Although she was thought to have participated in a number of other military operations, when peace was finally declared England and France in 1514, the Mary Rose, along with a number of other warships was said to have been placed in the reserves, maintained, but not on active service, a situation the continued to be the case until 1522, when the two countries once again found themselves at war with one another. However, apart from participating in the transportation of troops across the English Channel, the Mary Rose was thought to have seen little direct action and was returned to the reserves from 1522 until 1545, during which time she was said to have been refitted and maintained in readiness for her future use. In May 1545 though, Henry heard reports that the French were assembling a fleet in readiness for an invasion of England, forcing him to recall all of his naval reserves back into frontline service, including the newly updated Mary Rose, which subsequently joined the other English ships, including the king's newest warship, the Henri Grace a Dieu, in the waters of the Solent where they awaited the arrival of the extremely large and well equipped French fleet. Initially becalmed by the lack of wind, the English navy was forced to rely on its small number of oared galleys to confront the French vessels, although a sudden change in conditions and a favourable wind allowed the English carracks to move out against the enemy ships, with the Mary Rose and the Henri Grace a Dieu taking the lead, much to the relief of the smaller English ships. Unfortunately, as she prepared to engage the French galleys, the Mary Rose was seen to lean heavily to her starboard side, allowing water to rush in through her open gun ports and swamping the ship within a matter of moments. Unable to correct the problem, many of Mary Rose' crew were said to have simply abandoned her, anxious to avoid the rigging and anti-boarding nets that might easily entangle them and drag them to their deaths. With the fated ship heeling over, many of the large cannons, stove and other metal implements were thought to have caused mayhem amongst the panic stricken crew and soldiers, killing and maiming those who were unlucky enough to be standing in their way. It was thought to be as a result of this confused situation and the presence of the anti-boarding nets that less than forty men managed to escape from the Mary Rose alive, which was less than 10% of her total crew. Later reports of the catastrophe, all seemed to indicate that a number of factors had caused the loss of the Mary Rose, rather than one single incident or oversight, such as the gun ports being open as the ship attempted to turn. The most widely accepted theory is that a combination of too much weight on the upper decks, added to an unexpected breeze and the open gun ports all combined to allow water to enter the ship and ultimately seal its fate. Although several attempts were made to raise the wreck in the days and years following the disaster, eventually some of her cannons and other equipment were salvaged from the site, but a full scale rescue of the Mary Rose proved to be beyond the capabilities of the time and over time the site of the wreck was forgotten and the Mary Rose herself passed into history.

Although built after the Mary Rose, the Henri Grace a Dieu (Henry Grace of God), or more popularly known as the "Great Harry" was said to have been ordered by Henry VIII as a direct response to the launch of the Scottish Carrack, the "Great Michael", which was built at Newhaven, Edinburgh in 1511. Reportedly twice the size of Henry's flagship, the "Mary Rose", the "Great Michael" was reported to be around two hundred and forty feet in length, thirty five feet in width, weighed an estimated one thousand tons, had four masts and carried around seventy guns, as well as carrying a crew of three hundred seamen and several hundred troops, making her one of the most formidable warships in the whole of Europe. Not to be outdone by his northerly neighbours, Henry VIII was said to have ordered the construction of the Great Harry in 1512, with the work being undertaken at the Woolwich Dockyards, between 1512 and 1514, creating a carrack type ship that was around one hundred and sixty five feet long and weighing somewhere between one thousand and fifteen hundred tons, with a forecastle four storeys high and the capability to carry up to an estimated one thousand men. Built with specially designed gun ports, in total the Great Harry was reported to have carried nearly two hundred guns, both light and heavy, twenty of which were said to be of the new bronze type cannons that allowed a catastrophic broadside to be delivered against enemy ships. By the time of its launch in 1514, the Tudor warship was thought to have been the most heavily armed European fighting ship of the age, although within forty years was thought to have ended her days as a rotting hulk on the banks of the River Thames, although according to some other reports she was said to have been destroyed by fire whilst moored at Woolwich in 1553.

16th Century Ship

Mary Rose

Henri Grace a Dieu

A small number of English ports were thought to have been responsible for building many of England's early warships and cargo carriers, including Portsmouth, Woolwich, Convoys Wharf, Chatham and Devonport, with Portsmouth reportedly being the oldest of these major shipbuilding centres, the Roman's having used the city as their main naval base in the 3rd century AD. Some six centuries later, the Anglo Saxon monarch, Alfred the Great, was reported to have employed the city as one of the principal bases for his fledgling English fleet, raised to fight the dual maritime menace of the Vikings and seaborne raiders, who regularly attacked his kingdom's coastline. Centred round the ancient Roman camp of Portchester, England's Anglo Saxon monarchs were thought to have continued to use the site as a naval station right through to the 11th century invasion of the country by the Norman forces of William the Conqueror. However, despite the changes introduced by the Norman invaders, Portsmouth was said to have retained its importance as a naval base, so much so that by the beginning of the 13th century the Plantagenet monarch, King John, was reported to have ordered a dock to be built there, where the royal ships might be berthed and repaired, although the new dock was later said to have been inundated by the sea and lost by 1228. Despite this however, by 1265, the city was thought to have regained much of its importance as a major maritime base, to the extent that in 1265 parts of Portsmouth were deliberately burnt by the Baron's of the neighbouring Cinque Ports who were concerned about the increasing importance of the city; and its ability to attract many of the shipwrights and skilled craftsmen away from their own ports.

Although the port was thought to have received less support from later English monarchs, when Henry Tudor ascended the throne in 1485, he was said to have begun a program of rebuilding the English fleet, a part of which was reported to have included the construction of a new dry dock at Portsmouth, a project that was finally begun in 1495. Comprising a timber built dry dock, in the area of today's HMS Victory, this new shipbuilding facility was said to have included inner and outer gates that allowed water to be pumped in and out of the dock, using a new water engine which employed a number of iron buckets. The first English ship to use these new dry dock facilities was reported to be the "Sovereign", which was berthed at Portsmouth on 25th May 1496, presumably the same previously mentioned vessel that would eventually disappear from the official records after 1520. Even though Henry Tudor is credited with being the monarch who reorganised the financing and building of the English fleet, for most historians it was his son and royal successor, Henry VIII, who was largely responsible for the expansion and rearmament of England's fighting ships, with some eighty five different vessels reportedly being ordered by the king during his reign, including the likes of the Mary Rose. It was also said to be during Henry VIII's extensive reign that Portsmouth was officially appointed as England's main royal dockyards, becoming a centre of maritime excellence that would go on to build some of the nations biggest and most iconic warships right through to the 20th century.

The first English dockyard ordered by Henry VIII, was reported to be the one founded at Woolwich in 1512, ostensibly to complete the construction of the king's own warship, the Henri Grace a Dieu, at the time of its completion in 1514, the largest vessel of its type in all of Europe. Initially chosen because of its convenient location to Henry's royal palace at

Greenwich, over time, Woolwich would grow to include two of the largest dry docks in the country, along with an assortment of shipbuilding facilities, including ironworks that could produce the necessary metalwork for the numerous ships that would be built there, such as their anchors, etc. A large number of notable English ships were thought to have been built at Woolwich, beginning with the Henri Grace a Dieu (1514), right through to the HMS Beagle (1820), although as ships grew larger and the Thames began to suffer from increasing levels of silting, the dockyards at Woolwich were thought to have become less and less viable, leading to their eventual closure in 1869. A similar fate was reported to have occurred to the neighbouring royal dockyards at Deptford, which were said to have been founded by Henry VIII in 1513 as the King's Yard, but became more commonly known as Convoys Wharf. Developing into one of Tudor England's biggest and most important shipyards, it was said to have become inextricably linked to some of the most notable incidents of England's maritime history, including the knighting of Francis Drake by Elizabeth I and the despatching of English warships to confront the Spanish Armada. By the beginning of the 18th century though, a combination of increasing ship sizes, silting of the Thames and the greater suitability of other English dockyards to undertake naval work, had left both Woolwich and Deptford virtually obsolete, causing both of them to be closed in 1864, bringing an end to over 300 years of naval history on the two sites.

Although Portsmouth, Deptford and Woolwich remained the three most important shipyards in England up until 1544, with Deptford carrying out most of the important repairs on the king's ship, within three years yet another location had been added to this relatively short list of strategically important harbours. Gillingham Water as Chatham was more commonly known, was reported to have been established as a royal dockyard by Queen Elizabeth I in 1567 and by the 17th century was said to have become the largest refitting and repair dockyard in all of England. However, changes in the country's political and military priorities, along with the growth of the Royal Navy bases at Portsmouth and Plymouth, all contrived to reduce Chatham's importance as a major refitting centre and forced it to move from refitting vessels to actually constructing them. As part of this same reorganisation and in order to account for the increasing silting of the River Medway, the dockyards operations were said to have been relocated, allowing for the construction of much needed Royal Navy vessels, such as HMS Victory, which was launched from the yard in 1765. Following its move in 1622 and right through to 1885 the dockyards were said to have continued to expand, including the construction of four new dry dock facilities, much of which were thought to have been built using convict labour and causing a significant growth in the areas brick building industry that was asked to supply the necessary materials. Chatham's fortunes were further improved in 1869, following the closure of the two historic royal dockyards at Woolwich and Deptford, an event that was thought to have helped Chatham retain its position as a major shipbuilding centre all the way through to the 20th century. For much of its later history, the dockyards were reported to have been redeveloped in order to build and refit Royal Navy submarines, a role that it was thought to have first undertaken in 1908 and which continued uninterrupted until 1981, when the yard was earmarked for closure within three years. However, despite the yards being closed as a working Royal Navy facility in 1984, significant parts of the site were later saved by the establishment of the Chatham Historic Dockyards Trust, a society dedicated to the preservation of the historic site.

Although a fifth Royal dockyard would eventually be added to the list of England's great maritime centres, the important naval base of Devonport would only finally be constructed in 1690, a little over a century after England had finally secured her place as one of Europe's leading naval powers, following her defeat of the Spanish Armada in 1588. It was said to be this single historic event that inexorably linked the city of Plymouth to England's Royal Navy, despite the fact that the city itself was rejected as the site for the later naval base, largely because it was deemed to be unsuitable for the construction of the large dry dock facilities that were planned for the new royal dockyards. Despite these later issues however, the city was still remembered as the place where England's Royal Navy ships sailed out through the mouth of the River Plym to begin the military engagement that would not only secure Queen Elizabeth's position within her own kingdom, but also mark the start of a journey that would see her country achieve almost complete military supremacy over the high seas for well over three centuries. As with any great achievement though, Elizabeth's famous naval victory over the forces of the Roman Catholic monarch, Philip of Spain, was only really accomplished through a combination of circumstances, including those that affected the weather, personnel and of course the numbers and types of ships that each of the two sides deployed during the pivotal maritime confrontation.

Relations between England and Spain were thought to have been uneasy since the reign of Henry VIII, who not only created a schism with the Catholic Church, but also with the Spanish Court over his treatment of his first wife, Catherine of Aragon, the mother of Henry's first legitimate child, Mary, who the English king subsequently divorced in order to marry Anne Boleyn. It was said to be as a direct result of the Tudor monarch's actions that future relations between England and Spain would become fractious, with first Mary, the daughter of Catherine of Aragon ascending the English throne, to be followed by Elizabeth, the daughter of Anne Boleyn, one a Roman Catholic and the other a Protestant. Having reformed the English Church over a period of years during the 1530's, which resulted in him being excommunicated from the Church of Rome on at least two occasions, when Henry VIII died in 1547, he left behind three children, two of which were Protestants and the other a Roman Catholic, creating a situation that would cause decades of religious conflict, not only in England, but in Europe generally. Henry's immediate successor, Edward VI, was only nine years old when he inherited the English throne and as a consequence the religious fate of the country was left in the hands of his royal advisers and protectors, most of whom were vehement Protestants and staunch anti-Catholics who persecuted anyone who failed to share their faith. However, when Edward died in 1553 and despite an attempt to put Lady Jane Grey on the English throne, it was Henry VIII's oldest daughter, Mary, daughter of Catherine of Aragon and a staunch Roman Catholic who ascended as the next legitimate Tudor monarch, creating a complete reversal of the country's religious position, with Protestants feeling the full wrath of Mary's royal disfavour. From a Spanish perspective, the ascension of the Catholic Mary I to the English throne was thought to have come as a welcome relief, as a result of which Philip II of Spain subsequently married the English queen, not only to produce a Roman Catholic heir for England and therefore prevent Mary's half sister, Elizabeth, from inheriting the Crown, but also to provide Spain with influence in the English Court. Unfortunately for the Catholic cause, events elsewhere in Europe and Mary's deteriorating health ensured that there would be no royal heir for the English queen and her Spanish consort, a personal unhappiness that might well have incited Mary and her advisers to restore a series of medieval heresy laws that were used to suppress the Protestant faith in England and elsewhere, leading to hundreds of devout believers being burnt at the stake under the terms of what became known as the Marian Persecutions. Such was the scale of the anti-Protestant campaigns ordered by the English queen that she quickly earned herself the epithet of "Bloody Mary", a title that even some four hundred and sixty years later still attaches itself to her short and bloody reign. Even though during her time on the English throne, Mary I was said to have restored much of the Catholic Church's status, authority, lands and wealth, ultimately it proved to be of little long term use to the followers of her faith, as when she died childless in 1558, she was immediately followed to the English throne by her half sister, Elizabeth, as staunch a Protestant, as Mary had been Roman Catholic.

Restoring many of the Protestant rights that had been removed and suppressed under her royal predecessor, Elizabeth was said to have been the monarch who was responsible for completing the religious divisions between England and Rome that had been begun by her father Henry VIII. Although she was said to have been generally more tolerant to the Roman Catholic faith than Mary had been to Protestants, Elizabeth was reported to have been the sovereign who first accepted the appointment as the Supreme Governor of the Church of England, without actually declaring herself as the Head of the Church, as is the case today. It was also Elizabeth who oversaw the widespread removal of ornamentation from English churches, the dismissal of leading Roman Catholics from the Privy Council and the enforced attendance of her subjects in Anglican churches, where they would be expected to read from the Book of Common Prayer. However, despite the introduction of such laws, the Protestant queen was seen as being far more liberal towards other faiths, although outside of England itself, the restoration of the Protestant church and even Elizabeth's right to rule were thought to be the subject of far less reasoned debates, with some Catholic rulers and the leadership of the church in Rome calling for her removal. One of the most outspoken and vociferous of Elizabeth's enemies was the Catholic monarch Philip II of Spain, who despite having previously spoken out for Elizabeth when she was threatened by Mary I, had ultimately come to regard the young Protestant queen as not only illegitimate, but also as a heretic. Anxious to see England return to the Catholic fold, Philip was known to have involved himself in a number of plots against Elizabeth, most notably, in the support he showed for Elizabeth's cousin and potential royal successor, Mary Queen of Scots, who allowed herself to become involved in a plan to assassinate the English queen and as a result found herself facing the royal executioner. When Elizabeth had Mary executed in 1587, for the Roman Catholic community in Europe and particularly the Spanish, the death of their favoured candidate and regal relative proved to be the final straw for Philip who immediately began to plan for the military invasion of England, in order to settle the matter once and for all.

Mary's execution aside, there were thought to be a number of reasons why Philip was anxious to invade England and bring an end to Elizabeth's reign, not least of which was her support for those Dutch forces who were resisting Spain's conquest of the Low Countries, as well as English Privateer's continuing attacks on the Spanish treasure ships that regularly travelled across the Atlantic between Europe and the New World. Even though Elizabeth was reported to have publicly condemned the actions of such privateers, in reality many of these same ships were thought to have carried official papers authorising them to carry out such actions, with the English Crown receiving its fair share of the various prizes that were seized by the likes of Drake and Hawkins, etc. Assembling a large fleet of ships from Spain, Portugal and Naples, King Philip planned to send his enormous armada northward, into the English Channel, where Spanish troops in the Netherlands would be embarked on the fleets numerous ships and barges, before being delivered to the coast of Kent, to begin their military invasion of England. Unfortunately for the Spanish monarch, the fleet commander who he had originally appointed to lead his great religious crusade, the Marquis de Santa Cruz, was reported to have died in February 1588, leaving Philip II with no obvious replacement and forcing him to appoint the generally unsuitable Duke of Medina Sidonia, a nobleman with absolutely no previous naval or military experience whatsoever. Perhaps recognising his own limited abilities and the weight of expectation being placed on him personally, the Duke was reported to have asked the Spanish king to excuse him the appointment, but Philip was said to have refused the nobleman's request and ordered him to take command of the armada that had been assembled at Lisbon.

Philip II of Spain   Queen Mary I   Catherine of Aragon

From a number of contemporary reports, the Spanish Armada was said to have been composed of a number of different types of ships, most of which were entirely suitable for the planned venture, but others that were not, having been specifically designed to travel in the much calmer waters of the Mediterranean, rather than the heavier Atlantic seas. A case in point was said to be the Neapolitan Galleys that had been included in the Spanish monarch's fleet, extremely long ships that were propelled by oarsman, with such low sides that a number of them were said to have foundered in the heavy waters of the Atlantic coastline, forcing the remainder to return to port. Reportedly totalling some one hundred and sixty ships, the great Spanish Armada was said to have included a mixture of the maritime vessels of the age, from caravels to carracks, from galleons to hulks, in fact any sort of sea going vessel that was capable of delivering Spanish troops onto English soil. The principal vessels of Philip's armada were thought to have been the Portuguese Galleons, extremely large sailing ships that rode high in the water and which included prominent forecastles and aftcastles that were generally employed as fighting towers, from where sharpshooters and archers could fire down on the crew of an enemy ship. These huge ships and their large crews would typically use their guns to try and disable an enemy ship, before moving in close to board the enemy vessel and overpower its personnel, a form of naval warfare that was said to have existed for hundreds of years. Other types of vessels that were thought to have formed part of the large Spanish fleet included a number of ships that were primarily identified by their region, rather than by their type, being known as Biscayans, Castilians, Andalusians and Levantines, all of which were reported as being galleons of one sort or another. In addition to these ships, there was thought to be a number of hulks, large cargo vessels that were used to ferry soldiers and stores, as well as oared galleasses and xbecs, a small three masted sailing vessel that was commonly employed in the waters of the Mediterranean. Virtually all the Spanish ships were known to have been armed with cannons, from the smallest xbec, right up to the mightiest galleon, with the likes of the Sao Martinho carrying fifty guns, Santa Ana thirty guns, San Christobal thirty six guns, Nuestra Senora del Rosario forty six guns, whilst some of the larger galleys and galleasses were said to have carried anything up to fifty guns onboard. According to one source, by the time it set out on its journey towards the English Channel, the great armada was said to have been composed of one hundred and forty individual ships, nearly nine thousand sailors, some twenty two thousand soldiers and oarsmen numbering some two thousand convicts.

Opposing this enormous Spanish fleet was said to have been an equally impressive English naval force, which according to some sources was thought to have numbered as many as two hundred vessels, comprising some thirty-odd full-time royal navy ships, a dozen or so privateers, owned by the likes of Drake, Hawkins, Frobisher and Lord Howard of Effingham, along with an estimated one hundred and fifty vessels, which were reported to be English cargo vessels, coasters and barks specifically commandeered for the coming battle, but owned by various merchants and trading companies. Said to have been much smaller in size to the great Spanish galleons, over a period of time and thanks largely to the likes of Hawkins and Drake, many of England's Elizabethan warships were said to have been deliberately redesigned to make them smaller, more stable and considerably faster than their European counterparts, a shipbuilding trend that would ultimately prove to be pivotal for the supposedly outgunned and outnumbered English navy. Unlike the Spanish and the Portuguese, English ship designers had chosen to remove the towering forecastles and aftcastles from their vessels, not only making them smaller, but also lighter and faster, forcing English mariners to adopt new tactics, other than seeking to simply board enemy vessels to seize them. Instead English sea captains began to employ their cannons to greater effect, standing off from the bigger enemy ships and bombarding them into submission or destruction; and only boarding them as the final act of a sea battle. Comprising the likes of the Ark, Revenge, Victory, Triumph and Swallow, the English fleet was thought to have remained in home waters, save for a short-lived expedition to the Bay of Biscay in July 1588 where the English Admiral, Lord Howard of Effingham hoped to attack the armada at Corunna harbour, although weather conditions prevented him from carrying out the raid, leaving him with little option but to return to Plymouth and wait for the Spanish fleet to arrive in the Channel. It was only later in July that the captain of the Golden Hinde was reported to have spotted the vanguard of the Spanish armada off the south east coast of England and immediately turned his ship towards Plymouth to alert the English fleet. Arriving back in port, Captain Fleming announced the sighting of the enemy ships, whilst Drake and his fellow officers were enjoying a game of bowls on the Ho, high above the harbour. Having been given the news Drake was said to have calmly continued the game, creating a national legend for himself that would continue to exist right through to the present day. However, by the evening of the 19th July 1588, Lord Howard and a small contingent of around twenty English ships were thought to have sailed out of Plymouth and into the Channel, where the following morning they were joined by thirty-odd more warships, ready to face the mighty fleet that was still making its way northward. By the following evening, Howard and Drake were reported to have caught sight of the Spanish fleet, beginning a week long game of cat and mouse, with the English ships choosing to shadow their adversaries, rather than just engage them outright. However, as the days passed and the Spanish vessels became detached from one another, the English sailors were thought to have practiced their gunnery skills against the occasional enemy ship that came within range, most notably at Eddystone and the Isle of Portland, although there were no reports of any ship being seriously damaged or destroyed by the English ship's hit and run tactics. It was reported though that two of the Spanish ships had accidentally collided with one another whilst they were being pursued by the English fleet, as a result of which the two ships, the carrack Rosario and the galleon San Salvador were said to be so badly damaged that both were subsequently abandoned by their crews. Having witnessed the incident, the English privateer, Sir Francis Drake, was said to have returned to the two abandoned vessels with the intention of looting any supplies of gunpowder, weapons or treasure that had been left behind on the Spanish warships, but in doing so had to extinguish the lanterns that were guiding the English fleet, causing them to become separated in the darkness of the Channel.

The Spanish king's plan for the invasion of England was thought to have called for the Duke of Medina Sidonia to bring the armada to the south coast of England, where it would be met by a second fleet, which was to have been despatched from the Netherlands by the Spanish commander there, Alexander Parnese, the Duke of Parma. Unfortunately, the Duke of Parma was thought to have been experiencing problems of his own, being faced by a combined Dutch and English army in the Netherlands, which had reduced both the numbers and effectiveness of the troops that he was supposed to send to England as part of the invasion force. Seemingly a good deal more intuitive than his king, Philip II, Parma was said to have recognised the potential danger that the English fleet posed to his own forces and was therefore reluctant to despatch any troops to England before the English navy had been fully eliminated by Sidonia's ships, a task that he believed to be beyond the ability of the Spanish vessels. As a result, Parma had no intention of setting sail from Dunkirk before the armada were able to provide him and his men with safe conduct across the Channel, a decision that ensured that neither he, nor his forces were waiting off the south coast of England when the armada arrived in the area. Consequently, the Duke of Medina Sidonia was forced to detour to the French side of the Channel to try and embark Parma and his men, a decision that ultimately proved to be a fruitless exercise in the light of later events. According to a number of historians, this enforced detour and the reluctance of Parma to fully support the planned invasion were just two of many reasons why the Spanish armada had been doomed to failure ever since the idea was first conceived by Philip II of Spain.

First and foremost Philip was said to have underestimated the strength, abilities and determination of the English navy, believing it to be inferior to that of his own nation, despite the fact that the likes of Drake, Raleigh and Hawkins had consistently got the better of Spanish forces in the preceding years. Even leaving that matter aside though, perhaps the Spanish monarch's greatest error had been to plan the campaign, not only in haste, but also whilst he was in an emotional state over the death of Mary, Queen of Scots, which almost inevitably ensured that the invasion that he envisioned was not only badly planned and insufficiently supplied, but also poorly executed and understood. As has been previously noted, Spanish warfare techniques onboard ship differed markedly from those of the English, in that Spain's warships relied more heavily on close quarter, hand-to-hand combat, with their heavy ship's cannons being used sparingly, with victory generally being determined by the ship's crew seizing an enemy vessel, rather than destroying or damaging it from a distance, as was often the case with England's warships. Notably, when the wrecks of Spanish armada ships were later investigated, it was said to be noticeable that many of them still contained large numbers of cannonballs, indicating that most of them had fired relatively few salvoes at the English warships, which by contrast were reported to have run out of ammunition in their attacks against the Spanish galleons. In a related matter, it has also been suggested that many of the cannonballs aboard the Spanish ships had been so badly made that it was likely that most of those that were fired at the English carracks would have shattered after being fired, or as they struck the hardened oak timbers of the English ships, causing little if any damage to the structure of the vessels themselves. It has also been suggested that many of the guns on the great Spanish galleons were unable to be used in the first place, as later archaeological investigations were thought to have revealed that in numerous cases the munitions aboard the ships did not match the cannon themselves, indicating that even if the crews onboard the Spanish warships had wanted to fire their guns, in all likelihood they would have been unable to do so. The problems with the armaments aside, it was also thought that many of the stores placed aboard the Spanish ships for the lengthy expedition were either rotten, or inedible, with water barrels leaking so badly that more men were said to have been lost to disease, starvation and thirst than were lost to the weaponry of the English fleet. Added to these many logistical problems, Philip of Spain was also thought to have been labouring under a number of misconceptions regarding the people of Britain themselves, most notably his belief that Roman Catholic's throughout

England, Wales and Scotland would rise up to support his planned invasion, an event that was never likely to occur. In fact, it was reported that some of the first men to rush to England's defence were Roman Catholics, who along with their Protestant countrymen were appalled at the very thought of a Spanish invasion and certainly had no desire to live under a foreign monarch.

Having left Lisbon on 28th May 1588 the large Spanish fleet was said to have travelled north along the Portuguese coast at a relatively low rate of knots, its speed dictated by the slowest of the great ships that often found themselves struggling to cope with the weather conditions of the North Atlantic. Having reportedly taken some three weeks to navigate their way along the coast of Portugal, from Lisbon to Cape Finisterre, by the time they arrived at the Spanish port of Corunna, many of the sailors and soldiers onboard the ships were said to be suffering from hunger, thirst and disease, causing the Duke Medina Sidonia to relay his concerns over the suitability of the armada to King Philip II once again, although as before, the monarch was said to have ignored his naval commander's fears and ordered the venture to go ahead as planned. As if to reinforce Sidonia's concerns, as the huge fleet lay offshore, waiting to be re-provisioned, a severe Atlantic storm was said to blown in, scattering many of the vessels and causing the remainder to run for the port of Corunna, where it was feared they might pose a potential target for English fire ships. However, with little choice but to wait for the armada to be reassembled, the Duke of Medina was thought to have had little option but to remain in port for the best part of a month, giving the Spanish authorities plenty of time to carry out repairs and restock the fleet's spoiled and inadequate provisions. Having recovered most of the vessels that had been dispersed by the storm and with the armada now fully re-supplied, by the middle of July 1588 the Spanish fleet was reported to have left Corunna, narrowly avoiding the small English flotilla that Lord Howard of Effingham had brought to the Spanish coast to try and intercept the invasion force. Reaching the Scilly Isles on the 19th July 1588, the armada then travelled northward along the English coastline towards its planned meeting with the invasion barges of the Duke of Parma, who as previously noted, had not even despatched his forces from the Netherlands, leaving the Duke of Medina with little option but to cross the Channel and try and link up with Parma's troops on the European side of the waterway. Unfortunately, as Sidonia's naval commanders were largely unfamiliar with Dutch waters and his ships at risk from the Dutch navy, the Duke of Medina was said to have made the decision to sail to the French port of Calais, a harbour that might afford his fleet safe anchorage, from where he could contact the Duke of Parma directly.

Duke Medonia Sidonia

Portuguese Galleon

Duke of Palma

Even as he made the decision to head for Calais, the Duke of Medina recognised the potential dangers of gathering his enormous naval fleet within the French port, especially from the threat of English fire ships, which he knew might be one of the possible tactics employed by the likes of Drake or Hawkins, who were said to have been shadowing the armada ever since it had arrived off the English coastline on the 20th July. By the 27th of the month the Spanish fleet was reported to have been anchored in Calais, ostensibly while it waited for the Duke of Parma to inform them of his own intentions regarding the provision of the thousands of troops that were necessary for the planned invasion of England, although as it transpired, eventually he informed the Duke of Medina that he was unable to supply the men immediately, forcing the Spanish plans to be amended once again. Unfortunately, as they waited for Parma to make a decision, the fleet remained at risk from the English navy that was said to be patrolling off the French coast and who were reported to have been conducting raids against and bombardments of the tightly packed Spanish vessels in Calais, a continuing threat that undoubtedly forced Sidonia's hand somewhat. However, for the Spanish commanders, the greatest menace was the possible use of fire ships by the English navy, who were said to have brought a number of such vessels with them, as they pursued their Spanish quarry across the Channel, including the likes of the Hope, Thomas, Elizabeth and Angel. Filled with pitch, gunpowder and a mixture of combustible materials, on the evening of the 28th July 1588 eight English fire ships were thought to have been sailed into the harbour at Calais, where they were set ablaze by the handful of English sailors who were aboard each of the vessels, who then allowed them to drift into the packed ranks of the Spanish fleet. Although Sidonia and his commanders had planned for such a raid and had posted a number of picket ships to intercept any English fire ships that were sent into the French port, according to some witnesses only one of the eight fire boats was successfully intercepted, leaving the other seven to continue their passage unhindered and forcing Spanish commanders to cut their anchor lines, in order to escape the floating conflagrations. Even though it was not immediately obvious at the time, the decision by some captains to sever their anchor lines would ultimately prove to be fatal, as it robbed the vessels of their only method of saving themselves when caught in stormy weather, something that would eventually lead to the loss of half of the Spanish fleet and the deaths of thousands of their seamen and soldiers.

As pandemonium broke out amongst the armada's numerous vessels, the waiting English ships were reported to have begun a full scale attack on the fleeing Spanish fleet, which had begun to scatter in all directions, beginning what later became known as the Battle of Gravelines. Learning lessons from their earlier naval engagements with the huge galleons, galleasses and hulks of the armada, this time, the smaller, faster English carracks were said to have used their superior speed and agility to move amongst the slower moving Spanish ships and employed their superior gunnery skills to fire broadside after broadside of English shot into the sides of the increasingly defenceless Spanish and Portuguese vessels. Some of the English ships were said to have fired so many volleys into these nautical giants that they eventually ran out of ammunition, but rather than desist from their attacks, were reported to have gathered together any metalwork and chains that they could find; and used them to cause further damage to their naval adversaries. Realising the hopelessness of their situation and the superiority of the English tactics, it soon became clear to most of the Spanish commanders at sea that there was little hope of achieving their principal goal, of landing an invasion force in England, leaving them with little option but to flee for home, although even that relatively easy sounding task was not without its own problems. With the wind and weather both reportedly set against them, rather than face the threat of a rampant English navy, or the equally effective Dutch, the vast majority of the armada ships were reported to have sailed northward, in an attempt to reach home, after first having navigated the treacherous waters of the North Sea and then travelled around the equally dangerous northern coastlines of Scotland and Ireland, before sailing along the west coast of Ireland and on to Spanish waters.

Unfortunately, not only were most of the Spanish ships ill-equipped and insufficiently provisioned for such an arduous journey, with many commanders lacking maps of British waters, but many of them were also lacking their sea anchors, a vital piece of equipment in the storm wracked northern coasts of Scotland and Ireland. Typically, vessels of the time that were caught in violent storms would attempt to seek shelter by anchoring themselves off the coast of the nearby land, with the sea anchor helping to secure them in a fixed position, reducing the possibility of the craft being driven ashore and beached, or wrecked on coastal rocks. For those Spanish vessels that had been forced to cut away their sea anchors, during the English fire ship attack on Calais, without the benefit of that vital piece of equipment, most were thought to have eventually been driven onto the reefs and rocks of northern Scotland and Ireland. However, even those Spanish mariners and soldiers who managed to survive the wrecking and sinking of their vessels, even after they reached land, their fate remained uncertain, especially in Ireland, where the English authorities in Dublin were reported to have ordered the execution of hundreds of survivors, ostensibly to prevent them fomenting unrest amongst the native Roman Catholic communities. Out of the estimated thirty thousand Spanish mariners and soldiers who began their journey as part of the armada, by the time the last surviving ships returned home in September 1588, some twenty thousand men were thought to have been lost, with most of the country's nobility having lost at least one member of their family to the disastrous royal enterprise. It is also worth noting perhaps that virtually all of the hundreds of horses and mules that had been embarked on the armada, for use in the invasion of England, were subsequently thrown overboard by the ships crews, who being desperately short of fresh water, were not prepared to share their limited resources with their fellow creatures, choosing instead to abandon them to the violent waters of the British coastline.

For the Spanish, the results of the failed invasion plan would continue to haunt them for years, as large numbers of the survivors were thought to have returned home stricken by injuries and diseases that would affect them for the rest of their lives. Interestingly, one of those who did survive the dreadful journey was the Duke of Medina Sidonia, the man who had been tasked with achieving the almost impossible invasion of England and who had never wanted the appointment to begin with, but who had tried his best nonetheless. On his return to Spain, Sidonia was said to be in such physical health that he had to be carried back to his family estates and although he was initially blamed for the fiasco by Philip II, the monarch later forgave his elderly commander, despite the fact that the failure was almost entirely of the Spanish king's own making.

For England, its navy and especially for its monarch, Elizabeth I, the failure of the Spanish armada was regarded as a national victory, as well as a confirmation of the work done by the likes of Drake, Hawkins, Frobisher and Lord Howard in helping to reorganise and redevelop the English navy into one of Europe's leading seapowers, allowing their nation to begin its long journey to maritime supremacy. At the Battle of Gravelines, although the English fleet had only managed to destroy and seize a handful of Spanish vessels, many more were thought to have been so badly damaged by English cannon that it effectively neutralised any future threat to England and forced those remaining Spanish ships to undertake a perilous journey that would eventually culminate in their later destruction. Ships such as the La Maria Juan were thought to have been so badly damaged by English guns that they sank below the waters of the English Channel, whilst the Falcon Blanco Mayor was eventually taken as a prize by Sir Francis Drake, although for the most part few of the armada ships were thought to have fallen into English hands. In the immediate aftermath of Gravelines, the English navy was said to have contented itself with harrying the surviving Spanish ships as they travelled up into the North Sea, with other English warships remaining on station along the south coast in the event that any subsequent attack might be launched from the continent. Even though no single English vessel was sunk by enemy actions, save for the eight fire ships deliberately set ablaze by the English themselves, significant numbers of English mariners were reported to have perished, mostly from diseases, such as typhus and dysentery, caused by having to spend so much time onboard ship, as opposed to any injuries caused by enemy fire.

Following the failure of the Spanish plan for the invasion of England and no doubt in the belief that Spain's remaining ships would be unable to resist them, in 1589 the English authorities were said to have planned their own naval expedition against Spain, which has subsequently become known as either the Drake-Norris Expedition, or the English Armada. Despatched on the orders of Elizabeth I, who was anxious to exploit Spanish weaknesses in the aftermath of the armada's large scale destruction, ostensibly the aims of the Drake-Norris expedition were said to be fourfold, to destroy the remaining Spanish naval forces, to foment rebellion in Portugal, to seize the islands of the Azores and to capture the Spanish treasure fleets sailing back to Spain from the New World. However, right from the outset the expedition was said to have encountered problems, including its failure to attract large enough numbers of seasoned soldiers to fight the enemy, a shortage of heavy siege guns to carry out ground assaults, insufficient stores to feed the expedition's soldiers and sailors over the course of the extensive sea voyage and a failure by the Dutch authorities to provide the additional warships necessary for the venture. In fact, according to some later reporters of the expedition, the leaders of the English armada, Sir Francis Drake and Sir John Norris, were equally guilty of repeating exactly the same sorts of mistakes that had proved to be so catastrophic for the earlier Spanish fleet, but undeterred by these shortages and setbacks they determined that the expedition should go ahead anyway.

Comprising a fleet of an estimated 150 English and Dutch vessels, which were said to have carried some 25,000 soldiers, sailors and adventurers between them, the English armada was thought to have finally sailed out, sometime in May or June of 1589, with the intention of attacking the Spanish ports of Corunna, San Sebastian and Santander, where most of the great Spanish ships were reported to have been based. However, due to the delays caused whilst waiting in England, the leaders of the English expedition were said to have made the fateful decision to by-pass the port of Santander, where a significant number of Spanish galleons were being repaired following their arduous journey around the north coasts of Britain and Ireland the previous year. Seemingly unaware of the opportunity that they were missing, to deal a deadly blow against Spain's great warships, the Drake-Norris fleet sailed on by, determined instead to attack the Spanish port of Curunna, where they were reported to have launched a raid against the local garrison, killing some five hundred Spanish soldiers and destroying a dozen or more merchant ships, as well as looting the ports wine cellars. However, having completed their attack on the lower part of the town and whilst waiting for a favourable wind to carry them to their next target, the English forces were said to have tried unsuccessfully to besiege the fortified section of Corunna, a fairly pointless action that was reported to have cost the lives of several hundred English troops and caused a number of the Dutch ships to abandon the expedition and return home. Eventually though, with little else to be gained at Corunna and having favourable winds that would carry them to the Portuguese port of Lisbon, the English armada was said to have continued its journey southward, in the full expectation of achieving a fairly easy victory over what they were led to believe was the disaffected military garrison at Lisbon. Unfortunately, any hopes that Drake, Norris or the Earl of Essex might have had regarding the support of the local population, or indeed the state of local garrison, were very quickly dispelled once they arrived in Lisbon's harbour. Rather than welcoming the English fleet, the local people and military were thought to have taken shelter behind their recently reinforced defences, a task that was said to have been undertaken while Drake and his fleet had been busy raiding the wine cellars of Corunna. With no great siege guns to overcome the gates and walls of the city; and no doubt facing the prospect of eventually being confronted by much larger local forces, in the short term, the leader of the English land forces, the Earl of Essex, was reported to have contented himself with poking his sword at the city's main gates, daring the defenders to come out and face him. Despite such foolishness however, the English were able to destroy a number of the city's vitally important granaries, whilst Drake and his naval commanders were said to have seized a number of neutral merchant vessels that were anchored in the nearby harbour, which he claimed had deliberately broken the English blockade, thereby making them legitimate targets for his own ships.

When the first reports began to filter back to England, about the failure of the expedition to achieve two of its main objectives, the destruction of the remaining Spanish fleet; and the start of an uprising within Portugal itself, Elizabeth I was said to be so furious that she immediately summoned the Earl of Essex to return to England. Although she was quite prepared to support a national rebellion initiated by the Portuguese people, she had no intention of authorising a full scale military invasion of the country by English forces, leaving her with little option but to withdraw her land forces and the seemingly incapable Essex. Perhaps to try and save the financial costs of the venture, the English monarch was said to have given her permission for the remaining objectives to be pursued, namely the seizure of the Azores and the capture of the Spanish treasure fleet from the Americas, both of which were subsequently placed in the hands of Drake and Norris. Unfortunately, by the time the two English commanders were instructed to pursue these two final objectives, their fleet of ships were said to have been at sea for some considerable time and were becoming increasingly diminished by disease, food shortages and losses to enemy actions, leaving the English armada with only about 10% of its original strength. With an estimated fighting force of some 2-3,000 men, it quickly became apparent that any military invasion of the Azores would almost certainly be doomed to failure, forcing Drake and Norris to abandon that particular goal and settle instead for the capture of the famed Spanish treasure fleet. Whilst Drake took all of the physically fit men aboard a fleet of some twenty vessels, in order to track down the Spanish fleet, Norris was said to have gathered the remaining ships together, along with the thousands of sick and injured Englishmen and transported them back to England. Once again though, ill fortune struck the remainder of the English fleet, as a huge Atlantic storm was reported to have damaged a number of the vessels, including Drake's own ship, the Revenge, which was said to be leaking so badly that it very nearly foundered. With little choice but to return home, Drake was reported to have turned his remaining ships towards England, arriving in Plymouth a desperately disappointed man and with little more than £30,000 and a couple of hundred captured enemy cannon to show for their highly costly and unsuccessful naval adventure.

Martin Frobisher

Lord Howard

Sir John Norris

Ultimately, the abject failure of the Drake-Norris expedition to fulfil any single one of its planned objectives proved to have a number of adverse effects, the most important of which was the damage done to the reputations of Elizabeth I, Sir Francis Drake, the Earl of Essex and to a lesser extent, that of the English navy itself. Notwithstanding the negative effects that the disastrous venture had on the public standing of these individual persons and organisation, it had also led to the unnecessary loss of thousands of English seamen and soldiers, vitally important warships and upwards of some £80,000 that had been spent in financing the expedition, some of which was eventually recovered through the sale of captured Spanish prizes. Those matters aside though, in the aftermath of the abortive raids, the central core of the Spanish fleet remained intact, Portugal was still ruled by Philip II of Spain, the Azores were still in Spanish hands and the great American treasure fleet eventually managed to deliver its fabulous riches to the court of King Philip, a journey it would continue to make far into the future, after the rebuilding of the great Spanish galleons had been completed at Santander. However, the one great benefit that England did derive from the failed Drake-Norris expedition was that it forced Spain to concentrate almost entirely on its South American possessions, which had to be protected with an even bigger, more expensive royal fleet that not only put an enormous strain on the Spanish exchequer, but also allowed England to focus on the colonisation and exploitation of North America, as well as the Caribbean, helping to create the basis for its later worldwide empire. Additionally, both the successful defeat of the Spanish armada and the failure of the English armada, inexorably led to greater royal spending on and widespread development of a much more specialist and professional English fleet, one that was built around greater armaments, increasingly effective gunnery skills and superior naval tactics, features that would continue to distinguish the English navy from other European forces for many years to come.

However, following the death of Elizabeth I in 1603, the English navy was thought to have fallen into disrepair during the reign of her royal successor, James I, who was eager to conclude a peace treaty with the Spanish Empire and therefore saw no need for a strong and well equipped English force. It was only after 1625 and with the ascent of Charles I that the English navy became a priority again, although it's financing and employment by the highly divisive Stuart king proved to be a matter of some anger amongst the public and one of the root causes of the First English Civil War that erupted in 1642 and lasted until 1645. King Charles' decision to impose a nationwide levy, known as a "Ship Tax" or "Ship Money" was reported to have caused great resentment amongst the great and the good of England, creating a schism that quickly evolved into a campaign that pitted the monarch against England's elected representatives, over who exactly ruled the country, the king or the Commons. During the English Civil War, the majority of England's warships were thought to have supported the Parliamentary cause, although the Royalist army was known to have had a small number of ships that regularly blockaded Parliamentary ports and harbours, as well as being used to re-supply besieged Royalist bases having successfully evaded Parliamentary blockades. During the Second English Civil War, which was fought between 1648 and 1651, Charles I not only managed to conclude a deal with Scottish forces, but was also said to have been joined by small numbers of mutinous English ships, which between them, hoped to defeat the English navy. Unfortunately for them and the ill-fated King Charles, the Parliamentary navy was said to have included a new generation of English mariners, whose skills would help to regenerate the fortunes of the English navy, including the man regarded by many as one of the founders of the modern navy, the Parliamentary General at sea, Robert Blake.

One of thirteen children of a Somerset merchant, Blake was born in 1599 and along with his siblings was said to have received a reasonable level of education, attending the Bridgwater Grammar School for boys, before completing his studies at Wadham College, Oxford. Despite wanting to pursue an academic career, which he was unable to do; Blake was reported to have spent most of his formative years building a commercial career, before finally returning to his hometown in 1638, where he made the decision to stand for Parliament. Elected to Westminster in 1640, as the member for Bridgwater, he was reported to have attended Parliament throughout the period of upheaval caused by the political and constitutional crises, which erupted between the House of Commons and the Stuart king, Charles I. Failing to be re-elected to Parliament, as the conflict between the king and his Parliament reached its height, Blake was then said to have enlisted into the New Model Army as a Captain with Alexander Popham's regiment, where he was said to have distinguished himself sufficiently to earn a promotion to the rank of Lieutenant Colonel. By the following year he was reported to have performed so well during the Siege of Lyme, in April 1644 that he was promoted once again, this time to the rank of Colonel and for the next year was thought to have gained some national recognition for his military abilities and his sheer tenacity.

The year after the Second English Civil War had broken out in 1648, Blake was appointed to the post of General at sea, a rank equivalent to that of Admiral, but never used in the Parliamentary army, beginning a career that would ultimately earn him greater recognition than he would ever have achieved as a regular army officer. As part of the wider conflict, in January 1649 the Royalist leader, Prince Rupert of the Rhine, was reported to have brought a flotilla of ships to the port of Kinsale in Southern Ireland, intent on preventing the Parliamentary leader, Oliver Cromwell, from bringing English troops into the country to suppress the Roman Catholic backed Royalist cause there. In responding to the danger posed by Prince Rupert's fleet, in May 1649, general at sea, Robert Blake was said to have introduced a blockade of Kinsale harbour, to prevent these potentially dangerous royalist forces from intercepting a second English fleet, carrying Cromwell's troops, which was due to travel across the Irish Sea, to the main Irish port at Dublin. However, having trapped Rupert's ships for some five months, in October 1649 a violent Atlantic storm was said to have scattered Blake's blockading ships, allowing Rupert and his fleet to escape from Kinsale harbour, following which he was said to have travelled across the Bay of Biscay to the Portuguese port of Lisbon. Even though the royalist flotilla no longer represented an immediate threat to the Parliamentary forces in Ireland, Blake was reported to have reassembled his ships and set off in pursuit of the European noblemen, tracking him to the port of Lisbon, where the English general at sea anchored his vessels off the coast, before beginning to try and persuade the Portuguese authorities to expel the royalist fleet from their coastal waters, although his attempts ultimately proved to be unsuccessful.

Maarten Tromp   Witte de With   Michiel de Ruyter

Despite having been anchored off the Portuguese coast for some weeks, Blake was reluctant to leave the area, knowing full well that when he did, Prince Rupert would simply employ his ships in the royalist cause once again, thereby presenting a danger to any Parliamentary ships that they might encounter on their travels. However, as he maintained his blockade of Lisbon, Blake was reported to have been joined by a further four English warships under the command of Edward Popham, who brought with him authority for the English fleet to make war against Portugal itself, a development that later resulted in Blake and his ships fighting a number of sea battles with elements of the Portuguese navy. It was also said to be during one of these engagements that Blake captured a number of enemy ships which he was then forced to escort to Cadiz, lifting the English blockade on Lisbon and allowing Prince Rupert and his handful of ships to escape, although only temporarily. By the beginning of November 1649 Blake was said to have caught up with the small royalist fleet, capturing one and forcing the rest to be driven ashore, bringing an end to the royalist threat at sea and securing Parliamentary supremacy of the waters that surrounded Britain and Ireland. Rewarded handsomely by the English Parliament in 1651, in June of the same year Blake and his naval forces were reported to have secured the Isles of Scilly for Parliament, the last remaining base of the by now defeated royalist navy.

Having successfully eradicated the last remaining elements of the royalist navy by June of 1651, Blake and his fellow generals at sea were thought to have enjoyed a relatively short period of peace, before they were once again called into action, in order to face the equally capable, but less well-equipped Dutch fleet, as part of the wider Anglo-Dutch War of 1652 to 1654. Ostensibly a dispute over trading rights in the East Indies, the war was said to have begun because of English seizures of Dutch merchant ships, actions that were said to have received the implicit approval of Oliver Cromwell, following Dutch support for Charles I, the Stuart monarch that the Parliamentarians had been forced to execute. Although peaceful relations had been maintained and developed both before and after Charles' execution, many within the English establishment deeply envied and distrusted the Dutch, largely because they were England's most direct competitor in foreign trade. In order to curtail their influence within English controlled territories, Parliament had introduced the Navigation Act of 1651, which forbade the importation of goods into England, other than on English ships, or on vessels from where the goods were sourced, essentially depriving the Dutch merchant fleet from supplying goods directly into England. As part of enforcing this new Navigation Act, the English navy had begun to seize any ship that was contravening this new legislation, which was said to have led to some hundred or more Dutch ships being arrested by the English authorities, an action that was not easily tolerated by the Dutch authorities. As a result, in March 1652 the Dutch authorities in Holland began to equip a large number of converted cargo ships as armed convoys, which were intended to protect Dutch merchant vessels from English interference, although as it turned out, hostilities between the two countries were thought to have broken out over the issue of a flag, rather than anything to do with the carriage of goods. According to most sources, as a Dutch and English fleet passed one another in the waters of the North Sea, on the 29th May, the Dutch ships were slow to dip their flags in salute, an historic act that had been revived by Cromwell, causing the commander of the English fleet, Robert Blake, to open fire on the Dutch vessels, beginning what later became known as the Battle of Goodwin Sands, the opening act of the First Anglo-Dutch war, with war being formally declared by the English Parliament on 10th July 1652.

With England seemingly determined to pursue a military solution to the trade dispute, despite the best efforts of the Dutch to find an equitable political solution, by the middle of 1652 a large English fleet, under Blake's command, was reported to be at sea attempting to suppress the Netherland's trade with the East Indies and the Baltic States, leaving the Dutch authorities with little option but to assemble a battle fleet of its own with which it might confront Robert Blake's sixty ship taskforce. Under the command of the Dutch Admiral, Maarten Tromp, a one hundred strong fleet was assembled with the intention of confronting the English general at sea, Blake, who Tromp and his commanders were said to have pursued northward to the Shetlands, where an Atlantic storm was said to have scattered the huge Dutch flotilla, preventing them from confronting the Parliamentary forces. In the light of his obvious failure to meet and defeat the English navy, Tromp, was subsequently replaced as commander of the Dutch ships by Witte de With, who almost immediately put in place plans to confront the English at the mouth of the Thames, in what became known as the Battle of Kentish Knock, which took place on the October 8th 1652. Although the large Dutch force was reported to have been beaten back by Blake's superior Parliamentary ships, the English authorities subsequently made the fateful decision to weaken the fleet by sending twenty of its warships to the Mediterranean, in the mistaken belief that the Dutch navy had been fundamentally defeated, a judgement that would later be proved to be completely wrong. For the Dutch Admiral, Witte de With, the Battle of Kentish Knock was said to have proved to be too much and he was later reported to have had a nervous breakdown, forcing the Dutch authorities to once again call on the skills and experience of Maarten Tromp, the Admiral who had earlier been replaced after his failure to confront the English fleet in the Shetlands. However, with the Parliamentarian navy now weakened by the loss of the twenty warships sent to the Mediterranean, Recognising the opportunity for an overwhelming Dutch victory, Tromp quickly assembled a fleet of some ninety Dutch warships and went in search of the reduced English navy, which was reported to have numbered some forty-odd vessels, only half that of the Dutch Admiral's.

Having spent a week escorting a Dutch convoy through the English Channel, on the 9th December 1652, the Dutch and English fleets encountered one another off the coast of the Kentish Downs, an historic anchorage, where English fleets traditionally laid up before beginning their journey up into the North Sea. Seemingly unaware of the size of the Dutch fleet and forced by the prevailing winds towards Dover, Blake was reported to have kept his English flotilla close to shore, while the Dutch ships shadowed them, waiting for their enemy to be forced out to sea by the local sandbanks and reefs. Eventually, on the afternoon of the following day, Blake's naval units were forced away from the coastline and into a direct confrontation with the Dutch, with later reporters describing the scene as both sides opened fire on one another with round after round of explosive broadsides. Luckily for the English fleet, Tromp's flotilla was reported to be so large and inexperienced that many of his ships were unable to engage Blake's warships, although by the end of the battle the English were still said to have lost five of their vessels, two of which were later taken as prizes by the Dutch navy. As darkness fell, Blake and his remaining ships were able to withdraw to the comparative safety of the Kentish Downs, leaving the Dutch Admiral Tromp to rue the missed opportunity to inflict a devastating blow against the English navy. For Robert Blake though, the English navy's near humiliating defeat at the Battle of Dungeness, proved to be a turning point, not only for him as a commander, but also for the country's whole approach to the organisation of its naval forces, with a series of important changes being introduced as a direct consequence of this particular military defeat.

For Blake, his most serious complaints were said to have centred round the historic practice of the English navy to commandeer private merchant ships and leaving their civilian captains in charge, despite the fact that many had no military experience and were not easily inclined to involve their vessel in a situation where it might be damaged or destroyed, effectively making them of little use as a fighting ship. It was also reported that many of these civilian commanders would often come and go as they pleased, either to seize an enemy ship as a prize, or simply to re-provision their vessel, much of which was done without the permission of the overall commander, who had little practical control over the ships that he was supposedly leading. It was also thought that sometimes the sheer numbers of ships within an English fleet made it almost impossible for a general at sea to communicate effectively with every ship captain, meaning that all too often commanders were unclear or confused over exactly what the aims and objectives of the fleet were to begin with. Angered by the inefficiencies and lack of control within the Parliamentary navy, Blake was said to have reported his concerns to the authorities at Westminster and threatened to resign his post if steps were not taken to address these vitally important issues. Fortunately, most representatives within the English Parliament were sympathetic to Blake's concerns and as a result a new set of ordinances were drafted that would help to address many of the problems identified by their leading naval commander. As a result of the review, in future all private merchant vessels commandeered for national service would be commanded by a captain appointed by the authorities, fleets would be broken down into smaller squadrons and groups, thereby increasing the level of command and control within the fleet and finally, a clear set of rules would be issued to all captain's, ensuring that they all clearly understood the orders and intentions of the fleet's commander.

In the short term however, these later changes to the military command structure of the English navy, did little to help either Blake's forces in England, or indeed the twenty ships that had earlier been despatched to the Mediterranean, ostensibly to help reinforce the small naval force that was stationed there to interrupt the Dutch trade routes. Having previously forced the English fleet to withdraw to the Kentish Downs, following the Battle of Dungeness in December 1652, the Dutch authorities were then thought to have reinforced their units in the Mediterranean, under the command of Commodore Johan van Galen, who, along with a fleet of some sixteen ships, was reported to have tracked down a small

English flotilla of six vessels to the Italian port of Livorno in March 1653, where he immediately implemented a naval blockade to prevent the English squadron leaving harbour. The English commander, Captain Henry Appleton, aware that a second English squadron was reported to be at Elba, attempted to break the Dutch blockade, in order to link up with the second English force of eight warships, under the command of Captain Richard Badiley, which he hoped might help him to confront the Dutch ships on an equal footing. Unfortunately, rather than waiting for Badiley to arrive offshore, to confront the Dutch in a united front, Appleton was said to have led his seriously outnumbered squadron into battle against the blockading Dutch ships, as a result of which three of his ships were captured, two destroyed and only the remaining vessel managing to escape. As Badiley's flotilla of eight English ships finally arrived in the area, they too now found themselves outnumbered and were subsequently forced to withdraw, handing a second major sea victory to the Dutch navy within the space of four months. Sadly for the Dutch commander, Van Galen, he did not live long enough to see the long term fruits of his victory over the English, which gave his country temporary control of the Mediterranean, as he was reported to have died of the wounds he received at the Battle of Livorno, on March 23rd 1653. As if to underpin the concerns that were expressed by Robert Blake in his later report to the English Parliament, regarding the inherent weaknesses within the English navy, four of the six ships in Appleton's squadron were said to have been private merchant ships commandeered by the navy, whilst at least half of Badiley's vessels were also thought to have been privately owned, suggesting that such commercial ships and their captains were indeed ill-suited to be employed as frontline military vessels.

Robert Blake   George Monck   Samuel Pepys

With the Dutch navy having gained temporary control of the Mediterranean, the North Sea and the English Channel, the outlook for England's maritime trade looked extremely bleak and with the English navy appearing to be unable to confront their Dutch counterparts in any meaningful way, even Cromwell was beginning to talk about securing a peace deal, something that the Dutch authorities were said to be eager to pursue. Fortunately, or unfortunately, depending on what side of the argument one was on, during the winter months of 1652-3, one of England's most able Commonwealth strategists and planners, Robert Blake was said to have completed his Sailing and Fighting Instructions, a highly detailed explanation of naval tactics, which was said to have included the first modern use of the line of battle, a naval tactic that allowed for concentrated fire from a line of ships, without the risk of hitting any friendly vessels. Building on traditional English skills in gunnery and seamanship, Blake's new tactical directives quickly spread throughout the country's naval communities, ensuring that both the men and the captains of England's maritime forces could work together in a more effective way. These new tactics, allied to the previously mentioned naval ordinances, which put experienced military commanders in charge of England's fighting ships, not only increased the threat posed by England's ships, but caused a general rise in confidence amongst those men who were employed in the service. As a result, in spite of the earlier defeats and setbacks suffered by the English navy between December 1652 and March 1653, by June of 1653 England had once again regained control of the English Channel, following the Battle of Portland and was now pressing to restore its naval supremacy over the waters of the North Sea. Around the 12th June, the two fleets were reported to have encountered one another off the coast of Suffolk at a place known as Gabbard Bank, with the English fleet said to consist of around one hundred ships and the Dutch ninety eight. The English navy was reported to have been led by the likes of George Monck, Richard Deane and William Penn, all of whom were experienced soldiers, although Penn especially was thought to have been the most experienced mariner of the three Parliamentary leaders. On the Dutch side, the previously noted and highly experienced Dutch Admirals, Maarten Tromp and Witte de With were both once against charged with leading the fight against the English fleet, in the hope that they could repeat their earlier victories over England's maritime forces.

On the first day of the battle, the Dutch fleet, which was reported to have been divided into five separate squadrons, attacked first, but were immediately faced by the English ships adopting Robert Blake's new line of battle tactics, which forced the Dutch to withdraw after a number of their ships were damaged or lost. For the remainder of the day and throughout the following night the two navies were thought to have avoided one another, although the next day, on the 13th June the battle was resumed, with Tromp once again choosing to attack the English ships, despite reportedly being sort of ammunition. However, it was said to be as the winds changed that Tromp and his ships were suddenly and unexpectedly stalled, leaving him and his ships beneath the English guns, which very quickly began to cause carnage amongst the Dutch fleet and forcing them to flee for their home waters. As they retreated, large numbers of the Dutch ships were said to have been overtaken and captured by the pursuing English warships, with around a dozen Dutch vessels taken as prizes and a further half dozen sunk by English guns, bringing an end to what later became known as the Battle of Gabbard, a victory that was later celebrated by the naming of a Royal Navy vessel, HMS Gabbard. The most notable casualty on the English side was said to have been Richard Deane, although not a single English vessel was thought to have been lost to Dutch guns, in the engagement that ultimately gave England supremacy over the North Sea once again, restoring some pride to the English navy and its people. For the Dutch though, the outcome was thought to have been entirely different as their remaining ships were chased all the way back to their home ports, where they were subsequently blockaded, creating a military and financial disaster for the country that would only finally be relieved in 1654 when England and Holland agreed to a peace accord. Historically, the final naval engagement of the First Anglo-Dutch War was the Battle of Scheveningen, which occurred between the 8th and 10th August 1653 and was an engagement initiated by the Dutch in an attempt the lift the punishing English blockade of the Dutch ports, begun after the Battle of Gabbard. However, throughout the course of this major sea battle, both the English and Dutch fleets were reported to have sustained substantial damage, with the Dutch Admiral Maarten Tromp being killed during the fight, although in the aftermath of the battle both sides were said to have claimed victory. From the Dutch perspective, even though their ships were forced to withdraw once again, the damage they inflicted on a number of the English warships was thought to have been so severe that they too were compelled to return home, thereby lifting the English blockade of the Netherlands, the principal objective for the Dutch ships. However, regardless of the differing claims of who had, or had not won, following the highly destructive and expensive war, both England and Holland were keen to bring an end to the dispute, with Cromwell and the Dutch leader, Johan de Witt eventually agreeing to sign the Treaty of Westminster in 1654, bringing an end to the hostilities between the two Protestant states.

Having conducted a two year long and highly expensive conflict with the Dutch, which was finally settled to England's advantage, Cromwell was then reported to have turned his attention to another of England's commercial rivals, Spain, which apart from posing a threat to England's maritime trade, was also a Roman Catholic state and therefore a legitimate threat to his country's continuing prosperity and an affront to his own personal religious beliefs. Although both sides were thought to have engaged in commercial piracy against one another's ships, most notably in the New World, it was only in 1654 that these often minor skirmishes and engagements eventually escalated to all out war, especially when the Lord Protector launched his Western Design, a plan which called for the English annexation of Spanish held territories in the Caribbean. From a purely commercial point of view the development of the Caribbean's highly lucrative sugar industries was thought to be one of the major reasons for England's planned expansion within the central American region and one that Cromwell was more than happy to pay for, both in terms of English lives and finances. The first English fleet despatched to the Caribbean was reportedly sent in 1654 and was commanded by Sir William Penn, the father of the man who would later found the American State of Pennsylvania and who was said to have been accompanied across the Atlantic by another highly experienced officer, General Robert Venables. As part of this large English invasion force the fleet was reported to have included several thousand marines, whose numbers would be further strengthened by troop already present on England's existing Caribbean territories, including places such as Barbados and St Kitts. However, despite the size of the Parliamentary fleet and its associated land forces, ultimately the expedition to the Caribbean was deemed to have been a failure, as few of the objectives set out by the two commanders were actually realised, save for the capture of the Spanish held island of Jamaica, which in the first instance Cromwell himself regarded as being generally unimportant and uneconomic. It was only sometime later and after he had ordered both Penn and Venables to be imprisoned for their failures that the Parliamentary leader began to see the strategic importance of Jamaica and took increasingly expensive actions to ensure it remained in English hands.

The seizure of Jamaica was said to have caused the formal declaration of war between England and Spain in 1655, with Robert Blake once again playing a pivotal role in making sure that English sea power was brought to bear against Spanish interests. Almost as soon as hostilities began, Blake was reported to have brought a fleet to the Spanish coast, in order to blockade the major port of Cadiz, which not only prevented commercial traffic to the port, but also prevented Spanish warships from gaining access to the Atlantic. At the same time, another English commander, Captain Richard Stayner was said to have intercepted a Spanish treasure fleet, making the return journey across the Atlantic, which he relieved of its valuable cargo before sending virtually all of the vessels to the bottom of the ocean. Some months later, in April 1657, Blake himself was said to have captured yet another major Spanish convoy, at the Battle of Santa Cruz de Tenerife, which he likewise destroyed, although not before the ships had managed to land their valuable cargo on the Spanish mainland. Despite losing the treasure, Blake's actions were thought to have delayed its delivery to the Spanish treasury, causing problems for its war effort, a result that earned Blake great respect and praise throughout much of Europe. On the whole though, this phase of the war was thought to have proved to be extremely expensive for England, as just as many English merchant ships were said to have been seized and destroyed by the Spanish navy, making the whole exercise pretty pointless, as both countries suffered equal amounts of commercial and financial misery. However, from an English point of view, the situation was thought to have improved significantly in March 1657 when England and France signed the Treaty of Paris, which joined the two countries in a concerted effort against the military forces of Spain. In return for French ships supporting the English campaign at sea, Cromwell offered support to the French in their continuing war against Spain that was being fought in Flanders. As part of the treaty, some 6,000 English soldiers and the English fleet would be employed against the Flemish bases at Dunkirk, Mardyck and Gravelines, all three of which were subsequently captured by the Anglo-French forces.

Whilst cruising off the Spanish coast again, Blake was reported to have been taken ill as the result of an old wound and despite the best efforts of the ship's commander to return him home to Plymouth, the great Parliamentary Admiral was said to have died before reaching England. Despite this, once his ship had reached home, Blake's body was transferred to the Queens House in Greenwich where it lay in state for some time, before being transported to Westminster Abbey for a state funeral and burial, an event attended by Oliver Cromwell and members of the Council of State. Following the restoration of Charles II in 1660, Blake's remains were reportedly removed from their final resting place, only to be dumped in a common grave adjoining the Abbey, a sad end for one of England's greatest military leaders, who is often acclaimed as the father of the modern Royal Navy.

Following the restoration of the Stuart family to the English throne in 1660, Charles II and his new political administration were thought to have inherited a much improved English navy, albeit one that still required significant work and proper administrative organisation. The two men largely responsible for bringing some sort of order to the building, manning and provisioning England's navy were said to be Sir William Coventry and the much more famous Samuel Pepys, who despite being much more notable for his diary, was said to have been a pivotal figure in reorganising the administrative structures of the military service, helping it to become one of world's most professional and well run naval forces. William Coventry's part in the reorganisation and restructuring of the English navy was reported to have begun in 1660, when the prospect of a restored Stuart dynasty was first suggested, causing him to travel to Breda in the Netherlands where Charles Stuart, later Charles II, was based, where he received an appointment as a secretary to Charles' younger brother, James, Duke of York, who subsequently became the Lord High Admiral of England. In 1661 Coventry was elected to the Restoration Parliament as the member for Great Yarmouth and in the following year was reported to have been appointed as a Commissioner for the navy, a post that was thought to have given him enormous authority over the whole of the service, allowing him to push through a number of significant changes. Despite being accused of wrongdoing by his political opponents, with some suggesting that he was corrupt, his more notable contemporary, Samuel Pepys, who later held the post of First Secretary to the Navy, publicly acclaimed Coventry's dedication to his work, commending him both for his personal enthusiasm and his economic prudence.

One of the reasons for these later attacks on his character was thought to have been his involvement with the outbreak of a Second Anglo-Dutch War in 1665, which although starting well for England, was subsequently marked by notable disasters that were thought to have been caused by gross financial mismanagement and ill-advised appointments, both of which had little to do with Coventry himself. As with the First Anglo-Dutch War of 1652 to 1654, tensions between England and the Netherlands centred round international trade and the transportation of goods from part of the world to the other, which the Dutch were said to have dominated, much to England's extreme irritation. However, despite such matters having largely been resolved with the signing of the Treaty of Westminster in 1654 and even though Charles II was personally indebted to the Dutch authorities for the support they had showed him and his family during the English Commonwealth period, commercial tensions still existed within each countries commercial communities and only required the right sort of issue to reignite them into a full military conflict. In England, the chief instigators of this second great naval conflict was reported to be Lord Arlington, an adviser to the king and the monarch's younger brother, James, the Duke of York, who had his own personal financial reasons for initiating a military conflict between England and the Netherlands. As the major shareholder in the private merchant company, the Royal African Company and as the Lord High Admiral of England, James was perfectly placed to not only wage a war against the Dutch commercial fleet, but also to benefit financially from a successful outcome, with the expectation that many of the possessions controlled by the rival Dutch East Indies Company would almost inevitably fall into his own company's hands. For Charles II himself, the prospect of achieving some sort of military victory over one of his European neighbours was said to have been appealing, if only to give him greater credibility and status, not just in England, but also in mainland Europe, where he was often regarded as an extravagant and highly ineffective ruler. With his brother James, Lord Arlington and the English Ambassador to The Hague, George Downing, all advising the monarch to take affirmative action against the Dutch, Charles was said to have baulked at the prospect of declaring all out war, so instead, left it to others to try and provoke the Dutch into taking the first offensive action.

In the North Sea and the English Channel, English captains were instructed not to return the agreed salute to passing Dutch ships, a form of national insult that was not lost on the various Dutch seafarers, who were instructed by their government to bear the offence, rather than retaliate and risk armed conflict. When this provocation failed, the Duke of York was said to have instructed his agents in Africa to capture the trading posts of the Dutch East Indies Company along the west coast of Africa, in the hope that this too might provoke an attack, although eventually it was said to be English actions on the other side of the Atlantic that ultimately forced the Dutch authorities to react. In June 1664 English forces in North America were ordered to attack the Dutch held territories known as New Netherlands, which now form part of the modern day American states of New York, New Jersey, Delaware, Connecticut, Pennsylvania and Rhode Island, most of which had been seized by the end of October 1664. For the Dutch government, although they were prepared to accept the loss of the odd ship to English privateers, or the occasional insult at sea, the potential loss of their highly lucrative African outposts, so vital to their national economy and the seizure of their American colonies proved to be the final straw, forcing them to assemble a large naval force, under the command of Michiel de Ruyter, to recover all of the lost territories and possessions. Having arrived off the coast of West Africa, De Ruyter and his forces subsequently regained control of their former trading posts and also captured a number of English outposts as well, before setting off across the Atlantic to repeat the exercise in North America. While the Dutch fleet made its way across the Atlantic in late 1664, an English naval force was reported to have attacked a smaller Dutch flotilla at the port of Izmir in Turkey, although for the most part it was said to have caused little damage, other than to harden Dutch attitudes towards their English rivals. Having arrived off the east coast of North America in January 1665, De Ruyter was reported to have instructed his ship's captains to open fire on any English warships that they considered to be a threat to the Dutch colonies there, an order that Charles II was said to have used as an excuse for formally declaring war against the Dutch Republic in March 1665, marking the official start of the Second Anglo-Dutch War.

George Ayscue

Cornelius Tromp

Arthur Herbert

According to some sources, following the restoration of Charles Stuart to the English throne in 1660, although some highly capable people, such as Sir William Coventry, had been appointed to oversee the development of the English navy, there were also said to be large numbers of generally inept royalist supporters who held positions of authority within the service, who not only had little knowledge of military matters per se, but were also thought to have enriched themselves at the expense of England's fighting forces. It was also said to be the case that many of those responsible for maintaining the country's numerical superiority over its European rivals had failed to recognise that many of its naval competitors had also learned the lessons and tactics put forward by the likes of the great Commonwealth general at sea, Robert Blake, with the Dutch themselves being some of his most ardent students. In the aftermath of the First Anglo-Dutch War, military leaders in the Netherlands had begun a new round of shipbuilding, developing warships and military tactics that could rival the supposedly superior English fleets, a fact that was apparently overlooked by many of those responsible for the English navy and more especially those within the royal court who were determining the country's naval policies. Not only had the Dutch navy rebuilt its military forces with a larger number of heavy ships, but as in England, their naval commanders were typically drawn from the ranks of the very best mariners, making the Dutch fleet of the 1660's a much more dangerous enemy than had been the case nearly a decade before.

Fortunately for England perhaps, in the first major engagement between the two great European fleets, not only were the Dutch thought to have been without some of its most modern warships, but were also said to be missing some of their most experienced and able military commanders, many of whom, including the notable Michiel de Ruyter, were reported to be still on the other side of the Atlantic, fighting the English in North America. The Battle of Lowestoft on 13th June 1665 was ultimately an English victory that initially dealt a severe blow to the Dutch navy's confidence, although the inability of the English fleet to capitalise on the victory, the large numbers of new Dutch ships being launched, plus the return of De Ruyter from North America quickly restored Dutch belief in their naval forces, at exactly the same time that a lack of money, fiscal control and shipbuilding output was beginning to adversely affect the English navy. With the real possibility of the Dutch fleet being able to overturn England's naval superiority, Charles II was thought to have tried to arrange a military coalition against the Netherlands, although with Europe still largely divided by differing political and religious royal houses, such an alliance proved difficult to arrange, especially as England was deemed to be in such a precarious financial position, unlike the Dutch. Towards the end of 1665, the authorities in The Hague were said to have formed an anti-English military alliance, between themselves, France and Denmark, whilst at the same time a potential English ally, Bernhard Von Galen, the ruler of Munster in Lower Saxony, tired of waiting for English financial support and declared a separate peace with the anti-English alliance. As a result of these events, England not only faced a much better equipped and more professionally led Dutch fleet, but also one that now had strategic support from two other European states, leaving Charles Stuart with little option but to try and make peace with his adversaries on the best possible terms, although for the Dutch matters had gone too far to make another conflict unavoidable.

However, despite the odds being stacked against them and their position appearing to be impossible, in May 1666 the English fleet of some eighty ships was reported to have sailed out from the Kentish Downs to confront their Dutch rivals, with the veteran Commonwealth general at sea, George Monck, in overall command of the English flotilla. Having reached open water, the Civil War royalist leader, Prince Rupert of the Rhine, was then reported to have taken a group of some twenty ships southward to confront a French naval squadron that had arrived in the English Channel, which he believed was planning to join the Dutch fleet further north. With his remaining sixty vessels, Monck was said to have set out to find the Dutch fleet, which he later discovered lying at anchor, giving him the opportunity to begin a headlong attack against the enemy vessels and beginning a naval engagement that was said to have lasted for four full days, one of the longest naval battles in history. As both sides jostled for position, ships from each navy were said to have engaged one another with their vast array of cannons, guns and muskets, both of them striking hard at their adversaries throughout the day and leaving many vessels burning and broken by the time darkness brought an end to the day's hostilities. According to some reports, by dawn of the second day Monck was said to have lost around one third of his fleet, but despite this, he was said to have resumed the attack against De Ruyter's forces, ordering a number of passes to be made against the enemy and on each one delivering and receiving the full weight of each ship's weaponry, to the point where many of the English vessels were said to be in such poor condition that they were forced to withdraw, with the Dutch ships in hot pursuit.

The third day of the sea battle was thought to have been relatively unremarkable, apart from the fact that Monck was reported to have used his heavily damaged ships to cover those that were still in reasonably good order, until such time as the previously absent Prince Rupert, was said to have rejoined Monck's fleet having previously sailed south to confront a French squadron that failed to rendezvous with the Dutch, if indeed that had been their intention. Now reinforced with Prince Rupert's twenty ships, Monck was said to be far more confident about confronting De Ruyter's fleet, although the day was said to have been marked by the surrender of the Prince Royal, one of England's great warships, by its commander, Vice-Admiral George Ayscue, who gained notoriety as the last English Admiral to surrender his vessel in battle, although he paid for his actions by spending a significant period of time in a Dutch prison. On the fourth and final day of the battle, despite having been reinforced by the twenty new ships, the English fleet was reported to have got the worst of the day's engagements, with the Dutch Admiral, De Ruyter, repeatedly breaking the English lines and reportedly forcing Monck and his forces to withdraw, although he later claimed that he had done so in response to an earlier Dutch retreat, a difference of opinions that would continue to be argued over in succeeding years. Either way, by the time the four day sea battle had been concluded, the English fleet was reported to have lost a total of ten ships, as opposed to the four vessels lost by the Dutch, making it an English defeat, if only in numerical terms.

A month later, the final sea battle of the Second Anglo-Dutch War was said to have been fought off the Kentish coast, near North Foreland, in what became known as the Saint James' Day Battle, which was fought on the 25th and 26th July 1666, between the English and Dutch fleets. Believing that they had been victorious at the four day sea battle in the previous month and that they had superiority over the English ships, the Dutch fleet were said to have set out to confront their rivals off the southern coast of England, in order to settle the conflict between the two countries once and for all. As the two fleets finally encountered one another off the Kent Downs on the 25th, the commander of the English force, Prince Rupert was said to have encountered some unexpectedly good fortune, as the Dutch fleet, which was trying to gain the advantage suddenly found itself caught in a lull and unable to manoeuvre, leaving some of its ships at the mercy of the passing English guns, which were said to have unleashed a terrible barrage against them, decimating everyone and everything that lay in front of them. The Dutch Admiral, De Ruyter, unable to bring his main body of ships into the battle because of the prevailing winds was said to have been forced to watch helplessly as a number of his ships were shot to pieces, before simply drifting away with the dead and the dying left onboard to an uncertain fate. However, before long, De Ruyter's own ship and the centre of his battle line was said to have come under sustained attack from the English fleet, with the Dutch Admiral's flagship reportedly being attacked by two of the larger English warships, which were reported to have inflicted considerable damage on De Ruyter's ship, forcing him to withdraw from the area. Despite the damage caused to the front and centre of the Dutch battle line, the rearguard of the fleet, commanded by Admiral Cornelis Tromp, was said to have largely escaped the misfortune of his comrades and was thought to have managed to inflict some heavy damage on the ships of the English rearguard, including the Resolution, which was destroyed by a fireship and the disabling of the Loyal London, which was said to have been so badly damaged that it had to be towed back to England.

As dawn broke on the 26th July 1666, the Dutch Admiral, Cornelis Tromp initially believed that although his fleet had been victorious, he and his handful of ships were the only survivors of what had been a devastating sea battle, which seemed to have claimed virtually all of the other combatants, both English and Dutch. However, as the morning wore on, he quickly began to realise that there were significant numbers of enemy ships on the horizon, leading him to believe that him and his few ships were all that remained of the Dutch fleet and causing him to panic as to how exactly he was going to get his remaining vessels back to Dutch waters and safety. Within a short time though his good sense was said to have returned, allowing him to use his experience to safely navigate a course through the patrolling English ships, to the comparative safety of the port of Flushing, where to the Dutch crews delight they discovered the rest of the survivors from the Dutch fleet, including their commander, Michiel de Ruyter. Unfortunately, the English fleet too had discovered their safe haven and having put a blockade in place, immediately began to initiate a bombardment against the trapped Dutch ships, which was reported to have caused a great of damage, but failed to destroy them outright. As a consequence of the bad luck they had experienced and the losses they had suffered, De Ruyter was said to have temporarily lost his usual composure, blaming others and then himself, for the disaster, although eventually he was reported to have regained his senses and tried to find a way of escaping the situation they were in. Fortunately for the Dutch seamen, within a comparatively short time, the winds that had brought them so much misery during the engagement was said to have changed direction and allowed them to escape from Flushing and the English blockade, to their main harbours further north.

However, despite winning this final sea battle of the Second Anglo Dutch War, the conflict itself was said to have continued well beyond the St James' Day Battle in July 1666 and began to involve military attacks on both the commercial infrastructure and national territories of both the Netherlands and England. This dramatic escalation in attacks was thought to have been initiated by the English commander, Admiral Robert Holmes, who was said to have led a raid on the Dutch mainland, during which an estimated 140 merchant ships and the township of West Terschelling were deliberately burnt by the attacking English forces. Although in the aftermath of the St James' Day Battle, most of the Dutch navy and the country's merchant fleet were thought to have withdrawn to their larger and better defended major ports, this left the English fleet with little option but to maintain a regular blockade of the Dutch coastline, in the hope that this might force the country's leadership to accede to English peace demands. However, maintaining such a cordon around the coastline was often problematic and expensive for England, as ships not only needed to return home to be re-provisioned, which was a continuing expense for an already impoverished English exchequer, but such regular absences also made a complete blockade impossible and therefore generally ineffective. For some people within England, the only way to defeat the Dutch was to destroy its highly valuable commercial fleet, the source of the country's economic strength and one of the root causes of the ongoing disputes between England and the Netherlands. Having agreed that some sort of affirmative action should be taken against Dutch naval assets, rather than just sitting offshore and trying to blockade the coast, English leaders then set about trying to organise a raid against any Dutch ships that were safely anchored inland, but might still represent a potential target. Unfortunately, most of the great capital ships of the Dutch navy and some of the larger cargo vessels were thought to have been anchored in some of the Netherland's most heavily defended harbours, making access to them almost impossible. Eventually though and with the help of a rebel Dutch sea captain, the English authorities were finally able to identify a Dutch fleet of over one hundred ships that was anchored at Harlingen, on the Vlie estuary, which they believed would make a legitimate target for a potential military raid. Planned as a combined land and sea-based attack, having recruited some six hundred sailors and around three hundred soldiers, with experience of fighting from ships, a small flotilla of some eight English frigates and a handful of ketches and fireships were assembled under the command of Rear Admiral Robert Holmes, a reasonably experienced naval officer, who was reported to have risen to prominence after the restoration of Charles II.

HMS Victory   HMS Royal Charles   Queen Mary II

Bearing in mind that at the time English mariners were not only sailors, but also were also expected to fight on land, as and when necessary, Holmes was thought to have had a total fighting force of around a thousand men, which were reported to have been divided into eleven separate companies, each of which was commanded by different officers or noblemen. Although the principal aim of the military expedition was said to have been to attack the Dutch ships at Harlingen, as was usual during the period, another objective was to seize whatever valuables, stores and armaments presented themselves, which given the dire state of the English exchequer was said to have been given additional importance. Reportedly reaching the Dutch coast on the 18th August 1666, Holmes was said to have sent out reconnaissance parties to ensure which particular waterway was best for his small flotilla of ships, before deciding to enter the Vlie estuary and make his way towards the port of Harlingen. Having captured a local Dutch pilot, the English ships slowly made their way along the estuary anxiously expecting to be attacked by local forces, although for the most part the English flotilla was said to have sailed along unhindered, until at last they arrived at Harlingen where they discovered around one hundred and forty Dutch cargo ships, defended only be two small Dutch frigates. However, rather than commit is own frigates in a direct fight with the outnumbered warships, Holmes was reported to have employed his handful of fireships against the large numbers of cargo vessels that were moored in the harbour, causing an enormous conflagration to erupt which forced most of their passengers and crews to flee in terror. In the midst of all this confusion Holmes and his forces were reported to have despatched a number of crewmen to deliberately set fire to those Dutch ships that had somehow managed to escape the fireships, causing even greater damage and destruction within Harlingen, until at last an estimated one hundred and thirty of the Dutch vessels were reported to have been burnt and destroyed.

Even though the English raid had caused considerable damage to the Dutch commercial fleet at Harlingen, by the end of the 19th August, it soon became clear that the large warehouses at West Terschelling remained intact and they were one of Holmes' main military objectives he ordered a land attack to be made early on the following morning. Bringing several hundred troops ashore to the by now largely deserted Dutch town, Holmes ordered the great commercial warehouses in the town to be set ablaze, an order that was quickly implemented by the English forces. Unfortunately, given the types and numbers of men who had been set ashore, Holmes was said to have struggled to keep effective control of the entire party, leaving a large numbers of sailors and soldiers free to loot the unattended houses in the town. Recognising that Dutch forces would eventually arrive in the area to confront them, Holmes was said to have ordered large parts of the town to be burnt, in order to force his own men back to their ships, an act that caused even greater damage to the Dutch township. Eventually though, most of his men were forced to retire to the landing vessels, save for a handful who were so busy looting that they failed to see the arrival of local Dutch forces and were subsequently captured by the locals, who were said to have exacted their own retribution against the English raiders. By the following morning, on the 21st August 1666, Holmes and most of his men were said to have rejoined the main English flotilla and was able to report that an estimated one hundred and forty Dutch vessels had been destroyed, the warehouses and town of West Terschelling had been similarly burnt and that he had managed to capture a small Dutch vessel, along with its dozen or so cannon. Even though few prizes had been gained from the raid, the fact that an English force had managed to successfully carry out such a raid was said to have caused great celebrations in England, where Charles II was reported to have ordered the lighting of bonfires around the country, an act of celebration that might well have led to the raid later being recalled as Holmes' Bonfire, an event that had far reaching consequences within the Dutch Republic itself, although none of the celebratory. With the country still coming to terms with the St James' Day defeat by the English navy the previous month, this second national humiliation was said to have caused rioting in many of the Republic's biggest towns and cities, with the country's government and leading military figures being held personally accountable for these national failures, although in the end the Dutch leadership were able to harness this anger into a form of rampant nationalism that helped them gain the support of the Dutch population. As part of this later patriotic fervour, the Dutch leader, Johan de Witt was reported to have organised a nationwide pamphleting campaign that detailed the various atrocities committed by the English forces at the sackings of Terschelling and Harlingen, including the claims that numerous Dutch civilians had been barbarically killed by the English troops, events that had in fact never occurred. For De Witt's purposes however, the truth of the matter remained largely irrelevant, as the campaign itself proved to be worthwhile, in that it strengthened anti-English feelings within Holland and allowed him the time to initiate a military operation that he had been planning for some time, a raid that would impose a humiliating defeat on England and force its recalcitrant monarch Charles II to come to the negotiating table with a much more submissive attitude and reasonable demands.

Being aware of England's perilous financial situation and its subsequent decision to lay up a number of its biggest capital ships at the Royal dockyards in Chatham, in order to reduce spending on the English navy, the Dutch leader, Johan de Witt, was said to have seen English naval weakness as a perfect opportunity to exploit his country's own maritime strength. However, in the light of the St James' Day defeat and the later English raid on the port of Harlingen, during which significant numbers of Dutch ships and their crews were lost, De Witt was forced to consider adopting a much more aggressive policy towards England's naval strength, a strategy that was undoubtedly reinforced by the news that so many great English warships were being forced to remain anchored at Chatham, rather than patrolling the English coastline, or promoting English sea power throughout Western Europe. Despite the effective loss of these naval assets, from a Parliamentary and royal perspective England was entirely safe from attack; having few enemies that could launch a large scale co-ordinated military assault on the country, save for the Dutch, who most Englishmen considered unwilling to engage in such a foolhardy expedition. However, following its raid on the port of Harlingen and the wholesale destruction of the Netherlands commercial fleet in the Vlies estuary, any previously held restrictions on military assaults, especially those on each other's sovereign territories had been swept away and for the Dutch government all English territories, at home and abroad, were now considered to be legitimate targets for their naval forces. As a result, in June 1657 De Witt ordered his main naval commander, Admiral Michiel de Ruyter, to launch a full scale attack on the River Medway at the mouth of the Thames, with the intention of sending a mixed naval and land force along the river and across country to assault and destroy the Royal dockyards at Chatham, as well as any and all vessels that were anchored there. Using his numerous warships and large contingent of marines, De Ruyter's fleet quickly overcame the English fort at Sheerness, which they destroyed and continued unopposed, until they reached the defensive chain at Gillingham that was designed to prevent such an attack. Quickly overcoming the obstacle, by the 13th of the month the Dutch fleet was reported to have reached Chatham and were being confronted by the laid up and largely defenceless English ships, which they began to attack with both fire and shot, with the result that some fifteen ships, including three of the great capital vessels, the Royal Oak, Loyal London and Royal James were sunk by the Dutch forces. Worse still for the English navy, the biggest of their great battleships, the English flagship, HMS Royal Charles, was abandoned by its skeleton crew and captured by the Dutch, only to be towed back to Holland, where parts of its structure, including its Royal Crest, are still publicly displayed in the Rijksmuseum. Fortunately for England, the normally fearless De Ruyter was thought to have suffered from a sudden attack of cautiousness and withdrawn many of his forces before the Dutch marine force could set about destroying the royal dockyards, which was thought to have been one of the raids principal aims. Despite this failure however, upon their return to Holland with a number of prizes, including the HMS Unity and HMS Royal Charles, De Ruyter and his fellow commanders were treated as national heroes by their countrymen, who regarded their actions as fair compensation for the earlier English raid at Harlingen. Back in England though, the opposite was true, with the repercussions of the successful Dutch raid being felt for a number of years and increasing the public antipathy towards Charles II to previously unknown and almost alarming levels.

As a direct result of the attack and the loss of the English ships, England was forced to withdraw many of its previously unreasonable demands in order to achieve a final peace settlement with the Netherlands, as well as modifying some of the more troublesome terms of the previously agreed Navigation Act, which proved to be such a highly divisive issue for the two countries. As a result of these more pragmatic discussions between the two nations, on the 31st July 1667 the Treaty of Breda was signed bringing a formal end to the Second Anglo-Dutch War, although the agreement did not prevent the two nations from going to war with one another twice more in the future, in 1672 and 1780, both of which were thought to have been caused by territorial disputes and trading rights. The financial losses caused by the Dutch raid on the Medway was said to have mounted to some £250,000 at the time, although this might have been much worse had the three sunken capital ships, the Royal Oak, Loyal London and Royal James, not been salvaged and repaired at a later date. In the years immediately following the Dutch raid, England was reported to have lagged behind the Dutch in terms of maritime power, although twenty five years later, a new shipbuilding program and the Glorious Revolution of 1688 had seen England restored as the pre-eminent European sea power of the age, a position that it would continue to hold right through to the 20th century.

In part, the successful development of the English navy, from a leading European maritime power to a world superpower was undoubtedly helped by the religious and political conflicts of the late 17th century, which saw the Roman Catholic James II undermined and subsequently replaced by his Protestant son-in-law, William of Orange. Despite being a Roman Catholic, when James ascended the English throne in 1685, he was widely accepted as the legitimate successor to his older brother Charles II, just as long as he agreed to maintain the religious and political status quo that respected Parliamentary authority and the pre-eminence of the Anglican Church. It was also said to be an important factor that at the time of his accession to the English, Scottish and Irish Crowns, James did not have a son and therefore upon his death, the English throne would almost certainly pass to a Protestant successor, a far more acceptable situation for England's political elite. However, James' position and authority was thought to have become increasingly threatened by his own reckless actions, which saw him deliberately challenge the authority of Parliament and the Church of England, in an attempt to secure full Catholic emancipation, a dangerous development for many of England's Protestant legislators. Not content with making unpopular political alliances that might secure this personal goal, James then began to dismiss those Bishops and Commissioners who held opposing views to his own and replaced them with candidates that were either Roman Catholics, or those more easily disposed to supporting the king's campaign. Throughout the three kingdoms of England, Scotland and Ireland, James was reported to have purged any and all political and religious opponents in an attempt to "jerrymander" the country's Parliamentary executive, a move that was said to have caused many to recall the reign of the ill-fated Charles I and the resulting English Civil War. The situation was said to have become even more strained in 1688, when James not only raised a royal army led by Catholic commanders, without Parliament's permission, but also became a father once again, after his second wife, Mary of Modena, delivered him a son, James Francis Edward Stuart, who later became known as the Old Pretender.

For many Protestants within the English establishment, the prospect of a continuing Roman Catholic Stuart dynasty on the throne of England, was too serious to contemplate, causing many of England's leading politicians to seek alternatives to the increasingly autocratic rule of James II. However, rather than risk yet another Civil War, with the country divided between King and Parliament, leading Protestant politicians and Parliamentarians began to look for a legitimate royal alternative to James, with the most obvious candidate being his daughter, Mary Stuart, the consort of the Dutch ruler, William of Orange, both of whom were staunch supporters of the Protestant faith. For much of the first part of 1688, both sides were said to have become polarised in their positions, with each of them reportedly lobbying and making promises to the large numbers of independently neutral parties that could make or break the individual causes, until in the end, the country was said to have become divided between those who supported James II, those who supported Parliament and those who were prepared to wait and see how things developed. In the meantime though, a group of England's leading Protestant politicians were reported to have communicated privately with William of Orange in the Netherlands requesting that he rescue them from the growing absolutism of his father-in-law, James II and guaranteeing him and his consort, Mary Stuart, some sort of involvement in the future rule of a Protestant England. According to some sources, as Europe's leading Protestant monarch and no doubt with the prospect of England's military forces being put at his disposal in any future conflict with the Roman Catholic King, Louis XIV of France, eventually William was persuaded to bring his formidable professional army to England in order to confront the Catholic James II. However, before he would launch his invasion to supposedly free England from the Catholic tyranny of King James, William was keen to receive assurances that the not only would the English nobility and people support such a foreign intervention, but more importantly, the English navy and army too, which he was assured would not interfere in his planned military expedition to England.

Lord Arlington **Sir George Downing** **Sir Edward Popham**

Having spent some weeks preparing his invasion fleet and assembling the land forces that he intended to bring to England, William was also said to have arranged for pamphlets to be prepared which would be distributed throughout the country assuring the English population that he was merely acting to protect the Protestant faith and the authority of the English Parliament, both of which were being threatened by the policies and actions of the Catholic monarch, James II. For his part, King James was said to have finally realised the seriousness of the situation in England by the middle of 1688, although it was only in the August that he eventually began to see the possibility of his son-in-law, William of Orange, launching a military invasion to deprive him of his throne, an act that he initially believed he could resist by force of arms. Unfortunately for him, like his brother, James' ability to launch and maintain a large naval force to patrol the borders of his kingdoms was said to have been compromised by the country's perilous finances, which only allowed him to field a relatively small and generally out of date navy, which would not have been much of a match for the much larger and better equipped Dutch fleet that William had at his disposal. In light of this disparity between the two naval forces, James' limited number of ships were reported to have been positioned near the River Medway, presumably to guard against a similar attack that had occurred in 1657, when a number of the English navy's capital ships had been sunk by the Dutch fleet at Chatham. According to some reports, James II was also said to have been under the illusion that William of Orange would first have to attack the French fleet of the Catholic king, Louis XIV, before the Protestant prince could hope to attack England, an assumption that he was wrong to have made, as William's first target was always going to be the invasion of England, simply to gather additional forces with which he could eventually confront his Roman Catholic enemy.

Setting sail in October 1688, William was said to have assembled a fleet of nearly five hundred ships and an army of some forty thousand men with which to complete his invasion of England, although much still depended on the plans and actions of the English navy and the tens of thousands of soldiers that James II was said to have gathered to his cause. However, within days of having sailed, the huge Dutch fleet was said to have been scattered by a violent storm, which not only delayed its journey to England, but also led some English commanders to believe that the invasion would have to be postponed until the following Spring, bringing temporary relief to James' supporters who hoped to be given extra time to prepare an adequate defence. Unfortunately for them and their monarch, rather than cancel the operation, William was said to have continued on, recognising that had he failed to complete his promised invasion, then much of his support within England itself might well disappear, preventing him from achieving his long term objective of having English forces support him in his forthcoming war with the French king, Louis XIV. According to some reporters, as William's enormous fleet emerged into the English Channel, it was said to have assembled itself into a vast square formation, some twenty five ships deep that could be easily seen from both the English port of Dover and the French port of Calais. For the waiting English fleet, the prospect of attacking this extremely large Dutch armada was thought to have been daunting and it was said to have caused much relief amongst the English crews that the prevailing winds subsequently prevented them from interfering with its planned crossing to Torquay, where the Dutch forces were intending to land. Unfortunately, sea fog was thought to have caused the Dutch fleet to sail right past their intended destination, forcing them to come ashore at Torbay in Kent, where William and his commanders ordered their regiments of cavalry, foot soldiers and artillery units to disembark. At the same time that the thousands of mercenary troops were being unloaded by the Dutch ships, the English navy was reported to have been forced back to Portsmouth by the prevailing winds, preventing them from offering any sort of armed resistance to the thousands of Dutch, English, German and Swiss troops that were steadily being unloaded on the south coast of England. Even though these troops were paid mercenaries fighting for William, his adversary, the English monarch, James II, was also said to have raised additional forces to help repel the foreign invaders, although most of James' additional troops were thought to have been recruited in the largely Roman Catholic regions of Scotland and Ireland.

Having successfully landed his enormous army at Torbay, rather than going on the offensive and invading English territories, which may well have turned the population against him, William was reported to have simply encamped his military forces and forbade them to take any actions that might be deemed aggressive, even to the point of prohibiting his troops from foraging for supplies, a normal practice by most invading armies. By the 9th November 1688 and with no Roman Catholic army having confronted him, William was reported to have moved most of his forces to the town of Exeter, where his reception was said to have been muted, as the local population waited to see how the political situation developed, although reports were thought to have reached him that elsewhere in the country news of his arrival in the country had been well received, with increasing numbers of local noblemen, civic leaders and councillors, all declaring their support for the Protestant monarch and his English queen. Whilst such reports heartened William, at the same time they were said to have caused severe depression within the ranks of James' supporters, many of whom were thought to have lost hope with the Catholic monarch and subsequently switched their allegiances to the opposition, further undermining the resolution of the increasingly uncertain James II, who was thought to have used any excuse not to employ his sizeable Roman Catholic forces, much to the irritation and dismay of his still loyal military commanders. The crippling doubts that affected James so badly, so as to deter him from meeting Williams forces on the battlefield were thought to have continued for much of November, until the monarch convinced himself that his own army was not only unreliable, but generally unfaithful, leading him to order its disbandment and handing a largely bloodless victory to his Dutch son-in-law, William. In fact the only military engagement of note that took place between the two sides was said to have occurred at Reading, where the local townspeople, alarmed by the arrival of Irish forces who were loyal to James II, sent word to William requesting his help. The Dutch monarch immediately despatched a small force of regular Dutch troops into the town, who along with local Reading men, managed to drive the Irishmen out of the town, leaving around fifty or so of their number dead or wounded as they retreated.

By the 9th December 1688, it was abundantly clear to James that not only could he not resist William militarily, but neither could he rely on the support of the majority of the English population, many of whom had very little interest in becoming involved in what was rapidly becoming a private dispute between members of the Stuart family. For James especially, his greatest concern was thought to be that he might share the fate of his late father, Charles I, who was not only deposed by members of the English Parliament, but also lost his head to them, a fate he was not happy to repeat. As a result, on the evening of the 9th December, or the morning of the 10th, James' queen and newborn son were said to have left England for the final time, making their way to the court of the French monarch, King Louis XIV, the same Roman Catholic monarch who would subsequently find himself at war with the new joint English sovereigns, King William III and Queen Mary II. Although James II was thought to have tried to leave England at the same time, but by another route, he was subsequently captured at Sheerness by a group of local fishermen and later transported back to London, for a meeting with his son-in-law, William, who even at this late stage was anxious for James to formally abandon his kingdom, thereby giving the Dutch king, the moral authority for having invaded England, purely to save it from the uncertainty after being deserted by its lawful sovereign. In order to facilitate James' flight to the continent, William was even thought to have instructed his soldiers to keep a deliberately ineffective watch on the Stuart king, which allowed James to leave the country, without any obvious blame for his escape, attaching itself to the Dutch monarch or members of his entourage.

With James having effectively abandoned his kingdom through his escape to France, William and his wife, Mary Stuart, were then fully entitled to take control of the country through the formation of a provisional government, attended by many of the leading peers who had been instrumental in inviting William to invade England in the first place. As part of this same contingency plan, the new temporary ruler also called together all of those remaining members of Parliament who had held office during the reign of Charles II, thus excluding all of those members appointed by James II, most of whom were pro-Catholic and therefore opposed to William's presence in the country. However, even with a generally sympathetic Parliament to support him, the question of exactly who should rule the country and in which particular form, was said to have continued to vex the English legislature for a considerable period of time, so much so that William even threatened to leave the country if an equitable arrangement could not be agreed within a relatively short time. As a consequence, the Parliament eventually settled on a new arrangement that would see William and Mary rule England as joint sovereigns, William III and Mary II, although in practice Mary nearly always deferred to her husband, so William was thought to have ruled on an independent basis in most instances. However, as part of the same agreement that put William and Mary on the thrones of England, Scotland and Ireland, the English Parliament insisted on a number of constitutional changes that would bring an end to the practice of royal absolutism, the right of the sovereign to raise an army and prevent any Roman Catholic from sitting on the English throne ever again. The Bill of Rights which was passed by the English Parliament in December 1689 was said to have effectively enshrined the supremacy of both the Church of England and the English Parliament over the monarch, thereby preventing any future sovereign from usurping the power of the executive, or indeed the position of the Church of England. By the 13th February 1689, both William and Mary were thought to have agreed to accept the throne of England on these new terms and in recognition of their new constitutional status, both agreed to swear a coronation oath that saw them pledge to govern the peoples of England and its dominions according to the statutes of Parliament, creating the Parliamentary and monarchical systems that remain with us all through to the present day.

On balance, England was said to have benefited enormously from the Glorious Revolution, not just constitutionally, but financially, militarily and commercially, as the country became an integral part of a much greater and more powerful Anglo-Dutch alliance that William had always hoped to employ in his conflict with the French monarch, Louis XIV, who is often referred to as the "Sun King". Although the political and religious upheavals of mainland Europe had largely bypassed England, simply because of its island status and the presence of the reasonably powerful English navy, this situation did not prevent England from despatching its military forces to the European continent, as and when it believed that such an action was in its own national, political or religious interests. Such was said to be the case in the final years of the 17th century, following William and Mary's accession to the English throne, as the continuing royalist claims of the exiled James II, the imperial aims of the French king, Louis XIV and the ongoing disputes between the Roman Catholic and Protestant faiths, all combined to force much of Europe into a military conflict that would eventually become known as the Nine Years War, or the War of the Grand Alliance, which lasted from 1688 to 1697. Even though the conflict was said to have concerned the territorial ambitions of King Louis XIV of France, eventually it was said to have evolved into a Europe-wide dispute that would see Louis' kingdom confronted by an alliance of other European nations, including the Dutch Republic, England, Spain, Scotland, Sweden and the Holy Roman Empire. Although most of the fighting between the various combatants was said to have taken place in Europe and within its territorial waters, the island of Ireland was said to have been particularly affected by the conflict, as it was employed by the ousted Roman Catholic monarch, James II, to contest the right of the Protestant William III to sit on the throne of England, Scotland and Ireland. And it was said to be in Ireland that James Stuart, along with his accompanying French and Irish forces, were finally defeated by William and his Dutch commanders, being forced to retreat back to France, leaving behind them a legacy of division and religious intolerance that continues to exist within parts of Ireland's Catholic and Protestant communities, right through to the modern day.

Admiral John Byng

Admiral Edward Hawke

Lord Sandwich

For its part, the newly enlarged Anglo-Dutch navy was thought to have played a significant role in the suppression of the Irish Catholic revolt, being used to transport men and weaponry to the northern provinces of Ireland, from where they were able to drive James' Jacobite army southward and eventually to their final stronghold at Limerick, where they were eventually forced to capitulate to the forces of the new English monarch. However, despite their enlarged naval forces, the Anglo-Dutch navy still experienced the occasional setback and defeat, as was the case at the Battle of Beachy Head on the 10th July 1690, where the French fleet managed to destroy eleven coalition ships without loss, handing temporary control of the English Channel to the French, although this situation was said to have been very quickly reversed. The English commander of the Anglo-Dutch forces, Admiral Arthur Herbert, Lord Torrington, was heavily criticised for his performance during the battle and despite being court martialled for the defeat, he was later acquitted, although he was later dismissed by William III, who regarded his behaviour as completely unacceptable. Significantly though, this notable defeat, which was said to have caused widespread panic in England, largely because people believed it heralded a planned invasion of the country by France, was very quickly followed by the news of William's victory at the Battle of the Boyne in Ireland, an event that helped to steady nerves within the general population. Additionally, it has also been suggested by some historians that the defeat at Beachy Head forced the English authorities to begin planning for the wholesale rebuilding and modernisation of the English navy, an expensive undertaking that led to the establishment of the Bank of England in 1694, initially as a private institution, to raise revenue for the creation of a new naval force, with over one million pounds being raised in a little under two weeks, to begin the process. Although naval warfare was still a relatively small part of international warfare, due in part to the limitations of the available technologies, which saw ships of the line commonly used to defend each country's national coastlines, where sea battles did take place, it was generally the side with the largest number of ships, or those that benefited from good fortune that won most of these sea based engagements. It was largely through the acceptance of such thinking that over the course of the Nine Years War both England and the Netherlands made sure to out build their French adversaries, allowing them to gain naval supremacy of the world's oceans by the time the war came to an end in 1697.

MARINERS, MERCHANTS AND THE MILITARY TOO

11. THE MAKING OF A MODERN NAVY

For much of the next fifty or sixty years, England's navy continued to thrive, being engaged in not only protecting the country's rapidly expanding trade routes, but also playing a full role in a number of European military alliances that were raised in answer to one or other conflict, such as the War of the Spanish Succession, which was fought between 1702 and 1713; and during which the navy captured the valuable Spanish territories of Gibraltar and Minorca. Over the course of the same period, English ships were reported to have made significant gains from the declining Spanish Empire, particularly in the transatlantic slave trade and by annexing several of the Iberian kingdoms historic territories, including Sicily and Panama, helping to progress England's reputation from that of a European sea power to that of a world power, often at a direct cost to its immediate neighbours. The period was also marked by the Act of Union, the legislative treaty that formally united the kingdoms of England and Scotland, into the single nation of Great Britain and Ireland, essentially uniting these three historic kingdoms and their ancient crowns into a single political, commercial and constitutional state, a creation that continued to exist well into the first half of the 20th century. However, the next great conflict that was thought to have tested the skills, ships and men of the British Royal Navy was the Seven Years War, which once again pitted French warships against those of Britain and that was notable for the British navy because of the death of Admiral John Byng, who was executed on the deck of his own flagship. A highly experienced naval officer, Byng was said to have been given the relatively straightforward task of reinforcing the English garrison at Fort St Philip on Minorca, which had been besieged by French troops in 1756, but without being given adequate ships, stores and men with which to complete the task. Rather than being provided with well equipped front line vessels and a large enough landing force of marines to undertake a successful attack on the island and the French forces there, instead, the unfortunate English commander was said to have been given a fleet of ten largely unseaworthy ships and then had his specially trained marines replaced by regular troops, who were ill-suited to face an opposed landing. According to some sources, Byng was said to have made his concerns known to his superiors, but despite his obvious reservations was ordered to carry out his orders regardless, in a sense helping to create the situation that almost inevitably ensued.

Sailing first to the British military base at Gibraltar, Byng was said to been refused additional troops by the Governor there, a fact that he was also said to have reported to the Admiralty, before continuing his journey to Minorca. Arriving off the coast of the island around the middle of May, on the 19th of the month, the English commander was reported to have begun communicating with the trapped English garrison at Fort St Philip, before he landed any troops on the island, discussions that were said to have been interrupted the following morning when a French naval squadron suddenly appeared on the scene. Unfortunately, either through poor planning or just plain bad luck, as Byng ordered his flotilla to engage the French fleet, it was said to have approached at such a steep angle of attack that it left his leading ships exposed to enemy fire and without the support of the rest of the British battle line, an oversight that led some of his leading vessels being seriously damaged by French guns. As they watched these events unfold, it was reported that one of his subordinates suggested to Byng that he move his own flagship in closer, so as to entice the enemy fleet, but the English commander rejected the idea, for fear of inviting even greater damage to his own ships. Even though the French fleet was only thought to have been equal to his own, there was a suggestion that Byng appeared to be undecided as to the best course of action to pursue, causing a delay that ultimately allowed the enemy ships to simply sail away undamaged, leaving Byng and his vessels sitting off the coast of Minorca for the next four days. Even though the Admiral later reported that he had been trying to observe and communicate with the English garrison during that time, in the end he finally made the fateful decision to sail back to Gibraltar to have his damaged ships repaired, rather than attempting any sort of reinforcement of Minorca. Having successfully returned his fleet to Gibraltar, Byng was reported to be in the process of replacing those men who were sick or injured when news arrived from England that he had been replaced as the commander of the fleet and ordering him to return home, where he was subsequently placed in custody to face a court martial. It was said to be as a result of Byng's reluctance to reinforce the garrison on Minorca that on the 29th June 1756 the British troops there were forced to surrender to the besieging French forces, before being transported back to England.

The later humiliating loss of Fort St Philip on Minorca, undoubtedly caused a great deal of public anger to be levelled against Admiral Byng personally, although ultimately it was a series of changes in the Royal Navy's own Articles of War that would prove to be so fateful for the English commander. Where in earlier times, a senior military officer might well have escaped serious censure by a board of his peers, the fact that junior officers might often suffer a death sentence, because of a senior officer's orders or actions, who then escaped a similar fate because of his high rank, had caused the Articles of War to be much more stringently enforced by the various court martial panels. Charged with cowardice, disaffection and failing to do his utmost against the enemy, Byng was subsequently acquitted of the first two charges, but convicted of the third, in that he failed to pursue and confront the French fleet at Minorca, thereby protecting his own, a clear contravention of the Royal Navy's own Articles and one that was punishable by death. Even though some members of the court martial had been inclined to recommend clemency for Admiral Byng, subsequent appeals to the monarch, King George, all proved to be fruitless, as the Royal Navy, Parliament and the King sought to find somebody to blame for the humiliating loss of Minorca. In fact, the only allowance made by the monarch was for the unfortunate Byng to be executed on the quarterdeck of a Royal Navy vessels, the HMS Monarch, which was stationed in the Solent, where on the 14th March 1757 Admiral John Byng was led from below decks, allowed to kneel and make his peace with God, before being shot to death by a platoon of Marines. Throughout much of the country, the execution of John Byng was thought to have caused enormous outrage, especially as the public became increasingly aware of the poor condition of the ships that he had been provided with by the Admiralty. However, for others, the fact that such severe punishment was likely to be applied to any and all such servicemen, who failed to do their duty, or who showed cowardice in the face of the enemy, was said to have made the nations fighting men much more resolved to do their duty, as it was generally seen to be better to face the enemy, rather than face the gallows or the firing squad.

It is probably worth remembering that at the time Admiral Byng was executed, the British navy was operating under a set of rules that would be considered to be particularly brutal by modern standards, although in terms of the times in which they were first practiced, they were undoubtedly meant to be so. Unlike today, where service in the nations military services are almost entirely optional, for the most part, general seamen who served in the English and later British navy between the 16th and 19th centuries, were in most cases some of the basest human beings in the country. As a consequence, fairly severe measures were required to moderate their behaviour, in order to limit the opportunity for men to demonstrate their disobedience and disorderliness. According to some sources, navy discipline was governed by a set of rules, laid down in the Admiralty's Black Book, which assigned a particular punishment for a specific offence and that were supplemented in times of war, by the previously mentioned Articles of War, which have commanders additional rights and powers. The first of these Articles of War were said to have been issued in 1661 during the reign of Charles II, although most were thought to have been general outlines that had to be interpreted by individual commanders and it was only in the 1730's that more formal written regulations were introduced by the Admiralty, bringing some sort of uniformity to the country's naval service. Interestingly, it was around the same time that the traditional form of punishment, known as keel-hauling was finally outlawed by the British navy; and the number of lashes that a man could receive as punishment was limited to one dozen for any single offence. Clearly, the most serious form of punishment was to be hung from the yardarm, a penalty usually handed down for really serious offences such as mutiny or murder and generally carried out in full view of the nation's fleet, if only to deter other would-be offenders. Rather than the judicial hanging that we associate with a professional executioner, who is skilled enough to snap the condemned prisoners neck, in most cases, a guilty seaman would be simply hoisted up by a number of his crewmates, using any available block and tackle, to be strangled to death rather than being effectively hanged.

Following the loss of Minorca to the French and the associated execution of Admiral John Byng, the British navy was reported to have enjoyed substantially more success against their French adversaries, particularly in November 1759, when a British fleet commanded by Admiral Sir Edward Hawke, confronted a French fleet of some twenty one ships at Quiberon Bay in Brittany, as it prepared to embark an invasion force that it intended to transport to Scotland. In the battle that followed, a significant number of the French ships were either sunk or run aground, effectively undermining French naval strength for the next decade and helping to turn the tide of the Seven Years War in Britain's favour. Even though Spain later entered into a coalition with France against Britain, its involvement was said to have ultimately cost it control of its territories in Cuba and the Philippines, lands that were only later returned to them at the end of the war, but at the cost of their lands in modern day Florida. By the time that peace was declared in 1763, Britain was reported to have achieved significant territorial gains from their European adversaries, although the mistrust and national enmity the country would engender within France and Spain would have made even the most ardent English imperialist question whether the cost was actually worthwhile. Within a dozen or more years of gaining victory over their two European competitors, Britain soon found herself fighting the same countries once again, although this time in a much more one-sided conflict, as France and Spain, along with a number of other European states chose to ally themselves with Britain's rebellious American colonists, in what has become commonly known as the American Revolutionary War, which began in 1775.

Admiral Lord Howe

Comte D'Estaing

Augustus Keppel

Although the root causes of the American Revolution or the American War of Independence have been well documented elsewhere, it is probably worth noting that even though the conflict first erupted over the subjects of taxation and representation, eventually it became a military confrontation driven by political intransigence, commercial opportunism, petty national jealousies and competing territorial interests. Despite being regarded as Europe's leading maritime power, by the time Britain's American colonies decided to sever their ties to Parliament and the Crown, the Royal Navy was not only still comparatively small, but also in a generally poor condition, given that little investment had been made in new ships, since the end of the Seven Years War some twelve years earlier. Similarly, according to some sources, at the outbreak of the war Britain was reported to have had a standing army of around forty thousand men, most of who were employed in protecting the country's worldwide possessions, from Canada to the Caribbean, from Ireland to India, a seemingly impossible task given the size of the territories and the travelling distances involved. From a purely military point of view, the Royal Navy of the time was not only expected to protect Britain's extensive trade routes, but also its various imperial possessions, as well as delivering military forces to anywhere in the world and helping to support the nations diplomatic and political efforts throughout the globe, a truly monumental task for such a comparatively small force. Just prior to the outbreak of hostilities with the North American colonists, the Royal Navy was reported to have had less than two hundred warships at its disposal, only a quarter of which were thought to have been in a battle ready condition, a ridiculously insufficient number, given that the service was expected to patrol the world's oceans and seas. In the run-up to the North American War, the man principally responsible for Britain's naval services, Lord Sandwich, the First Lord of the Admiralty, was reported to have had great plans for the Royal Navy, many of which had not been realised by the time his vessels were forced to confront a coalition of American, French, Spanish and Dutch ships that would eventually face the British fleet. Unfortunately, according to some sources, Lord Sandwich was said to have been a poor replacement for his predecessor, Sir Edward Hawke, who was reported to have not only been an outstanding military commander, but a first rate naval administrator, who brought great credit on himself and the British fleet during his extensive service. For his part, Lord Sandwich was not thought to have been so successful during his third spell at the Admiralty, when he served as First Lord, as he was later accused of incompetence by some of his contemporaries, who were said to have blamed him personally for the poor condition and performance of the Royal Navy during the American War of Independence. One such critic was reported to be, Admiral Lord Howe, who was said to have resigned his post in 1778 and refused to serve again, while Sandwich remained First Lord of the Admiralty, although Howe was eventually persuaded to return to active service in 1782, playing an active part in helping to relieve the siege of Gibraltar, which was a related action during the course of the American Revolution.

In the first months of what was primarily a land-based conflict, the limited Royal Navy forces were reported to have been used in a number of different roles, but principally as a support service for the British army units that were operating on the American mainland. Employed in supplying stores and carrying reinforcements across the Atlantic, Royal Navy vessels were also said to have been used in a more effective way, by patrolling the east coast of America in order to prevent arms supplies from being brought into the country for the rebellious colonists and to enforce the terms of the various British trade acts, which had caused many of the American settlers to revolt in the first place. Although the colonial forces were reported to have had a small number of their own naval vessels with which to confront the Royal Navy blockades and roving patrols, for the most part such ships were operated almost entirely as privateers, with the individual captains sailing under American colours, carrying cargoes and capturing prizes for and on behalf of the colonial authorities, but ostensibly for their own financial reward. Unable to continuously patrol the eastern seaboard of America through a lack of available vessels, English commanders often decided to employ their naval assets in support of the land forces, stationing them offshore to bombard specific coastal targets, or using them to land troops that would then move against particular settlements, towns, or rebel bases. Because of the relatively small numbers of ground troops employed within the thirteen colonies, it was often the case that British sailors, accompanied by their ships detachment of marines would be landed to attack individual targets, as was said to be the case in the coastal town of Portland in Maine, where the navy was reported to have burnt parts of the settlement down in October 1775, through the use of incendiaries and landing parties. Interestingly, it was said to be as a result of such attacks that American Congressional leaders were thought to have ordered the establishment of a proper Continental Navy, in order to prevent such seaborne attacks from happening in the future.

As a direct response to Britain's restrictions on its commercial trade with Europe, which Parliament and the Crown hoped would strangle the rebellion financially, the emerging Continental Navy, still mostly comprised of privateers, was thought to have begun conducting similar raids against English cargo vessels in European waters, thereby forcing the Royal Navy to redeploy some of its hard pressed warships back to home waters. Able to operate from sympathetic French, Spanish and Dutch ports, these American privateers were reported to have played havoc with Britain's commercial trade, raiding into the Irish and North Seas, the English Channel and using their European bases to intercept British cargo ships that were making their way to and from Africa and Asia. As a result of such attacks and the increasing losses of both valuable cargoes and ships, the British authorities were said to have been forced to implement a convoy system to protect their valuable merchant trade, at a direct cost to the military efforts being made in North America and the Caribbean. However, despite the strains on its limited resources, in the year following the outbreak of the rebellion, the Royal Navy still managed to assemble a sizeable naval force to carry a large contingent of an estimated twenty thousand ground troops across the Atlantic, which were successfully landed in New York in June of 1776. For the most part, similar operations were thought to have been the main part of the Royal Navy's role for the next three years, as it was used on both sides of the Atlantic to support British ground troops, suppress the raiding activities of the fledgling Continental Navy and act as protection for the numerous British cargo vessels that travelled the High Seas. Although the American navy continued to be a commercial nuisance for Britain, due to its size and composition it failed to pose a serious threat to the more powerful Royal Navy, save for the occasional raid that individual colonial commanders were thought to have conducted against British interests. Despite later reports, which have suggested that that these American privateers posed a real danger to Britain's military campaign in North America, in reality the most obvious threat to Britain's naval superiority only really arose after 1778, when the great fleets of France, Spain and the Netherlands were finally brought to bear against the ships of the Royal Navy.

In the aftermath of the Seven Years War, which had cost France many of its North American territories, later to become the provinces of Canada, it was hardly surprising perhaps that the European state would seek to exploit the divisions caused by the outbreak of the American Revolutionary War. With little to lose and much to gain from a successful colonial uprising, France was said to have been particularly keen to support any cause that might undermine British control of the Americas, especially in the Caribbean, where Britain had managed to achieve significant territorial gains over previous centuries, often at a cost to their leading commercial European rivals, France and Spain. Initially, Britain's traditional enemies were thought to have contented themselves with simply providing financial and logistical aid to the colonial authorities, until such time as they could determine the likely outcome of the dispute, which to their surprise Britain failed to resolve in a relatively short time. By the beginning of 1778, the French government was reported to have made the decision to formally ally itself to the American cause, assembling a French fleet under the command of Comte D'Estaing, which they were said to have despatched to America in April of the same year. In order to ensure that this flotilla did not face the entire strength of the Royal Navy, the French authorities were also thought to have assembled a second fleet of ships that were to remain stationed in and around the English Channel, forcing Britain to divide its own limited naval resources between Europe and the New World; thereby weakening its hold on its valuable Caribbean possessions. In response, the Admiralty was reported to have despatched a separate British fleet across the Atlantic to safeguard its American territories, whilst at the same assembling and sending out to sea, a second naval squadron under the command of Augustus Keppel, which was tasked to seek out and confront the French fleet in European waters. Sailing south, Keppel's ships were said to have sighted the second French fleet off the coast of France, near Brest, although apart from bombarding one another from a distance, no close quarter action was taken by either commander, a failure that would later result in a number of the British officers facing a courts martial and Augustus Keppel resigning from the service.

On the opposite side of the Atlantic however, the various British and French commanders were thought to have been far more adventurous and aggressive, although ultimately the weather was said to have played just as pivotal a role, as did the individual sea captains themselves. The existing British fleet in North America was said to have been commanded by Admiral Lord Howe, who upon hearing that the French fleet of Comte D'Estaing was approaching American waters, was said to have assembled his small force of ships along the coast near New Jersey, where he hoped to confront his adversary. Unfortunately, the French commander was said to have sailed past Howe's force and carried on to Rhode Island, where he hoped to meet up with a colonial force to launch an attack on the British garrison there. Pursued by Howe, who had now been reinforced by other military units, the two fleets were reported to have prepared to engage one another, but a storm blew in and scattered the various ships, preventing a decisive engagement from taking place. Having reassembled his fleet, D'Estaing was then reported to have headed for Boston, whilst Howe was eventually joined by elements of the second British squadron that had been sent from England, under the command of John Byron. Reportedly frustrated by the course of the war, as well as the quality and numbers of the ships being assigned to him, which he blamed Lord Sandwich, the First Lord of the Admiralty for, Admiral Lord Howe was reported to have resigned his post on the 25th July 1778 and passed all responsibility to his successor, John Byron. However, even the American colonists were thought to have suffered some degree of frustration, as the French fleet was reported to have subsequently travelled south to the Caribbean, rather than waiting to support planned American attacks on the British bases in the north of the country, specifically around Halifax and Newfoundland. For his part though, D'Estaing was only seeking to pursue his own country's interests, which revolved around the British held West Indies, arguably some of the most valuable territories in the New World, given the financial importance of the regions sugar producing industry. For the remainder of the year, the French fleet, along with those French forces stationed in the West Indies were reported to have played cat-and-mouse with the two British naval commanders, William Hotham and Samuel Barrington, who had been ordered to protect British interests and territories in the region.

By the beginning of 1779 Spain was reported to have joined the coalition with France and the American colonial authorities, like France having its own historic reasons for opposing Britain's naval power and territorial holdings in the New World. Having gathered a highly impressive fleet with which to attack and harass British ships, as they travelled to and from their home ports, the Admiralty were reported to have assembled a fairly inferior force under the command of Sir Charles Hardy to try and contest control of Europe's main trade routes, although ultimately poor weather, adverse winds, outbreaks of disease and the general state of the Royal Navy ships was said to have forced Hardy to retire to his home ports. Fortunately for the country, by the latter part of the year, the weather conditions and the absence of targets was said to have caused this Franco-Spanish fleet to retire as well, leaving the seaways relatively open for those that were brave enough to risk the wintry waters of the Atlantic. Throughout the year, the Royal Navy was thought to have adopted a reactive strategy, rather than a proactive one, its hands generally being tied by the limited number of seaworthy vessels it had at its disposal at any one time. British interests were said to have been well served by the general ineptitude of the French and Spanish commanders who singularly failed to exploit their numerical advantage, in dogged pursuance of their own national policies, which often had little to do with achieving the American aims of becoming independent of British rule.

Admiral John Byron

Samuel Barrington

Sir George Rodney

By the start of 1780 however and perhaps having finally recognised that the American cause required more obvious means of support, the French authorities were reported to have sent a fleet across the Atlantic, carrying several thousand much needed regular troops, to help support the colonial militia's who assembled the main part of the Continental Army. From a purely naval perspective however, in the waters of North America, the rest of the year and well into 1781 was reported to have been fairly uneventful, with both sides operating in and around their main naval bases, but without engaging one another in any meaningful way. Elsewhere though, during the first few months of 1780 Britain was said to have suffered a major military reverse in the southern states, following a successful Spanish invasion of West Florida, a loss that ultimately prevented British forces from bringing pressure to bear on the main colonial armies further north. Despite this setback however, a few months earlier, the Admiralty was said to have sent a large naval force to sea under the command of Sir George Rodney, with specific instructions to relieve the garrison on Gibraltar, re-provision the British garrison on Minorca, before crossing the Atlantic to link up with other Royal Navy units in the West Indies. As he travelled to Gibraltar, Rodney's force was reported to have not only intercepted and captured a Spanish trade convoy, but also met and defeated a second squadron of enemy ships, before continuing their journey to relieve the besieged garrison on Gibraltar and prior to setting sail across the Atlantic to the West Indies. By March of 1780 Rodney was said to have arrived at Saint Lucia, from where he was said to have tried on several occasions to bring the French fleet to battle, but failed to engage them in any sort of definitive action, leaving the military situation generally unresolved. Later in the year, as the Caribbean hurricane season dawned, Rodney was reported to have travelled north to New York in the hope of confronting the enemy forces, but again he was said to have been unable to engage the French or Spanish fleets decisively, forcing him to return to the West Indies empty handed.

Having been informed that the Netherlands had now joined the colonial coalition, Rodney began to take steps to seize any Dutch vessels that his ships encountered in the Americas, as well as capturing a number of the smaller Dutch trading posts in the region. Although the Dutch merchant fleet and its military forces were said to have been seriously reduced since the late 17th century, when they had contested control of the seas with Britain, the fact that they had chosen to support the revolutionary cause, forced British commanders to use valuable resources to track down, confront and seizing those Dutch vessels that were being employed in supporting the American's revolution. As with France and Spain though, the Netherlands principal motivation for opposing Britain in its fight with the colonies, was not so much a deep-seated desire to see the American settlers achieve their freedom from Britain, but was simply a combination of earlier military accords, along with national and commercial opportunism. Even though the Dutch had few territorial possessions in the New World, save for a handful of trading posts and well established trading routes, as part of the wider conflict, the Dutch were keen to protect and expand upon the territories that they held on the Indian subcontinent and in Asia. Consequently, any actions that might reduce Britain's influence in these regions was always likely to be supported by the Netherlands and France, who had much to gain from a general British defeat, although according to most reports, both countries subsequently failed to achieve any significant gains in India and the Far East, as a result of their actions in the Americas.

By the beginning of 1781, Royal Navy units in the Caribbean, under Admiral George Rodney, were thought to have been so busy maintaining control of the region that they failed to properly prepare for the arrival of a new French fleet, under the command of the Count de Grasse, which was reported to have been despatched to help relieve the French held territory of Martinique. Although Rodney was said to have been aware of the fleet's impending arrival, according to some sources he failed to allow his second-in-command, Rear Admiral Sir Samuel Hood, to take proper action to confront De Grasse's fleet, resulting in a successful French reinforcement of Martinique and in Hood's relatively ineffective force being driven off by the French commander. However, even after Rodney himself became involved in the struggle to confront De Grasse' fleet, the French commander was said to have skilfully avoided a full-scale confrontation with the Royal Navy, something that not only frustrated Rodney and Hood personally, but also ensured that Britain's military operations in America would ultimately be doomed to failure. As was normal at the time, during the Caribbean hurricane season, the British fleet moved north to the calmer waters of the American east coast, although in the early months of 1781, Admiral Rodney, who was said to have become ill, was reported to have returned to Britain with half of his fleet, leaving the rest of the British force under the command of Rear Admiral Hood. Still determined to confront the French fleet of De Grasse', Hood and his ships were said to have moved north, unaware that the French commander was attempting to link up with other French warships based at Newport on the east coast of America, which when combined with his own would give the French navy a numerical superiority over the British. Seemingly unaware of the French commander's strategy, Admiral Hood was reported to have headed for the British naval station at New York, where a second Royal Navy squadron was based, commanded by Admiral Thomas Graves, who had recently taken over the post from his predecessor Admiral Arbuthnot. However, before Hood and his fleet ever reached New York, Admiral Graves was said to have been informed that the entire resident French fleet at Newport had left harbour and was sailing south towards Chesapeake Bay, forcing the newly installed British commander to assemble his forces and set off in pursuit. In the meantime, the skilful De Grasse had brought his own fleet to Chesapeake Bay, by a much more circuitous route, surprising not only Admiral Graves, but also Admiral Hood who had subsequently arrived in the area as he made his way north towards New York. With Admiral Rodney having earlier withdrawn half of the British ships to Europe, Admirals Graves and Hood now found themselves grossly outnumbered by the combined French forces, who very quickly engaged the Royal Navy fleets and forced them to withdraw to the comparative safety of their bases at New York, leaving De Grasse free to bring reinforcements and siege equipment into Chesapeake Bay. For the French commander, his victory over the Royal Navy, in what later became known as the Battle of the Chesapeake was vital, in that it completed the encirclement of the British land army at Yorktown, effectively forcing the British commander there, Lord Cornwallis, to surrender his position and forcing the British authorities to seek a political settlement, rather than an outright military solution. Interestingly, even after he was forced to withdraw his forces to New York, Admiral Thomas Graves was reported to have begun assembling a relief force to break the siege of Yorktown, although just two days before the rescue fleet was due to sail, news arrived that Cornwallis had surrendered to French and American forces, making any such expedition relatively pointless.

Despite Cornwallis' surrender at Yorktown, which was thought to have marked the start of what became a lengthy peace process, elsewhere in the Americas, much still remained to be resolved, especially between the main European protagonists, who were all still trying to consolidate their positions in preparation for the almost inevitable peace negotiations. For the highly adept French architect of the Chesapeake Bay victory, the Count de Grasse, having played his part in besieging Yorktown, he was later reported to have taken his fleet south once again to the waters of the Caribbean, closely followed by the British commander, Admiral Hood, who was keen to overturn the outcome of their previous meeting. However, in the French fleet's first few weeks back in the West Indies, De Grasse' forces were thought to have retained their advantage, successfully recovering a number of Dutch possessions previously acquired by Britain and also conquering the British held island of St Christopher. However, actions by Hood and the newly returned Admiral Rodney, prevented any further territorial gains by the French, who had intended to launch a full scale attack against the island of Jamaica, but were hampered in their efforts by the strategies of the British commanders who finally managed to engage De Grasse' fleet at the Battle of the Saintes, which despite preventing the invasion of Jamaica, has often been deemed to be a failure, in that Rodney failed to order a pursuit of the remaining French ships that might well have been captured or destroyed if he had acted quickly enough. For the most part though, for the remainder of the time, from the surrender of Yorktown in 1781, through to the formal signing of the Treaty of Paris in 1783, all of the combatants were thought to have spent their time and energies consolidating the gains that they had made as a direct result of the conflict. In the final analysis though, apart from the loss of the thirteen colonies, which many in Britain saw as an unnecessary expense to the national exchequer, Britain was thought to have suffered few territorial losses in the New World, save for those that they had actually acquired through seizure and subsequently handed back to France, Spain and the Netherlands, as part of the Treaty of Paris 1783. As has been previously been mentioned elsewhere, although there were some within the American leadership that would have preferred to see Britain driven out of North America completely, as in the case of the War of 1812, ultimately this objective was not achieved, as successive British governments asserted and defended their rights to retain its Caribbean and North American territories, most of which have subsequently become independent states in their own right.

It was thought to be as a result of the failures and successes of the American Revolution that over the period of the next decade, from 1783 to 1793, the Royal Navy emerged as a bigger, stronger and much more professional military service, one that was better able to confront the continuing threat posed by its European neighbours, France and Spain. Unlike Britain where an emerging constitutional monarchy provided a relatively stable political system, the France of King Louis XVI was said to have been in crisis since 1789, largely as a result of the monarch's own powers, the growing divisions between the nobility, the church and the common people, as well as the growth of revolutionary fervour, which many believed had its roots in the earlier American Revolutionary War of 1775 to 1783. It was certainly said to be the case that one of the main causes of the French Revolution was the financial collapse of the economy, due in no small part to the enormous amounts of money that France had spent in supporting its earlier involvement in the Seven Years War and the American Revolutionary War, with little to show for its investment. As a consequence, the French economy was reported to have declined into poverty, causing great hardship amongst the very poorest of the population, whose resentment was easily exploited by those political rabble rousers who were eager to see an end to the country's nobility, who they regarded as being the architects of France's national decline. One of the earliest and most infamous representations of this public anger was said to have been the Storming of the Bastile, which occurred on the 14th July 1789 and that was undertaken to demonstrate the public's feelings, rather than to free any of the prisoners incarcerated within its walls, of which there were only seven. As the weeks passed the situation was reported to have become increasingly tense and unmanageable, with various military units being used to guard one another, rather than to protect the capital, a situation that almost inevitably led to occasional fighting between different military units, leading to most of them being regarded as unreliable and therefore remaining unused by the authorities who were struggling to impose order on the city.

Unfortunately, as the situation in France continued to deteriorate, rumour and innuendo was said to have been added to by deliberate politically driven propaganda, which sought to further divide the mass of the people from Church leaders and the local nobility, both of whom were accused of attempting to use the military to put down the popular uprising, making them targets for local agitators, or the generally misinformed. It was also thought to be as a result of such malicious gossip and propaganda that many local towns and villagers began to form their own citizen committees and militia's in the belief that central government had collapsed and that the country was in danger of being invaded by a foreign army, helping to create a widespread mood that became commonly known as the Great Fear. Even though a

National Assembly had been created to help address the many pressing issues affecting the country, King Louis XVI and his queen, Marie Antoinette, had been keen to avoid giving the assembly any sort of legitimacy for fear of appearing to give it too much authority, at the cost of their own, although by October 1789 the situation was said to have become so grave that they were compelled to relocate themselves from their palace at Versailles to Paris, thereby granting implicit authority to the new National body. However, as the course of the general unrest continued and the new assembly began to introduce even more radical changes to a proposed new constitution, Louis was thought to have become increasingly alarmed about the way events were unfolding, causing him to reconsider his decision to remain in Paris. As a result, he was said to have left the capital in June 1791 in disguise, with the entire royal family being dressed in servants clothes, as they made their way to Montmedy Castle in the Lorraine region of France, although they were subsequently recognised whilst at Varennes and transported back to Paris, where the National Assembly suspended Louis and ordered the entire royal family to be held under guard.

Count De Grasse

Admiral Samuel Hood

Admiral Thomas Graves

Initially, even some of the most hardened anti-monarchists in France were content for Louis to remain on the throne, albeit as an entirely constitutional monarch, one that was governed by a national assembly, but with few if any real powers, as was the case across the Channel in England. However, with the king and his family still being held under guard, the new French authorities were thought to have begun to come under increasing pressure from the royal houses of Europe to release and reinstate Louis, or face the prospect of a military invasion to restore the monarchy. Despite such threats though, the French assembly continued with its efforts to restore Louis, but on their own terms, something that the king himself was said to have been willing to accept, much to the delight of many Frenchmen. Unfortunately, the constitution agreed in October 1791 and the new assembly that resulted from it were said to have lasted less than a year, before it degenerated into a chaotic shambles, where the competing political factions refused to agree anything with one another, causing the country and its armed forces to remain insecure and unreliable. In a scene that would be repeated in Russia some hundred and twenty years later, on the 10th August 1792 a group of dissidents were reported to have attacked the royal family's apartments in Paris and imprisoned them, before arranging for a emergency session of the National Assembly to be held, which temporarily suspended the monarchy as an institution. Almost inevitably, the imprisonment of the royal family, the suspension of the monarchy, the social fragmentation of the kingdom and the danger that this new republicanism posed to the other royal houses of Europe, ensured that within a short time France found itself at war with two of its leading neighbours, Austria and Prussia. However, despite the many problems within the borders of France, with competing factions fighting to determine the future direction of the fledgling revolution, the French military were reported to have maintained their discipline and despite many expectations, not only managed to repel the armies of Austria and Prussia, but perhaps surprisingly, were even able to achieve victory over them, at least in the short term. Although the French conquest of some Austrian and Prussian territories was thought to have been a matter of concern for some of Europe's other leading military powers, including Britain and Spain, for the British authorities, the two most worrying developments was the French annexation of parts of the southern Netherlands and the fate of the usurped French monarch Louis XVI and his family. Perhaps recognising that the imprisoned king and his family would remain a constant threat to their new republic, providing a figurehead behind whom the great powers could rally together, in January 1793 the new French government made the fateful decision to bring Louis XVI to trial, on charges of conspiring with France's enemies. Found guilty by a majority of the tribunal members, within a matter of days, King Louis XVI, now known simply as Citizen Louis Capet, was transported to the guillotine, in what is now the modern day Place de la Concord; and was executed before a howling revolutionary crowd, beginning a bloody campaign of terror that was estimated to have cost anything up to forty thousand lives.

From an entirely British perspective, the unwarranted killing of the French king, his queen and a significant part of the French nobility, not only created outrage amongst Britain's own leading citizens, but also the worry that such revolutionary ideals might easily be carried across the English Channel to the great cities of mainland Britain and the island of Ireland. Although many thousands of fleeing French refugees were thought to have been welcomed to Britain, as they tried to escape the Great Terror that began to be unleashed against the French population, the British authorities were careful to guard against any attempt by the new French republican administration to transport their ideals beyond their own national borders. Following the executions of Louis XVI and Marie Antoinette, all diplomatic ties between the two countries had been severed and on the 1st February 1793, the French government formally declared war on both Britain and its ally, the Dutch Republic. From a purely military perspective, Britain escaped many of the effects of the war, simply because of its separation from the European continent by the English Channel, which was itself protected by the Royal Navy, still a potent force, despite the pressures put on it by the sheer extent of the country's widespread imperial possessions. Britain's Channel Fleet was specifically tasked with confronting France's republican navy, although for the most part both naval forces managed to avoid any major engagement for most of 1793, save for occasional seizures of one another's cargo vessels, as each sides commercial companies struggled to maintain their vitally important trade links. The only action of note was thought to have been the large-scale evacuation of British, Spanish and other allied troops from the port of Toulon in December 1793, which was in danger of being captured by French republican troops, a relatively successful operation that was said to have been marked by the destruction of a sizeable portion of the French fleet and the local arsenal, both of which were subsequently denied to France's republican cause. It was also in this particular action that a young French artillery officer, Major Napoleon Bonaparte, was said to have played such a vital role in forcing the allies to withdraw from Toulon that he was subsequently promoted to the rank Brigadier General and began to make a name for himself within the French republican hierarchy. Perhaps fortunately for Bonaparte, he did not suffer a similar fate to that of a number France's most able military officers, who were reported to have been purged from the nations military services, often because their loyalty to the new republican regime was in doubt, resulting in many hundreds of them ending their days as victims of the guillotine, or as prisoners in France's most notorious prisons.

With a widespread European war to fight, France's enormous military forces were thought to have become a significant drain on the nations natural resources, most notably its arable land, which in normal times would have been used to grow the food, to feed its large population, much of which was reported to have been ruined by the extensive warfare, or simply abandoned by the rural workers who had been driven off their lands because of the ongoing conflict. As a result of the food shortages at home and the economic losses caused by the revolution and its associated conflicts, France had been forced to look elsewhere for supplies of food, finance and raw materials, including the lands of its former transatlantic ally, the United States. In order to feed, pay and arm its vast revolutionary army and its civilian populace, the French government was said to have sourced many of its requirements from the eastern states of America, most of which were transported across the Atlantic in huge convoys of merchants ships that were protected by a large contingent of warships, making them legitimate targets for its main maritime adversary, Britain's Royal Navy, who were ordered to intercept such convoys, as they made their way from the New World to the French Atlantic ports. Although the Royal Navy was known to have been numerically superior to the French fleet, in terms of individual ships, the French warships were reported to have been bigger, stronger and better armed than their British counterparts, giving them a distinct advantage when equal numbers of each country's vessels met at sea. For its part however, Britain's navy was said to have adopted a much more industrial approach to the construction, provisioning and arming of its battle fleet, lessons that it had learned as a result of Britain's military defeat in America, where the Royal Navy had failed to successfully support its land forces, resulting in the military siege and then surrender at Yorktown. Unfortunately, the rapid expansion of the Royal Navy had not been matched by a similar increase in the numbers of experienced seamen required to man these vast numbers of vessels, leading to the introduction of the infamous Royal Navy press-gangs, groups of sailors employed to abduct any able bodied man that happened to cross their paths, regardless of whether he had any experience at sea or not. Consequently, not only was the skill base of the Royal Navy itself diluted, but morale amongst most ships crews was said to have noticeably diminished, as increasing numbers of dissolute, unskilled and generally antagonistic seamen were added to the British navy's ranks.

However, despite such personnel issues, the Royal Navy still had the added benefit of training and maintaining a cadre of highly professional and generally experienced officers and commanders, who could be relied upon to fight a military engagement in the most effective manner, regardless of the calibre of men under his command. Unfortunately, this was not the case for many French vessels, which had been systematically deprived of some of their most experienced captains and commanders by virtue of the revolutionary zeal that had swept through the French navy, replacing experienced sea captains with less qualified mariners, many of whom had never commanded a warship, let alone fight a battle at sea. The first great test of the fighting abilities of the two opposing navies was reported to have occurred in 1794, when a large French convoy began its return journey across the Atlantic, having been loaded with much needed grain and other commodities in Chesapeake Bay, Virginia, before sailing out to meet the flotilla of French warships that would accompany it back home to Europe. Around the same time, a Royal Navy fleet, under the command of Admiral of the fleet, Richard Howe, the 1st Lord Howe, who was said to be one of the foremost English sea commanders of the age. Leading a flotilla of some twenty six ships of the line, Howe was reported to have taken his force to the Bay of Biscay in May 1794, firstly to check on the presence of a second French squadron at Brest, but secondly and more importantly to await the arrival of the great French grain convoy as it made its way back from Virginia. However, as he waited for the convoy to arrive, Howe was said to have become distracted by the second French squadron, which was operating in and around the Bay of Biscay and the eastern Atlantic, capturing a number of British and Dutch cargo vessels that Howe was desperate to recover. Eventually, the Royal Navy was reported to have tracked down the second French fleet and began to give chase, allowing themselves to be drawn away from the expected route of the more important French grain convoy, which was sailing closer to European waters. Perhaps believing that he could attack both French targets, Howe ultimately decided to engage the French ships that he had been pursuing in the first place, rather than disengaging and going in search of the grain convoy. As a result of this decision, on the morning of the 1st June 1794, the two fleets confronted one another in the waters of the Atlantic, with Howe determining to adopt a new attacking formation, which had it worked would undoubtedly have brought about the almost complete destruction of the French fleet. At the time, most European navy's employed a straight battle line, which involved combatants sailing in parallel to one another, often at a considerable distance and then each side simply bombarding one another with their guns and cannons, in the hope that sufficient damage might be caused to disable or destroy the enemy ships, forcing them to sink, withdraw or allow them to be boarded and taken as prizes. However, Admiral Howe adopted a strategy that would have seen each of his vessels sail between the individual French ships, delivering broadsides that would have struck both the front and rear of the French warships at the same moment, causing catastrophic damage to each of them instantly. Unfortunately, because a number of his less experienced commanders failed to follow his instructions the strategy failed to work in the most effective way, although by the end of the comparatively short battle a significant number of French vessels were reported to have been disabled by the British guns. There were said to have been significant losses on both sides by the end of the bloody engagement, but according to most sources the French side suffered the loss of some seven ships, which were either captured or sunk, as well as losing several thousand sailors, who were captured, injured or killed. For their part, the Royal Navy lost none of their ships in the battle, although several hundred seamen were reportedly injured or killed during the engagement that later became known as the Glorious First of June. In a purely military sense, the sea battle was deemed to be a resounding success for the British, with the French navy suffering one of its worst defeats in its naval history, although the fact that the vitally important grain shipment from the United States safely reached the new French republic virtually intact resulted in the overall events being hailed as a victory for France and its new republican administration.

In 1796, Republican France was said to have been joined in a new military coalition with the kingdom of Spain and the recently annexed Dutch states, which were adopted as the Batavian Republic, a satellite of the French republic. By combining the forces of these three disparate nations, the French Republic hoped to be the equal of the British Royal Navy at sea and especially in the Mediterranean where the Spanish were reported to have had a fleet, more than twice the size of Britain's regional squadron. Estimated at some forty ships of the line, this Spanish flotilla was said to have represented such a threat to the dozen or so Royal Navy warships stationed in the Mediterranean that the British were inexorably forced to withdraw from the region and had to operate from in and around their fortress at Gibraltar and the wider Iberian Peninsula. In January 1797, a large fleet of Spanish ships of the line was reported to have sailed from the port of Cartagena, with the intention of escorting a commercial convoy from there to the Spanish port of Cadiz, before sailing north to join the main French fleet at Brest, where they could assemble to try and confront the Royal Navy. However, unbeknownst to them, the British Mediterranean fleet was said to have temporarily stationed itself close to the River Tagus on the Spanish coastline, with the expressed intention of intercepting the Spanish flotilla as it made its way northward, in order to prevent it linking up with the French. The British fleet, under the command of Admiral John Jervis, despite only numbering ten ships of the line, expected to be joined within days by a second squadron of five warships, commanded by Admiral William Walker, which had previously been detached from the Channel Fleet, with the intention of reinforcing Jervis' force. With Walker arriving on station by the 6th February, the combined Royal Navy squadron was forced to wait for several days as the Spanish flotilla slowly made its way from Cartagena to Cadiz, where it safely delivered the convoy of cargo vessels that it had been escorting. Prevented from sailing immediately because of a dense fog, the Spanish naval force was said to have remained off the coast of Cadiz, unaware that the British frigate Minerve, under the command of Commodore Horatio Nelson had passed amongst them, as he made his way north to join the waiting English forces. Having safely navigated his way through the enemy ships, Nelson was subsequently able to advise Admiral's Jervis and Walker as to the exact location of the Spanish fleet, allowing them to plan for an attack on the enemy force, even though they still remained unclear as to the exact numbers of enemy ships that they might have to face in the forthcoming battle.

Within hours of Nelson advising them of the Spanish fleet's position, Jervis had ordered the British squadron to set sail for the location he had been given, his impending approach forcing the Spanish commanders to move away from the Iberian coastline and into the heavier waters of the Atlantic. By the early hours of the 14th February and with a heavy sea fog obscuring both fleet's view of the enemy, the British squadron was said to be listening out for any sound from the Spanish ships that might guide Jervis and his flotilla to their quarry, until at last they were reported to have heard the familiar sound of the signal guns that kept the Spanish vessels in touch with one another. Even though he had no clear idea of the size of the fleet that was facing him, Jervis signalled for his commanders to prepare their attack against the enemy, using the two distinct battle lines that he had previously agreed with his ship's captains, which he was pleased to see still remained intact in spite of the heavy waters and the blinding sea fog. As dawn approached, so the mists began to clear, allowing Jervis to receive reports from the various lookouts, who successively called out the increasing numbers of enemy sails that began to appear into view. By around nine o'clock in the morning, the British commanders had clear sight of their enemy, who had been formed into loose battle lines, one of about nine ships and the other of about eighteen, the smaller formation being closer to the British fleet and the first to prepare an attack on Jervis' flotilla. With both of the Spanish battles lines sailing in a generally parallel formation, Jervis signalled his ships to fall into a single line behind his own flagship, Victory, with the intention of sailing in between the two Spanish forces, making the most of his own gun's opportunity to launch simultaneous broadsides against the passing Spanish vessels on either side of the British line. Much to everyone's surprise, the Spanish ships were said to have been largely unprepared for the British ships as they sailed between the two Spanish columns, resulting in very little damage being done to the Royal Navy battle line. As the last of the British warships passed through the Spanish columns, the leading Royal Navy ships had already swung about to pass the Spaniards once again, not only to deliver another catastrophic broadside, but also in order prevent the Spanish fleet from escaping the battle, which they were almost certain to do, if given the opportunity.

Admiral Arbuthnot Admiral John Jervis Admiral Lord Nelson

As they tried to make a run for open water, Commodore Nelson was reported to have used his own initiative to interpret Jervis' standing orders and in doing so helped to bring the individual warships to battle with one another, guaranteeing that the Battle of Cape Saint Vincent would inevitably become a pivotal engagement for both the British and Spanish fleets, with the loser being forced to concede supremacy of the high seas to their winning opponent. Horatio Nelson, not content with having loosely interpreted his commander's orders, was also reported to have taken on some of the most dangerous actions of the ensuing battle, placing his own ship, Captain, in some of the most impossible situations, as he sought to confront some of the largest and most heavily armed Spanish warships, with no apparent concern for his own safety, or that of his crew. Having had her wheel and most of her sails and rigging shot away by enemy fire, Nelson was then thought to have led his men in an attack to board and capture one enemy ship, but also a second that was lying along side it, with the result that he and his crew captured both vessels, a highly unusual action that not only brought him great personal credit, but also helped to create the myth of Horatio Nelson, a hero of the British Empire. By around five o'clock in the afternoon of the 14th February 1797 the battle as such was over, save for a certain amount of skirmishing that took place on a number of captured Spanish ships, as the British prize crews arrived to prepare the vessels for their journey back to Britain. Remarkably, given the scale of the battle, less than a hundred British seamen were thought to have been killed during the engagement, with a further two hundred or so seriously injured. By the time the battle had been completed, the fact that a Royal Navy fleet of some fifteen ships had managed to comprehensively defeat a Spanish flotilla of twice that number was not only seen as remarkable, but almost miraculous, given that they were not only heavily outnumbered, but also seriously outgunned by their Spanish adversaries.

Unfortunately, despite the Royal Navy's continuing supremacy over the high seas and vital trade routes, elsewhere in Europe, the military alliance established to oppose the new French Republic's territorial expansion was slowly beginning to fall apart, as one by one the various countries were either overcome, or chose to settle their differences with France. In April 1797 the Austrian government sued for peace and in the following months Germany, Belgium and Venice were all annexed by the republic, leaving Britain as the only potential threat to France's military dominance of the European mainland. However, by the start of 1798, despite Britain herself remaining safe behind the protective screen provided by the Royal Navy, neither could she muster sufficient resources to launch an all out attack on mainland Europe, leaving military operations in that particular theatre at a virtual standstill. For their part, the French authorities had now gained control over, or reached agreement with most of Europe's leading nations, although in spite of their dominance over the mass of the continent, their lack of an effective naval force, with which to confront the Royal Navy, ensured that the French Republic remained largely contained. Perhaps to exploit perceived British weaknesses elsewhere, in 1798, France's leading military commander, the seemingly brilliant, General Napoleon Bonaparte, was said to have conceived a plan to launch an attack on the Mediterranean and North Africa, before potentially moving on to attack British interests on the Indian subcontinent. Taking with him a large number of the country's remaining warships and a land army of an estimated thirty thousand men, Bonaparte was reported to have sailed from the port of Toulon, to the Egyptian city of Alexandria, from where his forces moved on to the capital Cairo, where his professional European army met and easily defeated a local Muslim army, in what Napoleon himself later dubbed as the Battle of the Pyramids.

However, Napoleon's military expedition to the Mediterranean and North Africa had not gone unnoticed by the British Admiralty, who had instructed the by now Rear Admiral Horatio Nelson, attached to the Royal Navy fleet based on the River Tagus, to pursue the French forces, to determine its objectives and if possible engage it in battle. As he tracked the French fleet into the Mediterranean, in the short term, Nelson was said to have been unable to get close enough to the enemy forces in order to properly engage them, ostensibly because Bonaparte was said to have been careful to ensure strict secrecy over the destination of his fleet, leaving the Royal Navy with little option but to speculate about its exact location. It was only when the French expedition had finally arrived in Egypt and attacked Alexandria and Cairo that Admiral Nelson was finally able to identify the general position of Bonaparte's forces, allowing him to begin preparing a strategy for bringing the French ships into battle. Eventually, after many days searching, the British fleet of thirteen ships of the line was reported to have sighted the slightly larger French flotilla of seventeen vessels at Aboukir Bay, some twenty-odd miles from Alexandria, where its commander, Admiral Francois-Paul Brueys D'Aigalliers, had stationed his forces in order to support Bonaparte's land based campaign. Although the original intention had been for the French flotilla to anchor in the comparatively safe waters of Alexandria harbour, the sheer size of the large French warships had prevented this, forcing Admiral D'Aigalliers to look for an alternative anchorage nearby, with Aboukir Bay proving to be the most suitable in terms of depth and close proximity to Napoleon's land forces. Unfortunately, the choice of location was not thought to have been universally accepted by all of D'Aigalliers captains, some of whom believed that its general layout and position left them highly susceptible to attack by an enemy fleet, although despite such concerns, the French fleet commander still elected to remain there, albeit having taken some strategic measures to counter any such unforeseen enemy assault. Rather than having his ships anchored in a widely dispersed formation, which might render them likely to attack and prevent them from forming the standard battle line in the shortest time possible, D'Aigalliers was reported to have ordered his ships to line up and anchor in their formal battle formation, a decision that he would later have cause to regret.

Having initially sailed to Alexandria to ascertain whether or not the French warships had established themselves there, Nelson was reported to have been disappointed to find only the French troop barges there, although he quickly realised that the main French battle fleet must still be in the area, at some as yet unidentified location. However, within a matter of hours, one of his own ships, HMS Zealous, was reported to have sighted the French flotilla at Aboukir Bay and raced back to Nelson's formation to advise him of their discovery. As Nelson ordered his ships to change course to Aboukir Bay, at least three of his vessels were still detached from the main force, having previously been investigating other possible locations for the missing French fleet, so their commanders were forced to try and sail at full speed in order to catch up to the main British flotilla. As they approached the French force at about four o'clock in the afternoon on the 1st August 1798, Admiral Nelson was said to have ordered his ships to slow down, so that the three vessels trailing behind might catch up with the main body of his flotilla, before a full British attack on the French fleet began. Significantly, the French commander, D'Aigalliers, was reported to have ordered a meeting of his fleet commanders, onboard his flagship, Orient, where he would set out his orders for the forthcoming engagement, although even at this point he was said to have been undecided as to what action to take, first ordering his ships to prepare to sail and then subsequently rescinding the order. D'Aigalliers was also thought to have yet more problems to face, not least of which was the absence of large numbers of experienced sailors and soldiers who had earlier been sent ashore to gather provisions, causing a shortage of manpower amongst those ships that might soon be forced to go into battle against a highly experienced Royal Navy. Having witnessed Nelson's ships slow down as they approached his position, D'Aigalliers was thought to have convinced himself that there would be no battle before the following morning, allowing him the possibility to pass by the British fleet under the cover of darkness and avoid risking his ships in what would then be an unnecessary battle with the Royal Navy.

Although from an objective perspective, the choice of Aboukir Bay as a safe anchorage for the French fleet might well have been questionable, for an experienced mariner like D'Aigalliers it was an ideal location to try and hoodwink a less experienced adversary, who might well have overlooked the presence of French gun positions above the bay, the hidden shoals that lay beneath its waters and the strategic planning of a highly able French commander. By carefully positioning his battle line along one side of the bay and tying those ships together with cables strung from each ships bow and stern, D'Aigalliers hoped to create an impenetrable wall of guns on one side and an impassable channel on the other, leaving the Royal Navy with little option but to run aground on the hidden shoals, or to face a concentrated barrage from the hundreds of French guns that would be levelled against any passing vessels. Unfortunately for the French Admiral, the failure of some of his captains to fully secure their own ships to the vessels in front and behind, the absence of up to twenty percent of his men, who were reportedly still ashore and his own decision to call a meeting just as the Royal Navy arrived in the area, all contrived to defeat the best laid plans of the French commander. Of course, D'Aigalliers was also beaten by the planning and strategic ability of the Royal Navy commander, Admiral Horatio Nelson, who was not only equal to his French counterpart in terms of naval experience, but also a master tactician, who was able to instantly weigh the risks of any given situation and turn it to his own advantage. Despite being regarded as a reckless gambler by some of his less able and charitable contemporaries, even by the time of his military engagement with Napoleon's French fleet in Egypt, Nelson had proven on more than one occasion that he was prepared to sacrifice himself in order to ensure a British victory, having previously lost the use of one eye in Corsica in 1794 and one of his arms in the Battle of Santa Cruz de Tenerife in July 1797.

Despite the hopes of D'Aigalliers however, Nelson had no intention of waiting until the following morning to engage the French fleet, realising that in all likelihood they would try and pass him during the night, causing him to miss the opportunity to deliver a devastating military defeat on the new French Republic. With dusk approaching, he ordered all of his ships to display a signal of four horizontal lights on their topmost masts, along with both the white ensign and union jack, so that they might instantly identify one another in the forthcoming battle, where the gloom and smoke might easily disguise the nationality of each of the individual vessels. Sending out one of his smaller, lower draught frigates, D'Aigalliers attempted to draw Nelson's bigger warships onto the hidden shoals where they might become grounded and present themselves as an easy target for the French guns, but Nelson's commanders were not to be so easily misguided and simply ignored the efforts of the decoy ships, continuing with their course to confront the large French warships that remained in the bay. Unfortunately, a number of the French vessels that had not been secured properly began to drift out in the centre of the bay, allowing the Royal Navy squadron to manoeuvre on both sides of the French battle line, catching them in a devastating crossfire, which was said to have ripped through the vanguard and centre ships of the French formation. As they passed by and in between the single file of the French battle line, the various British warships were said to have delivered simultaneous broadsides against the enemy vessels, many of which lacked the experienced gun crews to fire back, allowing the Royal Navy to draw even closer in and deliver even greater punishment to the French superstructures. For all of the evening and well into the following morning the two fleets were reported to have battled one another, with the great French warships often being attacked by numbers of British vessels and as a result being steadily reduced as broadside, after broadside was fired across and into their decks, causing their masts to fall and their crews to abandon their posts. The most significant loss for the French though, was the flagship Orient, which having received several broadsides was reported to have burst into flames, after British shot ignited the stores of paint and spirits that had been left on deck just prior to the battle. As the fire caught hold of the Orient's sails and superstructure, so British warships stationed nearby continued to pound the vessel, until the conflagration was so severe that it was obvious that the ship was lost. As they moved further away from the burning wreck, almost inevitably the fire reached the great warship's magazine, causing an explosion that caused the Orient to disintegrate into thousands of burning pieces that were scattered over much of the bay, starting secondary fires on other ships that were located close by.

Admiral D'Aigallier   Lord Spencer   Admiral Calder

By late morning of the 3rd August 1798, the Battle of the Nile was over, save for some peripheral actions that were taking place, as the Royal Navy personnel attempted to take some of the surviving French ships as prizes. As Nelson began to take account of the losses incurred by his own forces, it was reported that an estimated two hundred British seamen had been killed and several hundred wounded, although some of these were later known to have perished as a result of their injuries, despite the best efforts of the various ships surgeons. Even the British commander himself was said to have been wounded, but was said to have been more concerned about the loss of his own captains and junior officers, of which some twenty were said to be dead and wounded by the end of the battle. However, British losses were significantly smaller than those on the French side, with some two thousand killed and more than one thousand injured as a result of the bloody engagement, with one of the most notable victims being Admiral D'Aigalliers aboard the flagship Orient. Of the fifteen British vessels that had been involved in the battle, none were lost or destroyed, although several were reported to have been either de-masted or suffered significant hull damage, most of which was repaired in the weeks after the battle. For the French fleet however, the outcome of the battle was far more serious, as two ships of the line were reported to have been completely destroyed, including the Orient, whilst a further two smaller frigates were also lost to the Royal Navy, along with nine other vessels that were subsequently captured as prizes by the British fleet. Of the seventeen French ships that had been present in Aboukir Bay on the 2nd August 1798, only four managed to escape the carnage relatively intact, with much of the blame for the defeat reportedly being levelled against those who survived, rather than the now deceased D'Aigalliers. Back in Britain, with no news having been received regarding Nelson's actions, in the short term the British commander was said to have been heavily criticised for his apparent failure to confront and destroy the French naval force. However, as reports began to filter back several weeks later, so his reputation began to be restored and finally in October 1798 Nelson's own dispatches eventually reached England, causing Lord Spencer, the head of the Admiralty, to pass out, after he read the reports regarding the astonishing British victory. As news of the engagement spread throughout the country, bonfires were ordered to be lit throughout the land, in order to celebrate the outcome of the battle, with Nelson and many of his subordinate officers all receiving titles, gifts, medals and promotions, as reward for their participation in what ultimately became the pivotal naval engagement of the French revolutionary period.

Not only did the Royal Navy's victory at Aboukir Bay deprive the French Republic of a much needed naval force, essentially handing control of the Mediterranean to Britain, but also caused a resumption of the European opposition to the armies of the French Republic, with Austria, Russia and the Ottoman Empire all latterly choosing to become part of a second allied coalition that declared war against France in 1799, although this united front ultimately failed to free Europe from French domination, but did achieve some measure of success in North Africa and the Middle East. In 1799, Napoleon was reported to have returned to France, in order to deal with an emerging military and political crisis in the country, leaving his French army in Egypt under the command of Jean Baptiste Kleber, who was later assassinated by an Egyptian student in Cairo in June of the following year. In the meantime, Bonaparte was said to have managed to avoid the Royal Navy ships that were now regularly patrolling the Mediterranean in search of French vessels and managed to make his way back to Paris, where the crises he had been informed about had passed. However, even though the republic itself was secure, politically the country's government was reported to have been in turmoil, ostensibly because France was bankrupt, making life hard for its citizens and the governing administration was becoming increasingly unpopular with the French population at large. Approached by a number of the country's politicians, who were planning to stage a coup, Bonaparte was said to have seen his chance to seize power as First Consul of the republic, using French troops to suppress any opposition that might try and prevent him taking over the government of the country. With his position as First Consul secured, in 1800 Bonaparte was reported to have taken yet another French army across the Alps to invade Italy, which had previously been freed from French control by Austrian troops, whilst Bonaparte was engaged in Egypt. Despite his ultimate victory there however, the campaign was said to have been a very close call for the French leader, who was thought to have been close to defeat until military reinforcements arrived to allow him to claim victory at the defining Battle of Marengo. Emboldened by his victory in Italy, Napoleon then demanded that Austria formally recognise his territorial rights over France's new territorial acquisitions, which the Austrian's refused to do, resulting in French forces being used to compel Austria into compliance through force of arms, with the resulting Treaty of Luneville, being signed in February 1801.

Back in Britain, the subsequent and successive surrenders of both Russia and Austria to the forces of the French Republic was said to have been greeted with dismay, although with the country safe from attack, its vital trade routes secured and having gained control of the Mediterranean, much of which was the result of a dominant Royal Navy. As a result, in 1801 the British government was said to have been more than content to sign a peace agreement with the new French authorities, although for both sides, the resulting Treaty of Amiens, was only ever likely to be a temporary arrangement and one that would be broken as soon as it suited one or other party. Although both Britain and France had freely agreed to the terms of the Treaty of Amiens, ultimately neither side was willing to surrender any of the territorial gains that they had made in the preceding years, or to withdraw their military forces from a number of disputed areas, causing relations between the two countries to descend into a campaign of charge and counter-charge. In March 1803 Bonaparte was reported to have begun assembling a large invasion force on the French coast, ostensibly with the aim of crossing the English Channel and conquering Britain once and for all, although quite how he expected his fleet of invasion barges to avoid the ships of the Royal Navy remains unclear. With France generally bankrupt and facing the prospect of fighting yet another expensively long war against Britain, in April 1803 Napoleon was also reported to have begun talks with the United States regarding the sale of the last great French territory in North America, Louisiana. Having recognised that such a large and distant territory would be prohibitively expensive, if not impossible, to defend, Bonaparte was said to have made the decision to sell this last great American possession, which would not only provide France with much needed revenue, but also limit his country's military responsibilities. Perhaps prophetically, as the more commonly known Louisiana Purchase was completed by agents from France and the United States, Napoleon was reported to have stated that he believed the completion of the sale would inexorably lead to the creation of a country, which would eventually challenge Britain's control of the high seas, a clear reference to the almost inevitable emergence of the United States as a major military power. Such fortune telling apart however, Bonaparte's decision to raise capital through such extraordinary means, the assembling of troops along the French coast and the ongoing disputes over the terms of the Treaty of Amiens, all helped to convince members of the ruling British executive that not only was Napoleon untrustworthy, but that another war was almost unavoidable, a view that led the government of the day to declare war against France in May 1803. Despite facing the prospect of fighting a third war against Britain and whatever European allies she could rally against him, Bonaparte still managed to find the time and the money to crown himself as Emperor Napoleon I on the 2nd December 1804 at Notre Dame, where his consort Josephine, was subsequently crowned as Empress, thereby creating a form of hereditary monarchy, which would finally bring an end to the claims of the earlier Bourbon dynasty.

With Britain having already declared war against France in May 1803 and with the newly crowned Emperor Napoleon I increasing his political and military stranglehold over much of Western Europe, by the beginning of 1805, both Austria and Russia had once again been persuaded to join yet another military coalition against the French. However, with Britain representing the greatest threat to his wider ambitions, Bonaparte continued to pursue his ambitious plans for the invasion of England, much of which centred round a proposal to lure the Royal Navy away from its defence of the English Channel, allowing his invasion barges to cross the waterway unhindered and land on the south coast of Britain. The kernel of the plan, was for his remaining French warships, then blockaded at the ports of Toulon and Brest, to somehow escape the cordon of British naval vessels lying offshore, sail across the Atlantic to the Caribbean and begin attacking Britain's possessions in the West Indies, forcing the Royal Navy to send their own warships to defend these territories and leaving the British mainland exposed to attack. Unfortunately, even though such a plan was unlikely to succeed in the first place, given that the Royal Navy would not relinquish its defence of the English Channel entirely, its ultimate success would depend on the qualities and abilities of the French commanders who would have to carry out the plan. As it turned out, only a small part of the French fleet managed to evade the British blockade of the French coast, which having joined up with a number of Spanish vessels, then set out across the Atlantic to the Caribbean. However, rather than menacing or attacking any of Britain's vitally important territories there, the French and Spanish ships were thought to have spent much of their time intercepting British treasure ships and cargo vessels, before simply turning around and heading back to Europe. Intercepted by a Royal Navy squadron on the 22nd July 1805, at what later became known as the Battle of Cape Finisterre, the Franco-Spanish fleet did not suffer any great loss during the engagement, save for two ships of the line that were later captured by the British flotilla, although its commander ultimately chose to seek refuge in the Spanish port of Cadiz, where the flotilla presented little threat to the Royal Navy, or indeed to wider British interests. From Britain's perspective, the indecisive naval engagement at Cape Finisterre was regarded as a missed opportunity, largely because the British fleet commander, Vice Admiral Robert Calder, had failed to actively pursue the enemy flotilla, choosing instead to wait, so that he might engage them the following day, by which time it was too late. It was a military decision that Admiral Calder would later have cause to regret, as he was subsequently recalled to England, where he was relieved of his command, brought before a court martial and severely reprimanded for his failure to engage the French fleet, a judgement that effectively ended his naval career.

With his plans for an invasion of Britain in tatters and with a growing threat emerging from both Austria and Russia, Bonaparte was left with little option but to withdraw his one hundred and fifty thousand strong army from the French coast, sending them eastward to help his armies that were about to confront the massing Austrian troops. However, the British Admiralty remained concerned about the presence of the remaining French and Spanish warships that were stationed at Cadiz and Brest, which still presented a significant threat to Britain, despite the fact that for the most part they were securely blockaded by the Royal Navy. In order to try and bring these Franco-Spanish forces to battle, in August 1805 Admiral Sir William Cornwallis was reported to have detached some twenty ships of the line from the Channel Fleet to make the journey south, where he hoped to confront those enemy forces still in Spanish waters, although in doing so was said to have left the main Channel squadron with only one third of its usual number. This reduced flotilla, temporarily under the command of the previously mentioned Admiral Calder, was then reported to have moved south towards the Spanish port of Cadiz, where it was subsequently joined by a second larger force of Royal Navy ships, commanded by Admiral Lord Nelson, who had been given overall control of the British naval forces in the area. Upon Nelson's arrival, Calder was subsequently sent back to Britain, to face charges over his failure to properly confront the French and Spanish fleets at the Battle of Finisterre some weeks earlier, so played no significant part in the battle that would eventually ensue.

According to most sources, unlike many British naval commanders who employed a very tight blockade on enemy ports, thereby reducing the chances of enemy vessels sneaking through their lines, Admiral Nelson often utilised a very loose form of cordon, allowing belligerent vessels to sail out into open waters, where they might be confronted in an all out battle, which the British commander considered to be a more effective use of his forces. As a result, having arrived off the coastline of Cadiz, Nelson was reported to have withdrawn all of his heavier battleships out of sight of the mainland, leaving only his smaller, lighter armed frigates to patrol the coastal waters, ostensibly in the hope that their presence might encourage the larger Franco-Spanish warships to venture out into open waters, where he could finally engage them. By the beginning of October 1805, this relatively small force of seven British frigates, under the command of a Captain Blackwood, was said to have been operating as the eyes and ears of Nelson's main fleet, watching the entrance to Cadiz harbour, in the hope that the French and Spanish vessels might eventually decide to risk their luck, against what appeared to be a rather nominal British blockade. However, as the days and weeks passed, rather predictably, provisioning such a large fleet at sea was thought to have presented a number of logistical problems for British commanders, although for the most part, Nelson was able to source supplies from the British base at Gibraltar, with regular trips being made which helped him maintain the efficiency of his fighting forces. Perhaps surprisingly, the French fleet at Cadiz was also thought to be experiencing similar problems with their supplies, generally because of the lengthy British blockade and their shortage of funds to purchase stores locally, increasing the pressure on the Franco-Spanish fleet to put out to sea and make their way to safer, better provisioned waters. However, despite Nelson's best efforts to entice his enemy out into open waters, the French and Spanish captains were said to have been aware of the British fleet's presence and were obviously reluctant to place themselves in a situation where they might be forced to confront an equally matched, or possibly superior naval force. Ultimately though and despite any personal reservations they might have had, the French commanders were thought to have received orders from Napoleon himself, which instructed the French commander, Admiral Villeneuve to set out to sea at his earliest convenience, sail to Cartagena, where he would meet a squadron of Spanish ships, before sailing for Naples, where he was to disembark the French ground troops that were aboard his vessels.

Admiral Cornwallis **Captain Blackwood** **Admiral Villeneuve**

Although Villeneuve himself was thought to have been initially reluctant to leave harbour, as were a number of his French and Spanish commanders, in October 1805, he was said to have heard reports that Napoleon had become so exasperated at the lack of action that the Emperor had appointed another Admiral to take over command of the fleet. Rather than face the humiliation of being replaced, Villeneuve was said to have decided to take his Franco-Spanish forces out to sea before his successor arrived in Cadiz, presumably in the hope that such a course of action might rescue his shattered reputation with Bonaparte. Unfortunately, during the time that his fleet had been anchored in Cadiz, many of his ships were said to have fallen into disorder, largely as a result of their crews being generally inexperienced, or having become indifferent to the usual shipboard routines. As a result, it was said to have taken some time for the vessels to be prepared for sea, during which their preparations had been observed and then reported to the Royal Navy fleet lying offshore. It has also been suggested that a number of the captains, who had previously voted to remain in Cadiz, were thought to be so irritated by Villeneuve's subsequent order to sail that they deliberately ignored many of his standing orders and strategies, causing the flotilla to leave the harbour in such a haphazard manner that Villeneuve was unable to maintain his usual battle line formation, making his vessels more susceptible to an attack from an enemy force. Leaving harbour in three separate columns, Villeneuve set a course for the Straits of Gibraltar to the South East and despite one of his ships reported sighting the British fleet, which forced him to order his flotilla to form a single battle line, it was thought to have been so far away that it presented little danger to Villeneuve's ships on the first leg of their journey. However, by the morning of the second day, the 21st October 1805, one of his ships again reported a sighting of the Royal Navy fleet, this time approaching fast from the northwest and with the wind behind them. Inexplicably, the French commander was reported to have signalled his ships to fall into three columns, although as they began to do so, he ordered them back to a single battle line, causing the whole flotilla to descend into one confused mess. Perhaps realising that his fleet were no match for the approaching Royal Navy flotilla and that flight was impossible, Admiral Villeneuve was then reported to have ordered the entire fleet to turn about, with the intention of returning it to the comparative safety of Cadiz.

For the pursuing British fleet, the sudden reversal of the Franco-Spanish ships was thought to have caught Nelson unawares, as his own battle line was turned around, leaving the vanguard as the rearguard; and the rearguard as the vanguard, with only the centre ships remaining intact, albeit in a slightly different fighting order. From a British perspective, this sudden change of direction caused few problems, other than to reverse its sailing order, but for the largely inexperienced French crews, sailing into relatively light winds was said to have been problematic, causing a number of their ships to fall behind and wander off course, making the actual formation of the Franco-Spanish flotilla even more fragmented and therefore easier to attack. As Nelson observed the enemy fleet, despite the fact that it was out of formation, he was still acutely aware of the danger that it posed to his own forces, not least because of its greater numbers of men, ships and more importantly guns, all of which could help to turn the forthcoming battle in the Franco-Spanish favour. As the two fleets closed with one another, the Franco-Spanish flotilla, sailing northward, was said to have merged into a crescent shaped formation, made up of a scattered line of ships that were loosely gathered together into two distinct groups. With the coastline to the east, the Royal Navy was reported to have been approaching Villeneuve's fleet from the west in two parallel squadrons, each of which was headed into the centre of the enemy formation, with the intention of dividing Villeneuve's forces into three separate groups, the vanguard, the centre and the rearguard. The northernmost British column was led by Nelson in Victory, whilst the southernmost British column led by Vice Admiral Cuthbert Collingwood, aboard the Royal Sovereign, was reported to have breached the Franco-Spanish line first, unleashing several broadsides that within a matter of minutes were said to have caused such damage to the Spanish Admiral's flagship, Santa Ana that it began to sink almost immediately. The southern British battle line was said to have engaged the enemy first, having taken a good deal of damage from the French and Spanish guns as they approached them, although despite this, once close enough their better seamanship and superior gunnery skills soon began to tell. As

Collingwood's ships cut through the enemy battle line, so Nelson's northern line intercepted the French and Spanish ships, receiving significant cannonfire from the enemy before the supporting British vessels arrived to offer some cover to Nelson's flagship. Having lost her steering temporarily, Victory was subsequently able to fire a devastating broadside through the gun decks of Villeneuve's flagship, killing and wounding large numbers of its gunnery crews, before sailing on past to engage yet another of the large French warships. It was said to be as Victory locked masts with this second French battleship, the Redoubtable that a sniper from the enemy vessel, firing from the mizzen mast, aimed his musket at Lord Nelson and fired, hitting the British commander in the left shoulder. As the musket round penetrated his shoulder, it then passed through his spine and came to rest around two inches below his right shoulder blade, causing Nelson to collapse, after which he was carried below decks by the flag officers who had rushed to his aid.

With Victory at risk of being boarded by the crew and French marines aboard the Redoubtable, every man onboard the British flagship was called up on deck to repel an attack, save for those who were tending to the fatally wounded Nelson. However, just as it seemed that Victory would be captured by the French, the British warship, Temeraire, which had been immediately behind Nelson's vessel, approached the Redoubtable at the bow and delivered a devastating blast from a cannon across the exposed deck of the French warship, killing and wounding many of the sailors and marines who were set to board Victory. In fact, the Temeraire's volley was said to have been so effective that within a short time, the commander of the Redoubtable, was said to have surrendered himself and his ship to the British forces, along with the hundred or so men left fit and able onboard the vessel. As Victory's crews were able to return to their duties, manning the guns and sailing the ship, so Nelson's flagship found herself engaged in battle once more, this time in conjunction with Temeraire, both British warships confronting Admiral Villeneuve's own flagship, Bucentaure, which was eventually overwhelmed by the increasing numbers of Royal Navy ships that chose to target her with their guns. By the time all of the British warships were engaged in the battle, most of the Franco-Spanish fleet was already under sustained attack by Nelson's fleet, save for the ships of the enemy flotilla's vanguard, which had been ahead of the British ships as the Royal Navy began its assault. According to contemporary reports of the time, having made some half-hearted attempts to drive off the British fleet and perhaps recognising that the main body of the Franco-Spanish force was lost, instead they turned away and made good their escape. By the time the sounds of battle had begun to subside, a total of some twenty two French and Spanish vessels were reported to have been lost or captured, with no single loss on the British side, although the wounding and subsequent loss of their iconic commander, Lord Nelson, was said to have had a disheartening effect on many within the British fleet. With the battle won, the dying Admiral was reported to have thanked God for being allowed to do his duty for his country, before quietly passing away on Victory at four-thirty on the afternoon of the 21st Otober 1805, some three hours after the fatal round had struck him.

Vice Admiral Cuthbert Collingwood subsequently took command of the British fleet and almost immediately countermanded Nelson's final order to anchor the fleet and their prizes at sea, despite the fact that a storm was expected to strike the area. As a result, a number of the more badly damaged enemy vessels were either sunk or ran aground on the local shoals, although one or two of these were recovered at a later date. Of the forty one French and Spanish ships that had set out from Cadiz the previous day, only eleven were said to have escaped back to the port, with only five of their number being considered seaworthy. These were thought to have been the same vessels that remained contained in the harbour until 1806 when Napoleon invaded Spain, causing these ships to be seized by the Spanish and subsequently used by them against the French. Although it is generally accepted that the Battle of Trafalgar had little impact on the land campaigns undertaken by Napoleon Bonaparte in Europe, the complete defeat of the Franco-Spanish fleet at sea, ultimately reinforced Britain's position as the leading European sea power of the age and ensured that the British Empire and its many overseas territories remained relatively untroubled by the armies of Emperor Napoleon I. With no significant enemy naval force to confront them, in the years following their success at Trafalgar, the Royal Navy was thought to have been employed in helping to isolate Napoleonic France from its supporters and suppliers outside of the European mainland. However, at the same time that Britain was trying to interrupt trade with the French Republic, most notably from the New World, Napoleon Bonaparte was said to have responded by closing most European ports to British commercial shipping, both sides helping to create a much wider trade war, which almost inevitably came to involve other generally neutral countries, the most important of which was the United States. In order to successfully prosecute its trade war against France and its European allies though, the British authorities quickly realised that the Royal Navy's fleets of large battleships were generally unsuitable for the task, lacking the speed and manoeuvrability necessary to properly intercept and capture the large numbers of merchant vessels that were crossing the Atlantic on an almost daily basis. Consequently, Britain's naval authorities were said to begun a fairly extensive program of either buying or building a new range of faster, much more manoeuvrable ships, the Bermuda sloop, or schooner, which is thought to be the basis for many of the modern day racing yachts. Although the terms sloop and schooner are thought to refer to a general type of vessel, with the number of masts determining their identification as either a sloop, or as a schooner, for the most part the Royal Navy was reported to have referred to all of its ships as sloops, the first of which were thought to have been HMS Dasher, Driver and Hunter. All three of these vessels were said to have weighed in the region of two hundred tons and were armed with a dozen or so cannons, giving them the speed and firepower to counter many of the French privateers that had been licensed by Napoleon Bonaparte to prey on any British ships. However, although these new vessels proved to be invaluable in helping to suppress privateering by French captains, along with helping Britain to add new territories to its already extensive imperial possessions, from a manpower perspective, this widespread expansion of the Royal Navy's forces proved to be highly problematic. More ships, meant more men; and with a limited number of experienced seamen at their disposal, the introduction of new naval vessels inevitably resulted in the Royal Navy being forced to use generally inexperienced men to man its ships, which not had only a detrimental effect on the ships overall performance, but also a marked a serious decline in the professionalism of the country's naval forces.

It was thought to be as a result of this decline in standards amongst its crews that in the short term the Royal Navy's new class of patrol vessel, the sloops, often found themselves outclassed and outmanoeuvred by many of the foreign vessels that they attempted to intercept in the waters of the Atlantic and Caribbean, causing a great deal of frustration back in Britain. An added problem for the Royal Navy's authorities was the almost regular desertion of experienced British mariners, who would often take the opportunity to jump ship at their earliest convenience, to find better paid and more rewarding employment aboard foreign vessels that happened to be in port at the same time. Even in usual times, desertion from Royal Navy vessels was regarded as an extremely serious offence, not just from the point of view of losing the services of a particular individual, but rather that the individual in question, had not only failed to do their duty, but had deliberately abandoned their ship, their comrades and their country. It was thought to be as a result of the increasing numbers of desertions that eventually the Admiralty began to instruct its ships captains to stop and search any and all foreign vessels for deserters, a course of action that was reported to have caused particular irritation amongst American ship-owners, who regularly found their vessels intercepted by the Royal Navy, who were on the lookout for contraband cargoes and missing British seamen. The excuse of trying to find these naval deserters also provided the Royal Navy with a legitimate reason to search American ships that were crossing the Atlantic, in order to ensure that they were not misusing their country's declared neutral status to provide military assistance to the forces of Napoleon Bonaparte, which might well have been regarded as an act of war by Britain and her allies. However, one of the most notable of these incidents was said to have occurred on the 22nd June 1807, in the area of Chesapeake Bay, off the coast of Virginia, when the British warship HMS Leopard, attacked and boarded the American frigate, Chesapeake, in search of a number of British sailors who had previously deserted their Royal Navy vessels that were blockading two French warships in the Bay. Believing that the missing crewmen had taken refuge on the American vessel, the commander of HMS Leopard, Captain Salusbury Pryce Humphreys, asked the commander of the Chesapeake, Commodore James Barron, for permission to board his vessel, a request that the American captain refused outright, causing Humphreys to fire a broadside into the American vessel, killing three and injuring eighteen onboard, including Barron himself. Striking his colours and surrendering the vessel, Commodore Barron fully expected to have his ship seized, although Humphreys had little interest in the ship itself and was said to have simply ordered a party of men to board Chesapeake, to search for the missing British seamen. Finding four Royal Navy deserters on the American ship, these men were seized and Humphreys boarding party retired to HMS Leopard with their prisoners. As it transpired, of the four men seized, only one of them, Jenkins Ratford, was British born and therefore liable to the ultimate sanction for desertion, being hung from the yardarm of HMS Halifax, on the 31st August 1807. The three remaining prisoners were all Royal Navy deserters, but as they were American born, they were immune from the usual death sentence and were subsequently sentenced to five hundred lashes each, although these sentences were not thought to have been carried out. The British warship's attack on the Chesapeake was said to have caused a great deal of public resentment and indignation in America, with a number of its leading politicians demanding that the Royal Navy withdraw from American territorial waters, desist from searching US vessels and to pay compensation for the damage and losses caused to the Chesapeake, which was the only demand actually met by the British authorities. Although not directly accountable for the later War of 1812, which pitched the United States into another military conflict with Britain, the incident in Chesapeake Bay was thought to have been used by some anti-British factions in the United States administration as a reason for the later attack on Britain's remaining North American territories, which later became the modern day states of Canada.

Largely fought over continuing American expansionism into the north and northwest states bordering Britain's remaining North American territories (Canada), the War of 1812 was said to have had a number of causes, including the trade restrictions imposed by Britain on American trade goods being sent to France, British support for the native Indian tribes of North America whose homelands were under threat from American expansionism and the public humiliation the United States was said to have suffered because of Britain's military and political actions. However, for some reporters, the continuing presence of British forces in both North America and the Caribbean was also thought to have been a hindrance to the United States' own plans for expansion and domination of the American continent, a program of financial, political and military control that has continued right through to the present day. Perhaps believing that Britain lacked the political and military will to fully defend its then still existing North American territories, given that many of her resources were engaged with confronting the forces of Emperor Napoleon I in Europe, on the 18th June 1812, the American President, James Madison, officially signed the declaration of war between Britain and the United States.

Admiral Collingwood   **Denis Papin**   **John Ericsson**

From a purely naval perspective, most of the engagements during the War of 1812 tended to centre around the intercepting and capturing of each sides smaller warships or cargo vessels, rather than larger set-piece battles, as had earlier been the case between the Royal Navy and the Franco-Spanish alliance, ostensibly because the United States had no large-scale naval force to speak of. What few warships the new republic did possess were often sent out to operate as raiders or privateers, targeting the smaller naval sloops and warships that were patrolling the Atlantic, many of which were undermanned or crewed by generally inexperienced seafarers, commonly known as "landsmen". As a consequence, many British commanders, especially those in charge of smaller military craft were instructed to avoid direct confrontation with any much larger, better armed American vessels, unless they were accompanied by additional Royal Navy ships. It was also thought to be the case that as Britain began to develop its naval facilities in the Caribbean, most notably at Bermuda, so these forces in conjunction with those already present in British North America (Canada) were able to mount a number of highly effective blockades and patrols along the full length of the American east seaboard, effectively confining many of the United States' warships to their home waters. The three year conflict, which has been reported elsewhere, ultimately achieved little, other than officially ratifying the land borders between today's United States and Canada, allowing successive American governments to displace and annihilate many of the First Nation tribes of the Northern States, as well as bringing about the humiliating destruction of Washington DC by a British marine and naval force in August 1814. As has been previously mentioned, most independent historians have a number of different opinions on the actually outcome of the 1812 War, although most agree that the real losers in the conflict were the First Nation tribes, whose homelands were eventually incorporated into the territories of the United States. Many reporters also conclude that America lost the conflict, in that it failed to accomplish any of its initial goals, the basis of the country's declaration of war, including the trade restrictions that were being imposed by the British authorities at the time and the seizure of British sailors from American vessels, both of which were only resolved after the conflict came to an end. For the British, although it made no further territorial gains, which was not a objective for Britain in the first place, its ability to retain virtually all of its existing North American possessions, whilst at the same time continuing with the trade sanctions that ultimately helped Britain defeat Napoleon Bonaparte, are all generally regarded as victories for the British side.

With both the Napoleonic and the 1812 Wars resolved by 1815, the Royal Navy was seen to be the world's leading military naval force, with few if any real rivals anywhere, allowing the British Empire to employ its great fleets to any continent in support of Britain's wider financial, political and military objectives, with the Indian Ocean, the Far East and the Pacific Ocean, all of particular interest to successive British governments. Often being used to underpin Britain's diplomatic efforts or demands, through what was commonly referred to as "gunboat diplomacy", Royal Navy squadrons were often reported to have been used in unison with other allied navies to secure or suppress particular objectives, as in the case of an Anglo-Dutch fleet, which was used to bombard the city of Algiers on the 27th August 1816, in order to persuade the local ruler, or Dey, to outlaw the practice of slavery. Generally regarded as one of the bases for the much feared Barbary Pirates, who raided the coastlines of Europe for white Christian slaves, having previously forced neighbouring states to suppress the trade, the authorities in Algeria were thought to have agreed to the British and Dutch demands, but not before several hundred captive Europeans were slaughtered by Algerian troops, an atrocity that the Anglo-Dutch fleet was sent to avenge. As a result of this particular action, the Dey of Algiers agreed to sign a peace treaty on the 24th September 1816, part of which outlawed the taking of slaves, along with the subsequent release of over one thousand Christian slaves. Similarly, on the 20th October 1827 a combined British, French and Russian naval force was reported to have destroyed an Egyptian and Ottoman fleet at Navarino in Greece, as part of the Greek War of Independence, a military engagement that was said to have marked the final battle of Europe's great sailing warships.

By the time of the next great international conflict, the Crimean War, which formally began in October 1853, new technologies had started to change the look, size, performance and firepower of the world's leading navies, most notably those of Britain, France and the United States, with the irregular power of the wind, being replaced by the highly reliable mechanical output of man-made steam engines. Although rudimentary steam engines were thought to have been built and demonstrated from the very earliest times, most of those that were constructed, were reported to have been of little practical use, other than to illustrate their possible applications. It was only during the 18th and 19th centuries that the actual physical power and practical employment of the steam engine began to be fully utilised, helping to industrialise many of the processes that had previously been undertaken by sheer animal or human labour. However, despite the steam engines ability to remove the sheer physical drudgery of early manufacturing industries, pump away large inundations of unwanted water and help create Britain's early railway systems, it was some time before these new technologies were actually suitable for any sort of large scale maritime application. It was said to be the French inventor, Denis Papin, who produced the first practical steam powered paddle boat, as early as 1704, although his ideas failed to gain any sort of significant backing within Europe, so few new developments were made until the middle of the 18th century. Improvements in steam engine design, undertaken by the likes of James Watt, was thought to have allowed a number of inventors to make great strides in the development of a fully working steamship, which finally culminated in the construction of a commercially viable steamboat, by John Fitch of Pennsylvania in 1788, a vessel that was able to carry passengers along the Delaware River, albeit for a very short time.

Despite the lack of commercial success for the paddle steamer, Fitch having managed to build a working steamship, within a relatively short time, designers, shipbuilders and inventors elsewhere subsequently began to create similar types of vessels, often with a commercial application, rather than a military one. Over the next half century, paddle steamers were said to have become common sights in most of North America and parts of Europe, as the technology evolved, with bigger ships even managing to cross the vast expanse of the North Atlantic, a feat that was first achieved by the American paddle steamer, SS Savannah, in May and June of 1819, although records suggest that the vessel was also equipped with sail, in the event that her engines failed at a crucial moment. However, despite the commercial success of such ships, from a military perspective, most naval authorities were said to have been generally unimpressed with the idea of a paddle steamer as a warship, simply because the exposed paddles represented an inherent weakness to the defence of a warship, ostensibly because they were an easy target for an enemy's guns and once they were destroyed or damaged then the vessel would have no real means of propulsion. Furthermore, the placement of the paddle wheels, on one or both sides of the ship, meant that there was no room for guns to be installed, other than in front or aft of the wheel, which would have involved a serious reduction in the amount of firepower that such a ship might carry into battle, a serious issue for any prospective military vessel. Although a number of paddle steamers were known to have been introduced into military service by a number of the world's navies, including Britain's, ultimately they failed to find a permanent place in most military services, being used instead, as coastal patrol vessels, or employed in inland waterways.

The only alternative form of propulsion to the paddle wheel was thought to be the propeller screw, although up until 1835 not a single trial had proved the efficacy of the system, despite numerous design patents being registered by various designers, inventors and shipbuilders. The failure of successive trials to design an effective propeller system was thought to have contributed to the rise of the paddle steamer, which for most naval engineers of the time was far inferior to sail. It was only in 1835 that two entirely separate British inventors, John Ericsson and Francis Pettit Smith, both began to work on the problem of the screw propeller, without actually realising that they were both working to solve the same problem. For his part, Pettit Smith, a farmer by trade, who had a personal interest in screw propulsion, was reported to have designed and registered his own patent for a screw propeller, ideas that he initially trialled on a small canal boat called the Francis Smith on a local London waterway, where through good luck and careful observation he was able to refine his designs into a highly effective propulsion system. Meanwhile, Ericsson, an experienced engineer had arranged for the construction of a full scale screw driven steamship, which he called the Francis Ogden, after one of his financial backers. Believing that his designs would answer the problems of the screw propeller, in the middle of 1837 Ericsson arranged for the ship's propulsion system to be demonstrated to members of the British Admiralty, many of whom were reported to have been generally unimpressed with the speed and manoeuvrability offered by the craft. Having had his ideas rejected by the Royal Navy, Ericsson was then reported to have built a bigger craft, the Robert F Stockton, which he subsequently sent across the Atlantic to America, where his designs were thought to have been included in the construction of the US Navy's own first screw type warship, the USS Princeton.

Despite the level of disinterest shown by the Admiralty in the idea of screw propellers as a form of propulsion and with John Ericsson having sent his own vessel to the United States, the farmer, Francis Pettit-Smith was said to have continued with his efforts to try and persuade the Royal Navy that the screw propeller was both a viable and logical alternative to the generally unsuitable paddle steamer. In September 1837, Pettit-Smith was thought to have conducted a series of sea trials with his vessel, the Francis Smith, in the open waters between London and Hythe in Kent, during which his vessel was seen by a number of Royal Navy officers, who were reported to have been impressed by the ship's ability to make headway against the prevailing winds and currents. With interest being revived in the practical application of the screw propeller, in 1838 Pettit-Smith was then reported to have built a full-sized vessel, the Archimedes, which was subsequently trialled against a number of the Royal Navy's own vessels, during which Pettit-Smith's propeller driven ship was said to have performed extremely well. However, even though Archimedes was said to have suffered some minor setbacks, often as a result of mechanical breakdowns, which were to be expected given the early development of screw drive technology, it was the trials of May 1840 that would ultimately decide that future of the screw propeller. It was only then that Archimedes was finally tested against her technological rival, the paddle steamer, with the mail packets, Swallow and Widgeon, being two of those that were pitted against Pettit-Smith's vessel. Although Archimedes did not prove to be significantly faster than any of her rivals, the fact that she displayed equal speed and had none of the obvious military drawbacks, such as exposed paddle wheels and limited gun space, ensured that Pettit-Smith's designs received a highly positive report from those Royal Navy officers who had been monitoring her performance.

Francis Pettit Smith   Charles Parsons   Cowper Phipps Cole

For many reporters, even though the Archimedes had been preceded by Pettit-Smith's own Francis Smith and John Ericsson's two earlier propeller driven vessels, the fact that all of these had been intended for use on inland or coastal waters, rather than on the high seas, meant that they were boats, as opposed to ships, leaving Archimedes as the world's first screw driven ship. Following her successful sea trials for the Royal Navy, Archimedes was subsequently taken around Britain and parts of Europe to demonstrate the new propeller technology, with Isambard Kingdom Brunel being one of the many engineers, designers, architects and shipbuilders, who would not only help to improve and advance the drive system, but would inevitably bring an end to the age of the paddle steamers and the sailing ship. Ultimately, Archimedes herself was reported to have ended her days as a sailing ship, ostensibly because her commercial owners were either unwilling or unable to maintain her engines and propeller system, as a result of which, the part that she played in helping to create the modern navy's of the world is quite often overlooked. Despite Archimedes' generally inauspicious end however, her success was said to have resulted in the later construction and launch of the Royal Navy's first purpose built propeller driven warship HMS Rattler in April 1843. For much of the first two years of her life, Rattler was reported to have undergone a whole series of trials for her Royal Navy builders, who were keen to test her performance in all sorts of circumstances, in order to ensure that all future warships would maintain Britain's position as the world's leading naval force. For many however, HMS Rattler is best remembered for her tug-of-war competition with the paddle steamer Alecto, at Portsmouth in March 1845, a test to determine once and for all, which of the two propulsion systems was the better, a trial that Rattler ultimately won having towed Alecto backwards for some distance. For much of her limited naval service though, Rattler was reported to have been used as general purpose vessel, rather than as a frontline warship, although between 1849 and 1856 she was said to have seen service in anti-slavery operations in the waters off West Africa, before undertaking anti-piracy patrols in and around the South China seas. Surprisingly perhaps, in 1856 HMS Rattler was said to have returned to Britain where she was subsequently decommissioned by the Royal Navy and later broken up, bringing an end to a comparatively short thirteen year career, as Britain's first purpose built propeller driven sloop-of-war. However, with the benefits of the screw propeller having been proved, first by Archimedes and later by Rattler, from the middle of the 19th century most wooden Royal Navy ships were said to have been built with a steam engine, as well as a full set of masts and sails, allowing the vessel to travel the high seas regardless of the prevailing winds and tides. One of the earliest ships of the line to have been constructed by the Royal Navy was he HMS Sans Pareil, which was first ordered by the Admiralty in February 1843 and laid down in September 1845. Initially conceived as a conventional wooden warship, driven entirely by sail, the success of ships such as HMS Rattler was said to have caused the Admiralty to change the specifications of Sans Pareil in October 1848, so that a steam engine and screw propeller were added to the vessel in the following year. Formally launched in March 1851, HMS Sans Pareil marked the beginning of the period that saw Britain's Royal Navy warships, transformed from a straightforward sailing vessel, to a dual powered steam and fully rigged warship, albeit one that was mainly built of wood and therefore increasingly susceptible to developments in contemporary armaments.

At the time, the traditional wooden hulls of these vitally important warships were said to have become increasingly susceptible to advances in munitions, with self exploding and incendiary shells both posing a real danger to the highly flammable structure of ships at sea, where there was little hope of safely escaping any sort of inferno. These dangers were thought to have been far more acute where a ship came in range of land based targets, where much larger and increased numbers of gun batteries could be brought to bear against a single ship, or indeed an entire fleet. This was said to have been particularly evident during the Crimean War, where Russian gun batteries were thought to have outnumbered and outranged most of the Anglo-French ships that were lying offshore, forcing them to withdraw and therefore play little part in support of their ground offensives. Even relatively modern warships, including those that were fitted with steam engines to drive their paddle wheels or screw propellers were ill-equipped to resist the occasional self exploding shell, or mortar that might tear through their timber defences, causing devastation amongst those onboard, especially if fire caught hold, or the round struck the ship's magazine. It was said to be in response to these increasingly large land based gun batteries, with their newly rifled barrels, which offered far greater accuracy that the French navy of Napoleon III first introduced the idea of armoured barges, the forerunner of the later Ironclad warship. Designed as low draught platforms that carried their own heavy modern guns and which were themselves protected by armour shielding. Built and used by both Britain and France during the Crimean War, these enormous and extremely well protected gunships were reported to have been highly effective during the conflict, although the fact that they were slow and cumbersome, often having to be towed by their accompanying steamships, meant that they had little practical use, other than as stationary floating gun positions. However, the military advantages of developing a fully armoured warship was clearly evident to both the British and French navies, who were both reported to have spent much of the 1850's competing with one another to produce Europe's first properly equipped Ironclad warship. As a result, at the end of 1859, France finally managed to produce the world's first ocean going Ironclad warship, The Gloire, which despite having a wooden superstructure, was sheathed with iron plate up to four inches thick that was designed to protect the vessel from damage that might be caused by modern artillery. Powered by a steam engine, driving a screw propeller, The Gloire, was reported to have been able to travel at around thirteen knots and was said to have been armed with some thirty six modern guns, a truly formidable weapons platform, of which a further sixteen were thought to have been planned by the French navy.

For the Royal Navy, the possibility of being outdone by France in terms of modern frontline ships was thought to have been tempered by the need to produce a much faster, better armed and much more effective Ironclad warship than their European neighbours. As a result, Britain was happy to allow the French navy to take a temporary lead in naval superiority, seemingly confident that their earlier supremacy would subsequently be restored, once their own fleet of modern Ironclad warships began to be launched in the following year. The first of these new Royal Navy ships, Warrior, was formally identified as a frigate, rather than as a conventional ship-of-the-line, ostensibly because she carried her guns on a single upper deck, was extremely fast and manoeuvrable; and was generally used for patrolling, rather than forming part of a regular battle line, which was commonly the role fulfilled by the much larger and better armed battle ships. From an entirely British perspective, the development of these frigates, was thought to have given the Royal Navy a distinct advantage over their French neighbours, simply because the likes of the Warrior were judged to be bigger, faster and better armed than their French competitors, although by this time, most of Europe's leading seafaring nations were also thought to have been building their own Ironclad warships, most of which were said to have been similar in one way or another. However, the actual military usefulness of the Ironclad warship was only finally tested on the opposite side of the Atlantic, during the American Civil War, when the fleets of the Northern Union and Southern Confederacy met one another in battle, with often differing results. Although the idea of Ironclad ships was thought to have given various navy's an advantage in terms of both defence and attack, in reality, even though such vessels were harder to damage or sink because of their amour, their own lack of real firepower ensured that most wooden ships also survived relatively intact. In fact, the main method of destroying or damaging an enemy ship was said to have been through the use of ramming, a strategy that represented a complete reversal terms of naval warfare and something that was only finally done away with once ships were equipped with modern guns.

Earlier muzzle loading guns still remained in service during the early part of the 19th century, despite the fact that they were slow to load and aim, as well as being highly inefficient. The breech loader by contrast, was thought to be a much more effective weapon, in that the barrel did not have to be moved for a new shot to be loaded and they required fewer men to operate, making them faster and much more accurate. However, the main problem with the breech loader, was that the breech cover, the means by which a new shell or round was loaded, represented a weak point in the barrel itself, one where gases might escape, thereby reducing the velocity of the round, or more seriously, create a situation where the breech cover might be blown open or off, injuring the men that were immediately behind the gun. In light of such problems and because of the increasing size of guns, along with their associated shells, a great deal of time and effort was put into developing systems of sealing the breech, to prevent dangerous blowouts and hydraulic loading systems that could carry and load heavy artillery shells directly into the guns breech. It was only around 1880 that the Royal Navy finally made the transition to arm all of its ships with breech loading guns, although the increasing size of these armaments were said to have thrown up yet another set of problems, as they began to reach the limits that any vessel could actually carry, without threatening to destabilise or overwhelm the vessel itself. According to later sources, the fundamental problem for most shipbuilders of the time, was that most Ironclad ships were still designed to carry guns on either side of the vessel, so that the ship could still deliver its historic broadside, a blistering fusillade of shot from a number of weapons, which could be fired from both sides of the vessel, at the same time if necessary. Additionally, the continuing existence of sails and rigging was thought to have played a part in limiting any new developments in naval gunnery, simply because the masts, spars and sails which occupied the central part of the ship, ensured that no effective weaponry could be placed there, simply because their field of fire would have been limited by the placement of the mast and other sailing apparatus. Although various alternatives to the conventional side cannons were said to have been tried during the latter part of the 19th century, with revolving turrets and armoured boxes both being trialled by various navies, the use of such gun positions could still occasionally compromise the stability of the ship, which along with their limited fields of fire, ensured that such arrangements failed to achieve popularity amongst most ship designers.

Many of the problems faced by these early Ironclad warships were thought to have been inter-related, revolving around the issue of the materials employed in the construction of the vessel, the size, efficiency and output of the steam engines used and the amount of fuel that a ship could reasonably carry, all of which had a direct effect on the size of ship that could be built. Although wood had always been used for shipbuilding up until the early 19th century, several European navies had experimented with iron during the 1820's and 1830's, but given its brittle nature, especially when struck by a projectile, by the 1840's many countries had abandoned it as a likely replacement for more traditional timbers. However, continuing experimentation and a limited availability of seasoned wood, coupled with the falling price of iron and improvements in its manufacture, ultimately led to a number of navies persevering with the use of iron in their shipbuilding programs. Because both wood and iron had their own particular advantages and disadvantages, almost inevitably shipbuilders began to use combinations of the two materials in the construction of their naval vessels, at least until the early 1870's when steel finally began to emerge as a much more suitable material. Even though steel had been available for years, in the short term it was said to have lacked the strength to be used on its own and was therefore commonly employed in conjunction with iron or wood, or both, to form a composite that was stronger than any of its individual parts. It was only in the 1890's that steel began to be processed in such a way that it quickly replaced the earlier composites as the material of choice in naval shipbuilding, although the Royal Navy was said to have continued using a mixture of wood, iron and steel for some years before finally accepting that hardened steel was the best material for the task.

The other great development that took place during the second half of the 19th century was the evolution of the steam engine itself, without which, none of the other improvements could or would have been made. The two most significant events were the development of the triple-expansion steam engine and the later much more important creation of the steam turbine, both of which helped to generate increasing amounts of mechanical energy that could then be used to propel bigger and larger vessels, inexorably leading to the loss of the masts, sails and rigging that had previously been used to transport ships across the world's oceans. However, the down side of this particular development was that bigger and better steam engines, often meant that more fuel, in the form of wood and coal, had to be carried by each of these vessels, as they travelled across the globe, not only resulting in bigger, heavier vessels, but also a radical redesign of their layouts, with engine rooms and coal bunkers becoming an integral part of a ships internal structure. Invented by Charles Algernon Parsons in 1884, the steam turbine revolutionised marine travel, although it was reported to have taken a considerable amount of time to actually resolve many of the issues that arose because of the engines high speeds, which were said to have caused problems with the existing propeller technologies. However, Parsons eventually managed to overcome many of these mechanical challenges and in August 1894 launched the world's first steam turbine powered ship, the Turbinia, which he chose to publicly display in a particularly outrageous way. At the Royal Navy Review, held on the 26th June 1897, to celebrate Queen Victoria's Diamond Jubilee, Parson's unexpectedly arrived at Spithead and began to steer Turbinia in between the massed ranks of the Royal Navy's warships that were anchored there and despite the best efforts of the navy's fastest patrol boats, easily managed to avoid them, much to the amusement and shock of the local dignitaries and general public. For Parson's himself, the outrageous publicity stunt, ultimately proved to be worthwhile, as many of the British Admiralty's leading officers were said to have been so impressed with the Turbinia's performance that they immediately began to investigate the possible military potential of the new steam turbine. Two years later, the first Royal Navy destroyers, propelled by steam turbines were launched by British builders and even though, both HMS Viper and HMS Cobra were later lost in unrelated incidents, they were thought to have played at least a partial role in the later building of the first of the modern day battleships, HMS Dreadnought, which was eventually launched in 1906.

However, the final piece of the puzzle in creating the 19th century warship remained the issue of its armaments, marking the final move away from the traditional gun decks, with their large numbers of individual weapons which were located on either side of the ship, to the centralised gun turret, which could launch high explosive projectiles in almost any direction. For most designers, inventors and engineers of the age, the two most obvious solutions to the problem of naval weaponry was either the revolving turret, or the barbette, both of which were located along the centre line of the warship and acted in very similar fashions. The revolving turret, was as its name suggests, an armoured turret that revolved in its entirety, with its fixed guns being adjusted by moving the whole turret in a particular direction. The barbette was slightly different, in that the outer armoured housing was static, whilst the guns inside were movable and could be brought to bear on either side of the vessel. Although both systems were thought to have their supporters, neither of them could fire directly fore or aft, as the continuing presence of masts and rigging prevented this, forcing most warships to carry guns on their bows and sterns in order to cover these particular blind spots. However, even though such weaknesses in design would eventually be resolved through the later disappearance of the sailing equipment, because of developments in engine performance, a much more fundamental problem existed with many of these early turrets and barbettes, in that their weight and height seriously compromised the stability of the ship itself. One of the earliest British designers of the revolving gun turret was Captain Cowper Phipps Cole, who was reported to have patented his ideas as early as 1859 and subsequently persuaded the British Admiralty to adopt a number of his ideas into early Royal Navy warships. Although the resulting vessels were said to have been suitable for working in generally calmer coastal waters, other naval architects of the time were thought to have been unconvinced by Coles' overall designs and in some cases insisted that changes be made to offset the top-heaviness of the turrets. Seemingly unconvinced by any concerns regarding his designs, in 1866 Cole and his backers began to agitate and lobby for a turret-type warship which was unaltered by other naval architects, in order that he could prove the efficacy of his designs once and for all, as a result of which in March 1869 the HMS Captain was formally launched. Almost immediately Coles' design of the vessel was heavily criticised by experienced shipbuilders within the Admiralty, who questioned not only the weight of the gun turrets, but also the potential for flooding on the gun deck, both of which Cole and his supporters rejected outright. The First Lord of the Admiralty, Sir John Pakington, perhaps aware of the support that Cole had gained amongst some of the country's most influential people, was reported to have simply approved the ship for use, but attached the caveat that ultimately Cole and his shipbuilder, Laird's of Merseyside, would bear the responsibility if anything untoward were to happen to HMS Captain, once she entered service.

Sir John Pakington

Lord Salisbury

Sir John Fisher

Finally commissioned by the Royal Navy in April 1870, the Captain was said to have excelled during her sea trials, outperforming all of her naval contemporaries and leading people to believe that she was everything that Captain Cole had initially promised for his turret-type ship. With her critics silenced and having proved that she was everything that she was purported to be, by September 1870 HMS Captain was reported to have joined the Royal Navy's Channel Fleet and was cruising off the Iberian Coast, near Cape Finisterre. However, as the wind strengthened throughout the day and the seas became heavier, a number of those onboard Captain, were thought to have become increasingly concerned over the number of waves that were crashing over the sides of the vessel, a result of the ship lying too far down in the water, due to the weight of the gun platforms designed by Cole. As the weather worsened and wind strength increased, the crew of the Captain were reported to have reduced the amount of sail being used, which not only slowed the speed of the vessel, but also prevented the ship from being pushed too far sideways. Unfortunately, by midnight, the Captain was reported to have been heeling over by around eighteen degrees, much less than most ordinary sailing vessels and was felt to lurch quite heavily, causing the ship's commander to order all sails dropped, in an attempt to steady the vessel. However, as the crew raced to fulfil the order, the ship's eighteen degree list continued to increase until finally HMS Captain simply rolled over and capsized. Of those aboard the vessel when she foundered, nearly five hundred men perished, including Cole himself, although a handful somehow managed to save themselves by clinging to a lifeboat that had broken free from its moorings. In the resulting enquiry that followed the loss of HMS Captain, the obvious instability of the ship, along with its inferior righting angle was pointed to as the main causes of the tragedy and as had been forecast in the correspondence of the First Sea Lord, Sir John Pakington, Cole, along with his shipbuilders and supporters were generally blamed for having allowed such an unsuitable vessel to have been built in the first place.

The most radical changes in British warship design were thought to have been introduced by Sir Edward Reed, the Royal Navy's chief builder between 1863 and 1870; and one of those who had severely criticised Captain Cowper Phipps Cole design's of the naval turrets which were a contributing factor in the loss of HMS Captain. Taking lessons from the American warship designs of the previously noted naval engineer, John Ericsson, Reed was said to have incorporated many of the ideas of the US Monitor-class warships into future Royal Navy vessels, including the breastwork armouring that prevented ships from being swamped by waves breaking over their bows and sides. By enclosing the bridge, gun turrets, funnels and necessary openings within a central armoured shield, it essentially made the vessel safe from inundation by the sea and allowed for gun turrets to be mounted above deck height. In the same year that HMS Captain plunged to the ocean floor, taking with her nearly five hundred souls, the first of Sir Edward Reed's Devastation class destroyers, HMS Devastation, was being built for the Royal Navy, the first British battleship that did not carry any sails, or rigging. Designed to carry two twelve inch guns, each of which were protected behind a turret constructed of fourteen inches of armour, these weapons were thought to have had a 280 degree of fire, with only the presence of the bridge and funnels preventing them from turning full circle. Even though the warship was only ever intended for use in coastal and regional waters, because of its obvious reliance on refuelling with coal, HMS Devastation was tested for her suitability in heavier seas and to many people's surprise was thought to have performed well in handling waves of up to eight metres high, which only caused the ship to list by a highly manageable fourteen degrees. In order to ensure that these vessels did not suffer a similar fate to HMS Captain, additional accommodations were added to the ship and the protective breastwork was extended further around the vessel, reducing the possibility of the decks being swamped by heavy waves. Even though Reed was said to have adopted many of his ideas from the American Monitor-class warships, the improvements made to the basic designs were thought to have helped make the Royal Navy's Devastation-class warships, the most powerful battleships of the age, a fact that helped Britain maintain its naval superiority towards the end of the 19th century.

However, despite being the world's dominant naval power throughout much of the 19th century, according to some sources, the service itself was generally maintained on a very small national budget, with Royal Navy vessels being utilised long after they might normally have been replaced. Britain's unrivalled dominance of the high seas and the absence of any major international conflicts were thought to be just two of the reasons why spending was significantly reduced during the period, although the pacifist policies of various British politicians was also thought to have been another contributory factor. By 1889 though, this national reluctance to invest in the future strength of the Royal Navy was said to have come to an end, when the government of Lord Salisbury passed the Naval Defence Act in that same year, which determined that the Royal Navy should maintain a naval force equivalent to, if not greater than, the combined forces of the world's next two biggest navies, which at the time were France and Russia. Under the terms of the new legislation, an additional twenty million pounds was set aside for the expansion of the country's naval service, which was intended to spent on constructing a further ten battleships, forty new cruisers and a handful of new fast gunboats, all of which were necessary to maintain this numerical supremacy.

By the beginning of the 20th century and following sustained developments in naval gun technologies, a number of ship designers throughout the world were beginning to plan for and speculate about the future of naval battleships, with British, Japanese, American and even Italian architects proposing the idea of much larger, much more heavily armed vessels waging war from a considerable distance. The evolution of newer, bigger guns that could effectively and accurately deliver their shells to a target over distances of several miles meant that the very nature of naval warfare had changed, leading to the creation of semi autonomous, heavily armoured gun platforms, which were built around speed, defensive capability and firepower. According to a number of sources, the man responsible for creating Britain's new generation of heavy battleships, or Dreadnoughts, as they became commonly known, was Admiral Sir John Fisher, the First Sea Lord, who set up and chaired the naval committee that would ultimately determine the size, scale and capability of the next great Royal Navy ships during the early 1900's. However, although the much larger Dreadnoughts were the leviathans of the high seas, the period also marked the emergence of the smaller, but much faster moving cruisers, destroyers and corvettes, which sacrificed armour and firepower for speed in varying degrees. Being a highly experienced naval officer, as well as an avid student of seaborne warfare, when deciding upon the designs of the proposed new battleships, Fisher ensured that their weaponry and propulsion systems, along with their defensive capability were all designed to the highest possible specifications, whilst at the same time ensuring that the vessels were not so heavy as to be ineffective. The first of the great capital ships, HMS Dreadnought, was designed to be over five hundred and twenty feet in length, eighty two feet wide and would have a draught of some thirty feet, when fully loaded, as well as having a double bottom that might protect the ship from underwater objects, or even from torpedoes. Built with two pairs of steam turbines, rather than the older triple expansion steam engines, Dreadnought was driven by two propeller shafts, which were said to have allowed the vessel to reach speeds of over twenty-one knots per hour, making her more than fast enough to complete the role assigned to her. Although she relied on coal to fuel her eighteen boilers, the great ship also carried a load of fuel oil that was sprayed directly onto the coal in order to increase its burn rate, allowing HMS Dreadnought to travel a maximum of well over six and a half thousand nautical miles before she needed to restock her bunkers and refill her tanks.

HMS Dreadnought's main armaments was said to have comprised five main batteries, each containing two twelve inch guns, with three of the batteries located along the centre line of the ship, from bow to stern, whilst the two remaining batteries were located on either side of the vessel, halfway along the deck. As a result of this layout, when called upon to do so, the vessel could unleash a simultaneous broadside from eight of its guns, to either the left or right and similarly could fire six of its guns to the rear and six to the front, allowing the ship to deliver some sort of salvo in an almost complete 360 degree field of fire. In addition to these main weapons, which could launch a shell anything up to sixteen miles, Dreadnought was also reported to have carried a vast array of smaller guns, ranging from three inch naval guns, to Anti-Aircraft weapons, all the way down to heavy calibre machine guns, all of them being designed to attack different sized targets at completely different ranges. The other weapon of note that was said to have been carried by these new Dreadnought's were torpedoes, which were intended to be used against other enemy warships that might well escape normal shelling, or that were beyond the range of the smaller guns. Also, as one of the most modern warships of the period, Dreadnought was also said to have been equipped with the latest in range finding technology, designed to help gun crews identify and strike targets, regardless of their varying distances and saving time and money in the process. An integral part of this equipment was reported to be the Vickers Range Clock, designed by Percy Scott, which worked on the basis of spotters reporting any fall of shot against an enemy vessel and then adjustments being made to correct the short fall, until hopefully the target was struck and destroyed. The whole point of the fire control system, rather than offering a fully guaranteed targeting system, which even with today's modern technology can prove to be problematic, was to create a sighting and range finding system that linked spotters with the gunners, by way of voice pipes, thereby making the process of targeting enemy assets much more immediate and effective. The other significant development incorporated into the designs of HMS Dreadnought was the Krupps steel armour, which involved chromium being added to a nickel steel alloy to create a much harder metal and one that was ideally suited for protecting naval vessels of the late 19th and early 20th centuries.

Initially laid down on the 2nd October 1905, Admiral Fisher and his committee had always intended that HMS Dreadnought would be constructed within a year, as a result of which, significant amounts of materials were said to have been stockpiled in readiness for her building programme, ensuring that few delays occurred during her construction. Officially launched by King Edward VII on the 3rd October 1906, at the Royal Navy dockyards in Portsmouth, HMS Dreadnought subsequently underwent sea trials from October 1906 and was formally commissioned by the Royal Navy on 11th December 1906. However, despite her military purpose, Dreadnought was reported to have had few opportunities to display her naval might, simply because, during the most significant naval engagement of WWI, the Battle of Jutland, which was fought on 31st May 1916, she was being refitted and missed the only large scale sea battle between Britain and Germany's great warships. As a result, HMS Dreadnought spent much of her life serving purely as a deterrent and as the flagship of one or other British fleets, before being decommissioned and sold for scrap in May 1921. Even though HMS Dreadnought failed to prove herself in battle, her overall design, speed and armaments were thought to have been so radical that the name "Dreadnought" was generally applied to any ultra large battleship, which was built after 1906. As a result, different classes of Royal Navy Battleships, such as the Bellerophon, or the King George V, were all deemed to be Dreadnoughts, simply because they were built to the size and standards of the first ship to carry that name. The Bellerophon-class ships that followed HMS Dreadnought into service with the Royal Navy, of which three were subsequently built, were all reported to have been almost identical to HMS Dreadnought in construction, although some areas of the ship were improved as a result of advances in naval technology, or through practical application, but the same sort of vessel nonetheless. According to some historians, the British Admiralty's decision to built these new enormous battleships was thought to have marked the start of an Arms Race that would continue right through to the start of the Second World War and which would come to involve a large number of nations, including Britain, France, America, Germany, and Japan, to name but a few. However, Britain's decision to begin construction of these great leviathans was also thought to have been influenced by the emerging strength of the Russian, Japanese and American navies, all of whom were known to have been developing their own versions of the Dreadnought type battleship, presumably with the intention of becoming a major naval force in their own right. The growing threat of Japanese and Russian naval forces were already well known to the Royal Navy following the Battle of the Yellow Sea in August 1904 and the later Battle of Tsushima in May 1905, both of which saw the navies of these two countries confront one another over disputed territories. Ultimately, the victory of Japan's navy over Russia's was thought to have marked a pivotal moment in naval history, in that it was said to have encouraged many of Japan's military leaders that they could and should use their military strength to pursue expansionist policies throughout Asia, a decision that would almost inevitably bring them into direct conflict with the regions great colonial powers, including Great Britain. For their part, the American Navy were also known to have been planning a Dreadnought-type battleship, the South Carolina class, as early as 1902, although progress in construction was reported to have been slowed by excessive deliberations over the actual specifications of the planned vessels, meaning that they did not actually come into service until 1908.

Alfred Von Tirpitz **Roger Keyes** **Reginald Tyrwhit**

Although Britain, France and Holland had remained as the main colonial powers right through to the beginning of the 20th century, during the 19th century a number of other European nations were thought to have acquired overseas possessions in Africa, Asia and in the Pacific, the most notable of which was the reunified state of Germany. Despite having limited territorial waters, unlike the other more westerly countries whose coastlines abutted the North Atlantic, as a trading nation, Germany remained determined to retain access to the Atlantic and the Baltic via the North Sea, as well as protecting its extremely vital coastal ports of Kiel and Wilhelmshaven, along with its commercially important waterways like the Kiel Canal. Consequently, beginning in 1872 the German authorities started to undertake a ten year building programme to modernise their fleet, which aimed to produce a large number of frigates, corvettes, gunships and torpedo boats with which to protect its marine assets from the much larger and far more powerful British and French fleets. However, Germany's long term naval objectives were reported to have been substantially increased in 1888 when the new Kaiser, Wilhelm II, came to power, with the intention of creating a German Fleet that could rival the maritime power of Britain and France, helping to turn his country into a truly global superpower, with its own extensive overseas empire. As part of that wider ambition, in 1893 the German authorities were reported to have ordered four new warships, of the Brandenburg-class, which were the country's first ocean going battleships, although from a size and specification point of view were considered to be of little threat to the ships of the British and French navies. Two years later, the German government authorised the construction of five more warships, the Kaiser Friedrich III-class, which were said to have been far larger and more effective than the Brandenburg-class, although by the time they were all completed in 1901, they offered little that might threaten the world's other great naval powers. It was only after 1898 that a longer term view was adopted by the German authorities, which set out a fixed term plan to bring the German Navy's strength to a level, where it might rival the forces of the French and Russian fleets, but without the expectation of equalling the size of the British Royal Navy, at least not in the foreseeable future. However, even these highly optimistic naval targets were reported to have been dwarfed by the later objectives set by the German government, who first doubled and later trebled their planned numbers of warships over the period of some eleven years, from 1898 to 1909, with an expected total of some forty-eight large battleships alone being proposed by the end of 1909.

The German Secretary of the Navy, Rear Admiral Alfred Von Tirpitz, the main architect of Germany's naval expansion, was reported to have taken the view that his forces only had to reach some 60% of the Royal Navy's numbers, in order to offer a realistic threat to Britain's maritime supremacy, simply because British navy resources were so widely dispersed throughout the world, defending its far flung empire. Unfortunately for Tirpitz, the British Admiralty's First Sea Lord, Admiral Sir John Fisher, was equally aware of the dangers posed by the emerging German navy and was said to have tried to maintain the Royal Navy's superiority by gradually modernising his own fleet, a part of which involved the construction of the previously mentioned HMS Dreadnought, which essentially made every other warship in the world obsolete, when she was launched in 1906. Despite the construction of these great capital ships however, by the time Dreadnought was ready for sea, it was being suggested by some people within the British Admiralty that Germany had already built the second most powerful battle fleet in the world, making her, not only a threat to all of the smaller maritime nations of the world, but a potential rival to Britain's long held marine supremacy. The Royal Navy's greatest fear was that Germany might choose to ally herself with one or more of the smaller naval powers, thereby creating a real military threat to Britain's control of the high seas, which could then threaten the country's vitally important trade routes, including its essential supplies of food and raw materials. Between 1899 and 1908 several classes of heavily armoured warships were reported to have been built by the German navy, each successive class being heavier and better armed than its predecessor, with the Scharnhorst and Gneisnenau representing the pinnacle of German battleship construction by the time both were completed in 1908.

For much of the period from 1908 through to 1914 and the outbreak of the First World War, both Germany and Great Britain were reported to have tried to outmatch one another in terms of modern warships, an exercise that the Royal Navy was always likely to win for a number of reasons. Not only had Britain started from an improved position in the first place, having a well established shipbuilding industry to begin with and having few of the logistical problems that Germany was facing, in terms of restrictive inland waterways and having to develop the necessary infrastructure to fully support their new battle fleet. It was also reported that the increasing costs of building and maintaining these great capital ships caused a great deal of dissent within Germany itself, as an increasing proportion of the nation's wealth began to be used, to try and compete with Britain and its navy, a situation that was said to have come to a head in 1909, when leading German politicians began to resign over the matter. Those that were aghast at the growing costs of naval development attempted to reach an agreement with the British government to limit both country's naval spending, but with Britain determined to maintain its two power standard and with the British public insisting that the Royal Navy must retain its numerical superiority, any hopes of mutual agreement over the subject of warships would prove to be futile. Although Admiral Sir John Fisher would later resign his post as First Sea Lord over a row involving the cost of outbuilding any other nation, his successor, Winston Churchill, was thought to have been an even greater militarist than Fisher, who made sure that the Royal Navy did indeed maintain their superiority over other nations, regardless of the financial cost.

Europe had always been dominated and shaped by military conflict and towards the end of the 19th century peace was being maintained largely by a series of individual treaties, which saw several coalitions of like-minded countries allying themselves together, in order to protect one another from other military alliances. In 1873, Russia, Germany and the Austro Hungarian Empire were said to have allied themselves in what became known as the League of the Three Emperors, although this coalition ultimately failed due to disagreements over the future of the Balkans, leaving Germany, Italy and the Austro-Hungarian Empire to form what later known as the Triple Alliance. As a deterrent to these particular alliances, France was reported to have signed treaties with a number of its European neighbours, including the Franco-Russian Alliance in 1892 and the Entente Cordiale with Britain in 1904, both of which were designed to guarantee its future security from any members of the Triple Alliance. With these military and political coalitions in place, for many people of the age, it was never a case of whether war would break out again, but rather when it would occur, a fateful opinion that was said to have been widely held in Germany, where military leaders were always thought to be preparing such an eventuality. However, it was one of Germany's allies, the Austro-Hungarian Empire, which ultimately set the stage for the next great European conflict, when it decided to formally annexe the former Ottoman territories of Bosnia Herzegovina in October 1908. Over the next few years political manoeuvring by a number of the regions leading powers, including Russia, Germany, Serbia, etc. was said to have turned the area into a powder keg, requiring only one single act to set the whole of Europe alight, as all sides struggled to impose their own solutions in what became an increasingly hostile atmosphere. The single act of madness that almost inevitably set the various European states on the road to war with one another, occurred on the 28th June 1914, when a Bosnian Serb student called Gavrilo Princip assassinated the heir to the Austro-Hungarian throne, the Archduke Franz Ferdinand in Sarajevo, Bosnia. However, rather than simply blaming the individual responsible, the Austro-Hungarian Empire was reported to have blamed the Balkan state of Serbia, which it believed was interfering in Bosnian politics. The Austro-Hungarian authorities were said to have then delivered a series of demands to the Serbian government, which it knew the Serbs could and would not agree to, allowing the Austrian state to legitimately declare war on Serbia on the 28th July 1914. In response to this declaration and in support of its most important Balkan ally, on the 29th July 1914 Russia ordered a partial mobilisation of its own forces, causing Germany to begin its own military response two days later. With Germany threatening to attack Russia, France subsequently began to mobilise its own army units on the 1st August 1914 and three days later, Great Britain formally declared war on Germany and its allies, setting in motion a bitter European conflict that would last for the next four years and cost the lives of an estimated thirty seven million people around the world, both military and civilian.

At the outbreak of the First World War, the Royal Navy's first priority was to blockade the German High Seas Fleet in the area of the North Sea and Baltic, at their home ports of Kiel and Wilhelmshaven, thereby preventing them from posing a threat to Britain and her vast overseas empire and its vitally important trade routes. Although a significant number of German warships were reported to have been scattered throughout the globe, the main core of the Kaiser's battle fleet was thought to have been stationed in and around the North Sea, where it was intended for use in confronting the British Grand Fleet directly. However, for the most part, the German fleet was reported to have remained safely anchored in home waters, protected by a screen of mines that prevented the Royal Navy from approaching their home ports, or indeed coming close enough to bombard Germany's warships into submission. Apart from a small number of major naval engagements that took place between the two navies, including the Battles of Heligoland Bight, Dogger Bank, Jutland and the Second Battle of Heligoland Bight, for the most part, military engagements between the great battleships of Germany and Great Britain were generally unremarkable and indecisive, with no outright winner or loser. Ultimately though, the Royal Navy's main strategy, of mounting a tight blockade of Germany's ports and harbours, thereby depriving that country of much needed supplies, eventually proved to be the most effective method of not only defeating German militarism, but also protecting British interests from the possible threat posed by Germany's impressive High Seas Fleet. Surprisingly, although many of Germany's heavily armed surface raiders failed to get much beyond their own territorial waters, the one part of the country's naval force that did manage to some degree of success was the German submarine service, which was known to have mounted a relatively successful campaign against merchant shipping in the North Atlantic during the War. Unfortunately, it was members of this same service who was responsible for attacking and sinking the passenger liner RMS Lusitania on the 7th May 1915, which not only led to the deaths of some twelve hundred of the two thousand people aboard the vessel, as it passed the Old Head of Kinsale in Southern Ireland, a large number of who were American citizens. Although this particular atrocity remains a matter of debate over the legitimacy of the Lusitania as a military target, ultimately the outrage is regarded as one of the root causes of American participation in World War I, an involvement that finally helped bring about an Allied victory over Germany and her partners in November 1918.

The first notable sea engagement between elements of the Royal Navy and the German High Seas Fleet was reported to have occurred on the 28th August 1914, in what later became known as the First Battle of Heligoland Bight. In the run up to war, the Royal Navy had adopted a strategy of patrolling the North Sea, rather than mounting a static blockade of Germany's northern ports, which may well have resulted in British ships being attacked or destroyed by German U-boats or mines. By representing a distant threat to Germany's capital ships, the British Admiralty hoped to tempt them to leave the relative safety of Kiel and Wilhelmshaven, thereby bringing them into the open waters of the North Sea where they might be engaged and destroyed by the superior forces of the Royal Navy. However, the German leadership, although confident of their own navy's abilities, were thought to have been reluctant to fight an outright sea battle with the British fleet, which they knew to be superior in terms of numbers and guns, so instead, satisfied themselves with sending out regular patrols of destroyers and cruisers, in the hope that these might intercept and destroy any smaller British forces that they happened to come across. Perhaps recognising that they would never persuade the whole German High Fleet to come out to sea, in early August 1914, two Royal Navy officers, Commodore Roger Keyes and Commodore Reginald Tyrwhitt were said to have conceived a plan to intercept the German destroyer and cruiser force, as it made one of its regular patrols into the waters of the North Sea. The plan called for three British submarines to deliberately expose themselves to the German patrol, so that the destroyers and cruisers were drawn out to sea, allowing a second British naval force, of submarines and destroyers to position themselves behind the German line of retreat, thereby blocking their way back to the safety of Kiel and Wilhelmshaven. Unfortunately, although the plan was subsequently approved by the First Lord of the Admiralty, Winston Churchill, in reality much depended on the agreement of the Admiralty's Chief of Staff, Vice-Admiral Sturdee who refused to order the British Grand Fleet southward to support the operation, but did provide two separate cruiser forces to participate in the plan.

Admiral Sturdee   Admiral John Jellicoe   Admiral Franz Hipper

With the operation planned for the 28th August 1914, Keyes and Tyrwhitt, along with their combined force of thirty two destroyers, seven cruisers and twelve submarines began to position themselves, ready to set the trap for the unknown number of German vessels that were expected to venture out on patrol. However, as the individual Royal Navy units began to take up their various stations, the commander of Britain's Grand Fleet, Admiral John Jellicoe, only received information about the proposal on the 26th August and immediately requested permission to bring his forces southward to support the action. He too though was instructed to only send cruisers to support Keyes and Tyrwhitt's operation and although he subsequently despatched a force of three battle cruisers and a further six light cruisers to support the action, Admiral Jellicoe obviously remained concerned, as he very quickly assembled the remainder of the Grand Fleet, ordered them out of Scapa Flow and headed them south towards Keyes and Tyrwhitt's waiting warships. At seven o'clock in the morning of the 28th August 1914 the British light cruiser HMS Arethusa, spotted the leading German destroyer, G-194, at a distance, causing both commanders to immediately begin signalling their closest vessels to report the enemy contact. For their part and as expected, the German commander, Admiral Franz Hipper, was reported to have ordered his cruisers, many of which were based on the Ems and Jade Rivers in the Heligoland Bight region, to move forward to protect the German destroyers, at the same engaging the British warships that were seen to be threatening them. The first vessel attacked by the Royal Navy was reported to be the destroyer, G-149, which was said to have been engaged by at least four British destroyers, whose gunfire was said to have alerted the remainder of the German destroyers who very quickly turned for home and the comparative safety of their cruiser squadron that they assumed would be coming to save them. Commodore Reginald Tyrwhitt, aboard HMS Arethusa, was then reported to have spotted a second flotilla of ten German destroyers that he subsequently ordered he own squadron to pursue, although due to their position and speed he was unable to intercept and engage, eventually being forced to call off the pursuit after the German vessels reached their home waters, where they were protected by submarines and mines. Meanwhile, two German cruisers were thought to have appeared in the area and although one of them retired, as all of their destroyers were now safe, the second vessel, the light cruiser, Frauenlob, entered into a firefight with HMS Arethusa, during which both warships were said to have sustained considerable battle damage.

With at least four German destroyers lost or damaged during the engagement and the remainder heading for home, the Battle of Heligoland Bight then became a contest between the bigger warships, the light cruisers and the heavier battle cruisers, both of which were capable of inflicting catastrophic damage against the smaller British destroyers that were still on the scene. At least four German cruisers were reported to have sailed out to investigate the attack upon their ships, still seemingly unaware of the size of the Royal Navy force, or indeed its dispersal, forcing them to sail individual routes in order to find the British ships. The already seriously damaged HMS Arethusa was said to have been confronted by the cruiser, Strassburg, from which she received further damage, before the German battleship was driven off by supporting British destroyers that fired their torpedoes at her. However, the arrival of these bigger German warships also heralded the introduction of the Royal Navy's own force of light cruisers and battle cruisers, which had been asked to reinforce the main British taskforce and were beginning to steam into the area. Prior to their arrival though, the mixed squadron of British destroyers and cruisers, were still forced to contend with the German battleships that were nearby, including the German cruiser, Mainz, which quickly found itself surrounded by HMS Arethusa and her supporting destroyers, who subsequently attacked the isolated German vessel with shells and torpedoes, forcing her captain to abandon his ship, before scuttling her. Two other German cruisers, the Strassburg and Koln, were then reported to have attacked the British flotilla together, no doubt hoping that their combined firepower would turn the battle in their favour, although any such hopes were very quickly shattered by the arrival of the Royal Navy's reserves of light and heavy cruisers that had been making their way into the areas. Strassburg was said to have disengaged from the battle immediately, but Koln was not so fortunate and was subsequently attacked by the much larger British battleships, although her destruction was said to have been delayed somewhat by the unexpected arrival of yet another German cruiser Ariadne, which was almost immediately attacked and sunk by the British ships, as was the Koln.

Ultimately, the Battle of Heligoland Bight in 1914 represented an outright naval victory for the Royal Navy's Grand Fleet, over Germany's High Seas Fleet, which was only ever used again in a very sparing way; given that the Kaiser was loathe to lose even more of his highly prized warships to Britain's naval forces. However, it is worth pointing out that Germany's armed forces were far more successful in entirely land based operations and that their extremely limited numbers of U-boats proved to be a far more effective weapons systems than did their large numbers of highly expensive and generally underused surface raiders. It is also worth making the point perhaps that the Royal Navy was highly fortunate that human ineptitude did not prove to be far more costly in the battle, as the failure to advise commanders about the presence of other friendly units in the area, could so easily have resulted in Royal Navy units attacking and destroying one another, with the loss of much needed men and equipment. Such occasional lapses in Britain's military effectiveness did not always just affect the men that served in her armed forces, but could also prove to be fatal to the civilian population, especially those people who lived in the coastal regions of the country and relied on the Royal Navy to protect Britain's territorial waters. Perhaps due to the fact that the British navy was renowned as the world's leading maritime power; and due to the earlier defeats of the German fleet at Heligoland Bight and in the Falkland Islands, a certain amount of overconfidence had been allowed to develop, which would eventually prove to have fateful results for people living along the east coast of England.

Admiral Von Spee

Admiral Cradock

Admiral David Beatty

The Battle of the Falkland Islands was reported to have occurred on the 8th December 1914, some three months after the First Battle of Heligoland Bight; and was generally thought to have represented the single major engagement between Germany's fleet of roving surface raiders and elements of the Royal Navy, tasked with protecting the Empire's extensive trade routes. Although the flotilla of German naval ships, under the command of Admiral Graf Maximilian Von Spee were primarily regarded as the German East Asia Squadron, which had been ordered to raid in the area of the Indian Ocean, the loss of their normal home port of Tsingtao in China, had brought those vessels to the other side of the world, where they joined up with a number of other German vessels on the Chilean coast. Von Spee had already achieved some degree of success against the Royal Navy at the beginning of November 1914, when his squadron of five vessels, including the heavy cruisers Scharnhorst and Gneisenau, plus three light cruisers Leipzig, Dresden and Numberg, had met and defeated an ageing Royal Navy taskforce, largely manned by naval reservists. Prior to what became known as the Battle of Coronel, the British commander, Admiral Sir Christopher Cradock, had been deprived of the more modern and more experienced battle cruiser HMS Defence, which was diverted elsewhere, leaving the British force both outgunned and easily outmanoeuvred by the superior German squadron. Rather than face the enemy with the larger guns of the much more powerful, but far slower battle cruiser, HMS Canopus, Admiral Cradock was reported to have employed his lighter warships against the better equipped German battleships, as a result of which his forces were subsequently decimated by the heavier guns of the enemy vessels. By the end of the battle, the British squadron was reported to have lost two heavy battleships, including Cradock's own flagship, HMS Good Hope and a second vessel, HMS Monmouth, both of which were sunk with most of their crews, a total of some sixteen hundred men.

In the aftermath of this defeat, the first of a Royal Navy squadron in more than a century, the Admiralty assembled a second, much larger and more modern naval force to hunt down Admiral Graf Von Spee's flotilla, which was known to be still operating in the South Atlantic. However, their decisive victory over the Royal Navy at Coronel was thought to have left the German fleet short of both ammunition and fuel, forcing them to look elsewhere for supplies of both, with the British supply base at Stanley, on the Falkland Islands, appearing to be the most obvious source of coal for Von Spee's fuel hungry fleet. In the meantime though, the second British squadron that had been sent to the South Atlantic, under the command of Admiral Doveton Sturdee, comprising the battle cruisers, HMS Invincible and HMS Inflexible, had arrived off the east coast of South America, where they met up with other Royal Navy ships, including HMS Glasgow, a survivor from Coronel. Anticipating that Von Spee would take his flotilla to the Falkland Islands, Admiral Sturdee announced his intention to take his Royal Navy squadron to the British held territories in order to force an armed confrontation with the German fleet, which in terms of ships, guns and speed was now thought to be inferior to his own. Accompanied by the heavy battle cruisers HMS Invincible and HMS Inflexible, Sturdee also had the armoured cruisers HMS Kent, Carnarvon and Cornwall at his disposal, as well as the light cruisers HMS Glasgow and Bristol, all of which were thought to have arrived in Stanley Harbour, on or around the 7th December 1914.

The following morning, on the 8th December 1914, the German fleet of Admiral Graf Von Spee was reported to have approached the Falklands, just as most of Sturdee's vessels were undertaking minor repairs, or refuelling their coal bunkers, making them an easy target, if the German commander had decided to launch an attack at that particular moment. Unfortunately for Von Spee, the sight of the large number of British cruisers in Stanley Harbour was thought to have unnerved the German Admiral, who very quickly ordered his own ships to run for the open sea, in the generally forlorn hope that they might outrun or evade the better armed and much faster British warships. Reminiscent of the sort of attitude shown by Drake at the time of the armada, Admiral Sturdee, knowing that his ships could easily outpace the German fleet, was said to have allowed his crews to enjoy their breakfast's, whilst his warships were prepared for sea, before sailing out of Port Stanley at around ten o'clock in the morning. In the time that it had taken the Royal Navy squadron to get underway, Von Spee's ships were thought to have widened the gap between the two naval forces, to an estimated fifteen miles, although with much of the day in front of them Sturdee was confident that by the end of the day he would have the German's within his grasp. By one o'clock in the afternoon, the faster British cruisers had closed the distance sufficiently to begin firing at Von Spee's vessels, forcing the German commander to make the decision to stand and fight with his own cruisers, in the hope that his slower, less well armed vessels might escape capture or destruction. Although the two great German battleships, Scharnhorst and Gneisenau, were thought to have found the range of the British ships quite quickly, their shells were thought to have had little effect on the heavily armoured hulls of HMS Invincible and Inflexible, which were beginning to bring their own big guns to bear on the two German battle cruisers. Generally outgunned by the two Royal Navy vessels, Von Spee was thought to have had little option but to mount a headlong attack on them, during which Scharnhorst received numerous strikes from the British guns, causing her to list and then sink, at four o'clock in the afternoon. Scharnhorst's sister ship, Gneisenau, was thought to have survived a little longer, until she too was overwhelmed by the combined guns of Invincible and Inflexible, which forced the exhausted German crew to finally abandon their vessel and deliberately sink her in open water.

At the same time that Scharnhorst and Gneisenau were being subjected to fire from HMS Invincible and Inflexible, the lighter German cruisers Numberg and Liepzig were being pursued by their Royal Navy counterparts, HMS Kent, Cornwall and Glasgow, which were said to have overcome the two German warships by the early evening of the same day. By the end of the naval engagement, some two thousand German sailors, including Admiral Graf Von Spee had perished, whilst a further two hundred seamen had been rescued by the ships of the Royal Navy, who suffered ten men killed and nineteen wounded, without the loss of a single British vessel. The only German warship to escape destruction in what became known as the Battle of the Falkland Islands, was the light cruiser Dresden, which was reported to have roamed the waters of the South Atlantic and Pacific, before being confronted by a Royal Navy squadron off the Chilean coast in March 1915, when her commander scuttled the vessel rather than see her fall into British hands. As a result of the Battle of the Falklands, most of Germany's traditional surface raiders had been removed from the high seas and with the prospect of losing more warships if they put to sea, for the most part, the German navy was thought to have contented itself with converting merchant ships into commercial raiders, although these generally failed to have the same sort of impact as their predecessors had done.

Some two weeks after the Battle of the Falklands however; and with elements of the Royal Navy still making their way back from the South Atlantic, the German navy did undertake one of its most infamous maritime actions against Great Britain, when a large flotilla of their warships launched a bombardment against the north east coast of England, striking the towns of Scarborough, Whitby and Hartlepool. Designed principally as a hit-and-run raid that would draw local Royal Navy ships into a confrontation with the much bigger eighty five strong German squadron, this attack on the British mainland was reported to have been approved by the Kaiser himself, although had been planned by Admiral Franz Von Hipper, the same German commander who had seen his ships devastated at the First Battle of Heligoland Bight. The British Admiralty were thought to have been aware that a naval raid of some sort was being planned by Germany, having previously captured code books from enemy ships, but they had no clear idea where the raid itself was to take place, so were forced to rely on listening out for radio traffic, or reports of German ships being made by various passing vessels. As a consequence, the British commander of the Grand Fleet at Scapa Flow, Admiral John Jellicoe was reported to have ordered a squadron of four battle cruisers and six modern Dreadnoughts to begin patrolling the North Sea, to try and find the German flotilla; and in the event that they did, to bring them to battle. At the same time, the Admiralty was also thought to have instructed Commodores Tyrwhitt and Keyes, two other highly experienced commanders, to take their squadrons of cruisers, destroyers and submarines to sea, in order to try and trace the German warships.

Around the same time, Hipper and his large naval force were said to have left the safety of the Jade River on the morning of the 15th December 1914 and slowly made their way into the North Sea, being careful to avoid unnecessary radio traffic that might alert the Royal Navy's Grand Fleet, which was based further north in Scapa Flow. However, as they made their way into the North Sea, Hipper was reported to have lost a handful of his ships, some of which had become detached from the main flotilla and others that the German commander had ordered home for some unknown reason. Despite these handful of losses though, the German force still represented a formidable threat by the time Hipper began to divide his ships on the morning of the 16th December 1914, sending some to Hartlepool and others to Scarborough, whilst others began to lay mines off the British coast, in the hope that Royal Navy warships or commercial shipping might be damaged, if not destroyed. At eight o'clock in the morning, two of the three German cruisers sent to Scarborough began to shell the town, hitting the town's castle, its main hotel and a number of surrounding buildings, causing the local population to flee to the local railway station and to take to the roads in an effort to escape the barrage. However, after some ninety minutes, the shelling was said to have stopped, as the two German warships moved off, travelling next to the town of Whitby, where at around ten o'clock in the morning they began to open fire on their second coastal target, where they were known to have caused considerable damage to a coastguard station and to historic Whitby Abbey. Around the same time, a second detachment of three German cruisers had arrived off the coast of Hartlepool, a much more important military target, given the presence of its docks, factories and naval vessels, which were said to have been defended by three six inch guns that were positioned along the seafront. Hartlepool was also known to be home to a local troop garrison, the Durham Light Infantry, who had been alerted to the possibility of a German attack and had been supplied with live ammunition, in order to repel any land based assault. Unfortunately, a similar warning had not been passed on to the Royal Navy units that were charged with patrolling the local waters, resulting in two light cruisers and a submarine remaining in the harbour, whilst the four Royal Navy destroyers that were at sea, were said to have been ill-equipped to deal with the much larger German cruisers and having shown token resistance, were forced to retire out of harms way. Although one of the moored British cruisers did attempt to steam out to meet the enemy ships, having been struck by German gunfire, its commander was forced to beach his vessel, in order to prevent it from sinking.

By eleven o'clock in the morning of the 16th December 1914, nearly one hundred and forty people had been killed and around six hundred others had been wounded during the German raid on the east coast of England, most of whom were entirely innocent civilians going about their daily lives. Having completed their bombardment of the three towns, the two detachments of German cruisers were reported to have withdrawn to meet up with the remainder of the fleet that was thought to have been stationed in and around the Dogger Bank, where they hoped to ambush any pursuing Royal Navy vessels. Unfortunately for both sides, a combination of bad weather, poor communications and heavy seas, all contrived to prevent the two sides confronting one another in any sort of meaningful or decisive manner. Although it was later reported that both sides very nearly fell into traps, placed by their adversaries, once again poor judgement, bad communications and possibly a little bit of luck, helped the Royal Navy maintain its numerical superiority over the Germans, following the naval raids on Scarborough, Hartlepool and Whitby. Save for the minimal damage caused to three German cruisers and that done to three British destroyers, neither side suffered any significant losses during the incident, other than the land based casualties and the loss of prestige incurred by Britain and her Royal Navy, which ultimately led to the relocation of some warships, to ensure that such a humiliating raid could not reoccur again. More importantly perhaps, was the effect that the resulting civilian deaths had on the psyche of the British nation as a whole, with posters proclaiming "Remember Scarborough" being used to encourage the country's young men to enlist in her armed forces and to seek revenge on Germany. It was undoubtedly such incidents, as well as the later bombing of civilian centres, through the use of airships that helped create the national antagonism between the native peoples of Britain and Germany, which would continue to exist right through to the present day.

From an entirely German point of view, the successful raid on the east coast of England was regarded as a victory, even though the large military fleet only managed to kill and wound a large number of civilians, as well as damage three Royal Navy destroyers, which were quickly repaired or replaced. The German commander of the expedition, Admiral Franz Von Hipper was said to have been extremely keen to repeat the exercise, this time by planning to attack the British fishing fleet which regularly located itself around Dogger Bank in the North Sea, right in between Germany's northern ports and the British mainland. However, once again though, the British Admiralty's intelligence services were aware of the proposed raid, which was planned for 23rd January 1915 and began to move Royal Navy cruiser units into the area from both Rosyth and Harwich, in the hope that Hipper's ships could be caught in between the two British squadrons. Having sighted the foremost vessels of the German flotilla at around seven o'clock in the morning of the 24th January, one of the Royal Navy squadrons, under the command of Admiral David Beatty, immediately steamed towards the enemy vessels, sighting the larger German battle cruisers about an hour later. As the Royal Navy's cruiser squadron came into view on the horizon, Hipper was reported to have ordered his ships to turn for home, although at least one of his older ships was thought to have been so slow that she lagged behind the rest, causing her to come into the range of British guns before any of the others. At just after nine o'clock in the morning, the German cruiser SMS Blucher, which was positioned at the rear of the four enemy ships, had already come within range of the British guns and was in serious danger of being hit by Royal Navy shells. With Admiral Beatty having five heavy cruisers to Hipper's four, the British commander was determined that none of the German ships should escape and set off in hot pursuit of the faster enemy vessels in an attempt to bring them to battle, when he could use his bigger guns to bombard them from a safe distance. Unfortunately, by eleven o'clock in the morning Hipper had already made the decision to leave SMS Blucher to her fate and ordered his three remaining cruisers, one of which was severely damaged, to run for home with Beatty's ships close behind. Once again though, ill-fortune and poor communication resulted in the Royal Navy squadron breaking off its pursuit of the three German battle cruisers, who all subsequently managed to reach the safety of German waters, albeit in a state of some disrepair, leaving SMS Blucher to face the full weight of the Royal Navy's guns alone. However, despite being heavily damaged, the German ship continued to fight, even though she was reported to have been struck up to fifty times by British shells, although in the end it was two torpedoes that caused her to capsize and sink, taking with her some eight hundred members of her crew.

Admiral Horace Hood   Admiral R Arbuthnot   Admiral Scheer

Although not a outright defeat for the German navy, the loss of SMS Blucher and her crew was thought to have been heavily criticised by Kaiser Wilhelm himself, who subsequently instructed the head of his navy to avoid confronting the Royal Navy when there was little certainty of a German victory, an approach that had been already been adopted by the leadership of the High Seas Fleet. However, the fact that the Royal Navy's gunnery had been so inaccurate during the Battle of Dogger Bank and that the German battleships had proved to be so resistant to damage from British shells, gave them hope of achieving more positive results in any future engagements with the British Grand Fleet. Even in the light of German failures at Dogger Bank, the Kaiser's navy continued to mount operations in and around the North Sea, in the hope of luring smaller British forces into a sea battle with superior German numbers, although for the most part and with the Royal Navy regularly intercepting German radio messages, such traps were rarely sprung. However, the single most definitive naval engagement between the two navies throughout the entire period of the First World War was said to have occurred between the 31st May 1916 and the 1st June 1916, in what became known as the Battle of Jutland. Once again, the German plan called for Admiral Franz Von Hipper's fast battle cruisers to sail out of their safe harbours, to try and tempt a smaller and less well armed Royal Navy squadron into a position, where it could be annihilated by the ships of the German High Seas Fleet. Unfortunately, with the British Admiralty being able to intercept and read German radio signals, even before the plan was put into action, Royal Navy commanders were aware that some sort of major naval operation was being planned and the British Grand Fleet, under the command of Admiral John Jellicoe, was brought to a state of readiness. The fact that the Royal Navy was aware of an impending naval action was thought to have caught German navy units relatively unaware, allowing Jellicoe to take his enormous naval force eastward towards Norway, to a position where he might reasonably expect to confront the bulk of Germany's High Seas Fleet and destroy them. Having arranged a rendezvous with Admiral David Beatty and his squadron of fast battle cruisers on the afternoon of May 30th 1916, Jellicoe had instructed Beatty to move forward towards the advancing German fleet, even though they were largely unaware of the size and numbers of the enemy forces that they might encounter. By the afternoon of the following day, Beatty's battle cruisers were reported to be still moving forward towards German waters, when they spotted the leading elements of Hipper's battle cruiser squadron, causing the British commander to order his ships to engage the enemy, a fateful decision that would result in the subsequent loss of two British warships, HMS Indefatigable and HMS Queen Mary, whose thin armour, proved to be little defence against the more accurate German gunnery. Initially, Beatty's forces had been prepared to pursue Hipper's ships southward, with the intention of engaging the enemy until the battle was decided one way or another, which was exactly what the German commander wanted, as he tried to draw Beatty and his vessels closer to Scheer and the main body of the German Grand Fleet. However, at around four thirty in the afternoon, one of Beatty's scout ships was said to have sighted the vanguard of Scheer's fleet, causing the British commander to order his remaining ships to complete a one hundred and eighty degree turn, with the intention of leading Scheers ships back towards Jellicoe and the waiting Royal Navy's Grand Fleet. With four of his battleships providing a screen for his withdrawal, the British commander was said to have continued acting as a decoy for the larger enemy fleet, all the time drawing Admiral Hipper's cruisers and the main body of the German High Seas Fleet, under Admiral Reinhard Scheer, closer and closer to an all out battle with Admiral John Jellico and the waiting Grand Fleet.

Although neither of the two large naval fleets could see one another, by round four o'clock in the afternoon, Admiral Jellicoe was said to have been aware that the German High Seas Fleet was approaching his position and that Beatty's squadron, despite having been badly mauled by Hipper's vessels, was steadily leading the enemy into his grasp. In order to support Beatty, Jellicoe was reported to have instructed Rear Admiral Horace Hood to take his squadron of battle cruisers south to try and find Beatty and his ships, so that he might help strengthen Beatty's position, which he finally managed to do at around five thirty in the afternoon. Perhaps buoyed by Hood's arrival and his own improving strategic position, just before six o'clock in the evening, Beatty was thought to have re-engaged with Hipper's cruisers that were still pursuing him, forcing the German commander to turn his flotilla south where he hoped to link up with the main body of the German High Seas Fleet, which was still slowly being brought northward by Admiral Scheer. Unfortunately for Jellicoe, even though he was thought to have caught sight of Beatty's ships approaching from the south, Scheer's main fleet was still out of view, leaving the British commander in a bit of a quandary, as to where and how he should deploy his vessels in readiness for the coming engagement. Despite signalling Beatty for information regarding the German disposition, the fact that Beatty could not see the main German fleet made the situation even more confusing, especially when Jellicoe began to receive unconfirmed reports of German ships in entirely different positions. As it turned out, Jellicoe was left with little option but to move his ships into a position that was largely based on his own military instincts and the best strategic position, which ultimately proved to be the correct choice, as moving the Grand Fleet eastward, put in him the ideal position to confront Scheer and his large naval flotilla.

By six thirty of the evening of the 31st May 1916, both battle fleets, comprising around two hundred and fifty warships in total, were reported to have sighted one another, marking the start of a series of ferocious engagements that would prove to be extremely costly for both fleets, but more especially for the Royal Navy. With several different squadrons all trying to get into the best position for attacking the enemy, it was reported that several Royal Navy ships came close to colliding with one another, whilst others were said to have been reckless enough to put themselves in danger from German guns, including the armoured cruisers HMS Defence and HMS Warrior. Commanded by Rear Admiral Robert Arbuthnot, these lightly armoured cruisers were thought to have been unsuitable for the coming battle, which was expected to be dominated by the guns of the much larger and more heavily armed Dreadnoughts. However, despite this, Arbuthnot was said to have ordered his flagship, HMS Defence, and her sister ship, HMS Warrior, to attack the crippled German warship Weisbaden, which was drifting under the gun sights of the fast approaching High Seas Fleet, inevitably bringing the two British cruisers within range of the enemy guns. According to contemporary reports, almost as soon as HMS Defence moved in to attack the crippled ship, she began to come under sustained fire from both Scheer's and Hipper's bigger battleship's, one of which fired a shell that struck HMS Defence's magazine, causing the Royal Navy warship to blow up with the loss of all of her nine hundred strong crew. HMS Warrior also came under withering fire from the same German battleships and was only saved from almost certain destruction by the timely arrival of the British Dreadnought, HMS Warspite, which was thought to have made a much better target for the German gunners, than her lighter ally. Despite the loss of HMS Defence and the continuing gunfire from the large German warships, Beatty's cruisers and Hood's battle cruiser squadron returned fire as best they could, even though their strategic position started to become increasingly untenable. A further disaster for the Royal Navy occurred just after six thirty in the evening, when Admiral Hood's flagship, HMS Invincible, was struck by shells fired by two different German warships, which caused her magazine to explode and the ship to break in two, causing the deaths of all but six of the thousand strong crew that were aboard her, including Admiral Hood himself.

For both Scheer and Hipper the course of the battle was going exactly as they expected, in that they believed they had managed to lure, first Beatty's and then Hood's Royal Navy squadrons into a well laid trap, where a numerically superior German fleet had been able to confront and subsequently defeat them. Believing that the second part of the operation was well underway, especially following the destruction of HMS Indefatigable, Queen Mary, Defence, Warrior and Invincible, the possibility of catching and destroying even more Royal Navy ships proved to be too much of a temptation for the two German commanders, who drove their ships on, right into the guns of the waiting Admiral John Jellicoe and the British Grand Fleet. As the German fleet emerged through the light sea mist and the smoke of battle, a number of the Royal Navy's biggest warships, including Jellicoe's flagship Iron Duke, were said to have fired a salvo of shells towards the leading German ships, striking the foremost German Dreadnought Konig several times, although none of these hits were thought to have fatally wounded the great battleship. Taken completely by surprise by the presence of the Grand Fleet, which he had assumed was still anchored in Scapa Flow, Scheer immediately ordered his fleet to turn about, an expertly performed manoeuvre that was undoubtedly helped by the increasing mists that were descending on the area. However, rather than pursue the fleeing German warships directly south, Jellicoe was said to have moved his forces slightly east, so that he could shadow the movement of Scheer's vessels, perhaps to intercept the German fleet later in the evening. Unfortunately, Scheer was equal to Jellicoe as a strategist and rather than maintain a direct course south, where he could be attacked from the stern, the German commander was reported to have ordered his ships to double back, in an attempt to evade Jellicoe, or at least gain the advantage over him. As it turned out however, the British admiral had already foreseen this manoeuvre, establishing his battle line in such a way that Scheer's fleet would once again sail directly onto the Royal Navy's waiting guns, which they did at seven o'clock in the evening. Unlike the first time, when most of the British ships had failed to fire when they had the German fleet under their guns, this time Scheer's flotilla was reported to have been hit by a barrage of Royal Navy shells that damaged a number of the leading German vessels, whilst only one British ship, the Colossus, received minor damage from enemy fire. Once again though, Scheer was able to employ his about turn tactics, taking his outnumbered and outmatched ships away from the British force, although it was only after a number of his destroyers and cruisers intervened that he was able to withdraw his bigger, more valuable battleships. Facing a fusillade of shells fired by up to eighteen British battleships, these German cruisers and destroyers were reported to have thrown themselves in the way of the intense barrage, during which many of the heavy cruisers were struck numerous times, although thanks to their heavier armour, for the most part they managed to survive the onslaught, giving Scheer the time he needed to withdraw his great capital ships to safety.

In normal circumstances Jellicoe's fleet would have simply pursued Scheer, but with German destroyers launching wave after wave of torpedoes against his forces, the British commander was forced to watch as his vessels scattered to avoid being sunk by them, which none of them were. However, by the time the Royal Navy fleet had been reassembled into some sort of order, valuable time had been lost and the opportunity to destroy Scheer's fleet missed. Although some of the faster British cruisers set out in pursuit, they were said to have been met by a screen of heavy German warships, which had been positioned to protect the German rear, during which contact, both sides exchanged shots with one another, without inflicting any terminal losses. With darkness having fallen, by nine o'clock in the evening of the 31st May 1916, Jellicoe was said to have been reluctant to engage in a major sea battle with the rest of the German fleet until the following morning, when daylight might help them in their cause. However, he still made the decision to steam south with the intention of blocking the German's line of retreat, although he also remembered to position a screen of cruisers and defenders some miles behind the Grand Fleet to ensure that he was not attacked from the rear, in the event that he passed Scheer during the night. Unfortunately, the gap between Jellicoe and his rear screen was thought to have become so big that it allowed Scheer and the entire German High Seas Fleet to simply break through the overstretched line of British destroyers, attacking those that happened to get in their way, who for some unknown reason failed to contact Jellicoe's main Royal Navy force to advise him of Scheer's actual position. Other British commanders were thought to have refrained from confronting the German ships because they received no orders to do so, whilst others did not report their sightings of enemy vessels because they did not want to break radio silence, all of which resulted in Jellicoe's Grand Fleet observing individual sea battles from a distance, without having the vaguest idea of which particular ships were involved. It was during the individual battles between German and Royal Navy ships, the ones observed from a distance by Jellicoe and his fleet that additional vessels from both sides were attacked, damaged and destroyed, although for the most part such defeats and victories occurred in relative isolation, only being recognised in the cold light of day, when the loss of individual ships was finally recognised. Between midnight and six o'clock in the morning of the 1st June 1916, several more British ships were said to have been lost and damaged, whilst German losses were relatively light, in part because other Royal Navy commanders refused to engage enemy ships that were within their sights, ostensibly to prevent their position being given away.

Almost as soon as the German High Seas Fleet had returned to its home ports, the German authorities were publicly announcing the success of their naval forces against the Royal Navy, which given the total number of losses on both sides was an entirely reasonable conclusion. For their part, the British press were already beginning to report the heavy losses suffered by Admiral Jellicoe's forces, although it was already being suggested that the losses were entirely due to the fact that smaller Royal Navy units had engaged a much larger and better armed German fleet, implying that they had deliberately taken on a superior force and suffered heavy casualties as a result. However, the reality was entirely different, as the British Grand Fleet was reported to have outnumbered the German High Seas Fleet by some one hundred and fifty ships to one hundred respectively, yet lost significantly more ships to German arms than they managed to destroy themselves. Many of these differences in military performance were thought to have been the result of better German technologies in the fields of shipbuilding, armaments, range finding and night equipment, all of which were markedly superior to their British counterparts. However, such obvious advantages aside, the British Admiralty's continuing habit of failing to pass on vitally important information to its commanders and the failure to remove incompetent officers from positions of authority, especially at sea, remained a significant drawback in the country's efforts to maintain its historic superiority over other emerging naval powers. Despite all of these shortcomings though, following the Battle of Jutland, Britain's Grand Fleet still managed to maintain its numerical advantage over the German High Seas Fleet, at least in terms of the heavy Dreadnoughts that both navies possessed. Within a matter of weeks, both British and German fleets were reported to have replaced their lost vessels, seemingly bigger, stronger and wiser than they had been before, although such changes made little difference to the many thousands of sailors from both sides who actually perished in the generally indecisive Battle of Jutland. For its part, total Royal Navy losses during the short, but devastating sea battle led to six cruisers and eight destroyers being lost, along with over six thousand British seamen, whilst Germany lost one battleship, five cruisers, five torpedo boats and an estimated two and a half thousand crewmen, less than half of the Royal Navy's total losses. The marked difference in casualty figures between the two sides was almost certainly caused by the previously mentioned flaws within the Royal Navy itself, including lack of armouring on gun turrets, handling and storage of munitions by the ships crews, a general failure to maintain safety protocols and the growing number of British captain's, who failed to engage an enemy ship, unless expressly instructed to do so by a superior officer. Although a number of these weaknesses were subsequently resolved, with additional armour being added to turrets and decks, along with changes in the storage and composition of munitions, ultimately bad decision making and tactics by some less competent Royal Navy officers continued to occur right through to the end of the Second World War, by which time Britain's supremacy of the high seas was already coming to an almost inevitable end.

Capt William Tennant

Admiral Ramsay

Philippe Petain

By the end of the First World War, Britain still retained the largest naval forces in the world, but was being closely followed by the navies of the United States and the emerging Japanese Empire, with all three nations undertaking significant shipbuilding programs in the immediate post-war era. With the United States declaring its intention to have the biggest and best navy in the world, the Japanese enlarging its naval forces to help support its own far eastern expansionism, Britain was left with little option but to embark on a massive program of rebuilding, if it was to retain its status as the world's pre-eminent naval power. Recognising the dangers of this unfolding arms race, by the early 1920's politicians on both sides of the Atlantic were reported to have been calling for international restraint, as a result of which, in 1921 the world's five leading naval powers, Great Britain, the United States, France, Italy and Japan, all met in America, to discuss ways of bringing the naval arms race to an equitable end. The resulting Washington Naval Treaty, which was signed by all five countries on the 6th February 1922, was designed to limit the numbers and size of warships that any of the signatories could build, in an attempt to prevent any single country from gaining an insurmountable advantage over the others, especially one that might be used in a time of war. Although all five nations initially agreed to the various terms of the treaty, such was the ever changing nature of naval warfare, in terms of new ship designs and weapons development that the actual terms of the treaty were known to have been subsequently modified, both in 1930 and in 1936. For the Royal Navy specifically, the signing of the Washington Naval Treaty in 1922 was reported to have led to the cancelling of a whole new range of battleships, which had been intended to replace many of the vessels that had been built prior to World War I, but which now had to be refitted, in order to maintain the Empire's strategic trade routes and supply lines. Although for the most part, all five nations were thought to have signed the treaty in good faith, throughout the 1920's and 1930's, most of the signatories were reported to have found ways of circumventing the strict terms of the agreement, simply to give their own ships some form of advantage over their international competitors. However, despite the best intentions of the Washington Naval Treaty and the two subsequent London Naval Treaties, by the middle of the 1930's the path to a second world war was already being laid, by the rise of the National Socialist Party in Germany and military hardliners within the Japanese government, both of which led to the agreements effectively becoming void, especially after Japan withdrew from the treaties in 1936.

Despite having been restricted by the terms of the various naval agreements, signed in 1922, 1930 and 1936, during that same period, Britain was still able to build a range of new warships with which to defend its worldwide Empire and vitally important trade routes, including its series of Illustrious and Implacable class aircraft carriers, along with a number of Nelson class battleships, all of which would play their part in the impending international conflict. A total of four Illustrious class carriers were reported to have been constructed between 1939 and 1940, including HMS Illustrious, Formidable, Victorious and Indomitable, just in time for the outbreak of the Second World War, whilst the two Implacable class carriers, HMS Implacable and Indefatigable were both launched in December 1942, at the height of the worldwide conflict. In addition to these new aircraft carriers, which would ultimately prove to be the most important type of naval craft during World War II, the Royal Navy also ordered the construction of two Nelson class warships, HMS Nelson and Rodney, as reinforcements for the Revenge class warships that had first been introduced in 1913. Although both vessels went on to play important roles throughout the course of the Second World War, given their limitations due to the terms of the Washington and London Naval Treaties of the interwar period, they were fairly quickly superceded by the newer King George V class battleships, which were first introduced into the Royal Navy in 1940, with the commissioning of HMS George V. Other King George V battleships commissioned around the same period included HMS Prince of Wales in 1941, HMS Duke of York in 1941, HMS Howe in 1942 and HMS Anson in 1942.

However, in the initial stages of the Second World War, when Britain and her allies were only facing the military threat of Nazi Germany and her Axis cohorts, many of the Royal Navy's assets were spread around the globe, helping to form part of the various imperial fleets, which Britain had assigned to protect its various overseas territories. Apart from the Home Fleet which was tasked with protecting Britain's home waters, from the Scottish Isles to the English Channel, the Royal Navy was also compelled to assign significant assets to the Mediterranean, where the British bases of Gibraltar, Malta and the ports of North Africa needed to be protected from the threat of Axis attack. Similarly, British colonies in the Far East were reported to have been protected by the naval assets attached to the China and East India Stations, which were later reformed as the Eastern Fleet and tasked with safeguarding the numerous imperial territories in and around the Indian and Pacific Oceans. The final Royal Navy vessels operating well away from Britain were those ships that were charged with protecting British interests in the Caribbean and the South Atlantic, which were collectively known as the North American and West Indies Station, who were charged with patrolling the vitally important trade routes from the Americas to Europe and that were reported to have acted in conjunction with the American and Canadian navies, effectively protecting the entire east coast of the New World from enemy attacks.

Although the Royal Navy was deployed in most areas of the world, for the most part, much of its service was thought to have taken place in the Atlantic, the Mediterranean and in the Indian Ocean, with the Pacific theatre largely featuring the considerable naval assets of the United States, Australia and New Zealand, who were occupied with confronting the military threat posed by the Imperial Japanese Navy. Right from the outbreak of the Second World War, the Royal Navy was said to have been compelled to defend Britain's vital trade routes, one of the most important being that which stretched across the vastness of the Atlantic, from the great eastern seaports of North America, to the western harbours of Britain, representing the last crucial lifeline between the New World and the now largely subjugated European continent. However, in the first stages of World War II, rather than being able to take an entirely offensive approach against Nazi Germany and her facist allies, Britain's navy was forced to undertake a number of reactive operations against the growing German threat, the two most notable being the rescue of the Allied armies from Dunkirk between the 27th May and the 4th June 1940 and the deliberate destruction of the captive French fleet at Mers-el-Kebir on the 3rd July 1940.

The first of these pivotal naval undertakings, the evacuation of the British Expeditionary Force and their French allies from the European continent, which was more formally known as Operation Dynamo, later came to symbolise the spirit of the entire British nation during World War II, largely because of the heroism, stoicism and selflessness that was shown by many of those involved in what was first and foremost a humbling military retreat. Having been pushed back towards the English Channel by the seemingly unstoppable German army, which had largely outmanoeuvred the allies at every turn, for most observers it seemed likely that the entire allied army, comprising some four hundred thousand men would simply be surrounded and forced to surrender by the advancing German troops. However, despite seemingly having the allies at their mercy, on the 24th May 1940 the German advance was suddenly and inexplicably halted, allowing British and French leaders to plan for the limited evacuation of some of their soldiers, which in the first instance was intended to be around forty five thousand troops, approximately 10% of the total force that was said to have been trapped around the French port of Dunkirk. Interestingly, at the time it was reported that the German advance had been stopped on the direct orders of Adolph Hitler, who it was claimed was eager to secure a peace treaty with Britain and was willing to release the British Expeditionary Force, in order to achieve that political goal. However, later investigations in the post war period revealed that it was one of Hitler's leading field commanders, General Von Rundstedt, who had called a halt, in order to allow German infantry to move forward, who could then confront the thousands of allied soldiers who were protecting the area around Dunkirk. Eager to protect his vitally important mechanised forces, including the infamous Panzer tanks, Von Rundstedt was said to have consulted with Hitler before ordering a temporary halt on the 24th May 1940, instructing his tank commanders to simply blockade the routes in and out of the allied held areas. It was only on the 27th May that sufficient German infantry and artillery units were brought within range of Dunkirk and the military assault began once again, although by this time Winston Churchill and allied planners back in London had decided to try and attempt a generally small scale evacuation by sea. Although Operation Dynamo officially began at around 7.00pm on the 26th May 1940, given what was left of the day, most historians tend to identify the 27th May as the first full day of the evacuation, even though a small number of passenger ships arrived in Dunkirk to ferry away the first allied soldiers, who were then returned to Britain. It was only on the 27th that a Royal Navy officer, Captain Tennant, arrived in Dunkirk and began to properly organise the evacuation, arranging for the troops to be embarked on the various passenger ships and Royal Navy destroyers that were slowly but surely arriving from the English south coast ports. Constantly running the risk of being attacked by German artillery and aircraft, on the first full day of operations just fewer than eight thousand allied troops were snatched from Dunkirk harbour, a tiny proportion of the four hundred thousand men, who were said to have been trapped within the increasingly dangerous military bubble.

By the start of the second full day of Operation Dynamo, the 28th May 1940, the system of evacuating the servicemen, organised by Tennant, was reported to have picked up speed, as organisers around the beaches and harbour got to grips with the systems of selecting and boarding the various military units that were scattered throughout the area. Although one of the larger passenger ships was said to have been lost to enemy action, the arrival of a large number of Dutch fishing vessels and coastal crafts, which had managed to avoid German forces were said to have added significantly to the evacuation process, as their shallow draught allowed them to come close inshore and rescue large numbers of troops directly from the open French beaches. By the end of the second full day, an estimated twenty thousand soldiers were said to have been rescued, although with all of the naval activity, so the incidents of ship losses were reported to have increased, a fact that was said to have led to the withdrawal of the Royal Navy's more valuable modern destroyers on the third day of operations, on the 30th May 1940, by which time the number of rescued servicemen was estimated to have reached some eighty thousand men. However, the large numbers of men being embarked from both Dunkirk harbour and its surrounding beaches was said to have been helped by the vagaries of the weather conditions, which helped to obscure much of the area and limit the abilities of the German Luftwaffe to fly over the port and attack the allied ships that were busily trying to load their battered and weary passengers. Unfortunately, as the conditions changed, so did the numbers of attacks by enemy aircraft, assaults that were only moderately reduced by the Royal Air Force fighter pilots which were having to operate from airfields in the south of England, but who did what they could to reduce German air attacks, often at great cost to themselves. By the 30th May 1940 and following the intervention of Admiral Ramsey, the man responsible for running Operation Dynamo, the Royal Navy's modern destroyers were returned to the area, in order to offer support to the older warships and numerous civilian craft that were still employed in trying to rescue as many allied soldiers as possible, before the outlying defences of the Dunkirk bubble were overcome and the port was eventually overcome by the pressing German forces.

Admiral Darlan   **Admiral Genoul**   **Admiral Somerville**

By Sunday the 2nd June 1940 it was estimated that only six thousand British and some seventy thousand French troops remained in and around Dunkirk, a remarkable figure when one considers that some four hundred thousand troops had been packed into the relatively small allied enclave less than a week before. Even though the evacuation had managed to rescue previously unimaginable hundreds of thousands of men, the British authorities simply refused to abandon any troops, until such time as there was no hope left to rescue them from Dunkirk. Consequently, even as late as the evening of the 3rd June and into the late morning of the 4th June, a further twenty six thousand mainly French troops were lifted from Dunkirk, until at last at 10.30am in the morning, the last British ships sailed out from Dunkirk, bringing an end to Operation Dynamo, one of the greatest seaborne evacuations that had ever been undertaken. By the time that the final figures were calculated by the British authorities, and estimated three hundred and thirty eight thousand allied soldiers had been safely delivered from almost certain death or imprisonment, an almost unbelievable number of men, given that the intention had only ever been to rescue around forty five thousand, when the operation was first proposed by allied planners. For British Prime Minister, Winston Churchill, the "Miracle of Dunkirk" represented mixed fortunes, in that, despite the fact that over three hundred thousand men had been saved, another seventy thousand allied troops had either been killed, wounded or taken prisoner, losses which had gained the nation absolutely no advantage whatsoever. In addition to these human losses, the British Expeditionary Force was also reported to have lost virtually all of its equipment, including thousands of artillery pieces, tens of thousands of vehicles and millions of pounds worth of munitions and other stores, all of which had been abandoned in Nazi controlled Europe. Those losses aside, hundreds of much needed fighter aircraft had been lost both before and during the evacuation at Dunkirk, whilst some twenty or more Royal Navy destroyers were reported to have been lost or damaged, in addition to several hundred other naval vessels lost before and during the operation. It was thought to be as a partial result of these equipment losses and the need to replace them that inevitably set Britain on the road to national paucity, which resulted in the country having to borrow significant amounts of money, often in the form of loans from the likes of the United States.

Despite Churchill describing the failure of the British Expeditionary Force in France as a great military disaster, it was his early belief that the whole root, core and brain of the British Army had been stranded in Europe that was said to have concerned him the most, especially as these men might well have been lost to the actual defence of Britain itself, leaving the country open to invasion. Although the civilian population were initially unaware of the disaster unfolding in France, as concerns grew within the establishment and national leaders, including the King and the Archbishop of Cantebury, called for prayers to be said for British troops, it quickly became evident that things were becoming increasingly desparate for the British soldiers fighting in France. The willingness of the British public to play their own part in the fight against facism was publicly demonstrated by the crews of the dozens of "little boats" which made their way across the

English Channel to help ferry many thousands of British and French troops from the beaches of Dunkirk, to the larger passenger ships and Royal Navy vessels that were lying offshore, ready to return them to Britain. Lifeboats, fishing vessels and pleasure craft from the entire length of the country were reported to have made their way south, to help shuttle the stranded servicemen from the shoreline, to the larger ships lying off the French coast, their shallow draughts allowing them to come close in to the lines of soldiers, many of whom had been waiting for many hours in freezing cold water, in the hope of being picked up by one of the smaller boats. With the operation completed successfully, Churchill's earlier warning to the British Parliament, telling them to expect hard and heavy tidings, was later tempered by what he himself described as a miracle. However, Churchill also recognised that Dunkirk was a military withdrawal, a retreat and should not therefore be regarded as a victory in any sense, although the fact that so many vitally important British troops had been returned to Britain was said to have given the country a huge boost of confidence, at a time when so much of the news was extremely bleak. Despite having lost so much of their equipment in the evacuation from Dunkirk, the soldiers themselves were the irreplaceable assets that Churchill had feared losing most of all, but with so many troops having been returned, he was now confident that Hitler's forces would never be able to launch a successful invasion of the British Isles. With that belief once again restored, the Prime Minister was not only able to bolster British resistance to Nazi Germany both within his own war cabinet and in the country generally, but also felt confident enough to state;

"Even though large tracts of Europe and many famous States have fallen or may fall into the grip of the Gestapo and all the odious apparatus of Nazi rule, we shall not flag or fail. We shall go on to the end. We shall fight in France, we shall fight in the seas and oceans, we shall fight with growing confidence and growing strength in the air; we shall defend our Island, whatever the cost may be. We shall fight in the fields and in the streets, we shall fight in the hills; we shall never surrender; and even if, which I do not for a moment believe, this Island, or a large part of it were subjugated and starving, then our Empire beyond the seas, armed and guarded by the British Fleet, would carry on the struggle, until, in God's good time, the New World, with all its power and might, steps forth to the rescue and the liberation of the Old."

When France was first threatened by Nazi Germany, it was hoped that the combined British and French armies might be able to repulse Hitler's forces, although having attacked France on the 10th May 1940, within a matter of weeks the combined allied armies had been thrown back towards Dunkirk, Paris had been abandoned by the French government and the newly appointed French Premier, Philippe Petain had been forced to request an armistice from the German leadership, which was signed on the 22nd June 1940. With the Fall of France, British leaders, both political and military, were reported to have become increasingly concerned over the future of France's naval assets, which were then stationed at the port of Mers-el-Kebir in French controlled Algeria and at the French port of Toulon. With the possibility of these military resources being seized by Nazi Germany and subsequently used against the allied cause, Britain's Prime Minister, Winston Churchill, was said to have demanded that the Admiral Darlan, the commander of the French fleet, should issue orders to his crews that all of the remaining ships should either be brought over to the British side, or that they should be put beyond the use of the German's, possibly by scuttling all of the remaining vessels. Even though Darlan was thought to have given Churchill his personal assurance that his ships would not be allowed to fall into German hands, a pledge that later led to the deliberate scuttling of French ships at Toulon, the British war leader was said to have remained unconvinced by Darlan's assurances and so initiated a plan to ensure that those warships stationed at Mers-el-Kebir could not be used against Britain or the Royal Navy. Prior to the operation that was launched against the French fleet in Algeria, Churchill also ordered that all French naval vessels anchored in British ports should be seized by local military forces, in order to prevent them leaving port and perhaps falling into enemy hands, although the seizures themselves were reported to have been resisted by their French crews, who having been overcome were subsequently given a choice of either joining the Free French navy, or being repatriated back to France, where they would almost certainly be interned as Prisoners of War. A particularly vociferous critic of the British actions regarding the seizure of the French ships was said to have been the leader of the Free French Forces, General Charles de Gaulle, a highly antagonistic and troublesome individual, who was said to have been deeply suspicious of the British leadership and of Britain generally.

However, despite the resistance of De Gaulle and other opponents, Churchill was determined to resolve the issue of the remaining French naval forces that were stationed in Algeria; and as a result ordered Admiral James Somerville, of the Royal Navy's Force H, which was anchored at Gibraltar, to deliver an ultimatum to the commanders of the French naval forces in Mers-el-Kebir. With his heavily armed British squadron lying offshore, Somerville was said to have sent one of his French speaking flag officers, Captain Cedric Holland, into the port to deliver the British ultimatum to the French commanders. Making it clear that Britain still regarded France as an important military ally, the communiqué was said to have informed the French naval commanders that they could either deliver their vessels into British hands, transport them to the French West Indies, where they would be away from any sort of German threat, but that they could not remain at Mers-el-Kebir where they remained a possible acquisition for the German Navy. In the event that the French commanders were not willing to accept either of the suggested solutions, then the British ultimatum also advised them that unless a decision was made within six hours then the Royal Navy would have no other option but to open fire on the French fleet and put the vessels beyond use through military means. Unfortunately, with the ultimatum being delivered to the senior French commander at Mers-el-Kebir, Admiral Gensoul, who then had to relay the communiqué to his superior, Admiral Darlan, it has been reported that only parts of the ultimatum were delivered to Darlan, which made no mention of the fleet being delivered to a neutral Caribbean port, a solution that the French authorities had already considered, if their naval vessels came under threat of being seized. Instead, Darlan was said to have been informed that the Royal Navy had given French commanders two simple options, either to willingly put their vessels beyond use themselves, or have them disabled through the use of British military force. Clearly for the French, the very idea of deliberately disabling or destroying their country's naval forces was not an option that the French commanders were prepared to consider, unless they came under direct threat of seizure by the German Navy. As the hours passed it became increasingly clear that neither side was prepared to compromise and so Admiral Somerville was left with little option but to confirm the orders he had received from Churchill's War Cabinet and having done so, began to position his squadron in readiness for attacking those French warships which lay in the Algerian port.

Codenamed Operation Catapult, the naval attack on the French fleet at Mers-el-Kebir, was not universally welcomed by many of those British sailors who had been ordered to carry out the assault, Admiral Somerville being one of the most public critics of the plan. However, for Winston Churchill, the need to prove Britain's military resolve, even in the most testing circumstances, was far more important than the worry of offending French national pride, especially if it resulted in the Germans being deprived the highly prized French naval assets that were stationed in Algeria. It is worth recalling perhaps that at the same time that Britain stood alone, the American President, Franklin D Roosevelt, was already being informed by many within his administration that Britain could not stand against Nazi Germany and would almost certainly fall victim to Hitler's armed forces within a relatively short time, an assessment that Churchill was determined to disprove. By demonstrating to the rest of the Free World, to Britain's enemies and to those nations held under the Nazi heel that Britain would go to any lengths in order to defeat facism, Churchill proved in the most public way possible that he was prepared to prosecute the war by whatever means were necessary, even if that meant upsetting some of Britain's closest military allies.

Admiral Lutjens   Captain Lindemann   Admiral Erich Raeder

Beginning at around 6.00pm on the 3rd July 1940, the Royal Navy's Force H, comprising the battleships HMS Hood, Valiant and Resolution, along with the aircraft carrier HMS Ark Royal were reported to have launched their initial assault against the French vessels anchored in Mers-el-Kebir, which included the battleships Provence and Bretagne, the battle cruisers, Dunkerque and Strasbourg, along with a handful of smaller destroyers and associated support ships. With the French warships limited by the confines of the harbour, when the Royal Navy's battleships finally opened fire on the early evening of the 3rd July, French commanders found themselves unable to fully respond, simply because they could not reposition their vessels in time. Within minutes of being targeted by the British guns, the French battleship Bretagne was reported to have been struck by a salvo which ignited her magazine, causing the ship to sink with the loss of nearly a thousand men, a dreadful loss of life in any circumstances, made worse by the fact that they had been caused by a former allies weapons. In less than an hour, the French warships Provence, Dunkerque and at least two destroyers had been badly damaged, or deliberately run aground to prevent them sinking. By the end of the attack a total of some thirteen hundred French servicemen were reported to have been killed, some four hundred injured and seven French warships had been either sunk, damaged or run aground, whilst the Royal Navy suffered minimal losses, comprising six aircraft lost and two servicemen killed. In the immediate aftermath of the attack, Anglo-French relations were said to have been severely strained and there was a great deal of anger amongst certain sections of the French population, who were outraged to hear about the destruction of their naval vessels by their supposed ally. In response to the attack, a few days later French aircraft were reported to have launched a retaliatory assault against Royal Navy ships based in Gibraltar, although according to most sources it has been suggested that these raids were undertaken purely as a token military response, rather than any real intention to cause damage to the Royal Navy's assets. However, despite the British assault, the French warships Dunkerque, Provence and Mogadore were able to be repaired and returned to the French port of Toulon, where in an ironic twist they later became targets for the German Navy, who were anxious to acquire them for their war against the allies, although as promised, all three ships were subsequently scuttled by their French crews to prevent them falling into enemy hands.

During the initial phases of the Second World War, much of the news for Britain's besieged population was reported to have been bad, especially when Germany launched their air assault against the country, in what became commonly known as the Battle of Britain, a campaign that was eventually won by the young aviators, who Churchill later immortalised as "The Few". At sea, the Royal Navy had managed to survive their losses at Dunkirk and was busily building a new range of warships and aircraft carriers to carry the fight forward, despite the fact that the German Navy remained a relatively small, but still dangerous, maritime threat to Britain's long established supply lines. As early as the beginning of the 1930's, when the National Socialist's first came to power in Germany, the new Nazi regime had begun to rebuild their country's shattered military forces, including its navy. However, rather than trying to construct a fleet that could match the British, in terms of size and numbers, instead German planners were reported to have concentrated their efforts in producing a relatively small number of extremely powerful surface raiders, the pocket battleships, which were not only designed to interrupt British trade routes, but also to confront and destroy any British naval asset that they might come across in the vast expanse of the Atlantic Ocean. One of the most formidable of these German raiders was the pocket battleship Bismarck, which had first been laid down in 1936, launched in 1939 and brought into service in August 1940, just in time to begin a raiding campaign, against a by then, largely isolated Britain. Although there had been an intention to construct a significant number of these extremely fast, highly manoeuvrable and heavily armed warships, the outbreak of the Second World War and the demands that it placed on Germany's industry and economy, was said to have ensured that large numbers of such ships were never ctually built.

Having undergone extensive sea trials in the comparatively safe waters of the Baltic, by May 1941, Bismarck was ready to begin her first foray into the North Atlantic, where she would be accompanied by the heavy German battlecruiser Prinz Eugen. Although it had originally been intended that Bismarck would be joined by the warships Scharnhorst, Gneisenau, or even her sister ship Tirpitz, problems and unforeseen delays with all three of these vessels was said to have made their attendance impossible, forcing the two great German battleships to set out together, with a small number of destroyers and support craft, rather than as part of a much larger naval force. However, despite these setbacks, the overall commander of the German expedition, Admiral Gunther Lutjens was said to have been supremely confident that the two warships and their escorts were more than capable of carrying out their mission, to disrupt British supply lines, destroy any British ships that they encountered and to divert Royal Navy resources from other vitally important theatres of operations. However, with the British being aware of the threat posed by the likes of Bismarck, Prinz Eugen and Germany's other great capital ships, a careful watch was said to have been kept on the two most obvious routes that such vessels might use to enter the North Atlantic, including the Kiel Canal and the routes in and out of the Baltic. Even though the Admiralty was reported to have been monitoring German communications, it was reported to have been largely due to the observations of a Norwegian or Swedish informant that the Royal Navy eventually became aware of the German battle group, which was making its way into the North Atlantic and thereby presenting itself as a potential threat to British interests. As a result the Royal Navy was said to have despatched an aircraft to reconnoitre the Norwegian coast, where it positively identified the two German battleships on the afternoon of the 21st May 1941, as they lay close to the main port of Bergen. Having received photographic evidence of the German battle groups position, the Admiralty were then reported to have sent orders for the battleships, HMS Prince of Wales, Hood and a number of British destroyers to make their way northward, to the area of the Denmark Straits and Faroe Islands, where they might reasonably expect to intercept the two German raiders and bring them to battle.

As Bismarck and Prinz Eugen made their way towards the Denmark Straits, the channel that lies between Iceland and Greenland; and which offered the safest route into the North Atlantic shipping lanes, even more Royal Navy vessels were reported to be converging on the area, including the British cruisers HMS Suffolk and Norfolk, as well as the battleship HMS King George V and the aircraft carrier HMS Victorious. However, being generally unaware of these facts, Admiral Lutjens and his two great warships were said to have continued with their journey regardless; and even when unexpectedly confronted by the two British cruisers, HMS Suffolk and Norfolk, on the evening of the 23rd May 1941, such was the superior firepower of the two German battleships, they were able to very quickly drive the two British warships away. However, in the early hours of the following morning, Saturday the 24th May 1941, as the two German vessels emerged from the Denmark Straits they suddenly found themselves confronted by two unidentified ships, which as it turned out was the British capital ships HMS Prince of Wales and the much older, World War I battleship, HMS Hood. As both pairs of ships stood off from one another at a distance of some twelve miles, it was the British ships that were reported to have opened fire first, concentrating their guns on the leading German ship, which they incorrectly believed to be Bismarck, but that was in fact Prinz Eugen. Perhaps assessing the threat that confronted him, Captain Lindemann, the commander of Bismarck was reported to have initially held his fire, until finally bringing his main guns to bear on the leading British battleship, which just happened to be the ageing HMS Hood. As the two sides began to close the distance between one another, both Bismarck and Prinz Eugen were said to have targeted HMS Hood with their guns and before long the British battleship was reported to have been struck by at least one shell, which caused a major fire near the centre of the ship that her crew struggled to extinguish. Despite the fire onboard though, HMS Hood continued to fire at Prinz Eugen, whilst HMS Prince of Wales was said to busily targeting Bismarck, which now began directing its fire towards the second, much more modern British warship. As the range continued to close between the two forces, Hood continued to fire salvo after salvo against the German ships, with her final shots reportedly being fired as around 6.00am on the 24th May 1941. As the battle raged, Hood was said to have turned to port, in an effort to bring all of her guns to bear on the leading German warship, when quite suddenly a huge plume of flame was said to have erupted from the vessel, followed by a deafening explosion, which saw the ship rise up and split into two, raining debris down on the crew of HMS Prince of Wales, which was reported to have been forced to veer away, to avoid being struck by pieces of the shattered vessel. Out of the fourteen hundred plus men who were said to have been aboard HMS Hood during her final battle, only three were said to have survived her destruction, a catastrophic loss of life in almost any circumstances. However, despite the initial shock of losing the almost legendary Hood and so many comrades, those aboard HMS Prince of Wales now had to look towards their own safety, although now being confronted by both German raiders, her captain was left with little option but to turn away and simply satify himself with shadowing the enemy battleships from a safe distance. Two later inquiries into the loss of HMS Hood, during what was commonly known as the Battle of the Denmark Straits, both concluded that the mighty vessel had been lost, ostensibly because of an explosion in one of her main ammunition magazines, which in all likelihood was caused by a German shell penetrating her armour, an event that was thought to have been caused in part by the warships last turn to port, which may or may not have made the battleship more susceptible to enemy fire. Additionally, it was also suggested that the earlier deck fire, which had occurred on Hood just prior to her loss and that was said to have been the result of anti-aircraft ammunition being ignited by enemy fire, may have also played a significant part in her loss. Either way though, no blame was subsequently attached to any of those who perished on the warship, but there were doubts raised over whether such an ageing battleship should have been used in the first place, given that in order to compete with the modern battleships of the time, she was known to have required a major refit, something that had already been planned for, but which had been delayed due to the prevailing military situation.

Even though the German force had achieved a notable victory with the destruction of HMS Hood, they were also reported to have paid a significant price for it, in that British gunfire was thought to have caused generally minor structural damage, but also caused a water leak that was slowly contaminating Bismarck's vital fuel oil, forcing her to reduce speed and require repairs. Although the Germans were said to have been jubilant over their destruction of the Hood, for the British Admiralty, what had initially been an operation to hunt down and confront two German surface raiders, had suddenly become a national crusade to avenge the loss of the legendary Hood and its hundreds of crewmen. Mobilising every resource at its disposal, the Admiralty was reported to have despatched additional ships and aircraft to track down the exact location of Bismarck and Prinz Eugen, so that they could be attacked and destroyed by the Royal Navy. Unfortunately, what was not immediately apparent to their British pursuers was that the two German raiders had already separated, with Bismarck intending to sail to the occupied French port of St Nazaire, whilst Prinz Eugen had been ordered to carry out her original mission, to disrupt the trade routes and supply lines that were helping to sustain the British war effort. For the British authorities however, the fact that the two German raiders had separated from one another was relatively unimportant, as their entire focus was levelled against Bismarck, the vessel which was judged to be responsible for the destruction of HMS Hood and therefore the main target for British vengeance.

Even though an initial attempt to attack the Bismarck at sea was said to have been made by aircraft operating from the Royal Navy carrier, HMS Victorious, the assault was thought to have been largely unsuccessful, other than causing minor damage to its superstructure and slowing the great battleship down somewhat. However, due to incompetence by one of the British naval commanders at sea and through the suspicions of Admiral Lutjens, onboard Bismarck, during the 25th and 26th May 1941 his battleship was somehow able to evade the shadowing British forces and disappear into the vastness of the North Atlantic, off the west coast of Ireland. Fortunately for the Royal Navy however, during the 26th May, a Catalina Patrol aircraft, operating from a British base in Northern Ireland was said to have spotted the oil slick emanating from Bismarck and was subsequently able to track the ship and report its proper position to the Admiralty. With the Bismarck's position known, the Royal Navy immediately advised all of its ships in the area to converge on the enemy battleship's position, with elements of the Gibraltar based Force H being brought further north to help confront the still immensely powerful German warship. Comprising the aircraft carrier HMS Ark Royal and the battleships HMS Sheffield and Renown, Force H, with its carrier borne aircraft was thought to have represented the most potent threat to Bismarck, although the plane's first attempted assault against the German battleship was said to have almost ended in disaster, when their pilots incorrectly identified HMS Sheffield as the target and began to attack it by mistake. Fortunately for everyone concerned, the detonators on the aircraft's torpedoes were reported to have been faulty, causing them to detonate as soon as they were dropped by the aircrews, ensuring that HMS Sheffield remained intact. Forced to return to HMS Ark Royal to rearm with contact detonators, rather than the faulty magnetic ones, on their second mission against Bismarck the British aircraft were reported to have successfully located and attacked Bismarck, but without causing any sort of major structural damage to the vessel or its dangerous main armaments. Despite the failure to seriously damage or destroy Bismarck though, at least one of the British torpedoes was said to have struck the warship's vital steering mechanism, making the vessel almost impossible to manoeuvre and ensuring that she was forced to steam in a widely arcing circle, which brought her back towards the British warships, HMS King George V and Rodney, which had been shadowing the pocket battleship for some time. However, despite its limited steering, Bismarck and its highly accurate guns still represented a major threat for any of the following British warships, so it was left to the Royal Navy destroyers and their torpedoes to launch the first assault against the crippled German vessel, with HMS Cossack, Sikh, Maori, Zulu and Piorun all participating in the first engagement against the stranded enemy battleship.

Karl Doenitz Sir Thomas Phillips Captain Langsdorff

For both Lutjens and Lindemann, the fate of their prized warship was clear, as the Royal Navy battle fleet continued to converge on their position and the hope that help might arrive in the shape of German U-boats began to disappear. However, rather than consider surrendering his ship, or scuttling her, as was later the case with the German raider Graf Spee, Lutjens and his subordinate were reported to have made the choice that they and their crew would go down fighting, rather than just meekly submit to the demands of the British forces that were slowly surrounding them. On the morning of the 27th May 1941, two of the Royal Navy warships, HMS King George V and Rodney, were reported to have begun positioning themselves to fire their guns at Bismarck, although both were said to have maintained station around twenty miles distance from the enemy battleship, from where it was hoped that their great guns could pummel her into submission. As the Royal Navy ships began their bombardment of Bismarck at around nine o'clock in the morning, the German gunners aboard the circling pocket battleship were said to have returned fire, even though their own limited manoeuvrability made it difficult for them to accurately target the British vessels that were attacking them. Now joined by other warships, including HMS Norfolk and Dorsetshire, within a matter of minutes the first British shells were thought to have struck Bismarck's superstructure, disabling and destroying a number of her vital gun batteries and control centres, thereby reducing her ability to defend herself from the increasingly accurate British salvoes. Just after nine o'clock in the morning, yet another Royal Navy burst was said to have destroyed the bridge area of the Bismarck, killing most of the senior officers onboard and essentially leaving the ship without anyone in overall command, or to make the decision to signal the vessel's surrender, causing the British to continue firing, even after the battleship was effectively finished as a potential threat. With no sign of the enemy warship being prepared to yield and in some minds still representing a threat to the British ships, HMS Rodney was reported to have closed with Bismarck in order to more accurately lay down fire on the stricken ship, although it quickly became evident that the vessel was no longer capable of defending itself and the Royal Navy warships HMS Rodney, King George V and their destroyer escorts were withdrawn and ordered back to base. The coup de grace was said to have been left to the British warship HMS Dorsetshire, which was said to have launched its remaining torpedoes against Bismarck, with the intention of sending her to the bottom of the sea, although it has also been suggested that the pocket battleship was actually scuttled by her remaining crew, who chose to sink the vessel rather than see their ship fall into British hands. After Bismarck finally slipped below the waves of the North Atlantic at around 10.30am on the 27th May 1941, HMS Dorsetshire and the destroyer HMS Maori were both reported to have stopped to pick up Bismarck's surviving crew, but were forced to abandon the operation after a submarine was detected in their general vicinity. According to some reports, out of the two thousand, two hundred crewmen who were said to have been aboard Bismarck at the time of her loss, only around two hundred survived her sinking, indicating that very nearly two thousand German mariners died in that one instance alone, a tragedy to rank alongside that suffered by the Royal Navy's own battleship, HMS Hood, which had been lost a few days earlier.

Although major surface actions between the Royal Navy and the German Fleet were said to have been few and far between, the much larger Battle of the Atlantic, which was generally fought between the Royal Navy's surface craft and Germany's U-boat's was a far more sustained campaign; and one that could easily have been won by either side. However, one of the few notable German raiders that did manage to successfully conduct maritime operations against Britain's vital commercial trade routes was the battleship, Admiral Graf Spee, which was reported to have conducted a brief, but highly effective campaign against allied shipping, before being deliberately scuttled by her crew in Montevideo Harbour, Uruguay, on the 17th December 1939. First laid down in October 1932, launched in 1934 and brought into service in 1936, the Graf Spee was thought to be one of the most heavily armed warships of her age, as well as being one of the lightest and most technologically advanced battleships ever built. Even before the outbreak of the Second World War, precipitated by Hitler's invasion of Poland, the Graf Spee, under the command of the highly experienced Captain Hans Langsdorff, was said to have been ready to conduct naval raids against British trade routes and only required official confirmation from Berlin to begin offensive operations against allied shipping, which Langsdorff was said to have received on the 26th September 1939. Travelling with her supply vessel, Altmark, the Graf Spee was said to have steamed towards the extremely busy shipping lanes of the South Atlantic, where he planned to intercept allied merchant vessels, which were bringing much needed commodities from various South American countries. Between the 30th September and the 22nd October 1939, Graf Spee was reported to have attacked and sunk at least four allied ships, whilst assaulting another, but retaining it as a prison ship, for some of the allied seamen who were captured by Graf Spee and her crew.

Eager to avoid being tracked by the Royal Navy, Langsdorff was reported to have sailed back across the Atlantic and into the shipping lanes of the Indian Ocean by the end of October 1939, where she attacked and sank the British tanker Africa Shell on the 15th of November. However, rather than remaining in the area, Langsdorff was then said to have taken Graf Spee back into the South Atlantic, where between the second half of November and the middle of December, the German battleship was said to have sunk a further three commercial vessels and taken their crews prisoner. Unsurprisingly perhaps, the Royal Navy became increasingly concerned over the losses of these allied vessels, although initially they were reported to have been unsure of the identity of the German raider that was responsible for the attacks, as Langsdorff was said to have ordered his ships carpenter to construct wooden facades, which were used to disguise the outline of the battleship and cause confusion amongst any would-be reporters. Establishing a number of Royal Navy patrols in both the Atlantic and Indian Oceans, the British Admiralty ordered these units to hunt down and confront the German raider, although it was only on the 13th December 1939 that a Royal Navy group, comprising the cruisers HMS Exeter, Ajax and Achilles, finally caught sight of the Graf Spee and positioned themselves to confront her, With her far superior weaponry, armour and speed, in normal circumstances, Graf Spee was more than able to defeat any one of the individual cruisers, possibly even two of them, but with three different targets splitting his fire, the situation was said to have become increasingly difficult for Langsdorff and his crew. Despite inflicting significant damage on HMS Exeter, which caused the Royal Navy ship to turn away, gunfire from both HMS Ajax and Achilles was reported to have caused their own extensive damage to Graf Spee's deck area, but it was only when a shell penetrated her armour, causing damage inside the ship that Langsdorff was finally persuaded to turn about and run for cover.

By the morning of the 14th December 1939, Graf Spee and her crew found themselves in Montevideo Harbour, Uruguay, whilst the pursuing Royal Cruisers, HMS Ajax and Achilles, along with HMS Cumberland, which had replaced the heavily damaged HMS Exeter, waited offshore, in the event that the German battleship decided to make a run for the open sea. However, although not immediately obvious at the time to those observers who studied Graf Spee from the shore, apart from the damage inflicted on the ships upper decks, the shell reportedly fired by HMS Exeter, which had pierced the German battleships armour had caused significant damage to Graf Spee's fuel system that would have required major work being undertaken, something that could not be undertaken in the seventy two hours available to them, under the terms of the Hague Convention, governing the treatment of military vessels in a neutral port. Left with few options but to either have his vessel interned, face the Royal Navy warships that were waiting for him offshore, or to deliberately scuttle his battleship in the waters of the River Plate, Langsdorff was said to have consulted with his superiors in Berlin, as well as with Hitler directly, as to what action he should take, given his situation. Although there was a general belief that the Royal Navy was bringing heavier battleships to confront Graf Spee, in the event that Langsdorff chose to make a fight of it, in reality it was thought that the three British warships waiting offshore, HMS Ajax, Achilles and Cumberland, were in fact the only British units capable of intercepting Graf Spee and even they could not guarantee that the German battleship would not escape them. As it turned out however, having used up most of the seventy two hours available to him, before his vessel was interned, on the evening of the 17th December 1939, Langsdorff and his crew were said to have begun steaming out of Montevideo Harbour, leaving many guessing as to what his actual intentions were. As the great battleship reached a particular point in the river's estuary, the remaining crew were taken off the ship by a coastal tender and the German warship was scuttled, settling on the soft bottom, with large parts of her upper structures remaining visible above the waves, until they too disappeared over time. For the surviving members of Graf Spee's crew, those who had survived the confrontation with the Royal Navy cruisers, which some thirty odd German seamen had not, their long term fate was to remain as internees in Uruguay, where most continued to be held until the war was over. Sadly for Graf Spee's commander, Captain Hans Langsdorff, who many of the captured allied seamen reported as being both generous and friendly, the loss of his ship and his subsequent failure to engage the waiting enemy warships, ostensibly to protect the lives of his own sailors, was said to have ended his own life some three days after his ship sank below the waters of the South Atlantic.

As an island nation and a major importer of basic commodities, Britain had always been reliant on the sea and the various trade routes that brought these vital necessities into the country, a multi-million pound trade, which any foreign enemy could and would be expected to exploit, which in itself explained the need for a large and highly effective naval force. Although in terms of surface craft, there were few nations to compete with the Royal Navy and even though the German High Seas Fleet had attempted to blockade and defeat Britain during the First World War, for the most part, it had failed to overcome the Royal Navy through conventional actions, but had enjoyed a measure of success through the use of its then fledgling submarine force, the fearsome U-boats. In light of these earlier successes, during the 1914-1918 conflict, the Royal Navy had fully expected these types of craft to be employed against British military and mercantile fleets during the Second World War, although possibly few strategists would have expected their use to have developed into a major part of the single longest military campaign of the entire war, the Battle of the Atlantic, which was waged from the outbreak of hostilities in September 1939, right through to the defeat of Nazi Germany in May 1945. Although the previously mentioned surface battleships, such as the Admiral Graf Spee, Prinz Eugen and the ill-fated Bismarck, along with the likes of Deutchland, Tirpitz, Admiral Scheer and Lutzow were intended to form the cutting edge of the German Navy at sea, ultimately the overall failure of these raiders to seriously damage British trade and developments in submarine technologies also ensured that the U-boats would play a far more significant role in the sea campaign than had originally been intended. From an allied perspective and despite having confronted the menace of these generally unseen raiders during the First World War, very little work was thought to have been undertaken to counter the threat of these undersea killers, so that in the first couple of years of the Atlantic campaign, the Royal Navy and their allies were said to have struggled to cope with the effects of the U-boat peril.

At the outbreak of war, those German surface raiders and submarines already at sea were simply authorised to begin attacking allied vessels, whilst British and French warships began blockading Germany's main sea routes, both in an attempt to limit German trade, but also to hinder the passage of it generally small, but highly effective naval assets. However, as with the likes of the Graf Spee, a significant number of German U-boats were already at sea and were busily attacking allied vessels, forcing the British and their French allies to divert elements of their own navies, to track down and destroy these battleships and submarines. Unfortunately, unlike conventional warships, which were comparatively easy to see on the surface, submarines were far more difficult to identify, largely because no-one knew they were there until they had launched their torpedoes against an allied target, or surfaced to attack a merchant vessel with its deck gun. As a result, rather than scouring the oceans for an unseen target, the allies were said to have resorted to employing a convoy system for the larger commercial fleets of ships that were sailing across the Atlantic and Indian Oceans; and who were the main target for the German U-boat commanders. In the first two years of the maritime conflict, both sides were thought to have experienced notable successes and failures, as the navies of Nazi Germany and Facist Italy, tried to interrupt the vital supply lines that kept Britain and its vast Empire fed and provisioned. With such huge distances involved, even the Royal Navy, formally the world's greatest marine force, found itself struggling to cope with the ever present threat of the German and Italian submarine menace, which were often able to operate with impunity in some areas of the globe, as the danger of invasion forced Britain to withdraw some of its valuable naval resources to home waters. Unfortunately, by stationing some of its limited numbers of corvettes and destroyers in and around the British mainland, they were then within easy reach of German fighters and bombers, which regularly targeted the Royal Navy ships for destruction, in the hope of weakening Britain's impenetrable naval shield, which had safeguarded the country for hundreds of years. The fall of France and the use of its Atlantic ports by the German Navy, made the situation even more perilous for British ships, as the loss of the powerful French Navy and the extended reach of the German U-boats both combined to make allied shipping even more susceptible to enemy attack, forcing the Admiralty to allocate even greater resources to protecting British shipping lanes and its coastal waters.

However, the most striking aspects of the Battle of the Atlantic, was the invention and development of new strategic planning and technological devices by both sides in the conflict, which helped to shift the balance of power between the two sides, throughout the entirety of the five year campaign. For their part and despite the reluctance of Admiral Erich Raeder to fully embrace the effectiveness of the German submarine fleet, its leading proponent, Commodore Karl Donitz, was reported to have developed the idea of the "Wolf Pack", a maritime strategy that would prove to be so devastating for allied shipping and which might well have helped starve Britain into submission, had it not been for divisions amongst the German military leadership. Although individual U-boats continued to attack allied ships alone, with some success, Donitz and some of his leading submarine captains, quickly realised the benefits of attacking the allied convoys en-masse, allowing the "packs" to inflict much more significant damage than might be caused by a single German U-boat and sharing the risk of being attacked by the convoy's naval escorts. Although Britain and her allies were reported to have established a number of anti-submarine task forces, to scour the oceans for the German U-boat menace, ultimately it was thought to be the development of the ASDIC system, maritime sonar equipment; and the breaking of the German Enigma codes, which proved to be the turning point for the allied navies, allowing them to track down and destroy individual submarines, but not before the German U-boat fleet as a whole had very nearly brought Britain and its people to the brink of submission. Although Britain's merchant marine suffered enormous losses during the period of the Battle of the Atlantic, it is generally accepted that the outcome of the conflict might have been entirely different, had it not been for the involvement and bravery of the Canadian, Norwegian and American navies, who all played a pivotal role in helping to overcome the threat of the German U-boat.

King George VI

Kaiser Wilhelm II

King Edward VII

Elsewhere in the world, the Royal Navy continued to find itself under pressure, from the Italian Navy in the Mediterranean and later, the Japanese Imperial Navy in the Far East, with the British forces suffering significant losses in both theatres. Despite the threat of the French Mediterranean Fleet having been neutralised at Mers-el-Kebir on the 3rd July 1940, for the British Admiralty, the Italian Navy was and remained a potential danger to Royal Navy assets in the Mediterranean, one that British military leaders were determined to remove, as quickly as possible. With Italian forces actively employed in North Africa against the allies and with British trade routes potentially exposed to Italian intervention, even before the official outbreak of the Second World War in September 1939 and Italy's own declaration of war, British planners had already made preparations to attack Mussolini's surface fleet. As a result of Italy's confederation with Nazi Germany, on the 12th November 1940, a Royal Navy taskforce, comprising the aircraft carrier HMS Illustrious, four cruisers and four destroyers, took up position some two hundred miles off the port of Taranto, on the Greek island of Cephalonia and prepared their Swordfish aircraft for the assault on the Italian fleet that was moored in the harbour. Said to have consisted of six battleships, nine cruisers and a number of destroyers, by the end of the airborne assault, one battleship had been destroyed, two others had been damaged and several hundred Italian servicemen had been killed or wounded. British losses during the attack were said to have been light, with the aircrew from two Fairey Swordfish aircraft being captured or killed after their planes were shot down by Italian ground fire. However, despite having suffered comparatively little damage overall, the assault by the Royal Navy was said to have forced the Italian Navy to withdraw its remaining ships back to the Italian port of Naples, where they were reported to have remained until Italy's unilateral surrender to the allies in 1943. Significantly, the British airborne assault on the Italian Navy at Taranto was said to have been used as a model by the Imperial Japanese Navy, when planning for their own aircraft carrier led strike against the American Fleet at Pearl Harbour in the following year.

Unfortunately, any lessons that were learned by the British military authorities, regarding the emerging dominance of the aircraft carrier at sea, seemed to have either been forgotten or ignored when dealing with the expansionist threat of the Japanese Empire in the Far East. As has been previously mentioned elsewhere, for the most part, British military strategy in the East was thought to have centred around the insurmountable defences of the Empire's great naval base at Singapore, which had once been described by Winston Churchill as the "Gibraltar of the East", implying that it could never be overcome by an enemy force. However, other planners were far more cautious, believing that the base needed to be substantially reinforced with capital ships, men and weapons, in order for it to act as a true counter to the evolving Japanese threat. Sadly, with Britain itself under threat, for Prime Minister Winston Churchill, there were few resources available to reinforce Singapore, a situation that would prove to have disastrous results for Britain's overseas dominions, many of which were dependant on the Royal Navy for their own defence. Although eventually a small contingent of British warships were allocated to the protection of Singapore, an aircraft carrier, a heavy cruiser, a battleship and four destroyers, for most military experts of the time this relatively small marine force was woefully inadequate for the task at hand, a point of view that was not shared by Churchill himself. Almost from the outset though, the planned naval reinforcement of Singapore began to unravel, as the intended aircraft carrier, the comparatively new HMS Indomitable, was reported to have run aground in the Caribbean and was therefore unable to join the other Royal Navy units, leaving the British ships without any meaningful air cover.

Designated as Force Z, the taskforce that arrived at Singapore on the 2nd December 1941 was reported to have included the relatively modern battleship HMS Prince of Wales, the WWI Battlecruiser HMS Repulse and the four destroyers HMS Electra, Encounter, Express and Jupiter. Along with these newly arrived Royal Navy assets, a number of other warships were reported to have been in Singapore at the time, including six assorted cruisers, five other British destroyers and at least four American destroyers that were said to be visiting the base. The link between British and American naval forces in the Pacific was said to have played a major part in both countries strategic planning regarding Japanese expansionism in the region, with the intention being that each nation would support the other, in the event that armed conflict with Japan ever arose. Unfortunately for these well laid plans, Japanese military strategists were equally aware of the allies mutual defence pact and had devised an offensive plan which would completely undermine both the American and British positions. According to most sources, it had always been assumed that if the Japanese launched any sort of offensive strike against British interests in the Far East, then the American Pacific Fleet would sail to Singapore from their main base at Pearl Harbour and help reinforce the Royal Navy's main port. Unfortunately, no amount of pre-war planning had anticipated that it would be the American base at Pearl Harbour which would be struck first, crippling most of their main capital ships, thus preventing them from rendering any sort of aid to Singapore, when it too was finally attacked. For Admiral Sir Thomas Phillips, the overall commander of the newly designated Force Z, the 8th December 1941 began with the news that the American Pacific Fleet at Pearl Harbour had been attacked and severely damaged by units of the Japanese Imperial Navy, which had launched wave after wave of carrier based aircraft carrying bombs and torpedoes. Not only had the assault effectively wiped out the American's immediate strike capability, but also put paid to any suggestion that the United States would be able to support the Royal Navy in the event that British interests were attacked by Japanese forces, which they were on the very same morning, the 8th December 1941. With Singapore being bombed by Japanese bombers and fighters; and with Imperial troops starting to land in Malaya, it quickly became clear to Admiral Phillips that not only had the arrival of his Force Z failed to deter Japanese aggression, but also that his naval armada lacked the vital air cover with which to confront the Japanese forces which were converging on his position. However, despite these problems, Admiral Phillips was said to have ordered his fleet out to sea, determined to try and intercept those Japanese invasion forces that were reported to be approaching the Malay Peninsula.

For some reason known only to himself, Phillips was thought to have failed to arrange for his naval squadron to be given adequate air cover by the land based aircraft that were actually available to him, presumably believing that his ships had sufficient anti-aircraft weaponry with which to deal with any Japanese warplanes that might try and attack his flotilla. Unfortunately for the Royal Navy's Eastern fleet and especially for Phillips' flagship, HMS Prince of Wales, the regions humidity was said to have caused problems, both with his vessels onboard radar and with the ammunition for the warships anti-aircraft guns, reducing the battleship's fighting abilities by some margin. Despite these issues though, Phillip's was said to have carried on regardless, taking his squadron out to sea, on the late afternoon of the 8th December 1941 and setting a northward course, towards the Thai port of Singora, where a Japanese invasion force was said to have been landing in preparation for an all out assault on British held Malaysia. As the Royal Navy squadron steamed north, their position was reported to have been constantly monitored by Japanese aircraft and submarines, which had been instructed to look out for the British taskforce, relaying their exact whereabouts to the Japanese military authorities in French Indo-China, now Vietnam. Despite knowing exactly where the British ships were for most of the time, the Japanese were thought to have been unable to launch any sort of direct assault against the Royal Navy ships; and so for much of the next day or so, both sides were said to have simply engaged in a game of cat and mouse with one another, with no direct confrontation resulting from the exercise. It was only on the 10th December 1941 and after Admiral Phillips had made the decision to return to Singapore that the two sides finally came into conflict with one another, when Japanese bombers operating from their base in Saigon, were reported to have launched an attack on the British flotilla. At around eleven o'clock in the morning of the 10th December, three waves of Japanese bombers began an assault on the fleet, although for the most part this attack was unsuccessful, save for starting a small deck fire onboard HMS Repulse, which was quickly extinguished. It was the later, second attack by Japanese bombers that would prove to be so catastrophic for the British ships, as these enemy aircraft were armed with torpedoes, which were used with devastating results by their pilots. Phillips' flagship, HMS Prince of Wales, was reported to have been struck by at least four enemy torpedoes, which caused such extensive damage that the battleship could not be saved, despite valiant efforts by her crew to get the crippled vessel underway once again. With the ship listing heavily as tons of seawater poured through the breach in her hull, the Royal Navy gunnery crews were said to have continued firing at the enemy bombers, even though the angle of the slowly sinking ship prevented them from bringing their guns to bear on the Japanese aircraft.

With HMS Prince of Wales fatally damaged, the Japanese bombers were then thought to have concentrated their attack on the fleets other warships, including the ageing HMS Repulse, which was reported to have avoided being struck by around twenty enemy torpedoes, before finally running out of room and luck; eventually being hit by three or four torpedoes that fatally damaged her. Recognising the situation, Repulse's commander, Captain Tennant was said to have ordered his crew to abandon the vessel, although her relatively rapid foundering was said to have caused significant losses amongst the crew all the same. With HMS Repulse slipping beneath the waves at twenty five past twelve in the afternoon of the 10th December 1941, she was followed to the seabed around an hour later by HMS Prince of Wales, about the same time that a squadron of allied warplanes arrived on the scene, having been despatched from RAF Sembawang in Singapore as air cover for the ill-fated British battleships. Over eight hundred crewmen were thought to have been lost on the two British warships, including Admiral Phillips, who chose to go down with his flagship HMS Prince of Wales, whilst most of the survivors were subsequently rescued by Royal Navy destroyers that had formed part of Force Z. Along with the American's, the British military authorities quickly came to recognise through bitter personal experience the emergence of air power as the most potent form of military weaponry, even in the vastness of the world's great oceans. With its two powerful warships destroyed and with no replacements immediately at hand, the British land fortress at Singapore was left to its own devices to try and stem the Japanese advance throughout Asia, something that it singularly failed to do, largely as a result of poor strategic planning and even worse personal judgements, failures that almost certainly played a part in the loss of HMS Prince of Wales and HMS Repulse. Being unable to maintain any sort of effective naval presence in the Far East, most of the Royal Navy's remaining assets were said to have been withdrawn to the area of the Indian Ocean and East Africa, where they were joined in the following year by a number of replacement warships, although it was only in the later part of World War II that British ships once again returned to the Pacific in any meaningful way and only then in conjunction with the American's. According to some commentators, the real weakness in the Royal Navy's Pacific operations was its inability to operate without land bases, something that American warships were able to do. As a former global power, Britain's navy had become accustomed to travelling from one military base to another, carrying sufficient stores to complete that particular journey and then restocking at the next available port. Unfortunately, when war broke out, many of these former bases and ports became unavailable to them, as the likes of Hong Kong, Singapore, etc were subsequently captured by the Japanese, thereby limiting the area of operations for Royal Navy units in the region. Unlike the Americans, Germans and even the Japanese, little thought had been given to reprovisioning Royal Navy ships at sea, so that by the time armed conflict had broken out in the Far East, the British military authorities were unable to keep their ships at sea for an extended of time. It was only in the latter stages of World War II and largely with the support of the US Navy that Royal Navy warships were able to remain at sea, being restocked and rearmed by a fleet of attendant supply ships.

The other vitally important area of operations for the Royal Navy was the Mediterranean, where enormous efforts and extensive assets were made and invested in order to protect allied interests in the region, particularly the strategically important island fortress of Malta. Because of its geographical position in relation to North Africa, where the allies were fighting the Italians and Rommel's famed Afrika Corps, the British held island of Malta was a pivotal base from where the allies could interrupt Axis supply lines, with the intention of depriving German and Italian troops of the much needed fuel, food and ammunition that they needed to continue their fight. Ostensibly used as an airbase from where allied aircraft could locate and destroy vital German supply convoys, unfortunately, Malta's isolated position also make it relatively easy to blockade and to target with German bombers and fighter aircraft. In common with their adversaries, any allied ships that sailed into the Mediterranean automatically became a target for Axis aircraft based in Egypt and Crete, making it incredibly difficult for Malta to be resupplied with foodstuffs, aviation fuel and ammunition, all of which were necessary to carry out the military campaigns against enemy forces in North Africa. In the event that supplies could not be delivered to the island, then allied planners knew that the Maltese population and the allied servicemen there would eventually be starved into submission, effectively handing Malta over to the Germans, from where they could then control much of the Mediterranean and North Africa. Clearly such an outcome was completely unacceptable to the allied leadership, who subsequently took the view that any and all means must be used to safeguard the island's position, regardless of the cost in ships, material and men that achieving such an objective might render. Successive supply convoys were despatched to reprovision the island, although as time passed and the Axis blockade was tightened, so the number of allied losses were said to have substantially grown, with increasing numbers of vessels being lost to German aircraft and submarines. The situation was reported to have become so severe that by the middle of 1942, the RAF bases on Malta only had sufficient fuel, ammunition and weaponry for a matter of weeks, whilst the entire population, both civil and military, were said to be suffering severe shortages in terms of foodstuffs and medicines.

Charles De Gaulle   **HMS Dreadnought**   **HMS Iron Duke**

In response to this perilous situation, allied planners began to organise some of the largest and most heavily armed supply convoys of the entire war, which were designed to break through the extensive enemy blockade and bring the much needed aid to Malta and its inhabitants. Although the most important allied convoy of the campaign was reported to be Operation Pedestal, which took place in August 1942, this convoy was preceded by the joint naval operations, Harpoon and Vigorous that took place in June 1942, but which ultimately failed to fully relieve the situation on Malta, largely as a result of German aircraft and Italian surface ships. Operations Harpoon and Vigorous, which sailed from Gibraltar and Alexandria respectively, were reported to have included a total of seventeen merchant ships, which were being protected by a large number of British warships, including aircraft carriers, battleships, cruisers and numerous destroyers, along with aircraft supplied by the two carriers. However, despite this protection Operation Vigorous was ultimately cancelled after it was attacked by Italian warships and German aircraft, which inflicted substantial losses on the convoy, including the destruction of one Royal Navy cruiser, three destroyers and two merchant vessels, as well as seriously damaging two merchantmen, three cruisers and a number of destroyers. Operation Harpoon sailing from Gibraltar was said to have suffered even greater losses, as a result of enemy action, including the loss of four of the six merchant vessels that had been despatched to Malta, the most important of which was the oil tanker Kentucky, which was lost, along with its valuable cargo of fuel oil. Royal Navy vessels accompanying the convoy were equally unlucky, with two destroyers sunk, a further half dozen damaged and at least two cruisers hit by enemy fire. Although two of Operation Harpoon's merchant vessels were reported to have survived the journey and their cargoes greatly welcomed by the island of Malta, ultimately the failure to deliver the much needed fuel oil simply deepened the concerns over the island's continuing viability as a front line military base.

Because of the failure of Operations Harpoon and Vigorous, allied planners were left with little option but to organise yet another supply convoy for the beleaguered island, one that would include the much needed fuel supplies, which would help the RAF to continue its own operations against the Axis supply lines. The most important merchant ship of the fourteen that were due to be despatched was the American owned, but British crewed tanker Ohio, which was chosen for its large capacity and basic speed, helping it to keep up with the warships that would be accompanying it on the journey. Possibly in view of earlier tactical issues, a great deal of strategic planning was said to have been put into organising Operation Pedestal, in order to ensure that the civilian merchantmen remained as safe as possible in the Mediterranean, with the convoys aircraft carriers, battleships, destroyers and aeroplanes all training with one another to help ensure their complete combat readiness. Unfortunately the preparations for and participation of so many naval vessels in the build up to Pedestal almost certainly forewarned the Axis forces that some sort of allied fleet was making its way into the Mediterranean, so that both German and Italian military units were well prepared for the allied ships as they made their way into the area. The fact that HMS Eagle, one of the convoy's four planned for aircraft carriers had been attacked and sunk on the morning of the operation meant that the military strength of the convoy had been seriously reduced, but the allied fleet pressed on in spite of the loss. Almost as soon as the ships passed into the Mediterranean they were reported to have come under sustained attack by enemy aircraft and submarines, although damage to the Royal Navy convoy was said to have been negligible, with no ships lost in the first part of the journey.

However, as the convoy moved closer to the Axis held territories of Sardinia and Sicily, so it came under increasing attacks from the enemy aircraft that were based there, most of which were successfully confronted by the aircraft operating from the British carriers. At the same though, several Italian cruisers and a dozen or more destroyers from Taranto were said to have sailed out to intercept the British convoy, hoping to repeat their earlier successes during the ill-fated Harpoon and Vigorous Operations. However, as it turned out the most effective Axis weapon against the Royal Navy ships and their civilian charges proved to be the Italian submarines and German E-boats which had been shadowing the convoy, both of which were reported to have gained some notable successes as night fell over the Mediterranean. Two cruisers, HMS Cairo and Nigeria were both reported to have been hit by enemy torpedoes, whilst the vitally important Ohio was also struck, forcing a number of destroyers to abandon their defensive positions and take up station alongside the damaged vessels, thereby depriving the convoy of part of its defensive screen. With the ships becoming increasingly separated from one another, as those that were damaged were slowed, whilst others pushed forward at speed, so the gaps in the defensive shield began to grow, offering the German and Italian attackers even more opportunities to carry out their assault. The first merchantman to succumb to enemy attack was thought to be the Empire Hope, which was struck by enemy bombs, before sinking beneath the waves, followed a short time later by a second cargo ship which was hit by a torpedo. Royal Navy units too were becoming to fall victim to the ongoing attacks, with the destroyer HMS Foresight had been lost and a number of other warships were said to have been so badly damaged that they were forced to turn around and head back to Gibraltar, along with a number of other destroyers who were charged with their protection.

HMS Hood

HMS Ark Royal

HMS Repulse

As the remnants of the battered allied convoy pressed on towards Malta, with growing numbers of the ships becoming separated from one another, so the surviving merchant ships became easier targets for the Axis E-boats, submarines and bombers that were still launching wave after wave of attacks against them. On the 13th August 1942, the third full day of the operation, three more of the precious cargo vessels were reportedly lost to enemy actions, whilst yet another Royal Navy cruiser, HMS Manchester, was torpedoed, then restarted, but later scuttled by her crew, most of whom were either transferred to other British ships, or were taken prisoner by Vichy-French supporters in Tunisia, when the ship was deliberately sunk. Later the same morning, more allied vessels fell victim to enemy actions, including yet another merchantman, which was completely destroyed and several others that were heavily damaged. The priceless oil tanker Ohio was attacked on numerous occasions but simply refused to surrender to the assaults, although by the middle of the morning the damage was said to have been so severe that she was left dead in the water, after her boilers had been ruptured by enemy action. However, as the day wore on and the gap between the convoy and British fighters on Malta closed, so there was some respite for the remaining allied ships, as increasing numbers of friendly aircraft began to appear in the skies to attack the German bombers and surface craft that had taken such a heavy toll on the allied ships. It was thought to be the arrival of these fighter bombers that finally persuaded many of the Italian craft to withdraw from the area, as they lacked the necessary air cover to protect themselves from the RAF attacks, even though German bombers continued with their assault on the dwindling allied convoy. By the morning of the 13th August the first three of the remaining merchant ships, Rochester Castle, Melbourne Star and Port Chalmers finally limped into Valetta harbour, to be greeted by a large crowd, who were anxious to see just how many of the ships had survived the horrifying journey to their tiny island home. The following morning the penultimate ship, The Brisbane Star made its way into port, its lower bow almost torn off by the enemy torpedo that had very nearly cost the ship its life, but it had survived nonetheless, to deliver its vital stores to the Maltese people. Perhaps the greatest cheer though was reserved for the stricken tanker, Ohio, which arrived in port on the morning of the 15th August 1942, shepherded by the Royal Navy warships, HMS Bramham and Penn, which had tied the crippled cargo carrier to their sides, in order to ensure its safe arrival in Valetta harbour, to deliver the vital fuel oil that would allow Malta to keep on fighting for a few more weeks.

Of the fourteen commercial vessels that had set out to participate in Operation Pedestal, nine of them were lost, whilst of the five that completed the journey, Ohio was said to be so badly damaged that as soon as her valuable fuel was unloaded, she sank into the harbour, damaged beyond repair. In addition to these material losses, the Royal Navy escorts too was reported to have suffered significant damage, losing one aircraft carrier, two cruisers, one destroyer and having one aircraft carrier, two cruisers and several destroyers damaged by enemy fire. Although the outcome of the operation was seen as a tactical victory for the Axis forces, in that they prevented the main part of the cargo from reaching Malta, as well as inflicting significant losses on the Royal Navy, ultimately that counted for little in the overall scope of things. The strategic and morale boosting effect of the partially successful operation not only helped to ensure that Malta remained a viable front line military base against Axis forces in the region, but also ensured that further supply convoys would be undertaken, although not on the scale of Pedestal. The safe delivery of the vital fuel oil also ensured that RAF units on Malta could continue to operate against Axis forces in North Africa, helping to interrupt the necessary supplies that Rommel and his troops required, if they were ever to overwhelm the allies in the region, which they were never able to do. It is also perhaps worth remembering that many of the seamen who served aboard the fourteen merchant vessels were civilians and as such were granted the greatest respect by their Royal Navy counterparts, who were humbled by the bravery and sheer determination of the Merchant Marine personnel who undertook such a perilous journey, often at the cost of their own lives, in order to break through the enemy's blockade and keep the inhabitants of Malta supplied for just a few weeks more. In dealing with this particular episode of the Royal Navy's glorious history, it is also worth recalling that the people of Malta themselves, along with the allied garrison were similarly honoured for their own sacrifice during this period of the Second World War. In recognition of their bravery and fortitude, in April 1942, the British monarch, King George VI, conferred the George Cross on the isolated Mediterranean island and its people, granting the award in the following manner *"To honour her brave people, I award the George Cross to the Island Fortress of Malta, to bear witness to a heroism and devotion that will long be famous in history."*

Although the Royal Navy participated in innumerable campaigns and operations during the Second World War, of which the ones mentioned are just a few, one of the final major naval operations involving the Royal Navy and the Royal Canadian Navy was Operation Overlord, or the D-Day Landings, which took place on the 6th June 1944 and signified the beginning of the final allied assault against the Nazi regime of Adolph Hitler's Germany. According to some reporters, approximately two-thirds of the five thousand or so ships and landing craft employed during the operation were provided by the Royal Navy and the Royal Canadian Navy. However, in the wider and long-term context the Second World War was significant in that it signalled the end of Britain's position as a great imperial power, both in military and economic terms. As had been the case in the earlier 1914-18 conflict, by the end of the war in 1945, Britain found itself almost bankrupt, much of its infrastructure shattered, but now with the added problem of indigenous nationalism raging through many of its overseas dominions, most especially within the Indian subcontinent. Of course other factors would help to determine post war Britain's place in the world, not least of which was the development of the atomic bomb, the emergence of the United States and Russia as the world's pre-eminent military super-powers and a diminishing British Empire, which undermined the need for a large and powerful Royal Navy surface fleet. Added to this, were the technological advances, including the development of the jet fighters, which would eventually break through the sound barrier, the ICBM that could travel from one side of the world to another in a matter of minutes, both of which helped to make national boundaries, or traditional defensive positions largely obsolete.

It is precisely this sort of thinking that continues to inform government thinking right through to the present day, helping to create the current situation where Britain is without an effective aircraft carrier force for the first time in decades. Although the advent of the modern jet fighter bombers and other supersonic missile systems are said to have rendered the aircraft carrier generally obsolete, this was spectacularly disproved in 1982, when Britain was compelled to cobble together a naval taskforce, including aircraft carriers, destroyers and troop transports to take back the Falkland Islands, which had been illegally occupied by Argentinian troops. Although the mission was eventually accomplished by the British forces, the action itself was not without problems and losses, some of which were thought to have been as a direct result of defence spending cuts and poor strategic planning by successive British governments. With the widely held view that a national nuclear deterrent was and is of paramount importance to the United Kingdom's protection, the almost prohibitive cost of maintaining this generally unuseable strike capability, has seen Britain's more conventional military forces reduced to their bare minimum. However, what the modern day Royal Navy lacks in numbers and types of vessels, it is thought to make up for in terms of technology, being one of the most advanced naval forces in the world, in terms of modern weaponry, training and equipment design. According to some sources, Britain's navy remains one of the largest by way of total tonnage, but has now shifted its emphasis from a reliance on larger warships and carriers, to the much smaller, faster types of frigates and destroyers, which would be largely unsuitable for any sort of large scale conflict at sea. Even though the Royal Navy is now largely devoid of aircraft carriers, due to yet another round of severe defence spending cuts and poor planning by the Ministry of Defence, two new vessels, the Queen Elizabeth class carriers, HMS Queen Elizabeth and HMS Prince of Wales, are due to be brought into service within the next decade, thereby restoring a mobile fighting platform to the Royal Navy's equipment list, albeit ten years too late. As of the present day and not including those vessels operated by the Royal Fleet Auxiliary, the Royal Navy is reported to consist of around eighty front line vessels, although only some twenty-odd destroyers and frigates, eleven submarines and a handful of support craft, including assault ships and helicopter platforms, could be truly regarded as militarily offensive. Whilst the declared intent of both major political parties in Britain, the Conservatives and the Labour Party has been to rebuild the Royal Navy as a truly "Blue Water" force, one that can operate independently in any of the world's high seas, it is generally accepted that the Royal Navy cannot achieve this without the presence of a standalone aircraft carrier, around which the associated fleet can assemble, something that will not happen again until 2020, when the new Queen Elizabeth carriers come into service.

MARINERS, MERCHANTS AND THE MILITARY TOO

12. THE THIN RED LINE

Prior to the arrival of the Roman army in the 1st century AD, Britain did not have any sort of large standing military force with which to defend the country, but rather a collection of individual tribal groups, who would periodically fight one another in disputes over territory, mineral deposits, water rights, or other such valuable commodities. It was thought to be as a result of one of these inter-tribal disputes, between the Catuvellauni people and their neighbours, the Atrebates that eventually led to the military invasion of Britain by the legions of the Roman Empire in 43 AD. Dispossessed of his kingdom by the Catuvellauni princes, Caratacus and Togodumnus, who were seeking to extend their own territorial influence, the Atrebate ruler, Verica, was reported to have travelled to Rome, where he pleaded with the new Roman Emperor, Claudius, for military support in regaining his tribal homelands. Fortunately for the ousted British king, his pleas for military aid came at a convenient time, given that Claudius was reportedly desperate to stamp his own authority on a Roman Empire, which had been severely damaged by the actions of his predecessor, the Emperor Caligula, whose madness was said to have brought the empire to the edge of destruction.

Britain at that time was reportedly composed of a large number of regional tribes, including the likes of the Catuvellauni, Atrebates, Iceni, Silures, Ordovices, et cetera, who were commonly ruled by a single high born individual, or members of a particular household, or clan, whose decisions were often informed by their closest and most experienced advisers. Each of these pre-Roman societies were thought to have been slightly distinct from one another, with some having tribal capitals, whilst others did not, others produced their own coinage, whereas others relied almost entirely on barter, some tribes grew crops, others bred and traded horses. However, even though each of these peoples were thought to have regarded themselves as being entirely distinct from the other surrounding British tribes, many of the smaller, more peaceful tribes were thought to have shared a common enemy in the form of the larger, more militaristic societies, such as the Catuvellauni, who used their martial strength to impose their demands or their territorial ambitions on their smaller, weaker neighbours. Consequently, when the four Roman legions of Aulus Plautius landed at Richborough in Kent in 43 AD, many of the smaller tribes were reported to have generally welcomed their arrival, simply because the Roman's military presence promised to curtail the expansionist policies of the stronger British tribes. It was precisely because of Britain's fragmented and regionalised tribal system that the estimated forty thousand Roman legionaries, who arrived in the summer of 43 AD, were able to successfully land on the British mainland and establish their first bases there. According to most contemporary sources, both Caratacus and Togodumnus, the rulers of the Catuvellauni were reported to have been in the vanguard of the British resistance to the European invaders and despite lacking the military strength to confront the Roman legions directly, were said to have conducted a highly effective guerrilla campaign against Rome's military forces, using hit-and-run, as well as a scorched earth policy to slow down the legion's inexorable advance into the centre of the country. Unfortunately, the Catuvellauni princes' decision to rely on the Rivers Medway and Thames to hold back the advancing Roman legions ultimately proved to be a mistake, as the highly experienced legionaries quickly overcame both natural barriers and were able to confront and defeat the British defenders, with Togodumnus reportedly being killed shortly after the battle on the Thames.

Anglo Saxons   Anglo Saxon Fyrd   Edward the Confessor

Unlike his brother, Caratacus was reported to have avoided being killed or seriously injured at the battle on the Thames, although with much of his army killed or captured by the Roman's, he was said to have been left with little choice but to retire westward, in the hope of finding new military forces with which to resist the invaders. In the short term however, Aulus Plautius and his four legions were content to request Claudius to come from Rome, so that he could triumphantly enter the Trinovantes capital of Camulodunum (Colchester), at the head of his triumphant Roman army, where he was said to have received the submissions of eleven British tribal leaders, mostly from the south of the country, who were keen to show their allegiance to the new military administration. Having established their hold on the south east of the country, over the next four years the Roman legions were reported to have pushed further west, imposing client relationships with those willing to accept their rule and conquering those that were not. For those that were able to escape the Roman's military expansion, almost inevitably they were forced back into the Welsh homelands of the Silures and Ordovices people, who controlled much of the territory there. Although both of these British tribes were reported to have resisted increasing Roman expansion within Britain, especially along their own regional borders, with what would later become known as England, it was only in 47 AD that the Roman authorities began to plan for the large scale invasion of the unconquered western regions of the country, when the new Roman Governor of Britain, Publius Ostorius Scapula, began a series of military campaigns against the peoples of Wales and northwest England. However, despite the experience and professionalism of his legionary forces, Scapula was reported to have found it difficult to suppress the fighting men of the Silures and the Ordovices, both of whom were said to have been led at some point by the renegade Catuvellauni prince Caratacus, who was thought to have organised British resistance to Rome, right the way through to 51 AD, when his forces were finally defeated at the Battle of Caer Caradoc. Although he managed to escape once again, following the battle, Caratacus' wife and children were all reportedly captured by the Roman's, who were said to have used them as hostages, in order to force the British prince's surrender, but all to no avail. Unfortunately for the rebel prince, having fled Wales, he then made the mistake of fleeing north, to the kingdom of the Brigante's and the court of their queen, Cartimandua, a client ruler of the Roman Empire. Duty bound to seize Caratacus, Cartimandua was reported to have ordered him chained and handed over to the Roman authorities, who subsequently arranged for the rebel prince and his family to be taken to Rome in chains, where Caratacus would be publicly displayed, before being executed. However, according to the Roman historian Tacitus, the British prince was permitted to make a speech before the Senate, which so impressed the Roman Emperor Claudius that Caratacus and his family were released from their imprisonment and allowed to settle in Rome, where they were said to have remained for the rest of his life.

The second great British insurrection against Roman rule was thought to have occurred around ten years after Caratacus had finally been captured by the Brigante's client ruler, Cartimandua; and was brought about in part by Rome's own laws and the overbearing attitude of some of the Roman officer's stationed in Britain. The Iceni people, who occupied the area of Britain, now marked by the modern day county of Norfolk, were reported to have been a generally successful tribe of horse breeders and traders, whose ruler, King Prasutagus and his wife Boudica, had taken a fairly pragmatic view towards the Roman invasion of Britain and as a result had maintained a significant amount of independence within the new Roman province of Britannia. However, as part of their increasing political and commercial links with the Empire, Prasutagus not only incurred a considerable amount of debt through Roman money lenders, but was also obliged to accept the Empire's strict inheritance laws, which would transfer all of his rights and properties to Rome upon his death and that strictly forbade any of his female relative from inheriting his estates when he finally died. Unfortunately, when Prasutagus finally did die in around 60 AD, his will ordered that all of his estates should be divided between the Roman Empire and his two daughters, in what was a clear breach of Roman Law, but perfectly legitimate under traditional British rules. However, the Roman authorities in Britain, no doubt encouraged by many of the money lenders who were keen to recover their loans, decided to ignore the Iceni king's last will and testament; and simply annexed the whole kingdom, bringing it under their own direct military control. When the late king's wife, Boudica, publicly protested their actions, according to some contemporary sources, she was publicly flogged and her daughters were raped, as punishment for daring to challenge the Roman authority's decision. It was an outrage that the Roman's would subsequently have cause to regret, as the Iceni queen soon began plotting with other neighbouring tribes to bring their military forces together and drive the Roman's out of Britain forever. To best illustrate the difference between the two societies, the fact that this particular British army chose to accept Queen Boudica as their war leader, was completely at odds with Rome's social norms, where women were held in little regard, save for those few that achieved noble status. For the ancient Briton's however, women were generally granted similar status to their menfolk in terms of commerce, political power and leadership; and as in the case of Boudica herself, were sometimes attributed with having magical powers that were largely unknown to men.

Rallying her military forces, Boudica's first target was reported to have been the Roman settlement of Calumodunum, now Colchester, which had once been the tribal capital of the Trinovantes people, but had since been colonised by Roman migrants, merchants and former soldiers. Some of these ex-legionaries were reported to have treated the local Briton's with great disrespect and had not only stolen their lands and possessions, but had also forced the local population to bear the cost of building a brand new temple dedicated to the former Roman emperor Claudius, which quickly became the target for the Briton's latent anger. Perhaps believing that the presence of these former legionaries would protect the settlement from any sort of attack, according to some sources, Calumodunum lacked any great defensive features and as a result was quickly overrun by Boudica's army, who were reported to have butchered everybody in the city, regardless of their nationality, or their reason for being there. The great temple that had been built to celebrate Claudius was said to have become the final refuge for many of the town's terrified residents, who huddled inside its protective walls for a number of days, before finally succumbing to the vengeance of the native British army. Modern day archaeological excavations in the city, suggest that having overcome the local defences Boudica's forces then systematically demolished the settlement, taking away only those items that were easily transported, whilst destroying and burning those that were not. Having spent several days razing the entire settlement, Boudica and her army were reported to have prepared to move on to their next target, the relatively new Roman settlement of Londinium, which was said to have become an extremely important administrative and commercial centre for the Roman authorities. However, having been delayed at Calumodunum, a handful of survivors were thought to have escaped the town and alerted the nearest legionary commanders about the raid, who quickly despatched members of the 9th Hispanic Legion into the area, in an effort to confront the Boudican army, before it managed to attack and destroy another Roman settlement. Unfortunately for the 9th Legion's commander, Quintus Petillius Cerialis, the forces that he managed to assemble at fairly short notice, were reported to have been completely inadequate for the task presented to them and were subsequently annihilated by Boudica's army, which then simply continued with its relentless march on Londinium.

Meanwhile, the Roman Governor of Britain, Gaius Suetonius Paulinus, who had been busy campaigning against the Druids on the island of Anglesey was informed about the razing of Calumodunum and the later defeat of the 9th Hispanic Legion, forcing him to bring his own legions south, in an effort to try and save the settlement of Londinium. Unfortunately, given the distances involved and his lack of seasoned troops, Paulinus was reported to have essentially sacrificed the new Roman settlement, for the sake of confronting the Iceni queen and her army at a place of his own choosing; and where the conditions would favour his smaller, but more professional troops. As a result, Boudica and her army quickly overran the defences of Londinium, putting everyone to the sword and forcing many hundreds of Roman administrators, traders and visitors to flee the city in terror. Even today, evidence of the widespread destruction wrought by the Boudican army remains beneath the modern day streets of the English capital, with a thick red layer of burnt debris testifying to the wholesale devastation that took place there nearly two thousand years ago. Once again, the British army was reported to have spent several days pursuing those residents who had failed to leave the city beforehand, slaughtering many thousands in the most barbaric way, whilst tearing down and burning anything that the Roman's had built, leaving the whole settlement as a bloody burning memory of the British horde's passing visitation. With both Camulodunum and Londinium destroyed, Boudica then led her army to the Roman settlement of Verulamium, now St Alban's, where once again the local population were slaughtered and their town destroyed, with particular attention being paid to any high bred woman who happened to fall into the rebel army's hands. According to some later reports, such women had one of their breasts cut off, which was then sewn into their mouths, before the unfortunate victim was impaled on a wooden stake, although such reports may simply have been horror stories invented by Roman historians in order to justify the equally brutal actions that the Roman legions would subsequently employ in the aftermath of the bloody Boudican revolt.

Having devastated Verulamium, Boudica's native army was then reported to have moved north, along the route of the main Roman highway, Watling Street, which would have taken them to the area of Britain now commonly known as The Midlands. Whether or not the Iceni queen intended to take her forces to attack yet another major Roman settlement is unclear, but it is known that as they moved north, the Roman Governor, Suetonius Paulinus, was beginning to assemble his own military forces to try and intercept the British army. Supported by an estimated ten thousand legionaries, Paulinus was said to have carefully chosen the site where he would finally confront Boudica and her native army, selecting a site that would favour his own men and disadvantage the war chariots of the Iceni warriors that he knew would be used against him. Although the exact site of the resulting battle has been lost over time, according to some contemporary reports Paulinus was careful to choose a location that not only prevented the encirclement of his forces by the much larger British army, but also ensured that Boudica's battle line was only equal to his own, by choosing a site that essentially limited the amount of space available to the soldiers from both side. Despite being several times larger than Paulinus' military force of ten thousand men, the Boudican army was reported to have been so large that it was virtually uncontrollable, which ultimately resulted in a lack of coordinated actions being taken by the Iceni queen and her military commanders, who were unable to oversee or control the actions of their massed troops, with the result that any attacks on the Roman lines were chaotic at best. For the highly experienced and professional Roman legionaries however, the months and years of drilling, training and fighting had formed them into a highly cohesive military force that could fight and die on any terrain, or in any conditions, simply by following the lead of their closest comrades, or the instructions given by their immediate superior, which they followed without question. Whilst the native British troops rushed headlong to meet their adversaries, the Roman legionaries were said to have calmly stood their ground and launched volley after volley of javelins into their enemy's rapidly advancing ranks, killing and wounding thousands before the two sides even got within arms length of one another. Even when the two armies did come together in hand-to-hand combat, the interlinked shields of the Roman phalanx and the skilfully employed legionary swords and spears were thought to have caused significant levels of death and destruction amongst the generally ill disciplined British ranks. As more and more British warriors rushed to attack the Roman lines, so those at the front were forced onto the legionnaire's swords and spears, causing even greater numbers of casualties amongst the native fighters, with no escape available even if they had wished to withdraw from the battle. Almost inevitably perhaps, as more and more of their fighters fell to the Roman weapons, so the British attack began to weaken and fail, until eventually increasing numbers of Boudica's army began to fall back, relieving the pressure on the Roman lines and allowing them to move forward, in pursuit of the retreating British fighters. However, in what subsequently proved to be a major tactical error, the Boudican army's line of retreat was reported to have been blocked by their own caravan of carts and chariots that contained their families and the many looted treasures that had been stolen from the Roman settlements of Camulodunum, Londinium and Verulamium. With no clear escape route and with their families now at risk from the rapidly advancing Roman forces, many of the British fighters, along with their wives and children, were reported to have been slaughtered by the vengeful Roman legionaries, whose commander, Suetonius Paulinus was determined to teach the native Briton's the human cost of rebelling against Roman military rule. Although some later historians have reported that as many as eighty thousand Briton's lost their lives in this final bloody engagement, it seems likely that this figure had been exaggerated, by both Roman and British recorders, often for their own particular political ends. As for the Iceni leader Boudica and her daughters, according to some later reports, she was reported to have committed suicide, rather than face the humiliation and pain of being take prisoner by the Roman army, although as with all such historic events, such reports are almost always speculative at best. However, it is generally accepted that Boudica's rebellion was the last great British revolt against Rome during their four centuries of military occupation of the British Isles.

With Britain under Roman military occupation and protection for the best part of four hundred years and with a number of the country's former military tribal powers having been forcibly disarmed by the legions of Rome, by the time the Roman's decided to withdraw from Britain at the beginning of the 5th century, the nation had few native military forces with which to defend its territorial borders. Although several contingents of both Roman legionaries and auxiliaries were reported to have remained in Britain following the withdrawal of Rome's legions by around 410 AD, they were thought to have been few and far between, given the growing level of threat that the country was facing from beyond its national borders. Quite apart from the Scottish tribes, such as the Caledonii, Cornovii, Gaels and Picts who lived in the far north, well beyond Roman control, other native tribes, including the Errain, Laigin, Deisi and the Dal Riata tribes from Ireland were said to have made their way across the Irish Sea and conquered parts of Western Britain. To the east, northern European tribes such as the Saxons and Vikings were said to have regularly raided around the British coast, stealing away people and possessions, as well as bringing death and destruction to numerous coastal settlements of Britain. The Votadini people, from the region of southern Scotland, were reported to have acted as a local auxiliary force to the regular Roman army during its occupation of Britain, although following the Roman abandonment of the country in the 5th century, a significant number of Votadini tribesmen were also said to have travelled south to the region of North Wales, where they established themselves as a defence against Irish raiders. However, such occurrences were rare and with Britain increasingly at risk from numerous foreign raiders, Romano-British leaders, including Ambrosius Aurelianus, were thought to have enlisted military aid from the European continent, in the form of Anglo-Saxon mercenaries, including the Angles, Saxons, Frisians and Jutes, who were promised both land and pay, in return for their military services. Unfortunately, before long, the Romano-British leadership were reported to have failed to pay the agreed monies, causing the mercenaries to launch their own full scale invasion of the country. In response, the British leadership appealed to the still surviving Western Roman Empire, whose leading military commander, Flavius Aetius, refused to send any of his remaining legions to Britain, informing the British leaders that they should look to their own resources to defend the country. For much of the period from 410 AD to 500 AD, large parts of Britain were reported to be in almost constant turmoil as the various competing factions, Britons, Angles, Jutes, Picts and Vikings all fought for control of particular regions of the country, a situation that was only temporarily halted in 500 AD, when the native Britons managed to defeat a combined Anglo-Saxon army, at the Battle of Mount Badon.

Unfortunately, despite this generally rare outright victory for the native British forces, many parts of the country continued to remain under foreign control, with the counties of Sussex, Kent, East Anglia and areas of Yorkshire all coming under Anglo Saxon control over a period of time, establishing the basis for the seven kingdoms that would come to dominate England right the way through to the 9th century. This Heptarchy of Anglo Saxon realms would eventually comprise Northumbria, Mercia, East Anglia, Essex, Sussex, Kent and Wessex, although all of these separate kingdoms would eventually be absorbed into the English nation, a geographical, political and cultural union first envisaged by King Alfred the Great in the 10th century. Parts of northern England, those controlled by the Viking's Danelaw, were reported to have remained outside of a unified England until 1013, when the whole of the country fell under Danish control, although Anglo Saxon rule was subsequently restored in 1042, when Edward the Confessor ascended the English throne. Although in part the Anglo Saxon invasion of post-Roman Britain represented a military takeover of the country, it was thought to have taken so long and happened so gradually that the two societies, British and Anglo-Saxon, essentially merged together to form a new, better and stronger Britain, one that embraced the best of its various characteristics from the Ancient Britons, Romans, Vikings and the Anglo Saxons, creating a new culture, traditions, national identity and even a new language. Those early Briton's who refused to adapt and embrace these new changes were thought to have been forced further west, creating the unique cultural identities of Cornwall, Wales and Cumbria that still exist to this present day, albeit in smaller numbers and in a much altered form. However, for the new Anglo Saxon England, one of the most significant advances, was thought to have been the development of centralised government and administration, which allowed the country to be ruled as a single political, financial and military union, allowing national policies, institutions and defence forces to be organised, both for the benefit of individual regions, as well as the country as a whole. No longer tribal or regional, England eventually began to emerge onto the European stage as a national entity in its own right, governed by a single monarch and administered by a collection of nationally appointed officials who brought the king's laws, justice and security to every corner of the country.

Many of the changes introduced during England's Dark Age military development are said to be directly attributable to the Anglo Saxon warriors who first sailed to Britain in the early 5th and 6th centuries, intent on conquering and settling the lands that lay across the English Channel. According to a number of sources, the Germanic Anglo Saxons of Western Europe were a highly disciplined martial society, whose fighting forces were typically divided into individual war bands, often comprising some thirty to forty men, who could fight and raid on their own, or as part of a much larger combined army. Each of these bands was thought to have been led by a war chief, who in turn was supported by a small cadre of full time warriors, who would serve, protect and die for that particular leader, much the same as the later Anglo Saxon Earls or Lords who maintained their own staff of knights or men at arms who served that individual nobleman alone. It was said to be these professional soldiers who were thought to have made up the vanguard of any Anglo Saxon army, with the younger, part time and older warriors making up the remainder of the fighting force that followed close behind. As the shock troops of the Anglo Saxon war band, the full time professional soldiers were reported to have been the most heavily armed, generally carrying a spear, shield, long sword, dagger and any other weapon that they could comfortably wield in battle, whilst at the same time being protected by a full metal helmet and chain-mail body armour. Supporting troops were thought to have been less well armed and protected than those who went into battle first, although most would have carried a shield, spear and double edged short sword that could be used during close quarter fighting. It has also been suggested that in common with the Spartan, Greek and Roman armies of earlier times, Anglo Saxon troops were regularly drilled in fighting formations, so that both small war bands and much larger military units could combine together, not only for their mutual defence, but also as part of a tactical offensive strategy. When a number of these individual war bands combined together to form a much bigger army unit, it has been suggested that this larger force was put under the command of the most senior leader, the Althing, who all of the other war chiefs would defer to in matters relating to military operations or strategies. Although it has been speculated that many Anglo Saxon armies may well have been relatively small contingents of men, as few as a couple of hundred at a time, it seems unlikely that such small numbers would have been able to play a significant role in conquering, let alone holding new territories, which suggests that larger numbers of Anglo Saxon warriors could and would be gathered together as and when the need arose.

Earl of Manchester   Sir Thomas Fairfax   Sir Philip Skippon

As Britain became increasingly settled in the post-Roman period, with a new Anglo-Saxon society beginning to be created throughout much of England, so many parts of the country began to be governed and protected by a new class of feudal Earls, who held individual territories for and on behalf of the English king. As part of their duties, each of these English noblemen was reported to have been responsible for the appointment of the local Sheriffs, Magistrates and Tax Collectors, who not only maintained the Earldom's legal and financial systems, but also ensured that their own area of the country was able to enjoy the King's Peace. These new Anglo Saxon Earls were also held to be responsible for ensuring the military security and defence of their individual regions through the creation of a local field force known as the "Fyrd", a local militia that could be called upon to take up arms and defend the country from any outside threat. The idea of regional armies had first been proposed and initiated by the Anglo Saxon king of Wessex, Alfred the Great, during the late 9th century, when he introduced the concept of the defensive "Burh" or "Burg", heavily defended towns and cities, which not only provided a safe haven for the local population, but also acted as military bases for the areas own Anglo Saxon defence forces. Typically, each of these burgs and their surrounding regions would be protected by the Earls own professional troops, as well as male members of the local population, many of whom were thought to have been granted lands in exchange for a given number of days of military service. According to some sources, service within the local militia, or Fyrd, was a highly regulated affair, which not only ensured that a sizeable local fighting force was available throughout the year, but that each man had sufficient time to work on his own lands, growing the crops and supplies that the country needed to survive. It has also been suggested that when members of the local militia, or Fyrd, were not engaged in military operations, then they would be used to defend the regions borders, strategic targets, or were undergoing additional military training, to improve their fighting capabilities with the shield, sword and spear that they would commonly carry into battle. A significant feature of the Fyrd was thought to have been its composition, most notably, the widely accepted view that it was a lightweight field army, one that consisted almost entirely of lightly armed infantrymen and archers, rather than a traditional mixture of light cavalry and heavily armed foot soldiers, as had often been the case with other historic armies, such as the Romans.

Although the English king was reported to have had his own personal military retinue, made up of armed retainers, full-time men at arms and members of the royal household, in order to put a large English army into the field against a foreign enemy, he continued to rely on the support of the new English nobility and their regional militia's to grant him their services. However, such support was not always guaranteed and on more than one occasion an English king was forced to rally his own military forces against those of an insubordinate nobleman who was either unwilling or unable to comply with the monarch's royal wishes. Such was thought to be the case in the middle of the 11th century, when the reigning English monarch, Edward the Confessor, either by accident or by design, was said to have caused dissention throughout the country, by reportedly nominating two entirely different men to be his legitimate heir, Harold Godwinsson and Duke William of Normandy, whilst at the same time, a third candidate, King Harald Hardrada of Norway, insisted on pursuing his own claim to the English throne. Consequently, when Edward died in 1066, all three candidates claimed to be the dead Anglo Saxon monarch's legitimate successor and although Harold Godwinsson found support amongst the majority of the English nobility and was subsequently crowned King of England, both Duke William and Harald Hardrada were reported to have received significant levels of support from a number of other leading nobles within the country. It was said to be as a result of such divisions that when the Norwegian army of Harald Hardrada landed on the east coast of England in 1066 in order to pursue Hardrada's claim against the English throne, Harold Godwinsson was forced to bring a fairly limited Fyrd, or field army with him to confront the foreign invaders, some of his nobles having previously switched their allegiances to Hardrada, whilst others simply chose to await the outcome of the Battle at Stamford Bridge, before deciding which side to support. However, despite the many obstacles that might well have prevented him from overcoming the Norwegian army, ultimately Harold Godwinsson and his Anglo Saxon Fyrd were said to have gained a victory over the invaders, whose leader, Harald Hardrada, was reported to be the most notable victim of the bitter and bloody engagement. Unfortunately for King Harold of England and his generally exhausted troops, almost as soon as they had overcome the Norwegian invaders, reports began to arrive informing them that the Norman leader, Duke William had landed at Pevensey with yet another invasion army, forcing Harold and his limited field force to march some two hundred and fifty miles south to confront this new military threat to their Anglo Saxon kingdom.

For many historians, the two armies that faced one another at the Battle of Hastings in 1066 were not that different to one another, save for the mounted Norman cavalry and the previously unseen motte and bailey castle, which would subsequently become such a regular feature in the British landscape. However, despite these advantages, ultimately the victory of William the Conqueror's Norman army over Harold Godwinsson's Anglo Saxon Fyrd was as much the result of extreme good fortune as much as anything else, with the misfortune of the Anglo Saxon's helping to hand victory to their Norman adversaries. Although no independent records from the time of Hastings are thought to exist, other than those produced by the two protagonists, who both have largely biased views on the course and outcome of the battle, for many historians the two sides were very evenly matched and it was only the ill-timed death of Harold Godwinsson that finally swung the engagement in Duke William' favour. With no clear royal successor, or prominent military commander to look to for leadership, the till then undefeated ranks of the Anglo Saxon Fyrd were thought to have dissipated through the actions of its men, rather than the attacks of William's cavalry and infantry. However, as their protective interlocked shields began to fragment, so the individual Anglo Saxon warriors became increasing susceptible to the lances of the Norman knights, the spears of the Norman foot soldiers and the arrows of the Norman archers, who quickly began to shatter the defensive lines, which the Fyrd relied upon for its protection. Even though William the Conqueror and his troops eventually managed to overcome this first English army and having fought their way to London, subsequently taking the Crown of England, within the wider country there were still thought to be sufficient fighting men to meet and defeat the Norman Lord, had they had an effective political and military commander who was popular enough to lead them. Unfortunately, rather than form a national alliance, which might confront the Norman invaders, many Anglo Saxon Earls and noblemen were thought to have sworn fealty to the new foreign monarch, whilst other chose to defend their territories independently, thereby guaranteeing their own demise and the end of Britain as an entirely Anglo Saxon kingdom.

Ascending the English throne in December 1066, despite having received the submissions of most of the Anglo Saxon nobility shortly after the Battle of Hastings, the new King, William I of England, was thought to have remained a relatively unpopular figure with a significant portion of the population, especially amongst the remaining Anglo Saxon nobility who had much to lose to a new Norman administration. Northern England and Wales were both thought to have been major centres of resistance to the rule of the new Norman king, forcing William to travel north with his huge armed retinue to begin what became known as the "Harrying of the North", a bloody campaign that saw numerous settlements razed, crops destroyed and thousands of innocent civilians driven from their lands. By 1070, just four years after his army had first landed in England, most of the country was thought to have been under the military control of Duke William, with only isolated pockets of resistance holding out in Wales, Scotland, Cornwall, Cumbria and East Anglia, although eventually these too were either defeated or isolated by the Norman king. In the aftermath of his successful invasion and occupation of England, the vast majority of Anglo Saxon noblemen and landowners were subsequently deprived of their lands and properties, which were then simply handed to the Norman knights, foreign mercenaries, financiers and Churches, who had either supported King William's great venture, or whose prayers were necessary for his continued good fortune. However, despite wearing the Crown of England and heading the largest military force in the country at that time, William's hold on his new English kingdom was thought to have remained tenuous at best, not least because of the relatively small numbers of Norman troops that were expected to guard the far reaches of his new realm. Even though fresh forces might occasionally be brought over from Normandy to supplement or replace those troops already stationed in England, King William did not have an inexhaustible supply of soldiers for his suddenly expanded territories and was therefore forced to look for alternative methods of securing his new lands. The system that he ultimately chose to employ, was the same one that had worked so well in Europe, where the country was broken down into individual regions, each of which was controlled by a nobleman of the king's choice, who would rule that particular Barony, or Earldom, for and on behalf of the Norman monarch, much the same as the Anglo Saxon king's had done before him. In turn, these newly created Norman Barons and Earls would be supported by their own cadre of sub-lieutenants, or knights, who would help control specific areas of the individual Baron or Earl's territories, ensuring that they remained safe and secure, at the same time ensuring that rents were paid and taxes collected.

As an occupying army, especially one that was comparatively small, the Norman forces of William the Conqueror were forced to consider their own personal safety as a matter of some priority, leading to the widespread introduction of the Norman motte and bailey castle to the English landscape. Initially constructed as a temporary timber redoubt, which was designed as a short term defensive shelter for the Norman troops, their horses and their possessions, almost inevitably, these early structures were later replaced by the much more permanent and far larger stone built castles, which continue to litter the British countryside to the present day. Although these early fortresses offered some level of protection to the new Norman elite, ultimately these relatively small numbers of foreign aristocrats found themselves isolated amongst a predominantly Anglo Saxon population, who carried on with their lives, entirely regardless of the foreign nobility who ruled over them. According to most informed sources, just like the Anglo Saxons before them, these new Norman incomers, rather than fundamentally altering the language, traditions and customs of the native British people, instead found themselves and their own heritage being absorbed by and added to what would eventually become the basis of the modern British character, a combination of Ancient Briton, Celtic, Viking, Anglo Saxon and Norman. Similarly, necessity was also thought to have brought about the creation of a new English fighting force, one that was bought and paid for by individual Norman nobles, who needed to expand their own household troops, not only to protect their own extensive possessions, but also to offer military support to the English King, in regional disputes, foreign wars, or even on crusades to the Holy Land. According to some records, King William I even took some English troops with him when he returned to continental Europe after securing his hold in his new kingdom of England, suggesting that a number of Anglo Saxon troops had already transferred their allegiance to the Norman Duke, either before or shortly after the Battle of Hastings in October 1066. Whatever the case, the fact that William I was reported to have brought an estimated twenty thousand men with him from Normandy, many of whom were reported to have died from battle wounds and disease, would seem to indicate that a large number of English born Anglo Saxon troops, must have played a part in helping the Norman Duke to secure his new territories.

The practice of protecting England through local troops raised by a series of regional Barons, Earls and other noblemen, who owed their title and position to one or other English monarch, undoubtedly had its roots in the Anglo Saxon period, although similar arrangements were thought to have operated elsewhere, following the demise of the Roman Empire. However, a number of problems presented themselves with regard to such locally raised forces, not least the fact that most of the individual soldiers were linked to the local community and were often loathe to operate outside of their home areas, preventing them from being used on a national, much less an international basis. Although such attitudes would change over the coming centuries, ultimately such troops remained tied and generally loyal to the particular nobleman who employed them, rather than to whichever monarch happened to be sitting on the English throne at that period of time. As a result, the military and political power of individual nobles could often outweigh the authority of a king and it was often the case that royal decisions were almost entirely dictated to and by the will of a particular Earl or Baron, who had the support of his own private army and whose wishes could not therefore be overlooked. Throughout the 12th and early 13th centuries, there were thought to be numerous instances of the future of the English Crown being decided by a handful of England's most powerful noblemen, who had the military might to insist that a particular candidate was placed on the throne, or that a king modify his behaviour, as in the case of King John and the Magna Carta in 1215. Even two of England's most able and militaristic Plantagenet monarch's Henry III and his son, the later Edward I, were said to have found themselves held hostage by a number of these powerful noblemen, whose revolt was only finally brought to an end after Henry and Edward managed to persuade or bribe some of the rebel Lords to once again support the royalist cause, thereby restoring authority to the English Crown. However, in order to gain the support of these former rebels, Henry and Edward were thought to have granted them even more titles and lands, essentially turning them into an even greater potential threat to the English monarchy, a situation that would inevitably lead to more military conflicts in later years. For the remainder of the Plantagenet period and on through the Lancastrian and Yorkist eras, England was thought to have suffered a series of royal disputes, which saw the various private armies of kings and nobles fight one another, not only for control of the country, but also for the Crown of England itself.

Civil War Dragoon

Civil War Pikemen

Civil War Musketeers

By the beginning of the 16th century, most of the large private armies, previously under the personal control of England's leading Earls and Barons had not only been outlawed, but had been largely replaced by a series of militias, local forces who were under the direct control of the monarch's representative, the Lord Lieutenant, who was responsible for the defence and security of his local region. Although the requirement for young men to defend their homeland was known to have existed since Anglo Saxon times, it was only finally placed into law in 1285 when the Statute of Winchester legally obliged any man between the ages of fifteen and sixty to take up arms as and when required to do so. The Act was reported to have taken account of the differing social and financial standings of each man, with the common worker expected to arm himself with a scythe or a knife, while the rich man was instructed to provide himself with a horse and armour. In many towns and cities, compulsory weapons training was reported to have become the norm, with the young men of the city, town or village obliged to attend archery and drill classes, so that they were able to defend their local region, as and when the need arose. Often the Lord Lieutenant deferred the training of such militias to the local Mayor and Sheriffs, who not only knew the local population, but would have been aware of the local geography, ensuring that any strategic targets and highways would have been protected during time of war. Each eligible man within a town, city or parish was thought to have been recorded on a local muster roll, so that numbers could be calculated and men identified as and when required, with those called to service being expected to attend a rallying or muster point along with his comrades. However, just like the Fyrd many centuries earlier, many of these local volunteers were thought to have been unwilling to serve outside of the own home areas, once again restricting their use to that of a regional force, rather than representing any sort of national army. A number of England's largest towns and cities were said to have been more fortunate than most, in that they could muster very large numbers of men who were prepared to meet and train regularly, helping to form the basis for the more established trained bands, or militias that would defend Britain's biggest towns and cities right through to the late 19th century. As has been mentioned elsewhere, the principal defender's of the British Isles for many centuries was the English, later the British Navy, who in nearly all circumstances would have been in the front line of defending the country from enemy invasion. The fact that the much larger English fleet of King Harold Godwinsson had been withdrawn to port for re-provisioning, just prior to the Norman invasion of England by William the Conqueror, perfectly illustrated the reliance placed on the nations navy and what might happen when that naval force was no longer there to protects England's coastline.

It was thought to be the inefficiencies and strategic limitations of local militias and trained bands during the early 17th century, most notably during the first months of the English Civil War that caused certain Parliamentary leaders to reconsider the efficacy of such armed forces. Although most of Parliaments troops were reported to have been raised through local Associations, as with the earlier Fyrd and Militias, most of their men were either unwilling or unable to be used far from home, making them tactically useless to the Parliamentary cause. By the middle of 1644, the fact that these local forces were being commanded by a mixture of Parliamentary General's who all had their own strategic religious and political objectives, some favouring peace with the Crown, whilst others the complete removal of the monarch, Charles I, it was becoming increasingly clear to a few leaders that little would be achieved if the military situation remained the same. Eventually, Parliament was reported to have divided into two distinct factions, with the Earl of Manchester's side demanding that Parliament should seek the best possible terms with the king, whilst hardliners such as Oliver Cromwell were determined to inflict a complete military defeat on the royalist cause, before dictating terms to the monarch. The divisions between the two political factions was said to have reached crisis point following the Second Battle of Newbury in October 1644, when the Earls of Essex and Manchester failed to destroy the kings forces, despite having the opportunity to do so. By the following month, a Parliamentary committee was formed to oversee the conduct of the war, as a result of which the Self Denying Ordinance was eventually passed by both Houses of Parliament, a statute which forbade all members of the Commons and Lords from holding any sort of military office and essentially removing the Earls of Manchester, Essex, as well as other royalist sympathisers from their commands. By January of 1645 the same committee was also reported to have laid out the basis for a New Model Army and appointed Sir Thomas Fairfax as the Captain General of this brand new military force, whilst Sir Philip Skippon was appointed as the Sergeant Major General of Foot. Although Oliver Cromwell was forbidden by the new Self Denying Ordinance from continuing to hold his military post, within a short time, Sir Thomas Fairfax was said to have made a special request for Cromwell to be allowed to hold a military command and within weeks he had been granted a temporary exception, which permitted him to take control of a cavalry regiment. Although he was given a three month allowance to hold his temporary military command, in practice this exemption was thought to have been continually renewed, allowing Cromwell and three other Members of Parliament to retain his military command throughout the entire period of the English Civil War.

Initially, Parliament's New Model Army was said to have comprised some twenty-odd thousand troops, made up of nearly seven thousand cavalrymen, fourteen thousand foot soldiers and an additional one thousand dragoons, many of which had been taken from the earlier regiments commanded by the Earls of Manchester and Essex, who were no longer involved in the military conduct of the war. Unlike the earlier militias and associations, the New Model Army was run along new and uniform lines, so that each infantryman, dragoon and cavalryman knew his rights, duties and conditions of service, with a centralised system being put in place, to ensure that each soldier was fed, clothed and more importantly, paid for his military service. Another peculiar feature of this new English national army was thought to have been its insistence that only the ablest soldiers should be recruited and retained, regardless of their rank or indeed their financial status, recognising perhaps that in many cases that the richest men did not always make the best soldiers, something that later governments often seemed to overlook. However, regardless of an individual soldiers social standing or wealth, according to some reports the New Model Army managed to retain rich and poor alike, as each in his turn was said to have been driven by the ideals of the Parliamentary cause, irrespective of his own particular circumstances. The elite troops of the New Model Army was said to be the cavalry regiments, whose behaviour and battlefield tactics were determined by the rules laid down by commander's such as Oliver Cromwell, who insisted that these mounted troops should be the most highly disciplined and determined of their age. Unlike their royalist counterparts and earlier cavalry forces, Cromwell's cavalry regiments were reported to have been trained to work alongside the New Model Army's infantry, musketeers, Dragoons and artillery units, marking the beginning of what would inevitably become the sort of modern warfare that would be fought in future years. For their part the thousand strong Dragoon force were often regarded and used as mounted infantry or skirmishers, which could be used to intercept any sort of enemy force, or even to assault enemy positions, holding them until reinforced by the main infantry body. But perhaps the most significant military force within the New Model Army was the infantry, which was reported to have been a mixed body, comprising two thirds musketeers and one third pikemen, comparable to anything that the royalist army of Charles I had at that particular time. However, unlike earlier English armies, which had generally been made up of half-trained, poorly equipped and often dissatisfied militias, the musketeers and pikemen of the new Parliamentary army were reported to have been highly trained, very well equipped and constantly motivated by their commanders, making them a far superior force to the one being fielded by the royalist cause.

The New Model Army was said to have first been used in May 1645 when elements of the new force attempted to break the royalist siege of Taunton, where the famous General-at-sea, then simply Colonel Robert Blake, was reported to have been blockaded in the town, along with his relatively small Parliamentary garrison. Unfortunately, these initial attempts to break the siege were said to have been largely unsuccessful, ostensibly because most of the New Model Army was being prepared for the forthcoming Battle of Naseby, which finally took place on the 14th June 1645. According to some contemporary reports of this decisive Civil War engagement, the battle itself proved to be a baptism of fire for the new professional Parliamentary army, simply because the royalist army of Charles I was said to have contained some of the monarch's most experienced and battle-hardened soldiers, men who would not have been concerned by the prospect of facing enemy infantry or cavalry. However, unlike Cromwell's mounted troops, who were both well trained and highly disciplined, elements of the royalist cavalry were reported to have been in such a rush to pursue retreating Parliamentary horsemen, that they left the field, thereby handing a tactical advantage to Oliver Cromwell's remaining mounted troops, which helped secure a Parliamentary victory over the king. This battle was also thought to have been marked by a number of murderous incidents, where Fairfax's and Cromwell's troops were reported to have slaughtered several hundred royalist supporters, including a hundred or so women who were part of the captured royalist baggage train. According to some sources, the women were killed, ostensibly because they were believed to be Irish, suggesting that even at this point in time; some English troops had such a deep inbred hatred of the Irish and their perceived Roman Catholic faith that they were prepared to commit cold blooded murder to satisfy their own racial and religious intolerance. Although the Battle of Naseby did not bring an end to the First English Civil War, most historians are thought to take the view that this particular engagement did mark the beginning of the end for the royalist cause, mainly because of the loss of so many of King Charles' highly experienced troops. It was said to be in the aftermath of Naseby that Thomas Fairfax was subsequently able to sent troops to lift the royalist siege of Taunton and take control of most of the West Country at the same time. The last great military engagement of the First English Civil War was the Battle of Langport which took place just outside Bristol on the 10th July 1645 and which resulted in the New Model Army defeating the last remaining royalist field force in England, an action that not only forced King Charles I to surrender himself to the Scottish army, but also brought an end to hostilities between Parliament and the English Crown.

However, having won the First English Civil War, discontent and disagreements then began to spread throughout Parliament, the New Model Army's military commanders and even amongst the rank and file members of the victorious English army, as to what should happen to the country in the aftermath of the bitter national conflict. For most of the common soldiers employed by Parliaments new army, their greatest cause of resentment was said to be the fact that they had not been paid for some time and with rumours of them being sent to Ireland to suppress royalist unrest there, many of these same English troops, were thought to be extremely angry about their treatment by Parliament. Within the army itself there was also thought to be many social and political agitators who not only wanted to see an end to the English monarchy, but also wanted to see new democratic and religious freedoms introduced, including universal male suffrage, a redrawing of the existing electoral boundaries and a reorganisation of the country's legal systems, much of which was proposed by a group called the Levellers. Members of a political movement, which was dedicated to the abolition of corruption in public office, the introduction of religious tolerance towards all faiths, as well as the translation of the law into the common tongue, it was reported to be members of the Levellers who proposed a new constitution for the country, which would have included many of these core demands. However, at the same time that the Levellers were trying to force their own demands on the English Parliament, many representatives, both in the Commons and the Lords, were trying to lobby for a complete restoration of the king's constitutional position, without any sort of reforms taking place, something that was totally unacceptable to most of the soldiers who had risked their lives in order to bring about change. In order to try and resolve these issues, in 1647 a new committee called the Army Council met for the first time, a consultative body which was reported to have drawn representatives from all of the different groups within the army, in the hope to find an agreeable solution to the many and varied demands that were being proposed. Unfortunately, even though this new council was said to have met several times in order to find a solution, ultimately it was thought to be as a result of lobbying by senior officers within individual regiments that brought about a solution, although even this was thought to have been resisted by some troops, causing Oliver Cromwell to use armed force to suppress the minor military mutiny.

During the time that Parliament and the army were busily debating the subject of soldiers pay, future constitutions and the use of English troops in Ireland, the English king, Charles I was said to have been busy negotiating with any party that might help restore him to the English throne. With four major power blocks operating in the country, the royalists, the New Model Army, the English Parliament and the Scottish Parliament, Charles hoped to be able to make some form of alliance with one or more of these parties which might allow him to seize back the political and military initiative, which would then allow him to dictate terms to the other sides in the ongoing dispute. Having first surrendered himself to the Scots, Charles was subsequently handed over to the English Parliament, many of whose members were keen to see the monarch restored to the throne, but on their own terms, rather than those of the king or indeed the army. However, before long, the monarch was said to have been snatched away from Parliamentary custody by a young army officer who served under the army's military commander, Sir Thomas Fairfax, causing both English and Scottish Parliaments to begin making preparation for a fresh civil war, this time against the English legislatures own creation, the New Model Army. In the first instance though, the English Parliament was said to have tried other methods to undermine the army's position, firstly by attempting to disband it, then trying to send it abroad on foreign service, before finally threatening to withhold its pay, all of which simply hardened the army's attitude and made them even more determined to bring about some sort of political change. As relations between Parliament and the army leadership became increasingly fraught, so Charles I was thought to have played his own part in ensuring that the divisions grew deeper and deeper, to the point that the Parliament made the fateful decision to ally itself with the remaining royalist factions in the country, along with supporters of the Scottish Parliament, resulting in the outbreak of the Second English Civil War in February 1648.

Duke of Hamilton

Richard Cromwell

Coldstream Regiment

Fortunately for Cromwell and the other leading New Model Army officers, the constitution that had been imposed by Fairfax, which dealt with many of the English soldiers political, social and religious grievances, had ensured that the New Model Army remained a viable fighting force, even up to and beyond the outbreak of the second civil conflict. However, the uncertainty that had arisen after the First English Civil War, as to the future of the king himself and the possible introduction of new social, political and religious freedoms was thought to have caused some Parliamentary commanders to reconsider their positions, causing some of them to switch sides on the outbreak of the Second English Civil War, much to the alarm and annoyance of Thomas Fairfax and Oliver Cromwell. Although not all royalists supported the king's second military campaign against Parliament, ultimately the Second English Civil War proved to a much more one-sided affair, simply because the English Parliament very quickly withdrew from the conflict, as their tacit support for the king's cause made such representatives highly unpopular with the general public, a fact that commanders such as Cromwell exploited to great effect. With limited resources of their own and with no outside military aid available to their cause, the royalist forces that participated in this Second English Civil War very quickly came under increasing pressure from the better armed, equipped and much more professional New Model Army, which during the first half of 1648 effectively crushed King Charles' remaining military support in England. By June of the same year, it was a Scottish Engager Army, a force fielded by the Scottish Parliament and led by the Duke of Hamilton which was said to have crossed the border to pursue Charles' royal ambitions in England, although the fact that it was comprised mostly of raw recruits and largely inexperienced officers meant that it posed little threat to the New Model Army and its battle hardened troops. The defining military engagement in the north of England was said to have taken place at Preston, between the 17th and 19th August 1648, when a twenty thousand strong Scottish army was met and defeated by Oliver Cromwell's force of around eight thousand seasoned soldiers, during which, some two thousand Engagers were reported to have been killed, as against the hundred or so members of the New Model Army who were said to have perished. Although there were thought to have been several more attempts to revive the royalist cause in England and Wales, ultimately all of them came to nothing and by the end of August 1648 the fighting had come to an end once again. However, for King Charles himself, his failure to overturn the outcome of the First English Civil War and his later decision to initiate yet another conflict in his kingdom, ensured that the calls for him to be removed permanently would become increasingly loud, leading to him later being charged, tried, sentenced and executed as a tyrant and traitor on the 30th January 1649.

In August 1649, elements of the New Model Army were reported to have been landed in Ireland to help suppress a combined Royalist-Roman Catholic insurrection that was taking place in the country, beginning a campaign which would not only heighten the divisions between the various faith communities there, but also create a legacy of hatred towards the English commander of those forces, Oliver Cromwell. The various military campaigns of Cromwell's forces in Ireland have been dealt with in an entirely separate chapter of this book, but suffice to say the New Model Army's campaigns in Ireland ultimately proved to be extremely costly affairs, both in terms of national unity and for the tens of thousands of people, military and civilian who were reported to have perished as a result of them. At the same time that English troops were involved in bitter fighting with the Royalists and Roman Catholic rebels in Ireland, other units of the New Model Army were reported to have been involved in what has been called the Third English Civil War, fighting Scottish Covenanters, who had allied themselves to the royalist cause of the late English king's son and heir, King Charles II. Agreeing to support Charles II claim to the English, Scottish and Irish thrones, which had been usurped by the Parliamentary cause, the Covenanters were thought to have been an alliance of Presbyterian's who were happy to lend their military support to Charles Stuart's campaign, in return for guaranteeing future religious reforms, both in Scotland and England. Unfortunately for the new Charles II and his Scottish allies, despite outnumbering the New Model Army units sent to suppress their activities, the English forces under the command of Oliver Cromwell ultimately proved to be superior to the Covenanter's forces, defeating them first at the Battle of Dunbar and later at the Battle of Inverkeithing. Despite these reversals, the ousted Stuart monarch, Charles II, still managed to lead a Scottish army into England, before being met and defeated at the Battle of Worcester, on the 3rd September 1651, which proved to be the final battle of the three English Civil Wars. In the aftermath of the Scottish royalist rebellion, the English army was reported to have maintained a significant presence in the north of the country, not only to guard against any future royalist revolts, but also to offer some degree of protection against highland raiders who were thought to have become more troublesome during the same period. Elsewhere on the British mainland, units of the New Model Army were thought to have been used to suppress various outbreaks of violence and insurrection in the country, although no serious threat to their authority was thought to have occurred following the royalist uprisings in Scotland, save for the ongoing disputes that were said to have continued in Ireland. Internationally, in 1654 the new English Commonwealth was reported to have declared war on the formidable Spanish Empire, as a result of which units of the English army were despatched to the Caribbean, to try and take control of Spanish possessions there, including the island of Hispaniola, now marked by the modern states of Haiti and the Dominican Republic. Unfortunately for the Parliamentarian forces sent to accomplish this task, tropical diseases, inclement weather and large numbers of highly experienced Spanish troops were all thought to have contrived to thwart the planned invasion of Hispaniola, although these same English forces did eventually manage to invade and maintain control of the island of Jamaica, which ultimately became one of Britain's most prized overseas assets.

The New Model Army was reported to have thrived during the Protectorate of Oliver Cromwell, who held the unique constitutional position of Lord Protector from December 1653 until his death in September 1658, after which the army's very existence began to be questioned by a newly resurgent Parliament and the many royalist representatives who held power there. Although Oliver Cromwell had initially been succeeded to the office of Lord Protector by his son Richard, unlike his father, the younger Cromwell was seemingly unable to cope with the increasing political and constitutional pressures that the office brought with it and was reported to have resigned the post in May 1659. With the army apparently fragmented under the leadership of various popular military commanders, for the new English Parliament there was a real fear that the country might well descend into yet another round of civil wars, as each military grouping sought to place themselves and their own local commanders in the most advantageous position. However, for other army leaders, including those who recognised the need to a central figure at the heart of the British constitution, the most obvious solution was for the English monarchy to be restored, something that they would not dared to have suggested during the lifetime of Oliver Cromwell. One such military leader though, General George Monck, who had been put in charge of the New Model Army units in Scotland, was reported to have recognised the dangers of the country fragmenting under different military leaders and as a result brought his forces south to London, to help support the restoration of the Stuart family, in the person of Charles II, who was officially crowned King of England on the 29th May 1660. Perhaps mindful of the risks posed by having a large standing army at home that might well be exploited by the new monarch, Parliament, or by some or other party, following the succession of Charles II to the English throne, most of the New Model Army regiments were subsequently disbanded, save for General Moncks own troops which subsequently evolved into the Coldstream Guards and the Regiment of Cuirassiers, which eventually became the Royal Horse Guards, both of which are reported to be two of the oldest serving regiments in the British Army. The Coldstream Guards were said to have been formally founded at Coldstream in Scotland in 1650, by their then commander General George Monck and now form part of the Household Division, being only one of two English regiments that can trace its ancestry all the way back to the New Model Army. The second British military unit that shares that particular history is the Royal Horse Guards, which has since been renamed as the Blues and Royals, but which was originally founded as the Royal Cuirassiers by Sir Arthur Haselrig at Newcastle upon Tyne in August 1650, on the orders of Oliver Cromwell. After the restoration of Charles II in 1660, the unit was renamed as the Earl of Oxford's Regiment and was reported to have been attired in a blue tunic, giving rise to the nickname the "Oxford Blues", leading to their later identification simply as "The Blues". It was only in 1969 that this earlier corp. was amalgamated with the Royal Dragoons, helping to create the regiment that is much more familiar today as the "Blues and Royals".

Although the British Army has only existed since the Act of Union was signed in 1707, which amalgamated the then English and Scottish Parliaments into a single political legislature, the earliest and therefore the oldest military regiment in Britain is reported to be the Royal Scots, or the Royal Regiment of Scotland, which has existed since 1633, a decade or more before the New Model Army of England was first raised by the English Parliament. The Royal Scots was said to have been founded by Sir John Hepburn on the orders of the monarch, King Charles I, ostensibly for service in France and was thought to have been made up of Scottish and Swedish mercenaries, who served almost exclusively in Europe, until 1661 when the regiment was finally recalled to Britain, to help secure the reign of the recently restored English monarch, Charles II. From a military perspective, the Royal Scots were thought to have represented the model upon which all subsequent British infantry regiments were based, even though elements of the Royal Scots were reported to have been sent to France during the 1660's and 1670's, although Royal Scots troops were also said to have responded to the Dutch naval raid on the Medway in June 1667, the sound of their drums helping to reassure frightened English residents that Scottish troops were coming to their aid. By 1680, the regiment was thought to have been withdrawn from European service once and for all, although they were subsequently despatched to Tangiers to take possession of the territory, which had been granted to Charles II as part of his wedding dowry acquired through his marriage to the Portuguese princess, Catherine of Braganza. Having spent some four years protecting the city from the native Moroccan Berbers, who wanted to reclaim the territory from the British, in 1684 the Royal Scots, now renamed as His Majesty's Royal Regiment of Foot were recalled to Britain, just in time to participate in the highly divisive Monmouth Rebellion, which took place in southwest England in 1685. When Charles II died on the 2nd February 1685, his younger brother James II succeeded to the English, Scottish and Irish thrones, although his right to rule the kingdoms was immediately contested by James Scott, the 1st Duke of Monmouth, who was an illegitimate son of the late monarch, Charles II. However, despite Monmouth's royal bloodline and his protestant faith, he failed to gain any widespread support for his royal claims, which resulted in his ill-equipped forces being easily defeated by James II's far better armed and much more experienced troops, including the Royal Scots. In the year following the suppression of Monmouth's claim, the regiment was reported to have been increased in size when a second battalion was added to their ranks, possibly illustrating King James II increasing concerns over the security of his own reign, which was said to have come under increasing threat largely because of his Roman Catholic faith and his habit of appointing fellow Catholics to important government posts. Almost inevitably, with Parliament and the monarch at odds with one another, a number of England's leading nobles and members of Parliament were reported to have approached James' son-in-law, William of Orange, to invade the country, in order to remove King James II from power. According to some sources, His Majesty's Royal Regiment of Foot, the Royal Scots, were said to be the only British regiment that actually remained faithful to the unpopular Stuart king, to the point that when James finally abandoned the country in favour of William and Mary in December 1688, members of the Royal Scots mutinied rather than serve the new foreign monarchs and as a result had to be forcibly disarmed. It was also reported that as a direct result of the army's faithfulness to the monarch, as opposed to the people through Parliament, one major piece of legislation passed by the English legislature was the Bill of Rights 1689, which finally put an end to a British monarch's right to raise a standing national army and placing control of such military forces firmly in the hands of the country's political representatives, a situation that remains in force to the present day.

Over the period of the next half century or so, the administration and formation of the British military was reported to have been reorganised, so that the power to raise, arm, feed, pay and deploy the country's land forces was placed into the hands of several trustworthy officials, rather than being at the disposal of one individual. New departments and official government offices were created to oversee this new professional military force, including the likes of the War Office, Board of Ordnance and the Commissariat, all of which were directly responsible for the general administration, arming, feeding and transportation of the nations infantry, along with its cavalry, artillery and the various auxiliary services that were necessary to help the army function on a day-by-day basis. Ultimately though, all of the various heads of departments, who controlled the various aspects of maintaining the British military, were reported to have been answerable to the Secretary of State for War, the Minister, or Lord, who was appointed to act as the link between the legislature and the military themselves. It was also during the same period that the names and identifications of the various regiments and local militias began to be rationalised, so that individual regiments, which had previously been named after their founders, began to be identified by seniority, with a "First" regiment typically being the oldest of its type, whether they were infantry, cavalry, or artillery units. Although local regiments or militias might commonly retain their original titles within their home areas, the adoption of the new numerical ranking system not only helped administer the growing lists of army units, but also ensured that there was no likelihood of one or more regiment sharing a common name, a situation that would undoubtedly have caused enormous administrative confusion within government and elsewhere.

Sir Arthur Haselrig

Major Roger Roberts

British Redcoats

Within late 17th and early 18th century Britain, several military conflicts were reported to have raged around the attempts of the exiled Stuart family to regain their rightful place on the thrones of England, Scotland and Ireland, a royal claim that was only finally extinguished by the Act of Settlement 1701, which was intended to ratify the right of succession to the Three Kingdoms, ensuring that only Protestant heirs or relations of William and Mary could ascend to the monarchy of the various kingdoms and that Roman Catholic heirs could not. Although this particular piece of legislation had not been passed by the time the ousted king, James II, attempted to recover his throne through the support of Roman Catholic's in Ireland, all of the subsequent Jacobite rebellions that took place in Ireland and Scotland ultimately proved to be military disasters for the Stuart cause. Despite the fact that the Stuart family were of Scottish descent and should therefore have had a great deal of support amongst the native peoples there, the apparently high handed and indifferent attitudes of James' predecessor's, including James I, Charles I, Charles II and even James II himself was thought to have divided Scottish public opinion, over whether or not the ousted monarch should be supported. For most of the Scottish people and their traditional tribal leaders, the ascension of William of Orange and his Stuart Wife, Mary, to the English and Scottish thrones was thought to have been generally acceptable, bearing in mind that for most of them James II's reign had not been that beneficial. However, when a number of Jacobite supporters rebelled against the new Protestant king and queen in 1689, bringing death and destruction to the Highlands of Scotland, William and Mary felt compelled to demand that all Clan leaders should subsequently swear an oath of allegiance to the new king and queen in front of an appointed magistrate. Although most Clan leaders were content to swear the oath, those who had allied themselves to the Jacobite cause found it necessary to ask James II's permission to do so, a process which was said to have taken some time, bearing in mind that James Stuart had retired back to France after his humiliating military defeats in Ireland. Unfortunately, this requirement for pro-Jacobite clans to take the oath was reported to have been exploited by their Scottish enemies, who were eager to settle long standing disputes, at least one of which was said to have led to the Glencoe Massacre of 13th February 1692, which saw thirty eight men of the McDonald clan murdered by British troops, including men from the rival

Campbell clan, who were staying there as guests. In addition to those that were killed outright by the soldiers, a further forty or more men, women and children were reported to have died from starvation and exposure, after they were driven out of their homes in order to escape the murderous onslaught. Although no single individual ever faced charges for what was later deemed to be murder by a Scottish court of inquiry, the outrage was even reported to have cast a shadow over the reign of the monarch's William and Mary, as well as helping to harden the attitudes of those Jacobites who would continue to fight for the Stuart family's cause for the next sixty years or more. However, for Britain's evolving military forces, this particular period of Scottish history was reported to have been incredibly valuable, with a significant number of loyalist regiments being raised, which would go on to play a vitally important role in helping to create the British Empire, by imposing Britain's political will around the globe, guarding its overseas territories from foreign enemies and helping some of their regiments achieve almost legendary status in some of history's bloodiest conflicts.

As the Stuart family's campaign to reclaim their royal heritage inexorably declined, so Britain found itself increasingly engaged in the political upheavals of continental Europe, the Indian sub-continent, the Caribbean and North America, all of which put great strains on the limited military manpower that the country had relied upon historically. As a result, the British Army found itself having to recruit increasing numbers of new British born troops and local native levies, many of whom were poor quality candidates and in some cases were the very worst members of society, thieves and cut-throats who saw enlistment as a way of avoiding the law. It was thought to be as a result of such inferior recruitment that discipline within the army was reported to have become much harsher, in order to ensure that such base individuals could be properly managed by the military authorities and the officers who were charged with controlling the growing numbers of ex-convicts, lawbreakers and miscreants, who were regularly being drafted into some British Army regiments. Much of the problem for the army as an employer was that it also had to contend with the various merchant companies who regularly recruited the very best soldiers and officers for their own private armies, in order to impose its commercial will on the native population of the Indian subcontinent and elsewhere. Although these private armies were thought to have performed reasonably well when faced with most native forces, who were less well trained and well-equipped, in 1756 Britain found itself at war with its traditional European adversary, France, which was reported to have had a much larger and more effective land army. Known formally as the Seven Years War, this military conflict has occasionally been called the "First World War", simply because it involved the two sides waging war against one another in Europe, Asia and North America, as well as on the high seas, becoming one of the most extensive conflicts that had ever been fought up until that time. Driven by the competing imperial ambitions of Britain, France and their respective European allies, for the most part, Britain's military forces were reported to confronted their adversaries in North America, including the territories of Canada, India, the Caribbean and West Africa, as well as in the world's great oceans, where the Royal Navy continued to reign relatively unchallenged. However, in the initial stages of the conflict, British land forces were reported to have fared comparatively badly, often failing to match the effectiveness of their French enemies and regularly falling victim to the many unknown diseases that plagued many of Britain's overseas territories. As a result, British officials were often forced to raise additional native levy forces, who were not only less prone to outbreaks of disease, but who knew the local terrain far better than the incoming foreign soldiers and in some cases proved to be far more successful troops than their British counterparts.

Although Britain did not supply significant numbers of ground troops to the European theatres during the Seven Years War, Royal Navy ships and raiding parties were reported to have played an important role in attacking French interests along the coast, thereby diverting French troops from more important uses. For its part, the ships of the Royal Navy were also known to have thwarted a number of planned Franco-Spanish naval operations that were intended to be launched against Britain and her allies, including a military invasion of Britain, which was finally undone after the Royal Navy defeated a combined Franco-Spanish fleet at Quiberon Bay on the 20th November 1759. However, Britain only sent its first land forces into the European theatre in April 1758 when some nine thousand men were despatched to support the Hanoverian army of Duke Ferdinand of Brunswick, who was reported to have made significant gains over the French before being forced back by a much larger enemy force. As the war dragged on with advances and reversals on both sides, almost inevitably the conflict caused other neighbouring European states to become involved, with Spain allying itself with the French cause and Portugal choosing to support the British side, a development that forced Britain to declare war against Spain in January 1762. Almost immediately Spain was said to have launched a military attack against Portugal, causing Britain to despatch even more of her own troops to the European continent in defence of Portugal's territorial borders, which they eventually managed to secure after several weeks of bitter fighting. For the most part however, Britain's major military undertakings were reported to have centred on its colonial possessions, the vast territories which helped to finance the burgeoning Empire's military and industrial expansion. Although Britain's campaigns in North America had had a less than auspicious start, as time progressed and additional military resources were introduced to the continent, so slowly but surely, Britain's land forces were able to turn around many of the reversals that the colonial authorities had initially suffered. As in Britain, the defence of many of Britain's overseas townships, cities and regions was reported to have been left in the hands of local militias, who could be supported as and when necessary by regular troops who were commonly garrisoned at a small number of centrally located forts or camps, which were within easy reach of most of the early eastern settlements. However, just as the French had traditionally allied themselves to a number of indigenous Indian tribes in North America, so too did Britain, forming alliances with any and all anti-French communities in the north of the continent, providing them with whatever stores were required to carry out hit and run raids against French commercial and military interests. The Seven Years War was also thought to have seen the birth and development of the first specialist American militias who were able to conduct armed campaigns against those native Indian tribes who were actively supporting the French cause in North America. Units such as Rogers' Rangers were reported to have been independent light infantry companies that were used for reconnaissance and special operations against both French and hostile Indian forces during the period of the Seven Years War, which is often referred to in North America as the French and Indian War. Founded in 1755 by Major Robert Rogers, although they were thought to have been regarded by most British commanders as little more than a local militia, the fact that these units could and would fight in the most atrocious conditions and were responsible for countless attacks against enemy forces undoubtedly made them one of the most effective fighting forces of the entire conflict, regardless of the fact that the British authorities singularly failed to recognise their achievements. However, the greatest benefit that the British enjoyed throughout the seven year conflict was the presence of the Royal Navy, which not only provided much needed armed support for troops who were attacking coastal objectives, but whose ships were able to replace stores and men on a fairly regular basis, unlike the French fleet which was reluctant to put to sea and face an all out battle with Britain's superior naval forces. Despite such advantages though, it was only in the late 1750's that British forces began to make serious inroads into the French domination of the American continents most northerly states, which they had named New France, but later evolved into modern day Canada. In September 1759, British forces commanded by General Wolfe, were reported to have captured the French city of Quebec and in September of the following year, the other great French possession, Montreal, also fell into British hands, after it had been temporarily besieged by a much larger British force. Although France was reported to have made several determined efforts to try and recover some of their lost North American territories during 1762, ultimately they were said to have lacked the military capability to forcibly remove the British troops who now held almost the entire eastern seaboard of North America, including the former French-held regions of Newfoundland, Hudson Bay and Acadia.

Although France was reported to have tried to undermine British interests in India, mostly through the actions of their local native allies, who were becoming increasingly concerned by Britain's growing influence within the subcontinent, France's reluctance, or inability to provide significant numbers of regular troops to support such native resistance, almost inevitably ensured that the British East India Company would go on to successfully suppress all such French inspired campaigns. Although French agents were reported to have tried to foment anti-British feeling throughout much of India, for the most part such campaigns were largely unsuccessful and it was only in the region of Bengal where they achieved some degree of success, encouraging their traditional ally, Siraj-ud-Daulah, to take up arms against British interests. The most infamous incident connected with this particular Indian Nawab, or ruler, was reported to be that of the Black Hole of Calcutta, where captured British and Anglo-Indian prisoners from the captured Fort William in Calcutta, were said to have been held overnight in such cramped conditions that many of them died as a result of crushing, suffocation and exhaustion. Although some later reports would claim that well over one hundred and twenty prisoners had died as a result of their incarceration, in all probability only some forty-odd people died because of the conditions, which had little to do with Siraj-ud-Daulah himself, who was said to have been unaware of the prisoner's physical predicament. However, Siraj' initial attack on Fort William, along with the subsequent incarceration and deaths of the British prisoners was said to have been used as part of a much wider campaign to remove Siraj-ud-Daulah from power and have him replaced by a more pro-British leader. Eventually, both French and British campaigns in the region were thought to have culminated in the Battle of Plassey which took place on 23rd July 1757, an engagement that resulted in a decisive military victory for the British East India Company, commanded by the then Colonel Robert Clive, who later became commonly known as "Clive of India". Although Siraj-ud-Daulah was reported to have been supported by a small number of regular French troops during the notable engagement, ultimately it was thought to be the desertion of one of the Nawab's most capable military commanders, Mir Jafar, which handed victory to Robert Clive and his Anglo Indian forces, setting the seal on Britain's domination of the entire subcontinent for the best part of the next two centuries. Even though a number of other major battles against French forces in India would finally bring an end to France's interests on the subcontinent, the British victory at Plassey is still regarded as the single most pivotal event in Britain's commercial and political campaigns to take control of the untold riches of India and her continental neighbours. By 1761 French interests in India, as with those in North America, were said to have largely disappeared, ostensibly because of the pressures that the country had to face in India, North America, as well as in Europe, all of which was said to have had a highly detrimental effect both on her economy and on her troops, forcing the French king, Louis XV to look for a final and equitable settlement to the international conflict. Having made diplomatic approaches to Britain and her allies, the Seven Years War was only formally ended with the signing of the Treaty of Paris 1763, which saw a number of France's lost colonies and possessions returned to her, including the economically vital sugar producing islands of Guadaloupe and Martinique. However, as part of the same agreement France was also reported to have surrendered its North American territory of Louisiana, which was ceded to her military ally Spain, in compensation for the Spanish lands of Florida that had been captured by Britain during the war. Additionally, France was also compelled to formally grant possession of its remaining New France territories in North America to Britain, thereby creating the basis for the later state of Canada, which Britain managed to retain following the later American Revolutionary War that brought an end to Britain's ownership of her thirteen American colonies. Even in India, France was reported to have lost control of many of its pre-war possessions, although she was granted the return of her former trading posts, allowing her to recover much of the commercial business that she had once enjoyed, but without having the military and political influence that had proved to be so troublesome to Britain's own interests. Finally, in the European theatre, national boundaries were said to have reverted to their earlier limits, although Prussia, one of Britain's leading allies, was reported to have gained substantial influence in continental Europe, establishing the basis for the later unified German state, which Britain and numerous other European nations would have cause to confront in future decades.

Redcoat Infantry

General Thomas Gage

Margaret Gage

It is probably worth remembering that for most British soldiers during the 18th century, a career in the military, army or navy, would not have been a preferred choice, but was often one that was dictated by circumstance, either through poverty, by foolishness, or by judicial dictate. Unlike today, where a military career is not only a legitimate and honourable form of employment, one which is entirely determined by personal choice, during the 18th century most soldiers were thought to have enlisted because they had little or no choice in the matter. With a vast imperial Empire to defend and with the Royal Navy actively trying to recruit able-bodied men for the nation's defence, like the infamous naval press gangs, British army regiments too, were known to have employed recruitment gangs, who would regularly visit Britain's towns and villages, with the intention of enlisting any suitable volunteers that might catch their eye. Typically, these seasoned soldiers would regale any potential candidate with talk of the comradeship and adventures that they had experienced in some or other military campaign, often failing to mention the hardship and brutality that formed part of the same military service. In most cases, young recruits would agree to join particular regiments, having been regally entertained in a local tavern and having consumed more alcohol than was good for them, would wake up the following morning to find that they had inadvertently taken the "King's shilling" and with little chance of escaping the bargain that they had made the previous evening. Alternatively, new recruits could often be found amongst the local criminal classes, with local magistrates and judges giving convicted miscreants the choice of serving time in prison, being transported overseas, or saving themselves by serving in the nation's military forces. As a consequence of having an army that was largely made up of conscripts, discipline within the various regiments was reported to have been severe, with public lashings, starvation, imprisonment and even capital punishment used to exercise control over the growing ranks of generally poorly educated, badly paid, overworked and often highly disaffected men who made up the majority of the British armed forces.

The officers who were chosen to lead, what the Duke of Wellington would later refer to as the "scum of the earth", or the British soldier, were often little better than the common men that they led, save for the fact that they were better educated and had significantly more money, or at least their wealthy families did. In common with their lowest soldier, many of these supposedly professional officers were often paid a pittance for their military service, monies that were generally in arrears and that were insufficient to cover the running costs of having to provide much of their own military equipment, including a horse, if they happened to be commissioned within a cavalry unit. As a result of the practice of individuals being able to buy their commissions, almost inevitably this was thought to have had a damaging effect on the overall performance of the British army, with significant numbers of badly trained, foolhardy and even cowardly officers being responsible for leading British regiments into battle against enemy forces. It is fair to say though that amongst both the officer corps and the common ranks there were any number of highly capable and extremely proficient soldiers, whose own military experience not only helped to maintain discipline, but also ensured that each regimental community managed to function efficiently and effectively.

A peculiarly historic tradition of the British army that was said to have continued right through to the 18th century was the habit of some soldier's families, who were chosen through a secret ballot, being able to accompany their menfolk on various campaigns, whether at home or abroad. Such baggage trains, caravans or even static married quarters were thought to have existed since the very earliest times, not only helping to retain the individual soldier's services by preventing homesickness, but also providing an unpaid supply of nurses, cooks and seamstresses for an army on the move. According to some sources the cost of transporting, feeding and housing the wives and children of the fighting men was said to have been borne by the War Office, who regarded the costs as worth bearing, if it kept the troops happy and content. Bearing in mind that very often military campaigns could commonly last for a number of years, had these married men not been able to bring their families with them, then it seems likely that desertions would have become a much more common occurrence, as men simply abandoned their regimental duties, in order to return to their wives and children. However, despite helping to maintain the family, the lives of the soldier's womenfolk and their children was reported to have been fairly harsh, with the civilians suffering similar hardships as the troops themselves, with many of the followers perishing from the same sorts of diseases and privations that often claimed the lives of their fighting men. As a military community, the family quarters were also thought to have been governed by a whole series of rules and regulations, which ensured that the civilian camp remained calm and peaceful, vital requirements in a community that was often bristling with weaponry and where personal scores could quite easily be settled by the use of deadly force. In order to maintain discipline, especially in an environment where the presence of women might cause personal rivalries or jealousies, most regiments were thought to have arranged their own procedures for dealing with such incidents, with men who were found guilty of attempting to covet another man's wife reasonably expecting to face the most severe form of censure, right up to being executed for his actions. Likewise, those who the regimental commanders felt might be a cause of disunity within the civilian camp, such as an erstwhile husband or wife, a disruptive teenager, or a young man who did not want to enlist alongside his father, would often be ordered to leave the camp, their behaviour, or refusal to serve, being regarded as reason enough for the army to stop feeding, housing or transporting them. In most cases though, according to some records, most young men either chose to enlist with their fathers, or were otherwise found an apprenticeship with some or other local tradesman, whilst soldier's daughters were either found some form of domestic employment, or were married off to a suitable partner, who may or may not have been part of the camp community.

One of the most traditional aspects of these early British army units was undoubtedly the russet red tunics that had first been adopted during the English Civil War by units of the New Model Army, a result of the newly raised military force being clothed, armed, fed and paid by the English Parliament. Although previous royal regiments were reported to have been dressed in varieties of red ever since the late 15th century, often in conjunction with other royal colours, the emergence of a standardised uniform, for a brand new professional English army was thought to have marked the beginning of a British army look that would continue right through to the late 19th century, when most regiments were outfitted with the much more practical khaki colours of the Indian subcontinent. One of the greatest myths surrounding the adoption of the famous British red coat, was that the colour was chosen in order to hide any bloodstains that might result from wounds received during battle, a feature that might appear to make the wearer impervious to the musket balls, pikes, swords and daggers, which they might commonly face in any military engagement. In fact, all of these early red uniforms were reported to have turned a blackish colour when they came into contact with any sort of blood, endorsing the more likely explanation that British uniforms were red, simply because it was the simplest, fastest and cheapest colour to use, an important consideration for any government that was having to bear the cost of producing tens of thousands of such garments on a fairly regular basis. Although from a purely financial perspective, the introduction of the new red uniforms was said to have been generally welcomed, amongst many regional regiments and militias; the loss of their often traditionally distinctive tunics was thought to have been unpopular, leading to the later introduction of different coloured cuffs, collars and lapels, which could be used to identify the various regiments from one another within a much larger military force. By modern standards of course, red uniforms would seem to be the most impractical sort of tunic to wear, given that today's weaponry is far more lethal and far more accurate than those that were employed during the 17th and 18th centuries. Unlike today, where battles are often conducted from a distance and through the use of specialised weaponry such as missiles, tanks, drones and fixed wing aircraft, the battlefields of the 17th, 18th and 19th centuries were often highly confusing places to be, with deafening noise, poor visibility and close quarter combat being regular features of such military engagements. The sorts of weaponry available to most infantrymen of the period, were reported to have included various types of muskets, such as the heavy Wheel lock and Matchlock guns that were fired from a movable stand, to the lighter Flintlocks and Cap locks that could be carried and fired by hand whilst on the move, as well as having a detachable bayonet that could be used in hand-to-hand combat. However, the biggest drawback of these early firearms was that they lacked any sort of accuracy, only being reliable over comparatively short distances, often as little as fifty yards, thereby presenting little danger to soldiers beyond that range, whether they were wearing red uniforms or not.

However, as battle was joined between facing armies, the smoke and noise caused by the firing from dozens of cannons and many hundreds, possibly thousands of muskets would have quickly seen the immediate area enveloped by swirling clouds of gun smoke, making it hard for the already confused and often frightened soldiers to find their bearings in a cauldron of competing sights, smells and sounds. However, the presence of familiar red tunics would no doubt have provided some sense of security for the British troops that were awaiting the advance of enemy troops, or those who were ordered to move forward against the massed ranks of their adversaries already fixed positions. With hundreds or thousands of red uniformed British soldiers moving towards an enemy line, it was said to have offered some degree of comfort to many of the troops that they were simply one amongst several hundreds potential targets, for the enemy musketeers, making their own death or survival little more than a chance event, which was regarded as being one of the major advantages of wearing the famous red tunics. Pride in the British uniform was very much at the forefront of military discipline, with a significant amount of each soldier's free time being given over to cleaning, repairing and maintaining his equipment in order to ensure that he looked his best when appearing on parade, his failure to so, being seen as a serious breach of discipline and often punishable with a beating, being put on fatigues, or being heavily fined. According to one source, many hours were spent shining the brass buttons on their uniforms, whitening the webbing that they wore about their shoulders and chests, as well as the belt around their waist, all of which were reported to have been brightened with white pipe clay. They were also expected to clean and maintain their own personal weapons and cartridge case, including their bayonet and dagger, as well as their musket, which each man was expected to clean and oil until it gleamed like new. For many reporters, not only did this insistence on maintaining a regiments presentation help to reinforce military discipline, but also helped to build and maintain the sort of esprit de corp. that became legendary amongst many early British military units. As most soldiers could expect to serve their entire working lives in the army, unless they were either killed or retired, the shared suffering, privations, defeats and victories, experienced by the men of particular units was said to have forged close bonds amongst the regular troops that were often akin to or superior than immediate family ties. It was said to be as a result of such close relationships and shared experiences that almost inevitably British regiments began to develop their own unique identities, becoming separate entities in their own right, which stored the collective memories of each units military history, a recording of campaigns that many British regiments continue to practice and in its most obvious form has previously led to the creation of individual regiment's colours or battle flags.

Significantly, at the time of the outbreak of the American Revolutionary Wars in 1775 the total military strength of the British army worldwide was reported to have numbered less than forty thousand men, most of who were scattered around the globe defending Britain's vast overseas possessions, including those on the Indian Subcontinent, West Africa, the Caribbean and North America. The man in charge of British forces in North America just prior to the outbreak of the Revolutionary War and whose actions were said to have precipitated the revolt, was General Thomas Gage, an individual, better suited to being a colonial administrator, rather than an outstanding military commander. According to some sources, Gage was thought to have gained his position as Commander-in-chief of British forces in North America largely through the lobbying of his well placed friends and relatives, as opposed to having attained it through his own abilities, a fact that would become all too evident, when he was finally faced with the prospect of imposing unpopular British legislation on a generally resistant and highly antagonistic colonial population. Unrest amongst the American population was reported to have begun around 1765 when the highly unpopular Stamp Act was first introduced by the British Parliament, a piece of legislation which insisted that a range of documents, including newspapers, magazines and legal papers should be printed on embossed or stamped paper, which was only manufactured in Britain and that could only be paid for with British currency, rather than colonial money. As has been previously mentioned, the intention of the tax was to try and recover some of the vast expenses that had been spent fighting the Seven Years War against France and her allies, particularly those campaigns which were fought in North America, from which the colonials had directly benefited. Although many colonial leaders had no formal objection to these new taxes being imposed, the fact that the American colonies had no political representation within the English Parliament and could not therefore argue against such tariffs was said to have caused a great deal of resentment amongst the American political elite. The Stamp Tax itself was said to have proved to be so unpopular, on both sides of the Atlantic that in 1766 the British Parliament was reported to have repealed the legislation, although by that time, significant damage had been done to the previously cordial relations which had existed between Britain and her American colonists. However, despite ending the divisive tax, at the same time, the British legislature was reported to have introduced the Declaratory Act of 1766, which formally asserted Parliaments right to enact legislation both on the British and American populations, essentially ignoring colonial demands for the sort of political representation that was enjoyed by the population of Britain. Around the same time that colonial leaders were becomingly increasingly irritated by the often high handed attitude of British Parliamentarians, the London based legislature also introduced the Quartering Act of 1765, which permitted British troops to be accommodated in private dwellings, irrespective of the individual householders permission, helping to add to the growing resentment felt by most of those colonists who happened to live in the towns and cities of America's eastern seaboard. It was said to be during General Thomas Gage's tenure as Britain's military commander-in-chief that local tensions were thought to have risen to such an extent that he ordered large numbers of British troops to withdraw from the frontier areas of British North America, back to some of the larger urban centres, including Boston and New York, both of which were said to have been inhabited by highly resentful and suspicious colonial populations.

Perhaps predictably, the large scale quartering of regular British troops in a number of America's largest cities was not generally welcomed by the local populations, who saw the move as a form of military occupation, which could only end in some form of bloody conflict, given the presence of large numbers of armed troops on their streets. Almost as soon as the British troops moved into Boston, tensions arose between them and the local population, which was generally characterised by a series of brawls and fights between men from both sides, although for the most part, such outbreaks of violence rarely resulted in any lives being lost. Tempers were thought to have been further inflamed by continuing press reports that concentrated on the mutual antagonisms, to the point that rather than helping to reduce the almost regular fights, the articles were thought to have heightened tensions further, although some regiments were withdrawn from Boston in order to prevent any serious outbreaks of disorder. However, despite the best efforts of all concerned, the almost inevitable loss of life, which many had feared would result from the ongoing tensions, was said to have occurred on the evening of the 5th March 1770. According to reports from the time, a British sentry, Private Hugh White, was guarding the local Customs House, when he witnessed a British officer, being publicly chastised by a local man, Edward Gerrish, who claimed that the Captain had not paid his employer, a local wigmaker, for items supplied to the officer. As it happened the British Captain had indeed paid his bill in full, but rather than remonstrate with Gerrish in the middle of the street, simply ignored the young colonial's charges. Seemingly not content with being ignored, Edward Gerrish was then reported to have left the scene, only to reappear sometime later with a group of friends and recommenced his verbal assault on the officer, at the same time exchanging insults with Private White who was still guarding his post. Unfortunately for the verbally abusive American, White was said to have been far less tolerant than his senior officer and having taken quite enough abuse from Gerrish, stepped forward and struck the young colonists on the side of his head with the butt of his musket. Almost immediately Gerrish's companions began to argue with Private White and his officer, challenging them to a fight and raising such a commotion that before long a large crowd was said to have gathered around the two British soldiers. Another British officer, Captain Preston, who happened to be close by and who had witnessed the confrontation, then ordered a detachment of one NCO and seven soldiers to go and retrieve Private White and the Captain from the increasingly angry crowd, although as they moved towards the two men, they themselves were said to have become hemmed in by the crowd, which by now was thought to have grown to well over several hundred angry citizens. Believing their lives to be at risk, the detachment of troops was reported to have loaded their weapons and aimed them in the direction of the slowly encroaching crowd, who rather than retreating from the small band of soldiers, were reported to have started pelting them with snowballs and whatever else they could lay their hands on. One member of the crowd however, a local innkeeper called Richard Holmes, was said to have escalated matters by rushing forward and striking one of the soldiers, a Private Hugh Montgomery, on the side of the head with a club. As he recovered his senses, the young soldier was reported to have discharged his musket into the crowd, but without hitting anyone with the shot, even though he later admitted to firing the weapon deliberately. However, as if to goad the remaining soldiers into repeating Montgomery's actions, the crowd reportedly began to chant "Fire" at the group of soldiers and having repeated the chant several times, the troops did exactly that, hitting eleven members of the crowd with the volley, killing three of them instantly. Two more civilians would subsequently perish in the aftermath of the shooting, bringing the total number of fatalities to five, for which Captain Preston and his eight soldiers were charged with murder on 27th March 1770. As a direct result of the incident, all of the remaining British troops were said to have been withdrawn from the city and were relocated to billets on Castle Island in Boston Harbour, whilst Captain Preston and his co-accused were remanded in custody to stand trial at Suffolk County Courthouse in October and November 1770.

John Adams   Benjamin Franklin   Colonial Minuteman

Captain Preston and the eight accused British soldiers were reported to have been tried separately and after a delay of several months, in order that local tensions might be eased before any sort of jury trials took place. Initially however, it was said to have proved extremely difficult to find a local lawyer who was prepared to defend the soldiers, mainly because it was felt that to do so would have a highly detrimental effect on any attorney's career, leading to many simply refusing to accept the papers. Eventually though, John Adams, one of the areas leading lawyers, colonial leaders and later America's second freely elected President, agreed to take the case, mainly to ensure that all of the accused men received a fair trial and that justice was seen to be served. At Captain Preston's subsequent trial, the basis of Adams' defence was that the British officer had not actually ordered his men to fire their weapons into the crowd and was therefore not responsible for the actions that led to the deaths of the five colonial civilians, an argument that was eventually accepted by the jury after a trial lasting some six days. The second trial, which involved the eight British soldiers, who were accused of firing into the crowd, took place in November 1770 and centred round Adams' main argument that the troopers had opened fire on the crowd ostensibly because they felt their own live were at risk from the large and extremely angry civilian crowd. Even though he was thought to have taken little personal satisfaction from his task, being publicly criticised for his decision to defend the British soldiers, Adam's was still able to demonstrate to the American jury that six of the soldiers had indeed been in fear for their lives, when confronted by the crowd, which Adams himself described as "a motley rabble of saucy boys, negroes, mulattoes, Irish Teagues and outlandish Jack Tars". Although two of the British troopers were subsequently found guilty of manslaughter, because it was felt that they had deliberately fired into the body of the crowd, rather than over it, Adams was still able to employ a historic loophole by invoking the benefit of clergy for the two men, which was a legal mechanism that allowed first time offenders to receive a lesser sentence for certain crimes, simply by proving that they had some form of clerical status by reading from the Holy Bible.

It was incidents, such as what later became known as the "Boston Massacre" and the introduction of a new "Tea Act" in May 1773 that were said to have created even greater divisions between the British Parliament and the colonial leadership in America, which inevitably led to the conflict that the British establishment regarded as a rebellion, but that most colonists saw as a war of independence, the American Revolutionary War. One of the most notable events that led to the outbreak of war between Britain and its American colonists was said to have been the Boston Tea Party of December 1773, the criminal destruction of several tons of tea by colonists, reportedly because the cargoes would have been taxed without their consent, if indeed the tea had ever been officially landed, which was not the case. Even the likes of Benjamin Franklin were reported to have been outraged by the actions of the colonists, who were said to have disguised themselves as native Indians to carry out the raid and a number of local American merchants even offered to compensate Britain for the loss of the cargo, although all such offers were subsequently refused. Today the Boston Tea Party is widely regarded as being symbolic of the American revolutionary cause and its opposition to the supposedly overbearing and illegal taxation imposed by a wholly unrepresentative British government, significantly a viewpoint that was only widely promoted some fifty or sixty years after the raid first took place. However, even though the "Tea Party" itself was thought to be little more than an aggravating assault on a single British tea clipper and its cargo, the action of the so-called patriots who carried the raid, was said to have had a far more serious consequences for the wider colonial community. As a direct result of the attack, the British Parliament was said to have been so incensed that they immediately introduced a series of legislative Acts, which were not only designed to punish the port of Boston and its population for the destruction of the tea, but also to reinforce the generally held view of the elected assembly that Parliament's authority was absolute, not only in Britain, but throughout its colonial Empire.

Later known as the Intolerable Acts, the various pieces of legislation passed by the British Parliament included the Boston Port Act, which essentially closed the city's port until such time as the cost of the destroyed cargo was repaid to the British East India Company and that the city itself proved that good order had been restored. The Massachusetts Government Act was reported to have unilaterally altered the colony's system of government, in order to bring it under the direct control of the British authorities, who could then control the appointment of local officials, essentially removing any sort of democratic accountability from the colony. The Administration of Justice Act was yet another legal instrument which removed any form of control from colonial Massachusetts, specifically in matters relating to those royal officials or agents who might be charged with a serious offence, who could subsequently be removed to another British colony, or back to Britain to face trial, rather than facing a jury made up of ordinary Massachusetts colonists. By imposing these Acts on the people of Massachusetts, the British Parliament had, in the view of many American colonists, violated their basic rights, not only constitutionally, but also under the terms of the colonial charters which had been used to establish the British settlements in the first place. Even outside of Massachusetts, the introduction of these new Acts was reported to have caused outrage amongst the colonial population, especially amongst those who believed that a formal American separation from Britain was the only legitimate way forward and who used the imposition of such unfair legislative Acts to underpin their own argument for full American independence. In response to these new measures many American colonies were reported to have sent representatives to the First Continental Congress, a meeting of colonial leaders, who agreed to form the Continental Association, an arrangement which called for the wholesale boycott of British made goods being brought into America. More importantly however, at the same meeting, colonial leaders also agreed to support Massachusetts in the event that the colony was attacked by British forces, a pledge that would ultimately be tested when the British commander-in-chief in North America, General Thomas Gage, sent troops into the towns of Lexington and Concord in April 1775, with orders to seek and destroy armaments that were being held by local colonial militias.

As a response to the introduction of the previously mentioned Intolerable Acts, a number of local militias within Massachusetts had begun to store large quantities of arms, just in case the political situation continued to deteriorate and in the event that any sort of armed action was taken against the local population by the estimated three thousand British troops that were said to have been stationed in the colony. Aware that the colonists were storing arms and ammunition, General Gage, who was generally seen as being sympathetic to the colonial cause, mainly because he had an American wife, undertook his duty as a British officer all the same and was said to have made plans for seizing the American arms caches in the most effective and quietest way possible. Rather than sending entire battalions or regiments to seek out and seize the arms dumps, Gage was reported to have planned for relatively small contingents of British troops to spread out throughout the countryside, search for and seek out information regarding the various weapons stores and to intercept and detain any rebel messengers or leaders that they might come across. Unfortunately, these roving military patrols and search parties were said to have been so unusual that before long their purpose was a well known fact amongst most of the local population, who quickly informed militia leaders about them, allowing the arms stores to be removed to other more secret locations. A notable colonial leader in Massachusetts at the time, Paul Revere, later achieved some degree of fame within American revolutionary circles for his reported ride to the city of Concord, where he alerted the local population to the impending arrival of British troops, to seize the militias arms, allowing the weapons to be removed and safely stored in other nearby towns. Likewise, other colonists were said to have received secret information that was supposedly unknown to anyone but General Gage himself, leading some historians to speculate that Gage's American wife, Margaret, was actually acting as a fifth-columnist for the colonial cause, passing along her husband's secret orders and allowing the colonial forces to be forewarned about future military operations and troop movements, although her actual involvement was never positively proved.

Colonel Smith

Major John Pitcairn

Earl Hugh Percy

The intention of Gage's military expedition of the 18th April 1775 was for a force of around seven hundred regular British troops to leave their main military bases in Boston and make towards the colonial centre of Concord, where they expected to search for and seize the militias arms depots, as well as arresting a number of colonial leaders, whose activities were deemed to be suspect by the British authorities. Drawing men from a number of the elite infantry regiments that were billeted in and around Boston, rather than taking command of the expedition himself, Gage was reported to have assigned a Colonel Smith would take overall command of the force, with a Major Pitcairn as his immediate subordinate. By the time that Gage was announcing the military operation to his junior officers, the general was said to have been completely unaware that large parts of the plan had already been leaked to the local colonial forces, either by Margaret Gage, or other sympathisers within the British camp, essentially rendering most of the proposal useless from a strategic point of view. He would have also have been unaware that by the time he began to instruct his officers on the morning of the 18th April 1775, many colonial militias were already being assembled by their leaders, in readiness for the British advance on Concord, giving the American forces plenty of time to prepare for the regular troop's arrival. Unfortunately, even though most of the British infantrymen were highly experienced soldiers, due to the way that Gage's forces were constituted, many of the more senior officers who were charged with commanding each of the various battalions and regiments were said to have been drawn from other units and were therefore largely unknown to the men that they were expected to lead on the vitally important expedition. However, regardless of such issues, on the evening of the 18th April, the various British troops were ordered to prepare themselves to leave Boston by boat, for the comparatively short journey to Lechmere Point on the other side of the Bay, where they would join up with the main route to Concord. However, even though the boat journey was said to have been largely uneventful, the fact that most of the troops were forced to stand during the trip and were then asked to wade through waist deep freezing cold water to come ashore, was thought to have been a less the favourable start to a campaign, which left many of the men and their equipment soaking wet.

Advance units of the British force were said to have been sent forward to the first major colonial settlement on the road to Concord, the town of Lexington, where the six units of regular soldiers were reported to have been confronted by a smaller eighty-strong militia force, who were in the process of forming up on the town's common. Known locally as minuteman companies, the local militia leader was said to have ordered his men to stand fast at the sight of the oncoming

British troops, whose Royal Marine vanguard was thought to have positioned themselves so as to try and contain the militia, with following units taking up a battle line formation, while they waited for their officers to come forward and address the local minutemen. When one of the British officers called for the militia to lay down their arms and disperse, there was said to have been a great deal of confusion, as the militias own leaders were shouting along with the British officers, creating a scenario where pretty much anything might happen. With uncertainty overcoming good order on both sides, almost inevitably someone discharged their weapon, although most reporters later agreed that the shot had not been fired by any of the men on the common, but rather by somebody away from the scene, with both sides subsequently accusing one another's supporters for the first sign of aggression. Initially only a few shots were exchanged between the two sides, but perhaps due to their better training, the British troops were reported to have begun to fire almost regular volleys of shot into the American ranks, without having been given any sort of order to fire, according to later American reports. As the minuteman company began to withdraw with some haste, the British regulars were said to have moved forward with their bayonets fixed, purportedly killing and wounding several more members of the militia, who were trying to escape the scene. According to British reports of the incident, much of the soldier's confusion was caused by a lack of information and leadership by their officers, who seemed to have been taken as much by surprise as was everybody else, leading to a temporary loss of command, during which the troops followed their normal practice. It was only when a more seasoned officer, Colonel Smith, came forward from the main column that some form of order was restored and the troops were ordered to reassemble.

Having left Lexington in relatively good order, the British force continued on its journey to Concord, no doubt aware that their earlier actions and the deaths of the local minutemen had already been reported to the main militia headquarters. For their part, local colonial forces were reported to have been generally undecided as to what action to take, whether to withdraw from the town, remain at their current posts, or march out to meet the British troops that were fast approaching the town. According to most sources, the decision was made to march out and confront the regular troops, although having left Concord, within a short distance they were said to have met the vanguard of the seven hundred-strong British force, realised they were outnumbered by three to one and subsequently marched back the way they had just come. Arriving back in the town with the British troops a short distance behind, rather than face a similar fate as their comrades in Lexington, militia leaders then made the decision to withdraw from Concord to a position just north of the town, where they could monitor the British troops, before deciding on any further action. As they arrived in the town, Colonel Smith was reported to have despatched a contingent of soldiers to guard the bridge at the north end of town, in order to protect the main body of troops from the militia forces that were known to be gathering in that general area. Likewise the British commander also detached a number of men to protect their line of retreat if that should become necessary, before ordering the remainder of his soldiers to begin searching the town for the weapons that were believed to be stored there. The main stockpile, which was said to have been located at a nearby farm, was fairly quickly found, containing three large artillery pieces and numerous pieces of shot which were subsequently destroyed and disposed of by the troops, who also ruined a significant amount of foodstuffs that were considered to be unusually high and might well have provided sustenance to an enemy force. Although the British troops were reported to have ruthless in their pursuit of any contraband items, for the most part they were thought to have been reasonable in their treatment of the local population, reimbursing the local businesses for any items of food and drink that were consumed during their search of the town.

In the meantime, the three to four hundred local minutemen who had taken up positions just north of the town were said to have been joined by large numbers of other local militia men who had been summoned by messengers, increasing their numbers significantly. The militia's commander's seemingly emboldened by the additional reinforcements, were then reported to have moved towards the town, forcing the regular troops who had been ordered to protect the British force's northern flank, from the high ground that they had initially occupied, to much lower ground just in front of the local bridge, essentially handing the militia the tactically superior position. With only an estimated one hundred regular troops to protect his position, it quickly became clear to the British commander in charge of the northern sector, Captain Parsons that not only was he vastly outnumbered, but he was also in a highly questionable position, given that he was now overlooked by a much larger enemy force. However, rather than attacking the regular troops from a distance, which would have proved largely ineffective, the militia commanders were reported to have ordered their forces to advance on the bridge, but cautioned them not to open fire, unless they were fired upon first. With a much larger enemy force approaching, the British infantrymen were ordered back across the bridge and told to adopt a street fighting position, a tactic which was completely unsuitable for the situation that they now found themselves in. As they rushed to assemble in their ranks, at least one soldier was said to have fired his weapon in the direction of the advancing militia, causing a handful of his comrades to do the same, as a result of which, at least two minutemen were killed and wounded, causing both sides to open fire on one another. Limited by the width of the road that they were walking down, the first few ranks of minutemen were reported to have fired around one another, killing and wounding a large number of the British troops who had been incorrectly gathered into a relatively tight group, making one big target for the minutemen to aim at. With most of their officers and senior NCO's killed or seriously wounded, the remaining British troops were said to have taken to their heels, abandoning their wounded comrades at the bridge and leaving behind the other British troops that were still searching the immediate area for the militia's secret arms supplies. As they fled back towards the town, the flight of the soldiers was only brought to a halt by the arrival of two Grenadier companies, under the command of Colonel Smith, who had moved forward towards the bridge having heard the exchange of gunfire that had taken place between his troops and the minutemen. However, having observed that members of the local militia were content to remain in a defensive position and not open fire on his troops, Smith was reported to have rounded up all of the search parties who had been looking for the hidden arms caches and retired back to Concord, where the main British force was said to have continued searching for weapons, before finally reassembling to make their way back to Boston.

According to some sources, having killed and wounded a number of the British troops that were holding the northern bridge, members of the militia were thought to have acted in a variety of different ways, with some retiring back up the hill, others advancing over the bridge, whilst a handful of others left the scene entirely. However, most of them remained nearby and simply waited for orders to be issued, as to what action they should take next, retreat, advance or hold their ground, although with no command to fire being given, as the advancing British Grenadier companies arrived at the bridge, the minutemen simply waited to see what action the troops would take. As the British soldiers retired back towards Concord, having recovered their scattered search parties and the wounded troops from the bridge, so the militia were left in control of the immediate area, later moving towards the town as the British forces moved out, on their way back to Boston, their mission having been largely accomplished. Most historical reports suggest that as the regular troops travelled back along the main road to Lexington and then Boston, their every move was shadowed by a growing number of colonial militia, who were intent on attacking the British party at every opportunity, a tactic which was said to have been expected by Colonel Smith, who put out flankers on both sides of the main column, in order to deter any large scale and unexpected attack on his main body of troops. However, when crossing bridges, these protective flankers were forced back towards the main column, allowing the American minutemen to close the distance between themselves and the regulars, near enough for them to fire coordinated volleys against the British ranks, killing and wounding a handful of the retiring soldiers, who were said to have continued on in good order nonetheless. By the time the British column had reached Meriam's Corner, only a quarter of the way back to Lexington, the militia forces were reported to have been increased some five-fold, from four hundred men to well over two thousand, giving them a three to one advantage over the British regulars, who continued with their withdrawal undaunted by the increasing numbers of colonials who were thought to have been pressing along both flanks of the column. At Brook's Hill, a contingent of some several hundred militia were reported to have tried to block the British advance along the road, but rather than being impeded by this sizeable threat, the vanguard of the column was said to have moved forward to try and drive the militia-men off, during which they were said to have incurred significant casualties. However, no sooner had the British troops cleared one militia position and began to move forward again, than they would encounter further ambushes laid by the minutemen, who rather than engage in a traditionally straightforward line of battle, which they would almost certainly have lost, employed guerrilla type hit and run attacks on the regulars, who were ill-equipped to deal with such repeated and lengthy diversions. Each of these militia ambushes, set up by the various colonial units who had been drawn into the area, were thought to have steadily reduced the British force, which lost handfuls and then dozens of men to each and every assault, but were still able to push forward, overcoming each and every enemy position that was placed in their way. However, by the early afternoon of the 19th April 1775 and having been on their feet for very nearly seventeen hours straight, during which they had been soaked, shot at and seen many of their friends and comrades killed or wounded, even some of the surviving British officers were beginning to find it difficult to keep their men encouraged.

Fortunately for Colonel Smith and his remaining troops, just as it seemed that they would be unable to continue with their journey, the arrival of a second larger British contingent, numbering around a thousand troops, who were equipped with cannon, was thought to have saved the day. Under the command of Earl Hugh Percy, although this second British force was reported to have been ill-provisioned for any sort of large scale expedition, ostensibly because Percy was in such a rush to make his way to Lexington, ultimately their arrival was said to have saved Colonel Smith's original force from being captured or destroyed by the colonial militia, which would have been a complete disaster for the British authorities. Having arrived at the town of Lexington, Percy was thought to have dispersed his troops and his cannon, so as to offer support for Smith's forces, which he expected to arrive from Concord sometime during the 19th April 1775, although as it happens, it was only an hour or so later that the vanguard of Colonel Smith's generally exhausted and demoralised forces first came into view, with units of the colonial militia in close pursuit. Ordering his cannon to fire at extreme range, Percy was able to disperse the local minutemen, before ensuring that Smith and his exhausted troops were finally able to rest and to get something to eat and drink. With his own soldiers securing the immediate area and with the threat of cannon discouraging further militia incursions, Percy was able to take stock of the situation, taking a report from Colonel Smith and arranging for Smith's wounded soldiers to be tended to in a quickly assembled field hospital. Having seen to the men's needs, after a couple of hours Percy was said to have taken formal command of both forces and began to make arrangements for the entire force to begin an orderly withdrawal back to Boston.

Although the colonial forces were thought to have been initially been stalled by the arrival of Percy's military column and its cannons, within a relatively short time they were said to have adapted their strategies, so that they shadowed the now much larger British force at a distance, occasionally firing into the ranks of the military column, with the expectation that their shot would kill or wound somebody. The fact that they refused to engage the British troops in a more formal battle line, was said to have irritated many of the regular officers and soldiers, as did the colonial's habit of using trees, walls and even private houses as firing positions, a custom that would inevitably lead to civilians being caught up in the increasingly bitter march. As the British column moved closer to its ultimate objective, their military base at Boston, so the numbers and formation of the militia was said to have grown, making them more of an obvious target for Earl Percy's cannons, which were said to have been used to great effect on the latter part of the journey, with many minutemen being killed and wounded by the British artillery. Apparently aware that the colonial's would attempt to ambush him on the final part of his march to Boston, Percy was reported to have moved his column along a much more circuitous route and away from a large militia force, who subsequently found themselves unable to intercept the regular troops, much to their own frustration. Although the detour was said to have taken the British troops into the neighbouring town of Charlestown, rather than Boston itself, the settlement still allowed the exhausted British troops to take up a series of well-defended positions from where they could be reinforced by other British infantry units and protected by the guns of HMS Somerset which was stationed in the nearby harbour. For many of Colonel Smith's surviving troops, those who had participated in the original operation against Concord, their undertaking had proved to be a remarkable feat of military strength and discipline. Not only had they gone nearly two days without sleep, but had also travelled well over forty miles on foot, a good deal of the time under direct enemy fire, something that few military units of the time would have been able to cope with. Despite the British positions though, the militias were reported to have continued to gather on the outskirts of Boston, with an estimated fifteen thousand minutemen assembled there by the morning of the 20th April 1775, although virtually all of these forces were said to have been withdrawn, once it became clear that the city was generally unassailable, without a huge loss of life.

Although some sources tend to regard this initial battle as largely unimportant, when compared to the later, much larger military engagements that formed part of the wider American Revolutionary War, other historians have claimed the actions at Lexington and Concord represented the first military victory of the colonial forces over the British army, even if only a tactical one. However, the fact that the British troops carried out their primary objective, of locating the arms and munitions that were being held at Concord, would seem to make any such assumption a highly questionable one. In fact, it is probably true to say that the only tactical victory achieved by the colonials was that that was accomplished through the efforts of the sympathisers, messengers and supporters who managed to arrange for the weapons to be removed to a place of safety, before the British troops actually arrived to seize them. From a purely military point of view and in terms of the actions that were subsequently fought between the colonial minutemen and their British adversaries suggesting any sort of victory by one side or another is a extremely difficult, given that both sides sustained losses and that neither surrendered outright. Like it or not, the British regulars completed the task that was assigned to them, of marching to Concord, where they were ordered to seize and destroy any colonial arms that they might find, which is exactly what they accomplished, regardless of the fact that most of the weapons had been removed beforehand. The fact that mistakes were made by individual British officer's in the deployment of their men, as was the case at the bridge located to the north of Concord and which resulted in a number of regulars being killed or injured, had little to do with colonial military strategy, but more to do with a highly inexperienced British officer. Likewise, the withdrawal of the troops from Concord was simply the result of the British forces having completed the task assigned to them, rather than any sort of pressure exerted by the colonial militia, who for the most part seem to have remained on the outskirts of the town, awaiting additional reinforcements who then took up position along the British column's line of withdrawal. Bearing in mind that throughout much of the journey from Concord to Lexington and then on to Charlestown, the British troops were in plain sight, unlike many of the minutemen who were hiding themselves behind walls, trees and nearby buildings, obviously unwilling or unable to expose themselves to direct and sustained British fire. It is also worth recalling that at one point during the day the British troops were thought to have been outnumbered by some three or four to one and yet the colonial militia still did not feel confident enough to stand toe to toe with their adversaries.

General William Howe   **George Washington**   **Paul Revere**

If the colonial's did secure any sort of tactical victory over the British in respect of this very early military engagement, then it was almost entirely political in nature, especially given the fact that the colonial leadership was particularly adept at producing and distributing highly misleading propaganda, which could be used to proclaim their own version of events to the wider world. Unlike the British authorities, who were known for being particularly bad at reporting or justifying specific events, often because they felt no need to do so, the colonial leadership saw the need for and benefit of being the victim in the ongoing dispute, not only to sell such an idea to their own population, but more importantly to sell it to the wider world, to countries like France, Spain and the Netherlands, who would later go on to support America's colonial cause. As part of what became a carefully prepared story for the outside world, details relating to the colonist's preparations for war, intelligence gathering and some of the less palatable aspects of their militia's behaviour during the Battle of Lexington and Concord, including the reported scalping of a British soldier and the use of civilian properties to launch attacks, were deliberately suppressed by colonial leaders, whereas every infringement, real or invented, which had purportedly been carried out by British troops, was meticulously reported to the watching world.

In the days following the engagements at Lexington and Concord, although the British forces under General Gage were reported to have held Boston quite securely, the outskirts of the city, where the vast majority of the colonial population was located was deemed to be unsafe for regular forces, largely because of the presence of the militias who had proved so troublesome to Colonel Smith and Lord Percy. With blood having been spilt by both sides during these initial battles, it was fairly evident to all of the various leaders that a line had been crossed and that a resolution would only be reached by force of arms, even though some leaders still hoped to find a peaceful solution. For the British commander-in-chief, General Gage, his most immediate priority was to request reinforcements for his beleaguered forces in Boston, one that was met in May 1775, when an additional three thousand troops arrived in the city, bringing his total troop strength up to six thousand regular soldiers and their officers. With these fresh troops having been brought in by sea, Gage was said to have felt confident enough to try and extend the British sphere of influence, before moving out to confront the main militia forces which were reported to have assembled around the town of Roxbury. Part of Gage's plan was thought to have called for his forces to take and secure a number of Boston's surrounding hills, including Breed's Hill and Bunker Hill, both of which were part of the larger Dorchester Height's that overlooked Boston to the south and might therefore represent a threat to British interests, if they happened to be taken by the colonials. Unfortunately for General Gage, once again an unknown source was said to have disclosed British plans to the colonial militia, who decided to place their own forces on top of Dorchester Height's, thereby preventing British troops from taking control of the vitally important range. On the night of June 16th 1775, an estimated twelve hundred colonial's were said to have made their way up Breed's Hill with the intention of placing artillery at its peak, which could then be used to target British targets in Boston harbour below, with some minor work being undertaken on the nearby Bunker Hill.

Although the British were said to have been aware of the colonial's presence on the hills above Boston, for the most part they were said to have been relatively unconcerned, although several vessels in the harbour were reported to have fired at them, but with little real effect. Eventually though, General Gage was said to have become concerned enough to order an attack against the position, which he was assured, would be easily overcome. As tended to be the case with the highly organised British forces, much time was said to have been lost while sufficient infantrymen were found to be used for the attack, after which they had to be inspected and then marched down to the harbour where they then had to wait to be embarked on the boats that would carry them to their target. However, having landed their forces, it was said to have come to one of the British commander's attention that more colonials might be present, than had first been thought, so he sent back for reinforcements, allowing his fifteen hundred soldiers to rest and eat while they waited for these additional troops to arrive. With the British forces below them making it plain that they intended to attack, the colonial militia at the top of the hills immediately sent back for their own reinforcements and whilst they waited, arranged for their newly built redoubt, to be further strengthened in readiness for the forthcoming attack.

It was only by the middle of the afternoon of the 17th June 1775 that all of the British troops had finally been assembled and were ordered to begin their advance on Breed and Bunker Hills. Unfortunately, with the militia holding the slightly higher ground and having the benefit of their recent fortifications to hide behind and steady their weapons on, as the first British assault was made on the colonial positions, their volley fire was reported to have been so effective that it forced the regular troops back, with significant losses. As the walking wounded made their way back to the rear, so they were reported to have got in the way of the second assault wave which had been sent forward by British commanders, only to suffer a similar fate to the soldiers from the first unsuccessful assault, with even more regular troops being injured and killed by the colonial volleys. However, as fresh troops arrived from Boston to help support the assault, British commanders were said to have initially struggled to assemble their forces for one final push on the colonial positions, with some officers actively encouraging their walking wounded to return to the front line, in order to help overcome the enemy positions. Eventually, as this third and final attack was made on the militias defensive redoubt, the colonial volley fire was reported to have caused significant losses amongst the advancing British line, but not to the point where the assault was stalled and with some colonials running low on ammunition and others keen to escape the scene, this time the regulars were able to close with the militia forces. With bayonets fixed, the surviving British marines and infantrymen quickly began fierce hand to hand fighting with the colonists who were eventually driven off both Breed and Bunker Hill's and back towards their main base at Cambridge. However, by the end of the bloody and costly engagement, which is generally known as the Battle of Bunker Hill, the British forces were reported to have sustained exceptionally high numbers of casualties, with over two hundred men dead and more than eight hundred wounded. According to some contemporary reports, British officers were thought to have suffered a disproportionate number of fatalities during the engagement, ostensibly because they were often leading their men from the front, putting themselves at greater risk of being killed or wounded by the guns of the colonial militia.

Sir Henry Clinton   Lord George Germain   Frederick II

Although the Battle of Bunker Hill was generally deemed to be a British victory, largely because they managed to remove a potential military threat to the city of Boston, ultimately the way in which they achieved that victory and the losses that they suffered as a result of it, proved to have much wider and longer lasting repercussions for Britain's interests there. Not only was General Thomas Gage subsequently replaced as the senior British military commander in America, but attitudes on both sides of the Atlantic were said to have hardened as a result of the ongoing conflict, with some political and military leaders becoming increasingly sympathetic to the colonial cause, whilst others adopted a much more hard line approach, believing that any and all means should be used to crush the rebellious militias and their political leadership. Unfortunately, the military commander appointed to replace Gage, General William Howe, was said to have been the commander who was directly responsible for the unnecessary losses at Bunker Hill, a man whose reticence was widely known and whose reluctance to secure victory at any cost would ultimately prove to have catastrophic results for the British cause in America. It was said to have been Howe's failure to properly support John Burgoyne's Saratoga Campaign in 1777 that essentially handed a military victory to the American colonists, which was thought to have persuaded France to add her own considerable military forces to the fight for American independence, making Britain's continuing control of the thirteen colonies an almost impossible task. For some historians, it was thought to have been the heavy losses suffered at Bunker Hill, as a result of his orders which turned a reasonably adept military leader, into a highly ineffective one, one who spent much of his valuable time pursuing social activities, to the detriment of his highly important command duties. Amongst his many most notable mistakes was said to have been his decision to allow the colonial forces, under the command of General George Washington to make a second, this time successful attempt to place artillery on the hills overlooking Boston, which eventually resulted in Howe withdrawing British forces to New York, where he planned a new offensive against Washington's new Continental Army. Unfortunately, having successfully landed his forces in New York and carried out a military campaign that might have put the colonial army at his mercy, Howe once again refused the opportunity to storm the American's well prepared positions, giving Washington and his forces the chance to escape over the East River, thereby saving the colonial troops from being captured or destroyed by British forces. Although Howe was thought to have been fairly successful at achieving straightforward military goals, many of his critics, who included a number of his immediate subordinates, accused him of lacking the imagination to adapt to a rapidly changing battlefield, being so fixed on his ultimate objective that nothing could distract him from achieving that one single aim. As the war started to work in the colonial's favour, Howe was reported to have begun to blame others for his failures, to the extent that in October 1777 the disgruntled commander was said to have submitted his resignation to London, although it was not finally accepted until April of 1778, when Sir Henry Clinton took over the post as British commander in chief.

One of the first orders that General Clinton was said to have received upon taking over from Howe as Britain's overall commander in America, was for him to withdraw his regular troops from Philadelphia and send some five thousand regulars to the Caribbean, in preparation for any French attacks that might be directed there by the colonial's newest European ally. With his land forces dramatically reduced and with little expectation that they would be replaced from Britain or elsewhere, Clinton was initially instructed to hold whatever grounds he could, without seeking to expand his areas of control. However, as a highly able military commander, Clinton was reported to have ignored his instructions and despatched what troops he had, to a number of theatres, often with mixed results, as he lacked the numbers to successfully suppress colonial activities outside of the main British held enclaves. As a highly experienced military commander, Clinton's actions were almost always directed against an enemy army, rather than against the civilian population that might be associated with them, a distinction that was not always shared by his political masters back in London. However, with hostilities largely at an impasse by the end of 1778 Clinton was said to have found his position undermined by the British government's regular habit of refusing his requests for specific military commanders, who he believed might make a marked contribution to his campaign. Unfortunately, many of those who were provided were often political appointees, those who could be relied upon to support the government's plans, rather than those of Clinton himself, who was the commander on the ground. As a consequence, Clinton often found it difficult to cultivate good working relationships with some of these commanders, a situation that was inevitably exacerbated by the fact that the British authorities remained unwilling or unable to send him fresh troops which might reinforce his limited and often exhausted forces. It was said to be as a result of these poor relations and the limited resources at Clinton's disposal that when military manoeuvrings did take place between the British and Continental armies, Clinton's troops often got the worst of them, helping to add to the criticism of his actions by his political enemies back in Britain. After the thirteen American colonies were effectively lost, following the successful siege of Yorktown by the Continental Army and their French allies at sea, Clinton was heavily criticised for his failure to fully support the beleaguered British commander, Lord Cornwallis, who Clinton believed had deliberately ignored many of his orders, ostensibly on the advice of Lord George Germain, the then Secretary of State for America.

A number of Britain's leading admirals and generals who would have been vitally important to Britain's war effort in America, were reported to have resigned, rather than participate in what was often regarded as an unnecessary and unwanted conflict with American settlers, many of whom originated from British stock. Even some of the senior officers who directed the course of the war in America, were said to have been unhappy about the situation, but excused their own involvement by insisting that they were simply following orders and as serving soldiers had little say in exactly where they served. However, the divisions caused by the outbreak of the American Revolutionary War, was said to have had a marked effect on the levels of recruitment undertaken by the British government, forcing the authorities to rely on other sources for troops, including mercenaries from the European state of Hesse-Kassel, whose ruler, Frederick II, was said to have hired out many of his own troops to his nephew, King George III, for the war in America, earning themselves the nickname "Hessians" in the process. Up to thirty thousand of these hired troops were thought to have been employed during the American Revolutionary War, along with an estimated fifty thousand British troops, as well as an unknown number of freed black African slaves and the loyalist settlers who were said to have taken up arms in Britain's cause. Opposing them, a reported thirty five thousand Americans were said to have joined the Continental Army, often serving anything between one and three years depending on their personal circumstances, whilst this regular force was said to have been supported by another forty five thousand militiamen, who tended to fight on a state by state, or engagement by engagement basis. Added to these American forces, something like ten thousand regular French troops were reported to have fought on American soil, although many more were thought to have attacked British interests around the globe, including in the Caribbean, India and Europe, forcing Britain to divert much needed troops away from the American theatre, in order to protect these overseas territories from French, Dutch and Spanish attacks. Ultimately though, there were thought to have been any number of decisions that contrived to defeat the British Army in America, few of which had little to do with the military capability of the Continental Army and its leaders directly.

Although many political mistakes were undoubtedly made which caused the outbreak of the American Revolution, from a purely military perspective, the regular troops that were charged with suppressing the rebellion, did very little wrong, given that they were thousands of miles from home, of limited number and faced an adversary that chose to fight them in a completely novel way. For a regular army, trained to fight set-piece battles, where hundreds or thousands of troops might face one another across an open battlefield, the potential dangers posed by a largely guerrilla force that could hit and run from a distance, prevented British regulars employing their greatest weapons, discipline and well practiced volley fire that might usually be employed against a similar military force. Given the size and scope of the thirteen colonies, which covered many thousands of square miles of generally unknown territories, there was never any real possibility of regular British troops being able to suppress such a widespread rebellion, simply because they lacked the numbers to do so effectively. With reasonably well trained colonial militias in most areas of the thirteen British colonies, most of whom had been raised to fight and defend against Indian attacks, although they lacked the uniform discipline of regular troops, they were ideally suited to fight an extended guerrilla war against any sort of enemy, whether European or native. This ability to launch highly effective hit and run raids against an enemy force was said to have been well demonstrated during the British journey back from Lexington and Concord, when colonial minutemen were reported to have taken a heavy toll on the regular troops, as well as managing to raise a total force of some several thousand men by journey's end. For the British forces to have suppressed such activity, they would almost certainly have needed to occupy substantial areas of the country, which given their limited numbers would have been almost impossible, unless of course Britain had prepared to commit hundreds of thousands of troops and carry out a highly repressive occupation of the territories, neither of which solution was possible for, or indeed acceptable to the British government of the day.

It was also thought to be the case that a number of the military commanders who were given overall control of the American colonies, seriously underestimated the ability of the colonial militias to stand up against British regulars, which of course, they very rarely did. General Thomas Gage was said to have been the first commander to misjudge the mood and fighting ability of the colonials, with his own personal character traits and the possible connivance of his wife, both helping to alert the colonists to most of the military proposals that Gage intended to implement. It was said to have been a combination of Gage's and General Howe's poor judgement which allowed the fiasco at Bunker Hill to occur and Howe alone that permitted the colonials to force him out of Boston, a sea port that the British forces would have been well advised to defend with a little more vigour. Howe's successor, General Clinton, despite being a highly capable and quite successful strategist was said to have helped create the final defeat of the British forces in America, by ordering his immediate subordinate, Lord Cornwallis, to establish a secure base at Yorktown in Virginia, an order that would prove to be catastrophic, when the enclave was later besieged by French and American forces. Although he was surrounded by enemy forces and with a French fleet blockading Chesapeake Bay, it was Lord Cornwallis who took the final and most humiliating decision of the entire American Revolutionary War, when he decided to surrender his forces of an estimated eight thousand men rather than be starved and bombarded into submission by the waiting enemy troops. Although a second British naval force was being prepared to relieve Yorktown, Cornwallis was said to be either unaware of the fact, or indifferent to it, leaving him with little option but to open negotiations with the besieging Continental forces and seek the best possible terms, marking an end to British control in the thirteen American colonies. Although up to thirty thousand regular troops were thought to be stationed along the eastern seaboard of America, with Cornwallis' surrender on 19th October 1781, the British government were thought to have taken the decision to suspend any further military actions there, essentially bringing an end to the war itself and Britain's control of the thirteen American colonies.

However, even though hostilities between British and American forces were not brought to a end until April 1782, when the British Parliament voted to end the war in America, the wider conflict involving the likes of France, Spain and the Netherlands, nations that had supported the American cause, were only finally concluded with the signing of the Treaties of Paris and Versailles in September 1783. Although no definitive figures exist regarding the numbers of British land troops who died of wounds received during the fighting, a basic estimate would seem to suggest that anything between seven and ten thousand soldiers died as a direct result of the conflict, but with far more dying as a result of the various diseases that all sides were exposed to during the same period. For many of the men who survived the war, especially those soldiers specifically recruited to oppose the colonial cause, the British defeat resulted in a significant number of British regiments either being amalgamated or disbanded entirely, their former members having being transferred to other units or discharged back into the civilian community. However, with the territories of British North America, later the state of

Canada, still in Britain's possession, large numbers of troops were said to have been retained in order to protect these British held lands, along with the Empire's other overseas territories including those in the Caribbean, West Africa and the Indian subcontinent. Even though the fate of the thirteen American colonies and the attached western frontier had been decided by the outcome of the Revolutionary War, ownership of the more northerly territories would remain a source of contention between Britain and America for the next twenty nine years, until it erupted into armed conflict between the two sides in what became known as the War of 1812, which has been discussed elsewhere.

In the short term, the next great military conflict that the British Army found itself involved in, was the French Revolutionary War, which was said to have had its roots in France's ill-fated decision to support the American colonials in their conflict with Britain, as a result of which, the European state essentially ended up bankrupting itself. As previously mentioned, in the section relating to the history of Britain's Royal Navy, the French Revolution was said to have been marked by the execution of the French monarch, King Louis XVI and his queen Marie Antoinette, as well as the rise of a young artillery officer called Napoleon Bonaparte. Although no large scale land engagements were thought to have taken place between British and French forces, for the most part, the war was fought at sea, with the Royal Navy actively attacking and blockading French ships and ports, in an attempt to starve the French Republican government into submission. However, as part of the wider conflict, French forces were reported to have been despatched to Ireland, in an attempt to support a rebellion led by the United Irishmen in 1798, which brought elements of both European armies into contact with one another, albeit in a relatively small way. An earlier French invasion of Ireland was said to have been thwarted in 1796, when atrocious weather conditions were thought to have scattered a large French fleet which had tried to land troops in Ireland, during which many thousands of French soldiers and sailors were said to have drowned, when their vessels were wrecked or simply inundated by the heavy seas. As has been previously noted in the chapter relating to Ireland's long history, the British authorities there were thought to have been well aware of the intentions of the United Irishmen and were generally well prepared to deal with any sort of rebellion that might occur there. However, it was only some two months after the bloody uprising began that French troops were finally despatched to Ireland, with an estimated one thousand soldiers, under the command of General Humbert, landing at Kilcummin in County Mayo, where they met a five thousand strong rebel force on the 22nd August 1798. Unfortunately, even though this mixed force was said to have enjoyed limited initial success against the British and Loyalist forces that stood against them, within three weeks the rebel army had been met and defeated by an extremely large British force commanded by Lord Cornwallis, the same military leader who had previously surrendered Yorktown in America. Although most of the French troops who were captured, were subsequently returned to France, many of the Irish born rebels were not so fortunate, with many of their leaders being hunted down and executed for their part in the rebellion, with a few others managing to avoid capture and continuing to oppose British rule in Ireland for the rest of their lives. It was said to have been the same year that Britain and Austria began to raise a new European military alliance to confront France, the previous coalition having collapsed, although from a British perspective her most active campaigns against the French continued to be fought at sea, with few land troops being committed to the cause until 1801, when British and Ottoman troops were used to force the French out of Egypt. However, by 1802 and with both Britain and France becoming exhausted by the ongoing dispute, the new First Consul of France, Napoleon Bonaparte was reported to have begun negotiations with the British government that resulted in the Treaty of Amiens being signed by both sides in 1802.

Hessian Troops

King George III

King Louis XVI

Even though both sides were thought to have regarded the Treaty of Amiens as a temporary arrangement, one that might allow them to reorganise and reinforce their individual armed forces, between 1802 and 1804 soldiers of the British East India Company were said to have continued to undermine French interests on the subcontinent, largely through the military suppression of those native tribesmen that were regarded as being favourable to France and its new national leader, Napoleon Bonaparte. It was said to be during this period that Major General Arthur Wellesley, later the Duke of Wellington, began to fashion the military career that would eventually bring him to national prominence in England, When war did officially break out once again between Napoleonic France and Great Britain, initially the conflict was said to have been fought in and around the Caribbean, involving a number of the West Indian islands that the two European neighbours had been arguing over for many decades. In Europe however, Britain presented a much greater threat to Napoleon's dominance in the west, simply because it remained beyond the reach of his vast armies and the Royal Navy continued to rule most of the world's seaways uncontested, limiting the French ruler's ability to impose his will anywhere outside of the European continent. Perhaps more importantly though, Britain remained as a centre of opposition to Napoleon's rule, helping to arm and finance those states that might be persuaded to join an anti-French alliance, leaving Napoleon with little option but to consider carrying out a full scale military invasion of Britain. However, as previously reported in the history of Britain's Royal Navy, despite positioning a large land army at Boulogne, which he intended to send to Britain, the failure of his Franco-Spanish fleet to overcome Admiral Nelson at the Battle of Trafalgar, ensured that not a single one of these French troops would ever place his foot on English soil. With most major military engagements between the two sides taking place only at sea, when French and Spanish ships dared to challenge the Royal Navy, Britain was able to employ a significant number of its land forces in defending its British North American territories during the War of 1812, as well as sending troops to participate in the Peninsula War of 1808 to 1814, where they fought alongside the soldiers of Spain and Portugal.

Representing the first significant involvement of British land troops in fighting the French forces of Napoleon Bonaparte, the Peninsula War was said to have begun in 1807, when French troops were reported to have crossed into Spain, on their way to suppress Portugal, which as one of the two remaining neutral European nations of the time, had refused to adopt Napoleon's clearly stated trade sanctions on British goods. Although in the first instance, the Spanish authorities had made no objections to the French invasion of Portugal, largely because they expected to benefit from the occupation, when elite French troops were subsequently sent into Spain, with orders to seize a number of the country's most important fortresses, it quickly became apparent to the Spanish leadership that Napoleon intended to occupy the entire Iberian peninsula, not just Portugal. With the Spanish monarchy almost immediately put under threat by French intrigues, which ended with Napoleon's older brother, Joseph Bonaparte, taking the throne, most of the Spanish army was said to have been left leaderless and generally scattered, preventing it from offering any sort of meaningful resistance to the highly efficient and professional French troops that were taking control of their country. Although some Spanish troops and local guerrillas were able to resist the French occupiers, for the most part, these full-time forces were said to have been fairly widespread; and so it was left to the large urban populations to demonstrate Spanish resistance to the invasion of their country, instances which were often suppressed in the most brutal fashion. Eventually though, some form of command and control began to be organised between the scattered Spanish forces, resulting in a much more structured resistance movement to develop, which saw regional and provincial Spanish units, publicly declare war against Napoleon and his occupying armies.

As part of the campaign against Napoleon's domination of Europe, initially Britain had had to content herself with conducting occasional raids in and around the European coastline, using Royal Navy ships to launch hit and run attacks against French interests that for the most part proved to be an irritation rather than any sort of serious military threat. It was only when France chose to invade neutral Portugal that this situation was fundamentally changed, as it not only altered Portugal's status in terms of the wider conflict, but also provided Britain with a number of European ports that could be used to land and re-supply British land forces, which were despatched to the Iberian Peninsula for the first time in August 1808. Initially under the command of Lieutenant-General Arthur Wellesley, later the Duke of Wellington, British troops, along with their Portuguese allies, were reported to have halted French advances in large parts of the country, although their destruction was said to have been prevented when Wellesley was replaced as British commander by a much less determined officer, who allowed the French forces to withdraw from Portugal without significant loss. In neighbouring Spain, local Spanish forces were also reported to have made significant gains over the French, to the extent that Napoleon himself was said to have become increasingly concerned over the fate of the country, forcing him to return there to take personal command of his armies in order to secure Spain once and for all. In part, the French leader was said to have been aided by problems within the Spaniard's own ranks, with social divisions beginning to appear amongst the various Spanish forces and logistical problems besetting the British army based in Portugal, all of which allowed Napoleon to secure much of Spain and its main cities by the end of 1808.

At the same time that an estimated two hundred and fifty thousand French troops were suppressing Spain, in neighbouring Portugal, the new British commander, General Sir John Moore, was said to have been making preparations for bringing his relatively small British army, of around thirty-odd thousand men across the shared border into Northwest Spain. Ostensibly a move to try and save the surviving Spanish nationalist forces, by distracting the larger French army with the British incursion, ultimately the strategy proved to be a failure, as not only was Moore forced to withdraw to the Spanish coast, where his army had to rescued by the Royal Navy, but the Spanish forces he had tried to save were subsequently destroyed anyway, making the thousands of British casualties an extraordinary and unnecessary sacrifice in the overall scheme of things. However, the actions of Moore's forces, those of his Spanish allies and the resistance of the remaining Spanish cities which had refused to surrender to Napoleon were all thought to have bought valuable time for the Portuguese army and the other British troops that were busily preparing themselves for the inevitable French assault on Portugal. While Napoleon's army had been crushing all opposition in Spain, Portugal's armed forces had been restructured by a cadre of British officers, who had not only rebuilt a regular army of some twenty thousand men, but also raised and trained various militias numbering a further thirty-odd thousand soldiers, which would help to confront the seasoned French army that would almost inevitably be sent against them. In March 1809, the first of Napoleon's forces were reported to have crossed the frontier, intent on re-establishing French control over Portugal, but were said to have met with stiff resistance from the Portuguese defenders who were able to prevent the French troops from extending their influence much beyond the north of the country. By April 1809, Arthur Wellesley was thought to have returned to Portugal, to take command of the combined Anglo-Portuguese forces and with these newly formed troops was said to have driven Napoleon's army out of the country for good, securing the country for its absent monarchy. Advancing into Spain, Wellesley was able to link up with General Gregorio de la Cuesta, one of the country's most prominent military commanders, with the intention of making a direct assault on the French held city of Talavera de la Reina, located on the River Tagus, where Wellesley expected to confront a French army commanded by Marshall Claude Victor and Major General Horace Sebastiani. Unfortunately, as Wellesley's twenty thousand soldiers prepared to move forward, the Spanish troops of General de la Cuesta were reported to have remained fast, reportedly refusing to fight on a Sunday; and it was only on the next day that they finally agreed to move forward with their British allies, a delay that was said to have proved to be very costly for the Wellesley and his forces. During the 24 hours that De la Cuesta had delayed his forces, the French army of Marshall Victor, was said to have not only been reinforced by other military units, but had also been allowed time to redeploy his forces so that they could more easily attack the British and Spanish flanks. Initially the allied forces were reported to have come under sustained pressure from the highly experienced French troops, although towards the end of the first day, the equally disciplined British force was said to have re-established its control over its area of the battlefield, forcing the enemy to retire to its previous position. However, at the beginning of the second day's fighting, Napoleon's troops once again attacked the allied positions, but were finally repulsed when British infantrymen moved forward to carry out a bayonet charge against the advancing French soldiers, causing their lines to break and their men to retire. With their soldiers repulsed, the French commander's were said to have employed cannon to try and reduce the allied ranks, a bombardment that was reported to have lasted from noon right through to the early evening and into the night, when the French made one final attempt to take the British and Spanish positions using their ground troops, an assault that was once again repulsed by the allies. During the later part of the evening, both sides were thought to have used their field guns to try and reduce each others armies, although by the following morning it quickly became evident to both Wellesley and De la Cuesta that the French cannon fire had actually been a ruse, to allow their main body of troops to retire, leaving only artillery units and wounded soldiers in the field, who were subsequently taken prisoner by the allied forces. During the Battle of Talavera, Wellesley's British forces were reported to have suffered significant losses with anything up to 25% of his soldiers, some five thousand men, being killed or wounded by the French opposition, who were themselves said to have lost over seven thousand troops. As it turned out, a fast moving column of British Light Infantry, numbering some three thousand men, had been sent to reinforce Wellesley's command and having famously marched some forty miles in just over twenty four hours, they were able to replace some of the losses that the British forces had suffered at the Battle of Talavera.

Having withdrawn their troops from the battlefield, French commanders was reported to have marched his forces south, with the intention of blocking the allied line of retreat over the Targus River, a move that compelled Wellesley to move his own forces eastward in an attempt to both protect his line of retreat and confront the enemy column, which the British commander believed to be smaller than his own. However, in order to move at speed, Wellesley was forced to leave his wounded soldiers in the care of his Spanish allies, who would subsequently abandon them to the mercy of the French, an act of betrayal that would continue to sour the relationship between Wellesley and his Spanish counterparts in later campaigns. Unfortunately, rather than finding himself facing a French army of around fifteen thousand men, as he had first assumed, Wellesley suddenly found himself confronting a much larger enemy force of some thirty thousand French troops, which was fifty percent bigger than his own. Quickly recognising the danger he faced if the French army reached the main river crossing before his own, Wellesley was reported to have despatched a flying infantry column ahead of his main force in order to secure the bridge before the French arrived there, which they were said to have done with hours to spare. Although Wellesley and his British troops were thought to have continued campaigning in Spain for several months after the battle at Talavera, the relationship between the two sides was said to grown increasingly tense, often because Spanish commanders failed to deliver the military and logistical support that they had promised to the British. It was said to be because of these problems, the shortage of supplies and continuing pressures from the large French armies that eventually forced Wellesley to withdraw his troops back to Portugal in the closing months of 1809, in order that they might be rejuvenate themselves for the spring campaigns of the following year.

Marie Antoinette

Duke of Wellington

Gen Sir John Moore

Fearing that the French might attempt yet another invasion of Portugal, Anglo-Portuguese commanders were reported to have begun the construction of a highly fortified defensive position, the Lines of Torres Vedras, which was composed of a series of blockhouses, redoubts and trenches, designed to repulse any sort of large scale enemy incursions. In July of 1810, the French duly fulfilled the allied expectations by crossing the border into Portugal, where they were said to have achieved some notable gains during the first months of their campaign, although by October their advance was permanently stopped at the Lines of Torres Vedras, which had only just been completed. With the French forces contained, the Anglo-Portuguese armies were said to have been substantially strengthened by the arrival of fresh regular troops from Britain, allowing the allies to begin their own successful offensive against the French, which resulted in Napoleon's forces being pushed back into Spain by May 1811. The British commander of the Portuguese army, Marshall William Beresford, was said to have been particularly successful in these Spanish campaigns, which once again saw the local Spanish guerrillas adding their own unique hit and run tactics to the allied cause. It was said to be as a direct result of the guerrillas activities that large numbers of French troops were permanently tied down guarding their own supply lines and military assets, rather than being used to engage the British, Portuguese and Spanish forces in much more traditional military operations and battles. With Napoleon's army in Spain seemingly unable to curtail the activities of the guerrillas and assigning substantial military resources to suppressing that particular aspect of the Peninsula War, the allied commanders, including Wellesley, were able to make significant gains against the overstretched French armies. Advancing further into Spain, by the start of 1812 the allies were reported to have recovered a number of Spanish towns from their French occupiers, including the historic city of Salamanca, in the west of the country, which was retaken in June 1812, just before a large French force arrived to relieve the city's garrison. Because the French army of Marshall Marmont was substantially larger than those at Wellesley's disposal, initially the Anglo-Portuguese was reported to have been forced to withdraw, with their enemy following behind, waiting for their chance to strike at the allied forces. Fortunately for Wellesley though, the left flank of Marshall Marmont's forces were said to have become detached from the main body of his army, offering the allied cavalry an opportunity to deliver a devastating blow to these isolated French troops, which resulted in Marmont's left wing being completely routed, at the same time that the French commander and his immediate subordinate were both wounded by flying shrapnel. Although the French army's third in command, Bertrand Clausel, was said to have ordered an immediate counterattack to the allied advance, Wellesley too was reported to have sent reinforcements forward, which helped to repulse the French assault and forced Clausel's troops to retire. Fought on the 22nd July 1812, the bitter and bloody engagement that is often referred to as the Battle of Salamanca, was reported to have cost the British some three thousand casualties, the Portuguese an estimated two thousand men, whilst the French losses were thought to have numbered around thirteen thousand troops, seven thousand of which were simply taken prisoner, rather than being killed or wounded during the military action. With much of their left wing annihilated, the main French force, under the nominal command of General Bertrand Clausel, was said to have withdrawn, being closely followed by Wellesley and his Portuguese allies, who were said to have temporarily liberated the city of Madrid, as a direct result of their victory, but were later forced to withdraw to Portugal once the French army had been reformed and reinforced by its commanders.

Although the allied victory at Salamanca had gained them little in terms of actual territory, the continuing see-sawing of the war was said to have compelled the French leadership in Spain, to not only reorganise their forces, but also to withdraw troops from less important regions, such as Andalucia and Asurias, effectively handing them back to local Spanish control. However, the most inexplicable French decision taken during 1812, was that of the Emperor, Napoleon Bonaparte, who committed the fatal mistake of not only forcing his armies to fight on two separate fronts, but also denuded the ranks of his army in Spain by an estimated thirty thousand highly experienced soldiers, who were subsequently sent to reinforce his ill-fated Russian adventure, a mistake that would be repeated some hundred and thirty years later by another European dictator, one Adolph Hitler. With the French army in Spain catastrophically weakened by the loss of these highly seasoned troops, Britain and her Iberian allies were reported to have re-doubled their efforts in

Spain during 1813, slowly but surely pushing the retreating French forces towards the Pyrenees, scoring a series of spectacular military victories over the ever reducing ranks of Joseph Bonaparte's army of occupation. By early July 1813, most of the French troops were reported to have been pushed back to the Franco-Spanish border, where Marshall Soult, one of Napoleon's most experienced commanders was given complete command of the retreating French army and began initiating a series of counterattacks which managed to stall the allied advance in the short term. Unfortunately, with the tide of war generally moving against him, these French victories were unable to prevent the almost inevitable allied progress towards driving Soult and his soldiers out of Spain forever, most especially after they were decisively beaten at the Battle of Sorauren on the 30th July 1813. As the allied armies pursued Soult and his men across the border into France itself, Napoleon was said to have tried to divide the allied cause by offering to make a separate peace with Spain, an offer that was quickly rejected by the Spanish authorities, who had learned through bitter experience that the word of the French Emperor could never be accepted again.

As the Peninsular War came to an end and both Spain and Portugal looked forward to rebuilding their countries after the conflict, so the battle against Napoleonic France moved into central Europe, where a growing coalition of leading powers and subject states began to work together to bring an end to Bonaparte's vast European empire. Although the French Emperor still had an estimated six hundred thousand troops under his nominal command, in reality only about a quarter of a million men were under his direct control, a number that was said to have been reduced each and every time that they fought against a coalition of western nations that between them could often muster several times that number. Despite these odd however, Bonaparte's sheer military brilliance and daring was thought to have turned a large number of military engagements from a likely French defeat to an inevitable French victory, often to the complete exasperation of those allied commanders who believed that they were on the brink of defeating Napoleon on several occasions, only to see events turned around by the strategy of the French commander. Throughout much of 1813, a number of pivotal battles were fought which resulted in the French gaining either a tactical and strategic advantage over their allied adversaries, many of which were subsequently wasted by the limited abilities of Napoleon's own commanders, who failed to capitalise on the gains that their leader had given them. As a consequence, over the period of the year, rather than managing to hold the territories, which had cost the lives of so many French soldiers, Napoleon's armies were forced further and further back towards Paris, where on the 30th March 1814 allied troops finally managed to enter the city to demand the surrender of the French leader. The following month Napoleon was forced to abdicate his throne, before being exiled to the island of Elba, after which the coalition helped to restore the Bourbon heir Louis XVI to the throne of France, before sitting down to initiate the Congress of Vienna and to redraw the map of Western Europe.

Held prisoner on the Mediterranean island of Elba until the beginning of 1815, Napoleon was reported to have landed at Cannes on 1st March 1815, along with most of his retinue who had accompanied him into exile and very quickly began to collect large numbers of recruits as he made his way through the French countryside, on his way to Paris. Having reached the capital with a sizeable military force, Bonaparte was said to have deposed the newly restored Bourbon monarch, Louis XVIII, before beginning to issue decrees calling for army veterans and new recruits to be raised in preparation for the allied invasion that he knew would result from his unauthorised and unexpected return to the country. Managing to assemble an estimated quarter of a million troops, including a large number of those who had fought for him in earlier campaigns, Napoleon was reported to have divided his forces into a number of distinct armies, with the intention of conscripting a further two and a half million men with which to recover his lost empire and defend it against the European coalition that he knew would be raised against him. For their part, Europe's leading nations were thought to have raised an estimated three quarters of a million men in the first instance, with the intention of increasing that number to well over one million men under arms, as the campaign progressed. The first major engagement, between the allies and the revived Napoleonic army was said to have taken place in June 1815, when Bonaparte himself was said to have taken his ninety thousand strong Northern Army to the Belgium border, with the intention of launching a pre-emptive assault against the allied forces, which he assumed would still be organising themselves in readiness for their own advance into France. As it happened, the coalition forces were still scattered, giving Napoleon the opportunity to engage the Prussian army first, before he turned his attention to meeting the Anglo-Dutch army commanded by Arthur Wellesley. Taking the main body of his army into battle against the Prussian army, commanded by Gebhardt von Blucher, Bonaparte ordered one of his most trusted lieutenants, Marshall Michel Ney, to detach his troops from the left flank of the Northern Army, in order to prevent Wellesley and his Anglo-Dutch forces from coming to Blucher's aid. Although Ney was said to have failed to prevent the Anglo-Dutch troops from advancing, when Bonaparte routed the Prussians at Ligny on the 16th June 1815, Wellesley had little choice but to withdraw his troops, retiring them to a defensive position that he had previously identified, just outside the small Belgium town of Waterloo.

Intent on confronting Wellesley's force, Bonaparte was said to have brought his Northern Army reserves to the front, after ordering another of his subordinates, Marshal Grouchy to detach his forces on the right wing of the Northern Army and pursue the retreating Prussian troops of Gebhardt Blucher, a strategic mistake that would ultimately prove to be catastrophic for the French leader. Without realising it, Blucher's Prussian forces had already begun to regroup and were reported to have begun a fairly leisurely and circuitous route to the town of Waterloo, where Wellesley had already stationed his Anglo-Dutch army. On the evening before the decisive Battle of Waterloo, heavy rain was said to have poured down on the area, soaking the ground and turning the earth into a muddy quagmire, an event that forced Napoleon to postpone the onset of the battle until midday of the June 18th, as he waited for the ground to dry out. With Wellesley having positioned his allied army along the top of a fairly low lying ridge, Bonaparte's strategy was thought to have involved attacking and destroying the three distinct sections of the coalition forces, the right wing, left wing and centre, one at a time, before Wellesley could be reinforced by the Prussian forces of Field Marshal Blucher, which Napoleon knew still posed a significant threat to his French forces. The right flank of Wellesley's forces were reported to have been positioned just to the rear of the Chateau d' Hougoumont, a farmhouse that lay at the bottom of the ridge where most of the coalition forces were stationed and which had previously been occupied by a number of allied battalions, including men from various British Guards regiments. Marking a position that would allow its occupants a clear field of fire against any French advance, the farmhouse and its surrounding grounds immediately became a strategic target for Bonaparte, who ordered a brigade of infantry to attack the position, in order that it could be used as a firing position for French artillery and snipers. However, although the French troops were said to have advanced through the chateau's grounds fairly easily, the heavy artillery and musket fire of the coalition defenders within the main parts of the house was said to have caused enormous casualties amongst the French infantry, who still managed to get close enough to the allied redoubt, to force open the north gate of the defensive compound, leaving its allied garrison open to further assaults. Fortunately for the British troops and their coalition partners, although a party of some thirty to forty French soldiers managed to break through to the central courtyard of the chateau, an allied soldier managed to secure the gateway once again, leaving the enemy troops at the mercy of the British Guards, who were reported to have killed all but one of the trapped French soldiers in fierce hand to hand fighting. Although Napoleon's forces outside of Château d' Hougoumont continued their assault against the property, the later arrival of additional British troops, including units of the Coldstream Guards was said to have finally dispersed the first major French attack, although throughout the remainder of the day the post continued to come under sustained attack by Bonaparte's forces. It was only when it became clear that his troops could not take the house through the use of infantry alone that Bonaparte ordered the chateau to be bombarded, to help drive the allied troops out of the building once and for all, even though the attack itself was said to have destroyed most of the house in the process. According to some historians, both Bonaparte and Wellesley were thought to have regarded the Chateau d' Hougoumont as being pivotal to the outcome of the wider battle, so much so that both commanders were said to have devoted significant human resources to either holding or capturing the house. However, for other reporters of the engagement, the fighting around Hougoumont was almost entirely a distraction which resulted from Napoleon's limited view of the battlefield, which made him believe that the building was of a far greater strategic value than it actually was, causing him to waste valuable time and resources in capturing the position.

At the same time that Napoleon's soldiers were struggling to overcome the allied defenders at Hougoumont, in the centre of the battlefield the French leader was unleashing his artillery against the main body of Wellesley's allied force that was occupying the Ridgeway, immediately facing Bonaparte's own army. Unfortunately for him, the French Emperor's decision making was said to have been heavily influenced by his own personal opinion of Arthur Wellesley, who Bonaparte considered to be a less than adequate leader, who commanded an allied army that was inferior to his own, a view not shared by many of his generals, especially those that had first hand knowledge of facing the British commander in the field. According to some sources, Wellesley was renowned for choosing positions that allowed him to utilise the reverse slopes of hills and ridges, thereby protecting his troops from the dangers of enemy artillery, a fact that was apparently unknown to Bonaparte, who had never faced Wellesley directly. As he ordered his guns to open fire on the coalition troops facing him, the sodden conditions of the open ground was said to have further played into the allies hands, as the cannonballs, shot and shells that were fired by the French guns were largely absorbed by the soft muddy earth, causing far less death and destruction that might normally have been the case, leaving the allied lines largely intact. Having done little real damage to the allied battle line, at around one o'clock in the afternoon of the 18th June, an hour or so after the fighting first commenced, Napoleon was said to have ordered his first infantry units forward to attack the coalition centre. Aware of Wellesley's usual battlefield tactic of employing heavy and coordinated musket volleys to decimate tightly packed enemy infantry formations, French commanders were said to have reorganised their ranks so that they were further apart and then sent them forward toward the allied lines. With the main part of his force on the reverse slope of the hill, initially the advancing French infantrymen were able to push the allied soldiers back, not realising that as they did so, they were walking towards the coalitions own guns. Having reached a particular point on the ridge, allied commanders were reported to have ordered their soldiers to stand up and unleash a devastating volley of shot against the French infantry, although this initial fusillade did not stop Napoleon's troops, who not only managed to return fire, but continued with their advance up the hill and moved towards the waiting British troops. However, just as it seemed that the allied lines would break, British heavy cavalry units were reported to have moved forward in support of the infantry, driving the French soldiers back down the hill and continuing their charge along the lines of the still advancing enemy infantry, until they found themselves confronted by hastily formed defensive squares, which their horses would not approach. With the British cavalry having put themselves at risk, by galloping too far ahead of their own lines, Bonaparte was said to have ordered his own highly experienced and well equipped Dragoons and Lancers forward to confront the allied horsemen, who were reported to have suffered heavy losses at the hands of the mounted French troops.

General De La Cuesta

Marshall Wm Beresford

Gebhardt Von Blucher

However, despite the unexpected loss of their British heavy cavalry regiments through ill-discipline, the coalition army remained relatively intact and with the anticipated arrival of Field Marshall Blucher and his Prussian troops, the balance of power was reported to have most decidedly swung against Bonaparte, who from the very outset had underestimated the ability and strategy of the coalition commanders. Recognising that he had to defeat Wellesley and his British troops first, if he was to have any chance of turning the battle in his favour, Napoleon, or perhaps his most faithful commander, Marshal Michel Ney, was then reported to have made yet another ill-conceived tactical mistake. As allied casualties were carried to the rear, Ney believed that the entire coalition force was being withdrawn from the battlefield and in his eagerness to achieve a complete victory, made the fateful decision to attack Wellesley's forces with cavalry alone, rather than with the support of his remaining infantry. Charging towards the coalition's lines with an estimated five thousand cavalrymen, on seeing their approach allied commanders simply ordered their troops to form into defensive squares, which provided them with the sort of protection that was used against enemy cavalry charges. Time and time again Ney's horsemen tried to break the allied squares, but without the support of artillery or infantry they were unable to break through the almost impenetrable lines of musket ball and bayonets, yet all the time the numbers of French cavalrymen were reduced by the highly disciplined volleys of allied gunfire. Seemingly unable to comprehend the futility of his mounted assault, rather than withdrawing, Ney was reported to have simply ordered even more cavalry units to sacrifice themselves against the allied square, until at last the final French cavalry units had wrecked themselves on the coalition positions. Each and every time Napoleon's horsemen retired to regroup for yet another charge against the battle squares, so allied gunners would rush out to reload their guns and decimate the approaching lines of French horsemen, wreaking carnage amongst the ranks of horses and riders alike, leaving the battlefield littered with the dead and dying, in scenes that shocked even the most hardened professional soldiers. Rather belatedly, French commanders were said to have arranged for a combined attack by cavalry, infantry and artillery, which initially proved to be highly effective, causing significant losses amongst a number of allied regiments, although ultimately the casualties suffered by the French forces earlier in the battle eventually began to tell on Napoleon's limited resources.

By four thirty in the afternoon, the first units of Field Marshal Blucher's Prussian forces began to arrive in the area, helping to reinforce the left flank of the allied army and attempting to attack the rear of Bonaparte's battle line. With the arrival of these fresh coalition troops, Napoleon had little choice but to send out more of his own limited forces to try and neutralise this Prussian threat, beginning yet another engagement which was centred around the settlement of Plancenoit and that would involve successive assaults on the town by both sides. However, by around seven thirty in the evening and having sent some twenty thousand infantrymen to secure the township, Napoleon determined that this was the perfect opportunity to launch one last major offensive against Wellesley's centre, with the intention of rolling it back and forcing his coalition allies to withdraw from the battlefield. Having kept back some of his most experienced infantry regiments, including the Young, Middle and Old Guards, which made up his own Imperial Guard Regiment's, Bonaparte was reported to have ordered some four regiments of his Middle Guards to advance on the allied position, which they did, regardless of the heavy fire they received. However, having reached the ridge and pushed the allies front line back, the French Guards then came under sustained attack from both infantry and artillery fire, which caused enormous losses amongst their ranks, although it was only a charge by a Dutch division and a well timed volley by a British infantry unit that finally caused the battered French line to break and withdraw. As the Middle Guard lines began to fall back, the sight of them retreating was said to have had a highly negative effect on the other French infantry units, who very quickly followed their example, whilst Wellesley was reported to have urged his own troops to push forward and pursue them. According to some sources, most French troops were said to have made for Bonaparte's headquarters which was based around the village of La Belle Alliance, where the two remaining regiments of Old Guards, who were the Emperor's Imperial bodyguards, were still located. As the French retreat turned into a rout, Bonaparte still hoped to rally his remaining forces behind his Old Guard, although eventually he was persuaded by members of his retinue that the battle was lost and that he should retire to Paris, leaving his soldiers to make whatever peace they could.

The Battle of Waterloo was said to have cost Arthur Wellesley an estimated seventeen thousand men, killed, wounded or missing, of which around two and a half thousand were said to have died during the battle itself, with hundreds of others dying in the following days and weeks. Unlike his main ally, the Prussian commander, Field Marshal Blucher, Wellesley did not hurry to pursue the remnants of the French Army back to Paris, but instead was reported to have allowed his own troops to regain their strength, before marching them across the border into France. Despite believing that he could still defeat the coalition, eventually Napoleon was forced to accept that his position was now untenable and he agreed to abdicate his throne for a second time, on the 24th June 1815, after which the Bourbon monarch King Louis XVIII was restored as the ruler of France. Fortunately for Bonaparte, rather than falling into Prussian hands, the French leader was said to have surrendered himself to a British officer, Captain Frederick Maitland, the commander of HMS Bellerophon, on the 15th July 1815, allowing him to be held in relatively safe custody until such time as his fate was decided by the victorious allied authorities. Following the signing of the Treaty of Paris on the 20th November 1815, Napoleon was exiled to St Helena, a volcanic island in the middle of the Atlantic Ocean, which was administered by Great Britain and that was commonly used as a place of exile for a number of high profile political prisoners, right through to the beginning of the 20th century. Brought to the island in October 1821, in order to guarantee his future security, a significant British garrison of several hundred men was said to have been maintained there, in addition to the cordon of Royal Navy vessels that patrolled the waters offshore. However, these arrangements were thought to have only been in place until the 5th May 1821, when Napoleon passed away as a result of the stomach cancer that was thought to have affected him in the final years of his life. Interestingly, one of Britain's most famous infantry regiments, the Grenadier Guards, who were directly involved in helping to defeat Napoleon's army at the Battle of Waterloo, as the 1st Foot Guards, were said to have adopted their now traditional bearskin headgear as a tribute to the Napoleonic Grenadiers that they met and defeated during that famously bitter military engagement.

With the defeat of Napoleon Bonaparte in June 1815, the series of European conflicts that had dogged the continent for the best part of twenty-odd years, were brought to an end, allowing much of Western Europe to settle down into a period of comparative peace, during which Britain was able to concentrate its efforts on overseeing and expanding its vast overseas Empire. However, even though Europe itself remained relatively peaceful from 1815, until the outbreak of the Crimean War in 1853, Britain's armed forces were known to have been involved in a number of military conflicts, especially in and around the Indian subcontinent, where British interests faced an almost constant threat from native rulers, some or all of whom were supported by agents of the Russian Empire, in what commonly became known as the "Great Game". Unfortunately, apart from changes in tactics, armaments and regimental titles, following the successful outcome of the Battle of Waterloo, for the most part, very little was thought to have changed within the ranks of Britain's land forces and it remained a military service dominated by squalid conditions, social inequality, overbearing cruelty and poor leadership. Apart from the common soldiers who were required to serve in the most onerous circumstances, in theatres from Ireland to Afghanistan, the widespread habit of selling commissions to the sons of well-to-do families, regardless of their abilities, ensured that very often the best troops might be led by the very worst officers, creating levels of distrust and antipathy that doubtless had a negative effect on the army's morale and performance. Promotion within the service was also said to have been earned on the basis of time served, meaning that it was often the worst sorts of candidates, those who had nowhere else to go, were prepared to wait, or had the right sort of connections, were often promoted above those that were far more capable military leaders. Units that were posted abroad were said to have been generally well thought of by the British public, but with no formal Police force to speak of, civil unrest within Britain itself was usually dealt with by the military, either local militias, or regular units who happened to be stationed within the immediate areas. However, being largely untrained for civilian policing duties, where troops were used in suppressing local unrest, it was often the case that their actions were severe and unjustified, undermining their reputation amongst the civilian population and illustrating the need for an community based law enforcement agencies, or regional Police forces. The role of the military within Britain's towns and cities was said to have been particularly questionable in places like Ireland, where a strong and widespread nationalist movement ensured that regular troops and local militias were regularly brought into conflict with the civilian population, resulting in almost inevitable tragedies which helped to divide the two sides even further.

Outside of Britain and in British India particularly, regular army units were thought to have played a secondary role to the private commercial forces of the British East India Company, which up until 1858, was the body charged with administering the country, for and on behalf of the British authorities. Apart from its own European officers and men, who were generally recruited and trained in Britain, the East India Company relied very heavily on the numerous native levies that were recruited from the various regions and states of India, where the company already had commercial interests. Before 1858, military rule within India was exercised by one or all of the Company's three native armies, which were centred round the organisations main commercial centres, or Presidencies, of Madras, Bombay and Bengal. Even within these private armies though, the same British class structures existed, with native soldiers being unable to progress much beyond the ranks of NCO's and the British officers who led these native troops often acquiring their promotion, as a result of time served, rather than through any sort of personal ability. However, having managed to secure large parts of the country over the previous centuries, largely through political manoeuvrings, military alliances and even plain bribery, by the start of the 19th century, the British East India Company were not only eager to protect the gains that they had made thus far, but were keen to continue their expansion in the wider subcontinent. It was as part of these dual objectives and whilst Napoleon Bonaparte was still exiled on Elba that the British company began a dispute with the kingdom of Nepal, a conflict which would bring them into contact with the Gorkha, or Ghurkha people, who would later go on to serve with such distinction within the ranks of the regular British Army. Believing that the Ghurkha people represented a threat to their operations in India and with the Ghurkha leadership refusing to be intimidated by the might of the British East India Company, almost inevitably Britain's representatives were said to have taken the decision to attack Nepal, rather than wait for the Ghurkhas to launch their own offensive against the Company's interests. In October 1814, a British force, comprising mostly Indian troops, but commanded entirely by British officers, was said to have crossed the border into Nepal with the intention of capturing the strategic targets of Katmandu and Dehra Dun, along with the important fortress at Jaithak. Over the course of the next five months and despite the hardship of the terrain, the British led Indian Sepoy's were said to have made significant advances within Nepal, although the unfamiliarity of the region was thought to have slowed their progress, to such a degree that they were unable to achieve any sort of outright victory against the determined Ghurkha forces. However, towards the end of April 1815 two of the smaller British military columns sent into the country were said to have achieved some success against the Nepalese fighters and these losses, coupled with the death of their main military leader was said to have compelled the Ghurkhas to seek terms with the British, ostensibly bringing an end to the conflict in April 1815.

Unfortunately, although the military leadership had agreed to a peace settlement, the Nepalese national council was reported to have failed to ratify the treaty by November 1815, causing the British to send a second, larger military force into the country, once again made up mainly of Indian Sepoy's. However, rather than risk having to face the Ghurkha troops head on, the British commander, Lord Moira, was said to have sent his forces in a much more circuitous route, which allowed them to attack the Ghurkhas from the rear, inflicting a heavy defeat on the native Nepalese army. With their army defeated and the British forces being supported by other anti-Nepalese factions, Lord Moira was able to successfully launch attacks on the Ghurkha strongholds of Makwanpur and Hariharpur, at the same time threatening the capital of Katmandu, which compelled the Nepalese national council to accept the earlier peace treaty without further delay. It was said to be as a result of their determined defence of their homelands that Ghurkha fighters had displayed during their resistance to the Company forces that their martial abilities were first recognised by British commanders, who were keen to recruit such high calibre warriors into their own ranks and incorporated the right to recruit Ghurkhas as part of the Treaty of Segauli in 1815. Initially founded as the Nusseree Battalion under the command of a Lieutenant Ross in April 1815, these first Ghurkha recruits later evolved into the 1st King George's Own Ghurkha Rifles and this force, along with subsequent Ghurkha regiments later became an intrinsic part of the British Indian Army.

Michele Ney

Captain F Maitland

Lord Moira

Securing and expanding its control within the wider Indian subcontinent remained a priority for the British East India Company during the first half of the 19th century and any possible threat to its continuing commercial exploitation of the region was always likely to be treated extremely seriously. Just as the Company had responded vigorously to the perceived danger posed by the Gorkha people of Nepal, so the growing influence of the expanding Russian Empire in both Afghanistan and Persia was thought to have caused enormous concerns in India, where the British Governor-General, Lord Auckland, was said to have become increasingly anxious about the intentions of Russia and its envoys. Having convinced himself of Russia's hostile intentions, Auckland was reported to have sent his own representatives to Kabul in order to try and form an alliance with the Afghan ruler, Dost Muhammad, against Russia, which ultimately proved to be fruitless, as Muhammad wanted British forces to help him recover the city of Peshawar from the Sikh Empire, something that Britain was unable to do. With the East India Company's refusal, the Afghan leader resumed talks with his new Russian allies, causing Lord Auckland to take the view that in order to prevent Russian expansion in the region, then Afghanistan would have to be conquered and its native leadership replaced with a more sympathetic regime. His proposals, which in normal circumstances might well have faced significant opposition back in London, were thought to have been made far more justifiable in 1838, when relations between the Afghan leadership and Russian diplomats broke down, leading to an outbreak of violence between Russian backed Persian forces and Afghan troops over the ownership of the city of Herat, which both countries claimed as their own. Using this incident to support his own claims that Russia represented a direct threat to British India, Auckland was reported to have ordered some twenty thousand Company troops into Afghanistan to not only drive out the Persian and Russians forces, but at the same time install his preferred pro-British candidate, Shuja Shah Durrani, as the new ruler of Afghanistan. Arguing that Durrani was a legitimate candidate for the Afghan throne, Auckland publicly refuted any suggestion that his actions represented an unwarranted invasion of Afghanistan and stated that British forces would be withdrawn from the country once Durrani was successfully installed as its new ruler.

Enthroned as the new Afghan ruler in August 1839, Durrani and his British supporters were reported to have been deeply unpopular with the majority of the native tribesmen; making the remaining eight thousand Company troops feel increasingly anxious about their ability to retain control of the vast and generally lawless country. Although the former ruler, Dost Muhammad and his supporters attempted to drive the British garrison out of the country, ultimately his tribal army was no match for the much more effective Company forces and having been captured by the British in 1840 was subsequently exiled to India shortly afterwards. With such a large military garrison to support, rather than risk housing their troops in a number of existing Afghan forts, British commanders were reported to have ordered the construction of one single large military encampment on the outskirts of Kabul, which was said to have been so extensive that it was virtually impossible for its inhabitants to fully protect the entire perimeter. As time passed and with the Company troops becoming more and more disenchanted with their enforced occupation of the country, the British agent in Kabul, William Hay MacNaghten was said to have granted permission for his soldiers to bring their families to Kabul, in an attempt to stave off the loneliness and tensions that such prolonged separations were likely to cause within the military ranks. However, by 1841, nearly two years after the British had first arrived in Afghanistan; the country was still thought to have remained generally unsettled, with increasing numbers of local tribal leaders choosing to support the cause of Dost Muhammad's son, Mohammed Akbar Khan, who continued to oppose the rule of Durrani, who he regarded as simply a puppet of the British East India Company. It was reported to be in November 1841 that this deep-seated native resistance to the British presence in the country first exhibited itself, when a British officer and his aides were killed by an angry mob in Kabul, although MacNaghten's subsequent failure to hand out any sort of communal punishment for the deaths was said to have merely emboldened local resistance fighters. However, rather than just make an example to the local population, the British envoy was reported to have tried to divide the local tribes against Akbar Khan, with some reports suggesting that he had even tried to have the Afghan leader assassinated in an effort to unite the country behind his own candidate, Shuja Shah Durrani. Unfortunately for MacNaghten, as the British situation deteriorated, with a growing number of attacks on their assets and personnel, Akbar Khan was said to have been informed about the envoy's attempts to have him assassinated, ensuring that attitudes on both sides became increasingly hardened and preventing any sort of compromise from being reached between the two parties. However, matters were said to have come to a head in December 1841, when much to MacNaghten's surprise a face to face meeting was arranged between the envoy and his Afghan opponent, just outside the limits of the large British encampment. Unfortunately, as MacNaghten and his three officers came forward to meet Akbar Khan and his party, all four Company men were seized by the Afghan's and subsequently murdered, with the envoy's body being dragged through the streets of Kabul as a demonstration of the Afghan leader's power and British weakness.

The man in charge of the British armed forces in Afghanistan, Major General William Elphinstone, a sixty-year-old Company officer, was not thought to have been widely respected by most of his immediate subordinates, many of whom regarded him as totally unsuitable for the post that he held, with some reports describing him as incompetent, weak and indecisive, personal qualities which were exacerbated by a generally sickly disposition. By the time that William Hay MacNaghten and his three aides had been murdered by Akbar Khan on the 23rd December 1841, Elphinstone was already said to have lost control of some of his troops, a contributing factor in the death of MacNaghten, when British soldiers assigned to protect the envoy simply failed to arrive, leaving him and his small party defenceless. However, even following MacNaghten's murder, Elphinstone failed to take any sort of retribution against the Afghan tribesmen, but instead agreed to a form of surrender that forced him to hand over all of his army's gunpowder reserves, their very latest muskets and most of their cannons, in return for being granted safe conduct out of the country. As his garrison assembled itself on the 6th January 1842, to begin its journey back across the border into British India, Elphinstone was said to have headed a column of some seven hundred British soldiers, three and a half thousand Indian Sepoys and over twelve thousand civilians, including large numbers of women and children, the families of the Company's troops, who had been allowed to come to Kabul by MacNaghten. Any wounded Company personnel who could not undertake the retreat were reported to have been left behind in Kabul, on the understanding that they would be cared for by Akbar Khan and his followers, although in reality, as soon as Elphinstone left the city virtually all of those who were left behind were killed and their bodies disposed of.

Intending to take his garrison to the city of Jalalabad, some ninety-odd miles from Kabul, even as the long journey began, Elphinstone was reported to have failed to take proper measures in order to fully protect his troops and their dependants, by neglecting to put out scouts that might forewarn him of any potential danger. In addition to this obvious failure, the British commander was also thought to have allowed the column to travel at such a slow rate that any enemy wishing to pursue them, could have done so quite easily, which was exactly what happened later in the day. As they travelled towards the Khord Kabul Pass, which marked the route through to India, large numbers of Afghan tribesmen were said to have passed the British column and taken up position in the hills and settled down to await the arrival of the slow moving refugees. As they walked through the pass, the local Afghans were reported to have fired down on the fleeing troops and refugees, with some of these native fighters using the modern muskets which Elphinstone had previously agreed to surrender to Akbar Khan, yet another incompetent decision which had been made by the British commander. Suffering significant losses to the Afghan tribesmen's guns, eventually Elphinstone's column managed to make its way into the mountains, although the bitter winter snows and plunging temperatures were said to have killed many hundreds of the refugees, as they tried to survive the rigorous conditions, as best as they could. Having only travelled some ten miles in less than three days and perhaps fearful of Elphinstone's increasingly poor leadership, a large number of his troops were said to have deserted the main column, in the hope that they might survive more easily, if they rid themselves of the slow moving civilians. Unfortunately for them, the shadowing Afghan warriors were aware of their departure and eventually hunted down all of those that attempted to abandon their posts. As the refugee caravan grew weaker and more desperate, so Akbar Khan was said to have sent out envoys to try and persuade the British members of the column to surrender themselves, promising them fair treatment, in return for their use as hostages in any future negotiations. On the 11th January, some five days after they had been forced to leave Kabul, a large number of the women and children were said to have been surrendered to the Afghan leader's care, although it later transpired that only the European families survived, as they had some intrinsic value, unlike those of the Indian Sepoys, whose families were not and were subsequently murdered as a result. Later the same day, Elphinstone himself and his second-in-command, Major Shelton were also reported to have surrendered themselves to Akbar Khan, in the mistaken belief that this would guarantee their own lives and those of the surviving column, which it did not. Kept as a prisoner for a number of days, the extremely ill and completely disillusioned British commander was said to have survived until the 23rd January 1841, when he finally died, still a prisoner of his Afghan adversary.

What remained of the British column was said to have continued on, trying to reach Jalalabad, although as they approached the village of Gandamack, they were reported to have faced a large force of Afghan tribesmen, who were blocking their way, forcing the Company troops to fight a bloody advance that claimed many more of their numbers. Only around forty men were thought to have survived this bitter engagement and those that did quickly found themselves surrounded by a large body of enemy fighters, who demanded that they should surrender and be taken prisoner. Being aware of the fate that awaited them, despite a desperate shortage of food, water and ammunition the British officer leading this last surviving contingent was reported to have rejected the Afghan calls for their surrender and carried on fighting. According to some reports, only nine men survived this final encounter, all of whom were subsequently captured by the Afghan tribesmen who then took them as hostages. The only man to have escaped the carnage of the retreat from

Kabul was thought to have been a British doctor, Assistant Surgeon William Brydon, who had somehow survived this last great battle, despite having part of his skull sheared off by an Afghan sword. Reportedly rescued by a local shepherd, who gave him refuge, once the Afghan fighters had left the area, he placed the injured surgeon on his horse and set him on his way, unsure of whether or not the British officer would survive long enough to reach the base at Jalalabad. Although other individual native Sepoys were said to have survived the destruction of Elphinstone's army, for the most part, Brydon's account of the deadly journey was the generally accepted account and the one that would be used to inform public opinion, both in India and more importantly back in London, where the authorities were said to have been shocked and outraged by the treatment meted out by the Afghan leader, Akbar Khan.

The chief architect of the Afghan invasion, the British Governor-General, Lord Auckland was said to have collapsed from a stroke upon hearing the news that nearly seventeen thousand men, women and children had been annihilated by the Afghan leader and his tribal supporters. Almost immediately, Auckland's successor, Lord Ellenborough, put plans in place to raise an "Army of Retribution" that would be sent into Afghanistan to exact full revenge against those who were deemed to be responsible for the action, an army that was already on the move by August 1842. Under the command of Generals Nott and Pollock, two heavily armed British military columns were said to have set out from Kandahar and Jalalabad heading for Kabul, where they quickly overcame Akbar Khan's forces. Having secured the release of the few remaining British hostages, those who were fortunate to have survived the massacre, Nott and Pollock set about levelling Kabul as an act of vengeance against the Afghan people. Although Khan himself escaped being killed by the British, in 1847 he was reported to have died in fairly mysterious circumstances, possibly as a result of his being poisoned by his father, Dost Muhammad who was released by the British authorities at the end of 1842, after they had already decided to play no further part in the country's internal power struggles. According to some reports, Akbar Khan was said to have incited his tribesmen to kill every member of the retreating British garrison, even though he must have known that the British authorities would send a second, much larger military expedition to avenge such an atrocity. However, the fact that William Elphinstone was deemed to be the main culprit behind the disaster, which had led to one of Britain's most humiliating and catastrophic defeats, ensured that British reprisals were quite restrained; bearing in mind the losses that had been suffered by the East India Company in the first place. Interestingly, even though British forces were subsequently withdrawn from Afghanistan, the authorities in London having determined that Britain should play no further part in the running of the country, the creeping encroachment of the Russian Empire in and around the borders of Afghanistan, continued to represent a threat to British influence in the wider region, forcing London to send yet another military expedition, of an estimated forty thousand men, into Afghanistan in 1878. However, having fought a series of bloody, but otherwise generally successful campaigns against the various Afghan tribesmen, Britain was said to have achieved most of its primary objectives, including the enthronement of its preferred native candidate as ruler of the country and control of Afghanistan's foreign policy, which then allowed all British forces to be withdrawn from the country for the second and final time by the end of 1880.

William McNaghten

General Elphinstone

Lord Auckland

Having withdrawn all of their forces from Afghanistan by the end of 1842, the British East India Company were reported to have continued to expand their sphere of influence within the subcontinent, bringing them ever closer to the borders of the independent Sikh kingdom of the Punjab. Ruled by the Maharaja Ranjit Singh until his death in 1839, up until that time relations between the East India Company and Ranjit Singh were said to have been cordial, but cautious, with the Sikh ruler maintaining a relatively strong native army in order to defend his kingdom from all potential enemies, including the British, if that ever became necessary. However, Ranjit Singh was not simply content to hold and defend his existing territories, but like other native rulers was always ready to exploit any obvious weakness amongst his immediate neighbours, which might allow him to annexe additional or disputed lands. During his reign, Ranjit Singh was reported to have conquered and incorporated a number of disputed regions into his own Punjabi kingdom, including the Afghan province of Peshawar and the neighbouring states of Jammu and Kashmir, all of which helped to further enlarge his already powerful and expansive independent kingdom. However, when he died in 1839, he was said to have been succeeded by his legitimate heir, Kharak Singh, who was said to have been so ineffective and unpopular that within a matter of months he had not only been overthrown, but had also died in fairly mysterious circumstances. Replaced by his own son, Kanwar Singh, he too was reported to have died quite suddenly, leaving the kingdom without any sort of legitimate royal heir to succeed to the throne, as a result of which an illegitimate son of Ranjit Singh, Sher Singh, was said to have been put forward as the most legitimate candidate. Unfortunately, his ascension to the Punjabi throne was thought to have divided the kingdom, allowing extremists and zealots within the extremely powerful Punjabi army to take control of certain units and bring the entire country to the brink of almost complete anarchy.

As the Punjab teetered on the edge of the abyss, which would result in an out and out civil war between the various rival factions, the assassinations of various military and political leaders in the region, was said to have compelled the British East India Company to station increasing numbers of its own troops along the border of the Punjab, ostensibly to ensure that the conflict did not spread into British India itself. However, even though the East India Company was thought to have lacked the resources to simply invade the Punjab and to take control of the country, the very fact that it had stationed large numbers of troops and military equipment on the edges of the kingdom was thought to have caused even greater tensions to arise within the royal courts. In response to British troop movements in the border region, the Punjabi army began to mobilise its own well trained units towards the same area, which almost inevitably led to the two armies facing one another and the prospect of fighting breaking out between them becoming an increasing possibility. Having crossed the Sutlej River on the 11th December 1845, an act that British commanders felt to be overtly hostile, the first clash between the two sides was said to have occurred at the Battle of Mudki on the 18th December, during which the British units were reported to have suffered heavy casualties, especially amongst its infantry officers, but still managed to drive the Punjabi forces from the battlefield and secure the immediate area. The following day, the same British column was reported to have confronted a much larger Punjabi force at the village of Ferozeshah and although the British commander, Sir Hugh Gough, was keen to assault the enemy troops as quickly as possible, the Governor-General of Bengal, Sir Henry Hardinge, who was accompanying the Company's forces was said to have insisted that Gough wait for reinforcements to arrive, before beginning any attack. Forced to wait for a full two days, for a second British division to arrive, by the 21st December 1845, both Gough and Hardinge were said to have been convinced that they now had the forces to overcome the enemy position and in the late afternoon of the 21st began their advance towards the Punjabi village of Ferozeshah. As they approached in the dimming light, the British troops were reported to have come under sustained attack by the well trained Punjabi artillery units, which caused significant casualties amongst the British and Indian troops who were advancing against their gun emplacements. However, despite the shot rained down on them, the British infantry continued on and by nightfall some units were even said to have overcome the Punjabi artillery's forward positions, even though other British infantrymen had been forced back to their own lines. By the next morning though, Gough and Hardinge were able to encourage their men forward once again, until this time they were able to force the Punjabi army from the field once and for all. Even though he and his men were exhausted by the bloody battle, Sir Hugh Gough was determined to hold his ground, until such time as his position was reinforced by additional British troops, which is exactly what he did, despite repeated efforts by the Punjabi army to dislodge him from his position and sever his lines of communication.

Whilst the British managed to rest their troops and consolidate their position, awaiting even more reinforcements from British India, the defeated Punjabi army units were said to have withdrawn further west to a place called Sobraon, where they too, were reported to have been joined by additional troops, including a number of their most formidable soldiers. Intent on constructing an insurmountable obstacle to the British forces that would subsequently attempt to conquer the whole of Punjab, Sikh military leaders were said to have constructed their final redoubt along the banks of the Sutlej River, on the same side as the British forces. Although their defensive position was said to have been formidable, the fact that their only line of retreat required them to cross a single pontoon bridge, which had been subjected to torrential rain and heavy river waters made their strategy risky at best and completely disastrous for any Punjabi troops who failed to cross the bridge, before it was finally swept away by the raging river. By the 10th February 1846 and having been reinforced by yet another British division under the command of Sir Harry Smith, Sir Hugh Gough was ready to begin his final assault against the Punjabi positions at Sobraon, a ground attack that was said to have been preceded by a two hours artillery exchange between the two sides, during which large numbers of soldiers from both armies were thought to have been killed or wounded. Having previously reconnoitred the Punjabi position, Gough ordered three separate divisional advances to be made against them, two of which were said to have been diversionary, whilst the third under the command of Major General Henry Dick, was said to have attacked the weakest point of the Punjabi defences. Although initially achieving some level of success, Dick's forces were eventually driven back by the Sikh troops and the British commander killed, causing his men to fall back even further. However, the British advance was said to have been resumed as Bengali, Ghurkha and British troops began to successfully assault the entire Punjabi line, breaking through in several places and forcing the Sikh soldiers to withdraw back towards the pontoon bridge over the Sutlej River. Unfortunately, as the retreat turned into a rout, the increasing numbers of Sikh and other Punjabi troops on the already weakened crossing point was said to have caused the bridge to collapse, allowing it to be swept away and trapping some twenty thousand of their troops on the same side of the river as the advancing British forces. Left with little option but to either surrender, or to fight to the death, most of the Sikh units were reported to have chosen the latter, although large numbers were also said to have tried to swim across the river to safety and were subsequently swept away, or simply shot by the British troops positioned along the river bank. Whichever choice these Punjabi troops made, according to some contemporary reports of the Battle of Sobraon, an estimated ten thousand Sikh and Punjabi soldiers were said to have been killed or wounded during the engagement, as opposed to the two thousand or so British troops, who were reported to have died or been injured.

In the aftermath of the Battle at Sobraon, the Punjabi army was said to have been largely destroyed, even though significant numbers of Sikh troops were thought to have survived beyond the disaster to continue the conflict, had they been ordered to do so. However, the Punjab's native leadership, in the form of the Lahore "Durbar" or council was reported to have chosen to seek terms with the British, rather than risk seeing their kingdom utterly destroyed by an even larger British army that would almost certainly result from continuing native resistance. As part of the Treaty of Lahore, which was signed by both sides on the 9th March 1846, the kingdom of Punjab agreed to surrender certain vitally important agricultural lands to the British East India Company, reimburse the company for its financial losses and permit British agents to be stationed in all of its major cities. Unfortunately, as was often the case with generally unequal peace treaties of the time, almost inevitably they would be refuted by one or other party, either because the terms of the agreement were thought to be too severe, or otherwise too lenient. So it was with the Treaty of Lahore that was signed in 1846, which not only allowed the British East India Company to place agents in every major city within the Punjab, but also ensured that a British Resident was installed in Kabul, who could essentially dictate the policy of the entire country. This loss of native power was said to have been exacerbated by the loss of the Kashmir region to the Maharajah of Jammu, Gulab Singh, who was reported to have paid seven and a half million rupees for the territory, all of which was said to have been paid to the East India Company, as part of the Treaty of Amritsar, which was signed in March 1846. With the Company holding almost complete control of the country and the running of the Punjab left almost entirely in the hands of British officers and agents, resentment towards British rule was said to have increased steadily after 1846, to the point that individual tribal leaders were reported to have begun conspiring together to rise up against the Company and force them out of the Punjab. Even though the British agent, James Abbot, was said to have been concerned about the possibility of an uprising in the Sikh region of Hazara, the new British Resident in Kabul, Frederick Currie, was said to have ignored Abbot's concerns and taken no affirmative action to address any of the widespread discontent. His apparent indifference to the growing native resentment within the country was reported to have culminated in him replacing a well established and very popular Hindu Governor, with a new Sikh Governor, in the city of Multan, which not only caused the death of the two British officers sent to oversee the process, one of whom was later decapitated, but also led to large numbers of Sikh soldiers deserting their posts in order to join the rebellion that was about to erupt throughout the kingdom.

Although other British East India Company officers were said to have taken steps to put down the initial outbreak of disorder, when the two British officers were murdered, it was said to have taken several weeks for the Company forces to fully confront the rebels and even then some of the rebellious Sikh troops were said to have withdrawn to the fortified city of Multan, where they were beyond the reach of the British soldiers. However, the uprising in and around Multan was said to have finally compelled the British Resident in Kabul, Sir Frederick Currie, to take some form of affirmative action in response to the unrest, although even then he was said to have simply contented himself with contacting Sir Hugh Gough, the military commander in Bengal, requesting additional Company units to be sent into the region. Unfortunately, given the time and money involved in launching such a major military expedition, both Gough and his immediate superior, the Governor-General, Lord Dalhousie, both refused to despatch any sort of large scale force into the region and settled for a much smaller contingent of Bengal troops to be sent in to the Punjab to support Currie. Commanded by a General Whish, this mixed force of British and native troops were reported to have made their way to Multan to join the siege of the city fortress, although it quickly became clear that the rebellion had the potential to become a much wider ranging dispute, if it was not handled in the most effective and judicious manner. In several other towns throughout the Punjab, other potential rebellions were reported to have been prevented, or at least delayed, by the proactive approach of local British officers, who were thought to have had the experience and initiative to carry out pre-emptive actions against potential rebels, thereby preventing the possible rebellion from engulfing the entire Punjab.

Lord Ellenborough   General William Nott   General George Pollock

The two main leaders of the Sikh rebellion were reported to have been Chattar Singh Attariwalla, the Sikh Governor of Hazara and his son, Sher Singh, both of whom were members of the Sikh nobility and experienced military commanders, who felt aggrieved about the continuing control of their country by the British East India Company and its agents. In the months following the murder of the two British officers at Multan in April 1848; and before any significant Company forces could be brought into the Punjab to suppress the wider rebellion, large numbers of Sikh commanders and soldiers were said to have joined Sher Singh's rebel army, which was reported to have been rallying in the centre of the Punjab. It was only towards the end of 1848, after the seasonal monsoons had ended that Sir Hugh Gough was able to bring elements of his Bengal Army into the Punjab in order to try and confront Sher Singh and his still growing native army, although this did not prove to be as straightforward as British commanders had first hoped. In the first military engagement between the two armies, the British were said to have failed to make an opposed crossing over the Chenab river, giving Sher Singh's army their first victory over the British and compelling Gough to undertake a much more risky river crossing, which not only delayed his advance, but also allowed Sher Singh and his army to melt away into the surrounding countryside. During December 1848, the Sikh leadership were also thought to have formed an alliance with the ruler of neighbouring Afghanistan, Dost Muhammad, the former British prisoner, who had been released by the East India Company following the end of the First Anglo-Afghan War in 1842. Although reluctant to ally his own country to the Sikh cause, for fear of British reprisals, Dost Muhammad was thought to have been persuaded to help Sher Singh's rebellion, in exchange for the return of the city of Peshawar, which had been seized by the Sikh ruler, Sanjit Singh, in earlier years. As part of the agreement made between Sher Singh and Dost Muhammad, the Afghan ruler agreed to provide several thousand mounted fighters to attack the British controlled fort at Attock, which was preventing Sher Singh's father, Chattar Singh, from bringing his own native forces out of Hazara, to meet up with the army headed by his son. However, when the British garrison in Attock, who were mainly Muslim troops, saw the approach of Dost Muhammad's large mounted force approaching their position, they simply put down their arms and agreed to join Sher Singh's rebel army, allowing Chattar Singh and his own troops to march out of Hazara and meet up with their fellow rebels.

Upon hearing about the surrender of the garrison at Attock, the British Governor-General, Lord Dalhousie, immediately sent word to Gough to locate and attack Sher Singh's army, before it could grow into an even greater threat to the Punjab. In the late afternoon of the 13th January 1849, the British commander was reported to have unexpectedly stumbled across Sher Singh's formidable army, but rather than wait until the following day to launch his assault, the rather "bullish" Gough was said to have ordered his forces to advance, just as the light was beginning to fade. The resulting Battle of Chillianwala turned out to be something of a disaster for the British forces, which were said to have been sent forward through fairly dense undergrowth and into well prepared enemy defences, which included artillery positions that decimated the British ranks with round after round of grapeshot. At the forefront of Gough's assault against Sher Singh's positions was the British infantry brigade, the 24th Foot, which had only just arrived in the country and although they were reported to have reached the Sikh positions, such were their casualties that they were subsequently forced to withdraw. Not only were they thought to have lost over five hundred of their number, either dead or wounded from enemy actions, but were also said to have lost their regimental colours, which was a humiliating loss for any British infantry unit. Although some of Gough's cavalry forces were thought to have successfully breached the Sikh lines, the failure of other supporting units to achieve similar successes, was said to have allowed the Sikh's to reorganise themselves and drive back the British horsemen, some of whom were reported to have fled with great haste. Seeing that his main assault was largely unsustainable, Gough was thought to have ordered a general withdrawal to his own lines, leaving many hundreds of British troops, both British and native, wounded and abandoned in the surrounding undergrowth, many of whom were reported to have been subsequently murdered by roving bands of Sikh fighters, who were scouring the surrounding countryside. By the end of the battle, both sides were reported to have retired to their initial positions, although sometime during the following hours, Sher Singh was said to have withdrawn north to meet up with his father, Chattar Singh, while Gough's troops were said to have maintained their positions for the next few days, as they tried to recover their dead and wounded from around the battlefield.

In the immediate aftermath of the Battle of Chillianwala, which was fought on the 13th January 1849, an estimated two and a half thousand British troops were said to have been killed, wounded, or were missing as a result of the fighting, some six hundred of which were British born men from the 24th Foot. On the other side, an estimated three and a half thousand Sikh soldiers were said to have been killed or wounded during the engagement, helping to enhance their reputation as highly determined fighting men, who were more than a match for any modern European army, including those fielded by the British East India Company. However, even though the Sikh army had sustained slightly higher losses than his own, Gough's reckless tactics, culminating in the deaths of over seven hundred men and the loss of various regimental colours, was reported to have caused the British authorities to relieve Gough of command and replace him with General Charles Villiers, who happened to be in England at the time. As it turned out though, by the time that Villiers had been despatched from Britain, to take over command of the army in the Punjab, Gough had already been reinforced by troops who had previously been employed in the Siege of Multan, which General Whish had successfully completed, bringing the city and its fortress back under British control. With these additional forces at his disposal, Hugh Gough, then advanced in pursuit of Sher Singh, who had already moved north to link up with the Sikh troops commanded by his father Chattar Singh, who had previously escaped from Hazara, with the help of the Afghan ruler Dost Muhammad. Father and son were reported to have joined up at Rawalpindi, but quickly found their large force was unable to find sufficient stores in the area that might sustain them for any period of time, forcing Sher and Chattar Singh to contemplate facing their enemy once again, in the hope of defeating them once and for all. Unfortunately, Sher Singh's original plan to flank the British column and attack it from the rear, proved to be impossible, as the Chenab river, which they intended to cross, was too swollen to allow them safe passage and was also being patrolled by British native cavalry. With few other options open to him and his army, Sher Singh was said to have withdrawn his Sikh army to the city of Gujerat, where he hoped to draw Gough and his forces into another well laid trap, assuming that the British commander adopted his usual headlong rush to attack. Unfortunately for the Sikh leader, Gough's approach was thought to have been tempered by the disaster at Chillianwala and no doubt stung by the criticism he had received within India, from Lord Dalhousie and the decision to replace him with Charles Villiers, which had been taken back in London. Rather than employing his ground troops to assault the Sikh positions at Gujerat, instead Gough determined to attack his enemy with the artillery pieces that he had brought with him and the large siege guns that had previously been employed in breaching the fortress walls at Multan.

Even though Sher Singh had his own cannons, which had been used to great effect at Chillianwala, this time they were not only outranged by Gough's heavy siege guns, but also outnumbered by them, so that by the end of the three hour artillery exchange, the Sikh gunners had been forced to abandon their cannon and retire from the battlefield. With Sher Singh's artillery neutralised, Gough was reported to sent his infantry forward, quickly followed by his artillery, which once again began bombarding the Sikh positions further back, until eventually they broke and began to retire at speed. With his foot soldiers being used to overcome the Sikh lines, Gough was then reported to have ordered his cavalry units and Dragoons forward to pursue the Sikh troops who were said to have fallen back over a significant distance. During the next ten days or so, Sher Singh's forces were thought to have been ruthlessly pursued by Gough's British troops, until eventually both Sher and Chattar Singh were left with little option but to surrender themselves and their remaining troops to the British East India Company. This particular battle was also thought to have been marked by the bloody retribution exacted by those British soldiers who had fought at Chillianwala and whose wounded comrades had been killed by the Sikh's after the battle was over. At Gujerat, there was very little pity shown to those injured Sikh troops who happened to be discovered by the British soldiers, even though in later years both sides would serve together to save India from the turmoil caused by the Sepoy Mutiny of 1857. Perhaps more significantly for the whole of Punjab, the main outcome of the Second Anglo-Sikh War was the complete annexation of the region by the British East India Company, the lifelong exile of Sher Singh from his homeland and the deposition of the Punjabi boy king, Duleep Singh, who was subsequently exiled to Britain and forced to hand over his kingdom's greatest treasure, the Kohinoor Diamond, to Queen Victoria in 1850, which later became and remains part of, the British Crown Jewels. In an ironic twist of fate, although the British East India Company essentially conspired to take over the kingdom of the Punjab, despite incurring the wrath of the Sikh people, as with the Gorkha tribesmen of Nepal, ultimately these particular native troops became some of the most valiant and faithful servants of the British Crown, not just during the catastrophic Indian Sepoy Mutiny of 1857, but also in the years up to and including the granting of Indian Independence in 1947. The famous Ghurkha regiments too were not only retained by the modern state of India after 1947, to help form an integral part of their own national army, but also by the regular British Army, which even today regards these tough fighting men as some of the most elite military troops in the world.

Although India was and remained the Jewel of Britain's vast overseas empire, British forces remained committed to other parts of the world, including neighbouring Europe, where the continent had been regularly convulsed by numerous wars and conflicts for hundreds of years. However, by the end of the Napoleonic Wars in 1815, much of Europe had remained relatively peaceful, as international conventions and treaties were employed to bring about some semblance of peace to the many and varied states, which had first been conquered and then freed by military might. It was said to have been the nephew of the first Napoleon Bonaparte, Charles Louis Napoleon Bonaparte, who began the next great European conflict, when he initiated a coup d'etat against the government of the Second French Republic in 1851, before declaring himself and ascending the French throne as Emperor Napoleon III on the 2nd December 1852. Intent on being granted sovereign authority over all of the Christian places in the Holy Land, which were then controlled by the Turkish Ottoman Empire, Napoleon III was said to have applied significant diplomatic pressure to the Ottoman leadership, even though previous treaties had granted the same authority to the Russian Empire, in the form of its own Orthodox Christian Church. However, not to be refused, Napoleon was said to have used bribery and even the threat of military force to try and persuade the Ottoman ruler in the region, Sultan Abdul Mecid I, to grant him control of the various vitally important Christian sites, including the Church of the Nativity, which the French ruler intended to pass into the care of the Roman Catholic Church. Under enormous pressure, eventually the Ottoman Sultan agreed to a new treaty that would place the shrines into Napoleon's care, with the result that Tsar Nicholas I put his own military forces on alert. Prepared to confront the Ottoman Empire through force of arms if necessary, Nicholas was keen to ensure that in the event he attacked the Ottoman's over the issue, that neither Britain, nor France would interfere in the conflict, or indeed ally themselves together to attack Russia. Despite their best efforts to find a diplomatic solution to the increasingly escalating situation, as tensions rose between the French, Ottomans and Russians, Britain's apparent refusal to deploy Royal Navy assets to help reduce any threat of armed conflict was thought to have convinced the Tzar that Britain would not interfere in any future conflict. On that basis and in the belief that Austria would have no real objections to him seizing the Ottoman controlled regions of Moldavia and Wallachia, along the Danube, Nicholas was reported to have sent Russian troops into the two areas, ostensibly on the basis of forcing the Ottomans to restore the Russian Church's protection of Christianity's most holy places.

Unfortunately, even though Britain had tried to force the Ottoman Empire to reject its new treaty with France, the fact that Russia had invaded the Ottoman held territories in Europe, which Britain regarded as a defence against future Russian expansion, proved to be too much for the British authorities in London, who subsequently sent a Royal Navy fleet to the

Dardanelles, as a show of force. Even at this late stage, the other four great powers in Europe, Britain, France, Austria and Prussia tried to find some form of mutual agreement that might be acceptable to the Ottoman ruler, Sultan Abdul Mecid I and the Russian Emperor, Tzar Nicholas I. Unfortunately, having reached a form of words that was acceptable to one side, the other party objected, ensuring that no real meaningful progress was made and convincing both Britain and France that additional negotiations would prove to be equally fruitless. In spite of Austrian and Prussian demands that further talks should take place between the two sides, almost inevitably one of the parties, in this case the Ottoman ruler Sultan Abdul Medid I, was reported to have lost patience with the Russians and on the 23rd October 1853 formally declared war on the Russian Empire. Ordering his Ottoman forces to attack Tzar Nicholas' troops along the Danube and in the Caucasus, in these initial engagements the Ottoman's were reported to have achieved some degree of success, largely as a result of two notable military commanders, Omar Pacha along the Danube and Imam Shamil in the Caucasus. However, the Russian leader, seemingly undeterred by these early setbacks was said to have ordered a number of his warships to attack and destroy Ottoman naval patrols in and around the Black Sea, in what became known as the Battle of Sinop which occurred on the 30th November 1853. It was thought to have been the destruction of the Ottoman frigates, which gave Britain and France the basis for declaring war against Russia, although it was only when Tzar Nicholas refused to withdraw his forces from Moldavia and Wallachia that the two countries finally lost patience with the Russian Emperor and formally declared war on his country. Unable to rely on the neutrality of other European states, which might just ally themselves to the French, British and Ottoman cause, Nicholas was said to have relented and withdrawn his troops from the disputed territories along the Danube, including Moldavia and Wallachia, essentially removing the cause of Britain and France's declaration of war. Unfortunately, having compelled the Tzar to comply with their initial demands, the two allies were then reported to have issued even more demands for the cessation of hostilities, some of which the Russian ruler found to be completely unacceptable, thereby setting the Crimean War in motion.

Raja Ranjit Singh

Sir Henry Hardinge

Lord Dalhousie

The first overtly hostile action that took place between British and Russian forces was said to have occurred in March 1854 when Russian guns, based in the port of Odessa, fired on the Royal Navy frigate HMS Furious, which was patrolling the waters just outside of the harbour. Returning fire, the Royal Navy fleet was reported to have caused considerable damage to the port and its surrounding buildings, before withdrawing back into the Black Sea to resume its task of protecting and re-supplying allied forces in the region. British naval units were also reported to have helped transport land troops to the Bulgarian city of Varna in June 1854, although with Russian forces having been withdrawn from that particular area around the same time, most of these same British forces were later re-embarked and transported to the Crimea, to begin a siege of Sevastopol. As the main city port for the Russian Black Sea fleet, Sevastopol was always likely to be a primary target for allied forces, whose own navies and land forces quickly enforced a blockade of the city, both on land and at sea. With their fleet trapped in Sevastopol harbour and therefore of little practical use, Russian commanders were said to have scuttled a number of their warships and relocated both their guns and crews to other positions, where they might be better employed in the defence of the city. British and French troops were said to have been initially landed at Eupatoria, just north of Sevastopol in September 1854 and having assembled there, were reported to have moved south, crossing the River Alma, before laying siege to Sevastopol and its vitally important port. In order to enforce the land blockade of the city, British and French engineers were thought to have been brought from their base at Balaclava, to begin constructing a series of redoubts, gun emplacements and trenches to the south of city, which would not only prevent movement in and out of Sevastopol, but would also allow allied artillery to bombard the city and its defenders. Unfortunately, just before the allies managed to complete their encirclement of the city, most of the Russian army was said to have retreated into the hinterland of the country, leaving an estimated forty thousand sailors, militia, engineers and artillery personnel to face the allied forces who were besieging Sevastopol. Having taken several weeks to construct their siege works, by the middle of October 1854, the allies were thought to have had well over one hundred heavy guns to begin bombarding the city, although the Russian defenders were said to have had at least three times as many, most of which had been taken from their naval vessels that the Russians had previously scuttled. Beginning on the 17th October 1854, the siege of Sevastopol began with devastating artillery barrages fired by both sides, but within a matter of days, was said to have developed into the sort of grinding trench warfare that would only be repeated some sixty years later, on the battlefields of Flanders.

At the same time that British and French engineers were building their siege works outside of Sevastopol, additional British troops commanded by Lord Raglan, were reported to have been making their way further south, well to the east of Sevastopol, in order to position themselves for an attack on the city's southern defences and to take advantage of the other regional port facilities that would allow them to be re-supplied. As they made their way south however, Raglans forces, along with the accompanying French and Ottoman troops were said to have been badly affected by the oppressive heat, shortage of fresh water and regular outbreaks of cholera, all of which were thought to have been endemic to this particular region. Moving towards the relatively small port of Balaclava, the entire allied force was said to have been too large to be accommodated there, so the British, French and Ottoman commanders decided between themselves who would occupy Balaclava and the nearby ports of Kasich and Kamiesch, with Lord Raglan being advised to choose Balaclava. As they settled down to await the final construction of the siege works at Sevastopol, Lord Raglan and the other allied commanders set about securing the immediate areas surrounding their own positions, apparently aware that the main Russian army, which had previously been withdrawn from Sevastopol, was stationed to the east of their own positions and therefore posed a significant danger to the allied army which was now accommodated at the three southern Russian ports. Unfortunately for Raglan, having chosen Balaclava as his main port, the fact that it lay furthest east and therefore closer to the Russian army quickly began to dawn on him, forcing him to establish additional defensive positions and draw upon his dwindling forces, in order to protect his British troops from a direct enemy attack.

To the east of Balaclava, the Russian army, commanded by Alexander Menshikov, had now been joined by more infantry reserves and more importantly, by four artillery batteries, which Menshikov now decided to use against the British forces, which were stationed in what he believed to be a highly vulnerable position. With defensive redoubts positioned well ahead of the main allied lines and therefore not easily reinforceable, Menshikov believed that these positions could be quickly overcome by his own Russian troops and on the 23rd October 1854 Menshikov despatched some sixteen thousand experienced troops to attack and capture these outlying allied positions. Although Lord Raglan and his commanders had been warned about possible Russian incursions, having initially reacted to every incident and report, eventually the often sick and exhausted allied troops stopped reacting to such alerts, making them easy targets for the Russians when they finally did launch an attack on the morning of the 25th October 1854. Beginning at around six o'clock in the morning, the outlying village of Kamara and a number of other allied sentry posts were assaulted by the first elements of the Russian force and it was only the quick reactions of one or two sentries who managed to signal the enemy attack, which prevented the Russian advance going unnoticed until it was far too late. These early warning, not only allowed some of the outlying sentries to retreat to the much more formidable defensive redoubts, but also gave sufficient notice to the British commanders back in Balaclava that a large scale enemy attack was underway. As the Ottoman guns on the hills overlooking the port, opened up on the advancing Russian troops, British commanders in Balaclava, including Lord Lucan, the commander of the British cavalry, were reported to have mustered their forces in order to repulse the enemy assault. Taking command of his Heavy Brigade, Lucan was said to have ordered his mounted troops forward in an attempt to discourage the Russian attack, but seeing that his attempt at intimidating the enemy soldiers was having no real effect, Lucan simply wheeled his men around and rode back to his original starting position, close to the Light Brigade. Bringing their own heavy guns to bear, the Russian artillery were thought to have targeted the allied guns that were firing on them from the hills, as well as the allied redoubts that were blocking the route to Balaclava, both of which were said to have suffered significant damage from the Russian gunners and riflemen, who were firing on their positions. It was thought to be as a result of the much heavier Russian guns that the Ottoman and British artillery were very quickly damaged or forced to withdraw, leaving those allied troops who were charged with holding the forward redoubts vulnerable to enemy assaults, which began at around seven thirty in the morning and by eight o'clock had forced the allied troops to retreat back to Balaclava.

With all of the forward redoubts and trenches having been captured or abandoned, the allied forces at Balaclava, as well as those besieging the southern suburbs of Sevastopol, were now at risk from the advancing Russian army, forcing Lord Raglan to order infantry units from Sevastopol to march eastward, in order to help support the remaining allied troops at Balaclava. Unfortunately, given the distances involved, these British infantry units would have to complete a gruelling two hour march to relieve Balaclava, during which time, the beleaguered allied troops at the port, comprising just over two thousand men, would have to defend Balaclava as best as they could. Just before eight o'clock in the morning, the Earl of Cardigan, commander of the British Light Brigade was reported to have joined his troops, just in time to receive orders from Lord Raglan to move his cavalry to the left hand side of the valley, which fronted Balaclava and to remain there, whilst Lord Lucan's Heavy Brigade, were positioned on the right. However, no sooner had Cardigan arrived on the western side of the valley, than Raglan changed his mind again and ordered units of the Heavy Brigade to relocate themselves to a position that supported the Turkish infantry, who had been posted a little bit closer to Balaclava. Even though Lord Lucan was said to have been confused by the order to split his cavalry, nonetheless he complied with Raglan's order and detached four regiments of his mounted troops back towards Balaclava, under the command of one of his subordinates, General James Scarlett.

At the northern end of the valley, the Russian commanders were said to have watched as the allied forces repositioned themselves ready for their assault and having identified the position of the British Highland infantry regiment, which had been posted to prevent the enemy advance, some four hundred Russian Hussars were ordered forward to attack the British infantry line. As the Russian cavalry thundered towards them, the Highlander's commander, Colin Campbell was said to have informed his troops that there would be no retreat and that if necessary they must die where they stood, compelling one observer of the scene to describe the legend of the "thin red line", a view of British troops that eventually achieved almost mythical status in later years. However, even though several hundred mounted Russian Hussars were bearing down on them at speed, Campbell's men never threatened to break, but merely fired volley after volley into the advancing Russian line, until at last, it was they that broke, retiring back up the hill in some disorder. At the same time that the Russian Hussars withdrew, so the remainder of the Russian cavalry, thought to have comprised around two thousand horsemen, plus a number of field guns, were finally identified by the commander of the British Heavy Brigade, General James Scarlett. Ordering his four mounted regiments into two lines facing the Russian cavalry, once they were in perfect alignment, Scarlett was said to have instructed his trumpeter to sound the charge, sending his two lines of heavy horse towards the enemy positions. However, as the British mounted troops advanced, so their Russian adversaries began to move towards them, ensuring that neither force were riding at full speed when the two sides finally met in the field. With their superior training and more than an element of good fortune, as the opposing cavalrymen struggled for dominance over one another, slowly but surely, Scarlett's British cavalrymen began to gain control of the engagement, cutting and hacking their way through the Russian ranks, until finally the first few enemy Hussars began to fall back, until eventually it became a full scale retreat. As the Russians retired, many of their men were reported to have passed close to the British Light Brigade, commanded by the Earl of Cardigan, who rather than ordering his troops to attack the enemy cavalry, was said to have instructed them to maintain their positions, thereby allowing the Russians to escape the field relatively intact.

Considered by many of the British officers in the field as a missed opportunity, Cardigan's decision not to inflict even greater casualties on the retiring Russian cavalry by attacking them with his Light Brigade, was reported to have caused much criticism of him as a military leader, although it was his actions later on in the day, which would guarantee his being regarded as one of the most incompetent British commanders of the age. Despite having seen their cavalry repulsed by the British infantry and heavy cavalry, the Russian commanders still held the allies outer defences and therefore controlled the main routes in and out of Balaclava, positions that they now began to consolidate with their artillery, foot soldiers and remaining cavalry units. Anxious to ensure that the Russians were not given time to construct an impenetrable defence and lacking the infantry, which were still on their way from Sevastopol, Lord Raglan had little choice but to order his cavalry to advance, ostensibly in the hope that the threat of a mounted charge, might persuade the Russian commanders to withdraw their forces. Informing Lord Lucan, the commander of the cavalry that his forces were to advance with the support of infantry, which was still to arrive from Sevastopol, Raglan's order was thought to have been so ambiguous that it caused confusion amongst British cavalry commanders, who assumed that they should first move forward, but then wait for infantry support, before engaging the enemy directly. However, as the Heavy Brigade were positioned to move forward in one direction and the Light Brigade in another, Russian movements on the hills overlooking Balaclava forced Raglan to issue yet another vague command, this time instructing Lord Lucan to move his cavalry forward to prevent the Russians removing the allied guns that had been abandoned on the hilltop redoubts. Unfortunately, by the time the message had been delivered to Lord Lucan, the precise location of the guns being referred to was unclear and with no artillery in plain sight, it was reported to have been Raglan's messenger who pointed Lucan in the direction of the Russian gun emplacements at the far end of the valley, rather than those guns that were still being dragged away from the top of the hills.

As he looked down towards the Russian positions, which had guns to the front and on both sides of the valley, Lucan knew that for cavalry to attack such a position was likely to be a suicidal task, but despite his reservations, he was reported to have ridden over to the Light Brigade's position and spoke to its commander, the Earl of Cardigan. Both men recognised the dangers of such an assault, although believing that this was what Lord Raglan had intended, were prepared to follow their orders, regardless of the risks involved. Forming his Brigade up into two lines of attack facing the enemy guns, at around eleven o'clock in the morning of the 25th October 1854, Cardigan ordered his Lancers and Dragoons to move forward, beginning their journey into what later became known as the "Valley of Death". For those British observers watching Cardigan's advance from an elevated position, it quickly became clear that the Light Brigade were intent on charging the Russian batteries at the far end of the valley, rather than pursuing the captured allied guns, which were still being removed from the hilltops, but by then, it was far too late for anyone to prevent the suicidal cavalry assault. With Cardigan's horsemen breaking into a trot and then into a canter, there was little anyone could do, other than to watch as the British Brigade rode into the shellfire, which began to rain down from the equally astonished Russian gunners positioned on the sides of the valley. As the Light Brigade moved forward, Lord Lucan then ordered the men of his own Heavy Brigade to begin their advance and almost immediately began to receive fire from the same enemy gunners and sharpshooters that had already devastated Cardigan's troops. Fortunately for Lucan's force, the timely intervention of French cavalry, who attacked and overran a number of the Russian positions, helped to limit the damage to the Heavy Brigade, but far too late to prevent hundreds of British Lancers and Dragoons being blown to bits as they steadfastly advanced towards the Russian batteries waiting at the end of the valley. However, the saving grace for Lucan's Heavy Brigade, was the British commander himself, who was said to have finally realised the futility of the British assault, which had already cost the lives of the Light Brigade and might very easily cost him every one of his own men. Bringing his Heavy Brigade to a sudden stop, Lucan was thought to have looked down the valley, perhaps momentarily regretting that he could not offer any further support to those surviving members of Cardigan's Brigade, who even then were beginning their final charge towards the waiting Russian ranks.

Dost Mohammad

Napoleon III

Omar Pasha

With less than a quarter of a mile to the Russian guns, the Earl of Cardigan was reported to have ordered the surviving men of his Light Brigade to begin their final charge towards the enemy positions, their mounts now brought to a full gallop of around thirty to forty miles an hour. The Lancers and Dragoons brought their weapons to bear, causing many of the Russian gunners to fire their final rounds into the British ranks before starting to abandon their guns, which they expected to be overwhelmed by the British cavalrymen. Finally reaching the main Russian batteries only seven or eight minutes after they had first been ordered to advance, the surviving members of the Light Brigade quickly found themselves involved in bitter hand-to-hand fighting with the Russian gunners, infantry and cavalry, who had not abandoned their positions at the first sight of the fast approaching British horsemen. In the immediate aftermath of having overcome the main Russian position, the survivors of the Light Brigade were reported to have continued with their attack, forcing the Russian cavalry units to withdraw, in what might have easily become a resounding allied victory, but one that was thwarted by the absence of Lord Lucan's Heavy Brigade, which had since retired back to the main British lines. With no reinforcements to bolster their position and with the Russian's quickly realising that they outnumbered the Light Brigade by some margin, Cardigan and his surviving troops were left with little option but to escape along the same perilous route that they had previously advanced down. With Russian Lancers and Hussars now blocking their line of retreat; and enemy sharpshooters firing down on them from the nearby hills, the British cavalrymen were left with little choice but to fight their way out of the Russian trap, in an attempt to get back to the safety of their own lines. Such was the valour of the members of the Light Brigade that even those men who were wounded refused to surrender to the Russians and as a result dozens of them were said to have perished, rather than be taken prisoner by the enemy.

By the time the last members of the Light Brigade had managed to get back to the allied lines, less than an hour after their initial advance had begun, just under a half of the unit were reported to have been lost, having been killed, wounded or taken prisoner during the engagement. Quite apart from representing a completely useless waste of life, given the mix up between Raglan, Lucan and Cardigan, the loss of the Light Brigade as an effective fighting unit was said to have limited Raglan in his attempts to force the Russian army to retire and compelled him to use his much needed infantry units from Sevastopol to guard the allied lines against further Russian assaults. Interestingly though, none of the three British commanders involved in the disastrous charge was publicly held accountable for the loss of life, with Cardigan seen as being generally blameless, as he had simply been following orders given to him by his immediate superior, Lord Lucan. Lord Raglan and Lucan were reported to have blamed one another for the disaster, although ultimately neither of them was publicly censured for their part in the event, but Lucan was never to see active service again, despite being promoted to the rank of General and then Field Marshal in later life. The men of the Light Brigade were subsequently immortalised by Britain's then Poet Laureate, Alfred, Lord Tennyson in 1854 when he wrote his "The Charge of the Light Brigade", which not only celebrated the valour of the individual soldiers, but also the futility of the action itself. The Crimean War was also thought to have been the first major conflict that was covered by correspondents from the national newspapers and as such, was the first time that individual acts of heroism could be reported to the British public. Prior to this point in time, awards for heroism, especially amongst the lower ranks were thought to have been limited to mentions in despatches and were sparingly used by the military. However, due to the publicity generated by the new war correspondents, Queen Victoria was said to have authorised the creation of a new military award for bravery, which could be given for any act of valour, regardless of the persons rank. Instituted in January 1856, the Victoria Cross outranks any other medal awarded by Britain's Armed Forces and since its inception has been awarded just over thirteen hundred times. During the previously mentioned Charge of the Light Brigade alone, some nine Victoria Crosses were subsequently awarded to members of the British Light and Heavy Brigades, including John Berryman, Alexander Dunne, John Farrell, James Grieve, Joseph Malone, James Mouat, Samuel Parkes, Henry Ramage and Charles Wooden. As a matter of record, the first man to officially receive the new Victoria Cross was Charles Davis Lucas, an Irish born sailor, who was serving aboard HMS Hecla in the Baltic during June 1854, when a live enemy shell landed on the deck of his ship, threatening to cause significant damage to the vessel and its British crew. Having been ordered to lay flat on the deck, in order to escape serious injury, Lucas was said to have rushed forward, scooped the shell up in his hands and then threw it overboard, where it exploded, just before hitting the water. In recognition of his selfless action, Lucas was granted an immediate promotion to Lieutenant and over the period of his following career with the Royal Navy was reported to have achieved the rank of Rear Admiral, as well as being recognised for his bravery with the receipt of the Victoria Cross.

Although the Russians would make yet another attempt to capture the British held port of Balaclava, in order to undermine the allied siege of Sevastopol, ultimately their attempts to defeat the British forces and to retain possession of their main base would prove to be unsuccessful, as Sevastopol fell to the allied armies in September 1856, having been blockaded and attacked for the best part of a year. During that same period, the two sides were said to have fought one another in a number of theatres, including the Baltic, Pacific, Caucasus and in Europe, although the Russian's largely conscript army, with its inferior training and weaponry, ultimately struggled to cope with the generally professional and mainly volunteer armies of the western allies. With their country's military and economy on the verge of collapse, in 1856 Tsar Nicholas' son and successor, Alexander II, was said to have decided to find a peaceful solution to the conflict, which culminated in the Treaty of Paris that was signed by all parties in the same year. Although much of Europe continued to remain unsettled due to the later rise of the German and the Austro-Hungarian Empires, for Great Britain, the end of the conflict was said to have been marked by a period of reflection, not only about the war itself, but also the many changes that had been brought about in modern weaponry, military tactics, the structure of Britain's armed forces and the role of women on the battlefield.

Unlike today, where nursing is generally seen as a mainstream professional career and one that is governed by pay and conditions, during the 19th century, medicine was very much regarded as an entirely masculine area of expertise, with women playing very much a peripheral role. On the battlefield, most casualties would have been treated by whatever surgeon or male medical assistant happened to be available and only after a battle had been lost or won, allowing the dead and injured to be transported back to the nearest field hospital. Although female camp followers, or wives and daughters are thought to have nursed injured soldiers for hundreds of years, the first official female nurses employed by the British Army were the thirty eight volunteers trained by Florence Nightingale and her aunt, Mai Smith, who were asked to tend to those soldiers injured during the Crimean War, by the British Secretary of State for War, Sidney Herbert, who was a close personal friend of Nightingale. Having taken the decision to become a nurse in 1844, when she was about twenty four years old, Florence was said to have undertaken extensive studies to achieve her aim, including periods of training in a number of medical institutions to gain practical experience. By 1853 she was reported to have been appointed as the Superintendent of the Institute for the Care of Sick Gentlewomen in London, where she began a nursing program to train new nurses. It was said to be a number of these same nurses that she took with her to Turkey in October 1854 to take care of the allied wounded who were being held at the main military hospital in Scutari, which is now known as Uskadar in modern day Istanbul. Finding thousands of badly injured allied soldiers being treated there, often in the most atrocious conditions, Nightingale and her volunteers attempted to improve their situation by ensuring that the patients were properly fed and that their surroundings were kept clean and tidy. Unfortunately, despite their best efforts, the lack of vital medication, poor sanitation and ineffective ventilation meant that large numbers of men continued to die, forcing the British authorities to send an inquiry team to the camp, to try and identify the underlying causes. Having identified the hazardous drains and poor ventilation as two of the major reasons for the regular outbreaks of dysentery, typhus, typhoid and cholera, once these problems had been resolved; death rates amongst the patient population began to drop. Although the underlying causes of these highly communicable diseases had been unknown to Florence and her nurses prior to their arrival in the Crimea, in the aftermath of the Crimean War, the evidence that she and others collected, very quickly identified poor sanitation as a major cause of the high death rates, allowing her to incorporate this knowledge into her later training programs back in Britain.

Although not involved with Florence Nightingale and her original group of volunteer nurses, an equally important nursing figure during the Crimean War was a Jamaican herbalist and carer, called Mary Seacole, who not only helped to save the lives of countless allied soldiers, but did so entirely at her own expense. So overwhelmed by the suffering of people during the Crimean conflict, Seacole was reported to have borrowed enough money to travel to the region and offer whatever help she could to soldiers from both sides of the argument. Even though she had offered her nursing services to the British War Department when they requested volunteers for the Crimea, it seems likely that because of her colour, she was refused any sort of employment position or financial aid, simply because of the racial prejudice that existed within the corridors of power at that time. However, not to be discouraged, Seacole was said to have formed a partnership with a business acquaintance and set out to establish what would later become the British Hotel, a place where allied servicemen could buy themselves a range of goods, have a meal, or simply a well earned rest, as well as receiving treatment for a range of medical ailments. Not simply trying to profit from the conflict by selling commodities to the thousands of soldiers who were posted around the region, according to most reports Seacole would regularly travel around the various allied defensive positions, helping to treat the injured soldiers, who had recently been wounded, or those suffering from ailments that the military did not consider to be serious enough to justify hospitalisation. Unfortunately, when the war came to a sudden end in 1856, Seacole was said to have found herself in a fairly dire financial circumstances, which resulted in her having to rely on her supporter's generosity to get her back to Britain, where she was said to have achieved a degree of celebrity for the nursing work that she had undertaken in the Crimea. Counting a number of Britain's leading figures as personal friends and acquaintances, in subsequent decades her humanitarian achievements during the conflict were reported to have been largely overshadowed by the service of Florence Nightingale and her nursing staff, although in recent years, the selflessness of Seacole is finally beginning to be recognised by a much wider audience.

Towards the end of the 19th century and as a result of the British Army's performance during the Crimean War and the later Indian Mutiny of 1857, a full scale review of Britain's land forces was undertaken by a Royal Commission, which helped to produce what became known as the Cardwell Reforms. Beginning in 1858, the intention of the Commission, led by Jonathan Peel, the Secretary of State for War was to investigate the various incidents of incompetence and malfeasance that were known to have occurred during the two great events and to review the performance of Britain's standing army of twenty five thousand men, which had only just managed to fulfil its role during the Crimean War and the Indian Mutiny, both of which had very nearly brought Britain's armed forces to near total collapse. Completed by 1862, the resulting report from Jonathan Peel, was reported to have produced no real change in the short term, largely because of the efforts of both the British East India Company which wanted to retain its own military forces and a number of highly placed officers within the British Army, who felt that any reform of the army was unnecessary and possibly dangerous. On the basis of Peel's report however; and the real fear that Britain's land forces lacked the numbers to withstand any future military confrontation, Parliament was said to have authorised the enlargement of the army by around twenty thousand men and an increase in the War Department's budget to cover the cost of these extra troops. However, the report itself was thought to have produced no real reforms as to the treatment and training of Britain's soldiers, a fact that Edward Cardwell, the Secretary of State for War from 1868 onwards was determined to introduce. Amongst the reforms introduced by Cardwell, was the abolition of flogging during peacetime, a measure that was strongly opposed by most officers, who believed that corporal punishment was a necessary measure to retain discipline within the ranks. In Cardwell's opinion though, the outlawing of flogging during peacetime would help to attract a better quality of recruit to the army, men that would otherwise be dissuaded from enlisting if they thought that such brutality was a normal part of everyday life within the service, although Cardwell was forced to retain flogging as a regular form of punishment during wartime. His second great reform was to withdraw regular British soldiers from many of Britain's overseas colonies, replacing them with locally raised troops, which would not only reduce the cost to the British exchequer, make these new troops more acceptable to the local indigenous populations, but also make the lives of the British troops far easier, allowing them to spend more time closer to their immediate family and friends. His third reform was to outlaw the practice of bounties for military recruiters and regular re-enlisters, as well as making it easier for the military authorities to discharge those individuals whose character or personal habits were unwanted by Britain's armed forces, including both army and navy. In later years, further reforms were said to have been introduced, including the abolition of branding as an acceptable form of punishment within the army, as well as ending the practice of selling commissions within the forces, a system that had undoubtedly brought much dishonour and distrust to the British army in previous years.

Lord Raglan   Lord Lucan   Lord Cardigan

In addition to the reforms introduced by Cardwell, the Secretary of State for War, was also reported to have drafted two specific pieces of legislation, which were not only designed to improve the lives of the individual servicemen, but also to bring some sort of order to the actual recruitment of Britain's fighting men. The Army Enlistment (Short Service) Act of 1870 was an attempt by Cardwell to rationalise the length of time that any individual soldier was forced to spend in frontline service, which as a rule could often be for a ten or twelve year period, perhaps longer if the man kept re-enlisting after each period of service. As a result of such practices, Britain's army was thought to have been manned by large numbers of older soldiers, who lives and health had often be blighted by years of arduous service and who had few skills that would allow them to pursue a civilian career, as and when their enlistment came to an end. For many young potential recruits, the idea of having to sign up for ten or twelve years of unremitting military service, half of which would be served in foreign lands, was thought to have been such an unattractive prospect for many of the country's young men that only the very worst or most desperate candidates would choose to enlist within the British forces. In Cardwell's view, the way forward was to offer new recruits the opportunity to vary their terms of service, so that although they would still serve ten or twelve years in the army, a significant part of that time might just as easily be spent as part of a reserve force, where soldiers were paid a part time wage, for their part time service, something akin to our modern day territorial army services. Caldwell thought that such arrangements would not only help the country to develop a fighting reserve, a force that could be called upon in a national emergency, but also that these new "short term" enlistments would help attract greater numbers of better quality candidates into the army's ranks, a view that later proved to be the case, as the number of new recruits climbed steadily after the Act was passed in 1870.

The second piece of legislation, the Regulation of the Forces Act 1871, was intended to address the problems caused by the "General Service" employment status of all new military recruits, one that failed to guarantee them a posting to a local regiment and which was thought to have been a major concern for many young men, who might otherwise have considered joining the British forces. In order to resolve this problem, Cardwell proposed that the whole country should be divided into sixty six regimental districts based around county boundaries and population centres, within which the various military forces, including local militias, would be amalgamated and reorganised to form a single regiment, composed of anything up to three battalions. Each of these sixty six regiments were to be based at a central training depot and were expected to recruit new troops from within their own geographical area, helping to ensure that most new soldiers were located in and around their home areas, retaining the social, cultural and linguistic heritage that were so important to new recruits during their first few months of service. Cardwell also proposed that each British regiment should have a minimum of two battalions, one that would be stationed at home, helping to train recruits, while the second battalion could be posted abroad to help protect one or more of the Empire's many overseas territories, a situation which also allowed the different battalions to be switched around after a given period of time. Although these measures were said to have been resisted by many within the British army, ostensibly because it removed their own ability to send new recruits to any part of the country, in the end the changes were introduced and with far fewer problems than had first been suggested by those that were fundamentally opposed to the new legislation. The changes introduced by Cardwell were reported to have been added to a decade later by those introduced by another Secretary of State for War, Hugh Childers, in 1881, all of which were said to have turned Britain's poorly motivated, badly organised and generally exhausted armed forces, into a highly professional and well organised military force, one that was well suited for its role in protecting the British Empire's vast imperial possessions.

Following the end of the Crimean War in 1856, even though Britain's armed forces would play no further part in the political and military upheavals in Europe for the next fifty-odd years, during the same period, Britain's soldiers and sailors still found themselves involved in a number of military conflicts, in Africa, the Indian subcontinent and in the Far East. Beginning with the Indian Mutiny of 1857, which resulted in regular troops having to be rushed to the subcontinent, in order to suppress the widespread native rebellion, the uprising there not only marked the end of the British East India Company, but also the start of ninety years of direct imperial rule which would only be brought to an end in 1947, leading to the creation of the modern day states of both India and Pakistan. Also, in the same year that the war in the Crimea came to an end, British military units, both army and navy were reported to have been committed to the Second Opium War against China, a conflict that was only finally ended in 1860, Britain having achieved most of its political objectives. Three years later, British troops were once again fighting on foreign soil, this time in the second of four wars that the British Empire would have to fight against the Ashanti peoples of Africa, the first from 1823 to 1831, the second from 1863 to 1864, the third from 1873 to 1874 and the fourth from 1894 to 1896. The African continent remained a major theatre for British interests throughout the 19th century, as part of the wider European colonisation and exploitation of the region, which is commonly referred to as the "Scramble for Africa" and which involved most of the leading European nations of the age, including Britain, France, Germany, Holland and even Belgium. In 1868 British troops were reported to have been sent on a punitive expedition into Abyssinia, not only to rescue a number of European hostages who were being held by the Ethiopian Emperor, Tewodros II, but also to teach the native leader the dangers of threatening any European who happened to be resident in his kingdom. Britain's colonisation and exploitation of Africa was also thought to have been the root cause of at least four major conflicts during the final twenty years of the 19th century, including the Anglo-Zulu War of 1879, the First Anglo-Boer War of 1880 to 1881 and the Second Anglo-Boer War of 1899 to 1902, all of which were said to have helped to fundamentally change the tactics, structures, attitudes and even the uniforms of the British Army. The final major conflict in the region was the Anglo-Sudanese War which was said to have occurred between 1881 and 1899, although for the most part, British forces were only involved in the latter stages of the conflict, acting in support of the Egyptians, who were reported to have controlled the country during most of the same period. Outside of Africa itself, the only other two major military conflicts involving British forces were the Third Anglo-Burmese War of 1885, which was reported to have been little more than a policing action, the country having previously been conquered in the two wars fought between 1823 to 1856, whilst the Boxer Rebellion of 1899 to 1901 was eventually suppressed by a multi-national force supplied by Britain, France, America and a number of other countries.

As a major industrial power and a nation possessed with its own fair share of gifted inventors, engineers, scientists and designers, allied to the improvements made to the soldiery themselves, advances in weaponry and military equipment generally, was thought to have played a major part in the success of Britain's armed forces throughout the 19th century. Where previously British troops were thought to have sweltered in the heavy red and scarlet uniforms of the Empire, after the Crimean war, much more practical, lightweight and neutral colours were used to outfit those soldiers serving in warmer climates, making their lives a little more comfortable and the men a little less obvious to the guns of enemy sharpshooters. Khaki, the Urdu word for "dust" was the name given to the sandy coloured uniforms used by some Indian forces during the 1850's and which eventually became the standard colour for all British troops serving in India and in Africa during the latter half of the 19th century. Similarly British weapons were improved and superseded over the period of the same half century, with breech loading rifles replacing the muzzle loaders of previous years, whilst at the same time the weapons barrels were rifled, improving the range and accuracy of individual firearms to previously undreamt of levels of performance. Field artillery too was likewise improved, with the earlier muzzle loaders giving way to breech loaders with their rifled barrels and self detonating shells, all of which made the practice of killing and injuring the enemy far more effective and much more distant. Unfortunately, although Britain could often mass produce such weapons of mass destruction, the British governments characteristic unwillingness to spend money on their proper development and supply, often resulted in such weaponry either being inferior to, or available in much smaller quantities, than those supplied to the enemy forces, resulting in greater numbers of British troops being killed or wounded than was absolutely necessary. Although such things rarely mattered when facing a native force that was armed with basic weapons, it was an entirely different situation when British troops were forced to confront an equally, or better armed adversary, such as the Boer people of South Africa. Skilled marksmen with far superior rifles, significant numbers of British troops were thought to have been killed or wounded, purely as a result of the better weapons and tactics employed by these highly skilled farmers and settlers. It was thought to be as a direct result of facing these irregular commandoes that Britain's ground troops were finally forced to embrace the sorts of changes to their tactics, weapons and dress that they would carry forward into the 20th century, in readiness for the wholesale slaughter that they would face some twelve years later in the trenches of the First World War.

At the beginning of 1914, the British Army was thought to have consisted of some four hundred thousand men, all of whom were volunteers, two hundred and fifty thousand of which served in the regular forces, while the remaining one hundred and fifty thousand, formed part of the country's territorial reserve. Ostensibly raised and maintained to protect Britain and its vast overseas Empire, since the end of the Crimean War in 1856, the force had been systematically altered and improved by a succession of inquiries and reports, including the previously mentioned Cardwell and Childwell Reforms of the late 19th century, along with the Esher Report of 1904 and the Haldane Reforms of 1907. In addition to the main body of four hundred thousand men who were stationed at home and abroad, a further two hundred thousand men were thought to have formed part of a special reserve, largely made up of men who had previous military experience, but who were not legally obliged to serve as in any sort reserve capacity. However, out of this total of an estimated seven hundred thousand men, only some eighty five thousand were available for any sort of immediate combat operations, so that when the First World War broke out in August 1914, under the terms of the Entente Cordiale, it was these soldiers that were used to make up the British Expeditionary Force, which was subsequently sent across the English Channel to help reinforce France. Earning themselves the nickname the "Old Contemptibles", after the German Kaiser was reputed to have ordered his commanders to annihilate the "contemptible little British army", this initial force was said to have included a significant number of men from the Indian army, many of whom would subsequently perish in their effort to prevent a German advance into French territory. Although a comparatively small force, the regular British army of the early 20th century was thought to have been one of the most effective, mobile and professional armies in the world, largely as a result of the wars that it had previously fought against the Boers of South Africa. Tactics learned during those conflicts had become a regular part of army training, so that Britain's troops were taught how to flank, encircle and surreptitiously approach enemy positions, rather than just attacking them head on in relatively straight lines. They were educated as to how to take advantage of the local ground conditions, so that any depression, outcrop of rocks, or native foliage might be used to hide themselves from enemy fire, as well as offering a position from where they could snipe at their adversaries. In addition, regular troops and their associated reserve forces were trained to shoot rapidly and accurately from any sort of position, standing, kneeling or lying prone on the floor, with the expectation that even the average British soldier would be able to fire around fifteen rounds per minute and hit his target with a fair degree of accuracy. In fact, most British regiments were said to have been able to produce a large number of expert marksmen, who could consistently hit their target over distances of three hundred metres and more. However, perhaps the greatest drawback for these highly mobile troops was the creation of the trench warfare which came to dominate the battlefields of France, defensive redoubts that not only robbed the British troops of their traditional manoeuvrability, but also ensured that the First World War was won through a process of human attrition, rather than through the sort of professional soldiery that the regular British Army was said to have excelled at.

Alexander Menshikov   Colin Campbell   Alfred Lord Tennyson

In order to match the enormous armies of both Germany and France, the British government quickly began mobilising those reserves it could spare, as well as recruiting new volunteers from the general population. When the war first began in August 1914 enthusiasm for the war effort was said to have been so widespread, so that the authorities were confident that their calls for a further five hundred thousand volunteers would be easily met, which it was, with some three quarters of a million men answering the original call to arms. In fact, the desire to participate in the war against Germany and her allies was said to be so high that the army had little trouble achieving the numbers that were required, with an estimated one million men enlisting by January 1915, most notably amongst the younger generations in Britain. In order to maintain the enthusiasm for the cause, a number of the country's leading public figures, including Lord Derby, proposed the idea of forming "Pals Battalions", units comprised entirely of men from the same town, city, workplace, social clubs, in fact any sort of business or organisation where large numbers of young men were brought together on a regular basis. The basis for the creation of the "Pals" regiments was thought to have been formed as a result of the earlier army reforms, which had created regional recruiting stations, where men from a specific part of the country could train, live, fight and possibly die with others from the same communities. Although this was undoubtedly good for the unit's morale, the major problem with the creation of these Pals battalions, was that such units often ran the risk of being completely annihilated, leaving individual villages, towns and other communities completely bereft of all their young men, an event which did occasionally happen during the carnage of the First World War. However, after the first flush of patriotic fervour, by the middle of 1915, the numbers of new recruits was reported to have declined markedly, to the extent that the government began to actively campaign for new volunteers using a variety of methods, including even publicly shaming suitable young men who were not in a reserved occupation. By the beginning of 1916, the lack of new volunteers and the increasing casualty figures amongst the allied nations, was thought to have been so serious that the authorities in London were left with little alternative but to consider conscription as a means of reinforcing the British Army. Introduced in January 1916 the Military Service Bill was initially designed to allow for the compulsory enlistment of single young men between the ages of 18 and 41 years old, although this was later amended to allow for the recruitment of married men as well from May 1916 onwards. Unfortunately, despite such measures, the numbers of men recruited during successive years continued to fall, as increasing numbers of candidates were rejected either because of poor health, through religious conviction, or because their employment prevented them from being conscripted. However, with so many inexperienced young men to train, the British Army had little choice but to forego many of the regular infantry techniques that had been taught to its troops in the years following the Boer Wars, the same training and techniques which had made Britain's land forces some of the very best in the world. As a result, with large numbers of generally inexperienced young officers being asked to lead units of equally raw recruits into battle, most of the infantry training, which had previously helped to make British regiments so formidable, were quickly abandoned, to be replaced with the rigid, head-on, wave formations, which would lead to many of their ranks being completely decimated by the German soldiers who awaited them on the Western Front.

In Europe, the British Expeditionary Force's first formal engagement against the German army was said to have taken place on the 23rd August 1914 just outside of the Belgium town of Mons, where they were ordered to defend the Mons-Conde Canal from the advancing enemy forces. However, having initially inflicted heavy casualties on the German troops, the subsequent withdrawal of the French Fifth Army, ostensibly to prevent its encirclement and possible destruction by the Germans, forced the British Expeditionary Force to retreat as well, all the way back to the outskirts of Paris. The French General responsible for the tactical withdrawal of the Fifth Army, Charles Lanrezac, was said to have been so critical of his country's military leadership that he was subsequently replaced as commander of his army and spent the rest of the war in virtual retirement. Outnumbered by their German adversaries by some three to one, the British were reported to have suffered some sixteen hundred casualties, killed or wounded during this first encounter, although they were also said to have inflicted at least three times that number on the Germans forces, even though the engagement was widely regarded as a strategic victory for the Kaiser's army. Despite having been forced back to the outskirts of Paris though, both French and British commanders were said to have taken advantage of a tactical error committed by the

Germans, which allowed them to force the Kaiser's troops back to the Aisne River, where the Germans eventually decided to dig themselves in. The Battle of the Marne, which began on the 5th September 1914, is sometime referred to as the Miracle of the Marne, and was a week long engagement fought between the allied armies and the Germans which not only brought an end to the month long German offensive, but also helped to establish the basis for the following four years of exhausting trench warfare that both sides would have to endure. Outnumbered by a German army of an estimated one and a half million men, the million strong allied armies were reported to have suffered over two hundred and sixty thousand casualties during the engagement, whilst the Kaiser's forces were said to have lost around two hundred and twenty five thousand men killed, wounded, or taken prisoner.

The resulting Battle of the Aisne, which first began in September 1914, is generally thought to mark the beginning of the four years of entrenched warfare that would become symbolic of the First World War, as well as leading to the creation of what is now called the "Western Front". Even though none of the participating armies had expected to engage in trench warfare, as the allied and German positions became increasingly fixed, so the Germans were thought to have adapted more readily to the static nature of their lines, incorporating equipment and weaponry into their redoubts, with which they could more readily observe and attack the allied armies from a distance. Unable to move forward, so both sides began to extend their positions sideways, creating networks of trenches, or subterranean walkways, which were often defended by machine gun posts, mortars and field guns, as well as incorporating sleeping quarters, first aid positions, feeding stations and bomb shelters. For most frontline soldiers, the trench systems became a second home, a place where they ate, slept, lived and died alongside their regimental comrades who shared the ever present danger of being targeted by an enemy sniper, or becoming the victim of an unexpected enemy artillery shell. Commonly infested with lice and rats, which fed on the dead and the dying, some allied trenches were said to have turned into quagmires that pulled and sucked at the men who lived in them twenty four hours a day and who regularly fell victim to trench foot, frostbite or heat exhaustion depending on the time of year. For most soldiers, life in the trenches was thought to have been an exercise in tedium, with their daily routines dictated by the regular chores that had to be carried out in order to keep them as safe and secure as possible. Digging and emptying latrines, keeping their weapons and equipment clean, as well as themselves, collecting and eating their rations, were all necessary tasks that each and every soldier had to do, along with taking their turn on sentry duty and participating in the occasional attack on the enemy lines. Initially, it was suggested that the various trench systems had begun as attempts by both sides to encircle their enemy, by outflanking them, although as each army responded to the other, within a matter of months the trench systems were thought to have extended for well over four hundred miles. As these positions moved steadily northward, towards the Belgium coastline, so British leaders, including Winston Churchill were said to have become increasingly alarmed about the prospect of the Germans seizing the major port at Antwerp and using it as a base for their warships, to assault allied shipping in the English Channel. Consequently, the main area of British military operations was shifted north, to try and ensure the safety of allied shipping in the English Channel, by protecting those Belgium territories in and around the ancient town of Ypres. The so-called First Battle of Ypres, which was said to have raged from the 19th October to the 22nd November 1914, was not in fact a single battle, but rather a series of individual military engagements, fought by various units, in and around the Belgium city of Ypres, all of which were originally intended to deprive the Germans access to the valuable Channel ports. It was said to be during this particular five week battle that the vast majority of Britain's Old Contemptibles, the eighty five thousand regular troops, who had first been sent to France in August 1914, were said to have been largely destroyed during the battle, only to be replaced by larger numbers of those enthusiastic young men who had answered Britain's call to arms, once war had been declared. Even though this First Battle of Ypres is generally regarded as an allied victory, it was said to have come at a considerable human cost, with over fifty thousand British troops reportedly being killed, wounded or missing in action as a result of the battle, nearly one third of the one hundred and sixty five thousand British soldiers who were reported to have been deployed in the Flanders region at that particular point in time.

Unfortunately, as the German and Allied lines became fixed in the landscape, being reinforced and defended by increasing amounts of barbed wire, sandbags and weapons of all descriptions, so it became significantly harder and more costly for one side to take territory from the other. Although particular sections of the various defences and individual positions could be targeted by each sides artillery regiments, ultimately such places could only be attacked and occupied by infantrymen, who were prepared to advance across the open spaces known as "no mans land", where they would be exposed to the withering fire of the enemy's machinegun positions. An additional result of these static front lines, was that large numbers of troops on both sides had to be stationed along their entire length, which not only tied these forces down, but also made it increasingly difficult for these same men to be used elsewhere along the battle front. As one of the smallest armies on the Western Front, Britain's deployment in the trenches of Flanders was thought to have seen a significant proportion of its total force tied down within the region, preventing its troops being used elsewhere, most especially, when some or other offensive was planned by the allied authorities. However, with neither side being able to deliver a knockout blow to the other and with thousands of troops dying or being debilitated by a variety of contagious diseases, it became imperative for the allies to try and drive the Germans out of France and Belgium once and for all. At a meeting held in December 1915 Allied strategists were reported to have put forward plans for a major military offensive against the German lines in the area of the Somme Region of France, close to the river of the same name. Having agreed on the offensive for the middle of 1916, an unexpected German assault on the French town of Verdun in January of that same year was reported to have changed the allied plans, resulting in Britain's troops having to take the lead in the planned offensive, which turned out to be one of the bloodiest and most costly campaigns of the entire First World War. Beginning on the 1st July 1916 and lasting until the 18th November of the same year, an estimated six hundred and twenty five thousand allied troops, including men from Britain, France, Canada, Australia, New Zealand, South Africa and Newfoundland were reported to have been killed, wounded, or taken prisoner, sixty thousand of whom were said to have been lost on the first day alone. During the entire Somme campaign, the regular British Army was said to have suffered some nineteen thousand fatalities, whilst another forty thousand men were reported to have been wounded, some of whom were able to return to active service, although many were returned to Britain to be invalided out of the service. As with the First Battle of Ypres, the Battle of the Somme was said to have comprised a series of individual engagements and strategic objectives, many of which were undertaken by individual regiments, or military units, with the likes of the Canadians, Australians, British, etc. all being given their own specific areas of operations, or particular military targets. However, by the end of the four month long offensive, very little had been achieved by either side, other than the loss of over half a million soldiers by each of the competing armies, with a staggering one million combatants reportedly being killed, injured, taken prisoner or simply disappearing over the course of this one offensive alone. It is perhaps worth noting that on the first day of the Battle of the Somme, the men of the 1st Newfoundland Regiment, were reported to have suffered catastrophic losses within the first few hours of the offensive having started, with over five hundred of their eight hundred-strong force either dead or dying by the end of the first day, a unimaginable level of loss, not only for the survivors themselves, but also for their families and communities back home in Newfoundland.

Perhaps with such large numbers of men at their disposal, the strategic planners on both sides failed to fully recognise the massive effect that such huge human losses would have, not only on those who served and survived, but also on the native populations of the various countries that participated in the wholesale slaughter of an entire generation, but who would also have to live with their losses forever. Almost inevitably, as carefully crafted strategic planning came to nothing in the face of well prepared trench warfare, so the only available option to help bring about any sort of victory was the age old tactic of fighting a war of human attrition, seeing which side was prepared to sacrifice the greatest numbers of its young men in order to achieve their overall aims. With the German leadership either unwilling or unable to withdraw its forces from France and Belgium, the allies were left with option, but to use whatever measures were necessary to force them to retreat, even if that meant losing millions of its young men to achieve that objective. As a result, the Battle of the Somme and its hundreds of thousands of casualties simply became one of a number of battles, which would come to symbolise the futility of such warfare, as well as the fragility, selflessness and valour of the human spirit. By the beginning of 1917, the Germans were reported to have begun withdrawing to new defensive positions along the much more formidable Hindenburg Line, which allied troops would subsequently have to assault later in the year, as part of the Arras Offensive, which would result in a further one hundred and sixty thousand British and Dominion troops being killed, wounded, going missing or being taken prisoner. On the 31st July 1917, the Battle of Passchendale began in Belgium, as allied soldiers, including British, French and Dominion troops, tried once again to dislodge the German army from its well defended positions, resulting in a three month battle that achieved very little territorially, but led to an estimated four hundred thousand allied casualties, while the Germans were thought to have suffered similar losses. As with the First Battle of the Somme, the Battle of Passchendale was not one single continuous action between the two sides, but was a series of phased encounters, including the notable engagements of Messines Ridge, Polygon Wood and Broodseinde, all of which were incorporated into the much larger and better known campaign of Passchendale.

In the final year of the Great War, both sides still believed that they could win an outright victory over their opponents and in March 1918 the German military leadership were said to have launched a major spring offensive, which initially forced the British to fall back in a number of areas, to the extent that British commanders were reported to have ordered their troops to fight to the last man. However, despite these initial German successes, the allies quickly regrouped their forces and began recovering much of the ground they had lost over the previous months, so that by August 1918 they were in a position to launch their own offensive against the Germans. Beginning on the 8th August 1918, the allies began the Hundred Days Offensive, which involved a general advance throughout the entire length of the allied front line, a push that was said to have continued right through to the announcement of the Armistice on the 11th November 1918, which brought a formal end to the First World War after four years of fighting. This peace settlement, not only brought an end to the conflict within France itself, but also to those numerous parts of the world where the allies had fought Germany and her own military partners, including the Dardanelles, Africa, the Middle East and the Balkans. Despite being more commonly associated with the sacrifice and heroism of the Anzac's, the soldiers from Australia, New Zealand and the South Pacific, the Gallipoli Campaign was also a significant theatre of war for Britain's troops, with an estimated twenty one thousand English, Irish, Scottish and Welsh soldiers reportedly perishing during the eight month long campaign, whilst another fifty two thousand were said to have been wounded, although enemy action, accidents and disease were all contributory factors to these overall figures. However, by the time that peace was declared in 1918, the British Army was said to have suffered a total loss of around six hundred and seventy three thousand men, killed or missing, although most of those reported as missing, were in fact already dead, but had not been found or correctly identified by the wars end. In addition to these losses, more than one and a half million men were thought to have been wounded during the four year conflict, thousands of whom were said to have been left with physical and psychological handicaps that would continue to affect them for the remainder of their lives.

With the war in Europe at an end, slowly but surely, the great allied armies were withdrawn from the continent, returned to their various homelands and demobilised, with most of their fighting men simply going back to the lives, families and careers that they had left several years before. However, with millions of men having been killed and even larger numbers having been physically injured or psychologically damaged by the fighting, most of the governments involved in overseeing the war immediately recognised that such unsustainable losses would not be acceptable in any future conflicts. Having emerged victorious in the war against Germany and her allies, Britain's leaders very quickly set about demobilising the millions of conscripts and volunteers who were anxious to resume their lives, up to four million of whom were returned to civilian life by the end of 1919. However, with the Empire still largely intact and needing to be safeguarded by a regular professional army, even as tens of thousands of men were being demobbed, so a core force of some eight hundred thousand troops was said to have been retained in order to ensure the Empire's short-term security. Reduced to under four hundred thousand men by the early 1920's, the British Army that emerged from the First World War was established as a highly mobile mechanised force, which could be transported to any part of the world by the Royal Navy; and where it could be supported by units from the newly evolving Royal Air Force, which had first begun to show its military value high above the battlefields of Western Europe. Perhaps foolishly believing that the Great War would end all such wars, the British government were said to have followed the guideline, known as the Ten Year Rule, which called for the country's armed forces to base their military requirements, on the assumption that the British Empire would not be involved in any major conflict for the period of at least ten years. Essentially bringing about ongoing reductions to the country's military budget, caused by the staggeringly large national debt that had been caused by the cost of fighting the First World War, it was perhaps, only through good fortune that no major conflict erupted during the inter-war period, permitting the now much smaller British Army to be employed in protecting Britain's vast imperial possessions. It was as a result of these fairly savage cost cutting measures, which continued throughout the 1920's and up until the early 1930's that the armed forces were generally reorganised, leading to smaller, much more specialised units being created, whilst the same time the Royal Air Force and Royal Navy were also re-equipped and modernised in preparation for their future roles. It was also during the inter-war years that the British Army was called upon to carry out support and policing duties in a number of theatres, including an allied intervention in Russia, following the Bolshevik Revolution there, as well as supplying a small number of men during the Polish-Soviet War, which was fought between 1919 and 1921. As part of Britain's responsibilities under the Treaty of Versailles, British troops were also stationed in Germany as the British Army of the Rhine, enforcing the terms that the victorious allies had imposed on the defeated country, as punishment for their having started the First World War, although all of these soldiers had been completely withdrawn by 1929. Regular army units, as well as Para-military forces such as the Black and Tans and Auxiliaries were all involved in the Anglo-Irish War that began in 1919 and was only finally brought to an end in July 1921, when negotiations were started between the two sides. Ultimately resulting in the creation of the Irish Free State in the same year, the same treaty also led to the division of the country into Northern and Southern Ireland, a situation which remains in place through to the present day.

However, by the early 1930's and following the emergence of right wing extremist parties in both Italy and Germany, the Ten Year Rule, which had governed British military spending after the First World War was finally abandoned, although the previous years of chronic under investment had left Britain lagging behind many of its European neighbours, including its most likely military adversary, Nazi Germany. Increasingly bitter over its treatment following the end of World War I, Germany, along with many other European states was said to have found itself in a state of political and economic flux, with a variety of disparate parties, theorists, economists and politicians all contriving to divide entire nations along racial, religious or political lines, with the result that the entire continent became relatively unstable. With the existing, more mainstream parties failing to deliver political and economic stability, so more extreme parties were said to have come to the fore, where they were widely welcomed by national electorates desperate for change and a restoration of their national pride. Tapping into the national dissatisfaction caused by the largely unfair settlement incorporated into the Treaty of Versailles and the widespread belief that Germany had been betrayed by its own leadership, often at the behest of the Jews and Communists, Adolph Hitler and his Socialist Party were able to successfully exploit the despair of the German people, in order to achieve their political aims. Choosing to believe that no European nation would wish to repeat the catastrophic mistakes that had led to the outbreak of the first Great War, as the Nazi's began their inexorable rise to power, so most of Europe's leading democratic leaders were thought to have found their own reasons not to confront many of the infringements of the Versailles Treaty, which ultimately helped to convince Adolph Hitler that no-one would stand in his way. Although both France and Britain were said to have been alarmed by the re-armament and modernisation of Germany's armed forces, neither country was thought to have felt able to confront the new German leadership militarily, naively believing perhaps that the new German Fuhrer would be true to his word, when he stated that he had no designs outside of Germany itself. Fortunately for Britain and the rest of Europe, despite the hope that the world would remain relatively peaceful; and regardless of the fact that Britain's land forces remained comparatively small and under funded, both the Royal Navy and the Royal Air Force had continued to receive sufficient funding for them to maintain some form of technological parity with the German's, if not in terms of sheer numbers. As in the First World War, Britain's superiority in battleships remained a formidable barrier to any conquest of the British Isles, although in the inter-war years, this formidable military force had been added to with developments in aircraft design and performance, allowing Britain to boast some of the most effective fighter aircraft and heavy bombers in the world at that time.

John Berryman VC   Charles Lucas VC   Florence Nightingale

However, as Nazi Germany's expansionist ambitions became more apparent during the late 1930's, with their re-occupation of the Rhineland, annexation of Austria and the Sudetenland, as well as the later occupation of the remaining parts of Czechoslovakia, so it became increasingly obvious that Europe was heading towards yet another war. Despite being initially reluctant to confront Germany, when Hitler began to make claims on the Polish city state of Danzig, Britain and France were left with little option but to guarantee the independence of Poland; and threaten war on Germany if Hitler dared to invade the country. However, convinced that the allies would not take action in defence of the Poles, on the 1st September 1939, German forces invaded Poland, leaving Britain and France with no alternative but to formally declare war on the 3rd September 1939, thereby marking the start of the Second World War, a conflict which would not only last for nearly six years and extend right across the globe, but also cost the lives of an estimated seventy million people worldwide. At the time that war was declared on the 3rd September 1939, the British Army remained a relatively small Imperial force, of around two hundred and fifty thousand men, which was intended to police and defend Britain's vast overseas territories from the threat of native rebellions, or foreign insurgencies, but was largely unsuitable for fighting any sort of major military conflict. Although, as in previous years Britain was said to have retained a reasonably sized territorial and regular reserve of around four hundred thousand men, as with the other regular land forces, earlier spending cuts had helped to ensure that many of these troops lacked the equipment and training, which might otherwise have allowed them to be brought into service straight away. It was also thought to be the case that the regular army was some sixty thousand men short of its preferred strength, largely because the service was less popular amongst new military recruits, most of whom chose to enlist with the Royal Navy or the Royal Air Force, both of which were deemed to be more exciting, as well as offering a higher public status. However, in order to compensate for the country's modest land forces, at the same time that Britain officially declared war on Nazi Germany, the government of the day also passed into law, the National Service (Armed Forces) Act of 1939, which was intended to conscript as many new troops as were necessary, in order to confront the growing Nazi danger that Europe now faced. Although conscription had never been a preferred method of recruiting British servicemen, except in times of war, the growing realisation that Britain and her Empire might well face yet another great military threat, allied to the fact that male unemployment within Britain remained stubbornly high, both provided justification for the passing of National Service Act in 1939.

With France and Britain finally recognising the threat of Hitler's new Germany, but being reluctant to confront it militarily in the short term, both governments were reported to have discussed the possibility and likelihood of Britain having to send yet another Expeditionary Force to the continent, much the same as it had done during the First World War. With a theoretical British army numbering some seven hundred thousand men, which was made up of regulars, regular reserves and the territorial's, but not including the one hundred thousand British troops who were stationed overseas, when war was declared on the 3rd September 1939, Britain immediately began to send the first elements of its one hundred and sixty thousand strong British Expeditionary Force across the Channel to France. By the beginning of October 1939 virtually all of these troops had been landed on the continent and along with their necessary transports and equipment were sent to help defend the French border near Belgium, as well as being employed along the Maginot Line, the fortifications which had been built to protect France from any future German aggression in the years following World War I. Unfortunately, even though these massive fortifications would have been virtually impregnable to the tactics and weaponry employed during the earlier conflict, in the intervening years both had changed markedly, to the extent that without realising it, the almost mythical Maginot Line had in fact become obsolete and would offer little protection against the fast moving, mechanised armies that Germany now possessed. In what commonly became known as the Phoney War, between October 1939 and May 1940 British and French forces simply consolidated their positions along the French borders and defences, whilst at the same time Britain continued to send additional materials and reinforcements across the Channel, in preparation for the forthcoming conflict with Germany.

As German forces massed along the French and Belgium borders, any hopes that they might withdraw, or that the Maginot Line would prevent an invasion of French territory, very quickly evaporated on the 10th May 1940, when German aircraft and land forces began their "blitzkrieg" assault on France, sending troops through the Ardenne region of Belgium and simply bypassing the Maginot Line, tactics which had not been anticipated or indeed planned for by allied commanders. Along the entire length of the allied defensive line, British and French troops were unable to offer any sort of real opposition to the heavily armed and well trained German forces, many of whom had been seasoned in the invasions of Czechoslovakia and Poland and who were supported by a large number of tanks and heavy field guns. Employing tactics which had first been honed during the Spanish Civil War, the German Airforce, the Luftwaffe, were reported to have targeted allied tanks, troop trains, supply depots, in fact anything that might be used to aid the allies advance, or indeed their almost inevitable defeat. As the allied lines inexorably collapsed, British and French commanders were thought to have ordered their forces to fall back towards the French coastline, often abandoning much of their equipment in certain areas, as steady withdrawals turned into routs. Some allied units chose to stand and fight, but quickly found themselves unable to resist the German advance and were either destroyed or taken prisoner. Having seen the French Army and the British Expeditionary Force prove to be largely ineffective against the might of the German Army and Airforce, allied commanders were left with little option but to consider evacuating the surviving troops from western France, choosing the port of Dunkirk as the most suitable point for their withdrawal. However, with the few port facilities there having been destroyed by German aircraft and the coastline being too shallow to allow large ships to easily embark the surviving troops, the Royal Navy was ordered to devise a method of rescuing the surviving French and British armies, who were still being driven back towards Dunkirk. In what was later regarded as a miracle, hundreds of small boats of every description were mobilised by the Royal Navy and were brought across the Channel, often in the hands of their civilian owners, to rescue handfuls or dozens of the allied soldiers, who were then put aboard larger transports, or taken back across the water to England. With very nearly four hundred thousand allied soldiers at risk of being killed or captured by the Germans, over the course of a week, from the 27th May 1940 to the 3rd June 1940, an estimated three hundred and thirty thousand allied troops were rescued from the coastline of France, many of whom would later form the core of the British Army, which along with its western allies would return to the continent in June 1944 to help release Europe from the Nazi menace. For many people the "miracle of Dunkirk" was the result of a number of factors, not least of which, was the bravery and selflessness of those private boat owners and civilians who put their own lives at risk, to help rescue allied troops from almost certain destruction. The sailors of the Royal Navy also played their part in the vital evacuation of the surviving allied troops, despite the fact that many of their larger ships almost inevitably became targets for the German bombers that were circling overhead and which were reported to have sunk and damaged significant numbers of Royal Navy ships, along with their crews. It is also worth remembering perhaps that large numbers of British, French and Belgium troops also remained behind to man the outer defences of the Dunkirk enclave, giving their comrades the time and space that was needed to effect their evacuation to England, a task that would ultimately lead to their own deaths, injury or capture by the advancing German armies.

Sidney Herbert Mary Seacole Edward Cardwell

With the core of the British army having been successfully rescued from mainland Europe, albeit in a relatively demoralised and dishevelled state, many of the soldiers were sent back to their home bases to begin the process of rebuilding, retraining and rearming, ready for future military operations elsewhere. However, with most of the European continent unassailable and with other areas of the British Empire coming under threat from German and Italian forces, large numbers of British and Dominion troops were eventually despatched to various overseas theatres, including the Mediterranean, the Middle East and Africa, where imperial interests were being directly threatened by the Axis Powers. Those that remained in Britain were thought to have been employed in the defence of the country, along with the large numbers of Canadian troops who had been sent across the Atlantic to help the mother country confront the Nazi menace and who would have been in the front line of the fighting had the Germans managed to launch a successful land invasion of Britain. Fortunately for everyone concerned though, the failure of the Luftwaffe to defeat the Royal Air Force and its cadre of young fighter pilots, during what became known as the Battle of Britain, ultimately prevented any sort of enemy landings taking place, although the damage done by the German airforce during their assault on the country was both prolonged and severe. However, despite the stoicism, ingenuity and resilience shown by the population during the period of the "Blitz", militarily, the first years of the Second World War were reported to have been marked by a series of disasters that might have crushed the fighting spirit of many other nations, but that were borne with great fortitude by Britain and its closest allies. Although many countries, including the administration of Franklin D Rooseveldt in the United States, had expected Britain to fall, others, such as William Mackensie King of Canada were said to have been far more certain about Britain's ability to resist Hitler's armed forces and willingly committed his own country's young men to fight against the Facist menace.

From the outset of the Second World War in September 1939, Britain's Armed Forces had little to celebrate, as what began as the "Phoney War", subsequently developed into a bitter military conflict, which quickly demonstrated the unpreparedness of the allied armies. Suffering major losses of both men and material in Western Europe, Britain's civilian population were also faced with notable casualties at sea, including HMS Royal Oak, which was reported to have been sunk by enemy action as early as the 14th October 1939. Within weeks of having rescued the last allied troops from France, Britain and its people found themselves watching the skies, as the German Luftwaffe struggled to overcome the ranks of the Royal Air Force and the international group of pilots who had travelled from every corner of the Empire to play their own personal part in the fight. This first part of the air war, which is commonly referred to as the Battle of Britain was waged between the 10th July 1940 to the 31st October and having been won by the "Few", was reported to have been immediately followed by the German bombing campaign, which became known as the "Blitz", a systematic attempt to destroy the public morale, infrastructure and manufacturing capability of Britain's major centres that continued from the 7th September 1940, all the way through to the 10th May 1941. However, just as the Blitz was coming to its end, British leaders were said to have been rocked by the loss of the iconic warship HMS Hood, which was destroyed in the Battle of Denmark Straits in May 1941, after the ageing battleship had been ordered to intercept the German surface raiders, Bismarck and Prinz Eugen that were making their way into the Atlantic to attack Britain's supply lines. The loss of the vessel and over fourteen hundred men was reported to have had a devastating effect on the country generally, but perhaps helped to prepare the population for the later reverses that the nation's Armed Forces would suffer in the coming months and years. Although the British mainland had managed to survive the enemy onslaught, as Adolph Hitler's gaze turned eastward, towards the lands of Communist Russia, so any hope that the British Empire had escaped relatively unscathed quickly evaporated, as Imperial Japan made the decision to attack western interests in the Far East and Pacific region. Within days of their unannounced and unprovoked air assault on Pearl Harbour, during which they temporarily crippled the US Pacific Fleet, Japanese air units had also attacked and destroyed two of the Royal Navy's biggest warships in the region, including HMS Prince of Wales, reputedly one of the most modern battleships of the period. Along with the much older warship HMS Repulse, the destruction of these vessels was said to have been notable, in that it represented the first time that two great capital ships had been sunk at sea, purely by airborne means, a fact that would provide cold comfort for the millions of British subjects, who would subsequently be subjugated by the Japanese, partly as a result of these two ships being lost.

Despite its great size and breadth, the British Empire was not protected by an enormous standing army, but rather by numbers of small individual contingents of regular troops, who were reinforced by local native forces, but who could be strengthened by additional British troops, as and when required, often with the Royal Navy helping to transport these additional soldiers, as well as bringing their own enormous armaments into play. However, little strategic planning seemed to have been made for the Empire having to fight in several theatres, all at the same time, which is exactly what happened during the course of World War II. Aside from Western Europe, where Britain itself was brought under direct threat of assault and invasion, the conflict itself very quickly spread to all parts of the European continent, the Mediterranean, North Africa, the Middle East, the Indian Subcontinent, Far East, South Atlantic and to much of the Pacific Ocean. Even the comparatively safe areas of North America were reported to have been threatened, although for the most part the danger there was thought to have been almost entirely naval in nature, as the dreaded German U-boats sought to exploit the susceptibility of the largely defenceless commercial fleets that were regularly travelling across the Atlantic. Prior to December 1941 and the unprovoked Japanese attack on the American Fleet at Pearl Harbour, Britain and her dominions had only been faced with the prospect of fighting Nazi Germany and her facist allies, including Italy, which publicly declared war against Britain and France on the 10th June 1940, the same month that the British Expeditionary Force had been forced to withdraw from mainland Europe. No doubt keen to exploit perceived British military weaknesses and to benefit from their pact with Germany, during the summer months of 1940 Italian units in Libya were reported to have begun carrying out a series of raids against British interests in neighbouring Egypt, possibly to test their defensive capabilities. With the intention of capturing the Suez Canal, finally in September 1940 and largely at the behest of their leader, Benito Mussolini, the Italian forces in Libya were said to have launched a full-scale invasion of Egypt with an army of some 150,000 men, against the estimated 30,000 British and Dominion troops who were charged with defending the North African country and its vitally important international waterway. As they advanced into Egypt, the Italians were reported to have made good progress, as many of the smaller British units they encountered initially fell back, rather than risk being annihilated by the much larger enemy force. However, unknown to the Italian's, the British commander in Egypt, General Archibald Wavell, had already noted weaknesses within the Italian disposition of their troops and was making secret plans for an all out assault against them.

With the Italian forces scattered throughout Egypt and Libya, beginning on the 7th December 1940, the combined British, Indian and Australian force began attacking the various Italian camps and bases, which had been established in both North African countries, in what became a series of individual battles, including those at Marmarica, Nibeiwa, Maktila, Sidi Barrani and Tobruk. By the time the allied advance was halted on the direct orders of Winston Churchill in February 1941, over 120,000 Italian troops had been taken captive, along with hundreds of their tanks and more than one thousand of their artillery pieces, although the curtailment of the operation, in order to send British and Dominion troops to help Greece, would ultimately prove to be a costly misjudgement by the British leadership. With a large number of Italian troops remaining in and around the area of Tripoli; and with a large number of allied troops being sent to reinforce the Greeks, the Italian leadership were reported to have subsequently reinforced their troops in Libya and accepted an offer of additional forces from Nazi Germany, including those men who would later achieve distinction as the Afrika Corp, who were led by their iconic commander, Erwin Rommel. Within days of Rommel and his German troops having arrived in North Africa, the allied held base at Al Agheila had been captured and by the 3rd April 1941 the port of Benghazi was reported to have been captured by the Axis forces. Lacking the men and equipment to fully confront the heavier armed Afrika Corp, who were supported by numbers of Panzer tanks, for much of 1941 the allies were said to have been pushed further and further back towards the Egyptian border, whilst the British held garrison at Tobruk was said to have been closely besieged by German and Italian forces, who easily repulse allied efforts to relieve the blockade on the city. During May 1941, the allied leadership were thought to have planned a number of large scale military operations to try and gain a tactical advantage over Rommel and his forces, but for the most part operations such as Brevity and Battleaxe were said to have been unsuccessful, despite the best efforts of the British, Indian, Australian, New Zealand and South African troops who tried to implement them.

However, by the end of November 1941, allied troops were beginning to hold their own against the Axis forces and even enjoyed some notable successes against them, as in the case of Indian soldiers who managed to destroy the 5th Panzer Division at Sidi Omar, on the 25th November 1941. Unfortunately such victories quickly proved to be few and far between and during the following month, December 1941, German Panzer units were said to have had a devastating effect on allied troops, most notably the New Zealand units charged with defending the town of Sidi Rezegh, who were reported to have suffered heavy casualties as a result of the German assault. Despite such reverses though the allied forces were reported to have continued with their military operations regardless of the cost in men and material, showing such determination that by the 7th December they had managed to relieve the siege of Tobruk and were even managing to repel a number of German counter attacks, causing such damage that Rommel was forced to withdraw his forces, such were the scale of his losses. Although in a subsequent battle between the two sides armoured divisions, Rommel's forces were said to have got the best of the fight, by the close of 1941, the front line of the battlefield was said to have returned to the town of Al Agheila, the same place where the desert war had first started some nine months before. The following year, 1942, was thought to have followed a similar pattern to that of 1941, with both sides suffering some notable reverses, whilst at the same time enjoying some degree of success, although the allied situation was said to have been markedly improved by two significant events, the appointment of Bernard Montgomery as leader of the allied Eighth Army and the participation of the United States in the war against Germany. By the second half of 1942, the allies were reported to be improving their situation, as the allies under Montgomery, launched Operation Lightfoot, thereby beginning the Second Battle of El Alamein, whilst at the same time the allied command launched Operation Torch, the invasion of Morocco and Algeria, under the leadership of General Eisenhower, the same man who would later oversee the allied invasion of mainland Europe in what became known as the D-Day landings.

Hugh Childers   Emperor Tewodros II   Adolph Hitler

By the end of 1942 and into the start of 1943, allied forces in North Africa continued to press the Axis Powers in the region, who were said to have been suffering supply problems thanks in part to the RAF pilots based on Malta, who regularly interrupted German convoys trying to bring food, fuel, spares and weapons to Rommel's increasingly embattled forces. By the end of January 1943 most of the major ports and cities, including Tobruk, Derna, Benghazi and Tripoli were back in allied hands, despite the best efforts of the Axis forces to throw them back. Although Rommel's troops remained a real threat to the allies, scoring notable victories at Terbouba and Medjez al Bab, ultimately their failing supply lines and lack of reinforcements were both said to have made their position in North Africa generally unwinnable, although it was only on the 13th May 1943 that the remaining Axis forces finally and formally surrendered to the allies, bringing an end to this particular area of conflict. The Second Battle of El Alamein is generally regarded as the pivotal allied victory of the Western Desert Campaign, largely because all of the allied forces involved acted in unison with one another and very few mistakes were made by those controlling the operation. Air power, artillery, mechanised vehicles and ground forces all worked together to produce an advance that was virtually unstoppable, especially against an enemy that seemingly failed, or was unable to unify its armed forces in a similar way. According to most historians, the one great mistake of El Alamein was the failure of the allies to pursue the Axis forces, when they finally withdrew from the battlefield, which undoubtedly caused the conflict in North Africa to drag on for many more months and led to additional losses on all sides. That fact aside however, for the besieged population of Britain, the news of the allied victory in the deserts of North Africa, the first real military triumph of the Second World War, was thought to have caused great rejoicing throughout the country. British Prime Minister Winston Churchill was said to have later commented *"Before El Alamein we never had a victory, but after El Alamein, we never suffered a defeat"*, although he also reportedly cautioned the British people at the time *"This is not the end, neither is it the beginning of the end, but it is perhaps, the end of the beginning"*.

The allied victory in North Africa helped offer some sort of antidote to the humiliating fall of Singapore, which had taken place in February 1942, when some 80,000 British, Indian and Australian troops were delivered into Japanese hands by the military commander of Singapore, Lieutenant General Arthur Percival, in what Winston Churchill later described as the *"worst and largest capitulation in British military history"*. Although the completely unexpected surrender of Singapore, the "Gibraltar of the East", has been dealt with in those sections relating to Malaya and Singapore itself, it is perhaps worth reiterating the causes of its failure, especially those relating to the incidents of poor strategic planning and ineffective leadership, which resulted in an allied garrison of some 80,000 men, being defeated by a numerically inferior military force. The most obvious and basic failure of course, was thought to have been committed by those architects and military planners who failed to envisage any sort of land based assault being made by an enemy force, choosing instead to believe that any sort of attack would come from the sea, which proved to be completely wrong. The same stategists also seem to have adopted the view that the jungles of Malaya would provide an impenetrable barrier to any land assault, thereby preventing heavy equipment and tanks from being brought to bear on the outskirts of the colony, yet another mistake that would prove to be a costly mistake for the population of the port city. Allied planners also seem to have underestimated the abilities and performance of the Japanese military, which was not only able to infiltrate large numbers of their troops directly into the Malay Peninsula and also had aircraft and crews that were far superior to those available to the allied garrison, which for the most part was said to have been equipped with out of date aeroplanes that could offer little competition to their Japanese adversaries, had they been ordered to do so. The fourth major mistake made by British planners was undoubtedly the over reliance on the United States Pacific Fleet, which was based at Pearl Harbour and that the Japanese military effectively crippled on the 7th December 1941, purely through the use of carrier based aircraft. Seemingly indifferent to the danger that such aircraft might pose to a warship at sea, as well as those in harbour, the British government, not only despatched an incomplete naval taskforce, without a carrier that could offer air support, but also mistakenly announced the despatch of their capital ships, in the hope that the announcement might somehow deter the Japanese from any sort of aggressive actions, yet another assumption that proved to be totally incorrect. Even though it remains questionable whether or not a carrier force, comprising ageing aircraft, a state of the art battleship, older cruisers and a handful of destroyers might have saved Singapore from eventual capture, the fact remains that the failure of the aircraft carrier to make the journey and the loss of HMS Prince of Wales and HMS Repulse to enemy aircraft, ultimately forced the remaining naval vessels to withdraw from Singapore, essentially abandoning the garrison there to a largely uncertain fate and leaving Malaya's extensive coastline exposed to further Japanese amphibious landings.

For the allied garrisons in Malaya and Singapore, the withdrawal of the Royal Navy not only removed any possibility of evacuation, but also left the task of defending the areas coastline as their responsibility, an almost impossible task given the number of beaches and coves, where enemy troops could be landed. An added problem for those troops charged with defending the peninsula, was the vast expanse of jungle and mountainous terrain, which although often inaccessible, might well have been used by the Japanese to gain access to different parts of the country. With many of the allied troops unfamiliar with what later became known as jungle warfare and in the mistaken belief that enemy troops would not be able to bring artillery and tanks across such rugged terrain, for the most part British defences were thought to have been fairly static affairs, which were easily avoided by the experienced Japanese troops, who simply outflanked the allied soldiers and either attacked them from the rear, or simply by-passed them completely. With the British forces having few heavy weapons to help support their defence of the country, the Japanese with their light tanks and field artillery, along with their bicycles were not only able to overcome the allied defensive positions, but move easily and quickly throughout the country using roads and tracks. The Japanese were reported to have begun their invasion of Malaya on the 8th December 1941 and by the 10th February 1942 Winston Churchill was ordering the British military leadership in the Far East, in the person of General Wavell that there was no question of the Singapore garrison surrendering and that they should fight to the last, a message that Wavell later passed on to his subordinate, General Arthur Percival, who was trapped in Singapore. For Churchill and many others back in London, the fact that some 80,000 allied troops in Malaya were confronting 30,000 Japanese troops was a pretty straightforward military equation, which he expected Wavell and Percival to understand, although these troop numbers took little account of the actual reality of the situation on the ground, where both the garrison and civilian population were being bombed on a daily basis and supplies of food, water and other supplies were beginning to run out. Although Percival was unaware of it at the time, the Japanese commander, Tomoyuki Yamashita, recognised the weakness of his own situation but decided to bluff and bully the allied leadership into surrendering their much larger forces, by permitting certain acts of terror to be carried out, such as the Alexandra Hospital Massacre and the bombing of civilian centres. Even though such actions were supposedly a ruse by the Japanese commander, ultimately they proved to be effective, as on the morning of the 15th February 1942, General Percival sent a deputation to the Japanese military headquarters to arrange the terms for the allied garrison's surrender. Although he clearly did not recognise it at the time, by agreeing to surrender the garrison and the colony to Japanese control, Percival had inadvertently signed the death warrants for many thousands of the allied troops who were under his command, along with thousands of Chinese residents who were brutally murdered by the occupying Japanese forces.

When Winston Churchill had ordered a halt to the allied advance in North Africa in February 1941, just when it seemed that the remaining Italian troops stationed there might be forced out of Libya for good, a number of the British, Australian and New Zealand units who had been fighting there were subsequently withdrawn to counter Italian aggression in Greece. However, having been posted to mainland Greece and repulsed the first Italian attempts to invade the country, the subsequent intervention of German troops in April 1941, very quickly saw the local Greek and Allied forces overwhelmed by the Axis powers and then had to be evacuated by the Royal Navy, who were ordered to deliver some of these same Commonwealth troops to Crete, where they were to be used to defend the strategic island from enemy attack. Numbering some 30,000 British, Australian and New Zealand soldiers, along with an additional 10,000 Greek troops, the hope was that Crete could be held, much the same as Malta, as a forward allied airbase from where Axis supply lines and convoys could be disrupted by Royal Air Force units, especially the deliveries of Romanian oil, which were helping to underpin the German and Italian war efforts. Unfortunately, even though German planners were thought to have been occupied with arranging the invasion of the Soviet Union, which is generally referred to as Operation Barbarossa, commanders of the Luftwaffe were said to have been eager to carry out an airborne assault against the allied held enclave, if only to gain some form of retribution for their earlier defeat during the Battle of Britain, which many Luftwaffe commanders were still humiliated by. Although given approval by Hitler to carry out the operation against Crete, it was said to be on the strict understanding that the operation should not interfere with the timetable of Operation Barbarossa, something that was agreed to by the German Airforce planners.

Unlike mainland Britain, which was relatively well defended by Radar stations, Anti-Aircraft guns and numerous fighter squadrons, the island of Crete and its comparatively small number of bases and aircraft could offer scant resistance to the regular waves of German bombers that were sent over the island to systematically reduce its air defences. Despite having such a large military garrison on the island, with both the RAF and the Royal Navy at daily risk from air assault, it very quickly became evident to allied planners that their position on Crete was becoming largely unsustainable, especially after the remaining Royal Air Force units were subsequently withdrawn to Egypt, in order to prevent them falling victim to the increasing German bombing raids. However, with the operation under Luftwaffe control and rather than risk landing German forces on the island by ship, which might well be intercepted by the Royal Navy, eventually it was decided to launch an invasion of Crete from the air, using the same sort of paratroopers, who had proved so effective in the German assaults on Denmark, Belgium, the Netherlands and France. Even though such airborne soldiers were largely unknown to the allies, given their successes in several theatres of operation, the idea of such troops was very quickly adopted by most allied armies ad eventually led to the development of some of the world's most elite fighting troops including the British Army's own Parachute Regiment and the US Airborne Divisions. Beginning on the 20th May 1941 the first waves of German troops were dropped onto the island, with large numbers of these first soldiers being killed outright as they parachuted into a hail of bullets and mortar fire put up by the defending allied troops. However, for many of the German paratroopers who landed away from the island's heavily defended airfields, military bases and civilian centres, they were very quickly able to assemble themselves into an effective fighting force and then set out to attack their various military objectives. For the allied commanders on Crete the generally unexpected arrival of thousands of German parachutists all over the island was reported to have caused a great deal of confusion, not least because much of their earlier defensive strategy had been based on the theory that any large scale invasion would come from the sea, where they might be susceptible to attack by the Royal Navy. However, despite being an airborne force, the German troops were said to have been well armed and highly organised; and in most instances were able to confront the allied defenders with an equal level of firepower, something that allied commanders had not anticipated. With no air cover to speak of and with the Royal Navy at risk from roving Luftwaffe patrols, it soon became apparent to the allied leadership that Crete was at serious risk of being overrun by German forces.

Even though the German troops were reported to have performed extremely well in the first couple of days of their airborne assault, by the end of the second day, sheer exhaustion and a shortage of supplies was beginning to hamper their efforts, forcing German commanders to bring in their reserves, which up until that point had been held back. With their numbers reinforced, so they were able to consolidate their gains and push forward, despite the best efforts of the allied defenders to overwhelm the enemy force, which by now had managed to establish fairly insurmountable defensive lines, which the British, Australian and New Zealand troops were finding increasingly difficult to overcome. Poor disposition of their own forces and a shortage of heavy weapons and ammunition were all said to have combined to prevent the allied defenders from attacking the German paratroopers in any sort of significant way, whilst at the same time even more enemy reinforcements were being brought onto the island by German gliders and transport aircraft that used any and all open areas to deposit their troops on the ground, including beaches and fields. Still hoping to rescue the situation, allied commanders were said to have ordered the Royal Navy into the area, in order to ensure that the German forces could not be resupplied by sea, but almost inevitably their presence offshore brought them within range of German fighters and bombers that were now able to roam at will, resulting in a significant number of Royal Navy ships being damaged and destroyed by enemy aircraft. With German troops tightening their grip on large parts of the island and with the Luftwaffe enjoying air superiority over Crete, by the evening of the 26th May 1941 allied leaders were said to be already discussing options for the wholesale evacuation of the Commonwealth military garrison there, a decision that was then conveyed to the allied commander on Crete, Major General Freyberg, the following day.

William Mackensie King

Benito Mussolini

General Archibald Wavell

As part of the planned evacuation of Crete, Layforce, a British commando unit, designed to operate in North Africa were reported to have been brought into Crete on the evening of the 26th May, to help act as a defence for the withdrawing allied garrison. These Special Forces were said to have been aided in part by the young men from the 8th Greek Regiment, who despite being poorly trained and inadequately armed were reported to have battled valiantly against units of the much better equipped German paratroopers and over the period of several days were said to have repulsed several enemy assaults, helping to provide valuable time, during which allied troops were successfully evacuated from the island by the Royal Navy. According to some historians, it was thought to be largely as a result of the bravery of these young and inexperienced Crete nationals that so many Commonwealth troops were able to be withdrawn, to be used elsewhere in the wider global conflict. Elsewhere on the island, other allied forces, including units from the ANZAC's, most notably the 28th Maori Battalion, were thought to have fought a fighting retreat to the coast, as they attempted to protect the main body of allied troops that were heading for the handful of beaches, bays and coves, where boats could ferry them out to the waiting Royal Navy warships and transports. Despite representing a highly risky strategy, one that might well have resulted in the loss of invaluable naval assets, when questioned about the possibility of losing ships for the sake of the embattled military garrison, Admiral Andrew Cunningham, was said to have replied "We must not let the Army down. It takes three years to build a ship, but it takes three centuries to build a tradition". Similarly gritty and resolute determination was said to have been held by many of the allied servicemen stationed on Crete, who were loathe to leave the island in such circumstances, believing that they were in some way betraying their Greek allies, large numbers of whom had been prepared to make the ultimate sacrifice in defence of their homeland. However, regardless of such personal sentiments, over the period of four days, from the 28th to the 31st May, an estimated 20,000 allied soldiers were rescued by the Royal Navy and delivered safely back to Egypt, whilst the remaining British, Australian and New Zealand troops, along with thousands of their Greek comrades were left behind to carry on the fight as best as they could. In total the Battle for Crete was said to have cost the allies some six thousand men who were either dead or wounded, as well as an additional 17,000 who were subsequently captured by the victorious Axis forces. The same operation was also thought to have cost the Royal Navy nearly two thousand lives, as well as some two hundred wounded and cost them nine ships sunk, with a further sixteen vessels damaged. Ironically perhaps, even though the Germans managed to successfully capture Crete, along with a large number of allied troops and remove the military threat from their southern flank, for many within the Nazi leadership, the cost had been extremely high, with an estimated six thousand men lost in the operation, many of whom were elite soldiers, which was said to have discouraged Hitler from using them in future similar operations, a fact that was thought to have had a highly negative effect on Germany's military effectiveness. The defeat on Crete was also said to have taught the allies a number of important lessons, not least of which was the need for a dedicated defence force for the RAF's military bases, as a result of which the Royal Air Force Regiment was officially founded in February 1942 with responsibility for protecting RAF's bases, a role that it continues to fulfil today.

Although the British Army had had a number of what might termed elite military units throughout its three hundred year history, regiments that were intended, or which could be used to overcome even the most obdurate defence, the elite or special forces that we recognise today are almost entirely the product of the specialised units, which were formed during the Second World War. Although the likes of the previously mentioned Layforce and their contemporaries, the Long Range Desert Group are generally accepted as the predecessors of the modern day Special Air and Boat Services, most of these early groups can be classed as commandoes, in one form or another. However, the first formal commando units were only thought to have been founded following the issuing of orders by the British Prime Minister, Winston Churchill, who asked the British military to create a dedicated force that could carry out raids against the Axis in occupied Europe. Initially, most of the men who volunteered to join the new commando force were reported to have been members of Britain's pre-existing elite regiments, including the likes of the various Guards regiments and some of the country's other frontline units, men who craved the sort of action and adventure that the new commando force seemed to offer. Unfortunately, not all the members of the British Army's senior staff welcomed the creation of these new commando units, which they considered to be little more than a distraction, along with encouraging the very best soldiers to leave their elite British regiments, thereby weakening them as a whole. According to some reporters, some commanding officers were even said to have refused permission for their own soldiers to volunteer for these new commando brigades, although when this became an obvious problem, most were ordered to release those men who were keen to join the new units. Although it was said to have taken some time for these new fighting brigades to become effective, within a month of their founding, the first units of commandoes were reported to have been carrying out their first operations, although thanks to largely inaccurate intelligence, bad luck and poor judgement, for the most part these early operations were generally unsuccessful.

The Layforce commando units that were sent to North Africa in the first few weeks of 1941 were reported to have been reasonably successful there, creating havoc amongst the Italian and German lines, although the local allied leadership's failure to fully understand, or indeed embrace the commando concept was thought to have resulted in the force being given meaningless, or almost impossible missions. However, where Layforce was employed properly and having an element of luck on their side they proved themselves to be a highly effective force, one that the Axis was compelled to guard against by employing increasing numbers of its own troops to protect its valuable supply lines and bases. Despite their vital activities in North Africa and the Middle East though, when the decision was made to evacuate the embattled allied garrison on Crete, a large number of the commandoes were subsequently despatched to the island to help rescue the allied troops there, a task that was reported to have led to over 75% of the force being lost to enemy action. In the following June, the remaining few hundred commandoes from Layforce were once again employed in a high risk operation, this time participating in an allied offensive against the Vichy French held regions of Syria and Lebanon, an action that was said to have cost the British commandoes over 25% of their fighting strength, which with the losses suffered in Crete, was said to have essentially destroyed the commandoes as an effective fighting force and the decision was subsequently made to disband Layforce entirely. Fortunately perhaps, even though Layforce had been disbanded and most of its survivors returned to their original units, enough of the commandoes were thought to have remained in the region to help found the succeeding Special Forces units, such as the Long Range Desert Group and the later Special Air Service, as well as its navy equivalent, the Special Boat Squadron, all of which helped to maintain and build on the traditions started by the now defunct Layforce.

Back in Western Europe though, the commando experiment was still alive and well, with occupied Europe being the main target for these highly specialised and increasingly effective elite troops, especially those areas of German held France that were deemed to be susceptible to British military infiltration. Determined to undermine the German war effort, both militarily and economically, commando units were reported to have been used for a wide variety of purposes, including kidnapping, sabotage, economic warfare and attacking any target that was deemed to be useful to the Nazi war effort. Aside from attacking industrial targets, such as Fish Oil factories, such raids were also intended to spread fear through the enemy ranks, especially at those isolated, but important outposts, which often had to be reinforced with extra troops, thereby depriving the German war effort of these highly valuable human resources. Of course not all of the commando raids launched from Britain resulted in such relatively low level rewards, although as was often the case with such military operations occasionally they could either go exceptionally well, or catastrophically wrong, depending on how much planning had been done, as well as how much luck the participants had on their side. Two cases in point were the commando raids on St Nazaire and on Dieppe, both of which were thought to have been reasonably well planned, suffered from a great deal of misfortune, resulted in high casualty rates for the troops who were involved, yet one ended up being hailed as a brilliant success, whilst the other was regarded as an unmitigated disaster.

The first of the two commando raids, Operation Chariot, which was carried out against the huge German held dry dock facility at St Nazaire, on the French Atlantic coast, was undertaken in March 1942, by a combined force of just over six hundred commandoes and sailors, who sailed to their target in an assortment of ships, including a former American destroyer, HMS Cambeltown, which had been converted into a floating bomb. Not only had the former warship had her bow filled with several tons of explosive, which was set on a timer in order to inflict the greatest damage to the port facility, had most of her internal fittings and weapons removed to lighten her weight, but had also had her outline disguised, so that she could be safely sailed past the German harbour defences. Along with the modified destroyer the strike force was also accompanied by a number of motor launches and gunboats that were intended to carry the commandoes and sailors back to Britain, once their mission had been accomplished. Unfortunately, almost as soon as they arrived off the French coast things started to go wrong, as a planned RAF bomber raid, which was intended to distract the German defenders of the port, simply alerted them to the possibility that something unusual was going on and made them even more suspicious about any unexpected arrivals in the port, including that of HMS Cambeltown and her attendant launches. Even though some confusion within the German ranks allowed the old destroyer enough time to ram the enormous dry dock gates, her intended target, the presence and alertness of large numbers of German troops was said to have resulted in the smaller British launches almost immediately being hit by enormous amounts of vicious enemy gunfire, which caused many of them to burst into flames and sink to the harbour floor.

Fortunately, those commandoes tasked with blowing up the dry dock's machinery, power plant and other essential equipment, had been aboard the heavily armoured Cambeltown and so were able to disembark from the vessel and make their way across the quays and into the surrounding buildings, where they placed explosives designed to destroy the vital dock machinery. However, by the time all of their primary objectives had been achieved, not only were most of their motor launches and support vessels destroyed, but increasing numbers of German troops were arriving at the docks to help defend the facility from the British assault. Ordered by their remaining officers to try and get away, as best as they could, most of the surviving commandoes and sailors were reported to have continued fighting until their ammunition ran out, at which time they surrendered themselves to the enemy forces. Of the six hundred strong contingent who had set out on the raid, only just over 30% of them managed to make their way back home, whilst just under 30% were said to have been killed and the remaining 30-odd percent were eventually captured by the Germans and subsequently became prisoners-of-war. Despite believing that the raid had been a failure and that the allied plan to batter down the dry dock gates at St Nazaire was an extreme folly, what the German defenders were completely unaware of was that HMS Cambeltown's cargo of explosive had been rigged with an eight hour delay fuse. As a result and completely unknown to the dozens of German officers who were busily investigating the ship on the morning following the raid, when the high explosive did finally explode, it not only killed everyone on board, but also wrecked the huge dock gates, which would only be repaired following Germany's defeat, as well as sinking several other enemy vessels that happened to be in the harbour at the same time. Even though the raid on the St Nazaire dry dock achieved little practical advantage for the allied military cause, save for depriving Germany of the strategically important Atlantic facility; and despite the fact that so many brave men were lost in carrying out the mission, perhaps more importantly the psychological effect that the raid had, both on the people of Britain and France was inestimable, in that it proved beyond doubt that Britain still retained the military ability to reach out and strike the Germans in their European fortress. In fact, Adolph Hitler was said to have been so worried by the potential military threat that he ordered the Atlantic coastal defences to be strengthened, in order that such an event could not happen again.

The next large scale allied raid that was launched against Hitler's European fortress was Operation Rutter, the codename given to the assault on the French port of Dieppe, which was carried out on the 19th August 1942, by a combined force of commandoes and Canadian infantry. The main objectives of the allied assault were said to have been, to capture and hold a major continental port for a specific period of time, measure German response to the assault, collect whatever intelligence was available, including capturing enemy personnel and to destroy any coastal defences, strategic facilities and port structures that might be of use to the German forces. With Dieppe lying within reach of allied fighter cover, significant RAF, Royal Navy and Army resources were reported to have been put into the operation, including several hundred aircraft, over two hundred naval vessels and some six thousand frontline soldiers, five thousand of which were Canadians, who were to form the core of the amphibious assault and whose leaders were keen for them to play their part in the attack on occupied Europe. Unfortunately, allied intelligence gatherers and military planners, those directly responsible for assessing and scrutinising the suitability of the Dieppe coastline for such an amphibious assault and who were tasked with estimating the likely German response, were said to have not only miscalculated the strength and determination of the enemy defenders, but also the difficulty of the obstacles that the allied troops would face, once they actually landed on the French coast.

Initially, it was intended that allied paratroopers would be used to assault the German gun emplacements that were defending the French coastline and which would almost certainly be used against the Canadian troops as they came ashore. However, for one reason or another these comparatively new parachute units were not available and so the task of neutralising these enemy gun positions was said to have been given to the commandoes, who were asked to land by boat, make their way to the gun posts, then assault and destroy the artillery pieces before they could be brought to bear against the allied forces at Dieppe. Unfortunately, the fact that the allies were said to have been so interested in the French port and its surrounding area, was thought to have alerted the German leadership, to the possibility that some form of allied action was being planned there, which resulted in their local garrisons being reorganised and strengthened in order to counter any proposed allied raid. Whether or not the military planners back in Britain were aware of the sudden surge in German activity is unclear, but regardless of whether they were or not, ultimately the planned assault was to go ahead as planned, with the forward elements of the attack force leaving the south coast of England on the evening of the 18th August 1942 to begin making its way across the Channel.

Erwin Rommel　　　　　Bernard Montgomery　　　　　Major General Freyberg

Some of the first troops to cross the Channel were the two groups of allied commandoes, who were charged with neutralising the coastal gun emplacements that would undoubtedly pose a threat to the allied vessels slowly approaching the French coastline. Unfortunately, one of the commando groups, the one tasked with eliminating the Goebbels battery at Berneval, was said to have been unlucky enough to be discovered by a German flotilla, which quickly attacked the commando's vessels and causing significant losses to the allied force, before they were finally driven off. Only around eighteen commandoes from this unit finally made it to shore, whilst many others were either forced to return Newhaven, were picked up by the approaching allied ships, or were killed or wounded in the firefight. Despite their losses however, those few men who did make it ashore were reported to have carried on with their mission, even though they lacked the weaponry to completely destroy the gun battery and launched a diversionary attack on the German guns, until such time as they were eventually driven back by superior enemy forces. Fortunately, the second group of commandoes, tasked with eliminating the gun battery near Varengeville and that included a detachment of US Rangers, was said to have been far more successful and were able to fully neutralise the enemy gun emplacement, before finally withdrawing at around seven o'clock in the morning of the 19th August, as the main allied taskforce came ashore.

Allied planners had divided the Dieppe coastline into four separate beachheads, which were designated as Blue, Red, White and Green beaches, each of which was assigned to the various British and Canadian units involved in the raid. However, rather than facing light resistance from what should have been a highly surprised German garrison, earlier British interest in the area and the noise of the firefight between the allied commandoes and the German flotilla which had taken place offshore, had both ensured the German defenders were wide awake and alert to any sort of unexpected event. With the allied taskforce running slightly behind time, so that the early morning darkness was fading, the German gunners waiting in positions above the high sea wall, simply waited for the Canadian troops to disembark from their landing craft, before delivering a murderous hail of bullets against the allied soldiers, who found themselves unable to escape the beaches, because of the sheer size of the sea defences that were confronting them. On Blue beach, where the Royal Regiment of Canada and the Canadian Black Watch were landed, over half of the Royal Regiment was said to have been killed or wounded, whilst the remainder were subsequently taken prisoner by the Germans. Similar failures were said to have been encountered on Green beach, where the South Saskatchewan Regiment and Cameron Highlanders of Canada, were not only meeting heavy opposition, but had also landed in the wrong place, which forced them to move inland and then try to reach their original objective by entering the town of Pourville. The only problem was that to go through the town the Canadian troops were required to cross a bridge which had been refortified by the German defenders and successive attempts to cross it, were reported to have caused significant casualties amongst the allied soldiers. Unable to move forward and with fresh enemy troops being brought in to confront them, the Canadians were left with little option but to withdraw to the beaches, resulting in even more casualties for the allied forces. By the time they finally reached their landing craft and began to embark, only a few hundred men were said to have made it back to the coast, with the remainder having been killed, wounded or taken prisoner by the Germans.

The main focus of the allied assault, the beaches designated as Red and White, which were centred in and around the port of Dieppe itself, were reported to have fared equally badly, as whatever could go wrong invariably did, although clearly some of these issues were undoubtedly the result of poor planning and bad intelligence. Comprising two infantry regiments, the Essex Scottish and Hamilton Light, which in turn were supported by the 14th Canadian Armoured Division equipped with Churchill tanks, a delay in the arrival of these armoured units resulted in to two allied infantry regiments having to assault the heavily defended port and beaches with comparatively light weapons, with the obviously horrendous results. With the same high sea wall blocking their advance and with German gunners pouring thousands of rounds into their ranks, both regiments were reported to have suffered significant losses. Unfortunately, even when the first Churchill tanks began to arrive on the beaches, offering the hope of salvation, only around thirty of these vital weapon platforms actually arrived, half of which quickly became stranded in the soft sand and shingle beaches. Those tanks that did manage to traverse the beach then found themselves unable to advance any distance, as obstacles positioned by the Germans blocked their way, forcing them to return to the beach, where they tried their best to offer support to the heavily embattled ground troops, who were now retreating back toward their landing craft. Although they were thought to be largely unaware of the unfolding disaster, simply because of the smokescreen being laid down by allied aircraft, allied commanders were then reported to have compounded their problems, by sending in the reserve troops that were still being held offshore, including Fusiliers Mont-Royal and a contingent of Royal Marines, both of which were subsequently added to the casualty lists, as they were met by increasing amounts of German gunfire and shelling from the port and beaches. Finally, as the scale of the unmitigated disaster became clear to the allied commanders offshore, the decision was eventually made to recall those units that could be saved, an operation that was finally completed by two o'clock in the afternoon, on the 19th August 1942, some nine hours after the main assault had first begun.

By the time a full and frank reckoning was carried out by allied planners regarding the raid on Dieppe, it was generally estimated that more than half of the ground troops involved in the operation had either been killed, wounded, or captured by the Germans, with the Canadian's losing the vast majority of that number, around 3,400 men. Some three hundred allied commandoes were also lost, as well as over five hundred Royal Navy personnel, along with more than a hundred Royal Air Force planes, most of which were Spitfires and Hurricanes. For their part, German losses were thought to have been relatively light, with an estimated six hundred troops dead or wounded, as well as around fifty aircraft destroyed, most of which were thought to have been bombers. Although it had been hoped that the RAF would be able to inflict heavy damage on the local Luftwaffe units, as it transpired this was not thought to have been the case and although the allied aircraft did offer some support to the embattled ground forces, ultimately the lack of a cohesive ground support strategy at the time, resulted in the RAF units being able to offer only limited support to the allied soldiers who were fighting for their lives at Dieppe.

A related aside to the case of the allied assault on Dieppe and the use of commandoes to carry out such raids, was the later introduction of the Commando Order to German forces, reportedly issued by Adolph Hitler on the 18th October 1942, but almost certainly drafted by his subordinate, Army Chief of Staff, Alfred Jodl, who would later be charged with its implementation by the allied authorities and pay for it with his life. Ostensibly, the order issued by Hitler accused the allies of employing highly illegal and brutal means in direct contravention of the Geneva Convention regarding the treatment of military prisoners, with allied commandoes being specifically identified as the worst perpetrators of these illegal actions. According to some German reports, allied commandoes who were involved in the raid on Dieppe and on the island of Sark had not only shackled German prisoners, but also subsequently killed some of them whilst they were still bound, something that was never admitted to by the allies, or indeed proved by the German authorities. However, Hitler was said to have been so outraged by this reported treatment of his armed forces that he later authorised the shackling of allied prisoners, especially a large number of those Canadians captured after the abortive raid on Dieppe. Inevitably, these actions were said to have led to a tit-for-tat approach by the Canadian authorities, who regularly began to shackle German POW's who were in their custody, something that was said to have outraged the German dictator even more. Eventually, the Swiss Red Cross were said to have become involved in the international dispute and after a good deal of negotiation with both sides, the practice was said to have been quietly dropped by both Germany and Canada.

It was said to be after these incidents and possibly as a result of the effectiveness of the allied commandoes that in October 1942 and having discussed the matter with members of his senior staff that Hitler insisted that the highly secretive Commando Order was employed by all of his armed forces. Essentially these highly illegal orders instructed all military and civilian leaders to either hand over any commandoes to the Gestapo, or if that was not possible to eliminate them at the earliest convenience, regardless of whether they were wearing allied uniforms or not. This particular point was said to be the one that made the Commando Order illegal in the eyes of the law, as the wearing of a uniform essentially guaranteed the combatant protection under the terms of the Geneva Convention. In order to ensure compliance by all of Germany's military forces and the civilian authorities, the new order also made it an offence for anyone to fail to report a potential commando to the relevant German authorities, or indeed to eliminate an allied commando when in a position to do so. Although the likes of Erwin Rommel and other traditional commanders chose to ignore such illegal orders, many officers did not and it was said to be as a direct result of the instruction that many hundreds of commandoes and allied agents were deliberately killed by the Nazi authorities, many in the most brutal way possible. Numerous incidents of Royal Marine commandoes who were captured by the German military and later executed were reported to have been documented, as well as hundreds more of OSS, SOE and Resistance fighters, who were brutally interrogated and then spent their last few days surrounded by the horrors of the Nazi concentration camp system, where they were either killed by firing squad, or by a lethal injection. However, despite his best efforts to eradicate the military threat of the uniformed commandoes, or any of the other Special Forces that operated against his regime, ultimately the men and women of the SAS, SBS, OSS and SOE continued with their work, eventually helping to bring an end to one of the most brutal and destructive governments that the world had ever seen. The allied commandoes especially continued to be a thorn in the Nazi's side right through from their creation in 1940 to the end of the Second World War in 1945, fighting in virtually every military theatre and building their fearsome reputation at places like St Nazaire, Dieppe, Crete, Algeria, Tunisia, Sicily, Burma and finally in numerous operations behind enemy lines following Operation Overlord, the allied invasion of mainland Europe in June 1944.

As the Second World War slowly drew to its inevitable end, with Germany surrendering on the 7th May 1945 and the Japanese on the 2nd September 1945, bringing a conclusion to a worldwide conflict that was estimated to have cost anything up to 60 million lives in total, including the six million Jews destroyed by the Nazi's as part of their ethnic cleansing program known as the "Final Solution". In almost similar fashion several million Russians and Chinese nationals were reported to have perished as a result of German and Japanese racism, leaving a legacy of mistrust and even hatred that would last for decades afterwards. For Great Britain and its vast imperial Empire, the Second World War also proved to be a watershed, as having fought to free the world from facism and tyranny, it could not therefore in good conscience, simply expect to resume its role as ruler of dozens of foreign nations whose indigenous peoples were crying out for, if not demanding self determination and independent rule. Outside of mainland Britain, which was said to have suffered some 382,000 military casualties during World War II, the British Empire's greatest treasure, India, was reported to have sacrificed the largest numbers of its people, with an estimated 87,000 military casualties being suffered as a direct result of the conflict. Many of the other British Commonwealth countries, which formed part of the then still existent British Empire, were also reported to have lost large numbers of their young fighting men, including Australia with some 40,000, Canada with 45,000, New Zealand with 12,000 and South Africa with 12,000, plus several thousand more from around the Empire, who were reported to have volunteered for military service with British Forces, including the Regular Army, Royal Air Force and Royal Navy.

Dieppe Commandoes

Alfred Jodl

Royal Marines

As Britain's historic Empire began to be dismantled by its various post war governments, so the need for numerous overseas military garrisons became largely unnecessary, as the likes of India, Pakistan and Burma became entirely responsible for their own defence and security. Although significant numbers of British troops were reported to have remained in Western Europe, as part of the allied occupation forces, within a relatively short time, this British Army of the Rhine was to become part of a bulwark against Russian expansionism, which saw the Soviet leadership divide the entire European continent in two, using what Winston Churchill later described as an "Iron Curtain", behind which many of the former independent European states would subsequently become subject to Soviet influence and control. During the period of the "Cold War", the political, ideological and territorial battle between East and West, which continued unabated for much of the next forty-five years, both the United States and Russia came to dominate the international scene as military super-powers, each developing arsenals of weapons that could annihilate millions of people in an instant, in what became commonly known as the Mutually Assured Destruction, or MAD scenario. It was said to be as part of this wider confrontation, between the East and West, communism and western style democracy that the conflict known as the Korean War was fought, which pitched the communist dictatorships of China, Russia and North Korea, against the various western democracies, including the United States, Great Britain, Australia, France, Canada and South Korea, along with a number of others, who came together under the auspices of the United Nations. During this three year conflict, Britain was reported to have supplied elements from all three of its armed forces and by the time hostilities had ended in July 1953, an estimated three and a half thousand men had been killed or wounded, whilst a further thousand soldiers were posted as missing in action, or being held as prisoners of war.

For Britain and her people, the years following World War II were thought to have been dominated, not only by the threat of Soviet attack, or the privations caused as a direct result of the war itself, but also by a series of insurgencies in a number of the Empires still existent colonies and overseas territories. British troops were called upon to deal with a number of rebellions, upheavals and disorder in places such as Aden, Kenya, Cyprus and Malaya, whilst still helping to safeguard those nations whose independence had already been agreed, but which still required British military support to help develop their own national security forces. For much of the thirty year period, from the 1960's through to the 1990's Britain's armed forces became increasingly specialised, as advances in weapons technology and a changing political climate not only reduced the potential for traditional large scale military wars, but created the possibility of smaller, much more numerous, regional conflicts arising, ones where highly mobile and well armed front line troops would become the norm. For much of that same thirty year period the British Army also found itself embroiled in the bitter religious rivalries of Northern Ireland, where paramilitary groups from both Roman Catholic and Protestant communities very nearly brought the province to the brink of civil war. Ostensibly sent there to protect the Roman Catholic community from Protestant intolerance and bigotry, within a comparatively short time, Republican groups such as the IRA had chosen to misrepresent the presence of British forces for their own political purposes, the generally unachievable objective of a united Ireland, an argument that had already been decided some fifty years before. Despite carrying out a particularly bloody campaign against British troops, their Protestant rivals and even members of their own Roman Catholic community, ultimately such bloodshed afforded them little, other to make them realise that a peaceful political solution was the only way for both religious groups to achieve real social parity in the province. Although a Peace Process was eventually agreed by those on both sides of the argument, with the help of national and international arbiters, the very fact that hundreds of British soldiers, Irish policemen and innocent Irish civilians had had to die for the warring parties to recognise that fact, perfectly illustrates the utter futility of the various paramilitary campaigns.

Although there is little doubt that the British Army would have preferred not to be involved in Northern Ireland in the first place, given that the streets of Belfast, etc. were not the ideal locations for armed troops, some of the strategies and tactics employed in the province have since become regular practice for Britain's frontline soldiers. It is thought to be largely as a result of the lessons learned there that British forces have become adept at policing large urban areas, techniques that they have been able to utilise when serving in a number of foreign theatres, including the likes of Iraq, Afghanistan, Sierre Leone and Bosnia. However, despite developing such people friendly skills and being able to operate in most sorts of environments, for the most part, the modern day British Army is a well trained, extremely professional and highly mobile offensive force, which is capable of operating in any theatre and at relatively short notice. Often though, where the British Army does fall down, this is often as a result of political interference, rather than through any fault with the troops themselves, who are not only highly regarded by other nation's soldiers, but more importantly by the British public, who continue to appreciate the level of sacrifice that Britain's young men and women are willing to make each and every day, especially in support of international campaigns, such as Bosnia, Iraq and Afghanistan. The legitimacy of individual campaigns, such as the one recently fought in Iraq, is not the responsibility of those young men and women who are asked to fight it, but is a matter for the politicians who authorise Britain's armed forces to carry it out in the first place. Some three and a half centuries after Britain's first national army was formed, with the raising of the New Model Army by the English Parliament, it is perhaps worth recalling that without her armed forces, the Royal Navy, the British Army and even the comparatively new Royal Air Force, the former British Empire could never have existed in the first place; and therefore books such as this might never have been written.

www.ingramcontent.com/pod-product-compliance
Lightning Source LLC
Chambersburg PA
CBHW080910230426
43666CB00013B/2658